Readings in Philosophy and Cognitive Science

Readings in Philosophy and Cognitive Science

edited by
Alvin I. Goldman

A Bradford Book

The MIT Press
Cambridge, Massachusetts
London, England

This book was set in Palatino by DEKR Corporation and was printed and bound in the United States of America.

Library of Congress Cataloging-in-Publication Data

Readings in philosophy and cognitive science / edited by Alvin
  I. Goldman,
        p.   cm.
    "A Bradford book."
    Includes bibliographical references and index.
    ISBN 0-262-07153-3. — ISBN 0-262-57100-5 (pbk.)
    1. Philosophy and cognitive science.   I. Goldman, Alvin I., 1938–
B67.R43   1993
100—dc20   93-1739
                                                                      CIP

Contents

Contributors

Irving Biederman
Department of Psychology
University of Southern California

Ned Block
Department of Linguistics and
Philosophy
MIT

Gary L. Bradshaw
Department of Psychology
University of Colorado

Tyler Burge
Department of Philosophy
UCLA

Susan Carey
Department of Brain and
Cognitive Sciences
MIT

Noam Chomsky
Department of Linguistics and
Philosophy
MIT

Patricia S. Churchland
Department of Philosophy
University of California at
San Diego

Paul M. Churchland
Department of Philosophy
University of California at
San Diego

Andy Clark
School of Cognitive and
Computing Sciences
University of Sussex

Antonio R. Damasio
Department of Neurology
University of Iowa

Hanna Damasio
Department of Neurology
University of Iowa

Daniel C. Dennett
Center for Cognitive Studies
Tufts University

Fred I. Dretske
Department of Philosophy
Stanford University

Owen Flanagan
Department of Philosophy
Duke University

Jerry A. Fodor
Departments of Philosophy
Rutgers University and CUNY
Graduate Center

Alvin I. Goldman
Department of Philosophy
University of Arizona

Alison Gopnik
Department of Psychology
University of California at
Berkeley

C. L. Hardin
Department of Philosophy
Syracuse University

Martin L. Hoffman
Department of Psychology
New York University

John H. Holland
Departments of Psychology and
Computer Science and
Engineering
University of Michigan

Keith J. Holyoak
Department of Psychology,
UCLA

Ray Jackendoff
Program in Linguistics and
Cognitive Science
Brandeis University

Philip N. Johnson-Laird
Department of Psychology
Princeton University

Daniel Kahneman
Department of Psychology
University of California at
Berkeley

Hilary Kornblith
Department of Philosophy
University of Vermont

Pat Langley
Department of Computer Science
University of California at Irvine

James L. McClelland
Department of Psychology
Carnegie Mellon University

Richard E. Nisbett
Department of Psychology
University of Michigan

Hilary Putnam
Department of Philosophy
Harvard University

Zenon W. Pylyshyn
Center for Cognitive Science
Rutgers University

David E. Rumelhart
Department of Psychology
Stanford University

Daniel L. Schacter
Department of Psychology
Harvard University

John R. Searle
Department of Philosophy
University of California at
Berkeley

Herbert A. Simon
Department of Psychology
Carnegie Mellon University

Paul Smolensky
Department of Computer Science
University of Colorado

Nancy N. Soja
Department of Psychology
Northeastern University

Elizabeth S. Spelke
Department of Psychology
Cornell University

Stephen P. Stich
Department of Philosophy and
Center for Cognitive Science
Rutgers University

Paul R. Thagard
Department of Philosophy
University of Waterloo

Amos Tversky
Department of Psychology
Stanford University

Karen Wynn
Department of Psychology
University of Arizona

Jan M. Zytkow
Department of Computer Science
Wichita State University

Introduction

Alvin I. Goldman

The cognitive revolution has had its impact on philosophy. Major portions of the philosophy of mind, and to a lesser extent epistemology and philosophy of language, have felt the impact of the scientific studies of mind and brain. Beyond these three fields, however, there is limited recognition of the philosophical relevance of cognitive science. No previous anthology samples the messages that can be extracted from cognitive science to a broad range of philosophical subjects. The time seems ripe to expand our horizons, to see how cognitive science bears on most of the major branches of philosophy. This collection is intended to encourage such broadening of horizons by making pertinent literature available that is organized by philosophical field.

The present collection was initially conceived as a companion to a little book I had written in a similar spirit: *Philosophical Applications of Cognitive Science* (1993). That text contains chapters on the relevance of cognitive science to five areas of philosophy: (1) epistemology, (2) philosophy of science (and mathematics), (3) philosophy of mind, (4) metaphysics, and (5) ethics. This book of readings complements that text by featuring the same five topics and by inclusion of many works discussed in *Philosophical Applications*. The present volume is entirely independent, however, and contains a great deal of unrelated material. Two further topics have also been added, one on language and one on conceptual foundations. The latter reflects a slightly different interface between philosophy and cognitive science, viz., philosophy scrutinizing the underpinnings and theoretical prospects of cognitive science. Both introduce more technical literature, though without serious sacrifice in accessibility.

The choice of readings here was guided by several desiderata. First, I have sought to provide representative works in the relevant research traditions, so that readers not already well acquainted with the cognitive literature can get a good sense of the various styles, problems, and methodologies. Second, because I am interested in philosophically significant findings and methodologies, I have gravitated toward selections where the philosophical morals are either expressly stated or are easily discernible. Chapters by philosophers usually draw explicitly on research in cognitive science, or develop a perspective congenial to the spirit thereof. The number of selections by philosophers and by cognitive scientists are about equal. Third, although I have not aimed to achieve an even balance among the several cognitive disciplines, quite a few are well represented: cognitive psychology (passim), vision (chapters 1, 6, 7, 19), developmental psychology (chapters 10, 15, 16, 19, 20), the psychology of judgment (chapters 2, 3, 4), social psychology (chapters 29, 30, 31), artificial intelligence (chapters 8, 9, 24, 35), linguistics (chapters 21, 23, 25), and neuroscience (chapters 18, 27, 34). (This includes philosophical chapters that report findings from these fields.) My working conception of cognitive science has been ecumenical, encompassing some specimens of psychology that would not ordinarily be identified as cognitive science (e.g., the work on empathy discussed in chapters 29 and 30). Most of the material, however, is cognitive science by anybody's standard.

The best guide to the individual parts, at least the five parts that parallel *Philosophical Applications*, is the latter text itself, which is intended as an introduction to this subject matter. Here I shall merely sketch the main themes by which the several parts are organized, and otherwise let the chapters speak for themselves.

Epistemology, Part I, is often characterized as a study of the sources and prospects for human knowledge. The five selections in Part I address these sources and prospects with reference to cognitive processes. Chapter 1, by Irving Biederman, presents a model of visual classification of objects. This model sheds light on the reliability of visual classification. Which parts of an object must be visible for a person to succeed in identifying it correctly? The next two chapters address human reasoning powers. What are people's native inferential skills? How good are they at detecting logical and probabilistic relations? Chapter 2, by John Holland, Keith Holyoak, Richard Nisbett, and Paul Thagard, discusses deductive reasoning, and chapter 3, by Amos Tversky and Daniel Kahneman, examines probabilistic reasoning. Chapter 4, by Hilary Kornblith, also discusses human capacities for probabilistic reasoning, but presents a more optimistic picture which contrasts with Tversky and Kahneman's pessimism. In chapter 5, Alvin Goldman's discussion is heavily meta-epistemological; it argues for the role of cognitive science in helping to 'analyze' folk epistemic concepts (e.g., the concept of *justification*), and defends epistemic reliabilism using this methodology.

Part II, Science and Mathematics, begins with the question of whether observation is theory laden, an issue that has troubled philosophers of science for three decades. In chapter 6, Jerry Fodor defends the modularity of perception, and concludes that observation is not penetrated by the relevant body of theory. Paul Churchland disputes these conclusions in chapter 7, presenting evidence for the plasticity of perception. Chapters 8 and 9 illustrate how artificial intelligence tries to model scientific reasoning. Paul Thagard (chapter 8) develops a model of scientific theory acceptance, and implements it with a connectionist program, and in chapter 9, Pat Langley et al. explain how the systems they have designed can discover scientific laws, given a body of data. Chapter 10, by Karen Wynn, presents evidence of an innate understanding of number and counting by humans and animals. This sheds new empirical light on controversies in the epistemology of mathematics which are as old as Plato.

Part III, Mind, begins with Ned Block's (chapter 11) exposition of functionalism and troubles that functionalism encounters with the phenomenological or 'qualitative' aspect of mental life. In chapter 12, Paul Churchland agrees with functionalism that mental states are commonsensically understood in terms of a network of laws; but Churchland questions the scientific value of these laws, and envisages a scenario in which the folk adherence to propositional attitudes is totally abandoned. Fodor (chapter 13) surveys theoretical options concerning the attitudes, plumping for realism and his 'representational' (language-of-thought) theory of mind, which is seen as highly congenial to cognitive science. In chapter 14, Fred Dretske addresses the problem of representation, meaning, or content from the perspective of an information-theoretic or correlational approach. Alison Gopnik introduces a more empirical angle in chapter 15, but addresses a very philosophical question: How do we know our own mental states? Appealing to experiments on children's reports of mental states, she argues against introspective access and in favor of an inferential, or 'theory theory', model. Addressing the same question in chapter 16, Alvin Goldman develops a pro-introspectionist account. He argues that commonsense functionalism (or the theory theory) has trouble accommodating self-attribution of mental states. A better cognitivist account of the ordinary understanding of mental states should make reference to phenomenology or 'qualia'. But is phenomenology a legitimate construct for cognitive science? In chapter 17, Daniel Dennett challenges its legitimacy by raising numerous puzzles about qualia. Does this mean that the notion of consciousness, understood as subjective awareness, should be jettisoned from the arsenal of cognitive science? Daniel Schacter answers in the negative in chapter 18. Schacter presents evidence from implicit memory and a variety of agnosias that there is a consciousness system in the mind. Whether and when information enters this system, thereby generating subjective awareness, is a matter that can be studied empirically.

Part IV, Metaphysics, proceeds on the assumption that one aim of metaphysics is to describe the nature and source(s) of our ordinary conception of the world. A basic ingredient of this conception is the idea of 'bodies', or physical objects. Elizabeth Spelke, in chapter 19, explores our (apparently) innate idea of physical objects through experiments on infants. In chapter 20, Nancy Soja, Susan Carey, and Elizabeth Spelke also use studies on children to identify primitive on-

tological assumptions. They argue, contrary to Quine, that certain ontological categories are not learned *through* language but are available
prior to language. In chapter 21, Ray Jackendoff examines a range of
ontological categories to which our language seems to be committed.
Jackendoff sketches a scheme for integrating these categories by viewing
some as the products of generalization from spatial to abstract domains.
Metaphysics is not exhausted by description of ordinary conceptions of
the world. It is also concerned with whether these conceptions are *right*.
In chapter 22, C. L. Hardin asks whether the ordinary conception of
color is right, and suggests a negative answer. Color science, at least
part of which is cognitive science, seems to invite the conclusion that
our ordinary, objectivist conception of color is a misguided artifact of
human biology.

Part V, Language, is in effect divided into two segments. The first
addresses the epistemology of language, that is, how language is
learned, especially whether this learning features the acquisition of
rules. Chapter 23 is a recent overview by Noam Chomsky of his influential rule-based perspective. In chapter 24, David Rumelhart and James
McClelland pose the connectionist challenge to the rule-based approach,
and chapter 25, by Andy Clark, presents the core of Steven Pinker and
Alan Prince's critique of Rumelhart and McClelland. The second segment of Part V is concerned with meaning and the representation of
meaning in the mind-brain. Chapter 26, by Philip Johnson-Laird, gives
a psychologist's perspective on the representation of word meaning,
and chapter 27, by Antonio Damasio and Hanna Damasio, provides
neuroscientific insights into the niche that language occupies in the
brain's network of concepts. In chapter 28, Hilary Putnam challenges
the notion that meaning is (wholly) determined by what's in the head;
he argues for the importance of environment and society in fixing
reference and meaning.

Part VI, Ethics, is a short one, reflecting the comparative paucity of
work at this interface. In chapter 29 Goldman identifies three aspects
of moral thought and experience that cognitive science might illuminate:
(A) the mental representation of moral categories and the possibility of
innate constraints on moral thought; (B) the determinants of subjective
judgments of well-being and happiness; and (C) empathy as a possible
source of moral principles and moral behavior. In chapter 30, Martin
Hoffman explores the phenomenon of empathy in greater depth, discussing both empirical and philosophical issues. Chapter 31, by Owen
Flanagan, reviews some striking literature in social psychology that
sheds light on the power of one's situation to influence moral decisions.

Part VII, Conceptual Foundations, begins by juxtaposing the rival
'internalist' versus 'externalist' approaches to the conceptualization of
psychological properties. In chapter 32, Stephen Stich presents the internalist, or 'individualist', position, according to which only purely
internal properties should be invoked in psychological explanation. In

chapter 33, Tyler Burge defends the contrary, 'anti-individualist,' position, as a faithful account of actual psychological practice. Patricia Churchland, in chapter 34, champions a 'co-evolutionary', or integrative, methodology in the study of mind, emphasizing contributions from neuroscience. She also casts a doubtful eye on the sententialist (language-of-thought) paradigm for the mind-brain. Chapters 35 and 36 display the continuing dispute over the theoretical viability of connectionism. In chapter 35, Paul Smolensky elucidates and defends it, while Jerry Fodor and Zenon Pylyshyn attack it in chapter 36. Finally, one very popular framework for cognitive science, the computational framework, is expounded by Ned Block in chapter 37 and challenged by John Searle in chapter 38.

A few words are in order about the instructional uses of this text. Its first and most natural home would be a course in philosophy and cognitive science (or philosophy and psychology). Large chunks of the text could be read in a one-semester course, or the entire volume in a two-semester sequence. Second, there are ample readings (at least 16 in all) that make it appropriate for a philosophy of mind course: the eight chapters of Part III, the seven chapters of Part VII, and chapter 28. (Additional chapters could also fit into philosophy of mind, depending on one's construal of its scope.) Third, part of a course in epistemology, especially "naturalistic" epistemology, could be built around Parts I and II, with further additions from the materials on language learning (chapters 23–25), knowledge of one's own mental states (chapters 15 and 16), and conceptual endowments (chapters 19, 20, and 21). The anthology might even find a congenial niche in a philosophy of science course, where Parts I, II, and VII would all be relevant. Finally, within any course various "modules" might be constructed from materials that cut across the volume's main divisions. For example, a little module on connectionism and its applications could be assembled from chapters 8, 24, 25, 35 and 36.

For specific help in assembling this group of readings, I am indebted to Mike Harnish, Ned Block, and David Silver. Harnish and Block offered valuable suggestions for Parts V and VII respectively. Silver provided excellent research assistance, both philosophical and editorial. The Society for Philosophy and Psychology and the Cognitive Science program at the University of Arizona have indirectly contributed to the end-product, by calling my attention to various researchers and lines of research that might otherwise have escaped my notice.

References

Goldman, A. I. (1993). *Philosophical Applications of Cognitive Science*. Boulder: Westview Press.

I

Epistemology

1 Visual Object Recognition

Irving Biederman

Try this demonstration. Turn on your TV with the sound off. Now change channels with your eyes closed. At each new channel, blink quickly. As the picture appears, you will typically experience little effort and delay (though there is some) in interpreting the image, even though it is one you did not expect and even though you have not previously seen its precise form. You will be able to identify not only the textures, colors, and contours of the scene but also the individual objects and the way in which the objects might be interacting to form a setting or scene or vignette. You will also know where the various entities are in the scene, so that you would be able to point or walk to any one of them should you be transported into the scene itself. Experimental observations confirm these subjective impressions (Intraub 1981; Biederman, et al. 1982). In a 100-millisecond exposure of a novel scene, people can usually interpret its meaning. However, they cannot attend to every detail; they attend to some aspects of the scene—objects, creatures, expressions, or actions–and not others. In this chapter we will primarily focus on our ability to recognize a pattern in a single glance and our limitations in attending to simultaneous entities in our visual field.

The Problem of Pattern Recognition

The Nature of Object Recognition
Object recognition is the activation in memory of a representation of a ✳ stimulus class—a chair, a giraffe, or a mushroom—from an image projected by an object to the retina. We would have very little to talk about in this chapter if every time an instance of a particular class was viewed it projected the same image to the retina, as occurs, for example, with the digits on a bank check when they are presented for reading by an optical scanner.

From I. Biederman, Higher-level vision, in D. N. Osherson et al., eds., *Visual cognition and action: An invitation to cognitive science,* vol. 2 (1990). Cambridge, MA: MIT Press. Reprinted by permission.

But there is a fundamental difference between reading digits on a check and recognizing objects in the real world. The orientation in depth of an object can vary so that any one three-dimensional object can project an infinity of possible images onto a two-dimensional retina. Not only might the object be viewed from a novel orientation, it might be partially occluded behind another surface, or it might be broken into little pieces, as when viewed behind light foliage or drapes, or it might be a novel instance of its class, as for example when we view a new model of a chair. But it is precisely this variation—and the apparent success of our visual system and brain in achieving recognition in the face of it—that makes the problem of pattern recognition so interesting.

Two major problems must be addressed by any complete theory of object recognition. The first is how to represent the information in the image so that it could activate a representation in memory under varied conditions. Here we will focus on the representation of three-dimensional objects, because the problems of stimulus representation have been most extensively studied for such inputs. The second problem is how that stimulus representation is matched against—or activates—a representation in memory.

Representing the Image
Over half a century ago the Gestalt psychologists noted that there is strong agreement among observers concerning the organization of a given pattern. Their observations led to the development of several principles of perception, such as the principle of good continuation, which holds that points that are aligned in a straight line or a smooth curve are interpreted as belonging together, and the law of Prägnanz or good figure, which holds that patterns are seen in such a way that the resulting structure is as simple as possible. The Gestalt demonstrations have become standard fare in most introductory books in psychology and perception.

For decades the Gestalt principles of perceptual organization stood as a curious phenomenon in most treatises on perception, with no explicit link to pattern recognition. Recently there has been considerable success in interpreting these organizational phenomena as special cases of *constraints* imposed by the visual system that (1) allow a solution to the problem of interpreting a three-dimensional world from the two-dimensional image, even when that image is perturbed by noise, and (2) reveal the part structure of an image. These constraints may offer a basis for the construction of a theory of object recognition.

Viewpoint-invariant image properties play a significant role in the task of interpreting a three-dimensional world from a two-dimensional image. Figure 1.1 illustrates several properties of image edges that are extremely unlikely to be a consequence of the particular alignment of eye and object. If the observer changes viewpoint or the edge or edges change orientation, assuming that the same region of the object is still

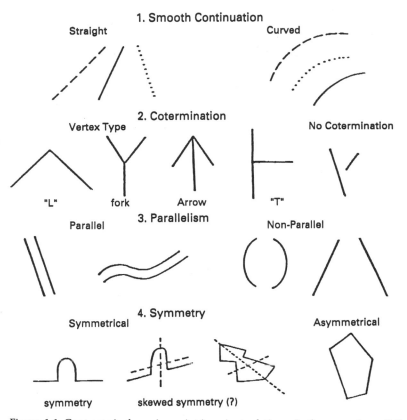

Figure 1.1 Contrasts in four viewpoint-invariant relations. In the case of parallelism and symmetry, biases toward parallel and symmetrical percepts when images are not exactly parallel are evidenced. (Adapted from Lowe 1984 by permission of the author.)

in view, the image will still reflect that property. For example, a straight edge in the image is perceived as being a projection of a straight edge in the three-dimensional world. The visual system ignores the possibility that a (highly unlikely) accidental alignment of eye and a curved edge was projecting the image. Hence, such properties have been termed *nonaccidental* (Lowe 1984). On those rare occasions when an accidental alignment of eye and edge does occur, for example, when a curved edge projects an image that is straight, a slight alteration of viewpoint or object out of the plane will readily reveal that fact.

Figure 1.1 illustrates several nonaccidental properties. In the two-dimensional image, if an edge is straight (collinear) or curved, then it is perceived as a straight or curved edge, respectively. These two constraints imply, of course, the Gestalt principle of good (or smooth) continuation. If two or more two-dimensional image edges terminate at a common point, or are approximately parallel or symmetrical, then the edges projecting those images are similarly interpreted. For reasons that will be apparent when we consider a theory of object recognition, figure 1.1 presents these viewpoint-invariant properties as dichotomous *con-*

trasts. Given an edge, it can be characterized as straight or curved. For two or more edges, the relation can be described as coterminating or noncoterminating, parallel or nonparallel, symmetrical or asymmetrical. The number of coterminating edges and whether they contain an obtuse angle also does not vary with viewpoint and can serve as a viewpoint-invariant classification of vertex type: **L, Y, T,** or arrow (or their curved counterparts). In a strict sense, parallelism and symmetry will vary with viewpoint and orientation, as occurs, for example, with perspective convergence. But there is a clear bias toward interpreting approximately parallel or symmetrical edges as parallel or symmetrical (Ittelson 1952; King et al. 1976). Within a tolerance range defined by the cues for surface slant, pairs of image edges that *could be* parallel or symmetrical, given uncertainty about the actual orientation of the edges to the eye, are interpreted as parallel or symmetrical (King et al. 1976). . . .

Complex visual entities almost always invite a decomposition of their elements into simple parts. We readily distinguish the legs, tail, and trunk of an elephant or the shade and the base of a lamp. This decomposition does not depend on familiarity with an object or on differences in surface color or texture, as shown by the fact that it is readily performed on a line drawing. Even nonsense shapes elicit strong agreement among observers concerning their part decomposition. . . .

RBC: A Theory of Object Recognition

The theory of object recognition known as *recognition-by-components* (RBC) (Biederman 1987, 1988) explains how the edges that have been extracted from an image could activate an entry-level representation of that object in memory.

Entry level is a term coined by Jolicoeur, et al. (1984) to refer to the initial classification of individual visual entities—for example, a chair, a giraffe, or a mushroom—that share a characteristic shape. Often the term that represents this classification (*chair, giraffe, mushroom*) will be the first that enters the child's vocabulary, and it will be used to a much greater extent than any other term to describe that entity. Entry-level classification is to be distinguished from *subordinate* classification, as for example when a particular subspecies of giraffe is specified. It is also to be distinguished from *superordinate* classification, in which shape descriptions are not specified; *mammal* and *furniture* are terms used at this level. If an entity is not typical for its class, such as penguins and ostriches for the class of birds, then entry-level classification is assumed to be at the individual level; that is, we would first classify the image as penguin before we determined that it was a bird. Biederman (1988) has estimated that there are approximately 3,000 common entry-level terms in English for familiar concrete objects.

The central assumption of RBC is that a given view of an object is represented as an arrangement of simple primitive volumes, called *geons* (for *geometrical ions*). Five (of the 24) geons are shown in figure 1.2. The relations among the geons are also specified, so that the same geons in different relations will represent different objects (see the cup and pail in figure 1.2). The geons have the desirable properties that they can be distinguished from each other from almost any viewpoint and that they are highly resistant to visual noise. The objects shown in figure 1.2 also illustrate a derivation from the theory: An arrangement of three geons will generally be sufficient to classify any object. We will consider in greater detail the segmenting of the image into regions that will be matched to geons, the description of the image edges in terms of viewpoint-invariant properties, and the geon arrangement that emerges from the parsing and edge processing.

Geons from Viewpoint-Invariant Edge Descriptions

According to RBC, each segmented region of an image is approximated by a geon. Geons are members of a particular set of convex or singly concave volumes that can be modeled as *generalized cones*, a general formalism for representing volumetric shapes (Binford 1971; Brooks 1981). A generalized cone is the volume swept out by a cross section moving along an axis. Marr (1977) showed that the contours generated

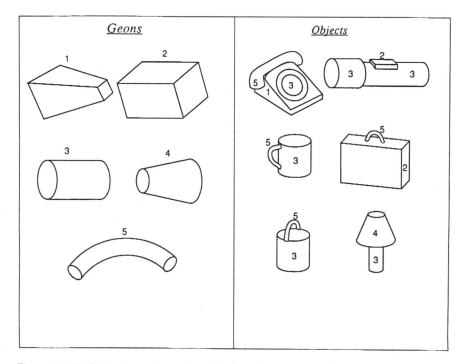

Figure 1.2 (Left) A given view of an object can be represented as an arrangement of simple primitive volumes, or geons, of which five are shown here. (Right) Only two or three geons are required to uniquely specify an object. The relations among the geons matter, as illustrated with the pail and cup.

by any smooth surface could be modeled by a generalized cone with a convex cross section.

The set of geons is so defined that they can be differentiated on the basis of dichotomous or trichotomous contrasts of viewpoint-invariant properties to produce 24 types of geons. The contrasts of the particular set of nonaccidental properties shown in figure 1.2 were emphasized because they may constitute a basis for generating this set of perceptually plausible components. Figure 1.3 illustrates the generation of a subset of the 24 geons from contrasts in the nonaccidental relations of four attributes of generalized cones. Three of the attributes specify characteristics of the cross section: *curvature* (straight versus curved), *size variation* (constant (parallel sides), expanding (nonparallel sides), expanding and contracting (nonparallel sides with a point of maximum convexity)), and *symmetry* (symmetrical versus asymmetrical). One attribute specifies the axis: straight versus curved.

When the contrasts in the generating functions are translated into image features, it is apparent that the geons have a larger set of distinctive nonaccidental image features than the four that might be expected from a direct mapping of the contrasts in the generating function. Figure 1.4 shows some of the nonaccidental contrasts distinguishing a

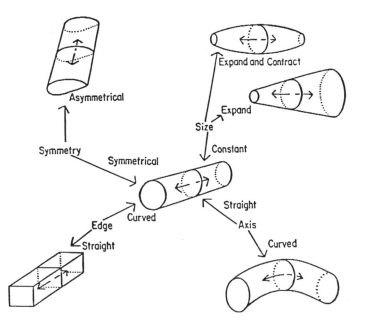

Figure 1.3 An illustration of how variations in three attributes of a cross section (curved versus straight edges, constant versus expanded versus expanded and contracted size, symmetrical versus asymmetrical shape) and one attribute of the shape of the axis (straight versus curved) can generate a set of generalized cones differing in nonaccidental relations. Constant-sized cross sections have parallel sides; expanded or expanded and contracted cross sections have sides that are not parallel. Curved versus straight cross sections and axes are detectable through collinearity or curvature. Shown here are the neighbors of a cylinder. The full family of geons has 24 members. (Adapted from Biederman 1985 by permission of the publisher, Academic Press.)

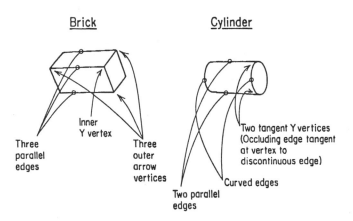

Brick   Cylinder

Inner
Y vertex

Three
parallel
edges

Three
outer
arrow
vertices

Two tangent Y vertices
(Occluding edge tangent
at vertex to
discontinuous edge)

Curved edges

Two parallel
edges

Figure 1.4 Some nonaccidental differences between a brick and a cylinder. (Adapted from Biederman 1987 by permission of the publisher. © 1987 by the American Psychological Association.)

brick from a cylinder. The silhouette of a brick contains a series of six vertices, which alternate between Ls and arrows, and an internal Y vertex. By contrast, the vertices of the silhouette of the cylinder alternate between a pair of Ls and a pair of tangent Ys. The internal Y vertex is not present in the cylinder (or any geon with a curved cross section). These differences in image features would be available from a general viewpoint and thus could provide, along with other contrasting image features, a basis for discriminating a brick from a cylinder. The geons are modal types. It is possible that a given region of the image might weakly activate two or more geons if some of the distinguishing image features (vertices and edges) were missing or ambiguous.

Being derived from contrasts in viewpoint-invariant properties, the geons themselves will be invariant under changes in viewpoint. Because the geons are simple (namely, convex or only singly concave), lack sharp concavities, and have redundant image properties, they can be readily restored in the presence of visual noise. Therefore, objects that are represented as an arrangement of geons will possess the same invariance to viewpoint and noise. Since geon activation requires only categorical classification of edge characteristics, processing can be completed quickly and accurately. A representation that would require fine metric specification, such as the degree of curvature or length of a segment, cannot be performed with sufficient speed and accuracy by humans to be the controlling process for object recognition.

Geon Relations and Three-Geon Sufficiency

According to RBC, the capacity to represent the tens of thousands of object images that people can rapidly classify derives from the employment of several viewpoint-invariant relations among geons (for example, TOP-OF, SIDE-CONNECTED, LARGER-THAN). These relations are defined for joined pairs of geons such that the same geons represent different objects if they are in different relations to each other, as with the cup and the pail in figure 1.2. How the relations among the parts of an object are to be described is still an open issue. The current version of RBC specifies 108 possible combinations of six types of relations. Also specified is a categorization of the relative aspect ratio of the geon (axis larger than, smaller than, or equal to the cross section).

With 24 possible geons, the variations in relations and aspect ratio can produce 186,624 possible two-geon objects ($24^2 \times 108 \times 3$). A third geon with its possible relations to another geon yields over 1.4 billion possible three-geon objects.

Although there are only about 3,000 common entry-level object names in English, people are probably familiar with approximately ten times that number of object models in that (1) many objects require a few models for different orientations and (2) some entry-level terms (such as *lamp* and *chair*) have several readily distinguishable object models (Biederman 1988). An estimate of the number of familiar object models would thus be on the order of 30,000. If these familiar models were distributed homogeneously throughout the space of possible object models, then the extraordinary disparity between the number of possible two- or three-geon objects and the number of objects in an individual's object vocabulary—even if the estimate of 30,000 was short by an order of magnitude—means that an arrangement of two or three geons would almost always be sufficient to specify any object.

The theory thus implies a principle of *geon recovery:* If an arrangement of two or three geons can be recovered from the image, objects can be quickly recognized even when they are occluded, rotated in depth, novel, extensively degraded, or lacking customary detail, color, and texture.

Stage Model

Figure 1.5 presents an overall architecture for RBC. An initial edge extraction stage, responsive to differences in surface characteristics, such as sharp changes in luminance or texture, extracts the edges in the image. The image is then segmented at matched concavities and its edges characterized in terms of their viewpoint-invariant properties. (RBC also specifies additional, albeit weaker, principles for parsing (Biederman 1987). For example, a change in viewpoint-invariant property, such as the change in parallelism from the base cylinder to the nose cone of a rocket, can also provide a [weaker] basis for parsing.) The geons and their relations are then activated, and this representation in turn activates a like representation in memory. RBC assumes that the activation of the geons and relations occurs in parallel, with no loss in capacity when matching objects with a large number of geons. Partial activation is possible, with the degree of activation assumed to be proportional to the overlap in the geon descriptions of a representation of the image and the representation in memory. Thus, an object missing some of its parts would produce weaker activation of its representation.

A Geometric visual sounder code

Biederman

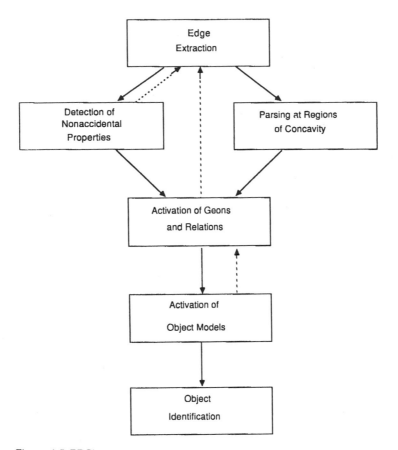

Figure 1.5 RBC's processing stages for object recognition. Possible top-down routes are shown with dashed lines. (Adapted from Biederman 1985 by permission of the publisher, Academic Press.)

An image from which it was difficult to determine the geons—for example, because of low contrast—would suffer a delay in the activation of its geons. However, once the geons are activated, the activation of the object models in memory should proceed as with a sharp image. . . .

Empirical Studies of Object Recognition

A number of experiments have been performed exploring human object recognition in general and various aspects of RBC in particular. In most of these experiments the subject names briefly presented object pictures (where "briefly" is, say, 100 milliseconds). The flash of the picture is followed by a *mask*, an array of meaningless straight and curved line segments, to reduce persistence of the image. Naming reaction times and errors are the primary dependent variables.

1. *Partial objects.* When only two or three geons of a complex object (such as an airplane or elephant) are visible, recognition can be fast and accurate (though, predictably, not as fast as when the complete image

is available). This supports the principle of three-geon sufficiency. You can try this for yourself by covering up parts of pictures of common objects. See whether the object remains recognizable to a friend (who did not see the original) if three geons remain in view.

2. *Effect of object complexity.* Complex objects, defined as those such as an airplane or elephant that require six or more geons to appear complete, do not require more time for their recognition than simple objects such as a flashlight or cup (Biederman 1987). This lack of a disadvantage for complex objects is consistent with a model positing parallel activation of the geons rather than a serial trace of the contours of the object. Often a single-geon model is appropriate for several entry-level objects. Other information such as surface color or texture, small details, or context is then required to classify these objects (Biederman and Ju 1988). For example, distinguishing among a peach, a nectarine, and a plum requires that surface color and texture be specified. RBC would predict that identifying such objects would require more time than identifying objects with distinctive geon models.

3. *When does an object become unrecognizable?* Images can be rendered unrecognizable if the contour is deleted so that the geons cannot be recovered from the image. One technique is to delete the cusps to the point where the remaining contours would bridge the cusp through smooth continuation, as with the handle of the cup in figure 1.6a. Another technique is to alter vertices, as with the stool, and suggest inappropriate ones, as with the watering can. If the same amount of contour is deleted but in regions where the geons can still be activated, as shown in figure 1.6b, objects remain identifiable. Actually, even more contour can be removed from the images in figure 1.6b and they will still remain recognizable. You can test this for yourself by covering up parts of an object (say, the right or left half) and determining whether you or a friend who has not seen the original version can still identify the object. . . .

4. *An extension to scene perception.* The mystery about the perception of scenes is that the exposure duration an observer requires to have an accurate perception of an integrated real-world scene is not much longer than what is typically required to perceive individual objects. Recognizing a visual array as a scene requires not only identifying the various entities but also semantically specifying the interactions among the objects and providing an overall semantic specification of the arrangement.

However, the perception of a scene is not necessarily derived from an initial identification of the individual objects making up that scene (Biederman 1988). That is, in general we do not first identify a stove, refrigerator, and coffee cup, in specified physical relations, and then conclude that we are looking at a kitchen.

Some demonstrations and experiments suggest that RBC may provide a basis for explaining rapid scene recognition. Mezzanotte (described

Figure 1.6 Example of five stimulus objects in the experiment on the perception of degraded objects. Column (a) shows the original intact versions. Column (b) shows the recoverable versions. The contours have been deleted in regions where they can be replaced through collinearity or smooth curvature. Column (c) shows the nonrecoverable versions. The contours have been deleted at regions of concavity so that collinearity or smooth curvature of the segments bridges the concavity. In addition, vertices have been altered (for example, from Ys to Ls). (Adapted from Biederman 1985 by permission of the publisher, Academic Press.)

in Biederman 1988) has shown that a readily interpretable scene can be constructed from arrangements of single geons that just preserve the overall aspect ratio of the objects, such as those shown in figure 1.7a. In this kind of scene none of the entities, when shown in isolation, could be identified as anything other than a simple volumetric body, such as a brick. Most important, such settings could be recognized sufficiently quickly to interfere with the identification of intact objects that were inappropriate to the setting.

It is possible that quick understanding of a scene is mediated by the perception of *geon clusters*. A geon cluster is an arrangement of geons from different objects that preserves the relative size, aspect ratio, and relations of the largest visible geon of each object. In such cases the individual geon will be insufficient to allow identification of the object. However, just as an arrangement of two or three geons almost always allows identification of an object, so an arrangement of two or more geons from different objects may produce a recognizable combination. The cluster acts very much like a large object. Figure 1.7b shows possible geon clusters for the scenes in figure 1.7a. If this account is correct, fast scene perception should only be possible in scenes where such familiar object clusters are present. This account awaits rigorous experimental test, but you may try to gauge it for yourself with the TV "experiment" described in the opening paragraph of this chapter. Are there some

(a)

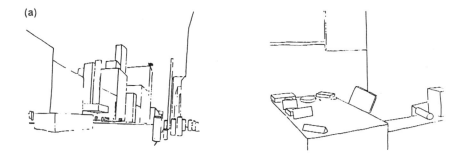

(b)

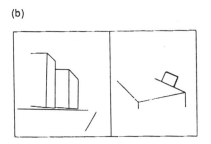

Figure 1.7 (a) Two of Mezzanotte's scenes: "City Street" and "Office." (b) Possible geon clusters for the scenes in (a).

scenes that you cannot identify from a single glance? My own experience is that such scenes are those where a familiar geon cluster is not present.

Note

The writing of this chapter was supported by grants 86-0106 and 88-0231 from the Air Force Office of Scientific Research.

References

Biederman, I. (1985). Human image understanding: Recent research and a theory. *Computer Vision, Graphics, and Image Processing* 32, 29–73.

Biederman, I. (1987). Recognition-by-Components: A theory of human image understanding. *Psychological Review* 94, 115–147.

Biederman, I. (1988). Aspects and extensions of a theory of human image understanding. In Z. Pylyshyn, ed., *Computational processes in human vision: An interdisciplinary perspective*. Norwood, NJ: Ablex.

Biederman, I., and G. Ju (1988). Surface vs. edge-based determinants of visual recognition. *Cognitive Psychology* 20, 38-64.

Biederman, I., R. J. Mezzanotte, and J.C. Rabinowitz (1982). Scene perception: Detecting and judging objects undergoing relational violations. *Cognitive Psychology* 14, 143–177.

Binford, T. O. (1971). Visual perception by computer. Paper presented at IEEE Systems Science and Cybernetics Conference, Miami, December.

Brooks, R. A. (1981). Symbolic reasoning among 3-D models and 2-D images. *Artificial Intelligence* 17, 205–244.

Intraub, H. (1981). Identification and naming of briefly glimpsed visual scenes. In D. F. Fisher, R. A. Monty, and J. W. Senders, eds., *Eye movements: Cognition and visual perception*. Hillsdale, NJ: Erlbaum Associates.

Ittelson, W. H. (1952). *The Ames demonstrations in perception*. New York: Hafner.

Jolicoeur, P., M. A. Gluck, and S. M. Kosslyn (1984). Pictures and names: Making the connection. *Cognitive Psychology* 16, 243–275.

King, M., G. E. Meyer, J. Tangney, and I. Biederman (1976). Shape constancy and a perceptual bias towards symmetry. *Perception and Psychophysics* 19, 129–136.

Lowe, D. G. (1984). Perceptual organization and visual recognition. Doctoral dissertation, Department of Computer Science, Stanford University, Stanford.

Marr, D. (1977). Analysis of occluding contour. *Proceedings of the Royal Society of London* B197, 441–475.

2 Deductive Reasoning

John H. Holland, Keith J. Holyoak, Richard E. Nisbett, and Paul R. Thagard

Teaching Logical Rules

How do ordinary people reason about problems that the logician can solve by applying formal syntactic rules? One answer, since Aristotle, has been that ordinary people themselves use formal syntactic rules. According to both philosophers and psychologists (including Piaget and his followers) who are sympathetic to the syntactic view, these deductive rules are either known a priori or induced by everyone in the course of normal development because of their manifest utility in problem solving.

We will review evidence for an alternative view, based on the proposal that everyday reasoning typically relies on sets of inferential rules that constitute pragmatic reasoning schemas (Cheng and Holyoak 1985; Cheng et al. 1986). First, however, we will critically examine earlier proposals.

Problems with the Syntactic View

It has always been known, of course, that people make errors when attempting to reason logically, but this fact usually has not been regarded as fatal to the syntactic view. Errors are often presumed to reflect vagaries in the interpretation of the material from which one reasons, including changes such as the addition or omission of premises (Henle 1962). For example, it has been pointed out that different conversational contexts invite different pragmatic assumptions (Fillenbaum 1975, 1976; Geis and Zwicky 1971). The sentence "If you mow the lawn, I'll give you five dollars," for instance, clearly invites the inference "If you don't mow the lawn, I won't give you five dollars." Such an inference, although fallacious according to formal logic (it is functionally equivalent

From J. Holland, K. Holyoak, R. Nisbett, and P. Thagard, *Induction: Processes of inference, learning, and discovery* (1986). Cambridge, MA: MIT Press. Reprinted by permission.

to the fallacy of Denying the Antecedent), is actually pragmatically valid within its context.

There is abundant evidence for such invited pragmatic inferences, but interpretive mistakes of that kind cannot account for typical patterns of errors produced by college students in a variety of deductive reasoning problems employing *arbitrary* symbols and relations. (See Evans 1982 for a review.) The best known of these problems is Wason's (1966) selection task. In this task subjects are informed that they will be shown cards that have numbers on one side and letters on the other, and are given a rule such as "If a card has an *A* on one side, then it has a 4 on the other." Subjects are then presented with four cards, which might show an *A*, a *B*, a 4, and a 7, and are asked to indicate all and only those cards that must be turned over to determine whether or not the rule holds. The correct answer in this example is to turn over the cards showing *A* and 7. More generally, the rule used in such problems is a conditional, "if *p* then *q*," and the relevant cases are *p* (because if *p* is the case it must be established that *q* is also the case) and *not-q* (because if it is not the case that *q* then it must be established that it is also not the case that *p*). When college students are presented with such problems in an abstract form, it is usually found that fewer than ten percent of them can produce the correct answer.

Each of the four alternatives in the selection task corresponds to the minor premise in one of the four possible inference patterns (two valid and two invalid) for the conditional. Selection of *p* corresponds to the minor premise in the valid rule of *modus ponens*:

If *p* then *q*

p

_____

Therefore, *q*.

Selection of *not-q* corresponds to the valid rule *modus tollens:*

If *p* then *q*

not-q

_____

Therefore, *not-p*.

Selection of *not-p* corresponds to the fallacy of Denying the Antecedent:

If *p* then *q*

not-p

_____

Therefore, *not-q*.

Selection of *q* corresponds to the fallacy of Affirming the Consequent:

If *p* then *q*

q

_____

Therefore, *p*.

Holland, Holyoak, Nisbett, and Thagard

From a logical perspective it might seem that subjects in these experiments mistakenly interpret the rule as a biconditional (that is, *p if and only if q*), which requires that all four cards to be turned over. In fact, however, this error is rare. Instead, most subjects select patterns that are irreconcilable with any logical interpretation, choosing, for example, *A* and 4 (that is, *p* and *q*). One of the errors in such an answer is omission of the card showing 7, indicating a failure to see the equivalence of a conditional statement and its contrapositive (that is, "If a card does not have a 4 on one side, then it does not have an *A* on the other"). Other errors include the fallacies of Affirming the Consequent (which corresponds to insistence on examining 4, which is unnecessary because the rule does not specify anything about the obverse of cards with a 4 on one side) and Denying the Antecedent (which corresponds to insistence on examining *B*, which also is unnecessary because the rule does not specify anything about cards that do not have an *A* on one side). Such errors suggest that typical college students do commit fallacies due to errors in the deductive process itself, at least with abstract ✳ materials.

Abstract Rules versus Specific Knowledge
Other research, however, has shown that subjects can solve problems that are formally identical to the selection task if they are presented in "realistic", "thematic" contexts. Johnson-Laird et al. (1972), for example, took advantage of a now-defunct British postal rule requiring that sealed envelopes have more postage than unsealed envelopes. They asked their subjects to pretend that they were postal workers sorting letters and had to determine whether rules such as "If a letter is sealed, then it had a 5*d.* stamp on it" were violated. The problem was cast in the frame of a standard Wason selection task. The percentage of correct responses for this version was 81, whereas only 15 percent of the responses given by the same subjects to the "card" version were correct.

In contrast, younger subjects in more recent studies, unfamiliar with the old postal rule, turn out to perform no better on the envelope version of the task than they do on the card version (Griggs and Cox 1982; Golding 1981). This pattern of results has suggested to some that the source of facilitation in the experiment by Johnson-Laird and colleagues was prior experience with a rule, particularly prior experience with counterexamples. It has been argued that subjects familiar with the postal rule do well because the falsifying instance—a sealed but understamped letter—would be available immediately through the subjects' prior experience. Several theorists have generalized this interpretation, suggesting that people typically do not reason using the rules of formal logic at all, but instead rely on memory of specific experiences or content-specific empirical rules (D'Andrade 1982; Griggs and Cox 1982; Manktelow and Evans 1979; Reich and Ruth 1982). This is a position of extreme domain specificity, which holds that subjects do not possess general and abstract inferential rules at all, but instead possess only rules covering specific, concrete content domains and an ability to check for counterexamples in those domains to ensure that the rule obtains.

The syntactic view has not been abandoned by all theorists, however (Braine 1978; Braine et al. 1984; Rips 1983). Braine (1978), for example, has proposed that there is a *natural* logic, different in its content from standard logic, but computationally complete and "mappable" onto a valid logical rule system. Natural logic is different from standard logic in that the connectives capture essential syntactic and semantic properties of the corresponding English words. Particular rules present in most standard logics—for example, *modus tollens*—are simply not represented in natural logic.

Work by Braine and his colleagues (1984) shows that people who have not been tutored in logic can indeed solve purely arbitrary problems with great accuracy. For example, subjects can solve problems of the following form:

If there's a D or a J, then there's not a Q
There is a D
Is there a Q?

According to Braine and his colleagues, subjects solve this problem by means of sequential application of their inference schemas P7 and P3 (out of a total of 16 schemas):

P7   IF p_1 OR . . . p_n THEN q
      p_i
      _____

      q
P3 p;
      False that p
      _____

      INCOMPATIBLE

The fact that people are quite accurate in solving problems like those presented by Braine, Reiser, and Rumain poses problems for positions at the empirical extreme. Subjects cannot be plausibly held to have empirical rules, or memories for counterexamples, for problems involving Ds and Qs.

A quite different approach, which can be viewed as an attempt to merge the extreme positions represented by specific knowledge and abstract syntactic rules, has been taken by Johnson-Laird (1982, 1983). He has proposed that people possess a set of procedures for modeling the relations in deductive reasoning problems so as to reach conclusions about possible states of affairs given the current model of relations among elements. In Johnson-Laird's theory, mental models are constructed using both general linguistic strategies for interpreting logical terms such as quantifiers, and specific knowledge retrieved from memory. The modeling procedures themselves are general and domain-independent.

Pragmatic Reasoning Schemas

The approach advocated by Cheng and her colleagues is based on a type of knowledge structure qualitatively different from those postulated by other theories of logical reasoning. This approach assumes that people often reason using neither formal syntactic rules nor memories of specific experiences, but rather pragmatic reasoning schemas, which are knowledge structures at an intermediate level of abstraction. Pragmatic reasoning schemas are highly abstract rule systems, inasmuch as they potentially apply to a wide range of content domains. Unlike syntactic rules, however, they are constrained by particular inferential goals and event relationships of certain broad types. Although pragmatic reasoning schemas are related to Johnson-Laird's (1983) concepts of mental models, some important differences are evident. For example, whereas Johnson-Laird focuses on limitations in working-memory capacity as an explanation of reasoning errors, the schema approach explains errors (as defined by the dictates of formal logic) in terms of the ease of mapping concrete situations into pragmatic schemas, as well as the degree to which the evoked schemas generate inferences that in fact conform to standard logic.

Cheng and Holyoak (1985) obtained several empirical findings that speak strongly for the existence of reasoning schemas. In one experiment using the selection paradigm, they compared the effect of direct experience to the effect of simply adding a rationale to rules that might otherwise seem arbitrary. Groups of subjects in Hong Kong and in Michigan were presented with both the envelope problem described earlier and another problem having to do with rule following. In the latter problem passengers at an airport were required to show a form, and it was necessary to check whether the rule "If the form says 'ENTERING' on one side, then the other side includes cholera among the list of diseases" was violated by each of four different cases corresponding to *p, q, not-p,* and *not-q*.

There was no reason to expect subjects in either location to have experience with the cholera rule. But because a version of the envelope rule had been in effect in Hong Kong until shortly before the experiment, subjects in Hong Kong were expected to have relevant specific experience to draw on. In addition, half the subjects in each location received brief rationales for the two rules. The stated rationale for the postal rule was that a sealed envelope defined first-class mail, for which the post office wished to receive more revenue; the rationale for the cholera rule was that the form listed diseases for which the passenger had been inoculated, and that a cholera inoculation was required to protect the entering passengers from the disease. It was anticipated that in both cases the rationale would trigger a "permission schema", or set of rules having to do with circumstances under which action Y is required if action X is to be permitted (for example, higher postage must be paid if a letter is to mailed first class).

The results of the experiment are depicted in figure 2.1. As expected, in the absence of a stated rationale only the Hong Kong subjects given the envelope problem performed particularly well. All groups, however, performed very well when an appropriate rationale was provided. For subjects lacking experience with a rule, the solution rate went from about 60 percent without the rationale to about 90 percent with the rationale.

This benefit conveyed by provision of a rationale is inexplicable according to either the domain-specificity view or the syntactic view. Except for the Hong Kong subjects given the envelope problem, subjects had no experience with the specific content in question and hence no memory for counterexamples to the rule. Thus improvement due to the rationale cannot be attributed to processes advocated by proponents of the domain-specificity view. On the other hand, improvement cannot

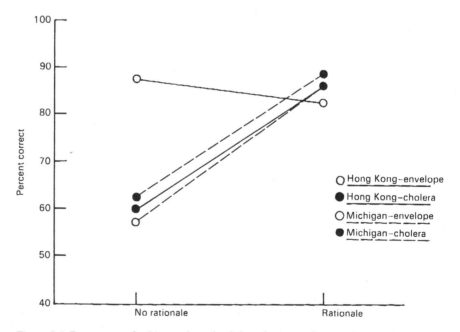

Figure 2.1 Percentage of subjects who solved the selection task correctly in each condition as a function of provision of a rationale. (Adapted from Cheng and Holyoak 1985 by permission of the publisher, Academic Press.)

Holland, Holyoak, Nisbett, and Thagard

be plausibly attributed to manipulation of the formal properties of the problems either, since the added rationale did not affect the logical structure of the problems.

These results are understandable, however, in terms of pragmatic reasoning schemas. The rules attached to such schemas are not abstract syntactic rules, but general rules or heuristics for solving problems of rather broad types. The schemas summarize habitually encountered relations among events of various kinds and rules for solving problems involving pragmatically important types of relations. Examples of pragmatic reasoning schemas include schemas for various types of regulations, such as "permissions," of which both the postal rule and the cholera rule are instances. Provision of a rationale for an otherwise arbitrary rule facilitated subjects' performance by supplying a cue that elicited a relevant reasoning schema for evaluating permissions.

The permission schema is particularly useful in performing the selection task because the rules that comprise it map well onto the rules of the logical conditional. The core of the permission schema is a rule of the form "If one is to do X" (for instance, buy liquor), "then one must satisfy precondition Y" (be over 21), together with an implicit or explicit justification for the regulation. Since satisfying precondition Y generally does not dictate doing X, the biconditional assumption is ruled out in this context. Moreover, the concept of permission stresses that one will not be allowed to do X if one violates precondition Y. Consequently, the contrapositive, "If one does not satisfy precondition Y, then one cannot do X," seems to be part of the permission schema, rather than derived by some indirect means such as the general logical rule of contraposition that states the equivalence of "If p than q" and "If not-q then not-p." Since an analysis of a problem in terms of a permission schema should dictate the same choices as would the conditional in formal logic, invocation of such a schema should especially facilitate performance on problems of the selection type.

In contrast, an arbitrary rule, being unrelated to typical life experiences, does not evoke any reasoning schemas. Subjects confronted with such a rule would therefore have to draw upon their knowledge of abstract reasoning principles to arrive at a correct solution. Only a small percentage of college students apparently knows the logical conditional well enough to use *modus tollens*. Instead, some might draw on some nonlogical strategy such as "matching" (that is, selecting the terms mentioned in the rule regardless of whether or not they are negated), as observed by Reich and Ruth (1982) and Manktelow and Evans (1979), among others.

Cheng and Holyoak (1985) obtained further evidence for the facilitative effect of a permission schema by presenting subjects with a selection problem based on an abstract description of a permission situation: "If one is to take action A, then one must first satisfy precondition P."

Subjects were also given the arbitrary card problem. About 60 percent of the subjects solved the abstract permission problem correctly when it was presented first, versus only about 20 percent who correctly solved the card version of the selection problem when it was presented first. The fact that a purely abstract description of a permission situation produces facilitation supports the schema hypothesis over the hypothesis that domain-specific knowledge is necessary to obtain high levels of performance.

Purely Formal versus Pragmatically Based Training

A series of training studies by Cheng et al. (1986) provides additional evidence differentiating the syntactic and pragmatic views. If people do not naturally reason using purely formal operations that are analogous to those of standard logic, and hence do not know how to map the terms in the abstract rules onto concrete cases, then it should be difficult or impossible to teach them effectively by purely abstract means. That is, it should be difficult to teach the rules in such a way that they actually are used in problems other than those that are presented during logic training. (It has long been known, of course, that teaching logic results in learning logic defined as manipulating the exact sorts of symbols presented in logic classes.) If, on the other hand, people typically do reason using purely abstract logical rules, then direct training in manipulating such rules according to standard logic might improve people's ability to reason in accord with logical requirements, just as purely abstract instruction in statistical rules has been shown to have substantial effects on people's ability to reason in accord with statistical principles (Fong et al. 1986).

Cheng and her colleagues argued that the pattern of results for training in the logic of the conditional would not be comparable to that found by Fong, Krantz, and Nisbett for training in the law of large numbers, because the full logic of the conditional has no counterpart in natural reasoning processes. They predicted instead that abstract training in logic would by itself have little or no impact on people's ability to reason about the Wason selection task, whether the task was presented in arbitrary form or in a form intended to evoke pragmatic reasoning schemas. They anticipated, however, that training in abstract logic would facilitate performance if it were coupled with training on how to model selection problems in terms that would facilitate the application of the conditional. Learning an abstract rule of logic and learning how to apply it to a particular type of problem may be separate requisites for correctly solving a reasoning problem by means of formal logic. If so, and if people typically do not naturally possess either requisite, then effective training for most people will require training both on the rule itself and on techniques for applying it. Only a small minority, who either are able to induce the relevant abstract rule from specific instances of it or are especially adept in applying newly learned rules, would benefit from training on either component alone.

Abstract Rule Training and Concrete Example Training   The first experiment by Cheng and colleagues was designed to assess the influence of a permission schema on performance in the selection task, as well as the usefulness of various training procedures based on abstract logic and/or examples of selection problems. Subjects who received abstract training read a seven-page booklet consisting of an exposition of conditional statements, followed by an inference exercise. The exposition consisted of an explanation of the equivalence between a conditional statement and its contrapositive, as well as an explanation of the two common fallacies of Affirming the Consequent and Denying the Antecedent. The contrapositive was explained in part by the use of a truth table, in part by Venn diagrams that used concentric circles to show the relations between a conditional statement and its contrapositive, and in part by an illustrative conditional statement, which expressed a realistic causal relation. Similarly, the fallacies were explained in part by diagrams and in part by alternative possible causes related to the illustrative statement.

Subjects who received examples training were requested to attempt to solve two selection problems. Neither problem bore any obvious surface similarities to the later test problems. Feedback was given about the subjects' success, and they were shown how to set up and solve the problem in terms dictated by the logic of the conditional. The correct answer for each example was explained in terms specific to the particular problem. Rule-plus-examples training consisted of the materials for the abstract condition followed by those for the examples condition. The only further addition was that for these subjects the explanation of the correct answer for each example was couched in terms of the abstract rules they had just learned.

The subjects were given a test that presented two types of problems involving a conditional rule—problems expressing an arbitrary relation and problems expressing a permission situation. (Other types of problems were also included, but these will not be discussed here.) Each problem took the form of a brief scenario, within which were embedded a conditional rule, a question asking the subject to determine the correctness of the rule, and a list of the four possible cases (p, not-p, q, and not-q) from which the subject was to select.

Two measures of performance were analyzed for each task—whether the subject made the correct selection (p and not-q) and whether the subject made any of the four possible kinds of errors. The four kinds of errors in the selection task were failing to select p, failing to select not-q, selecting q, and selecting not-p. These errors correspond respectively to errors on *modus ponens*, *modus tollens*, Affirming the Consequent, and Denying the Antecedent.

As expected, performance was much more accurate for the permission problems than for the arbitrary problems (66 percent versus 19 percent correct). Permission problems produced fewer errors of all four types than did arbitrary problems. It is particularly noteworthy that the permission problems yielded more accurate performance even for the choice of p, which corresponds to *modus ponens*, perhaps the most plausible of all the syntactic inference rules that Braine (1978) posited as components of natural logic.

A comparison of the two permission problems provided a test of the domain-specificity hypothesis, which claims that only rules with which subjects have prior familiarity will yield good performance. One of the two rules was a "drinking age" rule ("If a customer is drinking an alcoholic beverage, then he or she must be over 21"), which was presumably quite familiar to the college subjects. The other rule was a version of the "cholera rule," which was presumably less familiar. Although the percentage of subjects making a correct selection was marginally higher for the more familiar rule (71 percent versus 61 percent), even the relatively unfamiliar rule produced a much lower error rate than did either arbitrary problem. Thus subjects were able to reason in accord with standard logic even for a relatively unfamiliar rule if it evoked a permission schema. These results indicate that while specific experiences may play a role in reasoning, they cannot possibly provide a full account of reasoning performance.

The impact of the various training conditions, collapsed over type of selection problem, is indicated by the data in table 2.1. Abstract training coupled with examples training significantly decreased the frequencies of three types of errors—failure to select p, failure to select *not-q*, and erroneous selection of q. The frequency of correct selections increased from 25 percent for the control condition to 61 percent for the group given abstract training plus examples. Neither abstract training nor examples training alone decreased error frequencies significantly. This pattern suggests that knowledge of abstract rules of logic and the ability to apply them are two separate skills and that college students typically have not yet acquired either of them. Because the confidence intervals for pairwise differences between means were quite wide, however, the null hypothesis that neither abstract training nor examples training

Table 2.1 Performance as a function of training condition (after Cheng et al. 1986)

Training condition	Percent correct	Percent errors of each type			
		p	*not-p*	q	*not-q*
Abstract plus examples	61	5	27	28	8
Abstract only	35	14	48	33	7
Examples only	38	10	45	37	12
Control	25	18	51	44	14

Holland, Holyoak, Nisbett, and Thagard

alone yielded any benefit cannot be accepted with confidence on the basis of this experiment alone.

The Effects of a Logic Course   The results of the above experiment indicated that training in standard logic, when coupled with training on examples of selection problems, leads to improved performance on subsequent selection problems. In contrast, logic training without such examples failed to significantly improve performance. An obvious possibility is that the experimental "microcourse" on the logic of the conditional was simply too minimal to convey much benefit. To assess this possibility, Cheng and colleagues (1986) performed a second experiment that examined the impact of a much broader and more prolonged abstract training condition, namely a one-semester undergraduate course in standard logic.

Two introductory logic courses, one at the Ann Arbor campus of the University of Michigan and one at the branch campus at Dearborn, provided subjects. Both courses covered topics in propositional logic, including *modus ponens, modus tollens,* Affirming the Consequent, and Denying the Antecedent, and the distinction between the conditional and the biconditional. In both courses the treatment of the valid and invalid inference patterns was primarily formal. While meaningful conditional sentences were introduced in lectures to illustrate the inference rules and fallacies, the emphasis was on formal logical analyses (truthtable analyses and construction of proofs). Neither course provided any exposure to the selection task or other psychological research on deductive reasoning.

A pretest was given in the first week of class before any discussion of the conditional had taken place; a post-test was given in the final week of the semester. To generate matched test materials, the selection problems used in the previous experiment were divided into two matched sets.

The results provided little comfort for the notion that formal instruction in logic is sufficient to improve reasoning performance as measured by the selection task. No significant improvement was obtained in the percentage of problems solved correctly; the mean improvement was a bare 3 percent. Indeed, the only apparent influence of a one-semester logic course was a small (10 percent) decrease in the tendency to make the error corresponding to Affirming the Consequent (that is, selecting the q alternative).

Training Based on a Pragmatic Schema   The ineffectiveness of abstract instruction in formal logic supports our contention that formal syntactic rules are not the vehicle for everyday reasoning. If this role is in fact played by pragmatic reasoning schemas, it should be possible to develop an effective training method that focuses on the elaboration of preexisting schemas. To test this possibility, Cheng and colleagues

(1986) performed a further experiment in which one group of college students was given training about *obligations*. Obligations are a type of regulation closely related to permissions. As the instructions pointed out, "Obligations can often be stated in an 'If . . . then' form. For example, the following regulation specifies an obligation: 'If a student is a psychology major, then the student must take an introductory psychology course.' More generally, if we call the initial situation *I* and the action *C*, an obligation has the form 'If *I* arises, then *C* must be done'."

The obligation instructions went on to describe four rules related to the fulfillment of obligations. The rule for checking *p*, for example, was explained to subjects as follows: "If *I* occurs, then it is obligatory to do *C*. Clearly, if *I* arises, then failure to take the required action would constitute a violation of the obligation. To use our example, if a student is a psychology major, then that student must take an introductory psychology course." The four rules discussed were directly related to the rules governing the formal conditional: rule 1 is analogous to *modus ponens*, rule 2 rejects Denying the Antecedent, rule 3 rejects Affirming the Consequent, and rule 4 is analogous to *modus tollens*. The instructions were of a highly procedural nature, focusing on the conditions under which an obligation may or may not be violated. Except for the use of the single example about the psychology major, obligations were described only in abstract terms. No examples of selection problems were provided (unlike the "examples" conditions of the training study described earlier).

Other subjects were given training on the same checking procedures that obligation schema subjects were. They were shown how to reason about "contingencies" using precisely the same example about psychology majors. The training never made mention, however, of the notion of situations in which obligation arises, or indeed of any semantic interpretation at all.

Subjects who received instruction, as well as control subjects, were given a series of selection problems. Some of the problems contained conditional rules that could readily be interpreted as obligations, whereas others were relatively arbitrary.

The results are presented in table 2.2. It may be seen that, as usual, untrained control subjects solved more schema-interpretable problems than arbitrary problems. Even though both training packages presented the same formal checking procedures, the schema-based obligation training was more effective than the syntactic contingency training. Indeed, the nonsignificant trend was for the obligation training to be more effective even for the arbitrary problems. It is important to note that the syntactic contingency training had no effect at all on subjects' solutions to the semantically meaningful problems. This bolsters our view that pragmatic reasoning schemas are dominant wherever a semantic interpretation can be applied. Even when subjects have just

Holland, Holyoak, Nisbett, and Thagard

Table 2.2 Percent correct as a function of problem type and training condition (after Cheng et al. 1986)

Problem type	Training condition			$\overline{X}$
	Control	Contingency	Obligation	
Arbitrary	27	45	55	42
Obligation	64	66	92	74
$\overline{X}$	46	55	73	

been shown the exact checking procedures to be applied, they do not use them for the semantically meaningful problems. In our view, this is because a semantic interpretation will always lead to a search for reasoning schemas rather than for syntactic rules.

It should be noted that the obligation instruction used in this experiment forms an important contrast to the teaching of new empirical rules for physics and social psychology. Whereas instruction in the latter case competes with rules the student already possesses, instruction in pragmatic reasoning schemas builds upon and supports prior knowledge. In our view, instruction in purely syntactic rule systems lies between the two extremes in that it neither competes with nor builds upon preexisting knowledge. On the other hand, because it is an alien type of rule system for understanding actual events in the world, it also will not add to the individual's effective repertoire of pragmatic rules.

Induction, Deduction, and Default Hierarchies

The results just reviewed provide support for the view that people typically reason using knowledge structures at a level intermediate between the extreme localism implied by the domain-specificity view and the ultra-generality implied by the formal view. Subjects reasoned in closer accord with standard logic when thinking about problems intended to evoke regulation schemas (permissions and obligations) than when thinking about purely arbitrary elements and relations. These results on problem types are incompatible with the domain-specificity view because experience with the precise rules referred to in the regulation problems was not necessary for successful performance. The results are incompatible with the formal view because all problem types were stated in syntactically equivalent forms. The results from the training studies are also incompatible with the formal view. An entire course in standard logic had no effect on the avoidance of error (save for a slight reduction in the fallacy of Affirming the Consequent). A brief training session, of a type shown to produce substantial effects on people's ability to reason in accord with the law of large numbers (Fong et al. 1986), had no significant effect on subjects' ability to use *modus ponens* or *modus tollens* or to avoid the error of Affirming the

Consequent or Denying the Antecedent. This was not simply because the training was inherently useless: when it was combined with examples training, subjects were able to make substantial use of the abstract training.

The near-total ineffectiveness of purely abstract training in logic contrasts starkly with the ready ease with which people seem able to apply a naturally acquired pragmatic reasoning schema. For example, after one semester's training in standard logic, students solved only 11 percent of the arbitrary problems correctly, whereas the same students solved 62 percent of the permission problems correctly before receiving any formal training. The generality of the benefit apparently conveyed by evocation of a permission schema is also striking. The permission problems yielded significantly fewer errors of all types, including not only the common error of failing to select *not-q* (equivalent to *modus tollens*) but also the much less frequent error of failing to select *p* (equivalent to *modus ponens*).

In contrast to the benefit conveyed by the evocation of a permission schema, a course in logic produced no significant reduction in either of these errors. The failure to reduce the frequency of errors for *modus ponens* cannot be attributed to a floor effect, since evocation of the permission schema did reduce the frequency of errors for the *p* alternative. This failure of abstract training to facilitate the use of *modus ponens* suggests that even this rule may not be a general rule of logic for at least a substantial fraction of subjects. Evidence that *modus ponens* can be overridden by a matching strategy (Manktelow and Evans 1979; Reich and Ruth 1982) also supports this hypothesis. If *modus ponens* is not a robust rule of natural logic, as our results suggest, it is difficult to imagine any formal deductive rule that is universally held and widely used for the solution of problems with meaningful content.

The primacy of pragmatic reasoning schemas received further support from the final training study performed by Cheng and colleagues (1986), which demonstrated that brief instruction about the pragmatics of obligations greatly improved performance both on selection problems involving clear obligations and on problems involving relatively arbitrary rules. Instructional methods based on appropriate preexisting pragmatic knowledge appear to be far more effective than those based directly on syntactic rules.

A Default Hierarchy of Deductive Rules
The results we have reviewed speak strongly for the existence of pragmatic schemas at an intermediate level of abstraction, since the findings are inexplicable according to either the domain-specificity view or the formal view. Nonetheless, the findings need not be interpreted as evidence against the very possibility of the two extreme modes of reasoning. It is conceivable that these three modes coexist within a population

Holland, Holyoak, Nisbett, and Thagard

and even within an individual. In fact, the results are consistent with this interpretation.

First, as in other reasoning studies, most of the subjects' inferences were in accordance with *modus ponens*, whereas very few were in accordance with *modus tollens*. Although *modus ponens* may not be universal, the results do not exclude the possibility that many people may in fact reason with this formal rule—or even that all people may use it under particularly favorable circumstances. The same individuals who use *ponens* as a formal rule may use a rule corresponding to *tollens* only within the context of certain intermediate-level schemas.

Second, familiarity with a rule may in itself sometimes facilitate performance, as suggested by the marginal difference in selection performance between the two permission problems used in the first experiment by Cheng and colleagues (1986). The presumably more familiar drinking-age rule yielded slightly better performance than did the cholera-inoculation rule. Familiarity may facilitate indirectly by evoking an appropriate schema more reliably, or it may do so more directly by providing relevant specific knowledge, as hypothesized by proponents of the domain-specificity view.

If multiple levels of concepts relevant to reasoning coexist, within a population as well as within an individual, how are the levels related to each other and what determines the level of abstraction attained? Our pragmatic approach to induction suggests a possible answer. As we have emphasized [in this book], the process of induction from experience across many different domains results in a default hierarchy of rules. Rules are used to make predictions about regularities in environmental inputs to the cognitive system. Successive levels in the default hierarchy are related in that the more abstract level comprises a set of default categories and rules, relative to which the more specific level comprises a set of exception categories and rules. The default rules are generally predictive and are consequently followed in most circumstances, except when they are overridden by more specific exception rules.

Basic inductive processes, such as generalization and specialization, are applied to environmental inputs to produce a default hierarchy that has predictive utility in achieving the learner's problem-directed goals. If induction proceeds in a bottom-up, experience-driven manner, then successively more abstract concepts and associated rule schemas will be formed by generalization on the basis of constancies observed in inputs. Increasingly abstract default levels will emerge as long as concepts capturing significant regularities with predictive utility can be formed.

Let us consider how induction might proceed in the domains relevant to conditional logic. At the most specific level, experience with particular contingencies between events (such as the relationship between touching a stove and feeling pain, or between a request for assistance and help from a parent) will accrue to the learner. The concepts and rules induced in the process of dealing with specific contingency situations will be of the kind assumed by the domain-specificity hypothesis. At this point the person will be able to reason effectively in familiar situations and in those highly similar to them, but not elsewhere.

As experience with a range of contingency situations accrues, people will, through the operation of generalization mechanisms, induce a more abstract set of default concepts and rules. Many important subtypes of contingency situations will emerge, involving such concepts as causation, regulation, and set inclusion. This is a level at which pragmatic reasoning schemas emerge. Each schema will consist of a cluster of rules for dealing with a particular type of contingency situation. Because the concepts at this level are quite abstract, rules for dealing with situation types as general as "deterministic causation," for example, will be applicable to novel situations with little superficial resemblance to those from which the concepts were originally induced.

Kelley's (1972, 1973) *causal schemas*, it should be noted, are excellent examples of the kind of constructs we wish to include under the rubric of pragmatic reasoning schemas. Kelley proposed that people have very general rules for dealing with causality that are attached to particular kinds of causal relationships. People have, for example, a schema for reasoning about relationships that they take to involve a single determining cause, that is, those in which only a single cause can produce the effect and if present it invariably does so. They also have a schema for reasoning about multiple-cause, probabilistic relationships, namely, those in which many factors can produce the effect but the presence of any one of the factors does not entail certainty that the effect will occur. These causal schemas exist at a purely abstract level, independent of any content domain.

Eventually, constancies across various types of reasoning schemas may, through the same inductive mechanisms, produce yet more abstract concepts and rules at the level of a natural formal logic. The results we have reviewed suggest that this level of abstraction in conditional reasoning is seldom attained; and at any rate, rules at that level are probably only rarely applied to semantically meaningful material.

Why Formal Deductive Rules Are Difficult to Induce
In view of our negative conclusion regarding the prevalence of a natural logic based on syntactic rules, an obvious question arises: Why are such rules so difficult to induce? Or at least, why are they seldom used for reasoning about real events? Logicians through the centuries have assumed the existence, and the everyday use, of a natural repertoire of purely abstract logical rules, as have psychologists such as Piaget. We contend that although Piaget was right in believing that people develop and heavily use a schema corresponding to the inductive rule system

embodied in the law of large numbers, he was wrong in believing that they make much use of formal operations of deductive logic.

The reason for the difficulty in inducing rules for deductive logic appears to be that too few reliable, useful constancies in deductive rules hold at such abstract levels. In particular, the material conditional—the abstract formal conditional taught in elementary logic courses—has limited pragmatic value. The various pragmatic reasoning schemas differ from each other in many important ways. For example, in a causal statement of the form "If *cause,* then *effect,*" the cause temporally precedes the effect. In the corresponding form of a permission statement, "If *action,* then *permission required,*" the action typically *follows* the necessary permission. The individuating aspects of pragmatic reasoning schemas are far more important to successful problem solving than their commonalities. In order for the conditional to be employed in assessing causal claims, for example, extensive interpretation of problems in terms of causal direction, number of possible causes, certainty of effects given causes, and so on, is required. For most lay purposes the formal conditional therefore may not be an economical default rule.

Of the various syntactic rules associated with the formal conditional, virtually none have general utility. The formally valid contrapositive transformation cannot by itself solve many pragmatic problems that are expressible in its terms, because substantial interpretation concerning causality and other matters is required before it can be applied. Moreover, the "fallacies" of Denying the Antecedent and Affirming the Consequent often lead to pragmatically useful inferences in many contexts (Fillenbaum 1975, 1976; Geis and Zwicky 1971). For example, abduction of a hypothesis A to explain B using the rule "If A then B" is formally equivalent to the deductive fallacy of Affirming the Consequent but can be an inductively important form of inference.

Not only is contraposition lacking in positive utility, in some important cases it actually fails. Lewis (1973) points out that contraposition fails for counterfactual conditionals, in which the antecedent is known to be false. For example, it may be true that if the power hadn't failed, dinner would have been on time; but it does not follow that if dinner had not been on time, then the power would have failed (Ginsberg 1985). Our ability to determine the truth of counterfactual conditionals depends on special knowledge about causality in the world, of the sort that pragmatic reasoning schemas can encapsulate. It thus seems that only *modus ponens* constitutes a plausibly pragmatic abstract rule of inference, although the results of Cheng and colleagues (1986) suggest that even *modus ponens* may not be available as a fully abstract rule for purposes of everyday reasoning. It may be that rather than inducing an isolated abstract rule, many people maintain a more specific rule analogous to *modus ponens* within each of a number of pragmatic reasoning schemas.

In contrast to people's apparent failure to induce some abstract deductive rules, we have seen evidence that they do induce some abstract *inductive* rules, such as simple versions of the law of large numbers. This difference has a ready explanation within the present framework. Unlike deductive rules such as *modus tollens,* the law of large numbers is an excellent default rule (or set of rules) that does not require extensive domain-specific interpretation in order to be made applicable. Given (codable) uncertainty, the rule system in its totality has potential relevance. Consequently, everyday learning conditions will be favorable to induction of the law of large numbers at the highest level of generality and abstraction.

We are led, then, to the surprising possibility that the mechanisms of induction may result in the induction of various abstract inductive rules, but not certain abstract deductive rules, for the good reason that many abstract inductive rules are more obviously useful than some of their deductive counterparts in formal logic.

References

Braine, M. D. S. (1978). On the relation between the natural logic of reasoning and standard logic. *Psychological Review* 85, 1–21.

Braine, M. D. S., B. J. Reiser, and B. Rumain (1984). Some empirical justification for a theory of natural propositional logic. In G. H. Bower, ed., *The psychology of learning and motivation,* vol. 18. New York: Academic Press.

Cheng, P. W., and K. J. Holyoak (1985). Pragmatic reasoning schemas. *Cognitive Psychology* 17, 391–416.

Cheng, P. W., K. J. Holyoak, R. E. Nisbett, and L. M. Oliver (1986). Pragmatic versus syntactic approaches to training deductive reasoning. *Cognitive Psychology* 18, 293–328.

D'Andrade, R. (1982). Reason versus logic: Paper presented at the Symposium on the Ecology of Cognition: Biological, Cultural, and Historical Perspectives, Greensboro, North Carolina.

Evans, J. St. B. T. (1982). *The psychology of deductive reasoning.* London: Routledge and Kegan Paul.

Fillenbaum, S. (1975). If: Some uses. *Psychological Research* 37, 245–260.

Fillenbaum, S. (1976). Inducements: On phrasing and logic of conditional promises, threats and warnings. *Psychological Research* 38, 231–250.

Fong, G. T., D. H. Krantz, and R. E. Nisbett (1986). The effects of statistical training on thinking about everyday problems. *Cognitive Psychology* 18, 253–292.

Geis, M. C., and A. M. Zwicky (1971). On invited inferences. *Linguistic Inquiry* 2, 561–566.

Ginsberg, M. L. (1985). Counterfactuals. In *Proceedings of the Ninth Joint Conference on Artificial Intelligence*. Los Altos, CA: Kaufmann.

Golding, E. (1981). The effect of past experiences on problem solving. Paper presented at the Annual Conference of the British Psychological Association, Surrey.

Griggs, R. A., and J. R. Cox (1982). The elusive thematic-materials effect in Wason's selection task. *British Journal of Psychology* 73, 407–420.

Henle, M. (1962). On the relation between logic and thinking. *Psychological Review* 69, 366–378.

Johnson-Laird, P. N. (1982). Ninth Bartlett memorial lecture. Thinking as a skill. *Quarterly Journal of Experimental Psychology* 34A, 1–29.

Johnson-Laird, P. N. (1983). *Mental models*. Cambridge, MA: Harvard University Press.

Johnson-Laird, P. N., P. Legrenzi, and M. Legrenzi (1972). Reasoning and a sense of reality. *British Journal of Psychology* 63, 395–400.

Kelley, H. H. (1972). Causal schemata and the attribution process. In E. E. Jones, D. E. Kanouse, H. H. Kelley, R. E. Nisbett, S. Valins, and B. Weiner, eds., *Attribution: Perceiving the causes of behavior*. Morristown, NJ: General Learning Press.

Kelley, H. H. (1973). The process of causal attribution. *American Psychologist* 28, 107–128.

Lewis, D. K. (1973). *Counterfactuals*. Oxford: Blackwell.

Manktelow, K. I., and J. St. B. T. Evans (1979). Facilitation of reasoning by realism: Effect or non-effect? *British Journal of Psychology* 70, 477–488.

Reich, S. S., and P. Ruth (1982). Wason's selection task: Verification, falsification and matching. *British Journal of Psychology* 73, 395–405.

Rips, L. J. (1983). Cognitive processes in propositional reasoning. *Psychological Review* 90, 38–71.

Wason, P. C. (1966). Reasoning. In B. M. Foss, ed., *New horizons in psychology*. Harmondsworth: Penguin.

3 Probabilistic Reasoning

Amos Tversky and Daniel Kahneman

Judgment under Uncertainty: Heuristics and Biases

Many decisions are based on beliefs concerning the likelihood of uncertain events such as the outcome of an election, the guilt of a defendant, or the future value of the dollar. These beliefs are usually expressed in statements such as "I think that . . .," "chances are . . .," "it is unlikely that . . .," and so forth. Occasionally, beliefs concerning uncertain events are expressed in numerical form as odds or subjective probabilities. What determines such beliefs? How do people assess the probability of an uncertain event or the value of an uncertain quantity? This article shows that people rely on a limited number of heuristic principles which reduce the complex tasks of assessing probabilities and predicting values to simpler judgmental operations. In general, these heuristics are quite useful, but sometimes they lead to severe and systematic errors.

The subjective assessment of probability resembles the subjective assessment of physical quantities such as distance or size. These judgments are all based on data of limited validity, which are processed according to heuristic rules. For example, the apparent distance of an object is determined in part by its clarity. The more sharply the object is seen, the closer it appears to be. This rule has some validity, because in any given scene the more distant objects are seen less sharply than nearer objects. However, the reliance on this rule leads to systematic errors in the estimation of distance. Specifically, distances are often overestimated when visibility is poor because the contours of objects are blurred. On the other hand, distances are often underestimated when visibility is good because the objects are seen sharply. Thus, the reliance on clarity as an indication of distance leads to common biases.

First half from A. Tversky and D. Kahneman, Judgment under uncertainty: Heuristics and biases, *Science* 185, 1124–1131 (1974). Copyright 1974 by the AAAS. Second half from A. Tversky and D. Kahneman, Extensional versus intuitive reasoning: The conjunction fallacy in probabilistic reasoning, *Psychological Review* 90, 293–315 (1983). Copyright 1983 by the American Psychological Association. Reprinted by permission.

Such biases are also found in the intuitive judgment of probability. This article describes three heuristics [one omitted here—Ed.] that are employed to assess probabilities and to predict values. Biases to which these heuristics lead are enumerated, and the applied and theoretical implications of these observations are discussed.

Representativeness

Many of the probabilistic questions with which people are concerned belong to one of the following types: What is the probability that object A belongs to class B? What is the probability that event A originates from process B? What is the probability that process B will generate event A? In answering such questions, people typically rely on the representativeness heuristic, in which probabilities are evaluated by the degree to which A is representative of B, that is, by the degree to which A resembles B. For example, when A is highly representative of B, the probability that A originates from B is judged to be high. On the other hand, if A is not similar to B, the probability that A originates from B is judged to be low.

For an illustration of judgment by representativeness, consider an individual who has been described by a former neighbor as follows: "Steve is very shy and withdrawn, invariably helpful, but with little interest in people, or in the world of reality. A meek and tidy soul, he has a need for order and structure, and a passion for detail." How do people assess the probability that Steve is engaged in a particular occupation from a list of possibilities (for example, farmer, salesman, airline pilot, librarian, or physician)? How do people order these occupations from most to least likely? In the representativeness heuristic, the probability that Steve is a librarian, for example, is assessed by the degree to which he is representative of, or similar to, the stereotype of a librarian. Indeed, research with problems of this type has shown that people order the occupations by probability and by similarity in exactly the same way (Kahneman and Tversky, 1973). This approach to the judgment of probability leads to serious errors, because similarity, or representativeness, is not influenced by several factors that should affect judgments of probability.

Insensitivity to Prior Probability of Outcomes   One of the factors that have no effect on representativeness but should have a major effect on probability is the prior probability, or base-rate frequency, of the outcomes. In the case of Steve, for example, the fact that there are many more farmers than librarians in the population should enter into any reasonable estimate of the probability that Steve is a librarian rather than a farmer. Considerations of base-rate frequency, however, do not affect the similarity of Steve to the stereotypes of librarians and farmers. If people evaluate probability by representativeness, therefore, prior probabilities will be neglected. This hypothesis was tested in an experiment where prior probabilities were manipulated (Kahneman and Tversky, 1973). Subjects were shown brief personality descriptions of several individuals, allegedly sampled at random from a group of 100 professionals—engineers and lawyers. The subjects were asked to assess, for each description, the probability that it belonged to an engineer rather than to a lawyer. In one experimental condition, subjects were told that the group from which the descriptions had been drawn consisted of 70 engineers and 30 lawyers. In another condition, subjects were told that the group consisted of 30 engineers and 70 lawyers. The odds that any particular description belongs to an engineer rather than to a lawyer should be higher in the first condition, where there is a majority of engineers, than in the second condition, where there is a majority of lawyers. Specifically, it can be shown by applying Bayes' rule that the ratio of these odds should be $(.7/.3)^2$, or 5.44, for each description. In a sharp violation of Bayes' rule, the subjects in the two conditions produced essentially the same probability judgments. Apparently, subjects evaluated the likelihood that a particular description belonged to an engineer rather than to a lawyer by the degree to which this description was representative of the two stereotypes, with little or no regard for the prior probabilities of the categories.

The subjects used prior probabilities correctly when they had no other information. In the absence of a personality sketch, they judged the probability that an unknown individual is an engineer to be .7 and .3, respectively, in the two base-rate conditions. However, prior probabilities were effectively ignored when a description was introduced, even when this description was totally uninformative. The responses to the following description illustrate this phenomenon:

Dick is a 30 year old man. He is married with no children. A man of high ability and high motivation, he promises to be quite successful in his field. He is well liked by his colleagues.

This description was intended to convey no information relevant to the question of whether Dick is an engineer or a lawyer. Consequently, the probability that Dick is an engineer should equal the proportion of engineers in the group, as if no description had been given. The subjects, however, judged the probability of Dick being an engineer to be .5 regardless of whether the stated proportion of engineers in the group was .7 or .3. Evidently, people respond differently when given no evidence and when given worthless evidence. When no specific evidence is given, prior probabilities are properly utilized; when worthless evidence is given, prior probabilities are ignored (Kahneman and Tversky 1973).

Insensitivity to Sample Size   To evaluate the probability of obtaining a particular result in a sample drawn from a specified population, people typically apply the representativeness heuristic. That is, they assess the likelihood of a sample result, for example, that the average height in a random sample of ten men will be 6 feet (180 centimeters), by the similarity of this result to the corresponding parameter (that is, to the average height in the population of men). The similarity of a sample statistic to a population parameter does not depend on the size of the sample. Consequently, if probabilities are assessed by representativeness, then the judged probability of a sample statistic will be essentially independent of sample size. Indeed, when subjects assessed the distributions of average height for samples of various sizes, they produced identical distributions. For example, the probability of obtaining an average height greater than 6 feet was assigned the same value for samples of 1000, 100, and 10 men (Kahneman and Tversky 1972). Moreover, subjects failed to appreciate the role of sample size even when it was emphasized in the formulation of the problem. Consider the following question:

A certain town is served by two hospitals. In the larger hospital about 45 babies are born each day, and in the smaller hospital about 15 babies are born each day. As you know, about 50 percent of all babies are boys. However, the exact percentage varies from day to day. Sometimes it may be higher than 50 percent, sometimes lower.

For a period of 1 year, each hospital recorded the days on which more than 60 percent of the babies born were boys. Which hospital do you think recorded more such days?

The larger hospital (21)
The smaller hospital (21)
About the same (that is, within 5 percent of each other) (53)

The values in parentheses are the number of undergraduate students who chose each answer.

Most subjects judged the probability of obtaining more than 60 percent boys to be the same in the small and in the large hospital, presumably because these events are described by the same statistic and are therefore equally representative of the general population. In contrast, sampling theory entails that the expected number of days on which more than 60 percent of the babies are boys is much greater in the small hospital than in the large one, because a large sample is less likely to stray from 50 percent. This fundamental notion of statistics is evidently not part of people's repertoire of intuitions.

A similar insensitivity to sample size has been reported in judgments of posterior probability, that is, of the probability that a sample has been drawn from one population rather than from another. Consider the following example:

Imagine an urn filled with balls, of which ⅔ are of one color and ⅓ of another. One individual has drawn 5 balls from the urn, and found that 4 were red and 1 was white. Another individual has drawn 20 balls and found that 12 were red and 8 were white. Which of the two individuals should feel more confident that the urn contains ⅔ red balls and ⅓ white balls, rather than the opposite? What odds should each individual give?

In this problem, the correct posterior odds are 8 to 1 for the 4:1 sample and 16 to 1 for the 12:8 sample, assuming equal prior probabilities. However, most people feel that the first sample provides much stronger evidence for the hypothesis that the urn is predominantly red, because the proportion of red balls is larger in the first than in the second sample. Here again, intuitive judgments are dominated by the sample proportion and are essentially unaffected by the size of the sample, which plays a crucial role in the determination of the actual posterior odds (Kahneman and Tversky, 1972). In addition, intuitive estimates of posterior odds are far less extreme than the correct values. The underestimation of the impact of evidence has been observed repeatedly in problems of this type (W. Edwards, 1968; Slovic and Lichtenstein 1971). It has been labeled "conservatism."

Misconceptions of Chance People expect that a sequence of events generated by a random process will represent the essential characteristics of that process even when the sequence is short. In considering tosses of a coin for heads or tails, for example, people regard the sequence H-T-H-T-T-H to be more likely than the sequence H-H-H-T-T-T, which does not appear random, and also more likely than the sequence H-H-H-H-T-H, which does not represent the fairness of the coin (Kahneman and Tversky, 1972). Thus, people expect that the essential characteristics of the process will be represented, not only globally in the entire sequence, but also locally in each of its parts. A locally representative sequence, however, deviates systematically from chance expectation: it contains too many alternations and too few runs. Another consequence of the belief in local representativeness is the well-known gambler's fallacy. After observing a long run of red on the roulette wheel, for example, most people erroneously believe that black is now due, presumably because the occurence of black will result in a more representative sequence than the occurrence of an additional red. Chance is commonly viewed as a self-correcting process in which a deviation in one direction induces a deviation in the opposite direction to restore the equilibrium. In fact, deviations are not "corrected" as a chance process unfolds, they are merely diluted.

Misconceptions of chance are not limited to naive subjects. A study of the statistical intuitions of experienced research psychologists (Tversky and Kahneman 1971) revealed a lingering belief in what may be called the "law of small numbers," according to which even small samples are highly representative of the populations from which they are drawn. The responses of these investigators reflected the expectation that a valid hypothesis about a population will be represented by a statistically significant result in a sample—with little regard for its size. As a consequence, the researchers put too much faith in the results of small samples and grossly overestimated the replicability of such results. In the actual conduct of research, this bias leads to the selection of samples of inadequate size and to overinterpretation of findings.

Insensitivity to Predictability   People are sometimes called upon to make such numerical predictions as the future value of a stock, the demand for a commodity, or the outcome of a football game. Such predictions are often made by representativeness. For example, suppose one is given a description of a company and is asked to predict its future profit. If the description of the company is very favorable, a very high profit will appear most representative of that description; if the description is mediocre, a mediocre performance will appear most representative. The degree to which the description is favorable is unaffected by the reliability of that description or by the degree to which it permits accurate prediction. Hence, if people predict solely in terms of the favorableness of the description, their predictions will be insensitive to the reliability of the evidence and to the expected accuracy of the prediction.

This mode of judgment violates the normative statistical theory in which the extremeness and the range of predictions are controlled by considerations of predictability. When predictability is nil, the same prediction should be made in all cases. For example, if the descriptions of companies provide no information relevant to profit, then the same value (such as average profit) should be predicted for all companies. If predictability is perfect, of course, the values predicted will match the actual values and the range of predictions will equal the range of outcomes. In general, the higher the predictability, the wider the range of predicted values.

Several studies of numerical prediction have demonstrated that intuitive predictions violate this rule, and that subjects show little or no regard for considerations of predictability (Kahneman and Tversky 1973). In one of these studies, subjects were presented with several paragraphs, each describing the performance of a student teacher during a particular practice lesson. Some subjects were asked to *evaluate* the quality of the lesson described in the paragraph in percentile scores, relative to a specified population. Other subjects were asked to *predict*, also in percentile scores, the standing of each student teacher 5 years after the practice lesson. The judgments made under the two conditions were identical. That is, the prediction of a remote criterion (success of a teacher after 5 years) was identical to the evaluation of the information on which the prediction was based (the quality of the practice lesson). The students who made these predictions were undoubtedly aware of the limited predictability of teaching competence on the basis of a single trial lesson 5 years earlier; nevertheless, their predictions were as extreme as their evaluations.

The Illusion of Validity   As we have seen, people often predict by selecting the outcome (for example, an occupation) that is most representative of the input (for example, the description of a person). The confidence they have in their prediction depends primarily on the degree of representativeness (that is, on the quality of the match between the selected outcome and the input) with little or no regard for the factors that limit predictive accuracy. Thus, people express great confidence in the prediction that a person is a librarian when given a description of his personality which matches the stereotype of librarians, even if the description is scanty, unreliable, or outdated. The unwarranted confidence which is produced by a good fit between the predicted outcome and the input information may be called the illusion of validity. This illusion persists even when the judge is aware of the factors that limit the accuracy of his predictions. It is a common observation that psychologists who conduct selection interviews often experience considerable confidence in their predictions, even when they know of the vast literature that shows selection interviews to be highly fallible. The continued reliance on the clinical interview for selection, despite repeated demonstrations of its inadequacy, amply attests to the strength of this effect.

The internal consistency of a pattern of inputs is a major determinant of one's confidence in predictions based on these inputs. For example, people express more confidence in predicting the final grade-point average of a student whose first-year record consists entirely of B's than in predicting the grade-point average of a student whose first-year record includes many A's and C's. Highly consistent patterns are most often observed when the input variables are highly redundant or correlated. Hence, people tend to have great confidence in predictions based on redundant input variables. However, an elementary result in the statistics of correlation asserts that, given input variables of stated validity, a prediction based on several such inputs can achieve higher accuracy when they are independent of each other than when they are redundant or correlated. Thus, redundancy among inputs decreases accuracy even as it increases confidence, and people are often confident in predictions that are quite likely to be off the mark (Kahneman and Tversky 1973).

Misconceptions of Regression   Suppose a large group of children has been examined on two equivalent versions of an aptitude test. If one selects ten children from among those who did best on one of the two versions, he will usually find their performance on the second version to be somewhat disappointing. Conversely, if one selects ten children from among those who did worst on one version, they will be found, on the average, to do somewhat better on the other version. More generally, consider two variables X and Y which have the same distribution. If one selects individuals whose average X score deviates from the mean of X by k units, then the average of their Y scores will usually deviate from the means of Y by less than k units. These observations illustrate a general phenomenon known as regression toward the mean, which was first documented by Galton more than 100 years ago.

In the normal course of life, one encounters many instances of regression toward the mean, in the comparison of the height of fathers and sons, of the intelligence of husbands and wives, or of the performance of individuals on consecutive examinations. Nevertheless, people do not develop correct intuitions about this phenomenon. First, they do not expect regression in many contexts where it is bound to occur. Second, when they recognize the occurrence of regression, they often invent spurious causal explanations for it (Kahneman and Tversky 1973). We suggest that the phenomenon of regression remains elusive because it is incompatible with the belief that the predicted outcome should be maximally representative of the input, and hence, that the value of the outcome variable should be as extreme as the value of the input variable.

The failure to recognize the import of regression can have pernicious consequences, as illustrated by the following observation (Kahneman and Tversky 1973). In a discussion of flight training, experienced instructors noted that praise for an exceptionally smooth landing is typically followed by a poorer landing on the next try, while harsh criticism after a rough landing is usually followed by an improvement on the next try. The instructors concluded that verbal rewards are detrimental to learning, while verbal punishments are beneficial, contrary to accepted psychological doctrine. This conclusion is unwarranted because of the presence of regression toward the mean. As in other cases of repeated examination, an improvement will usually follow a poor performance and a deterioration will usually follow an outstanding performance, even if the instructor does not respond to the trainee's achievement on the first attempt. Because the instructors had praised their trainees after good landings and admonished them after poor ones, they reached the erroneous and potentially harmful conclusion that punishment is more effective than reward.

Thus, the failure to understand the effect of regression leads one to overestimate the effectiveness of punishment and to underestimate the effectiveness of reward. In social interaction, as well as in training, rewards are typically administered when performance is good, and punishments are typically administered when performance is poor. By regression alone, therefore, behavior is most likely to improve after punishment and most likely to deteriorate after reward. Consequently, the human condition is such that, by chance alone, one is most often rewarded for punishing others and most often punished for rewarding them. People are generally not aware of this contingency. In fact, the elusive role of regression in determining the apparent consequences of reward and punishment seems to have escaped the notice of students of this area.

Availability

There are situations in which people assess the frequency of a class or the probability of an event by the ease with which instances or occurrences can be brought to mind. For example, one may assess the risk of heart attack among middle-aged people by recalling such occurrences among one's acquaintances. Similarly, one may evaluate the probability that a given business venture will fail by imagining various difficulties it could encounter. This judgmental heuristic is called availability. Availability is a useful clue for assessing frequency or probability, because instances of large classes are usually reached better and faster than instances of less frequent classes. However, availability is affected by factors other than frequency and probability. Consequently, the reliance on availability leads to predictable biases, some of which are illustrated below.

Biases Due to the Retrievability of Instances   When the size of a class is judged by the availability of its instances, a class whose instances are easily retrieved will appear more numerous than a class of equal frequency whose instances are less retrievable. In an elementary demonstration of this effect, subjects heard a list of well-known personalities of both sexes and were subsequently asked to judge whether the list contained more names of men than of women. Different lists were presented to different groups of subjects. In some of the lists the men were relatively more famous than the women, and in others the women were relatively more famous than the men. In each of the lists, the subjects erroneously judged that the class (sex) that had the more famous personalities was the more numerous (Tversky and Kahneman 1973).

In addition to familiarity, there are other factors, such as salience, which affect the retrievability of instances. For example, the impact of seeing a house burning on the subjective probability of such accidents is probably greater than the impact of reading about a fire in the local paper. Furthermore, recent occurrences are likely to be relatively more available than earlier occurrences. It is a common experience that the subjective probability of traffic accidents rises temporarily when one sees a car overturned by the side of the road.

Biases Due to the Effectiveness of a Search Set   Suppose one samples a word (of three letters or more) at random from an English text. Is it more likely that the word starts with r or that r is the third letter? People approach this problem by recalling words that begin with r (road) and words that have r in the third position (car) and assess the relative frequency by the ease with which words of the two types come to mind. Because it is much easier to search for words by their first letter than by their third letter, most people judge words that begin with a given consonant to be more numerous than words in which the same consonant appears in the third position. They do so even for consonants, such as *r* or *k*, that are more frequent in the third position than in the first (Tversky and Kahneman 1973).

Different tasks elicit different search sets. For example, suppose you are asked to rate the frequency with which abstract words *(thought, love)* and concrete words *(door, water)* appear in written English. A natural way to answer this question is to search for contexts in which the word could appear. It seems easier to think of contexts in which an abstract concept is mentioned *(love* in love stories) than to think of contexts in which a concrete word (such as *door*) is mentioned. If the frequency of words is judged by the availability of the contexts in which they appear, abstract words will be judged as relatively more numerous than concrete words. This bias has been observed in a recent study (Galbraith and Underwood 1973) which showed that the judged frequency of occurrence of abstract words was much higher than that of concrete words, equated in objective frequency. Abstract words were also judged to appear in a much greater variety of contexts than concrete words.

Biases of Imaginability   Sometimes one has to assess the frequency of a class whose instances are not stored in memory but can be generated according to a given rule. In such situations, one typically generates several instances and evaluates frequency or probability by the ease with which the relevant instances can be constructed. However, the ease of constructing instances does not always reflect their actual frequency, and this mode of evaluation is prone to biases. To illustrate, consider a group of 10 people who form committees of k members, $2 \leq k \leq 8$. How many different committees of k members can be formed? The correct answer to this problem is given by the binomial coefficient $\binom{10}{k}$ which reaches a maximum of 252 for $k = 5$. Clearly, the number of committees of k members equals the number of committees of $(10 - k)$ members, because any committee of k members defines a unique group of $(10 - k)$ nonmembers.

One way to answer this question without computation is to mentally construct committees of k members and to evaluate their number by the ease with which they come to mind. Committees of few members, say 2, are more available than committees of many members, say 8. The simplest scheme for the construction of committees is a partition of the group into disjoint sets. One readily sees that it is easy to construct five disjoint committees of 2 members, while it is impossible to generate even two disjoint committees of 8 members. Consequently, if frequency is assessed by imaginability, or by availability for construction, the small committees will appear more numerous than larger committees, in contrast to the correct bell-shaped function. Indeed, when naive subjects were asked to estimate the number of distinct committees of various sizes, their estimates were a decreasing monotonic function of committee size (Tversky and Kahneman 1973). For example, the median estimate of the number of committees of 2 members was 70, while the estimate for committees of 8 members was 20 (the correct answer is 45 in both cases).

Imaginability plays an important role in the evaluation of probabilities in real-life situations. The risk involved in an adventurous expedition, for example, is evaluated by imaging contingencies with which the expedition is not equipped to cope. If many such difficulties are vividly portrayed, the expedition can be made to appear exceedingly dangerous, although the ease with which disasters are imagined need not reflect their actual likelihood. Conversely, the risk involved in an undertaking may be grossly underestimated if some possible dangers are either difficult to conceive of, or simply do not come to mind.

Illusory Correlation   Chapman and Chapman (1969) have described an interesting bias in the judgment of the frequency with which two events co-occur. They presented naive judges with information concerning several hypothetical mental patients. The data for each patient consisted of a clinical diagnosis and a drawing of a person made by the patient. Later the judges estimated the frequency with which each diagnosis (such as paranoia or suspiciousness) had been accompanied by various features of the drawing (such as peculiar eyes). The subjects markedly overestimated the frequency of co-occurrence of natural associates, such as suspiciousness and peculiar eyes. This effect was labeled illusory correlation. In their erroneous judgments of the data to which they had been exposed, naive subjects "rediscovered" much of the common, but unfounded, clinical lore concerning the interpretation of the draw-a-person test. The illusory correlation effect was extremely resistant to contradictory data. It persisted even when the correlation between symptom and diagnosis was actually negative, and it prevented the judges from detecting relationships that were in fact present.

Availability provides a natural account for the illusory-correlation effect. The judgment of how frequently two events co-occur could be based on the strength of the associative bond between them. When the association is strong, one is likely to conclude that the events have been frequently paired. Consequently, strong associates will be judged to have occurred together frequently. According to this view, the illusory correlation between suspiciousness and peculiar drawing of the eyes, for example, is due to the fact that suspiciousness is more readily associated with the eyes than with any other part of the body.

Lifelong experience has taught us that, in general, instances of large classes are recalled better and faster than instances of less frequent classes; that likely occurrences are easier to imagine than unlikely ones;

and that the associative connections between events are strengthened when the events frequently co-occur. As a result, man has at his disposal a procedure (the availability heuristic) for estimating the numerosity of a class, the likelihood of an event, or the frequency of co-occurrences, by the ease with which the relevant mental operations of retrieval, construction, or association can be performed. However, as the preceding examples have demonstrated, this valuable estimation procedure results in systematic errors. . . .

The Conjunction Fallacy in Probabilistic Reasoning

. . . The laws of probability derive from extensional considerations. A probability measure is defined on a family of events and each event is construed as a set of possibilities, such as the three ways of getting a 10 on a throw of a pair of dice. The probability of an event equals the sum of the probabilities of its disjoint outcomes. Probability theory has traditionally been used to analyze repetitive chance processes, but the theory has also been applied to essentially unique events where probability is not reducible to the relative frequency of "favorable" outcomes. The probability that the man who sits next to you on the plane is unmarried equals the probability that he is a bachelor plus the probability that he is either divorced or widowed. Additivity applies even when probability does not have a frequentistic interpretation and when the elementary events are not equiprobable.

The simplest and most fundamental qualitative law of probability is the extension rule: If the extension of A includes the extension of B (*i.e.*, $A \supset B$) then $P(A) \geq P(B)$. Because the set of possibilities associated with a conjunction $A\&B$ is included in the set of possibilities associated with B, the same principle can also be expressed by the conjunction rule $P(A\&B) \leq P(B)$: A conjunction cannot be more probable than one of its constituents. This rule holds regardless of whether A and B are independent and is valid for any probability assignment on the same sample space. Furthermore, it applies not only to the standard probability calculus but also to nonstandard models such as upper and lower probability (Dempster 1967; Suppes 1975), belief function (Shafer 1976), Baconian probability (Cohen 1977), rational belief (Kyburg 1983), and possibility theory (Zadeh 1978).

In contrast to formal theories of belief, intuitive judgments of probability are generally not extensional. People do not normally analyze daily events into exhaustive lists of possibilities or evaluate compound probabilities by aggregating elementary ones. Instead, they commonly use a limited number of heuristics, such as representativeness and availability (Kahneman et al. 1982). Our conception of judgmental heuristics is based on *natural assessments* that are routinely carried out as part of the perception of events and the comprehension of messages. Such natural assessments include computations of similarity and representativeness, attributions of causality, and evaluations of the availability of associations and exemplars. These assessments, we propose, are performed even in the absence of a specific task set, although their results are used to meet task demands as they arise. For example, the mere mention of "horror movies" activates instances of horror movies and evokes an assessment of their availability. Similarly, the statement that Woody Allen's aunt had hoped that he would be a dentist elicits a comparison of the character to the stereotype and an assessment of representativeness. It is presumably the mismatch between Woody Allen's personality and our stereotype of a dentist that makes the thought mildly amusing. Although these assessments are not tied to the estimation of frequency or probability, they are likely to play a dominant role when such judgments are required. The availability of horror movies may be used to answer the question, "What proportion of the movies produced last year were horror movies?," and representativeness may control the judgment that a particular boy is more likely to be an actor than a dentist.

The term *judgmental heuristic* refers to a strategy—whether deliberate or not—that relies on a natural assessment to produce an estimation or a prediction. One of the manifestations of a heuristic is the relative neglect of other considerations. For example, the resemblance of a child to various professional stereotypes may be given too much weight in predicting future vocational choice, at the expense of other pertinent data such as the baserate frequencies of occupations. Hence, the use of judgmental heuristics gives rise to predictable biases. Natural assessments can affect judgments in other ways, for which the term *heuristic* is less apt. First, people sometimes misinterpret their task and fail to distinguish the required judgment from the natural assessment that the problem evokes. Second, the natural assessment may act as an anchor to which the required judgment is assimiliated, even when the judge does not intend to use the one to estimate the other.

Previous discussions of errors of judgment have focused on deliberate strategies and on misinterpretation of tasks. The present treatment calls special attention to the processes of anchoring and assimiliation, which are often neither deliberate nor conscious. An example from perception may be instructive: If two objects in a picture of a three-dimensional scene have the same picture size, the one that appears more distant is not only seen as "really" larger but also as larger in the picture. The natural computation of real size evidently influences the (less natural) judgment of picture size, although observers are unlikely to confuse the two values or to use the former to estimate the latter.

The natural assessments of representativeness and availability do not conform to the extensional logic of probability theory. In particular, a conjunction can be more representative than one of its constituents, and instances of a specific category can be easier to retrieve than instances of a more inclusive category. The following demonstration illustrates the point. When they were given 60 sec to list seven-letter words of a specified form, students at the University of British Columbia (UBC) produced many more words of the form _ _ _ _ i n g than of the form _ _ _ _ _ n _, although the latter class includes the former. The average numbers of words produced in the two conditions were 6.4 and 2.9, respectively, $t(44) = 4.70$, $p < .01$. In this test of availability, the increased efficacy of memory search suffices to offset the reduced extension of the target class.

Our treatment of the availability heuristic (Tversky and Kahneman 1973) suggests that the differential availability of *ing* words and of _ n _ words should be reflected in judgments of frequency. The following questions test this prediction.

In four pages of a novel (about 2,000 words), how many words would you expect to find that have the form _ _ _ _ i n g (seven-letter words that end with "ing")? Indicate your best estimate by circling one of the values below:

0   1–2   3–4   5–7   8–10   11–15   16+

A second version of the question requested estimates for words of the form _ _ _ _ _ n _. The median estimates were 13.4 for *ing* words ($n = 52$), and 4.7 for _ n _ words ($n = 53$, $p < .01$, by median test), contrary to the extension rule. Similar results were obtained for the comparison of words of the form _ _ _ _ _ l y with words of the form _ _ _ _ _ l _; the median estimates were 8.8 and 4.4, respectively.

This example illustrates the structure of the studies reported in this article. We constructed problems in which a reduction of extension was associated with an increase in availability or representativeness, and we tested the conjunction rule in judgments of frequency or probability. In the next section we discuss the representativeness heuristic and contrast it with the conjunction rule in the context of person perception. The third section describes conjunction fallacies in medical prognoses, sports forecasting, and choice among bets. In the fourth section we investigate probability judgments for conjunctions of causes and effects and describe conjunction errors in scenarios of future events. Manipulations that enable respondents to resist the conjunction fallacy are explored in the fifth section, and the implications of the results are discussed in the last section. [The third through fifth sections are omitted.—Ed.]

Representative Conjunctions

Modern research on categorization of objects and events (Mervis and Rosch 1981; Rosch 1978; Smith and Medin 1981) has shown that information is commonly stored and processed in relation to mental models, such as prototypes and schemata. It is therefore natural and economical for the probability of an event to be evaluated by the degree to which that event is representative of an appropriate mental model (Kahneman and Tversky 1972, 1973; Tversky and Kahneman, 1971, 1982). Because many of the results reported here are attributed to this heuristic, we first briefly analyze the concept of representativeness and illustrate its role in probability judgment.

Representativeness is an assessment of the degree of correspondence between a sample and a population, an instance and a category, an act and an actor or, more generally, between an outcome and a model. The model may refer to a person, a coin, or the world economy, and the respective outcomes could be marital status, a sequence of heads and tails, or the current price of gold. Representativeness can be investigated empirically by asking people, for example, which of two sequences of heads and tails is more representative of a fair coin or which of two professions is more representative of a given personality. This relation differs from other notions of proximity in that it is distinctly directional. It is natural to describe a sample as more or less representative of its parent population or a species (e.g., robin, penguin) as more or less representative of a superordinate category (e.g., bird). It is awkward to describe a population as representative of a sample or a category as representative of an instance.

When the model and the outcomes are described in the same terms, representativeness is reducible to similarity. Because a sample and a population, for example, can be described by the same attributes (e.g., central tendency and variability), the sample appears representative if its salient statistics match the corresponding parameters of the population. In the same manner, a person seems representative of a social group if his or her personality resembles the stereotypical member of that group. Representativeness, however, is not always reducible to similarity; it can also reflect causal and correlational beliefs (see, e.g., Chapman and Chapman 1967; Jennings et al. 1982; Nisbett and Ross 1980). A particular act (e.g., suicide) is representative of a person because we attribute to the actor a disposition to commit the act, not because the act resembles the person. Thus, an outcome is representative of a model if the salient features match or if the model has a propensity to produce the outcome.

Representativeness tends to covary with frequency: Common instances and frequent events are generally more representative than unusual instances and rare events. The representative summer day is warm and sunny, the representative American family has two children, and the representative height of an adult male is about 5 feet 10 inches. However, there are notable circumstances where representativeness is at variance with both actual and perceived frequency. First, a highly specific outcome can be representative but infrequent. Consider a numerical variable, such as weight, that has a unimodal frequency distribution in a given population. A narrow interval near the mode of the distribution is generally more representative of the population than a wider interval near the tail. For example, 68% of a group of Stanford University undergraduates ($N = 105$) stated that it is more representative for a female Stanford student "to weigh between 124 and 125 pounds" than "to weigh more than 135 pounds". On the other hand, 78% of a different group ($N = 102$) stated that among female Stanford students there are more "women who weigh more than 135 pounds" than "women who weigh between 124 and 125 pounds." Thus, the narrow modal interval (124–125 pounds) was judged to be more representative but less frequent than the broad tail interval (above 135 pounds).

Second, an attribute is representative of a class if it is very diagnostic, that is, if the relative frequency of this attribute is much higher in that class than in a relevant reference class. For example, 65% of the subjects ($N = 105$) stated that it is more representative for a Hollywood actress "to be divorced more than 4 times" than "to vote Democratic." Multiple divorce is diagnostic of Hollywood actresses because it is part of the stereotype that the incidence of divorce is higher among Hollywood actresses than among other women. However, 83% of a different group ($N = 102$) stated that, among Hollywood actresses, there are more "women who vote Democratic" than "women who are divorced more than 4 times." Thus, the more diagnostic attribute was judged to be more representative but less frequent than an attribute (voting Democratic) of lower diagnosticity. Third, an unrepresentative instance of a category can be fairly representative of a superordinate category. For example, chicken is a worse exemplar of a bird than of an animal, and rice is an unrepresentative vegetable, although it is a representative food.

The preceding observations indicate that representativeness is nonextensional: It is not determined by frequency, and it is not bound by class inclusion. Consequently, the test of the conjunction rule in probability judgments offers the sharpest contrast between the extensional logic of probability theory and the psychological principles of representativeness. Our first set of studies of the conjunction rule were conducted in 1974, using occupation and political affiliation as target attributes to be predicted singly or in conjunction from brief personality sketches (see Tversky and Kahneman 1982, for a brief summary). The studies described in the present section replicate and extend our earlier work. We used the following personality sketches of two fictitious individuals, Bill and Linda, followed by a set of occupations and avocations associated with each of them.

Bill is 34 years old. He is intelligent, but unimaginative, compulsive, and generally lifeless. In school, he was strong in mathematics but weak in social studies and humanities.

Bill is a physician who plays poker for a hobby.
Bill is an architect.
Bill is an accountant. (A)
Bill plays jazz for a hobby. (J)
Bill surfs for a hobby.

Bill is a reporter.
Bill is an accountant who plays jazz for a hobby. (A&J)
Bill climbs mountains for a hobby.

Linda is 31 years old, single, outspoken and very bright. She majored in philosophy. As a student, she was deeply concerned with issues of discrimination and social justice, and also participated in anti-nuclear demonstrations.

Linda is a teacher in elementary school.
Linda works in a bookstore and takes Yoga classes.
Linda is active in the feminist movement. (F)
Linda is a psychiatric social worker.
Linda is a member of the League of Women Voters.
Linda is a bank teller. (T)
Linda is an insurance salesperson.
Linda is a bank teller and is active in the feminist movement. (T&F)

As the reader has probably guessed, the description of Bill was constructed to be representative of an accountant (A) and unrepresentative of a person who plays jazz for a hobby (J). The description of Linda was constructed to be representative of an active feminist (F) and unrepresentative of a bank teller (T). We also expected the ratings of representativeness to be higher for the classes defined by a conjunction of attributes (A&J for BIll, T&F for Linda) than for the less representative constituent of each conjunction (J and T, respectively).

A group of 88 undergraduates at UBC ranked the eight statements associated with each description by "the degree to which Bill (Linda) resembles the typical member of that class." The results confirmed our expectations. The percentages of respondents who displayed the predicted order (A > A&J > J for Bill; F > T&F > T for Linda) were 87% and 85%, respectively. This finding is neither surprising nor objectionable. If, like similarity and prototypicality, representativeness depends on both common and distinctive features (Tversky 1977), it should be enhanced by the addition of shared features. Adding eyebrows to a schematic face makes it more similar to another schematic face with eyebrows (Gati and Tversky 1982). Analogously, the addition of feminism to the profession of bank teller improves the match of Linda's current activities to her personality. More surprising and less acceptable is the finding that the great majority of subjects also rank the conjunctions (A&J and T&F) as more *probable* than their less representative constituents (J and T). The following sections describe and analyze this phenomenon.

Indirect and Subtle Tests   Experimental tests of the conjunction rule can be divided into three types: *indirect* tests, *direct-subtle* tests and *direct-transparent* tests. In the indirect tests, one group of subjects evaluates the probability of the conjunction, and another group of subjects evaluates the probability of its constituents. No subject is required to compare a conjunction (e.g., "Linda is a bank teller and a feminist") to its constituents. In the direct-subtle tests, subjects compare the conjunction to its less representative constituent, but the inclusion relation between the events is not emphasized. In the direct-transparent tests, the subjects evaluate or compare the probabilities of the conjunction and its constituent in a format that highlights the relation between them.

The three experimental procedures investigate different hypotheses. The indirect procedure tests whether probability judgments conform to the conjunction rule; the direct-subtle procedure tests whether people will take advantage of an opportunity to compare the critical events; the direct-transparent procedure tests whether people will obey the conjunction rule when they are compelled to compare the critical events. This sequence of tests also describes the course of our investigation, which began with the observation of violations of the conjunction rule in indirect tests and proceeded—to our increasing surprise—to the finding of stubborn failures of that rule in several direct-transparent tests.

Three groups of respondents took part in the main study. The statistically *naive* group consisted of undergraduate students at Stanford University and UBC who had no background in probability or statistics. The *informed* group consisted of first-year graduate students in psychology and in education and of medical students at Stanford who were all familiar with the basic concepts of probability after one or more courses in statistics. The *sophisticated* group consisted of doctoral students in the decision science program of the Stanford Business School who had taken several advanced courses in probability, statistics, and decision theory.

Subjects in the main study received one problem (either Bill or Linda) first in the format of a direct test. They were asked to rank all eight statements associated with that problem (including the conjunction, its separate constituents, and five filler items) according to their probability, using 1 for the most probable and 8 for the least probable. The subjects then received the remaining problem in the format of an indirect test in which the list of alternatives included either the conjunction or its separate constituents. The same five filler items were used in both the direct and the indirect versions of each problem.

Table 3.1 presents the average ranks (R) of the conjunction R(A&B) and of its less representative constituents R(B), relative to the set of five filler items. The percentage of violations of the conjunction rule in the direct test is denoted by V. The results can be summarized as follows: (a) the conjunction is ranked higher than its less likely constituents in all 12 comparisons, (b) there is no consistent difference between the ranks of the alternatives in the direct and indirect tests, (c) the overall incidence of violations of the conjunction rule in direct tests is 88%, which virtually coincides with the incidence of the corresponding pattern in judgments of representativeness, and (d) there is no effect of statistical sophistication in either indirect or direct tests.

Table 3.1 Tests of the conjunction rule in likelihood rankings

Subjects	Problem	Direct test				Indirect test		
		V	R (A & B)	R (B)	N	R (A & B)	R (B)	Total N
Naive	Bill	92	2.5	4.5	94	2.3	4.5	88
	Linda	89	3.3	4.4	88	3.3	4.4	86
Informed	Bill	86	2.6	4.5	56	2.4	4.2	56
	Linda	90	3.0	4.3	53	2.9	3.9	55
Sophisticated	Bill	83	2.6	4.7	32	2.5	4.6	32
	Linda	85	3.2	4.3	32	3.1	4.3	32

Note. V = percentage of violations of the conjunction rule; R (A & B) and R (B) = mean rank assigned to A & B and to B, respectively; N = number of subjects in the direct test; Total N = total number of subjects in the indirect test, who were about equally divided between the two groups.

The violation of the conjunction rule in a direct comparison of B to A&B is called the *conjunction fallacy.* Violations inferred from between-subjects comparisons are called *conjunction errors.* Perhaps the most surprising aspect of Table 3.1 is the lack of any difference between indirect and direct tests. We had expected the conjunction to be judged more probable than the less likely of its constituents in an indirect test, in accord with the pattern observed in judgments of representativeness. However, we also expected that even naive respondents would notice the repetition of some attributes, alone and in conjunction with others, and that they would then apply the conjunction rule and rank the conjunction below its constituents. This expectation was violated, not only by statistically naive undergraduates but even by highly sophisticated respondents. In both direct and indirect tests, the subjects apparently ranked the outcomes by the degree to which Bill (or Linda) matched the respective stereotypes. The correlation between the mean ranks of probability and representativeness was .96 for Bill and .98 for Linda. Does the conjunction rule hold when the relation of inclusion is made highly transparent? The studies described in the next section abandon all subtlety in an effort to compel the subjects to detect and appreciate the inclusion relation between the target events.

Transparent Tests This section describes a series of increasingly desperate manipulations designed to induce subjects to obey the conjunction rule. We first presented the description of Linda to a group of 142 undergraduates at UBC and asked them to check which of two alternatives was more probable:

Linda is a bank teller. (T)

Linda is a bank teller and is active in the feminist movement. (T&F)

The order of alternatives was inverted for one half of the subjects, but this manipulation had no effect. Overall, 85% of respondents indicated that T&F was more probable than T, in a flagrant violation of the conjunction rule.

Surprised by the finding, we searched for alternative interpretations of the subjects' responses. Perhaps the subjects found the question too trivial to be taken literally and consequently interpreted the inclusive statement T as T&not-F; that is, "Linda is a bank teller and is *not* a feminist." In such a reading, of course, the observed judgments would not violate the conjunction rule. To test this interpretation, we asked a new group of subjects ($N = 119$) to assess the probability of T and of T&F on a 9-point scale ranging from 1 (extremely unlikely) to 9 (extremely likely). Because it is sensible to rate probabilities even when one of the events includes the other, there was no reason for respondents to interpret T as T&not-F. The pattern of responses obtained with the new version was the same as before. The mean ratings of probability were 3.5 for T and 5.6 for T&F, and 82% of subjects assigned a higher rating to T&F than they did to T.

Although subjects do not spontaneously apply the conjunction rule, perhaps they can recognize its validity. We presented another group of UBC undergraduates with the description of Linda followed by the two statements, T and T&F, and asked them to indicate which of the following two arguments they found more convincing.

Argument 1. Linda is more likely to be a bank teller than she is to be a feminist bank teller, because every feminist bank teller is a bank teller, but some women bank tellers are not feminists, and Linda could be one of them.

Argument 2. Linda is more likely to be a feminist bank teller than she is likely to be a bank teller, because she resembles an active feminist more than she resembles a bank teller.

The majority of subjects (65%, $n = 58$) chose the invalid resemblance argument (Argument 2) over the valid extensional argument (Argument 1). Thus, a deliberate attempt to induce a reflective attitude did not eliminate the appeal of the representativeness heuristic.

We made a further effort to clarify the inclusive nature of the event T by representing it as a disjunction. (Note that the conjunction rule can also be expressed as a disjunction rule $P(A \text{ or } B) \geq P(B)$). The description of Linda was used again, with a 9-point rating scale for judgments of probability, but the statement T was replaced by

Linda is a bank teller whether or not she is active in the feminist movement. (T*)

This formulation emphasizes the inclusion of T&F in T. Despite the transparent relation between the statements, the mean ratings of likelihood were 5.1 for T&F and 3.8 for T* ($p < .01$, by t test). Furthermore, 75% of the subjects ($n = 75$) committed the conjunction fallacy by rating T&F higher than T*, and only 16% gave a lower rating to T&F than to T*.

The violations of the conjunction rule in direct comparisons of T&F to T* are remarkable because the extension of "Linda is a bank teller whether or not she is active in the feminist movement" clearly includes the extension of "Linda is a bank teller and is active in the feminist movement." Many subjects evidently failed to draw extensional inferences from the phrase "whether or not," which may have been taken to indicate a weak disposition. This interpretation was supported by a between-subjects comparison, in which different subjects evaluated T, T*, and T&F on a 9-point scale after evaluating the common filler statement, "Linda is a psychiatric social worker." The average ratings were 3.3 for T, 3.9 for T*, and 4.5 for T&F, with each mean significantly different from both others. The statements T and T* are of course extensionally equivalent, but they are assigned different probabilities. Because feminism fits Linda, the mere mention of this attribute makes T* more likely than T, and a definite commitment to it makes the probability of T&F even higher!

Modest success in loosening the grip of the conjunction fallacy was achieved by asking subjects to choose whether to bet on T or on T&F. The subjects were given Linda's description, with the following instruction:

If you could win $10 by betting on an event, which of the following would you choose to bet on? (Check one)

The percentage of violations of the conjunction rule in this task was "only" 56% ($n = 60$), much too high for comfort but substantially lower than the typical value for comparisons of the two events in terms of probability. We conjecture that the betting context draws attention to the conditions in which one bet pays off whereas the other does not, allowing some subjects to discover that a bet on T dominates a bet on T&F.

The respondents in the studies described in this section were statistically naive undergraduates at UBC. Does statistical education eradicate the fallacy? To answer this question, 64 graduate students of social sciences at the University of California, Berkeley, and at Stanford University, all with credit for several statistics courses, were given the rating-scale version of the direct test of the conjunction rule for the Linda problem. For the first time in this series of studies, the mean rating for T&F (3.5) was lower than the rating assigned to T (3.8), and only 36% of respondents committed the fallacy. Thus, statistical sophistication produced a majority who conformed to the conjunction rule in a transparent test, although the incidence of violations was fairly high even in this group of intelligent and sophisticated respondents.

Elsewhere (Kahneman and Tversky, 1982), we distinguished between positive and negative accounts of judgments and preferences that violate normative rules. A positive account focuses on the factors that produce a particular response; a negative account seeks to explain why the correct response was not made. The positive analysis of the Bill and Linda problems invokes the representativeness heuristic. The stubborn persistence of the conjunction fallacy in highly transparent problems, however, lends special interest to the characteristic question of a negative analysis: Why do intelligent and reasonably well-educated people fail to recognize the applicability of the conjunction rule in transparent problems? Postexperimental interviews and class discussions with many subjects shed some light on this question. Naive as well as sophisticated subjects generally noticed the nesting of the target events in the direct-transparent test, but the naive, unlike the sophisticated, did not appreciate its significance for probability assessment. On the other hand, most naive subjects did not attempt to defend their responses. As one subject said after acknowledging the validity of the conjunction rule, "I thought you only asked for my opinion."

The interviews and the results of the direct transparent tests indicate that naive subjects do not spontaneously treat the conjunction rule as decisive. Their attitude is reminiscent of children's responses in a Piagetian experiment. The child in the preconservation stage is not altogether blind to arguments based on conservation of volume and typically expects quantity to be conserved (Bruner 1966). What the child fails to see is that the conservation argument is decisive and should overrule the perceptual impression that the tall container holds more water than the short one. Similarly, naive subjects generally endorse the conjunction rule in the abstract, but their application of this rule to the Linda problem is blocked by the compelling impression that T&F is more representative of her than T is. In this context, the adult subjects reason as if they had not reached the stage of formal operations. A full understanding of a principle of physics, logic, or statistics requires knowledge of the conditions under which it prevails over conflicting arguments, such as the height of the liquid in a container or the representativeness of an outcome. The recognition of the decisive nature of rules distinguishes different developmental stages in studies of conservation; it also distinguishes different levels of statistical sophistication in the present series of studies. . . .

Cognitive Illusions   Our studies of inductive reasoning have focused on systematic errors because they are diagnostic of the heuristics that generally govern judgment and inference. In the words of Helmholtz (1881/1903), "It is just those cases that are not in accordance with reality which are particularly instructive for discovering the laws of the processes by which normal perception originates." The focus on bias and illusion is a research strategy that exploits human error, although it neither assumes nor entails that people are perceptually or cognitively inept. Helmholtz's position implies that perception is not usefully analyzed into a normal process that produces accurate percepts and a distorting process that produces errors and illusions. In cognition, as in perception, the same mechanisms produce both valid and invalid judgments. Indeed, the evidence does not seem to support a "truth plus error" model, which assumes a coherent system of beliefs that is perturbed by various sources of distortion and error. Hence, we do not share Dennis Lindley's optimistic opinion that "inside every incoherent person there is a coherent one trying to get out" (Lindley, personal communication 1980), and we suspect that incoherence is more than skin deep (Tversky and Kahneman, 1981).

It is instructive to compare a structure of beliefs about a domain, (e.g., the political future of Central America) to the perception of a scene (e.g., the view of Yosemite Valley from Glacier Point). We have argued that intuitive judgments of all relevant marginal, conjunctive, and conditional probabilities are not likely to be coherent, that is, to satisfy the constraints of probability theory. Similarly, estimates of distances and angles in the scene are unlikely to satisfy the laws of geometry. For example, there may be pairs of political events for which $P(A)$ is judged greater than $P(B)$ but $P(A/B)$ is judged less than $P(B/A)$—see Tversky and Kahneman (1980). Analogously, the scene may contain a triangle ABC for which the A angle appears greater than the B angle, although the BC distance appears to be smaller than the AC distance.

The violations of the qualitative laws of geometry and probability in judgments of distance and likelihood have significant implications for the interpretation and use of these judgments. Incoherence sharply restricts the inferences that can be drawn from subjective estimates. The judged ordering of the sides of a triangle cannot be inferred from the judged ordering of its angles, and the ordering of marginal probabilities cannot be deduced from the ordering of the respective conditionals. The results of the present study show that it is even unsafe to assume that $P(B)$ is bounded by $P(A\&B)$. Furthermore, a system of judgments that does not obey the conjunction rule cannot be expected to obey more complicated principles that presuppose this rule, such as Bayesian updating, external calibration, and the maximization of expected utility. The presence of bias and incoherence does not diminish the normative force of these principles, but it reduces their usefulness as descriptions of behavior and hinders their prescriptive applications. Indeed, the elicitation of unbiased judgments and the reconciliation of incoherent assessments pose serious problems that presently have no satisfactory solution (Lindley et al. 1979; Shafer and Tversky 1983).

The issue of coherence has loomed larger in the study of preference and belief than in the study of perception. Judgments of distance and angle can readily be compared to objective reality and can be replaced by objective measurements when accuracy matters. In contrast, objective measurements of probability are often unavailable, and most significant choices under risk require an intuitive evaluation of probability. In the absence of an objective criterion of validity, the normative theory of judgment under uncertainty has treated the coherence of belief as the touchstone of human rationality. Coherence has also been assumed in many descriptive analyses in psychology, economics, and other social sciences. This assumption is attractive because the strong normative appeal of the laws of probability makes violations appear implausible. Our studies of the conjunction rule show that normatively inspired theories that assume coherence are descriptively inadequate, whereas psychological analyses that ignore the appeal of normative rules are, at best, incomplete. A comprehensive account of human judgment must reflect the tension between compelling logical rules and seductive non-extensional intuitions.

Note

Research on the second half of this chapter was supported by Grant NR 197-058 from the U.S. Office of Naval Research.

References

Bruner, J. S. (1966). On the conservation of liquids. In J. S. Bruner, R. R. Oliver, and P. M. Greenfield et al., eds., *Studies in cognitive growth*. New York: Wiley.

Chapman, L. J., and J. P. Chapman (1967). Genesis of popular but erroneous psychodiagnostic observations. *Journal of Abnormal Psychology* 73, 193–204.

Chapman, L. J. and J. P. Chapman (1969). Illusory correlation as an obstacle to the use of valid psychodiagnostic signs. *Journal of Abnormal Psychology* 74, 271–280.

Cohen, L. J. (1977). *The probable and the provable*. Oxford: Clarendon Press.

Dempster, A. P. (1967). Upper and lower probabilities induced by a multivalued mapping. *Annals of Mathematical Statistics*. 38, 325–339.

Edwards, W. (1968). Conservatism in human information processing. In B. Kleinmuntz, ed., *Formal representation of human judgment*. New York: Wiley.

Galbraith, R. C., and B. J. Underwood (1973). Perceived frequency of concrete and abstract words. *Memory and Cognition* 1, 56–60.

Gati, I., and A. Tversky (1982). Representations of qualitative and quantitative dimensions. *Journal of Experimental Psychology: Human perception and Performance* 8, 325–340.

Helmholtz, H. von (1881/1903). *Popular lectures on scientific subjects*, trans. E. Atkinson. New York: Green.

Jennings, D., T. Amabile, and L. Ross (1982). Informal covariation assessment. In D. Kahneman, P. Slovic, and A. Tversky, eds., *Judgment under uncertainty: Heuristics and biases*. New York: Cambridge University Press.

Kahneman, D., P. Slovic, and A. Tversky, eds. (1982). *Judgment under uncertainty: Heuristics and biases*. New York: Cambridge University Press.

Kahneman, D., and A. Tversky (1972). Subjective probability: A judgment of representativeness. *Cognitive Psychology* 3, 430–454.

Kahneman, D., and A. Tversky (1973). On the psychology of prediction. *Psychological Review* 80, 237–251.

Kahneman, D., and A. Tversky (1982). On the study of statistical intuitions. *Cognition* 11, 123–141.

Kyburg, H. E. (1983). Rational belief. *Behavioral and Brain Sciences* 6, 231–273.

Lindley, D. V., A. Tversky, and R. V. Brown (1979). On the reconciliation of probability assessments. *Journal of the Royal Statistical Society* 142, 146–180.

Mervis, C. B., and E. Rosch (1981). Categorization of natural objects. *Annual Review of Psychology* 32, 89–115.

Nisbett, R. E., and L. Ross (1980). *Human inference: Strategies and shortcomings of social judgment.* Englewood Cliffs, NJ: Prentice-Hall.

Rosch, E. (1978). Principles of categorization. In E. Rosch and B. B. Lloyd, eds., *Cognition and categorization.* Hillsdale, NJ: Erlbaum.

Shafer, G. (1976). *A mathematical theory of evidence.* Princeton, NJ: Princeton University Press.

Shafer, G., and A. Tversky (1983). Weighing evidence: The design and comparison of probability through experiments. Unpublished manuscript, Stanford University, Stanford.

Slovic, P. and S. Lichtenstein (1971). Comparison of Bayesian and regression approaches to the study of information processing in judgment. *Organizational Behavior and Human Performance* 6, 649–744.

Smith, E. E., and D. L. Medin (1981). *Categories and concepts.* Cambridge, MA: Harvard University Press.

Suppes, P. (1975). Approximate probability and expectation of gambles. *Erkenntnis* 9, 153–161.

Tversky, A. (1977). Features of similarity. *Psychological Review* 84, 327–352.

Tversky, A., and D. Kahneman (1971). Belief in the "law of small numbers." *Psychological Bulletin* 76, 105–110.

Tversky, A., and D. Kahneman (1973). Availability: A heuristic for judging frequency and probability. *Cognitive Psychology* 5, 207–232.

Tversky, A., and D. Kahneman (1980). Causal schemas in judgments under uncertainty. In M. Fishbein, ed., *Progress in social psychology.* Hillsdale, NJ: Erlbaum.

Tversky, A., and D. Kahneman (1981). The framing of decisions and the psychology of choice. *Science* 211, 453–458.

Tversky, A., and D. Kahneman (1982). Judgments of and by representativeness. In D. Kahneman, P. Slovic, and A. Tversky, eds., *Judgment under uncertainty: Heuristics and biases*. New York: Cambridge University Press.

Zadeh, L. A. (1978). Fuzzy sets as a basis for a theory of possibility. *Fuzzy Sets and Systems* 1, 3–28.

4   Our Native Inferential Tendencies

Hilary Kornblith

Boyd's Account of Kinds: Homeostatic Property Clusters

Richard Boyd (1988, 1991) has suggested that natural kinds should be viewed as homeostatic property clusters. The underlying idea here is quite simple. Organisms are so structured as to maintain themselves in certain states. For example, many animals have systems to maintain their body temperature within certain limits; plant cells have cell walls which are designed to maintain the pressure from inside the wall in equilibrium with the pressure from outside. In general, what we see in these cases of homeostasis is a cluster of properties which work together so as to maintain themselves, even in the face of changes in the environment. Boyd suggests that this account of self-maintenance in organisms may provide a model for all natural kinds. A natural kind is a cluster of properties which, when realized together in the same substance, work to maintain and reinforce each other, even in the face of changes in the environment.

It is precisely because there are clusters of properties which enjoy this homeostatic relationship that there are the "gaps or chasms" which Locke required for the existence of natural kinds. Consider, for example, the chemical cases with which Locke frequently concerned himself. Why is it that groups of observable properties are found clustered together in samples of stuff, and one does not find samples which differ from one another by as many or as few properties as one likes? Why, in short, are there gaps or chasms between the various clusters of properties, and thus differences in kind, rather than continuous differences of degree? The explanation for this phenomenon is to be found at the level of unobservables. The salient observable properties which draw our attention to chemical kinds are a product of underlying unobservables, or as Locke would put it, the arrangement of insensible parts.

From H. Kornblith, *Inductive inference and its natural ground* (1993). Cambridge, MA: MIT Press. Reprinted by permission.

Not just any arrangement of insensible parts, however, is stable. One may not just slap together protons, neutrons and electrons in any ~~configuration whatsoever; only certain arrangements will form stable~~ configurations in a homeostatic relationship. By understanding the details of the arrangements of the insensible parts, we may come to understand why it is that these precise arrangements are possible and others not. Thus, for example, when we come to understand how chemical bonds are formed, we see why H_2O is a possible molecule, but HO_2 is not. The clustering of observable properties is a by-product of the stable configurations which are possible at the unobservable level.

If this account is on the right track, then we have the beginnings of an explanation of what it is about the world that makes it knowable. Because there are natural kinds, and thus clusters of properties which reside in homeostatic relationships, we may reliably infer the presence of some of these properties from the presence of others. In short, natural kinds make reliable inductive inference possible, because were it not for the existence of these homeostatic clusters, the presence of any set of properties would be fully compatible with the presence of any other. In investigating the nature of natural kinds, we are thereby investigating the natural ground of inductive inference.

In what follows, I develop Boyd's very fertile suggestion about the nature of natural kinds with an eye toward epistemological themes. . . .

Pessimism about Inferential Tendencies

The literature on human inferential tendencies which began to emerge in the early 1970s had a strikingly pessimistic tone. Tversky and Kahneman, in an early and extremely influential paper (1971), argued that our "intuitive expectations are governed by a consistent misperception of the world" (p. 31). Nisbett and Borgida spoke of their experiments as having "bleak implications for human rationality" (1975, 935). The catalog of inferential errors which we are naturally inclined to commit seemed limitless: we routinely violate the probabilistic law of large numbers by confidently making judgments about populations on the basis of extremely small samples (Tversky and Kahneman 1971); we judge the objective likelihood of an event on the basis of the ease with which we may recall events of that type, even when there is very good reason to think that the latter is no indication whatever of the former (Tversky and Kahneman 1973); we have an unseemly attachment to our beliefs, holding on to them even when our evidence has been completely undermined (Ross et al. 1975); we seem subject to an illusion of power over events which are clearly not within our control (Langer and Roth 1975); our degree of confidence in our own judgments far outstrips our objective reliability (Oskamp 1965). The list goes on and on.[1] Were a visiting anthropologist from another planet to read these studies, the only conclusion could be that we are a pathetic lot, fortunate to be able to muddle through our daily lives without serious mishap.

That this was the obvious conclusion to draw from the literature surely suggests that this work presented a one-sided picture of our inferential abilities. Nisbett and Ross report that a colleague of theirs commented, on reading a draft of their review of the literature, "If we're so dumb, how come we made it to the moon?" (1980, 249). This question points in the direction of a legitimate challenge to the starkly pessimistic tone of much of this work. It is not surprising then that the early work met with some strong reactions, many of which were even more optimistic about our inferential abilities than the early work was pessimistic. Indeed, there is a large body of literature arguing, on a priori grounds, that we reason perfectly well: the experimental evidence, it was argued, must have been misinterpreted.

I cannot possibly review all of this literature here, nor would it be profitable to examine all of the arguments offered on every side of this debate. There is, however, an emerging consensus that the early literature was far too pessimistic. What I want to do here is give an extended illustration of how this work may be illuminated by examining our inferential tendencies in light of the metaphysical picture and our conceptual categories offered earlier. I do not believe that all aspects of human inference are illuminated by this perspective, nor do I believe that, when properly understood, all inferences which come naturally to us are good ones. I do believe, however, that a great deal can be understood about human inference by seeing it in its proper metaphysical and conceptual setting, and that so understood, a great deal of human inference turns out to be extraordinarily well adapted to giving us an accurate picture of our environment. My goal in this chapter is to show how human inference may be illuminated by this perspective.

Inferential Error and Perceptual Error

I have said that the early literature on inference had an extremely pessimistic tone. This pessimism is most striking when the literature on inference is compared with the literature on perception. Everyone working on the mechanisms of perception is familiar with the various perceptual illusions, yet no one takes these systematic errors as even prima facie evidence of the unreliability of the senses. In the literature on inference, however, the discovery of a systematic pattern of errors was taken by many investigators to be far more than prima facie evidence of unreliability; it was taken as nearly conclusive evidence of the unreliability of human inference. The first step toward a proper perspective on human inference, to my mind, comes in seeing how perceptual psychologists view the standard illusions and errors, and recognizing the relevance of this to the topic of inference.

The standard perceptual illusions are of theoretical interest not because they show how badly we process perceptual information, but rather because they offer us clues about how we succeed in processing perceptual information so well. We understand how it is that the perceptual mechanisms work precisely by seeing how they go wrong in nonstandard environments. When we see that the senses can be fooled by contrived situations, we see what assumptions are built in to our perceptual processing, and, at least in the typical case, we come to understand how we are able to process information so quickly and so easily in situations which are not contrived.

Consider, for example, the phi phenomenon. Numerous highway signs, of the 'Eat at Joe's' variety, have an illuminated arrow composed of a large number of light bulbs. The bulbs are turned on and off sequentially: first the rightmost are on, then they are shut off and the ones immediately to their left are illuminated; then these are turned off and the ones immediately to their left are illuminated; and so on. The result is the illusion of motion: the arrow seems to be moving toward Joe's Diner, beckoning the unsuspecting traveler to a memorable meal. As with other perceptual illusions, knowing that there is such an illusion does nothing to change its effect. One has an irresistible impression of motion, even when one knows that nothing is, in fact, moving.

This illusion reveals something important about the way in which we process visual information.[2] We have a deep-seated bias in favor of object constancy: we tend to assume the existence of medium-sized physical objects in our environment, and any sensory stimulation which comes close to supporting such an interpretation is interpreted in just that way. Now, in fact, most of the sensory stimulation we get which can be read in a way consistent with object constancy is, indeed, caused by objects moving in our environment. Our bias in favor of interpreting sensory stimulation in this manner thus serves us well. By limiting the hypotheses we consider in the interpretation of our sensory stimulation, the presupposition of object constancy does not just make the task of visual information processing faster and easier than it would otherwise be, but rather, it makes it possible where it otherwise would be impossible. Trying to impose an order on our sensory stimulation without any constraining hypotheses at all about the environment would create an information-processing task of insurmountable complexity.

The cost of building in such presuppositions about the environment is that it brings with it a pattern of errors. Errors caused by breakdown of the perceptual mechanism are, of course, inevitable, for like any other physical mechanism, the equipment may sometimes malfunction. But errors such as those occasioned by the phi phenomenon are not a result of breakdown; instead, they are a product of the smooth operation of the mechanism, working in exactly the way in which it was designed to work. The processing of visual information occurs in the way it does because it builds in a presupposition of object constancy; it presupposes that the environment is populated with medium-sized physical objects having more or less rigid boundaries. When this presupposition is false, as in the 'Eat at Joe's' sign, the resulting interpretation of the sensory stimulation is in error. But this kind of error is a small price to pay for the speed and accuracy with which we are able to process information in standard conditions. More than that, it is the cost of being able to process information in standard conditions at all.

As a result, it would be a mistake, and a mistake which no one makes,[3] to look upon the visual illusions as providing reason to deny the reliability of our perceptual mechanisms. Far from offering evidence of unreliability, the illusions explain how the striking reliability of perception is achieved. This way of looking at the visual illusions is, indeed, simply standard (see, e.g., Rock 1983).

Now this kind of perspective may be brought to the data on human inference. The discovery of a pattern of inferential errors should not automatically lead us to conclude that our inferences are unreliable. Instead, such a pattern may offer us insight into how it is that we are able to arrive at accurate conclusions about the world so quickly and easily. The errors which we make may allow us to appreciate features of our standard environment which are presupposed by our inferential mechanisms, and which, when absent, lead to mistaken conclusions. Just as our perceptual mechanisms are well adapted to the environment in which they typically operate and build in presuppositions about the environment which are typically true, so our inferential mechanisms may also be built around presuppositions about standard environments which allow us to gain information about those environments both quickly and accurately. There is, of course, no a priori guarantee that this is the right perspective on human inference, and we should not try to force the data into such a mold. We would be foolish, however, if we did not consider the possibility that the pattern of inferential errors which have been discovered are a product of just such presuppositions.

This suggestion about how to view the literature on inference is not original with me. Nisbett and Ross make this suggestion in the preface to their survey of the literature.

People's inferential failures are cut from the same cloth as their inferential successes are. Specifically, we contend that people's inferential strategies are well adapted to deal with a wide range of problems, but that these same strategies become a liability when they are applied beyond that range. . . . We should warn the reader that the following pages give relatively more attention to shortcomings, and less to triumphs, than any balanced survey would justify. This emphasis on error follows from much the same premise that leads many of our colleagues to study the perceptual illusions or thinking disorders—the belief that the nature of cognitive structures and processes can be revealed by the defects which they produce. (1980, xii)

Although this approach has thus been available for some time now, it is well worth emphasizing. Far too much of the literature on inference fails to be informed by this method. A great deal can be learned about human inference when it is approached in this way.

What I hope to show is that our inferential mechanisms, like our conceptual categories, build in substantive assumptions about the causal structure of the world. We approach the world by presupposing that it contains natural kinds. Our inferences depend on this presupposition, and they make sense only if we recognize that a structure of natural kinds is in fact presupposed. This presupposition thus gives us a built-in advantage in understanding what the world is like, and thereby makes inductive understanding of the world a real possibility.

The Law of Small Numbers

Tversky and Kahneman (1971) investigated how people draw conclusions about a population on the basis of random sampling. Their findings were not encouraging for those who would like to believe that our inferences are fairly reliable.

Our thesis is that people have strong intuitions about random sampling; that these intuitions are wrong in fundamental respects; that these intuitions are shared by naive subjects and by trained scientists; and that they are applied with unfortunate consequences in the course of scientific inquiry. (p. 24)

The phenomenon which prompted this assessment involved projecting the traits of a population from very small samples. Subjects confidently drew conclusions about a population when the size of their sample gave no statistical grounds for such a conclusion. Moreover, having arrived at a conclusion about a population on the basis of an undersized sample, subjects then expected other small samples of the population to exhibit similar traits. This flies in the face of good statistical inference, for the smaller the sample size, the less reason there is to have confidence in the representativeness of the sample. Tversky and Kahneman compare the psychological law at work here with the probabilistic law of large numbers.

The law of large numbers guarantees that very large samples will indeed be highly representative of the population from which they are drawn. . . .[4] People's intuitions about random sampling appear to satisfy the law of small numbers, which asserts that the law of large numbers applies to small numbers as well. (1971, 25)

The study done by Tversky and Kahneman involved fairly technical questions about sampling and experimental design, and were administered to members of the American Psychological Association. It was, at a minimum, disappointing to find that researchers who routinely are called upon to make judgments about the representativeness of samples seem to perform so badly. More disappointing still was the result that members of the mathematical psychology group, whose skills with such problems might reasonably be thought to exceed those of the average member of the American Psychological Association, did not do much better (Tversky and Kahneman 1971, 27–28).

The phenomenon exhibited in this experiment proves to be remarkably robust. It is not limited to the performance of subjects, however technically skilled, on complex problems involving sample size in experimental design. It is, instead, an important component of the way in which ordinary people reason in their daily lives. Nisbett and Ross (1980, chapter 3) document the influence of the vividness of data upon inductive inference. Vividly described cases, or vivid experiences, have a tremendous impact on the inferences people draw; statistical information, which is typically more revealing but less vividly presented, does not have nearly the same degree of influence on our judgment. People are remarkably willing to draw conclusions about a population on the basis of a few vivid examples, and, indeed, frequently do so on the basis of a single vivid instance, thereby flouting the law of large numbers in a particularly dramatic way. There is some evidence, moreover, that people are more likely to make such hasty and apparently unwarranted inferences in cases which are of special importance to them; vivid data have the greatest distorting effect, it seems, just where the conclusion matters most (Nisbett and Ross 1980, 59).

Part of the upshot of this work, and a result which every teacher knows, is that from the point of view of producing conviction, a good example is worth a thousand arguments. I would thus be remiss if I did not at least present some examples of the kind of effect which Nisbett and Ross document. Hamill, Wilson, and Nisbett (1979) examined the effect of statistical information about welfare recipients, and compared it with the effect of a vivid description of a single, but unrepresentative, case. Although subjects believed upon entering the study that the average stay on welfare is approximately ten years, the statistical information showed that this is very far from the truth; the median time is in fact only two years. The vivid case study which some subjects read described but one family, and better fit the stereotype which many subjects had on entering the study.

The central figure was an obese, friendly, emotional, and irresponsible Puerto Rican woman who had been on welfare for many years. Middle-aged now, she had lived with a succession of "husbands," typically also unemployed, and had borne children by each of them. Her home was a nightmare of dirty and dilapidated plastic furniture bought on time at outrageous prices, filthy kitchen appliances, and cockroaches walking about in the daylight. Her children showed little promise of rising above their origins. They attended school off and on and had begun to run afoul of the law in their early teens, with the older children now thoroughly enmeshed in a life of heroin, numbers-running, and welfare. (Nisbett and Ross 1980, 57)

The results of the study were striking.

The surprising-but-pallid statistical information . . . had no effect on subjects' opinions about welfare recipients. In contrast, the vivid description of one particular welfare family prompted subjects to express more unfavorable attitudes toward recipients than control subjects did. Thus highly probative but dull statistics had no effect on inferences, whereas a vivid but questionably informative case history had a substantial effect on inferences. (Nisbett and Ross 1980, 57–58)

This particular study deals with the influence of new information on a belief already held, but vivid information is just as effective in creating beliefs as it is in reinforcing them, and the effect of statistical information pales by comparison. To cite a single case, the wives of the president and the vice-president of the United States both required mastectomies in the fall of 1974. Immediately thereafter, the number of visits to cancer detection clinics increased dramatically. Statistics on the importance of pre-cancer screening had previously been publicized quite widely, but had never had a comparable effect (Nisbett and Ross 1980, 56). It is clear both from controlled studies and from a large number of cases like the mastectomy case, where experimental control is impossible, that vivid information drives inductive inference far more effectively than does statistical information, and thereby leads to routine violation of the law of large numbers. We tend to draw inductive inferences on the basis of extraordinarily small samples.

How should we evaluate this tendency? What effect does it have on the accuracy of our beliefs? Tversky and Kahneman give an unequivocal assessment of this kind of inference.

The true believer in the law of small numbers commits his multitude of sins against the logic of statistical inference in good faith. The [resulting inferential tendency is] a cognitive or perceptual bias, which operates regardless of motivational factors. . . . His intuitive expectations are governed by a consistent misperception of the world. (1971, 31)

Although this assessment does, I admit, seem called for by the data, we would be hasty, and, I think, unjustified, to accept it without further consideration. The question of the reliability of this particular pattern of inference turns out to be far more subtle that Tversky and Kahneman recognize. We will need to examine this issue at greater length.

There are two questions I want to address here. First, what effect does the law of small numbers have on the accuracy of prediction? Tversky and Kahneman seem to take for granted that predictions which derive from an application of the law of small numbers will be significantly worse than predictions which might otherwise be made. We will see that such an assumption is both a distortion and an oversimplification of the facts. The issues involved here are addressed in the next section. Second, Tversky and Kahneman compare the logical form of our inferences with the logic of statistical inference, and on that basis, declare us sinners. Given the standards of proper statistical inference, our inferences receive a failing grade. But is the logic of statistical inference a reasonable standard against which to measure our own inferences? This question is addressed in the section [on standards of statistical inference.] I argue that this seemingly natural standard of comparison grossly distorts the phenomenon of human inference. Instead of illuminating our inferential errors, this kind of comparison encourages us to ignore features of human inference which are essential to its proper evaluation.

Predictions Based on the Law of Small Numbers

Suppose you and I must each predict whether the next ball drawn from an urn will be black or white.[5] We are each allowed to look at as many balls from the urn in advance as we like, although neither of us knows how many the other has examined. You decide to examine every ball in the urn; you predict black just in case there are more black balls than white. I sample a single ball. Being hasty to generalize, I jump to the conclusion that the urn is filled almost entirely with black balls if I choose black; almost entirely with white balls if I choose white. I make my prediction accordingly. Your prediction is made on grounds that would be favored by the principles of statistical inference;[6] mine is not. How much more successful will your prediction be than mine? If we play this game only once, there is likely to be very little difference.

Consider a simple case. Suppose the urn is filled with 10 percent black balls and 90 percent white ones. You count them all out, and, predicting that the next ball will be the color of the majority, you predict that it will be white. You will be right, of course, 90 percent of the time. I pull out a single ball and, because I believe that nearly all of the balls are of that color, I predict that the next ball drawn will be of that color as well. My chances of being correct are $((.90 \times .90) + (.10 \times .10)) = 82$ percent. This is not a very large difference. Chances are (81 percent) we will both be right in our predictions. You will be right and I wrong only 9 percent of the time.[7] there is even some chance (1 percent) that I will be right and you wrong.

What if the ratio of black balls to white is more nearly even? Consider the limiting case where the urn is half filled with black balls and half filled with white. You predict that the next ball to be drawn will be white (since you predict black just in case there are more black balls than white), and you will be correct 50 percent of the time. My prediction will be correct $((.5 \times .5) + (.5 \times .5)) = 50$ percent of the time.

When your prediction and mine differ, you and I will each be right half the time. No advantage is gained, in this case, by making the statistically ~~reasonable prediction.~~

Intermediate cases do not show large advantages for proper statistical prediction either. The fact is that when predictions are made about a single case, prediction based on the law of small numbers is not very much inferior to the best statistical methods. Indeed, from a practical point of view, use of the law of small numbers may frequently be preferred. If the cost of gaining additional information is high, the trade-off of reliability for ease of information gathering may be altogether reasonable, especially given the small loss of reliability and the possibility of having to search a very large sample space. In the case of making a single prediction about a population, beliefs based on the law of small numbers are thus nearly as accurate as any of the available alternatives.

I would not, however, wish to see a defense of the law of small numbers rest on this kind of argument. Although it is well worth pointing out that the gap between the reliability of predictions based on large samples and the reliability of those based on small samples is, in many cases, much smaller than one might have expected, this entire approach concedes far too much to those who condemn this inferential tendency. Like those who reject the law of small numbers as faulty, this limited defense of it presupposes that the standards of statistical inference are the appropriate ones against which to measure human inference. It is this presupposition which needs to be examined next.

The Standards of Statistical Inference

Tversky and Kahneman take for granted that predictions based on small samples are less reasonable than those based on larger samples. Why do they assume this? The answer is straightforward: the principles of statistical inference tell us that the degree of confidence we may assign to predictions based on small samples is typically less than, and never greater than, the degree of confidence we may assign to predictions based on larger samples. But why should we assume that the principles of statistical inference thereby set the appropriate standards?

When a population is uniform with respect to some property, inferences from small samples, and indeed, from a single case, are perfectly reliable. If I note that a sample of copper conducts electricity and straightaway conclude that all copper conducts electricity, then I will do just as well as someone who insists on checking a very large number of copper samples for their conductivity. Now to say that human beings have a deep-seated tendency to follow the law of small numbers is not to say that whenever someone comes to believe that some individual meets a certain description, that person will thereby come to believe that all individuals of the same type also meet that description. Such a suggestion would require that on coming to see a platypus for the first time, I thereby infer that all such animals have every property that the one before me has. It is clear enough that no one has such a tendency, and it is also clear enough that Tversky and Kahneman do not mean to be suggesting that anyone has such a tendency. What then are they suggesting? What does the law of small numbers amount to?

Although Tversky and Kahneman are not explicit about this, I think it is not unreasonable to attribute the following view to them. Human beings do not have a tendency to project just any description whatsoever. Although on viewing a single platypus lay eggs, I am likely to infer that all (female) platypuses lay eggs, viewing a single platypus in a zoo does not at all incline me to believe that all platypuses live in zoos. I am thus inclined to project certain descriptions and not others. Moreover, there are some descriptions which I am inclined to project of one class of individuals, but not of another. Seeing one black crow may incline me to believe that all crows are black, but seeing one black book does not at all incline me to believe that all books are black. Giving an account of which descriptions are likely to be projected at all, and, in the case of those which are sometimes projected, what determines whether the description will be projected in a particular case, is obviously an important and difficult psychological project. The law of small numbers, however, makes no contribution to this project. I take it that what the law of small numbers does require is just this: on those occasions when we do project some description, we have a tendency to make such projections on the basis of very small samples.

But it should be clear that this, by itself, tells us nothing about the reliability of such a tendency.[8] If we are sensitive to the situations in which a population is uniform with respect to some property, then making inferences on the basis of very small samples will be a reliable and efficient way to gain information about a population. If, on the other hand, we are entirely insensitive to the uniformity of traits in a population, or worse, if we tend to project descriptions which are unrepresentative of a population, then behaving in accord with the law of small numbers will tend to produce false beliefs. The fact that making inferences from small samples violates canons of good statistical inference, however, is simply irrelevant to assessing how well or badly we are served by such a tendency. Any assessment of the effects this tendency has must be predicated upon an account of the descriptions we project, and the situations in which we project them.

There can be no doubt that the literature is replete with examples, such as the one cited in the section [on the law of small numbers], in which we make predictions about a population on the basis of a small sample, where the description projected does not pick out a property which is representative of the entire population. This shows that we are not perfectly sensitive to the relevant features of our environment for making accurate inductive inferences. Of course, in this respect, inductive inference is no different from any other belief-generating mechanism: we are not perfectly sensitive to anything at all in our environment. What we need to examine is whether our errors here show that we are largely insensitive to the relevant features of the environment, or whether instead we are roughly responsive to those important features. I will argue that there is reason here to be optimistic.

Small Numbers and Natural Kinds: What Needs to Be Shown

The work reviewed earlier showed that we have a sensitivity and a responsiveness to natural kinds. We have a natural tendency to classify objects in a way which presupposes that kinds have essences, and that the observable features of objects are only a rough-and-ready guide to the properties which make a kind the kind it is. These features of our conceptual repertoire will play a crucial role in the assessment of our inferential tendencies. Here is what I wish to argue. When our inductive inferences are guided by our intuitive grasp of the real kinds in nature, and when we project those properties which we intuitively recognize to be essential to those kinds, our tendency to make inferences in accord with the law of small numbers serves us well. Our conceptual and inferential tendencies jointly conspire, at least roughly, to carve nature at its joints and project the features of a kind which are essential to it. This preestablished harmony between the causal structure of the world and the conceptual and inferential structure of our minds produces reliable inductive inference.

This is not to say, by any means, that there is natively a perfect match between our conceptual and inferential structure, on the one hand, and the causal structure of the world, on the other. If there were such a perfect match, we would never make any inductive mistakes. Moreover, hard-won empirical knowledge of the world would be unnecessary for the elaboration and refinement of our conceptual categories and inductive inferences; a system of concepts and inferences in perfect harmony with the causal structure of the world would need neither elaboration nor refinement. What we do have natively, I want to argue, is a set of dispositions which incline us in the right direction: a tendency to carve the world into kinds in ways which presuppose a certain causal structure; a tendency to look beyond the superficial characteristics of objects in classifying them into kinds; a sensitivity to those features in objects which tend to reside in homeostatic clusters; and a tendency to project those characteristics which are indeed essential to the real kinds in nature. The first two of these claims, about our classificatory tendencies, have already been argued for previously. The second pair of claims, about our sensitivity to properties which are homeostatically clustered and our tendency to project those very properties within the kinds to which they are essential, remain to be established here.

The sensitivity to homeostatic clusters can only be had if we are reasonably accurate detectors of covariation. We need not be able to reason well about covariation explicitly, but what is needed is a sensitivity to properties which tend to be found together. Without this, we would be insensitive to the existence of natural kinds. Without a sensitivity to the existence of natural kinds, inferences driven by the law of small numbers would be unreliable. If we are to defend the reliability of our use of the law of small numbers, we will thus need to address our capacities to detect covariation.

This does not put me in a terribly attractive position. Our ability to detect covariation has been widely attacked, and those who would defend our reliability on this score have an uphill battle. There is, undeniably, a good deal of evidence that we are not particularly adept in detecting covariation. This bad news is summarized in the next section. There is, however, some encouraging news as well, and this is discussed in [the following section on covariation]. Were the evidence on the detection of covariation merely mixed, I would hardly be in a good position to defend my thesis about the reliability of our inferential tendencies. I will argue, however, that the evidence is not mixed. We are not very good at detecting certain kinds of covariation. There is some evidence, however, that detecting covariations of a specific sort is well within our abilities. It is these, I will argue, that provide us with a sensitivity to the real kinds in nature.

Tolerably accurate detection of covariation, however, is not enough to provide a defense of the law of small numbers. It must also be shown that we have a tendency to project the properties which are found to covary, and that we project them in the right situations. This task is taken on later in this chapter. The result, then, all told, is a defense of the reliability of our use of the law of small numbers.

Detection of Covariation: The Bad News

The bad news about the detection of covariation falls into two categories: cases of theory-driven belief and cases of data-driven belief. In the theory-driven cases, antecedently held views are shown to swamp all the available data, so that covariation is believed to be present even when it is not, and is believed to be absent even when it is present. The influence of antecedently held belief is thus so strong as to make judgments of covariation entirely worthless. Data-driven cases are not a great deal more encouraging. Data which are relevant are typically ignored. Relevant data which are used are radically misinterpreted and stripped of the context which would make their proper interpretation possible. Nisbett and Ross are thus led to the following assessment:

There is mounting evidence that people are extremely poor at performing . . . covariation assessment tasks. In particular, it appears that a priori theories or expectations may be more important to the perception of covariation than are the actual observed data configurations. That is, if the layperson has a plausible theory that predicts covariation between two events, then a substantial degree of covariation will be perceived, even if it is present only to a very slight degree or even if it is totally absent. Conversely, even powerful empirical relationships are apt not to be detected or to be radically underestimated if the layperson is not led to expect such a covariation. (1980, 10)

Let us examine the work which prompted this assessment.

Consider, first, cases of data-driven assessments of covariation: that is, cases in which there are no antecedently held views about the degree of covariation of the variables at issue. One kind of experiment involves the use of 2 × 2 contingency tables. For example, subjects are asked to assess the likelihood that a certain symptom is indicative of a particular disease. They are presented with information about cases in the form of a 2 × 2 matrix indicating the number of patients found in a random sample with and without the symptom, and with and without the disease. Thus, subjects might be presented with a table such as the following (after Nisbett and Ross 1980, 91).

	DISEASE A	
	Present	Absent
Present	20	10
SYMPTOM X		
Absent	80	40

Although the only way to make proper use of such a table requires drawing on the data in each of the four cells, virtually none of the subjects in these experiments regard all four cells as relevant.

Almost exclusive reliance on the "present/present" cell seems to be a particularly common failing. Many subjects say that symptom X is associated with disease A simply because many people with the disease do in fact have the symptom. Other subjects pay attention only to two cells. Some of these will conclude that the relationship is positive because more people who have the disease have the symptom than do people who do not have the disease. Others conclude that the relationship is negative because more people with the disease do not have symptom X than have it. (Nisbett and Ross 1980, 91)

The standard strategies used for evaluating the data in these matrices are not even remotely reliable (see Smedslund 1963; Ward and Jenkins 1965; Peterson and Beach 1967; Nisbett and Ross 1980; Jennings et al. 1982). Although these contingency tables obviously present data in a manner quite different from that in which they are normally encountered, there are many respects in which the task of assessing covariation is made easier by the artificial form in which it is represented. Moreover, many of the errors made here generalize to other cases in which data are presented in a more natural setting (Nisbett and Ross 1980, 92; Jennings et al. 1982, 213).

In addition, the 2 × 2 matrix is not the only device used for the assessment of our powers of data-driven covariation assessment. Jennings, Amabile, and Ross (1982) asked subjects to assess the strength of covariation between a number of pairs of variables. In one case, subjects were given ten pairs of numbers and asked whether the relationship among the pairs was positive (i.e., the larger the first number, the larger the second), negative (the larger the first number, the smaller the second), or zero (no relationship). Subjects were then asked to rate the strength of the relationship on a 100-point scale. In another case, subjects were shown stick-figure drawings of men carrying walking sticks; they were asked to assess the direction and strength of covariation in the height of the men and the length of the walking sticks. The results were as follows.

the function relating mean subjective estimates to objective correlations . . . was a rather smooth one. More specifically, there seems to be a sharply accelerating function relating the two variables. Thus, relationships [which are significant but weak] (i.e., r = .2 to .4) are barely detectable, yielding mean estimates in the range of 4 to 8 on the 100-point scale. [An Accurate assessment here would have been in the 20 to 40 range.] Even relationships considered very strong . . . (i.e., r = .6 to .8) result in rather modest subjective estimates of covariation. Objective correlations of .7, for instance, [which should receive a rating of 70] produced a mean subjective estimate of 34—a rating midway between the points labelled "rather weak" and "moderate" on the 100-point subjective scale. Only when the objective correlations approached the .85 level did the group mean reach the midpoint of the subjective scale, and only beyond that point did subjects consistently rate the relationships as strongly positive. (Jennings et al. 1982, 221)

To put the point in more qualitative terms, we may fairly say that the degree of covariation between variables had to be strong before it was even detected; at very high levels of objective covariation, subjects believed the degree of covariation to be low. It was only when the degree of covariation was nearly perfect that subjects' ratings of covariation were remotely accurate. This is not good news.

But the news about the detection of covariation gets far worse when one considers cases in which subjects approach the data with some antecedently held views about where the correlations might lie. Devastatingly bad news about human performance was discovered by Loren Chapman and Jean Chapman (1967, 1969, 1971). In a widely used psychodiagnostic test called Draw-a-Person, or DAP, a patient is asked to execute a drawing, and features of the drawing are used to aid in diagnosis. For example, paranoid individuals are said to give emphasis to the eyes; those worried about intelligence are said to draw larger heads; those concerned about their sexual identity give prominence to genital areas. Although the test is widely used, it has been experimentally confirmed time after time that the allegedly diagnostic features of the pictures are not, in fact, diagnostic. It is simply untrue, for example, that paranoid individuals tend to draw pictures of people with prominent eyes. None of the allegedly diagnostic features of the drawings have been found to hold up in experimental tests. Nevertheless, many clinicians still use these tests.[9] One clinical psychologist told the Chapmans, "I know that paranoids don't seem to draw big eyes in the research labs, but they sure do in my office" (Chapman and Chapman 1971, 240).

The Chapmans were interested in discovering why it is that clinicians continue to use these tests, in spite of their widely documented invalidity. A questionnaire was sent to clinicians who use DAP to determine what features of the drawings they use to aid in diagnosis. There was a good deal of consensus among them on the relevant features. Undergraduates ignorant of the use of DAP were then shown a series of 45 drawings, each of which was paired with some alleged diagnosis. Careful measurements of the drawings were done in advance to guarantee that there was no correlation whatsoever between the labels on the drawings and the diagnostic signs used by the clinicians. Thus, for example, the drawings which were allegedly done by paranoids had eyes which were no more prominent than those in the other drawings. The students were then asked whether they noticed any correlation between the diagnoses and any features at all of the drawings. Even though no such correlation was there to be found, the students saw such correlations, and in fact, they saw the very same correlations which the clinicians did. A tendency to see such correlations was reduced, but not eliminated, when students were supplied with rulers and given as much time to study the drawings as they liked. Similarly, when students were given drawings which objectively had a negative correlation with the allegedly diagnostic features, the tendency to see a positive correlation was reduced, but not eliminated.

Not surprisingly, the Chapmans found that there is a strong tendency to associate intelligence with the head, paranoia with the eyes and so on. Word association tests given to undergraduates ignorant of DAP revealed the very associations which clinicians claim to see represented in the drawings of their patients. This wholly useless diagnostic instrument is thus a product of common association, and the fact that we tend to associate certain clinical problems with features of the body gives rise to the illusory correlation. The illusion is obviously quite strong. The tendency to see correlations when they are not there, and even when there is in fact a negative correlation, is striking.

The bad news then about our ability to detect covariation is just this. When we antecedently hold no views about a correlation, and are thus influenced only by the data available, we tend to do badly at covariation detection tasks. Only when the degree of covariation is nearly perfect do we seem to be even roughly accurate at discovering the strength of covariation. Nevertheless, our performance in data-driven covariation experiments is excellent by comparison with the cases of theory-driven covariation; in theory-driven cases, it seems, we have a very strong tendency to project covariations onto the data which conform to our antecedently held beliefs, regardless of the extent to which the data support or undermine those beliefs.

Detection of Covariation: The Good News

It is important to put the bad news about covariation detection in perspective. First, when the degree of covariation is nearly perfect, we do quite well in detecting it. This is important in helping us detect natural kinds, for there are many cases where the degree of covariation of features is indeed perfect. Samples of iron, for example, will all be dense; they will all conduct electricity; they will all participate in the same chemical combinations. There is no reason to think that we would have any difficulty at all detecting these covariations. Nevertheless, it is not sufficient for the recognition of natural kinds that we be good detectors of perfect covariation. Many features of natural kinds which do covary do not covary to degree 1. In the case of dogs, for example, a large number of properties are found to covary to a degree far short of perfection. If we are to be able to recognize natural kinds, we must be able to detect covariations such as this. The bad news cited above seems to reflect on our ability to recognize natural kinds because the cases in which natural kinds display significant covariations short of 1 are ubiquitous.

The studies which suggest that we have significant shortcomings in detecting covariation, however, are strikingly artificial. A degree of artificiality is inevitable in controlled experiments, but there is a partic-ular feature of these studies which bears scrutiny. In each of the exper-iments involving data-driven detection of covariation, a single pair of features covaried and it was these that subjects were supposed to detect. But in the case of natural kinds, there are a large number of properties which are clustered together and which jointly covary, rather than a single isolated pair. It may seem that if we are not very good at detecting covariation in a single pair of properties, it is unlikely that we will do better when we need to detect multiple covariations. On the other hand, the very clustering of properties which is characteristic of natural kinds could make the detection of covariation easier in the multiple case than it is in the isolated case. This is clearly a matter which needs to be looked into, and the experiments discussed under the heading of "bad news" fail to address it.

Work by Dorrit Billman (Billman 1983, summarized in Holland et al. 1986, 200–204; Billman and Heit 1988) suggests that we are, indeed, quite good detectors of multiple, clustered covariation, in spite of our limitations when it comes to detecting isolated cases. This work divides into two parts. In the first, Billman developed a computer model de-signed to detect cases of clustered covariation; the model illustrates how the very fact of clustering can make detection of covariation easier than it is in isolated cases (Billman and Heit 1988). In the second, Billman offered evidence that the computer model accurately represents human abilities (Billman 1983; Billman and Heit 1988). We will need to examine both parts of this project.

Billman used a technique in her computer model called *focused sampling*. The idea here is quite simple. Imagine an extremely large group of objects, each of which is characterized by a large number of properties. We are assigned the task of detecting covariations among the various properties exhibited by the objects. Because the number of objects is so large, and because the number of properties each object has is so large, a complete inventory of objects and properties proves to be a practical impossibility. As a result, we must try to discover the existing covariations by taking samples from the universe of objects and making our projections from them. There are familiar techniques available for discovering covariations under these conditions; these test the predictive success of hypothesized covariations and modify the hypotheses as more objects in the universe are sampled (see, e.g., Rumelhart et al. 1986). What focused sampling does is this: rather than randomly search the universe of objects, it is more likely to examine a particular object if it has properties which figure in hypotheses which have proven successful. Thus, if properties P and Q have been found to covary in the sample searched, objects with property P and those with property Q will be more likely to be examined. If there are additional properties which covary with both P and Q, this technique will dramatically increase the speed with which such covariation is detected. This result is known as *clustered feature facilitation* (Billman and Heit 1988, 593).

Billman and Heit note that this technique is effective only in certain environments.

Focused sampling benefits learning only when the structure to be learned is consistent with the bias that focused sampling assumes. It does not benefit rule learning if the structure of input does not afford intercorrelated features. If regularities are scattered through the system, predictions that a feature will be used in additional rules because it is used in one will not be sound. However, psychologically natural categories typically provide the correlational coherence assumed by focused sampling. Within a domain, if a feature participates in one regularity it is likely to participate in others. For example, singing predicts having feathers, flying and living in trees. Instances picked out by one predictive rule are much the same set as instances picked out by other rules in the cluster. For a learner equipped with focused sampling, noticing that many singing creatures fly would increase attention to the characteristics involved—singing, and perhaps vocalization as well, depending on the representation. This in turn increases the chance of noticing, say, that singing creatures live in trees. (Billman and Heit 1988, 593–594)

Although Billman and Heit note that the kind of learning environment on which focused sampling is effective involves psychologically natural categories, what is most important for us here is that real kinds in nature have this very structure as well. Precisely because real kinds have properties clustered in homeostatic relationships, a technique of focused sampling will be highly effective in detecting natural kinds. To put the point another way: the presuppositions of focused sampling describe the causal structure of a world which contains natural kinds.

Focused sampling would thus be a good technique to use in coming to understand the world, given its causal structure. But is there any evidence that we do indeed use anything like this technique? Is there evidence that, in spite of our well-documented difficulties in detecting isolated cases of covariation, we are adept at detecting clustered covariation? There is indeed such evidence. Billman (1983) constructed a number of artificial languages which she then attempted to teach to experimental subjects. One of the languages contained three properties (the shape of objects referred to by nouns; the vowel in the noun's stem; and the vowel in the noun's ending) which jointly covaried; any of the three properties was sufficient for predicting the remaining two. The other languages, containing the same basic elements, contained only a single regularity, rather than the clustered regularities of the first language. As a result, there was more to be learned in acquiring the first language, and a greater degree of redundancy as well. After a period of learning, subjects were asked to complete various sentences, parts of which had been omitted. Holland et al. summarize the results.

Billman found that subjects were significantly better able to learn the individual regularities related to noun categories if they formed part of a cluster. This result was obtained both when each relationship between two properties was entirely regular and when exceptions were introduced. Thus, multiple, interrelated associations are learned more readily than single associations, both when the associations are deterministic and when they are merely probabilistic. (1986, 202–203)

As Holland et al. rightly point out, this is an especially significant result.

The superior learning of a rule that formed part of a cluster is particularly noteworthy because there were of course more rules to be learned in the clustered condition. Consequently, one might have supposed that any particular rule would receive less attention than if it were the only regularity. Billman's results, in contrast, clearly support the assumption that human mechanisms for induction are designed to facilitate the acquisition of such interrelated groups. It can be easier to learn many things at once than to learn a single isolated regularity. (1984, 204)

The results Billman obtained with her artificial languages are consistent with what is known about the acquisition of natural language as well. In Hebrew, for example, gender is marked in a way which involves a clustered pattern of regularities, rather than the isolated regularities governing gender in Germanic and Slavic languages. The cluster of regularities governing gender in Hebrew is typically mastered before the age of two, whereas a mastery of the syntax of gender is not typically achieved in Germanic and Slavic languages until much later (Billman and Heit 1988, 622). Here again, learning is facilitated by the clustering of regularities characteristic of natural kinds.

We may now look back at the results which prompted the initial negative assessment of our ability to detect covariation. The bad news about covariation detection proves to be far more limited than first appearances would indicate. It is not the case, as many once concluded, that we are simply inept at detecting covariation. Our weakness lies in the detection of isolated cases of covariation when the strength of covariation is less than 0.8. We do perfectly well at detecting isolated cases of covariation which are stronger than 0.8, and, more importantly, we are accomplished detectors of multiple, clustered patterns of covariation. As with Billman and Heit's computer simulation, which is adapted, by way of focused sampling, to a certain kind of structured environment, we too have skills which are well adapted to certain specific environments, skills which give the illusion of incompetence when they are applied outside of the environments to which they are well adapted. This would be cold comfort if the environments to which our skills are adapted were rare. But nothing like this is the case. The causal structure of the natural world, a world of kinds whose properties are homeostatically clustered, is a structure which plays to our strengths. The covariations which we are best able to detect are built right in to the structure of natural kinds. The covariations which elude or deceive us, like the illusion of motion in the phi phenomenon and the other visual illusions, are the atypical case, which, in spite of their atypicality, point the way toward a better understanding of our cognitive skills.

What then should we say about the work of Chapman and Chapman on theory-driven detection of covariation? This work must also be seen as a small part of a larger picture. Human beings have a very strong tendency toward belief perseverance: once we acquire a certain belief, there is a strong tendency to hold on to it, even in the face of undermining evidence (see Nisbett and Ross 1980, 167–192). What the Chapmans discovered then was not so much a fact about the way in which we detect covariation in particular, as a fact about the way in which existing beliefs affect subsequent information processing in general. This is a large topic, and one which is not, so far as I can tell, related directly to the structure of natural kinds. Instead, the phenomenon of belief perseverance seems best explained by understanding its role in our large-scale cognitive economy (see Harman 1986, 29–42). It is undeniable that belief perseverance operates, in the context investigated by the Chapmans, in a way which interferes with a proper understanding of the world. But it would be unwise to assume without further investigation that this is typical of the way in which belief perseverance operates. Mistaken beliefs will, as a result of belief perseverance, taint our perception of new data. By the same token, however, belief perseverance will serve to color our perception of new data when our preexisting beliefs are accurate. Although this latter case involves bias just as much as the former, the bias involved here is one which informs and instructs, rather than one which distorts or misleads. It is only on narrowly foundationalist accounts of proper belief acquisition that our theories should be a product of the data alone, and our perception of the data should be uninfluenced by background theory. Allowing our background beliefs to influence our perception of the data when those background beliefs are true can only contribute to a better understanding of the world. If, overall, our belief-generating mechanisms give us a fairly accurate picture of the world, then the phenomenon of belief perseverance may do more to inform our understanding than it does to distort it.[10]

It is thus safe to say that we have a sensitivity to the features of objects which reside in homeostatic clusters. Indeed, the way in which we detect covariation is precisely tailored to the structure of natural kinds.

Projecting the Right Features of Natural Kinds

One more thing needs to be shown in order to complete my defense of our use of the law of small numbers: namely, that we have a tendency to project the right features of natural kinds, those features which, in fact, are universally shared by the kind. In order to defend this claim, I will need to review a bit of what has been shown thus far.

I argued earlier that natural kinds have essential properties which are universally shared by the members of the kind, and that these properties reside in a homeostatic relationship. If we have a tendency to project the essential properties of a kind, then even though our inferences are guided by the law of small numbers, such inferences will be reliable. Indeed, if we do have this tendency to project essential properties, the law of small numbers is itself an important aid to efficient understanding of the natural world. We certainly have the ability, as I have just argued, to detect the homeostatic clustering of properties characteristic of natural kinds. The question facing us now is whether our inferences are appropriately driven by this ability to detect covariation. I will argue that they are.

I want to return to the theme of psychological essentialism. The suggestion was made by Douglas Medin (1989; Medin and Ortony 1989) that we tend to presuppose the existence of underlying essences, and that our concepts build in this presupposition from the very beginning.

Medin and Ortony say that "people act as if their concepts contain essence placeholders that are filled with 'theories' about what the corresponding entities are" (1989, 186). The theories which fill these essence placeholders are subject to modification over time, as more information is obtained about a kind, and as misinformation is corrected. What I want to suggest is that the information which fills these essence placeholders drives inductive inference: the properties we take to be essential to a kind are those we project. Indeed, the function of the essence placeholder in our cognitive economy just is to drive inductive inference: we conceptualize kinds in such a way in order to separate the properties of the members of a kind which are projectable from those which are not. We are aided in this task by our ability to detect clustered covariation.

Why should we think this? The work of Gelman and her co-workers (Gelman and Markman 1986, 1987; Wellman and Gelman 1988; Gelman and Coley 1990; Gelman and Wellman 1991) is relevant here. It was found not only that children tend to classify objects on the basis of underlying properties rather than superficial similarities, but also that their inductive inferences are guided by underlying properties rather than superficial similarities. Children expect members of a kind to share deep similarities rather than superficial properties. This is not to say that children always have an accurate understanding of what those deep similarities are. Of course, they do not. Sometimes they are completely ignorant of the deep similarities which unite a kind, and sometimes they have mistaken views about those similarities. Nevertheless, they presuppose, from the very beginning, that the features which unite a kind are underlying rather than more superficial ones. But it is precisely those underlying properties which form the essence of natural kinds. In having our inferences driven by a sensitivity to the deeper properties which unite a kind, we are thereby drawing on what we know about the kind's essence. Insofar as that knowledge is accurate, our inductive inferences will be reliable.

The essence placeholder, which stands at the center of our conceptual structure, thus turns our sensitivity to clustered covariation into a medium for reliable inductive inference. The law of small numbers, like these other features of our cognitive repertoire, is carefully attuned to the causal structure of natural kinds.

Conclusion

I have argued that important features of our inferential tendencies may best be understood by seeing how they dovetail with the causal structure of the world. The law of small numbers, which is often assumed to be a paradigm of misguided inference, may be defended by seeing precisely how it is applied. Attempts to compare our inductive strategies with the probability calculus have been argued to be inappropriate, for such comparisons lead away from the crucial questions of which properties we tend to project, and under which circumstances we tend to project them. As it turns out, I have argued, we are quite adept at detecting the very features of natural kinds which are essential to them, and our conceptual structure places these essential features in the position of driving inductive inference. As a result, when the law of small numbers goes to work, we typically project the properties of natural kinds which are universally shared by their members. It is thus that our inductive inferences are tailored to the causal structure of the world, and thus that inductive understanding of the world is possible.

Notes

1. A large body of the papers which created this picture are collected in Kahneman et al. 1982. The literature is carefully reviewed in Nisbett and Ross 1980. More recent though less comprehensive reviews of various parts of the literature may be found in Holyoak and Nisbett 1988; Schustack 1988; Rips 1988; Fischhoff 1988; Osherson 1990; Slovic 1990; and Holyoak 1990.

2. Actually, the phi phenomenon is not limited to the processing of visual information. It can be produced tactilely as well (Wyburn et al. 1968, 20). This fact about it is striking confirmation of the explanation offered in the text. It shows how deep the presupposition of object constancy goes.

3. Some might think that this mistake has routinely been made by philosophers of a skeptical turn of mind, or at least that these philosophers, and others who take skepticism seriously, have spent a good deal of time considering whether perceptual illusions make a good case for the unreliability of the senses. This is not, however, correct. Although skeptical philosophers, and those who take skepticism seriously, have frequently considered whether perceptual illusions give us reason to doubt the reliability of the senses, there is a very large gap between such a doubt and the conviction that the senses are unreliable. No one, to my knowledge, has suggested that perceptual illusions give us reason to believe that the senses are unreliable.

4. This is not actually true. The law of large numbers states that the larger the sample of a population, the more likely it is to reflect the actual frequency of traits in the population as a whole. Large samples, however, so long as they do not merely coincide with the entire population, do not guarantee representativeness.

5. The first three paragraphs of this section are drawn from Kornblith 1983, 42–43, with little alteration, although this material was used there to argue for a different conclusion. The example is adapted from Nisbett and Ross 1980, 256–260.

6. Strictly speaking, what statistical inference licenses is not a prediction, or a sampling technique, but rather a degree of confidence in a prediction given a sampling technique. When I speak of the sampling techniques which statistical inference would license, strictly speaking what I should say is that these are the sampling techniques which would allow for the highest degree of confidence. The more informal language in the text will not, I expect, be at all misleading.

7. This figure was given incorrectly in Kornblith 1983.

8. This is just another way of putting Goodman's (1955) point that there can be no formal inductive logic.

9. So Chapman and Chapman reported in 1971. In discussion with a number of clinicians, I have discovered that this is still true.

10. I do not pretend to have given a full defense of belief perseverance. Such a defense would, I am well aware, require much further discussion. It is important to recognize, however, that the work of the Chapmans is not so much an attack on our ability to detect covariation as it is a challenge to a much broader cognitive phenomenon. I hope these gestures in the direction of a defense of that phenomenon go some way toward making this much clear: it is not obvious that belief perseverance is a bad thing.

References

Billman, D. O. (1983). *Procedures for learning syntactic categories: A model and test with artificial grammars.* Doctoral dissertation, University of Michigan, Ann Arbor.

Billman, D. O. and E. Heit (1988). Observational learning from internal feedback: A simulation of an adaptive learning method. *Cognitive Science* 12, 587–625.

Boyd, R. N. (1988). How to be a moral realist. In G. Sayre-McCord, ed., *Essays on moral realism.* Ithaca: Cornell University Press.

Boyd, R. N. (1991). Realism, anti-foundationalism and the enthusiasm for natural kinds. *Philosophical Studies* 61, 127–148.

Chapman, L. J., and J. P. Chapman (1967). Genesis of popular but erroneous diagnostic observations. *Journal of Abnormal Psychology* 72, 193–204.

Chapman, L. J., and J. P. Chapman (1969). Illusory correlation as an obstacle to the use of valid psychodiagnostic signs. *Journal of Abnormal Psychology* 74, 271–280.

Chapman, L. J., and J. P. Chapman (1971). Test results are what you think they are. Reprinted in D. Kahneman, P. Slovic, and A.Tversky, eds. (1982). *Judgment under uncertainty: Heuristics and biases.* Cambridge: Cambridge University Press.

Fischhoff, B. (1988). Judgment and decision making. In R. J. Sternberg, and E. E. Smith, eds., *The Psychology of Human Thought.* Cambridge: Cambridge University Press.

Gelman, S. A., and J. D. Coley (1990). The importance of knowing a Dodo is a bird: Categories and inferences in 2-year-old children. *Developmental Psychology* 26, 796–804.

Gelman, S. A., and E. M. Markman (1986). Categories and induction in young children. *Cognition* 23, 183–208.

Gelman, S. A., and E. M. Markman (1987). Young children's inductions from natural kinds: The role of categories and appearances. *Child Development* 58, 132–141.

Gelman, S. A., and H. M. Wellman (1991). Insides and essences: Early understanding of the non-obvious. *Cognition* 38, 213–244.

Goodman, N. (1955) *Fact, fiction and forecast.* Cambridge, MA: Harvard University Press.

Hamill, R., T. D. Wilson, and R. E. Nisbett (1979). Ignoring sample bias: Inferences about collectivities from atypical cases. Unpublished manuscript.

Harman, G. (1986). *Change in view: Principles of reasoning*. Cambridge, MA: MIT Press.

Holland, J. H., K. J. Holyoak, R. E. Nisbett, and P. R. Thagard (1986). *Induction: Processes of inference, learning, and discovery*. Cambridge, MA: MIT Press.

Holyoak, K. J. (1990). Problem solving. In Osherson and Smith, eds., *Thinking: An invitation to cognitive science*, vol. 3, Cambridge, MA: MIT Press.

Holyoak, K. J. and R. E. Nisbett (1988). Induction. In R. J. Sternberg and E. E. Smith, eds., *The Psychology of Human Thought*. Cambridge: Cambridge University Press.

Jennings, D. L., T. M. Amabile, and L. Ross (1982). Informal covariation assessment: Data-based versus theory-based judgments. In D. Kahneman, P. Slovic, and A. Tversky, eds., *Judgment under uncertainty: Heuristics and biases*. Cambridge: Cambridge University Press.

Kahneman, D., P. Slovic, and A. Tversky, eds. (1982). *Judgment under uncertainty: Heuristics and biases*. Cambridge: Cambridge University Press.

Kornblith, H. (1983). Justified belief and epistemically responsible action. *Philosophical Review* 92, 33–48.

Langer, E., and S. Roth (1975). Heads I win, tail's it's chance: The illusion of control as a function of the sequence of outcomes in a purely chance task. *Journal of Personality and Social Psychology*. 32, 951–955.

Medin, D. L. (1989). Concepts and conceptual structure. *American Psychologist* 44, 1469–1481.

Medin, D. L., and A. Ortony (1989) Comments on Part I: Psychological essentialism. In S. Vosniadou and A. Ortony, eds., *Similarity and analogical reasoning*. Cambridge: Cambridge University Press.

Nisbett, R. E., and E. Borgida (1975). Attribution and the psychology of prediction. *Journal of Personality and Social Psychology* 32, 932–943.

Nisbett, R. E., and L. Ross (1980). *Human inference: Strategies and shortcomings of social judgment*. Englewood Cliffs, NJ: Prentice-Hall.

Osherson, D. N. (1990). Judgment. In D. N. Osherson and E. E. Smith, eds., *Thinking: An invitation to cognitive science*, vol. 3. Cambridge, MA: MIT Press.

Oskamp, S. (1965). Overconfidence in case-study judgments. Reprinted in D.Kahneman, P. Slovic, and A. Tversky, eds., (1982). *Judgment under uncertainty: Heuristics and biases*. Cambridge: Cambridge University Press.

Peterson, C. R., and L. R. Beach (1967). Man as an intuitive statistician. *Psychological Bulletin* 68, 29–46.

Rips, L. J. (1988). Deduction. In R. J. Sternberg and E. E. Smith, eds., *The Psychology of Human Thought*. Cambridge: Cambridge University Press.

Rock, I. (1983). *The logic of perception*. Cambridge, MA: MIT Press.

Ross, L., M. R. Lepper, and M. Hubbard (1975). Perseverance in self-perception and social perception: Biased attributional processes in the debriefing paradigm. *Journal of Personality and Social Psychology* 32, 880–892.

Rumelhart, D. E., G. E. Hinton, and R. J. Williams (1986). Learning internal representations by error propagation. In D. E. Rumelhart, J. L. McClelland, and the PDP Research Group. *Parallel Distributed Processing*, vol. 1. Cambridge, MA: MIT Press.

Schustack, M. W. (1988). Thinking about causality. In R. J. Sternberg and E. E. Smith, eds., *The Psychology of Human Thought*. Cambridge: Cambridge University Press.

Slovic, P. (1990). Choice. In D. N. Osherson and E. E. Smith, eds., *Thinking: An invitation to cognitive science*, vol. 3. Cambridge, MA: MIT Press.

Smedslund, J. (1963). The concept of correlation in adults. *Scandinavian Journal of Psychology* 4, 16–173.

Tversky, A., and D. Kahneman (1971). Belief in the law of small numbers. Reprinted in D. Kahneman, P. Slovic, and A. Tversky, eds. (1982). *Judgment under uncertainty: Heuristics and biases*. Cambridge: Cambridge University Press.

Tversky, A., and D. Kahneman (1973). Availability: A heuristic for judging frequency and probability. Reprinted in D. Kahneman, P. Slovic, and A. Tversky, eds. (1982). *Judgment under uncertainty: Heuristics and biases*. Cambridge: Cambridge University Press.

Ward, W. D., and H. M. Jenkins (1965). The display of information and the judgment of contingency. *Canadian Journal of Psychology* 19, 231–241.

Wellman, H. M. and S. A. Gelman (1988). Children's understanding of the nonobvious. In R. J. Sternberg, ed., *Advances in the psychology of human intelligence*, vol. 4. Hillsdale, NJ: Erlbaum.

Wyburn, C. M., R. W. Pickford, and R. J. Hirst (1968). *Human senses and perception*. Toronto: University of Toronto Press.

5 Epistemic Folkways and Scientific Epistemology

Alvin I. Goldman

I

What is the mission of epistemology, and what is its proper methodology? Such meta-epistemological questions have been prominent in recent years, especially with the emergence of various brands of "naturalistic" epistemology. In this paper, I shall reformulate and expand upon my own meta-epistemological conception (most fully articulated in Goldman 1986), retaining many of its former ingredients while re-configuring others. The discussion is by no means confined, though, to the meta-epistemological level. New substantive proposals will also be advanced and defended.

Let us begin, however, at the meta-epistemological level, by asking what role should be played in epistemology by our ordinary epistemic concepts and principles. By some philosophers' lights, the sole mission of epistemology is to elucidate commonsense epistemic concepts and principles: concepts like knowledge, justification, and rationality, and principles associated with these concepts. By other philosophers' lights, this is not even part of epistemology's aim. Ordinary concepts and principles, the latter would argue, are fundamentally naive, unsystematic, and uninformed by important bodies of logic and/or mathematics. Ordinary principles and practices, for example, ignore or violate the probability calculus, which ought to be the cornerstone of epistemic rationality. Thus, on the second view, proper epistemology must neither *end* with naive principles of justification or rationality, nor even *begin* there.

My own stance on this issue lies somewhere between these extremes. To facilitate discussion, let us give a label to our commonsense epistemic concepts and norms; let us call them our *epistemic folkways*. In partial agreement with the first view sketched above, I would hold that *one*

From A. Goldman, Epistemic Folkways and Scientific Epistemology, in *Liaisons: Philosophy meets the cognitive and social sciences* (1992). Cambridge, MA: MIT Press. Reprinted by permission.

proper task of epistemology is to elucidate our epistemic folkways. Whatever else epistemology might proceed to do, it should at least have its roots in the concepts and practices of the folk. If these roots are utterly rejected and abandoned, by what rights would the new discipline call itself 'epistemology' at all? It may well be desirable to reform or transcend our epistemic folkways, as the second of the views sketched above recommends. But it is essential to preserve continuity; and continuity can only be recognized if we have a satisfactory characterization of our epistemic folkways. Actually, even if one rejects the plea for continuity, a description of our epistemic folkways is in order. How would one know what to criticize, or what needs to be transcended, in the absence of such a description? So a first mission of epistemology is to describe or characterize our folkways.

Now a suitable description of these folk concepts, I believe, is likely to depend on insights from cognitive science. Indeed, identification of the semantic contours of many (if not all) concepts can profit from theoretical and empirical work in psychology and linguistics. For this reason, the task of describing or elucidating folk epistemology is a *scientific* task, at least a task that should be informed by relevant scientific research.

The second mission of epistemology, as suggested by the second view above, is the formulation of a more adequate, sound, or systematic set of epistemic norms, in some way(s) transcending our naive epistemic repertoire. How and why these folkways might be transcended, or improved upon, remains to be specified. This will partly depend on the contours of the commonsense standards that emerge from the first mission. On my view, epistemic concepts like knowledge and justification crucially invoke psychological faculties or processes. Our folk understanding, however, has a limited and tenuous grasp of the processes available to the cognitive agent. Thus, one important respect in which epistemic folkways should be transcended is by incorporating a more detailed and empirically based depiction of psychological mechanisms. Here too epistemology would seek assistance from cognitive science.

Since both missions of epistemology just delineated lean in important respects on the deliverances of science, specifically cognitive science, let us call our conception of epistemology *scientific epistemology*. Scientific epistemology, we have seen, has two branches: *descriptive* and *normative*. While descriptive scientific epistemology aims to describe our ordinary epistemic assessments, normative scientific epistemology continues the practice of making epistemic judgments, or formulating systematic principles for such judgments.[1] It is prepared to depart from our ordinary epistemic judgments, however, if and when that proves advisable. . . . In the remainder of this paper, I shall sketch and defend the particular forms of descriptive and normative scientific epistemology that I favor.

II

Mainstream epistemology has concentrated much of its attention on two concepts (or terms): knowledge and justified belief. . . . This essay focuses on the latter. We need not mark this concept exclusively by the phrase 'justified belief'. A family of phrases pick out roughly the same concept: 'well-founded belief', 'reasonable belief', 'belief based on good grounds', and so forth. I shall propose an account of this concept that is in the reliabilist tradition, but departs at a crucial juncture from other versions of reliabilism. My account has the same core idea as Ernest Sosa's *intellectual virtues* approach, but incorporates some distinctive features that improve its prospects.[2]

The basic approach is, roughly, to identify the concept of justified belief with the concept of belief obtained through the exercise of intellectual virtues (excellences). Beliefs acquired (or retained) through a chain of "virtuous" psychological processes qualify as justified; those acquired partly by cognitive "vices" are derogated as unjustified. This, as I say, is a *rough* account. To explain it more fully, I need to say things about the psychology of the epistemic evaluator, the possessor and deployer of the concept in question. At this stage in the development of semantical theory (which, in the future, may well be viewed as part of the "dark ages" of the subject), it is difficult to say just what the relationship is between the meaning or "content" of concepts and the form or structure of their mental representation. In the present case, however, I believe that an account of the form of representation can contribute to our understanding of the content, although I am unable to formulate these matters in a theoretically satisfying fashion.

The hypothesis I wish to advance is that the epistemic evaluator has a mentally stored set, or list, of cognitive virtues and vices. When asked to evaluate an actual or hypothetical case of belief, the evaluator considers the processes by which the belief was produced, and matches these against his list of virtues and vices. If the processes match virtues only, the belief is classified as justified. If the processes are matched partly with vices, the belief is categorized as unjustified. If a belief-forming scenario is described that features a process not on the evaluator's list of either virtues or vices, the belief may be categorized as neither justified nor unjustified, but simply *non*justified. Alternatively (and this alternative plays an important role in my story), the evaluator's judgment may depend on the (judged) *similarity* of the novel process to the stored virtues and vices. In other words, the "matches" in question need not be perfect.

This proposal makes two important points of contact with going theories in the psychology of concepts. First, it has some affinity to the *exemplar* approach to concept representation (cf. Medin and Schaffer 1978; Smith and Medin 1981; Hintzman 1986). According to that approach, a concept is mentally represented by means of representations of its positive instances, or perhaps types of instances. For example, the representation of the concept *pants* might include a representation of a particular pair of faded blue jeans and/or a representation of the type *blue jeans*. Our approach to the concept of justification shares the spirit of this approach insofar as it posits a set of examples of virtues and vices, as opposed to a mere abstract characterization—e.g., a definition—of (intellectual) virtue or vice. A second affinity to the exemplar approach is in the appeal to a similarity, or matching, operation in the classification of new target cases. According to the exemplar approach, targets are categorized as a function of their similarity to the positive exemplars (and dissimilarity to the foils). Of course, similarity is invoked in many other approaches to concept deployment as well (see E. E. Smith 1990). This makes our account of justification consonant with the psychological literature generally, whether or not it meshes specifically with the exemplar approach.

Let us now see what this hypothesis predicts for a variety of cases. To apply it, we need to make some assumptions about the lists of virtues and vices that typical evaluators mentally store. I shall assume that the virtues include belief formation based on sight, hearing, memory, reasoning in certain "approved" ways, and so forth. The vices include intellectual processes like forming beliefs by guesswork, wishful thinking, and ignoring contrary evidence. *Why* these items are placed in their respective categories remains to be explained. As indicated, I plan to explain them by reference to reliability. Since the account will therefore be, at bottom, a reliabilist type of account, it is instructive to see how it fares when applied to well-known problem cases for standard versions of reliabilism.

Consider first the demon-world case. In a certain possible world, a Cartesian demon gives people deceptive visual experiences, which systematically lead to false beliefs. Are these vision-based beliefs justified? Intuitively, they are. The demon's victims are presented with the same sorts of visual experiences that we are, and they use the same processes to produce corresponding beliefs. For most epistemic evaluators, this seems sufficient to induce the judgment that the victims' beliefs are justified. Does our account predict this result? Certainly it does. The account predicts that an epistemic evaluator will match the victims' vision-based processes to one (or more) of the items on his list of intellectual virtues, and therefore judge the victims' beliefs to be justified.

Turn next to Laurence BonJour's (1985) cases in which hypothetical agents are assumed to possess a perfectly reliable clairvoyant faculty. Although these agents form their beliefs by this reliable faculty, BonJour contends that the beliefs are not justified; and apparently most (philosophical) evaluators agree with that judgment. This result is not predicted by simple forms of reliabilism.[3] What does our present theory predict? Let us consider the four cases in two groups. In the first three cases (Samantha, Casper, and Maud), the agent has contrary evidence that he or she ignores. Samantha has a massive amount of apparently cogent evidence that the president is in Washington, but she nonetheless believes (through clairvoyance) that the president is in New York City. Casper and Maud each has large amounts of ostensibly cogent evidence that he/she has no reliable clairvoyant power, but they rely on such a power nonetheless. Here our theory predicts that the evaluator will match these agent's belief-forming processes to the vice of ignoring contrary evidence. Since the processes include a vice, the beliefs will be judged to be unjustified.

BonJour's fourth case involves Norman, who has a reliable clairvoyant power but no reasons for or against the thesis that he possesses it. When he believes, through clairvoyance, that the president is in New York City, while possessing no (other) relevant evidence, how should this belief be judged? My own assessment is less clear in this case than the other three cases. I am tempted to say that Norman's belief is *non*justified, not that it is thoroughly *un*justified. (I construe unjustified as "having negative justificational status", and nonjustified as "lacking positive justificational status".) This result is also readily predicted by our theory. On the assumption that I (and other evaluators) do not have clairvoyance on my list of virtues, the theory allows the prediction that the belief would be judged neither justified nor unjustified, merely nonjustified. For those evaluators who would judge Norman's belief to be *un*justified, there is another possible explanation in terms of the theory. There is a class of putative faculties, including mental telepathy, ESP, telekinesis, and so forth that are scientifically disreputable. It is plausible that evaluators view any process of basing beliefs on the supposed deliverances of such faculties as vices. It is also plausible that these evaluators judge the process of basing one's belief on clairvoyance to be *similar* to such vices. Thus, the theory would predict that they would view a belief acquired in this way as unjustified.[4]

Finally, consider Alvin Plantinga's (1988) examples that feature disease-triggered or mind-malfunctioning processes. These include processes engendered by a brain tumor, radiation-caused processes, and the like. In each case Plantinga imagines that the process is reliable, but reports that we would not judge it to be justification conferring. My diagnosis follows the track outlined in the Norman case. At a minimum, the processes imagined by Plantinga fail to match any virtue on a typical evaluator's list. So the beliefs are at least nonjustified. Furthermore, evaluators may have a prior representation of pathological processes as examples of cognitive vices. Plantinga's cases might be judged (relevantly) similar to these vices, so that the beliefs they produce would be declared unjustified.

In some of Plantinga's cases, it is further supposed that the hypothetical agent possesses countervailing evidence against this belief, which he steadfastly ignores. As noted earlier, this added element would strengthen a judgment of unjustifiedness according to our theory, because ignoring contrary evidence is an intellectual vice. Once again, then, our theory's predictions conform with reported judgments.

Let us now turn to the question of how epistemic evaluators acquire their lists of virtues and vices. What is the basis for their classification? As already indicated, my answer invokes the notion of reliability. Belief-forming processes based on vision, hearing, memory, and ("good") reasoning are deemed virtuous because they (are deemed to) produce a high ratio for true beliefs. Processes like guessing, wishful thinking, and ignoring contrary evidence are deemed vicious because they (are deemed to) produce a low ratio of true beliefs.

We need not assume that each epistemic evaluator chooses his/her catalogue of virtues and vices by direct application of the reliability test. Epistemic evaluators may partly inherit their lists of virtues and vices from other speakers in the linguistic community. Nonetheless, the hypothesis is that the selection of virtues and vices rests, ultimately, on assessments of reliability.

It is not assumed, of course, that all speakers have the same lists of intellectual virtues and vices. They may have different opinions about the reliability of processes, and therefore differ in their respective lists.[5] Or they may belong to different subcultures in the linguistic community, which may differentially influence their lists. Philosophers sometimes seem to assume great uniformity in epistemic judgments. This assumption may stem from the fact that it is mostly the judgments of philosophers themselves that have been reported, and they are members of a fairly homogeneous subculture. A wider pool of "subjects" might reveal a much lower degree of uniformity. That would conform to the present theory, however, which permits individual differences in catalogues of virtues and vices, and hence in judgments of justifiedness.

If virtues and vices are selected on the basis of reliability and unreliability, respectively, why doesn't a hypothetical case introducing a novel reliable process induce an evaluator to add that process to his list of virtues, and declare the resulting belief justified? Why, for example, doesn't he add clairvoyance to his list of virtues, and rule Norman's beliefs to be justified?

I venture the following explanation. First, people seem to have a trait of *categorial conservatism*. They display a preference for "entrenched" categories, in Nelson Goodman's (1955) phraseology, and do not lightly supplement or revise their categorial schemes. An isolated single case is not enough. More specifically, merely imaginary cases do not exert much influence on categorial structures. People's cognitive systems are responsive to live cases, not purely fictional ones. Philosophers encounter this when their students or nonphilosophers are unimpressed with science fiction-style counterexamples. Philosophers become impatient with this response because they presume that possible cases are on a par (for counterexample purposes) with actual ones. This phenomenon testifies, however, to a psychological propensity to take an invidious attitude toward purely imaginary cases.

To the philosopher, it seems both natural and inevitable to take hypothetical cases seriously, and if necessary to restrict one's conclusions about them to specified "possible worlds". Thus, the philosopher might be inclined to hold, "If reliability is the standard of intellectual virtue, shouldn't we say that clairvoyance is a virtue *in the possible worlds* of BonJour's examples, if not a virtue in general?" This is a natural thing for philosophers to say, given their schooling, but there is no evidence that this is how people naturally think about the matter. There is no evidence that "the folk" are inclined to relativize virtues and vices to this or that possible world.

I suspect that concerted investigation (not undertaken here) would uncover ample evidence of conservatism, specifically in the normative realm. In many traditional cultures, for example, loyalty to family and friends is treated as a cardinal virtue.[6] This view of loyalty tends to persist even through changes in social and organizational climate, which undermine the value of unqualified loyalty. Members of such cultures, I suspect, would continue to view personal loyalty as a virtue even in *hypothetical* cases where the trait has stipulated unfortunate consequences.

In a slightly different vein, it is common for both critics and advocates of reliabilism to call attention to the relativity of reliability to the domain or circumstances in which the process is used. The question is therefore raised, what is the relevant domain for judging the reliability of a process? A critic like John Pollock (1986, 118–119), for example, observes that color vision is reliable on earth but unreliable in the universe at large. In determining the reliability of color vision, he asks, which domain should be invoked? Finding no satisfactory reply to this question, Pollock takes this as a serious difficulty for reliabilism. Similarly, Sosa (1988, 1991) notes that an intellectual structure or disposition can be reliable with respect to one field of propositions but unreliable with respect to another, and reliable in one environment but unreliable in another. He does not view this as a difficulty for reliabilism, but concludes that any talk of intellectual virtue must be relativized to field and environment

Neither of these conclusions seems apt, however, for purposes of *description* of our epistemic folkways. It would be a mistake to suppose that ordinary epistemic evaluators are sensitive to these issues. It is likely—or at least plausible—that our ordinary apprehension of the intellectual virtues is rough, unsystematic, and insensitive to any theoretical desirability of relativization to domain or environment. Thus, as long as we are engaged in the description of our epistemic folkways, it is no criticism of the account that it fails to explain what domain or environment is to be used. Nor is it appropriate for the account to introduce relativization where there is no evidence of relativization on the part of the folk.

Of course, we do need an explanatory story of how the folk arrive at their selected virtues and vices. And this presumably requires some reference to the domain in which reliability is judged. However, there may not be much more to the story than the fact that people determine reliability scores from the cases they personally "observe." Alternatively, they *may* regard the observed cases as a sample from which they infer a truth ratio in some wider class of cases. It is doubtful, however, that they have any precise conception of the wider class. They probably don't address this theoretical issue, and don't do (or think) anything that commits them to any particular resolution of it. It would therefore be wrong to expect descriptive epistemology to be fully specific on this dimension.

A similar point holds for the question of process individuation. It is quite possible that the folk do not have highly principled methods for individuating cognitive processes, for "slicing up" virtues and vices. If that is right, it is a mistake to insist that descriptive epistemology uncover such methods. It is no flaw in reliabilism, considered as descriptive epistemology, that it fails to unearth them. It may well be desirable to develop sharper individuation principles for purposes of normative epistemology (a matter we shall address in section III). But the missions and requirements of descriptive and normative epistemology must be kept distinct.

This discussion has assumed throughout that the folk have lists of intellectual virtues and vices. What is the evidence for this? In the moral sphere ordinary language is rich in virtues terminology. By contrast, there are few common labels for intellectual virtues, and those that do exist—'perceptiveness', 'thoroughness', 'insightfulness', and so forth— are of limited value in the present context. I propose to identify the relevant intellectual virtues (at least those relevant to *justification*) with the belief-forming capacities, faculties, or processes that would be accepted as answers to the question "How does X know?" In answer to this form of question, it is common to reply, "He saw it," "He heard it," "He remembers it," "He infers it from such-and-such evidence," and so forth. Thus, basing belief on seeing, hearing, memory, and (good) inference are in the collection of what the folk regard as intellectual virtues. Consider, for contrast, how anomalous it is to answer the question "How does X know?" with "By guess-work," "By wishful thinking," or "By ignoring contrary evidence." This indicates that *these* modes of belief formation—guessing, wishful thinking, ignoring contrary evidence—are standardly regarded as intellectual *vices*. They are not ways of obtaining knowledge, nor ways of obtaining justified belief.

Why appeal to "knowledge"-talk rather than "justification"-talk to identify the virtues? Because 'know' has a greater frequency of occurrence than 'justified', yet the two are closely related. Roughly, justified belief is belief acquired by means of the same sorts of capacities, faculties, or processes that yield knowledge in favorable circumstances (i.e., when the resulting belief is true and there are no Gettier complications, or no relevant alternatives).

To sum up the present theory, let me emphasize that it depicts justificational evaluation as involving two stages. The first stage features the acquisition by an evaluator of some set of intellectual virtues and vices. This is where reliability enters the picture. In the second stage, the evaluator applies his list of virtues and vices to decide the epistemic status of targeted beliefs. At this stage, there is no direct consideration of reliability.

There is an obvious analogy here to rule utilitarianism in the moral sphere. Another analogy worth mentioning is Saul Kripke's (1980) theory of *reference-fixing*. According to Kripke, we can use one property to fix a reference to a certain entity, or type of entity; but once this reference has been fixed, that property may cease to play a role in identifying the entity across various possible worlds. For example, we can fix a reference to heat as the phenomenon that causes certain sensations in people. Once heat has been so picked out, this property is no longer needed, or relied upon, in identifying heat. A phenomenon can count as heat in another possible world where it doesn't cause those sensations in people. Similarly, I am proposing, we initially use reliability as a test for intellectual quality (virtue or vice status). Once the quality of a faculty or process has been determined, however, it tends to retain that status in our thinking. At any rate, it isn't reassessed each time we consider a fresh case, especially a purely imaginary and bizarre case like the demon world. Nor is quality relativized to each possible world or environment.

The present version of the virtues theory appears to be a successful variant of reliabilism, capable of accounting for most, in not all, of the most prominent counterexamples to earlier variants of reliabilism.[7] The present approach also makes an innovation in naturalistic epistemology. Whereas earlier naturalistic epistemologists have focused exclusively on the psychology of the epistemic agent, the present paper also highlights the psychology of the epistemic evaluator.

III

Let us turn now to *normative* scientific epistemology. It was argued briefly in section I that normative scientific epistemology should preserve continuity with our epistemic folkways. At a minimum, it should rest on the same types of evaluative criteria as those on which our commonsense epistemic evaluations rest. Recently, however, Stephen Stich (1990) has disputed this sort of claim. Stich contends that our epistemic folkways are quite idiosyncratic and should not be much heeded in a reformed epistemology. An example he uses to underline his claim of idiosyncracy is the notion of justification as rendered by my "normal worlds" analysis in Goldman 1986. With hindsight, I would agree that that particular analysis makes our ordinary notion of justification look pretty idiosyncratic. But that was the fault of the analysis, not the analysandum. On the present rendering, it looks as if the folk notion of justification is keyed to dispositions to produce a high ratio of true beliefs in the actual world, not in "normal worlds"; and there is nothing idiosyncratic about that. Furthermore, there seem to be straightforward reasons for thinking that true belief is worthy of positive valuation, if only from a pragmatic point of view, which Stich also challenges. The pragmatic utility of true belief is best seen by focusing on a certain subclass of beliefs, viz., beliefs about one's own *plans of action*. Clearly, true beliefs about which courses of action would accomplish one's ends will help secure these ends better than false beliefs. Let proposition P = "Plan N will accomplish my ends" and proposition P' = "Plan N' will accomplish my ends." If P is true and P' is false, I am best off believing the former and not believing the latter. My belief will guide my choice of a plan, and belief in the true proposition (but not the false one) will lead me to choose a plan that *will* accomplish my ends. Stich has other intriguing arguments that cannot be considered here, but it certainly appears that true belief is a perfectly sensible and stable value, not an idiosyncratic one.[8] Thus, I shall assume that normative scientific epistemology should follow in the footsteps of folk practice and use reliability (and other truth-linked standards) as a basis for epistemic evaluation.

If scientific epistemology retains the fundamental standard(s) of folk epistemic assessment, how might it diverge from our epistemic folkways? One possible divergence emerges from William Alston's (1988) account of justification. Although generally sympathetic with reliabilism, Alston urges a kind of constraint not standardly imposed by reliabilism (at least not process reliabilism.) This is the requirement that the processes from which justified beliefs issue must have as their input, or basis, a state *of which the cognizer is aware* (or can easily become aware). Suppose that Alston is right about this as an account of our folk conception of justification. It may well be urged that this ingredient needn't be retained in a scientifically sensitive epistemology. In particular, it may well be claimed that one thing to be learned from cognitive science is that only a small proportion of our cognitive processes operate on consciously accessible inputs. It could therefore be argued that a reformed conception of intellectually virtuous processes should dispense with the "accessibility" requirement.

Alston aside, the point of divergence I wish to examine concerns the psychological units that are chosen as virtues or vices. The lay epistemic evaluator uses casual, unsystematic, and largely introspective methods to carve out the mental faculties and processes responsible for belief formation and revision. Scientific epistemology, by contrast, would utilize the resources of cognitive science to devise a more subtle and sophisticated picture of the mechanisms of belief acquisition. I proceed now to illustrate how this project should be carried out.

An initial phase of the undertaking is to sharpen our conceptualization of the types of cognitive units that should be targets of epistemic evaluation. Lay people are pretty vague about the sorts of entities that qualify as intellectual virtues or vices. In my description of epistemic folkways, I have been deliberately indefinite about these entities, calling them variously "faculties," "processes," "mechanisms," and the like. How should systematic epistemology improve on this score?

A first possibility, enshrined in the practice of historical philosophers, is to take the relevant units to be cognitive *faculties*. This might be translated into modern parlance as *modules*, except that this term has assumed a rather narrow, specialized meaning under Jerry Fodor's (1983) influential treatment of modularity. A better translation might be (cognitive) *systems* e.g., the visual system, long-term memory, and so forth. Such systems, however, are also suboptimal candidates for units of epistemic analysis. Many beliefs are the outputs of two or more systems working in tandem. For example, a belief consisting in the visual classification of an object ("That is a chair") may involve matching some information in the visual system with a category stored in long-term memory. A preferable unit of analysis, then, might be a *process*, construed as the sort of entity depicted by familiar flow charts of cognitive activity. This sort of diagram depicts a sequence of operations (or sets of parallel operations), ultimately culminating in a belief-like output. Such a sequence may span several cognitive systems. This is the sort of entity I had in mind in previous publications (especially Goldman 1986) when I spoke of "cognitive processes."

Even this sort of entity, however, is not a fully satisfactory unit of analysis. Visual classification, for example, may occur under a variety of degraded conditions. The stimulus may be viewed from an unusual orientation; it may be partly occluded, so that only certain of its parts are visible; and so forth. Obviously, these factors can make a big difference to the reliability of the classification process. Yet it is one and the same process that analyzes the stimulus data and comes to a perceptual "conclusion." So the same process can have different degrees of reliability depending on a variety of parameter values. For purposes of epistemic assessment, it would be instructive to identify the parameters and parameter values that are critically relevant to degrees of reliability. The virtues and vices might then be associated not with processes per se, but with processes operating *with specified parameter values*. Let me illustrate this idea in connection with visual perception.

Consider Irving Biederman's (1987, 1990) theory of object recognition, recognition-by-components (RBC). The core idea of Biederman's theory is that a common concrete object like a chair, a giraffe, or a mushroom is mentally represented as an arrangement of simple primitive volumes called *geons* (*geometrical ions*). These geons, or primitive "components" of objects, are typically symmetrical volumes lacking sharp concavities, such as blocks, cylinders, spheres, and wedges. A set of twenty-four types of geons can be differentiated on the basis of dichotomous or trichotomous contrasts of such attributes as curvature (straight versus curved), size variation (constant versus expanding), and symmetry (symmetrical versus asymmetrical). These twenty-four types of geons can then be combined by means of six relations (e.g., top-of, side-connected, larger-than, etc.) into various possible multiple-geon objects. For example, a cup can be represented as a cylindrical geon that is side-connected to a curved, handle-like geon, whereas a pail can be represented as the same two geons bearing a different relation: the curved, handle-like geon is at the top of the cylindrical geon.

Simplifying a bit, the RBC theory of object recognition posits five stages of processing. (1) In the first stage, low-level vision extracts edge characteristics, such as L's, Y-vertices, and arrows. (2) On the basis of these edge characteristics, viewpoint-independent attributes are detected, such as curved, straight, size-constant, size-expanding, etc. (3) In the next stage, selected geons and their relations are activated. (4) Geon activation leads to the activation of object models, that is, familiar models of simple types of objects, stored in long-term memory. (5) The perceived entity is then "matched" to one of these models, and thereby identified as an instance of that category or classification. (In this description of the five stages, all processing is assumed to proceed bottom-up, but in fact Biederman also allows for elements of top-down processing.)

Under what circumstances, or what parameter values, will such a sequence of processing stages lead to *correct*, or *accurate*, object identification? Biederman estimates that there are approximately 3,000 common basic-level, or entry-level, names in English for familiar concrete objects. However, people are probably familiar with approximately ten times that number of object models because, among other things, some entry-level terms (such as *lamp* and *chair*) have several readily distinguishable object models. Thus, an estimate of the number of familiar object models would be on the order of 30,000.

Some of these object models are simple, requiring fewer than six components to appear complete; others are complex, requiring six to nine components to appear complete. Nonetheless, Biederman gives theoretical considerations and empirical results suggesting that an arrangement of only *two* or *three* geons almost always suffices to specify a simple object and even most complex ones. Consider the number of possible two-geon and three-geon objects. With twenty-four possible geons, Biederman says, the variations in relations can produce 186,624 possible two-geon objects. A third geon with its possible relations to another geon yields over 1.4 billion possible three-geon objects. Thus, if the 30,000 familiar object models were distributed homogeneously throughout the space of possible object models, Biederman reasons, an arrangement of two or three geons would almost always be sufficient to specify any object. Indeed, Biederman puts forward a *principle of geon recovery:* If an arrangement of two or three geons can be recovered from the image, objects can be quickly recognized even when they are occluded, rotated in depth, novel, extensively degraded, or lacking in customary detail, color, and texture.

The principle of three-geon sufficiency is supported by the following empirical results. An object such as an elephant or an airplane is complex, requiring six or more geons to appear complete. Nonetheless, when only three components were displayed (the others being occluded), subjects still made correct identifications in almost 80 percent of the nine-component objects and more than 90 percent of the six-component objects. Thus, the reliability conferred by just three geons and their relations is quite high. Although Biederman doesn't give data for recovery of just one or two geons of complex objects, presumably the reliability is much lower. Here we presumably have examples of parameter values—(1) number of components in the complete object, and (2) number of recovered components—that make a significant difference to reliability. The same process, understood as an instantiation of one and the same flow diagram, can have different levels of reliability depending on the values of the critical parameters in question. Biederman's work illustrates how research in cognitive science can identify both the relevant flow of activity and the crucial parameters. The quality (or "virtue") of a particular (token) process of belief-acquisition depends not only on the flow diagram that is instantiated, but on the parameter values instantiated in the specific tokening of the diagram.

Until now reliability has been my sole example of epistemic quality. But two other dimensions of epistemic quality—which also invoke truth or accuracy—should be added to our evaluative repertoire. These are *question-answering power* and *question-answering speed.* (These are certainly reflected in our epistemic folkways, though not well reflected in the concepts of knowledge or justification.) If a person asks himself a question, such as "What kind of object is that?" or "What is the solution to this algebra problem?," there are three possible outcomes: (A) he comes up with *no answer* (at least none that he believes), (B) he forms a belief in an answer which is *correct*, and (C) he forms a belief in an answer which is *incorrect*. Now reliability is the ratio of cases in category (B) to cases in categories (B) and (C), that is, the proportion of true beliefs to beliefs. Question-answering *power*, on the other hand, is the ratio of (B) cases to cases in categories (A), (B), and (C). Notice that it is possible for a system to be highly reliable but not very powerful. An object-recognition system that never yields outputs in category (C) is perfectly reliable, but it may not be very powerful, since most of its outputs could fall in (A) and only a few in (B). The human (visual) object-recognition system, by-contrast, is very powerful as well as quite reliable. In general, it is power and not just reliability that is an important epistemic desideratum in a cognitive system or process.

Speed introduces another epistemic desideratum beyond reliability and power. This is another dimension on which cognitive science can shed light. It might have been thought, for example, that correct identification of complex objects like an airplane or an elephant requires more time than simple objects such as a flashlight or a cup. In fact, there is no advantage for simple objects, as Biederman's empirical studies indicate. This lack of advantage for simple objects could be explained by the geon theory in terms of parallel activation: geons are activated in parallel rather than through a serial trace of the contours of the object. Whereas more geons would require more processing time under a serial trace, this is not required under parallel activation. . . .

IV

We have been treating scientific epistemology from a purely reliabilist, or veritistic (truth-linked), vantage point. It should be stressed, however, that scientific epistemology can equally be pursued from other evaluative perspectives. You need not be a reliabilist to accept the proposed role of cognitive science in scientific epistemology. Let me illustrate this idea with the so-called *responsibilist* approach, which characterizes a justified or rational belief as one that is the product of epistemically responsible action (Kornblith 1983; Code 1987), or perhaps epistemically responsible processes (Talbott 1990). Actually, this conception of justification is approximated by my own *weak* conception of justification, as presented in Goldman (1988). Both depict a belief as justified as long as its acquisition is *blameless* or *nonculpable*. Given limited resources and limited information, a belief might be acquired nonculpably even though its generating processes are not virtuous according to the reliabilist criterion.

Let us start with a case of Hilary Kornblith's. Kornblith argues that the justificational status of a belief does not depend exclusively on the *reasoning* process that produces that belief. Someone might reason perfectly well from the evidence he possesses, but fail to be epistemically responsible because he neglects to acquire certain further evidence. Kornblith gives the case of Jones, a headstrong young physicist eager to hear the praise of his colleagues. After Jones presents a paper, a senior colleague makes an objection. Unable to tolerate criticism, Jones pays no attention to the objection. The criticism is devastating, but it makes no impact on Jones's beliefs because he does not even hear it. Jones's conduct is epistemically irresponsible. But his reasoning process from the evidence he actually possesses—which does not include the colleague's evidence—may be quite impeccable.

The general principle suggested by Kornblith's example seems to be something like this. Suppose that an agent (1) believes *P*, (2) does not believe *Q*, and (3) would be unjustified in believing *P* if he did believe *Q*. If, finally, he is *culpable* for failing to believe *Q* (for being ignorant of *Q*), then he is unjustified in believing *P*. In Kornblith's case, *P* is the physics thesis that Jones believes. *Q* consists in the criticisms of this thesis presented by Jones's senior colleague. Jones does not believe *Q*, but if he did believe *Q*, he would be unjustified in believing *P*. However, although Jones does not believe *Q*, he is culpable for failing to believe it (for being ignorant of these criticisms), because he *ought* to have paid attention to his colleague and acquired belief in *Q*. Therefore, Jones's belief in *P* is unjustified.

The provision that the agent be *culpable* for failing to believe *Q* is obviously critical to the principle in question. If the criticisms of Jones's thesis had never been presented within his hearing, nor published in any scientific journal, then Jones's ignorance of *Q* would not be culpable. And he might well be justified in believing *P*. But in Kornblith's version of the case, it seems clear that Jones *is* culpable for failing to believe *Q*, and that is why he is unjustified in believing *P*.

Under what circumstances is an agent culpable for failing to believe something? That is a difficult question. In a general discussion of culpable ignorance, Holly Smith (1983) gives an example of a doctor who exposes an infant to unnecessarily high concentrations of oxygen and thereby causes severe eye damage. Suppose that the latest issue of the doctor's medical journal describes a study establishing this relationship, but the doctor hasn't read this journal. Presumably his ignorance of the relationship would be culpable; he *should* have read his journal. But suppose that the study had appeared in an obscure journal to which he does not subscribe, or had only appeared one day prior to this particular treatment. Is he still culpable for failing to have read the study by the time of the treatment?

Smith categorizes her example of the doctor as a case of *deficient investigation*. The question is (both for morals and for epistemology), What amounts and kinds of investigation are, in general, sufficient or deficient? We may distinguish two types of investigation: (1) investigation into the physical world (including statements that have been made by other agents), and (2) investigation into the agent's own storehouse of information, lodged in long-term memory. Investigation of the second sort is particularly relevant to questions about the role of cognitive science, so I shall concentrate here on this topic. Actually, the term 'investigation' is not wholly apt when it comes to long-term memory. But it is adequate as a provisional delineation of the territory.

To illustrate the primary problem that concerns me here, I shall consider two examples drawn from the work of Amos Tversky and Daniel Kahneman. The first example pertains to their study of the "conjunction fallacy" (Tversky and Kahneman 1983). Suppose that a subject assigns a higher probability to a conjunction like "Linda is a bank teller and is active in the feminist movement" than to one of its own conjuncts, "Linda is a bank teller." According to the standard probability calculus, no conjunction can have a higher probability than one of its conjuncts. Let us assume that the standard probability calculus is, in some sense, "right." Does it follow that a person is irrational, or unjustified, to make probability assignments that violate this calculus? This is subject to dispute. One might argue that it does not follow, in general, from the fact that M is an arbitrary mathematical truth, that anyone who believes something contrary to M is ipso facto irrational or unjustified. After all, mathematical facts are not all so transparent that it would be a mark of irrationality (or the like) to fail to believe one of them. However, let us set this issue aside. Let us imagine the case of a subject who has studied probability theory and learned the conjunction rule in particular. Let us further suppose that this subject would retract at least one of his two probability assignments if he recognized that they violate the conjunction rule. (This is by no means true of all subjects that Tversky and Kahneman studied.) Nonetheless, our imagined subject fails to think of the conjunction rule in connection with the Linda example. Shall we say that the failure to recover the conjunction rule from long-term memory is a *culpable omission*, one that makes his maintenance of his probability judgments unjustified? Is this like the example of Jones who culpably fails to learn of his senior colleague's criticism? Or is it a case of nonculpable nonrecovery of a relevant fact, a fact that is, in some sense "within reach," but legitimately goes unnoticed?

This raises questions about when a failure to recover or activate something from long-term memory is culpable, and that is precisely a problem that invites detailed reflection on mechanisms of memory retrieval. This is not a matter to which epistemologists have devoted much attention, partly because little has been known about memory retrieval until fairly recently. But now that cognitive science has at least the beginnings of an understanding of this phenomenon, normative epistemology should give careful attention to that research. Of course, we cannot expect the issue of culpability to be resolved directly by empirical facts about cognitive mechanisms. Such facts are certainly relevant, however.

The main way that retrieval from memory works is by *content addressing* (cf. Potter 1990). Content addressing means starting retrieval with part of the content of the to-be-remembered material, which provides an "address" to the place in memory where identical or similar material is located. Once a match has been made, related information laid down by previously encoded associations will be retrieved, such as the name or appearance of the object. For example, if you are asked to think of a kind of bird that is yellow, a location in memory is addressed where "yellow bird" is located. "Yellow bird" has previously been associated with "canary," so the latter information is retrieved. Note, however, that there are some kinds of information that cannot be used as a retrieval address, although the information is in memory. For example, what word for a family relationship (e.g., *grandmother*) ends in *w*? Because you have probably never encoded that piece of information explicitly, you may have trouble thinking of the word (hint: not *niece*). Although it is easy to move from the word in question (*nephew*) to "word for a family relationship ending in *w*," it is not easy to move in the opposite direction.

Many subjects who are given the Linda example presumably have not established any prior association between such pairs of propositions ("Linda is a bank teller and is active in the feminist movement" and "Linda is a bank teller") and the conjunction rule. Furthermore, in some versions of the experiment, subjects are not given these propositions adjacent to one another. So it may not occur to the subject even to *compare* the two probability judgments, although an explicit comparison would be more likely to address a location in memory that contains an association with the conjunction rule. In short, it is not surprising, given the nature of memory retrieval, that the material provided in the specified task does not automatically yield retrieval of the conjunction rule for the typical subject.

Should the subject deliberately search memory for facts that might retrieve the conjunction rule? Is omission of such deliberate search a culpable omission? Perhaps, not how much deliberate attention or effort ought to be devoted to this task? (Bear in mind that agents typically have numerous intellectual tasks on their agendas, which vie for attentional resources.) Furthermore, what form of search is obligatory? Should memory be probed with the question, "Is there any rule of probability theory that my (tentative) probability judgments violate?" This is a plausible search probe for someone who has already been struck by a thought of the conjunction rule and its possible violation, or whose prior experiences with probability experiments make him suspicious. But for someone who has not already retrieved the conjunction rule, or who has not had experiences with probability experiments that alert him to such "traps," what reason is there to be on the lookout for violations of the probability calculus? It is highly questionable, then, that the subject engaged in "deficient investigation" in failing to probe memory with the indicated question.

Obviously, principles of culpable retrieval failure are not easy to come by. Any principles meriting our endorsement would have to be sensitive to facts about memory mechanisms.

A similar point can be illustrated in connection with the so-called *availability heuristic*, which was formulated by Tversky and Kahneman (1973) and explored by Richard Nisbett and Lee Ross (1980). A cognizer uses the availability heuristic when he estimates the frequency of items in a category by the instances he can *bring to mind* through memory retrieval, imagination, or perception. The trouble with this heuristic, as the abovementioned researchers indicate, is that the instances one brings to mind are not necessarily well correlated with objective frequency. Various *biases* may produce discrepancies: biases in initial sampling, biases in attention, or biases in manner of encoding or storing the category instances.

Consider some examples provided by Nisbett and Ross: one hypothetical example and one actual experimental result. (1) (Hypothetical example) An Indiana businessman believes that a disproportionate number of Hoosiers are famous. This is partly because of a bias in initial exposure, but also because he is more likely to notice and remember when the national media identify a famous person as a Hoosier. (2) (Actual experiment) A group of subjects consistently errs in judging the relative frequency of words with R in first position versus words with R in third position. This is an artifact of how words are encoded in memory (as already illustrated in connection with *nephew*). We don't normally code words by their third letters, and hence words having R in the third position are less "available" (from memory) than words beginning with R. But comparative availability is not a reliable indicator of actual frequency.

Nisbett and Ross (1980, 23) view these uses of the availability heuristic as normative errors. "An indiscriminate use of the availability heuristic," they write, "clearly can lead people into serious judgmental errors." They grant, though, that in many contexts perceptual salience, memorability, and imaginability may be relatively unbiased and well correlated with true frequency or causal significance. They conclude: "The normative status of using the availability heuristic . . . thus depend[s] on the judgmental domain and context. People are not, of course, totally unaware that simple availability criteria must sometimes be discounted. For example, few people who were asked to estimate the relative number of moles versus cats in their neighborhood would conclude 'there must be more cats because I've seen several of them but I've never seen a mole.' Nevertheless, as this book documents, people often fail to distinguish between legitimate and superficially similar, but illegitimate, uses of the availability heuristic."

We can certainly agree with Nisbett and Ross that the availability heuristic can often lead to incorrect estimates of frequency. But does it follow that uses of the heuristic are often *illegitimate* in a sense that implies the epistemic *culpability* of the users? One might retort, "These cognizers are using all the evidence that they possess, at least *consciously* possess. Why are they irresponsible if they extrapolate from this evidence?" The objection apparently lurking in Nisbett and Ross's minds is that these cognizers *should* be aware that they are using a systematically biased heuristic. This is a piece of evidence that they *ought* to recognize. And their failure to recognize it, and/or their failure to take it into account, makes their judgmental performance culpable. Nisbett and Ross's invocation of the cat/mole example makes the point particularly clear. If someone can appreciate that the relative number of cats and moles *he has seen* is not a reliable indicator of the relative number of cats and moles in the neighborhood, surely he can be expected to appreciate that the relative number of famous Hoosiers *he can think of* is not a reliable indicator of the proportion of famous people who are Hoosiers!

Is it so clear that people *ought* to be able to appreciate the biased nature of their inference pattern in the cases in question? Perhaps it seems transparent in the mole and Hoosier cases; but consider the letter *R* example. What is (implicitly) being demanded here of the cognizer? First, he must perform a feat of meta-cognitive analysis: he must recognize that he is inferring the relative proportion of the two types of English words from his own constructed samples of these types. Second, he must notice that his construction of these samples depends on the way words are encoded in memory. Finally, he must realize that this implies a bias in ease of retrieval. All these points may seem obvious in hindsight, once pointed out by researchers in the field. But how straightforward or obvious are these matters if they haven't already been pointed out to the subject? Of course, we currently have no "metric" of straightforwardness or obviousness. That is precisely the sort of thing we need, however, to render judgments of culpability in this domain. We need a systematic account of how difficult it is, starting from certain information and preoccupations, to generate and apprehend the truth of certain relevant hypotheses. Such an account clearly hinges on an account of the inferential and hypothesis-generating strategies that are natural to human beings. This is just the kind of thing that cognitive science is, in principle, capable of delivering. So epistemology must work hand in hand with the science of the mind. The issues here are not purely scientific, however. Judgments of justifiedness and unjustifiedness, on the responsibilist conception, require assessments of culpability and nonculpability. Weighing principles for judgments of culpability is a matter for philosophical attention. (One question, for example, is how much epistemic culpability depends on voluntariness.) Thus, a mix of philosophy and psychology is needed to produce acceptable principles of justifiedness.

Notes

I wish to thank Tom Senor, Holly Smith, and participants in a conference at Rice University for helpful comments on earlier versions of this paper.

1. Normative scientific epistemology corresponds to what I elsewhere call *epistemics* (see Goldman 1986). Although epistemics is not restricted to the assessment of *psychological* processes, that is the topic of the present paper. So we are here dealing with what I call *primary epistemics.*

2. Sosa's approach is spelled out most fully in Sosa 1985, 1988, and 1991.

3. My own previous formulations of reliabilism have not been so simple. Both "What Is Justified Belief?" (Goldman 1979) and *Epistemology and Cognition* (Goldman 1986) had provisions—e.g., the non-undermining provision of *Epistemology and Cognition*—that could help accommodate BonJour's examples. It is not entirely clear, however, how well these qualifications succeeded with the Norman case, described in note 4.

4. Tom Senor presented the following example to his philosophy class at the University of Arkansas. Norman is working at his desk when out of the blue he is hit (via clairvoyance) with a very distinct and vivid impression of the president at the Empire State Building. The image is phenomenally distinct from a regular visual impression but is in some respects similar and of roughly equal force. The experience is so overwhelming that Norman just can't help but form the belief that the president is in New York. About half of Senor's class judged that in this case Norman justifiably believes that the president is in New York. Senor points out, in commenting on this paper, that their judgments are readily explained by the present account, because the description of the clairvoyance process makes it sufficiently similar to vision to be easily "matched" to that virtue.

5. Since some of these opinions may be true and others false, people's list of virtues and vices may have varying degrees of accuracy. The "real" status of a trait as a virtue or vice is independent of people's opinions about that trait. However, since the enterprise of descriptive epistemology is to describe and explain evaluators' judgments, we need to advert to the traits they *believe* to be virtues or vices, i.e., the ones on their mental lists.

6. Thanks to Holly Smith for this example. She cites Riding 1989 (chap. 6) for relevant discussion.

7. It should be noted that this theory of justification is intended to capture what I call . . . the *strong* conception of justification. The complementary conception of *weak* justification will receive attention in section IV of this essay.

8. For further discussion of Stich, see Goldman 1991.

References

Alston, W. P. (1988). An internalist externalism. *Synthese* 74, 265–283.

Biederman, I. (1987). Recognition-by-components: A theory of human image understanding. *Psychological Review* 94, 115–147.

Biederman, I. (1990). Higher-level vision. In D. N. Osherson, S. M. Kosslyn, and J. M. Hollerbach, eds., *Visual cognition and action: An invitation to cognitive science*. Cambridge, MA: MIT Press.

BonJour, L. (1985). *The structure of empirical knowledge*. Cambridge, MA: Harvard University Press.

Code, L. (1987). *Epistemic responsibility*. Hanover, NH: University Press of New England.

Fodor, J. A. (1983). *The modularity of mind*. Cambridge, MA: MIT Press.

Goldman, A. I. (1979). What is justified belief? In G. Pappas, ed., *Justification and Knowledge*. Dordrecht: Reidel.

Goldman, A. I. (1986). *Epistemology and cognition*. Cambridge, MA: Harvard University Press.

Goldman, A. I. (1988). Strong and weak justification. In J. Tomberlin, ed., *Philosophical perspectives*, vol. 2. Atascadero, CA: Ridgeview.

Goldman, A. I. (1991). Review of S. Stich, *The fragmentation of reason. Philosophy and Phenomenological Research* 51, 189–193.

Goodman, N. (1955). *Fact, fiction, and forecast*. Cambridge, MA: Harvard University Press.

Hintzman, D. (1986). 'Schema abstraction' in a multiple-trace memory model. *Psychological Review* 93, 411–428.

Kornblith, H. (1983). Justified belief and epistemically responsible action. *Philosophical Review* 92, 33–48.

Kripke, S. A. (1980). *Naming and necessity*. Cambridge, MA: Harvard University Press.

Medin, D. L., and M. M. Schaffer (1978). A context theory of classification learning. *Psychological Review* 85, 207–238.

Nisbett, R. E., and L. Ross (1980). *Human inference: Strategies and shortcomings of social judgment*. Englewood-Cliffs, NJ: Prentice-Hall.

Plantinga, A. (1988). Positive epistemic status and proper function. In J. Tomberlin, ed., *Philosophical Perspectives*, vol. 2. Atascadero, CA: Ridgeview.

Pollock, J. L. (1986). *Contemporary theories of knowledge*. Totowa, NJ: Rowman and Littlefield.

Potter, M. (1990). Remembering. In D. N. Osherson and E. E. Smith, eds., *Thinking: An Invitation to cognitive science*. Cambridge, MA: MIT Press.

Riding, A. (1989). *Distant neighbors: A portrait of the Mexicans*. New York: Vintage Books.

Smith, E. E. (1990). Categorization. In D. N. Osherson and E. E. Smith, eds., *Thinking: An Invitation to cognitive science*. Cambridge, MA: MIT Press.

Smith, E. E., and D. L. Medlin (1981). *Categories and concepts*. Cambridge, MA: Harvard University Press.

Smith, H. M. (1983). Culpable ignorance. *Philosophical Review* 92, 543–572.

Sosa, E. (1985). Knowledge and intellectual virtue. *The Monist* 68, 226–263.

Sosa, E. (1988). Beyond scepticism, to the best of our knowledge. *Mind* 97, 153–188.

Sosa, E. (1991). Reliabilism and intellectual virtue. In Sosa, *Knowledge in perspective*. Cambridge: Cambridge University Press.

Stich, S. P. (1990). *The fragmentation of reason*. Cambridge, MA: MIT Press.

Talbott, W. (1990). *The reliability of our cognitive mechanism: A mechanist account of empirical justification.* New York: Garland Publishing.

Tversky, A., and D. Kahneman (1973). Availability: A heuristic for judging frequency and probability. *Cognitive Psychology* 5, 207–232.

Tversky, A., and D. Kahneman (1983). Extensional versus intuitive reasoning: The conjunction fallacy in probability judgment. *Psychological Review* 90, 293–315.

II

Science and Mathematics

6 Observation Reconsidered

Jerry A. Fodor

Granny and I think that things have gone too far, what with relativism, idealism, and pragmatism at Harvard, graffiti in the subway station, and Lord knows what all next. Granny and I have decided to put our foot down and dig our heel in. Granny is particularly aroused with people playing fast and loose with the observation/inference distinction; and when Granny is aroused, she is terrible. "We may not have prayers in the public schools," Granny says, "but by G-d, we will have a distinction between observation and inference."

The observation/inference distinction according to Granny:

"There are," Granny says, "two quite different routes to the fixation of belief. There is, on the one hand, belief fixation directly consequent upon the activation of the senses (belief fixation 'by observation', as I shall say for short) and there is belief fixation via inference from beliefs previously held ('theoretical' inference, as I shall for short). This taxonomy of the means of belief *fixation* implies, moreover, a corresponding taxonomy of *beliefs*. For, the character of an organism's sensory apparatus—and, more generally, the character of its perceptual psychology—may determine that certain beliefs, if acquired at all, must be inferential and cannot be attained by observation. It is, for example, an accident (of our geography) that our beliefs about Martian fauna are non-observationally acquired. By contrast, it is *not* an accident that our beliefs about the doings of electromagnetic energy in the extreme ultraviolet are all inferential. If there are Martian fauna then were we close enough, we could observe some (unless Martians are *very* small). But making observations in the extreme ultraviolet would require alteration of our sensory/perceptual mechanisms; beliefs about the extreme ultraviolet *must*, for us, all be inferential.

"Some beliefs are thus nonobservational in the nature of things. (To a first approximation, no beliefs are noninferential in the nature of things; and belief *could* be fixed by inference excepting, maybe, tricky

*unless your cognition isn't closed

From J. Fodor, Observation reconsidered, *Philosophy of Science* 51, 23–43 (1984). Reprinted by permission.

ones of the 'I exist' variety.) Moreover, beliefs that are fixed by observation play an interesting and central role in the acquisition of knowledge. (Not, perhaps, so interesting and central as philosophers have sometimes supposed, but still. . . .) For one thing, observationally fixed beliefs tend, by and large, to be more reliable than inferentially fixed beliefs. This is primarily because the etiological route from the fact that P to the belief that P is metaphorically—and maybe literally—*shorter* in observation than in inference; less is likely to go wrong because there's less that *can* go wrong. And, because beliefs that are fixed by observation tend to be relatively reliable, our rational confidence in our knowledge claims depends very largely on their ability to survive observational assessment.

"Second, the observational fixation of belief plays a special role in the adjudication and resolution of clashes of opinion. When observation is *not* appealed to, attempts to settle disputes often take the form of a search for premises that the disputants share. There is, in general, no point to my convincing you that belief B is derivable from theory T unless T is a theory you endorse; otherwise, my argument will seem to you merely a reductio of its premises. This is a peculiarly nasty property of inferential belief fixation because it means that *the more we disagree about, the harder it will likely be to settle any of our disagreements*. None of this applies, however, when the beliefs at issue are observational. Since observation is not a process in which new beliefs are inferred from old ones, the use of observation to resolve disputes does not depend on a prior consensus as to what premises may be assumed. The moral, children, is approximately Baconian. Don't think; look. Try not to argue."

Also sprach Granny. Recent opinion, however, has tended to ignore these homely truths. In this paper, I want to claim that widely endorsed arguments against the possibility of drawing a principled observation/theory distinction have, in fact, been oversold. This does not amount quite to Granny's vindication, since I will not attempt to say in any detail what role the notion of observational belief fixation might come to play in a reasonable naturalized epistemology. Suffice it, for present purposes, to have cleared the way for such a reconstruction.

The claim, then, is that there is a class of beliefs that are typically fixed by sensory/perceptual processes, and that the fixation of beliefs in this class is, in a sense that wants spelling out, importantly theory neutral. As a first shot at what the theory neutrality of observation comes to: given the same stimulations, two organisms with the same sensory/perceptual psychology will quite generally observe the same things, and hence arrive at the same observational beliefs, *however much their theoretical commitments may differ*. This will get some pretty comprehensive refinement as we go along, but it's good enough to start from.

There are, as far as I know, three sorts of arguments that have been alleged to show that no serious observation/inference distinction can be drawn.[1] These are: ordinary language arguments, meaning holism arguments, and de facto psychological arguments. I propose to concentrate, in what follows, mostly on arguments of the third kind; I think that recent changes in the way (some) psychologists view sensory/perceptual processes have significant implications for the present philosophical issues. But it's worth a fast run-through to see why the first two sorts of arguments are also, to put it mildly, less than decisive.

1. The Ordinary Language Argument   The main contention of this paper is that there is a theory-neutral observation/inference distinction; that the boundary between what can be observed and what must be inferred is largely determined by fixed, architectural features of an organism's sensory/perceptual psychology. I'm prepared to concede, however, that this is *not* the doctrine that emerges from attention to the linguistic practices of working scientists. Scientists do have a use for a distinction between what is observed and what is inferred, but the distinction that they have in mind is typically relativized to the inquiry they have in hand. Roughly, so far as I can tell, what a working scientist counts as an experimental *observation* depends on what issue his experiment is designed to settle and what empirical assumptions the design of his experiment takes for granted. One speaks of telescope observations—and of the telescope as an instrument of observation—because the functioning of the telescope is assumed in experimental designs that give us observations of celestial events. One speaks of observed reaction times because the operation of the clock is assumed in the design of experiments when reaction time is the dependent variable. If, by contrast, it begins to seem that perhaps the clock is broken, it then becomes an issue whether reaction times *are* observed when the experimenter reads the numerals that the clock displays.

That way of using the observation/inference distinction is, of course, responsive to an epistemically important fact: not all the empirical assumptions of an experiment can get tested in the same design; we can't test all of our beliefs at once. It is perfectly reasonable of working scientists to want to mark the distinction between what's foreground in an experiment and what is merely taken for granted, and it is again perfectly reasonable of them to do so by relativizing the notion of an observation to whatever experimental assumptions are operative. But, of course, if *that* is what one means by the observation/inference distinction, then there is no interesting issue about whether scientific observation can be theory neutral. Patently, on that construal, the theory of the experimental instruments and the (e.g. statistical) theory of the experimental design will be presupposed by the scientist's observational vocabulary, and what the scientist can (be said to) observe will change as these background theories mature. We can *now* observe craters on Venus (small differences in reaction times) because we now have powerful enough telescopes (accurate enough clocks). On this way of drawing it, the observation/inference distinction is inherently heuristic; it is relativized not just to the sensory/perceptual psychology of the observer, but also to the currently available armamentarium of scientific theories and gadgets.

Much that is philosophically illuminating can, no doubt, be learned by careful attention to what working scientists use terms like 'observed' and 'inferred' to do; but naturalized epistemology is not, for all that, a merely sociolinguistic discipline. Though one of the things that these terms are used for is to mark a distinction that is beyond doubt theory-relative, that does *not* settle the case against Granny. For, it is open to Granny to argue like this:

"True, there is an epistemologically important distinction that it's reasonable to call 'the' observation/inference distinction, and that is theory-relative. And, also true, it is this theory-relative distinction that scientists usually use the terms 'observed' and 'inferred' to mark. But that is quite compatible with there being another distinction, which it is also reasonable to call 'the' observation/inference distinction, which is also of central significance to the epistemology of science, and which is *not* theory-relative. No linguistic considerations can decide this, and I therefore propose to ignore mere matters of vulgar dialectology henceforth."

In her advanced years, Granny has become quite bitter about ordinary language arguments.

2. Arguments from Meaning Holism   Think of a theory (or, mutatis mutandis, the system of beliefs a given person holds) as represented by an infinite, connected graph. The nodes of the graph correspond to the entailments of the theory, and the paths between the nodes correspond to a variety of semantically significant relations that hold among its theorems; inferential relations, evidence relations, and so forth. When the theory is tested, confirmation percolates from node to node along the connecting paths. When the theory is disturbed—eg., by abandoning a postulate or a principle of inference—the local geometry of the graph is distorted, and the resulting strains are distributed throughout the network, sometimes showing up in unanticipated deformations of the structure of the graph far from the initial locus of the disturbance.

That sort of picture has done a lot of work for philosophers since Quine wrote "Two Dogmas." Most famously, skeptical work. Since—so the story goes—everything connects, the unit of meaning—the minimal context, so to speak, within which the meaning of a theoretical postulate is fixed—appears to be *the whole theory.* It is thus unclear how two theories could dispute the claim that P (since the claim that P means something different in a theory that entails that P than it does in, say, a theory that entails its denial). And, similarly, it is unclear how two belief systems that differ anywhere can help but differ everywhere

(since a node is identified by its position in a graph, and since a graph is identified by the totality of its nodes and paths, it appears that only identical graphs can have any nodes in common.)

It is, of course, possible to accept this sort of holism (as, by the way, Granny and I do not) and still acknowledge *some* sort of distinction between observation and inference; eg. the distinction might be construed as epistemic rather than semantic. Suppose every sentence gets its *meaning* from its theoretical context; still, some sentences are closer to the 'edges' of the graph than others, and these might be supposed to depend more directly upon experience for their *confirmation* than sentences further inland do. Quine himself has some such tale to tell. However,—and this is what bears on the present issues—the holism story does suggest that observation couldn't be *theory neutral* in the way that Granny and I think it is. On the holistic account, what you can observe is going to depend comprehensively upon what theories you hold because *what your observation sentences mean depends comprehensively on what theories you hold.*

This is precisely the moral that a number of philosophers have drawn from Quinean holism. For example, here are some quotations from Paul Churchland's (1979) recent *Scientific Realism and the Plasticity of Mind:*

The meaning of the relevant observation terms has nothing to do with the intrinsic qualitative identity of whatever sensations just happen to prompt their non-inferential application in singular empirical judgements. Rather, their position in semantic space appears to be determined by the network of sentences containing them accepted by the speakers who use them. . . . (p. 12)

The view that the meaning of our common observation terms is given in, or determined by, sensation must be rejected outright, and as we saw, we are left with networks of belief as the bearers or determinants of understanding. . . . (p. 13)

a child's initial (stimulus-response) use of, say, 'white' as a response to the familiar kind of sensation, provides that term with no semantic identity. It acquires a semantic identity as, and only as, it comes to figure in a network of beliefs and a correlative pattern of inferences. Depending on what that acquired network happens to be, that term could come to mean *white* or *hot* . . ., or an infinity of other things. (p. 14)

And so forth. So Churchland holds, on holistic grounds, that an observation sentence might mean *anything* depending upon theoretical context.

I emphasize that this conclusion is equivalent to the claim that *anything might be an observation sentence* depending upon theoretical context; or, material mode, that *anything might be observed* depending upon theoretical context. For Churchland—as, of course, for many other philosophers—*you can change your observational capacities by changing your theories.* Indeed, Churchland sees in this a program for educational reform. "If our perceptual judgements must be laden with theory in any case, then why not exchange the Neolithic legacy now in use for the conception of reality embodied in modern-era science?" (p. 35). Really well brought up children would not

> sit on the beach and listen to the steady roar of the pounding surf. They sit on the beach and listen to the aperiodic atmospheric compression waves produced as the coherent energy of the ocean waves is audibly redistributed in the chaotic turbulence of the shallows. . . . They do not observe the western sky redden as the Sun sets. They observe the wavelength distribution of incoming solar radiation shift towards the longer wavelengths . . . as the shorter are increasingly scattered away from the lengthening atmospheric path that they must take as terrestrial rotation turns us slowly away from their source. . . . They do not feel common objects grow cooler with the onset of darkness, nor observe the dew forming on every surface. They feel the molecular KE of common aggregates dwindle with the now uncompensated radiation of their energy starwards, and they observe the accretion of reassociated atmospheric H_2O molecules as their KE is lost to the now more quiescent aggregates with which they collide. (p. 30)

Oh brave new world/that has such children in it.

Once again: the moral that Churchland (and others) draw from holistic semantic doctrines about beliefs/theories is that an observation sentence can mean anything depending on theoretical context; hence that anything can *be* an observation sentence depending on theoretical context; hence that *there could not be a class of beliefs that must be inferential regardless of what theories the believer espouses.* Churchland's way of putting this is, perhaps, misleading. After all, if the gathering of the dew *is* the accretion of atmospheric H_2O molecules, then of course we do, right now and without technological retraining, observe the accretion of atmospheric H_2O molecules whenever we observe the gathering of the dew; 'observe' is transparent to the substitutivity of identicals. But I don't really think that Churchland (or anybody else party to the present controversy) is seriously confused about this, and I don't propose to carp about it. Indeed, it's easy to fix up. What Churchland must be claiming, on grounds of holism, is that what you can see things *as*—what you can *observe that things are*—is comprehensively determined by theoretical context; so that, depending on context, you can, or can learn to, see anything as anything.

Granny and I doubt that you can learn to see anything as anything (that anything can be an observation sentence); but our reasons for doubting this will keep till Section 3. For present purposes, suffice it to repeat the lesson that causal semantic theories have recently been teaching us, viz. that holism may not be true. Specifically, it may not be true that (all) the semantical properties of sentences (/beliefs) are determined by their location in the theoretical networks in which they are embedded; it may be that some of their semantic properties are determined by the character of their attachment to the world (eg., by the character

Principle 3. Analogy.

(a) If P_1 explains Q_1, P_2 explains Q_2, P_1 is analogous to P_2, and Q_1 is analogous to Q_2, then P_1 and P_2 cohere, and Q_1 and Q_2 cohere.
(b) If P_1 explains Q_1, P_2 explains Q_2, Q_1 is analogous to Q_2, but P_1 is disanalogous to P_2, then P_1 and P_2 incohere.

Principle 4. Data Priority.

Propositions that describe the results of observation have a degree of acceptability on their own.

Principle 5. Contradiction.

If P contradicts Q, then P and Q incohere.

Principle 6. Acceptability.

(a) The acceptability of a proposition P in a system S depends on its coherence with the propositions in S.
(b) If many results of relevant experimental observations are unexplained, then the acceptability of a proposition P that explains only a few of them is reduced.

Principle 7. System Coherence.

The global explanatory coherence of a system S of propositions is a function of the pairwise local coherence of those propositions.

Discussion of the Principles
Principle 1, Symmetry, asserts that pairwise coherence and incoherence are symmetric relations, in keeping with the everyday sense of coherence as holding together. The coherence of two propositions is thus very different from the nonsymmetric relations of entailment and conditional probability. Typically, P entails Q without Q entailing P, and the conditional probability of P given Q is different from the probability of Q given P. But if P and Q hold together, so do Q and P. The use of a symmetrical relation has advantages that will become clearer in the discussion of the connectionist implementation below.

Principle 2, Explanation, is by far the most important for assessing explanatory coherence, because it establishes most of the coherence relations. Part (a) is the most obvious: If a hypothesis P is part of the explanation of a piece of evidence Q, then P and Q cohere. Moreover, if a hypothesis P_2 is explained by another hypothesis P_1, then P_1 and P_2 cohere. Part (a) presupposes that explanation is a more restrictive relation than deductive implication, because otherwise we could prove that any two propositions cohere; for unless we use a relevance logic (Anderson and Belnap 1975), P_1 and the contradiction P_2 and not-P_2 imply any Q, so it would follow that P_1 coheres with Q. It follows from Principle 2(a), in conjunction with Principle 6, that the more a hypothesis explains, the more coherent and hence acceptable it is. Thus, this principle subsumes the criterion of explanatory breadth (which Whewell, 1967, called "consilience") that I have elsewhere claimed to be the most important for selecting the best explanation (Thagard 1978, 1988).

Whereas part (a) of Principle 2 says that what explains coheres with what is explained, part (b) states that two propositions cohere if together they provide an explanation. Behind part (b) is the Duhem-Quine idea that the evaluation of a hypothesis depends partly on the other hypotheses with which it furnishes explanations (Duhem 1954; Quine 1961). I call two hypotheses that are used together in an explanation "cohypotheses." Again I assume that explanation is more restrictive than implication; otherwise it would follow that any proposition that explained something was coherent with every other proposition, because if P_1 implies Q, then so does P_1 and P_2. But any scientist who maintained at a conference that the theory of general relativity and today's baseball scores together explain the motion of planets would be laughed off the podium. Principle 2 is intended to apply to explanations and hypotheses actually proposed by scientists.

Part (c) of Principle 2 embodies the claim that if numerous propositions are needed to furnish an explanation, then the coherence of the explaining propositions with each other and with what is explained is thereby diminished. Scientists had to be skeptical of hypotheses that require myriad ad hoc assumptions in their explanations. There is nothing wrong in principle in having explanations that draw on many assumptions, but we should prefer theories that generate explanations using a unified core of hypotheses. I have elsewhere contended that the notion of *simplicity* most appropriate for scientific theory choice is a comparative one preferring theories that make fewer special assumptions (Thagard 1978; 1988). Principles 2(b) and 2(c) together subsume this criterion. I shall not attempt further to characterize "degree of coherence" here, but the connectionist algorithm described below provides a natural interpretation. Many other notions of simplicity have been proposed (e.g., Foster and Martin 1966; Harman et al. 1988), but none is so directly relevant to considerations of explanatory coherence as the one embodied in Principle 2.

The third criterion for the best explanation in my earlier account was analogy, and this is subsumed in Principle 3. There is controversy about whether analogy is of more than heuristic use, but scientists such as Darwin have used analogies to defend their theories; his argument for evolution by natural selection is analyzed below. Principle 3(a) does not say simply that any two analogous propositions cohere. There must be an explanatory analogy, with two analogous propositions occurring in explanations of two other propositions that are analogous to each other. Recent computational models of analogical mapping and retrieval show how such correspondences can be noticed (Holyoak and Thagard, 1989;

Thagard et al. 1990). Principle 3(b) says that when similar phenomena are explained by dissimilar hypotheses, the hypotheses incohere. Although the use of such disanalogies is not as common as the use of analogies, it was important in the reasoning that led Einstein (1952) to the special theory of relativity: He was bothered by asymmetries in the way Maxwell's electrodynamics treated the case of (1) a magnet in motion and a conductor at rest quite differently from the case of (2) a magnet at rest and a conductor in motion.

Principle 4, Data Priority, stands much in need of elucidation and defense. In saying that a proposition describing the results of observation has a degree of acceptability on its own, I am not suggesting that it is indubitable, but only that it can stand on its own more successfully than can a hypothesis whose sole justification is what it explains. A proposition Q may have some independent acceptability and still end up not accepted, if it is only coherent with propositions that are themselves not acceptable.

From the point of view of explanatory coherence alone, we should not take propositions based on observation as independently acceptable without any explanatory relations to other propositions. As BonJour (1985) argues, the coherence of such propositions is of a nonexplanatory kind, based on background knowledge that observations of certain sorts are very likely to be true. From past experience, we know that our observations are very likely to be true, so we should believe them unless there is substantial reason not to. Similarly, at a very different level, we have some confidence in the reliability of descriptions of experimental results in carefully refereed scientific journals.

Principle 5, Contradiction, is straightforward. By "contradictory" here I mean not just syntactic contradictions like P & not-P, but also semantic contradictions such as "This ball is black all over" and "This ball is white all over." In scientific cases, contradiction becomes important when incompatible hypotheses compete to explain the same evidence. Not all competing hypotheses incohere, however, because many phenomena have multiple causes. For example, explanations of why someone has certain medical symptoms may involve hypotheses that the patient has various diseases, and it is possible that more than one disease is present. Competing hypotheses incohere if they are contradictory or if they are framed as offering *the* most likely cause of a phenomenon. In the latter case, we get a kind of pragmatic contradictoriness: Two hypotheses may not be syntactically or semantically contradictory, yet scientists will view them as contradictory because of background beliefs suggesting that only one of the hypotheses is acceptable. For example, in the debate over dinosaur extinction (Thagard 1991), scientists generally treat as contradictory the following hypotheses:

(1) Dinosaurs became extinct because of a meteorite collision.
(2) Dinosaurs became extinct because the sea level fell.

Logically, (1) and (2) could both be true, but scientists treat them as conflicting explanations, possibly because there are no explanatory relations between them and their conjunction is unlikely.

The relation "cohere" is not transitive. If P_1 and P_2 together explain Q, while P_1 and P_3 together explain not-Q, then P_1 coheres with both Q and not-Q, which incohere. Such cases do occur in science. Let P_1 be the gas law that volume is proportional to temperature, P_2 a proposition describing the drop in temperature of a particular sample of gas, P_3 a proposition describing the rise in temperature of the sample, and Q a proposition about increases in the sample's volume. Then P_1 and P_2 together explain a decrease in the volume, while P_1 and P_3 explain an increase.

Principle 6, Acceptability, proposes in part (a) that we can make sense of the overall coherence of a proposition in an explanatory system just from the pairwise coherence relations established by Principles 1–5. If we have a hypothesis P that coheres with evidence Q by virtue of explaining it, but incoheres with another contradictory hypothesis, should we accept P? To decide, we cannot merely count the number of propositions with which P coheres and incoheres, because the acceptability of P depends in part on the acceptability of those propositions themselves. We need a dynamic and parallel method of deriving general coherence from particular coherence relations; such a method is provided by the connectionist program described below.

Principle 6(b), reducing the acceptability of a hypothesis when much of the relevant evidence is unexplained by any hypothesis, is intended to handle cases where the best available hypothesis is still not very good, in that it accounts for only a fraction of the available evidence. Consider, for example, a theory in economics that could explain the stock market crashes of 1929 and 1987 but that had nothing to say about myriad other similar economic events. Even if the theory gave the best available account of the two crashes, we would not be willing to elevate it to an accepted part of general economic theory. What does "relevant" mean here? As a first approximation, we can say that a piece of evidence is *directly* relevant to a hypothesis if the evidence is explained by it or by one of its competitors. We can then add that a piece of evidence is relevant if it is directly relevant or if it is similar to evidence that is relevant, where similarity is a matter of dealing with phenomena of the same kind. Thus, a theory of the business cycle that applies to the stock market crashes of 1929 and 1987 should also have something to say about nineteenth-century crashes and major business downturns in the twentieth century.

The final principle, System Coherence, proposes that we can have some global measure of the coherence of a whole system of propositions. Principles 1–5 imply that, other things being equal, a system S will tend to have more global coherence than another if

(1) S has more data in it;

(2) S has more internal explanatory links between propositions that cohere because of explanations and analogies; and

(3) S succeeds in separating coherent subsystems of propositions from conflicting subsystems.

The connectionist algorithm described below comes with a natural measure of global system coherence. It also indicates how different priorities can be given to the different principles.

Connectionist Models

To introduce connectionist techniques, I shall briefly describe the popular example of how a network can be used to understand the Necker cube phenomenon (see, for example Feldman and Ballard 1982; Rumelhart et al. 1986). Figure 8.1 contains a reversing cube: By changing our focus of attention, we are able to see as the front either face ABCD or face EFGH. The cube is perceived holistically, in that we are incapable of seeing corner A at the front without seeing corners B, C, and D at the front as well.

We can easily construct a simple network with the desired holistic property using *units,* crudely analogous to neurons, connected by links. Let Af be a unit that represents the hypothesis that corner A is at the front, while Ab represents the hypothesis that corner A is at the back. Similarly, we construct units Bf, Bb, Cf, Cb, Df, Db, Ef, Eb, Ff, Fb, Gf, Gb, Hf, and Hb. These units are not independent of each other. To signify that A cannot be both at the front and at the back, we construct an *inhibitory* link between the units Af and Ab, with similar links inhibiting Bf and Bb, and so on. Because corners A, B, C, and D go together,

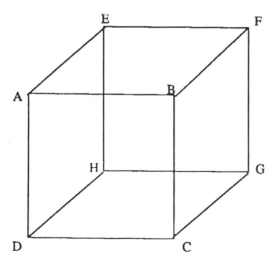

Figure 8.1 The necker cube. Either ABCD or EFGH can be perceived as the front.

we construct *excitatory* links between each pair of Af, Bf, Cf, and Df, and between each pair of Ab, Bb, Cb, and Db. Analogous inhibitory and excitatory links are then set up for E, F, G, and H. In addition, we need inhibitory links between Af and Ef, Bf and Ff, and so on. Part of the resulting network is depicted in figure 8.2. I have used solid lines to indicate excitatory links, and dotted lines to indicate inhibitory links.

Units can have varying degrees of *activation*. Suppose that our attention is focused on corner A, which we assume to be at the front, so that unit Af is activated. Then by virtue of the excitatory links from Af to Bf, Cf, and Df, these units will be activated. The inhibitory links from Af to Ab and Ef will cause those units to be deactivated. In turn, the excitatory links from Ab to Bb, Cb, and Db will deactivate them. Thus activation will spread through the network until all the units corresponding to the view that A, B, C, and D are at the front are activated, while all the units corresponding to the view that E, F, G, and H are at the front are deactivated.

Goldman has pointed out some of the attractive epistemological properties of this sort of network (Goldman 1986, Chap. 15; see also Thagard 1989). A proposition, represented by a unit, is accepted if it is part of the best competing coalition of units and its rivals are rejected. Uncertainty consists in the absence of a clear-cut winner. Goldman argues that the connectionist view that has units representing propositions settling into either on or off states is more psychologically plausible and epistemologically appealing than the Bayesian picture that assigns probabilities to propositions.

Echo

The Program
Let us now look at ECHO, a computer program written in Common LISP that is a straightforward application of connectionist algorithms to the

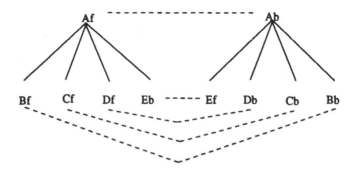

Figure 8.2 A connectionist network for interpreting the cube. Af is a unit representing the hypothesis that A is at the front, whereas Ab represents the hypothesis that A is at the back. Solid lines represent excitatory links; dotted lines represent inhibitory links.

problem of explanatory coherence. In ECHO, propositions representing hypotheses and results of observation are represented by units. Whenever Principles 1–5 state that two propositions cohere, an excitatory link between them is established. If two propositions incohere, an inhibitory link between them is established. In ECHO, these links are symmetric, as Principle 1 suggests: The weight from unit 1 to unit 2 is the same as the weight from unit 2 to unit 1. Principle 2(c) says that the larger the number of propositions used in an explanation, the smaller the degree of coherence between each pair of propositions. ECHO therefore counts the propositions that do the explaining and proportionately lowers the weight of the excitatory links between units representing coherent propositions.

Principle 4, Data Priority, is implemented by links to each data unit from a special evidence unit that always has activation 1, giving each unit some acceptability on its own. When the network is run, activation spreads from the special unit to the data units, and then to the units representing explanatory hypotheses. The extent of data priority—the presumed acceptability of data propositions—depends on the weight of the link between the special unit and the data units. The higher this weight, the more immune the data units become to deactivation by other units. Units that have inhibitory links between them because they represent contradictory hypotheses have to compete with each other for the activation spreading from the data units: The activation of one of these units will tend to suppress the activation of the other. Excitatory links have positive weights; best performance occurs with weights around .05. Inhibitory links have negative weights; best performance occurs with weights around $-.2$. The activation of units ranges between 1 and -1; positive activation can be interpreted as acceptance of the proposition represented by the unit, negative activation as rejection, and activation close to 0 as neutrality.

To summarize how ECHO implements the principles of explanatory coherence, we can list key terms from the principles with the corresponding terms from ECHO:

Proposition: unit

Coherence: excitatory link, with positive weight

Incoherence: inhibitory link, with negative weight

Data priority: excitatory link from special unit

Acceptability: activation

System coherence: See the function H defined in a later section.

The following are some examples of the LISP formulas that constitute ECHO's inputs:

1. (EXPLAIN (H1 H2) E1)

2. (EXPLAIN (H1 H2 H3) E2)

3. (ANALOGOUS (H5 H6) (E5 E6))

4. (DATA (E1 E2 E5 E6))

5. (CONTRADICT H1 H4)

Formula 1 says that hypotheses H1 and H2 together explain evidence E1. As suggested by the second principle of explanatory coherence proposed above, formula 1 sets up three excitatory links, between units representing H1 and E1, H2 and E1, and H1 and H2.[1] Formula 2 sets up six such links, between each of the hypotheses and the evidence, and between each pair of hypotheses, but the weight on the links will be less than those established by formula 1, because there are more cohypotheses. In accord with Principle 3(a), Analogy, formula 3 produces excitatory links between H5 and H6, and between E5 and E6, if previous input has established that H5 explains E5 and H6 explains E6. Formula 4 is used to apply Principle 4, Data Priority, setting up explanation-independent excitatory links to each data unit from a special evidence unit. Finally, formula 5 sets up an inhibitory link between the contradictory hypotheses H1 and H4, as prescribed by Principle 5.

Input to ECHO can optionally reflect the fact that not all data and explanations are of equal merit. For example, a data statement can have the form

(DATA (E1 (E2 .8))).

This formula sets up the standard link from the special unit to E1, but interprets the ".8" as indicating that E2 is not as reliable a piece of evidence as E1. Hence, the weight from the special unit to E2 is only .8 as strong as the weight from the special unit to E1. Similarly, explain statements take an optimal numerical parameter, as in

(EXPLAIN (H1) E1 .9).

The additional parameter, .9, indicates some weakness in the quality of the explanation and results in a lower than standard weight on the excitatory link between H1 and E1. In ECHO's applications to date, the additional parameters for data and explanation quality have not been used, because it is difficult to establish them objectively from the texts we have been using to generate ECHO's inputs. But it is important that ECHO has the capacity to make use of judgments of data and explanation quality when these are available.

Program runs show that the networks thus established have numerous desirable properties. Other things being equal, activation accrues to units corresponding to hypotheses that explain more, provide simpler explanations, and are analogous to other explanatory hypotheses. The considerations of explanatory breadth, simplicity, and analogy are smoothly integrated. The networks are holistic, in that the activation of every unit can potentially have an effect on every other unit linked to it by a path, however lengthy. Nevertheless, the activation of a unit is directly affected only by those units to which it is linked. Although complexes of coherent propositions are evaluated together, different hypotheses in a complex can finish with different activations, depending on their particular coherence relations. The symmetry of excitatory links means that active units tend to bring up the activation of units with which they are linked, whereas units whose activation sinks below 0 tend to bring down the activation of units to which they are linked. Data units are given priority, but can nevertheless be deactivated if they are linked to units that become deactivated. So long as excitation is not set too high, the networks set up by ECHO are stable: In most of them, all units reach asymptotic activation levels after fewer than 100 cycles of updating. The most complex network implemented so far, comparing the explanatory power of Copernicus's heliocentric theory with Ptolemy's geocentric one, requires about 210 cycles before its more than 150 units have all settled. To illustrate ECHO's capabilities, I shall describe some very simple tests that illustrate its ability to handle considerations of explanatory breadth, simplicity, and analogy. Later sections on scientific reasoning provide more complex and realistic examples.

Explanatory Breadth
We should normally prefer a hypothesis that explains more than alternative hypotheses. If hypothesis H1 explains two pieces of evidence, whereas H2 explains only one, then H1 should be preferred to H2. Here are four formulas given together to ECHO as input:

(EXPLAIN (H1) E1)
(EXPLAIN (H1) E2)
(EXPLAIN (H2) E2)
(CONTRADICT (H1 H2))
(DATA (E1 E2))

These formulas generate the network pictured in figure 8.3, with excitatory links corresponding to coherence represented by solid lines, and with inhibitory links corresponding to incoherence represented by dotted lines. Activation flows from the special unit, whose activation is clamped at 1, to the evidence units, and then to the hypothesis units, which inhibit each other. Because H1 explains more than its competitor H2, H1 becomes active, settling with activation above 0, while H2 is deactivated, settling with activation below 0. Notice that although the links in ECHO are symmetric, in keeping with the symmetry of the coherence relation, the flow of activation is not, because evidence units get activation first and then pass it along to what explains them.

 ECHO's networks have interesting dynamic properties. What happens if new data come in after the network has settled? When ECHO is given

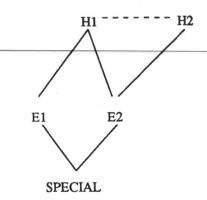

SPECIAL

Figure 8.3 Explanatory breadth. As in figure 8.2, solid lines represent excitatory links, whereas dotted lines represent inhibitory links. Evidence units E1 and E2 are linked to the special unit. The result of running this network is that H1 defeats H2.

the further information that H2 explains additional data E3, E4, and E5, then the network resettles into a reversed state in which H2 is activated and H1 is deactivated. However, if the additional information is only that H2 explains E2, or only that H2 explains E3, then ECHO does not resettle into a state in which H1 and H2 get equal activation. (It does give H1 and H2 equal activation if the input says that they have equal explanatory power from the start.) Thus ECHO displays a kind of conservatism also seen in human scientists.

Being Explained
Earlier we showed how Principle 2(a) leads ECHO to prefer a hypothesis that explains more than its competitors. The same principle also implies greater coherence, other things being equal, for a hypothesis that is explained. Consider the following input:

(EXPLAIN (H1) E1)
(EXPLAIN (H1) E2)
(EXPLAIN (H2) E1)
(EXPLAIN (H2) E2)
(EXPLAIN (H3) H1)
(CONTRADICT H1 H2)
(DATA (E1 E2))

Figure 8.4 depicts the network constructed using this input. Here, and in all subsequent figures, the special evidence unit is not shown. In figure 8.4, H1 and H2 have the same explanatory breadth, but ECHO activates H1 and deactivates H2 because H1 is explained by H3. ECHO thus gives more activation to a hypothesis that is explained than to a contradictory one that is not explained. If the above formulas did not include a CONTRADICT statement, then no inhibitory links would be

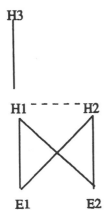

Figure 8.4 Being explained. H1 defeats H2 because it is explained by H3.

formed, so that all units would asymptote with positive activation. Because of the decay parameter, activation is still less than 1.

Refutation

According to Popper (1959), the hallmark of science is not the acceptance of explanatory theories but the rejection of falsified ones. Take the simplest case where a hypothesis H1 explains (predicts) some piece of "negative evidence" NE1, which contradicts data E1. Then E1 becomes active, deactivating NE1 and hence H1. Such straightforward refutations, however, are rare in science. Scientists do not typically give up a promising theory just because it has some empirical problems, and neither does ECHO. If in addition to explaining NE1, H1 explains some positive pieces of evidence, E2 and E3, then ECHO does not deactivate it. However, an alternative hypothesis H2 that also explains E2 and E3 is preferred to H1, which loses because of NE1. Rejection in science is usually a complex process involving competing hypotheses, not a simple matter of falsification (Lakatos 1970; Thagard 1988, Chap. 9).

Unification

The impact of explanatory breadth, being explained, and refutation all arise from Principle 2(a), which says that hypotheses cohere with what they explain. According to Principle 2(b), cohypotheses that explain together cohere with each other. Thus, if H1 and H2 together explain evidence E, then H1 and H2 are linked. This gives ECHO a preference for unified explanations, ones that use a common set of hypotheses rather than having special hypotheses for each piece of evidence explained. Consider this input, which generates the network shown in figure 8.5:

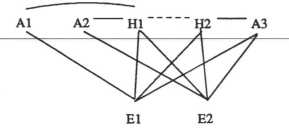

Figure 8.5 Unification. H2 defeats H1 because it gives a more unified explanation of the evidence.

(EXPLAIN (H1 A1) E1)
(EXPLAIN (H1 A2) E2)
(EXPLAIN (H2 A3) E1)
(EXPLAIN (H2 A3) E2)
(CONTRADICT H1 H2)
(DATA (E1 E2))

Although H1 and H2 both explain E1 and E2, the explanation by H2 is more unified in that it uses A3 in both cases. Hence ECHO forms a stronger link between H2 and A3 than it does between H1 and A1 or A2, so H2 becomes activated and H1 is deactivated. The explanations by H2 are not simpler than those by H1, in the sense of Principle 2(c), because both involve two hypotheses. ECHO's preference for H2 over H1 thus depends on the coherence of H2 with its auxiliary hypothesis and the evidence being greater than the coherence of H1 with its auxiliary hypotheses and the evidence. One might argue that the coherence between cohypotheses should be less than the coherence of a hypothesis with what it explains; ECHO contains a parameter that can allow the weights between cohypothesis units to be less than the weight between a hypothesis unit and an evidence unit.

Simplicity
According to Principle 2(c), the degree of coherence of a hypothesis with what it explains and with its cohypotheses is inversely proportional to the number of cohypotheses. An example of ECHO's preference for simple hypotheses derives from the input:

(EXPLAIN (H1) E1)
(EXPLAIN (H2 H3) E1)
(CONTRADICT H1 H2)
(DATA (E1))

Here H1 is preferred to H2 and H3 because it accomplishes the explanation with no cohypotheses. The generated network is shown in figure 8.6.

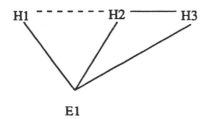

Figure 8.6 Simplicity. H1 defeats H2 because it gives a simpler explanation of the evidence.

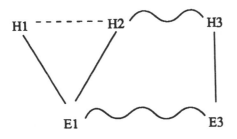

Figure 8.7 Analogy. The wavy lines indicate excitatory links based on analogies. H2 defeats H1 because the explanation it gives is analogous to the explanation afforded by H3.

Principle 2(c) is important for dealing with ad hoc hypotheses that are introduced only to save a hypothesis from refutation. Suppose that H1 is in danger of refutation because it explains negative evidence NE1, which contradicts evidence E1. One might try to save H1 by concocting an auxiliary hypothesis, H2, which together with H1 would explain E1. Such maneuvers are common in science: Nineteenth-century physicists did not abandon Newtonian mechanics because it gave false predictions concerning the notion of Uranus; instead, they hypothesized the existence of another planet, Neptune, to explain the discrepancies. Neptune, of course, was eventually observed, but we need to be able to discount auxiliary hypotheses that do not contribute to any additional explanations. Because the explanation of E1 by H1 and H2 is less simple than the explanation of NE1 by H1, the *ad hoc* maneuver does not succeed in saving H1 from deactivation.

Analogy
According to Principle 3(a), analogous hypotheses that explain analogous evidence are coherent with each other. Figure 8.7 shows relations of analogy, derived from the input:

(EXPLAIN (H1) E1)
(EXPLAIN (H2) E1)
(EXPLAIN (H3) E3)
(ANALOGOUS (H2 H3) (E1 E3))

(CONTRADICT H1 H2)
(DATA (E1 E3))

The analogical links corresponding to the coherence relations required by Principle 3 are shown by wavy lines. Running this example leads to activation of H2 and deactivation of its rival, H1. Figures 8.3–8.7 show consilience, simplicity, and analogy operating independently of each other, but in realistic examples these criteria can all operate simultaneously through activation adjustment. Thus ECHO shows how criteria such as explanatory breadth, simplicity, and analogy can be integrated. My most recent account of inference to the best explanation (Thagard 1988) included a computational model that integrated breadth and simplicity but left open the question of how to tie in analogy. Principle 3 and ECHO show how analogy can participate with consilience and simplicity in contributing toward explanatory power.

Evidence

Principle 4 asserts that data get priority by virtue of their independent coherence. But it should nevertheless be possible for a data unit to be deactivated. We see this both in the everyday practice of experimenters, in which it is often necessary to discard some of the data because they are deemed unreliable (Hedges 1987), and in the history of science where evidence for a discarded theory sometimes falls into neglect (Laudan 1976). Figure 8.8, which derives from the following input, shows how this might happen.

(EXPLAIN (H1) E1)
(EXPLAIN (H1) E2)
(EXPLAIN (H1) E3)
(EXPLAIN (H1) E4)
(EXPLAIN (H2) E2)
(EXPLAIN (H2) E5)
(EXPLAIN (H3) E3)

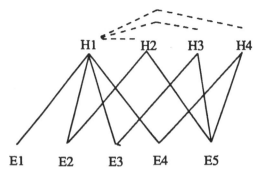

Figure 8.8 Downplaying of evidence. E5 is deactivated, even though it is an evidence unit, because it coheres only with inferior evidence.

(EXPLAIN (H3) E5)
(EXPLAIN (H4) E4)
(EXPLAIN (H4) E5)
(CONTRADICT H1 H2)
(CONTRADICT H1 H3)
(CONTRADICT H1 H4)

These inputs lead to the deactivation of E5, dragged down by the deactivation of the inferior hypotheses H2, H3, and H4. Because E5 coheres only with propositions that are themselves unacceptable, it becomes unacceptable too. Because H1 has four excitatory links, it easily deactivates the other three hypotheses, and their negative activation brings down the initially positive activation of E5 into the negative range.

Principle 6(b) also concerns evidence, undermining the acceptability of hypotheses that explain only a small part of the relevant data. Accordingly, ECHO automatically increases the value of a decay parameter in proportion to the ratio of unexplained evidence to explained evidence. A hypothesis that explains only a fraction of the relevant evidence will thus decay toward the beginning activation level of 0 rather than become activated.

Acceptability and System Coherence

If ECHO is taken as an algorithmic implementation of the first five principles of explanatory coherence, then it validates Principle 6, Acceptability, for it shows that holistic judgments of the acceptability of a proposition can be based solely on pairwise relations of coherence. A unit achieves a stable activation level merely by considering the activation of units to which it is linked and the weights on those links. Asymptotic activation values greater than 0 signify acceptance of the proposition represented by the unit, whereas negative values signify rejection.

ECHO also validates Principle 7, System Coherence, because we can borrow from connectionist models a measure H of the global coherence of a whole system of propositions at time t:

$$H(t) = \Sigma_i \Sigma_j w_{ij} a_i(t) a_j(t) \tag{8.1}$$

In this equation, w_{ij} is the weight from unit i to unit j, and $a_i(t)$ is the activation of unit i at time t. This measure or its inverse has been variously called the "goodness," "energy," or "harmony" of the network (Rumelhart et al. 1986, vol. 2, p. 13). For historical reasons, I prefer a variant of the last term with the alternative spelling "harmany" (Harman 1973). Thus ECHO stands for "Explanatory Coherence by Harmany Optimization."

Equation 1 says that to calculate the harmany of the network, we consider each pair of units a_i and a_j that are linked with weight w_{ij}.

Harmany increases, for example when two units with high activation have a link between them with high weight, or when a unit with high activation and a unit with negative activation have between them a link with negative weight. In ECHO the harmany of a system of propositions increases, other things being equal, with increases in the number of data units, the number of links, and the number of cycles to update activations to bring them more in line with the weights.

Parameters

The simulations just described depend on program parameters that give ECHO numerous degrees of freedom, some of which are epistemologically interesting. In the example shown in figure 8.3, the relation between excitatory weights and inhibitory weights is crucial. If inhibition is low compared to excitation, then ECHO will activate both H1 and H2, because the excitation that H2 gets from E1 will overcome the inhibition it gets from H1. Let the *tolerance* of the system be the absolute value of the ratio of excitatory weight to inhibitory weight. With high tolerance, the system will entertain competing hypotheses. With low tolerance, winning hypotheses deactivate the losers. Typically, ECHO is run with excitatory weights set at .05 and inhibition at −.2, so tolerance is .25. If tolerance is high, ECHO can settle into a state where two contradictory hypotheses are both activated. ECHO performs well using a wide range of parameters.

Other parameters establish the relative importance of simplicity and analogy. If H1 explains E1 by itself, then the excitatory link between H1 and E1 has the default weight .05. But if H1 and H2 together explain E1, then the weight of the links is set at the default value divided by 2, the number of cohypotheses, leaving it at .025. If we want to change the importance of simplicity as incorporated in Principle 2(c), however, then we can raise the number of cohypotheses to an exponent that represents the *simplicity impact* of the system. The greater the simplicity impact, the more weights will be diminished by having more cohypotheses. Similarly, the weights established by analogy can be affected by a factor representing *analogy impact*. If this is 1, then the links connecting analogous hypotheses are just as strong as those set up by simple explanations, and analogy can have a very large effect. If, on the other hand, analogy impact is set at 0, then analogy has no effect.

Another important parameter of the system is decay rate, represented by θ. We can term this the *skepticism* of the system, because the higher it is, the more excitation from data will be needed to activate hypotheses. If skepticism is very high, then *no* hypotheses will be activated. Whereas tolerance reflects ECHO's view of contradictory hypotheses, skepticism determines its treatment of all hypotheses. Principle 6(b) can be interpreted as saying that if there is much unexplained evidence, then ECHO's skepticism level is raised.

of us, and (b) the processing in which they play a role is insulated from any contrary assumptions or theories—indeed, from any *additional* assumptions whatever—that the perceiver may subsequently come to believe. Our perceptual processing is thus encapsulated; it delivers outputs to the higher cognitive centers, but it is impenetrable to any inputs from them. The result, according to Fodor, is that all humans are fated to share a common perceptual experience, an experience whose character is not subject to change as a function of any theories we may come to embrace. There is therefore an important sense, he concludes, in which human perception is neutral vis-à-vis the rough and tumble of competing theories. There is an unchanging perspective, on at least some parts of reality, that all human theorists must share in common.

The evidence in support of these claims is twofold. First, Fodor cites a number of experimental facts that illustrate, not the plasticity of perception, but rather the occasional rigidity of our perceptual deliverances (e.g., the persistence of certain illusions, such as the Müller-Lyer illusion) even in cases where we know them to be mistaken. Second, he claims that if perception is to be theory dependent in any epistemologically interesting sense, then the perceptual modules must have "*access to ALL (or anyhow, arbitrarily much) of the background information at the perceiver's disposal*" (130). Given the rigidity just cited, however, he concludes that the modules at issue lack such access, and hence that perception is not theory dependent in any interesting sense.

Let us suppose, for the moment, that our perceptual modules are indeed informationally isolated in the fashion claimed. That is, they embody a systematic set of endogenous or genetically implanted assumptions about the world, whose influence on perceptual processing is unaffected by any additional or contrary information.

Now this may be a recipe for a certain limited *consensus* among human perceivers, but it is hardly a recipe for theoretical *neutrality* and it is plain misleading to use this latter term to describe what encapsulation might secure. As conceived within the relevant dialectical tradition, an observation judgment is *theory neutral* just in case its truth is not contingent upon the truth of any general empirical assumptions, that is, just in case it is free of potentially problematic presuppositions. If an observation judgment does have such presuppositions, its theory-laden character will in no way be reduced by hardwiring those presuppositions into the process by which the judgment is produced, and by closing the process to all contrary information.

If everyone is a hopeless slave of the same hardwired theory, then what we have is a universal dogmatism, not an innocent Eden of objectivity and neutrality. The alleged cognitive impenetrability of our perceptual processing does nothing to reduce the extent to which the truth of our perceptual beliefs is contingent upon the truth of those background empirical assumptions or theories in which they are semantically embedded. Encapsulation does nothing to ensure the truth of our perceptual beliefs, not even their "truth in general" or their "truth under normal circumstances." Nor does it ensure their episte-mological integrity relative to competing interpretations of our sensory input. It merely dooms us to a single point of view, a point of view that is epistemologically just as problematic as any of the infinity of other sets of empirical assumptions that might have been hard-wired into us instead.

Fodor's premises, therefore, do not buy him anything like the theoretical neutrality of our perceptual judgments. An unchangeable set of prejudicial empirical assumptions is still a set of prejudicial empirical assumptions.

Fodor's premises may seem to solve, at least, the problem of incommensurability, by guaranteeing some effective communication, at the observation level, between ideologically diverse human theorists. But as we shall see at the end of this section, they fail to guarantee this also, since rigidity in our early perceptual processing is entirely consistent with plasticity at the level of conceptual apprehension and discursive judgment. And despite a popular misconception on this point, communication was never the real problem anyway. The epistemological problem of incommensurable alternatives arises most clearly and forcefully within a *single* individual, one who is "bitheoretical." Putting Fodor aside for a moment, consider someone who has internalized two competing theories, and has learned two correspondingly different ways of perceiving the relevant aspects of the world, but is torn over which of these two global packages to choose. It is not communication that is the problem here (he can perfectly well understand himself); the problem is theoretical evaluation and rational choice in the absence of a neutral touchstone.

I am not arguing at this point that Fodor's encapsulation thesis is false, only that it would not secure for us any theory-neutral foundation for knowledge, even were it true. Fodor's hardwired consensus is a sham neutrality: it mistakes the presumed universality of our prejudice for the absence of any prejudice. And hardwired or no, that consensus would last only until the first mutant or alien comes along, to confront us with a different perceptual point of view.

In fact, we begin to become such mutants or aliens ourselves when we change our sensory modalities by augmenting them with unusual instruments, such as phase-contrast microscopes, deep-sky telescopes, long-baseline stereoscopes, infrared scopes, and so forth. And the metamorphosis is completed when, after years of professional or amateur practice, we learn to see the world appropriately and efficiently with these new senses. This learning requires both that we suppress certain habits of processing "natural" to the naked eye and to the familiar world of middle-sized material objects, and that we learn to process the retinal data in novel ways, ways that are appropriate to the unfamiliar features one perceives by these novel means (e.g., interference patterns, diffraction rings, dark nebulae, fusion planes, temperature gradients, etc.). Reflections such as these do begin to challenge Fodor's factual claim of encapsulation or impenetrability. Let us therefore focus on the evidence he cites in support of that claim.

Is the Impenetrability Thesis Correct?

Visual illusions are good illustrations of the assumptions involved in early processing, since the illusion is often the result of the persistent operation of some assumption that is appropriate for most situations, but which is inappropriate for the particular situation at issue. Fodor cites the stubborn persistence of various visual illusions, even when we know that we are being misled, and even where we have the information about the inappropriate assumptions responsible for the illusory experience. Why, Fodor asks, doesn't *this* information affect the way we see the world, and thereby undo the illusion? His answer is that our perceptual processing is guided by mechanisms or assumptions that cannot be successfully overridden by contrary assumptions imposed from the outside.

A first response is just to point out the great many illusions and visual effects whose character shows that our visual modules are indeed penetrable by higher cognitive assumptions. Consider the wide range of ambiguous figures, such as the duck/rabbit, the old/young woman, the Necker cube, and the vase/faces. Such examples are ambiguous with respect to orientation, or scale, or perspective, or figure/ground, or any of a variety of other dimensions. But in all of these cases one learns very quickly to make the figure flip back and forth at will between the two or more alternatives, by changing one's assumptions about the ✱ nature of the object or about the conditions of viewing. At least some aspects of visual processing, evidently, are quite easily controlled by the higher cognitive centers.

One such reversible illusion is striking in that it extends even to changes in perceived *color*. Take a monochromatic birthday card or similar folded rectangle. Place it upright and oriented to the light so that one of the inside faces is in a very slight shadow relative to the other inside face. (Figure 7.1a illustrates the relevant configuration, but only a real card will support the illusion.) Despite this slight shadow, the two faces of the card will be perceived as having the same objective color. Now, closing one eye to defeat stereoscopic orientation cues, treat the object as a Necker cube and deliberately invert its orientation—in thought—so that the middle fold appears closer to you than the two outside edges. This will produce an obvious distortion in the perceived shape of the card: it will no longer look like a folded rectangle. And it will also produce a change in the perceived color of the shadowed and unshadowed areas of the card. In its original appearance, the slight contrast in luminance is suppressed by the visual system as a mere

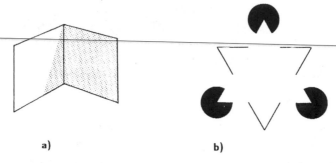

Figure 7.1 (a) Schematic preparation for illusory color contrast. (b) Illusory contours and brightness contrast.

shadow effect. But in the card's inverted configuration, the slight contrast in luminance is no longer consistent with a shadow hypothesis, and the contrast between the two areas is robustly interpreted as a sharp difference in their intrinsic colors. (I owe this example to Richard Gregory.)

Illusory contours provide a similar but contrasting example. The white background in figure 7.1*b* is, of course, entirely uniform. But most of us can see a slightly brighter triangular figure interposed between us and the three black circles, a figure with distinct rectilinear contours marked by a sharp change in luminance, even in the gap between the black circles. Here the eye-brain confers up luminance differences where in reality there are none. And again, the illusion is penetrable and reversible. Tell yourself that the circles have wedges cut out of them; see the elements of the diagram as six independent objects artfully arranged against a uniform background; center your attention on the two prongs of any V; and the illusory contours disappear.

These assembled examples compile a wide range of elements central to visual perception—contour, contrast, color, orientation, distance, size, shape, figure versus ground—all of which are cognitively penetrable. Collectively, they constitute a strong case against Fodor's claims of impenetrability for our perceptual processing.

But perhaps I am gathering evidence selectively or aiming it at an exaggerated version of Fodor's view. Perhaps many other elements of perceptual processing, even the dominant share, are *im*penetrable, despite these examples of a contrary cast. What examples does Fodor cite, then, in support of such a claim?

Only one, the Müller-Lyer illusion (figure 7.2*a*), though the class he has in mind is clear enough (it will include the Ponzo illusion, the Hering Illusion, and similarly persistent illusions). The Müller-Lyer, however, is an odd example for Fodor to be using, because the "textbook story" on how it works (a story apparently endorsed by Fodor, p. 128) explains it as the effect of our having *learned*, in judging absolute size with distance (fig. 7.2*b*.) That is, the illusion exists in the first place only

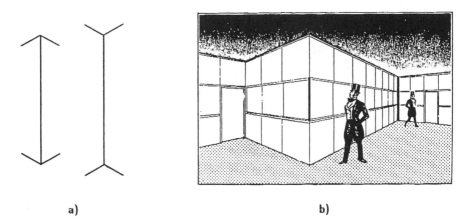

a)   b)

Figure 7.2 (a) The Müller-Lyer illusion. (b) The Müller-Lyer illusion in a realistic setting (bold, vertical lines).

because the relevant processing module is the well-trained victim of some substantial prior education—that is, of some penetration by cognitive activity. The Ponzo and the Hering illusions may have a similar origin. Accordingly, they are all of them poor examples on which to base a general claim of impenetrability.

Now I will grant that, its cognitive origins aside, the Müller-Lyer illusion cannot be overridden by any casual, fleeting, "voluntary" attempt to modify the character of one's visual experience. By itself, however, this means relatively little, for the issue is not whether visual processing is in general very *easily* or *quickly* penetrated by novel or contrary information; the issue is whether in general it is penetrable at all, where the acceptable means of penetration can include long regimes of determined training, practice, or conditioning. If the Müller-Lyer illusion is an incidental consequence of a long period of perceptual training on certain typical kinds of perceptual problems, then presumably a long period of training in an environment of a quite different perceptual character would produce a subject free from that particular illusion. Fodor, it seems to me, is in no position to insist otherwise, especially given examples of the following kind, which are not speculative, but real.

Recall the effects of chronically worn inverting lenses on the visual perception of normal humans. Such lenses have the effect of inverting the orientation of all visual information relative to the body's tactile and motor systems. In short, they turn the visual world upside down. (Kottenhoff 1957 provides a useful summary of this research.)

The initial effect is profoundly disorienting, but with little more than a week's practice, subjects adjust to the new perceptual regime. The subjects are not confined to a chair or bed for the duration of the experiment, but are forced by practical necessity to continue to interact with familiar objects and to engage in the normal forms of motor behavior. The result is that the subjects slowly manage to recoordinate their vision with the rest of their sensory and motor systems, and the illusion of the world's being upside down is said to fade away, all on a time scale of roughly a week.

When the lenses are first put on and the world is made to appear upside down, the subjects are of course quite aware of what the lenses are doing. They may even know how they do it. But the illusion is not banished by the mere possession of this information. It would clearly be wrong, however, to draw from this any conclusion about the impenetrability of our visual processors. A few weeks of steady practice and experience penetrates them quite nicely. And the degree to which that penetration is successful is further revealed when the lenses are finally removed: for a short time thereafter, the subjects suffer a disorientation illusion very much like that encountered when the lenses were first put on. Their visual processing, reconfigured by training to compensate for the lenses, continues to "compensate" after the lenses are gone.

In similar experiments on animals, training produces a reversal in the character of what one might have presumed to be endogenously specified reflexes, such as the vestibulo-ocular reflex, which directs one's eyes, when fixated on a target, to move an appropriate amount to the left or right in order to compensate for head movements in the opposite direction. Here the brain seems literally to rewire the relevant neural mechanism under the pressures imposed by left-right inverting lenses (see Gonshor and Jones 1976).

Cases like these are important, for they reflect the plasticity of some very deep "assumptions" implicit in visual processing, such as the specific orientation of the visual world relative to one's other sense modalities and to one's motor systems. If assumptions as deep as these can be reshaped in a week or two, then our perception begins to look very plastic and very penetrable indeed.

I expect Fodor to object, however, that examples such as these, dramatic though they may be, are not cases of the *cognitive* penetration of our peripheral modules. These perceptual changes are wrought not by the simple acquisition of certain beliefs, nor by reflecting on them in the relevant perceptual circumstances. Rather, they are wrought by some form of training, practice, or conditioning, often lengthy.

One way to turn this objection aside is to attack the integrity of the highly questionable dichotomy between "cognitive penetrability" and other forms of penetrability (see the commentaries on Pylyshyn 1980 in that work). But I shall not pursue this path here. There is a simpler and more direct response: Who ever claimed that the character of a scientist's perception is changed simply and directly by his embracing a novel belief? None of the theorists cited in Fodor's paper have defended such an unrealistic view. And all of us, at some point or other, have emphasized the importance of long familiarity with the novel idiom, of repeated practical applications of its principles, and of socialization within a like-minded group of researchers.

Kuhn is quite explicit (1962, chapters 5 and 10) that the enveloping paradigm that shapes the scientist's perception is not constituted solely by a set of explicit laws, but by an entire disciplinary matrix that includes standard ways of applying and using the resources of the paradigm, skills acquired during a long apprenticeship. And my own discussion of the plasticity of perception (1979, chapter 2) has the relevant community learning their nonstandard observational vocabulary from birth, in an ongoing *practical* setting where no other idiom is even contemplated.

I confess to having used one example where a temporary shift in perception can be made fairly swiftly: the example of reperceiving the organization of the solar system in a heliocentric rather than a geocentric fashion (1979, 30–34). This case is rather closer to the Necker cube in character than to the case of the inverting lenses. But even here it was emphasized that simply having the relevant Copernican beliefs is not enough; one must learn how to see the changing heavens as an unfolding instance of the Copernican organization, as viewed from our peculiar perspective within it. Having the relevant beliefs is one thing: we are all of us Copernicans, after all. Reshaping one's perception is quite another.

The point is a general one. A physics student does not come to see the motions of common objects in a new way simply by memorizing Newton's three laws. Most freshman physics students do memorize those laws, but relatively few have their perceptions much altered. The few who do are distinguished by having *practiced* the skills of applying those laws in a wide variety of circumstances. They do come to perceive a common pattern in the behavior of moving bodies that was hitherto invisible to them, but memorizing the laws was only the first step in a fairly lengthy process. There are sudden flashes of insight, to be sure, as when one first grasps how the pattern is instantiated in some typical case. But on the whole, the process of reshaping one's perception takes time, and it requires more than the mere adoption of a belief or three.

To summarize these points, if Fodor is attacking the view that perceptual processing always (or even usually) responds directly and immediately to changes in one's theoretical commitments, then he is attacking a straw man. This is not a view that anyone has defended. On the other hand, if Fodor is denying that perceptual processing is plastic in the face of more comprehensive and protracted kinds of pressures, such as the forced practical *use* of some novel perspective, then the empirical facts are against him. For by these means, even very basic aspects of visual processing can be overturned and reconfigured, as we saw with the visual-inversion experiments.

Some degree of "diachronic" penetrability is grudgingly conceded by Fodor, since the alternative is to hold that *all* of our adult perceptual capacities are *endogenously* specified. We know that they are not, since the development of so-called "normal" perception itself plainly involves a great deal of learning on the part of the growing infant. Our perceptual, practical, and social environment shapes our perceptual capacities mightily, especially in their early stages of development, and this suggests that different courses of learning would produce interestingly different perceptual capacities. Fodor attempts to play down this concession, however, by suggesting that the range of possible variation in perceptual development might be quite narrow.

Why he thinks this is left unexplained. The claim needs arguing, the facts suggest otherwise, and one need not turn to academic journals for shining examples. To see the nonstandard perceptual capacities that our native modalities can acquire, think of the following. In recent centuries most humans have learned to perceive speech not just auditorally but visually: We have learned to read. And some have learned to perceive speech by touch: They read Braille. And some of us have learned not just to hear music, but to see it: we have learned to sight-read musical notation. Now, neither the eyes nor the fingers were evolved for the instantaneous perception of those complex structures and organizations originally found in auditory phenomena, but their acquired mastery here illustrates the highly sophisticated and decidedly supernormal capacities that learning can produce in them. And if these capacities, why not others? Diachronic penetration, I assert, is not only possible and actual; it is commonplace.

Finally, there is neurophysiological evidence that suggests the systematic penetrability of the peripheral modules by the higher cognitive centers. Cell-staining techniques have allowed us to trace out a gross "wiring diagram" for many parts of the brain. When introduced into a neuronal body, certain chemical stains—notably, horseradish peroxidase—are transported down the entire length of its long fiber-like axon. This marks the axons visually, and the paths they trace through successive sections or slices of the brain can then be followed with an optical microscope. In the case of vision, for example, the dominant nervous pathway starts at the retina, and proceeds via the optic nerve to the lateral geniculate nucleus (LGN), and stepwise from there by other pathways to the primary visual cortex, to the secondary visual cortex, and from there to a variety of other areas even higher in the processing hierarchy.

But these "ascending" pathways are almost invariably matched by "descending" pathways that lead us stepwise back through the intermediate brain areas and all the way out to the earliest processing systems at the retina. The descending projections from the visual cortex back to the LGN, for example, are even greater in number than those in the ascending direction. And though the claim is not well established, there is some evidence that fully 10 percent of the axonal fibers in the human optic nerve are descending projections from the LGN back out to the retinal surface itself, the very first transducer in the processing hierarchy (Wolter 1965; Wolter and Lund 1968; Sacks and Lindenberg 1969).

There are similar chains of descending pathways—from the various areas topmost in the information-processing hierarchy, down through all of the intermediate processing stages, and all the way out to the periphery—for all of the other sensory modalities as well. This organizational pattern is typical in mammals and also in birds (Livingston 1978, 45–49). Prima facie, the function of these descending pathways is "centrifugal control." They allow for the modulation of lower level neural activity as a function of the demands sent down from levels higher in the cognitive hierarchy. Experimentation on their functional significance is so far limited, but lesions confined to the descending optic nerve pathways (from LGN to retina) are known to cause perceptual deficits in birds, even though the descending fibers in their case constitute only 1 percent of the optic nerve total. Lesioned birds are less able than intact birds to distinguish edible seeds from other minute objects in dim light (Rogers and Miles 1972).

If such descending pathways were always sharply confined close to the sensory periphery, or if they were to be found scattered only here and there in the information-processing hierarchy, then we might have some realistic hope of dismissing any backward loop as an element of what is still an "encapsulated module" from a functional point of view. But descending pathways are the rule in the processing hierarchy of the brain, not the exception. They appear to connect the upper levels in the hierarchy to most and perhaps to all of the lower ones, in each and every one of the sensory modalities. In sum, the wiring of the brain relative to its sensory periphery certainly does not suggest the encapsulation and isolation of perceptual processing. As with the psychological data discussed earlier, it strongly suggests exactly the opposite arrangement.

[Added in 1989: Two new pieces of neuroscientific evidence have recently emerged that bear on the questions of both plasticity and theory-ladenness. The first piece of evidence is theoretical and derives from the new connectionist models of information processing in the brain. Those models identify the general knowledge acquired by the organism with the acquired configuration of its myriad synaptic weights. Since on this model all cognitive processing, including perceptual processing, consists in vector transformations at the hands of those modifiable and much instructed weights, it would seem that all perceptual processing is inescapably laden with the legacy of general knowledge shaped by past experience.

The second piece of evidence is experimental and concerns the functional plasticity of auditory cortex. Sur et al. (1988) induced the axons in the optic nerve of neonate ferrets to project into the animals' auditory pathway (the medial geniculate nucleus or MGN) instead of to their normal visual pathway (the LGN). The result is an animal whose auditory cortex is now driven exclusively by information sent from the eyes. Such animals do develop significant visual function as they mature, and recordings from cells in the "auditory" cortex of adult animals show the cells to have developed the same directional sensitivity, orientation selectivity, and capacity for edge detection displayed by cells in the visual cortex of normal animals. This striking result suggests that the processing characteristics peculiar to our adult sensory systems are not endogenously specified, as Fodor's picture invites us to suppose, but rather are developed over time in a highly plastic system that is shaped by the long-term characteristics of the sensory input they receive from the periphery. This does not sit at all well with a picture of endogenously specified assumptions unique to each modality. This result is also exactly what one should expect if the connectionist models of learning and information processing just mentioned have any integrity.] . . .

Sensational Plasticity versus Conceptual Plasticity

One possible way to defend Fodor would be to concede the theory-dependent character of our observational concepts and judgments, and try to insist on no more than the theory-independent character of our *sensations*. Fodor himself seems to be sketching a position of this sort late in his paper when he urges the rigidity of "how things are judged to be" (p. 135).

But this defense will not take us any distance at all. For one thing, if all Fodor wishes to insist on is uniformity in the character of our sensations through changes in our doxastic commitments, then his argument is largely an *ignoratio*. It fails to address the major epistemological tradition at issue, whose central theme has always been the theory-laden character, not of our sensations, but of our observational concepts and observational judgments.

And there is a very good reason for the centrality of that theme. Thinkers in the tradition at issue (Popper, Feyerabend, Hanson, etc.) have been primarily concerned with the refutation or corroboration of theories. But sensations themselves neither confirm nor refute any theory. Sensations belong to the wrong logical space: It is only an observation *judgment*, or *belief*, or *report* that can be logically consistent or inconsistent with any theory (Popper 1959). Thus the chronic concern, throughout the positivist and postpositivist periods, with the possibility of a theory-neutral observation *vocabulary*. Whether sensations themselves might be infected or modified by theory was rarely, if ever, an issue.

My own 1979 position, to cite one target of Fodor's, simply assumes the generally constant character of our sensory responses to the environment. The plasticity that excited me there was confined to the conceptual frameworks within which we make our judgmental responses to the passing contents of our sensory manifold. Accordingly, if rigidity in the character of our sensations is all Fodor is concerned to defend, then I do not understand his objection to, and dismissal of, the alternative perceptual possibilities sketched in my 1979. For that sketch makes no assumptions about the plasticity of our sensations. It is *conceptual* plasticity that is there at issue.

To be sure, sensational plasticity would constitute an *additional* argument for the plasticity of perception. At least one author has cautiously advanced a claim of this kind (Kuhn 1962, 120–121). And I, for another, am now willing to defend it vigorously (recall the examples in figure 7.1). So there is a genuine point to attacking it, as Fodor does. But it is wrong to represent or regard this attack, successful or otherwise, as aimed at the principal arguments in favor of theory-ladenness. Those arguments have typically been based on other grounds entirely: on the plasticity of our conceptual responses to sensory activity. . . .

References

Bruner, J. (1973). On perceptual readiness. In J. Anglin, ed., *Beyond the information given.* New York: W. W. Norton.

Churchland, P. M. (1975). Two grades of evidential bias. *Philosophy of Science* 42, 250–259.

Churchland, P. M. (1979). *Scientific realism and the plasticity of mind.* Cambridge: Cambridge University Press.

Fodor, J. A. (1984). Observation reconsidered. *Philosophy of Science* 51, 23–43.

Gonshor, A., and G. M. Jones (1976). Extreme vestibulo-ocular adaptation induced by prolonged optical reversal of vision. *Journal of Physiology* 256, 381–414.

Gregory, R. (1970). *The intelligent eye.* New York: McGraw-Hill.

Gregory, R. (1974). *Concepts and mechanisms of perception.* New York: Charles Scribners and Sons.

Hanson, N. R. (1961). *Patterns of Discovery.* Cambridge: Cambridge University Press.

Kottenhoff, H. (1957). Situational and personal influences on space perception with experimental spectacles. *Acta Psychologica* 13, 79–97.

Kuhn, T. S. (1962). *The structure of scientific revolutions.* Chicago: University of Chicago Press.

Livingstone, R. B. (1978). *Sensory processing, perception, and behavior.* New York: Raven Press.

Popper, K. (1959). *The logic of scientific discovery*. New York: Harper & Row.

Pylyshyn, Z. (1980). Computation and cognition: Issues in the foundation of cognitive science. *Behavioral and Brain Sciences* 3, 111–134.

Rock, I. (1983). *The logic of perception*. Cambridge, MA: MIT Press.

Rogers, L. J., and F. A. Miles (1972). Centrifugal control of avian retina: Effects of lesions of the isthmo-optic nucleus on visual behavior. *Brain Research* 48, 147–156.

Sacks, J. G., and R. Lindenberg (1969). Efferent nerve fibers in the anterior visual pathways in bilateral congenital cyctic eyeballs. *American Journal of Ophthalmology* 68, 691–695.

Sur, M., P. Garraghty, and A. Roe (1988). Experimentally induced visual projections into auditory thalamus and cortex. *Science* 242, 1,437–1,441.

Wolter, J. R. (1965). The centrifugal nerves in human optic tract, chiasm, optic nerve, and retina. *Transactions of the American Ophthalmological Society* 63, 678–707.

Wolter, J. R., and O. E. Lund (1968). Reaction of centrifugal nerves in the human retina. *American Journal of Ophthalmology* 66, 221–232.

8 Explanatory Coherence

Paul R. Thagard

Introduction

Why did the oxygen theory of combustion supersede the phlogiston theory? Why is Darwin's theory of evolution by natural selection superior to creationism? How can a jury in a murder trial decide between conflicting views of what happened? This target article develops a theory of explanatory coherence that applies to the evaluation of competing hypotheses in cases such as these. The theory is implemented in a connectionist computer program with many interesting properties.

The problem of inference to explanatory hypotheses has a long history in philosophy and a much shorter one in psychology and artificial intelligence (AI). Scientists and philosophers have long considered the evaluation of theories on the basis of their explanatory power. In the late nineteenth century, Peirce discussed two forms of inference to explanatory hypotheses: *hypothesis*, which involved the acceptance of hypotheses, and *abduction*, which involved merely the initial formation of hypotheses (Peirce 1931–1958; Thagard 1988). Researchers in artificial intelligence and some philosophers have used the term "abduction" to refer to both the formation and the evaluation of hypotheses. AI work on this kind of inference has concerned such diverse topics as medical diagnosis (Josephson et al. 1987; Pople 1977; Reggia et al. 1983) and natural language interpretation (Charniak and McDermott 1985; Hobbs et al. 1988). In philosophy, the acceptance of explanatory hypotheses is usually called *inference to the best explanation* (Harman 1973, 1986). In social psychology, attribution theory considers how people in everyday life form hypotheses to explain events (Fiske and Taylor 1984). Recently, Pennington and Hastie (1986, 1987) have proposed that much of jury decision making can be best understood in terms of explanatory coherence. For example, to gain a conviction of first-degree murder, the prosecution must convince the jury that the accused had a preformed intention to kill the victim. Pennington and Hastie argue that whether the jury will believe this depends on the explanatory coherence of the prosecution's story compared to the story presented by the defense.

Actual cases of scientific and legal reasoning suggest a variety of factors that go into determining the explanatory coherence of a hypothesis. How much does the hypothesis explain? Are its explanations economical? Is the hypothesis similar to ones that explain similar phenomena? Is there an explanation of why the hypothesis might be true? In legal reasoning, the question of explaining the hypothesis usually concerns motives: If we are trying to explain the evidence by supposing that the accused murdered the victim, we will find the supposition more plausible if we can think of reasons why the accused was motivated to kill the victim. Finally, on all these dimensions, how does the hypothesis compare against alternative hypotheses?

This paper presents a theory of explanatory coherence that is intended to account for a wide range of explanatory inferences. I shall propose seven principles of explanatory coherence that encompass the considerations just described and that suffice to make judgments of explanatory coherence. Their sufficiency is shown by the implementation of the theory in a connectionist computer program called ECHO that has been applied to more than a dozen complex cases of scientific and legal reasoning. My account of explanatory coherence thus has three parts: the statement of a theory, the description of an algorithm, and applications to diverse examples that show the feasibility of the algorithm and help to demonstrate the power of the theory (cf. Marr 1982).

A Theory of Explanatory Coherence

Coherence and Explanation

Before presenting the theory, it will be useful to make some general points about the concepts of coherence and explanation, although it should be made clear that this paper does not purport to give a general account of either concept. The question of the nature of explanation is extremely difficult and controversial. Philosophers disagree about whether explanation is primarily deductive (Hempel 1965), statistical (Salmon 1970), causal (Salmon 1984), linguistic (Achinstein 1983), or pragmatic (van Fraassen 1980). In AI, explanation is sometimes thought of as deduction (Mitchell et al. 1986) and sometimes as pattern instantiation (Schank 1986). This paper does not pretend to offer a theory of explanation, but is compatible with any of the foregoing accounts (except van Fraassen's, which is intended to make explanation irrelevant to questions of acceptability and truth).

Nor does this paper give a general account of coherence. There are various notions of coherence in the literatures of different fields. We can distinguish at least the following:

- Deductive coherence depends on relations of logical consistency and entailment among members of a set of propositions.

- Probabilistic coherence depends on a set of propositions having probability assignments consistent with the axioms of probability.

- Semantic coherence depends on propositions having similar meanings.

BonJour (1985) provides an interesting survey of philosophical ideas about coherence. Here, I am only offering a theory of *explanatory* coherence.

Explanatory coherence can be understood in several different ways, as

(a) a relation between two propositions,

(b) a property of a whole set of related propositions, or

(c) a property of a single proposition.

I claim that (a) is fundamental, with (b) depending on (a), and (c) depending on (b). That is, explanatory coherence is primarily a relation between two propositions, but we can speak derivatively of the explanatory coherence of a set of propositions as determined by their pairwise coherence, and we can speak derivatively of the explanatory coherence of a single proposition with respect to a set of propositions whose coherence has been established. A major requirement of an account of explanatory coherence is that it show how it is possible to move from (a) to (b) to (c); algorithms for doing so are presented as part of the computational model described below.

Because the notion of the explanatory coherence of an individual proposition is so derivative and depends on a specification of the set of propositions with which it is supposed to cohere, I shall from now on avoid treating coherence as a property of individual propositions. Instead, we can speak of the *acceptability* of a proposition, which depends on but is detachable from the explanatory coherence of the set of propositions to which it belongs. We should accept propositions that are coherent with our other beliefs, reject propositions that are incoherent with our other beliefs, and be neutral toward propositions that are neither coherent nor incoherent. Acceptability has finer gradations than just acceptance, rejection, and neutrality, however: The greater the coherence of a proposition with other propositions, the greater its acceptability.

In ordinary language, to cohere is to hold together, and explanatory coherence is a holding together because of explanatory relations. We can, accordingly, start with a vague characterization:

Propositions P and Q cohere if there is some explanatory relation between them.

To fill this statement out, we must specify what the explanatory relation might be. I see four possibilities:

(1) P is part of the explanation of Q.

(2) Q is part of the explanation of P.

(3) P and Q are together part of the explanation of some R.

(4) P and Q are analogous in the explanations they respectively give of some R and S.

This characterization leaves open the possibility that two propositions can cohere for nonexplanatory reasons: deductive, probabilistic, or semantic. Explanation is thus sufficient but not necessary for coherence. I have taken "explanation" and "explain" as primitives, while asserting that a relation of explanatory coherence holds between P and Q if and only if one or more of (1)–(4) is true. *Incoherence* between two propositions occurs if they contradict each other or if they offer explanations that background knowledge suggests are incompatible.

The psychological relevance of explanatory coherence comes from the following general predictions concerning the acceptance of individual propositions:

If a proposition is highly coherent with the beliefs of a person, then the person will believe the proposition with a high degree of confidence.

If a proposition is incoherent with the beliefs of a person, then the person will not believe the proposition.

Principles of Explanatory Coherence

I now propose seven principles that establish relations of explanatory coherence and make possible an assessment of the global coherence of an explanatory system S. S consists of propositions P, Q, and $P_1 \ldots P_n$. Local coherence is a relation between two propositions. I coin the term "incohere" to mean more than just that two propositions do not cohere: To incohere is to *resist* holding together. The principles are as follows:

Principle 1. Symmetry.

(a) If P and Q cohere, then Q and P cohere.
(b) If P and Q incohere, then Q and P incohere.

Principle 2. Explanation.

If $P_1 \ldots P_m$ explains Q, then:

(a) For each P_i in $P_1 \ldots P_m$, P_i and Q cohere.
(b) For each P_i and P_j in $P_1 \ldots P_m$, P_i and P_j cohere.
(c) In (a) and (b), the degree of coherence is inversely proportional to the number of propositions $P_1 \ldots P_m$.

of the causal route from distal objects and events to the tokening of the sentence or the fixation of the belief.) The point is, of course, that their attachment to the world, unlike their inferential role, is something that symbols (/beliefs) can have *severally;* so that, when such attachments are at issue, the morals of holism need not apply.

At a minimum, this suggests a way out of Churchland's dilemma. It will have been clear from the fragments quoted above that Churchland's discussion relies heavily, if implicitly, on the following modus tollens: if the semantics of observation sentences is theory neutral, that must be because observation sentences get their meanings—somehow—from their connections with sensations. But we have good reason to deny that they get their semantics that way. The alternative is that observation sentences get their meanings from their theoretical contexts (from "networks of beliefs").

In fact, however, *neither* of these accounts of the semantics of observation sentences seems particularly attractive, least of all for color terms, although, as it happens, color terms are Churchland's favorite working examples. It tells against the first alternative that 'white' is typically used to refer to the color of objects, not to the color of sensations; and it tells against the second that the inferential roles of color terms tend to be isomorphic—hence inverted spectrum puzzles—so that color words provide the worst possible cases for 'functional role' theories of meaning. In fact, it looks as though the sensible thing to say about 'white' might be that it means what it does because of the special character of its association (not with a sensation or an inferential role but) *with white things.* To accept that, however, is to reject holism as, anyhow, the *whole* story about the semantics of color terms.

I don't suppose that there's anything much novel in this, and I certainly don't suppose it establishes that there *is* a viable, theory neutral, observation/inference distinction. The point I have been making is merely negative: meaning holism is unequivocally destructive of a theory-neutral notion of observation only if you suppose that *all* the semantic properties of sentences/beliefs are determined by their theoretical context; for, if some are not, then perhaps the essential semantic conditions for being observational can be framed in terms of these. The obvious suggestion would be, on the one hand, that what makes a term observational is that it denotes what is, by independent criteria, an observable property; and, on the other, that what a term denotes is nonholistically (perhaps causally) determined. In light of this, I propose simply not to grant that all the semantic properties of sentences/beliefs are determined by their theoretical context. And Granny proposes not to grant that too.

3. Psychological Arguments   Precisely parallel to the philosophical doctrine that there can be no principled distinction between *observation* and *inference* is the psychological doctrine that there can be no principled distinction between *perception* and *cognition*. The leading idea here is that "perception involves a kind of problem-solving—a kind of intelligence" (Gregory 1970, 30). Perception, according to this account, is the process wherein an organism assigns probable distal causes to the proximal stimulations it encounters. What makes the solution of perceptual problems other than mere routine is the fact that, as a matter of principle, any given pattern of proximal stimulation is compatible with a great variety of distal causes; there are, if you like, many possible worlds that would project a given pattern of excitation onto the sensory mechanisms of an organism. To view the mental processes which mediate perception as inferences is thus necessarily to view them as *nondemonstrative* inferences. "We are forced . . . to suppose that perception involves betting on the most probable interpretation of sensory data, in terms of the world of objects" (Gregory 1970, 29). It is worth stressing the putative moral: what mediates perception is an inference from effects to causes. The sort of mentation required for perception is thus not different in *kind*—though no doubt it differs a lot in conscious accessibility—from what goes on in Sherlock Holmes' head when he infers the identity of the criminal from a stray cigar band and a hair or two. If what Holmes does deserves to be called cognition, perception deserves to be called cognition too, or so, at least, some psychologists like to say.

Neither Granny nor I have heard of a serious alternative to this view of perception, so let's suppose, for purposes of argument at least, that these psychologists are right. It may then seem that the psychology of perception provides an argument—indeed, quite a direct argument—that observation can't be theory neutral. To see how such an argument might go, consider the following question: if, in general, there are many distal solutions compatible with the perceptual problem that a given sensory pattern poses, how is it possible that perception should ever manage to be univocal (to say nothing of *veridical*)? Why, that is, doesn't the world look to be many ways ambiguous, with one 'reading' of the ambiguity corresponding to each distal layout that is compatible with the current sensory excitation; (as, indeed, a Necker cube *does* look to be several ways ambiguous, with one term of the ambiguity corresponding to each of the possible optical projections from a three dimensional cube onto a two dimensional surface). Assuming, in short, that perception is problem solving, how on earth do perceptual problems ever get solved? As Gregory comments, "it is surely remarkable that out of the infinity of possibilities the perceptual brain generally hits on just about the best one" (1970, 29).

All psychological theories that endorse the continuity of perception with problem solving offer much the same answer to this question: viz. that though perceptual analyses are underdetermined by sensory arrays, it does not follow that they are underdetermined *tout court*. For, perceptual analyses are constrained not just by the available sensory information, but also by such prior knowledge as the perceiver may bring to the task. What happens in perceptual processing, according to this account, is that sensory information is interpreted by reference to the perceiver's background theories, the latter serving, in effect, to rule out certain etiologies as implausible causal histories for the present sensory array. Only thus is sensory ambiguity resolved; and, if perception is typically veridical, that's because the background theories that organisms exploit in perceptual analysis are, for the most part, true.

Accepting this account of the perceptual reduction of sensory ambiguity is, of course, fully compatible with stressing the analogy between perception and problem solving. There are many, many ways that the hairs and the cigar band could have come to where Holmes found them; many projections, if you like, of possible criminals onto actual clues. How, then, is it possible—even in principle—that Holmes should solve the crime? Answer: Holmes knows about the clues, but he knows a lot more too; and his background knowledge comes into play when the clues get unravelled. Jones couldn't have left brown hairs because Jones is blond; Smith couldn't have left the cigar band because he only smokes iced tea. Bentley, however, has brown hair and his dog collects cigar bands; so Bentley and his dog it must have been. The clues underdetermine the criminal, but the clues plus background knowledge may be univocal up to a very high order of probability. The trick—the trick that problem solving *always* amounts to—is having the right background information and knowing when and how to apply it. So too in the case of perception, according to the cognitivists.

What has all this to do with reconsidering observation? The point is that, if the present story is right, then the appeal to a background theory is *inherent* in the process of perceptual analysis. Perception wouldn't work without it because the perceptual problem is the reduction of sensory ambiguity, and that problem is solved only when one's sensory information is interpreted in the light of one's prior beliefs. So, the one thing that perception *couldn't* be, on this account of how it works, is theory neutral. Indeed, this is precisely the moral that a number of philosophers have drawn from the psychological texts. Thus, Thomas Kuhn remarks that "the rich experimental literature [in psychology] . . . makes one suspect that something like a paradigm is prerequisite to perception itself. What a man sees depends both upon what he looks at and also upon what his previous visual-conceptual experience has taught him to see" (Kuhn 1962, 113). Kuhn clearly thinks that, among the "visual-conceptual experiences" that can work such alterations in perception is the assimilation of scientific doctrine: "paradigm changes do cause scientists to see the world of their research-engagements differently. . . . It is as elementary prototypes for these transformations of the scientist's world view that the familiar demonstrations of a switch in visual gestalt prove so suggestive" (1962, 111). Nelson Goodman reads the experimental literature on perception in much the same way. "That we find what we are prepared to find (what we look for or what forcefully affronts our expectations), and that we are likely to be blind to what neither helps nor hinders our pursuits, are commonplaces . . . amply attested in the psychological laboratory. [See also Goodman's *Languages of Art,* where this view of perceptual psychology is strikingly in evidence.]" (Goodman 1978, 14).

In fact, however, it is unclear that that's what the psychological laboratory *does* attest, and thereby hangs a puzzle. For if we ought to be impressed by the degree to which perception is interpretive, contextually sensitive, labile, responsive to background knowledge and all that, we surely ought also to be impressed by the degree to which it is often bull headed and recalcitrant. In fact, many of the standard psychological demonstrations seem to point both morals at the same time. Consider the famous Müller-Lyer figures. The text-book story goes like this: when the arrow heads bend in, as in figure 6.1a, the figure is unconsciously interpreted in three dimensional projection as a convex corner with its edge emerging towards the viewer from the picture plane. Conversely, when the arrow heads bend out, as in 6.1b, the figure is unconsciously interpreted in three dimensional projection as a concave corner with its edge receding from the viewer. It follows that the center line is interpreted as *further from the observer* in 6.1b than in 6.1a. Since, however, the two center lines are in fact of the same length, their retinal projections are identical in size. This identity of retinal projection could be compatible with the three dimensional interpretation of the figures only if the center line is longer in figure b than in figure a; two objects at different distances can have the same retinal projection only if the more distant object is larger. So size constancy operates (to compensate, as one might say, for what appears to be the

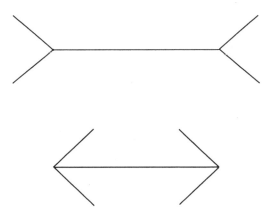

Figure 6.1 The Müller-Lyer illusion.

apparent effect of distance) and the two lines are perceived as differing in length. See what a nice regard for consistency the unconscious has, Freud to the contrary notwithstanding. There is abundant empirical evidence for this explanation including, notably, the fact that children, having had less experience with edges and corners than adults, are correspondingly less susceptible to the illusion.

The Müller-Lyer illusion thus appears to be, and is often cited as, a prime example of how background information—in this case a complex of assumptions about the relations between three-dimensional objects and their two-dimensional projections—can affect the perceptual analysis of a sensory array. 'What', one might ask, 'could be clearer evidence of the penetration of perception by information that is *not* available at the retina?' On the other hand, there's this: The Müller-Lyer is a *familiar* illusion; the news has pretty well gotten around by now. So, it's part of the 'background theory' of anybody who lives in this culture and is at all into pop psychology that displays like figure 6.1 are in fact misleading and that it always turns out, on measurement, that the center lines of the arrows are the same length. Query: *Why isn't perception penetrated by THAT piece of background theory?* Why, that is, doesn't *knowing* that the lines are the same length make it *look as though* the lines are the same length? (For that matter, since one knows perfectly well that figure 6.1 is a drawing in two dimensions, why doesn't *that* information penetrate perception, thereby blocking the three dimensional interpretation and cancelling the illusion?) This sort of consideration doesn't make it seem at all as though perception is, as it's often said to be, saturated with cognition through and through. On the contrary, it suggests just the reverse: that how the world looks can be peculiarly unaffected by how one knows it to be. I pause to emphasize that the Müller-Lyer is by no means atypical in this respect. To the best of my knowledge, all the standard perceptual illusions exhibit this curiously refractory character: knowing that they *are* illusions doesn't make them go away.[2]

I hope that the polemical situation is beginning to seem a little queer. On the one hand, reflection upon the impoverishment and ambiguity of sensory information leads, by a plausible route, to the analysis of perception as a form of problem solving in which proximal stimulations are interpreted in light of some background theory accessible to the perceiver. This makes it seem that how the world is perceived to be ought to depend very largely on the perceiver's prior beliefs and expectations; hence the perceptual effects of cognitive set that psychologists of the 'New Look' persuasion made a living by advertising. But, on the other hand, there are these curious and persuasive perceptual *im*plasticities, cases where knowing doesn't help seeing. It is, of course, reflection on examples of the second sort that keeps Granny going. These are the cases where the idea of theory-neutral observation can get a toe-hold. The problem is: Which sorts of cases ought we to believe? And, while we're at it, *how can a theory of perception accommodate the existence of both?*

We come to the main point at last. The New Look idea that perception is a kind of problem solving does not, all by itself, imply the theory dependence of observation. Philosophers who read that moral in the psychological texts read the texts too fast. (Granny says that a little psychology is a dangerous thing and inclineth a man to relativism.) To get from a cognitivist interpretation of perception to any epistemologically interesting version of the conclusion that observation is theory dependent, you need *not only the premise that perception is problem solving, but also the premise that perceptual problem solving has access to ALL (or, anyhow, arbitrarily much) of the background information at the perceiver's disposal.* Perceptual implasticities of the sorts we've just been noticing make it highly implausible, however, that this second premise is true.

All this suggests that we'd better distinguish between two questions that up 'til now we've been treating as the same: the question whether perception is a kind of problem solving (i.e., whether observation is inferential) and the question whether perception is comprehensively penetrated by background beliefs (i.e., whether observation can be theory-neutral). It is entirely possible—to put the point another way—to steer a middle course between Granny and Jerome Bruner: to agree with Bruner (as against Granny) that there is an important sense in which observation is a kind of inference, but also to agree with Granny (as against Harvard relativists) that there is, in perception, a radical isolation of how things look from the effects of much of what one believes.

Since it is the second issue, rather than the first, that raises all the epistemological questions, this seems to be a moral victory for Granny. If, for example, the inferential character of perception is, as I'm supposing, compatible with the theory neutrality of observation, then *nothing* follows from perceptual psychology about whether scientists who accept radically different theories can observe the same phenomena. In particular, on this view, it would *not* follow from the inferential character of perception that "the infant and the layman . . . cannot see what the physicist sees" (Hanson 1961, 17), or that "[when the physicist looks at an X-ray tube] . . . he sees the instrument in terms of electrical circuit theory, thermodynamic theory, the theories of metal and glass structure, thermionic emission, optical transmission, refraction, diffraction, atomic theory, quantam theory and special relativity" (pp. 15–16). Similarly, on this account, the inferential character of perception leaves it open that the children whom Churchland wants to teach not to see the gathering of the dew might, thank God, see things much the same way after they've learned physics as they did before. The argument for the relativity of observation requires, to repeat, not just the inferential character of perception, but the idea that *all* your background knowledge, including especially your scientific theories, is accessible as premises for perceptual integration. By contrast, if you think that perception, though inferential, is nevertheless encapsulated from much of what the perceiver believes, the common epistemic situation of the scientist and the layman starts to show through. There is, perhaps, just one perceptual world, though the experts sometimes know more about it than the amateurs.

What might the psychology of perception look like if observation is *both* inferential and theory neutral? I'll say a word about this before returning to the epistemological issues.

The view that perception is problem solving, though it takes the distinction between perception and *cognition* as heuristic, takes quite seriously the distinction between perception and *sensation*. Sensory processes, according to this account, merely register such proximal stimulations as an organism's environment affords. It's left to cognitive processes—notably the perceptual ones—to interpret sensory states by assigning probable distal causes. So we have the following picture: sensation is responsive solely to the character of proximal stimulation and is noninferential. Perception is both inferential and responsive to the perceiver's background theories. It is not, of course, an accident that things are supposed to line up this way; inference requires premises. Perceptual processes *can* be inferential because the perceiver's background theory supplies the premises that the inferences run on. Sensory processes *can't* be inferential because they have, by assumption, no access to the background theories in light of which the distal causes of proximal stimulations are inferred. The moral is that, if you want to split the difference between Granny and the New Look, you need to postulate a tertium quid; a kind of psychological mechanism which is both encapsulated (like sensation) and inferential (like cognition). The apparent contradiction between inference and encapsulation is resolved by assuming that the access to background theory that such mechanisms have is sharply delimited; indeed, delimited by the intrinsic character of the mechanisms.

I won't say much about this here since I've set out the psychological story at some length in a previous study (see Fodor 1983) and I'm anxious to return to the philosophical morals. Suffice it just to suggest, by way of a brief example, what the organization of such "modular" perceptual mechanisms might be like.

It's plausible to assume that the perceptual analysis of speech typically effects an assignment of sentence tokens to sentence types. One reason it's plausible to assume this is that it's obviously true. Another reason is that understanding what someone says typically requires knowing what form of words he uttered, and to assign an utterance to a form of words *is* to assign a token to a type. Cognitive psychology proceeds by diagnosing functions and postulating mechanisms to perform them; so let's assume that there is some psychological mechanism—a *parser*, let's call it—whose function is this: it takes sensory (as it might be, acoustic) representations of utterances as inputs and produces representations of sentence types (as it might be, linguistic structural descriptions) as outputs. No doubt this way of setting up the problem assumes a lot that a lot of you won't want to grant—for example, that there are psychological mechanisms, and that they are properly viewed as functions from one sort of representations onto another. However, remember the context: we've been wondering what current psychological theory implies about the observation/inference distinction. And the sort of psychological theory that's current is the one I've just outlined.

There is abundant empirical evidence—with which, however, I won't bother you—that parsing has all the properties that make psychologists want to say that perception is inferential. All the indications are that the acoustic character of an utterance significantly underdetermines its structural description, so the parser—if it is to succeed in its function—will have to know a lot of background theory. This isn't, by the way, particularly mysterious. Consider the property of being a noun—a sort of property that some utterances surely have and that adequate structural descriptions of utterances must surely mark. Patently, that property has no sensory/acoustic correspondent; there's nothing that nouns qua nouns sound like, or look like on an oscilliscope. So a mechanism that can recognize utterances of nouns as such must know about something more than the acoustic/sensory properties of the tokens it classifies; in this case, something about the language that it parses; i.e., it has to know which words in the language are nouns.

Well, then, what would it be like for the parser to be a module? A simple story might go like this; a parser for L contains a grammar of L. What it does when it does its thing is: it infers from certain acoustic properties of a token to a characterization of certain of the distal causes of the token (e.g. to the speaker's intention that the utterance should be a token of a certain linguistic type). Premises of this inference can include: whatever information about the acoustics of the token the mechanisms of sensory transduction provide, whatever information about the linguistic types in L the internally represented grammar provides, *and nothing else*. It is, of course, the closure condition that makes the parser modular.

Compare a New Look parser. In the extreme case, a New Look parser can bring to the process of assigning structural descriptions *anything that the organism knows* (or believes, or hopes, or expects . . . etc.). For example, a New Look parser knows how *very* unlikely it is that anyone would say, right smack in the course of a philosophical lecture on observation and inference: "Piglet gave Pooh a stiffening sort of nudge, and Pooh, who felt more and more that he was somewhere else, got up slowly and began to look for himself." So if someone *were* to say that, right smack in the middle of a philosophical lecture on observation and inference, a New Look parser would presumably have a lot of trouble understanding it; by definition, a New Look parser tends to hear just what it expects to hear. By the way, this example suggests one of the reasons why encapsulated perceptual modules might be quite a good thing for an organism to have: background beliefs, and the expectations that they engender, from time to time prove *not to be true*. That doesn't matter so much when they are background beliefs about observation and inference, or about Pooh and Piglet. When, however, they are background beliefs about Tigger, it's a different story. Tiggers bounce. And bite.

I won't try to convince you that the parser—or any other perceptual mechanism—actually *is* modular; what I want to urge, for present purposes, is just that *if* perception is modular (inferential but encapsulated), then that has serious implications for the putative psychological arguments against the theory neutrality of observation. I have a scattering of points to make about this.

First, and most important, if perceptual processes are modular, then, by definition, bodies of theory that are inaccessible to the modules *do not affect the way the perceiver sees the world*. Specifically, perceivers who differ profoundly in their background theories—scientists with quite different axes to grind, for example—might nevertheless see the world in *exactly* the same way, so long as the bodies of theory that they disagree about are inaccessible to their perceptual mechanisms.

Second, the modularity story suggests not only that something can be made of the notion of theory neutral observation, but also that something can be made of the notion of observation *language;* i.e., that—much current opinion to the contrary notwithstanding—there is a good sense in which some terms (like 'red', as it might be) are observational and others (like 'proton', as it might be) are not. Suppose that perceptual mechanisms are modular and that the body of background theory accessible to processes of perceptual integration is therefore rigidly fixed. By hypothesis, only those properties of the distal stimulus count as observable which terms in the *accessible* background theory denote. The point is, no doubt, entirely empirical, but I am willing to bet lots that 'red' will prove to be observational by this criterion and that 'proton' will not. This is, of course, just a way of betting that Hanson, Kuhn, Churchland, Goodman and Co. are wrong; that physics doesn't belong to the accessible background.

There are other, more exciting cases where we are already in a pretty good position to say which properties of distal objects will count as observable, hence which terms will count as observation vocabulary. The case of parsing is among these. This is because it is plausible to suppose that the background theory accessible to a modularized parser would have to be a grammar, and we know, more or less, what sorts of properties of sentences grammatical descriptions specify. So then, applying the present criterion to the present assumptions, the observable linguistic properties of utterances of sentences ought to include things like: being an utterance of a sentence, being an utterance of a sentence that contains the word 'the', being an utterance of a sentence that contains a word that refers to trees . . . and so forth, depending on details of your views about what properties of sentences linguistic structural descriptions specify. By contrast, what would *not* count as observable on the current assumptions are such properties of sentences as: being uttered with the intention of deceiving John; being ill-advised in the context, containing a word that is frequently used in restaurants where they sell hamburgers . . . and so forth. It should be noted in passing that this sort of account permits one to distinguish sharply between observable properties and *sensory* properties. If sensory properties are ones that *non*inferential psychological mechanisms respond to, then the sensory properties of utterances are plausibly all acoustic and almost all inaccessible to consciousness.

Third point: what I've been saying about modularity so far is equivalent to the claim that perceptual processes are 'synchronically' impenetrable by—insensitive to—much of the perceiver's background knowledge. Your current sophistication about the Müller-Lyer is inaccessible to the module that mediates visual form perception and does not, therefore, serve to dispel the illusion. But this leaves open the question whether perception may be 'diachronically' penetrable; in effect, whether experience and training can affect the accessibility of background theory to perceptual mechanisms.

To deny diachronic penetrability would be to claim, in effect, that *all* the background information that is accessible to modular perceptual systems is endogenously specified, and that is viewed as implausible even by mad dog nativists like me. For example, parsing may be modular, but children must learn *something* about their language from the language that they hear; why else would children living in China so often grow up speaking Chinese? The point about the diachronic penetrability of perception is, however, just like the point about its synchronic penetrability: it offers an argument for the continuity of perception with cognition only if just any old learning or experience can affect the way you see, and there is no reason at all to suppose that that is so. Perhaps, on the contrary, perception is diachronically penetrable only within strictly—maybe endogenously—defined limits. Not only do your current Copernican prejudices fail to much dispel the apparent motion of the Sun, it may be that there is *no* educational program that would do the trick; because it may be that the inaccessibility of astronomical background to the processes of visual perceptual integration is a consequence of innate and unalterable architectural features of our mental structure. In this case, our agreement on the general character of the perceptual world might transcend the particularities of our training and go as deep as our common humanity. Granny and I hope that this is so since common humanity is something that we favor.

I return now to more strictly epistemological concerns. Two points and I'll have done.

First, if Granny wants to appeal to modularity psychology as a way of holding onto theory-neutral observation, she is going to have to give a bit. In particular, she is going to have to distinguish between *observation* and *the perceptual fixation of belief*. It is only for the former that claims for theory neutrality have any plausibility.

Thus far, I've been emphasizing that psychological sophistication doesn't change the way the Müller-Lyer *looks*. Knowing that it's an illusion—even knowing how the illusion works—doesn't make the effect go away. But if one side of perception is about the look of things, the other side is about how things are judged to be; and it bears emphasis that how the Müller-Lyer looks doesn't, in the case of a sophisticated audience, much affect the perceptual beliefs that its observers come to have. I assume, for example, that you're not remotely tempted to suppose that the center line in figure b actually is longer than the center line in figure a; and the reason you're not is that *the mechanisms of belief fixation, in contrast to the presumptive perceptual modules, ARE in contact with background theory.* Belief fixation, unlike the fixation of appearances—what I'm calling observation—is a *conservative* process; to a first approximation, it uses everything you know.

Here is one way to conceptualize the situation: the fixation of perceptual belief effects a reconciliation between the character of current sensory stimulation, as analyzed by modular processors, and background theory. The modular systems might be thought of as proposing hypotheses about the distal sources of sensory stimulation; these hypotheses are couched in a restricted (viz., observational) vocabulary and are predicated on a correspondingly restricted body of information: viz. current sensory information together with whatever fragment of background theory the modules have access to. The hypotheses that modular systems propose are then compared with the rest of the organism's background theory, and the perceptual fixation of belief is consequent upon this comparison.

So, to a first approximation, the activity of the modules determines what you would believe if you were going on the appearances alone. But, of course, this is *only* a first approximation since, as remarked above, modules deal not only in a restricted body of background knowledge, but also in a restricted conceptual repertoire. There are some hypotheses that modules *never* offer because they have no access to a vocabulary in which to express them: hypotheses about the instantiation of nonobservable properties such as, for example, that what's currently on view is a proton. So one might better put it that the activity of modules determines what you would believe *about the appearances* if you were going just on the appearances. Less gnomically: modules offer hypotheses about the instantiation of observable properties of things, and the fixation of *perceptual belief* is the evaluation of such hypotheses in light of the totality of background theory. According to this usage, what you observe is related to what you believe in, something like the way that what you want is related to what you want on balance.

It should be clear from all this that even if Granny gets the theory-neutrality of observation, she is unlikely to get anything remotely like its infallibility. For starters, only a faculty of belief fixation can be infallible and, according to the present story, the psychological mechanisms that are informationally encapsulated do not, in and of themselves, effect the fixation of belief. Anyhow—beside this somewhat legalistic consideration—the infallibility of observation would presumably require the introspective availability of its deliverances; and, though I suppose one usually knows how things look to one, it seems to be empirically false that one always does. If, for example, the story I told about the Müller-Lyer is true, then the existence of the illusion turns on the fact that one sees the figures as three dimensional corners. But it is *not* introspectively obvious that one sees them that way, and the psychologists who figured out the illusion did so not by introspecting but by the usual route of theory construction and experimentation. (Similarly, a crucial issue in the history of the psychology of color perception was whether yellow looks to be a mixed hue. It is *now*—post-theoretically—introspectively obvious that it does not.)

'But look', you might say, growing by now understandably impatient, 'if the notion of observation we're left with is as attenuated as it now appears to be, what, epistemologically speaking, is it good for? Haven't you and your Granny really given away everything that the opposition ever wanted?'

I quote from Norwood Russell Hanson: "To say that Tycho and Kepler, Simplicius and Galileo, Hooke and Newton, Priestly and Lavoisier, Soddy and Einstein, De Broglie and Born, Heisenberg and Bohm all make the same observations but use them differently is too easy. This parallels the too-easy epistemological doctrine that all normal observers see the same things in x, but interpret them differently. It does not explain controversy in research science" (Hanson 1961, 13). (In Hanson's text, the second sentence appears as a footnote at the point where I have inserted it.) Now, on the view of science that Granny and I hold to, this is worse than the wrong answer; it's the answer to the wrong question. It is no particular puzzle, given the nondemonstrative character of empirical inference, that there should be scientific controversy. Rather, as the skeptical tradition in philosophy has made crystal clear, the epistemological problem *par excellence* is *to explain scientific consensus*; to explain how it is possible, given the vast and notorious underdetermination of theory by data, that scientists should agree about so much so much of the time.

What Granny and I think is that part of the story about scientific consensus turns crucially on the theory-neutrality of observation. Because the way one sees the world is largely independent of one's theoretical attachments, it is possible to see that the predictions—even of theories that one likes a lot—aren't coming out. Because the way one sees the world is largely independent of one's theoretical attachments, it is often possible for scientists whose theoretical attachments differ to agree on what experiments would be relevant to deciding between their views, and to agree on how to describe the outcomes of the experiments once they've been run. We admit, Granny and I do, that working scientists indulge in every conceivable form of fudging, smoothing over, brow beating, false advertising, self-deception, and outright rat painting—all the intellectual ills that flesh is heir to. It is, indeed, a main moral of this paper that, in many important ways, *scientists are a lot like us*. Nevertheless, it is perfectly obviously true that scientific observations often turn up unexpected and unwelcome facts, that experiments often fail *and are often seen to do so*, in short that what scientists observe isn't determined solely, or even largely, by the theories that they endorse, still less by the hopes that they cherish. It's *these* facts that the theory neutrality of observation allows us to explain.

The thing is: if you don't think that theory neutral observation can settle scientific disputes, you're likely to think that they are settled by appeals to coherence, or convention or—worse yet—by mere consensus. And Granny—who is a Realist down to her tennis sneakers—doesn't see how any of those could compel *rational* belief. Granny and I have become pretty hardened, in our respective old ages; but we're both still moved by the idea that belief in the best science is rational because it is objective, and that it is objective because the predictions of our best theories can be *observed to be true*. I'm less adamant than Granny is, but I don't find the arguments against the theory neutrality of observation persuasive, and I think that the theory neutrality of observation is a doctrine that Realists have got to hold onto. "Help stamp out creeping pluralism," Granny says; "give 'em an inch and they'll take a mile!" "Right on (with certain significant qualifications)!" say I.

Notes

1. Well, four really. But I shan't discuss *ontological* approaches which support a distinction between observation terms and others by claiming that only the former denote (eg., because whatever is unobservable is ipso facto fictitious). That the assumptions of the present discussion are fully Realistic with respect to unobservables will become entirely apparent as we proceed.

2. Interestingly enough, Jerome Bruner, in his foundational 'New Look' disquisition "On Perceptual Readiness", takes note of this point using, in fact, the same examples I have cited. But he makes nothing of it, remarking only that the persistence of illusions in face of contrary background knowledge, though it militates against the "utter indistinguishability of perceptual and more conceptual inferences . . . must not lead us to overlook the common feature of inference underlying so much of cognitive activity" (1973, 8). The issue, however, is not whether some inferences are "more conceptual" than others—

whatever, precisely, that might mean—or even whether perception is in some important sense inferential. What's at issue is rather: how much of what you know actually does affect the way you see. Failing to distinguish among these questions was, in my view, the original sin of New Look psychological theorizing.

References

Bruner, J. (1973). "On perceptual readiness." In J. Anglin, ed., *Beyond the information given*. New York: W. W. Norton.

Churchland, P. (1979). *Scientific realism and the plasticity of mind*. Cambridge: Cambridge University Press.

Fodor, J. (1983). *The modularity of mind*. Cambridge, MA: MIT Press.

Goodman, N. (1978). *Ways of worldmaking*. Indianapolis: Hackett.

Gregory, R. (1970). *The intelligent eye*. New York: McGraw-Hill.

Hanson, N. R. (1961). *Patterns of discovery*. Cambridge: Cambridge University Press.

Kuhn, T. (1962). *The structure of scientific revolutions*. Chicago: University of Chicago Press.

7 Perceptual Plasticity and Theoretical Neutrality: A Reply to Jerry Fodor

Paul M. Churchland

The idea that observational knowledge always and inevitably involves some theoretical presuppositions or prejudicial processing is an idea that has provoked much discussion in recent years, for its consequences are profound. If observation cannot provide a theory-neutral access to at least some aspects of reality, then our overall epistemic adventure contains both greater peril, and greater promise, than we might have thought. The first and perhaps the most important consequence is that we must direct our attention away from foundational epistemologies, and toward epistemologies that tell a more global story of the nature of theoretical justification and rational belief. A second consequence is that our current observational ontology is just one such ontology out of an indefinitely large number of alternative observational ontologies equally compatible with our native sensory apparatus. And a third consequence is that, since some theoretical frameworks are markedly superior to others, the quality of our observational knowledge is in principle improvable. If the conceptual framework in which our perceptual responses to the world are habitually framed were to be replaced by a more accurate and penetrating conception of physical reality, then our newly-framed perceptual judgments could be significantly more revealing of the structural properties and the dynamical details of our perceptual environment.

The motivation for such a view is not purely philosophical. Perceptual psychology provides supporting evidence in the form of experiments designed to illustrate both the inevitable ambiguity of perceptual situations and the cunning resolution of those ambiguities at the hands of general assumptions imposed by "higher" cognitive centers (Gregory 1970, 1974; Bruner 1973; Rock 1983). These "New Look" ideas, however, have recently come under interesting attack from within cognitive and computational psychology itself. The complaint is that these ideas have exaggerated the extent to which perceptual processing is under the

From P. Churchland, Perceptual plasticity and theoretical neutrality: A reply to Jerry Fodor, *Philosophy of Science* 55, 167–187 (1988). Reprinted by permission.

control of the higher cognitive centers. And the counterclaim is that the job of reducing ambiguity is conducted largely or entirely by peripheral "modules" whose activities are insulated from, and quite insensitive to, the fickle content of human belief.

It is here that Jerry Fodor enters the debate. In a recent paper (Fodor 1984), he marshalls the alleged modularity of our perceptual systems in criticism of various claims made by Hanson (1961), Kuhn (1962), Churchland (1979), and others concerning the theory-laden character of perceptual knowledge and the holistic nature of the human epistemic enterprise. My principal aim in this chapter is to show that Fodor's specific claims about the psychology of human perception are mostly irrelevant to the epistemological issues at stake here. His discussion serves more to muddy the waters than to clarify them, for even if the modularity/encapsulation thesis is correct—which almost certainly it is not—it contains no significant message concerning the traditional epistemological issues. It is, in short, a red herring. In what follows, I shall try to defend and expand on the specific claims, listed in my opening paragraph, against the several criticisms directed at them in Fodor's paper.

There are three principal ways in which any perceptual belief may fail of theoretical neutrality: in its causal history or *etiology*, in its *semantics*, and in the purely *extensional structure* of the ontology it presupposes. In his 1984 article, Fodor has much to say on the first topic, a little on the second, and he does not discuss the third. Since he does not address what I have called "extensional bias" (Churchland 1975), and space does not permit its exploration here, I shall merely emphasize its existence and move on. What follows will be focused on the first two loci of epistemic prejudice.

The Etiology of Perceptual Belief

Does Encapsulated Processing Buy Us Theory-Neutral Perceptions?
I shall pass over Fodor's opening discussion in order to address immediately what he describes as his main point. Fodor, of course, is quite aware that early perceptual processing very likely does involve many elements that resemble or correspond to general empirical "assumptions" about the world (e.g., the three-dimensionality of space, the spatial and temporal continuity of common objects, the sharp change of luminance at a body's boundaries, color constancy through changing environments, the occlusion of distant bodies by proximate ones, etc.), and to "inferences" drawn or "hypothesis selections" made in accordance with a system of such default assumptions. On this view, the etiology of perceptual beliefs looks highly, even dramatically, theoretical in character, as Fodor himself remarks.

But Fodor's view, to a first approximation at least, is that (a) the assumptions involved in early processing are endogenously fixed in all

Finally, we can vary the priority of the data by adjusting the weights to the data units from the special unit. *Data excitation* is a value from 0 to 1 that provides these weights. To reflect the scientific practice of not treating all data equally seriously, it is also possible to set the weights and initial activations for each data unit separately. If data excitation is set low, then, contrary to earlier discussion, new evidence for a rejected hypothesis will not lead to its adoption. If data excitation is high, then evidence that supports only a bad hypothesis will not be thrown out.

With so many degrees of freedom, which are typical of connectionist models, one might question the value of simulations, as it might seem that any desired behavior whatsoever could be obtained. However, if a fixed set of default parameters applies to a large range of cases, then the arbitrariness is much diminished. In *all* the computer runs reported in this paper, ECHO has had excitation at .05, inhibition at −.2 (so tolerance is .25), data excitation at .1., decay (skepticism) at .05, simplicity impact at 1, and analogy impact at 1. There is nothing special about the default values of the parameters: ECHO works over a wide range of values. In a full simulation of a scientist's cognitive processes, we could imagine better values being *learned*. Many connectionist models do not take weights as given, but instead adjust them as the result of experience. Similarly, we can imagine that part of a scientist's training entails learning how seriously to take data, analogy, simplicity, and so on. Most scientists get their training not merely by reading and experimenting on their own but also by working closely with scientists already established in their field; hence, a scientist can pick up the relevant values from advisors. In ECHO they are set by the programmer, but it should be possible to extend the program to allow training from examples. . . .

Application of ECHO to Scientific Reasoning

Theories in the philosophy of science, including computational ones, should be evaluated with respect to important cases from the history of science. To show the historical application of the theory of explanatory coherence, I shall discuss two important cases of arguments concerning the best explanation: Lavoisier's argument for his oxygen theory against the phlogiston theory, and Darwin's argument for evolution by natural selection. [Only the former is included in this edition.—Ed.] ECHO has also been applied to the following:

> Contemporary debates about why the dinosaurs became extinct (Thagard 1991);
> Arguments by Wegener and his critics for and against continental drift (Thagard and Nowak 1988);
> Psychological experiments on how beginning students learn physics (Ranney and Thagard 1988); and

Copernicus's case against Ptolemaic astronomy (Nowak and Thagard, 1991).

Additional applications are currently under development.

Lavoisier

In the middle of the eighteenth century, the dominant theory in chemistry was the phlogiston theory of Stahl, which provided explanations of important phenomena of combustion, respiration, and calcination (what we would now call oxidation). According to the phlogiston theory, combustion takes place when phlogiston in burning bodies is given off. In the 1770s, Lavoisier developed the alternative theory that combustion takes place when burning bodies combine with oxygen from the air (for an outline of the conceptual development of his theory, see Thagard 1990). More than 10 years after he first suspected the inadequacy of the phlogiston theory, Lavoisier mounted a fullblown attack on it in a paper called "Réflexions sur le Phlogistique" (Lavoisier 1862).

Tables 8.1 and 8.2 present the input given to ECHO to represent Lavoisier's argument in his 1783 polemic against phlogiston. Table 8.1

Table 8.1 Input propositions for Lavoisier (1862) example

Evidence

(proposition 'E1	"In combustion, heat and light are given off.")
(proposition 'E2	"Inflammability is transmittable from one body to another.")
(proposition 'E3	"Combustion only occurs in the presence of pure air.")
(proposition 'E4	"Increase in weight of a burned body is exactly equal to weight of air absorbed.")
(proposition 'E5	"Metals undergo calcination.")
(proposition 'E6	"In calcination, bodies increase weight.")
(proposition 'E7	"In calcination, volume of air diminishes.")
(proposition 'E8	"In reduction, effervescence appears.")

Oxygen hypotheses

(proposition 'OH1	"Pure air contains oxygen principle.")
(proposition 'OH2	"Pure air contains matter of fire and heat.")
(proposition 'OH3	"In combustion, oxygen from the air combines with the burning body.")
(proposition 'OH4	"Oxygen has weight.")
(proposition 'OH5	"In calcination, metals add oxygen to become calxes.")
(proposition 'OH6	"In reduction, oxygen is given off.")

Phlogiston hypotheses

(proposition 'PH1	"Combustible bodies contain phlogiston.")
(proposition 'PH2	"Combustible bodies contain matter of heat.")
(proposition 'PH3	"In combustion, phlogiston is given off.")
(proposition 'PH4	"Phlogiston can pass from one body to another.")
(proposition 'PH5	"Metals contain phlogiston.")
(proposition 'PH6	"In calcination, phlogiston is given off.")

Table 8.2 Input explanations and contradictions in Lavoisier (1862) example

Oxygen explanations
    (explain '(OH1 OH2 OH3) 'E1)
    (explain '(OH1 OH3) 'E3)
    (explain '(OH1 OH3 OH4) 'E4)
    (explain '(OH1 OH5) 'E5)
    (explain '(OH1 OH4 OH5) 'E6)
    (explain '(OH1 OH5) 'E7)
    (explain '(OH1 OH6) 'E8)

Phlogiston explanations
    (explain '(PH1 PH2 PH3) 'E1)
    (explain '(PH1 PH3 PH4) 'E2)
    (explain '(PHT5 PH6) 'E5)

Contradictions
    (contradict 'PH3 'OH3)
    (contradict 'PH6 'OH5)

Data
    (data '(E1 E2 E3 E4 E5 E6 E7 E8))

shows the 8 propositions used to represent the evidence to be explained and the 12 used to represent the competing theories. The evidence concerns different properties of combustion and calcination, while there are two sets of hypotheses representing the oxygen and phlogiston theories, respectively. These propositions do not capture Lavoisier's argument completely but do recapitulate its major points. (In a slightly more complicated simulation not presented here, I have encoded the attempt by the phlogiston theory to explain the increase in weight in combustion and calcination by the supposition that phlogiston has negative weight; Lavoisier argues that this supposition renders the phlogiston theory internally contradictory, because phlogiston theorists sometimes assumed that phlogiston has positive weight.)

Table 8.2 shows the part of the input that sets up the network used to make a judgment of explanatory coherence. The "explain" statements are based directly on Lavoisier's own assertions about what is explained by the phlogiston theory and the oxygen theory. The "contradict" statements reflect my judgment of which of the oxygen hypotheses conflict directly with which of the phlogiston hypotheses.

These explanations and contradictions generate the network partially portrayed in figure 8.9. Excitatory links, indicating that two propositions cohere, are represented by solid lines. Inhibitory links are represented by dotted lines. All the oxygen hypotheses are arranged along the top line and all the phlogiston hypotheses along the bottom, with the evidence in the middle. Omitted from the figure for the sake of legibility are the excitatory links among the hypotheses of the two theories and the links between the evidence units and the special unit. In addition to its displayed links to evidence, OH1 has excitatory links to OH2,

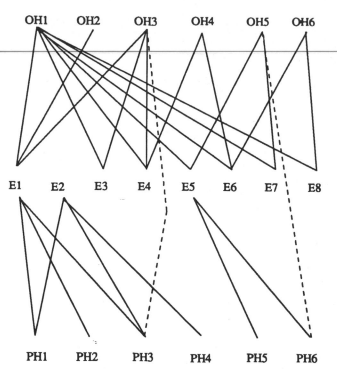

Figure 8.9 Network representing Lavoisier's (1862) argument. E1–E8 are evidence units. OH1–OH6 are units representing hypotheses of the oxygen theory; PH1–PH6 represent the phlogiston hypotheses. Solid lines are excitatory links; dotted lines are inhibitory.

OH3, OH4, OH5, and OH6. The link between OH1 and OH3 is particularly strong, because these two hypotheses participate in three explanations together. Figure 8.10, produced by a graphics program that runs with ECHO, displays the links to OH3, with excitatory links shown by thick lines and the inhibitory link with PH3 shown by a thin line. The numbers on the lines indicate the weights of the links rounded to three decimal places: In accord with Principle 2(c), weights are different from the default weight of .05 whenever multiple hypotheses are used in an explanation. If the hypotheses participate in only one explanation, then the weight between them is equal to the default excitation divided by the number of hypotheses; but weights are additive, so that the weight is increased if two hypotheses participate in more than one explanation. For example, the link between OH3 and E1 has the weight .017 (.0166666 rounded), because the explanation of E1 by OH3 required two additional hypotheses. The weight between OH3 and OH1 is .058 (.025 + .0166666 + .0166666), because the two of them alone explain E3, and together they explain E1 and E4 along with a third hypothesis in each case. OH1 and OH3 are thus highly coherent with each other by virtue of being used together in multiple explanations.

The numbers beneath the names in figure 8.10 indicate the final activation of the named units, rounded to three decimal places. When

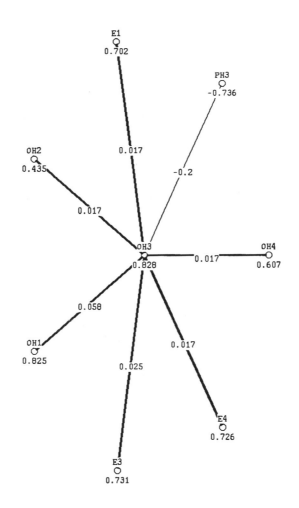

Figure 8.10 Connectivity of oxygen theory unit OH3. The numbers under the units are their activation values after the unit has settled. Thick lines indicate excitatory links; thin line indicates inhibitory link. Numbers on the lines indicate the weights on the links.

ECHO runs this network, starting with all hypotheses at activation .01, it quickly favors the oxygen hypotheses, giving them activations greater than 0. In contrast, all the phlogiston hypotheses become deactivated. The activation history of the propositions is shown in figure 8.11, which charts activation as a function of the number of cycles of updating. Figure 8.11 shows graphs, produced automatically during the run of the program, of the activations of all the units over the 107 cycles it takes them to reach asymptote. In each graph, the horizontal line indicates the starting activation of 0 and the y axis shows activation values ranging between 1 and -1. Notice that the oxygen hypotheses OH1–OH6 rise steadily to their asymptotic activations, while PH3 and PH6, which directly contradict oxygen hypotheses, sink to activation levels well below 0. The other phlogiston hypotheses that are not directly contradicted by oxygen hypotheses start out with positive activation but are dragged down toward 0 through their links with their deactivated cohypotheses. Thus the phlogiston theory fails as a whole.

The run of ECHO is biased towards the oxygen theory because it was based on an analysis of Lavoisier's argument. We would get a different network if ECHO were used to model critics of Lavoisier such as Kirwan (1789/1968), who defended a variant of the phlogiston theory. By the late 1790s, the vast majority of chemists and physicists, including Kirwan, had accepted Lavoisier's arguments and rejected the phlogiston theory, a turnaround contrary to the suggestion of Kuhn (1970) that scientific revolutions occur only when proponents of an old paradigm die off.

Lavoisier's argument represents a relatively simple application of ECHO, showing two sets of hypotheses competing to explain the evidence. But more complex explanatory relations can also be important. Sometimes a hypothesis that explains the evidence is itself explained by another hypothesis. Depending on the warrant for the higher-level hypothesis, this extra explanatory layer can increase acceptability: A hypothesis gains from being explained as well as by explaining the evidence. The Lavoisier example does not exhibit this kind of coherence, because neither Lavoisier nor the phlogiston theorists attempted to explain their hypotheses using higher-level hypotheses; nor does the example display the role that analogy can play in explanatory coherence. . . .

Conclusion

I conclude with a brief survey of the chief accomplishments of the theory of explanatory coherence offered here.

First, it fits directly with the actual arguments of scientists such as Lavoisier and Darwin who explicitly discuss what competing theories explain. There is no need to postulate probabilities or contrive deductive relations. The theory and ECHO have engendered a far more detailed

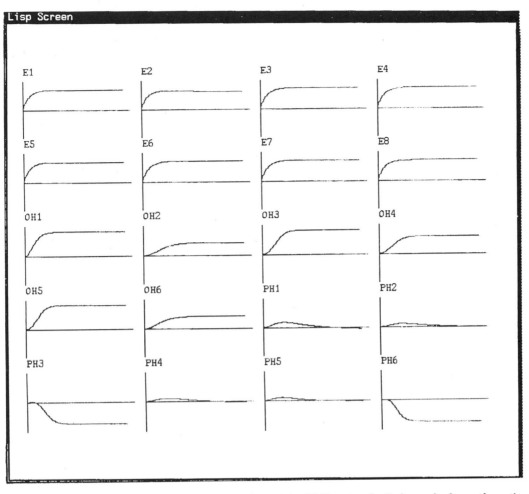

Figure 8.11 Activation history of Lavoisier (1862) network. Each graph shows the activation of a unit over 107 cycles of updating, on a scale of −1 to 1, with horizontal line indicating the initial activation of 0.

analysis of these arguments than is typically given by proponents of other accounts. . . .

Second, unlike most accounts of theory evaluation, this view based on explanatory coherence is inherently comparative. If two hypotheses contradict each other, they incohere, so the subsystems of propositions to which they belong will compete with each other. As ECHO shows, successful subsystems of hypotheses and evidence can emerge gracefully from local judgments of explanatory coherence.

Third, the theory of explanatory coherence permits a smooth integration of diverse criteria such as explanatory breadth, simplicity, and analogy. ECHO's connectionist algorithm shows the computability of coherence relations. The success of the program is best attributed to the usefulness of connectionist architectures for achieving parallel constraint satisfaction, and to the fact that the problem inherent in inference to the best explanation is the need to satisfy multiple constraints simultaneously. Not all computational problems are best approached this way, but parallel constraint satisfaction has proven to be very powerful for other problems as well—for example, analogical mapping (Holyoak and Thagard, 1989).

Finally, my theory surmounts the problem of holism. The principles of explanatory coherence establish pair-wise relations of coherence between propositions in an explanatory system. Thanks to ECHO, we know that there is an efficient algorithm for adjusting a system of propositions to turn coherence relations into judgments of acceptability. The algorithm allows every proposition to influence every other one, because there is typically a path of links between any two units, but the influences are set up systematically to reflect explanatory relations. Theory assessment is done as a whole, but a theory does not have to be rejected or accepted as a whole. Those hypotheses that participate in many explanations will be much more coherent with the evidence, and with each other, and will therefore be harder to reject. More peripheral hypotheses may be deactivated even if the rest of the theory they are linked to wins. We thus get a holistic account of inference that can nevertheless differentiate between strong and weak hypotheses. Although our hypotheses face evidence only as a corporate body, evidence and relations of explanatory coherence suffice to separate good hypotheses from bad.

Note

The development of the ideas in this paper has benefited from discussions with Gilbert Harman, Michael Ranney, Gregory Nowak, Frank Doring, and other members of a discussion group on explanatory coherence. For ideas about connectionist models, I am indebted to Keith Holyoak and Stephen Hanson. I am grateful to Ziva Kunda, Dan Hausman, Phil Johnson-Laird, Robert McCauley, Yorick Wilks, William Bechtel, James Hendler, Robin Dawes, Paul O'Rorke, and several anonymous referees for helpful comments on previous drafts. Thanks to Greg Nelson for the graphics program used for some of the figures, and to Robert McLean for writing a C version of ECHO. (LISP and C versions of ECHO are available on request.) This research was supported by a grant from the James S. McDonnell Foundation to Princeton University and by a contract from the Basic Research Office of the Army Research Institute for the Behavioral and Social Sciences.

1. From here on, I shall be less careful about distinguishing between units and the propositions they represent.

References

Achinstein, P. (1983). *The nature of explanation.* Oxford: Oxford University Press.

Anderson, A., and N. Belnap (1975). *Entailment.* Princeton: Princeton University Press.

BonJour, L. (1985). *The structure of empirical knowledge.* Cambridge, MA: Harvard University Press.

Charniak, E. and D. McDermott (1985). *Introduction to artificial intelligence.* Reading, MA: Addison-Wesley.

Duhem, P. (1954). *The aim and structure of physical theory,* trans. P. Wiener. Princeton: Princeton University Press.

Einstein, A. (1952). On the electrodynamics of moving bodies. In H. A. Lorentz, A. Einstein, H. Minkowski, and H. Weyl, eds., *The principle of relativity.* New York: Dover.

Feldman, J., and D. Ballard (1982). Connectionist models and their properties. *Cognitive Science* 6, 205–254.

Fiske, S., and S. Taylor (1984). *Social cognition.* New York: Random House.

Foster, M., and M. Martin, eds. (1966). *Probability, confirmation, and simplicity.* New York: Odyssey Press.

Goldman, A. (1986). *Epistemology and cognition.* Cambridge, MA: Harvard University Press.

Harman, G. (1973). *Thought.* Princeton: Princeton University Press.

Harman, G. (1986). *Change in view: Principles of reasoning.* Cambridge, MA: MIT Press.

Harman, G., M. Ranney, K. Salem, F. Doring, J. Epstein, and A. Jaworska (1988). A theory of simplicity. *Proceedings of the Tenth Annual Conference of the Cognitive Science Society.* Hillsdale, NJ: Erlbaum.

Hedges, L. (1987). How hard is hard science, how soft is soft science? *American Psychologist* 42, 443–455.

Hempel, C. (1965). *Aspects of scientific explanation.* New York: Free Press.

Hobbs, J., M. Stickel, P. Martin, and D. Edwards (1988). Interpretation as abduction. *Proceedings of the 26th Annual Meeting of the Association for Computational Linguistics.*

Holyoak, K., and P. Thagard (1989). Analogical mapping by constraint satisfaction. *Cognitive Science* 13, 295–355.

Josephson, J., B. Chandrasekaran, J. Smith, and M. Tanner (1987). A mechanism for forming composite explanatory hypotheses. *IEEE Transactions on Systems, Man and Cybernetics* 17, 445–454.

Kirwan, R. (1789/1968). *An essay on phlogiston and the constitution of acids.* London: Cass.

Kuhn, T. (1970). *The structure of scientific revolutions,* 2nd edition. Chicago: University of Chicago Press.

Lakatos, I. (1970). Falsification and the methodology of scientific research programs. In I. Lakatos and A. Musgrave, eds., *Criticism and the growth of knowledge.* Cambridge: Cambridge University Press.

Laudan, L. (1976). Two dogmas of methodology. *Philosophy of Science* 43, 585–597.

Lavoisier, A. (1862). *Oeuvres* (6 vols). Paris: Imprimerie Imperiale.

Marr, D. (1982). *Vision.* San Francisco: Freeman.

Mitchell, T., R. Keller, and S. Kedar-Cabelli (1986). Explanation-based generalization: A unifying view. *Machine Learning* 1, 47–80.

Nowak, G. and P. Thagard (1991). Copernicus, Newton, and explanatory coherence. In R. Giere, ed., *Cognitive models of science.* Minneapolis: University of Minnesota Press.

Peirce, C. S. (1931–1958). *Collected papers* (8 vols), ed. C. Hartshorne, P. Weiss, and A. Burks. Cambridge, MA: Harvard University Press.

Pennington, N., and R. Hastie (1986). Evidence evaluation in complex decision making. *Journal of Personality and Social Psychology* 51, 242–258.

Pennington, N., and R. Hastie (1987). Explanation-based decision making. *Proceedings of the Ninth Annual Meeting of the Cognitive Science Society.* Hillsdale, NJ: Erlbaum.

Pople, H. (1977). The formation of composite hypotheses in diagnostic problem solving. In *Proceedings of the Fifth International Joint Conference on Artificial Intelligence.* San Mateo: Morgan Kaufmann, 1030–1037.

Popper, K. (1959). *The logic of scientific discovery.* London: Hutchinson.

Quine, W. V. (1961). *From a logical point of view* (2d ed.). New York: Harper Torchbooks.

Ranney, M., and P. Thagard (1988). Explanatory coherence and belief revision in naive physics. *Proceedings of the Tenth Annual Conference of the Cognitive Science Society.* Hillsdale, NJ: Erlbaum.

Reggia, J., D. Nau, and P. Wang (1983). Diagnostic expert systems based on a set covering model. *International Journal of Man-Machine Studies* 19, 437–460.

Rumelhart, D. E., J. R. McClelland, and the PDP Research Group (1986). *Parallel distributed processing: Explorations in the microstructure of cognition* (2 vols). Cambridge, MA: MIT Press.

Salmon, W. (1970). Statistical explanation. In R. Colodny, ed., *The nature and function of scientific theories*. Pittsburgh: University of Pittsburgh Press.

Salmon, W. (1984). *Scientific explanation and the causal structure of the world*. Princeton: Princeton University Press.

Schank, R. (1986). *Explanation patterns*. Hillsdale, NJ: Erlbaum.

Thagard, P. (1978). The best explanation: Criteria for theory choice. *Journal of Philosophy* 75, 76–92.

Thagard, P. (1988). *Computational philosophy of science*. Cambridge, MA: MIT Press.

Thagard, P. (1989). Connectionism and epistemology: Goldman on winner-take-all networks. *Philosophia* 19, 189–196.

Thagard, P. (1990). The conceptual structure of the chemical revolution. *Philosophy of Science* 57, 183–209.

Thagard, P. (1991). The dinosaur debate: Explanatory coherence and the problem of competing hypotheses. In R. Cummins and J. Pollock, eds., *Philosophy and AI: Essays at the interface*. Cambridge, MA: MIT Press.

Thagard, P., K. Holyoak, G. Nelson, and D. Gochfeld (1990). Analog retrieval by constraint satisfaction. *Artificial Intelligence* 46, 259–310.

Thagard, P., and G. Nowak (1988). The explanatory coherence of continental drift. In A. Fine and J. Leplin, eds., *PSA 1988*, vol. 1. East Lansing, MI: Philosophy of Science Association.

Thagard, P., and G. Nowak (1990). The conceptual structure of the geological revolution. In J. Shrager and P. Langley, eds., *Computational models of discovery and theory formation*. Hillsdale, NJ: Erlbaum.

van Fraassen, B. (1980). *The scientific image*. Oxford: Clarendon Press.

9 Scientific Discovery

Pat Langley, Herbert A. Simon, Gary L. Bradshaw, and Jan M. Zytkow

What Is Scientific Discovery?

In the scientist's house are many mansions. Not only does science divide into innumerable disciplines and subdisciplines, but within any single discipline the progress of science calls for the most diverse repertoire of activities—activities so numerous and diverse that it would seem that any person could find one to his or her taste. Outsiders often regard science as a sober enterprise, but we who are inside see it as the most romantic of all callings. Both views are right. The romance adheres to the processes of scientific discovery, the sobriety to the responsibility for verification.

Histories of science put the spotlight on discovery. Everyone knows by what accident Fleming discovered penicillin, but only specialists can tell us much about how that discovery was subsequently put to the test. Everyone knows of Kekule's dream of the benzene ring, but only chemists can tell us why the structure of that molecule was problematic, and how and when it was finally decided that the problem had been solved. The story of scientific progress reaches its periodic climaxes at the moments of discovery; verification is the essential but not very glamorous aftermath—the sorting out of facts that comes after the tale's denouement and tells us that matters worked out all right (if only for a while, as in the story of phlogiston).

The philosophy of science has taken a very different tack than the discipline of the history of science. In the philosophy of science, all the emphasis is on verification, on how we can tell the true gold of scientific law from the fool's gold of untested fantasy. In fact, it is still the majority view among philosophers of science that only verification is a proper subject of inquiry, that nothing of philosophical interest can be said about the process of discovery.

From P. Langley, H. Simon, G. Bradshaw, and J. Zytkow, *Scientific discovery: Computational explorations of the creative processes* (1987). Cambridge, MA: MIT Press. Reprinted by permission.

In one respect the philosophers are right. What distinguishes science from the other works of the human imagination is precisely the insistence on testing, on subjecting hypotheses to the most intense scrutiny with the help of empirical evidence. If we are to distinguish science from poetry, we must have a theory of verification or confirmation that tells us exactly how to make that distinction.

But we believe that science is also poetry, and—perhaps even more heretical—that discovery has its reasons, as poetry does. However romantic and heroic we find the moment of discovery, we cannot believe either that the events leading up to that moment are entirely random and chaotic or that they require genius that can be understood only by congenial minds. We believe that finding order in the world must itself be a process impregnated with purpose and reason. We believe that the process of discovery can be described and modeled, and that there are better and worse routes to discovery—more and less efficient paths.

With that claim, we open ourselves to attack from the other flank. Do we think it is possible to write books of advice to poets? Are we not aware that writing poems (and making scientific discoveries) is a creative process, sometimes even calling for genius? But we can avoid dangerous terms like "genius" by asking more modest questions. We can at least inquire into the *sufficient* conditions for making a poem (or a discovery). If writing poetry calls for creativity, it also calls for craft. A poet becomes a craftsman (if not a creative poet) by long study and practice. We might aspire to distill and write down what a poet learns in this arduous apprenticeship. If we did that, we would have a book on the writing of poetry (there are some such on the library shelves). Perhaps its advice would take us merely to the level of superior doggerel, but we could determine that only after we had tested the advice by experiment—by writing poetry on its principles. Thus, the question of how poetry is written (or can or should be written) becomes a researchable question, one that can be approached with the standard methods of scientific inquiry.

This is no less true of scientific discovery than it is of poetry. Whether there is method in discovery is a question whose answer is open to scientific study. We may fail to find methods that account for discovery, or for the greater success of some would-be discoverers than of others, but we are free to look for them. And if we arrive at some hypotheses about them, then we must test these just as we test any other hypotheses in science.

The aims of this book are to give an account of some methods of scientific discovery and to demonstrate the efficacy of these methods by using them to make a number of discoveries (more accurate, rediscoveries). The methods we propose are embedded in a set of computer programs, and they are tested by providing the programs with data that they can explore in search of regularities.

The work has several motivations, which have already been hinted at in our introductory remarks.

First, it seeks to investigate the psychology of the discovery process, and to provide an empirically tested theory of the information-processing mechanisms that are implicated in this process. (However, it is mainly limited to finding a set of mechanisms that is sufficient to account for discovery. It will provide little in the way of detailed comparison with human performance.)

Second, it undertakes to provide some foundations for a normative theory of discovery—for the "how to make discoveries" book. Specifically, it proposes and evaluates a substantial number of heuristics that are designed to facilitate the discovery process and raise its efficiency over chance or blind trial-and-error search.

Third, it reexamines the relations between the processes of discovery and the processes of verification, finding that these two classes of processes are far more intimately connected than is generally suggested in the literature of philosophy of science.

Fourth, since most of the examples we use to test our hypotheses are drawn from the history of science, it suggests a methodology for examining the history of discoveries that may prove to be a useful addition to the repertoire of the historians of science.

Thus, this book enters a number of science's mansions, including cognitive psychology, artificial intelligence, the philosophy of science, and the history of science. We hope that it will excite the interest (and elicit the corrections) of practitioners in all these fields and of scientists working in other fields who are curious about their own cognitive processes. If it does that, it will have served its purpose: to contribute to the understanding of discovery in science.

Discovery as Problem Solving

A hypothesis that will be central to our inquiry is that the mechanisms of scientific discovery are not peculiar to that activity but can be subsumed as special cases of the general mechanisms of problem solving. The question whether this hypothesis is true, and to what extent, is properly postponed until we have reached the end of our exploration, for as we go along we shall be collecting just the materials that are needed to test it.

Our method of inquiry will be to build a computer program (actually a succession of programs) that is capable of making nontrivial scientific discoveries and whose method of operation is based on our knowledge of human methods of solving problems—in particular, the method of heuristic selective search.

The attractiveness of our approach lies precisely in the fact that it allows us to draw on a large body of knowledge that has been accumulated by research on human problem solving. We do not have to make our theories of discovery from whole cloth; rather, we can derive them from theories of problem solving that have already been tested extensively in the laboratory. Of course, if our hypothesis is wrong—if scientific discovery is something quite different from ordinary problem solving—our labor will be lost. But we have already peeked at the end of the book and know that matters did not work out too badly.

There is a second attraction in the hypothesis that scientific discovery is a species of normal problem solving: It meets our desire for parsimony. It minimizes the degree to which the work of discovery must be treated as the exercise of a special human faculty. It preserves a framework in which all forms of serious human thought—in science, in the arts, in the professions, in school, in personal life—may reveal their commonalities.

The thesis that scientific discovery is problem solving writ large, and that it can be simulated by computer, is not completely novel. It goes back at least as far as a paper delivered in 1958 by Newell, Shaw, and Simon (see Newell et al. 1962), and it was carried forward in additional investigations by Simon (1966, 1973) and Buchanan (1966) and in the construction of such computer programs as meta-DENDRAL (Buchanan and Mitchell 1978), AM (Lenat 1977), and EURISKO (Lenat 1983). Huesmann and Cheng (1973) described a program that induced numerical laws from data, and Gerwin (1974) described another such program. A decade earlier, Simon and Kotovsky (1963) had constructed a program that could find the pattern in letter sequences and extrapolate them. The research on BACON, the first of the simulation programs to be discussed in this book, began in the mid 1970s (see Langley 1978).

Of course, there are several respects in which scientific discovery is obviously different from other instances of problem solving. First, scientific inquiry is a social process, often involving many scientists and often extending over long periods of time. Much human problem solving, especially the sort that has been studied in psychology laboratories, involves a single individual working for a few hours. A second way in which scientific inquiry differs from much other problem solving is in the apparent indefiniteness of its goals. Consider the missionaries-and-cannibals puzzle: Three missionaries and three cannibals are trying to cross a river in a boat that holds no more than two persons. Everyone knows how to row. Missionaries may never be left on either bank with a larger number of cannibals, because the missionaries will then be eaten. How can the party cross the river? Here we know exactly what we want to achieve as a solution: We want a plan for transporting the missionaries and the cannibals across the river in the available small boat without any casualties from drowning or dining.

Some scientific discovery is like that. The mathematicians who found a proof for the four-color theorem knew exactly what they were seeking; so did Adams and Leverrier when they detected Neptune while searching for a celestial object that would explain anomalies in the orbits of the other planets. However, in much scientific inquiry—including some of the most important and challenging—the targets are less sharp. Initially, what were Darwin and his predecessors seeking more definite than a way of bringing order to the complex, confusing data of biology and fossil geology? Toward the end of the eighteenth century, just before the work of Lavoisier, exactly how would one have defined the "problem of combustion," and what would have been accepted as a satisfactory account of the phenomena to which that term was applied? Indeed, finding problems and formulating them is as integral a part of the inquiry process as is solving them, once they have been found. And setting criteria of goal satisfaction, so that indefinite goals become definite, is an essential part of formulating problems.

In spite of these differences between scientific inquiry and other problem solving, it is quite possible that the component processes of scientific discovery are not qualitatively distinct from the processes that have been observed in simpler problem-solving situations. Solving complex problems generally involves decomposing them into sets of simpler problems and attacking those. It could well be the case (and we will argue that it is) that the component problem solving involved in scientific discovery has no special properties to distinguish it from other problem solving.

Herein we will be concerned more with describing and explaining scientific discovery than with providing a normative theory of the process. Indeed, the very possibility of a normative theory has been challenged by many philosophers of science. However, if we succeed in producing a credible explanation of discovery, that explanation will itself constitute a first approximation to a normative theory. This is especially true if the explanation is constructive—if it exhibits a set of processes that, when executed, actually make scientific discoveries. The explanation we shall propose is of this constructive kind. . . .

Discovering Quantitative Empirical Laws

Since there are advantages in translating theories about information processing into running computer programs, we have followed this route in our research on scientific discovery. Our first efforts along these lines led to a sequence of computer programs collectively called BACON. The BACON systems (versions 1 through 6) are named after Francis Bacon, because they incorporate many of his ideas on the nature of scientific reasoning. The successive versions of BACON share a common approach to discovery, as well as a common representation of data and laws. The differences among the various systems lie in the discovery heuristics that each uses in its search for empirical laws. In general, later versions of BACON retain the heuristics of earlier versions, but also incorporate additional ones.

BACON.1 is the simplest of the systems and thus the easiest to describe and to understand. In addition, since the BACON.1 heuristics are used by later incarnations of the system, their description here will provide a solid foundation for what is to come. Later in this chapter we will describe BACON.3 in terms of amendments and additions to BACON.1. We will follow the same strategy in discussing BACON.4 and BACON.5 [omitted in the present edition—Ed.]. In each case, we describe the systems in terms of their heuristics and provide numerous examples of those heuristics in action.

BACON.1 uses a general representation and a few heuristics to discover an impressive range of empirical laws. The system is general in the same sense that the General Problem Solver of Newell, Shaw, and Simon (see Newell and Simon 1963) was general. That is to say, the basic methods of BACON make no reference to the semantic meaning of the data on which they operate and make no special assumptions about the structure of the data. BACON.1 also has much in common with the General Rule Inducer proposed by Simon and Lea (1974), since it searches a space of data and a space of rules and attempts to relate one to the other.

We have striven for generality in BACON because we wish to explore the role in scientific discovery of heuristics that may be relevant over a wide range of scientific disciplines and hence may contribute to our basic understanding of discovery wherever it may occur. In adopting this strategy, it is not our intention to deny the important role that discipline-specific knowledge and heuristics play in the work of science; rather, we want to see how far we can go initially with data-driven, semantically impoverished processes. Having clarified our bias toward general mechanisms, let us consider an example of how one might employ such mechanisms to discover an empirical law.

A Sample Protocol

In 1618, Johannes Kepler discovered his third law of planetary motion: The cube of a planet's distance from the Sun is proportional to the square of its period. This law can be restated as $D^3/P^2 = c$, where D is the distance, P is the period, and c is a constant.

How might one discover such a law? Here is a sample protocol that draws on three very simple heuristics:

· If the values of a term are constant, then infer that the term always has that value.

· If the values of two numerical terms increase together, then consider their ratio.

· If the values of one term increase as those of another decrease, then consider their product.

Langley, Simon, Bradshaw, and Zytkow

The value of these heuristics can best be seen in their operation. The three planets considered below, A, B, and C, obey a version of Kepler's law where the constant is 1. The discoverer must begin by gathering some data, selecting different values for the nominal variable (planet), and obtaining the values of the numerical terms (D and P):

When planet is A
What is P?   Answer: 1.0
What is D?   Answer: 1.0

When planet is B
What is P?   Answer: 8.0
What is D?   Answer: 4.0

When planet is C
What is P?   Answer: 27.0
What is D?   Answer: 9.0

D increases with P
so I'll consider their ratio.
I'll define Term-1 as the ratio of D and P [D/P].

Here the second heuristic has been applied. The distance and the period have been observed to increase together, so the new concept Term-1 has been defined as their ratio. Next, the values of this new term are calculated.

When D is:	1.0	4.0	9.0
and P is:	1.0	8.0	27.0
Term-1 is:	1.0	0.5	0.333

D increases as Term-1 decreases
so I'll consider their product.
I'll define Term-2 as the product
        of D and Term-1 [$D(D/P) = D^2/P$].

When D is:	1.0	4.0	9.0
and P is:	1.0	8.0	27.0
Term-2 is:	1.0	2.0	3.0

Term-1 increases as Term-2 decreases
so I'll consider their product.
I'll define Term-3 as the product
        of Term-1 and Term-2 [$(D/P)(D^2/P) = D^3/P^2$].

By this point, the third heuristic has been applied twice. Two more concepts have been defined: Term-2 as D^2/P and Term-3 as D^3/P^2. Since the latter of these is the most recently formed, we next examine its values:

When D is:	1.0	4.0	9.0
and P is:	1.0	8.0	27.0

Term-3 is: 1.0   1.0   1.0
Term-3 has the constant value 1.0

Finally, the first heuristic applies, for the new concept Term-3 (defined as D^3/P^2) has the constant value 1.0 for all three planets. The statement that this term is constant across planets is equivalent to Kepler's third law of planetary motion, and the above protocol is a plausible trace of how one might discover this law. In this example we used idealized data for the sake of clarity, but later in the chapter we will reconsider Kepler's law in the context of the original data.

BACON.1's Representation

The above protocol was actually generated by the BACON.1 program. Of course, BACON.1 was not designed to produce fluent English; we gave it the ability to generate simple protocols only in order to be better able to trace the path it travels toward discovery. Here we attempt to clarify the nature of the program still further by considering the representations it uses for its data and for its heuristics.

The Representation of Data

BACON.1 represents its data in terms of *data clusters*. A data cluster is a set of attribute-value pairs linked to a common node; it represents a series of observations that have occurred together. The program knows about two types of terms or attributes: *independent* and *dependent*. It has control over independent attributes; it can vary their values and request the corresponding values of the dependent attributes (i.e., the values that the system is trying to explain). Independent terms may take on either numerical or nominal (symbolic) values, whereas the version of BACON.1 described here allows only numerical values for its dependent terms. In the above example, the values of the independent term were the names of planets; the values of the dependent terms were the distances and periods of those planets.

Figure 9.1 shows three data clusters from the Keplerian example. In this case, there are three primitive (directly observable) attributes: the planet being observed, the planet's distance D from the sun, and the period P of the planet's orbit. However, much of BACON.1's power comes from its ability to define higher-level (theoretical) attributes in terms of more primitive ones. Thus, the clusters in figure 9.1 also show the values for three nonprimitive attributes: Term-1 (defined as D/P), Term-2 (defined as D^2/P), and Term-3 (defined as D^3/P^2). Since these terms include dependent terms in their definitions and thus cannot be manipulated by experiment or observation, they are considered dependent.

When BACON.1 defines a new term, it generates a name for the variable (e.g., "Term-1") and treats it in the same way it treats directly

Langley, Simon, Bradshaw, and Zytkow

observable terms. Defined terms can be used to define other new terms as well, so the process is recursive. The generation of higher-level attributes is useful mainly because it allows for parsimonious representation of the data; it permits complex laws to be stated as simple constancies. For instance, it is only because BACON.1 defines Term-3 as D^3/P^2 that it can state Kepler's third law in such a simple manner. As this example shows, BACON.1 can always restate the laws in terms of observables by replacing the theoretical terms with their definitions.

Although BACON.1's internal representation of data is much like the clusters shown in figure 9.1, it is more convenient to display these data in tabular form. Table 9.1 presents the same data as figure 9.1. Each column in the table lists the values for a given term, such as the planet, the distance D, and Term-1; each row corresponds to one of the data clusters shown in the figure. In the remainder of this chapter, we will use tabular rather than graphic notation for the data gathered by BACON. We will not mark higher-level terms explicitly to distinguish them from observables, but they will generally occur in the rightmost columns of tables.

The data used in this example were contrived to fit Kepler's law exactly. Except for rounding errors, BACON did not have to deal with any form of noise or imprecision in the numbers given to it. The BACON programs do have modest capabilities for handling imprecise data by ignoring small deviations from the predictions of the laws they hypothesize. The amount of noise that is accepted is controlled by parameters in the programs. We will have a little more to say later about the processing of inexact data, and about laws that are only approximate, but this will not be a main theme of our discussion.

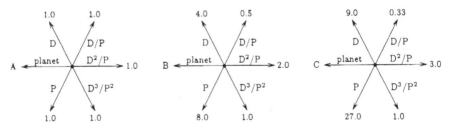

Figure 9.1 Three data clusters from the Keplerian example.

Table 9.1 Data obeying Kepler's third law of planetary motion

Planet	Distance (D)	Period (P)	Term-1 (D/P)	Term-2 (D^2/P)	Term-3 (D^3/P^2)
A	1.0	1.0	1.0	1.0	1.0
B	4.0	8.0	0.5	2.0	1.0
C	9.0	27.0	0.333	3.0	1.0

The Representation of Heuristics

BACON.1 is implemented in the production-system language PRISM, described in Langley and Neches 1981 and in Langley and Ohlsson 1984. In turn, PRISM is implemented in LISP, a list-processing language widely used in artificial-intelligence research.

A production-system program has two main components: a set of condition-action rules, or *productions,* and a dynamic *working memory.* A production system operates in cycles. On every cycle, the conditions of each production are matched against the current state of the working memory. From the rules that match successfully, one is selected for application. When a production is applied, its actions affect the state of the working memory, making new productions match. This process continues until no rules are matched or until a stop command is encountered.

BACON.1's discovery heuristics are stated as PRISM productions. Each rule contains a set of *conditions* describing the system's goals or specifying patterns that may occur in the data. In addition, each rule contains a set of *actions,* which are responsible for setting goals, formulating laws (e.g, that some term has a constant value), defining new terms, computing the values of these terms, and so forth. Conditions and actions can be written either directly in PRISM or as LISP functions. On each cycle, one of the matching rules is selected for application, and its associated actions are carried out. When two or more rules match, BACON.1 prefers the rule that matches against elements that have been added to memory most recently. This leads the system to pursue possibilities in a depth-first manner. That is, since the newest goals and data always receive the most attention, BACON continues each line of search until it is successful or until it peters out. In the latter case, the program returns to an earlier step and sets out on a new line of search in the same way.

Production systems were first proposed as a general framework for modeling human cognition by Newell and Simon (1972), who listed a number of advantages of these systems, some of which are particularly relevant to discovery systems. First, production systems carry out an essentially parallel search to determine which rules are applicable to the current situation. Thus, they seem well suited for searching a large set of data for constancies and trends. Second, production systems can be "data driven" in the sense that new data can strongly influence the course taken by a set of rules. At the same time, production rules can also incorporate information about the current goals of the system, so that a compromise between data-driven, bottom-up behavior and goal-driven, top-down behavior can be achieved. Finally, since each production is relatively independent of every other production, one can (with care) construct modular programs that continue to run after new rules have been inserted or old rules removed. This characteristic will allow us to add new heuristics to BACON without modifying the system in

Langley, Simon, Bradshaw, and Zytkow

other ways. . . . [Detailed specification of productions is omitted in this edition.—Ed.]

Testing Laws

In discussing the relations between discovering laws and testing them, we argued that these two processes are wholly intermingled. A law is not first discovered, in full and final form, and then tested for its validity. Usually the discovery process itself involves search, where each step that is taken is evaluated for progress. By the time the search has been completed and the discovery accomplished, the consistency of the proposed law with the data from which it has been induced has already been guaranteed by the generation process.

Thus, BACON.1, which is conservative in not announcing invariants until it has examined all the relevant evidence, does not require separate productions for testing the laws it has found. Other versions of BACON announce laws on the basis of partial evidence, but they are capable of revising their conclusions after examining new evidence and of qualifying their generalizations by specifying the conditions under which they hold.

The Discoveries of BACON.1

Here we shall trace BACON.1's steps in rediscovering three additional laws from the history of science: Boyle's law, Galileo's law of uniform acceleration, and Ohm's law. We shall also reconsider the discovery of Kepler's third law from noisy data. The derivation of Ohm's law follows a somewhat different path than the other derivations. The repetition of the Keplerian example illustrates BACON.1's methods for noting constants when noise is present.

Boyle's Law

Around 1660, Robert Boyle discovered that the pressure exerted by a given amount of gas varies inversely with its volume. This relation can be stated mathematically via the equation $PV = c$, where P is the pressure, V is the volume occupied by the gas, and c is a constant. As we shall see later in the chapter, the value of this constant is a function of other variables, such as the temperature of the gas; however, Boyle's discovery was limited to pressure and volume.

Table 9.2 presents the volume and pressure data from Boyle's 1662 book, converted to decimals from the fractional form that was commonly used in Boyle's time.[1] The data we have used may be found in Magie 1935 (p. 187, columns A and D). Despite the roughness of Boyle's data, BACON.1 has no difficulty discovering the law. Upon examining the data, the system notes that the volume increases as the pressure decreases, and so considers the product, PV, which has a mean value of 31.6.

Table 9.2 Boyle's original gas data

Volume (V)	Pressure (P)	PV
1.0	29.750	29.750
1.5	19.125	28.688
2.0	14.375	28.750
3.0	9.500	28.500
4.0	7.125	28.500
5.0	5.625	28.125
6.0	4.875	29.250
7.0	4.250	29.750
8.0	3.750	30.000
9.0	3.375	30.375
10.0	3.000	30.000
12.0	2.625	31.500
14.0	2.250	31.500
16.0	2.000	32.000
18.0	1.875	33.750
20.0	1.750	35.000
24.0	1.500	36.000
28.0	1.375	38.500
32.0	1.250	40.000

BACON's crude way of determining what deviations from constancy are acceptable to incorporate a maximum percentage deviation around the mean, Δ, and require all observations to fall in the interval $[M(1 - \Delta), M(1 + \Delta)]$. In this case, if Δ is set to 0.3, the values of PV will be judged to be constant. We hold no particular brief for this method (or for the specific value of Δ used here). It must be thought preferable, for example, to place a limit on the ratio of the standard deviation σ to the mean M, and to accept a value as constant if the absolute value of σ/M falls below Δ. (In Boyle's data, two-thirds of the observations of PV lie within about 10 percent of the mean.)

Of course, whether a particular degree of constancy is acceptable lies in the eye of the beholder. During the nineteenth century, there was great dispute among chemists as to whether the data supported or refuted William Prout's hypothesis that all atomic weights were integral multiples of the atomic weight of hydrogen. This was (nearly) true for many elements, but there were gross anomalies (e.g. chlorine, with a weight of 35.5 in hydrogen units). Some chemists were impressed by how many elements conformed to Prout's hypothesis, others by how many exceptions there were. Not until Francis Aston discovered isotopes was the dispute settled and a much amended and reinterpreted form of Prout's hypothesis generally accepted.

The Law of Uniform Acceleration
In his studies of motion, Galileo Galilei performed experiments with inclined planes and rolling balls to determine the laws governing ve-

locity and acceleration. (See Magie 1935, 11.) The result of these experiments was the law of uniform acceleration, which relates the distance D an object has fallen to the time T since it was dropped. The law may be stated as $D/T^2 = k$, where k is a constant and the ration D/T^2 is the acceleration of the object at each point in its downward path. In finding this law, BACON.1 varied the time T at which it obtained data on the position of the object, and recorded the distance D provided to it for each time. Table 9.3 presents some contrived (noise-free) values for observations in such an experiment.

Upon gathering the values for various time, BACON's trend detectors noticed that the values of D increased with the values of T. Since these quantities were not linearly related, the system defined the ration D/T and computed its values. Although these were not constant, they increased with increases in the values of D. However, since the resulting ratio D/TD would have been equivalent to $1/T$, the system abandoned this path and focused on a second regularity: that the values of D/T increased with those of the time T. On the basis of this relation, BACON.1 defined a second ratio, D/T^2, and computed a new set of values. These values appeared to have the constant value 9.8, leading BACON to infer that D/T^2 always has this value. This statement is equivalent to the inverse-square law described above.

Ohm's Law

In 1826, Georg Simon Ohm began a series of experiments on currents and batteries. (See Magie 1935, 456–472.) Finding the voltaic pile too unstable for his work, he built a version of the thermoelectric battery (invented by Seebeck only four years earlier). In this type of battery, the ends of a copper wire are attached to opposite ends of a bar of metal. If the two ends of the bar are kept at different temperatures, a current flows through the wire. Ohm found that the current I, as measured by the twist of a galvanometer needle, and the length of the wire L fit the equation $I = v/(r_i + L)$, where v and r_i are constants associated with a given experiment.

In order to let it discover this law, we gave BACON.1 experimental control over the length L of the wire in an electrical circuit and told it to examine the values of the current I for the same circuit. Table 9.4

Table 9.3 Idealized data obeying the law of uniform acceleration

Time (T)	Distance (D)	D/T	D/T^2
0.1	0.098	0.98	9.8
0.2	0.392	1.96	9.8
0.3	0.882	2.94	9.8
0.4	1.568	3.92	9.8
0.5	2.450	4.90	9.8
0.6	3.528	5.88	9.8

Table 9.4 Ohm's original data for electrical circuits

Length (L)	Current (I)	LI	Slope (Li, I)	Inter (Li, I)
2.0	326.75	653.5	−0.049	358.5
4.0	300.75	1,203.0	−0.049	358.5
6.0	277.75	1,666.5	−0.049	358.5
10.0	238.25	2,382.5	−0.049	358.5
18.0	190.75	3,433.5	−0.049	358.5
34.0	134.50	4,573.0	−0.049	358.5
66.0	83.25	5,494.5	−0.049	358.5
130.0	48.50	6,305.0	−0.049	358.5

Table 9.5 Borelli's data for Jupiter's satellites

Moon	Distance (D)	Period (P)	Term-1 (D/P)	Term-2 (D^2/P)	Term-3 (D^3/P^2)
A	5.67	1.769	3.203	18.153	58.15
B	8.67	3.571	2.427	21.036	51.06
C	14.00	7.155	1.957	27.395	53.61
D	24.67	16.689	1.478	36.459	53.89

presents some of Ohm's original data, converted to decimals, along with BACON's transformation of these data. (The data are given in Magie 1935, 469, first line of table.) The system began by noting that the values of I increased as those of L decreased. This led it to define the product LI. Although the values of this new term were not constant, they were linearly related to the values of I (assuming a relative noise limit of 0.15 above or below the mean). As a result, BACON.1 summarized the data with a line of the form $LI = aI + b$, with $a = −0.049$ and $b = 358.5$. Subtracting aI from both sides, factoring out I, and dividing both sides by $(L − a)$ yielded the expression $I = b/(L − a)$, which had the same form as Ohm's original law. (Ohm interpreted the constant b as measuring the voltage of the battery and interpreted the constant a as its internal resistance.)

Kepler's Law Revisited

Let us now return to a less idealized set of data for Kepler's third law. Table 9.5 presents data on the Galilean satellites of Jupiter. These data, originally reported by Giovanni Borelli, were used by Newton in the *Principia* as one basis for his empirical verification of Kepler's third law. The periods were originally given in days, hours, minutes, and seconds, and the distances in fractions, but we converted them to decimals for BACON's convenience. The distances are expressed as multiples of the radius of Jupiter.

As before, BACON noted that the distance D and the period P increased together, and defined the ratio D/P. This term decreased as the distance increased, leading BACON to define the product D^2/P. That term in-

Langley, Simon, Bradshaw, and Zytkow

creased as D/P decreased, and so the product D^3/P^2 was examined. This term had a mean value of 54.17. With Δ/M set at 0.075, BACON decided that all values were sufficiently close to the mean to be considered constant. (The data on the distances from the Sun and the periods of revolution of the planets that Kepler himself used to verify his third law were more precise; the maximum deviations from constancy of D^3/P^2 were less than 2 percent of the mean value. See Gingerich 1975.)

Laws Discovered by BACON.1

To summarize: The BACON.1 system has rediscovered a number of empirical laws involving two numerical terms, in several cases using actual data. Table 9.6 lists the names of these laws, along with their forms. As the table shows, the system's heuristics lead it to quite different laws, depending on the regularities they find in the data. In this sense, BACON.1 is a data-driven discovery system. The program has many limitations (some of which will be addressed in the following section), but its accomplishments are quite impressive in view of the small set of heuristics it employs. Although later versions of BACON inevitably increase in complexity as they gain in power, our concern with retaining simple, general models of the discovery process will remain.

The BACON.3 System

The methods described in the previous section can discover numerical relations between two variables; however, more complex relations are largely beyond their scope. For instance, one would like to have methods for discovering functions involving many terms, such as the ideal-gas law and Coulomb's law of electric attraction. In cases where one has experimental control over the independent terms, the traditional method of "varying one term at a time" can be used to separate the effects of each independent term on the dependent variables. We have implemented this basic approach in BACON.3, an extension of BACON.1 that can discover much more complex laws than its predecessor.[2] In our discussion of BACON.3 we will restrict ourselves to the naive version of this data-gathering method, in which all possible combinations of the independent terms are examined in turn so that a complete factorial design is generated. . . .

Table 9.6 Physical laws discovered by BACON.1

Boyle's law	$PV = c$
Kepler's third law	$D^3P^2 = k$
Galileo's law	$D/T^2 = g$
Ohm's law	$IL = -rI + v$

Levels of Description

The BACON.1 system made a sharp distinction between the data it had "observed" and the laws that summarized those data. As a result, the program could summarize the relation between two terms, but it could not apply its discovery heuristics recursively to those summaries as if they were data. In contrast, BACON.3 blurs the distinction between data and laws by allowing various *levels of description*. In the new system, regularities in one level of *descriptive clusters* lead to the creation of a descriptive cluster at the next higher level. In turn, this new cluster and its neighbors can lead to a yet higher level of description. A descriptive cluster is simply a conjunction of attribute-value pairs. (In the examples that will follow shortly, each row in a table corresponds to a single descriptive cluster.)

In order to take advantage of this new ability, BACON.3 also requires the ability to systematically gather data involving many independent terms. The system's approach to gathering data is straightforward. It begins by holding all but one of the terms constant and attempting to discover a specific law in that context. The constant values found in this situation are stored, along with the independent values for which they occurred. Different constants are found for different contexts. When enough constant values have been found, the system treats them as dependent values at a higher level of description and attempts to find a higher-level relation between independent terms and the newly defined dependent terms. The system employs the same method to find the second-level law that it used at the lower level. After a law at the second level has been found, the program recurses to still higher levels until all the independent terms have been incorporated into a unified law and all the data have been summarized. In short: BACON.3's search for laws is embedded within its search through the data space. An example should clarify the basic approach further, so let us examine its application to the discovery of the ideal-gas law.

An Example: The Ideal-Gas Law

BACON.3 can be viewed as searching two distinct problem spaces: the space of data and the space of laws. These searches interact in a complex manner. Before we examine this interaction, let us examine each of the search schemes independently, starting with search through the data space.

As already noted, BACON.3 is provided with a set of independent terms and with possible values for each term. Using these values, the system generates a complete factorial design involving all combinations of independent values and then examines the values of the known dependent terms for each combination. BACON.3's generation of all independent combinations can be viewed in terms of search through a space of states containing partially specified experimental combinations. The initial state has no independent values specified; the goal states include values for all the independent terms. The operator for moving through this space inputs a partially specified experimental combination and decides on the value for one of the unspecified terms. Search control is depth-first; however, since many combinations must be generated, the system must backtrack and explore many different paths.

Suppose that BACON.3 is given three independent terms—the pressure P on a gas, the temperature T of that gas in degrees Celsius, and the quantity N of the gas—and the single dependent term V, the volume of the gas. Suppose further that BACON.3 is told to examine N with values 1, 2, and 3, T with values 10, 20, and 30, and P with values 1,000, 2,000, and 3,000. In order to generate an experimental combination, the system begins with an initial state in which no values have been specified, which we may represent as [ ]. Next, BACON generates a new state in which the value of N is determined, say $[N = 1]$. In its next step, the system generates a third state in which the value of T is given, say $[N = 1, T = 10]$. On its third step through the data space, BACON.3 generates the complete experimental combination $[N = 1, T = 10, P = 1,000]$, and the program can report and record the volume associated with this combination.

However, if BACON.3 is to gather sufficient data on which to base its laws, it must continue the search. Accordingly, the system backs up to the previous state, $[N = 1, T = 10]$, and generates a second goal combination, $[N = 1, T = 10, P = 2,000]$. This allows data for a second value of the volume to be recorded and associated with an experimental combination. At this point, the system again backtracks to $[N = 1, T = 10]$ and then generates a third goal state, $[N = 1, T = 10, P = 3,000]$, thus gathering a third observation of the volume. Having exhausted the potential values of P, BACON.3 then backs up two steps to $[N = 1]$. From there it generates the states $[N = 1, T = 20]$ and, finally, $[N = 1, T = 20, P = 1,000]$—another complete experimental combination. BACON.3 continues in this fashion until it has generated all the experimental combinations of the independent values it was given and recorded the volumes associated with each combination. Figure 9.2 shows the tree that results from this search through the space of data; the numbers on the states represent the order in which the states are generated.

In directing its search through the space of laws and theoretical terms, BACON.3 employs the same heuristics as BACON.1, but now these have been generalized to operate at any level of description. Thus, the system looks for constant values and linear relations, and, failing this, considers monotonically increasing and decreasing relations. In each case, BACON attempts to relate the values of an independent term to those of some dependent term, though if multiple dependent terms are involved these may be related to one another as well.

Unlike BACON.1, however, the current system considers laws at each level in its search through the data space. Basically, BACON.3's search

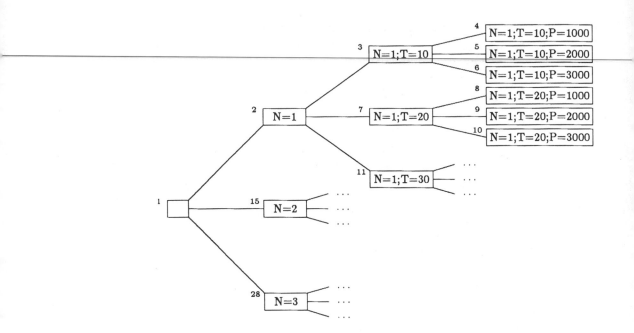

Figure 9.2 Tree generated by BACON.3 search.

for laws is embedded within its search through data. To understand this statement, let us return to figure 9.2, which presents the order in which BACON.3 gathers its data. Consider the topmost terminal nodes, $[N = 1, T = 10, P = 1,000]$, $[N = 1, T = 10, P = 2,000]$, and $[N = 1, T = 10, P = 3,000]$. For each of these combinations, the system records some value of the dependent volume V. When all three values have been noted, BACON.3 attempts to find a law relating them to the three values of the pressure P, using the regularity detectors from BACON.1. The results of this search are one or more theoretical terms and their constant values, which are stored at the next higher state in the data-search tree. For instance, for $P = 1,000$, 2,000, and 3,000, the recorded values for V would be 2.354, 1.177, and 0.785. Given these data, BACON notes that V decreases as P increases, considers the product $a = PV$, and notes that this term has the constant value 2,354.0. The value for a is stored with the state $[N =, 1, T = 10]$ for future use.

Upon requesting and recording a second set of values, BACON.3 attempts to find a second law. For the experimental combinations $[N = 1, T = 20, P = 1,000]$, $[N = 1, T = 20, P = 2,000]$, and $[N = 1, T = 20, P = 3,000]$, the system finds the values 2.438, 1.218, and 0.813 for the volume. Again the term $A = PV$ proves useful, this time with the value 2,438.0, and again this value is stored at a higher state, in this case $[N = 1, T = 20]$. Very similar events occur when the value of T is 30, giving the parameter value $a = 2,521.0$, which is stored with $[N = 1, T = 30]$. At this point (see table 9.7), BACON.3 has three sets of values for the higher-level dependent term a. Moreover, these values are stored

Langley, Simon, Bradshaw, and Zytkow

Table 9.7 Simulated data obeying the ideal-gas law

Moles (N)	Temperature (T)	Pressure (P)	Volume (V)	$a = PV$
1	10	1,000	2.354	2,354
1	10	2,000	1.177	2,354
1	10	3,000	0.785	2,354
1	20	1,000	2.438	2,438
1	20	2,000	1.218	2,438
1	20	3,000	0.813	2,438
1	30	1,000	2.521	2,521
1	30	2,000	1.265	2,521
1	30	3,000	0.840	2,521

Table 9.8 Second-level summary of the gas-law data

Moles (N)	Temperature (T)	$a = PV$	b	c
1	10	2,354	8.32	2,271.4
1	20	2,438	8.32	2,271.4
1	30	2,521	8.32	2,271.4
2	10	4,709	16.64	4,542.7
2	20	4,876	16.64	4,542.7
2	30	5,042	16.64	4,542.7
3	10	7,064	24.96	6,814.1
3	20	7,313	24.96	6,814.1
3	30	7,563	24.96	6,814.1

with the abstracted combinations $[N = 1, T = 10]$, $[N = 1, T = 20]$, and $[N = 1, T = 30]$. Given the values 10, 20, and 30 for T and the values 2,354.0, 2,438.0, and 2,521.0 for a, the program attempts to find a law relating these two terms. In this case, it finds the linear relation $a = bT + c$, with slope $b = 8.32$ and intercept $c = 2,271.4$. These values are stored with the next higher state in the data tree, $[N = 1]$, for future use (table 9.8).

This process is continued as more data are gathered. First, BACON.3 finds three additional laws relating the variables P and V. Then, on the basis of the resulting parameter values, analogous linear relations are found between a and T, this time with $b = 16.64$ and $c = 4,542.7$. These higher-level dependent values are stored with the state $[N = 2]$. Similar steps lead to three more laws involving the product $a = PV$, and then to a third law of the form $a = bT + c$. This time, BACON.3 finds the best fit with $b = 24.96$ and $c = 6,814.1$, and stores these values with $[N = 3]$.

Now the system has three values of N, along with three associated values of b and three of c (table 9.9). For each of these dependent terms, BACON.3 searches for some law, arriving at the two linear relations with zero intercepts: $b = dN$ and $c = eN$, in which $d = 8.32$ and $e = 2,271.4$. These two parameter values, which are stored at the initial data state

Table 9.9 Third-level summary of the gas-law data

Moles (N)	b	c	$d = b/N$	$e = c/N$
1	8.32	2,271.4	8.32	2,271.4
2	16.64	4,542.7	8.32	2,271.4
3	24.96	6,814.1	8.32	2,271.4

[ ], represent invariant parameters that do not depend on any independent terms.

Substituting these values into the forms found at each level in BACON.3's search, we arrive at the relation

$$PV = 8.32NT + 2,271.4N.$$

By factoring out 8.32N on the right-hand side, we arrive at

$$PV = 8.32N(T + 273),$$

which is the standard form of the ideal-gas law. Note that, in some way, BACON.3 has determined that the Celsius temperature scale is inconvenient for describing the relation among the four terms and has effectively introduced the Kelvin scale by adding 273 to the recorded Celsius values.

As this example shows, BACON.3 carries out as many searches through the law space as there are nonterminal states (figure 9.2) in the data space. Figure 9.3 summarizes the parameter values that result from each of these searches, along with the data states at which they are stored. The numbers next to the states represent the order in which the laws were discovered. Note that this order is different from the order in which the data space itself was searched. In an important sense, the search for data provides structure to BACON.3's search for laws, since it provides both direct observations and a place to store parameters so that they can be used as data at later stages. Thus, BACON.3's search through the data space can be viewed as providing top-down constraints on the types of laws that will be discovered (e.g., which variables are related). The system must still search (bottom up) through the resulting law space to determine the particular laws that best summarize the data.

Once BACON.3 discovers that a particular form of law is useful in one context, it uses that information to constrain search in similar contexts. For instance, when the system finds that the form $PV = a$ is useful when [$N = 1$, $T = 10$], it considers only this form when [$N = 1$, $T = 20$], [N] $= 1$, $T = 30$, and so forth. In other words, BACON.3 redefines its problem space in the light of its previous experience, so that considerably less search is required.

Table 9.10 summarizes the steps taken in rediscovering the ideal-gas law, comparing BACON's version of the law with the standard version,

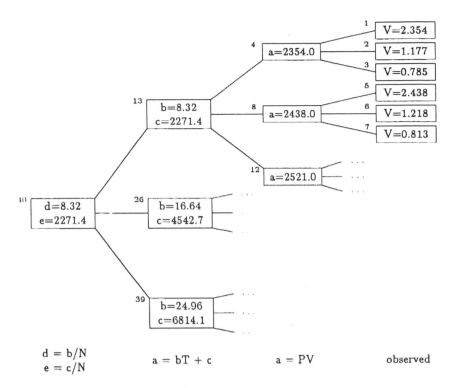

Figure 9.3 Parameter values resulting from searches.

Table 9.10 Summary of discovery of ideal-gas law

BACON's version	Standard version	Constant terms
$PV = a$	$PV = k$	T, N
$PV = bT + c$	$PV = k(T - 273)$	N
$PV = dNT + eN$	$PV = 8.32N(T - 273)$	

and showing the independent terms held constant at each level of description.

Notes

1. We have not found it possible to be wholly consistent in the number of significant (or insignificant!) figures we display in our tables. In cases like the present one, we have retained the full decimal equivalents of the published fractions, although the accuracy of the measurements may not go beyond two or three figures. In other tables too, unless the clutter became excessive, we have retained figures to facilitate the checking of our computations, even when the final digits are surely not significant.

2. The second incarnation of the system, BACON.2, employed somewhat different discovery methods than BACON.1. For example, it found empirical laws using a differencing method that searched for constant derivatives rather than considering products and ratios. The system could also solve sequence-extrapolation tasks, but it employed heuristics for noting recurring chunks rather than the periodicity detector of BACON.1A. We have chosen

to bypass the BACON.2 system for the same two reasons that we presented a simplified version of BACON.1: our concern with scientific discovery and our desire for continuity in our description of the BACON systems. A fuller description of BACON.2 is given in appendix B [omitted here—Ed.], and additional details can be found in Langley 1979a. BACON.3 was first described in Langley 1979b.

References

Buchanan, B. G. (1966). Logics of scientific discovery. AI Memo 47, Computer Science Department, Stanford University, Stanford.

Buchanan, B. G., and T. M. Mitchell (1978). Model-directed learning of production rules. In D. A. Waterman and F. Hayes-Roth, eds., *Pattern-directed inference systems*. New York: Academic Press.

Gerwin, D. G. (1974). Information processing, data inferences, and scientific generalization. *Behavioral Science* 19, 314–325.

Gingerich, O. (1975). The origins of Kepler's third law. In A. Beer and P. Beer, eds., *Kepler: Four Hundred Years*. Oxford: Pergamon.

Huesman,, L. R., and C. M. Cheng (1973). A theory of mathematical functions. *Psychological review* 80, 125–138.

Langley, P. (1978). BACON 1: A general discovery system. In Proceedings of the Second National Conference of the Canadian Society for Computational Studies.

Langley, P. (1979a). Descriptive Discovery Processes: Experiments in Baconian Science. Doctoral dissertation, Carnegie-Mellon University, Pittsburgh.

Langley, P. (1979b). Rediscovering physics with BACON 3. In *Proceedings of the International Joint Conference on Artificial Intelligence*.

Langley, P. and R. Neches (1981). R. PRISM User's Manual. Technical report, Department of Psychology, Carnegie-Mellon University, Pittsburgh.

Langley, P. and S. Ohlsson (1984). Automated cognitive modeling. In *Proceedings of the National Conference on Artificial Intelligence*.

Lenat, D. B. (1977). Automated theory formation in mathematics. In *Proceedings of the Fifth International Joint Conference on Artificial Intelligence*. San Mateo: Morgan Kaufmann.

Lenat, D. B. (1983). EURISKO: A Program that learns new heuristics and domain concepts. *Artificial Intelligence* 21, 61–98.

Magie, W. F. (1935). *A source book in physics*. New York: McGraw-Hill.

Newell, A., and H. A. Simon (1963). GPS, a program that simulates human thought. In E. A. Feigenbaum and J. Feldman, eds., *Computers and thought*. New York: McGraw-Hill.

Newell, A., and H. A. Simon (1972). *Human problem solving*. Englewood Cliffs, NJ: Prentice-Hall.

Newell, A., J. C. Shaw, and H. A. Simon (1962). The processes of creative thinking. In H. E. Gruber et al, eds., *Contemporary approaches to creative thinking.* New York: Atherton.

Simon, H. A. (1966). Scientific discovery and the psychology of problem solving. In R. Colodny, ed., *Mind and cosmos.* Pittsburgh: University of Pittsburgh Press.

Simon, H. A (1973). Does scientific discovery have a logic? *Philosophy of Science* 40, 471–480.

Simon, H. A., and K. Kotovsky (1963). Human acquisition of concepts for sequential patterns. *Psychological Review* 70, 534–546.

Simon, H. A., and G. Lea (1974). Problem solving and rule induction: A unified view. In L. W. Gregg, ed., *Knowledge and cognition.* Potomac, MD: Erlbaum.

10 Evidence against Empiricist Accounts of the Origins of Numerical Knowledge

Karen Wynn

Introduction

There have long been speculations, both in philosophy and psychology, about the origins of mathematical knowledge and numerical concepts. The standard empiricist explanation of how we possess such knowledge is that we acquire even the simplest understanding of numerical relationships from observations of the world. Within psychology, Piaget has argued that children cannot learn the compositional relationships between different numbers or engage in numerical reasoning until about seven years of age (Piaget 1952). Cooper (1984) proposes that infants' initial ability to discriminate between small numerosities (described below) does not include any understanding that the different numerosities "are information about the same kind of thing"; that is, infants' concepts of 'oneness' and 'twoness' are initially as unrelated to each other as are their concepts of, say, 'squareness' and 'blueness'. Infants learn that the numerosities belong to a single category by observing additions and subtractions on collections of objects, and noticing that these actions result in a change from one numerosity to another. Infants are provided with a basis for ordering the different numerosities when they go on to learn, from further such observation, that oneness is related to twoness in precisely the same way as twoness is to threeness, and so on.

This general account of the origins of numerical knowledge also exists in the philosophical literature. John Stuart Mill (1973), for example, held that we learn numerical truths, such as that one plus two equals three, by observing it to be true for sheep in one instance, for cookies in another instance, and so on, until finally we induce that it is true in all cases.

Kitcher (1984, 1988) is perhaps the contemporary philosopher who has spelled out in most careful detail an empiricist view of the origins

From K. Wynn, Evidence against empiricist accounts of the origins of numerical knowledge, *Mind and Language* 7, 315–332 (1992). Copyright 1992 by Blackwell Publishers. Reprinted by permission.

of numerical knowledge. Kitcher's proposal is that individuals learn the simplest mathematical facts from observing the results of their own actions, and learn the rest of mathematics from parents, teachers and other authorities, who obtain their knowledge from the current mathematics experts. The whole chain of knowledge, both for the individual and for the culture, is grounded in the activities of young children, who learn about the mathematical structure of reality through their actions and interactions with the physical world. We learn that one plus two equals three, for example, by performing the action of collecting one item, performing on different items the action of collecting two, and then performing the action of combining these collections, observing that the result is equivalent to the action of collecting three items. Children come to learn basic truths of arithmetic by engaging in such activities of collecting and segregating.

On the various versions of this kind of account, it remains to be spelled out in precise terms what kinds of actions and observations are the relevant kinds for giving us knowledge of numerical truths. If the actions of collecting and segregating must be overtly performed on physical objects by each individual acquiring the knowledge in question,[1] this would predict that paraplegics, for example, could not arrive at these numerical truths. If the relevant actions need only be mental actions (such as the collecting in our minds of 1 and 2 and observing the result), this would not be an empiricist theory, since it would be claiming that the relevant knowledge is all in the head, simply awaiting inspection. Similarly, if the individual can learn simply by observing the results of actions performed by *another* individual, it must be specified what kind of observation is the necessary sort—certainly it need not be tied to a particular modality, since congenitally blind, deaf, etc. people are capable of learning arithmetic. Thus, we need, on the empiricist account, some detailed specification of exactly what kinds of actions, combined with what forms of observation, are sufficient for acquiring numerical truths.

Even if this challenge is satisfactorily met, however, there is a principled objection to any account in which mathematical knowledge of the most basic sort is acquired via faculties of induction. It has not yet been shown how an inductive learning process could account for the apparent necessity of certain mathematical truths. Our intuition of the inevitability of one plus one equaling two goes far beyond our experience, even if our experience has been quite consistent in yielding the correct result. To take a well-worn example, it might be that every crow we have ever seen has been black; we may read scientists' claims that every crow that has ever existed has been black, and read their well-accepted and convincing theories for why this is so; yet we still can conceive of a non-black crow, and can believe that it *need not have been* the case that all crows are black. Yet we cannot conceive that in some possible world, however remote from our own, that one plus one equals three. Inductive processes can lead to beliefs of the nature that "such-and-such *is* the case," but there is no explanation for how they could ever give rise to beliefs of the kind that "such-and-such *must be* the case." Any empiricist theory must either account for how it is that certain mathematical statements have the psychological status of necessary truth rather than of empirical fact, or else argue that numerical truths such as one plus one equals two do not, in fact, enjoy a more privileged psychological status than other beliefs.[2]

There is also empirical evidence that some mathematical knowledge is not learned. Studies show that infants and non-human animals are sensitive to numerosity; they can distinguish between different numerosities and, moreover, can recognize numerical equivalence across perceptually distinct kinds of items. Further studies show that animals and infants also possess knowledge of some arithmetical relationships; that is, they are able to manipulate these number concepts in numerically meaningful ways.

The Empirical Findings

Infants' and Animals' Sensitivity to Number

Over the last 10 years it has been clearly shown that human infants are sensitive to number. For example, studies have shown that newborns (Antell and Keating 1983), 5-month-olds (Starkey and Cooper 1980), and 10-month-olds (Strauss and Curtis 1981) are able to discriminate small numerosities; they can tell *two* from *three* and, under certain conditions, *three* from *four*. These studies used a habituation technique, in which infants are repeatedly presented with (habituated to) different pictures showing a certain number of objects, until their looking time to each picture drops below a designated criterion (typically to half of what it was for the initial two or three pictures). They are then shown a picture either of that same number of objects again, or of a different number of objects. Some of these experiments used pictures of black solid circles arranged in different spacial configurations from trial to trial, while others used photographs of various household objects that were different in each picture; for example, one picture might consist of an orange and a glove arranged haphazardly, while the next might include a keychain and a banana. The test pictures might all consist of completely new items, such as a wallet, a cup, and a pair of sunglasses. Infants tend to look significantly longer at (to "dishabituate to") the picture depicting a new number of objects, indicating that they differentiate between the two numerosities.[3]

Furthermore, the knowledge underlying this ability is not local to visual perception; infants can recognize numerical equivalence across different perceptual modalities. For example, when six- to nine-month-old infants were played a tape recording of either two knocks or three knocks, and then shown simultaneously a picture of two items and a picture of three items, they preferred to look at the picture showing the number of items corresponding to the number of knocks heard (Starkey et al. 1983, 1990). Thus, the basis for infants' ability to recognize differences and equivalences between instances of small numbers is an abstract and conceptual representation of number. It is not simply an ability to recognize differences between sets of objects of the same kind, nor does it appear to be some kind of perceptual pattern-recognition (as has been proposed by Cooper 1984, for example).

Non-human animals, too, are sensitive to exact numerosities, as has been shown in many studies over a wide range of vertebrate species. A brief summary of some of these findings is given below. (For a far more extensive review and discussion, see Gallistel 1990, chap. 10.)

Rats are able to determine the number of times they have pressed on a lever, up to at least 24 presses, when trained to press a certain number of times on a particular lever before pressing a single time on a second lever for a reward. Furthermore, their response is clearly based on the *number* of presses rather than on elapsed time; when trained to press for a certain amount of time, they typically press for a certain extra *proportion* of the trained time in order to be sure that they have pressed the required amount (there is a penalty for pressing the second lever too early), but when trained to press a certain number of times, their response is typically to press a certain extra *constant number* of presses, independent of the required number (Mechner and Guevrekian 1962). Similar abilities have been shown in pigeons with a somewhat different task (Rilling 1967; Rilling and McDiarmid 1965). Rats have also been trained (Davis and Bradford 1986) to turn down the third, fourth, or fifth tunnel on the left in a maze, and once trained, will do so even when the spatial configuration of the maze is varied from trial to trial so that the distance between the tunnels changes each time, and a corner must be turned before the rewarded tunnel on the left is reached. Given this, the rats could not simply be running for a fixed length of time before turning left, or determining the extent to which they feel fatigued by the run. They must be encoding the numerosity of the tunnels on the left in order to succeed at the task.

Birds have shown similar abilities. In one experiment, canaries were trained to select an object based on its ordinal position in an array (Pastore 1961). Out of 10 cubicles spaced along a runway, the canaries had to walk along the runway and choose the cubicle that held, say, the fifth aspirin. The ordinal position of the cubicle containing the relevant aspirin varied from trial to trial, to rule out any regularity of distance from the starting point. Furthermore, to control for the possibility of the birds' using rhythm as the basis of their judgments, different numbers of aspirins were placed into each cubicle on different trials. Thus both the space between cubicles and the number of aspirins per cubicle varied. The birds were clearly succeeding on the basis of the ordinal position of the aspirin.

Animals can also discriminate different numerosities of simultaneously presented objects. In one study, a raccoon was taught to choose the plexiglass box containing three items, when presented with an array of three to five boxes each containing from one to five items; nonnumerical cues such as size, stimulus density, odor, and location of target box were controlled for (Davis 1984). In another study, Matsuzawa (1985) trained a chimpanzee to pick out the correct Arabic number symbol when presented with a set of a certain numerosity, for the numbers one through six. Pepperberg (1987) trained an African Grey Parrot to say the appropriate number word when presented with up to five objects. In all of these studies, results generalized to novel items.[4]

Adult humans, as well, possess some automatic process that determines the absolute and relative frequencies of entities. Studies have shown this for a range of different entities, including letters, words, colors, and even different kinds of lethal events (e.g., Attneave 1951; Hasher and Zacks, 1979; Hintzman 1969; Lichtenstein et al. 1978; Lund et al. 1983; Shapiro, 1969). It seems likely that we are born with a mechanism that computes event frequency (Hasher and Zacks, 1979). The most parsimonious theory is that humans possess the same mechanism that underlies other animals' determination of event frequency.

It has sometimes been claimed that it must have taken humans a long time historically to realize that a *brace* of pheasants, a *pair* of boots, and so on all have the abstracted concept of twoness in common (Fuson and Hall 1983 make a similar conjecture regarding the development of numerical concepts in young children). Several of the infant and animal studies, however, show possession of just such an abstracted concept; infants recognize the common attribute to twoness (for example) across different kinds of items (they do not dishabituate when shown a picture of two novel items), and animals will generalize a response to new kinds of items.[5] There is also evidence showing that not only are animals and infants sensitive to numerosity, but they can also perform basic arithmetical calculations over these numerosities.

Knowledge of Arithmetical Relationships in Animals and Infants
The most conclusive evidence of addition abilities in animals is shown in the following experiment. Boysen and Berntson (1989) taught a chimpanzee to associate the Arabic numerals "0" through "4" with their respective numerosities. Without further training, she was able to choose the numeral representing the sum of oranges hidden in two hiding places. Most impressive of all, when the sets of oranges in the hiding places were replaced with Arabic numerals, she was immediately able to choose the Arabic numeral representing the sum of these numerals. That is, without training, she was able to operate over two symbols representing numerosities in such a way as to arrive at the symbol representing their sum.

Evidence against Empiricist Accounts of the Origins of Numerical Knowledge

Rats have been shown to apparently anticipate when they are approaching the required number of presses, when they must press a certain number of times one lever before pressing another level to obtain a reward (Platt and Johnson 1971). When there is no penalty for pressing the second lever too early, rats will frequently press it before they have finished the required number of presses on the first lever, and upon finding that they are too early, will return to the first lever to increase their number of presses according to the following constraint—the greater their initial number of presses, the smaller their number of additional presses. That is, they appear to know roughly how close they are to the needed number, not only whether they have or have not reached that number yet.

In another study, Church and Meck (1984) trained rats to press the left lever if presented with either two sounds or two light flashes, and the right lever if presented with four sounds or four light flashes. They then presented the rats with two simultaneous sound/light-flash pairings. In this situation, the rats pressed the right lever, showing that they had computed that there were four stimuli altogether. The results from these experiments suggest that these animals possess representations of number that can be manipulated in the appropriate ways so as to determine the results of simple additions.

Studies recently conducted in my infant cognition laboratory suggest that young human infants can calculate the results of both additions and subtractions (Wynn 1992a). These studies tested five-month-old infants' knowledge that two is composed of one and one.

In one experiment, infants were divided into two groups. Those in the "1+1" group were shown a single item being placed into an empty display area. Then a small screen rotated up, hiding the item from view, and the experimenter brought a second identical item into the display area, in clear view of the infant. The experimenter then placed the second item out of the infant's sight behind the screen (this sequence of events is shown in Figure 10.1). Thus, infants could clearly see the nature of the arithmetical operation being performed, but could not see the result of the operation. Infants in the "2−1" group were similarly presented with a sequence of events depicting a subtraction of one item from two items (also shown in Figure 10.1). For both groups of infants, after the above sequence of events was concluded the screen rotated downward to reveal either one or two items in the display case. Infants' looking time to the display was then recorded. The prediction was that infants would be surprised by an apparently impossible result. Thus, the two groups should show significantly different looking patterns; infants in the "1+1" group should look longer when the result is one than when it is two, while infants in the "2−1" group should show the reverse pattern. (A pretest condition showed that infants in the two groups did not differ in their baseline looking patterns to one and two items.)

Test sequence of events: 1+1 = 1 or 2

1. Object placed in case	2. Screen comes up	3. Second object added	4. Hand leaves empty
		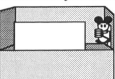	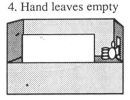

Then either: (a) Possible Outcome   **Or   (b) Impossible Outcome**

5. screen drops ...	6. revealing 2 objects	5. screen drops ...	6. revealing 1 object
		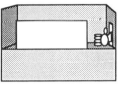	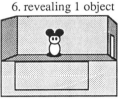

Test sequence of events: 2-1 = 1 or 2

1. Objects placed in case	2. Screen comes up	3. Empty hand enters	4. One object removed
			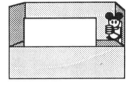

Then either: (a) Possible Outcome   **Or   (b) Impossible Outcome**

5. screen drops ...	6. revealing 1 object	5. screen drops ...	6. revealing 2 objects
			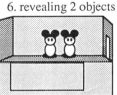

Figure 10.1 Schematic drawing of sequence of events shown to infants in Wynn (1992a). (Reprinted with permission from *Nature* 358, 749–750 (1992). Copyright (1992) Macmillan Magazines Limited.)

This was in fact the pattern of results obtained; infants in the two groups showed different patterns of looking in the test trials, but not in the pretest trials. Infants in the "1+1" group looked longer when the addition appeared to result in a single item than when it resulted in two items, while infants in the "2−1" group looked longer when the subtraction appeared to result in two items than when it resulted in a single item.

In another experiment, infants were shown an addition of one plus one where the outcome was either two or three objects. Again, the prediction was that infants would look longer at the apparently impossible outcome (three items) than at the expected outcome (two objects). (A pretest condition showed that infants looked equally long at two and at three objects). This, too, was the pattern of results obtained; infants were surprised when the addition appeared to result in three items, but not when it resulted in two items (they looked longer at three than at two).

The findings from these experiments concur with a recent experiment at Baillargeon, Miller, and Constantino (n.d.) that shows precise knowledge of simple addition in 10-month-olds. They showed infants a hand taking and depositing a single item out of sight behind a screen, then doing the same with a second item. They then lowered the screen, revealing to the infants either two or three items. The infants looked longer when shown three items behind the screen than when shown two, showing that they had been expecting only two. (They had previously demonstrated equal preference to look at two versus three items.) That is, from two distinct experiences, each of one item, they had constructed an expectation of two items.

The above results show that upon computing the numerosity of some set of items or events, animals can compare the symbol for the numerosity just determined with others stored in memory and compute some precise arithmetical relationships that obtain. Similarly, infants as young as five months are able to calculate the precise outcomes of simple additions and substractions. These results suggest that the mental number symbols over which animals and infants operate have a structure that allows them to abstract information of the precise numerical relationships between the numerosities; that is, the mental symbols for numerosities inherently embody the relationships between the numerosities. Below, I describe a theory of an innate representation of number that would entail such a structure for the mental number symbols.

The Accumulator Theory

Meck and Church (1983) suggest that a single mechanism underlies both animals' ability to determine numerosity (whether of events or of simultaneously presented items), and their ability to measure duration. Briefly, their proposed mechanism (based on a model for measurement of temporal intervals developed by Gibbon 1981) works as follows: a pacemaker puts out pulses at a constant rate, which can be passed into an accumulator by the closing of a mode switch. In its counting mode, every time an entity is experienced that is to be counted, the mode switch closes for a fixed interval, passing energy into the accumulator. Thus, the accumulator fills up in equal increments, one for each entity counted. In its timing mode, the switch remains closed for the duration of the temporal interval, passing energy into the accumulator continuously at a constant rate. The mechanism contains several accumulators and switches, so that the animal can count different sets of events and measure several durations simultaneously.

The final value in the accumulator can be passed into working memory, and there compared with previously stored accumulator values. In this way the animal can evaluate whether a number of events or the duration of an interval is more, less, or the same as a previously stored number or duration that is associated with some outcome, such as a reward. Thus, while the animal may not have access to the inner workings of the mechanism, the output values of its calculations are available for inferences and so constitute part of the animal's general conceptual system.

Evidence that the same mechanism underlies both animals' timing processes and their counting processes comes from several experiments (Meck and Church 1983). First of all, methamphetamine increases rats' measure of duration and of numerosity by the same factor, strongly suggesting that it is a single mechanism being affected. The effect would be explained on the model by the drug causing an increase in the rate of pulse generation by the pacemaker, leading to a proportionate increase in the final value of the accumulator regardless of the mode in which it was operating. Second, both numerical and duration discriminations transferred to novel stimuli equally strongly, when rats trained on auditory stimuli were then tested on mixed auditory and cutaneous stimuli. Finally, an experiment tested the following prediction: If the animal's decision is based on a comparison of the final value of the accumulator with a previously stored value of the accumulator, then one might expect there to be immediate transfer from making an evaluation on the basis of the output of the timing process to making an evaluation on the basis of the output of the counting process, so long as the final output value of the accumulator in the two cases was identical. For example, a count that yielded the same final fullness value in the accumulator as a previously trained duration might be responded to as if it were that duration. This prediction was confirmed: When rats were trained to respond to a specific *duration* of continuous sound, they immediately generalized their response when presented with a certain *number* of one-second sound segments that had been calculated by the experimenters to fill up the accumulator to the same level as the level for the duration the rats had been initially trained on. Meck and Church concluded that it was indeed the same mechanism underlying both counting and timing processes in rats.

An Alternative Theory of Innate Knowledge of Number

It is worth distinguishing the accumulator theory from another nativist theory of numerical knowledge. Rochel Gelman and colleagues (e.g., Gelman and Gallistel 1978; Gelman and Greeno 1989; Gelman and Meck 1983; Gelman et al. 1986) have proposed that young children possess an innate concept of numbers consisting of a set of counting principles that define correct counting, and a set of mental counting tags that are used in accordance with these principles. The three "how-to-count" principles are as follows: The *one-to-one correspondence* principle states that items to be counted must be put into one-to-one correspondence with members of the set of number tags that are used to count with (e.g., the child's innately given mental counting tags, or a set of number words); the *stable-order* principle states that the number tags must have a fixed order in which they are consistently used; and the *cardinality* principle states that the last number tag used in a count represents the cardinality of the items counted.

These principles can be viewed as an initial skeletal framework, which serves to shape and structure the developing body of numerical knowledge, both by defining the domain and by identifying relevant input (e.g., Gelman 1990). For example, the principles make it easier for children to learn the number words of their language and to map them onto their own innately given list of number tags, because the number words are used in accordance with the same principles as their mental number tags. They have a fixed order in which they are consistently used, and they are applied to items in one-to-one correspondence. Thus, the counting principles help children to identify early on the linguistic, culturally supported counting activity as *counting* (i.e., as the same kind of activity as their own innate, non-linguistic counting activity). Once children do so, the counting principles allow them to develop their skills in the overt, linguistic counting activity, by serving as guidelines for correct counting so that children can monitor their counting performance (e.g., Gelman and Greeno 1989; Gelman and Meck 1983; Gelman et al. 1986).

Differences between the Accumulator and Counting Models

It has been noted (Gallistel 1990) that the accumulator mechanism embodies the counting principles in the following way: There is a *one-to-one correspondence* between entities to be counted and increments of the accumulator; the states of the accumulator are arrived at in a *stable order* from count to count (the accumulator always reaches the level of two increments before that of three increments); and the final value of the accumulator represents the *cardinality* of the items counted.

There is, however, an important difference between this kind of counting mechanism and the linguistic counting system. It is the entire fullness of the accumulator, comprised of all the increments together, that represents the numerosity of the items counted. In the accumulator mechanism, numerosity is *inherently embodied in the structure of the representations*, which are themselves magnitude values (the output values of the accumulator). It is the entire fullness of the accumulator that represents the numerosity of the items 'counted'. Thus the relationships between the representations exactly reproduce the relationships between the quantities they represent. For example, four is one more than three, and the representation for four (the magnitude of fullness of the accumulator) is one more increment than the representation for three. Ten is 5 times as large as 2; the representation for 10 is 5 times as large as the representation for 2 (the accumulator has 5 times as many increments, is five times as full).

In linguistic counting, on the other hand, the final word alone represents the numerosity of the items counted. Thus number is not inherently represented in the structure of each individual linguistic symbol; rather, the symbols are inherently arbitrary and obtain their numerical meaning by virtue of their positional relationships with each other. They represent cardinalities with a system that does not directly reproduce, but is *analogous* to, the inherent relationships among the numerosities. The number words bear relationships to each other in their ordinality that are analogous to the relationships the numerosities themselves bear to each other in their cardinality. For example, the linguistic symbol for *six* occurs three positions later in the number word list than the linguistic symbol for *three*, or twice as far along; the numerosity *six* is three units larger than, or twice as large as, the numerosity *three*. In contrast, on the accumulator representation of number, the representations for the numerosities bear exactly the *same* relationship to each other as do the numbers themselves.

Consider the information implicit in a system where the symbols for the numerosities inherently represent number, rather than being "arbitrary" symbols; where the symbol for *one* is something like 'x', that for *two*, 'xx', that for *three*, 'xxx', and so on. A comparison of any two symbols will indicate whether the represented numerosities are the same or different. It will also reveal if one is larger or smaller than the other; furthermore, it will reveal *how much* larger or smaller one is from the other. Thus, the claim that animals and young children possess such a representation of numerosity accounts for their ability to determine more-than/less-than relations and to compute the results of additions and subtractions, provided they can operate over the representations in relatively straightforward ways.

Evidence against Empiricist Accounts of the Origins of Numerical Knowledge

For example, addition could be achieved by simply concatenating two (or more) representations (x+xx = xxx), or transferring the energy from two accumulators into an empty third accumulator. A more-than/less-than/equal-to comparison of two accumulators A and B could be achieved by transferring one increment from one of the accumulators (say A) into an empty third accumulator, and transferring one increment from the other accumulator (B) into an empty fourth accumulator. A and B are slowly emptied in this way, one decrement at a time, alternating between the two accumulators. If B becomes empty before A, then the number represented by B is smaller. If, when A becomes empty, the next decrement from B leaves B empty as well, then both accumulators represent the same number. If B is not empty after this decrement, then the number represented by B is larger. Determining how much larger one is than the other (subtraction) could be achieved by transferring the remaining energy from the fuller accumulator (say A) into another empty accumulator. The difference between the two values would be represented by the fullness value of this accumulator.[6] Thus, the accumulator theory could plausibly account for the ability of animals and infants to determine more/less than relations and compute the results of additions and subtractions.

On the other hand, consider what follows if animals possess a symbol for each numerosity that is arbitrary, such as 'x' for *one*, 'y' for *two*, 'z' for *three*, and so on. Many of the above experimental results could still be explained. The ability to press a lever a certain number of times for a reward, for example, could be accounted for as follows: After each press, the animal examines the symbol representing the current numerosity, compares it with the rewarded symbol retained in short-term memory, and stops when the two symbols match. (Again, it must be assumed that the animal can inspect the output value while keeping a running total). The ability of animals to pick out the set of items of a particular numerosity, or to say a word or choose a symbol describing a displayed numerosity, could similarly be explained by appeal to such symbol-matching procedures. However, animals' and infants' abilities to calculate the results of additions and subtractions would not be explained. A comparison of two such arbitrary symbols would not reveal whether one is larger or smaller than the other; there is nothing inherent to the symbol 'x', for example, that indicates how it should be ordered with respect to the symbol 'z'. The only information a comparison of such symbols would yield is whether the two represented numerosities are the same, or different. In order to account for the ability of animals and infants to calculate the results of additions and subtractions, added assumptions must be made about the kinds of operations animals and infants can perform on their list of mental number tags. For example, the ability to add and subtract could be explained by positing that animals and infants can count up or down along their list of mental number tags itself; to add two to three, the animal would start at the 'three' tag, and count two successive tags upward, observing that the tag arrived at is the 'five' tag. Thus, the capacity of animals and infants to add and subtract does not conclusively distinguish the two theories, although it would appear to require less complex processes on the accumulator model.

A clear prediction that follows from the difference between the two theories is that on the accumulator model of representation of number, it should not be a simple process for children to acquire the linguistic counting system, because they must learn the mapping between two very different representations—their own magnitudinal representations of number, and the ordinal representations inherent in the linguistic counting system. In contrast, the counting-principles theory predicts that it should be a relatively straightforward process for children to identify the ordered list of number words with their ordered list of mental number tags.

Several studies show that (a) children know how to perform the linguistic counting activity before they know how it determines numerosity (that is, knowledge of the linguistic counting activity is at first quite distinct from their knowledge of number), and (b) acquiring an understanding of the linguistic counting system is in fact quite a difficult process for children. In one study (Wynn 1990), 2½- to 3½-year-olds were given a "give-a-number" task, in which they were asked to give a puppet from one to six toy animals from a pile. If they understand how linguistic counting determines numerosity, they should be able to use counting to give the correct number. It turned out that children under about 3½ years of age were utterly unable to use counting to solve the task; they never counted items from the pile to give the correct number, even though they were quite good at linguistic 'counting'. For example, children who could count six items perfectly well were unable to give, say, three items from the pile. When asked for larger numbers, they just grabbed and gave a random number of items. When asked for smaller numbers (three and fewer), some children had apparently directly associated some of these number words with their correct numerosities and so could give the correct number just by looking, but without counting.[7] Thus, children had acquired considerable skill at the linguistic counting activity *before* connecting it with the hypothesized set of innate counting principles.

In another, longitudinal study (Wynn 1992b), children's understanding of aspects of the meanings of number words was examined. The results showed that by 2½ years of age children already know that each number word refers to a specific, unique numerosity, even though they do not know to *which* numerosity each word refers. This was determined by showing pairs of pictures to those children who already knew the meaning of the word "one" (those who, as in the previous study, had associated the word 'one' with its corresponding numerosity). For example, they would be shown one picture depicting a single blue fish,

Evidence against Empiricist Accounts of the Origins of Numerical Knowledge

and the other depicting four yellow fish, and asked, "Can you show me the four fish?" If children know the word 'four' is a number word, they should know it does not refer to a single item since they already have a word for the numerosity *one*. They should thus choose the correct picture by a process of elimination. It turned out that even the youngest children succeeded on this task (they were equally likely to point to either picture when asked a nonsense question, such as "Can you show me the *blicket* fish?"). However, despite this early knowledge, it took children nearly a year to learn the pattern behind *which* words refer to *which* numerosities. That is, it took the same children about a year more before they were able to correctly point out which of two pictures, one with three items and the other with four items, was the one depicting the four items. Even though they had learned the number word list beyond 'four' (at least to 'five' or 'six', which was the highest the experiment tested), and knew that these words each referred to a specific numerosity, they did not know which numerosity each word picked out. This would not be expected on the counting-principles theory, according to which children would know which word referred to each numerosity once they had connected the counting word list with their own number concepts.

These studies show that it is not until about 3½ years of age, long after children know that the number words refer to numerosities, that they come to understand how counting determines numerosity. This protracted period of learning, predicted by the accumulator theory, goes against the counting theory of representation of knowledge.

Conclusions

The experiments reviewed above show that human infants and other animals possess a sensitivity to numerosity, and an ability to determine the results of simple arithmetical operations. The fact that these abilities are evident in a wide range of species and at a very early age in human infancy suggests that we are innately equipped with such knowledge, rather than learning it through induction over experience.

How might this initial numerical understanding be related to the acquisition of more complex mathematical knowledge? There are obvious limitations on what mathematical knowledge could be obtained from the outputs of the accumulator model. It is unlikely that the notion of infinity could result from this mechanism, as all physical processes are limited and there is presumably some point beyond which the accumulator cannot measure. As well, numbers other than the positive integers cannot be represented—by its nature, the accumulator mechanism does not measure fractional values, negative values, imaginary values, and so on. Similarly, there are probably strict limits on the calculations that can be performed. Earlier I outlined some plausible procedures for calculating the results of simple additions and substractions. Although procedures for multiplication, division, exponentiation, and so on are also possible from a computational perspective, they require progressively more steps, and more accumulators to keep concurrent tallies of various iterations and working results. As the procedures become more complex, it becomes less plausible that they are physically instantiated in the mechanism.[8] Finally, on the accumulator model, number is inherently tied to the physical world—the model can only represent numbers *of things* (objects, sounds, events, etc.), whereas mathematics operates as an abstract system unconnected to the physical world.

However, it seems reasonable that our initial numerical knowledge *somehow* serves as a basis for the development of mathematics—after all, this initial knowledge embodies numerical relationships that follow the same laws that apply to the rest of finite mathematics (such as, for example, the commutativity and associativity of addition). Determining just how the transition from this initial basis to more abstract knowledge could be achieved is a major undertaking; and it is here, finally, that empiricist theories of the nature of mathematical knowledge may have much to contribute (such as, for example, Kitcher's (1984) proposal that mathematics is an empirical science and his account of how it has developed as such). A recurring question in the philosophy of mathematics is why mathematics as an abstract system applies so well to the physical world. At least part of the answer may be that the knowledge underlying its development arises from abilities designed to provide information of the physical world.

Notes

I would like to thank Paul Bloom, Susan Carey, David Galloway, Denise Cummins, Marcus Giaquinto, and Lynn Nadel for their discussions and comments. A version of this paper was presented at the 17th Annual Meeting of the Society for Philosophy and Psychology, San Francisco, 1991.

1. Kitcher does appear to be proposing this, e.g., 1984, p. 107: "Children come to learn the meanings of 'set', 'number', 'addition', and to accept basic truths of arithmetic by engaging in *activities* of collecting and segregating" (italics in the original).

2. This is not a challenge for an explanation of how mathematical facts obtained the logical status of necessary truths (if one's theory grants them such status), but rather, of how it is that some mathematical truths have for us the *psychological* inevitability that they do. (Not all mathematical truths hit our intuition as being necessary; for example, those untutored in mathematics are often astonished to learn that there are the same number of odd numbers as whole numbers.)

3. There is no tension between these studies and Frege's point that number is not an intrinsic property of a group of items (two decks of cards shuffled together serve as an instance of many different numerosities—two *decks*, 104 *cards*, 4 *suits*, 10^{25} *molecules*, etc.). There is evidence that, psychologically, we are predisposed to view the world in terms of individual, discrete physical objects. For example, the concept of physical object ap-

pears fundamental to the way infants perceptually and conceptually break up the world (e.g., Spelke 1991; 1988); and young children will persist in counting the individual, discrete physical objects in a pile, even when asked to count *parts* of objects such as the number of ears on a group of teddy bears, or asked to count the different *kinds* of objects represented in the pile rather than the individual objects themselves (Shipley and Shepperson 1990). The above infant number discrimination studies are themselves further evidence that a given collection of entities may *psychologically* serve as an instance of a particular numerosity.

4. These studies are particularly interesting because they show a sensitivity to the *cardinality* of a set of entities, while the previous group of experiments may have tapped a sensitivity to the *ordinality* of a single event—its position in a sequence of events. Presses on a lever are temporally sequential, physical events of the animal; similarly, when a rat must always turn down, say, the fifth tunnel in a maze, it could be the fifth "reaching-a-tunnel-on-the-left" event that is the relevant one. But the ability to, e.g., reliably distinguish a group of 3 objects from groups of 1 to 5 objects cannot rest in any way on some internal event-state of the animal itself; it must rest solely on the properties of the groups of items (their numerosities in particular).

5. This is not a claim that infants and animals are capable of considering the numbers as abstract objects, but simply that their concept of twoness (say) applies across perceptually different stimuli.

6. How such calculations are actually achieved is an empirical question. The descriptions are given here simply to show that there are procedures that could be plausibly instantiated in the accumulator mechanism to account for arithmetical abilities; they are not intended as definitive claims about how the procedures actually operate.

7. The ability to recognize small numbers without overt counting, called "subitization", has been shown in infants (e.g., Starkey et al. 1990; Strauss and Curtis 1981), children (e.g., Silverman and Rose 1980), and adults (e.g., Mandler and Shebo 1982). The upper limit appears to be between 3 and 5 for adults, and 3 for children.

8. Gallistel (1990) argues that animals can perform quite complex calculations: for example, rats can determine which of several foraging areas yields a better rate of return, which involves dividing the time spent in a location by the amount of food obtained; and honey bees make complex calculations using elapsed time along with the position of the sun to determine their trajectory homeward. While these abilities are impressive in their own right, it is likely that they do not generalize to other tasks, and are therefore not part of general numerical abilities.

References

Antell, S., and D. P. Keating (1983). Perception of numerical invariance in neonates. *Child Development* 54, 695–701.

Attneave, F. (1951). Psychological probability as a function of experimental frequency. *Journal of Experimental Psychology* 46, 81–86.

Baillargeon, R., K. Miller and J. Constantino (n.d.). Ms. under revision. Ten-month-old infants' intuitions about children. Department of Psychology. University of Illinois, Urbana-Champaign.

Boysen, S. T., and G. G. Berntson (1988). Numerical competence in a chimpanzee, *Pan troglodytes. Journal of Comparative Psychology* 103, 23–31.

Church, R. M., and W. H. Meck (1984). The numerical attribute of stimuli. In H. Roitblatt, T. G. Bever, and H. S. Terrence, eds., *Animal Cognition*. Hillsdale, NJ: Erlbaum.

Cooper, R. G. (1984). Early number development: Discovering number space with addition and subtraction. In C. Sophian, ed., *Origins of cognitive skills*. Hillsdale, NJ: Erlbaum.

Davis, H. 1984: Discrimination of the number three by a raccoon, *Procyon lotor. Animal Learning and Behavior* 12, 409–413.

Davis, H., and S. A. Bradford (1986). Counting behavior by rats in a simulated natural environment. *Ethology* 73, 265–280.

Fuson, K. G., and J. W. Hall (1983). The acquisition of early number word meanings: A conceptual analysis and review. In H. P. Ginsburg, ed., *The development of mathematical thinking*. New York: Academic Press.

Gallistel, C. R. (1990). *The organization of learning*. Cambridge, MA: MIT Press.

Gelman, R. (1990). First principles organize attention to and learning about relevant data: Number and the animate/inanimate distinction as examples. *Cognitive Science* 14, 79–106.

Gelman, R., and C. R. Gallistel (1978). *The child's understanding of number*. Cambridge: MA: Harvard University Press.

Gelman, R., and J. G. Greeno (1989). On the nature of competence: Principles for understanding in a domain. In L. B. Resnick, ed., *Knowing and learning: Issues for a cognitive science of instruction*. Hillsdale, NJ: Erlbaum.

Gelman, R., & E. Meck (1983). Preschoolers' counting: Principles before skill. *Cognition* 13, 343–359.

Gelman, R., E. Meck, and S. Merkin (1986). Young children's numerical competence. *Cognitive Development* 1, 1–29.

Gibbon, J. (1981). On the form and location of the psychometric bisection function for time. *Journal of Mathematical Psychology* 24, 58–87.

Hasher, L., and R. T. Zacks (1979). Automatic and effortful processes in memory. *Journal of Experimental Psychology: General* 108, 356–388.

Hintzman, D. L. (1969). Apparent frequency as a function of frequency and the spacing of repetitions. *Journal of Experimental Psychology* 80, 139–145.

Kitcher, Philip (1984). *The nature of mathematical knowledge*. Oxford: Oxford University Press.

Kitcher, Philip (1988). Mathematical naturalism. In W. Aspray and P. Kitcher, eds., *History and philosophy of modern mathematics*. Minneapolis: University of Minnesota Press.

Lichtenstein, S., P. Slovic, B. Fischoff, M. Layman, and B. Combs (1978). Judged frequency of lethal events. *Journal of Experimental Psychology: Human Learning and Memory* 4, 551–578.

Lund, A. M., J. W. Hall, K. P. Wilson, and M. S. Humphreys (1983). Frequency judgment accuracy as a function of age and school achievement (learning-disabled versus non-learning-disabled) patterns. *Journal of Experimental Child Psychology* 35, 236–247.

Mandler, G., and B. J. Shebo (1982). Subitizing: An analysis of its component processes. *Journal of Experimental Psychology: General* 11, 1–22.

Matsuzawa, T. (1985). Use of numbers by a chimpanzee. *Nature* 315, 57–59.

Mechner, F. M., and L. Guevrekian (1962). Effects of deprivation upon counting and timing in rats. *Journal of the Experimental Analysis of Behavior* 5, 463–466.

Meck, W. H., and R. M. Church (1983). A mode control model of counting and timing processes. *Journal of Experimental Psychology: Animal Behavior Processes* 9, 320–334.

Mill, J. S. (1973). A system of logic ratiocinative and inductive, 8th ed. In J. M. Robson, ed., *Collected works of John Stuart Mill*, vols. 7 and 8. Toronto: University of Toronto Press (originally published 1843).

Pastore, N. (1961). Number sense and "counting" ability in the canary. *Zeitschrift für Tierpsychologie* 18, 561–573.

Pepperberg, I. M. (1987). Evidence for conceptual quantitative abilities in the African Grey Parrot: Labelling of cardinal sets. *Ethology* 75, 37–61.

Piaget, J. (1952). *The child's conception of number*. New York: Norton.

Platt, J. R., and D. M. Johnson (1971). Localization of position within a homogeneous behavior chain: Effects of error contingencies. *Learning and Motivation* 2, 386–414.

Rilling, M. E. (1967). Number of responses as a stimulus in fixed interval and fixed ratio schedules. *Journal of Comparative and Physiological Psychology* 63, 60–65.

Rilling, M. E., and C. McDiarmid (1965). Signal detection in fixed ratio schedules. *Science* 148, 526–527.

Shapiro, B. J. (1969). The subjective estimation of relative word frequency. *Journal of Verbal Learning and Verbal Behavior* 8, 248–251.

Shipley, E. F., and B. Shepperson (1990). Countable entities: Developmental changes. *Cognition* 34, 109–136.

Silverman, I. W., and A. P. Rose (1980). Subitizing and counting skills in 3-year-olds. *Developmental Psychology* 16, 539–540.

Spelke, E. S. (1988). Where perceiving ends and thinking begins: The apprehension of objects in infancy. In A. Yonas, ed., *Perceptual Development in Infancy. Minnesota Symposium on Child Psychology*, vol. 20. Hillsdale, NJ: Erlbaum.

Spelke, E. S. (1990). Principles of object perception. *Cognitive Science* 14, 29–56.

Spelke, E. S. (1991). Physical knowledge in infancy: Reflections on Piaget's theory. In S. Carey and R. Gelman, eds., *The Epigenesis of Mind*. Hillsdale, NJ: Erlbaum.

Starkey, P., and R. G. Cooper Jr. (1980). Perception of numbers by human infants. *Science* 210, 1033–1035.

Starkey, P., E. S. Spelke, and R. Gelman (1983). Detection of intermodal numerical correspondences by human infants. *Science* 222, 179–181.

Starkey, P., E. S. Spelke, and R. Gelman (1990). Numerical abstraction by human infants. *Cognition* 36, 97–128.

Strauss, M. S., and L. E. Curtis (1981). Infant perception of numerosity. *Child Development* 52, 1146–1152.

Wynn, K. (1990). Children's understanding of counting. *Cognition* 36, 155–193.

Wynn, K. (1992a). Addition and subtraction by human infants. *Nature* 358, 749–750.

Wynn, K. (1992b). Children's acquisition of the number words and the counting system. *Cognitive Psychology* 24, 220–251.

III

Mind

11 Troubles with Functionalism

Ned Block

Functionalism, Behaviorism, and Physicalism

The functionalist view of the nature of the mind is now widely accepted.[1] Like behaviorism and physicalism, functionalism seeks to answer the question "What are mental states?" I shall be concerned with identity thesis formulations of functionalism. They say, for example, that pain is a functional state, just as identity thesis formulations of physicalism say that pain is a physical state.

I shall begin by describing functionalism, and sketching the functionalist critique of behaviorism and physicalism. Then I shall argue that the troubles ascribed by functionalism to behaviorism and physicalism infect functionalism as well.

One characterization of functionalism that is probably vague enough to be acceptable to most functionalists is: each type of mental state is a state consisting of a disposition to act in certain ways *and to have certain mental states*, given certain sensory inputs and certain mental states. So put, functionalism can be seen as a new incarnation of behaviorism. Behaviorism identifies mental states with dispositions to act in certain ways in certain input situations. But as critics have pointed out (Chisholm 1957, Geach 1957, Putnam 1963), desire for goal G cannot be identified with, say, the disposition to do A in input circumstances in which A leads to G, since, after all, the agent might not *know* that A leads to G and thus might not be disposed to do A. Functionalism replaces behaviorism's "sensory inputs" with "sensory inputs and mental states"; and functionalism replaces behaviorism's "dispositions to act" with "dispositions to act and have certain mental states." Functionalists want to individuate mental states causally, and since mental states have mental causes and effects as well as sensory causes

From N. Block, Troubles with functionalism, in C. W. Savage, ed., *Perception and cognition: Issues in the foundations of psychology* (1978). Minneapolis: University of Minnesota Press. © Copyright 1975 by the University of Minnesota. Reprinted by permission.

and behavioral effects, functionalists individuate mental states partly in terms of causal relations to other mental states. One consequence of this difference between functionalism and behaviorism is that there are possible organisms that according to behaviorism, have mental states but, according to functionalism, do not have mental states.

So, necessary conditions for mentality that are postulated by functionalism are in one respect stronger than those postulated by behaviorism. According to behaviorism, it is necessary and sufficient for desiring that G that a system be characterized by a certain set (perhaps infinite) of input-ouput relations; that is, according to behaviorism, a system desires that G just in case a certain set of conditionals of the form "It will emit O given I" are true of it. According to functionalism, however, a system might have these input-output relations, yet not desire that G; for according to functionalism, whether a system desires that G depends on whether it has internal states which have certain causal relations to other internal states (and to inputs and outputs). Since behaviorism makes no such "internal state" requirement, there are possible systems of which behaviorism affirms and functionalism denies that they have mental states.[2] One way of stating this is that, according to functionalism, behaviorism is guilty of *liberalism*—ascribing mental properties to things that do not in fact have them.

Despite the difference just sketched between functionalism and behaviorism, functionalists and behaviorists need not be far apart in spirit.[3] Shoemaker (1975), for example, says, "On one construal of it, functionalism in the philosophy of mind is the doctrine that mental, or psychological, terms are, in principle, eliminable in a certain way" (pp. 306–307). Functionalists have tended to treat the mental-state terms in a functional characterization of a mental state quite differently from the input and output terms. Thus in the simplest Turing-machine version of the theory (Putnam 1967; Block and Fodor 1972), mental states are identified with the total Turing-machine states, which are themselves *implicitly* defined by a machine table that *explicitly* mentions inputs and outputs, described nonmentalistically.

In Lewis's version of functionalism, mental-state terms are defined by means of a modification of Ramsey's method, in a way that eliminates essential use of mental terminology from the definitions but does not eliminate input and output terminology. That is, 'pain' is defined as synonymous with a definite description containing input and output terms but no mental terminology (see Lewis 1972).

Furthermore, functionalism in both its machine and nonmachine versions has typically insisted that characterizations of mental states should contain descriptions of inputs and outputs in *physical* language. Armstrong (1968), for example, says,

We may distinguish between 'physical behaviour', which refers to any merely physical action or passion of the body, and 'behaviour proper' which implies relationship to mind. . . . Now, if in our formula ["state of the person apt for bringing about a certain sort of behaviour"] 'behaviour' were to mean 'behaviour proper', then we would be giving an account of mental concepts in terms of a concept that already presupposes mentality, which would be circular. So it is clear that in our formula, 'behaviour' must mean 'physical behaviour'. (p. 84)

Therefore, functionalism can be said to "tack down" mental states only at the periphery—that is, through physical, or at least nonmental, specification of inputs and outputs. One major thesis of this article is that, because of this feature, functionalism fails to avoid the sort of problem for which it rightly condemns behaviorism. Functionalism, too, is guilty of liberalism, for much the same reasons as behaviorism. Unlike behaviorism, however, functionalism can naturally be altered to avoid liberalism—but only at the cost of falling into an equally ignominious failing.

The failing I speak of is the one that functionalism shows *physicalism* to be guilty of. By 'physicalism', I mean the doctrine that pain, for example, is identical to a physical (or physiological) state.[4] As many philosophers have argued (notably Fodor 1965, Putnam 1966, see also Block and Fodor 1972), if functionalism is true, physicalism is probably false. The point is at its clearest with regard to Turing-machine versions of functionalism. Any given abstract Turing machine can be realized by a wide variety of physical devices; indeed, it is plausible that, given any putative correspondence between a Turing-machine state and a configurational physical (or physiological) state, there will be a possible realization of the Turing machine that will provide a counterexample to that correspondence. (See Kalke 1969, Gendron 1971, and Mucciolo 1974, for unconvincing arguments to the contrary; see also Kim 1972). Therefore, if pain is a functional state, it cannot, for example, be a brain state, because creatures without brains can realize the same Turing machine as creatures with brains.

I must emphasize that the functionalist argument against physicalism does not appeal merely to the fact that one abstract Turing machine can be realized by systems of different *material composition* (wood, metal, glass, etc.). To argue this way would be like arguing that temperature cannot be a microphysical magnitude because the same temperature can be had by objects with *different* microphysical structures (Kim 1972). Objects with different microphysical structures, such as objects made of wood, metal, glass, etc., can have many interesting microphysical properties in common, such as molecular kinetic energy of the same average value. Rather, the functionalist argument against physicalism is that it is difficult to see how there *could be* a nontrivial first-order (see note 4) physical property in common to all and only the possible physical realizations of a given Turing-machine state. Try to think of a remotely plausible candidate! At the very least, the onus is on those who think such physical properties are conceivable to show us how to conceive of one.

One way of expressing this point is that, according to functionalism, physicalism is a *chauvinist* theory: it withholds mental properties from systems that in fact have them. In saying mental states are brain states, for example, physicalists unfairly exclude those poor brainless creatures who nonetheless have minds.

A second major point of this paper is that the very argument which functionalism uses to condemn physicalism can be applied equally well against functionalism; indeed, any version of functionalism that avoids liberalism falls, like physicalism, into chauvinism. . . .

More about What Functionalism Is

One way of providing some order to the bewildering variety of functionalist theories is to distinguish between those that are couched in terms of a Turing machine and those that are not.

A Turing-machine table lists a finite set of machine-table states, S_1 . . . S_n; inputs, I_1 . . . I_m; and outputs, O_1 . . . O_p. The table specifies a set of conditionals of the form: if the machine is in state S_i and receives input I_j, it emits output O_k and goes into state S_1. That is, given any state and input, the table specifies an output and a next state. Any system with a set of inputs, outputs, and states related in the way specified by the table is described by the table and is a realization of the abstract automaton specified by the table.

To have the power for computing any recursive function, a Turing machine must be able to control its input in certain ways. In standard formulations, the output of a Turing machine is regarded as having two components. It prints a symbol on a tape, then moves the tape, thus bringing a new symbol into the view of the input reader. For the Turing machine to have full power, the tape must be infinite in at least one direction and movable in both directions. If the machine has no control over the tape, it is a "finite transducer," a rather limited Turing machine. Finite transducers need not be regarded as having tape at all. Those who believe that machine functionalism is true must suppose that just what power automaton we are is a substantive empirical question. If we are "full power" Turing machines, the environment must constitute part of the tape.

One very simple version of machine functionalism (Block and Fodor 1972) states that each system having mental states is described by at least one Turing-machine table of a specifiable sort and that each type of mental state of the system is identical to one of the machine-table states. Consider, for example, the Turing machine described in table 11.1 (cf. Nelson 1975). One can get a crude picture of the simple version of machine functionalism by considering the claim that S_1 = dime-desire, and S_2 = nickel-desire. Of course, no functionalist would claim that a Coke machine desires anything. Rather, the simple version of

Table 11.1

	S_1	S_2
nickel input	Emit no output Go to S_2	Emit a Coke Go to S_1
dime input	Emit a Coke Stay in S_1	Emit a Coke and a nickel Go to S_1

machine functionalism described above makes an analogous claim with respect to a much more complex hypothetical machine table. Notice that machine functionalism specifies inputs and outputs explicitly, internal states implicitly (Putnam (1967, 434) says: "The S_i, to repeat, are specified only *implicitly* by the description, i.e., specified *only* by the set of transition probabilities given in the machine table"). To be described by this machine table, a device must accept nickels and dimes as inputs and dispense nickels and Cokes as outputs. But the states S_1 and S_2 can have virtually any natures (even nonphysical natures), so long as those natures connect the states to each other and to the inputs and outputs specified in the machine table. All we are told about S_1 and S_2 are these relations; thus machine functionalism can be said to reduce mentality to input-output structures. This example should suggest the force of the functionalist argument against physicalism. Try to think of a first-order (see note 4) physical property that can be shared by all (and only) realizations of this machine table!

One can also categorize functionalists in terms of whether they regard functional identities as part of a priori psychology or empirical psychology. The a priori functionalists (such as Smart, Armstrong, Lewis, Shoemaker) are the heirs of the logical behaviorists. They tend to regard functional analyses as analyses of the meanings of mental terms, whereas the empirical functionalists (such as Fodor, Putnam, Harman) regard functional analyses as substantive scientific hypotheses. In what follows, I shall refer to the former view as 'Functionalism' and the latter as 'Psychofunctionalism'. (I shall use 'functionalism' with a lowercase 'f' as neutral between Functionalism and Psychofunctionalism. When distinguishing between Functionalism and Psychofunctionalism, I shall always use capitals.)

Functionalism and Psychofunctionalism and the difference between them can be made clearer in terms of the notion of the Ramsey sentence of a psychological theory. Mental-state terms that appear in a psychological theory can be defined in various ways by means of the Ramsey sentence of the theory. All functional state identity theories . . . can be understood as defining a set of functional states . . . by means of the Ramsey sentence of a psychological theory—with one functional state corresponding to each mental state. The functional state corresponding to pain will be called the 'Ramsey functional correlate' of pain, with respect to the psychological theory. In terms of the notion of a Ramsey functional correlate with respect to a theory, the distinction between Functionalism and Psychofunctionalism can be defined as follows: Functionalism identifies mental state S with S's Ramsey functional correlate with respect to a *commonsense* psychological theory; Psychofunctionalism identifies S with S's Ramsey functional correlate with respect to a *scientific* psychological theory.

This difference between Functionalism and Psychofunctionalism gives rise to a difference in specifying inputs and outputs. Functionalists are restricted to specification of inputs and outputs that are plausibly part of commonsense knowledge; Psychofunctionalists are under no such restriction. Although both groups insist on physical—or at least nonmental—specification on inputs and outputs, Functionalists require externally observable classifications (such as inputs characterized in terms of objects present in the vicinity of the organism, outputs in terms of movements of body parts). Psychofunctionalists, on the other hand, have the option to specify inputs and outputs in terms of internal parameters, such as signals in input and output neurons.

Let T be a psychological theory of either commonsense or scientific psychology. T may contain generalizations of the form: anyone who is in state w and receives input x emits output y, and goes into state z. Let us write T as

$$T(S_1 \ldots S_n, I_1 \ldots I_k, O_1 \ldots O_m)$$

where the Ss are mental states, the Is are inputs, and the Os are outputs. The 'S's are to be understood as mental state *constants* such as 'pain', not variables, and likewise for the 'I's and 'O's. Thus, one could also write T as

$$T(\text{pain} \ldots, \text{light of 400 nanometers entering left eye} \ldots, \text{left big toe moves 1 centimeter left} \ldots)$$

To get the Ramsey sentence of T, replace the mental state terms—*but not the input and output terms*—by variables, and prefix an existential quantifier for each variable:

$$\exists F_1 \ldots \exists F_n T(F_1 \ldots F_n, I_1 \ldots I_k, O_1 \ldots O_m)$$

If 'F_{17}' is the variable that replaced the word 'pain' when the Ramsey sentence was formed, then we can define pain as follows in terms of the Ramsey sentence:

$$x \text{ is in pain} \Leftrightarrow \exists F_1 \ldots \exists F_n$$
$$T[(F_1 \ldots F_n, I_1 \ldots I_k, O_1 \ldots O_m) \text{ and } x \text{ has } F_{17}]$$

The Ramsey functional correlate of pain is the property expressed by the predicate on the right hand side of this biconditional. Notice that this predicate contains input and output constants, but no mental constants since the mental constants were replaced by variables. The Ramsey functional correlate for pain is defined in terms of inputs and outputs, but not in mental terms.

For example, let T be the theory that pain is caused by skin damage and causes worry and the emission of "ouch," and worry, in turn, causes brow wrinkling. Then the Ramsey definition would be:

x is in pain ⇔ There are 2 states (properties), the first of which is caused by skin damage and causes both the emission of "ouch" and the second state, and the second state causes brow wrinklng, and x is in the first state.

The Ramsey functional correlate of pain with respect to this "theory" is the property of being in a state that is caused by skin damage and causes the emission of "ouch" and another state that in turn causes brow wrinkling. (Note that the words 'pain' and 'worry' have been replaced by variables, but the input and output terms remain.)

The Ramsey functional correlate of a state S is a state that has much in common with S. Specifically, S and its Ramsey functional correlate share the structural properties specified by the theory T. But, there are two reasons why it is natural to suppose that S and its Ramsey functional correlate will be distinct. First, the Ramsey functional correlate of S with respect to T can "include" at most those aspects of S that are captured by T; any aspects not captured by T will be left out. Second, the Ramsey functional correlate may even leave out some of what T does capture, for the Ramsey definition does not contain the "theoretical" vocabulary of T. The example theory of the last paragraph is true only of pain-feeling organisms—but trivially, in virtue of its use of the word 'pain'. However, the predicate that expresses the Ramsey functional correlate does not contain this word (since it was replaced by a variable), and so can be true of things that don't feel pain. It would be easy to make a simple machine that has some artificial skin, a brow, a tape-recorded "ouch", and two states that satisfy the mentioned causal relations, but no pain.

The bold hypothesis of functionalism is that for *some* psychological theory, this natural supposition that a state and its Ramsey functional correlate are distinct is false. Functionalism says that there is a theory such that pain, for example, *is* its Ramsey functional correlate with respect to that theory.

One final preliminary point: I have given the misleading impression that functionalism identifies *all* mental states with functional states. Such a version of functionalism is obviously far too strong. Let X be a newly created cell-for-cell duplicate of you (which, of course, is functionally equivalent to you). Perhaps you remember being bar mitzvahed. But X does not remember being bar mitzvahed, since X never was bar mitzvahed. Indeed, something can be functionally equivalent to you but fail to know what you know, or [verb], what you [verb], for a wide variety of "success" verbs. Worse still, if Putnam (1975a) is right in saying that "meanings are not in the head," systems functionally equivalent to you may, for similar reasons, fail to have many of your other propositional attitudes. Suppose you believe water is wet. According to plausible arguments advanced by Putnam and Kripke, a condition for the possibility of your believing water is wet is a certain kind of causal connection between you and water. Your "twin" on Twin Earth, who is connected in a similar way to XYZ rather than H_2O, would not believe water is wet.

If functionalism is to be defended, it must be construed as applying only to a subclass of mental states, those "narrow" mental states such that truth conditions for their application are in some sense "within the person." But even assuming that a notion of narrowness of psychological state can be satisfactorily formulated, the interest of functionalism may be diminished by this restriction. I mention this problem only to set it aside.

I shall take functionalism to be a doctrine about all "narrow" mental states.

Homunculi-Headed Robots

In this section I shall describe a class of devices that are prima facie embarrassments for all versions of functionalism in that they indicate functionalism is guilty of liberalism—classifying systems that lack mentality as having mentality.

Consider the simple version of machine functionalism already described. It says that each system having mental states is described by at least one Turing-machine table of a certain kind, and each mental state of the system is identical to one of the machine-table states specified by the machine table. I shall consider inputs and outputs to be specified by descriptions of neural impulses in sense organs and motor-output neurons. This assumption should not be regarded as restricting what will be said to Psychofunctionalism rather than Functionalism. As already mentioned, every version of functionalism assumes *some* specification of inputs and outputs. A Functionalist specification would do as well for the purposes of what follows.

Imagine a body externally like a human body, say yours, but internally quite different. The neurons from sensory organs are connected to a bank of lights in a hollow cavity in the head. A set of buttons connects to the motor-output neurons. Inside the cavity resides a group of little men. Each has a very simple task: to implement a "square" of an adequate machine table that describes you. On one wall is a bulletin board on which is posted a state card; that is, a card that bears a symbol designating one of the states specified in the machine table. Here is what the little men do: Suppose the posted card has a 'G' on it. This alerts the little men who implement G squares—'G-men' they call themselves. Suppose the light representing input I_{17} goes on. One of the G-men has the following as his sole task: when the card reads 'G' and the

I_{17} light goes on, he presses output button O_{191} and changes the state card to 'M'. This G-man is called upon to exercise his task only rarely. In spite of the low level of intelligence required of each little man, the system as a whole manages to simulate you because the functional organization they have been trained to realize is yours. A Turing machine can be represented as a finite set of quadruples (or quintuples, if the output is divided into two parts): current state, current input; next state, next output. Each little man has the task corresponding to a single quadruple. Through the efforts of the little men, the system realizes the same (reasonably adequate) machine table as you do and is thus functionally equivalent to you.[5]

I shall describe a version of the homunculi-headed simulation, which has more chance of being nomologically possible. How many homunculi are required? Perhaps a billion are enough.

Suppose we convert the government of China to functionalism, and we convince its officials . . . to realize a human mind for an hour. We provide each of the billion people in China (I chose China because it has a billion inhabitants) with a specially designed two-way radio that connects them in the appropriate way to other persons and to the artificial body mentioned in the previous example. We replace each of the little men with a citizen of China plus his or her radio. Instead of a bulletin board, we arrange to have letters displayed on a series of satellites placed so that they can be seen from anywhere in China.

The system of a billion people communicating with one another plus satellites plays the role of an external "brain" connected to the artificial body by radio. There is nothing absurd about a person being connected to his brain by radio. Perhaps the day will come when our brains will be periodically removed for cleaning and repairs. Imagine that this is done initially by treating neurons attaching the brain to the body with a chemical that allows them to stretch like rubber bands, thereby assuring that no brain-body connections are disrupted. Soon clever businessmen discover that they can attract more customers by replacing the stretched neurons with radio links so that brains can be cleaned without inconveniencing the customer by immobilizing his body.

It is not at all obvious that the China-body system is physically impossible. It could be functionally equivalent to you for a short time, say an hour.

"But," you may object, "how could something be functionally equivalent for me for *an hour*? Doesn't my functional organization determine, say, how I would react to doing nothing for a week but reading the *Readers' Digest*?" Remember that a machine table specifies a set of conditionals of the form: if the machine is in S_i and receives input I_j, it emits output O_k and goes into S_1. These conditionals are to be understood *subjunctively*. What gives a system a functional organization at a time is not just what it *does* at that time, but also the counterfactuals true of it at that time: what it *would* have done (and what its state transitions would have been) had it had a different input or been in a different state. If it is true of a system at time t that it *would* obey a given machine table no matter which of the states it is in and no matter which of the inputs it receives, then the system is described at t by the machine table (and realizes at t the abstract automaton specified by the table), even if it exists for only an instant. For the hour the Chinese system is "on," it *does* have a set of inputs, outputs, and states of which such subjunctive conditionals are true. This is what makes any computer realize the abstract automaton that it realizes.

Of course, there are signals the system would respond to that you would not respond to—for example, massive radio interference or a flood of the Yangtze River. Such events might cause malfunction, scotching the simulation, just as a bomb in a computer can make it fail to realize the machine table it was built to realize. But just as the computer *without* the bomb *can* realize the machine table, the system consisting of the people and artificial body can realize the machine table so long as there are no catastrophic interferences, such as floods, etc.

"But," someone may object, "there is a difference between a bomb in a computer and a bomb in the Chinese system, for in the case of the latter (unlike the former), inputs as specified in the machine table can be the cause of the malfunction. Unusual neural activity in the sense organs of residents of Chungking Province caused by a bomb or by a flood of the Yangtze can cause the system to go haywire."

Reply: The person who says what system he or she is talking about gets to say what signals count as inputs and outputs. I count as inputs and outputs only neural activity in the artificial body connected by radio to the people of China. Neural signals in the people of Chungking count no more as inputs to this system than input tape jammed by a saboteur between the relay contacts in the innards of a computer counts as an input to the computer.

Of course, the object consisting of the people of China + the artificial body has *other* Turing-machine descriptions under which neural signals in the inhabitants of Chungking *would* count as inputs. Such a new system (that is, the object under such a new Turing-machine description) would not be functionally equivalent to you. Likewise, any commercial computer can be redescribed in a way that allows tape jammed into its innards to count as inputs. In describing an object as a Turing machine, one draws a line between the inside and the outside. (If we count only neural impulses as inputs and outputs, we draw that line inside the body; if we count only peripheral stimulations as inputs, . . . we draw that line at the skin.) In describing the Chinese system as a Turing machine, I have drawn the line in such a way that it satisfies a certain type of functional description—one that you *also* satisfy, and one that, according to functionalism, justifies attributions of mentality. Functionalism does not claim that every mental system has a machine table of a sort that justifies attributions of mentality with respect to *every* specification of inputs and outputs, but rather, only with respect to *some* specification.

Objection: The Chinese system would work too slowly. The kind of events and processes with which we normally have contact would pass by far too quickly for the system to detect them. Thus, we would be unable to converse with it, play bridge with it, etc.

Reply: It is hard to see why the system's time scale should matter. . . . Is it really contradictory or nonsensical to suppose we could meet a race of intelligent beings with whom we could communicate only by devices such as time-lapse photography? When we observe these creatures, they seem almost inanimate. But when we view the time-lapse movies, we see them conversing with one another. Indeed, we find they are saying that the only way they can make any sense of us is by viewing movies greatly slowed down. To take time scale as all important seems crudely behavioristic.

What makes the homunculi-headed system (count the two systems as variants of a single system) just described a prima facie counter-example to (machine) functionalism is that there is prima facie doubt whether it has any mental states at all—especially whether it has what philosophers have variously called "qualitative states," "raw feels," or "immediate phenomenological qualities." (You ask: What is it that philosophers have called qualitative states? I answer, only half in jest: As Louis Armstrong said when asked what jazz is, "If you got to ask, you ain't never gonna get to know.") In Nagel's terms (1974), there is a prima facie doubt whether there is anything which it is like to be the homunculi-headed system.[6]

Putnam's Proposal

One way functionalists can try to deal with the problem posed by the homunculi-headed counterexamples is by the ad hoc device of stipulating them away. For example, a functionalist might stipulate that two systems cannot be functionally equivalent if one contains parts with functional organizations characteristic of sentient beings and the other does not. In his article hypothesizing that pain is a functional state, Putnam stipulated that "no organism capable of feeling pain possesses a decomposition into parts which separately possess Descriptions" (as the sort of Turing machine which can be in the functional state Putnam identifies with pain). The purpose of this condition is "to rule out such 'organisms' (if they count as such) as swarms of bees as single pain feelers" (Putnam 1967, 434–435).

One way of filling out Putnam's requirement would be: a pain-feeling organism cannot possess a decomposition into parts *all* of which have a functional organization characteristic of sentient beings. But this would not rule out my homunculi-headed example, since it has non-sentient parts, such as the mechanical body and sense organs. It will not do to go to the opposite extreme and require that *no* proper parts be sentient. Otherwise pregnant women and people with sentient parasites will fail to count as pain-feeling organisms. What seems to be important to examples like the homunculi-headed simulation I have described is that the sentient beings *play a crucial role* in giving the thing its functional organization. This suggests a version of Putnam's proposal which requires that a pain-feeling organism has a certain functional organization and that it has no parts which (1) themselves possess that sort of functional organization and also (2) play a crucial role in giving the whole system its functional organization.

Although this proposal involves the vague notion "crucial role," it is precise enough for us to see it will not do. Suppose there is a part of the universe that contains matter quite different from ours, matter that is infinitely divisible. In this part of the universe, there are intelligent creatures of many sizes, even humanlike creatures much smaller than our elementary particles. In an intergalactic expedition, these people discover the existence of our type of matter. For reasons known only to them, they decide to devote the next few hundred years to creating out of *their* matter substances with the chemical and physical characteristics (except at the subelementary particle level) of *our* elements. They build hordes of space ships of different varieties about the sizes of our electrons, protons, and other elementary particles, and fly the ships in such a way as to mimic the behavior of these elementary particles. The ships also contain generators to produce the type of radiation elementary particles give off. Each ship has a staff of experts on the nature of our elementary particles. They do this so as to produce huge (by our standards) masses of substances with the chemical and physical characteristics of oxygen, carbon, etc. Shortly after they accomplish this, you go off on an expedition to that part of the universe, and discover the "oxygen," "carbon," etc. Unaware of its real nature, you set up a colony, using these "elements" to grow plants for food, provide "air" to breathe, etc. Since one's molecules are constantly being exchanged with the environment, you and other colonizers come (in a period of a few years) to be composed mainly of the "matter" made of the tiny people in space ships. Would you be any less capable of feeling pain, thinking, etc., just because the matter of which you are composed contains (and depends on for its characteristics) beings who themselves have a functional organization characteristic of sentient creatures? I think not. The basic electrochemical mechanisms by which the synapse operates are now fairly well understood. As far as is known, changes that do not affect these electrochemical mechanisms do not affect the operation of the brain, and do not affect mentality. The electrochemical mechanisms in your synapses would be unaffected by the change in your matter.[7]

It is interesting to compare the elementary-particle-people example with the homunculi-headed examples the chapter started with. A natural first guess about the source of our intuition that the initially described homunculi-headed simulations lack mentality is that they have *too much* internal mental structure. The little men may be sometimes bored, sometimes excited. We may even imagine that they deliberate about the best way to realize the given functional organization and make changes intended to give them more leisure time. But the example of the elementary-particle people just described suggests this first guess is wrong. What seems important is *how* the mentality of the parts contributes to the functioning of the whole.

There is one very noticeable difference between the elementary-particle-people example and the earlier homunculus examples. In the former, the change in you as you become homunculus-infested is not one that makes any different to your psychological processing (that is, information processing) or neurological processing but only to your microphysics. No techniques proper to human psychology or neurophysiology would reveal any difference in you. However, the homunculi-headed simulations described in the beginning of the chapter are not things to which neurophysiological theories true of us apply, and *if they are construed as Functional* (rather than Psychofunctional) simulations, they need not be things to which psychological (information-processing) theories true of us apply. This difference suggests that our intuitions are in part controlled by the not unreasonable view that our mental states depend on our having the psychology and/or neurophysiology we have. So something that differs markedly from us in both regards (recall that it is a Functional rather than Psychofunctional simulation) should not be assumed to have mentality just on the ground that it has been designed to be Functionally equivalent to us.

Is the Prima Facie Doubt Merely Prima Facie?

The Absent Qualia Argument rested on an appeal to the intuition that the homunculi-headed simulations lacked mentality or at least qualia. I said that this intuition gave rise to prima facie doubt that functionalism is true. But intuitions unsupported by principled argument are hardly to be considered bedrock. Indeed, intuitions incompatible with well-supported theory (such as the pre-Copernican intuition that the earth does not move) thankfully soon disappear. Even fields like linguistics whose data consist mainly in intuitions often reject such intuitions as that the following sentences are ungrammatical (on theoretical grounds):

The horse raced past the barn fell.
The boy the girl the cat bit scratched died.

These sentences are in fact grammatical though hard to process.[8]

Appeal to intuitions when judging possession of mentality, however, is *especially* suspicious. *No* physical mechanism seems very intuitively plausible as a seat of qualia, least of all a *brain*. Is a hunk of quivering gray stuff more intuitively appropriate as a seat of qualia that a covey of little men? If not, perhaps there is a prima facie doubt about the qualia of brain-headed systems too?

However, there is a very important difference between brain-headed and homunculi-headed systems. Since we know that *we are brain-headed systems*, and that *we* have qualia, we know that brain-headed systems can have qualia. So even though we have no theory of qualia which explains how this is *possible*, we have overwhelming reason to disregard whatever prima facie doubt there is about the qualia of brain-headed systems. Of course, this makes my argument partly *empirical*—it depends on knowledge of what makes us tick. But since this is knowledge we in fact possess, dependence on this knowledge should not be regarded as a defect.[9]

There is another difference between us meat-heads and the homunculi-heads: they are systems designed to mimic us, but we are not designed to mimic anything (here I rely on another empirical fact). This fact forestalls any attempt to argue on the basis of an inference to the best explanation for the qualia of homunculi-heads. The best explanation of the homunculi-heads' screams and winces is not their pains, but that they were designed to mimic our screams and winces.

Some people seem to feel that the complex and subtle behavior of the homunculi-heads (behavior just as complex and subtle—even as "sensitive" to features of the environment, human and nonhuman, as your behavior) is itself sufficient reason to disregard the prima facie doubt that homunculi-heads have qualia. But this is just crude behaviorism.

My case against Functionalism depends on the following principle: If a doctrine has an absurd conclusion which there is no independent reason to believe, and if there is no way of explaining away the absurdity or showing it to be misleading or irrelevant, and if there is no good reason to believe the doctrine that leads to the absurdity in the first place, then don't accept the doctrine. I claim that there is no independent reason to believe in the mentality of the homunculi-head, and I know of no way of explaining away the absurdity of the conclusion that it has mentality (though of course, my argument is vulnerable to the introduction of such an explanation). The issue, then, is whether there is any good reason to believe Functionalism. One argument for Functionalism is that it is the best solution available to the mind-body problem. I think this is a bad form of argument, but since I also think that Psychofunctionalism is preferable to Functionalism (for reasons to be mentioned below), I'll postpone consideration of this form of argument to the discussion of Psychofunctionalism.

The only other argument for Functionalism that I know of is that Functional identities can be shown to be true on the basis of analyses of the meanings of mental terminology. According to this argument, Functional identities are to be justified in the way one might try to justify the claim that the state of being a bachelor is identical to the state of being an unmarried man. A similar argument appeals to commonsense platitudes about mental states instead of truths of meaning. Lewis says that functional characterizations of mental states are in the province of "commonsense psychology—folk science, rather than professional science" (Lewis 1972, 250). (See also Shoemaker 1975; and Armstrong 1968. Armstrong equivocates on the analyticity issue. See Armstrong 1968, 84–85, 90.) And he goes on to insist that Functional characterizations should "include only platitudes which are common knowledge among us—everyone knows them, everyone knows that everyone else knows them, and so on" (Lewis 1972, 256). I shall talk mainly about the "platitude" version of the argument. The analyticity version is vulnerable to essentially the same considerations, as well as Quinean doubts about analyticity.

I am willing to concede, for the sake of argument, that it is possible to define any given mental state term in terms of platitudes concerning other mental state terms, input terms, and output terms. But this does not commit me to the type of definition of mental terms in which all mental terminology has been eliminated via Ramsification or some other device. It is simply a fallacy to suppose that if each mental term is definable in terms of the others (plus inputs and outputs), then each mental term is definable nonmentalistically. To see this, consider the example given earlier. Indeed, let's simplify matters by ignoring the inputs and outputs. Let's define pain as the cause of worry, and worry as the effect of pain. Even a person so benighted as to accept this needn't accept a definition of pain as *the cause of something*, or a definition of worry as *the effect of something*. Lewis claims that it is analytic that pain is the occupant of a certain causal role. Even if he is right about a causal role, specified in part mentalistically, one cannot conclude that it is analytic that pain is the occupant of any causal role, nonmentalistically specified.

I don't see any decent argument for Functionalism based on platitudes or analyticity. Further, the conception of Functionalism as based on platitudes leads to trouble with cases that platitudes have nothing to say about. Recall the example of brains being removed for cleaning and rejuvenation, the connections between one's brain and one's body being maintained by radio while one goes about one's business. The process takes a few days and when it is completed, the brain is reinserted in the body. Occasionally it may happen that a person's body is destroyed by an accident while the brain is being cleaned and rejuvenated. If hooked up to input sense organs (but not output organs) such a brain would exhibit *none* of the usual platitudinous connections between behavior and clusters of inputs and mental states. If, as seems plausible, such a brain could have almost all the same (narrow) mental states as we have (and since such a state of affairs could become typical), Functionalism is wrong.

It is instructive to compare the way Psychofunctionalism attempts to handle brains in bottles. According to Psychofunctionalism, what is to count as a system's inputs and outputs is an empirical question. Counting neural impulses as inputs and outputs would avoid the problems just sketched, since the brains in bottles and paralytics could have the right neural impulses even without bodily movements. Objection: There could be paralysis that affects the nervous system, and thus affects the neural impulses, so the problem which arises for Functionalism arises for Psychofunctionalism as well. Reply: Nervous system diseases can actually *change mentality*: for example they can render victims incapable of having pain. So it might actually be true that a widespread nervous system disease that caused intermittent paralysis rendered people incapable of certain mental states.

According to plausible versions of Psychofunctionalism, the job of deciding what neural processes should count as inputs and outputs is in part a matter of deciding *what malfunctions count as changes in mentality and what malfunctions count as changes in peripheral input and output connections*. Psychofunctionalism has a resource that Functionalism does not have, since Psychofunctionalism allows us to *adjust the line we draw between the inside and the outside of the organism so as to avoid problems of the sort discussed*. All versions of Functionalism go wrong in attempting to draw this line on the basis of only commonsense knowledge; "analyticity" versions of Functionalism go especially wrong in attempting to draw the line a priori.

Psychofunctionalism

In criticizing Functionalism, I appealed to the following principle: if a doctrine has an absurd conclusion which there is no independent reason to believe, and if there is no way of explaining away the absurdity or showing it to be misleading or irrelevant, and if there is no good reason to believe the doctrine that leads to the absurdity in the first place, then don't accept the doctrine. I said that there was no independent reason to believe that the homunculi-headed Functional simulation has any mental states. However, there *is* an independent reason to believe that the homunculi-headed *Psycho*functional simulation has mental states, namely that a Psychofunctional simulation of you would be Psychofunctionally equivalent to you, so any psychological theory true of you would be true of it too. What better reason could there be to attribute to it whatever mental states are in the domain of psychology?

This point shows that any Psychofunctional simulation of you shares your *non*-qualitative mental states. However, in the next section I shall argue that there is nonetheless some doubt that it shares your qualitative mental states.

Are Qualia Psychofunctional States?

I began this chapter by describing a homunculi-headed device and claiming there is prima facie doubt about whether it has any mental states at all, especially whether it has qualitative mental states like pains, itches, and sensations of red. The special doubt about qualia can perhaps be explicated by thinking about *inverted* qualia rather than *absent* qualia. It makes sense, or seems to make sense, to suppose that objects we both call green look to me the way objects we both call red look to you. It seems that we could be functionally equivalent even though the sensation fire hydrants evoke in you is qualitatively the same as the sensation grass evokes in me. Imagine an inverting lens which when placed in the eye of a subject results in exclamations like "Red things now look the way green things used to look, and vice versa." Imagine further, a pair of identical twins one of whom has the lenses inserted at birth. The twins grow up normally, and at age 21 are functionally equivalent. This situation offers at least some evidence that each's spectrum is inverted relative to the other's. (See Shoemaker 1975, note 17, for a convincing description of intrapersonal spectrum inversion.) However, it is very hard to see how to make sense of the analog of spectrum inversion with respect to nonqualitative states. Imagine a pair of persons one of whom believes that p is true and that q is false while the other believes that q is true and that p is false. Could these persons be functionally equivalent? It is hard to see how they could.[10] Indeed, it is hard to see how two persons could have only this difference in beliefs and yet there be no possible circumstance in which this belief difference would reveal itself in different behavior. Qualia seem to be supervenient on functional organization in a way that beliefs are not.

There is another reason to firmly distinguish between qualitative and nonqualitative mental states in talking about functionalist theories: Psychofunctionalism avoids Functionalism's problems with nonqualitative states—for example propositional attitudes like beliefs and desires. But Psychofunctionalism may be no more able to handle qualitative states than is Functionalism. The reason is that qualia may well not be in the domain of psychology.

To see this let us try to imagine what a homunculi-headed realization of human psychology would be like. Current psychological theorizing seems directed toward the description of information-flow relations among psychological mechanisms. The aim seems to be to decompose such mechanisms into psychologically primitive mechanisms, "black boxes" whose internal structure is in the domain of physiology rather than in the domain of psychology. (See Fodor 1968, Dennett 1975, and Cummins 1975; interesting objections are raised in Nagel 1969.) For example, a near-primitive mechanism might be one that matches two items in a representational system and determines if they are tokens of the same type. Or the primitive mechanisms might be like those in a digital computer—for example, they might be (a) *add 1 to a given register*, and (b) *subtract 1 from a given register, or if the register contains 0, go to the nth (indicated) instruction*. (These operations can be combined to accomplish any digital computer operation; see Minsky 1967, 206.) Consider a computer whose machine-language code contains only two instructions corresponding to (a) and (b). If you ask how it multiplies or solves differential equations or makes up payrolls, you can be answered by being shown a program couched in terms of the two machine-language instructions. But if you ask how it adds 1 to a given register, the appropriate answer is given by a wiring diagram, not a program. The machine is hard-wired to add 1. When the instruction corresponding to (a) appears in a certain register, the contents of another register "automatically" change in a certain way. The computational structure of a computer is determined by a set of primitive operations and the ways nonprimitive operations are built up from them. Thus it does not matter to the computational structure of the computer whether the primitive mechanisms are realized by tube circuits, transistor circuits, or relays. Likewise, it does not matter to the psychology of a mental system whether its primitive mechanisms are realized by one or another neurological mechanism. Call a system a "realization of human psychology" if every psychological theory true of us is true of it. Consider a realization of human psychology whose primitive psychological operations are accomplished by little men, in the manner of the homunculi-headed simulations discussed. So, perhaps one little man produces items from a list, one by one, another compares these items with other representations to determine whether they match, etc.

Now there is good reason for supposing this system has some mental states. Propositional attitudes are an example. Perhaps psychological theory will identify remembering that P with having "stored" a sentencelike object which expresses the proposition that P (Fodor 1975). Then if one of the little men has put a certain sentencelike object in "storage," we may have reason for regarding the system as remembering that P. But unless having qualia is just a matter of having certain information processing (at best a controversial proposal), there is no such theoretical reason for regarding the system as having qualia. In short, there is perhaps as much doubt about the qualia of this homunculi-headed system as there was about the qualia of the homunculi-headed Functional simulation discussed early in the chapter.

But the system we are discussing is *ex hypothesi* something of which any true psychological theory is true. *So any doubt that it has qualia is a doubt that qualia are in the domain of psychology*.

It may be objected: "The kind of psychology you have in mind is *cognitive* psychology, that is, psychology of thought processes; and it is no wonder that qualia are not in the domain of *cognitive* psychology!" But I *do not* have cognitive psychology in mind, and if it sounds that way, this is easily explained: nothing we know about the psychological processes underlying our conscious mental life has anything to do with qualia. What passes for the "psychology" of sensation or pain, for example, is (a) physiology, (b) psychophysics (that is, the study of the mathematical functions relating stimulus variables and sensation variables; for example, the intensity of sound as a function of the amplitude of the sound waves), or (c) a grab bag of description studies (see Melzack 1973, chap. 2). Of these, only psychophysics could be construed as being about qualia *per se*. And it is obvious that psychophysics touches only the *functional* aspect of sensation, not its qualitative character. Psychophysical experiments done on you would have the same results if done on any system Psychofunctionally equivalent to you, even if it had inverted or absent qualia. If experimental results would be unchanged whether or not the experimental subjects have inverted or absent qualia, they can hardly be expected to cast light on the nature of qualia.

Indeed, on the basis of the kind of conceptual apparatus now available in psychology, I do not see how psychology in anything like its present incarnation *could* explain qualia. We cannot now conceive how psychology could explain qualia, though we *can* conceive how psychology could explain believing, desiring, hoping, etc. (see Fodor 1975). That something is currently inconceivable is not a good reason to think it is impossible. Concepts could be developed tomorrow that would make what is now inconceivable conceivable. But all we have to go on is what we know, and on the basis of what we have to go on, it looks as if qualia are not in the domain of psychology.

It is no objection to the suggestion that qualia are not psychological entities that qualia are the very paradigm of something in the domain of psychology. As has often been pointed out, it is in part an empirical question what is in the domain of any particular branch of science. The liquidity of water turns out not to be explainable by chemistry, but rather by subatomic physics. Branches of science have at any given time a set of phenomena they seek to explain. But it can be discovered that some phenomenon which seemed central to a branch of science is actually in the purview of a different branch.

The Absent Qualia Argument exploits the possibility that the Functional or Psychofunctional state Functionalists or Psychofunctionalists would want to identify with pain can occur without any quale occurring. It also seems to be conceivable that the latter occur without the former. Indeed, there are facts that lend plausibility to this view. After frontal lobotomies, patients typically report that they still have pains, though the pains no longer bother them (Melzack 1973, 95). These patients show all the "sensory" signs of pain (such as recognizing pin pricks as sharp), but they often have little or no desire to avoid "painful" stimuli.

One view suggested by these observations is that each pain is actually a *composite* state whose components are a quale and a Functional or Psychofunctional state.[11] Or what amounts to much the same idea, each pain is a quale playing a certain Functional or Psychofunctional role. If this view is right, it helps to explain how people can have believed such different theories of the nature of pain and other sensations; they have emphasized one component at the expense of the other. Proponents of behaviorism and functionalism have had one component in mind; proponents of private ostensive definition have had the other in mind. Both approaches err in trying to give one account of something that has two components of quite different natures. . . .

Notes

I am indebted to Sylvain Bromberger, Hartry Field, Jerry Fodor, David Hills, Paul Horwich, Bill Lycan, Georges Rey, and David Rosenthal for their detailed comments on one or another earlier draft of this paper. Beginning in the fall of 1975, parts of earlier versions were read at Tufts University, Princeton University, the University of North Carolina at Greensboro, and the State University of New York at Binghamton.

1. See Fodor 1965; Lewis 1972; Putnam 1966, 1967, 1970, 1975b; Armstrong 1968; Locke 1968; perhaps Sellars 1968; perhaps Dennett 1969, 1978a; Nelson 1969, 1975 (but see also Nelson 1976); Pitcher 1971; Smart 1971; Block and Fodor 1972; Harman 1973; Grice 1975; Shoemaker 1975; Wiggins 1975.

2. The converse is also true.

3. Indeed, if one defines 'behaviorism' as the view that mental terms can be defined in nonmental terms, then functionalism *is* a version of behaviorism.

4. State type, not state token. Throughout the chapter, I shall mean by 'physicalism' the doctrine that says each distinct type of mental state is identical to a distinct type of physical state; for example, pain (the universal) is a physical state. Token physicalism, on the other hand, is the (weaker) doctrine that each particular datable pain is a state of some physical type or other. Functionalism shows that type physicalism is false, but it does not show that token physicalism is false.

By 'physicalism', I mean *first-order* physicalism, the doctrine that, e.g., the property of being in pain is a first-order (in the Russell-Whitehead sense) physical property. (A first-order property is one whose definition does not require quantification over properties; a second-order property is one whose definition requires quantification over first-order properties—and not other properties.) The claim that being in pain is a second-order physical property is actually a (physicalist) form of functionalism. See Putnam 1970.

5. The basic idea for this example derives from Putnam (1967). I am indebted to many conversations with Hartry Field on the topic. Putnam's attempt to defend functionalism from the problem posed by such examples is discussed in the section entitled Putnam's Proposal of this chapter.

6. Shoemaker (1975) argues (in reply to Block and Fodor 1972) that absent qualia are logically impossible; that is, that it is logically impossible that two systems be in the same functional state yet one's state have and the other's state lack qualitative content.

7. Since there is a difference between the role of the little people in producing your functional organization in the situation just described and the role of the homunculi in the homunculi-headed simulations this chapter began with, presumably Putnam's con-

dition could be reformulated to rule out the latter without ruling out the former. But this would be a most *ad hoc* maneuver.

8. Compare the first sentence with "The fish eaten in Boston stank." The reason it is hard to process is that 'raced' is naturally read as active rather than passive. See Fodor et al., 1974, 360. For a discussion of why the second sentence is grammatical, see Fodor and Garrett 1967, Bever 1970, and Fodor et al., 1974.

9. We often fail to be able to conceive of how somethng is possible because we lack the relevant theoretical concepts. For example, before the discovery of the mechanism of genetic duplication, Haldane argued persuasively that no conceivable physical mechanism could do the job. He was right. But instead of urging that scientists should develop ideas that would allow us to conceive of such a physical mechanism, he concluded that a *non*physical mechanism was involved. (I owe the example to Richard Boyd.)

10. Suppose a man who has good color vision mistakenly uses 'red' to denote green and 'green' to denote red. That is, he simply confuses the two words. Since his confusion is purely linguistic, though he says of a green thing that it is red, he does not *believe* that it is red, any more than a foreigner who has confused 'ashcan' with 'sandwich' believes people eat ashcans for lunch. Let us say that the person who has confused 'red' and 'green' in this way is a victim of Word Switching.

Now consider a different ailment: having red/green inverting lenses placed in your eyes without your knowledge. Let us say a victim of this ailment is a victim of Stimulus Switching. Like the victim of Word Switching, the victim of Stimulus Switching applies 'red' to green things and vice versa. But the victim of Stimulus Switching *does* have false color beliefs. If you show him a green patch he says *and believes* that it is red.

Now suppose that a victim of Stimulus Switching suddenly becomes a victim of Word Switching as well. (Suppose as well that he is a lifelong resident of a remote Arctic village, and has no standing beliefs to the effect that grass is green, fire hydrants are red, and so forth.) He speaks normally, applying 'green' to green patches and 'red' to red patches. Indeed, he is functionally normal. But his *beliefs* are just as abnormal as they were before he became a victim of Word Switching. Before he confused the words 'red' and 'green', he applied 'red' to a green patch, and mistakenly believed the patch to be red. Now he (correctly) says 'red', but his belief is still wrong.

So two people can be functionally the same, yet have incompatible beliefs. Hence, the inverted qualia problem infects belief as well as qualia (though presumably only qualitative belief). This fact should be of concern not only to those who hold functional state identity theories of belief, but also to those who are attracted by Harman-style accounts of meaning as functional role. Our double victim—of Word and Stimulus Switching—is a counter-example to such accounts. For his word 'green' plays the normal role in his reasoning and inference, yet since in saying of something that it "is green," he expresses his belief that it is *red*, he uses 'green' with an abnormal meaning. I am indebted to Sylvain Bromberger for discussion of this issue.

11. The quale might be identified with a physico-chemical state. This view would comport with a suggestion Hilary Putnam made in the late 1960s in his philosophy of mind seminar. See also chapter 5 of Gunderson 1971.

References

Armstrong, D. (1968). *A materialist theory of mind*. London: Routledge & Kegan Paul.

Bever, T. (1970). The cognitive basis for linguistic structures. In J. R. Hayes, ed., *Cognition and the development of language*. New York: Wiley.

Block, N. (1980). Are absent qualia impossible? *Philosophical Review*, 89, 257–274.

Block, N. and Fodor, J. (1972). What psychological states are not. *Philosophical Review*, 81, 159–181.

Chisholm, Roderick (1957). *Perceiving*. Ithaca: Cornell University Press.

Cummins, R. (1975). Functional analysis. *Journal of Philosophy* 72, 741–764.

Davidson, D. (1970). Mental events. In L. Swanson and J. W. Foster, eds, *Experience and theory*. Amherst: University of Massachusetts Press.

Dennett, D. (1969). *Content and consciousness*. London: Routledge & Kegan Paul.

Dennett, D. (1975). "Why the law of effect won't go away. *Journal for the Theory of Social Behavior* 5, 169–187.

Dennett, D. (1978a). *Brainstorms*. Montgomery, VT.: Bradford.

Dennett, D. (1978b). Why a computer can't feel pain. *Synthese* 38, 3.

Fodor, J. (1965). Explanations in psychology. In M. Black, ed., *Philosophy in America*. London: Routledge & Kegan Paul.

Fodor, J. (1968). The appeal to tacit knowledge in psychological explanation. *Journal of Philosophy*, 65, 627–640.

Fodor, J. (1975). *The language of thought*. New York: Crowell.

Fodor, J., T. Bever, and M. Garrett, (1974). *The psychology of language*. New York: McGraw-Hill.

Fodor, J., and M. Garrett, (1967). Some syntactic determinants of sentential complexity. *Perception and Psychophysics*, 2, 289–296.

Geach, P. (1957). *Mental acts*. London: Routledge & Kegan Paul.

Gendron, B. (1971). On the relation of neurological and psychological theories: A critique of the hardware thesis. In R. C. Buck and R. S. Cohen, eds, *Boston studies in the philosophy of science VIII*. Dordrecht: Reidel.

Grice, H. P. (1975). Method in philosophical psychology (from the banal to the bizarre). *Proceedings and Addresses of the American Philosophical Association*.

Gunderson, K. (1971). *Mentality and machines*. Garden City: Doubleday Anchor.

Harman, G. (1973). *Thought*. Princeton: Princeton University Press.

Hempel, C. (1970). Reduction: Ontological and linguistic facets. In S. Morgenbesser, P. Suppes, and M. White, eds, *Essays in honor of Ernest Nagel*. New York: St. Martins Press.

Kalke, W. (1969). What is wrong with Fodor and Putnam's functionalism? *Noûs* 3, 83–93.

Kim, J. (1972). Phenomenal properties, psychophysical laws, and the identity theory. *The Monist* 56(2), 177–192.

Lewis, D. (1972). Psychophysical and theoretical identifications. *Australasian Journal of Philosophy* 50(3), 249–258.

Locke, D. (1968). *Myself and others.* Oxford: Oxford University Press.

Melzack, R. (1973). *The puzzle of pain.* New York: Basic Books.

Minsky, M. (1967). *Computation.* Englewood Cliffs, NJ: Prentice-Hall.

Mucciolo, L. F. (1974). The identity thesis and neuropsychology, *Noûs*, 8, 327–342.

Nagel, T. (1969). The boundaries of inner space. *Journal of Philosophy* 66, 452–458.

Nelson, R. J. (1969). Behaviorism is false. *Journal of Philosophy*, 66, 417–452.

Nelson, R. J. (1975). Behaviorism, finite automata and stimulus response theory. *Theory and Decision* 6, 249–267.

Nelson, R. J. (1976). Mechanism, functionalism, and the identity theory. *Journal of Philosophy* 73, 365–386.

Pitcher, G. (1971). *A theory of perception.* Princeton: Princeton University Press.

Putnam, H. (1963). Brains and behavior. Reprinted in *Mind, language and reality: Philosophical papers*, vol. 2. London: Cambridge University Press, 1975.

Putnam, H. (1966). The mental life of some machines. Reprinted in *Mind, language and reality: Philosophical papers*, vol. 2. London: Cambridge University Press, 1975.

Putnam, H. (1967). The nature of mental states (originally published under the title "Psychological Predicates"). Reprinted in *Mind, language and reality: Philosophical papers*, vol. 2. London: Cambridge University Press, 1975.

Putnam, H. (1970). On properties. In *Mathematics, matter and method: Philosophical papers*, vol. 1. London: Cambridge University Press.

Putnam, H. (1975a). The meaning of 'meaning'. In *Mind, language and reality: Philosophical papers*, vol. 2. Cambridge: Cambridge University Press.

Putnam, H. (1975b). Philosophy and our mental life. In *Mind, language and reality: Philosophical papers*, vol. 2. Cambridge: Cambridge University Press.

Sellars, W. (1968). *Science and Metaphysics* (chap. 6). London: Routledge & Kegan Paul.

Shoemaker, S. (1975). Functionalism and qualia. *Philosophical Studies* 27, 271–315.

Smart, J. J. C. (1971). Reports of immediate experience. *Synthese* 22, 346–359.

Wiggins, D. (1975). Identity, designation, essentialism, and physicalism. *Philosophia* 5, 1–30.

12 Eliminative Materialism and the Propositional Attitudes

Paul M. Churchland

Eliminative materialism is the thesis that our commonsense conception of psychological phenomena constitutes a radically false theory, a theory so fundamentally defective that both the principles and the ontology of that theory will eventually be displaced, rather than smoothly reduced, by completed neuroscience. Our mutual understanding and even our introspection may then be reconstituted within the conceptual framework of completed neuroscience, a theory we may expect to be more powerful by far than the commonsense psychology it displaces, and more substantially integrated within physical science generally. My purpose in this paper is to explore these projections, especially as they bear on (1) the principal elements of commonsense psychology: the propositional attitudes (beliefs, desires, etc.), and (2) the conception of rationality in which those elements figure.

This focus represents a change in the fortunes of materialism. Twenty years ago emotions, qualia, and "raw feels" were held to be the principal stumbling blocks for the materialist program. With these barriers dissolving (Feyerabend 1963; Rorty 1965; Churchland 1979), the locus of opposition has shifted. Now it is the realm of the intentional, the realm of the propositional attitude, that is most commonly held up as being both irreducible to and ineliminable in favor of anything from within a materialist framework. Whether and why this is so, we must examine.

Such an examination will make little sense, however, unless it is first appreciated that the relevant network of commonsense concepts does indeed constitute an empirical theory, with all the functions, virtues, *and perils* entailed by that status. I shall therefore begin with a brief sketch of this view and a summary rehearsal of its rationale. The resistance it encounters still surprises me. After all, common sense has yielded up many theories. Recall the view that space has a preferred direction in which all things fall, that weight is an intrinsic feature of a body, that a force-free moving object will promptly return to rest, that

From P. Churchland, Eliminative materialism and the propositional attitudes, *Journal of Philosophy* 78, 67–90 (1981). Reprinted by permission.

the sphere of the heavens turns daily, and so on. These examples are clear, perhaps, but people seem willing to concede a theoretical component within common sense only if (1) the theory and the common sense involved are safely located in antiquity, and (2) the relevant theory is now so clearly false that its speculative nature is inescapable. Theories are indeed easier to discern under these circumstances. But the vision of hindsight is always 20/20. Let us aspire to some foresight for a change.

Why Folk Psychology Is a Theory

Seeing our commonsense conceptual framework for mental phenomena as a theory brings a simple and unifying organization to most of the major topics in the philosophy of mind, including the explanation and prediction of behavior, the semantics of mental predicates, action theory, the problem of other minds, the intentionality of mental states, the nature of introspection, and the mind-body problem. Any view that can pull this lot together deserves careful consideration.

Let us begin with the explanation of human (and animal) behavior. The fact is that the average person is able to explain, and even predict, the behavior of persons with a facility and success that is remarkable. Such explanations and predictions standardly make reference to the desires, beliefs, fears, intentions, perceptions, and so forth, to which the agents are presumed subject. But explanations presuppose laws—rough and ready ones, at least—that connect the explanatory conditions with the behavior explained. The same is true for the making of predictions, and for the justification of subjunctive and counterfactual conditionals concerning behavior. Reassuringly, a rich network of commonsense laws can indeed be reconstructed from this quotidian commerce of explanation and anticipation; its principles are familiar homilies; and their sundry functions are transparent. We understand others, as well as we do, because we share a tacit command of an integrated body of lore concerning the lawlike relations holding among external circumstances, internal states, and overt behavior. Given its nature and functions, this body of lore may quite aptly be called "folk psychology." (I shall examine a handful of these laws presently. For a more comprehensive sampling of the laws of folk psychology, see P. M. Churchland 1979. For a detailed examination of the laws that underwrite action explanations in particular, see P. M. Churchland 1970.)

This approach entails that the semantics of the terms in our familiar mentalistic vocabulary is to be understood in the same manner as the semantics of theoretical terms generally: The meaning of any theoretical term is fixed or constituted by the network of laws in which it figures. (This position is quite distinct from logical behaviorism. I deny that the relevant laws are analytic, and it is the lawlike connections generally that carry the semantic weight, not just the connections with overt behavior. But this view does account for what little plausibility logical behaviorism did enjoy.)

More important, the recognition that folk psychology is a theory provides a simple and decisive solution to an old skeptical problem, the problem of other minds. The problematic conviction that another individual is the subject of certain mental states is not inferred deductively from his behavior, nor is it inferred by inductive analogy from the perilously isolated instance of one's own case. Rather, that conviction is a singular *explanatory hypothesis* of a perfectly straightforward kind. Its function, in conjunction with the background laws of folk psychology, is to provide explanations/predictions/understanding of the individual's continuing behavior, and it is credible to the degree that it is successful in this regard over competing hypotheses. In the main, such hypotheses are successful, and so the belief that others enjoy the internal states comprehended by folk psychology is a reasonable belief.

Knowledge of other minds thus has no essential dependence on knowledge of one's *own* mind. Applying the principles of our folk psychology to our behavior, a Martian could justly ascribe to us the familiar run of mental states, even though his own psychology were very different from ours. He would not, therefore, be "generalizing from his own case."

As well, introspective judgments about one's own case turn out not to have any special status or integrity anyway. On the present view, a spontaneous introspective judgment is just an instance of an acquired habit of conceptual response to one's internal states, and the integrity of any particular response is always contingent on the integrity of the acquired conceptual framework (theory) in which the response is framed. Accordingly, one's *introspective* certainty that one's mind is the seat of beliefs and desires may be as badly misplaced as was the classical man's *visual* certainty that the star-flecked sphere of the heavens turns daily.

Another conundrum is the intentionality of mental states. The "propositional attitudes," as Russell called them, form the systematic core of folk psychology, and their uniqueness and anomalous logical properties have inspired some to see here a fundamental contrast with anything that mere physical phenomena might conceivably display. The key to this matter lies again in the theoretical nature of folk psychology. The intentionality of mental states here emerges not as a mystery of nature, but as a structural feature of the concepts of folk psychology. Ironically, those same structural features reveal the very close affinity that folk psychology bears to theories in the physical sciences. Let me try to explain.

Consider the large variety of what might be called "numerical attitudes" appearing in the conceptual frameworks of physical science: '. . . has a mass$_{kg}$ of n', '. . . has a velocity$_{m/s}$ of n', '. . . has a temperature$_K$ of n', and so forth. These expressions are predicate-forming expressions:

when one substitutes a singular term for a number into the place held by 'n', a determinate predicate results. More interesting, the relations between the various "numerical attitudes" that result are precisely the relations between the numbers "contained" in those attitudes. More interesting still, the argument place that takes the singular terms for numbers is open to quantification. All this permits the expression of generalizations concerning the law-like relations that hold between the various numerical attitudes in nature. Such laws involve quantification over numbers, and they exploit the mathematical relations holding in that domain. Thus, for example,

(1) $(x)(f)(m)[((x$ has a mass of $m)$ & $(x$ suffers a net force of $f))$
$\supset (x$ accelerates at $f/m)]$.

Consider now the large variety of propositional attitudes: '. . . believes that p', '. . . desires that p', '. . . fears that p', '. . . is happy that p', etc. These expressions are predicate-forming expressions also. When one substitutes a singular term for a proposition into the place held by 'p', a determinate predicate results, e.g., '. . . believes that Tom is tall'. (Sentences do not generally function as singular terms, but it is difficult to escape the idea that when a sentence occurs in the place held by 'p', it is there functioning as or like a singular term. More on this below.) More interesting, the relations between the resulting propositional attitudes are characteristically the relations that hold between the propositions "contained" in them, relations such as entailment, equivalence, and mutual inconsistency. More interesting still, the argument place that takes the singular terms for propositions is open to quantification. All this permits the expression of generalizations concerning the lawlike relations that hold among propositional attitudes. Such laws involve quantification over propositions, and they exploit various relations holding in that domain. Thus, for example,

(2) $(x)(p)[(x$ fears that $p) \supset (x$ desires that $\sim p)]$

(3) $(x)(p)[((x$ hopes that $p)$ & $(x$ discovers that $p))$
$\supset (x$ is pleased that $p)]$

(4) $(x)(p)(q)[((x$ believes that $p)$ & $(x$ believes that (if p then $q)))$
$\supset$ (barring confusion, distraction, etc., x believes that $q)]$

(5) $(x)(p)(q)[((x$ desires that $p)$ & $(x$ believes that (if q then $p))$
& $(x$ is able to bring it about that $q))$
$\supset$ (barring conflicting desires or preferred means,
x brings it about that $q)]$.

(If we stay within an objectual interpretation of the quantifiers, perhaps the simplest way to make systematic sense of expressions like ⌜x believes that p⌝ and closed sentences formed therefrom is just to construe whatever occurs in the nested position held by 'p', 'q', etc. as there having the function of a singular term. Accordingly, when the standard connectives occur between terms in that nested position, they must be construed as there functioning as operators that form compound singular terms from other singular terms, and not as sentence operators. The compound singular terms so formed denote the appropriate compound propositions. Substitutional quantification will of course underwrite a different interpretation, and there are other approaches as well. Especially appealing is the prosentential approach of Grover et al. 1975. But the resolution of these issues is not vital to the present discussion.)

Finally, the realization that folk psychology is a theory puts a new light on the mind-body problem. The issue becomes a matter of how the ontology of one theory (folk psychology) is, or is not, going to be related to the ontology of another theory (completed neuroscience); and the major philosophical positions on the mind-body problem emerge as so many different anticipations of what future research will reveal about the intertheoretic status and integrity of folk psychology.

The identity theorist optimistically expects that folk psychology will be smoothly *reduced* by completed neuroscience, and its ontology preserved by dint of transtheoretic identities. The dualist expects that it will prove *ir*reducible to completed neuroscience, by dint of being a nonredundant description of an autonomous, nonphysical domain of natural phenomena. The functionalist too expects that it will prove irreducible, but on the quite different grounds that the internal economy characterized by folk psychology is not, in the last analysis, a law-governed economy of natural states but an abstract organization of functional states, an organization instantiable in a variety of quite different material substrates. It is therefore irreducible to the principles peculiar to any one of them.

Finally, the eliminative materialist too is pessimistic about the prospects for reduction, but his reason is that folk psychology is a radically inadequate account of our internal activities, too confused and too defective to win survival through intertheoretic reduction. On his view, it will simply be displaced by a better theory of those activities.

Which of these fates is the real destiny of folk psychology, we shall attempt to divine presently. For now the point to keep in mind is that we shall be exploring the fate of a theory, a systematic, corrigible, speculative *theory*.

Why Folk Psychology Might (Really) Be False

Since folk psychology is an empirical theory, it is at least an abstract possibility that its principles are radically false and that its ontology is an illusion. With the exception of eliminative materialism, however, none of the major positions takes this possibility seriously. None of them doubts the basic integrity or truth of folk psychology (FP), and all of them anticipate a future in which its laws and categories are conserved. This conservatism is not without some foundation. After all, FP does enjoy a substantial amount of explanatory and predictive success. And what better grounds for confidence in the integrity of its categories?

What better grounds indeed. Even so, the presumption in favor of FP is spurious, born of innocence and tunnel vision. A more searching examination reveals a different picture. First, we must reckon not only with the successes of FP but also with its explanatory failures and with their extent and seriousness. Second, we must consider the long-term history of FP, its growth, fertility, and current promise of future development. And third, we must consider what sorts of theories are *likely* to be true of the etiology of our behavior, given what else we have learned about ourselves in recent history. That is, we must evaluate FP with regard to its coherence and continuity with fertile and well-established theories in adjacent and overlapping domains—with evolutionary theory, biology, and neuroscience, for example—because active coherence with the rest of what we presume to know is perhaps the final measure of any hypothesis.

A serious inventory of this sort reveals a very troubled situation, one which would evoke open skepticism in the case of any theory less familiar and dear to us. Let me sketch some relevant detail. When one centers one's attention not on what FP can explain, but on what it cannot explain or fails even to address, one discovers that there is a great deal. As examples of central and important mental phenomena that remain largely or wholly mysterious within the framework of FP, consider the nature and dynamics of mental illness, the faculty of creative imagination, or the ground of intelligence differences between individuals. Consider our utter ignorance of the nature and psychological functions of sleep, that curious state in which a third of one's life is spent. Reflect on the common ability to catch an outfield fly ball on the run, or hit a moving car with a snowball. Consider the internal construction of a three-dimensional visual image from subtle differences in the two-dimensional array of stimulations in one's respective retinas. Consider the rich variety of perceptual illusions, visual and otherwise. Or consider the miracle of memory, with its lightning capacity for relevant retrieval. On these and many other mental phenomena, FP sheds negligible light.

One particularly outstanding mystery is the nature of the learning process itself, especially where it involves large-scale conceptual change, and especially in its prelinguistic or entirely nonlinguistic form (as in infants and animals), which is by far the most common form in nature. FP is faced with special difficulties here, since its conception of learning as the manipulation and storage of propositional attitudes founders on the fact that how to formulate, manipulate, and store a rich fabric of propositional attitudes is itself something that is learned, and is only one among many acquired cognitive skills. FP would thus appear constitutionally incapable of even addressing this most basic of mysteries. (A possible response here is to insist that the cognitive activity of animals and infants is linguiform in its elements, structures, and processing right from birth. J. A. Fodor [1975] has erected a positive theory of thought on the assumption that the innate forms of cognitive activity have precisely the form here denied. For a critique of Fodor's view, see P. S. Churchland 1978.)

Failures on such a large scale do not yet show that FP is a false theory, but they do move that prospect well into the range of real possibility, and they do show decisively that FP is *at best* a highly superficial theory, a partial and unpenetrating gloss on a deeper and more complex reality. Having reached this opinion, we may be forgiven for exploring the possibility that FP provides a positively misleading sketch of our internal kinematics and dynamics, one whose success is owed more to selective application and forced interpretation on our part than to genuine theoretical insight on FP's part.

A look at the history of FP does little to allay such fears, once raised. The story is one of retreat, infertility, and decadence. The presumed domain of FP used to be much larger than it is now. In primitive cultures, the behavior of most of the elements of nature were understood in intentional terms. The wind could know anger, the moon jealousy, the river generosity, the sea fury, and so forth. These were not metaphors. Sacrifices were made and auguries undertaken to placate or divine the changing passions of the gods. Despite its sterility, this animistic approach to nature has dominated our history, and it is only in the last two or three thousand years that we have restricted FP's literal interpretation to the domain of the higher animals.

Even in this preferred domain, however, both the content and the success of FP have not advanced sensibly in two or three thousand years. The FP of the Greeks is essentially the FP we use today, and we are neglibly better at explaining human behavior in its terms than was Sophocles. This is a very long period of stagnation and infertility for any theory to display, especially when faced with such an enormous backlog of anomalies and mysteries in its own explanatory domain. Perfect theories, perhaps, have no need to evolve. But FP is profoundly imperfect. Its failure to develop its resources and extend its range of success is therefore darkly curious, and one must query the integrity of its basic categories. To use Imre Lakotos's terms, FP is a stagnant or degenerating research program and has been for millennia.

Explanatory success to date is, of course, not the only dimension in which a theory can display virtue or promise. A troubled or stagnant theory may merit patience and solicitude on other grounds, for example, on grounds that it is the only theory or theoretical approach that fits well with other theories about adjacent subject matters, or the only one that promises to reduce to, or to be explained by, some established background theory whose domain encompasses the domain of the theory at issue. In sum, it may rate credence because it holds promise of theoretical integration. How does FP rate in this dimension?

Eliminative Materialism and the Propositional Attitudes

It is just here, perhaps, that FP fares poorest of all. If we approach *Homo sapiens* from the perspective of natural history and the physical sciences, we can tell a coherent story of the species' constitution, development, and behavioral capacities that encompasses particle physics, atomic and molecular theory, organic chemistry, evolutionary theory, biology, physiology, and materialistic neuroscience. That story, though still radically incomplete, is already extremely powerful, outperforming FP at many points even in its own domain. And it is deliberately and self-consciously coherent with the rest of our developing world picture. In short, the greatest theoretical synthesis in the history of the human race is currently in our hands, and parts of it already provide searching descriptions and explanations of human sensory input, neural activity, and motor control.

But FP is no part of this growing synthesis. Its intentional categories stand magnificently alone, without visible prospect of reduction to that larger corpus. A successful reduction cannot be ruled out, in my view, but the explanatory impotence and long stagnation of FP inspire little faith that its categories will find themselves neatly reflected in the framework of neuroscience. On the contrary, one is reminded of how alchemy must have looked as elemental chemistry was taking form, how Aristotelian cosmology must have looked as classical mechanics was being articulated, or how the vitalist conception of life must have looked as organic chemistry marched forward.

In sketching a fair summary of this situation, we must make a special effort to abstract from the fact that FP is a central part of our current *Lebenswelt*, and serves as the principal vehicle of our interpersonal commerce. For these facts provide FP with a conceptual inertia that goes far beyond its purely theoretical virtues. Restricting ourselves to this latter dimension, what we must say is that FP suffers explanatory failures on an epic scale, that it has been stagnant for at least twenty-five centuries, and that its categories appear (so far) to be incommensurable with, or orthogonal to, the categories of the background physical science whose long-term claim to explain human behavior seems undeniable. Any theory that meets this description must be allowed a serious candidate for outright elimination.

We can, of course, insist on no stronger conclusion at this stage. Nor is it my concern to do so. We are here exploring a possibility, and the facts demand no more, and no less, than that it be taken seriously. The distinguishing feature of the eliminative materialist is that he takes it very seriously indeed.

Arguments Against Elimination

Thus the basic rationale of eliminative materialism: FP is a theory, and quite probably a false one; let us attempt, therefore, to transcend it.

The rationale is clear and simple, but many find it uncompelling. It will be objected that FP is not, strictly speaking, an *empirical* theory; that it is not false, or at least not refutable by empirical considerations; and that it ought not or cannot be transcended in the fashion of a defunct physical theory. In what follows I shall examine these objections as they flow from the most popular and best founded of the competing positions in the philosophy of mind: functionalism.

An antipathy toward eliminative materialism arises from two distinct threads running through contemporary functionalism. The first thread concerns the *normative* character of FP, or at least of that central core of FP that treats of the propositional attitudes. FP, some will say, is a characterization of an ideal, or at least a praiseworthy, mode of internal activity. It outlines not only what it is to have and process beliefs and desires, but also (and inevitably) what it is to be rational in their administration. The ideal laid down by FP may be imperfectly achieved by empirical humans, but this does not impugn FP as a normative characterization. Nor need such failures seriously impugn FP even as a descriptive characterization, for it remains true that our activities can be both usefully and accurately understood as rational *except* for the occasional lapse due to noise, interference, or other breakdown, which defects empirical research may eventually unravel. Accordingly, though neuroscience may usefully augment it, FP has no pressing need to be displaced, even as a descriptive theory; nor could it be replaced, *qua* normative characterization, by any descriptive theory of neural mechanisms, since rationality is *defined over* propositional attitudes like beliefs and desires. FP, therefore, is here to stay.

Daniel Dennett has defended a view along these lines. (He defended it most explicitly in 1981, but this theme of Dennett's goes all the way back to his 1971.) And the view just outlined gives voice to a theme of the property dualists as well. Karl Popper and Joseph Margolis both cite the normative nature of mental and linguistic activity as a bar to their penetration by any descriptive/materialist theory (Popper 1972; Popper and Eccles 1978; Margolis 1978). I hope to deflate the appeal of such moves below.

The second thread concerns the *abstract* nature of FP. The central claim of functionalism is that the principles of FP characterize our internal states in a fashion that makes no reference to their intrinsic nature or physical constitution. Rather, they are characterized in terms of the network of causal relations they bear to one another and to sensory circumstances and overt behavior. Given its abstract specification, that internal economy may therefore be realized in a nomically heterogeneous variety of physical systems. All of them may differ, even radically, in their physical constitution, and yet at another level they will all share the same nature. This view, says Fodor, "is compatible with very strong claims about the ineliminability of mental language from behavioral theories" (1968, 116). Given the real possibility of multiple instantiations in heterogeneous physical substrates, we cannot eliminate the functional characterization in favor of any theory peculiar to one such substrate. That would preclude our being able to describe the (abstract) organization that any one instantiation shares with all the others. A functional characterization of our internal states is therefore here to stay.

This second theme, like the first, assigns a faintly stipulative character to FP, as if the onus were on the empirical systems to instantiate faithfully the functional organization that FP specifies, instead of the onus being on FP to describe faithfully the internal activities of a naturally distinct class of empirical systems. This impression is enhanced by the standard examples used to illustrate the claims of functionalism: mousetraps, valve lifters, arithmetical calculators, computers, robots, and the like. These are artifacts, constructed to fill a preconceived bill. In such cases, a failure of fit between the physical system and the relevant functional characterization impugns only the former, not the latter. The functional characterization is thus removed from empirical criticism in a way that is most unlike the case of an empirical theory. One prominent functionalist, Hilary Putnam, has argued outright that FP is not a corrigible empirical theory at all (Putnam 1964, 675, 681ff). Plainly, if FP is construed on these models, as regularly it is, the question of its empirical integrity is unlikely ever to pose itself, let alone receive a critical answer.

Although fair to some functionalists, the preceding is not entirely fair to Fodor. On his view the aim of psychology is to find the *best* functional characterization of ourselves, and what that is remains an empirical question. Also, his argument for the ineliminability of mental vocabulary from psychology does not pick out current FP in particular as ineliminable. It need claim only that *some* abstract functional characterization must be retained, some articulation or refinement of FP perhaps.

His estimate of eliminative materialism remains low, however. First, Fodor plainly thinks that there is nothing fundamentally or interestingly wrong with FP. On the contrary, FP's central conception of cognitive activity—as consisting in the manipulation of propositional attitudes—turns up as the central element in Fodor's own theory of the nature of thought (1975). And second, there remains the point that, whatever tidying up FP may or may not require, it cannot be displaced by any naturalistic theory of our physical substrate, since it is the abstract functional features of the internal states that make a person, not the chemistry of his substrate.

All of this is appealing. But almost none of it, I think, is right. Functionalism has too long enjoyed its reputation as a daring and avant-garde position. It needs to be revealed for the shortsighted and reactionary position it is.

The Conservative Nature of Functionalism

A valuable perspective on functionalism can be gained from the following story. To begin with, recall the alchemists' theory of inanimate matter. We have here a long and variegated tradition, of course, not a single theory, but our purposes will be served by a gloss.

The alchemists conceived the "inanimate" as entirely continuous with animated matter in that the sensible and behavioral properties of the various substances are due to the ensoulment of baser matter by various spirits or essences. These nonmaterial aspects were held to undergo development, just as we find growth and development in the various souls of plants, animals, and humans. The alchemist's peculiar skill lay in knowing how to seed, nourish, and bring to maturity the desired spirits enmattered in the appropriate combinations.

On one orthodoxy, the four fundamental spirits (for "*in*animate" matter) were named "mercury," "sulfur," "yellow arsenic," and "sal ammoniac." Each of these spirits was held responsible for a rough but characteristic syndrome of sensible, combinatorial, and causal properties. The spirit mercury, for example, was held responsible for certain features typical of metallic substances: their shininess, liquefiability, and so forth. Sulfur was held responsible for certain residual features typical of metals, and for those displayed by the ores from which running metal could be distilled. Any given metallic substance was a critical orchestration principally of these two spirits. A similar story held for the other two spirits, and among the four of them a certain domain of physical features and transformations was rendered intelligible and controllable.

The degree of control was always limited, of course. Or better, such prediction and control as the alchemist possessed was owed more to the manipulative lore acquired as an apprentice to a master than to any genuine insight supplied by the theory. The theory followed, more than it dictated, practice. But the theory did supply some rhyme to the practice, and in the absence of a developed alternative it was sufficiently compelling to sustain a long and stubborn tradition.

The tradition had become faded and fragmented by the time the elemental chemistry of Lavoisier and Dalton arose to replace it for good. But let us suppose that it had hung on a little longer—perhaps because the four-spirit orthodoxy had become a thumb-worn part of everyman's common sense—and let us examine the nature of the conflict between the two theories and some possible avenues of resolution.

No doubt the simplest line of resolution, and the one that historically took place, is outright displacement. The dualistic interpretation of the four essences—as immaterial spirits—will appear both feckless and unnecessary given the power of the corpuscularian taxonomy of atomic chemistry. And a reduction of the old taxonomy to the new will appear impossible, given the extent to which the comparatively toothless old theory cross-classifies things relative to the new. Elimination would thus appear the only alternative—*unless* some cunning and determined defender of the alchemical vision had the wit to suggest the following defense.

Being "ensouled by mercury," or "sulfur," or either of the other two so-called spirits, is actually a *functional* state. The first, for example, is defined by the disposition to reflect light, to liquefy under heat, to unite with other matters in the same state, and so forth. And each of these four states is related to the others, in that the syndrome for each varies as a function of which of the other three states is also instantiated by the same substrate. Thus the level of description comprehended by the alchemical vocabulary is abstract: *various* material substances, suitably "ensouled," can display the features of a metal, for example, or even of gold specifically. For it is the total syndrome of occurrent and causal properties that matters, not the corpuscularian details of the substrate. Alchemy, it is concluded, comprehends a level of organization in reality that is distinct from, and irreducible to, the organization found at the level of corpuscularian chemistry.

This view might have had considerable appeal. After all, it spares alchemists the burden of defending immaterial souls that come and go; it frees them from having to meet the very strong demands of a naturalistic reduction; and it spares them the shock and confusion of outright elimination. Alchemical theory emerges as basically all right! Nor need the alchemists appear too obviously stubborn or dogmatic in this. Alchemy as it stands, they concede, may need substantial tidying up, and experience must be our guide. But we need not fear its naturalistic displacement, they remind us, since it is the peculiar orchestration of the syndromes of occurrent and causal properties that makes a piece of matter gold, not the idiosyncratic details of its corpuscularian substrate. A further circumstance would have made this claim even more plausible. For the fact is, the alchemists *did* know how to make gold, in this relevantly weakened sense of 'gold', and they could do so in a variety of ways. Their "gold" was never as perfect, alas, as the "gold" nurtured in nature's womb, but what mortal can expect to match the skills of nature herself?

What this story shows is that it is at least possible for the constellation of moves, claims, and defenses characteristic of functionalism to constitute an outrage against reason and truth, and to do so with a plausibility that is frightening. Alchemy is a terrible theory, well deserving of its complete elimination, and the defense of it just explored is reactionary, obfuscatory, retrograde, and wrong. But in historical context, that defense might have seemed wholly sensible, even to reasonable people.

The alchemic example is a deliberately transparent case of what might be called "the functionalist stratagem," and other cases are easy to imagine. A cracking good defense of the phlogiston theory of combustion can also be constructed along these lines. Construe being highly phlogisticated and being dephlogisticated as functional states defined by certain syndromes of causal dispositions; point to the great variety of natural substrates capable of combustion and calxification; claim an irreducible functional integrity for what has proved to lack any natural integrity; and bury the remaining defects under a pledge to contrive improvements. A similar recipe will provide new life for the four humors of medieval medicine, for the *archeus* or vital essence of premodern biology, and so forth.

If its application in these other cases is any guide, the functionalist stratagem is a smoke screen for the preservation of error and confusion. Whence derives our assurance that in contemporary journals the same charade is not being played out on behalf of FP? The parallel with the case of alchemy is in all other respects distressingly complete, right down to the parallel between the search for artificial gold and the search for artificial intelligence!

Let me not be misunderstood on this last point. Both aims are worthy aims: thanks to nuclear physics, artificial (but real) gold is finally within our means, if only in submicroscopic quantities, and artificial (but real) intelligence eventually will be. But just as the careful orchestration of superficial syndromes was the wrong way to produce genuine gold, so may the careful orchestration of superficial syndromes be the wrong way to produce genuine intelligence. Just as with gold, what may be required is that our science penetrate to the underlying *natural* kind that gives rise to the total syndrome directly.

In summary, when confronted with the explanatory impotence, stagnant history, and systematic isolation of the intentional idioms of FP, it is not an adequate or responsive defense to insist that those idioms are abstract, functional, and irreducible in character. For one thing, this same defense could have been mounted with comparable plausibility no matter *what* haywire network of internal states our folklore had ascribed to us. And for another, the defense assumes essentially what is at issue: it assumes that it is the intentional idioms of FP, plus or minus a bit, that express the *important* features shared by all cognitive systems. But they may not. Certainly it is wrong to assume that they do, and then argue against the possibility of a materialistic displacement on grounds that it must describe matters at a level that is distinct from the important level. This just begs the question in favor of the older framework.

Finally, it is very important to point out that eliminative materialism is strictly *consistent* with the claim that the essence of a cognitive system resides in the abstract functional organization of its internal states. The eliminative materialist is not committed to the idea that the correct account of cognition *must* be a naturalistic account, though he may be forgiven for exploring the possibility. What he does hold is that the correct account of cognition, whether functionalistic or naturalistic, will bear about as much resemblance to FP as modern chemistry bears to four-spirit alchemy.

Let us now try to deal with the argument, against eliminative materialism, from the normative dimension of FP. This can be dealt with rather swiftly, I believe.

First, the fact that the regularities ascribed by the intentional core of FP are predicated on certain logical regularities among propositions is not by itself grounds for claiming anything essentially normative about FP. To draw a relevant parallel, the fact that the regularities ascribed by the classical gas law are predicated on arithmetical relations between numbers does not imply anything essentially normative about the classical gas law. And logical relations between propositions are as much an objective matter of abstract fact as are arithmetical relations between numbers. In this respect, the law

(4) $(x)(p)(q)[((x$ believes that $p)$ & (x believes that (if p then $q)))$
$\supset$ (barring confusion, distraction, etc., x believes that $q)]$

is entirely on a par with the classical gas law

(6) $(x)(P)(V)(\mu)[((x$ has a pressure $P)$
& (x has a volume V) & (x has a quantity μ))
$\supset$ (barring very high pressure or density,
x has a temperature of $PV/\mu R)]$.

A normative dimension enters only because we happen to *value* most of the patterns ascribed by FP. But we do not value all of them. Consider

(7) $(x)(p)[((x$ desires with all his heart that $p)$
& (x learns that $\sim p$))
$\supset$ (barring unusual strength of character,
x is shattered that $\sim p)]$.

Moreover, and as with normative convictions generally, fresh insight may motivate major changes in what we value.

Second, the laws of FP ascribe to us only a very minimal and truncated rationality, not an ideal rationality as some have suggested. The rationality characterized by the set of all FP laws falls well short of an ideal rationality. This is not surprising. We have no clear or finished conception of ideal rationality anyway; certainly the ordinary man does not. Accordingly, it is just not plausible to suppose that the explanatory failures from which FP suffers are due primarily to human failure to live up to the standards it provides. Quite to the contrary, the conception of rationality it provides appears limping and superficial, especially when compared with the dialectical complexity of our scientific history or with the ratiocinative virtuosity displayed by any child.

Third, even if our current conception of rationality—and more generally, of cognitive virtue—*is* largely constituted within the sentential/

propositional framework of FP, there is no guarantee that this framework is adequate to the deeper and more accurate account of cognitive virtue that is clearly needed. Even if we concede the categorial integrity of FP, at least as applied to language-using humans, it remains far from clear that the basic parameters of intellectual virtue are to be found at the categorial level comprehended by the propositional attitudes. After all, language use is something that is learned, by a brain already capable of vigorous cognitive activity; language use is acquired as only one among a great variety of learned manipulative skills; and it is mastered by a brain that evolution has shaped for a great many functions, language use being only the very latest and perhaps the least of them. Against the background of these facts, language use appears as an extremely peripheral activity, as a biologically idiosyncratic mode of social interaction that is mastered thanks to the versatility and power of a more basic mode of activity. Why accept, then, a theory of cognitive activity that models its elements on the elements of human language? And why assume that the fundamental parameters of intellectual virtue are, or can be defined over, the elements at this superficial level?

A serious advance in our appreciation of cognitive virtue would thus seem to *require* that we go beyond FP, that we transcend the poverty of FP's conception of rationality by transcending its propositional kinematics entirely, by developing a deeper and more general kinematics of cognitive activity, and by distinguishing within this new framework which of the kinematically possible modes of activity are to be valued and encouraged (as more efficient, reliable, productive, or whatever). Eliminative materialism does not imply the end of our normative concerns. It implies only that they will have to be reconstituted at a more revealing level of understanding, the level that a matured neuroscience will provide.

What a theoretically informed future might hold in store for us, we shall now turn to explore. Not because we can foresee matters with any special clarity, but because it is important to try to break the grip on our imagination held by the propositional kinematics of FP. As far as the present section is concerned, we may summarize our conclusion as follows. FP is nothing more and nothing less than a culturally entrenched theory of how we and the higher animals work. It has no special features that make it empirically invulnerable, no unique functions that make it irreplaceable, no special status of any kind whatsoever. We shall turn a skeptical ear then, to any special pleading on its behalf. . . .

References

Churchland, P. M. (1970). The logical character of action explanations. *Philosophical Review* 79, 214–236.

Churchland, P. M. (1979). *Scientific realism and the plasticity of mind*. Cambridge: Cambridge University Press.

Churchland, P. S. (1978). Fodor on language learning. *Synthese* 38, 149–159.

Dennett, D. C. (1971). Intentional systems. *Journal of Philosophy* 68, 87–106.

Dennett, D. C. (1981). Three kinds of intentional psychology. In R. Healey, ed., *Reduction, Time, and Reality*. Cambridge: Cambridge University Press.

Feyerabend, P. K. (1963). Materialism and the mind-body problem. *Review of Metaphysics* 17, 49–66.

Fodor, J. A. (1968). *Psychological explanation*. New York: Random House.

Fodor, J. A. (1975). *The language of thought*. New York: Crowell.

Grover, D., J. Camp, and N. Belnap (1975). A prosentential theory of truth. *Philosophical Studies* 27, 73–125.

Margolis, J. (1978). *Persons and minds*. Dordrecht: Reidel.

Popper, K. R. (1972). *Objective knowledge*. New York: Oxford University Press.

Popper, K. R., and J. Eccles (1978). *The self and its brain*. New York: Springer Verlag.

Putnam, H. (1964). Robots: Machines or artificially created life? *Journal of Philosophy* 61, 668–691.

Rorty, R. (1965). Mind-body identity, privacy, and categories. *Review of Metaphysics* 19, 24–54.

13 Fodor's Guide to Mental Representation: The Intelligent Auntie's Vade-Mecum

Jerry A. Fodor

It rained for weeks and we were all *so* tired of ontology, but there didn't seem to be much else to do. Some of the children started to sulk and pull the cat's tail. It was going to be an *awful* afternoon until Uncle Wilifred thought of Mental Representations (which was a game that we hadn't played for *years*) and everybody got *very* excited and we jumped up and down and waved our hands and all talked at once and had a perfectly *lovely* romp. But Auntie said that she couldn't stand the noise and there would be tears before bedtime if we didn't please calm down.

Auntie rather disapproves of what is going on in the Playroom, and you can't entirely blame her. Ten or 15 years of philosophical discussion of mental representation has produced a considerable appearance of disorder. Every conceivable position seems to have been occupied, along with some whose conceivability it is permissible to doubt. And every view that anyone has mooted, someone else has undertaken to refute. This does *not* strike Auntie as constructive play. She sighs for the days when well-brought-up philosophers of mind kept themselves occupied for hours on end analyzing their behavioral dispositions.

But the chaotic appearances are actually misleading. A rather surprising amount of agreement has emerged, if not about who's winning, at least about how the game has to be played. In fact, everybody involved concurs, pretty much, on what the options are. They differ in their hunches about which of the options it would be profitable to exercise. The resulting noise is of these intuitions clashing. In this paper, I want to make as much of the consensus as I can explicit; both by way of reassuring Auntie and in order to provide new participants with a quick guide to the game: Who's where and how did they get there? Since it's very nearly true that you can locate all the players by their answers to quite a small number of diagnostic questions, I shall organize the discussion along those lines. What follows is a short projective test of the sort that self-absorbed persons use to reveal their hitherto unrecognized proclivities. I hope for a great success in California.

Reprinted from MIND Volume 94, 55–97 (1985) by permission of Oxford University Press and the author.

First Question: How Do You Feel about Propositional Attitudes?

The contemporary discussion about mental representation is intimately and intricately involved with the question of Realism about propositional attitudes. Since a goal of this essay is to locate the issues about mental representation with respect to other questions in the philosophy of mind, we commence by setting out this relation in several of its aspects.

The natural home of the propositional attitudes is in "commonsense" (or "belief/desire") psychological explanation. If you ask the Man on the Clapham Omnibus what precisely he is doing there, he will tell you a story along the following lines: "I wanted to get home (to work, to Auntie's) and I have reason to believe that there—or somewhere near it—is where this omnibus is going." It is, in short, untendentious that people regularly account for their voluntary behavior by citing beliefs and desires that they entertain; and that, if their behavior is challenged, they regularly defend it by maintaining the rationality of the beliefs ("Because it *says* it's going to Clapham") and the probity of the desires ("Because it's *nice* visiting Auntie"). That, however, is probably as far as the Clapham Omnibus will take us. What comes next is a philosophical gloss—and, eventually, a philosophical theory.

First Philosophical Gloss

When the ordinary chap says that he's doing what he is because he has the beliefs and desires that he does, it is reasonable to read the 'because' as a *causal* 'because'—whatever, exactly, a causal 'because' may be. At a minimum, common sense seems to require belief/desire explanations to support counterfactuals in ways that are familiar in causal explanation at large: If, for example, it is true that Psmith did A because he believed B and desired C, then it must be that Psmith would *not* have done A if either he had not believed B or he had not desired C. (Ceteris paribus, it goes without saying.) Common sense also probably takes it that if Psmith did A because he believed B and desired C, then—ceteris paribus again—believing B and desiring C is causally sufficient for doing A. (However, common sense does get confused about this since—though believing B and desiring C was what caused Psmith to do A— still it is common sense that Psmith could have believed B and desired C and *not* done A had he so decided. It is a question of some interest whether common sense can have it both ways.) Anyhow, to a first approximation the commonsense view is that there is mental causation, and that mental causes are subsumed by counterfactual–supporting generalizations of which the practical syllogism is perhaps the paradigm.

Closely connected is the following: Everyman's view seems to be that propositional attitudes cause (not only behavior but also) other propositional attitudes. Thoughts cause desires (so that thinking about visiting

Auntie makes one want to) and—perhaps a little more tendentiously—the other way around as well (so that the wish is often father to the thought, according to the commonsense view of mental genealogy). In the paradigm mental process—viz. thinking—thoughts give rise to one another and eventuate in the fixation of beliefs. That is what Sherlock Holmes was supposed to be so good at.

Second Philosophical Gloss

Common sense has it that beliefs and desires are semantically evaluable; that they have *satisfaction-conditions*. Roughly, the satisfaction-condition for a belief is the state of affairs in virtue of which that belief is true or false and the satisfaction-condition for a desire is the state of affairs in virtue of which that desire is fulfilled or frustrated. Thus, 'that it continues to rain' makes true the belief that it is raining and frustrates the desire that the rain should stop. This could stand a lot more sharpening, but it will do for the purposes at hand.

It will have occurred to the reader that there are other ways of glossing commonsense belief/desire psychology. And that, even if this way of glossing it is right, commonsense belief/desire psychology may be in need of emendation. Or cancellation. Quite so, but my purpose isn't to defend or criticize; I just want to establish a point of reference. I propose to say that someone is a *Realist* about propositional attitudes if (a) he holds that there are mental states whose occurrences and interactions cause behavior and do so, moreover, in ways that respect (at least to an approximation) the generalizations of commonsense belief/desire psychology; and (b) he holds that these same causally efficacious mental states are also semantically evaluable.

So much for commonsense psychological explanation. The connection with our topic is this: the full-blown Representational Theory of Mind (hereinafter RTM, about which a great deal presently) purports to explain how there *could be* states that have the semantical and causal properties that propositional attitudes are commonsensically supposed to have. In effect, RTM proposes an account of what the propositional attitudes *are*. So, the further you are from Realism about propositional attitudes, the dimmer the view of RTM that you are likely to take.

Quite a lot of the philosophical discussion that's relevant to RTM, therefore, concerns the status and prospects of commonsense intentional psychology. More, perhaps, than is generally realized. For example, we'll see presently that some of the philosophical worries about RTM derive from scepticism about the semantical properties of mental representations. Putnam, in particular, has been explicit in questioning whether coherent sense could be made of such properties. (See Putnam 1983, 1986.) I have my doubts about the seriousness of these worries (see Fodor 1985); but the present point is that they are, in any event, misdirected as arguments against RTM. If there is something wrong with meaning, what that shows is something *very* radical, viz. that there is something wrong with propositional attitudes (a moral, by the way, that Quine, Davidson, and Stich, among others, have drawn explicitly). That, and *not* RTM, is surely the ground on which this action should be fought.

If, in short, you think that common sense is just plain *wrong* about the aetiology of behavior—i.e., that there is *nothing* that has the causal and semantic properties that common sense attributes to the attitudes—then the questions that RTM purports to answer don't so much as arise for you. You won't care much what the attitudes are if you take the view that there aren't any. Many philosophers do take this view and are thus united in their indifference to RTM. Among these Anti-Realists there are, however, interesting differences in motivation and tone of voice. Here, then, are some ways of not being a Realist about beliefs and desires.

First Anti-Realist Option

You could take an *instrumentalist* view of intentional explanation. You could hold that though there are, *strictly speaking*, no such things as belief and desires, still talking as though there were some often leads to confirmed behavioral predictions. Everyman is therefore licensed to talk that way—to adopt, as one says, the intentional stance—so long as he doesn't take the ontological commitments of belief/desire psychology literally. (Navigators talk geocentric astronomy for convenience, and nobody holds it against them; it gets them where they want to go.) The great virtue of instrumentalism—here as elsewhere—is that you get all the goodness and suffer none of the pain: you get to use propositional-attitude psychology to make behavioral predictions; you get to 'accept' all the intentional explanations that it is convenient to accept; but you don't have to answer hard questions about what the attitudes *are*.

There is, however, a standard objection to instrumentalism (again, here as elsewhere): it's hard to explain why belief/desire psychology works so well if belief/desire psychology is, as a matter of fact, not true. I propose to steer clear, throughout this essay, of general issues in the philosophy of science; in particular of issues about the status of scientific theories at large. But—as Putnam, Boyd and others have emphasized—there is surely a presumptive inference from the predictive successes of a theory to its truth; still more so when (unlike geocentric astronomy) it is the *only* predictively successful theory in the field. It's not, to put it mildly, obvious why this presumption shouldn't militate in favor of a Realist—as against an instrumentalist—construal of belief/desire explanations.

The most extensively worked-out version of instrumentalism about the attitudes in the recent literature is surely owing to D. C. Dennett. (See the papers in Dennett (1978a), especially the essay "Intentional

Systems.") Dennett confronts the 'if it isn't true, why does it work?' problem (Dennett 1981), but I find his position obscure. Here's how I *think* it goes: (a) belief/desire explanations rest on very comprehensive rationality assumptions; it's only fully rational systems that such explanations could be literally true of. These rationality assumptions are, however, generally contrary to fact; *that's* why intentional explanations can't be better than instrumental. On the other hand, (b) intentional explanations *work* because we apply them only to evolutionary successful (or other "designed") systems; and if the behavior of a system didn't at least *approximate* rationality it wouldn't *be* evolutionarily successful; what it would be is extinct.

There is a lot about this that's problematic. To begin with, it's unclear whether there really is a rationality assumption implicit in intentional explanation and whether, it there is, the rationality assumption that's required is so strong as to be certainly false. Dennett says in "Intentional Systems" (Dennett 1978c) that unless we assume rationality, we get no behavioral predictions out of belief/desire psychology since without rationality any behavior is compatible with any beliefs and desires. Clearly, however, you don't need to assume *much* rationality if all you want is *some* predictivity; perhaps you don't need to assume more rationality than organisms actually have.

Perhaps, in short, the rationality that Dennett says that natural selection guarantees is enough to support *literal* (not just instrumental) intentional ascription. At a minimum, there seems to be a clash between Dennett's principles (a) and (b) since if it *follows from* evolutionary theory that successful organisms are pretty rational, then it's hard to see how attributions of rationality to successful organisms can be construed purely instrumentally (as merely a 'stance' that we adopt towards systems whose behavior we seek to predict).

Finally, if you admit that it's a matter of fact that some agents are rational to some degree, then you have to face the hard question of how they *can* be. After all, not *everything* that's "designed" is rational even to a degree. Bricks aren't, for example; they have the wrong kind of structure. The question what sort of structure is required for rationality does, therefore, rather suggest itself and it's very unclear that that question can be answered without talking about structures of beliefs and desires; intentional psychology is the only candidate we have so far for a theory of how rationality is achieved. This suggests—what I think is true but won't argue for here—that the rational systems are a species of the intentional ones rather than the other way around. If that is so, then it is misguided to appeal to rationality in the analysis of intentionality since, in the order of explanation, the latter is the more fundamental notion. With what one thing and another, it does seem possible to doubt that a coherent instrumentalism about the attitudes is going to be forthcoming.

Second Anti-Realist Option

You could take the view that belief/desire psychology is just plain false and skip the instrumentalist trimmings. On this way of telling the Anti-Realist story, belief/desire psychology is in competition with alternative accounts of the aetiology of behavior and should be judged in the same way that the alternatives are; by its predictive successes, by the plausibility of its ontological commitments, and by its coherence with the rest of the scientific enterprise. No doubt the predictive successes of belief/desire explanations are pretty impressive—especially when they are allowed to make free use of ceteris paribus clauses. But when judged by a second and third criteria, commonsense psychology proves to be a *bad* theory; 'stagnant science' is the preferred epithet (see Paul Churchland 1981; Stich 1983). What we ought therefore to do is get rid of it and find something better.

There is, however, some disagreement as to what something better would be like. What matters here is how you feel about Functionalism. So let's have that be our next diagnostic question.

(Is everybody still with us? In case you're not, see the decision tree in figure 13.1 for the discussion so far. Auntie's motto: a place for every person; every person in his place.)

Second Question: How Do You Feel about Functionalism?

(This is a twice-told tale, so I'll be quick. For a longer review, see Fodor 1981b; Fodor, 1981c.)

It looked, in the early 1960s, as though anybody who wanted psychology to be compatible with a physicalistic ontology had a choice between some or other kind of *behaviorism* and some or other kind of *property-identity theory.* For a variety of reasons, neither of these options seemed very satisfactory (in fact, they still don't) so a small tempest brewed in the philosophical teapot.

What came of it was a new account of the type/token relation for psychological states: psychological-state tokens were to be assigned to

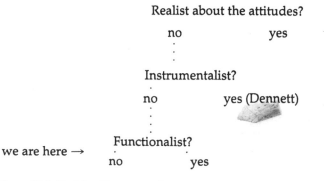

Figure 13.1 Decision Tree, stage 1.

psychological-state types *solely* by reference to their causal relations to proximal stimuli ('inputs'), to proximal responses ('outputs'), and to one another. The advertising claimed two notable virtues for this theory: first, it was *compatible* with physicalism in that it permitted tokenings of psychological states to be identical to tokenings of physical states (and thus to enjoy whatever causal properties physical states are supposed to have). Second, it permitted tokens of one and the same psychological-state type to differ arbitrarily in their physical kind. This comforted the emerging intuition that the natural domain for psychological theory might be physically heterogeneous, including a motley of people, animals, Martians (always in the philosophical literature, assumed to be silicon based), and computing machines.

Functionalism, so construed, was greeted with audible joy by the new breed of 'Cognitive Scientists' and has clearly become the received ontological doctrine in that discipline. For, if Functionalism is true, then there is plausibly a *level of explanation* between commonsense belief/desire psychology, on the one hand, and neurological (circuit-theoretic; generally 'hard-science') explanation on the other. 'Cognitive Scientists' could plausibly formulate their enterprise as the construction of theories pitched at that level. Moreover, it was possible to tell a reasonable and aesthetically gratifying story about the relations *between* the levels: commonsense belief/desire explanations *reduce* to explanations articulated in terms of functional states (at least the true ones do) because, according to Functionalism, beliefs and desires *are* functional states. And, for each (true) psychological explanation, there will be a corresponding story, to be told in hard-science terms, about how the functional states that it postulates are "realized" in the system under study. Many different hard-science stories may correspond to one and the same functional explanation since, as we saw, the criteria for the tokening of functional states abstract from the physical character of the tokens. (The most careful and convincing Functionalist manifestos I know are Block 1980; and Cummins 1983; q.v.)

Enthusiasm for Functionalism was (is) not, however, universal. For example, viewed from a neuroscientist's perspective (or from the perspective of a hard-line "type-physicalist") Functionalism may appear to be merely a rationale for making do with bad psychology. A picture many neuroscientists have is that, if there really are beliefs and desires (or memories, or percepts, or mental images or whatever else the psychologist may have in his grab bag), it ought to be possible to "find" them in the brain; where what *that* requires is that two tokens of the same *psychological* kind (today's desire to visit Auntie, say, and yesterday's) should correspond to two tokens of the same *neurological* kind (today's firing of neuron #535, say, and yesterday's). Patently, Functionalism relaxes that requirement; relaxes it, indeed, to the point of invisibility. Functionalism just *is* the doctrine that the psychologist's theoretical taxonomy doesn't need to look "natural" from the point of view of any lower-level science. This seems to some neuroscientists, and to some of their philosopher friends, like letting psychologists get away with murder. (See, for example, Churchland 1981, which argues that Functionalism could have "saved" alchemy if only the alchemists had been devious enough to devise it.) There is, for once, something tangible at issue here: who has the right theoretical vocabulary for explaining behavior determines who should get the grants.

So much for Functionalism except to add that one can, of course, combine *accepting* the Functionalist ontology with *rejecting* the reduction of belief/desire explanations to functional ones (for example because you think that, though *some* Functionalist psychological explanations are true, no commonsense belief/desire psychological explanations are). Bearing this proviso in mind, we can put some more people in their places: if you are Anti-Realist (and anti-instrumentalist) about belief/desire psychology *and* you think there is no Functional level of explanation, then probably you think that behavioral science is (or, anyhow, ought to be) neuroscience.[1] (A fortiori, you will be no partisan of RTM, which is, of course, way over on the other side of the decision tree.) The Churchlands are the paradigm inhabitants of this niche. On the other hand, if you combine eliminativist sentiments about propositional attitudes with enthusiasm for the functional individuation of mental states, then you anticipate the eventual *replacement* of commonsense belief/desire explanations by theories couched in the vocabulary of a Functionalist psychology; replacement rather than *reduction*. You are thus led to write books with such titles as *From Folk Psychology to Cognitive Science* and are almost certainly identical to Stephen Stich.

One more word about Anti-Realism. It may strike you as odd that, whereas instrumentalists hold that belief/desire psychology works so well that we can't do anything without it, eliminativists hold that it works so badly ("stagnant science" and all that) that we can't do anything *with* it. Why, you may ask, don't these Anti-Realists get their acts together?

This is not, however, a real paradox. Instrumentalists can agree with eliminativists that *for the purposes of scientific/serious explanation* the attitudes have to be dispensed with. And eliminativists can agree with instrumentalists that for *practical* purposes, the attitudes do seem quite indispensable. In fact—and here's the point I want to stress just now— what largely motivates Anti-Realism is something deeper than the empirical speculation that belief/desire explanations won't pan out as science; it's the sense that there is something intrinsically wrong with the intentional. This is so important that I propose to leave it to the very end.

Now for the other side of the decision tree. (Presently we'll get to RTM.)

If you are a Realist about propositional attitudes, then of course you think that there are beliefs and desires. Now, on this side of the tree too you get to decide whether to be a Functionalist or not. If you are not, then you are probably John Searle, and you drop off the edge of this paper. My own view is that RTM, construed as a species of Functionalist psychology, offers the best Realist account of the attitudes that is currently available; but this view is—to put it mildly—not universally shared. There are philosophers (many of whom like Searle, Dreyfus, and Haugeland are more or less heavily invested in Phenomenology) who are hyper-Realist about the attitudes but deeply unenthusiastic about both Functionalism and RTM. It is not unusual for such theorists to hold (a) that there *is* no currently available, satisfactory answer to the question 'how could there be things that satisfy the constraints that common sense places upon the attitudes?'; and (b) that finding an answer to this question is, in any event, not the philosopher's job. (Maybe it is the psychologist's job, or the neuroscientist's. See Dreyfus 1979; Haugeland 1978; Searle 1980.)

For how the decision tree looks now, see figure 13.2.

If you think that there are beliefs and desires, and you think that they are functional states, then you get to answer the following diagnostic question:

Third Question: Are Propositional Attitudes Monadic Functional States?

This may strike you as a *silly* question. For, you may say, since propositional attitudes are by definition relations to propositions, it follows that propositional attitudes are by definition not monadic. A propositional attitude is, to a first approximation, a *pair* of a proposition and a set of intentional systems, viz., the set of intentional systems which bear that attitude to that proposition.

That would seem to be reasonable enough. But the current (Naturalistic) consensus is that if you've gone this far you will have to go further. Something has to be said about the place of the semantic and the intentional in the natural order; it won't do to have unexplicated

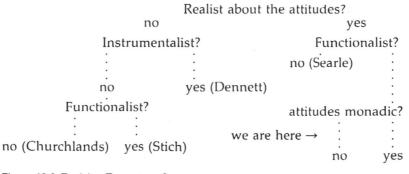

Figure 13.2 Decision Tree, stage 2.

"relations to propositions" at the foundations of the philosophy of mind.

Just *why* it won't do—precisely what physicalist or Naturalist scruples it would outrage—is, to be sure, not very clear. Presumably the issue isn't Nominalism, for why raise that issue *here*; if physicists have numbers to play with, why shouldn't psychologists have propositions? And it can't be worries about individuation since distinguishing propositions is surely no harder than distinguishing propositional attitudes and, for better or worse, we're committed to the latter on this side of the decision tree. A more plausible scruple—one I am inclined to take seriously—objects to unreduced *epistemic* relations like *grasping* propositions. One really doesn't want psychology to presuppose any of *those*; first because epistemic relations are preeminently what psychology is supposed to *explain,* and second for fear of "ontological danglers." It's not that there aren't propositions, and it's not that there aren't graspings of them; it's rather that graspings of propositions aren't plausible candidates for ultimate stuff. If they're real, they must be really something else.

Anyhow, one might as well sing the songs one knows. There *is* a reductive story to tell about *what it is* for an attitude to have a proposition as its object. So, metaphysical issues to one side, why not tell it?

The story goes as follows. Propositional attitudes are monadic, functional states of organisms. Functional states, you will recall, are type-individuated by reference to their (actual and potential) causal relations; you know everything that is essential about a functional state when you know which causal generalizations subsume it. Since, in the psychological case, the generalizations that count for type individuation are the ones that relate mental states to one another, a census of mental states would imply a network of causal interrelations. To specify such a network would be to constrain the nomologically possible mental histories of an organism; the network for a given organism would exhibit the possible patterns of causal interaction among its mental states (insofar, as least, as such patterns of interaction are relevant to the type individuation of the states). Of necessity, the actual life of the organism would appear as a path through this network.

Given the Functionalist assurance of individuation by causal role, we can assume that each mental state can be identified with a node in such a network: for each mental state there is a corresponding causal role and for each causal role there is a corresponding node. (To put the same point slightly differently, each mental state can be associated with a formula—e.g., a Ramsey sentence, see Block, 1980—that uniquely determines its location in the network by specifying its potentialities for causal interaction with each of the other mental states.) Notice, however, that while this gives a Functionalist sense to the individuation of propositional attitudes, it does not, in and of itself, say what it is for a propositional attitude to have the propositional content that it has. The present proposal is to remedy this defect by reducing the notion of propositional content to the notion of causal role.

So far, we have a network of mental states defined by their causal interrelations. But notice that there is also a network generated by the *inferential* relations that hold among *propositions*; and it is plausible that its inferential relations are among the properties that each proposition has essentially. Thus, it is presumably a noncontingent property of the proposition that Auntie is shorter than Uncle Wilifred that it entails the proposition that Uncle Wilifred is taller than Auntie. And it is surely a noncontingent property of the proposition that $P \& Q$ that it entails the proposition that P and the proposition that Q. It may also be that there are evidential relations that are, in the relevant sense, noncontingent; for example, it may be constitutive of the proposition that many of the G's are F that it is, ceteris paribus, evidence for the proposition that all of the G's are F. If it be so, then so be it.

The basic idea is that, given the two networks—the causal and the inferential—we can establish partial isomorphisms between them. Under such an isomorphism, *the causal role of a propositional attitude mirrors the semantic role of the proposition that is its object.* So, for example, there is the proposition that John left and Mary wept; and it is partially constitutive of this proposition that it has the following semantic relations: it entails the proposition that John left; it entails the proposition that Mary wept; it is entailed by the pair of propositions {John left, Mary wept}; it entails the proposition that somebody did something; it entails the proposition that John did something; it entails the proposition that either it's raining or John left and Mary wept . . . and so forth. Likewise there are, among the potential episodes in an organism's mental life, states which we may wish to construe as: (S^1) having the belief that John left and Mary wept; (S^2) having the belief that John left; (S^3) having the belief that Mary wept; (S^4) having the belief that somebody did something; (S^5) having the belief that either it's raining or John left and Mary wept . . . and so forth. The crucial point is that it constrains the assignment of propositional contents to these mental states that the latter exhibit an appropriate pattern of causal relations. In particular, it must be true (if only under idealization) that being in S^1 tends to cause the organism to be in S^2 and S^3; that being in S^1 tends to cause the organism to be in S^4; that being (simultaneously) in states (S^2, S^3) tends—very strongly, one supposes—to cause the organism to be in state S^1, that being in state S^1 tends to cause the organism to be in state S^5 (as does being in state S^6, viz. the state of believing that it's raining). And so forth.

In short, we can make nonarbitrary assignments of propositions as the objects of propositional attitudes because there is this isomorphism between the network generated by the semantic relations among propositions and the network generated by the causal relations among mental states. The assignment is nonarbitrary precisely in that it is constrained to preserve the isomorphism. And because the isomorphism is perfectly objective (which is not, however, to say that it is perfectly unique; see below), knowing what proposition gets assigned to a mental state—what the object of an attitude is—is knowing something useful. For, within the limits of the operative idealization, *you can deduce the causal consequences of being in a mental state from the semantic relations of its propositional object*. To know that John thinks that Mary wept is to know that it's highly probable that he thinks that somebody wept. To know that Sam thinks that it is raining is to know that it's highly probable that he thinks that somebody wept. To know that Sam thinks that it is raining is to know that it's highly probable that he thinks that either it is raining or that John left and Mary wept. To know that Sam thinks that it's raining and that Sam thinks that if it's raining it is well to carry an umbrella is to be far along the way to predicting a piece of Sam's behavior.

It may be, according to the present story, that preserving isomorphism between the causal and the semantic networks is *all* that there is to the assignment of contents to mental states; that nothing constrains the attribution of propositional objects to propositional attitudes *except* the requirement that isomorphism be preserved. But one need not hold that that is so. On the contrary, many—perhaps most—philosophers who like the isomorphism story are attracted by so-called 'two-factor' theories, according to which what determines the semantics of an attitude is not just its functional role but also its causal connections to objects 'in the world'. (This is, notice, still a species of functionalism since it's still causal role alone that counts for the type individuation of mental states; but two-factor theories acknowledge as semantically relevant 'external' causal relations, relations between, for example, states of the organism and *distal* stimuli. It is these mind-to-world causal relations that are supposed to determine the denotational semantics of an attitude: what it's about and what its truth-conditions are.) There are serious issues in this area, but for our purposes—we are, after all, just sightseeing—we can group the two-factor theorists with the pure functional-role semanticists.

The story I've just told you is, I think, the standard current construal of Realism about propositional attitudes.[2] I propose, therefore, to call it Standard Realism (SR for convenience). As must be apparent, SR is a compound of two doctrines: a claim about the 'internal' structure of attitudes (viz., that they are *monadic* functional states) and a claim about the source of their semantical properties (viz., that some or all of such properties arise from isomorphisms between the causal role of mental states and the implicational structure of propositions). Now, though they are usually held together, it seems clear that these claims are orthogonal. One could opt for monadic mental states without functional-role semantics; or one could opt for functional-role semantics together with some nonmonadic account of the polyadicity of the attitudes. My own view is that SR should be rejected wholesale: that it is wrong about both the structure *and* the semantics of the attitudes. But—such is the confusion and perversity of my colleagues—this view is widely thought to be eccentric. The standard Realistic alternative to Standard Realism holds that SR is right about functional semantics but wrong about monadicity. I propose to divide these issues: monadicity first, semantics at the end.

If, in the present intellectual atmosphere, you are Realist and Functionalist about the attitudes, but you don't think that the attitudes are *monadic* functional states, then probably you think that to have a belief or a desire—or whatever—is to be related in a certain way to a Mental Representation. According to the canonical formulation of this view: for any organism O and for any proposition P, there is a relation R and a mental representation MP such that: MP means that (expresses the proposition that) P; and O believes that P iff O bears R to MP. (And similarly, O desires that P iff O bears some *different* relation, R', to MP. And so forth. For elaboration, see Fodor 1975, 1978; Field 1978.) This is, of course, the doctrine I've been calling full-blown RTM. So we come, at last, to the bottom of the decision tree. (See figure 13.3.)

As compared with SR, RTM assumes the heavier burden of ontological commitment. It quantifies not just over such mental states as be-

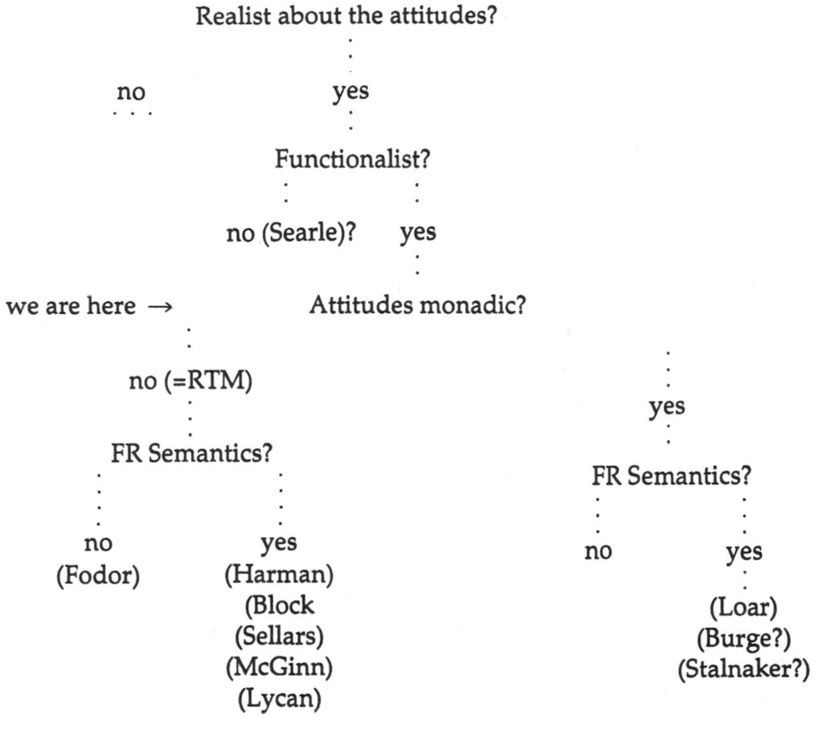

Realist about the attitudes?

no   yes

Functionalist?

no (Searle)?   yes

we are here →   Attitudes monadic?

no (=RTM)   yes

FR Semantics?   FR Semantics?

no   yes   no   yes
(Fodor)   (Harman)   (Loar)
         (Block   (Burge?)
         (Sellars)   (Stalnaker?)
         (McGinn)
         (Lycan)

Figure 13.3 Decision Tree, stage 3.

lieving that P and desiring that Q but also over mental representations; symbols in a "language of thought." The burden of proof is thus on RTM. (Auntie holds that it doesn't matter who has the burden of proof because the choice between SR and RTM isn't a *philosophical* issue. But I don't know how she tells. Or why she cares.) There are two sorts of considerations that, in my view, argue persuasively for RTM. I think they are the implicit sources of the Cognitive Science community's commitment to the mental representation construct.

First Argument for RTM: Productivity and Constituency

The collection of states of mind is productive: for example, the thoughts that one actually entertains in the course of a mental life comprise a relatively unsystematic subset drawn from a vastly larger variety of thoughts that one could have entertained had an occasion for them arisen. For example, it has probably never occurred to you before that no grass grows on kangaroos. But, once your attention is drawn to the point, it's an idea that you are quite capable of entertaining, one which, in fact, you are probably inclined to endorse. A theory of the attitudes ought to account for this productivity; it ought to make clear what it is about beliefs and desires in virtue of which they constitute open-ended families.

Notice that Naturalism precludes saying 'there are arbitrarily many propositional attitudes because there are infinitely many propositions' and leaving it at that. The problem about productivity is that there are arbitrarily many propositional attitudes that one can *have*. Since relations between organisms and propositions aren't to be taken as primitive, one is going to have to say what it is about organic states like believing and desiring that allows them to be (roughly) as differentiated as the propositions are. If, for example, you think that attitudes are mapped to propositions in virtue of their causal roles (see above), then you have to say what it is about the attitudes that accounts for the productivity *of the set of causal roles*.

A natural suggestion is that the productivity of thoughts is like the productivity of natural languages, i.e., that there are indefinitely many thoughts to entertain for much the same reason that there are indefinitely many sentences to utter. Fine, but how do natural languages manage to be productive? Here the outlines of an answer are familiar. To a first approximation, each sentence can be identified with a certain sequence of subsentential constituents. Different sentences correspond to different ways of arranging these subsentential constituents; new sentences correspond to new ways of arranging them. And the meaning of a sentence—the proposition it expresses—is determined, in a regular way, by its constituent structure.

The constituents of sentences are, say, words and phrases. What are the constituents of propositional attitudes? A natural answer would be:

other propositional attitudes. Since, for example, you can't believe that *P* and *Q* without believing that *P* and believing that *Q*, we could take the former state to be a complex of which the latter are the relatively (or perhaps absolutely) simple parts. But a moment's consideration makes it clear that this won't work with any generality: believing that *P* or *Q* doesn't require either believing that *P* or believing that *Q*, and neither does believing that if *P* then *Q*. It looks as though we want propositional attitudes to be built out of *something*, but not out of other propositional attitudes.

There's an interesting analogy to the case of speech-acts (one of many such; see Vendler 1972). There are indefinitely many distinct assertions (i.e., there are indefinitely many propositions that one can assert); and though you can't assert that *P* and *Q* without asserting that *P* and asserting that *Q*, the disjunctive assertion, *P* or *Q*, does not imply the assertion of either of the disjuncts, and the hypothetical assertion, if *P* then *Q*, does not imply the assertion of its antecedent or its consequent. So how do you work the constituency relation for *assertions*?

Answer: you take advantage of the fact that making an assertion involves using symbols (typically it involves *uttering* symbols); the constituency relation is defined for the symbols that assertions are made by using. So, in particular, the standard (English-language) vehicle for making the assertion that either John left or Mary wept is the form of words 'either John left or Mary wept'; and, notice, this complex linguistic expression *is*, literally, a construct out of the simpler linguistic expressions 'John left' and 'Mary wept'. You can assert that *P* or *Q* without asserting that *P* or asserting that *Q*, but you can't utter the form of words '*P* or *Q*' without uttering the form of words '*P*' and the form of words '*Q*'.

The moral for treatments of the attitudes would seem to be straightforward: solve the *productivity* problem for the attitudes by appealing to constituency. Solve the *constituency* problem for the attitudes in the same way that you solve it for speech-acts: tokening an attitude involves tokening a symbol, just as tokening an assertion does. What kind of symbol do you have to token to token an attitude? A mental representation, of course. Hence RTM. (Auntie says that it is crude and preposterous and *unbiological* to suppose that people have sentences in their heads. Auntie always talks like that when she hasn't got any arguments.)

Second Argument for RTM: Mental Processes

It is possible to doubt whether, as functional-role theories of meaning would have it, the propositional contents of mental states are reducible to, or determined by, or epiphenomena of, their causal roles. But what *can't* be doubted is this: the causal roles of mental states typically closely parallel the implicational structures of their propositional objects; and

Fodor's Guide to Mental Representation

the predictive successes of propositional-attitude psychology routinely exploit the symmetries thus engendered. If we know that Psmith believes that $P \rightarrow Q$ and we know that he believes that P, then we generally expect him to infer that Q and to act according to his inference. Why do we expect this? Well, because we believe the business about Psmith to be an instance of a true and counterfactual-supporting generalization according to which believing P and believing $P \rightarrow Q$ is causally sufficient for inferring Q, ceteris paribus. But then, *what is it about the mechanisms of thinking in virtue of which such generalizations hold*? What, in particular, could believing and inferring be, such that thinking the premises of a valid inference leads, so often and so reliably, to thinking its conclusion?

It was a scandal of midcentury Anglo-American philosophy of mind that though it worried a lot about the nature of mental states (like the attitudes) it quite generally didn't worry much about the nature of mental *processes* (like thinking). This isn't, in retrospect, very surprising given the behaviorism that was widely prevalent. Mental processes are causal sequences of mental states; if you're eliminativist about the attitudes you're hardly likely to be Realist about their causal consequences. In particular, you're hardly likely to be Realist about their *causal interactions*. It now seems clear enough, however, that our theory of the structure of the attitudes *must* accommodate a theory of thinking; and that it is a preeminent constraint on the latter that it provide a mechanism for symmetry between the inferential roles of thoughts and their causal roles.

This isn't, by any means, all that easy for a theory of thinking to do. Notice, for example, that the philosophy of mind assumed in traditional British Empiricism was Realist about the attitudes and accepted a form of RTM. (Very roughly, the attitudes were construed as relations to mental images, the latter being endowed with semantic properties in virtue of what they resembled and with causal properties in virtue of their associations. Mental states were productive because complex images can be constructed out of simple ones.) But precisely because the mechanisms of mental causation were assumed to be associationistic (and the conditions for association to involve preeminently spatio-temporal propinquity), the Empiricists had no good way of connecting the *contents* of a thought with the effects of entertaining it. They therefore never got close to a plausible theory of thinking, and neither did the associationistic psychology that followed in their footsteps.

What associationism missed—to put it more exactly—was the similarity between trains of thought and *arguments*. Here, for an example, is Sherlock Holmes doing his thing at the end of "The Speckled Band":

I instantly reconsidered my position when . . . it became clear to me that whatever danger threatened an occupant of the room could not come either from the window or the door. My attention was speedily drawn, as I have already remarked to you, to this ventilator, and to the bell-rope which hung down to the bed. The discovery that this was a dummy, and that the bed was clamped to the floor, instantly gave rise to the suspicion that the rope was there as a bridge for something passing through the hole, and coming to the bed. The idea of a snake instantly occurred to me, and when I coupled it with my knowledge that the Doctor was furnished with a supply of the creatures from India I felt that I was probably on the right track.

The passage purports to be a bit of reconstructive psychology, a capsule history of the sequence of mental episodes which brought Holmes first to suspect, then to believe, that the Doctor did it with his pet snake. Now, back when Auntie was a girl and reasons weren't allowed to be causes, philosophers were unable to believe that such an aetiology could be literally true. I assume, however, that liberation has set in by now; we have no philosophically impressive reason to doubt that Holmes's train of thoughts went pretty much the way that he says it did.

What is therefore interesting, for our purposes, is that Holmes's story isn't *just* reconstructive psychology. It does a double duty since it also serves to assemble *premises* for a plausible inference to the *conclusion* that the doctor did it with the snake. ("A snake could have crawled through the ventilator and slithered down the bell-rope," "the Doctor was known to keep a supply of snakes in his snuff box," and so forth.) Because this train of thoughts is tantamount to an argument, Holmes expects Watson to be *convinced* by the considerations that, when they occurred to him, caused Holmes's own conviction. (Compare the sort of mental history that goes, "Well, I went to bed and slept on it, and when I woke up in the morning, I found that the problem had solved itself." Or the sort that goes, "Bell-ropes always make me think of snakes, and snakes make me think of snake oil, and snake oil makes me think of doctors; so when I saw the bell-rope it popped into my head that the Doctor and a snake might have done it between them." That's mental causation perhaps; but it's not *thinking*.)

What connects the causal-history aspect of Holmes's story with its plausible-inference aspect is precisely the parallelism between trains of thought and arguments: the thoughts that effect the fixation of the belief that P provide, often enough, good *grounds* for believing that P. (As Holmes puts it in another story, "one true inference invariably suggests others.") Were this not the case—were there not this general harmony between the semantical and the causal properties of thoughts—there wouldn't, after all, be much profit in thinking.

What you want to make thinking worth the while is that trains of thoughts should be generated by mechanisms that are generally truth-preserving (so that "a true inference [generally] suggests other inferences *that are also true*"). Argument is generally truth-preserving; that, surely, is the teleological basis of the similarity between trains of thoughts and arguments. The associationists noticed hardly any of this;

and even if they had noticed it, they wouldn't have known what to do with it. In this respect, Conan Doyle was a far deeper psychologist—far closer to what is essential about the mental life—than, say, James Joyce (or William James, for that matter).

When, therefore, Rationalist critics (including, notably, Kant) pointed out that thought—like argument—involves judging and inferring, the cat was out of the bag. Associationism was the best available form of Realism about the attitudes, and associationism failed to produce a credible mechanism for thinking. Which is to say that it failed to produce a credible theory of the attitudes. No wonder everybody gave up and turned into a behaviorist.

Cognitive Science is the art of getting the cat back in. The trick is to abandon associationism and combine RTM with the "computer metaphor." In this respect I think there really has been something like an intellectual breakthrough. Technical details to one side, this is—in my view—the *only* respect in which contemporary Cognitive Science represents a major advance over the versions of RTM that were its eighteenth- and nineteenth-century predecessors.

Computers show us how to connect semantical with causal properties *for symbols*. So, if the tokening of an attitude involves the tokening of a symbol, then we can get some leverage on connecting semantical with causal properties *for thoughts*. Here, in roughest outline, is how the story is supposed to go.

You connect the causal properties of a symbol with its semantic properties via its syntax. The syntax of a symbol is one of its second-order physical properties. To a first approximation, we can think of its syntactic structure as an abstract feature of its (geometric or acoustic) *shape*. Because, to all intents and purposes, syntax reduces to shape, and because the shape of a symbol is a potential determinant of its causal role, it is fairly easy to see how there could be environments in which the causal role of a symbol correlates with its syntax. It's easy, that is to say, to imagine symbol tokens interacting causally *in virtue of* their syntactic structures. The syntax of a symbol might determine the causes and effects of its tokenings in much the way that the geometry of a key determines which locks it will open.

But, now, we know from formal logic that certain of the semantic relations among symbols can be, as it were, "mimicked" by their syntactic relations; that, when seen from a very great distance, is what proof-theory is about. So, within certain famous limits, the semantic relation that holds between two symbols when the proposition expressed by the one is implied by the proposition expressed by the other can be mimicked by syntactic relations in virtue of which one of the symbols is derivable from the other. We can therefore build machines which have, again within famous limits, the following property: the operations of such a machine consist entirely of transformations of symbols; in the course of performing these operations, the machine is sensitive solely to syntactic properties of the symbols; and the operations that the machine performs on the symbols are entirely confined to alterations of their shapes. Yet the machine is so devised that it will transform one symbol into another if and only if the symbols so transformed stand in certain *semantic* relations; e.g., the relation that the premises bear to the conclusion in a valid argument. Such machines—computers, of course—just *are* environments in which the causal role of a symbol token is made to parallel the inferential role of the proposition that it expresses.[3]

I expect it's clear how this is all supposed to provide an argument for quantifying over mental representations. Computers are a solution to the problem of mediating between the causal properties of symbols and their semantic properties. So *if* the mind is a sort of computer, we begin to see how you can have a theory of mental processes that succeeds where associationism (to say nothing of behaviorism) abjectly failed; a theory which explains how there could regularly be nonarbitrary content relations among causally related thoughts.

But, patently, there are going to have to be mental representations if this proposal is going to work. In computer design, causal role is brought into phase with content by exploiting parallelisms between the syntax of a symbol and its semantics. But that idea won't do the theory of *mind* any good unless there are *mental* symbols; mental particulars possessed of semantic *and syntactic* properties. There must be mental symbols because, in a nutshell, only symbols have syntax, and our best available theory of mental processes—indeed, the *only* available theory of mental processes that isn't *known* to be false—needs the picture of the mind as a syntax-driven machine.[4]

A brief addendum before we end this section: the question of the extent to which RTM must be committed to the 'explicitness' of mental representation is one that keeps getting raised in the philosophical literature (and elsewhere; see Dennett 1978b, Stabler 1983). The issue becomes clear if we consider real computers as deployed in Artificial Intelligence research. So, to borrow an example of Dennett's, there are chess machines that play as though they 'believe' that it's a good idea to get one's Queen out early. But there needn't be—in fact, there probably wouldn't be—anywhere in the system of heuristics that constitutes the program of such a machine a symbol that *means* '(try and) get your Queen out early'; rather the machine's obedience to that rule of play is, as it were, an epiphenomenon of its following many *other* rules, much more detailed, whose joint effect is that, ceteris paribus, the Queen gets out as soon as it can. The moral is supposed to be that though the contents of *some* of the attitudes it would be natural to attribute to the machine *may* be explicitly represented, none of them *have* to be, *even assuming the sort of story about how computational processes work that is supposed to motivate RTM.* So, then, what exactly *is* RTM minimally committed to by way of explicit mental representation?

Fodor's Guide to Mental Representation

The answer should be clear in light of the previous discussion. According to RTM, mental processes are transformations of mental representations. The rules which determine the course of such transformations may, but needn't, be themselves explicitly represented. But the mental contents (the 'thoughts', as it were) that get transformed *must* be explicitly presented or the theory is simply false. To put it another way: if the occurrence of a thought is an episode in a mental process, then RTM is committed to the explicit representation of the content of the thought. Or, to put it still a third way—the way they like to put it in AI—according to RTM, programs may be explicitly represented and data structures have to be.

For the sake of a simple example, let's pretend that associationism is true; we imagine that there is a principle of Association by Proximity in virtue of which thoughts of salt get associated with thoughts of pepper. The point is that even on the assumption that it subsumes mental processes, the rule 'associate by proximity' need not itself be explicitly represented; association by proximity may emerge from dynamical properties of ideas (as in Hume) or from dynamical properties of neural stuff (as in contemporary connectionism). But what *must* be explicit is the Ideas—of pepper and salt, as it might be—that get associated. For, according to the theory, mental processes are actually *causal sequences of tokenings of such Ideas;* so, no Ideas, no mental processes.

Similarly, mutatis mutandis, for the chess case. The rule 'get it out early' may be emergent out of its own implementation; out of lower-level heuristics, that is, any one of which may or may not itself be explicitly represented. But the representation of the board—of actual or possible states of play—over which such heuristics are defined *must* be explicit or the representational theory of chess playing is simply false. The theory says that a train of chess thoughts is a causal sequence of tokenings of chess representations. If, therefore, there are trains of chess thoughts but no tokenings of chess representations, it *follows* that something is not well with the theory.

So much, then, for RTM and the polyadicity of the attitudes. What about their semanticity? We proceed to our final diagnostic question:

Fourth Question: How Do You Feel about Truth-Conditions?

I remarked above that the two characteristic tenets of SR—that the attitudes are monadic and that the semanticity of the attitudes arises from isomorphisms between the causal network of mental states and the inferential network of propositions—are mutually independent. Similarly for RTM; it's not mandatory, but you are at liberty to combine RTM with functional-role (FR) semantics if you choose. Thus, you could perfectly well say: 'Believing, desiring, and so forth are relations between intentional systems and mental representations that get tokened (in their heads, as it might be). Tokening a mental representation has causal consequences. The totality of such consequences implies a network of causal interrelations among the attitudes . . . and so on to a functional-role semantics. In any event, it's important to see that RTM needs *some* semantic story to tell if, as we have supposed, RTM is going to be Realist about the attitudes and the attitudes have their propositional objects essentially.

Which semantic story to tell is, in my view, going to be *the* issue in mental representation theory for the foreseeable future. The questions here are so difficult, and the answers so contentious, that they really fall outside the scope of this paper; I had advertised a tour of an intellectual landscape about whose topography there exists some working consensus. Still, I want to say a little about the semantic issues by way of closing. They are the piece of Cognitive Science where philosophers feel most at home; and they're where the 'philosophy of psychology' (a discipline over which Auntie is disinclined to quantify) joins the philosophy of language (which, I notice, Auntie allows me to spell without quotes).

There are a number of reasons for doubting that a functional-role semantic theory of the sort that SR proposes is tenable. This fact is currently causing something of a crisis among people who would like to be Realists about the attitudes.

In the first place—almost, by now, too obvious to mention—functional-role theories make it seem that empirical constraints must underdetermine the semantics of the attitudes. What I've got in mind here isn't the collection of worries that cluster around the 'indeterminacy of translation' thesis; if that sort of indeterminacy is to be taken seriously at all—which I doubt—then it is equally a problem for *every* Realist semantics. There are, however, certain sources of underdetermination that appear to be built into functional-role semantics as such; considerations which suggest either that there is no unique best mapping of the causal roles of mental states on to the inferential network of propositions or that, even if there is, such a mapping would nevertheless underdetermine assignments of contents to the attitudes. I'll mention two such considerations, but no doubt there are others; things are always worse than one supposes.

Idealization
The pattern of causal dispositions actually accruing to a given mental state must surely diverge very greatly from the pattern of inferences characteristic of its propositional object. We don't, for example, believe all the consequences of our beliefs; not just because we haven't got time to, and not just because everybody is at least a little irrational, but also because we surely have some false beliefs about what the consequences of our beliefs are. This amounts to saying that some substantial idealization is required if we're to get from the causal dispositions that mental states actually exhibit to the sort of causal network that we would like

to have: a causal network whose structure is closely isomorphic to the inferential network of propositions. And now the problem is to provide a noncircular justification—one which does not itself appeal to semantical or intentional considerations—for preferring *that* idealization to an infinity or so of others that ingenuity might devise. (It won't do, of course, to say that we prefer that idealization because it's the one which allows mental states to be assigned the intuitively plausible propositional objects; for the present question is precisely whether anything besides prejudice underwrites our common-sense psychological intuitions.) Probably the idealization problem arises, in some form or other, for any account of the attitudes which proposes to reduce their semantic properties to their causal ones. That, alas, is no reason to assume that the problem can be solved.

Equivalence

Functionalism guarantees that mental states are individuated by their causal roles; hence by their position in the putative causal network. But *nothing* guarantees that *propositions* are individuated by their *inferential* roles. Prima facie, it surely seems that they are not, since equivalent propositions are ipso facto identical in their inferential liaisons. Are we therefore to say that equivalent propositions are identical? Not, at least, for the psychologist's purposes, since attitudes whose propositional objects are equivalent may nevertheless differ in their causal roles. We need to distinguish, as it might be, the belief that P from the belief that P and $(Q \vee \text{-}Q)$, hence we need to distinguish the *proposition* that P from the proposition that P and $(Q \vee \text{-}Q)$. But surely what distinguishes these propositions is not their inferential roles, assuming that the inferential role of a proposition is something like the set of propositions it entails and is entailed by. It seems to follow that propositions are not individuated by their position in the inferential network, hence that assignments of propositional objects to mental states, if constrained only to preserve isomorphism between the networks, ipso facto underdetermine the contents of such states. There are, perhaps, ways out of such equivalence problems; 'situation semantics' (see Barwise and Perry 1983) has recently been advertising some. But all the ways out that I've heard of violate the assumptions of FR semantics; specifically, they don't identify propositions with nodes in a network of inferential roles.

In the second place, FR semantics isn't, after all, much of a panacea for Naturalistic scruples. Though it has a Naturalistic story to tell about how mental states might be paired with their propositional objects, the semantic properties of the propositions themselves are assumed, not explained. It is, for example, an intrinsic property of the proposition that Psmith is seated that it is true or false in virtue of Psmith's posture. FR semantics simply takes this sort of fact for granted. From the naturalist's point of view, therefore, it merely displaces the main worry from: 'What's the connection between an attitude and its propositional object?' to 'What's the connection between the propositional object of an attitude and whatever state of affairs it is that makes the proposition true or false?' Or, to put much the same point slightly differently, FR semantics has a lot to say about the mind-to-proposition problem but nothing at all to say about the mind-to-world problem. In effect FR semantics is content to hold that the attitudes inherit their satisfaction-conditions from their propositional objects and that propositions have *their* satisfaction-conditions *by stipulation*.

And, in the third place, to embrace FR semantics is to raise a variety of (approximately Quinean) issues about the individuation of the attitudes; and these, as Putnam and Stich have recently emphasized, when once conjured up are not easily put down. The argument goes like this: according to FR semantic theories, each attitude has its propositional object in virtue of its position in the causal network: 'Different objects iff different loci' holds to a first approximation. Since a propositional attitude has its propositional object essentially, this makes an attitude's identity depend on the identity of its causal role. The problem is, however, that we have no criteria for the individuation of causal roles.

The usual sceptical tactic at this point is to introduce some or other form of slippery-slope argument to show—or at least to suggest—that there *couldn't be* a criterion for the individuation of causal roles that is other than arbitrary. Stich, for example, has the case of an increasingly senile woman who eventually is able to remember about President McKinley only that he was assassinated. Given that she has no *other* beliefs about McKinley—given, let's suppose, that the *only* causal consequence of her believing that McKinley was assassinated is to prompt her to produce and assent to occasional utterances of 'McKinley was assassinated' and immediate logical consequences thereof—is it clear that she in fact has *any* beliefs about McKinley at all? But if she *doesn't* have, *when, precisely, did she cease to do so*? How much causal role does the belief that McKinley was assassinated have to have to be the belief that McKinley was assassinated? And what reason is there to suppose that this question has an answer? (See Stich 1983; and also Putnam 1983.) Auntie considers slippery-slope arguments to be in dubious taste and there is much to be said for her view. Still, it looks as though FR semantics has brought us to the edge of a morass and I, for one, am not an enthusiast for wading in it.

Well then, to summarize: the syntactic theory of mental operations promises a reductive account of the *intelligence* of thought. We can now imagine—though, to be sure, only dimly and in a glass darkly—a psychology that exhibits quite complex cognitive processes as being constructed from elementary manipulations of symbols. This is what RTM, together with the computer metaphor, has brought us; and it is, in my view, no small matter. But a theory of the *intelligence* of thought does not, in and of itself, constitute a theory of thought's *intentionality*. (Compare such early papers as Dennett 1978c, where these issues are more or less comprehensively run together, with such second thoughts as Fodor 1981a, and Cummins 1983, where they more or less aren't.) If RTM is true, the problem of the intentionality of the mental is largely—perhaps exhaustively—the problem of the semanticity of mental representations. But of the semanticity of mental representations we have, as things now stand, no adequate account.

Here ends the tour. Beyond this point there be monsters. It may be that what one descries, just there on the farthest horizon, is a glimpse of a causal/teleological theory of meaning (Stampe 1977; Dretske 1981; Fodor 1990, 1984); and it may be that the development of such a theory would provide a way out of the current mess. At best, however, it's a long way off. I mention it only to encourage such of the passengers as may be feeling queasy.

"Are you finished playing now?"
"Yes, Auntie."
"Well, don't forget to put the toys away."
"No, Auntie."

Notes

1. Unless you are an eliminativist behaviorist (say, Watson) which puts you, for present purposes, beyond the pale.

While we're at it, it rather messes up my nice taxonomy that there are philosophers who accept a Functionalist view of psychological explanation and are Realist about belief/desire psychology, but who reject the reduction of the latter to the former. In particular, they do not accept the identification of any of the entities that Functionalist psychologists posit with the propositional attitudes that common sense holds dear. (A version of this view says that functional states "realize" propositional attitudes in much the way that the physical states are supposed to realize functional ones. See, for example, Matthews 1984.)

2. This account of the attitudes seems to be in the air these days, and, as with most doctrines that are in the air, it's a little hard to be sure exactly who holds it. Far the most detailed version is in Loar 1981, though I have seen variants in unpublished papers by Tyler Burge, Robert Stalnaker, and Hartry Field.

3. Since the methods of computational psychology tend to be those of proof theory, its limitations tend to be those of formalization. Patently, this raises the well-known issue about completeness; less obviously, it connects the Cognitive Science enterprise with the Positivist program for the formalization of inductive (and, generally, nondemonstrative) styles of argument. On the second point, see Glymour 1987.

4. It is possible to combine enthusiasm for a syntactical account of mental processes with any degree of agnosticism about the attitudes—or, for that matter, about semantic evaluability itself. To claim that the mind is a "syntax-driven machine" is precisely to hold that the theory of mental processes can be set out in its entirety without reference to any of the semantical properties of mental states (see Fodor 1981a), hence without assuming that mental states *have* any semantic properties. Stephen Stich is famous for having espoused this option (Stich 1983). My way of laying out the field has put the big divide between Realism about the attitudes and its denial. This seems to me justifiable, but

admittedly it underestimates the substantial affinities between Stich and the RTM crowd. Stich's account of what a good science of behavior would look like is far closer to RTM than it is to, for example, the eliminative materialism of the Churchlands.

References

Barwise, J., and J. Perry (1983). *Situations and attitudes.* Cambridge, MA: MIT Press.

Block, N. (1980). Troubles with functionalism. In N. Block, ed., *Readings in philosophy of psychology,* vol. 1. Cambridge, MA: Harvard University Press.

Churchland, P. M. (1981). Eliminative materialism and the propositional attitudes. *Journal of Philosophy* 78, 67–90.

Cummins, R. C. (1983). *The nature of psychological explanation.* Cambridge, MA: MIT Press.

Dennett, D. C. (1978a). *Brainstorms.* Cambridge, MA: Bradford Books.

Dennett, D. C. (1978b). A cure for the common code? In D. C. Dennett, *Brainstorms.* Cambridge, MA: Bradford Books.

Dennett, D. C. (1978c). Intentional systems. In D. C. Dennett, *Brainstorms.* Cambridge, MA: Bradford Books.

Dennett, D. C. (1981). True believers: The intentional stance and why it works. In A. F. Heath, ed., *Scientific explanation: Papers based on the Herbert Spencer Lectures given in the University of Oxford.* Oxford: Clarendon Press.

Dretske, F. I. (1981). *Knowledge and the flow of information.* Cambridge, MA: MIT Press.

Dreyfus, H. (1979) *What computers can't do.* New York: Harper & Row.

Field, H. (1978). Mental representation. *Erkenntnis* 13, 9–61.

Fodor, J. A. (1975). *The language of thought.* New York: Crowell.

Fodor, J. A. (1978). Propositional attitudes. *The Monist* 61, 501–523.

Fodor, J. A. (1981a). Methodological solipsism considered as a research strategy in cognitive psychology. *Behavioral and Brain Sciences* 3, 63–110.

Fodor, J. A. (1981b). The mind-body problem. *Scientific American* 244, 515–531.

Fodor, J. A. (1981c). *Representations.* Cambridge, MA: MIT Press.

Fodor, J. A. (1984). Semantics, Wisconsin style. *Synthese* 59, 231–250.

Fodor, J. A. (1985). Banish discontent. In J. Butterfield, ed., *Language, mind and logic.* Cambridge: Cambridge University Press.

Fodor, J. A. (1990). Psychosemantics, or where do truth conditions come from. In W. G. Lycan, ed., *Mind and Cognition: A Reader.* Oxford: Blackwell.

Glymour, C. (1987). Android epistemology and the frame problem. In Z. Pylyshyn, ed., *The robot's dilemma: The Frame Problem in Artificial Intelligence*. Norwood, NJ: Ablex.

Haugeland, J. (1978). The nature and plausibility of cognitivism. *Behavioral and Brain Sciences* 1, 215–226.

Loar, B. (1981). *Mind and meaning*. Cambridge: Cambridge University Press.

Matthews, R. (1984). Troubles with representationalism. *Social Research* 51, 1065–1097.

Putnam, H. (1983). Computational psychology and interpretation theory. In H. Putnam, *Realism and reason*. Cambridge: Cambridge University Press.

Putnam, H. (1986). Meaning holism. In L. Hahn and P. Schilpp, eds., *The Philosophy of W. V. Quine*. La Salle, IL: Open Court.

Searle, J. R. (1980) Minds, brains, and programs. *Behavioral and Brain Sciences* 3, 417–424.

Stabler, E. (1983). How are grammars represented? *Behavioral and Brain Sciences* 6, 391–402.

Stampe, D. (1977). Towards a causal theory of linguistic representation. In P. French, T. Uehling, and H. Wettstein, eds., *Midwest Studies in Philosophy*, vol. 2. Minneapolis: University of Minnesota Press.

Stich, S. P. (1983). *From folk psychology to cognitive science*. Cambridge, MA: MIT Press.

Vendler, Z. (1983). *Res cogitans*. Ithaca: Cornell University Press.

14 Misrepresentation

Fred Dretske

Epistemology is concerned with knowledge: how do we manage to get things right? There is a deeper question: how do we manage to get things wrong? How is it possible for physical systems to *misrepresent* the state of their surroundings?

The problem is not how, for example, a diagram, *d*, can misrepresent the world, *w*. For if we have another system, *r*, already possessed of representational powers, *d* can be used as an expressive extension of *r*, thereby participating in *r*'s representational successes and failures. When this occurs, *d* can come to mean that *w* is *F* when, in fact, *w* is not *F*, but *d*'s meaning derives, ultimately, from *r*. A chart depicting unemployment patterns over the past ten years can misrepresent this condition, but the chart's capacity for misrepresentation is derived from its role as an expressive instrument for agents, speakers of the language, who already have this power.

No, the problem is, rather, one of a system's powers of representation in so far as these powers do not derive from the representational efforts of another source. Unless we have some clue to how this is possible, we do not have a clue how naturally evolving biological systems could have acquired the capacity for belief. For belief is, or so I shall assume, a *non-derived* representational capacity the exercise of which *can* yield a misrepresentation.

The capacity for misrepresentation is a part, perhaps only a small part, of the general problem of meaning or intentionality. Once we have meaning, we can, in our descriptions and explanations of human, animal, and perhaps even machine behavior, lavish it on the systems we describe. Once we have intentionality, we can (to use Dennett's language) adopt the intentional stance.[1] But what (*besides* intentionality) gives us (and not, say, machines) the power to adopt this stance? Our ability to adopt this stance is an *expression*, not an analysis, of intentionality. The borrowed meaning of systems toward which we adopt

---

© Fred Dretske 1986. Reprinted from *Belief: Form, Content, and Function* edited by Radu J. Bogdan (1986) by permission of Oxford University Press and the author.

appropriate attitudes tells us no more about the original capacity for misrepresentation than does a misplaced pin on a military map. What we are after, so to speak, is *nature*'s way of making a mistake, the place where the misrepresentational buck stops. Only when we understand this shall we understand how grey matter can misrepresent the weather for tomorrow's picnic.

Natural Signs

Naturally occurring signs mean something, and they do so without any assistance from us.[2] Water does not flow uphill; hence, a northerly flowing river means there is a downward gradient in that direction. Shadows to the east mean that the sun is in the west. A sudden force on the passengers in one direction means an acceleration of the train in the opposite direction. The power of these events or conditions to mean what they do is independent of the way we interpret them—or, indeed, of whether we interpret or recognize them at all. The dentist may *use* the X-ray to diagnose the condition of your upper right molar, but the dark shadows mean extensive decay has occurred whether or not he, or anyone else, appreciates this fact. Expanding metal indicates a rising temperature (and in this sense means that the temperature is rising) whether or not anyone, upon observing the former, comes to believe the latter. It meant that *before* intelligent organisms, capable of exploiting this fact (by building thermometers), inhabited the earth. If we are looking for the ultimate source of meaning, and with it an understanding of a system's power of misrepresentation, here, surely, is a promising place to begin.

Natural signs are indicators, more or less reliable indicators, and what they mean is what they indicate to be so. The power of a natural sign to mean something—for example, that Tommy has measles—is under-written by certain objective constraints, certain lawful relations, between the sign (or the sign's having a certain property) and the condition that constitutes its meaning (Tommy's having measles). In most cases this relation is causal or lawful, one capable of supporting a counterfactual assertion to the effect that if the one condition had not obtained (if Tommy did not have measles), neither would the other (he would not have those red spots all over his face). Sometimes there are merely regularities, non-lawful but none the less pervasive, that help secure the connection between sign and significance. It is partly the fact, presumably not itself lawful, that animals (for example, squirrels or woodpeckers) do not regularly ring doorbells while foraging for food that makes the ringing bell *mean* that someone (i.e. some *person*) is at the door. If squirrels changed their habits (because, say, doorbells were made out of nuts), then a ringing doorbell would no longer mean what it now does. But as things *now* stand, we can (usually) say that the bell would not be ringing unless someone was at the door, that the bell indicates someone's presence at the door, and that, therefore, that is what it means. But this subjunctively expressed dependency between the ringing bell and someone's presence at the door is a reflection of a regularity which, though not conventional, is not fully lawful either. None the less, the doorbell retains its natural meaning as long as this regularity persists.

Beyond this I have nothing very systematic to say about what constitutes the natural meaning of an event or a condition.[3] I shall proceed with what I hope is a reasonably familiar notion, appealing (when necessary) to concrete examples. The project is to see how far one can go in understanding misrepresentation, the power of a condition (state, event, situation) r to mean (say, indicate) *falsely* that w is F (thereby misrepresenting w), in terms of a natural sign's meaning that w if F. Only when (or if) this project succeeds, or shows reasonable prospects of succeeding, will it, or might it, be necessary to look more carefully at what got smuggled in at the beginning.

Though natural meaning is a promising point of departure, it is hard to see how to get under way. Natural signs, though they mean something, though they can (in this sense) represent w (by indicating or meaning that w is F) are powerless to *misrepresent* anything. Either they do their job right or they don't do it at all. The spots on Tommy's face certainly can mean that he has measles, but they mean this *only* when he has measles. If he doesn't have measles, then the spots don't mean this. Perhaps all they mean is that Tommy has been eating too many sweets.

Grice expresses this point by saying that an occurrence (a tokening of some natural sign) means (in what he calls the natural sense of "meaning"—hereafter meaning$_n$) that P only if P.[4] He contrasts this sense of meaning with non-natural meaning where a sign can mean that P even though P is false. If we reserve the word 'meaning' (minus subscripts) for that species of meaning in which something can mean that w is F when w isn't F, the kind of meaning in which misrepresentation is possible, then meaning$_n$ seems a poorly qualified candidate for understanding meaning.

In speaking of signs and their natural meaning I should always be understood as referring to *particular* events, states or conditions: *this* track, *those* clouds, and *that* smoke. A sign type (for example, smoke) may be said to mean, in some natural sense, that there is fire even when every token of that type fails to mean$_n$ this (because, occasionally, there is no fire). But this type-associated meaning, whatever its proper analysis, does *not* help us understand misrepresentation unless the individual tokens of that type *have* the type-associated meaning, unless particular puffs of smoke mean$_n$ that there is fire when there is no fire. This, though, is not the case. A petrol gauge's registration of "empty" (this *type* of event) can signify an empty tank, but when the tank is not empty, no particular registration of "empty" by the gauge's pointer means$_n$ that the tank is empty. Hence, no particular registration of the gauge misrepresents the amount of gas in the tank (by meaning$_n$ that it is empty when it is not).

The inability of (particular) natural signs to misrepresent anything is sometimes obscured by the way we exploit them in manufactured devices. Interested as we may be in whether, and if so when, w becomes F, we concoct a device d whose various states are designed to function as natural signs of w's condition. Since this is how we use the device, we tend to say of some particular registration that d's being G (assuming this is the natural sign of w's being F) means that w is F even when, through malfunction or misuse, the system is failing to perform satisfactorily and w is not F. But this, clearly, is not what the particular pointer position means$_n$. This is what it is *supposed* to mean$_n$, what it was *designed* to mean$_n$, what (perhaps) tokens of type *normally* mean$_n$, but not what it *does* mean$_n$.

When there is a short circuit, the ring of the doorbell (regardless of what it was designed to indicate, regardless of what it normally indicates) does not indicate that the bellpush is being pressed. It still means$_n$ (indicates) that there is electric current flowing in the doorbell circuit (one of the things it always meant$_n$), but the latter no longer means$_n$ that the bellpush is being pressed. What the flow of current *now* means$_n$—and this is surely how we would judge if we could *see* the bellpush, *see that* it was *not* being pressed—is that the system is malfunctioning or that there is a short circuit somewhere in the wiring. The *statement*, "There is someone at the door," can mean that there is someone at the door even when no one is there, but the ringing doorbell cannot mean this when no one is there. Not, at least, if we are talking about meaning$_n$. If the bellpush is not being pressed, then we must look for something else for the ringing bell to mean$_n$. Often, we withdraw to some more proximal meaning$_n$, some condition or state of affairs in the normal chain of causal antecedents that *does* obtain (for example, the flow of current or the *cause* of the flow of current—for example, a short circuit) and designate it as the meaning$_n$ of the ringing bell.

Functional Meaning

Granted, one may say, the doorbell's ringing cannot mean$_n$ that someone is at the door when no one is there; still, in some related sense of meaning, it means this whether or not anyone is there. If this is not natural meaning (meaning$_n$), it is a close cousin.

Whether it is a cousin or not, there certainly is a kind of meaning that attaches to systems, or components of systems, for which there are identifiable *functions*. Consider, once again, the fuel gauge. It has a function: to pass along information about the amount of petrol in the tank. When things are working properly, the position of the needle is a natural sign of the contents of the tank. Its pointing to the left means$_n$ that the tank is empty. Its pointing to the right means$_n$ that the tank is full. And so on for the intermediate positions. But things sometimes go wrong: connections work loose, the battery goes dead, wires break. The gauge begins to register "empty" when the tank is still full. When this happens there is a tendency to say that the gauge misrepresents the contents of the tank. It *says* the tank is empty when it is not. It *means* (not, of course means$_n$, but still means in *some* sense) that the tank is empty.

When d's being G is, normally, a natural sign of w's being F, when this is what it normally means$_n$, then there is a sense in which it means this whether or not w is F *if it is the function of d to indicate the condition of w.* Let us call this kind of meaning *meaning$_f$*—the subscript indicating that this is a functionally derived meaning.

(M$_f$) d's being G means$_f$ that w is F = d's function is to indicate the condition of w, and the way it performs this function is, in part, by indicating that w is F by its (d's) being G

The position of the needle on the broken fuel gauge means$_f$ that the tank is empty because it is the gauge's function to indicate the amount of remaining fuel, and the way it performs this function is, in part, by indicating an empty tank when the gauge registers "empty."[5] And, for the same reason and in the same sense, the ringing doorbell says (i.e., means$_f$) that someone is at the door even when no one is there.

Whether or not M$_f$ represents any progress in our attempt to naturalize meaning (and thus understand a system's non-derivative power to misrepresent) depends on whether the functions in question can themselves be understood in some natural way. If these functions are (what I shall call) *assigned* functions, then meaning$_f$ is tainted with the purposes, intention, and beliefs of those who assign the function from which meaning$_f$ derives its misrepresentational powers.[6] We shall not have tracked meaning, in so far as this involves the power of misrepresentation, to its original source. We shall merely have worked our way back, somewhat indirectly, to *our own* mysterious capacity for representation.

To understand what I mean by an *assigned* function, and the way *we* (our intentions, purposes and beliefs) are implicated in a system's having such a function, consider the following case. A sensitive spring-operated scale, calibrated in fractions of a gram, is designed and used to determine the weight of very small objects. Unknown to both designers and users, the instrument is a sensitive indicator of altitude. By registering a reduced weight for things as altitude increases (note: a thing's weight is a function of its height above sea level), the instrument *could* be used as a crude altimeter if the user attached a standard weight and noted the instrument's variable registration as altitude changed.

Suppose, now, that under normal use in the laboratory the instrument malfunctions and registers 0.98 g. for an object weighing 1 g. Is it misrepresenting the *weight* of the object? Is it misrepresenting the *altitude* of the object? What does the reading of 0.98 g. mean? If we are talking about meaning$_n$, it clearly does not mean$_n$ that the object weighs 0.98 g. Nor does it mean$_n$, that the laboratory is 40,000 ft. above sea level. If we ask about meaning$_f$, though, it seems reasonable to say that the instrument's pointer says or indicates (i.e. means$_f$) that the object weights 0.98 g. It is the function of this instrument to tell us what objects weigh, and it is telling us (incorrectly, as it turns out) that this object weighs 0.98 g.

But is the altitude being misrepresented? No. It should be noticed that the instrument cannot be misrepresenting *both* the altitude and the weight since a representation (or misrepresentation) of one presupposes a *fixity* (hence, *non*-representation) of the other.[7] Although the instrument *could* be used as an altimeter, it *is not* used that way. That is not its function. Its function is to register weight. That is the function we assign to it, the reason it was built and the explanation why it was built the way it was. Had our purposes been otherwise, it might have meant$_f$ something else. But they were not and it does not.

We sometimes change an instrument's assigned function. When we calibrate it, for example, we do not use it to measure what it is normally used to measure. Instead, we apply it to known quantities in order to use its indication as a (natural) sign of possible malfunction or inaccuracy in the instrument itself. In this case, a reading of 0.98 g. (for a weight *known* to be 1 g.) indicates that the spring has changed its characteristics, the pointer is bent, or some other component is out of adjustment. We get a new functional meaning because our altered background knowledge (normally a result of different intentions and purposes) changes what the pointer's behaviour means$_n$. With *assigned* functions, the meanings$_f$ change as *our* purposes change.[8]

We sometimes use animals in the same way that we use instruments. Dogs have an acute sense of smell. Exploiting this fact, customs officers use dogs to detect concealed marijuana. When the dog wags it tail, barks, or does whatever it is trained to do when it smells marijuana, the dog's behaviour serves as a natural sign—a sign that the luggage contains marijuana. But this does not mean that the dog's behaviour (or the neural condition that triggers this behaviour) can misrepresent the contents of the luggage. The dog's behaviour may make the customs officer believe (falsely) that there is marijuana in the suitcase, but the dog's behaviour means$_f$ this only in a derived way. If the dog is particularly good at its job, barking only when there is marijuana present, we can say that its bark indicates (i.e. means$_n$) that there is marijuana present. Furthermore, it means$_n$ this whether or not anyone interprets it as meaning$_n$ this, whether or not we *use* this natural sign for our own investigative purposes. But when there is no marijuana present, when the dog barks at an innocent box of herbs, the bark does *not* mean$_n$ that there is marijuana present. Nor does it mean$_f$ this in any sense that is independent of *our* interpretative activities. We can, of course, say what the bark means *to us* (that there is marijuana in the suitcase), but this way of talking merely reveals our own involvement in the meaning assigned to the dog's behaviour. *We* assign this meaning because this is the information we are *interested* in obtaining, the information we *expect* to get by using the dog in this way, the information the dog was trained to deliver. But if we set aside our interests and purposes, then, *when there is no marijuana present,* there is *no* sense in which the dog's bark means that there is marijuana in the suitcase. The only kind of misrepresentation occurring here is of the derived kind we are familiar with in maps, instruments, and language.

Therefore, if M$_f$ is to serve as a naturalized account of representation, where this is understood to include the power of *mis*representation, then the functions in question must be *natural* functions, functions a thing has which are independent of *our* interpretative intentions and purposes. What we are looking for are functions involving a system of natural signs that give these signs a content, and therefore a meaning (i.e. a meaning$_f$), that is not parasitic on the way *we* exploit them in our information-gathering activities, on the way we choose to interpret them.[9]

We need, then, some characterization of a system's natural functions. More particularly, since we are concerned with the function a system of natural signs might have, we are looking for what a sign is *supposed* to mean$_n$ where the "supposed to" is cashed out in terms of the function of that sign (or sign system) in the organism's *own* cognitive economy. We want to know how *the dog* represents the contents of the luggage— what (if anything) the smell of the box means$_f$ *to it*.

Needs

The obvious place to look for natural functions is in biological systems having a variety of organs, mechanisms, and processes that were developed (flourished, preserved) *because* they played a vital information-gathering role in the species' adaptation to its surroundings. An information-gathering function, essential in most cases to the satisfaction of a biological need, can only be successfully realized in a system capable of occupying states that serve as natural signs of external (and sometimes *other* internal) conditions. If that cluster of photoreceptors we call the retina is to perform its function (whatever, exactly, we take this function to be), the various states of these receptors must mean$_n$ something about the character and distribution of one's optical surroundings. Just what the various states of these receptors mean$_f$ will (in accordance with M$_f$) be determined by two things: (1) what it is the function of this receptor system to indicate, and (2) the meaning$_n$ of the various states that enable the system to perform this function.

To illustrate the way M_f is supposed to work it is convenient to consider simple organisms with obvious biological needs—some thing or condition without which they could not survive. I say this is convenient because this approach to the problem of misrepresentation has its most compelling application to cognitive mechanisms subserving some basic biological need. And the consideration of *primitive* systems gives us the added advantage of avoiding that kind of circularity in the analysis that would be incurred by appealing to those kinds of "needs" (for example, my need for a word processor) that are derived from desires (for example, my desire to produce faster, cleaner copy). We cannot bring desires in at this stage of the analysis since they already possess the kind of representational content that we are trying to understand.

Some marine bacteria have internal magnets (called magnetosomes) that function like compass needles, aligning themselves (and, as a result, the bacteria) parallel to the earth's magnetic field.[10] Since these magnetic lines incline downwards (towards geomagnetic north) in the northern hemisphere (upwards in the southern hemisphere), bacteria in the northern hemisphere, oriented by their internal magnetosomes, propel themselves towards geomagnetic north. The survival value of magnetotaxis (as this sensory mechanism is called) is not obvious, but it is reasonable to suppose that it functions so as to enable the bacteria to avoid surface water. Since these organisms are capable of living only in the absence of oxygen, movement towards geomagnetic north will take the bacteria away from oxygen-rich surface water and towards the comparatively oxygen-free sediment at the bottom. Southern-hemispheric bacteria have their magnetosomes reversed, allowing them to swim towards geomagnetic south with the same beneficial results. Transplant a southern bacterium in the North Atlantic and it will destroy itself—swimming upwards (towards magnetic south) into the toxic, oxygen-rich surface water.

If a bar magnet oriented in the opposite direction to the earth's magnetic field is held near these bacteria, they can be lured into a deadly environment. Although I shall return to the point in a moment (in order to question this line of reasoning), this appears to be a plausible instance of misrepresentation. Since, in the bacteria's normal habitat, the internal orientation of their magnetosomes means$_n$ that there is relatively little oxygen in *that* direction, and since the organism needs precisely this piece of information in order to survive, it seems reasonable to say that it is the function of this sensory mechanism to serve the satisfaction of this need, to deliver this piece of information, to indicate that oxygen-free water is in *that* direction. If this is what it is *supposed* to mean$_n$, this is what it means$_f$. Hence, in the presence of the bar magnet and in accordance with M_f, the organism's sensory state misrepresents the location of oxygen-free water.

This is not to say, of course, that bacteria have *beliefs*, beliefs to the effect that there is little or no oxygen in *that* direction. The capacity for misrepresentation is only *one* dimension of intentionality, only *one* of the properties that a representational system must have to qualify as a belief system. To qualify as a belief, a representational content must also exhibit (among other things) the familiar opacity characteristic of the propositional attitudes, and, unless embellished in some way, meaning$_f$ does not (yet) exhibit *this* level of intentionality. Our project, though, is more modest. We are looking for a naturalized form of misrepresentation and, if we do not yet have an account of false *belief*, we do, it seems, have a naturalized account of false *content*.

Apart from some terminological flourishes and a somewhat different way of structuring the problem, nothing I have said so far is particularly original. I have merely been retracing steps, some very significant steps, already taken by others. I am thinking especially of Stampe's seminal analysis of linguistic representation in which the (possibly false) content of a representation is identified with what would cause the representation to have the properties it has under conditions of well-functioning;[11] Enc's development of functional ideas to provide an account of the intentionality of cognitive states;[12] Fodor's application of teleological notions in supplying a semantics for his "language of thought";[13] and Millikan's powerful analysis of meaning in terms of the variety of proper functions a reproducible event (such as a sound or a gesture) might have.[14] I myself have tried to exploit (vaguely) functional ideas in my analysis of belief by defining a structure's semantic content in terms of the information it was developed to carry (hence, acquired the function of carrying).[15]

The Indeterminacy of Function

Though this approach to the problem of meaning—and, hence, misrepresentation—has been explored in some depth, there remain obstacles to regarding it as even a promising sketch, let alone a finished portrait, of nature's way of making a mistake.

There is, first, the question of how to understand a system's ability to misrepresent something for which it has no biological need. If O does not need (or need to avoid) F, it cannot (on the present account) be the *natural* function of any of O's cognitive systems to alert it to the presence (absence, location, approach, identity) of F. And without this, there is no possibility of *mis*representing something *as* F. Some internal state could still mean$_n$ that an F was present (in the way the state of Rover's detector system means$_n$ that the luggage contains marijuana), but this internal state cannot *mean$_f$* this. What we have so far is a way of understanding how an organism might misrepresent the presence of food, an obstacle, a predator, or a mate (something there is a biological need to secure or avoid),[16] but no way of understanding how *we* can misrepresent things as, say, can-openers, tennis-rackets, tulips, or the jack of diamonds. Even if we suppose our nervous systems sophisticated enough to indicate (under normal conditions) the presence of such things, it surely cannot be the *natural* function of these neural states to signal the presence—much less, specific kinds—of kitchen utensils, sporting equipment, flowers, and playing cards.

I think this is a formidable, but *not* an insuperable, difficulty. For it seems clear that a cognitive system might develop so as to service, and hence have the natural function of servicing, some biological need without its representational (*and* misrepresentational) efforts being confined to these needs. In order to identify its natural predator, an organism might develop detectors of color, shape, and movement of considerable discriminative power. Equipped, then, with this capacity for differentiating various colors, shapes, and movements, the organism acquires, as a fringe benefit so to speak, the ability to identify (and, hence, misidentify) things for which it has no biological need. The creature may have no need for green leaves, but its need for pink blossoms has led to the development of a cognitive system whose various states are capable, because of their need-related meaning$_f$, to mean$_f$ that there are green leaves present. Perhaps, though having no need for such things, it has developed a taste for them and hence a way of representing them with elements that already have a meaning$_f$.

There is, however, a more serious objection to this approach to the problem of misrepresentation. Consider, once again, the bacteria. It was said that it was the function of their magnetotactic system to indicate the whereabouts of oxygen-free environments. But why describe the function of this system in this way? Why not say that it is the function of this system to indicate the direction of geomagnetic north? Perhaps, to be even more modest, we should assign to this sensor the function of indicating the whereabouts (direction) of magnetic (not necessarily *geo*magnetic) north. This primitive sensory mechanism is, after all, functioning perfectly well when, under the bar magnet's influence, it leads its possessor into a toxic environment. *Something* is going wrong in this case, of course, but I see no reason to place the blame on the sensory mechanism, no reason to say it is not performing *its* function. One may as well complain that a fuel gauge is not performing its function when the petrol tank is filled with water (and the driver is consequently misled about the amount of *petrol* he has left). Under such abnormal circumstances, the instrument is performing its duties in a perfectly satisfactory way—i.e., indicating the amount of liquid in the tank. What has gone wrong is something for which the instrument itself is not responsible: namely, a breakdown in the normal correlations (between the quantity of liquid in the tank and the quantity of petrol in the tank) that make the gauge serviceable as a *fuel* gauge, that allow it (when conditions are normal) to mean$_n$ that there is petrol in the tank. Similarly, there is nothing wrong with one's perceptual system when one consults a slow-running clock and is, as a result, misled about the time of day. It is the function of one's eyes to tell one what *the clock says*; it is the function of *the clock* to say what the time is. Getting things right about what you need to know is often a *shared* responsibility. You have to get G right and G has to get F right. Hence, even if it is F that you need, or need to know about, the function of the perceptual system may be only to inform you of G.

If we think about the bacterium's sensory system in this way, then *its* function is to align the organism with the prevailing magnetic field. It is, so to speak, the job of magnetic north to be the direction of oxygen-free water. By transplanting a northern bacterium in the southern hemisphere we can make things go awry, but *not* because a hemispheric transplant undergoes *sensory* disorientation. No, the magnetotactic system functions as it is supposed to function, as it was (presumably) evolved to function. The most that might be claimed is that there is some *cognitive* slip (the bacterium mistakenly "infers" from its sensory condition that *that* is the direction of oxygen-free water). This sort of reply, however, begs the question by presupposing that the creature *already* has the conceptual or representational capacity to represent something *as* the direction of oxygen-free water. Our question is *whether* the organism has this capacity and, if so, where it comes from.[17]

Northern bacteria, it is true, have no need to live in northerly climes *qua* northerly climes. So to describe the function of the bacterium's detectors in terms of the role they play in identifying geomagnetic north is not to describe them in ways that reveal *how* this function is related to the satisfaction of its needs. But we do not have to describe the function of a mechanism in terms of its possessor's ultimate biological needs.[18] It is the function of the heart to circulate the blood. Just *why* the blood needs to be circulated may be a mystery.

So the sticky question is: *given* that a system needs F, and *given* that mechanism M enables the organism to detect, identify or recognize F, *how* does the mechanism carry out this function? Does it do so by representing *nearby Fs as nearby Fs* or does it, perhaps, represent them merely *as nearby Gs*, trusting to nature (the correlation between F and G) for the satisfaction of its needs? To describe a cognitive mechanism as an F-detector (and, therefore, as a mechanism that plays a vital role in the satisfaction of an organism's needs) is not *yet* to tell the functional story by means of which this mechanism does its job. All we know when we know that O needs F and that m enables O to detect F is that M *either* means$_f$ that F is present *or* it means$_f$ that G is present where G is, in O's natural surroundings, a natural sign of F's presence (where G means$_n$ F).[19] If I need vitamin C, my perceptual-cognitive system should not automatically be credited with the capacity for recognizing objects *as* containing vitamin C (as meaning$_f$ that they contain vitamin C) just because it supplies me with the information required to satisfy this need. Representing things as oranges and lemons will do quite nicely.

The problem we face is the problem of accounting for the misrepresentational capacities of a system *without* doing so by artificially *inflating* the natural functions of such a system. We need some *principled* way of saying what the natural function of a mechanism is, what its various states not only *mean$_n$*, but what they *mean$_f$*. It sounds a bit far-fetched (to my ear at least) to describe the bacteria's sensory mechanism as indicating, and having the function of indicating, the whereabouts of oxygen. For this makes it sound as though it is not performing its function under deceptive conditions (for example, in the presence of a bar magnet). This is, after all, a *magneto*tactic, not a *chemo*tactic, sensor. But if we choose to describe the function of this sensor in this more modest way, we no longer have an example of a system with misrepresentational powers. A northern bacterium (translated in the southern hemisphere) will not be misrepresenting anything when, under the guidance of its magnetotactic sensor, it moves upwards (towards geomagnetic north) into the lethal surface water. The alignment of its magnetosomes will mean$_n$ what it has always meant$_n$, what it is its function to mean$_n$, what it is supposed to mean$_n$: namely, that *that* is the direction of magnetic north. The disaster can be blamed on the abnormal surroundings. Nor can we salvage some residual misrepresentational capacity by supposing that the bacterium, under the influence of a bar magnet, at least misrepresents the direction of geomagnetic north. For, once again, the same problem emerges: why suppose it is the function of this mechanism to indicate the direction of *geo*magnetic north rather than, simply, the direction of the surrounding magnetic field? If we describe the function only in the latter way, it becomes impossible to fool the organism, impossible to make it misrepresent anything. For its internal states only mean$_f$ that the magnetic field is pointing in *that* direction and (like a compass) this is always accurate.

Functional Determination

For the purpose of clarifying issues, I have confined the discussion to simple organisms with primitive representational capacities. It is not surprising, then, to find no clear and unambiguous capacity for misrepresentation at this level. For this power—and, presumably, the dependent capacity for belief—requires a certain threshold of complexity in the information-processing capabilities of a system. Somewhere between the single cell and man we cross that threshold. It is the purpose of this final section to describe the character of this threshold, to describe the *kind* of complexity responsible for the misrepresentational capabilities of higher organisms.

Suppose an organism (unlike our bacterium) has *two* ways of detecting the presence of some toxic substance F. This may be because the organism is equipped with two sense modalities, each (in their different way) sensitive to F (or some modally specific natural sign of F), or because a single sense modality exploits different external signs (or symptoms) of F. As an example of the latter, consider the way we might identify oak trees visually by either one of two ways: by the distinctive leaf pattern (in the summer) or by the characteristic texture and pattern of the bark (in winter). We have, then, two internal states or conditions, I_1 and I_2, each produced by a different chain of antecedent events, that are natural signs of the presence of F. Each means$_n$ that F is present. Suppose, furthermore, that, having a need to escape from the toxic F, these internal states are harnessed to a third state, call it R, which triggers or releases a pattern of avoidance behaviour. Figure 14.1 assembles the relevant facts. R, of course, is also a natural sign of F. Under normal circumstances, R does not occur unless F is present. f_1 and f_2 are properties typical of normal Fs. s_1 and s_2 are proximal stimuli.

If, now, we present the system with some ersatz F (analogous to the bar magnet with the bacteria), something exhibiting *some* of the properties of the real f (say f_1), we trigger a chain of events (s_1, I_1, R and avoidance) that normally occurs, and is really only appropriate, in the presence of F. If we look at the internal state R and ask what it means$_f$ under these deceptive conditions, we find ourselves unable to say (as we could in the case of the bacteria) that it means$_f$ anything short of (i.e., more proximal than) F itself. Even though s_1 (by means of I_1) is triggering the occurrence of R, R does not mean$_n$ (hence, cannot mean$_f$) that s_1 (or F_1) is occurring. R is analogous to a light bulb connected to switches wired in parallel *either* of whose closure will turn the light on. When the bulb lights up, it does not mean$_n$ that switch no. 1 is closed even when it is this switch's closure that causes the light to go on. It does not mean$_n$ this, because there is no regular correlation between the bulb lighting up and switch no. 1 being closed (50 per cent of the time it is switch no. 2).

If we think of the detection system described above as having the function of enabling the organism to detect F, then the multiplicity of ways of detecting F has the consequence that certain internal states (for example, R) can indicate (hence mean$_f$) that F is present without indi-

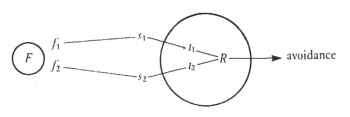

Figure 14.1

Misrepresentation

cating anything about the intermediate conditions (i.e., f_1 or s_1) that "tell" it that F is present. Our problem with the bacteria was to find a way of having the orientation of its magnetosomes mean$_f$ that oxygen-free water was in a certain direction without *arbitrarily* dismissing the possibility of its meaning$_f$ that the magnetic field was aligned in that direction. We can now see that, with the multiple resources described in figure 1, this possibility can be *non*-arbitrarily dismissed. R *cannot* mean$_f$ that f_1 or s_1 is occurring, because it *does not*, even under optimal conditions, mean$_n$ this. We can therefore claim to have found a non-derivative case of misrepresentation (i.e., R's meaning$_f$ that F is present when it is not) which cannot be dismissed by redescribing what R means$_f$ so as to eliminate the appearance of misrepresentation. The threatened inflation of possible meanings$_f$, arising from the variety of ways a system's natural function might be described, has been blocked.

Still, it will be said, we *need not* accept this as a case of genuine misrepresentation *if* we are prepared to recognize that R has a *disjunctive* meaning$_n$. The lighting up of the bulb (connected to switches wired in parallel) does not mean$_n$ that any particular switch is on, but it does indicate that *one* of the switches is on. Similarly, it may be said, even though it is the function of the mechanism having R as its terminal state to alert the organism to the presence of F, it does so by R's indicating, and having the function of indicating, the occurrence of a certain disjunctive condition—namely, that either f_1 or f_2 (or s_1 or s_2). Our hypothetical organism mistakenly withdraws from F, *not* because it misrepresents the ersatz F as F, but because what it correctly indicates (i.e. that the ersatz F is either f_1 or f_2) is no longer correlated in the normal way with something's being F.

No matter how versatile a detection system we might design, no matter how many routes of informational access we might give an organism, the possibility will always exist of describing its function (and therefore the meaning$_f$ of its various states) as the detection of some highly disjunctive property of the proximal input. At least, this will always be possible *if* we have a determinate set of disjuncts to which we can retreat.

Suppose, however, that we have a system capable of some form of associative learning. Suppose, in other words, that through repeated exposures to *cs* (a conditioned stimulus) in the presence of F, a change takes place. R (and, hence, avoidance behaviour) can now be triggered by the occurrence of *cs* alone. Furthermore, it becomes clear that there is virtually no limit to the kind of stimulus that can acquire this "displaced" effectiveness in triggering R and subsequent avoidance behaviour. Almost any *s* can become a *cs*, thereby assuming "control" over R, by functioning (in the "experience" of the organism) as a sign of F.

We now have a cognitive mechanism that not only transforms a variety of different sensory inputs (the s_i) into *one* output-determining state *(R)*, but is capable of modifying the character of this many-one mapping over time. If we restrict ourselves to the sensory inputs (the s_i of figure 14.1), R means$_n$ one thing at t_1 (for example, that either s_1 or s_2), something else at t_2 (for example, that either s_1 or s_2 or, through learning, cs_3), and something still different at a later time. Just *what R* means$_n$ will depend on the individual's learning history—on *what s_i* became cs_i *for it*. There is no *time-invariant* meaning$_n$ for R; hence, nothing that, through time, could be its function to indicate. In terms of the s_i that produce R, R can have no time-invariant meaning$_f$.

Of course, throughout this process, R continues to indicate the presence of F. It does so because by hypothesis, any new s_i to which R becomes conditioned is a natural sign of F. Learning is a process in which stimuli that indicate the presence of F are, in their turn, indicated by some relevant internal state of the organism (R in this case). Therefore, if we are to think of these cognitive mechanisms as having a time-invariant function at all (something that is implied by their continued—indeed, as a result of learning, more efficient—servicing of the associated need), then we *must* think of their function, not as indicating the nature of the proximal (even distal) conditions that trigger positive responses (the s_i and f_1), but as indicating the condition (F) for which these diverse stimuli are signs. The mechanism just described has, then, as its natural function, the indication of the presence of F. Hence, the occurrence of R means$_f$ that F is present. It does not mean$_f$ that s_1 or s_2 or . . . s_x obtains, even though, at any given stage of development, it will mean$_n$ this for some definite value of x.

A system at this level of complexity, having not only multiple channels of access to what it needs to know about, but the resources for expanding its information-gathering resources, possesses, I submit, a genuine power of misrepresentation. When there is a breakdown in the normal chain of natural signs, when, say, cs_7 occurs (a learned sign of F) under circumstances in which it does not mean$_n$ that F is present (in the way that the broken clock does not mean$_n$ that it is 3.30 a.m.), R still means$_f$ (though not, of course, means$_n$) that F is present. It means$_f$ this because that is what it is *supposed* to mean$_n$, what it is its natural function to mean$_n$, and there is available no other condition it can mean$_f$.

Notes

I am grateful to Berent Enc, Dennis Stampe, and Jerry Fodor for their helpful criticisms, both constructive and destructive, of earlier drafts of this essay.

1. See Dennett (1971).

2. This needs some qualification, but it will do for the moment. What a natural sign means often does depend on us, on what we *know* about relevant alternative possibilities or on how we *use* an associated device. But if we don't know anything, or if the sign occurs in the operation of a device having no normal use, the sign still means something—just not, specifically, what we say it means under epistemically (or functionally) richer conditions. I return to this point in note 8.

Misrepresentation

3. I give a fuller account of it in Dretske (1981), chaps. 1 and 2.

4. See Grice (1957).

5. I hope it is clear, that I am not here concerned with the word "empty" (or the letter "E") that might appear on the gauge. This symbol means empty whatever the gauge is doing, but this is purely conventional. I am concerned with what the pointer's position means$_n$ *whatever* we choose to print on the face of the instrument.

6. L. Wright (1973) calls these "conscious" functions.

7. A doorbell, for example, cannot mean$_n$ *both* that there is someone at the door *and* that there is a short circuit.

8. It isn't the change of purpose *alone* that changes what something means$_n$ (hence, means$_f$). It is the fact that this change in use is accompanied by altered background knowledge, and meaning$_n$ changes as background knowledge changes. If, for example, A depends on both B and C, a changing A can mean$_n$ that C is changing *if* we know that B is constant. If we know that C is constant, it can mean$_n$ that B is changing. If we know nothing, it only means that either B or C is changing. Natural meaning is relative in this sense, but derelativizing it (by ignoring what we know and how we use a device) does not eliminate natural meaning. It merely makes *less determinate* what things mean$_n$. For a fuller discussion of this point, see Dretske (1981), chap. 3.

9. I think much of our talk about the representational capacities of computers is of this assigned, hence derived, kind. It tells us nothing about the intrinsic power of a machine to represent or misrepresent anything. Hence, nothing about the cognitive character of its internal states. R. Cummins, I think, gets it exactly right by distinguishing *cognition (a version of *assigned* meaning) from genuine cognition. See Cummins (1983).

10. My source for this example is Blakemore and Frankel (1981).

11. See Stampe (1977).

12. Enc (1982) identified the content of a functional state with the (construction of the) properties of the event to which the system has the function of responding.

13. Fodor (1990).

14. See Millikan (1984).

15. See Dretske (1981), part 3.

16. Something for which there is, in Dennett's (earlier) language, an "appropriate efferent continuation": see Dennett (1969).

17. Fodor (in a circulated draft of "Why paramecia don't have mental representations") distinguishes organisms for which a representational theory of mind is not appropriate (paramecia, for example) and ones for which it is (us, for example) in terms of the latter's ability to respond to non-nomic stimulus properties (properties that are not transducer-detectable). We, but not paramecia, are capable of representing something as, say, a crumpled shirt, and *being a crumpled shirt*, is not a projectible property. In this article, Fodor is not concerned with the question of *where* we get this extraordinary representational power from (he suggests it requires inferential capacities). He is concerned only

with offering it as a way of distinguishing us from a variety of other perceptual and quasi-cognitive systems.

I agree with Fodor about the importance and relevance of this distinction, but my present concern is to understand *how* a system could acquire the power to represent something in this way. The power to represent something *as* a crumpled shirt (where this implies the correlative ability to misrepresent it as such) is certainly not innate.

18. Enc (1982) says that a photoreceptor in the fruit-fly has the function of enabling the fly to reach humid spots (in virtue of the correlation between dark spots and humid spots). I have no objection to describing things in this way. But the question remains: *how* does it perform this function? We can answer this question without supposing that there is any mechanism of the fly whose function it is to indicate the degree of humidity. The sensory mechanism can perform this function if there is merely something to indicate the luminosity—i.e., a photoreceptor. *That* will enable the fly to reach humid spots. Likewise, the bacteria's magnetotactic sense *enables* (and, let us say, has the *function* of enabling) the bacteria to avoid oxygen-rich water. But the way it does it (it may be argued) is by having a sensor that indicates, and has the function of indicating, the direction of the magnetic field.

19. In Fodor's way of putting the point (in "Psychosemantics"), this is merely a way of saying that his identification of the semantics of M (some mental representation) with entry conditions (relative to a set of normalcy conditions) still leaves some slack. We can say that the entry condition is the absence (presence) of oxygen *or* a specific orientation of the magnetic field. Appeal to the selectional history of this mechanism won't decide *which* is the right specification of entry conditions—hence, won't tell us whether the bacteria are capable of *mis*representing anything. Fodor, I think, realizes this residual indeterminacy and makes the suggestive remark (note 9) that this problem is an analog of the problems of specifying the perceptual object for theories of perception.

References

Blakemore, R. P., and R. B. Frankel (1981). Magnetic nativation in bacteria. *Scientific American* 245, 6.

Cummins, R. C. (1983). *Psychological explanation*. Cambridge, MA: MIT Press.

Dennett, D. C. (1969). *Content and consciousness*. London: Routledge and Kegan Paul.

Dennett, D. C. (1971). Intentional systems. *Journal of Philosophy* 68, 87–106.

Dretske, F. I. (1981). *Knowledge and the flow of information*. Cambridge, MA: MIT Press.

Enc, B. (1982). Intentional states of mechanical devices. *Mind* 91, 161–182.

Fodor, J. A. (1990). Psychosemantics, or where do truth conditions come from. In W. G. Lycan, ed., *Mind and Cognition: A Reader*. Oxford: Blackwell.

Grice, H. P. (1957). Meaning. *Philosophical Review* 66, 377–388.

Millikan, R. (1984). *Language, thought, and other biological categories*. Cambridge, MA: MIT Press.

Stampe, D. (1977). Toward a causal theory of linguistic representation. In P. French, T. Uehling, and H. Wettstein, eds., *Midwest Studies in Philosophy*, vol. 2. Minneapolis: University of Minnesota Press.

Wright, L. (1973). Functions. *Philosophical Review* 82, 139–168.

15   How We Know Our Minds: The Illusion of First-Person Knowledge of Intentionality

Alison Gopnik

The Problem of First-Person Knowledge

As adults all of us have a network of psychological beliefs. We believe that other people have beliefs, desires, intentions, and emotions and that these states lead to their actions. Moreover, we also believe that we ourselves have analogous beliefs and desires that are involved in our own decisions to act. And we believe, at least implicitly, that beliefs, desires, and so on are what philosophers would call "intentional" states; we believe that they are about the world. However, we also believe that our relations to our own beliefs and desires are different from our relations to those of others. We believe that we know our own beliefs and desires directly, but that we must infer the beliefs and desires of other people. Are we right?

In trying to understand our commonsense psychological beliefs, and to test whether they are correct, it is helpful to distinguish between two different ways we think about mental states such as beliefs and desires. We sometimes think of mental states as the underlying entities that explain our behavior and experience. Describing such states is the goal of scientific psychology. I will call these underlying entities "psychological states." These psychological states are similar to other physically or functionally defined objects and events in the world: atoms, species, word-processing programs, and so forth.

In addition, however, we use mentalistic vocabulary to talk about conscious experiences with a particular kind of phenomenology, the Joycean or Woolfian stream of consciousness. I will call these "psychological experiences." These experiences are phenomenologically distinct from other types of experience, such as our experiences of trees or rocks or colors. Our experiences of our own beliefs and desires are also phenomenologically distinct from our experiences of other people's.[1] In

From A. Gopnik, How we know our minds: The illusion of first-person knowledge of intentionality, *Brain and Behavioral Sciences* 16, 1–14 (1993). Copyright 1993 by Cambridge University Press. Reprinted with the permission of Cambridge University Press.

one sense, of course, all experience is first-person and psychological. In a different sense, however, we can use these terms to pick out a distinctive type of experience, for example, the experience I have as I sit motionless at my desk and thoughts, desires, emotions, and intentions fill my head.

The commonsense notion that our knowledge of our own minds is immediate and privileged can be construed in many ways. We can construe it simply as a claim about our psychological beliefs themselves. We might simply be saying that, as a matter of fact, most people do believe that we know our own minds. This means, for example, that they don't require justifications for first-person psychological assertions (see Davidson 1980). Construed this way, the claim is obviously true. We do have the beliefs outlined in the first paragraph and they form the background for the way we speak and act. Alternatively, we might construe the assertion of first-person privileged knowledge as a matter of phenomenology. It concerns the way our psychological experience feels to us. This assertion also seems incontrovertibly true.

We might, however, also construe the claim of first-person privileged knowledge as an epistemological, even a cognitive, one.[2] Common sense itself appears to make this stronger claim, which does not just concern the phenomenology of our psychological experiences but also their relation to underlying psychological states. According to this interpretation of first-person privilege, our beliefs about our own psychological states do not come from the same source as our beliefs about the psychological states of others. In the case of our own minds, there is a direct link leading from our underlying psychological states to our psychological experiences. It is easy enough to imagine how we might be so wired that whenever we were in a particular psychological state we would have a particular corresponding psychological experience. Because we have no experience of other minds, this link cannot exist in that case, and so our beliefs about the psychological states of others must be indirect. According to this interpretation, we note the behaviors that result from our own psychological states, known directly through psychological experience, and then infer that others have similar psychological states when they produce similar actions.

This is an intuitively plausible idea and one that underlies our commonsense understanding as well as many philosophical and psychological accounts. It is also, however, an empirical claim about the cognitive relation between our psychological states and experiences and our beliefs about them. Are psychological states, experiences, and beliefs actually related in this way?

The answer might be different for beliefs about different psychological states. For simple sensations, the commonsense conviction that our beliefs about ourselves and our beliefs about others come from different sources may be very strong. In other cases, for example, very abstract emotional states such as jealousy or guilt or love, we may feel less certain that this picture is correct. In particular, we may notice that there are cases of self-deception where our beliefs about ourselves, and even our psychological experiences of ourselves, prove to be consistently inaccurate.

In this target article, I will be concerned with one particular belief: the belief that psychological states are intentional. As ordinary, unphilosophical adults we believe that our beliefs are psychological entities that refer to the world but that they can also be misleading. We may not make this belief about beliefs fully explicit, but it is clearly apparent in our ability to understand the complexities of the relationship between the world and our beliefs about it, and particularly in our ability to understand cases of misrepresentation. How do we develop these beliefs about beliefs? Our adult intuitions suggest that knowledge of intentionality, like knowledge of sensations, comes directly and reliably from our psychological experience. I know that my beliefs refer to the world—but that they may be false, they may change, or they may come from many different sources—simply by experiencing these facts about them.

Alternatively, our commonsense intuitions might be wrong. My beliefs about the intentionality of my own mental states and those of others might have a very similar cognitive history. I will argue here that evidence from developmental psychology suggests that this is the case. As young children we have psychological states, we have psychological experiences, and we have beliefs about our psychological states. Our beliefs about at least some of those states, however, are consistently incorrect and differ from the beliefs we will have later. As far as we can tell, our experience of those states is also different. Young children do not seem to believe that their own psychological states are intentional, nor do they experience them as intentional, in the way adults do. Since we were all once such children, what we think we know about ourselves changes radically.

Perhaps more important, these changes reflect our knowledge about the psychological states of other people. When we are children and our understanding of others is incorrect, our understanding of ourselves, even our experience of ourselves, is incorrect in the same way. Empirical findings show that the idea of intentionality is a theoretical construct, one we invent in our early lives to explain a wide variety of evidence about ourselves and others. This theoretical construct is equally applicable to ourselves and others and depends equally on our experience of ourselves and others.

This conclusion may seem to leave us with a puzzle. If the origins of first-person knowledge of intentionality are not profoundly different from the origins of third-person knowledge, why do we as adults think they are? I will suggest an analogy between our impression that we experience our own psychological states directly and similar phenomena in cases of expertise. In the case of the expert, phenomenological immediacy may be divorced from cognitive directness. Experts experience their knowledge as immediate and perceptually based; in reality, however, it depends on a long theoretical history. Similarly, we, as experts in commonsense psychology, may experience our theoretical knowledge of the intentionality of our psychological states as if it were the result of direct perception. . . .

Developing an Understanding of the Minds of Others

The Evidence

In the last few years there has been a veritable explosion of interest in children's ideas about the mind (see Astington et al. 1988; Perner 1991; Wellman 1990; Whiten 1990; see also Astington and Gopnik 1991b; Gopnik 1990, for reviews). Much of this investigation has centered on the period between about 2½ and 5 years of age.[3] In this developmental period there are clear and consistent changes in the ways that children make inferences about the mental states of others. The area is a new one and there is some controversy over the details of various experiments. Nevertheless, there is also an emerging consensus about the general outlines of the developments.

By 18 months children show some capacity to generate representations that are not given to them perceptually, and to comment, implicitly or explicitly, on the fit between representations and reality. For example, they may use words like "no" to comment on the nonexistence of hypothetical objects, or (later) the falsity of hypothetical propositions; or they may use "uh-oh" to comment on the fact that their goals have not been realized (Gopnik 1982). In their pretend play they show the capacity to treat an object as something other than itself, and to demonstrate, by their laughter and delight, that they know they are doing this (Leslie 1988). These abilities suggest some very early capacity to distinguish between reality and representations, between physical objects and mental states.

During the second year children become increasingly able to refer to mental states linguistically (Shatz et al. 1983). By the age of 3, the capacity to understand the ontological difference between physical reality and mental states is clearly in place. The most dramatic evidence for this comes in a study by Wellman and Estes (1986). Three-year-old children were able to distinguish between dreams, images and thoughts, and real things. Moreover, as we might expect from the early emergence of pretend play, 3-year-olds appear to be able to differentiate other people's pretenses from reality. Flavell et al. (1987) found that 3-year-old children had little difficulty understanding that someone was pretending to be a dog yet was really a person.

At about the same time, children also show some ability to understand differences between their own mental states and the mental states of others. Children of this age seem to understand that there might be limits on how much of the world one might see or think of, and that these limits might differ for different people. For example, children as young as 2½ years appear to know that someone else may not be able to see something they themselves see, or vice versa (Flavell et al. 1981). (There is some evidence that this ability is itself gradually constructed in the second year; Lempers et al. 1977). Recent work by Wellman (1990) also suggests that young children may be able to make similar judgments about knowledge and belief. For example, 3-year-old children may know that if there are pencils in two locations, say, the shelf and the desk, and someone has only looked in the desk, they will not know about the pencils on the shelf.

An interesting, ambiguous case concerns children's ability to intentionally deceive others. Some have suggested that this ability might be a hallmark of general "metarepresentational" ability. However, it also appears difficult to distinguish genuine deception (an attempt to implant a particular false belief in the mind of another) from what one might call "behavioral deception," the acquisition of a pragmatic strategy for bringing about certain events, without a deeper understanding of the basis for that strategy. The developmental literature is also ambiguous. Some investigators have claimed to find deceptive behaviors in 3-year-olds (Chandler et al. 1989); others have failed to replicate these results (Sodian 1991).

These are impressive abilities in such very young children. However, the failures of these children are equally impressive. Three-year-old children consistently fail to understand certain other problems, or rather understand them in a way that is profoundly different from adult understanding. These problems involve very different questions and tasks but a common conceptual basis. All of them require that the child understand the complex representational process relating real objects and mental representations of those objects.

Two types of tasks have been extensively studied, the appearance-reality task (Flavell et al. 1986) and the false-belief task (Hogrefe et al. 1986; Perner et al. 1987; Wimmer and Perner 1983). In the appearance-reality task, children are presented with an object that appears to be one thing but is actually another: a "Hollywood rock" made of painted sponge; a "sucker egg" made of chalk; a green cat covered by a red filter that makes it look black. After extensive pretraining to ensure that they understand the questions, children are asked what the object looks like and what it really is. Typically, 3-year-olds give the same answer to both questions, saying that the object looks like a sponge, and really is a sponge or the cat looks black and really is black (whether they respond with the reality or the appearance depends on the particular object).

Flavell and his colleagues have gone to heroic lengths to ensure that the children's errors are genuinely conceptual and not merely linguistic. In one particularly convincing demonstration (Flavell et al. 1986) children are shown a white cardboard "flower" with a blue filter over it. The filter is placed over the flower and the children have a chance to see that the blue color is only apparent. The children say that the flower both appears blue and is really blue. The children next see the flower with the filter on top and see the experimenter cut away a small portion of the cardboard flower. They are then shown two pieces of cardboard, one white and one blue, and asked which piece came from the flower. Even though this question is not explicitly about appearance or reality, and only requires children to point to a piece, children err by choosing the blue patch.

In one version of the false-belief task, children are asked to predict how a deceptive object will appear to others. For example, children see a candy box, which turns out to be full of pencils (Perner et al. 1987). They are asked what someone else will think when they first see the box. Three-year-old children consistently say that the other person will think there are pencils in the box. They apparently fail to understand that the other person's beliefs may be false. Again, this finding has proved to be strikingly robust. Children make this error in many different situations, involving many different kinds of objects and events. They continue to make the error when they actually see the other person respond to the box with surprise, and even when they are explicitly told about the other person's false belief (Moses and Flavell 1990; Wellman 1990). Moreover, they make incorrect predictions about the other person's actions, which reflect their incorrect understanding of the other person's beliefs (Perner et al. 1987). They make similar errors in dealing with deceptive physical representations, such as misleading pictures or photographs (Zaitchik 1990).[4]

These are the best-investigated tasks, but there are also other indicators in the literature that an important conceptual change occurs at this point. One indication concerns children's ability to understand that people may see objects in different ways, what Flavell has called "level-2" perceptual perspective-taking. Three-year-olds, for example, appear to have difficulty understanding that a turtle on a table who looks right-side up to them may look upside-down to an observer on the other side of the table (Flavell et al. 1981).

There are also changes in children's ability to understand the sources of their beliefs. Wimmer has suggested that children have difficulty inferring where beliefs come from, knowing, for example, that someone who has had perceptual access to an object would know what it was, while someone who has not, could not (Wimmer, Hogrefe, and Perner 1988; Wimmer, Hogrefe, and Sodian 1988). Others have failed to replicate this finding, particularly where vision is involved (Pillow 1989). There is, however, other evidence that children have difficulty understanding where beliefs come from. O'Neill et al. (1992) tested whether children understood that only certain kinds of information could be obtained from particular types of sources. For example, children were shown two objects which could only be differentiated by touch and two others which could only be differentiated by sight; they were also shown a person who either saw or touched the objects. Three-year-olds had difficulty predicting which objects the other person would be able to differentiate.

There is also evidence that 3-year-olds have difficulty understanding the notion of subjective probability. Moore et al. (1990) found that 3-year-olds were unable to determine that a person who knew about an object was a more reliable source of information than one who merely guessed or thought. Similarly, 3-year-olds, in contrast to 4-year-olds, showed no preference for getting information from people who were sure they knew what was in a box rather than those who expressed uncertainty about their knowledge. These children seemed to divide cognitive states into full knowledge or total ignorance; they did not appreciate that belief could admit of degrees.

A final piece of evidence for a developing understanding of belief comes from investigations of children's spontaneous references to such events in their ordinary speech. Bartsch and Wellman (cited in Wellman 1990), following an earlier study by Shatz et al. (1983) analyzed extensive spontaneous speech samples from the CHILDES corpus and discovered that there were virtually no genuine references to belief or knowledge (as opposed to formulaic expressions such as "I don't know") before the third birthday. In contrast, there were many references to desire and perception in the earliest transcripts. After the third birthday, references to belief and even occasional references to false belief began to appear, and these increased markedly in the period from ages 3 to 4.

The understanding of perceptions, of false beliefs, and of sources and degrees of belief requires an understanding of what Searle has called mental states with a "mind-to-world" direction of fit; states where the mind is altered to fit the world (Searle 1983). An interesting question, only recently being investigated, concerns children's understanding of "world-to-mind" mental states, states such as desire and intention where the world is altered to fit the mind. Classical philosophical accounts often describe our everyday psychology as a "belief-desire" psychology and have argued that both belief and desire are always implicated in our explanations of action. Moreover, such states are considered to be intentional in most philosophical accounts; what we desire or intend (by and large) is not a thing itself but the thing as represented in a particular way. For example, if the chocolate cake I am intent on obtaining turns out to be made of carob and tofu, I will be frustrated. My desire was less for this piece of cake, than for this piece of cake as I first represented it to myself, full of sin and cholesterol. At the same time, the differences in direction of fit may make desires rather different from beliefs.

There is evidence that even 2-year-olds have a simple nonrepresentational concept of desire. They understand, for example, that desires may not be fulfilled (Astington and Gopnik 1991a; Wellman and Woolley 1990). There is also evidence, however, that other aspects of desire are more difficult to understand. One particularly interesting recent finding concerns children's understanding of differences in judgments of value, judgments more closely related to desires than to beliefs (Flavell et al. 1990). Children appear to be better able to make the correct judgment in these cases than in the standard false-belief task. They appear to be more willing to say, for example, that they might think a cookie was yummy whereas another person thought it was yucky than that they might think the box was full of pencils whereas the other thought it was full of candy. Nevertheless, a fair minority of 3 year-old children (between 30% and 40%) still made errors on these tasks.

Similarly, there is some evidence that children have difficulty understanding some aspects of intention. Intentions may be construed simply as desires. We might also think of intentions, however, as more complex states that mediate between beliefs and desires and actions. Three-year-old children appear to understand intentions in the first way but not the second, just as they have difficulty understanding how representations mediate between beliefs and desires and the world. Astington has found that children identify intentions with either actions or desires rather than understanding them as mental states following desires but preceding actions (Astington and Gopnik 1991a).

These abilities consistently appear at around age 4. Given appropriately simple tasks, 4-year-olds have little difficulty understanding false beliefs, appearance-reality contrasts, and the other concepts that give 3-year-olds difficulty. Moreover, there is evidence for an association among these tasks; children who do well on one are also likely to do well on the others. Flavell et al. (1986) found that the level-2 perceptual task (knowing that the turtle would appear upside down to the other viewer) was significantly correlated with performance on the appearance-reality task when age was controlled for. Similarly, we found that, with age controlled, performance on false-belief and appearance-reality tasks was significantly correlated (Gopnik and Astington 1988). Moore et al. (1990) replicated this result and also found that judgments of subjective probability were correlated with all these other developments.

The Shift to Representational Model of the Mind

How do we interpret these results? There is some consensus among these investigators that there is a quite general shift in the child's concept of the mind at around 3½ years. This shift involves central changes in the child's epistemological concepts, concepts of the relation between mind and world. The precise characterization of this shift has been a matter of some debate. Indeed it is difficult to know exactly how to characterize a view of the mind that is profoundly different from our own. The essential idea, however, is that the 3-year-old believes objects or events are directly apprehended by the mind. In Chandler's (1988) striking phrase, objects are bullets that leave an indelible trace on any mind that is in their path. Different theorists have captured this idea in different ways. Flavell (1988) talks about cognitive connections; Wellman (1990) talks about a "copy theory of representation"; Perner (1991) talks about connections to situations. We have suggested that it may be useful to think of this view as analogous to certain views of perception, such as a Gibsonian or Dretskean (Dretske 1981) view (Astington and Gopnik 1991a),[5] in which the relation between real things in the world and our perception of them is a direct causal link, almost a transference. Indeed, it seems plausible that children originally apply this model to perception and then extend it to belief.

For 3-year-olds, there are two kinds of psychological states. In true 3-year-old spirit, we might call them "silly states" and "serious states." Silly states include images, dreams, and pretenses, whereas serious states are similar to what adults would call perceptions, desires, and beliefs. For the 3-year-old, silly states have no referential or causal relation to reality; they are neither true nor false. They are completely divorced from considerations of the real world (which largely explains their charm). The 3-year-old versions of perception, desire, and belief, however, involve a completely accurate, if sometimes limited, apprehension of the way the world really is. Objects exist in the world and people see, want, or apprehend them. One way of putting it might be that for the 3-year-old, all serious psychological states are "transparent" (Quine 1956). That is, children think of belief the way we as adults sometimes construe perception or desire, as a matter of a direct relation between the mind and objects in the world, not a relation mediated by representations or propositions. They think we simply believe x, *tout court*, just as, even in the adult view, we may simply see or want x, *tout court*, rather than seeing, wanting, or believing *that* x.

This view of the mind allows children to make many predictions and solve many problems. It allows them to see that if a mind is not in the path of an object it will not apprehend the object and to understand how beliefs lead to action. It does not, however, allow them to understand cases of misrepresentation, such as false beliefs or misleading appearances (consider the similar difficulties for a Gibsonian [1979] or Dretskean account). In an important sense, if you cannot understand the possibility of misrepresentation, you do not understand representation at all. And this is not all this Gibsonian view fails to allow children to understand. It also, in a quite different way, makes it difficult to understand that beliefs may come from many different sources, that they may come in degrees, and that there are intermediate steps between the mind and the world.

Three-year-olds believe that cognitive states come in only two varieties, total knowledge, when the world is related to the mind, and absolute ignorance, when it is not. In cases of misrepresentation, there is one object in the world and two people are both related to that object, but differences in the relations between the minds and the world lead to different representations of that object. In the sources and subjective probability cases (see previous section entitled "The Evidence"), there is one object in the world and two people arrive at the same representation of that object, but the relations between each person and the world are different. To distinguish between degrees of belief and sources of belief we need to understand that people's cognitive relations to the world may differ in significant ways even when both their ultimate beliefs and the objects in the world are the same. To understand both misrepresentation and sources and subjective probability, requires "a representational model of the mind" (Forguson and Gopnik 1988). The absence of a representational model might also make it difficult for children to appreciate the intentionality of desire, the fact that objects are desired under a description, and that desires may vary as a result of variations in that description.

By the age of 4 or 5, children, at least in our culture, have developed something more like a representational model of mind. Accordingly, almost all psychological functioning in 5-year-olds is mediated by representations. Desires, perceptions, beliefs, pretenses, and images all involve the same basic structure, one sometimes described in terms of propositional attitudes and propositional contents. These mental states all involve representations of reality, rather than direct relations to reality itself. Perceiving, desiring, and believing become perceiving, desiring, and believing *that.* Rather than distinguishing different types of mental states with different relations to a real world of objects, the child sees that all mental states involve the same abstract representational structure. Many characteristics of all psychological states, such as their diversity and their tendency to change, can be explained by the properties of representations. This unified view provides predictions, explanations, and interpretations that were not possible earlier.

I have argued above and elsewhere (Gopnik 1990) that a representational model of the mind is an essential part of the commonsense adult notion of intentionality. Clearly, if we asked most adults whether their beliefs and desires were "intentional" they would not understand what we were talking about. The philosophical term is shorthand for a number of related commonsense beliefs. One of these is the belief that beliefs and desires are about things. More important we also believe that the contents of beliefs and desires are not the things themselves but what we think about those things. As a consequence, beliefs and desires may vary as our understanding of the world varies. The intuitions that are captured by philosophical notions like "opacity" or "propositional contents" or the rest (Quine 1956) concern the mediated nature of representation and the possibility of misrepresentation that results. If common sense were Gibsonian, if we all thought that cognition was direct and unmediated, then, I suggest, we would not think that psychological states were intentional.[6]

Developing an Understanding of Your Own Mind

So far, I have argued that there is evidence for a deep change in children's understanding of the psychological states of other people somewhere between the ages of 3 and 4. Is this change in the child's concept of the mind applicable only to others or to the self as well?

Suppose the commonsense and philosophical accounts of privileged first-person beliefs about the mind were correct. Then we should predict that, however erroneous children's views of the psychological states of others might be, they would not make similar errors in their understanding of their own psychological states. If they knew anything at all about their own minds, then what they knew ought to be substantially correct. This knowledge certainly should not be systematically and consistently wrong.

One could argue that the changes in the understanding of the mind we have described so far reflect the difficulties inherent in inferring the psychological states of other people, and indeed this argument has been made in the literature (Harris 1990; Johnson 1988). Children certainly seem to assume that their current beliefs about the object will be shared by others. There is a difficulty here, however, for our concept of what is real is constituted by our current beliefs. Children's errors might come from two rather different sources: They might believe (1) that everyone else believes what they do or (2) that everyone believes what is actually the case, where what is the case, for children as well as adults, is specified by their current beliefs. The problem with false beliefs might not be that children assume that particular beliefs are shared, but simply that they assume that others believe what is the case.

One way to differentiate between these possibilities is by looking at children's understanding of their immediately past beliefs or other psychological states, states they no longer hold. If children's problems genuinely stem from a kind of egocentrism, they should not have similar difficulties in understanding their own immediately past beliefs. These beliefs are, after all, as much their own as their current beliefs.

Moreover, our immediate recall of psychological states that occurred within the span of a few minutes ought to count as part of first-person psychological experience. Phenomenologically, first-person experience extends beyond the immediate moment (indeed it is hard to see how it could exist, or at least how we could know it did, otherwise). In adults, the span of introspection, as it were, is at least this long.[7] If I were to describe my psychological experience when I see a candy box and then discover that it is full of pencils, I would say that I experience my belief that the box is full of candy, and then the change in my belief that comes with the new discovery, with all its attendant phenomenological vividness and detail. The very psychological experience of the change in belief depends on the fact that I continue to remember the previous belief.

We have compared children's performance on "other minds" tasks like those we have just described with their performance on tasks that require them to report their own immediately past mental states. We find that children make errors about their own immediately past states that are similar to the errors they make about the states of others. This is true even though children ought to have direct first-person psychological evidence of these past states.

In our original experiment (Gopnik and Astington 1988) we presented children with a variety of deceptive objects, such as the candy box full of pencils, and allowed them to discover the true nature of the objects. We then asked the children both the false-belief question, "What will Nicky think is inside the box?" and the appearance-reality question, "Does it look as if there are candies in the box?" But we also asked children about their own immediately past beliefs about the box: "When you first saw the box, before we opened it, what did you think was inside it?" The pattern of results on all three tasks was similar: One-half to two-thirds of the 3-year-olds said they had originally thought there were pencils in the box. They apparently failed to remember their immediately previous false beliefs. Moreover, children's ability to answer the false-belief question about their own belief was significantly correlated with their ability to answer the question about the others' belief and the appearance-reality question, even with age controlled. This result was recently replicated by Moore et al. (1990), who also found significant correlations with children's understanding of subjective probability.

The children were given an additional control task. They saw a closed container (a toy house) with one object inside it, then the house was opened, the object was removed, and a different object was placed inside. Children were asked, "When you first saw the house, before we opened it, what was inside it?" This question had the same form as the belief question. It asked, however, about the past physical state of the house rather than about a past mental state. Children were only included in the experiment if they answered this question correctly, demonstrating that they could understand that the question referred to the past and remember the past state of affairs. Several different syntactic forms of the question were asked to further ensure that the problem was not a linguistic one.

Recently, this experiment has been replicated, with additional controls, by Wimmer and Hartl (1991) (who also draw similar philosophical conclusions). First, they phrased the control question as a "think" question: "When you first saw the box, before we opened it, what did you think was inside it?" ensuring that the additional syntactic complexity of the embedded clause was not confusing the children. Moreover, they used exactly the same materials and question in the control and belief tasks. In the control task, children were shown a box whose contents were subsequently changed. Three-year-olds were again fully capable of answering the question when it referred to an actual change in the world rather than a change in belief. Finally, in the belief task the children were explicitly asked to identify the object when they first saw it. All the children initially said they thought there was candy in the box, confirming that they did, in fact, have the false belief initially. The results were similar to the previous results.

In a second set of experiments (Gopnik and Graf 1988) we investigated children's ability to identify the sources of their beliefs, elaborating on a question first used by Wimmer, Hogrefe, and Perner (1988). Children found out about objects that were placed in a drawer in one of three ways; they either saw the objects, were told about them, or figured them out from a simple clue. Then we asked "What's in the drawer?" and all the children answered correctly. Immediately after this question we asked about the source of the child's knowledge: "How do you know there's an x in the drawer? Did you see it, did I tell you about it, or did you figure it out from a clue?" Again, 3-year-olds made frequent errors on this task. Although they knew what the objects were, they could not say how they knew. They might say, for example, that we had told them about an object, even though they had actually seen it. Their performance was better than chance but still significantly worse than the performance of 4-year-olds, who were almost error-free. In a follow-up experiment (O'Neill and Gopnik 1991) we used different and simpler sources (tell, see, and feel) and presented children with only two possibilities at a time. We also included a control task to ensure that the children understood the meaning of "tell," "see," and "feel." Despite these simplifications of the task, the performance of the 3-year-olds was similar to their performance in the original experiment.

In a more recent experiment we have investigated whether children could understand changes in psychological states other than belief (Gopnik and Slaughter 1991). When the child pretends an object is another object, or imagines an object, there need be no understanding of the relation between those representations and reality. For young children, pretenses and images are unrelated to reality: They cannot be false—or true, for that matter. And, as we have seen, these "silly" mental states are apparently well understood by 3-year-olds. Similarly, we have seen that even without an understanding of the representational process, 3-year-olds can tell that someone else may not see something they see themselves and vice versa. These simple perceptual judgments should also be possible for young children.

To test this we placed children in a series of situations in which they were in one psychological state and that state was changed, situations

How We Know Our Minds

comparable to the belief-change task. For example, we asked children to pretend that an empty glass was full of hot chocolate. Then the glass was "emptied" and the child was asked to pretend that it was full of lemonade. We then asked them, "When I first asked you, . . . what did you pretend was in the glass then?" We also asked them to imagine a blue dog and then a pink cat and asked them, "When I first asked you, . . . what did you think of then?" In both these cases, as in the belief-change case, the child is in one mental state and then another mental state, even though nothing in the real world has changed. In these cases, however, unlike the belief case, the mental states need not be interpreted as involving any representational relation to the real world. In a perceptual task, we placed the children on one side of a screen from which one object was visible and then moved them to the other side from which another object was visible and asked them to recall their past perception. The 3-year-olds were fully able to perform these tasks; only one out of 30, for example, failed to remember an earlier pretense. However, a majority of these same 3-year-olds were unable to perform the belief-change task.

We also tested children's understanding of changes in states with a direction of fit, such as desires and intentions. In three different tasks we presented children with situations in which their desires were satiated and so changed. Cases of satiation are particularly interesting because they induce both changes in desires themselves and changes in the representation of the desired object. Satiation not only changes our desires, it changes our very notion of whether the object is desirable. The delicious, tempting mousse becomes cloying and nauseating by the fourth portion, the exciting new toy becomes a bore. Moreover, these changes are not parasitic on belief changes but stem from the nature of the desire itself (see Astington and Gopnik 1991a, for discussion).

In all three tasks a sizable minority of 3-year-olds (30%–40%) reported that they had been in their final state all along. Thus, for example, hungry children were fed crackers at snack time until they were no longer hungry and were then asked "Were you hungry before we had snack?" A third of them reported that they were not.

Nevertheless, just as in the Flavell task, which measured children's understanding of the desires of others ("Does Ellie think the cookie is yummy or yucky?") (Flavell et al. 1990), so in our similar task ("Were you hungry before?") the children were better at reporting past desires than past beliefs. Indeed, the absolute levels of performance were strikingly similar in our task and Flavell's.

Finally, we examined children's ability to report their earlier intentions when they did not actually come to fruition. Children were given a red crayon and asked to draw a ball; halfway through the experimenter said, "Why that drawing looks like this big red apple, could you make it a big red apple?" Children complied. Then we asked the children to report their past intention; 50% of the 3-year-olds reported that they had originally intended to draw the apple.

Information-Processing Alternatives

Research with very young children raises the question of the information-processing demands of the tasks. Are tasks difficult for some reason other than a conceptual one? Such concerns are raised whenever a developmental study claims to have found an inability in children or a difference between children and adults. As Wellman has cogently argued (Wellman 1990), no individual task or experiment is immune from such criticisms. (For some recent examples of criticisms of individual experiments along these lines see Freeman et al. 1991; Lewis and Osborne 1991). We can, nevertheless, consider whether a pattern of results, taken across a number of studies, is best explained in terms of some difference in the information-processing ability of 3- and 4-year-olds or in terms of a conceptual difference. Let me consider a few such arguments that might be applied to particular experiments and show how they are incompatible with other pieces of evidence.

Understanding Questions about the Past

Wimmer and Hartl (1991) have shown that children can readily understand questions identical to those asked in the experiment ("What did you think was inside the box?") when they refer to changes in the actual world rather than to strictly mental changes. Moreover, in our experiments children are able to understand questions about their past psychological states such as pretenses even when they are syntactically identical to the belief questions ("What did you pretend was in the glass?" vs. "What did you think was in the box?").

Remembering Past Events

Common observation suggests that 3-year-old children can remember events that occurred minutes earlier. The control tasks and pretense, imagination, and perception task test this possibility experimentally. Children could understand the questions as well as recall the past mental states in these cases. Note that in the pretense, image, and perception tasks, there was no change of the objects in reality, only a psychological change. Children, nevertheless, had no difficulty remembering their past psychological states in these cases. Certainly, no simple memory problem can explain these results.

Reality Seduction

One might argue that children are subject to a kind of "reality seduction," feeling compelled to answer questions by referring to what is actually true, although they are intellectually able to appreciate false belief. Children are not "reality seduced," however, in the pretense or image tasks. In both these tasks they could answer the question by referring to the reality, the empty glass or the objects actually in front of them, but they do not. Nor are they "reality seduced" in the perception task, where they are able to report their earlier limited vision. Also, this objection does not apply to the sources or subjective probability tasks. The "How do you know?" question does not ask the child to say anything about appearance or reality but simply how two events, an event in the world and the belief that results, are related. Similarly, in the subjective probability tasks the children do not know what the real state of affairs is. Finally, the objection also fails to apply to the desire or intention tasks.

Embarrassment

To an adult, the most likely explanation for the results in the belief-change task is embarrassed deception or perhaps self-deception: The child was too ashamed to say he had been wrong (the most likely explanation for similar phenomena in adulthood). This explanation could not apply to any of the other belief tasks, such as the classic false-belief or appearance-reality tasks, on which children behave in similar ways at a similar time. Nor could it apply to the desire or intention tasks. Changing your mind does not entail an admission of a mistake or embarrassment; there is no obvious reason, for example, why you should be embarrassed that you are no longer hungry after you have a snack. Nor, finally, does it apply to the sources task; here, in fact, the children are quite willing to confess their ignorance.

No doubt the *BBS* commentators will supply other possibilities for particular tasks. What is important, however, is the pattern of development across a variety of tasks. To be parsimonious, an information-processing account would need to demonstrate some information-processing complication that was common to the difficult tasks (false-belief, appearance-reality, sources, desires, intentions [both for self and others] and subjective probability) and not common to the easy tasks (pretense, perception, imagination, physical-state change, both for self and others).

The conceptual account does provide such an explanation. Consider what a child with a Gibsonian (1979) model of the mind might and might not understand. Such children should understand that mental states may exist independently of physical ones (the image and pretense cases) and that such states are subject to change. They should understand that the spatial relation between a mind and a world may determine how much of the world the mind apprehends (the perception case). On the other hand, they should understand neither cases of misrepresentation (the false-belief cases) nor the mediated nature of cognition (the sources and subjective probability cases). In the mind-to-world cases they might fail to understand how satiation alters representation. In particular, they might see "desirability" as an objectively apprehended feature of the world. They might also fail to understand the way that intention mediates between desire and action (see Astington and Gopnik 1991a).

Developmental Evidence as Support for the "Theory-Theory"

The striking finding, from our present point of view, is the parallel between children's understanding of the psychological states of others and their understanding of their own immediately past psychological states. If the epistemological version of our commonsense intuitions is correct, the process of discovering our own psychological states is fundamentally different from the process of discovering someone else's states. We see the other person look in the box or feel inside it, or see him grimace at the taste of the cookie, and infer his beliefs, their sources and his desires. In our own case we simply report the changes in our psychological states, or their sources, by referring to our psychological experience. We need not infer them; we need not, indeed, use any theoretical account of the mind at all.

If our findings correctly reflect the experience of young children, the situation is very different. In each of our studies, children's reports of their own immediately past psychological states are consistent with their accounts of the psychological states of others. When they can report and understand the psychological states of others, in the cases of pretense, perception, and imagination, they report having had those psychological states themselves. When they cannot report and understand the psychological states of others, in the cases of false beliefs, and source, they report that they have not had those states themselves. In the source case, they simply say they do not know the answer, or they respond at random when pressed. In the belief case they report that they have always held their current belief. Moreover, and in some ways most strikingly, the intermediate cases, such as the case of desire, are intermediate both for self and other.

These findings are consistent with other findings in social psychology (Nisbett and Ross 1980; Nisbett and Wilson 1977) and in neuropsychology, such as cases of agnosia and amnesia, in which there are similar dissociations between subjects' behaviors and their report of their own psychological experience. The findings from other children also differ, however. The social psychological cases typically involve rather abstract reports of the motivations for particular actions. The subjects in the Nisbett and Wilson experiments, for example, can report their past desires perfectly accurately, though they are mistaken about the underlying reason for that desire. In these cases, even in the commonsense view, our adult psychological experience may be hazy or unclear or even nonexistent, and subjects may simply confabulate. The children, on the other hand, have first-person experiences different from those of adults in cases where the adult first-person experiences are crystal clear. Second, unlike the amnesics or agnosics, these children are perfectly capable of reporting their psychological states in some cases—precisely those that are consistent with their general theory of the mind.

The developmental evidence I have described here fails to support some views of the origins of commonsense psychology. In particular, there is little evidence that the commonsense psychological account of intentionality is an innately determined aspect of our understanding of the mind. Some aspects of commonsense psychology may indeed be innately given (see, for example, Baron-Cohen 1991; Hobson 1991; Meltzoff and Gopnik 1993). But other crucial aspects of that understanding, and particularly the idea of intentionality, appear to be constructed somewhere between 3 and 4. Before this point children's accounts of the mind may be very different from adult accounts.[8]

At the same time, the evidence does not support the position that our commonsense psychological ideas are simply stances we adopt: the view of Dennett (1987) and Davidson (1980). If this were true we would imagine that the process of acquiring those ideas would be less a process of knowledge construction than of enculturation. We would learn how to psychologize appropriately much the way we learn to eat politely or dress appropriately. This may indeed be the case for certain sophisticated esthetic or emotional states. It does not seem to be true, however, for the simple states we have investigated here. In particular, it is interesting that young children actually acquire an incorrect account of commonsense psychology, what we have called a Gibsonian or copy account. They adhere to this view with some stubbornness at about age 3, even in the face of error. This view is not the adult one; if it is a stance or what Wittgenstein calls a "form of life," it is one unique to 3-year-olds.

The developmental evidence, however, and particularly the evidence we have presented here, also fails to support the view that the intentionality of psychological states is discovered through first-person experience, as common sense, Searle's (1980, 1984, 1990) view, or the simulation view (Gordon 1986, 1992; Goldman 1989, 1992) would suggest. The evidence suggests that there is a dissociation between the psychological states that cause the children's behavior and their sincere conscious report of their psychological experience. Either we have to deny that 3-year-olds have psychological states like ours, or we have to deny that their experience of those states is like ours. If we take the second option, we must also deny that children learn about these psychological states through direct psychological experience, because their experience is wrong. Three-year-olds are the converse of "swamp-things": The swamp-things think they have intentional states even though they do not; the 3-year-olds think they do not even though they do. But, like swamp-things, they make the point that intentionality may be divorced from phenomenology.[9]

We could, of course, take the first option and deny that 3-year-olds have psychological states like ours at all, given that their experience of those states is so different from our own. In fact, Searle's (1990) most recent views suggest that he might take this position. We even might want to deny that the psychological states or experiences of children have anything to do with our states and experiences as adults. Children, like computers in Searle's view, might just fail to be the sorts of things to which intentionality could be attributed.

This argument might seem plausible when we are comparing human beings and machines. We have no prima facie reason to suppose that things made of silicon will have the same properties, or be explained in the same way, as things made of blood and bone. It seems much less plausible when we are considering creatures that are made out of exactly the same stuff that we are, creatures that are grown and not engineered or made, creatures that talk, that reflect, that answer questions, that even have much of the same commonsense psychological terminology that we do. Moreover, these creatures do seem to have accurate beliefs about some aspects of their own psychological states, precisely the ones that are consistent with their accounts of the minds of others. Indeed, the case is even stronger: These creatures are not just like us, they *are* us, they are Searle himself, and me, myself (the first-person consciousness who formulates these lines), a few years ago.

The current findings support the view that has come to be called the "theory-theory": commonsense psychological beliefs are constructed as a way of explaining ourselves and others. A number of investigators have recently proposed more general parallels between theory change in science and some kinds of cognitive development (Carey 1985, 1988; Gopnik 1984, 1988; Gopnik and Wellman n.d.; Karmiloff-Smith 1988; Karmiloff-Smith and Inhelder 1974; Keil 1987; Wellman and Gelman 1987). Some version of this theory is widely accepted among developmental psychologists investigating children's understanding of the mind (Flavell 1988; Forguson and Gopnik 1988; Perner 1991; Wellman 1990; though see Leslie, 1987, and Harris, 1990, for opposing views). The developmental evidence suggests that children construct a coherent, abstract account of the mind which enables them to explain and predict psychological phenomena. Although this theory is implicit rather than explicit, this kind of cognitive structure appears to share many features with a scientific theory. Children's theories of the mind postulate unobserved entities (beliefs and desires) and laws connecting them, such as the practical syllogism. Their theories allow prediction, and they change (eventually) as a result of falsifying evidence. (For a detailed exposition and justification of these claims see Gopnik and Wellman 1992; n.d.). Moreover, the child's theory of mind is equally applicable to the self and to others.

There may well be certain sorts of first-person psychological experience that serve as evidence for the commonsense psychological theory and are used in its construction. Unlike Ryle (1949), for example, I would not want to suggest that this theory is reducible to behavior, but more strongly, I would also deny that it is based on behavior. Some experiences might indeed be directly related to certain psychological states, as is perhaps the case with simple sensations. Whether this is the case, what types of first-person psychological experience are involved in theory construction and what role they play in the development of the theory of mind are empirical questions. The important point is that the theoretical constructs themselves, and particularly the idea of intentionality, are not the result of some direct first-person apprehension that is then applied to others. Rather, they are the result of cognitive construction. The child constructs a theory that explains a wide variety of facts about the child's experience and behavior and about the behavior and language of others.

The Illusion of Expertise

So far I have argued that our beliefs about our own intentional psychological states parallel our beliefs about the intentional psychological states of others. If the sources of the two kinds of beliefs are really similar, however, why do we also believe that there is such a profound difference between them? The move from the phenomenological claim that our first-person psychological experience feels direct and immediate to the epistemological claim that our first-person knowledge of our psychological states is direct and immediate seems compelling. Yet the evidence suggests that our adult beliefs about the origins of our beliefs about beliefs are just as mistaken as our 3-year-old beliefs about beliefs.

I will suggest a speculative analogy between the illusion of privileged knowledge of our own psychological states and what might be called the illusion of expertise. In the case of expertise, direct and immediate experience may be combined with a long, indirect (and theoretical) cognitive history.

We know that certain kinds of expertise appear to cause changes not just in knowledge, but in perception (Chi et al. 1982). Master chessplayers report that they no longer see the board in terms of individual pieces and squares but as a set of competing forces and powers. They need not calculate that an isolated king is vulnerable; they see he is (Chase and Simon 1973; De Groot 1978). The baseball player, asked why he got seven hits in a game, says he was seeing the ball well. Diagnosticians and fortune tellers see cancer in the face of a patient, or an unhappy marriage in the stance of a client. Dowsers feel the pull of water when, we believe, they are actually reading off subtle geographical cues. Expertise and immediacy go hand in hand.

Do the experts really perceive the king's strength or the cancer or the strike? The notion of perception is itself ambiguous in much the same way that other mental state concepts are. It might be used to capture a particular phenomenological quality, a sense of directness or immediacy. In this sense the chess-player *does* perceive the strength of the king. But it might also mean something about the cognitive relation between an experience and its object. It might mean that the experience is reliably, and reasonably directly, caused by the object. In the case of the expert, the experiences do not bear this cognitive relation to the objects they are about. In this second sense, the chess-player does not perceive the strength of the king, though he may think he does.

Consider this thought experiment: Suppose we lived in Kasparovia, a world in which everyone has been trained to play chess from an early age and has essentially mastered the game by age 5, and where chess is essential to any kind of social survival. Imagine that chess is so pervasive that no one can remember a time when the game did not exist. It seems rather likely that players in such a world would see their adult chess expertise in largely perceptual terms. They might indeed differentiate their knowledge of chess from their knowledge of other games like parcheesi, or dominoes, which they learn in a more ordinary way. They might say that when they choose the right move in parcheesi they calculate, infer, construct heuristics, and so on, but that when they choose the right move in chess they just see it on the board.

Our knowledge of our ordinary psychological states in this world might be like our hypothetical knowledge of chess in Kasparovia. As Ryle (1949) pointed out long ago, our expertise about minds and behavior is great, about our own minds and behavior, which after all, we live with every day, even greater. The force of this expertise might be such that our beliefs about psychological states, particularly our own, would appear to be perceptually immediate, noninferential, direct.

One story of the relation between expertise and perception might run as follows: In developing forms of expertise, we construct an implicit theory of the realm in which we are expert. Various kinds of genuine perception act as important evidence for that theory. In applying it, we rely on our genuine perception of particularly common or crucial pieces of such evidence. The diagnostician really does see the patient's pallor, feel the pulse, and so forth. The dowser really does see the hill contours. Given this evidence, or even a single piece of it, the diagnostician draws on vast, nonperceptual, theoretical knowledge to make implicit inferences about the patient. He quite appropriately applies the theory, "the patient has cancer." The diagnostician is engaging in the same cognitive processes that a less experienced medical student might engage in, but more quickly and surely. To the diagnostician, however, none of this may be going on at all. From his first-person view, the cancer may simply be perceived.

How might we apply this story in the case of psychological states? We saw that one possible source of evidence for the child's theory may be first-person psychological experiences that may themselves be the consequence of genuine psychological perceptions. For example, we may well be equipped to detect certain kinds of internal cognitive activity in a vague and unspecified way, what we might call "the Cartesian buzz." Given the recurrence of such experiences in adulthood, and other appropriate contextual and behavioral evidence, the adult may now apply the full theoretical apparatus of the theory of mind, including the idea of intentionality, and so draw conclusions or inferences about his own psychological states. These inferences lead to a psychological experience with a particular complex phenomenological character. Given the effects of expertise, we may be quite unaware of these inferences, and so interpret these complex, theory-laden experiences as direct perceptions of our psychological states.[10]

The fact that a particular ascription of an intentional psychological state is based in part on psychological experience may mislead us into thinking that the entire theoretical apparatus itself is so given. This fact might also be one element in our sense that beliefs about our own psychological states are direct or privileged. For example, our genuinely special and direct access to certain kinds of first-person evidence might account for the fact that we can draw some conclusions about our own psychological states when we are perfectly still and silent. We might not be able to draw similarly confident inferences about another person. This is the sort of fact that lends credence to the commonsense picture.

The crucial point, however, is that the theoretical knowledge in all these cases does not actually come from the experience, even if we feel it does. A chess novice, no matter how keen-sighted and quick-witted, would never be able to see the strength of the king. The patient's pallor or pulse, all by itself, does not spell cancer. No matter how certain the dowser may be that he feels a tug on his wand, our knowledge of the physical world suggests that he is really using implicit geographical knowledge. It would be wrong to say that in these cases the source of the expert's knowledge is direct perception, rather than implicit theoretical construction.

It might not be possible for experts, even when pressed, to tell which parts of their belief come from direct perceptual experiences and which are the result of theoretical knowledge. Experts' first-person experience alone may be simply insufficient to make this differentiation, though they might attempt a "rational reconstruction" of the source of the belief. To really answer this question we would need to know something about the developmental course of the expert's knowledge, how the diagnostician moved from fumbling medical student to assured expert. We would need a developmental account of the diagnostician's expertise.

The theoretical nature of the expert's experience is particularly clear when the theory is wrong. Suppose a chess-player had not yet learned about a particular gambit. We might expect that the player's perceptions would be equally affected, the knight that was, in fact, about to capture the king would appear misleadingly weak and helpless. A diagnostician who had failed to keep up with the most recent literature might see cancer where there was none. This kind of failure argues against a genuinely perceptual account of these beliefs. Surely, what these experts would say in such cases is that they believed that the king was strong or the patient had cancer, even that it looked as if the king was strong or the patient had cancer, but that further evidence proved that this was wrong.

Similarly, in the case of psychological beliefs, 3-year-olds' misleading beliefs about their psychological states apparently affect their experience of those states. Just as the chess-player or the diagnostician might be mistaken, so 3-year-old children are mistaken about their own psychological states. Even if we use some psychological experience as evidence for our psychological state ascriptions, we can and do clearly override that evidence with great ease. We do so, moreover, in cases other than that of self-deception. Perhaps some experiential evidence was available to the children in our tasks. That evidence, however, was clearly outweighed for them by theoretical convictions about the kind of position they were in and what they could or could not have known or believed. This is perfectly proper if, for them, "beliefs" and "desires" are theoretical terms that are, in principle, equally applicable to themselves and others. If they are theoretical terms for them, they are theoretical terms for us. Remember again that these children *are* us, when we knew less about the mind than we do now.

Why I Am Not a Behaviorist

One response to the sorts of arguments I have been making in this target article is to suggest that they are really old-fashioned behaviorism, but they need not imply behaviorism at all. I do not deny that there are internal psychological states; on the contrary, discovering the nature of such states is the fundamental task of psychology. Nor do I deny that there are full, rich, first-person psychological experiences of the Joycean or Woolfian kind. I even suggest that there may be cases in which psychological states *do* lead directly to psychological experiences, cases in which there is genuine perception of a psychological state.

What I do want to argue is that intentionality is not such a case. In this instance, the relationship between underlying psychological states, behavior, and experiences is rather different from what we had supposed. The commonsense picture proposes that we have intentional psychological states, then we have psychological experiences of the intentionality of those states, then we observe our own behavior that follows those states, and finally, we attribute the states to others with similar behavior. I suggest a different sequence: First we have psychological states, observe the behaviors and the experiences they lead to in ourselves and others, construct a theory about the causes of those behaviors and experiences that postulates intentionality, and then, in consequence, we have experiences of the intentionality of those states.

First-Person Knowledge and Cognitive Science Revisited

We return now to the question of the role of first-person psychological experience of intentionality in the development of cognitive science. I have suggested there is empirical evidence that this experience is the result of the construction of an implicit theory. One characteristic of such theoretical structures, in children as well as in scientists, is that they are "defeasible," subject to change and revision. They are neither fundamentally different from scientific psychological claims nor are they epistemologically privileged. Whether they require revision or replacement, whether "intentionality" will survive in some modified form or go the way of "phlogiston," is an open question, one more likely to be resolved by the actual progress of cognitive science than by a priori speculation.

Moreover, not only are theoretical structures themselves defeasible, but so are the decisions about the types of evidence that are relevant to the theory. As the theory develops, pieces of evidence that were crucial at one stage of its construction may turn out to be irrelevant later. To take a hackneyed example, it seems likely that such features of objects as color and texture were important in identifying chemical elements at one point. Thus the yellowness and shininess of gold played a part in the construction of theories of the nature of gold. Even now we might use these features as useful identifying marks, rough guides for when the application of the theoretical term "gold" is appropriate. Nevertheless, it would be wrong to say, now, that color and texture were essential to the concept of gold, or that something that was not yellow and shiny could not be gold.

In the same way, genuine first-person psychological perceptions might play a role in the formation of the commonsense theory of intentionality. As adults we might also use such evidence as a way of identifying the occurrence of some mental state. Nevertheless, the theory itself might be applied without that experience. In fact, 3-year-old psychologists already seem to be willing to apply the theory to themselves on the basis of contextual and behavioral evidence, even when it is not supported by first-person experience. They must do this, because their direct, first-person experience could not, presumably, tell them that they had believed there were pencils in the box before they opened it. As somewhat older and wiser scientific psychologists, we might similarly identify unconscious states, or the states of a computer, as intentional, in spite of the absence of psychological experience, in much the same way that we might identify colorless gases as gold.

The Moral: Listen to Children

The most important point of this target article is not that one account or another of first-person knowledge is the right one. Rather, it is that in deciding among the possibilities sketched by philosophers, and inventing new ones, we sought to consider much more than adult experience. Experience does not wear its epistemological history on its sleeve. If our goal is to say how we actually develop knowledge of the mind, or indeed knowledge of any kind, we must look beyond an analysis of the conceptual structures that we have as adults, or "just-so" stories about how those structures might have arisen. We must look to actual evidence about how we develop such knowledge.

The experiments I have reported here might have come out differently. Children might instead have proved to be accurate in reporting their own psychological states, and to develop an understanding of the states of others by analogy with those states. If this had been the case it would have provided evidence for the commonsense view of first- and third-person knowledge. The "theory-theory" would have been challenged by such evidence as, I have argued, the commonsense view is challenged by the actual evidence.

It is of course true that no single source of evidence, developmental, psychological, neurological, or conceptual, can answer epistemological questions definitively. Moreover, developmental facts may not always reflect the acquisition of knowledge; sometimes they may be the consequence of other factors: maturation, information-processing changes, enculturation, and so on. Children are nevertheless an important and often neglected source of information about where knowledge comes from. Studying them may force us to reexamine the deeply rooted assumptions of our adult common sense and provide us with new and surprising answers to ancient questions. Two thousand years ago in Plato's *Meno*, Socrates combined one of the first-recorded philosophical discussions of the genesis of knowledge with the first-recorded experiment in cognitive development. Perhaps it is time to try it again.[11]

Acknowledgments

The writing of this target article was supported by NSF grant no. BNS-8919916. The manuscript had the benefit of an unusually large number of unusually helpful comments. Earlier versions of the manuscripts were presented at the Berkeley Cognitive Science Seminar and at John Flavell's Children's Theory of Mind Seminar at Stanford University; I am grateful to all the participants in those seminars who commented on it. Particularly helpful were comments by Irvin Rock, Steve Palmer, Bert Dreyfus, John Searle, Tony Dardis, and Charles Siewert. Among developmentalists, Janet Astington, John Flavell, Henry Wellman, Simon Baron-Cohen, and Andrew Meltzoff all read drafts and made many helpful suggestions. I am grateful to them and to other theory-of-mind investigators, particularly Josef Perner, Paul Harris, Heinz Wimmer, and Alan Leslie for much stimulating work, thought, and conversation. On three separate occasions, Clark Glymour asked an apparently simple question which led me to rewrite the manuscript completely. I am grateful to him anyway.

Notes

1. Ordinary language embodies the assumptions of common sense. When we try to categorize our experiences phenomenologically we typically talk about "experiences of trees" or "experiences of our beliefs" or "experiences of others' desires," but these phrases already make assumptions about the relations between experiences and objects. For my purposes it would be more appropriate to say "tree-experiences" or "own-belief-experiences" or "others'-desire-experiences"—appropriate, but unfortunately, not English.

2. Throughout this article I am adopting the position that has been called "naturalistic epistemology" in the literature: the idea that an account of the naturalistic connections between world and mind (is the only thing that) can tell us how knowledge is acquired. I will not argue for this general position here. The philosophical accounts I will discuss do make claims about the nature of the world and the mind, and the connections between them. If these accounts are instead construed as claims about ordinary language or phenomenology, the evidence I will present might not be relevant to them. On the other hand, they would also not be relevant to psychology and cognitive science.

3. Exact ages are not crucial. In fact, according to the theory-theory, we would expect to find, as we indeed do, wide variation in the ages at which successive theories develop. We would expect to find similar sequences of development, however. I will use age as a rough way of referring to successive developments.

4. Very recently, a number of studies have appeared in which it is reported that, under some conditions, more 3-year-olds will produce the "right answer" in false-belief-like tasks than in the standard tasks (e.g., Freeman et al. 1991; Lewis and Osborne 1991; Siegal and Beattie 1991). The conditions are very varied and often the results are difficult to interpret (for a detailed discussion see Gopnik and Wellman n.d.). There are also questions about the replicability of some of these results. At best, it appears that there may be evidence of some fragile and fragmentary false-belief understanding in some 3-year-olds under some conditions, particularly when there is extensive contextual support. Some of this evidence suggests that children may have their first glimmerings of false belief when they are forced to confront counterevidence. Wellman and Bartsch (1988), for example, found that some 3-year-old children would, with prompting, produce some false-belief claims as explanations for anomalous behaviors. Similarly, in a recent study, Mitchell and Lacohée (1991) found that children in a belief-change task who selected an explicit physical token of their earlier belief (a picture of what they thought was in the box) were better able to avoid later misinterpretation of that belief. That is, these children seemed to recognize the contradiction between the action they had just performed (picking a picture of candies), which was well within the scope of their memory, and their theoretical prediction about their past belief. These results actually provide an interesting line of evidence in support of the "theory-theory." We have suggested that children may initially treat representation in general and false belief in particular as a kind of auxiliary hypothesis, invoked only to deal with particular anomalies (Gopnik and Wellman 1992).

This is in sharp contrast to the more powerful "theory-like" predictive and general understanding of pretenses, images, and perceptions in these children, and the powerful, predictive and general understanding of false belief in 4- and 5-year-olds.

5. According to the views of Gibson and Dretske, at least some kinds of perception are not viewed as representational in the usual sense. Instead, the idea is that there is a more direct causal link between the world and the mind. In Gibson's terminology, perception involves a kind of "resonance" between objects in the world and the organism; in Dretske's, information (in the technical sense) flows from the object to the organism. I suggest that 3-year-olds understand all relations between the world and the mind, including those that involve beliefs, in a similar way.

6. If we consider the philosophical stories that feature in discussions of intentionality, from the morning star and the evening star (Frege 1892), to Scott and the author of *Waverly* (Russell 1905), to Ortcutt the spy (Quine 1956), all of them involve cases of misrepresentation. In each case, an observer's initial beliefs about an object turn out to be misleading or seriously incomplete later on.

7. The "span of introspection" is probably longer. The first-person experience of, say, a patient with Korsakov's syndrome, who only has access to information within the short-term span, but not the long-term span, seems to be radically different from our own (see Tulving 1985).

8. One possibility might be that the 3- and 4-year-old shift is the result of the maturation of an innately determined capacity. A number of authors have suggested that the child's theory of mind is indeed partly based on various kinds of innately specified knowledge (Baron-Cohen 1991a; Hobson 1991; Leslie 1987; Meltzoff and Gopnik 1993). Leslie (1987) in particular has argued for an innate "theory of mind module" or, in his most recent work, two innate modules, one maturing at 9 months and another at 18 months. So far as I know no one actively working in the field, not even Leslie, has suggested that the 3- to 4-year-old shift is the result of the maturation of such a module. (For other arguments against this possibility see Astington and Gopnik 1991b; Gopnik and Wellman, in press).

9. The fact that 3-year-olds actually exist makes me think they are a more convincing example, but this may be an antiphilosophical prejudice.

10. An interesting problem concerns why, if the impression of perceptual immediacy comes from expertise, we do not extend this impression to our equally expert beliefs about other people. Two explanations come to mind. First, we do, I suggest, have precisely this impression when we are dealing with those we know very intimately, young children or lovers, for example. It is this experience that makes the notion of telepathy so plausible to common sense. There are others, however, who are genuinely strange to us, and with them, the impression of immediacy rapidly breaks down. The breakdown is then retroactively extended even to intimates. A second and related factor involves our commonsense notion of causality, which emphasizes spatial contact. In common sense, our own minds and brains, our psychological experiences and our psychological states, are located in the same place, inside our skins. Other people's minds are located in a different place. We assume that we cannot really see them because their skins get in the way. But no such difficulty arises with our own minds.

11. In the last 2,000 years we have had Socrates and Piaget. This discussion may sound Piagetian, and so it should. Almost all of Piaget's substantive claims about the child's conception of the mind have turned out to be wrong. The Piagetian notion of general stagelike, domain-independent changes is also not supported by the more recent research.

Piaget's general constructivist approach, however, informs both the empirical research and the theoretical position outlined here. I, for one (and, I suspect, others in the field), would be pleased to think of the "theory-theory" as the genuine inheritor of the tradition of genetic epistemology.

References

Astington, J. W., and A. Gopnik (1991a). Developing understanding of desire and intention. In A. Whiten, ed., *Natural theories of mind*. Oxford: Basil Blackwell.

Astington, J. W., and Gopnik, A. (1991b). Theoretical explanations of children's understanding of mind. *British Journal of Developmental Psychology* 9, 7–31.

Astington, J. W., P. L. Harris, and D. R. Olson, eds. (1988). *Developing theories of mind*. Cambridge: Cambridge University Press.

Baron-Cohen, S. (1991). Precursors to a theory of mind: Understanding attention in others. In A. Whiten, ed., *Natural theories of mind*. Oxford: Basil Blackwell.

Carey, S. (1985). *Conceptual change in childhood*. Cambridge, MA: MIT Press.

Carey, S. (1988). Conceptual differences between children and adults. *Mind and Language* 3, 3, 167–183.

Chandler, M. (1988). Doubt and developing theories of mind. In J. W. Astington, D. Olson, and P. Harris, eds., *Developing theories of mind*. Cambridge: Cambridge University Press.

Chandler, M. J., A. S. Fritz, and S. M. Hala (1989). Small scale deceit: Deception as a marker of 2, 3, and 4-year-olds' early theories of mind. *Child Development* 60, 1263–1277.

Chase, W. G., and H. A. Simon (1973). Perception in chess. *Cognitive Psychology*, 4, 55–81.

Chi, M., R. Glaser, and E. Rees (1982). Expertise in problem-solving. In R. J. Sternberg, ed., *Advances in the psychology of human intelligence*, vol. 1. Hillsdale, NJ: Erlbaum.

Davidson, D. (1980). *Essays on actions and events*. Oxford: Oxford University Press.

De Groot, A. (1978). *Thought and choice in chess*. The Hauge: Mouton.

Dennett, D. C. (1987). *The intentional stance*. Cambridge, MA: Bradford/MIT Press.

Dretske, F. (1981). *Knowledge and the flow of information*. Cambridge, MA: Bradford/MIT Press.

Flavell, J. H. (1988). The development of children's knowledge about the mind: From cognitive connections to mental representations. In J. W. Astington, P. L. Harris, and D. R. Olson, eds., *Developing theories of mind*. Cambridge: Cambridge University Press.

Flavell, J. H., B. A. Everett, K. Croft, and E. R. Flavell (1981). Young children's knowledge about visual perception: Further evidence for the Level 1-Level 2 distinction. *Developmental Psychology* 17, 99–103.

Flavell, J. H., E. R. Flavell, and F. L. Green (1987). Young children's knowledge about the apparent-real and pretend-real distinctions. *Developmental Psychology* 23, 6, 816–822.

Flavell, J H., E. R. Flavell, F. L. Green, and L. J. Moses (1990). Young children's understanding of fact beliefs versus value beliefs. *Child Development* 61, 915–928.

Flavell, J. H., F. L. Green, and E. R. Flavell (1986). *Development of knowledge about the appearance-reality distinction.* Monographs of the Society for Research in Child Development, No. 212, 51(1).

Forguson, L., and A. Gopnik (1988). The ontogeny of common sense. In J. W. Astington, P. L. Harris, and D. R. Olson, eds., *Developing Theories of Mind.* Cambridge: Cambridge University Press.

Freeman, N. H., C. Lewis, and M. J. Doherty (1991). Preschoolers grasp of a desire for knowledge in false-belief prediction: Practical intelligence and verbal report. *British Journal of Developmental Psychology.*

Frege, G. (1892). Über Sinn und Bedeutung (On sense and reference). *Zeitschrift für Philosophie und philosophische Kritik,* 25–50.

Gibson, J. J. (1979). *The ecological approach to perception.* Boston: Houghton Mifflin.

Goldman, A. (1989). Interpretation psychologized. *Mind and Language* 4, 161–185.

Goldman, A. (1992). In defense of the simulation theory. *Mind and Language* 7, 104–119.

Gopnik, A. (1982). Words and plans: Early language and the development of intelligent action. *Journal of Child Language* 9, 303–318.

Gopnik, A. (1984). Conceptual and semantic change in scientists and children: Why there are no semantic universals. *Linguistics* 20, 163–179.

Gopnik, A. (1988). Conceptual and semantic development as theory change. *Mind and Language* 3, 3, 197–217.

Gopnik, A. (1990). Developing the idea of intentionality: Children's theories of mind. *The Canadian Journal of Philosophy* 20, 1, 89–114.

Gopnik, A., and J. W. Astington (1988). Children's understanding of representational change and its relation to the understanding of false-belief and the appearance-reality distinction. *Child Development* 59, 26–37.

Gopnik, A., and P. Graf (1988). Knowing how you know: Young children's ability to identify and remember the sources of their beliefs. *Child Development* 59, 1366–1371.

Gopnik, A., and V. Slaughter (1991). Young children's understanding of changes in their mental states. *Child Development* 62, 98–110.

Gopnik, A., and H. Wellman (1992). Why the child's theory of mind really *is* a theory. *Mind and Language* 7, 145–171.

Gopnik, A., and H. Wellman (in press). The "theory theory" of cognitive development. In L. Hirschfield and S. Gelman, eds., *Domain specificity in culture and cognition*. New York: Cambridge University Press.

Gordon, R. (1986). Folk psychology as simulation. *Mind and Language* 4, 158–171.

Gordon, R. (1992). The simulation theory: Objections and misconceptions. *Mind and Language* 7, 11–34.

Harris, P. L. (1990). The work of the imagination. In A. Whiten, ed., *Natural theories of mind*. Oxford: Basil Blackwell.

Hobson, P. (1991). Against the theory of "Theory of Mind." *British Journal of Developmental Psychology* 9, 33–51.

Hogrefe, G. J., H. Wimmer, and J. Perner (1986). Ignorance versus false belief: A developmental lag in attribution of epistemic states. *Child Development* 57, 567–582.

Johnson, C. N. (1988). Theory of mind and the structure of conscious experience. In J. W. Astington, P. L. Harris, and D. R. Olson, eds., *Developing theories of mind*. New York: Cambridge University Press.

Karmiloff-Smith, A. (1988). The child is a theoretician, not an inductivist. *Mind and Language* 3, 3, 183–197.

Karmiloff-Smith, A., and B. Inhelder (1974). If you want to get ahead, get a theory. *Cognition* 3, 3, 195–212.

Keil, F. (1987). Conceptual development and category structure. In U. Neisser, ed., *Concepts and conceptual development*.

Lempers, J. D., E. R. Flavell, and J. H. Flavell (1977). The development in very young children of tacit knowledge concerning visual perception. *Genetic Psychology Monographs* 95, 3–53.

Leslie, A. (1987). Pretense and representation: The origins of "theory of mind." *Psychological Review* 94, 412–426.

Leslie, A. (1988). Some implications of pretense for children's theories of mind. In J. W. Astington, P. L. Harris, and D. R. Olson, eds., *Developing theories of mind*. Cambridge: Cambridge University Press.

Lewis, C., and A. Osborne (1991). Three-year-old's problem with false-belief: Conceptual deficit or linguistic artifact? *Child Development* 61, 1514–1519.

Meltzoff, A., and A. Gopnik (1993). The role of imitation in understanding persons and developing theories of mind. In S. Baron-Cohen, H. Tager-Flusberg, and D. Cohen, eds., *Understanding other minds: Perspectives on the theory of mind hypotheses in autism*. Oxford: Oxford University Press.

Mitchell, P., and H. Lacohée (1991). Children's early understanding of false belief. *Cognition* 39, 2, 107–127.

Moore, C., K. Pure, and D. Furrow (1990). Children's understanding of the modal expression of speaker certainty and uncertainty and its relation to the development of a representational theory of mind. *Child Development* 61, 722–730.

Moses, L. J., and J. H. Flavell (1990). Inferring false beliefs from actions and reactions. *Child Development* 61, 929–945.

Nisbett, R. E., and L. Ross (1980). *Human inference: Strategies and shortcomings of social judgment.* Englewood Cliffs, NJ: Prentice-Hall.

Nisbett, R. E., and T. D. Wilson (1977). Telling more than we can know: Verbal reports on mental processes. *Psychological Review* 84, 231–259.

O'Neill, D., J. W. Astington, and J. Flavell (1992). Young children's understanding of the role that sensory experiences play in knowledge acquisition. *Child Development* 63, 474–491.

O'Neill, D., and A. Gopnik (1991). Young children's understanding of the sources of their beliefs. *Developmental Psychology* 27, 390–397.

Perner, J., S. Leekam, and H. Wimmer (1987). 3-year-olds' difficulty understanding false belief: Cognitive limitation, lack of knowledge, or pragmatic misunderstanding. *British Journal of Developmental Psychology* 5, 125–137.

Perner, J. (1991). *Understanding the representational mind.* Cambridge, MA: Bradford/MIT Press.

Pillow, B. H. (1989). Early understanding of perception as a source of knowledge. *Journal of Experimental Child Psychology* 47, 1, 116–129.

Quine, W. V. O. (1956). Quantifiers and propositional attitudes. *Journal of Philosophy* 53, 117–187.

Russell, B. (1905). On denoting. *Mind* 14, 479–493.

Ryle, G. (1949), *The concept of mind.* New York: Barnes & Noble.

Searle, J. R. (1980). Minds, brains and programs. *Behavioral and Brain Sciences* 3, 417–457.

Searle, J. R. (1983). *Intentionality: An essay in the philosophy of mind.* Cambridge: Cambridge University Press.

Searle, J. R. (1984). *Minds, brains, and science.* Cambridge, MA: Harvard University Press.

Searle, J. R. (1990). Consciousness, explanatory inversion, and cognitive science. *Behavioral and Brain Sciences* 13, 585–642.

Shatz, M., H. M. Wellman, and S. Silber (1983). The acquisition of mental verbs: A systematic investigation of the first reference to mental state. *Cognition* 14, 301–321.

Siegal, M., and K. Beattie (1991). Where to look first for children's understanding of false beliefs. *Cognition* 3, 1–12.

Sodian, B. (1991). The development of deception in young children. *British Journal of Developmental Psychology* 9, 173–188.

Tulving, E. (1985). Memory and consciousness. *Canadian Psychology* 26, 1–12.

Wellman, H. M. (1990). *The child's theory of mind*. Cambridge, MA: Bradford/MIT Press.

Wellman, H. M., and K. Bartsch (1988). Young children's reasoning about beliefs. *Cognition* 30, 239–277.

Wellman, H. M., and D. Estes (1986). Early understanding of mental entities: A reexamination of childhood realism. *Child Development* 57, 910–923.

Wellman, H. M., and S. Gelman (1987). Children's understanding of the non-obvious. In R. Sternberg, ed., *Advances in the psychology of intelligence*, vol. 4. Hillsdale, NJ: Erlbaum.

Wellman H. M., and J. D. Woolley (1990). From simple desires to ordinary beliefs: The early development of everyday psychology. *Cognition* 35, 245–275.

Whiten, A. (ed.) (1990). *Natural theories of mind*. Oxford: Basil Blackwell.

Wimmer, H., and M. Hartl (1991). The Cartesian view and the theory view of mind: Developmental evidence from understanding false belief in self and other. *British Journal of Developmental Psychology* 9, 125–128.

Wimmer, H., G. Hogrefe, and J. Perner (1988). Children's understanding of informational access as source of knowledge. *Child Development* 59, 386–396.

Wimmer, H., J-G. Hogrefe, and B. Sodian (1988). A second stage in children's conception of mental life: Understanding sources of information. In J. W. Astington, P. L. Harris, and D. R. Olson, eds., *Developing theories of mind*. Cambridge: Cambridge University Press.

Wimmer, H., and J. Perner (1983). Beliefs about beliefs: Representation and constraining function of wrong beliefs in young children's understanding of deception. *Cognition* 13, 103–128.

Zaitchek, D. (1990). When representations conflict with reality: The preschooler's problem with false beliefs and "false" photographs. *Cognition* 35, 41–68.

16 The Psychology of Folk Psychology

Alvin I. Goldman

Introduction

The central mission of cognitive science is to reveal the real nature of the mind, however familiar or foreign that nature may be to naive preconceptions. The existence of naive conceptions is also important, however. Prescientific thought and language contain concepts of the mental, and these concepts deserve attention from cognitive science. Just as scientific psychology studies folk physics (Hayes 1985; McCloskey 1983), namely, the common understanding (or misunderstanding) of physical phenomena, so it must study *folk psychology*, the common understanding of mental states. This subfield of scientific psychology is what I mean by the phrase "the psychology of folk psychology."

The phrase "folk psychology" often bears a narrower sense than the one intended here. It usually designates a *theory* about mental phenomena that common folk allegedly hold, a theory in terms of which mental concepts are understood. In the present usage, "folk psychology" is not so restricted. It refers to the ordinary person's repertoire of mental concepts, whether or not this repertoire invokes a theory. Whether ordinary people have a theory of mind (in a suitably strict sense of "theory") is controversial, but it is indisputable that they have a folk psychology in the sense of a collection of concepts of mental states. Yet people may not have, indeed, probably do not have, direct introspective access to the contents (meanings) of their mental concepts, any more than they have direct access to the contents of their concepts of *fruit* or *lying*. Precisely for this reason we need cognitive science to discover what those contents are.

The study of folk psychology, then, is part of the psychology of concepts. We can divide the psychology of concepts into two parts: (a) the study of conceptualization and classification in general, and (b) the

---

From A. Goldman, The psychology of folk psychology, *Behavioral and Brain Sciences* 16, 15–28 (1993). Copyright 1993 by Cambridge University Press. Reprinted with the permission of Cambridge University Press.

study of specific folk concepts or families of folk concepts such as number concepts, material object concepts, and biological kind concepts. The study of folk psychology is a subdivision of (b), the one that concerns mental state concepts. It presupposes that mature speakers have a large number of mentalistic lexemes in their repertoire, such as *happy, afraid, want, hope, pain* (or *hurt*), *doubt, intend,* and so forth. These words are used in construction with other phrases and clauses to generate more complex mentalistic expressions. The question is: What is the meaning, or semantical content, of these expressions? What is it that people understand or represent by these words (or phrases)?

This target article advances two sorts of theses: methodological and substantive. The general methodological thesis is that the best way to study mental-state concepts is through the theoretico-experimental methodology of cognitive science. We should consider the sorts of data structures and cognitive operations involved in mental attributions (classifications), both attributions to oneself and attributions to others. Although this proposal is innocuous enough, it is not the methodology that has been followed, or even endorsed in principle, by philosophers who have given these questions the fullest attention. And even the cognitive scientists who have addressed these questions empirically have not used the specific methodological framework I shall recommend below.

In addition to methodological theses, this target article advances some substantive theses, both negative and positive. On the negative side, some new and serious problems are raised concerning the functionalist approach to mental-state concepts (as well as some doubts about pure computationalism). On the positive side, the article supports a prominent role for phenomenology in our mental-state concepts. These substantive theses are put forward tentatively because I have not done the kind of experimental work that my own methodological precepts would require for their corroboration; nor does existing empirical research address these issues in sufficient detail. Theoretical considerations, however, lend them preliminary support. I might state at the outset, however, that I am more confident of my negative thesis—about the problems facing the relevant form of functionalism—than of my positive theses, especially the role of phenomenology in the propositional attitudes.

Proposed Methodology

Philosophical accounts of mental concepts have been strongly influenced by purely philosophical concerns, especially ontological and epistemological ones. Persuaded that materialism (or physicalism) is the only tenable ontology, philosophers have deliberately fashioned their accounts of the mental with an eye to safeguarding materialism. Several early versions of functionalism (e.g., Armstrong 1968; Lewis 1966) were deliberately designed to accommodate type-physicalism,[1] and most forms of functionalism are construed as heavily physicalist in spirit. Similarly, many accounts of mental concepts have been crafted with epistemological goals in mind, for example, to avoid skepticism about other minds.

According to my view, the chief constraint on an adequate theory of ✸ our commonsense understanding of mental predicates is not that it should have desirable ontological or epistemological consequences; rather, it should be *psychologically realistic*: Its depiction of how people represent and ascribe mental predicates must be psychologically plausible.

An adequate theory need not be ontologically neutral, however. As we shall see in the last section, for example, an account of the ordinary understanding of mental terms can play a significant role in arguments about eliminativism.[2] Whatever the ontological ramifications of the ordinary understanding of mental language, however, the nature of that understanding should be investigated purely empirically, without allowing prior ontological prejudices to sway the outcome.

In seeking a model of mental-state ascription (attribution), there are two types of ascriptions to consider: ascriptions to self and ascriptions to others. Here we focus primarily on self-ascriptions. This choice is made partly because I have discussed ascriptions to others elsewhere (Goldman 1989, 1992a, 1992b), and partly because ascriptions to others, in my view, are "parasitic" on self-ascriptions (although this is not presupposed in the present discussion).

Turning now to specifics, let us assume that a competent speaker/ hearer associates a distinctive semantical representation with each mentalistic word, whatever form or structure this representation might take. This (possibly complex) representation, which is stored in long-term memory, bears the "meaning" or other semantical properties associated with the word. Let us call this representation the *category representation* (CR), since it represents the entire category the word denotes. A CR might take any of several forms (see Smith and Medin 1981), including: (1) a list of features treated as individually necessary and jointly sufficient for the predicate in question; (2) a list of characteristic features with weighted values, where classification proceeds by summing the weights of the instantiated features and determining whether the sum meets a specified criterion; (3) a representation of an ideal instance of the category, to which target instances are compared for similarity; (4) a set of representations of previously encountered exemplars of the category, to which new instances are compared for similarity; or (5) a connectionist network with a certain vector of connection weights. The present discussion is intended to be neutral with respect to these theories. What interests us, primarily, is the semantical "contents" of the various mentalistic words, or families of words, not the particular "form" or "structure" that bears these contents.

Perhaps we should not say that a CR bears the "meaning" of a mental word. According to some views of meaning, after all, naive users of a word commonly lack full mastery of its meaning; only experts have such mastery (see Putnam 1975). But if we are interested in what guides or underpins an ordinary person's use of mental words, we want an account of what *he* understands or represents by that word. (What the expert knows cannot guide the ordinary person in deciding when to apply the word.) Whether or not this is the "meaning" of the word, it is what we should be after.

Whatever form a CR takes, let us assume that when a cognizer decides what mental word applies to a specified individual, active information about that individual's state is compared or matched to CRs in memory that are associated with candidate words. The exact nature of the matching process will be dictated by the hypothesized model of concept representation and categorization. Because our present focus is self-ascription of mental terms, we are interested in the representations of one's own mental states that are matched to the CRs. Let us call such an active representation, whatever its form or content, an *instance representation* (IR). The content of such an IR will be something like, "A current state (of mine) has features $\phi_1, \ldots, \phi_n$." Such an IR will match a CR having the content: $\phi_1, \ldots, \phi_n$. Our aim is to discover, for each mental word M, its associated CR; or more generally, the sorts of CRs associated with families of mental words. We try to get evidence about CRs by considering what IRs are available to cognizers, IRs that might succeed in triggering a match.

To make this concrete, consider an analogous procedure in the study of visual object-recognition; we will use the work of Biederman (1987) as an illustration. Visual object-recognition occurs when an active representation of a stimulus that results from an image projected to the retina is matched to a stimulus category or concept category, for example, chair, giraffe, or mushroom. The psychologist's problem is to answer three coordinated questions: (1) What (high-level) visual representations (corresponding to our IRs) are generated by the retinal image? (2) How are the stimulus categories represented in memory (these representations correspond to our CRs)? (3) How is the first type of representation matched against the second so as to trigger the appropriate categories?

Biederman (1987) hypothesizes that stimulus categories are represented as arrangements of primitive components, namely, volumetric shapes such as cylinders or bricks, which he calls *geons* (for "geometrical ions"). Object recognition occurs by recovering arrangements of geons from the stimulus image and matching these to one of the distinguishable object models, which is paired with an entry-level term in the language (such as *lamp, chair, giraffe,* and so forth). The theory rests on a range of research supporting the notion that information from the image can be transformed (via edge extraction, etc.) into representations of geons and their relations. Thus, the hypothesis that, say, *chair* is represented in memory by an arrangement (or several arrangements) of geons is partly the result of constraints imposed by considering what information could be (a) extracted from the image (under a variety of viewing circumstances), and (b) matched to the memory representation. In similar fashion I wish to examine hypotheses about the stored representations (CRs) of mental-state predicates by reflecting on the instance representations of mental states that might actually be present and capable of producing appropriate matches.

Although we have restricted ourselves to self-ascriptions, there are still at least two types of cases to consider: ascriptions of *current* mental states—"I have a headache (now)"—and ascriptions of *past* states—"I had a headache yesterday." Instance representations in the two cases are likely to be quite different, obviously, so they need to be distinguished. Ascriptions of current mental states, however, have primacy, so these will occupy the center of our attention.

Problems for Functionalism

In the cognitive scientific as well as the philosophical community, the most popular account of people's understanding of mental-state language is the "theory of mind" theory, according to which naive speakers, even children, have a theory of mental states and understand mental words *solely* in terms of that theory. The most precise statement of this position is the philosophical doctrine of *functionalism*, which states that the crucial or defining feature of any type of mental state consists of its causal relations to (1) environmental or proximal inputs, (2) other types of mental states, and (3) behavioral outputs. (Detailed examples are presented below.) Since what is at stake is the ordinary understanding of the language of the mental, the doctrine is generally called *analytic*, or *commonsense, functionalism*. Another doctrine that fits under the label "functionalism" is scientific functionalism (roughly what Block [1978] calls "psychofunctionalism"), according to which it is a matter of scientific fact that mental states are functional states: That is, mental states have functional properties (causal relations to inputs, other mental states, and outputs) and should be studied in terms of these properties. I shall have nothing to say against scientific functionalism. I do not doubt that mental states have functional properties; nor do I challenge the proposal that mental states should be studied (at least in part) in terms of these properties. But this doctrine does not entail that ordinary people understand or represent mental words as designating functional properties and functional properties only. States designated by mental words might have functional properties without ordinary folk knowing this, or without their regarding it as crucial to the identity of the states. But since we are concerned here exclusively with the ordinary person's representations of mental states, only analytic functionalism is relevant to our present investigation.

Philosophers usually discuss analytic, or commonsense, functionalism quite abstractly, without serious attention to its psychological realization. I am asking us to consider it as a psychological hypothesis, that is, a hypothesis about how the cognizer (or his cognitive system) represents mental words. It is preferable, then, to call the type of functionalism in question *representational functionalism* (RF). This form of functionalism is interpreted as hypothesizing that the CR associated with each mental predicate M represents a distinctive set of functional properties, or functional role, F_M.[3] Thus, RF implies that a person will ascribe a mental predicate M to himself when and only when an IR occurs in him bearing the message, "role F_M is now instantiated." That is, ascription occurs precisely when there is an IR that matches the functional-role content of the CR for M. (This may be subject to some qualification. Ascription may not require perfect or complete matching between IR and CR; partial matching may suffice.) Is RF an empirically plausible model of mental self-ascription? In particular, do subjects always get enough information about the functional properties of their current states to self-ascribe in this fashion (in real time)?

Before examining this question, let us sketch RF in more detail. The doctrine holds that folk wisdom embodies a theory, or a set of generalizations, which articulates an elaborate network of relations of three kinds: (a) relations between distal or proximal stimuli (inputs) and internal states, (b) relations between internal states and other internal states, and (c) relations between internal states and items of overt behavior (outputs). Here is a sample of such laws from Churchland (1979). Under heading (a) (relations between inputs and internal states) we might have:

When the body is damaged, a feeling of pain tends to occur at the point of damage.
When no fluids are imbibed for some time, one tends to feel thirsty.
When a red apple is present in daylight (and one is looking at it attentively), one will have a red visual experience.

Under heading (b) (relations between internal states and other internal states) we might have:

Feelings of pain tend to be followed by desires to relieve that pain.
Feelings of thirst tend to be followed by desires for potable fluids.
If one believes that P, where P elementarily entails Q, one also tends to believe that Q.

Under heading (c) (relations between internal states and outputs) we might have:

Sudden sharp pains tend to produce wincing.
States of anger tend to produce frowning.
An intention to curl one's finger tends to produce the curling of one's finger

According to RF, each mental predicate picks out a state with a distinctive collection, or syndrome, or relations of types (a), (b), and/or (c). The term *pain*, for example, picks out a state that tends to be caused by bodily damage, tends to produce a desire to get rid of that state, and tends to produce wincing, groaning, and so on. The content of each mental predicate is given by its unique set of relations, or functional role, and nothing else. In other words, RF attributes to people a *purely relational* concept of mental states.

There are slight variations and important additional nuances in the formulation of functionalism. Some formulations, for example, talk about the *causal* relations among stimulus inputs, internal states, and behavioral outputs. Others merely talk about *transitional* relations, that is, one state following another. Another important wrinkle in an adequate formulation is the *subjunctive* or *counterfactual* import of the relations in question. For example, part of the functional role associated with desiring water would be something like this: If a desire for water were accompanied by a belief that a glass of water is within arm's reach, then (other things being equal) it would be followed by extending one's arm. To qualify as a desire for water, an internal state need not actually be accompanied by a belief that water is within reach, nor need it be followed by an extending of the arm. It must, however, possess the indicated subjunctive property: If it were accompanied by this belief, the indicated behavior would occur.

We are now in a position to assess the psychological plausibility of RF. The general question I wish to raise is, Does a subject who self-ascribes a mental predicate always (or even typically) have the sort of instance information required by RF? This is similar to an epistemological question sometimes posed by philosophers, namely, whether functionalism can give an adequate account of one's knowledge of one's own mental state. But the present discussion does not center on *knowledge;* it merely asks whether the RF model of the CRs and IRs in mental self-ascription adequately explains this behavior. Does the subject always have functional-role information about the target states—functional-role IRs—to secure a "match" with functional-role CRs?

There are three sorts of problems for the RF model. The first is *ignorance of causes and effects* (or predecessor and successor states). According to functionalism, what makes a mental state a state of a certain type (e.g., a pain, a feeling of thirst, a belief that $7 + 5 = 12$, and so forth) is not any intrinsic property it possesses but its relations to other states and events. What makes a state a headache, for example, includes the environmental conditions or other internal states that actually cause or precede it, and its actual effects or successors. There are situations, however, in which the self-ascription of *headache* occurs in the absence of any information (or beliefs) about relevant causes or effects, predecessors or successors. Surely there are cases in which a person wakes up with a headache and immediately ascribes this type of feeling to himself. Having just awakened, he has no information about the target state's immediate causes or predecessors; nor need he have any information about its effects or successors. The classification of the state occurs "immediately," without waiting for any further effects, either internal or behavioral, to ensue. There are cases, then, in which self-ascription occurs in the absence of information (or belief) about critical causal relations.

It might be replied that a person need not appeal to *actual* causes or effects of a target mental state to type-identify it. Perhaps he determines the state's identity by its subjunctive properties. This brings us to the second problem confronting the RF model: *ignorance of subjunctive properties*. How is a person supposed to determine (form beliefs about) the subjunctive properties of a current state (instance or "token")? To use our earlier example, suppose the subject does not believe that a glass of water is within arm's reach. How is he supposed to tell whether his current state would have produced an extending of his arm if this belief were present? It is extremely difficult to get information about subjunctive properties, unless the RF model is expanded in ways not yet intimidated (*infimated*) (a possible expansion will be suggest in the next section). The subjunctive implications of RF, then, are a liability rather than an asset. Each CR posited by RF would incorporate numerous subjunctive properties, each presumably serving as a necessary condition for applying a mental predicate. How is a cognizer supposed to form IRs containing properties that match those subjunctive properties in the CR? Determining that the current state has even one subjunctive property is difficult enough; determining many such properties is formidably difficult. Is it really plausible, then, that subjects make such determinations in type-identifying their inner states? Do they execute such routines in the brief timeframes in which self-ascriptions actually occur? This seems unlikely. I have no impossibility proof, of course; but the burden is on the RF theorist to show how the model can handle this problem.

The third difficulty arises from two central features of functionalism: (1) The type-identity of a token mental state depends exclusively on the type-identity of its relata, that is, the events that are (or would be) its causes and effects, its predecessors and successors, and (2) the type-identity of an important subclass of a state's relata, namely, other internal states, depends in turn on *their* relata. To identify a state as an instance of thirst, for example, one might need to identify one of its effects as a desire to drink. Identifying a particular effect as a desire to drink, however, requires one to identify *its* relata, many of which would also be internal states whose identities are a matter of *their* relata; and so on. Complexity ramifies very quickly. There is no claim here of any vicious circularity, or vicious regress. If functionalism is correct, the system of internal state-types is tacked down definitionally to independently specified external states (inputs and outputs) via a set of lawful relations. Noncircular definitions (so-called Ramsey definitions) can be

Goldman

given of each functional state-type in terms of these independently understood input and output predicates (see Block 1978; Lewis 1970, 1972; Loar 1981; Putnam 1967). The problem I am raising, however, concerns how a subject can determine which functional type a given state-token instantiates. There is a clear threat of combinatorial explosion: Too many other internal states will have to be type-identified in order to identify the target state.

This problem is not easily quantified with precision, because we lack an explicitly formulated and complete functional theory, hence we do not know how many other internal states are directly or indirectly invoked by any single functional role. The problem is particularly acute, though, for beliefs, desires, and other propositional attitudes, which under standard formulations of functionalism have strongly "holistic" properties. A given belief may causally interact with quite a large number of other belief tokens and desire tokens. To type-identify that belief, it looks as if the subject must track its relations to each of these other internal states, their relations to further internal states, and so on until each path terminates in an input or an output. When subjunctive properties are added to the picture the task becomes unbounded, because there is an infinity of possible beliefs and desires. For each desire or goal-state there are indefinitely many beliefs with which it could combine to produce a further desire or subgoal. Similarly, for each belief there are infinitely many possible desires with which it could combine to produce a further desire or subgoal, and infinitely many other beliefs with which it could combine to produce a further belief. If the type-identification of a target state depends on tracking *all* of these relations until inputs and outputs are reached, clearly it is unmanageably complex. At a minimum, we can see this as a challenge to an RF theorist, a challenge that no functionalist has tried to meet, and one that looks forbidding.

Here the possibility of partial matching may assist the RF theorist. It is often suggested that visual object identification can occur without the IR completely matching the CR. This is how partially occluded stimuli can be categorized. Biederman (1987, 1990) argues that even complex objects, whose full representation contains six or more geons, are recognized accurately and fairly quickly with the recovery of only two or three of these geons from the image. Perhaps the RF theorist would have us appeal to a similar process of partial matching to account for mental-state classification.

Although this might help a little, it does not get around the fundamental difficulties raised by our three problems. Even if only a few paths are followed from the target state to other internal states and ultimately to inputs and/or outputs, the demands of the task are substantial. Nor does the hypothesis of partial matching address the problem of determining subjunctive properties of the target state. Finally, it does not help much when classification occurs with virtually no information about neighboring states, as in the morning headache example. Thus, the simple RF model of mental self-ascription seems distinctly unpromising.

A Second Functionalist Model

A second model of self-ascription is available to the RF theorist, one that assumes, as before, that for each mental predicate there is a functional-role CR. (That is what makes an RF model functional.) This second model, however, tries to explain how the subject determines which functional role a given state-token exemplifies without appealing to on-line knowledge of the state's current relations. How, after all, do people decide which objects exemplify other dispositional properties, for example being soluble in water? They presumably do this by inference from the *intrinsic* and *categorical* (i.e., non-dispositional) properties of those objects. When a person sees a cube of sugar, he may note that it is white, hard, and granular (all intrinsic properties of the cube), infer from background information that such an object must be made of sugar, and then infer from further background information that it must be soluble in water (because all sugar is soluble in water). Similarly, the RF theorist may suggest that a subject can detect certain intrinsic and categorical properties of a mental state, and from this he can infer that it has a certain functional property, that is, a suitable relational and dispositional property.

Let us be a bit more concrete. Suppose that the CR for the word *headache* is the functional-role property F. Further suppose that there is an intrinsic (nonrelational) property E that mental states have, and the subject has learned that any state which has E also has the functional-role property F. The subject is in a position to classify a particular headache as a headache without any excessively demanding inference or computation. He just detects that a particular state-token (his morning headache, for example) has property E, and from this he infers that it has F. Finally, he infers from its having F that if can be labeled *headache*.[4]

Although this may appear to save the day for RF, it actually just pushes the problem back to what we may call "the learning stage." A crucial part of the foregoing account is that the subject must know (or believe) that property E is correlated with property F—that whenever a state has E it also has F. But how could the subject have learned this? At some earlier time, during the learning stage, the subject must have detected some number of mental states, each of which had both E and F. But during this learning period he did not already know that E and F are systematically correlated. So he must have had some other way of determining that the E-states in question had F. How did he determine that? The original difficulties we cited for identifying a state's functional properties would have been at work during the learning stage, and they would have been just as serious then as we saw them to be in the first model. So the second model of functionalist self-ascription is not much of an improvement (if any) over the first.

In addition, the second model raises a new problem (or question) for RF: What are the intrinsic properties of mental states that might play the role of property *E*? At this point let us separate our discussion into two parts, one dealing with what philosophers call *sensation* predicates (roughly, names for bodily feelings and percepts), and the other dealing with *propositional attitudes* (believing that *p*, hoping that *q*, intending to *r*, etc.). In this section we restrict our attention to sensation predicates; later we shall turn to predicates for propositional attitudes.

What kinds of categorical, nonrelational properties might fill the role of *E* in the case of sensations? In addition to being categorical and nonrelational, such properties must be accessible to the system that performs the self-ascription. This places an important constraint on the range of possible properties.

There seem to be two candidates to fill the role of *E*: (1) neural properties and (2) what philosophers call "qualitative" properties (the "subjective feel" of the sensation). Presumably any sensation state or event has some neural properties that are intrinsic and categorical, but do these properties satisfy the accessibility requirements? Presumably not. Certainly the naive subject does not have "personal access" (in the sense of Dennett 1969; 1978) to the neural properties of his sensations. That would occur only if the subject were, say, undergoing brain surgery and watching his brain in a mirror. Normally people do not see their brains; nor do they know much, if anything, about neural hardware. Yet they still identify their headaches without any trouble.

It may be replied that although there is no personal access to neural information in the ordinary situation, the system performing the self-ascription may have *subpersonal* access to such information. To exclude neural properties (i.e., neural concepts) from playing the role of *E* we need reasons to think that self-ascription does not use these properties of sensations. It goes without saying that neural events are involved in the relevant information processing; all information processing in the brain is, at the lowest level, neural processing. The question, however, is where the *contents* (meanings) encoded by these neural events are about neural properties. This, to repeat, seems implausible. Neural events process visual information, but cognitive scientists do not impute neural contents to these neural events. Rather, they consider the contents encoded to be structural descriptions, things like edges and vertices (in low-level vision) or geons (in higher-level vision). When connectionists posit neurally inspired networks in the analysis of, say, language processing, they do not suppose that configurations of connection weights encode neural properties (e.g., configurations of connection weights), but rather things like phonological properties.

There is more to be said against the suggestion that self-ascription is performed by purely subpersonal systems, which have access to neural properties. Obviously, a great deal of information processing does occur at subpersonal levels within the organism. But when the processing is purely subpersonal, no verbal labels seem to be generated that are recognizably "mental." There are all sorts of homeostatic activities in which information is transmitted about levels of certain fluids or chemicals; for example, the glucose level is monitored and then controlled by secretion of insulin. But we have no folk psychological labels for these events or activities. Similarly, there are information-processing activities in low-level vision and in the selection and execution of motor routines. None of these, however, are the subjects of primitive (pretheoretic) verbal labeling, certainly not "mentalistic" labeling. This strongly suggests that our spontaneous naming system does not have access to purely subpersonal information. Only when physiological or neurological events give rise to conscious sensations such as thirst, felt heat, or the like does a primitive verbal label get introduced or applied. Thus, although there is subpersonal detection of properties such as "excess glucose," these cannot be the sorts of properties to which the mentalistic verbal-labeling system has access.

We seem to be left, then, with what philosophers call "qualitative" properties. According to the standard philosophical view, these are indeed intrinsic, categorical properties that are detected "directly." Thus, the second model of functional self-ascription might hold that in learning to ascribe a sensation predicate like *itch*, one first learns the functional role constitutive of that word's meaning (e.g., being a state that tends to produce scratching, and so forth). One then learns that this functional role is realized (at least in one's own case) by a certain qualitative property: itchiness. Finally, one decides that the word is self-ascribable whenever one detects in oneself the appropriate qualitative property, or quale, and infers the instantiation of its correlated functional role. This model still depicts the critical IR as a representation of a functional role, and similarly depicts the CR to which the IR is matched.

We have found a kind of property, then, which might plausibly fill the role of E in the second functionalist model. But is this a model that a true functionalist would welcome? Functionalists are commonly skeptical about qualia (e.g., Dennett 1988, 1991; Harman 1990). In particular, many of them wish to deny that there are any qualitative properties *if these are construed as intrinsic, nonrelational properties*. But this is precisely what the second model of RF requires: that qualitative properties be accepted as intrinsic (rather than functional) properties of mental states. It is not clear, therefore, how attractive the second model would be to many functionalists.

A Qualitative Model of Sensation Representation

Furthermore, although the second functionalist model may retain some appeal (despite its problems with the learning stage), it naturally invites a much simpler and more appealing model: one that is wholly *nonfunctionalist*. Once qualitative properties are introduced into the psychological story, what need is there for functional-role components? Why not drop the latter entirely? Instead, we hypothesize that both the CR and the IR for each sensation predicate are representations of a qualitative property such as itchiness (or, as I suggest below, some microcomponents of the property of itchiness). This vastly simplifies our story, for both the learning phase and the ascription phase itself. All one learns in the learning phase is the association between the term *itch* and the feeling of itchiness. At the time of self-ascription, all one detects (or represents) is itchiness, and then matches this IR to the corresponding CR. This is a very natural model for the psychology of sensation self-ascription, at least to anyone free of philosophical prejudice or preconception. "The eternal cry of The philosophically pre-judiced"

Of course, some philosophers claim that qualitative properties are "queer," and should not be countenanced by cognitive science. There is nothing objectionable about such properties, however, and they are already implicitly countenanced in scientific psychology. One major text, for example, talks of the senses producing sensations of different "quality" (Gleitman 1981, 172). The sensations of pressure, A-flat, orange, or sour, for example, are sharply different in experienced quality (as Gleitman puts it). This use of the term *quality* refers to differences across the sensory domains, or sense modalities. It is also meaningful, however, to speak of qualitative differences within a modality, for example, the difference between a sour and a sweet taste. It is wholly within the spirit of cognitive science, then, to acknowledge the existence of qualitative attributes and to view them as potential elements of systems of representation in the mind (see Churchland 1985).

Although I think that this approach is basically on the right track, it requires considerable refinement. It would indeed be simplistic to suppose that for each word or predicate in the common language of sensation (e.g., *itch*) there is a simple, unanalyzable attribute (e.g., *itchiness*) that is the cognitive system's CR for that term. But no such simplistic model is required; most sensory or sensational experience is a mixture or compound of qualities, and this is presumably registered in the contents of CRs for sensations. Even if a person cannot dissect an experience introspectively into its several components or constituents, these components may well be detected and processed by the subsystem that classifies sensations.

Consider the example of pain. Pain appears to have at least three distinguishable dimensional components (see Campbell 1985; Rachlin 1985): intensity, aversiveness, and character (e.g., "stinging," "grinding," "shooting," or "throbbing"). Evidence for an intensity/aversive-ness distinction is provided by Tursky et al. (1982), who found that morphine altered aversiveness reports from chronic pain sufferers without altering their intensity reports. In other words, although the pain still hurt as much, the subjects did not mind it so much. Now it may well be that a subject would not, without instruction or training, dissect or analyze his pain into these microcomponents or dimensions. Nonetheless, representations of such components or dimensions could well figure in the CRs for *pain* and related sensation words; in particular, the sub-system that makes classification decisions could well be sensitive to these distinct components. The situation here is perfectly analogous to the phonological microfeatures of auditory experience that the phonologist postulates as the features used by the system to classify sequences of speech.

Granted that qualitative features (or their microcomponents) play some sort of role in sensation classification, it is (to repeat) quite parsimonious to hypothesize that such features constitute the contents of CRs for mental words. It is much less parsimonious to postulate functional-role contents for these CRs, with qualitative features playing a purely evidential or intermediate role. Admittedly, there are words in the language that do have a functional-style meaning, and their ascriptions must exemplify the sort of multistage process postulated by the complex version of functionalism. Consider the expression *can-opener*, for example. This probably means something like: device capable of (or used for) opening cans. To identify something as a can-opener, however, one does not have to see it actually open a can. One can learn that objects having certain intrinsic and categorical properties (shape, sharpness, and so on) also thereby exemplify the requisite functional (relational, dispositional) property. So when one sees an object of the right shape (etc.), one classifies it as a can-opener.

Although this is presumably the right story for *some* words and expressions in the language, it is not so plausible for sensation words. First, purely syntactic considerations suggest that *can-opener* is a functional expression, but there is no comparable suggestion of functionality for sensation words. Second, there are familiar difficulties from thought experiments, especially *absent-qualia* examples such as Block's Chinese nation (Block 1978).[5] For any functional description of a system that is in pain (or has an itch), it seems as if we can imagine another system with the same functional description but lacking the qualitative property of painfulness (or itchiness). When we do imagine this, we are intuitively inclined to say that the system is not in pain (has no itch). This supports the contention that no purely functional content exhausts the meaning of these sensation words; qualitative character is an essential part of that content.

On a methodological note, I should emphasize that the use of thought experiments, so routine in philosophy, may also be considered (with due caution) a species of psychological or cognitivist methodology, complementary to the methodology described earlier in this article. Not only do applications of a predicate to actual cases provide evidence about the correlated CR, but so do decisions to apply or withhold the predicate for imaginary cases. In the present context, reactions to hypothetical cases support our earlier conclusion that qualitative properties are the crucial components of CRs for sensation words.

Quite a different question about the qualitative approach to sensation concepts should now be addressed, namely, its compatibility with our basic framework for classification. This framework says that self-ascription occurs when a CR is matched by an IR, where an IR is a representation of a current mental state. Does it make sense, however, to regard an instance of a qualitative property as a *representation* of a mental state? Is it not more accurate to say that it *is* a mental state, not a representation thereof? If we seek a representation of a mental state, should we not look for something entirely distinct from the state itself (or any feature thereof)?

Certainly the distinction between representations and what they represent must be preserved. The problem can be avoided, however, by a minor revision in our framework. On reflection, self-ascription does not require the matching of an instance representation to a category representation; it can involve the matching of an instance itself to a category representation. The term *instance representation* was introduced because we wanted to allow approaches like functionalism, in which the state itself is not plausibly matched to a CR, only a representation of it. Furthermore, we had in mind the analogy of perceptual categorization, where the cognizer does not match an actual stimulus to a mental representation of the stimulus category but an inner representation of the stimulus to a category representation.

In this respect, however, the analogy between perceptual recognition and sensation recognition breaks down. In the case of sensation there *can* be a matching of the pain itself, or some features of the pain, to a stored structure containing representations of those features. Thus, we should revise our framework to say that categorization occurs when a match is effected between (1) a category representation and (2) either (a) a suitable representation of a state or (b) a state itself. Alternative (b) is especially plausible in the case of sensations, because it is easy to suppose that CRs for sensations are simply memory "traces" of those sensations, which are easily activated by reoccurrences of these same (or similar) sensations.

This new picture might look suspicious because it seems to lead to the much-disparaged doctrines of infallibility and omniscience about one's own mental states. If a CR is directly matched to an instance of a sensation itself, is all possibility of error not precluded? And would it not be impossible to be unaware of one's sensations, because correct matching is incvitable? Yet surely both error and ignorance are possible.

The proposed change implies neither infallibility nor omniscience. The possibility of error is readily guaranteed by introducing an assumption (mentioned earlier) of partial matching. If a partial match suffices for classification and self-ascription, there is room for inaccuracy. If we hypothesize that the threshold for matching can be appreciably lowered by various sorts of "response biases" (such as prior expectation of a certain sensation), this makes error particularly easy to accommodate. Ignorance can be accommodated in a different way, by supplementary assumptions about the role of attention. When attentional resources are devoted to other topics, there may be no attempt to match certain sensations to any category representation. Even an itch or a pain can go unnoticed when attention is riveted on other matters. Mechanisms of selective attention are critical to the full story of classification, but this large topic cannot be adequately addressed here.

Even with these points added, some readers might think that our model makes insufficient room for incidental cognitive factors in the labeling of mental states. Does not the work on emotions by Schachter and Singer (1962), for example, show that such incidental factors are crucial? My first response is that I am not trying to address the complex topic of emotions but restricting attention to sensations (in this section) and propositional attitudes. Second, there are various ways of trying to accommodate the Schachter-Singer findings. One possibility, for example, is to say that cognitive factors influence which emotion is actually felt (e.g., euphoria or anger) rather than the process of labeling or classifying the felt emotion (see Wilson 1991). So it is not clear that the Schachter-Singer study would undermine the model proposed here, even if this model were applied to emotions (which is not my present intent).

The Classical Functionalist Account of Self-Ascription

Classical functionalists such as Putnam (1960), Sellars (1956), and Shoemaker (1975) have not been oblivious to the necessity of making room in their theory for self-ascriptions or self-reports of mental states. They thought this could be done without recourse to anything like qualitative properties. How, then, does their theory go, and why do I reject it?

According to the classical account, it is part of the specification of a mental state's functional role that having the state guarantees a self-report of it; or, slightly better, that it is part of the functional specification of a mental state (e.g., pain) that it gives rise to a belief that one is in that state (Shoemaker 1975). If one adopts the general framework of RF that I have presented, however, it is impossible to include this specification. Let me explain why.

According to our framework, a *belief* that one is in state M occurs precisely when a *match* occurs between a CR for M and a suitable IR. (Since we are now discussing functionalism again, we need not worry about "direct" matching of state to CR.) But classical functionalism implies that part of the concept of being in state M (a necessary part) is having a belief that one is in M. Thus, no match can be achieved until the system has detected the presence of an M-belief. However, to repeat, what an M-belief is, according to our framework, is the occurrence of a match between the CR for M and an appropriate IR. Thus, the system can only form a belief that it is in M (achieve an IR-CR match) by first forming a belief that it is in M! Obviously this is impossible.

What this point shows is that there is an incompatibility between our general framework and classical functionalism. They cannot both be correct. But where does the fault lie? Which should be abandoned?

A crucial feature of classical functionalism is that it offers no story at all about *how* a person decides what mental state he is in. Being in a mental state automatically entails, or gives rise to, the appropriate belief. Precisely this assumption of automaticity has until now allowed functionalism to ignore the sorts of questions raised in this paper. In other words, functionalism has hitherto tended to assume some sort of "nonrecognitional" or "noncriterial" account of self-reports. Allegedly, you do not use any criterion (e.g., the presence of a qualitative property) to decide what mental state you are in. Classification of a present state does not involve the comparison of present information with anything stored in long-term memory. Just *being* in a mental state *automatically* triggers a classification of yourself as being in that state.

It should be clear, however, that this automaticity assumption cannot and should not be accepted by cognitive science, for it would leave the process of mental-state classification a complete mystery. It is true, of course, that we are not introspectively aware of the mechanism by which we classify our mental states. But we are likewise not introspectively aware of the classification processes associated with other verbal labeling, the labeling of things such as birds or chairs, leapings or strollings. Lack of introspective access is obviously no reason for cognitive scientists to deny that there is a microstory of how we make—or how our *systems* make—mental classifications. There must be some way a system decides to say (or believe) that it is now in a thirst state rather than a hunger state, that it is hoping for a rainy day rather than expecting a rainy day. That is what our general framework requires. In short, in a choice between our general framework and classical functionalism (with its assumption of automatic self-report), cognitive science must choose the former. Any tenable form of functionalism, at least any functionalism that purports to explain the content of naive mental concepts, must be formulated within this general framework. This is just how RF has been formulated. It neither assumes automaticity of classification nor does it create a vicious circularity (by requiring the prior detection of classification event—a belief—as a necessary condition for classification). So RF is superior to classical functionalism for the purposes at hand. Yet RF, we have seen, has serious problems of its own. Thus, the only relevant form of functionalism is distinctly unpromising. . . .

A Phenomenological Model for the Attitudes?

Returning to my positive theory, I have thus far only proposed a qualitative approach to *sensation* concepts. Let us turn now from sensations to propositional attitudes, such as believing, wanting, and intending. This topic can be divided into two parts (Fodor 1987): the representation of attitude *types* and the representation of attitude *contents*. Wanting there to be peace and believing there will be peace are different attitudes because their types (wanting and believing) are different. Intending to go shopping and intending to go home are different attitudes because, although their type is the same, their contents differ. In this section we consider how attitude types are represented; in the next we consider attitude contents.

Philosophical orthodoxy favors a functionalist approach to attitude types. Even friends of qualia (e.g., Block 1990b) feel committed to functionalism when it comes to desire, belief, and so forth. Our earlier critiques of functionalism, however, apply with equal force here. Virtually all of our antifunctionalist arguments (except the absent-qualia arguments) apply to all types of mental predicates, not just to sensation predicates. So there are powerful reasons to question the adequacy of functionalism for the attitude types. How, then, do people decide whether a current state is a desire rather than a belief, a hope rather than a fear?

In recent literature some philosophers use the metaphor of "boxes" in the brain (Schiffer 1981). To believe something is to store a sentence of mentalese in one's "belief box"; to desire something is to store a sentence of mentalese in one's "desire box"; and so on. Should this metaphor be taken seriously? I doubt it. It is unlikely that there are enough "boxes" to have a distinct one for each attitude predicate. Even if there are enough boxes in the brain, does the ordinary person know enough about these neural boxes to associate each attitude predicate with one of them (the correct one)? Fodor (1987) indicates that box-talk is just shorthand for treating the attitude types in functional terms. If so, this just reintroduces the forbidding problems already facing functionalism.

Could a qualitative or phenomenological approach work for the attitude types? The vast majority of philosophers reject this approach out of hand, but this rejection is premature. I shall adduce several tentative(!) arguments in support of this approach.

First a definitional point. The terms *qualia* and *qualitative* are sometimes restricted to sensations (percepts and somatic feelings), but we should not allow this to preclude the possibility of other mental events (beliefs, thoughts, etc.) having a phenomenological or experiential dimension. Indeed, at least two cognitive scientists (Baars 1988; Jackendoff 1987) have defended the notion that "abstract" or "conceptual" thought often occupies awareness or consciousness, even if it is phenomenologically "thinner" than modality-specific experience. Jackendoff appeals to the tip-of-the-tongue phenomenon to argue that phenomenology is not confined to sensations. When one tries to say something but cannot think of the word, one is phenomenologically aware of having requisite conceptual structure, that is, of having a determinate thought-content one seeks to articulate. What is missing is the phonological form: the *sound* of the sought-for word. The absence of this sensory quality, however, does not imply that nothing (relevant) is in awareness. Entertaining the conceptual unit has a phenomenology, just not a sensory phenomenology.

Second, in defense of phenomenal "parity" for the attitudes, I present a permutation of Jackson's (1982, 1986) argument for qualia (cf. Nagel 1974). Jackson argues that qualitative information cannot be captured in physicalist (including functionalist) terms. Imagine, he says, that a brilliant scientist named Mary has lived from birth in a cell where everything is black, white, or gray. (Even she herself is painted all over.) By black-and-white television she reads books, engages in discussion, and watches experiments. Suppose that by this means Mary learns all physical and functional facts concerning color, color vision, and the brain states produced by exposure to colors. Does she therefore know all facts about color? There is one kind of fact about color perception, says Jackson, of which she is ignorant: what it is like (i.e., what it feels like) to experience red, green, and so on. These qualitative sorts of facts she will come to know only if she actually undergoes spectral experiences.

Jackson's example is intended to dramatize the claim that there are subjective aspects of sensations that resist capture in functionalist terms. I suggest a parallel style of argument for attitude types. Just as someone deprived of any experience of colors would learn new things upon being exposed to them, namely, what it feels like to see red, green, and so forth, so (I submit) someone who had never experienced certain propositional attitudes, for example, doubt or disappointment, would learn new things on first undergoing these experiences. There is "something it is like" to have these attitudes, just as much as there is "something it is like" to see red. In the case of the attitudes, just as in the case of sensations, the features to which the system is sensitive may be microfeatures of the experience. This still preserves parity with the model for sensations.

My third argument is from the introspective discriminability of attitude strengths. Subjects' classificational abilities are not confined to broad categories such as belief, desire, and intention; they also include intensities thereof. People report how *firm* is their intention or conviction, how *much* they desire an object, and how satisfied or dissatisfied they are with a state of affairs. Whatever the behavioral predictive power of these self-reports, their very occurrence needs explaining. Again, the functionalist approach seems fruitless. The other familiar device for conceptualizing the attitudes—namely, the "boxes" in which sentences of mentalese are stored—would also be unhelpful even if it were separated from functionalism, since box storage is not a matter of degree. The most natural hypothesis is that there are dimensions of awareness over which scales of attitude intensity are represented.

The importance of attitude strength is heightened by the fact that many words in the mentalistic lexicon ostensibly pick out such strengths. *Certain, confident,* and *doubtful* represent positions on a credence scale; *delighted, pleased,* and *satisfied* represent positions on a liking scale. Since we apparently have introspective access to such positions, self-ascription of these terms invites an introspectivist account (or a quasi-introspectivist account that makes room for microfeatures of awareness).

One obstacle to a phenomenological account of the attitudes is that stored (or dispositional) beliefs, desires, and so on are outside awareness. However, there is no strain in the suggestion that the primary understanding of these terms stems from their activated ("occurrent") incarnations; the stored attitudes are just dispositions to have the activated ones.

A final argument for the role of phenomenology takes its starting point from still another trouble with functionalism, a trouble not previously mentioned here. In addition to specific mental words like *hope* and *imagine*, we have the generic word *mental*. Ordinary people can classify internal states as mental or nonmental. Notice, however, that many nonmental internal states can be given a functional-style description. For example, *having measles* might be described as a state that tends to be produced by being exposed to the measles virus and tends to produce an outbreak of red spots on the skin. So having measles is a functional state; although, it clearly is not a *mental* state. Thus, functionalism cannot fully discharge its mission by saying that mental states are functional states; it also needs to say *which* functional states are *mental*. Does functionalism have any resources for marking the mental/nonmental distinction? The prospects are bleak. By contrast, a plausible-looking hypothesis is that mental states are states having a phenomenology, or an intimate connection with phenomenological events. This points us again in the direction of identifying the attitudes in phenomenological terms.

Skepticism about this approach has been heavily influenced by Wittgenstein (1953, 1967), who questioned whether there is any single feeling or phenomenal characteristic common to all instances of an attitude such as intending or expecting. (A similar worry about sensations is registered by Churchland and Churchland 1981.) Notice, however, that our general approach to concepts does not require a single "defining characteristic" for each mental word. A CR might be, for example, a list of exemplars (represented phenomenologically) associated with the word, to which new candidate instances are compared for similarity. Thus, even if Wittgenstein's (and Churchland and Churchland's) worries about the phenomenological unity of mental concepts are valid, this does not exclude a central role for phenomenological features in CRs for attitude words.

Content and Computationalism

The commonsense understanding of the contents of the propositional attitudes is an enormous topic; we shall touch on it here only lightly. The central question concerns the "source" of contentfulness for mental states. Recent theories have tended to be externalist, claiming that content arises from causal or causal-historical interactions between inner states (or symbols in the language of thought) and external objects. It is highly doubtful, however, whether any of the most developed externalist theories gives an adequate account of the naive cognizer's understanding or representation of content.

Fodor currently advocates a complex causal-counterfactual account (Fodor 1987, 1990). Roughly, a mental symbol C means *cow* if and only if (1) C-tokens are reliably caused by cows, and (2) although noncows (e.g., horses) also sometimes cause C-tokens, noncows would not cause C-tokens unless cows did, whereas it is false that cows would not cause C-tokens unless noncows did. Clause (2) of this account is a condition of "asymmetric dependence" according to which there being non-cow-caused C-tokens depends on there being cow-caused C-tokens, but not conversely. It seems most implausible, however, that this sort of criterion for the content of a mental symbol is what ordinary cognizers have in mind. Similarly implausible for this purpose are Millikan's evolutionary account of mental content (Millikan 1984, 1986) and Dretske's (1988) learning-theoretic (i.e., operant conditioning) account of mental content. Most naive cognizers have never heard of operant conditioning, and many do not believe in evolution; nevertheless, the same subjects readily ascribe belief contents to themselves. So did our sixteenth-century ancestors, who never dreamt of the theory of evolution or operant conditioning. (For further critical discussion see Cummins 1989.) Perhaps Millikan and Dretske do not intend their theories as accounts of the *ordinary* understanding of mental contents. Millikan (1989), for one, expressly disavows any such intent. But then we are left with very few detailed theories that do address our question. Despite the popularity of externalist theories of content, they clearly pose difficulties for self-ascription. Cognizers seem able to discern their mental contents—what they believe, desire, or plan to do—without consulting their environment.[6]

What might a more internalist approach to contents look like? Representationalism, or computationalism, maintains that content is borne by the formal symbols of the language of thought (Fodor 1975, 1981, 1987; Newell and Simon 1976). But even if the symbolic approach gives a correct de facto account of the working of the mind, it does not follow that the ordinary concept of mental content associates it with formal symbols per se. I would again suggest that phenomenological dimensions play a crucial role in our naive view. Only what we are aware or conscious of provides the primary locus of mental content.

For example, psycholinguists maintain that in sentence processing there are commonly many interpretations of a sentence that are momentarily presented as viable, but we are normally aware of only one—the one that gets selected (Garrett 1990). The alternatives are "filtered" by the processing system outside of awareness. Only in exceptional cases such as "garden path" sentences (e.g., "Fatty weighed three hundred and fifty pounds of grapes") do we become aware of more than one considered interpretation. Our view of mental content is, I suggest, driven by the cases of which we are aware, although they may be only a minority of the data structures or symbolic structures that occupy the mind.

Elaboration of this theme is not possible in the present paper, but a brief comment about the relevant conception of "awareness" is in order. Awareness, for these purposes, should not be identified with accessibility to verbal report. We are often aware of contents that we cannot (adequately) verbalize, either because the type of content is not easily encoded in linguistic form or because its mode of cognitive representation does not allow full verbalization. The relevant notion of awareness, or consciousness, then, may be that of qualitative or phenomenological character (there being "something it is like") rather than verbal reportability (see Block 1990a, 1991).

The role I am assigning to consciousness in our naive conception of the mental bears some similarity to that assigned by Searle (1990). Unlike Searle, however, I see no reason to decree that cognitive science cannot legitimately apply the notion of content to states that are inaccessible (even in principle) to consciousness. First, it is not clear that the ordinary concept of a mental state makes consciousness a "logical necessity" (as Searle puts it). Second, even if *mental* content requires consciousness, it is inessential to cognitive science that the nonconscious states to which contents are ascribed should be considered *mental*. Let them be "psychological" or "cognitive" rather than "mental"; this does not matter to the substance of cognitive science. Notice that the notion of content in general is not restricted to *mental* content; linguistic utterances and inscriptions are also bearers of content. So even if mental content is understood to involve awareness, this places no constraints of the sort Searle proposes on cognitive science.

Empirical Research on the Theory-Theory

The idea underlying functionalism, that the naive cognizer has a "theory" of mind, goes increasingly by the label "the theory-theory" (Morton 1980). Although originally proposed by philosophers, this idea is now endorsed by a preponderance of empirical researchers, especially developmental psychologists and cognitive anthropologists. Does their research lend empirical support to the functionalist account of mental concepts?

Let us be clear about exactly what we mean by functionalism, especially the doctrine of RF (representational functionalism) that concerns us here. There are two crucial features of this view. The first feature is *pure relationalism*. RF claims that the way subjects represent mental predicates is by relations to inputs, outputs, and other internal states. The other internal-state concepts are similarly represented. Thus, every internal-state concept is ultimately tied to external inputs and outputs. What is deliberately excluded from our understanding of mental predicates, according to RF, is any reference to the phenomenology or experiential aspects of mental events (unless these can be spelled out in relationalist terms). No "intrinsic" character of mental states is appealed to by RF in explaining the subject's basic conception or understanding of mental predicates. The second crucial feature of RF is the appeal to *nomological* (lawlike) generalizations in providing the links between each mental-state concept and suitably chosen inputs, outputs, and other mental states. Thus, if subjects are to exemplify RF, they must mentally represent *laws* of the appropriate sort. Does empirical research on "theory of mind" support either of these two crucial features? Let us review what several leading workers in this tradition say on these topics. We shall find that very few of them, if any, construe theory of mind in quite the sense specified here. They usually endorse vaguer and weaker views.

Premack and Woodruff (1978), for example, say that an individual has a theory of mind if he simply imputes mental states to himself and others. Ascriptions of mental states are regarded as "theoretical" merely because such states are not directly observable (in others), and because such imputations can be used to make predictions about the behavior of others. This characterization falls short of RF, because it does not assert that the imputations are based on lawlike generalizations and does not assert that mental-state concepts are understood solely in terms of relations to external events.

Wellman's (1988, 1990) concept of the theory-theory (TT) is also quite a weak one. A body of knowledge is theory-like, he says, if it has (1) an interconnected ("coherent") set of concepts, (2) a distinctive set of ontological commitments, and (3) a causal-explanatory network. Wellman grants that some characterizations of theories specify commitments to nomological statements, but his own conception explicitly omits that provision (Wellman 1990, chap. 5). This is one reason why his version of TT falls short of RF. A second reason is that Wellman explicitly allows that the child's understanding of mind is partly founded on firsthand experience. "The meaning of such terms/constructs as *belief, desire* and *dream* may be anchored in certain firsthand experiences, but by age three children have not only the experiences, but the theoretical constructs" (Wellman 1990, 195). Clearly, then, Wellman's view is not equivalent to RF, and the evidence he adduces of his own version of TT is not sufficient to support RF.

Similarly, Rips and Conrad (1989) present evidence that a central aspect of people's beliefs about the mind is that mental activities are interrelated, with some activities being kinds or parts of others. For example, reasoning is a kind of thinking and reasoning is a part of problem solving. The mere existence of taxonomies and partonomies (part-whole hierarchies), however, does not support RF, since mental terms could still be represented in introspective terms, and such taxonomies may not invoke laws.

D'Andrade (1987) also describes the "folk model of the mind" as an elaborate taxonomy of mental states, organized into a complex causal system. This is no defense of functionalism, however, since D'Andrade expressly indicates that concepts such as emotion, desire, and intention are "primarily defined by the conscious experience of the person" (p. 139). The fact that laymen recognize causal relations among mental events does not prove that they have a set of laws. Whether or not belief in causal relations requires belief in laws is a controversial philosophical question. Nor does the fact that people use mental concepts to explain and predict the behavior of others imply the possession of laws, as we shall see below.

The TT approach to mental concepts is, of course, part of a general movement toward understanding concepts as theory-embedded (Carey 1985, 1988; Gopnik 1984, 1988; Karmiloff-Smith and Inhelder 1975; Keil 1989; Murphy and Medin 1985). Many proponents of this approach, however, acknowledge that their construal of "theory" is quite vague, or remains to be worked out. For example, Murphy and Medin (1985, 290) simply characterize a theory as "a complex set of relations between concepts, usually with a causal basis"; and Keil (1989, 279–280) says: "So far we have not made much progress on specifying what naive theories must look like or even what the best theoretical vocabulary is for describing them." Thus, commitment to a TT approach does not necessarily imply commitment to RF in the mental domain; nor would evidential corroboration of a TT approach necessarily corroborate RF.

A detailed defense of TT is given by Gopnik (1993), who specifically rejects the classical view of direct or introspective access to one's own psychological states. However, even Gopnik's view is significantly qualified and her evidential support far from compelling. First, although her main message is the rejection of an introspective or "privileged access" approach to self-knowledge of mental states, she acknowledges that we use some mental vocabulary "to talk about conscious experiences with a particular kind of phenomenology, the Joycean or Woolfian stream of consciousness, if you will." This does not sound like RF. Second, Gopnik seems to concede privileged access, or at least errorless performance, for subjects' self-attributions of *current* mental states. At any rate, all of her experimental data concern self-attributions of *past* mental states; nowhere does she hint that subjects make mistakes about their current states as well. How can errorless performance be explained on her favored inferential model of self-attribution? If faulty theoretical inference is rampant in children's self-attribution of past states, why do they not make equally faulty inferences about their current states? Third, there is some evidence that children's problems with reporting their previous thoughts are just a result of *memory* failure. Mitchell and Lacohée (1991) found that such memory failure could be largely alleviated with a little help. Fourth, Gopnik's TT does not explain satisfactorily why children perform well on self-attributions of past pretense and imaging. Why are their inferences so much more successful for those mental states than for beliefs? Finally, how satisfactory is Gopnik's explanation of the "illusion" of first-person privileged access? If Gopnik were right that this illusion stems from expertise, why should we not have the same illusion in connection with attribution of mental states to others? If people were similarly positioned vis-à-vis their own mental states and those of others, they would be just as expert for others as for themselves and should develop analogous illusions; but there is no feeling of privileged access to others' mental states.

At this point the tables might be turned on us. How are *we* to account for attributions to *others* if subjects do not have a theory, that is, a set of causal laws, to guide their attributions? An alternative account of how such attributions might be made is the "simulation," or role-taking, theory (Goldman 1989, 1992a, 1992b; Gordon 1986, 1992; Harris 1989, 1991, 1992; Johnson 1988), according to which one can predict another person's choices or mental states by first imagining himself in the other person's situation and then determining what he himself would do or how he would feel. For example, to estimate how disappointed someone would feel if he lost a certain tennis match or did poorly on a certain exam you might project yourself into the relevant situation and see how you would feel. You do not need to know any psychological laws about disappointment to make this assessment. You just need to be able to feed an imagined situation as input to some internal psychological mechanism that then generates a relevant output state. Your mechanism can "model" or mimic the target agent's mechanism even if you do not know any laws describing these mechanisms.

To compete with TT, the simulation theory (ST) must do as well in accounting for developmental data such as 3-year-olds' difficulties with false-belief ascriptions (Astington et al. 1988; Wimmer and Perner 1983). Defenders of TT usually postulate a major change in children's theory of mind: from a primitive theory—variously called a "copy theory" (Wellman 1990), a "Gibsonian theory" (Astington and Gopnik 1991), a "situation theory" (Perner 1991), or a "cognitive connection theory" (Flavell 1988)—to a full representational theory. Defenders of ST might explain these developmental data in a different fashion by positing not fundamental changes of theory but increases in flexibility of simulation (Harris 1992). Three-year-olds have difficulty in *imagining* states that run directly counter to their own current states; but by age four children's imaginative powers overcome this difficulty. ST also comports well with early propensities to mimic or imitate others' attitudes or actions such as joint visual attention and facial imitation (Butterworth 1991; Goldman 1992b; Harris 1992; Meltzoff and Moore 1977). Thus, ST provides an alternative to TT in accounting for attributions of mental states to others.

Psychological Evidence about Introspection and the Role of Consciousness

The positive approach to mental concepts I have tentatively endorsed has much in common with the classical doctrine of introspectionism. Does not this ignore empirical evidence against introspective access to mental states? The best-known psychological critique of introspective access is Nisbett and Wilson's (1977); so let us review briefly the question of how damaging that critique is and where the discussion now stands.

The first sentence of Nisbett and Wilson's abstract reads: "Evidence is reviewed which suggests that there may be little or no direct introspective access to higher order cognitive processes" (Nisbett and Wilson 1977, 231). At first glance this suggests a sweeping negative thesis. What they mean by "process," however, is *causal process*; and what their evidence really addresses is people's putative access to the *causes* of their behavior. This awareness-of-causes thesis, however, is one that no classical introspectionist, to my knowledge, has ever asserted. Moreover, Nisbett and Wilson explicitly concede direct access to many or most of the private states that concern us here and that concern philosophy of mind in general:

We do indeed have direct access to a great storehouse of private knowledge. . . . The individual knows a host of personal historical facts; he knows the focus of his attention at any given point of time; he knows what his current sensations are and has what almost all psychologists and philosophers would assert to be "knowledge" at least quantitatively superior to that of observers concerning his emotions, evaluations, and plans. (Nisbett and Wilson, 1977, 255)

Their critique of introspectionism then, is hardly as encompassing as it first appears (or as citations often suggest). As White (1988) remarks, "causal reports could turn out to be a small island of inaccuracy in a sea of insight" (p. 37).

Nisbett and Wilson's paper reviewed findings from several research areas including attribution, cognitive dissonance, subliminal perception, problem solving, and bystander apathy. Characteristically, the reported findings were of manipulations that produced significant differences on behavioral measures but not on verbal self-report measures. In Nisbett and Wilson's position-effect study, for example, passersby appraised four identical pairs of stockings in a linear display and chose the pair they judged of best quality. The results showed strong preference for the rightmost pair. Subjects did not report that position had influenced their choice and vehemently denied any such effect when the possibility was mentioned.

However, as Bowers (1984) points out, this sort of finding is not very damaging to any sensible form of introspectionism. As we have known since Hume (1748), causal connections between events cannot be directly observed; nor can they be introspected. A sensible form of introspectionism, therefore, would not claim that people have introspective access to causal connections, but this leaves it open that they do have introspective access to the mere occurrence of certain types of mental events.

Other critics, for example Ericsson and Simon (1980), complain that Nisbett and Wilson fail to investigate or specify the *conditions* under which subjects are unable to make accurate reports. Ericsson and Simon (1980, 1984) themselves develop a detailed model of the circumstances in which verbal reports of internal events are likely to be accurate. In particular, concurrent reports about information that is still in short-term memory (STM) and fully attended are more likely to be reliable than retrospective reports. In most of the studies reviewed by Nisbett and Wilson, however, the time lag between task and probe was sufficiently great to make it unlikely that relevant information remained in STM. A sensible form of introspectionism would restrict the thesis of privileged access to current states and not extend it to *past* mental events. But their direct access is then to these memories, not to the original mental events themselves.

In a more recent work, one of the two authors, T. D. Wilson, has been very explicit in accepting direct access. He writes: "People often have direct access to their mental states, and in these cases the verbal system can make direct and accurate reports. When there is limited access, however, the verbal system makes inferences about what these processes and states might be" (Wilson 1985, 16). He then explores four conditions that foster *im*perfect access, with the evident implication that good access is the default situation. This sort of position is obviously quite compatible with the one advocated in the present target article. . . .

Ontological Implications of Folk Psychology

These technical issues aside, the content of folk psychology may have significant ontological implications about the very existence of the mental states for which common speech provides labels. Eliminativists maintain that there are no such things as beliefs, desires, thoughts, hopes, and other such intentional states (Churchland 1981; Stich 1983). They are all, like phlogiston, caloric, and witches, the mistaken posits of a radically false theory, in this case a commonsense theory. The argument for eliminativism proceeds from the assumption that there is a folk *theory* of mind. This article counters the argument by denying (quite tentatively, to be sure) that our mental concepts rest on a folk theory.

It should be stressed that the study of folk psychology does not by itself yield ontological consequences. It just yields theses of the form: Mental (or intentional) states are ordinarily conceptualized as states of kind K. This sort of thesis, however, may appear as a premise in arguments with eliminativist conclusions, as we have just seen. If kind K features nomological relations R, for example, one can defend eliminativism by holding that no states actually instantiate relations R. On the other hand, if K just includes qualitative or phenomenological properties, it is harder to see how a successful eliminativist argument could be mounted. One would have to hold that no such properties are instantiated or even exist. Although qualitative properties are indeed denied by some philosophers of mind (e.g., Dennett 1988, 1991; Harman 1990), the going is pretty tough (for replies to Dennett and Harman, respectively, see Flanagan 1992, chap. 4, and Block 1990b). The general point, however, should be clear. Although the study of folk psychology does not directly address ontological issues, it is indirectly quite relevant to such issues.

Apart from ontological implications, the study of folk psychology also has intrinsic interest as an important subfield of cognitive science. This, of course, is the vantage-point from which the present discussion has proceeded.

Acknowledgments

I am grateful to the following people for very helpful comments and discussion: Kent Bach, Paul Bloom, Paul Boghossian, Robert Cummins, Carl Ginet, Christopher Hill, John Kihlstrom, Mary Peterson, Sydney Shoemaker, and Robert Van Gulick, as well as the BBS referees. I also profited from discussions of earlier versions of the paper at the Society for Philosophy and Psychology, the Creighton Club, CUNY Graduate

Goldman

Center, Cornell University, Yale University, University of Connecticut, and Brown University.

Notes

1. Type-physcialism is the doctrine that every mental state type is identical with some neurophysiological state type.

2. Eliminativism is the philosophical view that certain types of mental states invoked by everyday language, especially the propositional attitudes, would not appear in a fully mature science of the mind and should therefore be "eliminated" from our ontology.

3. Since a person does not have direct introspective access to the contents of his CRs, he may be unable to report or even recognize F_M as the content paired with M. This, at any rate, is what a defender of RF might point out. We do seem to have limited access, however, to the meanings or contents of our words. Hence, if ordinary people have no recognition whatsoever of functional roles as the meanings or contents of their mental predicates, this (in my opinion) would be *some* evidence, though not decisive evidence, against the hypothesis that these are their meanings or contents.

4. Note that our framework allows the RF theory to exclude E from the content of the CR for *headache* despite the fact that E is used as "evidence" for a headache. This shows that our framework is not verificationist: It does not equate something's being *evidence* for a type of mental state with its being in the CR for that type of mental state.

5. Block describes an imaginary scenario in which a system involving the entire Chinese nation (one billion people strong) is functionally equivalent for an hour to a single human mind. Although each Chinese person in this system has inner states with qualitative character, it is doubtful that the entire *system* in question would be conscious, or have inner states with qualitative character, despite the system's functional equivalence to an individual human mind.

6. Solutions to this apparent puzzle are proposed by Davidson (1987) and Burge (1988); but the former is less than transparent and the latter is convincingly shown by Boghossian (1989) to be inadequate. The considerations of this target article support Boghossian's contention, in contrast to Burge's, that knowledge of one's own mental contents cannot be merely automatic or "cognitively insubstantial" (as Boghossian puts it).

References

Armstrong, D. (1968). *A materialist theory of the mind.* New York: Humanities Press.

Astington, J., P. Harris, and D. Olson (1988). *Developing theories of mind.* Cambridge: Cambridge University Press.

Astington, J., and A. Gopnik (1991). Theoretical explanations of children's understanding of the mind. *British Journal of Developmental Psychology* 9, 7–31.

Baars, B. (1988). *A cognitive theory of consciousness.* Cambridge: Cambridge University Press.

Biederman, I. (1987). Recognition by components: A theory of human image understanding. *Psychological Review* 94, 115–147.

Biederman, I. (1990). Higher level vision. In D. Osherson, S. Kosslyn, and J. Hollerbach, eds., *Visual Cognition and Action*. Cambridge, MA: MIT Press.

Block, N. (1978). Troubles with functionalism. In C. Savage, ed., *Minnesota studies in Philosophy of Science,* vol. IX. Minneapolis: University of Minnesota Press.

Block, N. (1990a). Consciousness and accessibility. *Behavioral and Brain Sciences* 13, 596–598.

Block, N. (1990b). Inverted earth. In J. Tomberlin, ed., *Philosophical perspectives* 4. Atascadero, CA: Ridgeview.

Block, N. (1991). Evidence against epiphenomenalism. *Behavioral and Brain Sciences* 14, 670–672.

Boghossian, P. (1989). Content and self-knowledge. *Philosophical Topics* 17, 5–26.

Bowers, K. (1984). On being unconsciously influenced and informed. In K. Bowers and D. Meichenbaum, eds., *The unconscious reconsidered*. New York: John Wiley.

Burge, T. (1988). Individualism and self-knowledge. *The Journal of Philosophy* 85, 649–663.

Butterworth, G. (1991). The ontogeny and phylogeny of joint visual attention. In A. Whiten, ed., *Natural theories of mind*. Oxford: Basil Blackwell.

Campbell, K. (1985). Pain is three-dimensional, inner, and occurrent. *Behavioral and Brain Sciences* 8, 56–57.

Carey, S. (1985). *Conceptual change in childhood*. Cambridge, MA: MIT Press.

Carey, S. (1988). Conceptual differences between children and adults. *Mind and Language* 3, 167–181.

Churchland, P. M. (1979). *Scientific realism and the plasticity of mind*. Cambridge: Cambridge University Press.

Churchland, P. M. (1981). Eliminative materialism and the propositional attitudes. *The Journal of Philosophy* 78, 67–90.

Churchland, P. M. (1985). Reduction, qualia, and the direct introspection of brain states. *The Journal of Philosophy* 82, 8–28.

Churchland, P. M., and P. S. Churchland (1981). Functionalism, qualia, and intentionality. *Philosophical Topics* 12, 121–145.

Cummins, R. (1989). *Meaning and mental representation*. Cambridge, MA: MIT Press.

D'Andrade, R. (1987). A folk model of the mind. In D. Holland and N. Quinn, eds., *Cultural models in language and thought*. Cambridge: Cambridge University Press.

Davidson, D. (1987). Knowing one's own mind. *Proceedings and Addresses of the American Philosophical Association* 60, 441–458.

Dennett, D. (1969). *Content and consciousness*. New York: Humanities Press.

Dennett, D. (1978). *Brainstorms*. Cambridge, MA: MIT Press.

Dennett, D. (1991). *Consciousness explained*. Boston: Little, Brown.

Dretske, F. (1988). *Explaining behavior*. Cambridge, MA: MIT Press.

Ericsson, K., and H. Simon (1980). Verbal reports as data. *Psychological Review* 87, 215–251.

Ericsson, K., and H. Simon (1984). *Protocol analysis: Verbal reports as data*. Cambridge, MA: MIT Press.

Flanagan, O. (1992). *Consciousness reconsidered*. Cambridge, MA: MIT Press.

Flavell, J. (1988). The development of children's knowledge about the mind. In J. Astington, P. Harris, and D. Olson, eds., *Developing Theories of Mind*. Cambridge: Cambridge University Press.

Fodor, J. (1975). *The language of thought*. New York: Crowell.

Fodor, J. (1981). *Representations*. Cambridge, MA: MIT Press.

Fodor, J. (1987). *Psychosemantics*. Cambridge, MA: MIT Press.

Fodor, J. (1990). *A theory of content and other essays*. Cambridge, MA: MIT Press.

Gleitman, H. (1981). *Psychology*. New York: W. W. Norton.

Garrett, M. (1990). Sentence processing. In D. Osherson and H. Lasnik, eds., *Language*. Cambridge, MA: MIT Press.

Goldman, A. (1989). Interpretation psychologized. *Mind and Language* 4, 161–185.

Goldman, A. (1992a). In defense of the simulation theory. *Mind and Language* 7, 104–119.

Goldman, A. (1992b). Empathy, mind, and morals. *Proceedings and Addresses of the American Philosophical Association*.

Gopnik, A. (1984) Conceptual and semantic change in scientists and children: Why there are no semantic universals. *Linguistics* 20, 163–179.

Gopnik, A. (1988). Conceptual and semantic development as theory change. *Mind and Language* 3, 197–217.

Gopnik, A. (1993). How we know our minds: The illusion of first-person knowledge of intentionality. *Behavioral and Brain Sciences* 16, 1–14.

Gordon, R. (1986). Folk psychology as simulation. *Mind and Language* 1, 158–171.

Gordon, R. (1992) The simulation theory: Objections and misconceptions. *Mind and Language* 7, 11–34.

Harman, G. (1990) The intrinsic quality of experience. In J. Tomberlin, ed., *Philosophical Perspectives*, vol. 4. Atascadero, CA: Ridgeview.

Harris, P. (1989). *Children and emotion*. Oxford: Basil Blackwell.

Harris, P. (1991). The work of the imagination. In A. Whiten, ed., *Natural theories of mind*. Basil Blackwell.

Harris, P. (1992). From simulation to folk psychology: The case for development. *Mind and Language* 7, 120–144.

Hayes, P. (1985). The second naive physics manifesto. In J. Hobbs and R. Moore, eds., *Formal theories of the commonsense world*. Norwood, NJ: Ablex.

Hume, D. (1748). *An enquiry concerning human understanding*.

Jackendoff, R. (1987). *Consciousness and the computational mind*. Cambridge, MA: MIT Press.

Jackson, F. (1982). Epiphenomenal qualia. *Philosophical Quarterly* 32, 127–136.

Jackson, F. (1986). What Mary didn't know. *The Journal of Philosophy* 83, 291–295.

Johnson, C. (1988). Theory of mind and the structure of conscious experience. In J. Astington, P. Harris, and D. Olson, eds., *Developing Theories of Mind*. Cambridge: Cambridge University Press.

Karmiloff-Smith, A., and B. Inhelder (1975). If you want to get ahead, get a theory. *Cognition* 3, 195–212.

Keil, F. (1989). *Concepts, kinds, and cognitive development*. Cambridge, MA: MIT Press.

Lewis, D. (1966). An argument for the identity theory. *The Journal of Philosophy* 63, 17–25.

Lewis, D. (1970). How to define theoretical terms. *The Journal of Philosophy* 67, 427–446.

Lewis, D. (1972). Psychophysical and theoretical identifications. *Australasian Journal of Philosophy* 50, 249–258.

Loar, B. (1981). *Mind and meaning*. Cambridge: Cambridge University Press.

McCloskey, M. (1983). Naive theories of motion. In D. Gentner and A. Stevens, eds., *Mental Models*. Hillsdale, NJ: Lawrence Erlbaum.

Meltzoff, A., and M. Moore (1977). Imitation of facial and manual gestures by human neonates. *Science* 198, 75–78.

Millikan, R. (1984). *Language, thought, and other biological categories*. Cambridge, MA: MIT Press.

Millikan, R. (1986). Thoughts without laws, cognitive science with content. *Philosophical Review* 95, 47–80.

Millikan, R. (1989). In defense of proper functions. *Philosophy of Science* 56, 288–302.

Mitchell, P., and H. Lacohée (1991). Children's early understanding of false belief. *Cognition* 39, 107–127.

Morton, A. (1980). *Frames of mind*. Oxford: Oxford University Press.

Murphy, G., and D. Medin (1985). The role of theories in conceptual coherence. *Psychological Review* 92, 289–316.

Nagel, T. (1974). What is it like to be a bat? *Philosophical Review* 83, 435–450.

Newell, A., and H. Simon (1976). Computer science as empirical inquiry: Symbols and search. *Communications of the Association for Computing Machinery* 19, 113–126.

Nisbett, R., and T. Wilson (1977). Telling more than we can know: Verbal reports on mental processes. *Psychological Review* 84, 231–259.

Perner, J. (1991). *Understanding the representational mind*. Cambridge, MA: MIT Press.

Premack, D., and G. Woodruff (1978). Does the chimpanzee have a theory of mind? *Behavioral and Brain Sciences* 1, 515–526.

Putnam, H. (1960). Minds and machines. In S. Hook, ed., *Dimensions of mind*. New York: New York University Press.

Putnam, H. (1967). The mental life of some machines. In H. Castaneda, ed., *Intentionality, minds and perception*. Detroit: Wayne State University Press.

Putnam, H. (1975). The meaning of 'meaning'. In K. Gunderson, ed., *Language, mind and knowledge*. Minneapolis: University of Minnesota Press.

Rachlin, H. (1985). Pain and behavior. *Behavioral and Brain Sciences* 8, 43–53.

Rips, L., and F. Conrad (1989). Folk psychology of mental activities. *Psychological Review* 96, 187–207.

Schachter, S. and J. Singer (1962). Cognitive, social and physiological determinants of emotional state. *Psychological Review* 69, 379–399.

Schiffer, S. (1981). Truth and the theory of content. In H. Parret and J. Bouveresse, eds., *Meaning and Understanding*. Berlin: de Gruyter.

Searle, J. (1990). Consciousness, explanatory inversion, and cognitive science. *Behavioral and Brain Sciences* 13, 585–596.

Sellars, W. (1956). Empiricism and the philosophy of mind. In H. Feigl and M. Scriven, eds., *Minnesota studies in the philosophy of science*, vol. 1. Minneapolis: University of Minnesota Press.

Shoemaker, S. (1975). Functionalism and qualia. *Philosophical Studies* 27, 291–315.

Smith, E., and D. Medin (1981). *Categories and concepts*. Cambridge, MA: Harvard University Press.

Stich, S. (1983). *From folk psychology to cognitive science: The case against belief*. Cambridge, MA: MIT Press.

Tursky, B., L. Jamner, and R. Friedman (1982). The pain perception profile: A psycholophysical approach to the assessment of pain report. *Behavior Therapy* 13, 376–394.

Wellman, H. (1988). First steps in the child's theorizing about the mind. In J. Astington, P. Harris, and D. Olson, eds., *Developing Theories of Mind*. Cambridge: Cambridge University Press.

Wellman, H. (1990). The child's theory of mind. Cambridge, MA: MIT Press.

White, P. (1988). Knowing more about what we can tell: 'Introspective access' and causal report accuracy 10 years later. *British Journal of Psychology* 79, 13–45.

Wilson, M. (1991). Privileged access. Department of Psychology, University of California, Berkeley.

Wilson, T. (1985). Strangers to ourselves: The origins and accuracy of beliefs about one's own mental states. In J. Harvey and G. Weary, eds., *Attribution: Basic issues and applications*. New York: Academic Press.

Wimmer, H., and J. Perner (1983). Beliefs about beliefs: Representation and constraining function of wrong beliefs in young children's understanding of deception. *Cognition* 13, 103–128.

Wittgenstein, L. (1953). *Philosophical investigations*. New York: Macmillan.

Wittgenstein, L. (1967) *Zettel*, ed. G. Anscombe and G. von Wright. Oxford: Basil Blackwell.

17 Quining Qualia

Daniel C. Dennett

Corralling the Quicksilver

'Qualia' is an unfamiliar term for something that could not be more familiar to each of us: the *ways things seem to us*. As is so often the case with philosophical jargon, it is easier to give examples than to give a definition of the term. Look at a glass of milk at sunset; *the way it looks to you*—the particular, personal, subjective visual quality of the glass of milk is the *quale* of your visual experience at the moment. The *way the milk tastes to you then* is another, gustatory *quale*, and *how it sounds to you* as you swallow is an auditory *quale*. These various 'properties of conscious experience' are prime examples of *qualia*. Nothing, it seems, could you know more intimately than your own qualia; let the entire universe be some vast illusion, some mere figment of Descartes' evil demon, and yet what the figment is *made of* (for you) will be the *qualia* of your hallucinatory experiences. Descartes claimed to doubt everything that could be doubted, but he never doubted that his conscious experiences had qualia, the properties by which he knew or apprehended them.

The verb 'to quine' is even more esoteric. It comes from *The Philosophical Lexicon* (Dennett 1987b), a satirical dictionary of eponyms: 'quine, v. To deny resolutely the existence or importance of something real or significant'. At first blush it would be hard to imagine a more quixotic quest than trying to convince people that there are no such properties as qualia; hence the ironic title of this chapter. But I am not kidding.

My goal is subversive. I am out to overthrow an idea that, in one form or another, is 'obvious' to most people—to scientists, philosophers, lay people. My quarry is frustratingly elusive; no sooner does it retreat in the face of one argument than 'it' reappears, apparently innocent of all charges, in a new guise.

Which idea of qualia am I trying to extirpate? Everything real has properties, and since I do not deny the reality of conscious experience, I grant that conscious experience has properties. I grant moreover that each person's states of consciousness have properties in virtue of which those states have the experiential content that they do. That is to say, whenever someone experiences something as being one way rather than another, this is true in virtue of some property of something happening in them at the time, but these properties are so unlike the properties traditionally imputed to consciousness that it would be grossly misleading to call any of them the long-sought qualia. Qualia are supposed to be *special* properties, in some hard-to-define way. My claim—which can only come into focus as we proceed—is that conscious experience has no properties that are special in *any* of the ways qualia have been supposed to be special.

The standard reaction to this claim is the complacent acknowledgement that while some people may indeed have succumbed to one confusion or fanaticism or another, one's own appeal to a modest, innocent notion of properties of subjective experience is surely safe. It is just that presumption of innocence I want to overthrow. I want to shift the burden of proof, so that anyone who wants to appeal to private, subjective properties has to prove first that in so doing they are *not* making a mistake. This status of *guilty until proven innocent* is neither unprecedented nor indefensible (so long as we restrict ourselves to concepts). Today, no biologist would dream of supposing that it was quite all right to appeal to some innocent concept of *élan vital*. Of course one *could* use the term to mean something in good standing; one could use *élan vital* as one's name for DNA, for instance, but this would be foolish nomenclature, considering the deserved suspicion with which the term is nowadays burdened. I want to make it just as uncomfortable for anyone to talk of qualia—or 'raw feels' or 'phenomenal properties' or 'subjective and intrinsic properties' or 'the qualitative character' of experience—with the standard presumption that they, and everyone else, knows what on earth they are talking about.[1]

What are qualia, *exactly*? This obstreperous query is dismissed by one author ('only half in jest') by invoking Louis Armstrong's legendary reply when asked what jazz was: 'If you got to ask, you ain't never gonna get to know' (Block 1978, 281). This amusing tactic perfectly illustrates the presumption that is my target. If I succeed in my task, this move, which passes muster in most circles today, will look as quaint and insupportable as a jocular appeal to the ludicrousness of a living thing—a living thing, mind you!—doubting the existence of *élan vital*.

My claim, then, is not just that the various technical or theoretical concepts of qualia are vague or equivocal, but that the source concept, the 'pre-theoretical' notion of which the former are presumed to be refinements, is so thoroughly confused that, even if we undertook to salvage some 'lowest common denominator' from the theoreticians' proposals, any acceptable version would have to be so radically unlike the ill-formed notions that are commonly appealed to that it would be tactically obtuse—not to say Pickwickian—to cling to the term. Far better, tactically, to declare that there simply are no qualia at all.[2]

Rigorous arguments only work on well-defined materials, and, since my goal is to destroy our faith in the pre-theoretical or 'intuitive' concept, the right tools for my task are intuition pumps, not formal arguments. What follows is a series of fifteen intuition pumps, posed in a sequence designed to flush out—and then flush away—the offending intuitions. In the next section, I will use the first two intuition pumps to focus attention on the traditional notion. It will be the burden of the rest of the paper to convince you that these two pumps, for all their effectiveness, mislead us and should be discarded. In the following section, the next four intuition pumps create and refine a 'paradox' lurking in the tradition. This is not a formal paradox, but only a very powerful argument pitted against some almost irresistibly attractive ideas. In the next section, six more intuition pumps are arrayed in order to dissipate the attractiveness of those ideas, and the following section drives this point home by showing how hapless those ideas prove to be when confronted with some real cases of anomalous experience. This will leave something of a vacuum, and in the final section three more intuition pumps are used to introduce and motivate some suitable replacements for the banished notions.

The Special Properties of Qualia

Intuition pump 1: watching you eat cauliflower. I see you tucking eagerly into a helping of steaming cauliflower, the merest whiff of which makes me feel faintly nauseated, and I find myself wondering how you could possibly relish *that taste*, and then it occurs to me that, to you, cauliflower probably tastes (must taste?) different. A plausible hypothesis, it seems, especially since I know that the very same food often tastes different to me at different times. For instance, my first sip of breakfast orange juice tastes much sweeter than my second sip if I interpose a bit of pancakes and maple syrup, but after a swallow or two of coffee, the orange juice goes back to tasting (roughly? exactly?) the way it did with the first sip. Surely we want to say (or think about) such things, and surely we are not wildly wrong when we do, so . . . surely it is quite OK to talk of *the way the juice tastes to Dennett at time t*, and ask whether it is just the same as or different from *the way the juice tastes to Dennett at time t'* or *the way the juice tastes to Jones at time t*.

This 'conclusion' seems innocent, but right here we have already made the big mistake. The final step presumes that we can isolate the qualia from everything else that is going on—at least in principle or for the sake of argument. What counts as *the way the juice tastes to x* can be distinguished, one supposes, from what is a mere accompaniment, contributory cause, or byproduct of this 'central' way. One dimly imagines taking such cases and stripping them down gradually to the essentials, leaving their common residuum, the way things look, sound, feel, taste, smell to various individuals at various times, independently of how they are subsequently disposed to behave or believe. The mistake is not in supposing that we can in practice ever or always perform this act of purification with certainty, but the more fundamental mistake of supposing that there is such a residual property to take seriously, however uncertain our actual attempts at isolation of instances might be.

The examples that seduce us are abundant in every modality. I cannot imagine, will never know, could never know, it seems, how Bach sounded to Glenn Gould. (I can barely recover in my memory the way Bach sounded to me when I was a child.) And I cannot know, it seems, what it is like to be a bat (Nagel 1974), or whether you see what I see, colourwise, when we look up at a clear 'blue' sky. The homely cases convince us of the reality of these special properties—those subjective tastes, looks, aromas, sounds—that we then apparently isolate for definition by this philosophical distillation.

The specialness of these properties is hard to pin down, but can be seen at work in *intuition pump 2: the wine-tasting machine.* Could Gallo Brothers replace their human wine-tasters with a machine? A computer-based 'expert system' for quality control and classification is probably within the bounds of existing technology. We now know enough about the relevant chemistry to make the transducers that would replace taste buds and olfactory organs (delicate colour vision would perhaps be more problematic), and we can imagine using the output of such transducers as the raw material—the 'sense data' in effect—for elaborate evaluations, descriptions, classifications. Pour the sample in the funnel and, in a few minutes or hours, the system would type out a chemical assay, along with commentary: "a flamboyant and velvety Pinot, though lacking in stamina"—or words to such effect. Such a machine might well perform better than human wine-tasters on all reasonable tests of accuracy and consistency the wine-makers could devise,[3] but *surely* no matter how 'sensitive' and 'discriminating' such a system becomes, it will never have, and enjoy, what *we* do when we taste a wine: the qualia of conscious experience. Whatever informational, dispositional, functional properties its internal states have, none of them will be special in the way qualia are. If you share that intuition, you believe that there are qualia in the sense I am targeting for demolition.

What is special about qualia? Traditional analyses suggest some fascinating second-order properties of these properties. First, since one *cannot say* to another, no matter how eloquent one is and no matter how co-operative and imaginative one's audience is, exactly what way one is currently seeing, tasting, smelling, and so forth, qualia are *ineffable*—in fact the paradigm cases of ineffable items. According to tradition, at least part of the reason why qualia are ineffable is that they are *intrinsic* properties–which seems to imply *inter alia* that they are some- how atomic and unanalysable. Since they are 'simple' or 'homogeneous' there is nothing to get hold of when trying to describe such a property to one unacquainted with the particular instance in question.

Moreover, verbal comparisons are not the only cross-checks ruled out. *Any* objective, physiological, or 'merely behavioral' test—such as those passed by the imaginary wine-tasting system—would of necessity miss the target (one can plausibly argue), so all interpersonal compari- sons of these ways of appearing are (apparently) systematically impos- sible. In other words, qualia are essentially *private* properties. And, finally, since they *are* properties of *my experiences* (they are not chopped liver, and they are not properties of, say, my cerebral blood flow—or haven't you been paying attention?), qualia are essentially directly ac- cessible to the consciousness of their experiencer (whatever that means), or qualia are properties of one's experience with which one is intimately or directly acquainted (whatever that means), or 'immediate phenom- enological qualities' (Block 1978) (whatever that means). They are, after all, the very properties the appreciation of which permits us to identify our conscious states. So, to summarize the tradition, qualia are sup- posed to be properties of a subject's mental states that are

(1) ineffable

(2) intrinsic

(3) private

(4) directly or immediately apprehensible in consciousness.

Thus are qualia introduced onto the philosophical stage. They have seemed to be very significant properties to some theorists because they have seemed to provide an insurmountable and unavoidable stumbling block to functionalism or, more broadly, to materialism or, more broadly still, to any purely 'third-person' objective viewpoint or approach to the world (Nagel 1986). Theorists of the contrary persuasion have pa- tiently and ingeniously knocked down all the arguments, and said most of the right things, but they have made a tactical error, I am claiming, of saying in one way or another: "We theorists can handle *those qualia* you talk about just fine; we will show that you are just slightly in error about the nature of qualia." What they ought to have said is: "What qualia?"

My challenge strikes some theorists as outrageous or misguided be- cause they think they have a much blander and hence less vulnerable notion of qualia to begin with. They think I am setting up and knocking down a straw man, and ask, in effect: "Who said qualia are ineffable, intrinsic, private, directly apprehensible ways things seem to one?" Since my suggested fourfold essence of qualia may strike many readers as tendentious, it may be instructive to consider, briefly, an apparently milder alternative: qualia are simply 'the qualitative or phenomenal features of sense experience[s], in virtue of having which they resemble and differ from each other, qualitatively, in the ways they do' (Shoemaker 1982, 367). Surely I do not mean to deny *those* features.

I reply: it all depends on what 'qualitative or phenomenal' comes to. Shoemaker contrasts *qualitative* similarity and difference with 'intentional' similarity and difference—similarity and difference of the properties an experience represents or is 'of'. That is clear enough, but what then of 'phenomenal'? Among the non-intentional (and hence qualitative?) properties of my visual states are their physiological properties. Might these very properties be the qualia Shoemaker speaks of? It is supposed to be obvious, I take it, that these sorts of features are ruled out, because they are not 'accessible to introspection' (S. Shoemaker, personal communication). These are features of my visual *state*, perhaps, but not of my visual *experience*. They are not *phenomenal* properties.

But then another non-intentional similarity some of my visual states share is that they tend to make me think about going to bed. I think this feature of them *is* accessible to introspection—on any ordinary, pretheoretical construal. Is that a phenomenal property or not? The term 'phenomenal' means nothing obvious and untendentious to me, and looks suspiciously like a gesture in the direction leading back to ineffable, private, directly apprehensible ways things seem to one.[4]

I suspect, in fact, that many are unwilling to take my radical challenge seriously, largely because they want so much for qualia to be acknowledged. Qualia seem to many people to be the last ditch defence of the inwardness and elusiveness of our minds, a bulwark against creeping mechanism. They are sure there must be *some* sound path from the homely cases to the redoubtable category of the philosophers, since otherwise their last bastion of specialness will be stormed by science.

This special status for these presumed properties has a long and eminent tradition. I believe it was Einstein who once advised us that science could not give us the *taste* of the soup. Could such a wise man have been wrong? Yes, if he is taken to have been trying to remind us of the qualia that hide forever from objective science in the subjective inner sancta of our minds. There are no such things. Another wise man said so–Wittgenstein (1958, especially pp. 91–100). Actually, what he said was:

The thing in the box has no place in the language-game at all; not even as a *something*; for the box might even by empty.—No, one can 'divide through' by the thing in the box; it cancels out, whatever it is (p. 100);

and then he went on to hedge his bets by saying "It is not a *something*, but not a *nothing* either! The conclusion was only that a nothing would serve just as well as a something about which nothing could be said" (p. 102). Both Einstein's and Wittgenstein's remarks are endlessly amenable to exegesis, but, rather than undertaking to referee this War of the

Titans, I choose to take what may well be a more radical stand than Wittgenstein's.[5] Qualia are not even 'something about which nothing can be said'; 'qualia' is a philosophers' term which fosters nothing but confusion,[6] and refers in the end to no properties or features at all.

The Traditional Paradox Regained

Qualia have not always been in good odour among philosophers. Although many have thought, along with Descartes and Locke, that it made sense to talk about private, ineffable properties of minds, others have argued that this is strictly nonsense—however naturally it trips off the tongue. It is worth recalling how qualia were presumably rehabilitated as properties to be taken seriously in the wake of Wittgensteinian and verificationist attacks on them as pseudo-hypotheses. The original version of *intuition pump 3: the inverted spectrum* (Locke 1959) is a speculation about two people: how do I know that you and I see the same subjective colour when we look at something? Since we both learned colour words by being shown public coloured objects, our verbal behaviour will match *even if we experience entirely different subjective colours*. The intuition that this hypothesis is systematically unconfirmable (and undisconfirmable, of course) has always been quite robust, but some people have always been tempted to think technology could (in principle) bridge the gap.

Suppose, in *intuition pump 4: the Brainstorm machine*, there were some neuroscientific apparatus that fits on your head and feeds your visual experience into my brain (as in the movie, *Brainstorm*, which is not to be confused with the book, *Brainstorms*). With eyes closed I accurately report everything you are looking at, except that I marvel at how the sky is yellow, the grass red, and so forth. Would this not confirm, empirically, that our qualia were different? But suppose the technician then pulls the plug on the connecting cable, inverts it 180 degrees, and reinserts it in the socket. Now I report the sky is blue, the grass green, and so forth. Which is the 'right' orientation of the plug? Designing and building such a device would require that its 'fidelity' be tuned or calibrated by the normalization of the two subjects' reports—so we would be right back at our evidential starting point. The moral of this intuition pump is that no intersubjective comparison of qualia is possible, even with perfect technology.

So matters stood until someone dreamt up the presumably improved version of the thought experiment: the *intra*personal inverted spectrum. The idea seems to have occurred to several people independently (Gert 1965; Putnam 1965; Taylor 1966; Shoemaker 1969, 1975; Lycan 1973). Probably Block and Fodor (1972) have it in mind when they say "It seems to us that the standard verificationist counterarguments against the view that the 'inverted spectrum' hypothesis is conceptually incoherent are not persuasive" (p. 172). In this version, *intuition pump 5: the* *neurosurgical prank,* the experiences to be compared are all in one mind. You wake up one morning to find that the grass has turned red, the sky yellow, and so forth. No one else notices any colour anomalies in the world, so the problem must be in you. You are entitled, it seems, to conclude that you have undergone visual colour qualia inversion (and we later discover, if you like, just how the evil neurophysiologists tampered with your neurons to accomplish this).

Here it seems at first—and indeed for quite a while—that qualia are acceptable properties after all, because propositions about them can be justifiably asserted, empirically verified, and even explained. After all, in the imagined case, we can tell a tale in which we confirm a detailed neurophysiological account of the precise etiology of the dramatic change you undergo. It is tempting to suppose, then, that neurophysiological evidence, incorporated into a robust and ramifying theory, would have all the resolving power we could ever need for determining whether or not someone's qualia have actually shifted.

But this is a mistake. It will take some patient exploration to reveal the mistake in depth, but the conclusion can be reached—if not secured—quickly with the help of *intuition pump 6: alternative neurosurgery.* There are (at least) two different ways the evil neurosurgeon might create the inversion effect described in intuition pump 5:

1. Invert one of the 'early' qualia-producing channels, e.g. in the optic nerve, so that all relevant neural events 'downstream' are the 'opposite' of their original and normal values. *Ex hypothesi* this inverts your qualia.

2. Leave all those early pathways intact and simply invert certain memory-access links—whatever it is that accomplishes your tacit (and even unconscious) comparison of today's hues, with those of yore. *Ex hypothesi* this does *not* invert your qualia at all, but just your memory-anchored dispositions to react to them.

On waking up and finding your visual world highly anomalous, you should exclaim 'Egad! *Something* has happened! Either my qualia have been inverted or my memory-linked qualia reactions have been inverted. I wonder which!'

The intrapersonal, inverted spectrum thought experiment was widely supposed to be an improvement, since it moved the needed comparison into one subject's head. But now we can see that this is an illusion, since the link to earlier experiences, the link via memory, is analogous to the imaginary cable that might link two subjects in the original version.

This point is routinely—one might say traditionally—missed by the constructors of 'intrasubjective, inverted spectrum' thought experiments, who suppose that the subject's *noticing the difference*—surely a vivid experience is discovery by the subject—would have to be an instance of (directly? incorrigibly?) recognizing the difference *as a shift in qualia*. But as my example shows, we could achieve the same startling effect in a subject without tampering with his presumed qualia at all. Since *ex hypothesi* the two different surgical invasions can produce exactly the same introspective effects, while only one operation inverts the qualia, nothing in the subject's experience can favour one of the hypotheses over the other. So unless he seeks outside help, the state of his own qualia must be as unknowable to him as the state of anyone else's qualia: hardly the privileged access or immediate acquaintance or direct apprehension the friends of qualia had supposed 'phenomenal features' to enjoy!

The outcome of this series of thought experiments is an intensification of the 'verificationist' argument against qualia. *If* there are qualia, they are even less accessible to our ken than we had thought. Not only are the classical intersubjective comparisons impossible (as the *Brainstorm* machine shows), but we cannot tell in our own cases whether our qualia have been inverted—at least not by introspection. It is surely tempting at this point—especially to non-philosophers—to decide that this paradoxical result must be an artefact of some philosophical mis-analysis or other, the sort of thing that might well happen if you took a perfectly good pre-theoretical notion—our everyday notion of qualia—and illicitly stretched it beyond the breaking point. The philosophers have made a mess; let them clean it up; meanwhile we others can get back to work, relying as always on our sober and unmetaphysical acquaintance with qualia.

Overcoming this ubiquitous temptation is the task of the next section, which will seek to establish the unsalvageable incoherence of the hunches that lead to the paradox by looking more closely at their sources and their motivation.

Making Mistakes about Qualia

The idea that people might be mistaken about their own qualia is at the heart of the ongoing confusion and must be explored in more detail, and with somewhat more realistic examples if we are to see the delicate role it plays.

Intuition pump 7: Chase and Sanborn. Once upon a time there were two coffee-tasters, Mr Chase and Mr Sanborn, who worked for Maxwell House.[7] Along with half a dozen other coffee-tasters, their job was to ensure that the taste of Maxwell House coffee stayed constant, year after year. One day, about six years after Chase had come to work for Maxwell House, he confessed to Sanborn:

I hate to admit it, but I'm not enjoying this work anymore. When I came to Maxwell House six years ago, I thought Maxwell House coffee was the best-tasting coffee in the world. I was proud to have a share in the responsibility for preserving that flavour over the years. And we've done our job well; the coffee tastes just the same today as it tasted when I arrived. But, you know, I no longer like it! My tastes have changed. I've become a more sophisticated coffee drinker. I no longer like *that taste* at all.

Sanborn greeted this revelation with considerable interest. 'It's funny you should mention it,' he replied, 'for something rather similar has happened to me.' He went on:

When I arrived here, shortly before you did, I, like you, thought Maxwell House coffee was tops in flavour. And now I, like you, really don't care for the coffee we're making. But *my* tastes haven't changed; my . . . *tasters* have changed. That is, I think something has gone wrong with my taste buds or some other part of my taste-analyzing perceptual machinery. Maxwell House coffee doesn't taste to me the way it used to taste; if only it did, I'd still love it, for I still think *that taste* is the best taste in coffee. Now I'm not saying we haven't done our job well. You other tasters all agree that the taste is the same, and I must admit that on a day-to-day basis I can detect no change either. So it must be my problem alone. I guess I'm no longer cut out for this work.

Chase and Sanborn are alike in one way at least: they both used to like Maxwell House coffee, and now neither likes it. But they claim to be different in another way. Maxwell House tastes to Chase just the way it always did, but not so for Sanborn. But can we take their protestations at face value? Must we? Might one or both of them simply be wrong? Might their predicaments be importantly the same and their apparent disagreement more a difference in manner of expression than in experiential or psychological state? Since both of them make claims that depend on the reliability of their memories, is there any way to check on this reliability?

My reason for introducing two characters in the example is not to set up an interpersonal comparison between how the coffee tastes to Chase and how it tastes to Sanborn, but just to exhibit, side by side, two poles between which cases of intrapersonal experiential shift can wander. Such cases of intrapersonal experiential shift, and the possibility of adaptation to them, or interference with memory in them, have often been discussed in the literature on qualia, but without sufficient attention to the details, in my opinion. Let us look at Chase first. If we fall in for the nonce with the received manner of speaking, it appears at first that there are the following possibilities:

(a) Chase's coffee-taste qualia have stayed constant, while his reactive attitudes to those qualia, devolving on his canons of aesthetic judgment, etc., have shifted—which is what he seems, in his informal, casual way, to be asserting.

(b) Chase is simply wrong about the constancy of his qualia; they have shifted gradually and imperceptibly over the years, while his standards of taste have not budged—in spite of his delusions about having become more sophisticated. He is in the state Sanborn claims to be in, but just lacks Sanborn's self-knowledge.

(c) Chase is in some predicament intermediate between (a) and (b); his qualia have shifted some *and* his standards of judgment have also slipped.

Sanborn's case seems amenable to three counterpart versions:

(a) Sanborn is right; his qualia have shifted, due to some sort of derangement in his perceptual machinery, but his standards have indeed remained constant.

(b) Sanborn's standards have shifted unbeknownst to him. He is thus misremembering his past experiences, in what we might call a nostalgia effect. Think of the familiar experience of returning to some object from your childhood (a classroom desk, a tree-house) and finding it much smaller than you remember it to have been. Presumably as you grew larger your internal standard for what was large grew with you somehow, but your memories (which are stored as fractions or multiples of that standard) did not compensate, and hence, when you consult your memory, it returns a distorted judgment. Sanborn's nostalgia-tinged memory of good old Maxwell House is similarly distorted. (There are obviously many different ways this impressionistic sketch of a memory mechanism could be implemented, and there is considerable experimental work in cognitive psychology that suggests how different hypotheses about such mechanisms could be tested.)

(c) As before, Sanborn's state is some combination of (a) and (b).

I think that everyone writing about qualia today would agree that there are all these possibilities for Chase and Sanborn. I know of no one these days who is tempted to defend the high line on infallibility or incorrigibility that would declare that alternative (a) is—and must be—the truth in each case, since people just cannot be wrong about such private, subjective matters.[8]

Since quandaries are about to arise, however, it might be wise to review in outline why the attractiveness of the infallibilist position is only superficial, so it will not recover its erstwhile allure when the going gets tough. First, in the wake of Wittgenstein (1958) and Malcolm (1956, 1959), we have seen that one way to buy such infallibility is to acquiesce in the complete evaporation of content (Dennett 1976). "Imagine someone saying: 'But I know how tall I am!' and laying his hand on top of his head to prove it" (Wittgenstein 1958, 96). By diminishing one's claim until there is nothing left to be right or wrong about, one can achieve a certain empty invincibility, but that will not do in this case. One of the things we want Chase to be right about (if he is right) is that he is not in Sanborn's predicament, so if the claim is to be reviewed as infallible it can hardly be because it declines to assert anything.

There is a strong temptation, I have found, to respond to my claims in this chapter more or less as follows: "But after all is said and done, there is still something I know in a special way: I know *how it is with me right now.*" But if absolutely nothing follows from this presumed knowledge—nothing, for instance, that would shed any light on the different psychological claims that might be true of Chase or Sanborn—what is the point of asserting that one has it? Perhaps people just want to reaffirm their sense of proprietorship over their own conscious states.

The infallibilist line on qualia treats them as properties of one's experience one cannot in principle misdiscover, and this is a mysterious doctrine (at least as mysterious as papal infallibility) unless we shift the emphasis a little and treat qualia as *logical constructs* out of subjects' qualia judgements: a subject's experience has the quale F if and only if the subject judges his experience to have quale F. We can then treat such judgings as constitutive acts, in effect, bringing the quale into existence by the same sort of license as novelists have to determine the hair colour of their characters by fiat. We do not ask how Dostoevski knows that Raskolnikov's hair is light brown.

There is a limited use for such interpretations of subjects' protocols, I have argued (Dennett 1978a, 1979, especially pp. 109–110, 1982), but they will not help the defenders of qualia here. Logical constructs out of judgments must be viewed as akin to theorists' fictions, and the friends of qualia want the existence of a particular quale in any particular case to be an empirical fact in good standing, not a theorist's useful interpretive fiction, else it will not loom as a challenge to functionalism or materialism or third-person objective science.

It seems easy enough, then, to dream up empirical tests that would tend to confirm Chase and Sanborn's different tales, but if passing such tests could support their authority (that is to say, their reliability), failing the tests would have to undermine it. The price you pay for the possibility of empirically confirming your assertions is the outside chance of being discredited. The friends of qualia are prepared, today, to pay that price, but perhaps only because they have not reckoned how the bargain they have struck will subvert the concept they want to defend.

Consider how we could shed light on the question of where the truth lies in the particular cases of Chase and Sanborn, even if we might not be able to settle the matter definitively. It is obvious that there might be telling objective support for one extreme version or another of their stories. Thus if Chase is unable to re-identify coffees, teas, and wines in blind tastings in which only minutes intervene between first and second sips, his claim to *know* that Maxwell House tastes just the same to him now as it did six years ago will be seriously undercut. Alternatively, if he does excellently in blind tastings, and exhibits considerable knowledge about the canons of coffee style (if such there be), his claim to have become a more sophisticated taster will be supported. Exploitation of the standard principles of inductive testing—basically Mill's method of differences—can go a long way toward indicating what sort of change has occurred in Chase or Sanborn—a change near the brute perceptual processing end of the spectrum or a change near the ultimate reactive judgment end of the spectrum. And as Shoemaker (1982) and others have noted, physiological measures, suitably interpreted in some larger theoretical framework, could also weight the scales in favour of one extreme or the other. For instance, the well-studied phenomenon of induced illusory boundaries (see figure 17.1) has often been claimed to be a particularly 'cognitive' illusion, dependent on 'top-down' processes and hence, presumably, near the reactive judgment end of the spectrum, but recent experimental work (Von der Heydt et al. 1984) has revealed that 'edge detector' neurons *relatively* low in the visual pathways—in area 18 of the visual cortex—are as responsive to illusory edges as to real light-dark boundaries on the retina, suggesting (but not quite proving, since these might somehow still be 'descending effects') that illusory contours are not imposed from on high, but generated quite early in visual processing. One can imagine discovering a similarly 'early' anomaly in the pathways leading from taste buds to judgment in Sanborn, for instance, tending to confirm his claim that he has suffered some change in his basic perceptual—as opposed to judgmental—machinery.

But let us not overestimate the resolving power of such empirical testing. The space in each case between the two poles represented by possibility (a) and possibility (b) would be occupied by phenomena that were the product, somehow, of two factors in varying proportion: roughly, dispositions to generate or produce qualia and dispositions to react to the qualia once they are produced. (That is how our intuitive picture of qualia would envisage it.) Qualia are supposed to affect our action or behaviour only via the intermediary of our judgments about

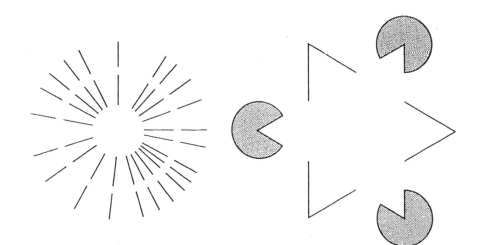

Figure 17.1 Induced illusory contours

them, so any behavioural test, such as a discrimination or memory test, since it takes acts based on judgments as its primary data, can give us direct evidence only about the *resultant* of our two factors. In extreme cases we can have indirect evidence to suggest that one factor has varied a great deal, the other factor hardly at all, and we can test the hypothesis further by checking the relative sensitivity of the subject to variations in the conditions that presumably alter the two component factors. But such indirect testing cannot be expected to resolve the issue when the effects are relatively small—when, for instance, our rival hypotheses are Chase's preferred hypothesis (a) and the minor variant to the effect that his qualia have shifted *a little* and his standards *less than he thinks*. This will be true even when we include in our data any unintended or unconscious behavioural effects, for their import will be ambiguous. (Would a longer response latency in Chase today be indicative of a process of "attempted qualia renormalization" or "extended aesthetic evaluation?")

The limited evidential power of neurophysiology comes out particularly clearly if we imagine a case of adaptation. Suppose, in *intuition pump 8: the gradual post-operative recovery*, that we have somehow "surgically inverted" Chase's taste bud connections in the standard imaginary way: post-operatively, sugar tastes salty, salt tastes sour, etc. But suppose further—and this is as realistic a supposition as its denial—that Chase has subsequently compensated—as revealed by his behaviour. He now *says* that the sugary substance we place on his tongue is sweet, and no longer favours gravy on his ice-cream. Let us suppose the compensation is so thorough that on all behavioural and verbal tests his performance is indistinguishable from that of normal subjects—and from his own pre-surgical performance.

If all the internal compensatory adjustment has been accomplished early in the process—intuitively, pre-qualia—then his qualia today are restored to just as they were (relative to external sources of stimulation) before the surgery. If on the other hand some or all of the internal compensatory adjustment is post-qualia, then his qualia have not been renormalized *even if he thinks they have*. But the physiological facts will not in themselves shed any light on where in the stream of physiological process twixt tasting and telling to draw the line at which the putative qualia appear as properties of that phase of the process. The qualia are the 'immediate or phenomenal' properties, of course, but this description will not serve to locate the right phase in the physiological stream, for, echoing intuition pump 6, there will always be at least two possible ways of interpreting the neurophysiological theory, however it comes out. Suppose our physiological theory tells us (in as much detail as you like) that the compensatory effect in him has been achieved by an *adjustment in the memory-accessing process* that is required for our victim to compare today's hues to those of yore. There are *still* two stories that might be told:

(I) Chase's current qualia are still abnormal, but thanks to the revision in his memory-accessing process, he has in effect adjusted his memories of how things used to taste, so he no longer notices any anomaly.

(II) The memory-comparison step occurs just prior to the qualia phase in taste perception; thanks to the revision, it now *yields* the same old qualia for the same stimulation.

In (I) the qualia contribute to the input; in effect, to the memory comparator. In (II) they are part of the output of the memory comparator. These seem to be two substantially different hypotheses, but the physiological evidence, no matter how well developed, will not tell us on which side of memory to put the qualia. Chase's introspective evidence will not settle the issue between (I) and (II) either, since *ex hypothesi* those stories are not reliably distinguishable by him. Remember that it was to confirm or disconfirm Chase's opinion that we turned to the neurophysiological evidence in the first place. We can hardly use his opinion in the end to settle the matter between our rival neurophysiological theories. Chase may think that he thinks his experiences are the same as before *because* they really are (and he remembers accurately how it used to be), but he must admit that he has no introspective resources for distinguishing that possibility from alternative (I), on which he thinks things are as they used to be *because* his memory of how they used to be has been distorted by his new compensatory habits.

Faced with their subject's systematic neutrality, the physiologists may have their own reasons for preferring (I) to (II), or vice versa, for they may have *appropriated* the term 'qualia' to their own theoretical ends, to denote some family of detectable properties that strike them as playing an important role in their neurophysiological theory of perceptual recognition and memory. Chase or Sanborn might complain—in the company of more than a few philosophical spokesmen—that these properties the neurophysiologists choose to call 'qualia' are not the qualia they are speaking of. The scientists' retort is: "If we cannot distinguish (I) from (II), we certainly cannot support either of your claims. If you want our support, you must relinquish your concept of qualia."

What is striking about this is not just that the empirical methods would fall short of distinguishing what seem to be such different claims about qualia, but that they would fall short *in spite of being better evidence than the subject's own introspective convictions.* For the subject's own judgments, like the behaviours or actions that express them, are the resultant of our two postulated factors, and cannot discern the component proportions any better than external behavioural tests can. Indeed, a subject's 'introspective' convictions will generally be *worse* evidence than what outside observers can gather. For if our subject is—as most are— a 'naive subject', unacquainted with statistical data about his own case or similar cases, his immediate, frank judgments are, evidentially, like any naive observer's perceptual judgments about factors in the outside world. Chase's intuitive judgments about his qualia constancy are no better off, epistemically, than his intuitive judgments about, say, lighting intensity constancy or room temperature constancy—or his own body temperature constancy. Moving to a condition inside his body does not change the intimacy of the epistemic relation in any special way. Is Chase running a fever or just feeling feverish? Unless he has taken steps to calibrate and cross-check his own performance, his opinion that his fever-perception apparatus is undisturbed is no better than a hunch. Similarly, Chase may have a strongly held opinion about the degree to which his taste-perceiving apparatus has maintained its integrity, and the degree to which his judgment has evolved through sophistication, but, pending the results of the sort of laborious third-person testing just imagined, he would be a fool to claim to know—especially to know directly or immediately—that his was a pure case (a), closer to (a) than to (b), or a case near (b).

Chase is on quite firm ground, epistemically, when he reports that *the relation* between his coffee-sipping activity and his judging activity has changed. Recall that this is the factor that Chase and Sanborn have in common: they used to like Maxwell House; now they do not. But unless he carries out on himself the sorts of tests others might carry out on him, his convictions about what has stayed constant (or nearly so) and what has shifted *must be sheer guessing*.

But then qualia—supposing for the time being that we know what we are talking about—must lose one of their 'essential' second-order properties: far from being directly or immediately apprehensible properties of our experience, they are properties whose changes or constancies are either entirely beyond our ken, or inferrable (at best) from 'third-person' examinations of our behavioural and physiological reaction patterns (if Chase and Sanborn acquiesce in the neurophysiologists' sense of the term). On this view, Chase and Sanborn should be viewed not as introspectors capable of a privileged view of these properties, but as autopsychologists, theorists whose convictions about the properties of their own nervous systems are based not only on their 'immediate' or current experiential convictions, but also on their appreciation of the import of events they remember from the recent past.

There are, as we shall see, good reasons for neurophysiologists and other 'objective, third-person' theorists to single out such a class of properties to study. But they are not qualia, for the simple reason that one's epistemic relation to them is *exactly* the same as one's epistemic relation to such external, but readily—if fallibly—detectable, properties as room temperature or weight. The idea that one should consult an outside expert, and perform elaborate behavioural tests on oneself to confirm what qualia one had, surely takes us too far away from our original idea of qualia as properties with which we have a particularly intimate acquaintance.

So perhaps we have taken a wrong turning. The doctrine that led to this embarrassing result was the doctrine that sharply distinguished qualia from their (normal) effects on reactions. Consider Chase again. He claims that coffee tastes "just the same" as it always did, but he admits—nay insists—that his reaction to "that taste" is not what it used to be. That is, he pretends to be able to divorce his apprehension (or recollection) of the quale—the taste, in ordinary parlance—from his different reactions to the taste. But this apprehension or recollection is itself a reaction to the presumed quale, so some sleight of hand is being perpetrated—innocently no doubt—by Chase. So suppose instead that Chase had insisted that precisely *because* his reaction was now different, the taste had changed for him. (When he told his wife his original tale, she said "Don't be silly! Once you add the dislike you change the experience"—and the more he thought about it, the more he decided she was right.)

Intuition pump 9: the experienced beer drinker. It is familiarly said that beer, for example, is an acquired taste; one gradually trains oneself— or just comes—to enjoy that flavour. What flavour? The flavour of the first sip? No one could like *that* flavour, an experienced beer drinker might retort:

Beer tastes different to the experienced beer drinker. If beer went on tasting to me the way the first sip tasted, I would never have gone on drinking beer! Or to put the same point the other way around, if my first sip of beer had tasted to me the way my most recent sip just tasted, I would never have had to acquire the taste in the first place! I would have loved the first sip as much as the one I just enjoyed.

If we let this speech pass, we must admit that beer is *not* an acquired taste. No one comes to enjoy *the way the first sip tasted.* Instead, prolonged beer drinking leads people to experience a taste they enjoy, but precisely their enjoying the taste guarantees that it is not the taste they first experience.[9]

But this conclusion, if it is accepted, wreaks havoc of a different sort with the traditional philosophical view of qualia. For if it is admitted that one's attitudes towards, or reactions to, experiences are in any way and in any degree constitutive of their experiential qualities, so that a change in reactivity *amounts to* or *guarantees* a change in the property, then those properties, those 'qualitative or phenomenal features', cease to be 'intrinsic' properties and in fact become paradigmatically extrinsic, relational properties.

Properties that 'seem intrinsic' at first often turn out on more careful analysis to be relational. Bennett (1965) is the author of *intuition pump 10: the world-wide eugenics experiment.* He draws our attention to phenolthio-urea, a substance which tastes very bitter to three-fourths of humanity, and as tasteless as water to the rest. Is it bitter? Since the reactivity to phenol-thio-urea is genetically transmitted, we could make it paradigmatically bitter by performing a large-scale breeding experiment: prevent the people to whom it is tasteless from breeding, and in a few generations phenol would be as bitter as anything to be found in the world. But we could also (in principle) perform the contrary feat of mass 'eugenics' and thereby make phenol paradigmatically tasteless— as tasteless as water—without ever touching phenol. Clearly, public bitterness or tastelessness is not an intrinsic property of phenol-thio-urea but a relational property, since the property is changed by a change in the reference class of normal detectors.

The public versions of perceptual 'qualia' all *seem* intrinsic, in spite of their relationality. They are not alone. Think of the 'felt value' of a dollar (or whatever your native currency is). "How much is that in *real* money?" the American tourist is reputed to have asked, hoping to translate a foreign price onto the scale of 'intrinsic value' he keeps in his head. As Elster (1985) claims, "there is a tendency to overlook the implicitly relational character of certain monadic predicates." Walzer (1985) points out that "a ten-dollar bill might seem to have a life of its own as a thing of value, but, as Elster suggests, its value implicitly depends on 'other people who are prepared to accept money as payment for goods'." But even as one concedes this, there is still a tendency to reserve something subjective, felt value, as an 'intrinsic' property of that ten-dollar bill. But as we now see, such intrinsic properties cannot be properties to which a subject's access is in any way privileged.

Which way should Chase go? Should he take his wife's advice and declare that since he cannot stand the coffee anymore, it no longer tastes the same to him (it used to taste good and now it tastes bad)? Or should he say that really, in a certain sense, it does taste the way it always did, or at least it sort of does—when you subtract the fact that it tastes so bad now, of course?

We have now reached the heart of my case. The fact is that we have to ask Chase which way he wants to go, and there really are two drastically different alternatives available to him *if we force the issue*. Which way would *you* go? Which concept of qualia did you "always have in the back of your mind," guiding your imagination as you thought about theories? If you acknowledge that the answer is not obvious, and especially if you complain that this forced choice drives apart two aspects that you had supposed united in your pre-theoretic concept, you support my contention that there is no secure foundation in ordinary 'folk psychology' for a concept of qualia. We *normally* think in a confused and potentially incoherent way when we think about the ways things seem to us.

When Chase thinks of 'that taste' he thinks equivocally or vaguely. He harkens back in memory to earlier experiences, but need not try— or be able—to settle whether he is including any or all of his reactions or excluding them from what he intends by 'that taste'. His state then and his state now are different—*that* he can avow with confidence—but he has no 'immediate' resources for making a finer distinction, nor any need to do so.[10]

This suggests that qualia are no more essential to the professional vocabulary of the phenomenologist (or professional coffee-taster) than to the vocabulary of the physiologist (Dennett 1978b). To see this, consider again the example of my dislike of cauliflower. Imagine now, in *intuition pump 11: the cauliflower cure,* that someone offers me a pill to cure my loathing for cauliflower. He promises that after I swallow this pill cauliflower will taste exactly the same to me as it always has, but I will like that taste. "Hang on," I might reply, "I think you may have just contradicted yourself." But in any event I take the pill and it works. I become an instant cauliflower-appreciator, but if I am asked which of the two possible effects (Chase-type or Sanborn-type) the pill has had on me, I will be puzzled, and will find nothing *in my experience* to shed light on the question. Of course I recognize that the taste is (sort of) the same—the pill has not made the cauliflower taste like chocolate cake, after all—but at the same time my experience is so different now that I resist saying that cauliflower tastes the way it used to taste. There is in any event no reason to be cowed into supposing that my cauliflower experiences have some intrinsic properties behind, or in addition to, their various dispositional, reaction-provoking properties.

"But in principle there has to be a right answer to the question of how it is, intrinsically, with you now, even if you are unable to say with any confidence" Why? Would one say the same about all other properties of experience? Consider *intuition pump 12: visual field inversion created by wearing inverting spectacles,* a phenomenon which has been empirically studied for years. (G. M. Stratton published the pioneering work in 1896, and J. J. Gibson and I. Kohler were among the principal investigators; for an introductory account, see Gregory 1977.) After wearing inverting spectacles for several days subjects make an astonishingly successful adaptation. Suppose we pressed on them this question: "Does your adaptation consist in your re-inverting your visual field or in your turning the rest of your mind upside-down in a host of compensations?" If they demur, may we insist that there has to be a right answer, even if they cannot say with any confidence which it is? Such an insistence would lead directly to a new version of the old inverted spectrum thought experiment: "How do I know whether some people see things upside-down (but are perfectly used to it), while others see things right-side-up?"

Only a very naive view of visual perception could sustain the idea that one's visual field has a property of right-side-upness or upside-downness *independent of one's dispositions to react to it*—'intrinsic right-side-upness' we could call it (see my discussion of the properties of the 'images' processed by the robot, SHAKEY, in Dennett 1982). So not all properties of conscious experience invite or require treatment as 'intrinsic' properties. Is there something distinguishing about a certain sub-class of properties (the 'qualitative or phenomenal' subclass, presumably) that forces us to treat them—unlike subjective right-side-upness—as intrinsic properties? If not, such properties have no role to play, in either physiological theories of experience, or in introspective theories.

Some may be inclined to argue this way: I can definitely imagine the experience of 'spectrum inversion' from the inside; after all, I have actually experienced temporary effects of the same type, such as the 'taste-displacement' effect of the maple syrup on the orange juice. What is imaginable, or actual, is possible. Therefore spectrum inversion or displacement (in all sensory modalities) is possible. But such phenomena just *are* the inversion or displacement of qualia, or intrinsic subjective properties. Therefore there must be qualia: intrinsic subjective properties.

This is fallacious. What one imagines and what one says one imagines may be two different things. To imagine visual field inversion, of the sort Stratton and Kohler's subjects experienced, is not necessarily to imagine the absolute inversion of a visual field (even if that is what it 'feels like' to the subjects). Less obviously, you imagining—as vividly as you like—a case of subjective colour-perception displacement is not necessarily you imagining what that phenomenon is typically called by philosophers: an inverted or displaced spectrum *of qualia*. In so far as that term carries the problematic implications scouted here, there is no support for its use arising simply from the vividness or naturalness of the imagined possibility.

If there are no such properties as qualia, does that mean that 'spectrum inversion' is impossible? Yes and no. Spectrum inversion as classically debated is impossible, but something like it is perfectly possible—something that is as like 'qualia inversion' as visual field inversion is like the impossible *absolute* visual image inversion we just dismissed.

Some Puzzling Real Cases

It is not enough to withhold our theoretical allegiances until the sunny day when the philosophers complete the tricky task of purifying the everyday concept of qualia. Unless we take active steps to shed this source concept, and replace it with better ideas, it will continue to cripple our imaginations and systematically distort our attempts to understand the phenomena already encountered.

What we find, if we look at the actual phenomena of anomalies of colour perception, for instance, amply bears out our suspicions about the inadequacy of the traditional notion of qualia. Several varieties of *cerebral achromatopsia* (brain-based impairment of colour vision) have been reported, and while there remains much that is unsettled about their analysis, there is little doubt that the philosophical thought experiments have underestimated or overlooked the possibilities for counterintuitive collections of symptoms, as a few very brief excerpts from case histories will reveal.

Objects to the right of the vertical meridian appeared to be of normal hue, while to the left they were perceived only in shades of gray, though without distortions of form. . . . He was unable to recognize or name any color in any portion of the left field of either eye, including bright reds, blues, greens and yellows. As soon as any portion of the colored object crossed the vertical meridian, he was able to instantly recognize and accurately name its color (Damasio et al. 1980).

This patient would seem at first to be unproblematically describable as suffering a shift or loss of colour qualia in the left hemifield, but there is a problem of interpretation here, brought about by another case:

The patient failed in all tasks in which he was required to match the seen color with its spoken name. Thus, the patient failed to give the names of colors and failed to choose a color in response to its name. By contrast, he succeeded on all tasks where the matching was either purely verbal or purely nonverbal. Thus, he could give verbally the names of colors corresponding to named objects and vice versa. He could match seen colors to each other and to pictures of objects and could sort colors without error (Geschwind and Fusillo 1966).

This second patient was quite unaware of any deficit. He "never replied with a simple 'I don't know' to the demand for naming a colour" (Geschwind and Fusillo 1966, 140). There is a striking contrast between these two patients: both have impaired ability to name the colours of things in at least part of their visual field, but, whereas the former is acutely aware of his deficit, the latter is not. Does this difference make all the difference about qualia? If so, what on earth should we say about this third patient?

His other main complaint was that 'everything looked black or grey' and this caused him some difficulty in everyday life. . . . He had considerable difficulty recognizing and naming colours. He would, for example, usually describe bright red objects as either red or black, bright green objects as either green, blue or black, and bright blue objects as black. The difficulty appeared to be perceptual and he would make remarks suggesting this; for example when shown a bright red object he said 'a dirty smudgy red, not as red as you would normally see red.' Colours of lesser saturation or brightness were described in such terms as 'grey' 'off-white' or 'black,' but if told to guess at the colour, he would be correct on about 50 per cent of occasions, being notably less successful with blues and greens than reds (Meadows 1974).

This man's awareness of his deficit is problematic to say the least. It contrasts rather sharply with yet another case:

One morning in November 1977, upon awakening, she noted that although she was able to see details of objects and people, colors appeared 'drained out' and 'not true.' She had no other complaint . . . her vision was good, 20/20 in each eye. . . . The difficulty in color perception persisted, and she had to seek the advice of her husband to choose what to wear. Eight weeks later she noted that she could no longer recognize the faces of her husband and daughter . . . [So in] addition to achromatopsia, the patient has prosopagnosia, but her linguistic and cognitive performances were otherwise unaffected. The patient was able to tell her story cogently and to have remarkable insight about her defects (Damasio et al. 1980).

As Meadows notes, "Some patients thus complain that their vision for colours is defective while others have no spontaneous complaint but show striking abnormalities on testing."

What should one say in these cases? When no complaint is volunteered but the patient shows an impairment in colour vision, is this a sign that his qualia are unaffected? ("His capacities to discriminate are terribly impaired, but, luckily for him, his inner life is untouched by this merely public loss.") We could line up the qualia this way, but equally we could claim that the patient has simply not noticed the perhaps gradual draining away or inversion or merging of his qualia revealed by his poor performance. ("So slowly did his inner life lose its complexity and variety that he never noticed how impoverished it had become.") What if our last patient described her complaint just as she did above, but performed normally on testing? One hypothesis would be that her qualia had indeed, as she suggested, become washed out. Another would be that in the light of her sterling performance on the colour discrimination tests, her qualia were fine; she was suffering from some hysterical or depressive anomaly, a sort of colour-vision hypochondria that makes her complain about a loss of colour perception. Or perhaps one could claim that her qualia were untouched; her disorder was purely verbal: an anomalous understanding of the words she uses to describe her experience. (Other startlingly specific, colour-word disorders have been reported in the literature.)

The traditional concept leads us to overlook genuine possibilities. Once we have learned of the curious deficit reported by Geschwind and Fusillo (1966), for instance, we realize that our first patient was never tested to see if he could still sort colours seen on the left or pass other non-naming, non-verbal, colour-blindness tests. Those tests are by no means superfluous. Perhaps he would have passed them; perhaps, *in spite of what he says*, his qualia are as intact for the left field as for the right—if we take the capacity to pass such tests as 'critical'. Perhaps his problem is 'purely verbal'. If your reaction to this hypothesis is that this is impossible, that must mean you are making his verbal, reporting behaviour sovereign in settling the issue—but then you must rule out a priori the possibility of the condition I described as colour-vision hypochondria.

There is no prospect of *finding* the answers to these brain-teasers in our everyday usage or the intuitions it arouses, but it is of course open to the philosopher to *create* an edifice of theory defending a particular set of interlocking proposals. The problem is that although normally a certain family of stimulus and bodily conditions yields a certain family of effects, any particular effect can be disconnected, and our intuitions do not tell us which effects are 'essential' to quale identity or qualia constancy (cf. Dennett 1978a, chap. 11.). It seems fairly obvious to me that none of the real problems of interpretation that face us in these curious cases are advanced by any analysis of how the concept of *qualia* is to be applied—unless we wish to propose a novel, technical sense for which the traditional term might be appropriated. But that would be at least a tactical error: the intuitions that surround and *purport* to anchor the current understanding of the term are revealed to be in utter disarray when confronted with these cases.

My informal sampling shows that some philosophers have strong opinions about each case and how it should be described in terms of qualia, but they find they are in strident (and ultimately comic) disagreement with other philosophers about how these 'obvious' descriptions should go. Other philosophers discover that they really do not know what to say—not because there are not enough facts presented in the descriptions of the cases, but because it begins to dawn on them that they have not really known what they were talking about over the years.

Filling the Vacuum

If qualia are such a bad idea, why have they seemed to be such a good idea? Why does it seem as if there are these intrinsic, ineffable, private, 'qualitative' properties in our experience? A review of the presumptive second-order properties of the properties of our conscious experiences will permit us to diagnose their attractiveness and find suitable substitutes (for a similar exercise, see Kitcher 1979).

Consider 'intrinsic' first. It is far from clear what an intrinsic property would be. Although the term has had a certain vogue in philosophy, and often seems to secure an important contrast, there has never been an accepted definition of the second-order property of intrinsicality. If even such a brilliant theory-monger as David Lewis can try and fail, by his own admission, to define the extrinsic/intrinsic distinction coherently, we can begin to wonder if the concept deserves our further attention after all. In fact Lewis (1983) begins his survey of versions of the distinction by listing as one option: "We could Quine the lot, give over the entire family as unintelligible and dispensable," but he dismisses the suggestion immediately: "That would be absurd" (p. 197). In the end, however, his effort to salvage the accounts of Chisholm (1976) and Kim (1982) are stymied, and he conjectures that "if we still want to break in we had best try another window" (p. 200).

Even if we are as loath as Lewis is to abandon the distinction, should we not be suspicious of the following curious fact? If challenged to explain the idea of an intrinsic property to a neophyte, many people would hit on the following sort of example: consider Tom's ball; it has many properties, such as its being made of rubber from India, its belonging to Tom, its having spent the last week in the closet, and its redness. All but the last of these are clearly *relational* or *extrinsic* properties of the ball. Its redness, however, is an intrinsic property. Except that this is not so. Ever since Boyle and Locke we have known better. Redness—public redness—is a quintessentially relational property, as many thought experiments about 'secondary qualities' show. [One of the first was Berkeley's [1713] pail of lukewarm water, and one of the best is Bennett's (1965) phenol-thio-urea.] The seductive step, on learning that public redness (like public bitterness, etc.) is a relational property after all, is to cling to intrinsicality ("*something* has to be intrinsic") and move it into the subject's head. It is often thought, in fact, that if we take a Lockean, relational position on objective bitterness, redness, etc., we *must* complete our account of the relations in question by appeal to non-relational, intrinsic properties. If what it is to be objectively bitter is to produce a certain effect in the members of the class of normal observers, we must be able to specify that effect and distinguish it from the effect produced by objective sourness and so forth.

What else could distinguish this effect but some intrinsic property? Why not another relational or extrinsic property? The relational treatment of monetary value does not require, for its completion, the supposition of items of intrinsic value (value independent of the valuers' dispositions to react behaviourally). The claim that certain perceptual properties are different is, in the absence of any supporting argument, just question-begging. It will not do to say that it is just obvious that they are intrinsic. It may have seemed obvious to some, but the considerations raised by Chase's quandary show that it is far from obvious that any intrinsic property (whatever that comes to) could play the role for the Lockean, relational treatment of the public perceptual properties.

Why not give up intrinsicality as a second-order property altogether, at least pending resolution of the disarray of philosophical opinion about what intrinsicality might be? Until such time the insistence that qualia are the intrinsic properties of experience is an empty gesture at best; no one could claim that it provides a clear, coherent, understood prerequisite for theory.[11]

What, then, of ineffability? Why does it seem that our conscious experiences have ineffable properties? Because they do have *practically* ineffable properties. Suppose, in *intuition pump 13: the osprey cry*, that I have never heard the cry of an osprey, even in a recording, but know roughly, from reading my bird books, what to listen for "a series of short, sharp, cheeping whistles, *cheep, cheep* or *chewk chewk*, etc; sounds annoyed" (Peterson 1947) (or words to that effect or better). The verbal description gives me a partial confinement of the logical space of possible bird cries. On its basis I can rule out many bird calls I have heard or might hear, but there is still a broad range of discriminable-by-me possibilities within which the actuality lies hidden from me like a needle in a haystack.

Then one day, armed with both my verbal description and my binoculars, I identify an osprey visually, and then hear its cry. "So *that's* what it sounds like," I say to myself, ostending—it seems—a particular mental complex of intrinsic, ineffable qualia. I dub the complex '*S*' (*pace* Wittgenstein), rehearse it in short-term memory, check it against the bird book descriptions, and see that, while the verbal descriptions are true, accurate, and even poetically evocative—I decide I could not do better with a thousand words—they still fall short of *capturing* the qualia complex I have called *S*. In fact, that is why I need the neologism, '*S*', to refer directly to the ineffable property I cannot pick out by description. My perceptual experience has pin-pointed for me the location of the osprey cry in the logical space of possibilities in a way verbal description could not.

But tempting as this view of matters is, it is overstated. First of all, it is obvious that from a single experience of this sort I do not—cannot—know how to generalize to other osprey calls. Would a cry that differed only in being half an octave higher also be an osprey call? That is an empirical, ornithological question for which my experience provides scant evidence. But moreover—and this is a psychological, not ornithological, matter—I do not and cannot know, from a single such experience, which physical variations and constancies in stimuli would produce an indistinguishable experience in me. Nor can I know whether I would react the same (have the same experience) if I were presented with what was, by all physical measures, a re-stimulation identical to the first. I cannot know the modulating effect, if any, of variations in my body (or psyche).

This inscrutability of projection is surely one of the sources of plausibility of Wittgenstein's scepticism regarding the possibility of a private language:

> Wittgenstein emphasizes that ostensive definitions are always in principle capable of being misunderstood, even the ostensive definition of a color word such as 'sepia'. How someone understands the word is exhibited in the way someone goes on, 'the use that he makes of the word defined'. One may go on in the right way given a purely minimal explanation, while on the other hand one may go on in another way no matter how many clarifications are added, since these too can be misunderstood (Kripke 1982, 83; see also 40–46).

But what is inscrutable in a single glance, and somewhat ambiguous after limited testing, can come to be justifiably seen as the deliverance of a highly specific, reliable, and projectible property detector, once it has been field-tested under a suitably wide variety of circumstances.

In other words, when first I hear the osprey cry, I may have identified a property detector in myself, but I have no idea (yet) what property my newfound property detector detects. It might seem then that I know nothing new at all—that my novel experience has not improved my epistemic predicament in the slightest. But of course this is not so. I may not be able to describe the property or identify it relative to any readily usable public landmarks (yet), but I am acquainted with it in a modest way: I can refer to the property I detected: it is the property I detected in *that* event. My experience of the osprey cry has given me a new way of thinking about osprey cries (an unavoidably inflated way of saying something very simple) which is practically ineffable both because it has (as yet for me) an untested profile in response to perceptual circumstances, and because it is—as the poverty of the bird book description attests—such a highly informative way of thinking: a deliverance of an informationally very sensitive portion of my nervous system.

In this instance I mean information in the formal information theory sense of the term. Consider *(intuition pump 14: the Jello box)* the old spy trick, most famously encountered in the case of Julius and Ethel Rosenberg, of improving on a password system by tearing something in two (a Jello box, in the Rosenberg's case), and giving half to each of the two parties who must be careful about identifying each other. Why does it work? Because tearing the paper in two produces an edge of such informational complexity that it would be virtually impossible to reproduce by deliberate construction. (Cutting the Jello box along a straight edge with a razor would entirely defeat the purpose.) The particular jagged edge of one piece becomes a *practically* unique pattern-recognition device for its mate; it is an apparatus for detecting the shape property M, where M is uniquely instantiated by its mate. It is of the essence of the trick that we cannot replace our dummy predicate 'M' with a longer, more complex, but accurate and exhaustive description of the property, for, if we could, we could use the description as a recipe or feasible algorithm for producing another instance of M or another M detector. The only *readily available* way of saying what property M is is just to point to our M detector and say that M is the shape property detected by this thing here.

And that is just what we do when we seem to ostend, with the mental finger of inner intention, a quale or qualia complex in our experience. We refer to a property—a public property of uncharted boundaries—via reference to our personal and idiosyncratic capacity to respond to it. That idiosyncracy is the extent of our privacy. If I wonder whether your blue is my blue, your middle C is my middle C, I can coherently be wondering whether our discrimination profiles over a wide variation in conditions will be approximately the same. And they may not be; people experience the world quite differently. But that is empirically discoverable by all the usual objective testing procedures.[12]

Peter Bieri has pointed out to me that there is a natural way of exploiting Dretske's (1981) sense of information in a reformulation of my first three second-order properties of qualia: intrinsicality, ineffability, and privacy. (There are problems with Dretske's attempt to harness information theory in this way—see my discussion in Dennett 1987a, chapter 8—but they are not relevant to this point.) We could speak of what Bieri would call 'phenomenal information properties' of psychological events. Consider the information—what Dretske would call the *natural meaning*—that a type of internal perceptual event might carry. That it carries that information is an objective (and hence, in a loose sense, intrinsic) matter since it is independent of what information (if any) the subject *takes* the event type to carry. Exactly what information is carried is (practically) ineffable, for the reasons just given. And it is private in the sense just given: proprietary and potentially idiosyncratic.

Consider how Bieri's proposed 'phenomenal information properties' (let us call them *pips*) would apply in the case of Chase and Sanborn. Both Chase and Sanborn ought to wonder whether their pips have changed. Chase's speech shows that he is under the impression that his pips are unchanged (under normal circumstances—all bets are off if he has just eaten horse-radish). He believes that the same objective things in the world—in particular, chemically identical caffeine-rich fluids—give rise to his particular types of taste experiences now as six years ago.

Sanborn is under the impression that his pips are different. He thinks his objective property detectors are deranged. He no longer has confidence that their deliverances today inform him of what they did six years ago. And what, exactly, did they inform him of then? If Sanborn were an ordinary person, we would not expect him to have an explicit answer, since most of us treat our taste detectors as mere M detectors, detecting whatever it is that they detect. (There are good reasons for this, analysed by Akins 1987.) But professional coffee-tasters are probably different. They probably have some pretty good idea of what kind of chemical-analysis transduction machinery they have in their mouths and nervous systems.

So far, so good. We could reinterpret Chase's and Sanborn's speeches as hypotheses about the constancies or change in the outputs of their perceptual information-processing apparatus, and just the sort of empirical testing we imagined before would tend to confirm or disconfirm their opinions thus interpreted. But what would justify calling such an information-bearing property 'phenomenal'?

Such a pip has, as the testimony of Chase and Sanborn reveals, the power to provoke in Chase and Sanborn acts of (apparent) re-identification or recognition. This power is of course a Lockean, dispositional property on a par with the power of bitter things to provoke a certain reaction in people. It is this power alone, however it might be realized in the brain, that gives Chase and Sanborn 'access' to the deliverances of their individual property detectors.

We may 'point inwardly' to one of the deliverances of our idiosyncratic, proprietary property detectors, but when we do, what are we pointing *at*? What does that deliverance itself *consist of*? Or what are its consciously apprehensible properties, if not just our banished friends the qualia? We must be careful here, for if we invoke an inner perceptual process in which we observe the deliverance with some inner eye and thereby discern its properties, we will be stepping back into the frying pan of the view according to which qualia are just ordinary properties of our inner states.

But nothing requires us to make such an invocation. We do not have to know how we identify or re-identify or gain access to such internal response types in order to be able so to identify them. This is a point that was forcefully made by the pioneer functionalists and materialists, and has never been rebutted (Farrell 1950; Smart 1959). The properties of the 'thing experienced' are not to be confused with the properties of the event that realizes the experiencing. To put the matter vividly, the physical difference between someone's imagining a purple cow and imagining a green cow *might* be nothing more than the presence or absence of a particular zero or one in one of the brain's 'registers'. Such a brute physical presence is all that it would take to anchor the sorts of dispositional differences between imagining a purple cow and imagining a green cow that could then flow, causally, from that 'intrinsic' fact. (I doubt that this is what the friends of qualia have had in mind when they have insited that qualia are intrinsic properties.)

Moreover, it is our very inability to expand on, or modify, these brute dispositions so to identify or recognize such states that creates the doctrinal illusion of 'homogeneity' or 'atomicity to analysis' or 'grainlessness' that characterizes the qualia of philosophical tradition.

This putative grainlessness, I hypothesize, is nothing but a sort of functional invariability: it is close kin to what Pylyshyn (1980, 1984) calls *cognitive impenetrability*. Moreover, this functional invariability or impenetrability is not absolute but itself plastic over time. Just as on the efferent side of the nervous system, *basic actions*—in the sense of Danto (1963, 1965) and others (see Goldman 1970)—have been discovered to be variable, and subject under training to decomposition (one can learn with the help of 'biofeedback' to will the firing of a particular motor neuron 'directly'), so what counts for an individual as the simple or atomic properties of experienced items is subject to variation with training.[13]

Consider the results of 'educating' the palate of a wine-taster, or 'ear training' for musicians. What had been 'atomic' or 'unanalysable' becomes noticeably compound and describable; pairs that had been indistinguishable become distinguishable, and when this happens we say *the experience changes*. A swift and striking example of this is illustrated in *intuition pump 15: the guitar string*. Pluck the bass or low E string open and listen carefully to the sound. Does it have describable parts or is it one and whole and ineffably guitarish? Many will opt for the latter way of talking. Now pluck the open string again and carefully bring a finger down lightly over the octave fret to create a high 'harmonic'. Suddenly a *new* sound is heard: 'purer' somehow and of course an octave higher. Some people insist that this is an entirely novel sound, while others will describe the experience by saying "the bottom fell out of the note"— leaving just the top. But then on a third open plucking one can hear, with surprising distinctness, the harmonic overtone that was isolated in the second plucking. The homogeneity and ineffability of the first experience is gone, replaced by a duality as 'directly apprehensible' and clearly describable as that of any chord.

The difference in experience is striking, but the complexity apprehended on the third plucking was *there* all along (being responded to or discriminated). After all, it was by the complex pattern of overtones that you were able to recognize the sound as that of a guitar rather than of a lute or harpsichord. In other words, although the subjective experience has changed dramatically, the *pip* has not changed; you are still responding, as before, to a complex property so highly informative that it practically defies verbal description.

There is nothing to stop further refinement of one's capacity to describe this heretofore ineffable complexity. At any time, of course, there is one's current horizon of distinguishability—and that horizon is what sets, if anything does, what we should call the primary or atomic properties of what one consciously experiences (Farrell 1950). But it would be a mistake to transform the fact that inevitably there is a limit to our capacity to describe things we experience into the supposition that there are absolutely indescribable properties in our experience.

So when we look one last time at our original characterization of qualia, as ineffable, intrinsic, private, directly apprehensible properties of experience, we find that there is nothing to fill the bill. In their place are relatively or practically ineffable public properties we can refer to indirectly via reference to our private property detectors—private only in the sense of idiosyncratic. And in so far as we wish to cling to our subjective authority about the occurrence within us of states of certain types or with certain properties, we can have some authority—not infallibility or incorrigibility, but something better than sheer guessing— but only if we restrict ourselves to relational, extrinsic properties like the power of certain internal states of ours to provoke acts of apparent re-identification. So contrary to what seems obvious at first blush, there simply are no qualia at all.

Acknowledgments

The first version of this paper was presented at University College, London, in November 1978, and in various revisions at a dozen other universities in 1979 and 1980. It was never published, but was circulated widely as Tufts University Cognitive Science Working Paper 7, December 1979. A second version was presented at the Universities of Adelaide and Sydney in 1984, and in 1985 to psychology department colloquia at Harvard and Brown under the title "Properties of conscious experience." The second version was the basis for my presentation at the workshop from which this book arises, and was circulated in pre-print in 1985, again under the title "Quining qualia." The present version, the fourth, is a substantial revision, thanks to the helpful comments of many people, including Kathleen Akins, Ned Block, Alan Cowey, Sydney Shoemaker, Peter Bieri, William Lycan, Paul Churchland, Gilbert Harman, and the participants at Villa Olmo.

Notes

1. A representative sample of the most recent literature on qualia would include Block 1980; Shoemaker 1981, 1982; Davis 1982; White 1985; Armstrong and Malcolm 1984; Churchland 1985; and Conee 1985.

2. The difference between 'eliminative materialism'—of which my position on qualia is an instance—and a 'reductive' materialism that takes on the burden of identifying the problematic item in terms of the foundational materialistic theory is thus often best seen not so much as a doctrinal issue but as a tactical issue: how might we most gracefully or effectively enlighten the confused in this instance? See my discussion of 'fatigues' in the Introduction to *Brainstorms* (Dennett 1978a) and, earlier, my discussion of what the enlightened ought to say about the metaphysical status of *sakes* and *voices* in *Content and consciousness* (Dennett 1969, chap. 1).

3. The plausibility of this concession depends less on a high regard for the technology than on a proper scepticism about human powers, now documented in a fascinating study by Lehrer (1983).

4. Shoemaker (1984, 356) seems to be moving reluctantly towards agreement with this conclusion: 'So unless we can find some grounds on which we can deny the possibility of the sort of situation envisaged . . . we must apparently choose between rejecting the functionalist account of qualitative similarity and rejecting the standard conception of qualia. I would prefer not to have to make this choice; but if I am forced to make it, I reject the standard conception of qualia'.

5. Shoemaker (1982) attributes a view to Wittgenstein (acknowledging that 'it is none too clear' that this is actually what Wittgenstein held) which is very close to the view I defend here. But to Shoemaker, 'it would seem offhand that Wittgenstein was mistaken' (p. 360), a claim Shoemaker supports with a far from offhand thought experiment—which Shoemaker misanalyses if the present paper is correct. (There is no good reason, contrary to Shoemaker's declaration, to believe that his subject's *experience* is systematically different from what it was before the inversion.) Smart (1959) expresses guarded and partial

approval of Wittgenstein's hard line, but cannot see his way clear to as uncompromising an eliminativism as I maintain here.

6. In 1979, I read an earlier version of this paper in Oxford, with a commentary by John Foster, who defended qualia to the last breath, which was: 'qualia should not be quined but fostered!' Symmetry demands, of course, the following definition for the most recent edition of *The philosophical lexicon* (Dennett 1987b): 'foster, v. To acclaim resolutely the existence or importance of something chimerical or insignificant.

7. This example first appeared in print in my reflections on Smullyan in *The Mind's I* (Hofstadter and Dennett 1981, 427–428).

8. Kripke (1982, 40) comes close when he asks rhetorically: 'Do I not know, directly, and *with a fair degree of certainty*, that I mean plus [by the function I call "plus"]?' [my emphasis]. Kripke does not tell us what is implied by a 'fair degree of certainty', but presumably he means by this remark to declare his allegiance to what Millikan (1984) attacks under the name of 'meaning rationalism'.

9. We can save the traditional claim by ignoring presumably private or subjective qualia and talking always of public tastes—such as the public taste of Maxwell House coffee that both Chase and Sanborn agree has remained constant. Individuals can be said to acquire a taste for such a public taste.

10. 'I am not so wild as to deny that my sensation of red today is like my sensation of red yesterday. I only say that the similarity can *consist* only in the physiological force behind consciousness—which leads me to say, I recognize this feeling the same as the former one, and so does not consist in a community of sensation.'—(Peirce, *Collected Works*, vol. V, 172 fn 2).

11. A heroic (and, to me, baffling) refusal to abandon intrinsicality is Sellars' (1981) contemplation over the years of his famous pink ice cube, which leads him to postulate a revolution in microphysics, restoring objective 'absolute sensory processes' in the face of Boyle and Locke and almost everybody since them (also see my commentary in Dennett 1981).

12. Stich (1983) discusses the implications for psychological theory of incommensurability problems that can arise from such differences in discrimination profiles (see, especially, chaps. 4 and 5).

13. See Churchland (1979, especially chap. 2) for supporting observations on the variability of perceptual properties, and for novel arguments against the use of 'intrinsic properties' as determiners of the meaning of perceptual predicates. See also Churchland (1985) for further arguments and observations in support of the position sketched here.

References

Akins, K. (1987). Information and organisms: or why Nature doesn't build epistemic engines. Unpublished PhD thesis, University of Michigan, Ann Arbor.

Armstrong, D. and N. Malcolm, ed. (1984). *Consciousness and causality.* Oxford: Blackwell Scientific.

Bennett, J. (1965). Substance, reality and primary qualities. *American Philosophical Quarterly* 2, 1–17.

Berkeley, G. (1713). *Three dialogues between Hylas and Philonous.* London.

Block, N. (1978). Troubles with functionalism. In C. W. Savage, ed., *Perception and cognition: Issues in the foundations of psychology.* Minneapolis: University of Minnesota Press.

Block, N. (1980). Are absent qualia impossible? *The Philosophical Review* 89, 257–274.

Block, N., and J. Fodor (1972). What psychological states are not. *The Philosophical Review* 81, 159–181.

Chisholm, R. (1976). *Person and object.* La Salle, IL: Open Court Press.

Churchland, P. M. (1979). *Scientific realism and the plasticity of mind.* Cambridge: Cambridge University Press.

Churchland, P. M. (1985). Reduction, qualia and the direct inspection of brain states. *Journal of Philosophy* 82, 8–28.

Conee, E. (1985). The possibility of absent qualia. *The Philosophical Review* 94 (3), 345–366.

Damasio, A., Yamada, T., Damasio, H., Corbett, J., and McKee, J. (1980). Central achromatopsia: behavioral, anatomic, and physiological aspects. *Neurology* 30, 1064–1071.

Danto, A. (1963). What we can do. *Journal of Philosophy* 60, 435–445.

Danto, A. (1965). Basic actions. *American Philosophical Quarterly* 60, 141–148.

Davis, L. (1982). Functionalism and absent qualia. *Philosophical Studies* 41 (2), 231–251.

Dennett, D. C. (1969). *Content and consciousness.* Andover: Routledge and Kegan Paul.

Dennett, D. C. (1976). Are dreams experiences? *The Philosophical Review* 73, 151–171.

Dennett, D. C. (1978a). *Brainstorms.* Cambridge, MA: MIT Press.

Dennett, D. C. (1978b). Two approaches to mental images. In D. C. Dennett, *Brainstorms.* Cambridge, MA: MIT Press.

Dennett, D. C. (1979). On the absence of phenomenology. In D. F. Gustafson and B. L. Tapscott, eds., *Body, mind, and method.* Dordrecht: D. Reidel.

Dennett, D. C. (1981). Wondering where the yellow went. *The Monist* 64, 102–108.

Dennett, D. C. (1982). How to study human consciousness empirically: Or nothing comes to mind. *Synthese* 53, 159–180.

Dennett, D. C. (1987a). *The intentional stance.* Cambridge, MA: MIT Press.

Dennett, D. C. (1987b). *The philosophical lexicon,* (8th ed.). Copy available from the American Philosophical Association, University of Delaware, Newark, DE.

Dretske, F. (1981). *Knowledge and the flow of information*. Cambridge, MA: MIT Press.

Elster, J. (1985). *Making sense of Marx*. Cambridge: Cambridge University Press.

Farrell, B. (1950). Experience. *Mind* 59, 170–198.

Gert, B. (1965). Imagination and verifiability. *Philosophical Studies* 16, 44–47.

Geschwind, N. and Fusillo, M. (1966). Color-naming defects in association with alexia. *Archives of Neurology* 15, 137–146.

Goldman, A. (1970). *A theory of human action*. Englewood Cliffs, NJ: Prentice-Hall.

Gregory, R. (1977). *Eye and brain* (3rd ed.). London: Weidenfeld and Nicolson.

Hofstadter, D., and D. C. Dennett (1981). *The mind's I: Fantasies and reflections on self and soul*. New York: Basic Books.

Kim, J. (1982). Psychophysical supervenience. *Philosophical Studies* 41, 51–70.

Kitcher, P. (1979). Phenomenal qualities. *American Philosophical Quarterly* 16, 123–129.

Kripke, S. (1982). *Wittgenstein on rules and private language*. Cambridge, MA: Harvard University Press.

Lehrer, A. (1983). *Wine and conversation*. Bloomington: Indiana University Press.

Lewis, D. (1983). Extrinsic properties. *Philosophical Studies* 44, 197–200.

Locke, J. (1959). *An essay concerning human understanding*, ed. A. C. Fraser. New York: Dover.

Lycan, W. (1973). Inverted spectrum. *Ratio* 15, 315–319.

Malcolm, N. (1956). Dreaming and skepticism. *The Philosophical Review*, 65, 14–37.

Malcolm, N. (1959). *Dreaming*. Andover: Routledge and Kegan Paul.

Meadows, J. C. (1974). Disturbed perception of colours associated with localized cerebral lesions. *Brain* 97, 615–632.

Millikan, R. (1984). *Language, thought and other biological categories*. Cambridge, MA: MIT Press.

Nagel, T. (1974). What is it like to be a bat? *The Philosophical Review*, 83, 435–451.

Nagel, T. (1986). *The view from nowhere*. Oxford: Oxford University Press.

Peirce, C. (1931–58). *Collected Works*, vol. V, ed., C. Hartshorne and P. Weiss. Cambridge MA: Harvard University Press.

Peterson, R. T. (1947). *A field guide to the birds*. Boston: Houghton Mifflin.

Putnam, H. (1965). Brains and behavior. In J. Butler, ed., *Analytical philosophy*, second series, Oxford: Blackwell Scientific.

Pylyshyn, Z. (1980). Computation and cognition: Issues in the foundations of cognitive science. *Behavioral and Brain Sciences* 3, 111–132.

Pylyshyn, Z. (1984). *Computation and cognition: Toward a foundation for cognitive science.* Cambridge, MA: MIT Press.

Sellars, W. (1981). Foundations for a metaphysics of pure process (the Carus Lectures). *The Monist* 64, 3–90.

Shoemaker, S. (1969). Time without change. *Journal of Philosophy* 66, 363–381.

Shoemaker, S. (1975). Functionalism and qualia. *Philosophical Studies* 27, 291–315.

Shoemaker, S. (1981). Absent qualia are impossible—A reply to Block. *The Philosophical Review* 90, 581–599.

Shoemaker, S. (1982). The inverted spectrum. *Journal of Philosophy* 79, 357–381.

Shoemaker, S. (1984). *Identity, cause, and mind.* Cambridge: Cambridge University Press.

Smart, J. C. (1959). Sensations and brain processes. *The Philosophical Review* 68, 141–156.

Stich, S. (1983). *From folk psychology to cognitive science: The case against belief.* Cambridge, MA: MIT Press.

Taylor, D. M. (1966). The incommunicability of content. *Mind* 75, 527–541.

Von der Heydt, R., Peterhans, E., and Baumgartner, G. (1984). Illusory contours and cortical neuron response. *Science* 224, 1260–1262.

Walzer, M. (1985). What's left of Marx. *The New York Review of Books,* 21 November, 43–46.

White, S. (1985). Professor Shoemaker and so-called 'qualia' of experience. *Philosophical Studies* 47, 369–383.

Wittgenstein, L. (1958). *Philosophical investigations.* Oxford: Blackwell Scientific.

18 Neuropsychological Evidence for a Consciousness System

Daniel L. Schacter

Understanding the relation between memory and consciousness would appear to be an essential task for both cognitive and neuropsychological theories of memory. Yet, as Tulving (1985b) has argued, modern memory researchers have taken surprisingly few steps toward such an understanding:

One can read article after article on memory, or consult book after book without encountering the term 'consciousness.' Such a state of affairs must be regarded as rather curious. One might think that memory should have something to do with remembering, and remembering *is* a conscious experience. . . . Nevertheless, through most of its history, including the current heyday of cognitive psychology, the psychological study of memory has largely proceeded without reference to the existence of conscious awareness in remembering. (p. 11)

One would be hard pressed to argue convincingly against the thrust of Tulving's claim: The relation between memory and consciousness has certainly not been near the top of, or even on, the agenda of most memory researchers. As Tulving (1985b) pointed out, this circumstance is not entirely surprising in view of the historical neglect of consciousness in many sectors of psychology.

In recent years, however, the "benign neglect" (Tulving, 1985b, p. 1) accorded the memory and consciousness issue has been replaced by growing interest. A good deal of this interest has been sparked by demonstrations of striking dissociations between memory and consciousness in normal subjects and amnesic patients: Performance on various tasks can be facilitated by recent experiences even though subjects may lack any conscious awareness or recollection of those experiences. The major purpose of the present chapter is to sketch a framework for conceptualizing the relation between memory and consciousness. The framework draws on, and attempts to integrate, findings and ideas from cognitive, neuropsychological, and neurophysiological studies of both memory and consciousness.

Before proceeding further, some discussion of terminology is necessary. It comes as no surprise to state that "consciousness" is one of the most ephemeral, difficult-to-define terms in all of psychology, and no formal definition is attempted here. It is possible, however, to provide guidelines concerning how the term is used. In this chapter, the terms "conscious" and "consciousness" are used interchangeably with terms such as "phenomenal awareness," to refer to what Dimond (1976) called "the running span of subjective experience" (p. 377). Thus, I do not use consciousness in reference to generalized states of arousal or alertness (e.g., sleep, coma, waking), but rather in reference to a person's ongoing awareness of specific mental activity.

The terms *implicit memory* and *explicit memory* (Graf and Schacter 1985; Schacter 1987) are also used frequently throughout the chapter. Explicit memory refers to intentional recollection of previous experiences as revealed on standard laboratory tests of recall and recognition. Explicit memory is roughly equivalent to "memory with consciousness" or "memory with awareness." Implicit memory, on the other hand, refers to situations in which previous experiences facilitate performance on tests that do not require intentional or deliberate remembering, such as word stem and fragment completion, word identification, and lexical decision. Implicit memory, as revealed by priming effects on such tests, need not and often does not involve any conscious memory for a prior experience. However, it is important to distinguish between two senses of "conscious memory" or "conscious recollection" that are often used interchangeably. On the one hand, conscious recollection can refer to the manner in which retrieval is *initiated*. When a subject intentionally attempts to "think back" to a prior experience, as required on standard recall and recognition tests, this voluntary and deliberate initiation of retrieval can be described as "conscious." On the other hand, conscious recollection can refer to a phenomenological quality of the *product* of the retrieval process—the presence of what Tulving (1983) has called "recollective experience" or "sense of pastness." It is this aspect of the memory/consciousness relation that is of primary interest here. To keep the foregoing distinction clear, I use the terms intentional/unintentional or voluntary/involuntary to refer to the manner in which retrieval is initiated, and only use the terms "conscious recollection" or "conscious remembering" to refer to subjects' recollective experience once the retrieval process has been completed (for further discussion, see Schacter et al. 1989.).

Implicit Memory and the Memory/Consciousness Relation:
A Brief Survey

Research on implicit memory indicates that the effects of previous experiences can be revealed in the absence of conscious recollection. I have reviewed implicit memory research in some detail elsewhere (Schacter 1987) and only highlight some key points here.

Consider first observations concerning patients with organic amnesia. Such patients have severe difficulties remembering recent experiences and learning many different kinds of new information despite normal intelligence, perception, and linguistic function (for review, see Cermak 1982; Hirst 1982; Squire and Cohen 1984; Weiskrantz 1985). However, beginning in the middle 19th century (e.g., Dunn, 1845; Korsakoff 1889), numerous investigators have reported that amnesic patients show implicit memory for experiences that they cannot recollect consciously. Thus, it has been demonstrated repeatedly that even profoundly amnesic patients, such as the well-known case H. M., can show normal or near-normal learning of various perceptual and motor skills without any conscious memory for the experiences of learning (e.g., Brooks and Baddeley 1976; Cohen and Squire 1980; Eslinger and Damasio 1985; Milner et al. 1968; Moscovitch 1982; Nissen and Bullemer 1987).

It has also been established firmly that, following a single exposure to an item, amnesic patients show intact priming effects on various implicit memory tests, including stem completion, word identification, free association, and lexical decision, despite the fact that they are frequently unable to recall or recognize the items on explicit memory tests (e.g., Cermak et al. 1985; Graf et al 1985; Graf et al. 1984; Moscovitch et al. 1986; Schacter 1985; Schacter and Graf 1986b; Shimamura and Squire, 1984; Warrington and Weiskrantz, 1968, 1974; for more extensive review, see Schacter 1987; Shimamura 1986). Priming in the foregoing studies was observed when patients studied old, familiar items that have pre-existing, unitized representations in memory, such as words, common idioms, and highly related paired associates. Priming of such familiar items in amnesic patients appears to be a relatively transient phenomenon, lasting only a couple of hours (Diamond and Rozin, 1984; Graf et al. 1984; Squire et al. 1987). In addition, several studies have found that amnesic patients do not show priming of pseudowords, which have no pre-existing memory representations (Cermak et al. 1985; Diamond and Rozin 1984), thereby suggesting that priming may be attributable to temporary activation of pre-existing representations (e.g., Cermak et al. 1985; Diamond and Rozin, 1984; Graf et al. 1984). In contrast, several studies have recently shown that some amnesic patients can show implicit memory for novel information that does not have any pre-existing, unitized representation in memory. Thus, Graf and Schacter (1985) reported that amnesic patients showed implicit memory for a newly acquired association between normatively unrelated words on a stem completion task. However, Schacter and Graf (1986b) found that this associative effect was observed only in mildly amnesic patients. Cermak and his colleagues (Cermak et al. 1988; Cermak et al. 1988) found that Korsakoff patients did not show implicit memory for new associations on the stem completion test, whereas a severely amnesic encephalitic patient (S.S.) did. Moscovitch et al. (1986) observed that even severely amnesic patients showed normal implicit memory for new associations between unrelated words on a test that involved reading degraded word pairs. McAndrews et al. (1987) showed patients sentences that were difficult to understand (e.g., "The notes were sour because the seams split") and provided a critical word that rendered the sentence comprehensible (e.g., *bagpipes*) when patients could not generate the word themselves. Sentences were re-presented after retention intervals of up to 1 week. Although severely amnesic patients did not explicitly recognize any of the old sentences, they showed a marked facilitation in generating the critical words even after a 1-week retention interval, thereby indicating that patients had implicit memory for these novel sentences. These kinds of observations suggest that some priming effects in amnesics may reflect the influence of newly established episodic representations.

Amnesic patients have shown implicit memory for recent experiences, together with a reduction or absence of conscious memory for those experiences, in numerous other tasks and situations that are only noted briefly here. These include classical conditioning (Weiskrantz and Warrington 1979), learning of new facts (Schacter et al. 1984), stories (Luria 1976), and complex computer commands (Glisky and Schacter 1987, 1988; Glisky et al. 1986), acquisition of preferences (Johnson et al. 1985), and detection of hidden figures (Crovitz et al. 1979). Of course, patients' performance is not entirely normal on all of these implicit tasks. The point to be stressed at this stage, however, is that amnesic patients have shown *some* implicit memory for just about every kind of experimental material that one could imagine.

There has also been a great deal of recent research on implicit memory in normal subjects, particularly within the domain of repetition priming. Although I will not undertake a detailed review of this work (see Schacter 1987), it should be noted that

1. Normal subjects, like amnesic patients, have shown implicit memory on a variety of tests.

2. Implicit and explicit memory have been dissociated experimentally (e.g., Graf and Mandler 1984; Graf and Schacter 1987; Jacoby and Dallas 1981; Roediger and Blaxton 1987; Schacter and Graf 1986a; Sloman et al. 1988; Tulving et al. 1982).

3. Implicit memory has been observed both for items that have integrated or unitized pre-existing memory representations, such as fa-

miliar words and idioms, and for new associations that were established for the first time during a study trial (e.g., Graf and Schacter 1985, 1987; McKoon and Ratcliff 1979, 1986; Schacter and Graf 1986a).

4. Some implicit effects are relatively short lived (e.g., Forster and Davis 1984; Graf et al 1984), whereas others persist for days, weeks, and months (e.g., Jacoby and Dallas 1981; Schacter and Graf, 1986a; Tulving et al 1982).

Although studies of amnesic patients demonstrate clearly that robust implicit memory can be observed without any conscious recollection of a prior experience, the data concerning normal subjects are not as clear cut. As argued elsewhere (Schacter 1987), it appears that normal subjects can show implicit memory without any conscious recollective experience when they are prevented, at the time of study, from encoding target material in an elaborative manner. This can be accomplished by presenting the target on an unattended channel (Eich 1984), giving extremely brief stimulus exposures that attenuate or eliminate conscious perception (Bargh and Pietromonaco 1982; Kunst-Wilson and Zajonc 1980; Mandler et al. 1987), or requiring subjects to perform nonsemantic orienting tasks (Graf and Mandler 1984). Under these conditions, robust implicit memory has been observed even though recall and recognition are at or near chance levels, thereby suggesting that subjects possess little or no conscious experience of remembering the information that is expressed on an implicit memory test. However, when subjects are given elaborative study tasks, recall and recognition performance are generally quite high, indicating that the kind of information necessary for conscious remembering is potentially available to subjects when they are performing an implicit memory task. Of course, the fact that subjects *can* consciously remember target material on an explicit test does not necessarily mean that they do so when performing an implicit test (Schacter 1987; Schacter et al. in press). It does suggest, however, that if elaborative study tasks are used, caution must be exercised when making inferences about whether normal subjects lack a conscious experience of remembering on an implicit memory test.

A recent study conducted in collaboration with Jeffrey Bowers (see Schacter et al. in press) provides some pertinent information. Subjects in that study were shown a list of common words, some under semantic encoding conditions (e.g., rating the pleasantness of a word) and some under non-semantic encoding conditions (e.g., counting vowels and consonants). The experimental group most relevant to the present concerns was told that the purpose of the experiment was to examine perception of words and other materials; no mention was made of a later memory test. A series of filler tasks was then given (e.g., generating names of countries and cities), followed by a stem completion test, which was presented as another filler task. Subjects were instructed to complete the stem with the first word that came to mind; they were not told that some of the stems could be completed with words from the earlier encoding task. Following the completion test, subjects were given a detailed questionnaire that probed whether they were aware that any of the completions represented previously studied items.

Analysis of the questionnaire responses revealed that even those subjects who expressed no awareness that any test items had been completed with previously studied items showed robust implicit memory. Twenty subjects were classified as unaware (they responded negatively to all questionnaire items), and 20 subjects were classified as aware (they responded positively to at least one questionnaire item). Overall level of implicit memory in aware (33%) and unaware (31%) subjects did not differ significantly. Following non-semantic encoding, aware subjects completed 23% of stems with study-list items, whereas unaware subjects completed 28% (baseline completion rate was 12%). Following semantic encoding, aware subjects completed more stems with list items (43%) than did unaware subjects (33%). The critical point, however, is that unaware subjects showed substantial implicit memory following semantic encoding. Because it seems reasonable to infer that these subjects did not consciously remember having studied any of the items that they provided as completions, these data would appear to indicate that normal subjects can show implicit memory, devoid of conscious recollective experience, even for items that have been encoded in a semantic or elaborative manner.

In summary, several types of implicit memory phenomena have been observed in amnesic and normal subjects: gradual acquisition of perpetual, motor, and cognitive skills; transient activation of pre-existing memory representations; and long-lasting effects of newly established episodic representations. Various theoretical ideas have been put forward to account for these manifestations of implicit memory, but none successfully accommodates all of them (see Schacter 1987). I consider some of these ideas later and attempt to integrate them into a general framework. Before turning to the theoretical issues, however, it is necessary to consider a series of phenomena that, in my view, provide key clues concerning the nature of the relation between memory and consciousness.

Implicit/Explicit Dissociations in Neuropsychological Syndromes

Recent studies of brain-damaged patients with specific perceptual and cognitive deficits have shown that patients have access to knowledge that they are not aware that they possess and cannot express consciously. Just as amnesic patients show implicit memory for information that they do not consciously remember, these patients show implicit knowledge of stimuli that, depending on the exact nature of their impairment, they either cannot perceive, identify, recognize, or understand consciously. The evidence for such dissociations has been reviewed and discussed in detail elsewhere (Schacter et al. 1988). For the present purposes, it suffices to present a few illustrative examples and then delineate their theoretical implications.

Consider first the phenomenon of prosopagnosia. Prosopagnosic patients have serious difficulties recognizing familiar faces, usually because of bilateral lesions to occipito-temporal cortex (e.g., Damasio 1985). Such patients typically report no familiarity with the faces of family, relatives, and friends. Despite the absence of any conscious experience that a face is familiar, recent data indicate that patients do have implicit knowledge of facial familiarity. In a psychophysiological study, Tranel and Damasio (1985) found that a severely prosopagnosic patient showed larger skin conductance responses to familiar than to unfamiliar faces—yet none of the faces seemed familiar to the patient. Also using the skin conductance response, Bauer (1984) reported a similar phenomenon in another prosopagnosic patient. De Haan et al. (1987) reported data from various behavioral measures that dovetail nicely with the psychophysiological evidence. Their patient was entirely unable to distinguish consciously between familiar and unfamiliar faces. Yet on a matching task that entailed same-different judgments about two simultaneously exposed faces, this patient, like control subjects, was faster to respond when a judgment was made about familiar than unfamiliar faces. In addition, the patient was subject to interference from familiar faces—even though he did not recognize them—on a Stroop-like naming task. De Haan et al. concluded that their patient had access to much the same information about familiarity that control subjects did; the critical difference was that the patient could not express it consciously (see also, Young 1988).

Results like those obtained with prosopagnosics have been reported in other neuropsychological syndromes. A great deal of experimental work has been directed at the phenomenon of *blindsight* (Weiskrantz 1986). Patients with lesions to striate cortex typically lack conscious perceptual experiences within their scotoma. Yet it has been consistently demonstrated that, when required to "guess," such patients can make above-chance forced-choice judgments concerning stimulus attributes (e.g., location) that they do not consciously "see" (e.g., Richards 1973; Weiskrantz 1977, 1980, 1986; Zihl 1980). Although some aspects of the blindsight phenomenon have been disputed and are subject to alternative interpretations (Campion et al. 1983), there are good reasons to believe that these patients can gain access implicitly to information that does not inform conscious visual experience (Schacter et al 1988; Weiskrantz 1986). Similar dissociations have been observed in the syndrome of alexia without agraphia. Alexic patients cannot read visually presented words unless they resort to a letter-by-letter decoding strategy. However, when words are presented at brief tachistoscopic exposures that prevent letter-by-letter decoding, such patients can make above-chance lexical decisions, semantic categorizations, and other judgments about words that they are unable to identify consciously (Coslett 1986; Landis et al. 1980; Shallice and Saffran 1986).

Implicit knowledge of information that is not accessible to consciousness has also been observed in patients with visual object agnosia (Margolin et al. 1983; Warrington 1975), Broca's and Wernicke's aphasia (Andrewsky and Seron 1975; Blumstein et al. 1982; Milberg and Blumstein 1981; Milberg et al., in press), and in studies of inter-hemispheric transfer in split-brain patients (Holtzman et al. 1981; Sergent 1987). This corpus of dissociations raises a number of conceptual and interpretive issues that have been dealt with elsewhere (Schacter et al. 1988). For the present purposes, however, two key points need to be stressed. The first concerns the *generality* and *diversity* of the dissociations: Similar patterns of results have been observed across different patient groups, experimental tasks, types of information, and perceptual/cognitive processes. This observation complements and extends the previously noted diversity of implicit memory phenomena. Second, the failures to gain access to consciousness observed in the various neuropsychological syndromes are selective or *domain specific*. By *domain specific*, I mean that patients do not have difficulties gaining conscious access to information outside the domain of their specific impairment. Thus, for example, prosopagnosic patients do not have the difficulties consciously reading words that alexic patients do, whereas alexic patients do not have the difficulties consciously recognizing familiar faces that prosopagnosic patients do. Similarly, amnesic patients do not have problems consciously perceiving visual stimuli, and blindsight patients are not characterized by difficulties in conscious recollection. The striking disruptions of conscious processes observed in these and other patients occur largely in the circumscribed bandwidth of cognition that is defined by their specific deficit. By the present view, the diversity and domain-specificity of these phenomena provide clues concerning the relation between memory and consciousness.

Dissociable Interactions and Conscious Experience

The dissociations discussed thus far indicate clearly that memory for recent experiences can be revealed in performance without any conscious experience of remembering, and also indicate that various kinds of knowledge can be expressed in the absence of conscious experiences of perceiving, identifying, or knowing. It is possible, of course, that the resemblance among these phenomena is entirely superficial, and that each dissociation demands a separate theoretical treatment. By this view, it would be uninformative and possibly misleading to approach the memory and consciousness issue in the context of the phenomena discussed in the previous section. Such a possibility cannot be ruled out with any certainty. However, I believe that it is worth exploring the idea that there is a theoretically significant relation among the dissociations. This belief is based in part on several of Tulving's admonitions concerning the proper approach to psychological issues that are highly familiar to his students and colleagues. First, the self-correcting nature of the scientific enterprise insures us that nothing much will be lost if the ideas put forward here turn out to be wrong (this can also be read as an excuse for speculation). Second, broad conceptual approaches are currently needed instead of premature formalism (I take this as an excuse for vagueness). Third, falsifiability is not the only criterion for a useful scientific idea (in other words, circularity can be excused). Fourth, all current ideas in psychology are wrong anyway, so why not give it a shot?

In conformity with the foregoing, I use the observations of implicit/ explicit dissociations in various neuropsychological syndromes to motivate a general framework for understanding the memory/consciousness relation. The main usefulness of the framework, in my view, is that it brings together a variety of phenomena and ideas that might not otherwise be related. The spirit of the present proposal is similar to Tulving's (1983) GAPS framework (General Abstract Processing System), which organizes and interrelates diverse phenomena via a small number of ideas, but does not offer detailed explanations or quantitative predictions. And just as the acronym GAPS reflected Tulving's acute awareness that his model was incomplete, I have chosen an acronym for the present approach—DICE—that reflects my awareness that attempting to relate diverse phenomena to one another is a gamble that involves considerable risk. In addition, as should become clear shortly, some of the central ideas to be put forward are captured in the words that the acronym represents: Dissociable Interactions and Conscious Experience. DICE draws on and attempts to integrate ideas that have been proposed by Baars (1983), Dimond (1976), Johnson-Laird (1983), Kihlstrom (1984), Marcel (1983), Mesulam (1981), Norman and Shallice (1986), Squire and Cohen (1984), Tulving (1985a, 1985b) and Weiskrantz (1977, 1980), among others.

DICE is built on a half-dozen or so main ideas:

1. Conscious experiences of remembering, perceiving, and knowing all depend on the involvement of a specific mechanism or system.

2. This system is normally activated by the outputs of various processing and memory modules, and the resulting *interaction* between a particular module and the conscious system defines a particular kind of conscious experience.

3. In some cases of neuropsychological impairment, specific processing and memory modules are *selectively disconnected* from the conscious system, thereby resulting in a domain-specific deficit of conscious experience.

4. Information that does not have access to the conscious system can still affect verbal/motor response systems.

5. The conscious system functions as a gateway to executive control systems.

6. Procedural knowledge does not normally have access to the conscious system.

I first flesh out these notions in a bit more detail, and then discuss evidence that suggests a neurophysiological basis for the various components of DICE. To aid the reader's understanding of the model, fig. 18.1 displays a schematic of its components and the relations among them.

Central to the present approach is the idea that conscious experiences of remembering, knowing, and so forth all depend on the functioning of a specific mechanism or system that is distinct from, but interacts with, modular mechanisms that process and represent various types of information. I refer to this system simply as the Conscious Awareness System (CAS). By the present view, activation at the modular level—in a particular perceptual or memory system, for example—is not sufficient to produce conscious awareness of the activated representation. Such

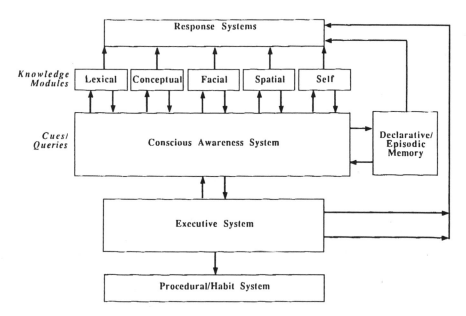

Figure 18.1 A schematic depiction of DICE. Knowledge modules represent various types of overlearned information; declarative/episodic memory subserves remembering of recent events and information; the procedural/habit system is involved in perceptual/motor skill learning. Phenomenal awareness of specific types of information depends on intact connections between the conscious awareness system and individual knowledge modules or declarative/episodic memory. The procedural/habit system does not have any connections with the conscious awareness system. The conscious awareness system serves as the gateway to the executive system, which is involved in initiation of voluntary activities.

awareness depends on the activation of CAS by the output of perceptual or memory modules. Thus, activation of CAS is held to occur at a relatively late stage in processing, only after information has been elaborated extensively at the modular level. However, activation of CAS represents just one output route from a particular module. It is also possible for information represented in a particular module to be expressed via output routes to verbal or motor response systems that do not involve CAS. When modular outputs affect response systems without activation of CAS, knowledge is expressed implicitly, in the absence of any phenomenal awareness or subjective experience of perceiving, remembering, or knowing. In the present scheme, CAS serves three functions. First, as implied previously, its activation is necessary for the subjective sense that one "remembers," "knows," or "perceives" something. Second, CAS can be viewed as a "global data base" (Baars 1983) that integrates the output of modular processes. Such an integrative mechanism is crucial in any modular system in which processing and representation of different types of information is handled in parallel by separate modules (Allport 1979; Baars 1983; Johnson-Laird 1983). Third, it is hypothesized that CAS sends outputs to an *executive system* that is involved in regulation of attention and initiation of such voluntary activities as memory search, planning, and so forth. Whereas CAS can be activated by inputs from various sources (i.e., modules), its major output is to the executive control system. Thus, CAS is not itself an executive system, but it outputs the kind of information that can be used by executive systems (cf. Baars 1983). The distinction between CAS and the executive system is central to the present view, and I attempt to justify it on neuropsychological grounds later in the chapter.

DICE incorporates a distinction between procedural and declarative memory systems, and also accepts a further distinction between types of declarative memory that is similar but not identical to Tulving's (1972, 1983) episodic/semantic distinction. I use the procedural/declarative distinction in the manner of Anderson (1976) and Winograd (1975), who were among the first to apply it to psychological issues—procedural memory entails "knowing how," and is involved primarily in various kinds of incremental skill learning, whereas declarative memory entails "knowing that," and involves primarily memory for words, events, facts, and so on (for a somewhat different use of the procedural/declarative distinction, see Squire 1987). "Procedural" is used here in a sense that is roughly equivalent to the notion of "habit" proposed by Mishkin and his colleagues (e.g., Mishkin et al. 1984), and so I refer to the system held to be involved in incremental skill learning as the procedural/habit system. An important postulate of DICE is that this system does not send input to CAS under *any* circumstances. It is frequently acknowledged that people do not have conscious access to psychological processes or procedures (e.g., Johnson-Laird 1983; Kihlstrom 1984; Kinsbourne and Wood 1982; Nisbett and Wilson 1977), and it seems reasonable to argue that people do not have conscious access to *modifications* of these processes (e.g., Cohen 1984; Squire 1986). The notion that the procedural/habit system does not have an input link to CAS, however, does not mean that this system is totally isolated. Clearly, it is possible to voluntarily *initiate* various acquired skills or procedures, and some procedural learning may require the allocation of attention (cf. Nissen and Bullemer 1987). Accordingly, DICE postulates that the executive system has an output link to procedural memory that permits the voluntary initiation of skills that depend on procedural systems. The critical point, however, is that the actual running off of a procedure, skill, or habit does not constitute input to CAS. The implication of this idea is that all manifestations of the procedural/habit system are implicit. With respect to the finding of normal skill learning in amnesic patients who do not explicitly remember learning any skills, the present account is much the same as that of Cohen and Squire (1980) or Mishkin et al. (1984): The procedural/habit system is assumed to be spared in organic amnesia.

If the data indicated that only perceptual and motor skills could be expressed without conscious awareness of remembering, it would be possible to argue that conscious memory is a property of the declarative memory system, and that whenever declarative memory is involved in task performance, remembering will be characterized by conscious recollective experience. However, it appears that implicit memory phenomena can be observed in tasks that involve memory for what many people would describe as declarative (i.e., representational) information—words, sentences, paired associates, facts, and so on. How can implicit memory for declarative information occur? By the present view, the answer to this question is to be found in the relation between CAS and declarative memory structures. CAS is assumed to have connections with two dissociable types of declarative memory. The first resembles what Tulving (1972) has termed *episodic* memory, in the sense that it is responsible for storing and retrieving *new* information. In the present scheme, however, this memory system is responsible for representing various types of new information (e.g., facts, associations, context, etc.), whereas Tulving (1983) restricts episodic memory to autobiographical information. In DICE, explicit remembering of a recent event depends on an *interaction* between the declarative/episodic system and CAS. Activation of a representation in declarative/episodic memory is not itself a sufficient condition for explicit remembering of a recent event. For explicit remembering to occur, the output of declarative/episodic memory must be able to gain access to CAS. If such access does not occur, an episodic representation may still affect verbal or motor response systems via alternative output routes that do not involve CAS. Under these conditions, however, information from declarative/episodic memory will affect performance implicitly, without any conscious experience of remembering.

The second class of declarative memory structures with access to CAS are those that represent highly overlearned and unitized information of various kinds—lexical, conceptual, autobiographical, spatial, visual, and so forth. These structures could be viewed either as a subset of declarative memory or as a distinct *semantic* memory system (Tulving 1983). For the present purposes, the critical point is that "semantic memory" appears to be composed of different modules that represent various types of information (e.g., Allport and Funnell 1981; Johnson-Laird 1983; Warrington and Shallice 1984). For descriptive purposes, I refer to these as "knowledge modules" or "semantic memory modules." Although no firm assumptions are made here regarding the specific nature of these modules, it is hypothesized that explicit knowledge of words, concepts, familiar faces, and so forth depends on an *interaction* between the appropriate knowledge module and CAS. Mere activation of a semantic memory representation is not sufficient to yield a conscious experience of knowing or identifying. The route from a particular module to CAS must also be functional in order for activated information to produce a conscious experience of knowing. If information represented in a specific module cannot gain access to CAS, it is postulated that the activated information can still affect verbal or motor response systems through routes that bypass CAS. When such routes are used, however, the output of a specific module will be expressed implicitly, without a conscious experience of knowing or identifying.

Whereas CAS can be activated by an "upstream" flow of input from knowledge modules or declarative/episodic memory, voluntary or deliberate access to information represented by a particular memory module depends on the executive system, which is assumed to have unidirectional "downstream" links to memory structures. The executive system can thus query various memory structures regarding the accessibility of sought-after information, a process that corresponds to the initiation of search or voluntary retrieval. If the sought-after information is activated, it can gain access to CAS and produce a conscious experience of remembering or knowing.

Within the context of the foregoing ideas, there are two ways in which implicit memory for declarative information can occur: (a) through transient activation of pre-existing representations in semantic memory modules, and (b) through the establishment of new declarative/episodic representations that are expressed through retrieval routes that do not involve CAS. Consider first the role of activation. Following relatively short retention intervals, a pre-existing representation that had been activated at the time of study may gain access to CAS when an appropriate cue is provided on an implicit memory test (e.g., a word stem), thereby resulting in the conscious experience of a familiar word "popping into mind." However, access of an activated representation to CAS does not provide any contextual information about the occurrence of a recent event, and therefore does not provide a basis for explicit remembering. For explicit remembering to occur, CAS must receive input from declarative/episodic memory. In normal subjects, this can happen when test instructions call for explicit remembering (e.g., Graf and Mandler 1984; Schacter and Graf 1986a), thereby initiating a "query" from the executive system to declarative/episodic memory that can produce an input to CAS. When appropriate information is available (i.e., following elaborative encoding), CAS will be activated, and remembering of the prior occurrence of a word in a study list will occur; however, when appropriate information is not available (i.e., following non-semantic encoding), CAS will not be activated, and thus explicit remembering will not occur.

This formulation can also be applied to the finding of normal priming of old or pre-existing knowledge in amnesic patients. Amnesic patients generally do not have difficulty gaining conscious access to highly overlearned information such as words and concepts. Therefore, it is reasonable to posit that such information can be activated normally and can gain access to CAS. However, amnesic patients do not remember explicitly the prior occurrence of an activated word. One possible reason for this is that amnesic patients do not store or retain new declarative information about an event, information whose retrieval is necessary for conscious recollection to occur. A second possibility, which is advocated here, is that at least some amnesic patients can "store" new declarative information, but such information is unable to gain access to conscious awareness. Why should one favor this notion over the idea that the declarative/episodic representations are simply unavailable? The main reason stems from the various demonstrations that some amnesic patients can show implicit memory for new, contextually specific information, such as unrelated paired associates (Cermak et al. in press; Graf and Schacter 1985; Moscovitch et al. 1986; Schacter and Graf 1986b), sentence puzzles (McAndrews et al. 1987), repeated spatio-temporal patterns (Nissen and Bullemer 1987), and some kinds of factual information (Glisky et al. 1986; Schacter et al. 1984). By the present view, such newly acquired declarative/episodic information can affect motor and verbal response systems via routes that bypass CAS. The fact that this newly learned information is not always retrieved *normally* in amnesic patients (e.g., Schacter et al. 1984; Squire 1986) can be accommodated by postulating some damage to the declarative/episodic system itself as well as disconnection from CAS.

The foregoing constitutes an overview of DICE and illustrates how some of its main ideas can be applied to various implicit/explicit dissociations. To evaluate the plausibility of this framework, however, it is necessary to examine in greater detail the nature of and empirical basis for these ideas. In the following section, I first discuss further the evidence for CAS, followed by consideration of the neuropsychology of the executive system and its relation to CAS. I then elaborate my view of modularity and the issue of multiple memory systems. Finally, I compare the present approach to other views of the memory/consciousness issue and then outline several predictions that are made by DICE. [The last few topics are omitted here.—Ed.]

Conceptions of CAS

Although a great many psychological and neurophysiological theories concerning the nature of conscious awareness have been advanced, two broad approaches to the problem can be distinguished. One has a *global* emphasis: Consciousness is identified with the sum total of all information processing activities or as an emergent property of diffuse brain or cognitive systems (e.g., Karmiloff-Smith 1986; Neisser 1976; Sperry 1969). The other has a *local* emphasis: Consciousness is identified with the activity of a specific psychological/neurological mechanism or system (e.g., Baars 1983; Dimond 1976; Hilgard 1977; Johnson-Laird 1983; Kihlstrom 1984; Posner 1978, 1980). As described in the previous section, the present approach has a decidedly, although not exclusively, local emphasis. Any attempt to identify conscious awareness with a specific mechanism or system immediately raises two interrelated problems. First, it is all too easy to endow such a system with homunculus-like properties that enable it to perform a host of activities that are casually grouped together under the heading of *conscious.* Part of the problem here is that the term *conscious* is often used to refer to a variety of psychological functions, including phenomenal awareness of mental activity, voluntary or intentional initiation of action, selection of stimuli for attention, and control of processing activity. To postulate a conscious mechanism and blithely assign it all of the foregoing capacities is not terribly helpful. Thus, to escape or at least minimize the homunculus charge, one must be quite specific about the properties and functions of any alleged conscious mechanism. I have attempted to do so by identifying CAS with one particular function: phenomenal awareness of ongoing mental activity. CAS is held to be activated by input from various modular processors, and to represent such information in a way that it can be output to executive systems. The present conception of CAS is close in spirit to Baars' (1983) notion that consciousness is a "global data base" that represents in an integrated manner the output of parallel modular systems. Of course, it could be argued that restricting one's conception of CAS in such a manner merely shifts the homunculus to the executive system. Although there may be some truth to this, there are also reasonably strong neuropsychological grounds for distinguishing between CAS and executive systems, as is argued in this and the next section.

The second main problem in attempting to identify conscious awareness with a specific mechanism or system is that this *description* could be mistakenly viewed as an *explanation*. Clearly, to postulate that conscious awareness depends on a specific mechanism in no way explains how consciousness is achieved or exactly what it is. Accordingly, one must guard against any tendency to reify the hypothetical conscious system or to imagine that the problem has been "solved" merely by postulating the existence of such a system. In the present formulation, the notion of CAS can be viewed as a convenient shorthand for the idea that conscious awareness of a specific bit of information requires processing beyond the modular level. Even if postulation of a conscious system amounts to no more than redefining the problem, this is not without value when the redefinition is useful (White 1982)—that is, when it suggests a fruitful line of approach to the phenomenon and raises questions that might not be investigated otherwise. If we hypothesize the existence of a system such as CAS, we are led to ask questions concerning the reasons for supporting its existence, how it interacts with other systems, the areas of the brain that are involved in CAS, what happens when these areas are damaged, and so forth. These questions are quite different than those that would be posed if consciousness were viewed as a global, emergent property of brain organization, and the next section addresses some of them.

The Neuroanatomy and Neuropsychology of CAS

If the notion of CAS is to be more than just a fanciful speculation that is invoked *post-hoc* to describe various implicit/explicit dissociations, it ought to be possible to cite evidence of its existence independently of the phenomena that led to the initial postulation of it. I believe that there are empirical grounds for inferring the existence of a system akin to CAS. More specifically, both neuroanatomical and neuropsychological evidence suggest that a posterior region of the cortex, critically involving the inferior parietal lobes, constitutes part of a circuit or system subserving conscious awareness (e.g., Dimond 1976; Mountcastle 1978).

Consider first the neuroanatomical basis for suggesting the involvement of posterior parietal cortex in conscious awareness. Two characteristics of CAS delineated earlier are that it is activated at a relatively late stage in the processing of a particular stimulus, and that it serves to integrate the output of various modules. A neural system that fits this description would be one with (a) access to information that has already been analyzed extensively at earlier stages of processing, and (b) access to highly processed information from a variety of sources (i.e., modules). Recent neuroanatomical evidence indicates that certain areas of the parietal lobes meet both of these criteria. For example, Mesulam and his colleagues (Mesulam et al. 1977) showed that the inferior parietal lobule in rhesus monkeys is uniquely characterized by the convergence of projections from all multimodal or higher-order association areas of the cortex, as well as from the limbic system. By contrast, the inferior parietal region receives relatively few projections from unimodal or low-level sensory areas. What this means is that the inferior parietal region takes as its input information which already has been processed to high levels in association areas, and it gets such input from multiple sources. As Mesulam (1985) stated, the inferior parietal lobule "could be considered an association area for high-order association areas" (p. 152). He noted further that "We have examined the connectivity of many other cortical areas . . . but we have not yet found an area that receives sensory input which is this extensively preprocessed" (1983, 395). Although some caution must be exercised when making inferences regarding human cortical organization from monkey data, the foregoing observations suggest that regions of parietal cortex have precisely the pattern of interconnections that would be necessary if they constituted part of a larger system with the hypothesized properties and functions of CAS.

The idea that parietal lobes form part of a system that underlies conscious awareness was noted and discussed in an important but little cited article by Dimond (1976). He proposed the existence of a "consciousness circuit" extending across a posterior section of the cortex, with the parietal lobes representing the lateral endpoints of the circuit. Other key neural structures that Dimond hypothesized to be part of this system include the posterior regions of the corpus callosum, particularly the cingulate area in the splenium of the callosum. If the circuit proposed by Dimond is even a rough approximation of the neuroanatomical substrate of CAS, it would be expected that lesions to the various components of the system should produce disorders of conscious awareness. Neuropsychological observations are consistent with this idea. Discussing literature on split-brain patients, Dimond noted that disturbances of awareness that are sometimes observed in such patients are found only following sectioning of the posterior third of the callosum—the part that links the parietal lobes and is thus an important component of the consciousness circuit. Patients in whom the anterior two thirds is sectioned and the posterior third is preserved do not show any disturbances of awareness (Gordon et al. 1971). Dimond also noted that severe disturbances of consciousness have been observed following lesions in the cingulate area, which also forms part of the bridge that links the parietal lobes. For example, the phenomenon of akinetic mutism has been observed in patients with cingulate lesions: They are unresponsive to external stimuli, apathetic, and do not voluntarily speak or move, although they are "awake" (i.e., eyes are open and reflexes are intact) and not considered to be comatose (e.g., Barris and Schuman 1953; Nielsen and Jacobs 1951). Cingulate lesions have also been associated with confusional states, which are characterized by disordered thought, severe disorientation, and a breakdown of selective attention—in short, a global disorder of conscious awareness (Amyes and Nielsen 1955; Whitty and Lewin 1960).

Several lines of evidence indicate that lesions to certain regions of the parietal lobes can produce disorders of conscious awareness. First, global confusional states have been reported in right parietal patients (Geschwind 1982; Mesulam and Geschwind 1978; Mesulam et al. 1976). Second, the syndrome of anosognosia—unawareness and denial of a neuropsychological deficit—is often associated with parietal damage (e.g., Bisiach et al. 1986; Critchley 1953; Frederiks 1985; Koehler et al. 1986; Warrington 1962; for review, see McGlynn and Schacter in press). Anosognostic patients may be unaware of motor deficits (e.g., hemiplegia), perceptual deficits (e.g., hemianopia and blindness), or cognitive deficits (e.g., jargon aphasia), and complete unawareness can be observed even when the primary deficit is severe (i.e., total blindness). Patients' subjective sense that their deficient function is normal can be extraordinarily compelling, and they often deny a deficit in the face of contrary evidence, resorting to rationalizations and confabulations. This dramatic disorder of awareness in parietal lobe patients implies a disruption of CAS.

Further relevant evidence is provided by the phenomenon of unilateral neglect. A large body of neuropsychological observations indicates that unilateral damage to the inferior parietal lobe, particularly in the right hemisphere, produces a striking disorder of attention or awareness (e.g., Bisiach et al. 1979; Brain 1941; Critchley 1953; Mesulam 1985; Vallar and Perani 1986): Neglect patients appear entirely unaware of the existence of the internal and external world contralateral to their lesion, even though basic sensory/perceptual function is intact. Such patients may fail to shave, wash, or dress the neglected side of the body, constantly bump into objects on the side of space contralateral to their lesion, and even fail to report the content of internally generated images from the contralateral side (Bisiach and Luzzati 1978; Bisiach et al. 1979). The apparent reason for this disorder is that patients are unable to shift attention away from the field ipsilateral to their lesion (Posner et al. 1987). Thus, it is possible that neglect ought not to be viewed as a disruption of CAS in the same way that such phenomena as confusional states, anosognosia, and akinetic mutism are. The disruption may be at the level of the output of CAS to attentional control systems. However, Dimond (1976) has suggested a way of conceptualizing neglect as a deficit of consciousness. He proposed that:

the patient with parietal lobe damage is deficient in the capacity for the production of consciousness. We believe that the cerebral disorder is such as to seriously restrict that which the patient can accommodate in consciousness; the individual now possesses only a narrowed and restricted channel through which the stuff of consciousness can pass with the result that much fails to enter. He is in other words deprived of one arm of the system for consciousness and like any one-armed individual is seriously restricted in what he can do. (p. 387)

It is also worth noting that lesions of the inferior parietal lobule in monkeys produce an inattention syndrome that is, in several respects, similar to neglect in humans (Lynch 1980; Mountcastle 1978). Noting the convergence from human and animal data, Mountcastle (1978) offered an interpretation similar to Dimond's (1976): "A patient with a parietal lobe lesion has a defect of conscious awareness, for he no longer has the capacity to attend to the contralateral world; for him it no longer exists. And the withdrawn self-isolation of a monkey after bilateral parietal lobe lesions suggests a reduction in his level of conscious awareness" (p. 48).

Taken together, the foregoing considerations provide reasonable grounds for postulating a neural circuit or system that corresponds to CAS. It must be emphasized, however, that the existing evidence can be regarded as no more than suggestive. For example, there are only a few empirical observations linking posterior regions of the corpus callosum—the heart of the consciousness circuit postulated by Dimond (1976)—with disorders of conscious awareness. Likewise, damage to inferior parietal regions, which constitute the lateral end-points of Dimond's system, does not inevitably result in a disruption of awareness, and in some instances produces other kinds of neuropsychological disturbances (e.g., Critchley 1953; Frederiks 1985). Nevertheless, the existing empirical clues are suggestive enough to merit serious consideration.

It should also be noted that some of the phenomena observed in conjunction with parietal lesions, such as neglect and anosognosia, have been observed in connection with frontal damage (see Stuss and Benson 1986). Although it is not clear whether the parietal and frontal manifestations of these phenomena are identical (McGlynn and Schacter in press; Stuss and Benson 1986), such observations have led to the suggestion that frontal lobes are critically involved in self-awareness (Stuss & Benson, 1986). It is possible that the posterior-based CAS described here interacts with frontal regions and thus forms part of a larger network concerned with various kinds of awareness (see Mesulam 1981, for a similar idea with respect to selective attention). The fact that there are strong reciprocal links between parietal and frontal lobes (e.g., Mesulam 1981; Nauta 1971) lends neuroanatomical plausibility to this suggestion. However, as described in the next section, the present approach emphasizes the involvement of frontal lobes in the closely related domain of executive formation and intentional retrieval.

I have distinguished several times between two ways in which the concept of consciousness has been used with respect to memory: to indicate phenomenal awareness of remembering or "recollective experience" on the one hand, or to refer to deliberate or intentional initiation of retrieval on the other. In outlining DICE, the latter activity was assigned an executive system that is distinct from CAS. In addition, it was suggested that when an activated representation gains access to CAS, it is made available to the executive system and can thus be used in intentional actions and behaviors that are controlled by the executive. By contrast, it was hypothesized that activated representations that do not gain access to CAS cannot be used by the executive. Such representations can only affect output systems involved in relatively automatic responding.

Recent ideas advanced by Norman and Shallice (1986; Shallice 1982) provide a basis for sharpening these suggestions and linking them to neuropsychological observations. Norman and Shallice described two mechanisms for the control of action. The first, referred to as *contention scheduling,* involves relatively automatic triggering of highly activated schemas by appropriate environmental information. This mechanism supports the execution of routine behaviors that run off without voluntary control and are determined solely by which schema is most strongly activated by an environmental trigger. Although it is an efficient means of controlling action, contention scheduling breaks down when nonroutine behaviors are demanded; an organism operating on the basis of contention schedule alone is susceptible to perseverative responding and involuntary "slips of action." For example, an intended action may not be performed because a strong, although inappropriate, schema is activated and "captures" response systems (e.g., a person walks through his back porch to get his car, and ends up putting on a jacket and boots for gardening; Reason 1979). In view of the shortcomings of contention scheduling, Norman and Shallice postulated a second mechanism, referred to as the Supervisory Attentional System (SAS), which is involved in intentional or deliberate control of action. SAS "contains the general programming or planning systems that can operate on schemas in every domain" (Shallice 1982, 20). It functions to bias the contention scheduling mechanism by adding additional activation to appropriate schemas and inhibiting inappropriate ones. SAS is thus crucial for various kinds of voluntary, non-routine behaviors.

What I have described as the executive system corresponds roughly to Norman and Shallice's SAS. As has been pointed out by Norman and Shallice and others (e.g., Luria 1966; Milner 1982; Stuss and Benson 1986), neuropsychological observations support the existence of such a system and tie it closely to prefrontal cortex. Beginning with the classic observation of Luria (1966), it has been reported repeatedly that patients with frontal lesions have difficulties in the programming, planning, and monitoring of behavior. Such patients can perform routine, stimulus-driven tasks well, but are impaired when a task requires self-initiated responses, active planning, sequential organization, or response monitoring (Milner 1982). These are all activities that can be roughly described as "executive functions."

The critical point of the foregoing is to suggest that there are reasonable grounds for distinguishing between intentional and unintentional control of behavior and action. In DICE, intentional initiation of retrieval is handled by the executive. In addition, only those activated representations that gain access to CAS can be used by the executive system and thus influence voluntary activities. Activated information that does not gain access to CAS can still influence response systems, along the lines suggested by Norman and Shallice in their discussion of contention scheduling. However, such implicitly expressed information cannot serve as a basis for formulating plans or other kinds of voluntary action. Consider, for example, an amnesic patient who has no conscious recollection of a recent experience, yet demonstrates retention of that experience via priming effects on an implicit memory test. Such a patient would likely be unable to use the information acquired during the episode as a basis for formulating future plans or strategies, although such information might affect the patient's automatic response in the presence of an appropriate environmental trigger. Thus, an amnesic patient in whom CAS is disconnected from declarative/episodic memory would have no "memory for the future" (Tulving 1985b), because recently acquired information is unavailable to the executive system. It is interesting to note in this regard that Marcel (1986) reported a similar observation in the case of a blindsight patient:

Cortically blind patients who have no phenomenal experience of an object in the blind field will nonetheless preadjust their hands appropriately to size, shape, orientation and 3-D location of that object in the blind field when forced to attempt to grasp it. . . . Yet such patients will make no spontaneous attempt to grasp a glass of water in their blind field even when thirsty. Voluntary actions often depend upon conscious perception. (p. 41)

[The concluding sections of this article are omitted.—Ed.]

Acknowledgments

This chapter was supported by a Special Research Program Grant from the Connaught Fund, University of Toronto, by Grant No. U0361 from the Natural Sciences and Engineering Research Council of Canada, and by a Biomedical Research Support Grant from the University of Arizona. I am grateful to Laird Cermak, Peter Graf, Larry Jacoby, John Kihlstrom, Bob Lockhart, Mary Pat McAndrews, Susan McGlynn, Morris Moscovitch, Lynn Nadel, Roddy Roediger, and Endel Tulving for helpful comments and discussion concerning many of the ideas presented in this chapter.

References

Allport, D. A. (1979). Conscious and unconscious cognition: A computational metaphor for the mechanism of attention and integration. In L.-G Nilson, ed., *Perspectives on memory research*. Hillsdale, NJ: Lawrence Erlbaum Associates.

Allport, D. A., and E. Funnell (1981). Component of the mental lexicon. *Philosophical Transactions of the Royal Society of London* B 295, 297–410.

Amyes, E. W., and J. M. Nielsen (1955). Clinicopathologic study of vascular lesions of the anterior cingulate region. *Bulletin of the Los Angeles Neurological Society* 20, 112–130.

Anderson, J. R. (1976). *Language, memory, and thought*. Hillsdale, NJ: Lawrence Erlbaum Associates.

Andrewsky, E. L., and X. Seron (1975). Implicit processing of grammatical rules in a classical case of agrammatism. *Cortex* 11, 379–390.

Baars, B. J. (1983). Conscious contents provide the nervous system with coherent, global information. In R. J. Davidson, G. E. Schwartz, and D. Shapiro, eds., *Consciousness and self-regulation*, vol. 3. New York: Plenum.

Bargh, J. A., and P. Pietromonaco (1982). Automatic information processing and social perception: The influence of trait information presented outside of conscious awareness on impression formation. *Journal of Personality and Social Psychology* 43, 437–449.

Barris, R. W., and H. R. Schuman (1953). Bilateral anterior cingulate gyrus lesions. *Neurology* 3, 44–52.

Bauer, R. M. (1984). Autonomic recognition of names and faces in prosopagnosia: A neuropsychological application of the guilty knowledge test. *Neuropsychologia* 22, 457–469.

Bisiach, E., and C. Luzzati (1978). Unilateral neglect of representational space. *Cortex* 14, 129–133.

Bisiach, E., Luzzati, C., and D. Perani (1979). Unilateral neglect, representational schema and consciousness. *Brain* 102, 609–618.

Bisiach, E., G. Vallar, D. Perani, C. Papagno, and A. Berti (1986). Unawareness of disease following lesions of the right hemisphere: Anosognosia for hemiplegia and anosognosia for hemianopia. *Neuropsychologia* 24, 471–482.

Blumstein, S. E., W. Milberg, and R. Shrier (1982). Semantic processing in aphasia: Evidence from an auditory lexical decision task. *Brain and Language* 17, 301–315.

Brain, W. R. (1941). Visual disorientation with special reference to lesions of the right cerebral hemisphere. *Brain* 64, 244–272.

Brooks, D. N., and A. D. Baddeley (1976). What can amnesic patients learn? *Neuropsychologia* 14, 111–122.

Campion, J., R. Latto, and Y. M. Smith (1983). Is blindsight an effect of scattered light, spared cortex, and near-threshold vision? *The Behavioral and Brain Sciences* 6, 423–486.

Cermak, L. S. (ed.) (1982). *Human memory and amnesia.* Hillsdale, NJ: Lawrence Erlbaum Associates.

Cermak L. S., S. P. Blackford, M. O'Connor, and R. P. Bleich (1988). The implicit memory ability of a patient with amnesia due to encephalitis, *Brain Cognition* 7, 145–156.

Cermak, L. S., R. P. Bleich, and S. P. Blackford (1988). Deficits in the implicit retention of new associations by alcoholic Korsakoff patients, *Brain Cognition* 7, 312–323.

Cermak, L. S., N. Talbot, K. Chandler, and L. R. Wolbarst (1985). The perceptual priming phenomenon in amnesia. *Neuropsychologia* 23, 615–622.

Cohen, N. J. (1984). Preserved learning capacity in amnesia: Evidence for multiple memory systems. In L. R. Squire and N. Butters, eds., *Neuropsychology of memory.* New York: Guilford Press.

Cohen, N. J., and L. R. Squire (1980). Preserved learning and retention of pattern-analyzing skill in amnesia: Dissociation of "knowing how" and "knowing that." *Science* 210, 207–209.

Coslett, H. B. (1986). *Preservation of lexical access in alexia without agraphia.* Paper presented at the 9th European Conference of the International Neuropsychological Society, Veldhoven, the Netherlands.

Critchley, M. (1953). *The parietal lobes.* New York: Hafner.

Crovitz, H. F., M. T. Harvey, and S. McLanahan (1979). Hidden memory: A rapid method for the study of amnesia using perceptual learning. *Cortex* 17, 273–278.

Damasio, A. R. (1985). Disorders of complex visual processing: Agnosias, achromatopsia, Balint's syndrome, and related difficulties of orientation and construction. In M. M. Mesulam, ed., *Principles of behavioral neurology.* Philadelphia: F. A. Davis.

de Haan, E. H. F., A. Young, and F. Newcombe (1987). Face recognition without awareness. *Cognitive Neuropsychology* 4, 385–415.

Diamond, R., and P. Rozin (1984). Activation of existing memories in the amnesic syndrome. *Journal of Abnormal Psychology* 93, 98–105.

Dimond, S. J. (1976). Brain circuits for consciousness. *Brain, Behaviour and Evolution* 13, 376–395.

Dunn, R. (1845). Case of suspension of the mental faculties. *Lancet* 2, 588–590.

Eich, J. E. (1984). Memory for unattended events: Remembering with and without awareness. *Memory & Cognition* 12, 105–111.

Eslinger, P. J., and A. R. Damasio (1985). Preserved motor learning in Alzheimer's disease. *Journal of Neuroscience* 6, 3006–3009.

Forster, K. I., and C. Davis (1984). Repetition priming and frequency attenuation in lexical access. *Journal of Experimental Psychology: Learning, Memory, and Cognition* 10, 680–698.

Frederiks, J. A. M. (1985). Disorders of the body schema. In J. A. M. Frederiks, ed., *Handbook of clinical neurology*, vol. 1. Holland: Elsevier.

Geschwind, N. (1982). Disorders of attention: A frontier in neuropsychology. *Philosophical Transactions of the Royal Society of London* B298, 173–185.

Glisky, E. L., D. L. Schacter, and E. Tulving (1986). Computer learning by memory-impaired patients: Acquisition and retention of complex knowledge. *Neuropsychologia* 24, 313–328.

Glisky, E. L. and D. L. Schacter (1987). Acquisition of domain-specific knowledge in organic amnesia: training for computer-related work. *Neuropsychologia* 25, 893–906.

Glisky, E. L., and D. L. Schacter (1988). Long-term retention of computer learning by patients with memory disorders. *Neuropsychologica* 26, 173–178.

Gordon, H. W., J. E. Bogen, and R. W. Sperry (1971). Absence of deconnexion syndromes in two patients with partial section of the neocommissures. *Brain* 94, 327–336.

Graf, P., and G. Mandler (1984). Activation makes words more accessible, but not necessarily more retrievable. *Journal of Verbal Learning and Verbal Behavior* 23, 553–568.

Graf, P., and D. L. Schacter (1985). Implicit and explicit memory for new associations in normal and amnesic subjects. *Journal of Experimental Psychology: Learning, Memory, and Cognition*, 11, 501–518.

Graf, P., and D. L. Schacter (1987). Selective effects of interference on implicit and explicit memory for new associations. *Journal of Experimental Psychology: Learning, Memory, and Cognition*, 12, 45–53.

Graf, P., A. P. Shimamura, and L. R. Squire (1985). Priming across modalities and priming across category levels: Extending the domain of preserved function in amnesia. *Journal of Experimental Psychology: Learning, Memory, and Cognition* 11, 385–395.

Graf, P., L. R. Squire, and G. Mandler (1984). The information that amnesic patients do not forget. *Journal of Experimental Psychology: Learning, Memory, & Cognition* 10, 164–178.

Hilgard, E. R. (1977). *Divided consciousness*. New York: Wiley.

Hirst, W. (1982). The amnesic syndrome: Descriptions and explanations. *Psychological Bulletin*, 91, 435–460.

Holtzman, J. D., J. J. Sidtis, B. T. Volpe, D. H. Wilson, and M. S. Gazzaniga (1981). Dissociation of spatial information for stimulus localization and the control of attention. *Brain*, 104, 861–872.

Jacoby, L. L., and M. Dallas (1981). On the relationship between autobiographical memory and perceptual learning. *Journal of Experimental Psychology: General* 110, 306–340.

Johnson, M. K., J. K. Kim, and G. Risse (1985). Do alcoholic Korsakoff's syndrome patients acquire affective reactions? *Journal of Experimental Psychology: Learning, Memory, and Cognition* 11, 27–36.

Johnson-Laird, P. (1983). *Mental models*. Cambridge: Harvard University Press.

Karmiloff-Smith, A. (1986). From meta-processes to conscious access: Evidence from children's metalinguistic and repair data. *Cognition* 23, 95–147.

Kihlstrom, J. F. (1984). Conscious, subconscious, unconscious: A cognitive perspective. In K. S. Bowers and D. Meichenbaum, eds., *The unconscious reconsidered*. New York: Wiley.

Kinsbourne, M., and F. Wood (1982). Theoretical considerations regarding the episodic-semantic memory distinction. In L. S. Cermak, ed., *Human memory and amnesia*. Hillsdale, NJ: Lawrence Erlbaum.

Koehler, P. J., L. J. Endtz, J. Te Velde, and R. E. M. Hekster (1986). Aware or non-aware. On the significance of awareness for the localization of the lesion responsible for homonymous hemianopia. *Journal of the Neurological Sciences* 75, 255–262.

Korsakoff, S. S. (1889). Etude médico-psychologique sur une forme des maladies de la mémoire. *Review Philosophique* 28, 501–530.

Kunst-Wilson, W. R., and R. B. Zajonc (1980). Affective discrimination of stimuli that cannot be recognized. *Science* 207, 557–558.

Landis, T., M. Regard, and A. Serrant (1980). Iconic reading in a case of alexia without agraphia caused by a brain tumor: A tachistoscope study. *Brain and Language* 11, 45–53.

Luria, A. R. (1966). *Higher cortical functions in man*. London: Tavistock.

Luria, A. R. (1976). *The neuropsychology of memory*. Washington: V. H. Winston.

Lynch, J. C. (1980). The functional organization of posterior parietal association cortex. *The Behavioral and Brain Sciences* 3, 485–534.

McAndrews, M. P., E. L. Glisky, and D. L. Schacter (1987). When priming persists: Long-lasting implicit memory for a single episode in amnesic patients. *Neuropsychologia* 25, 497–506.

McGlynn, S. M., and D. L. Schacter (in press). Unawareness of deficits in neuropsychological syndromes. *Journal of Clinical and Experimental Neuropsychology*.

McKoon, G., and R. Ratcliff (1979). Priming in episodic and semantic memory. *Journal of Verbal Learning and Verbal Behavior* 18, 463–480.

McKoon, G., and R. Ratcliff (1986). Automatic activation of episodic information in a semantic memory task. *Journal of Experimental Psychology: Learning, Memory, and Cognition* 12, 108–115.

McKoon, G., R. Ratcliff, and G. Dell (1986). A critical evaluation of the semantic/episodic distinction. *Journal of Experimental Psychology: Learning, Memory, and Cognition* 12, 295–306.

Mandler, G., Y. Nakamura, B. J. S. Van Zandt (1987). Nonspecific effects of exposure on stimuli that cannot be recognized. *Journal of Experimental Psychology: Learning, Memory, and Cognition* 13, 646–649.

Marcel, A. J. (1983). Conscious and unconscious perception: Experiments on visual masking and word recognition. *Cognitive Psychology* 15, 197–237.

Marcel, A. J. (1986). Consciousness and processing: Choosing and testing a null hypothesis. *The Brain and Behavioral Sciences* 9, 40–41.

Margolin, D., F. Friedrich, and N. Carlson (1983). Visual agnosia and optic aphasia: A continuum of visual-semantic dissociation. *Neurology* 33, 242.

Mesulam, M.-M. (1981). A cortical network of directed attention and unilateral neglect. *Annals of Neurology* 10, 309–325.

Mesulam M.-M. (1983). The functional anatomy and hemispheric specialization for directed attention—the role of the parietal lobe and its connectivity. *Trends in Neuroscience* 6, 384–387.

Mesulam, M.-M. (1985). Attention, confusional states, and neglect. In M.-M. Mesulam, ed., *Principles of behavioral neurology*. Philadelphia: F. A. Davis.

Mesulam, M.-M., and N. Geschwind (1978). On the possible role of neocortex and its limbic connections in the process of attention and schizophrenia: Clinical cases of inattention in man and experimental anatomy in monkey. *Journal of Psychiatric Research* 14, 249–259.

Mesulam, M.-M., G. W. Van Hoesen, D. N. Pandya, and N. Geschwind (1977). Limbic and sensory connections of the inferior parietal lobule (area PG) in the rhesus monkey: A study with a new method for horseradish peroxidase histochemistry. *Brain Research* 136, 393–414.

Mesulam, M.-M., S. G. Waxman, N. Geschwind, and T. D. Sabin (1976). Acute confusional states with right middle cerebral artery infarctions. *Journal of Neurology, Neurosurgery, and Psychiatry* 39, 84–89.

Milberg, W., and S. Blumstein (1981). Lexical decision and aphasia. Evidence for semantic processing. *Brain and Language* 14, 371–385.

Milberg, W., S. E. Blumstein, and B. Dworetzky (in press). Processing of lexical ambiguities in aphasia. *Brain and Language*.

Milner, B. (1982). Some cognitive effects of frontal lobe lesions in man. In D. E. Broadbent and L. Weiskrantz eds., *The Neuropsychology of cognitive function*. London: The Royal Society.

Milner, B., S. Corkin, and H. L. Teuber (1968). Further analysis of the hippocampal amnesic syndrome: 14 year follow-up study of H.M. *Neuropsychologia* 6, 215–234.

Mishkin, M., B. Malamut, and J. Bachevalier (1984). Memories and habits: Two neural systems. In J. L. McGaugh, G. Lynch, and N. M. Weinberger, eds., *Neurobiology of learning and memory*. New York: Guilford Press.

Moscovitch, M. (1982). Multiple dissociations of function in amnesia. In L. S. Cermak, ed., *Human memory and amnesia*. Hillsdale, NJ: Lawrence Erlbaum.

Moscovitch, M., G. Winocur, and D. McLachlan (1986). Memory as assessed by recognition and reading time in normal and memory-impaired people with Alzheimer's disease and other neurological disorders. *Journal of Experimental Psychology: General* 115, 331–347.

Mountcastle, V. B. (1978). Some neural mechanisms for directed attention. In P. A. Buser and A. Rougeul-Buser, eds., *Cerebral correlates of conscious experience*, INSERM Symposium No. 6. Amsterdam: North-Holland.

Nauta, W. J. H. (1971). The problem of the frontal lobe: A reinterpretation. *Journal of Psychiatric Research* 8, 167–187.

Neisser, U. (1976). *Cognition and reality: Principles and implications of cognitive psychology*. San Francisco: Freeman.

Nielsen, J. M., and L. J. Jacobs (1951). Bilateral lesions of the anterior cingulate gyri. *Bulletin of the Los Angeles Neurological Society* 16, 231–234.

Nisbett, R. E., and T. D. Wilson (1977). Telling more than we can know: Verbal reports on mental processes. *Psychological Review* 84, 231–259.

Nissen, M. J., and P. Bullemer (1987). Attentional requirements of learning: Evidence from performance measures. *Cognitive Psychology* 19, 1–32.

Norman, D. A., and T. Shallice (1986). Attention to action. Willed and automatic control of behavior. In R. J. Davidson, G. E. Schwartz, and D. Shapiro, eds., *Consciousness and self-regulation*, vol. 4. New York: Plenum Press.

Posner, M. I. (1978). *Chronometric explorations of mind*. Hillsdale, NJ: Lawrence Erlbaum.

Posner, M. I. (1980). Mental chronometry and the problem of consciousness. In P. W. Jusczyk and R. M. Klein, eds., *The nature of thought*. Hillsdale, NJ: Lawrence Erlbaum.

Posner, M. I., A. W. Inhoff, F. J. Friedrich, and A. Cohen (1987). Isolating attentional systems: A cognitive-anatomical analysis. *Psychobiology* 15, 107–121.

Reason, J. T. (1979). Actions not as planned. In G. Underwood and R. Stevens, eds., *Aspects of consciousness*. London: Academic Press.

Richards, W. (1973). Visual processing in scotomata. *Experimental Brain Research* 17, 333–347.

Roediger, H. L., III, and T. A. Blaxton (1987). Retrieval modes produce dissociations in memory for surface information. In D. S. Gorfien and R. R. Hoffman, eds., *Memory and cognitive processes: The Ebbinghaus centennial conference*. Hillsdale, NJ: Lawrence Erlbaum.

Schacter, D. L. (1985). Priming of old and new knowledge in amnesic patients and normal subjects. *Annals of the New York Academy of Sciences* 444, 41–53.

Schacter, D. L. (1987). Implicit memory: History and current status. *Journal of Experimental Psychology: Learning, Memory, and Cognition* 13, 501–518.

Schacter, D. L., J. Bowers, and J. Booker (1989). Intention, awareness, and implicit memory: The retrieval intentionality criterion. In S. Lewandowsky, K. Kirsner, and ~~J. Dunn, eds.,~~ *Implicit memory: theoretical issues.* Hillsdale, NJ: Lawrence Erlbaum.

Schacter, D. L., and P. Graf (1986a). Effects of elaborative processing on implicit and explicit memory for new associations. *Journal of Experimental Psychology: Learning, Memory, and Cognition* 12, 432–444.

Schacter, D. L., and P. Graf (1986b). Preserved learning in amnesic patients: Perspectives from research on direct priming. *Journal of Clinical and Experimental Neuropsychology* 8, 727–743.

Schacter, D. L., J. L. Harbluk, and D. R. McLachlan (1984). Retrieval without recollection: An experimental analysis of source amnesia. *Journal of Verbal Learning and Verbal Behavior* 23, 593–611.

Schacter, D. L., M. P. McAndrews, and M. Moscovitch (1988). Access to consciousness: Dissociations between implicit and explicit knowledge in neuropsychological syndromes. In L. Weiskrantz, ed., *Thought without language.* Oxford: Oxford University Press.

Sergent, J. (1987). A new look at the human split brain. *Brain* 110, 1375–1392.

Shallice, T. (1982). Specific impairments of planning. In D. E. Broadbent and L. Weiskrantz, eds., *The neuropsychology of cognitive function.* London: The Royal Society.

Shallice, T., and E. Saffran (1986). Lexical processing in the absence of explicit word identification: Evidence from a letter-by-letter reader. *Cognitive Neuropsychology* 3, 429–458.

Shimamura, A. P. (1986). Priming effects in amnesia: Evidence for a dissociable memory function. *Quarterly Journal of Experimental Psychology* 38A, 619–644.

Shimamura, A. P., and L. R. Squire (1984). Paired-associate learning and priming effects in amnesia: A neuropsychological study. *Journal of Experimental Psychology: General* 113, 556–570.

Sloman, S. A., C. A. G. Hayman, N. Ohta, and E. Tulving (1988). Forgetting and interference in fragment completion. *Journal of Experimental Psychology: Learning, Memory, and Cognition,* 14, 223–239.

Sperry, R. W. (1969). A modified concept of consciousness. *Psychological Review* 76, 532–536.

Squire, L. R. (1986). Mechanisms of memory. *Science* 232, 1612–1619.

Squire, L. R. (1987). *Memory and brain.* New York: Oxford University Press.

Squire, L. R., and N. J. Cohen (1984). Human memory and amnesia. In J. McGlaugh, G. Lynch, and N. Weinberger, eds., *Proceedings of the conference on the neurobiology of learning and memory.* New York: Guilford Press.

Squire, L. R., A. P. Shimamura, and P. Graf (1987). Strength and duration of priming effects in normal subjects and amnesic patients. *Neuropsychologia* 25, 195–210.

Stuss, D. T., and D. F. Benson (1986). *The frontal lobes.* New York: Raven Press.

Tranel, D., and A. R. Damasio (1985). Knowledge without awareness: An autonomic index of facial recognition by prosopagnosics. *Science* 228, 1453–1454.

Tulving, E. (1972). Episodic and semantic memory. In E. Tulving and W. Donaldson, eds., *Organization of memory.* New York: Academic Press.

Tulving, E. (1983). *Elements of episodic memory.* Oxford: The Clarendon Press.

Tulving, E. (1985a). Ebbinghaus's memory: What did he learn and remember? *Journal of Experimental Psychology: Learning, Memory, and Cognition* 11, 485–490.

Tulving, E. (1985b). How many memory systems are there? *American Psychologist* 40, 385–398.

Tulving, E., D. L. Schacter, and H. A. Stark (1982). Priming effects in word-fragment completion are independent of recognition memory. *Journal of Experimental Psychology: Learning, Memory, and Cognition* 8, 336–342.

Vallar, G., and D. Perani (1986). The anatomy of unilateral neglect after right-hemisphere stroke lesions. A clinical/CT-scan correlation study in man. *Neuropsychologia* 24, 609–622.

Warrington, E. K. (1962). The completion of visual forms across hemianopic field defects. *Journal of Neurosurgery and Psychiatry* 25, 208–217.

Warrington, E. K. (1975). The selective impairment of semantic memory. *Quarterly Journal of Experimental Psychology* 27, 635–657.

Warrington, E. K. and T. Shallice (1984). Category specific semantic impairments. *Brain* 107, 829–954.

Warrington, E. K., and L. Weiskrantz (1968). New method of testing long-term retention with special reference to amnesic patients. *Nature* 217, 972–974.

Warrington, E. K., and L. Weiskrantz (1974). The effect of prior learning on subsequent retention in amnesic patients. *Neuropsychologia* 12, 419–428.

Warrington, E. K., and L. Weiskrantz (1982). Amnesia: A disconnection syndrome? *Neuropsychologia* 20, 233–248.

Weiskrantz, L. (1977). Trying to bridge some neuropsychological gaps between monkey and man. *British Journal of Psychology* 68, 431–445.

Weiskrantz, L. (1980). Varieties of residual experience. *Quarterly Journal of Experimental Psychology* 32, 365–386.

Weiskrantz, L. (1985). On issues and theories of the human amnesic syndrome. In N. Weinberger, J. McGaugh, and G. Lynch, eds., *Memory systems of the brain: Animal and human cognitive processes.* New York: Guilford Press.

Weiskrantz, L. (1986). *Blindsight.* New York: Oxford University Press.

Weiskrantz, L., and E. K. Warrington (1979). Conditioning in amnesic patients. *Neuropsychologia*, 17, 187–194.

White, P. (1982). Beliefs about conscious experience. In G. Underwood, ed., *Aspects of consciousness*. London: Academic Press.

Whitty, C. W. M., and W. Lewin (1960). A Korsakoff syndrome in the post-cingulectomy confusional state. *Brain* 83, 648–653.

Winograd, T. (1975). Understanding natural language. In D. Bobrow and A. Collins, eds., *Representation and understanding*. New York: Academic Press.

Young, A. W. (1988). Functional organisation of visual recognition. In L. Weiskrantz, ed., *Thought without language*. London: Oxford University Press.

Zihl, J. (1980). 'Blindsight': Improvement of visually guided eye movements by systematic practice in patients with cerebral blindness. *Neuropsychologia* 18, 71–77.

IV

Metaphysics

19 Object Perception

Elizabeth S. Spelke

Problems of Perceiving Objects

The capacity to perceive objects is as intriguing as the capacity to perceive surfaces, and it raises new issues and problems. As adults, we perceive the surrounding world as a layout of persisting physical bodies. Perception of objects is usually immediate, effortless, and accurate. Object perception is a puzzling achievement, however, because visual information for objects is both incomplete and potentially misleading. Objects come to us in a continuous surface array in which they sit upon and beside each other. Objects also are partly hidden: the back of every opaque object is hidden by its front, and the front surfaces of most objects are partly hidden behind other objects (fig. 19.1). Finally, the images of objects continually enter and leave the visual field as we shift fixation and as objects move in relation to one another. Despite these complexities, we perceive objects as bounded bodies that are distinct from one another, as complete bodies that continue where they are hidden, and as persisting bodies that exist whether they are in or out of view.

Theories of Object Perception and Its Development

Like those who study surface perception, students of object perception have attempted to shed light on these abilities, in part, by turning to development. Two theories have dominated discussion. According to one thesis, again from the empiricist tradition, newborn perceivers experience just the momentarily visible surfaces in a scene. As children move around surfaces and manipulate them, they learn how different views of an object are related (Helmholtz 1866) and how object unity and boundaries can be predicted from certain properties of visible sur-

From E. Spelke, Origins of visual knowledge, in D. N. Osherson et al., *Visual cognition and action: An invitation to cognitive science*, vol. 2 (1990). Cambridge, MA: MIT Press, Reprinted by permission.

Figure 19.1 A typical visual environment (child's birthday party). Cups, plates, napkins, and chairs are recognizable, although each is partly occluded. Cups and plates are also seen as distinct, even when their images are adjacent.

faces such as their proximity, their similarity in texture and color, and the alignment of their edges (Brunswik and Kamiya 1953). This learning eventually allows children to infer complete and bounded objects from partial visual information.

The principal rival to empiricist theory has come from Gestalt psychology, an early twentieth-century movement that attempted to explain perception in terms of the intrinsic organizational properties of complex physical systems (see Koffka 1953; Köhler 1947). Because of its nature as a physical system, the brain was thought to tend toward a state of equilibrium. This physical tendency was thought to have a psychological counterpart: perceivers tend to confer the simplest, most regular, and most balanced organization on their experience. Thus, perceivers group together surfaces so as to form units that are maximally homogeneous in color and texture and maximally smooth and regular in shape (Wertheimer 1923; Koffka 1935). The tendency toward simplicity allows perceivers to apprehend the boundaries, the unity, and the persistence of most objects, because physical objects tend to be relatively homogeneous in substance and regular in form. Since the tendency toward simplicity follows from innate properties of the nervous system, learning was thought to play no essential role in the development of object perception.

Like theories of surface perception, these theories changed over the years as more was learned about perception, its physical basis, and its computational structure. The core of the debate between empiricist and Gestalt theories has remained alive, however, and it has stimulated research both on the modifiability of object perception in adults and on the development of object perception in infancy.

The Modifiability of Object Perception in Adults

Like Helmholtz, the Gestalt psychologists attempted to test their theory by studying the effects of experience on a mature perceiver's apprehension of objects. Their experiments appeared to show, however, that experience has little or no effect on object perception. In the most famous learning experiments (Gottschaldt 1926) subjects were repeatedly shown a complex figure, and then they were shown a simple figure that had been embedded within it (fig. 19.2a). They were asked if the simple figure looked familiar. Even after viewing the complex

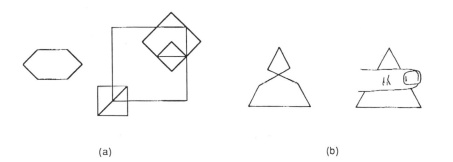

(a)   (b)

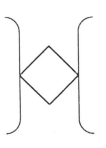

(c)

Figure 19.2 Some noneffects of knowledge or experience on perceptual organization: (a) after hundreds of exposures to a complex figure (right), subjects fail to recognize a simpler figure embedded within it (left) (after Gottschaldt 1926); (b) after viewing an irregular triangle, subjects still perceive a simple, complete figure when the irregular region is occluded, contrary to what they know is there (after Michotte et al. 1964); (c) a single abstract figure is perceived, despite the presence of the familiar embedded letters "M" and "W" (after Wertheimer 1923).

figure on hundreds of occasions, the subjects failed to recognize the simpler figure within it. What they learned from their encounters with the complex visual display appeared to depend on their organization of that display.

In a later demonstration (Michotte et al. 1964) Michotte showed subjects a triangle with an irregular center, and then he covered its irregular regions by a finger (see figure 19.2b). Asked what they saw when the figure was covered, Michotte's subjects reported a complete, regular triangle, despite what they had apparently learned about the display. Michotte concluded that intrinsic organizing tendencies are impervious to explicit knowledge or instruction. Demonstrations by Wertheimer (1923; fig. 19.2c) and by Kanizsa (1979) support the same conclusion.

These experiments have been thoroughly criticized. Just because learning cannot be demonstrated in one laboratory session with adults, it is argued, one cannot conclude that learning does not occur in infancy. Adults might learn to perceive objects differently if they were given more time in which to learn. Moreover, even if learning never occurred for adults, such learning might occur earlier in life. For example, most adults never learn to speak a second language without a detectable foreign accent. Accents are not innate, however; they are acquired by speakers as children. Demonstrations of a lack of plasticity in adults do not imply a lack of plasticity during development.

Nevertheless, a different lesson may be drawn from the Gestalt experiments: what one learns from a given experience depends on how one organizes that experience. This lesson comes originally from the work of the philosopher Immanuel Kant (1781). It was expounded forcefully by Köhler (1947) in a classic critique of the empiricist theory of object perception. Suppose, Köhler reasoned, that object perception is learned. How does this learning take place? An empiricist would reply that children learn to perceive objects by encountering them repeatedly, observing each object under various circumstances. For example, a child might learn to perceive a violin by encountering the violin on a table, in its case, in the hands of a violinist, and so forth. At different times the violin would appear at different distances and orientations and under different conditions of illumination. Eventually, each of these encounters would become associated with the others and with experiences such as hearing a violin sonata, touching the violin's strings, and hearing the word *violin*. Perception of the violin would emerge from this network of associations.

To proponents of such a theory, Köhler posed this question: How does the child determine which of his sensory experiences should be associated together to form the perceptual experience of a violin? What tells the child, for example, that the sight of a violin on a table should be linked to the sight of a violin in the hands of a violinist and not to the sight of a lamp on a table? In order to associate the violin's appearances with one another, one needs to perceive, somehow, that all those appearances are appearances of the same object—the violin. But that perceptual ability is just what the empiricists were attempting to explain by learning. The empiricist explanation seems to turn in a circle, presupposing the very ability that it seeks to explain: how one perceives a bounded, unitary, and constant violin from changing and varying arrays of light.

Köhler's argument suggests that what one learns from experience will depend on how one organizes that experience, and the demonstrations by Gottschaldt, Michotte, and Wertheimer appear to underline the point. Can this point be reconciled with the possibility that perceptual organization itself is subject to learning? I think it can, if the organization of surfaces into objects, like the perception of surfaces in depth, normally depends on multiple and redundant sources of information. If perceivers begin with a small set of mechanisms for detecting this organization, sufficient for recognizing objects under certain conditions, then they could learn to perceive objects by other means. But how do infants perceive objects initially, and how do they extend their initial abilities by learning? Developmental research can best address this question.

Object Perception in Infancy

Research on object perception in infancy began with studies of perception of partly occluded objects (Kellman and Spelke 1983). These studies used an experimental method, developed by Fantz (1961), that assesses infants' preferential looking at familiar and novel displays. When young infants are presented repeatedly with the same visual display, they tend to look at it less and less. If the infants are then presented with the original display and with a new display, they tend to look longer at the new display. This preference indicates that infants discriminate the two displays and detect the novelty of the second display. Fantz's method— often called the *habituation/dishabituation method*—has since been used to study a variety of perceptual capacities in infancy, including the capacity to perceive the complete shape of an object that is partly hidden.

Four-month-old infants were presented with an object whose top and bottom were visible but whose center was occluded by a nearer object (fig. 19.3). They saw this display repeatedly until their visual interest declined, and then they were shown a complete object, which corresponded to the display adults report seeing behind the occluder, and two object fragments, which corresponded to the visible surfaces of the partly hidden object. Infants were expected to look longer at whichever display appeared more novel to them. If they experienced the display as a mosaic of visible surface fragments, they should have looked longer at the complete object; if they organized the occlusion display into a single continuous unit, they should have looked longer at the fragmented object.

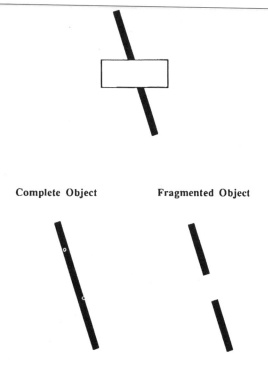

Figure 19.3 Habituation display (top) and test displays (bottom) for an experiment on infants' perception of partly occluded objects (after Kellman and Spelke 1983).

Like adults, infants were found to perceive a center-occluded object as a complete and continuous unit if the visible areas of the object moved in unison. Motion in depth was as effective as vertical or lateral motion—further evidence for depth perception in infancy. Unlike adults, however, infants did not perceive the completeness of a center-occluded, stationary object of a simple shape. Familiarization with such an object was followed by increased looking both at the complete and at the fragmented displays, with no preference between those displays. It appeared that the infants' perception of the stationary displays was indeterminate, as in an adult's perception of a stationary, center-occluded object with irregular coloring and form.

These studies provided evidence that motion specifies object unity to infants but that static configurational properties do not. Similar conclusions were suggested by investigations of young infants' perception of object boundaries. Three-to five-month-old infants were presented with displays of two objects, arranged so that their images overlapped at the infants' eyes. Perception of the objects' boundaries was tested in various ways, including preferential looking methods (for details, see Spelke

1985). All the studies provided evidence that infants perceived object boundaries by detecting the spatial arrangements of surfaces: two objects were perceived as distinct units if they were separated in depth. Infants also perceived object boundaries by detecting the relative motions of surfaces: two objects were perceived as distinct if they moved independently, even if they touched throughout their motion. Infants did *not* perceive object boundaries, however, by analyzing the static, configurational properties of surfaces: two adjacent, motionless objects were not perceived as distinct, even if they differed in color, texture, and shape. Unlike adults, young infants perceived neither the unity nor the boundaries of objects by analyzing the static, configurational properties of visual arrays.

Experiments by Schmidt (1985) have focused on the development of sensitivity to static configurational information for object unity. Children are sensitive to the properties of figural simplicity and color/texture similarity by 2 years of age. Sensitivity to these properties appears to emerge gradually; the development of gestalt perception is a slow process. For example, 7-month-old infants perceive a stationary, center-occluded object as a single, continuous unit if the object is three-dimensional and its visible surfaces are coplanar, with collinear edges and homogeneous coloring. If these same relationships indicate that two partly occluded surfaces lie on distinct objects, however, 7-month-old infants' perception of the occlusion display is indeterminate, in contrast to the perceptions of adults. These findings suggest that gestalt organization by the principles of good continuation and similarity is not a unitary phenomenon.

We have considered infants' perception of objects as unitary and bounded. What about their perception of objects as persisting over a succession of sporadic encounters? Experimenters have recently begun to investigate this ability, by means of the same preferential looking method. In one study 4-month-old infants were habituated to events in which one or two objects moved in and out of view behind one or two occluders (for details, see Spelke 1988). For different groups of subjects, the identity or distinctness of the object(s) was specified by the apparent continuity of the path of object motion, the apparent discontinuity of the path of object motion, the apparently constant speed of object motion, or the apparently irregular speed of object motion. Figure 19.4 depicts the displays for the first and second conditions. Perception of object identity or distinctness was assessed by presenting the infants, after habituation, with fully visible events involving one or two objects (fig. 19.4). Patterns of looking at these test events provided evidence that the infants perceived object identity by analyzing the spatiotemporal continuity of motion, as do adults: when object motion was discontinuous, infants perceived two objects, each moving continuously through part of the scene. In contrast to adults, infants did not perceive

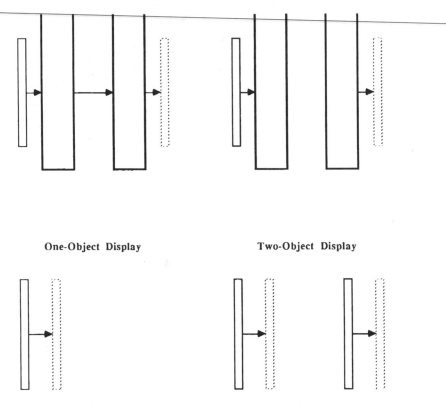

Figure 19.4 Habituation displays (top) and test displays (bottom) for an experiment on infants' apprehension of the identity of objects that leave and return to the field of view. An object's initial and final positions are indicated, respectively, by solid and dotted lines (after Spelke 1988).

object identity or distinctness by analyzing the apparent constancy or change of an object's speed of motion. The development of this last ability has not been investigated.

In summary, humans have some early-developing abilities to perceive the unity, the boundaries, and the identity of objects in visual scenes. These abilities are present before the onset of visually directed reaching or independent locomotion. Capacities to apprehend objects appear to emerge without benefit of trial-and-error motor learning.

Unlike adults, young infants fail to apprehend objects by analyzing the static configurational properties or the velocity relations of surfaces so as to form units that are maximally simple and homogeneous or that move in maximally regular ways. Some of the latter abilities have been shown to emerge quite early in development, however, before infants can locomote around objects or communicate with others about them. Capacities to perceive objects thus appear to be extended spontaneously over the course of early development.

Experiments on infants' perception of objects cast doubt on the two theories with which we began. Contrary to empiricist theory, infants can perceive the unity and boundaries of certain objects before they can reach for objects or locomote around them. Contrary to Gestalt theory, however, infants fail to perceive objects by organizing arrays of surfaces into units with the most regular shapes, colors, and textures. This failure is especially striking, because experiments provide evidence that infants do detect these configurational properties (for discussion, see Spelke 1988). Infants detect the static configurational properties of a visual scene, but they do not appear to use these properties when they divide the scene into objects. Young infants divide surfaces into objects only by analyzing the three-dimensional arrangements and motions of surfaces.

On the positive side, young infants appear to apprehend objects by analyzing the arrangements and the motions of surfaces so as to form units that are *cohesive* (the units are spatially connected and move as wholes), *bounded* (the units are spatially distinct from one another and move independently), and *spatiotemporally continuous* (the units exist continuously and move on connected paths). What kind of mechanism could accomplish this?

Two sets of experiments provide evidence that the mechanism of object perception is quite central. The first studies, by Kellman (see especially Kellman et al. 1987), investigated the conditions under which infants perceive object unity from surface motion. In particular, the experiments investigated whether infants perceive the unity of an object by analyzing the two-dimensional displacements of its images in a relatively low-level representation (such as Marr's primal sketch) or by analyzing the three-dimensional displacements of its surfaces in a higher-level representation (such as Marr's $2\frac{1}{2}$-D sketch).

Infants were presented with a center-occluded object under four conditions of motion (fig. 19.5). In the first condition both the infant and the object were stationary. In the second condition the infant was stationary and the object moved laterally, producing both image and surface displacements. In the third condition the infant was moved in an arc around the stationary object; the motion of the infant produced nearly the same two-dimensional displacement of the object's images as the object motion in the second condition, without any true displacement of the object's surfaces. In the fourth condition the infant again was moved in an arc but the object moved so as to cancel any two-dimensional displacement of the object's images. Infants were found to perceive the unity of the object in the second and fourth conditions, in which the object moved, but not in the first or third condition, in which it did not. Two-dimensional image displacements were neither necessary (fourth condition) nor sufficient (third condition) for perception of object unity. It appears, therefore, that mechanisms for perceiving objects take as input representations of the three-dimensional layout as it

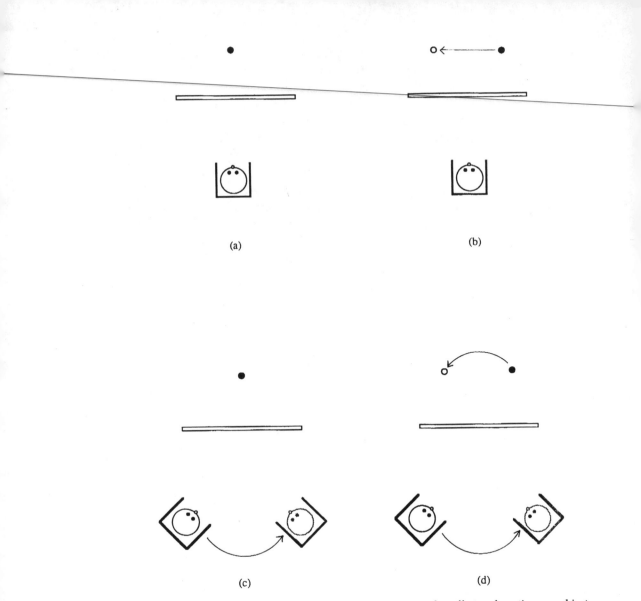

Figure 19.5 Habituation displays for experiments on the effects of motion on object perception, seen from above (after Kellman and Spelke 1983 and Kellman, Gleitman, and Spelke 1987). The displays present (a) neither image motion nor object motion, (b) both image motion and object motion, (c) image motion but no object motion, and (d) object motion but no image motion.

is perceived, rather than operating on more primitive, two-dimensional image representations. Representations of objects are constructed after, and on the basis of, representations of three-dimensional surface arrangements and motions.

The second series of studies, by Streri and Spelke (1988, 1989), investigated object perception in the tactile mode. In particular, the experiments investigated whether infants perceive the unity and boundaries of objects under the same conditions when they feel objects as when they see them. Four-month-old infants held two spatially separated rings, one in each hand, under a cloth that blocked their view of the rings and of the space between them (fig. 19.6). In different conditions the rings either could be moved rigidly together or could be moved independently, and they either shared a common substance, texture, and shape or differed on these dimensions. Perception of the connectedness or separateness of the rings was tested by means of a habituation-of-holding-time method similar to that used with visual displays (for details, see Streri and Spelke 1988).

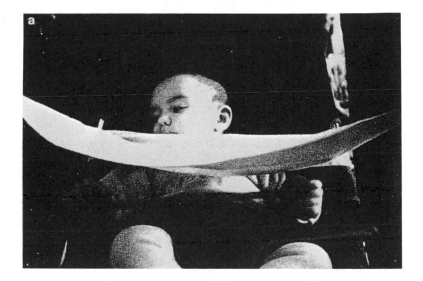

Figure 19.6 Habituation displays for an experiment on infants' perception of object boundaries through active touch. (Adapted from Streri and Spelke 1988 by permission of the publisher, Academic Press.)

The infants were found to perceive the two rings as a single unit that extended between their hands if the rings could only be moved rigidly together; they perceived the rings as two distinct objects separated by a gap if the rings could be moved independently. Perception was unaffected by the static configurational properties of the ring displays. These findings indicate that 4-month-old infants perceive object unity and boundaries under the same conditions in the visual and tactile modes. That finding, in turn, suggests that the mechanisms of object perception are amodal. Humans may not be endowed with visual and tactile mechanisms for perceiving objects; we may perceive objects by means of a single set of mechanisms, located more centrally in the brain, that operate on representations of surfaces derived from either sensory modality.

All these findings suggest that perceiving objects may be more akin to *thinking* about the physical world than to *sensing* the immediate environment (Spelke 1988). That suggestion, in turn, echoes suggestions from philosophers and historians of science that theories of the world determine the objects one takes to inhabit the world (Quine 1960; Kuhn 1962; Jacob 1970). Just as scientists may be led by their conceptions of biological activities and processes to divide living beings into organs, cells, and molecules, so infants may divide perceived surfaces into objects in accord with implicit conceptions that physical bodies move as wholes, separately from one another, on connected paths.

Overview

Before human infants can reach for objects to manipulate them, they can already perceive objects as bounded, as complete, and as persisting over occlusion, under certain conditions. As Köhler proposed, mechanisms for organizing the world into objects may be present and functional before infants learn about particular objects and their properties, and they may serve as a foundation for such learning.

Nevertheless, young infants do not appear to experience the same arrangements of objects that adults do. When they face a stationary array such as that in figure 19.1 they do not segment that array into objects by analyzing relationships such as edge and surface continuity, or color and texture similarity, in accord with a tendency to maximize figural goodness. The development of this tendency is not understood, but it appears to be a long and gradual process. Gestalt organizational phenomena may not depend, at any age, on general rules or wholistic processes but rather on a wealth of slowly accumulated knowledge about objects and their properties. If that is the case, then there are aspects of object perception in infancy that lend some support to empiricist conceptions of perceptual learning.

Research on the mechanisms of object perception in infancy suggests that those mechanisms are relatively central in two respects: they take as input a representation of the surface layout as it is perceived, rather than operating directly on more primitive sensory representations, and they are amodal, operating on representations derived from different perceptual systems. Object perception may depend on the same mechanisms for adults, despite the rapidity and the apparent "impenetrability" of the processes by which we as adults apprehend the things around us. Here is a case in which studies of infancy may shed light on mature cognitive processes: they may reveal processes that operate throughout life but that are hard to discern in adulthood beneath the layers of skills and knowledge that adults have acquired.

There is a second way in which studies of infants may shed light on the perceptual knowledge of adults. The properties that infants appear to find in the things around them—cohesion, bounds, and spatiotemporal continuity—are among the properties that are most central to our mature intuitive conceptions of physical bodies. Adults conceive quite easily of physical bodies with poor Gestalt properties: bodies that are irregular in shape (rocks), heterogeneous in substance (vacuum cleaners), and subject to complex patterns of motion (flags). We do not readily consider something as a physical body, however, if it lacks cohesion (a pile of leaves), bounds (a drop of water in a pool), or continuity (a row of flashing lights). The latter entities may be collections of objects or parts of objects, but they are not unitary and independent objects for us.

These observations suggest that the infant's first mechanisms for apprehending objects remain central to human perception and thought. As in the case of depth perception, early-developing capacities to apprehend objects may remain powerful capacities for adults. These capacities may be enriched but not fundamentally changed by the wealth of further abilities whose acquisition they support. Studies of infancy may help to reveal what these core capacities are.

References

Brunswik, E., and J. Kamiya (1953). Ecological cue-validity of "proximity" and of other Gestalt facts. *The American Journal of Psychology* 66, 20–32.

Ellis, W. D. (1939). *A source book of Gestalt psychology.* New York: Harcourt, Brace.

Fantz, R. L. (1961) The origin of form perception. *Scientific American* 204. 66–72.

Gottschaldt, K. (1926). On the influence of experience on the recognition of figures. *Psychologische Forschungen* 8, 261–317. (Edited and translated in Ellis 1939.)

Helmholtz, H. von (1866). *Treatise on physiological optics,* vol.III. (Translated by J. P. C. Southall, Optical Society of America, 1925.)

Jacob, F. (1970). *The logic of life.* Paris: Gallimard. (Translated by B. E. Spillman. New York: Pantheon, 1972.)

Kanizsa, G. (1979). *Organization in vision*. New York: Praeger.

Kant, I. (1781). Critique of pure reason. (Translated by N. Kemp Smith. London: Macmillan, 1929).

Kellman, P. J., H. Gleitman, and E. S. Spelke (1987). Object and observer motion in the perception of objects by infants. *Journal of Experimental Psychology: Human Perception and Performance* 13, 586–593.

Kellman, P. J., and E. S. Spelke (1983). Perception of partly occluded objects in infancy. *Cognitive Psychology* 15, 483–524.

Koffka, K. (1935). *Principles of Gestalt psychology*. New York: Harcourt, Brace.

Köhler, W. (1947). *Gestalt psychology*. London: Liveright.

Kuhn, T. S. (1962). *The structure of scientific revolutions*. Chicago: University of Chicago Press.

Michotte, A., R. Thinès, and G. Crabbé (1964). *The amodal completion of perceptual structures*. Louvain, Belgium: Publications Universitaires de Louvain.

Quine, W. V. O. (1960) *Word and object*. Cambridge, MA: MIT Press.

Schmidt, H. (1985). Gestalt perception in early childhood. Doctoral dissertation, Department of Psychology, University of Pennsylvania, Philadelphia, PA.

Spelke, E. S. (1985). Preferential looking methods as tools for the study of cognition in infancy. In G. Gottlieb and N. Krasnegor, eds., *Measurement of audition and vision in the first year of postnatal life*. Norwood, NJ: Ablex.

Spelke, E. S. (1988). Where perceiving ends and thinking begins: The apprehension of objects in infancy. In A. Yonas, ed., *Perceptual development in infancy. The Minnesota Symposia on Child Psychology, Vol. 20*. Hillsdale, NJ: Lawrence Erlbaum.

Streri, A., and E. S. Spelke (1988). Haptic perception of objects in infancy. *Cognitive Psychology* 20, 1–23.

Streri, A., and E. S. Spelke (1989). Effects of motion and figural goodness on haptic object perception in infancy. *Child Development* 60, 1111–1125.

Wertheimer, M. (1923). Principles of perceptual organization. *Psychologische Forschungen* 4, 301–350. (Edited and translated by M. Wertheimer in D. C. Beardslee and M. Wertheimer, eds., *Readings in perception*. Princeton, NJ: Van Nostrand, 1958.)

20 Ontological Categories Guide Young Children's Inductions of Word Meaning

Nancy N. Soja, Susan Carey, and Elizabeth S. Spelke

Introduction

Young children are word-learning wizards, acquiring new vocabulary at the prodigious rate of 8 to 10 items each day (Carey 1978; Miller 1977). Their achievement is especially intriguing at the early stages of word learning, when word meanings are most radically underdetermined by the evidence available to the child. When a child hears a word (say "George") while attending to an object (say a man), the word could refer to the individual (i.e., George himself), the type of object (e.g., person or man), an action involving the object (e.g., eating), a part of the object (e.g., ear), a property of the object (e.g., dirty), the substance of which the object is composed (e.g., skin), an abstraction that the object embodies (e.g., virtue), among countless other options. How do young children find their way through this labyrinth of possibilities to master the meanings of words?

Word Learning Prior to Ontological Commitments: Quine's View

Quine (1960) suggested that the youngest children do not master word meanings in ways that honor the above distinctions. Rather, ontological categories such as *object* and *substance* emerge as a consequence of language learning. Such distinctions therefore are not available to guide the acquisition process during the early stages of language learning.

More specifically, Quine suggested that children learn language by detecting contingencies between words and other perceptual experiences. Generalization of a word to a new experience is determined by global perceptual similarity within a "quality space" defined by the detectability and salience of perceptual dimensions. Because the young child has made no ontological commitments, each of his words refers only to "a history of sporadic encounters, a scattered portion of what goes on." Early words function most like mass nouns in the child's

From N. Soja, S. Carey, and E. Spelke, Ontological categories guide young children's inductions of word meaning, *Cognition* 38, 179–211 (1991). Reprinted by permission.

conceptual system.[1] For example, "book" refers to a portion of book experience, "mama" to a portion of mama experience (Quine 1960, 1969). Portions can be scattered—a portion of water can be distributed in drops over a table or collected in a cup. Similarly, portions of mama and book can be scattered or not. Children only begin to distinguish among different types of word meanings involving different types of quantification when they learn the syntax of quantification: determiners, plurals, and quantifiers such as "three," "some," and "another."

Quine's proposal actually embodies two separate, partially independent, claims. The first claim (hereafter Claim 1) is that until children have learned the syntax of quantification they do not conceptualize the world in terms of objects, non-solid substances, properties, and so on. That is, these ontological distinctions play no role whatsoever in the child's mental life. The child does not see a rock and a stick as inherently more similar to each other than a rock and a pile of mud.

According to the second claim children's perceptual/cognitive system may well pick out solid objects in the world, realizing, for example, the differing consequences of grasping objects versus non-solid substances. The concern of the second claim is how the child *quantifies* over these different types of entities. Quine's deep insight was that quantification is at the heart of the distinctions among different types of conceptual entities. Suppose children say "table" every time they see a table. We would not credit them with the same concept of *table* as we have if they could not represent the conceptual distinction between one table on different occasions and two different identical tables. This quantificational distinction underlies the difference between count nouns and proper names. Similarly, we would not credit them with the same concept of *table* as we have if they conceived of tables as any portions of experience that shared a common shape, or if they conceived of any part of a table as also a table. The language quantifies over tables differently from over sand or wood; tables are directly countable whereas sand and wood must be put into portions (cups of sand, sticks of wood) in order to be counted. Quine's second claim (hereafter Claim 2) is that until children have learned the syntax of quantification they lack any concepts of individuated whole objects, like "a table", or "Mama", and of portions of substances, like "this pile of sand" or "this stick of wood".[2]

According to Quine, then, when children hear a new word, the meaning they assign to it is determined by Procedure 0:

Procedure 0   Conclude that the word refers to aspects of the world that share salient properties of the perceptual experience when the word is used.

Psychologists have endorsed versions of Procedure 0 as well. Clark (1973), for example, conjectured that early words referred to salient perceptual properties. Landau et al. (1988) have added that the salient property that is weighted most strongly in this perceptual space is shape.

There is a problem with the mechanism Quine offers for how children come to share the ontological commitments of their language community. Consider, for example, the quantifiers that distinguish mass terms (e.g., "more water") from count terms (e.g., "another stick"). If a child already understood "water" to refer to portions of a kind of substance and "stick" to refer to individual whole objects, then he might discover the meanings of "more" and "another" by observing that each expression was used when an additional individual of the appropriate kind appeared ("another stick") or an additional portion of the appropriate kind appeared ("more water"). However, if the child understood "stick" to refer to a part of stick experience, it is not clear what would prevent him from concluding that "another stick" means *more stick stuff, more stick experience*. Although Quine (1960) hints at the ways in which children work out the syntax of quantification, no explicit or plausible account of the learning process has been given.

An Alternative: Ontological Commitments Prior to Word Learning

This problem motivates an alternative to Quine's view: children may approach the task of learning language with a pre-existing set of ontological categories. That is, from the earliest stages of language acquisition, ontological commitments embodying the quantificational system of natural language syntax may guide their learning of new words. If humans approach the task of learning language with the ontological categories of object and substance, then their learning of words might proceed as follows. As in Quine's account, a child would detect a contingency between a word and a perceived state of the world. The child would represent the relevant state of the world, however, as a solid object or a non-solid substance (Step 1 of Procedures 1 and 2), provided that his perception centered on an entity of the appropriate type. Generalization of the word to new states of the world would depend on this representation, according to Procedures 1 and 2. Step 1 of each procedure embodies a denial of Claim 1: Step 2 embodies a denial of Claim 2.[3]

Procedure 1   Step 1: Test to see if the speaker could be talking about a solid object: if yes,

Step 2: Conclude the word refers to individual whole objects of the same type as the referent.

Procedure 2   Step 1: Test to see if the speaker could be talking about a non-solid substance; if yes,

Step 2: Conclude the word refers to portions of substance of the same type as the referent.

With respect to Quine's first claim, research with young infants suggests that prelinguistic humans conceptualize solid objects in a way that distinguishes them from non-solid substances (Spelke 1985). For human infants, solid objects are bodies that are cohesive, bounded, spatiotemporally continuous, and solid or substantial; they move as connected wholes, independently of one another, on connected paths through unoccupied space. There is no research on infants' appreciation of non-solid substances, such as liquids, gels, and powders, in terms of the same parameters that define objects for infants. Non-solid substances are spatiotemporally continuous and substantial, but not cohesive or bounded; they do not retain either their internal connectedness or their external boundaries as they move and contact one another.

Even if infants make a principled distinction between objects and non-solid substances, it does not follow that they quantify over representations of entities of each type, nor that this distinction is relevant for word learning. Two quantificational distinctions are relevant to Procedures 1 and 2: that between individuated entities and portions of non-individuated entities and that between unique individuals and types. A given car could be conceptualized as a portion of metal and glass, as a car-shaped portion of experience, or as an individual whole object. Once it is so conceptualized, it could be thought of as a token of a type ("a hatchback," "chrome") or as a unique individual ("my own car Bessie," "my favorite pile of metal"). Notice that the quantificational distinction between individuals and portions of unindividuated entities is conceptually prior to the distinction between unique individuals and tokens of a type.

Methodological Issues and Problems

Despite the wealth of recent research on language acquisition, existing studies of children's word learning do not distinguish between Quine's thesis, embodied in Procedure 0, and the alternative outlined above, embodied in Procedures 1 and 2. The failure of research to distinguish these views is surprising, because many observations and experiments appear to suggest that the Quinean view is wrong.

For example, observations of child language during the one-word stage (i.e., before the productive use of syntax) reveal that children quickly gain productive command of object words such as "ball", substance words such as "milk", and non-referential expressions such as "hi". Nevertheless, these observations do not reveal whether such words have the same meanings for young children as they have for adults. Each might refer to a scattered portion of what goes on, consistent with Quine's view. In fact, other observations suggest that the Quinean interpretation may be correct. Many psychologists have argued that children's earliest word meanings are sometimes complexive (Bowerman 1978; Dromi 1987; Vygotsky 1962). That is, children appear to extend words to new referents on the basis of any of the salient perceptual properties of the original referent. These complexive uses often violate ontological categories, as when "paper" apparently refers to the act of cutting, to the act of drawing, to pens and pencils, and to paper (Dromi 1987). If such uses actually reflect attempts to name, rather than other speech acts, these observations support Quine's claim. Even after the decline of complexive overgeneralizations at about 18 months (Dromi 1987), we do not know whether words like "ball" refer to kinds of objects or perceptual properties like shape (see below).

Potentially better evidence that prelinguistic ontological commitments guide word learning comes from experimental studies of word learning. The distinction between objects and substances (or objects and parts) has been investigated in a number of experiments. Children have been taught a new word in the presence of an unnamed object and then tested on their generalization of the word to new objects. Children generalized words to new objects that adults would describe as whole individuated objects of the same type, rather than to perceptually similar entities that were not objects of the same type. For example, children generalized a word that was initially applied to one object to a new object of the same shape, in preference to a new object of a different shape but the same material, and in preference to a new object consisting only of a part of the original object (Markman and Wachtel 1988).

Unfortunately, these findings do not permit a choice between the Quinean view and its rival, for two reasons. First, the subjects in most of these studies were over $3\frac{1}{2}$, old enough to have mastered the relevant natural language syntax. It is not clear whether their ontological commitments preceded or followed their acquisition of the corresponding syntactic forms. Second and more seriously, these studies do not reveal whether children interpreted the new word as a term for a type of individuated object or in some other way more congenial to Quine's view. For example, Landau et al. (1988) have suggested that children's first nouns refer to shapes: "book" means *book-shaped*, "clock" means *clock-shaped*, etc. Unlike adults, that is, children may think that "clock" would refer to a clock-shaped pile of ashes and not to time-keeping devices that are not round. This suggestion will be discussed, and criticized, below (see General Discussion). It is consistent, however, with the Markman and Wachtel findings. Early learning of words for objects could depend exclusively on processes of contingency detection and generalization through a quality space in which shape is a highly salient dimension.[4]

A Better Method
These problems suggest what a better test of Quine's thesis requires. First, such a test must focus simultaneously on children's learning of words for entities in different ontological categories. If children generalize words to new situations on the basis of global perceptual similarity, then the same perceptual dimensions (such as shape) should govern

generalization regardless of the ontological category of the referent. In contrast, if ontological distinctions govern word learning, then generalization to new instances should depend on the ontological category of the entity to which the child first hears the word applied. Second, to capture how the child quantifies entities of different ontological categories, the choices offered to the child for generalization must reflect different quantificational options. Specifically, if the distinction between *portion* and *individual* is at issue, the options offered should vary in the numbers of pieces or piles the entity is broken into. Third, such a test must focus on children's inductions at the very beginning of language learning, before they begin to understand and use the quantificational syntax of mass terms and count terms.

The research reported here attempts to meet these requirements. Children were presented with two word-learning tasks. In one task, they were taught a new term for a solid object. In a second task, they were taught a new term for a non-solid substance. After learning the term, they were tested for generalization to two new instances: one instance that matched the original instance in *shape* and *number* but not *substance*, and one instance that matched the original instance in *substance* but not *shape* or *number*.

On object trials, a word was introduced in the presence of a solid object, and then children were tested for generalization to a new object of the same shape versus three pieces of the same substance. If the ontological category of "object" governs generalization then children should generalize to the new single object; the requirement that objects be cohesive (Spelke 1985) rules out the three spatially distinct bodies as one object. Additionally, if the subjects know that objects are quantified over individuals then they should rule out the three spatially distinct bodies as another individual object of the same type.

Nonetheless, selection of the new single object could as easily be explained by a Quinean quality space in which shape similarity or numerical similarity is more important than substance, color, or texture similarity. This possibility was tested by the substance trials. A word was introduced in the presence of a non-solid substance appearing in one (or several) piles. Children were then tested for generalization to the same substance in a different number of piles (several or one) versus a different substance in the same number and shape of piles as the original exemplar. If generalization depends on global perceptual similarity within a quality space free of ontological distinctions, then children should show the same generalization patterns for the substance trials as for the object trials. In contrast, if generalization is based on the categorization of an entity as an object or substance, and if substances are quantified over portions, then a different pattern of generalization should be seen. Children should generalize the substance word to the same substance in a new number of piles and not to the different substance in the same number of piles. The spatial distribution of parts of a portion of material are irrelevant to the identity of the material.

Our experiments were conducted with very young children, aged 2 years or 2 years, 6 months. Two-year-olds do not command count/mass syntax; 2½-year-olds are in the process of mastering it (Gordon 1982, 1985). Children's command of the relevant syntax was tested in two ways. First, comprehension of count/mass syntax was tested by teaching children the new words for objects and for substances under two conditions: a neutral syntax condition and an informative syntax condition. In the neutral syntax condition, the subcategorization of the word was ambiguous; in the informative syntax condition, selective count syntax was used with the term applied to the object and selective mass syntax was used with the term applied to the non-solid substance. If children comprehend the syntactic distinction, then their adherence to Procedures 1 and 2 should be greater in the informative syntax condition. Second, productive command of count/mass syntax was tested by obtaining speech production samples from each child and assessing his or her mastery of noun phrase syntax. If mastery of syntax leads to mastery of principles 1 and 2, as Quine proposed, then children who do not benefit from the informative syntax and who have not begun to produce the relevant count/mass syntax should fail to honor these principles.

Experiment 1

Method

Subjects   Subjects were 24 2-year-olds (mean age, 2;1), ranging from 1;10 to 2;3. They were recruited from the greater Boston area and randomly placed into two groups (neutral syntax and informative syntax) with equal numbers of boys and girls in each group. Testing was begun with three other subjects but not finished; these three had no understanding of the task and could not complete a trial. Testing was conducted at the subjects' homes. The subjects received $5.00 each for their participation.

Procedure and Stimuli   Each testing session began with two familiar trials: one object trial and one substance trial. The stimuli in the familiar object trial were a blue plastic cup, a white styrofoam cup, and cup pieces. The stimuli in the familiar non-solid substance trial were peanut butter and Play-doh. These trials followed the same format as the unfamiliar trials described below. The two familiar trials were followed by eight unfamiliar trials: four object trials and four substance trials which were intermingled. The subjects were tested on each trial on two separate occasions. Eight novel words were used: "blicket," "stad," "mell," "coodle," "doff," "tannin," "fitch," and "tulver." Each word was used to refer to substances and objects across subjects.

An Unfamiliar Object Trial in the Neutral Syntax Condition   The child was presented with an unfamiliar object (see fig. 20.1). Four different sorts of objects were used: apple corers (orange plastic and aluminum); plumbing fixtures shaped like a "T" (copper and white plastic); childhood toys often called cootie catchers or fortune tellers (orange acetate and silver paper) and honey dippers (wooden and clear plastic). The objects were given names. For example, the experimenter said "This is my blicket." The experimenter then continued to talk about the object using "my," "the," and "this" for determiners. She and the subject manipulated the object. The object was placed to the side and two other sets of objects were presented directly in front of the subject. One set contained one object that was the same sort of object as the original but made out of a different material. For example, if the original object was a metal "T", then the second object was a plastic "T". The other set of objects contained three or four chunks made of the same material as the original object. They were small and in arbitrary shapes. In the present example they would have been four small pieces of metal. The experimenter said, "Point to the blicket". Both objects of each type were used as the named object across subjects.

An Unfamiliar Substance Trial in the Neutral Syntax Condition   Figure 20.1 shows a sample unfamiliar substance trial. The child was shown one of the unfamiliar substances and was told, for example, "This is my stad." The experimenter referred to the substance using only "my," "the," and "this" for determiners. The substance was presented in a single pile for half of the trials and in three or four small piles for the other trials. The experimenter and the subject talked about the substance and played with it. In the presentation of test substances the subject was shown two substances, the original and the new one, and told "Point to the stad." The original substance was in the alternative configuration, whereas the new substance was in the configuration used

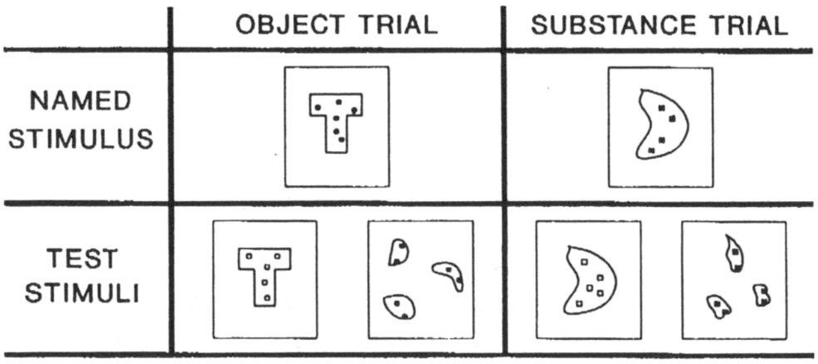

	OBJECT TRIAL	SUBSTANCE TRIAL
NAMED STIMULUS		
TEST STIMULI		

Figure 20.1 An example of an object trial and a substance trial in Experiment 1 (filled circles indicate metal, open circles indicate plastic, filled squares indicate Dippity-do, and open squares indicate lump Nivea).

originally with the named substance. There were four pairs of substances: (1) Dippity-do (a setting gel) and lumpy Nivea (a hand cream mixed with gravel); (2) coffee (freeze-dried) and orzo (a rice-shaped pasta); (3) sawdust and leather (cut into tiny pieces); and (4) Crazy Foam and clay. Of each pair one member was named and the other was used as the alternative to the original in the test presentation. Each member served in both roles across subjects.

The syntax used in the neutral condition determined that the new word was a noun, but did not indicate whether it was a count noun or a mass noun. However, if the subjects knew both count/mass syntax and its relation to objects and substances, half of the substance trials provided syntactic evidence about the referent, namely the substance trials in which the original substance was presented in multiple piles. To see why, consider "This is my glass." If the referent is a single glass made out of glass, the syntax is neutral as to whether the object or substance is the referent. However, if the referent is many glasses, then "glass" must be being used as a mass noun because only mass nouns are used with singular verbs and singular nouns when referring to multiple items.[5]

Object and Substance Trials in the Informative Syntax Condition   The informative syntax condition differed from the neutral syntax condition only in the determiners and quantifiers used when naming the original stimulus. The experimenter introduced an object trial in the informative syntax condition with "This is a blicket" and used "a blicket" and "another blicket" in subsequent discussion. Substance trials in the informative syntax condition were introduced with "This is stad" and in subsequent discussion the experimenter continued to omit determiners or use "some" or "some more." These determiners were chosen because in production they are among the earliest selective determiners used by 2-year-olds (Gordon 1982). Also, in comprehension, 3-year-olds can determine the subcategorization of a noun based on its previous occurrence with one of these determiners (Gordon 1985). The trials in the neutral and informative syntax conditions differed only in the introducing events: in both cases the test items were prefaced with the neutral "Which is the xxx?"

Before and after testing the experimenter played with the subject. The entire period of involvement with the subject was tape recorded, but only the productions from the play periods were used in the analyses of linguistic competence. Competence with count/mass syntax can be defined in different ways. One definition is that competence is achieved when the child's use of determiners and plural endings differs depending on the noun type. When children achieve this level of competence, they are using two different systems of individuation and quantification. It is this aspect of the count/mass distinction that reflects the object/substance distinction and that is relevant to Quine's argument. Therefore, a syntax score was found for each subject that reflected their ability to use determiners and plural endings differently for the two kinds of nouns.

Results and Discussion

Familiar Word Trials   The data are depicted in terms of the percentage of trials in which the child matched the shape and number of the originally named stimulus. Points above 50 indicate that the subjects chose the stimulus of the original shape and number, as predicted for the object trials. Points below 50 indicate that the subjects chose the stimulus of the original substance as predicted for the substance trials. The further a point is from 50 in either direction, the further it is from chance.

Not surprisingly, subjects in both conditions did well on the familiar object trials. That is, they said that the cup was the cup, rather than the group of pieces of a previously named cup (neutral syntax condition: 96%; informative syntax condition: 79%). They also did well on the familiar substance trials. That is, for example, they said that pieces of

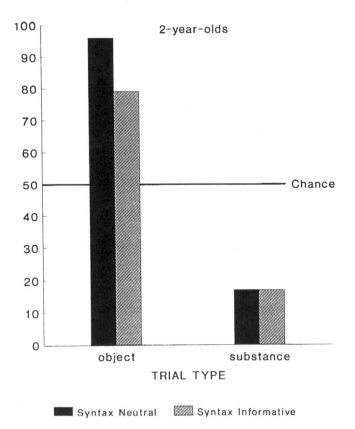

Figure 20.2 Mean percentage of responses by shape and number as a function of trial type (Experiment 1, familiar word trials).

Soja, Carey, and Spelke

Play-doh were Play-doh, rather than a single pile of peanut butter shaped like an earlier named pile of Play-doh (neutral syntax condition: 17%; informative syntax condition: 17%). A 4-way repeated-measure ANOVA compared the effects of session (First × Second), trial type (Object × Substance), syntax group (Neutral × Informative), and sex of subject (Female × Male). There was a significant main effect of trial type ($F(1,20) = 61.489$, $p < .001$). No other main effects or interactions were significant (all $Fs < 2.7$, $ps > .118$). The subjects' performance significantly differed from chance on both kinds of trials (object: $t(23) = 8.351$, $p < .001$, 2-tailed; substance: $t(23) = 5.826$, $p < .001$, 2-tailed). In sum, the subjects differentiated the object and substance trials, as predicted.

Word-Learning Trials Subjects differentiated the two types of trials. Responses were consistent with shape and number on the object trials (neutral syntax: 93%; informative syntax: 94%) and were not consistent with shape and number on the substance trials (neutral syntax: 24%; informative syntax: 38%).

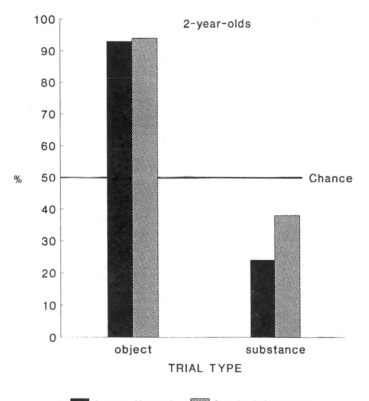

Figure 20.3 Mean percentage of responses by shape and number as a function of trial type (Experiment 1, word-learning trials).

Ontological Categories Guide Young Children's Inductions of Word Meaning

A 4-way repeated-measure ANOVA analyzed the effects of session (First × Second), stimulus pairs (the 8 different stimulus pairs—4 object and 4 substance), syntax group (Neutral × Informative), and sex of subject (Female × Male). The only significant effect was stimulus ($F(7,140) = 29.266$, $p < .001$: all other Fs < 1.992, ps > .174). A pre-planned contrast testing the difference between the object trials and the substance trials was significant ($F(1,140) = 202.105$, $p < .001$). In fact, 99% of the total sum of squares is attributable to this contrast. Performance on both the object trials and the substance trials was significantly different from chance (object: $t(23) = 23.3$, $p < .001$, 2-tailed; substance: $t(23) = 3.6$, $p < .002$, 2-tailed).

The subjects performed more consistently on the object trials than the substance trials. There was a significant difference between the degree to which the object scores differed from chance compared to the degree to which the substance scores differed from chance ($t(23) = 4.897$, $p < .001$, 2-tailed).

A separate ANOVA compared the substance trials in which the substance was named in one big pile and the trials in which it was named in three or four small piles. The two did not differ ($F(1,22) = .226$, $p = .64$).

In sum, the children chose according to object type when the stimulus was an object and according to substance type when the stimulus was a non-solid substance. However, the subjects were more consistent when the stimulus was a solid object than when it was a non-solid substance. There was no effect of the syntactic context: performance was neither facilitated nor hindered by the additional syntactic information. Performance also was not affected by the configuration of the named substance in the substance trials.

Production Data Productive competence was assessed for 22 of the 24 subjects. One subject was not yet talking and therefore had no productions to assess. Another subject had a cold—which greatly affected his desire to talk, but not his desire to do the experiment, which all children found fun.

Most nouns used were count nouns (1467 count noun tokens compared to 153 mass noun tokens). The children's count/mass syntax was not very developed. Determiners were usually omitted (55% of count noun tokens and 75% of mass noun tokens). Plural inflections were also infrequent (15% of count noun tokens and 2% of mass noun tokens).

Approximately half (52%) of the mass noun types were non-solid substance words. No solid substance words (e.g., "metal," "plastic") were used. The other mass nouns referred to abstract entities (e.g., "magic"), superordinate substances (e.g., "food," "stuff"), and entities ambiguous as to their status as solid or non-solid substances (e.g., "grass," "ground"). Although children may well first learn non-solid substance words through their experience with food, 25% of the non-solid substance types were not food words (e.g., "sand," "toothpaste").

In order to assess each child's productive command of count/mass syntax, we examined the use of selective count noun frames. Nouns that appeared in neutral syntactic frames (e.g., "the dog," "the mud," "my house," "Sandy's sand") were removed from the analysis (15% of the noun tokens). We then calculated for each subject the percentage of count nouns occurring in selective count noun contexts—"a (noun)," "one (noun)," "(noun)-s," "the (noun)-s," "some (noun)-s," and "two (or a higher number) (noun)-s." High scores should indicate good control of count syntax, except for the fact that some subjects used "a" indiscriminately with count nouns and mass nouns, which yielded a high score that was misleading. To correct for such indiscriminate use, we subtracted from that score the percentage of mass nouns used in selective count noun contexts. The resultant score could be as high as 1, indicating full command of count syntax and differentiation of count and mass nouns, or as low as 0, indicating no productive control of this syntactic distinction.[6] The scores ranged from 0 to .88 (mean .38). Thus, there was a considerable range of control of count syntax. The two groups (syntax neutral and informative syntax) did not differ (neutral: .30; informative: .47; $t(20) = 1.517$, $p > .14$, 2-tailed).

To test whether subjects who distinguish objects from substances in the word-learning task have better command of count/mass syntax, we also needed a measure for each subject that reflected the child's differentiation of the object and substance trials. We took the difference between the object and substance scores. Difference scores ranged from 0 to 100 (mean .59), with high scores reflecting good differentiation of object and substance trials. There was no correlation between the syntax scores derived from the analysis of the subjects' speech and the word-learning scores ($r = .06$, $p > .3$, 1-tailed).

The lack of correlation could reflect the fact that the variability in the word-learning score was primarily due to performance on the substance trials (because performance was essentially at ceiling on the object trials) while the syntax score reflected competence with *count* syntax. This was unavoidable; when children omit determiners and plurals, they produce a correct mass frame ("(noun)"), but many children of this age omit determiners and plurals from all nouns. Consequently, a syntax score based on the discriminating use of mass noun syntax would be essentially the same as the score we did use, since the variance would be due to count nouns used in count noun syntactic frames.[7] The score we used reflected the differentiation between count and mass nouns as well as the use of count noun syntax, and it correlated with the number of mass nouns used ($r = .54$, $p < .005$, 1-tailed). Thus, it does reflect the child's emerging command of count/mass syntax and can be used to explore Quine's conjecture.

Procedures 1 and 2 have two steps relevant to the two interpretations of Quine's claim. Step 1 requires that children represent the distinction between objects and substances, and condition their projection of word meaning upon classifying the referent as one or the other. Step 1 thus embodies the denial of Claim 1, namely that young children do not represent the ontological distinction between objects and non-solid substances. The data from Experiment 1 show that different inferences about the meaning of a newly heard word are drawn according to the ontological status of its referent. If the word refers to an object, the child's projection respects shape and number, and ignores texture, color, and substance. If the word refers to a non-solid substance, the child's projection ignores shape and number, respecting texture, color and substance.

The data do not support Quine's conjecture that children learn the ontological distinction between objects and substances through mastering syntactic devices for individuation and quantification. There was no effect of productive control of count/mass syntax on performance on this task, even though many of the subjects had no productive control. Perhaps children's language production underestimates their knowledge of count/mass syntax. With this in mind we assessed whether the syntactic context in which a newly heard word occurred constrained our subjects' hypotheses about its meaning. It did not; subjects in the informative syntax condition performed no better than those in the neutral syntax condition. This was even true of the substance trials, on which our subjects were not at ceiling. Further, there was no difference in performance between the substance trials in which the named substance was in one big pile and the substance trials in which the named substance was in multiple small piles. Apparently, 2-year-old children do not exploit the syntactic information derivable from the fact that mass nouns can be used with singular verbs to refer to scattered portions.

We will hold off discussion of how the child is *quantifying* over objects and substances (Step 2 of Procedures 1 and 2; Quine's second claim) until the general discussion. . . .

General Discussion

Claim 1: Step 1 of Procedures 1 and 2
We can reject Procedure 0 as the basis of young toddlers' fixation of word meanings. The present results show that presyntactic infants[8] do see the world as composed of objects and non-solid substances (among other ontological types, presumably), and do condition the projection of word meanings in terms of this distinction. The salient perceptual features—shape, texture, number of entities—were the same for object trials and non-solid substance trials. Indeed, in Experiment 2 [omitted here—Ed.] we made the shapes of the non-solid substances more com-

plex and salient than those of the objects. Yet the subjects did not project word meaning according to the same perceptual features across the two sets of trials. A single similarity space based on perceptual salience cannot explain the pattern of results. A more complex perceptual similarity space, in which salience of perceptual features is context dependent (e.g., if the referent is solid, then shape is salient) will be addressed in the discussion of Procedures 3 and 4 below.

On Ontology and Noun Meaning Landau et al. (1988) claim that adults, as well as children, ignore ontological categories in their inductive projection of noun meanings. Rather, they argue, shared shape is the basis of noun meanings. They support this claim with evidence that the extension of a single noun can include referents of different ontological types, in Sommers' (1963) sense. For example, "bear" can refer to the wild animal or to a stuffed toy. Moreover, they present evidence that young children generalize words applied to a single, solid inanimate object to new objects of the same shape.

Even if we grant Landau et al.'s examples[9] and evidence, it does not follow that nouns refer to shape. As the present studies show, 2-year-old children ignore shape when the referent of a newly heard noun is a non-solid substance, as do 3- to 5-year old children and adults (Dickinson 1988). Further, many nouns in the speech of young children refer to abstract entities for which shape is irrelevant. Perhaps Landau et al. meant that when the referent is a solid object, shape is the basis for determining the relevant kind. Even this is not so. Data from Keil (1989) show that adults, and even early elementary-aged children, are robustly sensitive to how an animal came to get its shape in deciding what that animal is. For example, adults and 10-year-olds are certain that if an antelope were to get a long neck by plastic surgery, it would not become a giraffe, even if the surgeon made it physically indistinguishable from a giraffe.

Suppose, however, that Landau et al. were correct that shape provides the taxonomic basis for noun meanings, *when the referents are solid objects*. Far from showing ontology is irrelevant to word meanings, this generalization has an ontological condition. While Keil's studies show that adults do not determine noun categories of objects, at least for natural kinds, on the basis of shape, Landau et al.'s work suggests a serious alternative to Procedures 1 and 2 as the basis for the projection of word meanings by very young children. Perhaps Procedures 3 and 4 underlie the projection of word meanings of the toddlers in Experiments 1 and 2.

Procedure 3 Step 1: Test to see if the speaker could be talking about a solid object; if yes,

Step 2: Conclude the word refers to shape.

Procedure 4   Step 1: Test to see if the speaker could be talking about a non-solid substance; if yes,

Step 2: Conclude the word refers to texture.

Are the data from the present studies consistent with Procedures 3 and 4? While these data do show that the young child's projections of word meanings are conditioned by the ontological status of the referent, they may not show anything about how the child is quantifying over the referent. The question we now turn to, then, is whether these data bear on Quine's Claim 2.

Claim 2: Step 2 of Procedures 1 and 2

Consideration of the crucial role of *number* in the present studies supports the conclusion that the children in our study are taking nouns to refer to objects quantified as individuals and to refer to non-solid substances quantified as portions. On each object trial, the choice that the child rejects (the distractor) consists of three or four chunks of the original material. If the child is following Procedure 3, then the child should perform equally well if the distractor consisted of a single intact object of the same material but a different shape from the target. This, however, is not the case. Two studies have found that 2-year-old children are much less likely to project noun meanings on the basis of shape under these circumstances (chance performance in Landau et al. 1988, 73% success in Soja 1987). In the present studies, therefore, shape alone did not account for the ceiling performance on the object trials. Instead, children evidently performed at ceiling because the distractor was something that could not be an object at all. The 2-year-old child appears to know that "blicket" must refer to individual whole objects of the same kind as the ostensively defined referent, but does not yet have very good ways of determining what properties are likely to determine "same kind."

Consider now the substance trials. Unlike the situation of the object trials, in which one of the choices is ruled out if the child is following Procedure 1, following Procedure 2 does not allow the child to rule out either choice. Portions of substance can be scattered—three piles of stad is as good an example of a portion of stad as is one big pile. Thus, the object trials and the substance trials are not entirely symmetrical. If children followed Procedures 1 and 2, then their performance should be perfect on object trials but not on non-solid substance trials. That is, of course, the consistent finding of Experiments 1 and 2.

A detailed comparison of the $2\frac{1}{2}$-year-olds in Soja (1987) and those of Experiment 2 supports this analysis. Soja used neutral syntax; the stimuli had complex shapes (as in Experiment 1 of the present study).[10] Subjects in Soja's experiment picked the object of the same shape as the target 73% of the time (as opposed to 93% performance in Experiment 2; $p < .002$, 2-tailed). Indeed the performance of the $2\frac{1}{2}$-year-olds

    Soja, Carey, and Spelke

on the substance trials of Experiment 2 (79%) did not differ from the performance of the subjects in Soja (1987) ($p > .5$, 2-tailed). We take this pattern of results to show that 2-year-olds are projecting word meanings from solid objects to individual whole objects of the same kind and from non-solid substances to portions of substance of the same kind, *without yet having very good methods of determining kinds of objects and substances*. In sum, the role number plays in the trials of Experiments 1 and 2 supports our conclusion that toddlers are following Procedures 1 and 2 and militates against the conclusion that they are following Procedures 3 and 4.

The Relation between Procedures 1 and 2 and Other Work on Word-Learning Constraints

Our focus here differs from most related work on the early constraints on word meanings. We have not here been concerned with contrast (Clark, 1987) or mutual exclusivity (Markman and Wachtel 1988) although we ensured that the objects and materials we used were unfamiliar to the child, so that contrast or mutual exclusivity would not influence the child's choices. Nor was the taxonomy constraint (Markman 1989; Markman and Hutchinson 1984) our focus. We assumed, following Markman, that the child was projecting noun meanings according to taxonomic categories. A taxonomy requires an ontology; our concern here was explicitly the ontology underlying the kinds children think nouns name.

We have argued that the quantificational distinction between objects and non-solid substances guides word learning from at least age 2, and is not induced from learning the explicit quantificational syntax of English. These studies leave open whether the conceptual distinction between objects and substances influences all of the child's inductive projections, just projections of word meanings, or just projections of noun meanings. Future research will establish the scope of the constraint.

Notes

The research reported here was part of the first author's doctoral dissertation in the Department of Brain and Cognitive Sciences at MIT. We thank Molly Potter, Sandy Waxman, Ned Block, Paul Bloom, Debbie Zaichik, and Sandeep Prasada for their helpful discussion and comments on earlier drafts. We also thank three anonymous reviewers for their insightful comments and criticisms. We appreciate the assistance of Laura Kotovsky, Jim Melton, Nancy Turner, Jean Piper, and Thomas Soja in the testing of subjects and the data analysis.

1. Of course, Quine himself would not speak of concepts, mental representations, or conceptual systems: in this discussion we are "cognitivizing" Quine's claims.

2. Some languages do not have a count/mass distinction. It is possible that there are languages with no syntactic devices at all for conveying the quantificational distinction

Ontological Categories Guide Young Children's Inductions of Word Meaning between individuated and non-individuated entities. According to Quine's position, people speaking these languages would not be able to make the ontological distinction between objects and substances.

3. The procedures children use include many additional components. For example, very young children are sensitive to whether they already know a word for the entity being named (Markman & Wachtel 1988), and very young children have procedures for deciding whether the word picks out a type or an individual (Gelman and Taylor 1984; Katz et al. 1974). Here we will focus on the object/substance distinction and the quantificational distinction between individuals and portions.

4. A classic study by Katz, Baker, and Macnamara (1974; see also Gelman and Taylor 1984) is relevant both to the quantificational distinction between types and individuals and to that between individuated entities and portions. Katz et al. showed that 17-month-old girls restricted a new proper noun "Dax" applied to an unfamiliar doll to that doll itself, while a new common noun "a dax" was generalized to other dolls of the same type. Unfortunately, this study also does not settle the argument against Quine. First, the children already knew the English syntax distinction between proper and common nouns, so it is possible, as Quine suggested, that they worked out the semantic distinction between unique individuated entities and types in the course of learning the syntax. Second, these data do not rule out the possibility that the dolls were being conceptualized as Quine said. For example, proper nouns might simply require a greater degree of similarity than common nouns on the same similarity space. To be Dax, like being Mama, means that the portions of experience so named must share more of the perceptually salient attributes than to be a dax or a woman.

5. Collective nouns are also used with singular verbs and refer to multiple items. For example, "family" is a count noun that is used with a singular verb to refer to multiple items in the sentence: "Everyone in the family is here". If the subjects interpret the noun as a collective noun referring to a particular arrangement of small piles, then on the test trials they should choose the other substance arranged similarly, and thus do *worse* on the non-solid substance trials in which the original stimulus is in small piles.

6. Negative scores were also possible—a child using "a" indiscriminately, but not all the time, could by chance use it on a higher proportion of mass nouns than count nouns. Since this reflects no productive control of the distinction, such scores, of which there were a total of 2, were converted to zeros.

7. We did construct such a score. The percentage of mass nouns appearing in the frames "(noun)" and "some (noun)" was found for each child. To ensure that the score reflected command of mass noun syntax and not the general omission of determiners, it was corrected by subtracting from it the percentage of count nouns appearing in the same frames. These scores ranged from 0 to .87 (mean: .34) and were nearly identical to the syntax score based on selective command of count noun syntax ($r = .99$, $p < .001$, 1-tailed). And there was again no correlation between this score and the word-learning score ($r = -.07$, $p > .3$, 1-tailed).

8. The subjects were "presyntactic" with respect to the count/mass distinction; obviously they mastered a good deal of syntax.

9. Actually, we do not agree that a toy bear is a bear; when we call a stuffed animal a "bear," the context allows us to drop the qualifier "stuffed" or "toy."

10. There were three conditions in Soja (1987). We are referring to the double-object condition. All three conditions involved objects; non-solid substances were not tested in that experiment.

References

Bowerman, M. (1978). The acquisition of word meaning: An investigation into some current conflicts. In N. Waterson and C. Snow, eds., *Development of communication.* New York: Wiley.

Carey, S. (1978). The child as word learner. In M. Halle, J. Bresnan, and G. A. Miller, eds., *Linguistic theory and psychological reality.* Cambridge, MA: MIT Press.

Clark, E. V. (1973). What's in a word? On the child's acquisition of semantics in his first language. In T. Moore, ed., *Cognitive development and the acquisition of language.* New York: Academic Press.

Clark, E. V. (1987). The principle of contrast: A constraint on language acquisition. In B. MacWhinney, ed., *Mechanisms of language acquisition.* Hillsdale, NJ: Erlbaum.

Dickinson, D. K. (1988). Learning names for materials: Factors constraining and limiting hypotheses about word meaning. *Cognitive Development* 3, 15–35.

Dromi, E. (1987). *Early lexical development.* London: Cambridge University Press.

Gelman, S. A., and M. Taylor (1984). How two-year-old children interpret proper and common names for unfamiliar objects. *Child Development* 55, 1535–1540.

Gordon, P. (1982). *The acquisition of syntactic categories: The case of the count/mass distinction.* Unpublished doctoral dissertation, Massachusetts Institute of Technology, Cambridge, MA.

Gordon, P. (1985). Evaluating the semantic categories hypothesis: The case of the count/mass distinction. *Cognition* 20, 209–242.

Katz, N., Baker, E., and J. Macnamara (1974). What's in a name? A study of how children learn common and proper names. *Child Development* 45, 469–473.

Keil, F. C. (1989). *Concepts, kinds, and cognitive development.* Cambridge, MA: MIT Press.

Landau, G., L. B. Smith, and S. S. Jones (1988). The importance of shape in early lexical learning. *Cognitive Development* 3, 229–321.

Markman, E. M. (1989). *Categorization and naming in children: Problems of induction.* Cambridge, MA: MIT Press.

Markman, E. M., and J. E. Hutchinson (1984). Children's sensitivity to constraints on word meaning: Taxonomic versus thematic relations. *Cognitive Psychology* 16, 1–27.

Markman, E. M., and G. F. Wachtel (1988). Children's use of mutual exclusivity to constrain the meanings of words. *Cognitive Psychology* 20, 121–157.

Miller, G. A. (1977). *Spontaneous apprentices: Children and language.* New York: Seabury.

Naigles, L. (1990). Children use syntax to learn verb meanings. *Journal of Child Language* 17, 357–374.

Quine, W. V. (1960). *Word and object.* Cambridge, MA: MIT Press.

Quine, W. V. (1969). *Ontological relativity and other essays.* New York: Columbia University Press.

Soja, N. N. (1987). *Ontological constraints on 2-year-olds' induction of word meanings.* Unpublished doctoral dissertation, Massachusetts Institute of Technology, Cambridge, MA.

Sommers, F. (1963). Types and ontology. *Philosophical Review* 72, 327–363.

Spelke, E. S. (1985). Perception of unity, persistence, and identity: Thoughts on infants' conception of objects. In J. Mehler and R. Fox, eds., *Neonate cognition: Beyond the blooming buzzing confusion.* Hillsdale, NJ: Erlbaum.

Vygotsky, L. S. (1962). *Thought and language.* Cambridge, MA: MIT Press.

21 Some Elements of Conceptual Structure

Ray Jackendoff

Ontological Claims: Some Major Categories of Concepts

Let us consider the ontological presuppositions of natural language—what sorts of entities inhabit the world as construed and are capable of being referred to by linguistic expressions.

One circumstance under which a speaker clearly construes there to be an entity in the world is when he refers to it by means of an expression like (21.1).

(21.1)   (*That* [pointing] *is a dog*).

In (21.1) the use of the demonstrative pronoun is accompanied by a gesture that serves as an invitation to the hearer to locate the entity in his own visual field. If the hearer cannot identify an entity of the appropriate sort, perhaps because he has his eyes shut, or the conversation is taking place over the telephone, or the speaker is pointing to something in a blurry photograph, the intended referent is unavailable to the hearer, and discourse cannot proceed. A demonstrative pronoun used in this fashion has been called a "pragmatic anaphor"; it takes its reference from nonlinguistic context.

So far this should be fairly unsurprising. The interest arises when we observe, as pointed out by Hankamer and Sag (1976), that pragmatic anaphora is possible not only to designated *objects*, as in (21.1), but also to entities best classified as *places* (21.2a), *paths* or *trajectories* (21.2b), *actions* (21.2c), *events* (21.2d), *sounds* (21.2e), *manners* (21.2f), *amounts* (21.2g), and *numbers* (21.2h).

(21.2) a. Your hat is here [*pointing*] and your coat is there [*pointing*].
     b. He went thataway [*pointing*].
     c. Can you do that [*pointing*]?
       Can you do this [*demonstrating*]?
     d. That [*pointing*] had better not happen in *my* house!

From R. Jackendoff, *Consciousness and the computational mind* (1987). Cambridge, MA: MIT Press. Reprinted by permission.

e. That [*gesturing*] sounds like Brahms.

f. You shuffle cards $\begin{Bmatrix} \text{like this} \\ \text{thus} \\ \text{this way} \end{Bmatrix}$ [*demonstrating*].

g. The fish that got away was $\begin{Bmatrix} \text{this} \\ \text{that} \\ \text{yay} \end{Bmatrix}$ [*demonstrating*] long.

h. Please bring back this many cookies [*holding up some number of fingers*].

The conditions on the interpretation of *that* in (21.1) also obtain with the pragmatic anaphors in (21.2). For instance, if the hearer is unable to see or figure out what goings-on the speaker is pointing at in (21.2d), he will not fully understand the utterance—he will not have received all the information he is intended to receive, and discourse cannot properly continue.

If, as seems uncontroversial, the pragmatic anaphor in (21.1) refers to a thing (or physical object), those in (21.2) must also refer, but to entities quite distinct from physical objects—namely, a place, a path, an action, an event, a sound, a manner, an amount, and a number, respectively. Thus, the world as construed must include such entities—a variety rarely recognized in extant semantic theories.

Other grammatical constructions also support this range of entities. One is the expression of identity and individuation with *same* and *different*. Compare (21.3), which expresses identity and individuation of physical objects, with (21.4a–f), which express identity and individuation of other entity types. (In some cases such sentences assert only that two distinct individuals belong to a common type—for instance, *Bill ate the same sandwich he always eats*, on the normal, nonregurgitation interpretation. But even these cases presuppose the existence of distinct individuals to be categorized.)

(21.3) $\begin{Bmatrix} \text{Bill picked up the same things } \begin{Bmatrix} \text{that} \\ \text{as} \end{Bmatrix} \text{ Jack did.} \\ \text{Bill picked up something different than Jack did.} \end{Bmatrix}$ [Object]

(21.4) a. Bill ate at $\begin{Bmatrix} \text{the same place as} \\ \text{a different place than} \end{Bmatrix}$ Jack did. [Place]

b. Bill went off $\begin{Bmatrix} \text{the same way as} \\ \text{a different way than} \end{Bmatrix}$ Jack did. [Path]

c. Bill did $\begin{Bmatrix} \text{the same thing as} \\ \text{a different thing than} \end{Bmatrix}$ Jack did. [Action]

d. $\begin{Bmatrix} \text{The same thing} \\ \text{A different thing} \end{Bmatrix}$ happened today $\begin{Bmatrix} \text{as} \\ \text{than} \end{Bmatrix}$ happened yesterday. [Event]

e. Bill heard $\begin{Bmatrix} \text{the same noise as} \\ \text{a different noise than} \end{Bmatrix}$ Jack did. [Sound]

f. Bill cooks meat $\left\{\begin{array}{l}\text{the same way (as)} \\ \text{a different way than}\end{array}\right\}$ he cooks eggs. [Manner]

Amounts and numbers are identified and individuated by different expressions than the other entities, but the semantic parallelism is clear.

g. $\left\{\begin{array}{l}\text{Bill is as tall as Jack is.} \\ \text{Bill is taller than Jack is.}\end{array}\right\}$ [Amount]

h. The trumpeter played $\left\{\begin{array}{l}\text{as many notes as} \\ \text{more notes than}\end{array}\right\}$ there were marks on the page. [Number]

In order for these sentences to say what they do, there must be entities of the requisite sort for the sentences to talk about, and conceptual structure must be capable of distinguishing among them. Accordingly, we introduce into conceptual structure a set of *ontological category features*, including at least [OBJECT], [PLACE], [PATH], [ACTION], [EVENT], [SOUND], [MANNER], [AMOUNT], and [NUMBER], as well as possible others such as [PROPERTY], [SMELL], and [TIME]. These can be thought of as elements that serve as primitive "parts of speech" of conceptual structure. Just as each syntactic constituent must be of a unique syntactic category, so a conceptual unit must be of a unique ontological category.

Each of these category features may be associated with either the [TOKEN] or the [TYPE] feature. For instance, a perceived object will be represented as an [OBJECT TOKEN], and a category of objects as an [OBJECT TYPE]. Similarly, a perceived event will be represented as an [EVENT TOKEN], and a category of events as an [EVENT TYPE].

Now consider how the ontological categories are expressed in language. Traditional grammar implies that the correspondence between syntactic categories and ontological categories is fairly obvious: a noun names a person, place, or thing; a verb names an action or state of being; and so on. Actually, the only simple case is [OBJECT], which seems always to be expressed by a noun. Otherwise, the situation is more complex. The standard expression of [EVENT] is as a Sentence; but [EVENT] can also be expressed by a noun (*earthquake*). The standard expression of [PROPERTY] is as an adjective (*red, tall*), but there are also idiomatic noun phrases (*a gas, a bummer*) and prepositional phrases (*out of luck*) that express [PROPERTIES]. And so on. This divergence shows the potential complexity of the correspondence rules between syntactic and conceptual structure. It is also important in showing that syntactic structure cannot be based entirely on semantics, as is sometimes assumed. (See Jackendoff 1983, chapter 4, Grimshaw 1979, and Jackendoff 1985 for discussion.)

Let us look next at nonlinguistic connections to conceptual structure. In order for the pragmatic anaphors in (21.2) to be interpreted, the visual system must deliver information that corresponds to the visibly distinguishable ontological categories in conceptual structure. For instance, to distinguish (21.5a) from (21.5b), the visual system must fill in the pragmatic anaphors with objects in one case and locations in the other.

(21.5) a. This is your coat, and that is your hat.
b. Here is your coat, and there is your hat.

To interpret (21.2e), the auditory system must deliver information that appears in conceptual structure as [SOUNDS]. In order to verify (21.4h), both the visual and the auditory systems must deliver information that appears in conceptual structure as [NUMBER].

Although perception of entities other than objects has not been prominent in the literature, the work I have encountered (for example, Michotte 1954 on causation; Jenkins et al. 1978 and Cutting 1981 on event-perception; remarks in Köhler 1929 on temporal grouping; Piaget 1952 and Gelman and Gallistel 1978 on amounts and numbers) reveals characteristics entirely parallel to the perception of physical objects, such as the Gestalt properties of proximity, closure, "good form," and the like. There seems no bar in principle to the perceptual systems delivering information about diverse ontological categories, using mechanisms similar to those for the perception of objects, if we think to look for it.

Besides giving evidence for an important class of primitives in conceptual structure, this section reinforces earlier arguments on the priority of Conceptual Semantics over Real Semantics. Even if we can refer to this variety of entities, and even if truth-conditions must involve them, we do not want to have to justify them as objective elements of physical reality. For instance, the continuous flow of matter in the physical world does not come neatly segmented into events, as language seems to imply; nor does it seem plausible that the Real World contains manners segregated from the actions whose manners they are; nor does it contain numbers except in some curious Platonic sense. The characteristics of these entities seem much less paradoxical if we regard them in terms of how humans structure the world—what is real *for us*. This in turn is determined by our capacity for mental representation, in particular, the properties of the ontological categories available in conceptual structure. Thus, the nature of the internal system of symbols that support meaning must be a primary focus of semantic inquiry.

Generalization of Spatial Concepts to Abstract Domains

We end our foray into conceptual structure with some further evidence from language that bears on the organization of conceptual primitives. (This material derives from the analysis in Gruber 1965 and is developed in greater detail in Jackendoff 1976, 1983, chaps. 9–10.)

Consider the English verbs of spatial position. These can be divided into three important classes, which I will call *GO verbs, BE verbs,* and *STAY verbs.* The sentences in (21.6) exemplify the class of GO verbs.

(21.6) a. The dog ran from the door to the table.
b. A meteor hurtled toward the earth.
c. The hawk flew over the prairie.

These sentences all express concepts that pick out types of physical motion. Following Gruber's (1965) terminology, I will refer to the object in motion as the *theme* of the sentence. In each sentence the theme travels along a path, which may, as in the first example, be further differentiated into a source, or initial point, and a goal, or final point. The semantic similarity between these sentences can be described by saying that the concepts they express are all specialized forms of the general concept [GO (X,P)], which represents the motion of some object X (the theme) along some path P. This concept belongs to the ontological category [EVENT]; it is something that happens over time. In turn, the variables X and P belong to the ontological categories [OBJECT] and [PATH], respectively. So the concept is more fully expressed as shown in (21.7). (In this and subsequent examples I will notate ontological category as a subscript.)

(21.7) $[_{\text{Event}}\ \text{GO}\ ([_{\text{Object}}\ X],\ [_{\text{Path}}\ P])]$

In turn, the expressions of path in (21.6) are composite. Each contains one or more *reference objects (the door, the table, the earth, the prairie)* plus a *path-function* that determines how the path is related to the reference object. The path-function expressed by the preposition *from* designates a path that begins at the reference object; that expressed by *to,* a path that ends at the reference object; that expressed by *toward,* a path that if extended would end at the reference object; that expressed by *over,* a path that passes through a point (or region) vertically above the reference object. Thus, the general form of these path-concepts is (21.8).

(21.8) $[_{\text{Path}}\ \text{PATH-FUNCTION}\ ([_{\text{Object}}\ y])]$

Combining (21.7) and (21.8), we get (21.9) as the general form of the conceptual structures expressed by the sentences of (21.6). ((21.6a) has two path-functions and reference objects in its path.)

(21.9) $[_{\text{Event}}\ \text{GO}\ ([_{\text{Object}}\ x],\ [_{\text{Path}}\text{PATH-FUNCTION}\ ([_{\text{Object}}\ y])])]$

BE verbs are exemplified in (21.10).

(21.10) a. Max was in Africa.
b. The cushion lay on the couch.
c. The statue stands in the woods.

These describe not motion but the location of an object. Thus, they express forms of a general concept [BE (X,L)], where X is the theme (the object being located) and L is a location. The ontological category of this concept is not [EVENT]: these are not things that happen but rather states of affairs. We will adopt the notation [STATE] for the requisite ontological category. The locations are of the ontological category [PLACE]; like paths, they can be decomposed into a *place-function* expressed by the preposition and a reference object expressed by the object of the preposition. Thus, the general form of the concepts expressed by (21.10) is (21.11).

(21.11)   [State BE ([Object x], [Place PLACE-FUNCTION ([Object y])])]

In addition to the verbs of location illustrated in (21.10), there is a second, smaller class of location verbs with rather different semantic properties, which I will call *STAY VERBS*.

(21.12) a. The bacteria stayed in his body.
         b. Stanley remained in Africa.

Like BE verbs, these express the location of an object in a place. But unlike them, they involve the maintenance of this location over a period of time; they cannot be attributed to a point in time such as *at six o'clock*.

(21.13) a. The bacteria $\left\{\begin{array}{l}\text{were}\\ \text{*stayed}\end{array}\right\}$ in his body at six o'clock.

         b. The cushion $\left\{\begin{array}{l}\text{lay}\\ \text{*remained}\end{array}\right\}$ on the couch at six o'clock.

Because of their temporal structure, they turn out to belong to the ontological categories [EVENTS]. Thus, like the GO verbs and unlike the BE verbs, they can occur after the phrase *what happened was*.

(21.14)   What happened was $\left\{\begin{array}{ll}\text{the dog ran to the table.} & \Big\}\, \text{GO}\\ \text{the hawk flew over the prairie.} & \\ \text{Stanley remained in Africa.} & \Big\}\, \text{STAY}\\ \text{the bacteria stayed in his body.} & \\ \text{*Max was in Siberia.} & \Big\}\, \text{BE}\\ \text{*the statue stood in the woods.} & \end{array}\right.$

The general conceptual form of (21.12) will therefore be decomposed as in (21.15).

(21.15)   [Event STAY ([Object x], [Place PLACE-FUNCTION ([Object y])])]

Given these three subfields of verbs of spatial position, let us consider another semantic field, verbs of possession. These can again be divided into three subfields, exemplified in (21.16), (21.17), and (21.18).

(21.16) a. Harry gave the book to Betty.
         b. Charlie bought the lamp from Max.
         c. Will inherited a million dollars.

(21.17) a. The book belonged to the library.
         b. Max owned an iguana.
         c. Bill had no money.

(21.18) a. The library kept the book.
 b. The iguana stayed in Max's possession.
 c. The leopard retained its spots.

In (21.16) the things described by the direct object of the sentence undergo a change in possession. The sentences in (21.17), however, express states of possession. The sentences in (21.18) also express a single unchanging possessor, but *at six o'clock* may be added only to (21.17), not to (21.18), and *what happened was* may be prefixed to (21.18) but not to (21.17).

Thus there is an important parallel between (21.16)–(21.18) on the one hand and (21.6), (21.10), and (21.12) on the other. Gruber (1965) represents this parallel by claiming that the verbs in (21.16) are also instances of [GO (X,P)], the verbs in (21.17) are instances of [BE (X,L)], and the verbs in (21.18) are instances of [STAY (X,L)]. The difference between (21.16)–(21.18) and (21.6), (21.10), and (21.12) is then expressed by a modifier on GO, BE, and STAY, picking out the proper semantic field. For physical motion and location, the field modifier is *Positional*; for possession, it is *Possessional*. For example, (21.6a) expresses something like (21.19a), (21.16a) something like (21.19b).

(21.19) a. [$_{Event}$ GO $_{Posit}$ ([$_{Object}$ DOG], [$_{Path}$ FROM ([$_{Object}$ DOOR]) TO ([$_{;Object}$ TABLE])])]
 b. [$_{Event}$ GO $_{Poss}$ ([$_{Object}$ BOOK], [$_{Path}$ FROM ([$_{Object}$ HARRY]) TO ([$_{Object}$ BETTY])])]

This now gives us a principle with which to organize a third important semantic field, verbs of predication or ascription. These verbs are used to describe properties of things. The same three-way division into subfields obtains.

(21.20) a. The coach changed from a handsome young man into a pumpkin.
 b. The metal turned red.
 c. The ice became mushy.

(21.21) a. The coach was a turkey.
 b. The metal was vermilion.
 c. The pumpkin seemed tasty.

(21.22) a. The poor coach remained a pumpkin.
 b. The metal stayed red.

The sentences of (21.20) describe changes of state; those of (21.21) describe a state; those of (21.22) describe persistence of a state. Of the two latter cases, (21.21) and (21.22), *at six o'clock* may be added only to (21.21) and *what happened was* may be prefixed only to (21.22). Thus, these three sets of verbs are further instances of the concepts GO, BE, and STAY, respectively. We will call the field modifier this time *Identificational*; locations and paths in this field make claims about what the theme is, rather than where it is, as in the Positional field, or whose it is, as in the Possessional field.

Let us look a little more closely at sentences that express Identificational concepts. The theme as usual is a noun phrase, but the phrase expressing the reference object may typically be either a "predicate nominal," as in (21.20a), (21.21a), and (21.22a), or an adjective phrase, as in the rest of the examples. The latter express [PROPERTIES]; what about the former? In Positional sentences the reference objects are particular (that is, token) objects; similarly in Possessional sentences. But Identificational sentences speak of category membership. This suggests that predicate nominals differ from ordinary noun phrases in that they express [TYPE] concepts rather than [TOKEN] concepts, a distinction we have so far ignored in this section. (This suggestion is worked out and defended in Jackendoff 1983, section 5.3.) For example, (21.20a) expresses something like (21.23a); (21.20b) expresses (21.23b). (I am assuming that the events and paths are particular (that is, TOKENS) here. For PROPERTIES the type-token distinction is harder to justify and may be absent altogether; I leave the feature blank in (21.23b).)

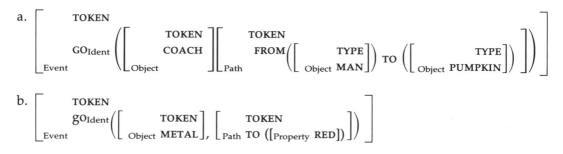

Thus, the three major concepts GO, BE, and STAY apply to three semantic fields that a priori have nothing to do with each other. This illustrates a phenomenon that might be called *cross-field generalization*. A basic notion of what it is to be "in a place" differs from one field to another. In the Positional field a location is a spatial position; in the Possessional field it is to be owned by someone; in the Identification field it is to have a property or be in a category. From any of these notions of location an entire field of verbs is elaborated out of instances of the three basic concepts GO, BE, and STAY, understood as they apply to that particular type of location.

As evidence that cross-field generalization is of genuine grammatical significance, observe that it is common for particular verbs to function in more than one semantic field, while still preserving their classification as GO, BE, or STAY verbs. Consider the examples in (21.24).

(21.24) a. The coach turned into a driveway.   (Positional)
             The coach turned into a pumpkin.   (Identificational)
         b. The train went to Texas.   (Positional)
             The inheritance went to Philip.   (Possessional)

c. Max is in Africa.	(Positional)
Max is a dog.	(Identificational)
d. Bill kept the book on the shelf.	(Positional)
Bill kept the book.	(Possessional)
e. The coach remained in the driveway.	(Positional)
The coach remained a pumpkin.	(Identificational)

In each pair the same verb is used in two different semantic fields. Since these uses are not a priori related, it is a significant generalization that a sizable number of verbs exhibit such behavior. The hypothesis proposed here claims that the relation between these uses is simple and nonaccidental: the verb stays fundamentally the same, changing only its semantic field via a cross-field generalization. One way in which words can extend their meanings, then, is by keeping all semantic structure intact except the part that picks out the semantic field.

In particular, the fundamental semantic function of categorization, called IS-AN-INSTANCE-OF, is now subsumed by the function BE$_{\text{Ident}}$. It is now seen to be, not a primitive function sui generis, but a composite formed from the intersection of the family of BE concepts and the family of Identificational concepts. This enables us to unify various uses of the verb *be* under a more general function; we do not have to say that in its use with expressions of location it means one thing, and in its use in categorization sentences it means something entirely different. As this generalization appears in many languages of the world besides English, we would like to ascribe it to something more than coincidence. The hypothesis of cross-field generalization makes possible a more enlightening approach. But is also removes categorization from the purely logical domain, in that it has come to be formally connected with concrete representations of spatial relations.

We are proposing, then, that among the set of conceptual primitives is a three-way opposition between GO, STAY, and BE and that the former two are associated with the ontological category EVENT and the third with the category STATE. However, the units cannot appear in isolation: they must co-occur with a field modifier in order to be realized as a well-formed concept. The class of field modifiers (the three given here plus at least a few others discussed in Jackendoff 1983) constitute a feature opposition that operates independently of the choice of GO/STAY/BE, of EVENT/STATE, and of TYPE/TOKEN. Thus, we have uncovered four fundamental oppositions in conceptual structure; these operate in many respects like phonological distinctive features—particularly in that they must be bundled together for a well-formed concept to be produced. For instance, the feature EVENT alone is meaningless, just like the feature [+ voiced].

The usual polemic applies to the pair of oppositions introduced in this section. There seems to be nothing intrinsic to the real world that requires possession and ascription of properties to be mentally represented in an algebraic system that parallels the representation of spatial events and states. Rather, the most appealing explanation of this parallelism (to me, at least) is that it is a reflection of the way human beings are constrained to construe the world. It is not that this is a true or false representation of the world—it is just the way we have. Again we are led to the necessity of an observer-based treatment of reference and truth, rather than one that depends on a preestablished Reality.

Similar cross-field generalizations having to do with notions of causality are hinted at by Jackendoff (1977) and developed in splendid detail by Talmy (1985). As it turns out, the conception of physical force and causation, as well as that of the resistance or acquiescence of one object to force applied by another object, find parallels in such domains as social coercion and resistance and in logical and moral necessity. The most abstract of these domains, that of logical relations, has often been regarded as a field isolated from human conceptualization, to be studied by purely mathematical techniques. On the other hand, analysis through cross-field generalization reveals that this domain, like categorization, has formal parallels to a very concrete semantic field having to do with pushing objects around in space. Although radically at variance with the philosophical tradition, this result makes a great deal of sense in the context of a theory of meaning as conceptualization. One can begin to see the principles of logic as abstractions away from the general algebraic form implicit in our understanding of the physical world, and through this one can begin to envision the evolutionary channels by which they might have developed in the computational mind.

(A personal note: it was the existence of cross-field generalizations that first led me to believe that linguistic evidence could motivate powerful hypotheses about the structure of thought. From them emerged the germ of all my present thinking on conceptual structure, the observer's construal of the world, and the observer-based notions of reference and truth. I mention this, not just as an anecdote about my own intellectual development (or degeneration, as the case may be), but primarily because these facts have played absolutely no role in more standard theories of semantics. It seems to me that they cry out for explanation and that, if taken seriously, they lead inescapably to a wholly mentalistic semantics of at least approximately the form presented here.) . . .

References

Cutting, J. (1981). Six tenets for event perception. *Cognition* 10, 71–78.

Gelman, R., and C. R. Gallistel (1978). *The child's understanding of number.* Cambridge, MA: Harvard University Press.

Grimshaw, J. (1979). Complement selection and the lexicon. *Linguistic Inquiry* 10, 279–325.

Gruber, J. S. (1965). Studies in lexical relations. Doctoral dissertation, MIT. Reprinted by Indiana University Linguistics Club, Bloomington. Reprinted (1976) as part of *Lexical structures in syntax and semantics*. Amsterdam: North-Holland.

Jackendoff, R. (1976). Toward an explanatory semantic representation. *Linguistic Inquiry* 7, 89–150.

Jackendoff, R. (1977). Toward a cognitively viable semantics. In C. Rameh, ed., *Georgetown University Round Table on Languages and Linguistics*. Washington, D.C.: Georgetown University Press.

Jackendoff, R. (1983). *Semantics and cognition*. Cambridge, MA: MIT Press.

Jackendoff, R. (1985). Multiple subcategorization and the T-criterion: The case of *climb*. *Natural Language and Linguistic Theory* 3, 271–295.

Jenkins, J. J., J. Wald, and J. B. Pittenger (1978). Apprehending pictorial events: An instance of psychological cohesion. In C. W. Savage, ed., *Perception and cognition: Issues in the foundations of psychology*. Minnesota Studies in the Philosophy of Science 9. Minneapolis: University of Minnesota Press.

Köhler, W. (1929). *Gestalt psychology*. New York: Liveright.

Michotte, A. (1954). *La perception de la causalité*. 2d ed. Louvain: Publications Universitaires de Louvain.

Piaget, J. (1952). *The child's conception of number*. New York: Norton.

Talmy, L. (1985). Force dynamics in language and thought. *Cognitive Science* 12, 49–100.

22 Color Subjectivism

C. L. Hardin

Imagine the following experiment. Before you is a spinning disk, illuminated by an ordinary incandescent lamp. If most people are asked what color they see on the face of the disk, they will unhesitatingly reply that they see a bluish green. But you, ever the skeptical and cagey philosopher, may hesitate, not because what you see doesn't look bluish green, for it very plainly does, but because you suspect a trick. And, indeed, this proves to be a trick of sorts. When the wheel is made to turn very slowly you see a half-black, half-white disk, with a slot through which a red lamp flashes. You saw no red at all before, and you can discern no bluish green now. The bluish green color the disk looked to have was entirely the color of an after-image, one that appeared to be the color of the surface of a physical object rather than the color of a free-floating patch. This particular after-image phenomenon is called Bidwell's ghost, after the early twentieth century psychologist who first discovered it.[1] When you view Bidwell's ghost, it is always open to you to deny that you are seeing bluish green, on the ground that after-images are not physical objects and only physical objects can have colors. But it is then fair to ask you what color you do see. Red? Gray? No color at all? None of these answers is intuitively very appealing.

If you are like most philosophers, you will nevertheless be inclined to say that Bidwell's ghost is a color illusion, and that when the disk is rapidly spinning, you don't see its true colors. But just what is a color illusion? Isn't it a failure of correspondence between the color that an object seems to have and the color that it does have? If it is, to characterize an object's apparent possession of a color as illusory is to presume that one knows what counts as the object's true color. In ordinary practice this presumption seems natural enough. But it is in fact quite difficult to justify in a principled fashion, especially if you happen to be a physicalist.

From C. L. Hardin, Color and illusion, in W. Lycan, ed., *Mind and cognition* (1990). Oxford: Blackwell Publishers. Reprinted by permission.

I shall argue that the facts about chromatic phenomena[2] make it very hard to construe colors as properties of physical objects or processes outside the body of the perceiver. I shall consider three attempts at a physicalistic reduction of colors: to wavelengths of light as Armstrong (1968) would have it; to the dispositions of objects appropriately to affect normal observers under standard conditions, a thesis defended by Smart (1975) and Lewis;[3] and to spectral reflectances, as proposed by Averill (1985) and Hilbert (1987). We shall have reason to suppose that all such reductions will fail, and thus to question the legitimacy of the conception of a color illusion.

We normally see color because light of certain wavelengths strikes the retina and excites the photoreceptors that dwell there. They in turn hyperpolarize, generating small electrochemical signals in other cells. The photoreceptors that are relevant to color vision are called *cones*. There are three types of cones, each sensitive to a particular range of the visible spectrum. They are often misleadingly labeled the blue, green and red cones. Let us call them instead the shortwave, middlewave and longwave cones. Their sensitivity curves are rather broad and overlap substantially. When a cone absorbs a photon of light of a particular wavelength, it generates a voltage, and the character of this voltage is independent of the wavelength of the photon that the receptor absorbed. Subsequent cells in the visual processing chain can only "know" that a receptor of a particular type has been excited, but they cannot "know" the wavelength of the photon that has caused it to become excited. Information about wavelength can only be gleaned by cells that are able to compare the outputs of cones of different types that are in the same retinal region. So chromatic information about the light in a particular retinal region that is conveyed to higher visual cells takes the form of the ratios of excitations of the three cones types in that region. The vast amount of wavelength information in the optical array that strikes a small retinal region is reduced to a three-termed cone excitation ratio right at the beginning of the visual processing chain. This is a massive information loss, and it has important consequences. In particular, any two stimuli of the same intensity that produce the same cone excitation ratios will be regarded as equivalent by the chromatic visual system. This is one of the most fundamental facts about color vision, since it means that for most perceptible light stimuli, there exist indefinitely many other stimuli, each with a physically distinct wavelength composition, that will evoke precisely the same perceived color. Color vision stimuli that are perceptually equivalent but physically inequivalent are known as *metamers*.

The existence of metamers might be expected to make trouble for a purported reduction of colors to combinations of wavelengths of light. The difficulty arises conspicuously in the case of white. It is often said that white is a combination of light of all colors. But this seems odd on the face of it. Although orange looks reddish as well as yellowish, and purple looks both reddish and bluish, white, far from looking reddish and greenish and yellowish and bluish, looks to have no chromatic colors in it at all. Had he the opportunity to do it all over again, the biblical Joseph would have doubtless preferred his coat of many colors to have been white.

You may reply that this misrepresents the intention of the specification of white, which is not to advance the claim that white is a combination of all other perceived colors, but to assert that perceptions of white are produced by light of all the visible wavelengths put together in the appropriate amounts. Now it is true that light that we call white is most often composed in this fashion, but it is also true that a white light can be generated from the superposition of as few as two monochromatic light sources, and there are infinitely many distinct pairs of such monochromatic sources. Furthermore, one can superimpose as many of these pairs as one likes, and still get light that looks white. On the other hand, each of these white-looking lights has, as we shall see, color-rendering properties that are different from the rest. Which of these, according to the account of color that identifies colors with wavelengths of light, is "real" white, and which is just "apparent" white? And by virtue of what principle does one make such choices?

Let us consider another example. It might seem plausible to identify "pure" yellow with a spectral wavelength that most people see as "pure" yellow—about 577 nm (a *nanometer* is a billionth of a meter)—and to suppose that anything that is yellow is such in virtue of sending light to the eye containing a component of 577 nm light. But what are we to say of a spot of light that has just two components: monochromatic 540 nm light (that most people see as green) and monochromatic 670 nm light (that most people see as red)? Such a spot will not only appear yellow, but will exactly match the appearance of a monochromatic yellow, although the one stimulus consists entirely of 577 nm light, whereas the other hasn't a trace of 577 nm light.

The reason that both stimuli look yellow is that they produce the same ratios of excitations in the three cone types. To find out what *looks* yellow, we obviously must attend to the operating characteristics of human visual systems. But the physicalist who would reduce real colors to wavelengths of light should be able to pick out the *real* colors on the basis of physical considerations alone.

Such physical considerations seem to fail entirely to give us a conceptual grip on the phenomenon of colored shadows, first described in detail by Count Rumford (Thompson 1802). One may illustrate colored shadows in a variety of ways, but a simple and striking way to do it is to arrange two slide projectors so that the light that they project falls on the same area of the screen. First turn them on separately. Let one projector carry a slide that consists of a piece of green celluloid on which is fixed a cross made of two strips of tape. The image that it projects is of a black cross on a green field. Let the second projector carry only the empty frame of a slide, so that it casts a rectangle of incandescent projector light on the screen. What will happen when the two images are superimposed? To the black cross and the green field, the second projector adds only some broadband, approximately white, light. According to the wavelength theorist, you should see nothing particularly remarkable, only a grayish cross on a somewhat washed-out green field. What you will in fact see is quite different: the cross will look bright pink. If you were to bring in a spectrophotometer, it would tell you that the spectrum of light reflected from the area of the screen on which the cross appears is only that which is characteristic of ordinary projector light, and not that which would have been there had you produced the effect by means of a red filter.

"Ah, but this is just another illusion," the wavelength theorist might reply. "What I am concerned to do is to give an account of the real colors of things, not a theory of the colors things seem to have in demonstrations of bizarre effects." Very well. But any theory of color that is to be of any interest must go beyond a set of raw stipulations to the effect that such-and-such wavelength combinations are to count as red, and that so-and-so wavelengths are to be cyan, and so on. Their proponents always claim that materialist theories of color fit into a scientific picture of the world (often The Scientific Picture of the World), so any such theory of color should provide the framework for a scientific theory of the color qualities that we see. At the very least, we can demand of a theory of color that it satisfactorily represent what is going on when we see red and brown and white and black in ordinary life. But in fact, a proper account of our everyday experience of black and brown requires an appeal to one of the fundamental phenomena—namely, simultaneous contrast—that is involved in colored shadows, so this so-called "illusion" is not as far removed from ordinary experience as one might have supposed.

Simultaneous contrast is ubiquitous and easily illustrated. The principle involved is, roughly speaking, that a large area of color tends to induce its complementary color into a neighboring area. Thus, an area of red makes adjacent areas look greener, blue makes a nearby region look more yellow, white induces black, and so on. The effect is rooted in the physiology of the visual system. The biological details are at least roughly understood and quite interesting, but they need not detain us now. The pink that appears on the cross in our colored shadow experiment is, roughly, the complement of the green in the field, and is induced by it.

Simultaneous contrast is consciously manipulated by painters, often to great effect. Delacroix once said "Give me mud, let me surround it as I think fit, and it shall be the radiant flesh of Venus." For examples of simultaneous contrast we do not strictly require either mud or the radiant flesh of Venus. Some experimentation with pieces of colored paper will soon persuade you that two squares cut from the same piece of colored paper can look very different from one another when placed on backgrounds that differ from each other in color.

With certain choices of background, the phenomenon is so strong that often people need to be specially persuaded that the specimen areas will indeed look the same when seen in isolation. When confronted with an effective example of simultaneous contrast, you can undo the effect by using a viewing tube or other device to replace the inducing surround by a neutral one. (It is well to bear in mind that what is "neutral" depends upon the color in question; there is no such thing as a universal neutral surround). It is easy to construct a tolerably useful viewing tube. Just roll up a piece of paper, preferably dark gray, into a tube and peer at the patch you wish to inspect, rolling the paper tightly enough to shut out the view of the ambient light and the surrounding regions. In the colored shadow experiment, if you look at the pink cross through a viewing tube, its pinkness disappears.

Now what does simultaneous contrast have to do with the everyday perception of black and brown? The answer, in brief, is that both blackness and brownness are always the products of simultaneous contrast. Nakedly stated, this seems implausible. But let us examine some of the evidence for it. Take black first, we are commonly told that black is the absence of light, a visual nullity. But in truth, what we see in the absence of visual stimulation is not black, but a dark gray; the blackest blacks arise as a result of contrast. You can see this for yourself by entering at night an unilluminated room containing a collection of objects that, by good light, range from white through the grays to black. Equip yourself with a lamp that is controlled by a dimmer. Go into the darkened room, slowly turn up the dimmer, and look at the contents. Notice that when you look at them under conditions of very dim light, the gray range is tightly compressed, with little visible lightness difference between the lightest and darkest objects. But as the light increases, the gray range expands in both directions: not only do the whites look whiter, the blacks look blacker. An increase in the total amount of light has increased blackness.

Another, more painful, way of seeing this is to watch some daytime television. Before you turn on the set, notice that the screen is, by daylight, a middle gray. Turn on the set, find a clear picture, and stand far enough away from it to minimize most of the remaining visual noise. Look for a good black, and mentally compare its lightness with the middle gray of the turned-off screen. (If you are sufficiently sinful to have two television sets, the comparison could be direct.) The black is obviously darker than the gray. But since television pictures are produced by generating light, not by subtracting it, the blackening of that area of the screen must be the result of contrast.

Browns are, for most people, a distinctive set of colors, as differentiated in character from reds and yellows as reds and yellows are differentiated from each other. But in fact, browns are simply blackened oranges and yellows, and their characteristic (or, to use the technical term, "dominant") wavelengths are the same as those of most orange and yellow objects. The spectral profile of a chocolate bar closely resembles that of an orange, but, under the same lighting conditions, the light reflected from the chocolate bar is of much lower intensity. The characteristic difference in appearance between the two depends entirely upon their perceived relationships to the ambient light.

To see this, you can first project an orange spot on a darkened screen, and then, using a second projector, surround the orange spot with bright projector light. The slides may be prepared in the following way. First, use a paper punch to cut a round hole in a piece of stiff paper, glue a piece of orange celluloid onto the paper, and cut the paper and its attached celluloid so that it will fit inside an empty slide frame. This gives you a projectable orange spot. The second slide, the one that is responsible for the bright surround and blackened center, is produced by gluing onto a piece of transparent celluloid the round piece of paper that was made when you cut out the hole with the punch when you were making the first slide. On the screen, line of the projected (orange) hole with the projected (shadow) disk, and try the experiment. The whiteness of the surround induces blackness into the orange, transforming it into a brown. Here, as before, the action of simultaneous contrast may be undone by the judicious use of a viewing tube. You might also like to use a viewing tube to examine a chocolate bar, or other brown object, in a bright light. It will lose its brownness, and look like a dim orange or yellow. In performing such experiments it is best to use a tube with a blackened interior, and to avoid looking at portions of the surface that contain highlights.

So to write off simultaneous contrast as something that need not enter into one's fundamental theory of colors is also to write off the possibility of giving a proper account of the nature of black and brown. This seems unacceptable, unless one is prepared to think of black and brown as "illusory" rather than as "real" colors.

We also ought to demand that a minimally adequate theory of color lend itself to an account of the elementary laws of color mixing. For example, since orange is visibly yellow-red (notice that it could not *fail* to be yellow-red), it has a red component and a yellow component. Furthermore, when color-normal observers look at *monochromatic* spectral light of 590 nm, they see orange. But how can this be on a wavelength theory that maintains that red *is* light of a wavelength of, say, 650 nm, and yellow *is* light of a wavelength of 577 nm? And what of the basic and simple relationships about the relations that colors bear to each other? How is it that we can see reddish blues—the purples—but no reddish greens? One will search the writings of wavelength theorists in vain to find persuasive answers to any of these questions. We might be tolerant of such shortcomings if nobody else had an explanation for color mixing and color compatibilities and incompatibilities—in short, if there were no such discipline as color science. In truth, visual scientists know a great deal about all of these matters. But they do not encumber themselves with the supposition that chromatic phenomena can be accounted for without an essential reference to eyes and brains.

Most philosophers are, indeed, not very sympathetic to a program such as wavelength reductionism. They are aware that a wide variety of distinct physical circumstances can be responsible for producing a given color appearance, and that because of the peculiarities of human perceptual mechanisms, the relationship between external physical conditions and what we see is not a simple one. "No matter," say they, "how physically diverse and, indeed, gerrymandered the class of red things may be, what makes them red is that they are disposed to look red to normal observers under standard conditions." According to the adherents of this position, colors are, to use Locke's term, *powers* of objects to cause us to be in particular perceptual states under particular circumstances. The perceptual states are not themselves to be thought of as colors or as being colored, but, rather, as signs or indices of certain dispositions in physical objects. The human perceptual apparatus is to be regarded as a stalking-horse to pick out and classify physical powers that are of interest to us and to creatures constituted like us, although those powers would not have been picked out or thought to form natural classes on the basis of purely physical considerations.

This way of approaching the problem has much to commend it. For a variety of purposes, the practitioners of that branch of color science known as colorimetry employ a statistically defined Standard Observer whose "receptoral" sensitivities are used in combination with various standard illuminants and viewing conditions to sort objects into classes according to such technical parameters as purity and dominant wavelength. In turn, these parameters are correlated with perceptual variables like saturation and hue. But unlike some philosophers, color scientists are well aware that, for example, hue is a quite different property from dominant wavelength, and that the correlation between the two is only approximate and is well-defined only under certain carefully specified standard viewing conditions. Furthermore, the standard viewing conditions to be employed will depend upon the purpose for which the measurement is being taken. There is, in color science, no set of conditions for determining the "true" or "real" colors of objects. As we shall now see, if they are construed non-pragmatically and in more than a rough-and-ready sense, the notions of "normal observer" and "standard condition" are philosophers' fictions.

Let's look more closely into these matters by returning to the centrally important phenomenon of metamerism. We have previously considered the metameric matches of spots of light. The conception can be extended to reflective surfaces. The wavelength distribution that strikes the eye depends upon the spectral characteristics of both the illumination and the surface that reflects it to the eye. A change in the spectral characteristics of either illumination or surface will often make a difference in what we see. If two spectrally distinct surfaces visually match under a given illuminant for a given observer, the surfaces are said to be metamers for that illuminant and that observer. But we must expect that since the two samples are spectrally different, that difference will be made visually apparent under some illuminant or other. It is not difficult in our age of synthetic colorants to find two color samples that are, for most people, a good match in daylight but when shifted to another illuminant—one or another variety of artificial light—fail to match. Furthermore, when we use first one, then another, illuminant to see a piece of white paper, the illuminants may look to be very similar or even identical, but they may give dramatically different results when they illuminate various pieces of chromatically colored paper.

These effects are well known to people who pay attention to colors. Many people know that it is advisable to see whether the coat and trousers that look so handsome together in the store are equally pleasing when taken into the natural light of the street. Photographers learn to their sorrow that a film that yields a proper color balance when used out of doors gives pictures with a markedly yellow tinge when the same subject is photographed under incandescent light.

It is perfectly true that if you saw the subject of such photographs, first in natural light, then in incandescent light, you would not be aware of such a profound shift in hue. In fact, you might not notice any difference at all if you weren't looking for it. The perceived colors of objects tend to remain relatively stable over a wide variety of changes in illumination. This is partly due to the fact that most people don't attend to relatively small color differences and possess poor color memories for even relatively large differences. But it is also because the eye, unlike a camera's film, adapts automatically to the character of the illuminant and, in large measure, successfully discounts illumination changes. We are more sensitive to the relationships of the colors in a scene than we are to their absolute values. A piece of white paper in shadow looks to us to be lighter than a piece of coal in sunlight, even though the coal sends more light to the eye than the paper does.

This stability across variations in ambient lighting has been called color constancy, and it has frequently been noted, theorized about, and its completeness exaggerated, especially by Land and his followers.[4] Although the phenomenon is robust, constancy is far from complete, even under the range of natural lighting conditions. Inconstancy becomes a very vexing problem with artificial colorants and illuminants, and color technologists wrestle with problems of metamerism every day. For instance, restorers of old paintings are often unable to replicate the original colorants. They create an excellent visual match with the old paint under the illumination of the workshop, only to find that when it is exhibited under the illumination of the gallery, the restoration is plainly visible. So even though adaptation may preserve color appearances for the most part, a change in illuminants that transforms a metameric match into a mismatch—especially a gross mismatch—will always be noticeable.

Let us now see what problems metamerism poses for a theory that would assign colors to objects on the basis of normal observers and standard conditions. First of all, consider two colorants that match metamerically under the standard illuminant. Because the match is metameric, the colorants will have different spectral characteristics and will thus fail to match under some other illuminant. Instead of saying that the two colorants have the same color because they match under the standard illuminant, shouldn't we say that they can't be the same color because under the other illuminant they look different to normal observers?

Although this objection certainly has some force, it is open to the proponent of the normal-observer and standard-condition thesis to stick by her guns, and insist that it is the comparison of samples under the standard illuminant that must decide the issue. But it is now necessary for her to specify the standard illuminant. Two frequently employed standards are sunlight and north daylight. But although some philosophers seem to be unaware of the fact, the spectral characteristics of the two are not the same. So we must expect—and it is in fact the case—that there will be colorants that will match under the one illuminant but not under the other. Then which illuminant is to be the standard? Are there any principled philosophical grounds—as opposed to the pragmatic considerations of color technologists—for choosing one over the other? And shall we let our illuminant have energy outside the visible range and take fluorescence into account, or use a band-limited source so as to exclude it?

There is much more to specifying a set of standard conditions than the choice of illuminant. What are we to do about simultaneous contrast? For many purposes, it makes sense to require that the sample be seen through a viewing tube or other aperture with a "neutral" surround. What counts as "neutral" will depend upon the sample itself, since dark surrounds will brighten light colors, and light surrounds will darken dark colors. There are no all-purpose neutral surrounds, just compromises of various degrees of utility. On the other hand, to insist on using an aperture for all determinations is to forbear categorizing objects as black or brown, since, as we have already seen, these are essentially contrast colors.

The next decision that must be made in assigning standard conditions concerns the angular size of the sample with respect to the eye of the observer. Both a ten-degree standard and a two-degree standard are in use in colorimetric practice. They don't give exactly the same results, and there is no agreed-upon recipe for converting from the one to the other. Color technologists will choose to use the one or the other, depending upon the purpose for which the measurement is to be made, but it never occurs to them to choose one rather than the other because it enables them to determine the "true" colors of material samples. Are we to conclude that color technologists lack a healthy sense of reality? Or do they understand something about standard conditions that philosophers don't?

Then there is the matter of the illuminant-sample-observer viewing angle. The colors we see from all manner of materials depend upon viewing angles, not only because some surfaces are glossy, but because much of the world's color is due to such physical mechanisms as scattering, refraction, interference and polarization, and these are typically angle-dependent. The colors of rainbows, oil films, and iridescent beetles are obvious examples. There are many others. For instance, crumple a piece of transparent cellophane and sandwich it between two sheets of polaroid material. Hold the sandwich up to a strong light, rotate one piece of the polaroid material relative to the other, and enjoy the spectacle of shifting colors. Many objects have transmission colors, which may be quite different from their reflection colors and may interact with them in surprising ways: gold is a notable example. Some objects are translucent, and there do not at the moment exist standards for determining their color characteristics. Then there are fluorescent objects, and self-luminous objects and the like. What are the standard conditions for viewing the colors of stars and bioluminescent fish? North daylight and six inches away?[5]

Still more might be said about viewing conditions, but we must cease beating this moribund horse. However, we should devote a moment to examining the remaining term of the equation, the "normal" observer. About six per cent of all males and a much smaller proportion of females are color deficient; doubtless some of the readers of the present volume fall into this category. Color-deficient people can make some visual discriminations that so-called "color normals" can't, a capability used by the military to penetrate camouflage that confuses color normals. Nevertheless, we, the majority, choose not to let them be the arbiters of the colors of things; we reserve this privilege for ourselves.

I have previously referred to the Standard Observer that is used in colorimetric determinations. The Standard Observer (also known as the Average Observer) is actually a standardized set of color matching curves that are based on average values obtained from the color matches made by fifty or so normal—that is, non-color-deficient—observers. The utility of having a standard observer so defined is scarcely to be doubted, but the fact remains that this is only an average taken over a range of people who vary significantly from each other in their visual performance. Indeed, the color matches made by the standard observer would not be fully acceptable to 90 per cent of the population, especially if they got more persnickity about the matches than they do in most everyday situations.

You might like to get an intuitive idea of the magnitude of the variation in color perception among normal observers. To do this, it will be helpful to look at a printed hue circle, such as may be found in textbooks on color for students of painting. Notice that all of the hues in the circle look to be either red, or yellow, or blue, or green, or some perceptual combination of two of them. Thus orange is a perceptual mixture of yellow and red, and turquoise is a perceptual mixture of blue and green. Now observe that some of the hues are more elementary than others. For instance, you can locate a red that is neither yellowish nor bluish, but you cannot find a purple that is neither reddish nor bluish; indeed a hue that was not reddish or not bluish could, for this reason alone, not count as purple. Visual scientists refer to hues such as purple and orange as *binary* hues, and to a non-binary hue such as the red that is neither yellowish nor bluish as a *unique* hue. It is easy to see that there are exactly four unique hues: there is a unique red, a unique yellow, a unique green, and a unique blue.

Do color-normal observers see unique hues at the same wavelength locations in the spectrum? Experimental investigations show that they do not. For example, Hurvich et al. (1968) did a study on the spectral location of unique green, a hue that is neither yellowish nor bluish. Under carefully controlled conditions, any individual observer can consistently locate his or her unique green on a spectrum with an error of plus or minus three nanometers. But the average settings for 50 normal observers spanned a range of almost *thirty* nanometers, from 490 nm to 520 nm. Most people will see this range of greens as consisting of several distinguishable hues, ranging from a bluish green at one end to a yellowish green at the other. If your library has the *Munsell Book of Color*, you can get some idea of the perceptual breadth of the range. Look at the medium Value, high Chroma color chips in the Hue sequence from 5 Blue-Green to 2.5 Green.

The moral that we can draw from this is that the variability between normal observers is distinctly larger than the accuracy with which any of them can make hue distinctions. Equally large variability holds for the other perceptual dimensions of color. It should not be surprising, then, that just as metameric matches vary with the spectrum of the illumination, they vary from one observer to the next under the same conditions of observation. We may conclude that she who would fix the colors of the surfaces of objects by appealing to the perceptions of a normal observer under standard conditions is obliged not only to specify which normal observer and which set of standard conditions she has in mind, but is also obliged to give us a set of principles that will justify her choices. Needless to say, the philosophical literature contains neither the specifications nor the justifications.

We must now consider the third of the theories we had set out to investigate. This theory maintains that the colors of the surfaces of physical objects are to be identified with the spectral reflectances of such surfaces. Because of the mechanisms of approximate color constancy, reflectance is a physically measurable (though of course non-fundamental) feature of objects that, under ordinary conditions, correlates better with what we see than does the wavelength of the light that strikes the eye. This is because color vision has evolved so that animals can distinguish reflectances from each other without being confused by illuminance changes. Furthermore, reflectance is what is typically picked out by the phrase 'physical color' when that is used by color scientists to refer to an attribute of the surfaces of objects. It is a consequence of the reflectance theory that if objects have distinct spectral reflectances, they must be accounted distinct colors, even though they may not look distinct under any but the most special and bizarre illuminants. So, for the reflectivists, a metameric color match is a match of apparent colors, but not a match of real ones. Therefore, the problems that metamerism poses for the normal-observer, standard-condition theory are not problems for the reflectance theory.

However, there are two tasks that remain to be carried out by the reflectivist before he can claim that his is an adequate theory of color. The first of them is to extend the theory to cover chromatic physical phenomena that do not depend upon the reflection of light. There are many of these, and their number has increased rapidly with the advent of technology. Holograms and color television are obvious examples. The extension of the theory to encompass some of these phenomena will be relatively easy, but rather more difficult in others. For instance, there is more than one basic way to produce color television pictures. One of them, not commercially successful because of ineradicable problems of low saturation and flicker, has the interesting property that it permits the reception of color pictures on "black-and-white" television sets! The picture to be transmitted must first be encoded by a device, the Butterfield encoder (Butterfield 1968), whose effect depends upon the ability of suitably sequenced achromatic pulses to stimulate differentially the color-perception mechanisms in the eye. The same principle is employed on a spinning wheel or top often sold as a novelty item. Psychologists know it as the "Benham disk."[6] The wheel has only a black-and-white pattern on it, but as it spins, you will, if you look at it closely and under a bright incandescent light, see rings of various desaturated colors, the hues of which depend upon the speed and direction of the rotation of the disk. If its inventor had succeeded in circumventing the limitations of the process, the Butterfield encoder might have become the industry standard. Would one then have been so easily tempted to regard these as "illusory" colors?

Let's suppose, though, that the reflectivist has successfully extended his account to cover the wide range of the physical causes of color perceptions. Has he thereby given us a theory of color? Surely he has not until he has told us about red, and green, and yellow, and blue.

These, after all, are what most of us have in mind when we think about colors. By avoiding the problems of metamerism as well as other products of the workings of our visual systems, the reflectivist has no resources within his theory for collecting reflectances into the hue classes that we find in experience. We recall that metamerism comes about because our chromatic information consists entirely of the excitation ratios of three cone types. This trivariant chromatic information is transformed into fourfold hue perception in consequence of the way that the outputs of the cones are subsequently summed and differenced to generate two chromatic channels. One chromatic channel carries information that is registered by the brain as redness or greenness, but not both at once, and the other carries information that is registered by the brain as yellowness or blueness, but not both at once. The four unique hues along with their binary perceptual mixtures arise from this postreceptoral processing, as does the mutual exclusion of color complements. (This is why there are reddish yellows—the oranges—but no reddish greens.) This fourfold color structure has no counterpart in physical structures outside the organism, and any attempt to assign reflectances to fourfold color classes will inevitably appeal to normal observers and standard conditions, with inevitable arbitrariness. But beyond all of that, the colors that we actually see depend upon many more factors than relative spectral reflectance, such as the intensity with which the receptors are stimulated, what is going on in surrounding receptors at the moment, and what went on in the receptors during the previous milliseconds.

Let's look for a moment at just one of these factors, the effect of the intensity of light upon hue. Take an ordinary incandescent bulb and hold it next to a white wall. Since the wall looks white, it ought to reflect pretty faithfully the spectrum of any light that is incident upon it. When it is illuminated by the bulb, the light that the wall reflects will have the same wavelength make-up of the light that comes to your eye directly from the bulb, although the reflected light will be significantly less intense. A piece of red celluloid placed between your eyes and the bulb will serve as a transmission filter that will reduce the intensity of light from both sources. Its wavelength selectivity will be exactly the same for both the direct and the reflected light. Now if hue were to depend only upon the spectrum of the light, the light from the wall should have the same hue as the light that comes directly from the filament of the bulb. But as you will see when you try the experiment, the light from the filament is significantly more yellowish than the light reflected from the wall, although a spectrophotometer would show that the spectral profile is the same for both. Visual scientists explain the effect—a shifting of hues toward yellows and blues as light levels are increased—as a consequence of an increase in sensitivity of the yellow-blue channel relative to the red-green channel as the intensity of the light increases.

So the redness, greeness, yellowness and blueness we see when we look at the surfaces of objects depend upon quite a few more variables than just their wavelength profile. The reflectivist theory, like the wavelength theory, suffers from an irremediable underdetermination: too many of the mechanisms essential to the production of the colors that we see lie within the bodies of perceivers.

This should not be an unwelcome conclusion, even to physicalists. Why should chromatic phenomena not depend essentially upon processes that take place within the confines of the head? The stuffings of the head are, after all, material, and the whole process of color perception is physical, determinate, and lawlike from beginning to end. Physical objects need not have colors of their own, in some special, elitist manner, in order to look colored. The world need contain only objects and "looks," and sometimes just the looks will do. In a spirit of chromatic democracy, we should be willing to embrace Bidwell's ghost, for its origins are not supernatural, but only out of the ordinary. It is no more, but also no less, illusory than all the rest of the world's colors.

Notes

1. See Bidwell (1901).

2. An excellent source for these facts about color and color vision is Hurvich (1981). Many of the chromatic phenomena likely to be of interest to philosophers are discussed in Hardin (1988).

3. David Lewis's view is described in Smart (1975).

4. For a brief discussion of the advantages and difficulties of Edwin Land's retinex theory of color vision, see the appendix to Hardin (1988).

5. See Austin (1962).

6. See Benham (1894).

References

Armstrong, D. M. (1968). *A materialist theory of the mind.* London: Routledge and Kegan Paul.

Austin, J. L. (1962). *Sense and Sensibilia.* Oxford: Oxford University Press.

Averill, E. W. (1985). Color and the anthropocentric problem. *Journal of Philosophy* 82, 281–303.

Benham, E. C. (1894). Notes. *Nature* 51, 113–114.

Bidwell, S. (1901). On negative after-images and their relation to certain other visual phenomena. *Proceedings of the Royal Society of London* B 68, 262–269.

Butterfield, J. F. (1968). Subjective (induced) color television. *Society of Motion Picture and Television Engineers Journal* 77, 1025–1028.

Hardin, C. L. (1988). *Color for philosophers*. Indianapolis: Hackett.

Hilbert, D. (1987). *Color and color perception: A study in anthropocentric realism*. Chicago: University of Chicago Press.

Hurvich, L. M. (1981). *Color vision*. Sunderland, MA: Sinauer Associates.

Hurvich, L. M., D. Jameson, and J. D. Cohen (1968). The experimental determination of unique green in the spectrum. *Perceptual Psychology* 4, 65–68.

Smart, J. J. C. (1975). On some criticisms of a physicalistic theory of colors. In C.-Y. Cheng, ed., *Philosophical aspects of the mind-body problem*. Honolulu: University of Hawaii Press.

Thompson, B. (Count Rumford) (1802). *Philosophical papers*, vol. 1. London: Cadell and Davies.

Part V

Language

23 On the Nature, Use, and Acquisition of Language

Noam Chomsky

For about thirty years, the study of language—or more accurately, one substantial component of it—has been conducted within a framework that understands linguistics to be a part of psychology, ultimately human biology. This approach attempts to reintroduce into the study of language several concerns that have been central to Western thought for thousands of years, and that have deep roots in other traditions as well: questions about the nature and origin of knowledge in particular. This approach has also been concerned to assimilate the study of language to the main body of the natural sciences. This meant, in the first place, abandoning dogmas that are entirely foreign to the natural sciences and that have no place in rational inquiry, the dogmas of the several varieties of behaviorism, for example, which seek to impose a priori limits on possible theory construction, a conception that would properly be dismissed as entirely irrational in the natural sciences. It means a frank adherence to mentalism, where we understand talk about the mind to be talk about the brain at an abstract level at which, so we try to demonstrate, principles can be formulated that enter into successful and insightful explanation of linguistic (and other) phenomena that are provided by observation and experiment. Mentalism, in this sense, has no taint of mysticism and carries no dubious ontological burden. Rather, mentalism falls strictly within the standard practice of the natural sciences and, in fact, is nothing other than the approach of the natural sciences applied to this particular domain. This conclusion, which is the opposite of what is often assumed, becomes understandable and clear if we consider specific topics in the natural sciences; for example, nineteenth-century chemistry, which sought to explain phenomena in terms of such abstract notions as elements, the periodic table, valence, benzene rings, and so on—that is, in terms of abstract

From N. Chomsky, On the nature, use and acquisition of language, in N. Chomsky, *Generative grammar: Its basis, development and prospects* (1987). Kyoto: Kyoto University of Foreign Studies; and N. Chomsky, *Language in a psychological setting, Sophia Linguistica* XII (1987). Tokyo: Sophia University. Reprinted by permission of the author.

properties of then-unknown, perhaps still unknown, physical mechanisms. This abstract inquiry served as an essential preliminary and guide for the subsequent inquiry into physical mechanisms. Mentalistic inquiry in the brain sciences is quite similar in approach and character to the abstract inquiry into properties of the chemical elements, and we may expect that this abstract inquiry too will serve as an essential preliminary and guide for the emerging brain sciences today; the logic is quite similar.

This work proceeds from the empirical assumption—which is well-supported—that there is a specific faculty of the mind/brain that is responsible for the use and acquisition of language, a faculty with distinctive characteristics that is apparently unique to the species in essentials and a common endowment of its members, hence a true species property.

These ideas have developed in the context of what some have called "the cognitive revolution" in psychology, and in fact constituted one major factor contributing to these developments. It is important, I think, to understand clearly just what this "revolution" sought to accomplish, why it was undertaken, and how it relates to earlier thinking about these topics. The so-called "cognitive revolution" is concerned with the states of the mind/brain that enter into thought, planning, perception, learning and action. The mind/brain is considered to be an information-processing system, which forms abstract representations and carries out computations that use and modify them. This approach stands in sharp contrast to the study of the shaping and control of behavior that systematically avoided consideration of the states of the mind/brain that enter into behavior, and sought to establish direct relations between stimulus situations, contingencies of reinforcement, and behavior. This behaviorist approach has proven almost entirely barren, in my view, a fact that is not at all surprising since it refuses in principle to consider the major and essential component of all behavior, namely, the states of the mind/brain.

Consider the problem of learning. We have an organism with a mind/brain that is in a certain state or configuration. The organism is presented with certain sensory inputs, leading to a change in the state of the mind/brain. This process is the process of learning, or perhaps more accurately, mental and cognitive growth. Having attained a new state as a result of this process, the organism now carries out certain actions, in part influenced by the state of the mind/brain that has been attained. There is no direct relation between the sensory inputs that led to the change of state of the mind/brain and the actions carried out by the organism, except under highly artificial, uninformative and very marginal conditions.

There is of course a relation of some kind between sensory inputs and behavior; a child who has not been presented with data of Japanese will not be able to carry out the behavior of speaking Japanese. Presented with appropriate data from Japanese, the child's mind/brain undergoes a significant change; the mind/brain comes to incorporate within itself knowledge of Japanese, which then enables the child to speak and understand Japanese. But there is no direct relation between the data presented to the child and what the child says, and it is hopeless to try to predict what the child will say, even in probabilistic terms, on the basis of the sensory data that led to acquisition of knowledge of Japanese. We can study the process by which the sensory data lead to the change of state of the mind/brain, and we may study at least certain aspects of how this attained knowledge is used. But an effort to study the relation between the sensory data and the actual behavior, avoiding the crucial matter of the nature of the mind/brain and the changes it undergoes, is doomed to triviality and failure, as the history of psychology demonstrates very well. The cognitive revolution was based in part on the recognition of such facts as these, drawing conclusions that really should not be controversial, though they are—a sign of the immaturity of the field, in my view. This change of perspective in the study of psychology, linguistics included, was surely a proper one in essence, and in fact was long overdue.

Not only was this change of perspective overdue, but it also was much less of a revolution than many believed. In fact, without awareness, the new perspective revived ideas that had been developed quite extensively centuries earlier. In particular, seventeenth-century science developed a form of cognitive psychology that was quite rich, and basically, I think, on the right track. Descartes's major scientific contribution, perhaps, was his rejection of the neoscholastic idea that perception is a process in which the form of an object imprints itself somehow on the brain, so that if you see a cube, for example, your brain has the form of a cube imprinted in it in some fashion. In place of this fallacious conception, Descartes proposed a representational theory of mind. He considered the example of a blind man with a stick, who uses the stick to touch in sequence various parts of a physical object before him, let us say a cube. This sequence of tactile inputs leads the blind man construct, in his mind, the image of a cube, but the form of the cube is not imprinted in the mind. Rather, the sequence of tactile inputs leads the mind to construct a mental representation of a cube, using its own resources and its own structural principles. Descartes argued that much the same is true of normal vision. A series of stimuli strike the retina, and the mind then forms ideas that provide a conception of the objects of the external world. The mind then carries out various computational processes, as the person thinks about these objects, including processes that enable the person to carry out certain actions involving them: for example, picking up the cube, rotating it, and so on. This is surely the right general approach. It has been revived in recent psychology and physiology, and by now something is known about how the process takes place, including even some understanding of the physical mechanisms involved in the coding and representation of stimuli.

Descartes also observed that if a certain figure, say a triangle, is presented to a person, then what the person will perceive is a triangle, though the presented image is certainly not a Euclidean triangle, but rather some far more complex figure. This will be true, he argued, even if the person is a child who has had no previous acquaintance with geometrical figures. In a certain sense the point is obvious, since true geometrical figures do not exist in the natural environment in which we grow and live, but we nevertheless perceive figures as distorted geometrical figures, not as exact instances of whatever they may happen to be. Why does the child perceive the object as a distorted triangle, rather than as the very complex figure that it actually is: with one of the lines slightly curved, with two sides not quite touching, and so on? Descartes' answer was that the Euclidean triangle is produced by the mind on the occasion of this stimulation, because the mechanisms of the mind are based on principles of Euclidean geometry and produce these geometrical figures as exemplars or models for the organization of perception, and for learning, drawing them from its own resources and structural principles.

In contrast, empiricists such as David Hume argued that we simply have no idea of a triangle, or a straight line, since we could not distinguish "perfect images" of such objects from the "defective ones" of the real world. Hume correctly drew the consequences of the empiricist principles that he adopted and developed: in particular, the principle that the mind receives impressions from the outside world and forms associations based upon them, and that this is all there is to the story (apart from the animal instinct underlying induction). But the consequences that Hume correctly drew from these assumptions are certainly false. Contrary to what he asserted, we do, indeed, have a clear concept of a triangle and a straight line, and we perceive objects of the world in terms of these concepts, just as Descartes argued. The conclusion, then, is that the empiricist assumptions are fundamentally wrong, as a matter of empirical fact; the properties of the mind/brain that are involved in determining how we perceive and what we perceive are crucially different from what was postulated in empirical speculation. It seems reasonable to resort to a representational theory of mind of the Cartesian sort, including the concept of the mind as an information-processing system that computes, forms and modifies representations; and we should also adopt something like the Cartesian concept of innate ideas as tendencies and dispositions, biologically determined properties of the mind/brain that provide a framework for the construction of mental representations, a framework that then enters into our perception and action. Ideas of this sort have been revived in the context of the cognitive revolution of the past generation.

Seventeenth-century psychologists, who we call "philosophers," went far beyond these observations. They developed a form of what much later came to be called "Gestalt psychology" as similar ideas were rediscovered during this century. These seventeenth-century thinkers speculated rather plausibly on how we perceive objects around us in terms of structural properties, in terms of our concepts of object and relation, cause and effect, whole and part, symmetry, proportion, the functions served by objects and the characteristic uses to which they are put. We perceive the world around us in this manner, they argued, as a consequence of the organizing activity of the mind, based on its innate structure and the experience that has caused it to assume new and richer forms. "The book of nature is legible only to an intellectual eye," as Ralph Cudworth argued, developing such ideas as these. Again, these speculations seem to be very much on the right track, and the ideas have been rediscovered and developed in contemporary psychology, in part within the context of the cognitive revolution.

The contemporary cognitive revolution has been considerably influenced by modern science, mathematics and technology. The mathematical theory of computation, which developed in the 1920s and 1930s particularly, provided conceptual tools that make it possible to address certain classical problems of representational psychology in a serious way, problems of language in particular. Wilhelm von Humboldt understood, a century and a half ago, that language is a system that makes infinite use of finite means, in his phrase. But he was unable to give a clear account of this correct idea, or to use it as the basis for substantive research into language. The conceptual tools developed in more recent years make it possible for us to study the infinite use of finite means with considerable clarity and understanding. Modern generative grammar, in fact, can be regarded in part as the result of the confluence of the conceptual tools of modern logic and mathematics and the traditional Humboldtian conception, inevitably left vague and unformed. A generative grammar of a language is a formal system that states explicitly what are these finite means available to the mind/brain, which can then make infinite, unbounded use of these means. Unfortunately, the classical ideas concerning language and representational psychology had long been forgotten when the cognitive revolution took place in the 1950s, and the connections I am now discussing were discovered only much later, and are still not widely known.

The development of electronic computers has also influenced the cognitive revolution considerably, primarily in providing useful concepts such as internal representation, modular structure, the software-hardware distinction and the like, and also, in areas such as vision at least, in making it possible to develop explicit models of cognitive processes that can be tested for accuracy and refined. It is worthy of note that much the same was true of the seventeenth-century cognitive revolution. The Cartesians were much impressed with the mechanical automata then being constructed by skilled craftsmen, which seemed to mimic certain aspects of the behavior of organisms. These automata were a stimulus to their scientific imagination much in the way that modern electronic computers have contributed to the contemporary cognitive revolution.

Some of these seventeenth-century ideas, which are now being rediscovered and developed in quite new ways, have much earlier origins. What is probably the world's first psychological experiment is described in the Platonic dialogues, when Socrates undertakes to demonstrate that a slave boy, who has had no instruction in geometry, nevertheless knows the truths of geometry. Socrates demonstrates this by asking the slave boy a series of questions, providing him with no information but drawing from the inner resources of the slave boy's mind, and in this way Socrates leads the slave boy to the point where he recognizes the truth of theorems of geometry. This experiment was understood, quite plausibly, to show that the slave boy knew geometry without any experience. Indeed, it is difficult to see what other interpretation can be given. The experiment was, presumably, a kind of "thought experiment," but if it were carried out rigorously, as has never been done, the results would probably be more or less as Plato presented them in this literary version of a psychological experiment.

The human mind, in short, somehow incorporates the principles of geometry, and experience only serves to bring them to the point where this innate knowledge can be used. This demonstration also poses a very crucial problem: the problem is to explain how the slave boy can have the knowledge he does have, when he has had no relevant experience from which he could derive this knowledge. Let us refer to this problem as "Plato's problem," returning to it directly.

The rise of generative grammar in the 1950s, a major factor in the cognitive revolution, also resurrected traditional ideas. The Cartesians, in particular, had applied their ideas on the nature of the mind to the study of language, which was commonly viewed as a kind of "mirror of mind." Subsequent study enriched these investigations in quite impressive ways, which we are now only beginning to understand. The cognitive revolution of the 1950s, then, should be understood, I believe, as having recovered independently the insights of earlier years, abandoning the barren dogmas that had impeded understanding of these questions for a very long period; and then applying these classical ideas, now reconstructed in a new framework, in new ways, and developing them along lines that would not have been possible in an earlier period, thanks to new understanding in the sciences, technology and mathematics.

From the point of view adopted in this "second cognitive revolution," the central problems of the study of language are essentially the following four:

The first question, a preliminary to any further inquiry, is this: What is the system of knowledge incorporated in the mind/brain of a person who speaks and understands a particular language? What constitutes the language that the person has mastered and knows? A theory concerned with this topic for a particular language is called "a grammar of that language," or in technical terms, "a generative grammar of the language," where the term "generative grammar" means nothing more than a theory of the language that is fully explicit, so that empirical consequences can be derived in it. Traditional grammars, in contrast, relied crucially on the knowledge of language of the reader of the grammar to fill in the enormous gaps that were left unstudied, and were not even recognized to be gaps; it is surprising, in retrospect, to see how difficult it was to recognize that even the simplest of phenomena pose rather serious problems of explanation. A traditional grammar, then, is not a theory of the language, but is rather a guide that can be followed by a person who already knows the language. Similarly, a pedagogic grammar of Spanish written in English is not a theory of Spanish but rather a guide to Spanish that can be used by a speaker of English who already knows the basic principles of language, though unconsciously, and can therefore make use of the hints and examples in the grammar to draw conclusions about Spanish. A generative grammar, in contrast, seeks to make explicit just what this knowledge is that enables the intelligent reader to make use of a grammar.

To the extent that we can provide at least a partial answer to the first problem, we can turn to a second problem: How is this knowledge of language used in thought or expression of thought, in understanding, in organizing behavior, or in such special uses of language as communication, and so on? Here we have to make a crucial conceptual distinction between (1) the language, a certain cognitive system, a system of knowledge incorporated in the mind/brain and described by the linguist's generative grammar; and (2) various processing systems of the mind/brain that access this knowledge in one or another way, and put it to use.

Still assuming some kind of answer to the problem of characterizing the knowledge attained, we can turn to a third problem: what are the physical mechanisms that exhibit the properties that we discover in the abstract investigation of language and its use; that is, the physical mechanisms of the brain that are involved in the representation of knowledge and in accessing and processing this knowledge? These are pretty much tasks for the future, and they are very difficult ones, primarily, because for very good ethical reasons, we do not permit direct experimentation that might enable scientists to investigate these mechanisms directly. In the case of other systems of the mind/brain, such as the visual system, the investigation of mechanisms has proceeded quite far. The reason is that we allow ourselves, rightly or wrongly, to carry out direct experimentation with cats, monkeys, and so on. Their visual systems are in many ways like our own, so a good deal can be learned about the physical mechanisms of the human visual system in this way. But it appears that the language faculty is a unique human possession in its essentials, and if we were to discover some other organism that shared this faculty in part, we would probably regard it as quasi-human and refrain from direct experimentation. Consequently, the study of physical mechanisms of the language faculty must be studied in much more indirect ways, either by non-intrusive experiments, or by "nature's experiments," such as injury and pathology. Part of the intellectual fascination of the study of language is that it must proceed in such indirect ways, relying very heavily on the abstract level of inquiry—a difficult and challenging task, but one that can be addressed and has much promise.

The fourth problem is to explain how the knowledge of language and ability to use it are acquired. This problem of acquisition arises both for the language—the cognitive system itself—and for the various processing systems that access the language. I will focus attention here on the first of these questions: on acquisition of language. Plainly, the question can be formulated only to the extent that we have some understanding of what is acquired—of what is a language—though as always, inquiry into the acquisition or use or physical basis of some abstract system can and should provide insight into its nature.

The fourth question is a special case of Plato's problem: How do we come to have such rich and specific knowledge, or such intricate systems of belief and understanding, when the evidence available to us is so meager? That was the problem that rightly troubled Plato, and it should trouble us as well. It is a question that for a long period did not trouble psychologists, linguists, philosophers, and others who thought about the matter, except for a few, who were rather marginal to the main intellectual tradition. This is a sign of the serious intellectual failings of the thought of this era, an interesting topic that I will not pursue here. If a rational Martian scientist were to observe what takes place in a single language community on earth, he would conclude that knowledge of the language that is used is almost entirely inborn. The fact that this is not true, or at least not entirely true, is extremely puzzling, and raises many quite serious problems for psychology and biology, including evolutionary biology.

Recall that Plato had an answer to the problem he posed: we remember the knowledge we have from an earlier existence. This is not a proposal that we would nowadays be inclined to accept in exactly these terms, though we should, in all honesty, be prepared to recognize that it is a far more satisfactory and rational answer than the ones that have been offered in the dominant intellectual traditions of recent centuries, including the Anglo-American empiricist tradition, which simply evaded the problems. To render Plato's answer intelligible, we have to provide a mechanism by which our knowledge is remembered from an earlier existence. If we are disinclined to accept the immortal soul as the mechanism, we will follow Leibniz in assuming that Plato's answer is on the right track, but must be, in his words, "purged of the error of preexistence." In modern terms, that means reconstructing Platonic "remembrance" in terms of the genetic endowment, which specifies the initial state of the language faculty, much as it determines that we will grow arms not wings, undergo sexual maturation at a certain stage of growth if external conditions such as nutritional level permit this internally directed maturational process to take place, and so on. Nothing is known in detail about the mechanisms in any of these cases, but it is now widely and plausibly assumed that this is the place to look. At least, it is widely assumed for physical growth. The fact that similar evidence does not lead to similar rational conclusions in the case of the mind/brain again reflects the serious intellectual inadequacies of recent thought, which has simply refused to approach problems of the mind/brain by the methods of rational inquiry taken for granted in the physical sciences. This is strikingly true, particularly, of those who falsely believe themselves to be scientific naturalists, and who see themselves as defending science against the obscurantists. Exactly the opposite is true, in my opinion, for the reasons that I have briefly indicated.

Putting aside various dogmas, let us approach questions of mind/brain, including questions of language, in the spirit of the natural sciences. Abstracting away from unknown mechanisms, we assume that the language faculty has an initial state, genetically determined, common to the species apart from gross pathology, and apparently unique to the human species. We know that this initial state can mature to a number of different steady states—the various attainable languages—as conditions of exposure vary. The process of maturation from the initial state to the steady state of mature knowledge is, to some extent, data-driven; exposed to data of English, the mind/brain will incorporate knowledge of English, not Japanese. Furthermore, this process of growth of the language faculty begins remarkably early in life. Recent work indicates that four-day-old infants can already distinguish somehow between the language spoken in their community and other languages, so that the mechanisms of the language faculty begin to operate and to be "tuned" to the external environment very early in life.

It is fairly clear that the process of maturation to the steady state is deterministic. Language learning is not really something that the child does; it is something that happens to the child placed in an appropriate environment, much as the child's body grows and matures in a predetermined way when provided with appropriate nutrition and environmental stimulation. This is not to say that the nature of the environment is irrelevant. The environment determines how the options left unspecified by the initial state of the language faculty are fixed, yielding different languages. In a somewhat similar way, the early visual environment determines the density of receptors for horizontal and vertical lines. Furthermore, the difference between a rich and stimulating environment and an impoverished environment may be substantial, in language acquisition as in physical growth—or more accurately, as in other aspects of physical growth, the acquisition of language being simply one of these aspects. Capacities that are part of our common human endowment can flourish, or can be restricted and suppressed, depending on the conditions provided for their growth.

The point is probably more general. It is a traditional insight, which merits more attention than it receives, that teaching should not be compared to filling a bottle with water, but rather to helping a flower to grow in its own way. As any good teacher knows, the methods of instruction and the range of material covered are matters of small importance as compared with the success achieved in arousing the natural curiosity of the students and stimulating their interest in exploring on their own. What the student learns passively will be quickly forgotten. What students discover for themselves, when their natural curiosity and creative impulses are aroused, will not only be remembered, but will be the basis for further exploration and inquiry, and perhaps significant intellectual contributions. The same is true in other domains as well. A truly democratic community is one in which the general public has the opportunity for meaningful and constructive participation in the formation of social policy: in their own immediate community, in the workplace, and in the society at large. A society that excludes large areas of crucial decision-making from public control, or a system of governance that merely grants the general public the opportunity to ratify decisions taken by the elite groups that dominate the private society and the state, hardly merits the term "democracy." These too are insights that were alive and vital during the eighteenth century, and have in recent years been largely forgotten or suppressed. The point was made, in another context, by Kant, defending the French Revolution during the period of the Terror against those who argued that the masses of the population "are not ripe for freedom." "If one accepts this proposition," he wrote, "freedom will never be achieved, for one can not arrive at the maturity for freedom without having already acquired it; one must be free to learn how to make use of one's powers freely and usefully . . . one can achieve reason only through one's own experience and one must be free to be able to undertake them. . . . To accept the principle that freedom is worthless for those under one's control and that one has the right to refuse it to them for ever, is an infringement of the rights of God himself, who has created man to be free." Reason, the ability to make use of one's powers freely and usefully, and other human qualities can be achieved only in an environment in which they can flourish. They cannot be taught by coercive means. What is true of physical growth holds quite generally of human maturation and learning.

Returning to the language faculty, learning of language, as noted, is something that happens to the child, without awareness for the most part, just as other processes such as sexual maturation happen to the child. A child does not decide to undergo sexual maturation because it sees others doing so and thinks this would be a good idea, or because it is trained or reinforced. Rather, the process happens in its own inner-directed way. The course of the process, its timing, and its detailed nature are in part influenced by the environment, by nutritional level for example, but the process itself is inner-directed in its essentials. The same appears to be true of language learning, and of other aspects of cognitive growth as well. The term "learning" is, in fact, a very misleading one, and one that is probably best abandoned as a relic of an earlier age, and earlier misunderstandings. Knowledge of language grows in the mind/brain of a child placed in a certain speech community.

Knowledge of language within a speech community is shared to remarkably fine detail, in every aspect of language from pronunciation to interpretation. In each of these aspects, the knowledge attained vastly transcends the evidence available in richness and complexity, and in each of these aspects, the fineness of detail and the precision of knowledge goes well beyond anything that can be explained on any imaginable functional grounds, such as the exigencies of communication. For example, children mimic the sounds of the language around them to a level of precision that is well beyond the capacity of adults to perceive, and in other domains as well, the precision of knowledge and understanding, as well as its scope and richness, are far beyond anything that could be detected in normal human interchange. These properties of normal language can often only be discovered by careful experiment. These are the basic and simplest elements of the problem we face.

We therefore conclude that the initial stage of the language faculty can be regarded as in effect a deterministic input-output system that takes presented data as its input and produces a highly structured cognitive system of a very specific form as its "output"—here the output is internalized, represented in the mind/brain; it is the steady state of knowledge of some particular language. The initial state of the language faculty can be regarded, in essence, as a language-acquisition device; in normal terms, a function that maps presented data into a steady state of knowledge attained. This general conclusion allows many specific variants, to some of which I will briefly return, but it is virtually inconceivable that it is wrong in any fundamental way. There has been much debate over this issue in the literature—more accurately, a one-sided debate in which critics argue that the idea has been refuted, with little response from its defenders. The reason for the lack of response is that the criticism must be based on profound confusion, and inspection of the arguments quickly reveals that this is the case, as it must be, given the nature of the problem.

The theory of the initial state—of the language acquisition device—is sometimes called "universal grammar," adapting a traditional term to a somewhat different conceptual framework. It is commonly assumed that universal grammar, so conceived, determines the class of attainable languages. Let me quote from a recent paper by the two leading researchers in the important new field of mathematical learning theory, a paper on models of language acquisition. They write that universal grammar

imposes restrictions on a [particular] grammar in such a way that the class of [particular] grammars admissible by the theory includes grammars of all and only natural languages, [where] the natural languages are identified with the languages that can be acquired by normal human infants under casual conditions of access to linguistic data.

The first of these propositions is a definition, and a proper and useful one, so it is not open to challenge: we may define a "natural language" as one that accords with the principles of universal grammar. But the second of these propositions need not be correct. The languages attainable under normal conditions of access are those that fall in the intersection of two sets: (1) the set of natural languages made available by the initial state of the language faculty as characterized by universal grammar, and (2) the set of learnable systems. If universal grammar permits unlearnable languages, as it might, then they simply will not be learned. Learnability, then, is not a requirement that must be met by the language faculty.

Similarly, parsability—that is, the ability of the mind/brain to assign a structural analysis to a sentence—is not a requirement that must be met by a language, contrary to what is often claimed. In fact, we know that the claim is false: every language permits many different categories of expressions that cannot be used or understood readily (or at all), though they are perfectly well-formed, a fact that in no way impedes communication. Furthermore, deviant expressions may be readily parsable, and are often quite properly used. In brief, it is a mistake to think that languages are "designed" for ease of use. In so far as their structure does not conform to functional requirements, their elements are not used.

In the case of learnability, the proposition that the natural languages are learnable may very well be true, but if so, that is not a matter of principle, but rather a surprising empirical discovery about natural language. Recent work in linguistics suggests that it probably is true, again, a surprising and important empirical discovery, to which I will briefly return.

There has been a fair amount of confusion about these matters, in part resulting from misinterpretation of properties of formal systems: for example, the well-known observation that unconstrained transformational grammars can generate all sets that can be specified by finite means, and results on efficient parsability of context-free languages. In both cases, entirely unwarranted conclusions have been drawn about the nature of language. In fact, no conclusions at all can be drawn with regard to language, language learning, or language use, on the basis of such considerations as these, though other directions of formal inquiry perhaps show more promise of potential empirical significance; for example, some recent work in complexity theory.

When the study of language is approached in the manner I have just outlined, one would expect a close and fruitful interaction between linguistics proper and the investigation of such topics as language processing and acquisition. To some extent this has happened, but less so than might have been hoped. It is useful to reflect a little about why this has been the case. One reason, I think, is the one just mentioned: misinterpretation of results about formal systems has caused considerable confusion. Other problems have arisen from a failure to consider carefully the conceptual relations between language and learnability, and between language and processing. One instructive example is the history of what was called "the derivational theory of complexity," the major paradigm of psycholinguistic research in the early days of the "cognitive revolution." This theory led to an experimental program. The experiments carried out were tests of a theory with two components: (1) assumptions about the rule systems of natural language; (2) assumptions about processing. Some of the experimental results confirmed this combination of theories, others disconfirmed it. But care must be taken to determine just which elements of the combination of theories were confirmed or disconfirmed. In practice, where predictions were disconfirmed, it was concluded that the linguistic component of the amalgam was at fault. While this might be true, and sometimes was as other evidence showed, it was a curious inference, since there was independent evidence supporting the assumptions about language but none whatsoever supporting the assumptions about processing, assumptions that were, furthermore, not particularly plausible except as rough first approximations. Failure to appreciate these facts undermined much subsequent discussion. Similar questions arise with language acquisition, and confirming evidence too, in both areas, is unclear in its import unless the various factors entering into the predictions are properly sorted out.

The history of the derivational theory of complexity illustrates other problems that have impeded useful interaction between linguistics and experimental psychology. Early experimental work was designed to test certain ideas about rule systems on the assumption that processing satisfies the conditions of the derivational theory of complexity. By the time the experimental program had been carried out, with mixed results, the theories of rule systems had changed. Many experimental psychologists found this disconcerting. How can we carry out experimental tests of a theory if it is not stable and is subject to change? These reactions led to a noticeable shift in focus to work in areas that are better insulated from theoretical modification elsewhere.

There are a number of problems with such reactions. One problem is a point of logic: to insulate one's work from theoretical modifications elsewhere is to keep to topics of limited significance, close to the surface of phenomena. If one's work is important enough to have consequences beyond its immediate scope, then it cannot be immune to new understanding outside of this scope. For example, it is likely that results on order of acquisition of function words or on turn-taking in conversation will be immune to discoveries and new understanding elsewhere; the reason is that the implications are very slight. Relevance, after all, is a two-way street. This reaction to the inevitable changes in theoretical assumptions in a discipline that is alive also reflects a far too limited conception of the work of the experimental psychologist, who is perceived as someone who tests ideas developed elsewhere but does not contribute otherwise to their proper formulation. But research into language should obviously be a cooperative enterprise, which can be informed and advanced by use of evidence of many different kinds. There is no privileged sector of this discipline that provides theories, which are tested by others. One sign that the discipline is approaching a higher level of maturity will be that research into language processing and language acquisition will yield conclusions about the structure of language that can be tested by linguists, using the tools of their specific approach to a common network of problems and concerns. The idea that linguistics should be related to psychology as theoretical physics is related to experimental physics is senseless and untenable, and has, I think, been harmful.

Theories of language have indeed undergone significant changes during the period we are now considering—which is to say that the discipline is alive. I think we can identify two major changes of perspective during this period, each with considerable ramifications for the study of language use and acquisition. Let me review these changes briefly, focusing on the three central questions that I mentioned earlier: (1) what is knowledge of language?; (2) how is it acquired?; and (3) how is it used?

Some thirty years ago the standard answers to these questions would have been something like this.

1. What is knowledge of language? Answer: it is a system of habits, dispositions and abilities. This answer, incidentally, is still widely held, notably by philosophers influenced by Wittgenstein and Quine.

2. How is language acquired? Answer: by conditioning, training, habit-formation or "general learning mechanisms" such as induction.

3. How is language used? Answer: language use is the exercise of an ability, like any skill; say, bicycle-riding. New forms are produced or

understood "by analogy" to old ones. In fact, the problem posed by production of new forms, the normal situation in language use, was barely noticed. This is quite a remarkable fact, first, because the point is obvious, and second, because it was a major preoccupation of the linguistics of the first cognitive revolution of the seventeenth century. Here we have a striking example of how ideology displaced the most obvious of phenomena from inquiry.

Attention to the simplest phenomena suffices to show that these ideas cannot be even close to the truth of the matter, and must simply be abandoned. Let me illustrate with a very simple example. Imagine a child learning English who comes to understand the sentence *John ate an apple*. The child then knows that the word *eat* takes two semantic roles, that of the subject (the agent of the action) and that of object (the recipient of the action); it is a typical transitive verb. Suppose that the child now hears the reduced sentence *John ate*, in which the object is missing. Since the verb is transitive, requiring an object, the child will understand the sentence to mean, roughly, "John ate something or other." So far everything is fairly straightforward if we assume the simple principle that when a semantically required element is missing, the mind interprets it to be a kind of "empty pronoun" meaning: something or other. Perhaps an empiricist linguist might be willing to suppose that this principle is available as an innate element of the language faculty.

Consider now a very simple but slightly more complex sentence. Suppose the child comes to understand such sentences as *John is too clever to catch Bill*. Here the verb *catch* also requires a subject and an object, but the subject is missing in this sentence. It therefore has to be supplied by the mind, in the manner of the object of *ate* in *John ate*. By the principle just assumed to account for *John ate*, the sentence should mean: John is so clever that someone or other will not catch Bill. That is a fine meaning, but it is not the meaning of *John is too clever to catch Bill*. Rather, the sentence means: John is so clever that he, John, will not catch Bill. The mind does not use the empty pronoun principle, but rather takes the subject of *catch* to be the same as the subject of *is clever*. Since this is known without instruction or evidence, we must attribute to the mind still a second principle, let us call it the principle of subject control: the missing subject of the embedded clause is understood to be the same as the subject of the main clause. Our assumptions about the innate resources of the mind must therefore be enriched.

Let us carry the discussion a step further. Suppose we delete *Bill* from the sentence *John is too clever to catch Bill*, so that we have *John is too clever to catch*. By the empty pronoun principle and the subject control principle, the sentence should mean: John is so clever that he, John, will not catch someone or other. But the child knows that it does not mean that at all; rather, it means that John is so clever that someone or other will not catch him, John. The child interprets the sentence by some other principle, call it the inversion principle, which tells us that the object of the embedded sentence is understood to be the same as the subject of the main verb, and the subject of the embedded sentence is an empty pronoun referring to someone or other.

We now have to attribute to the mind/brain three principles: the empty pronoun principle, the subject principle, and the inversion principle. Furthermore, some overarching principle of the mind/brain determines when these principles of interpretation are applied.

Turning to slightly more complicated examples, the mysteries deepen. Consider the sentence *John is too clever to expect anyone to catch*. English speakers at first may find this sentence a bit puzzling, but "on reflection" (whatever that involves), they understand it to mean that John is so clever that someone doesn't expect anyone to catch John; that is, it is interpreted by means of the empty pronoun principle and the inversion principle. But now compare this sentence with another that is roughly comparable in complexity: *John is too clever to meet anyone who caught*. Here all principles fail; the sentence is complete gibberish. We can parse the sentence with no difficulty; it just doesn't mean anything sensible. In particular, it is not understood "by analogy" to mean that John is so clever that no one met anyone who caught him, John.

Notice that none of this is the result of training, or even experience. These facts are known without training, without correction of error, without relevant experience, and are known the same way by every speaker of English—and in analogous constructions, other languages. Hence all of this must somehow derive from the inner resources of the mind/brain, from the genetically determined constitution of the language faculty. Clearly the answer cannot be that these resources include the empty pronoun principle, the subject principle, the inversion principle, some principle that determines how they operate, and a principle blocking the "analogy" in the last example. Rather, we would like to show that the observed facts follow from some deeper principles of the language faculty. This is a typical problem of science, and one that has, in fact, been rather successfully addressed in recent work. But the point here is that the facts show rather clearly that the standard answers to our questions that I have just mentioned cannot be on the right track.

Notice again that the concept of "analogy" does no work at all. By analogy to *John ate*, the sentence *John is too clever to catch* should mean "John is too clever to catch someone or other," but it does not. Notice also that such examples refute the conception of knowledge of language as a skill or ability. The child does not fail to provide the analogous interpretation because of a failure of ability—because it is too weak, or needs more practice. Rather, the computational system of the mind/ brain is designed to force certain interpretations for linguistic expressions. To put the matter in the context of the theory of knowledge, our knowledge that expression such-and-such means so-and-so is not justified or grounded in experience in any useful sense of these terms, is not based on good reasons or reliable procedures, is not derived by induction or any other general method. Since these are examples of ordinary propositional knowledge, knowledge that so-and-so, the standard paradigms of epistemology and fixation of belief cannot be correct, and investigation of further examples and other cognitive systems reveals exactly the same thing, so I believe.

I think that these are all important facts, insufficiently appreciated, with quite considerable import. We discover facts of this sort wherever we look, if we are not blinded or misled by dogma.

One notable feature of the widely held conceptions of knowledge and language in terms of ability, skill, habit, general learning mechanisms and analogy, is that they were entirely unproductive and without empirical consequences. One can hardly point to a single empirical result of the slightest significance that derived from these conceptions. The psychology of language of the time was almost completely barren. There was an empirical discipline, namely structural linguistics, which did profess these doctrines and did achieve empirical results and some theoretical understanding. But a closer look will show that in practice, research departed from the professed ideology at every crucial point. The general conceptual framework limited and impoverished the discipline, barring natural lines of inquiry, but otherwise was simply professed and abandoned in practice, though it did, I believe, have a serious and generally harmful impact on applied disciplines such as language teaching.

Recognition of the complete inadequacy of these conceptions led to the first major conceptual change, which was, in many respects, a return to traditional ideas and concerns that had been dismissed or forgotten during the long period when empiricist and behaviorist doctrines prevailed. This shift of focus provided a new set of answers to the central question:

1. What is knowledge of language? Answer: language is a computational system, a rule system of some sort. Knowledge of language is knowledge of this rule system.

2. How is language acquired? Answer: the initial state of the language faculty determines possible rules and modes of interaction. Language is acquired by a process of selection of a rule system of an appropriate sort on the basis of direct evidence. Experience yields an inventory of rules, through the language-acquisition device of the language faculty.

3. How is language used? Answer: the use of language is rule-governed behavior. Rules form mental representations, which enter into our speaking and understanding. A sentence is parsed and understood

by a systematic search through the rule system of the language in question.

The new set of answers constitutes a major component of the "cognitive revolution."

This was a significant shift of point of view: from behavior and its products to the system of knowledge represented in the mind/brain that underlies behavior. Behavior is not the focus of inquiry; rather, it simply provides one source of evidence for the internal systems of the mind/brain that are what we are trying to discover—the system that constitutes a particular language and that determines the form, structural properties and meaning of expressions, and more deeply, the innate structure of the language faculty. As I mentioned earlier, this shift towards an avowed mentalism is also a shift towards assimilating the study of language to the natural sciences, and opens up the possibility of a serious investigation of physical mechanisms.

This shift of focus was extremely productive. It led to a rapid decrease in the range of empirical phenomena that were brought under investigation, with many new empirical discoveries, such as those just illustrated, including very simple facts that had never been noticed. It also led to some degree of success in providing explanations for these facts. But serious difficulties arise at once. Basically, these relate to Plato's problem, the problem of acquisition of language. In essence, the problem is that there are too many possible rule systems. Therefore it is hard to explain how children unerringly select one such system rather than another. Furthermore, children seem to select very complex rule systems and systematically to avoid much simpler ones, a conclusion that makes no sense.

These problems set the research agenda since about 1960, within the framework I am considering here. I will not review the steps that were taken, but rather will turn to the result. In the past several years, a new and very different conception of language has emerged, which yields new answers to our three questions. The initial state of the language faculty consists of a collection of subsystems, or *modules* as they are sometimes called, each of which is based on certain general principles. Many of these principles admit of a certain limited possibility of variation. We may think of the system as a complex network associated with a switch box that contains a finite number of switches. The network is invariant, but each switch can be in one of several positions, perhaps two: on or off. Unless the switches are set, nothing happens. But when the switches are set in one of the permissible ways, the system functions, yielding the entire infinite array of interpretations for linguistic expressions. A slight change in switch settings can yield complex and varied phenomenal consequences as its effects filter through the network. There are no rules at all, hence no necessity to learn rules. For example, the possible phrase structures of a language are fixed by general principles and are invariant among languages, but there are some switches to be set. One has to do with order of elements. In English, for example, nouns, verbs, adjectives and prepositions precede their objects: in Japanese, the comparable elements follow their objects. English is what is called a "head-first" language, Japanese a "head-last" language. These facts can be determined from very simple sentences; for example, the sentences "John ate an apple" (in English) or "John an apple ate" (in Japanese). To acquire a language, the child's mind must determine how the switches are set, and simple data must suffice to determine the switch settings, as in this case. The theory of language use also undergoes corresponding modifications, which I cannot explore here.

This second conceptual change gives a very different conception of language and knowledge. To mention one example, notice that from the point of view of rule systems, there are an infinite number of languages, since there are infinitely many rule systems of the permissible form. But from the network-switch point of view, there are only finitely many languages, one for each arrangement of switch settings. Since each of the switch settings can be determined from simple data, each of these finitely many languages is learnable. Hence the general principle of learnability theory discussed earlier is in fact true: each natural language is learnable—though it is far from true that the learnable systems are all natural languages. As I mentioned, this is an empirical result, and a very surprising one, not a matter of principle. There is, incidentally, some intriguing work in mathematical learning theory which suggests that language acquisition is possible in principle under plausible conditions only if the set of natural languages is indeed "finite" (in a special sense).

This second conceptual change has, once again, led to a great increase in the range of empirical materials discovered and subjected to serious inquiry within generative grammar, now from a much wider range of languages.

Assuming that this change is pointing in the right direction, what are the consequences for the study of language acquisition? The problem will be to determine how the switches are set and to discover the principles of learning, or maturation, or whatever is responsible for carrying out the transition from the initial state of the language faculty to the steady state of adult competence; that is, for setting the switches of the language faculty. Recall that two factors enter into language acquisition: the nature of the language faculty, and the principles of learning theory or more properly growth theory, and any evidence about language acquisition must be assessed carefully to determine how it bears on one or the other of these two interacting factors. How can we proceed in studying this question?

Notice that the problem of assessment of evidence and explanation would plainly be simplified if one or the other of these two components—universal grammar or growth theory—does not exist. Each of these positions has been maintained, the first one quite vigorously, the second as a tentative working hypothesis.

Denial of the existence of universal grammar—that is, of the language faculty as an identifiable system of the human mind/brain—is implicit in the empiricist program and in some recent claims about mechanisms of "general intelligence" or "connectionism" or theory formation, mechanisms that are allegedly applied to yield our linguistic abilities and other intellectual achievements in an undifferentiated way. There has been no attempt to formulate these alleged mechanisms that seems to offer any real promise. The clearer formulations have been quickly refuted, in some cases refuted in principle, and for reasons that should be familiar, the prospects for this program seem very dim. Since there is nothing substantive to discuss, I will disregard this possibility and proceed to the second possibility: that growth theory is negligible or non-existent, so that language-acquisition simply involves switch setting on the basis of presented data, such as the sentences "John ate an apple" and "John an apple ate." Let us call this the "no-growth theory" of language acquisition.

Obviously, this cannot be literally true. During the first few months or perhaps weeks of life, an infant probably is exposed to enough linguistic data to set most switches, but plainly it has not done so. In fact, the process extends over quite a few years. So to maintain the no-growth theory we would have to argue that some independent and extrinsic change in cognitive capacities, say in memory or attention, accounts for the observed stages of growth.

Such ideas have been advanced with regard to stages of cognitive development in the sense of Jean Piaget, and also with respect to the stages of language growth. For example, it has been observed that the transition from so-called "telegraphic speech," lacking function words, to normal speech is quite rapid, and includes a number of different systems: questions, negations, tag questions, etc. Furthermore, in the telegraphic speech stage, children understand normal speech better than their own telegraphic speech, and if function words are introduced randomly, the results are unintelligible. This suggests that the children knew the facts of normal speech all along, and were using telegraphic speech because of some limitation of attention and memory. When this limitation is overcome in the course of normal growth and maturation, their already acquired knowledge of language can be manifested. But there are some serious problems in assuming this idea in other cases of regular stages of development: for example, the shift from semantic to syntactic categories, the use of color words, the appearance of a true verbal passive construction and other more complex structures, the emergence of semantic properties of control, and so on. Prima facie, it seems hard to explain these transitions without appeal to maturational processes that bring principles of universal grammar into operation on some regular schedule in a manner to be described and accounted for in a genetic theory. Of course, what is prima facie plausible is not necessarily correct, but the questions that arise are clear enough, and it is an important task to address them, as many investigators are now doing in important recent work.

There is, on the one hand, work by Yukio Otsu, Stephen Crain, and others that seems to show that principles of universal grammar are available as soon as constructions are used in which they would be manifested, and the delay in use of these constructions might be explained in terms of inherent complexity, hence extrinsic factors such as memory.

To take one complex example of much general interest, consider recent work of Nina Hyams on the null subject property that distinguishes languages like French and English, in which subjects must be overtly expressed, from languages such as Italian and Spanish, in which the subject may be suppressed in the phonetic output. Hyam's work indicates that at an early stage, all children treat their language as if it were a null subject language. The switch, she suggests, has what is called an "unmarked setting," or in the more usual terminology, the null subject parameter has an "unmarked value," a value selected in the absence of data, and this value provides a null subject language. Italian-speaking children maintain the unmarked value, while English-speaking children later change to the marked value of the parameter, setting the switch differently. The question then is: What triggers the change? There is good evidence that positive evidence suffices for language acquisition; that is, correction of error is unnecessary and probably largely irrelevant when it occurs. Assuming so, the answer to the question cannot be that the English-speaking children are explicitly corrected. Nor can the answer be that they never hear sentences without subjects, since they hear no evidence for most of what they know. Assuming a no-growth theory, Hyams suggests that the change is triggered by the presence of overt expletives in English, such elements as *there* in "there is a man in the room," elements that are semantically empty but must be present to satisfy some syntactic principle. The assumption is that universal grammar contains a principle implying that if a language has overt expletives, then it is not a null subject language. This is, incidentally, an example of a hypothesis about universal grammar deriving from language acquisition studies that might be tested by linguists, rather than the converse, as in the usual practice. It cannot be quite correct as it stands, but something similar might be true.

But now we have to ask why the English-speaking children delay in using this evidence. A possible answer (though not the one Hyams proposes) might be that extrinsic conditions of memory and attention render these expletives inaccessible at an early stage.

Pursuing a similar idea, Luigi Rizzi suggests that contrary to Hyams's initial conclusion, the unmarked value for the parameter is: overt subject. English-speaking children appear to violate this principle at an early stage, but only because extrinsic considerations suppress the production of such elements as unstressed subject pronouns. Italian-speaking children then select the marked value of the parameter on the basis of direct evidence of subjectless sentences.

A third approach is to reject the no-growth theory and to suppose that the null subject parameter only becomes available at a certain stage of maturation, and is set at the marked null subject value only if direct evidence of subjectless sentences is presented. At the moment, the question remains open, and these possibilities do not exhaust the options (for example, the null subject parameter might be further differentiated, or cast in different terms).

Notice that further clarification of these issues might well contribute to our knowledge of the principles and parameters of universal grammar—of the nature of the network and the switches—on the basis of evidence from language acquisition, as we should anticipate as the discipline progresses.

Consider a second example. Sascha Felix argues against the no-growth theory on the basis of evidence about use of negatives in several languages. Apparently, at the earliest stage, children use sentence-external negation, as in "not John likes milk." This fact (which, not surprisingly, is itself controversial) already raises problems for a no-growth theory, since natural languages rarely if ever exhibit sentence-external negation. At a later stage, the child shifts to sentence-internal negation, as in "John no likes milk," which is also inconsistent with the evidence from the adult language. Later, the correct form "John doesn't like milk" emerges. Felix points out that stage I, with sentence-external negation, is consistent with Dan Slobin's principle that the learner avoids interruption of linguistic units, and hence might be taken to support this principle. But he notes that that leaves unresolved the question why this principle becomes inoperative at stage II, and is even more radically abandoned at stage III. A maturational theory seems a possible candidate for an explanation. Again, further research should contribute to clarifying both the principles of language growth, if they exist, and the actual principles and parameters of universal grammar.

Consider finally a more complex example studied in some detail by Hagit Borer and Kenneth Wexler. They argue that the results in many languages on acquisition of passives can be explained by a maturational theory, which provides a more sophisticated version of the idea that transformations are acquired step-by-step during language acquisition. Their theory postulates that until a certain stage of development, phrases can only be interpreted in a canonical position in which semantic roles are assigned by principles of universal grammar, thus the position of abstract underlying deep structures, in effect. At this stage, a sentence such as "John was killed" is simply uninterpretable, since

John is displaced from its canonical position as object of *kill*. Apparent passive forms at this stage, they argue, are in fact adjectives, as in "the door is closed." Later, a device becomes available, through maturation, by which displaced elements can be interpreted through a so-called *chain* formed by a transformation, which links the displaced element to an empty *trace* in the canonical position. Such chains must then meet various conditions of universal grammar, which account for the possibilities of displacement. They argue that the range of available evidence about acquisition of passives can be largely explained on the basis of this assumption: that chains become available at a certain stage of maturation. Again, there are numerous empirical problems and consequences to be explored, and the results should bear directly on the principles of universal grammar as well as growth theory.

If Borer and Wexler are right, one might be tempted to explore a famous suggestion by Roman Jakobson that language acquisition and language loss in aphasia are mirror images: the earlier some items and structures are acquired in language learning, the later they are lost under brain injury. It would then follow that in some kinds of aphasia, we should find that chains are lost while other aspects of phrase structure remain. Evidence to this effect has in fact been presented by Yosef Grodzinsky. This again suggests what might prove to be an intriguing line of inquiry.

These examples barely scratch the surface. A wide range of intriguing questions arise at once if we think through the implications of the principles-and-parameters conception of universal grammar in terms of an invariant network and an associated set of switches, and if we ask how this conception might relate to possible principles of maturation involved in language growth, along with extrinsic factors in cognitive development. I have not had time to consider the question of language processing, but here too the questions look quite different when approached in these terms. And within the study of language proper, many new and exciting questions enter into the research agenda. If the principles-and-parameters approach is correct, it should be possible literally to deduce the properties of each natural language by setting the switches in one or another way and computing the consequences. Typological difference should be a matter of differences in switch-settings. Language change should be the result of a change in such a setting; note that a small change might yield a substantial phenomenal difference as its effects filter through the fixed network of modular principles. These are all questions that are now being addressed, in some cases with some success, in other cases with failures that are highly suggestive in opening up new lines of inquiry. Furthermore, the class of typologically different languages that have come under investigation, and that seem to be amenable to a coherent and uniform approach, has vastly extended, again, a promising sign.

There are, it seems, real grounds for considerable optimism about the prospects that lie ahead, not only for the study of language proper, but also for the study of cognitive systems of the mind/brain of which language is a fundamental and essential component, in the human species.

24 On Learning the Past Tenses of English Verbs

David E. Rumelhart and James L. McClelland

The Issue

Scholars of language and psycholinguistics have been among the first to stress the importance of rules in describing human behavior. The reason for this is obvious. Many aspects of language can be characterized by rules, and the speakers of natural languages speak the language correctly. Therefore, systems of rules are useful in characterizing what they will and will not say. Though we all make mistakes when we speak, we have a pretty good ear for what is right and what is wrong—and our judgments of correctness—or grammaticality—are generally even easier to characterize by rules than actual utterances.

On the evidence that what we will and won't say and what we will and won't accept can be characterized by rules, it has been argued that, in some sense, we "know" the rules of our language. The sense in which we know them is not the same as the sense in which we know such "rules" as "*i* before *e* except after *c*," however, since we need not necessarily be able to state the rules explicitly. We know them in a way that allows us to use them to make judgments of grammaticality, it is often said, or to speak and understand, but this knowledge is not in a form or location that permits it to be encoded into a communicable verbal statement. Because of this, this knowledge is said to be *implicit*.

So far there is considerable agreement. However, the exact characterization of implicit knowledge is a matter of great controversy. One view, which is perhaps extreme but is nevertheless quite clear, holds that the rules of language are stored in explicit form as propositions, and are used by language production, comprehension, and judgment mechanisms. These propositions cannot be described verbally only because they are sequestered in a specialized subsystem which is used in lan-

From D. Rumelhart and J. McClelland, On learning the past tenses of English verbs, in J. McClelland, D. Rumelhart, and the PDP Research Group, *Parallel distributed processing*, vol. 2 (1986). Cambridge, MA: MIT Press. Reprinted by permission.

guage processing, or because they are written in a special code that only the language processing system can understand. This view we will call the *explicit inaccessible rule* view.

On the explicit inaccessible rule view, language acquisition is thought of as the process of inducing rules. The language mechanisms are thought to include a subsystem—often called the *language acquisition device* (LAD)—whose business it is to discover the rules. A considerable amount of effort has been expended on the attempt to describe how the LAD might operate, and there are a number of different proposals which have been laid out. Generally, though, they share three assumptions:

· The mechanism hypothesizes explicit inaccessible rules.

· Hypotheses are rejected and replaced as they prove inadequate to account for the utterances the learner hears.

· The LAD is presumed to have *innate* knowledge of the possible range of human languages and, therefore, is presumed to consider only hypotheses within the constraints imposed by a set of *linguistic universals.*

The recent book by Pinker (1984) contains a state-of-the-art example of a model based on this approach.

We propose an alternative to explicit inaccessible rules. We suggest that lawful behavior and judgments may be produced by a mechanism in which there is no explicit representation of the rule. Instead, we suggest that the mechanisms that process language and make judgments of grammaticality are constructed in such a way that their performance is characterizable by rules, but that the rules themselves are not written in explicit form anywhere in the mechanism. An illustration of this view, which we owe to Bates (1979), is provided by the honeycomb. The regular structure of the honeycomb arises from the interaction of forces that wax balls exert on each other when compressed. The honeycomb can be described by a rule, but the mechanism which produces it does not contain any statement of this rule.

In our earlier work with the interactive activation model of word perception (McClelland and Rumelhart 1981, Rumelhart and McClelland 1981, 1982), we noted that lawful behavior emerged from the interactions of a set of word and letter units. Each word unit stood for a particular word and had connections to units for the letters of the word. There were no separate units for common letter clusters and no explicit provision for dealing differently with orthographically regular letter sequences—strings that accorded with the rules of English—as opposed to irregular sequences. Yet the model did behave differently with orthographically regular nonwords than it behaved with words. In fact,

Rumelhart and McClelland

the model simulated rather closely a number of results in the word perception literature relating to the finding that subjects perceive letters in orthographically regular letter strings more accurately than they perceive letters in irregular, random letter strings. Thus, the behavior of the model was lawful even though it contained no explicit rules.

It should be said that the pattern of perceptual facilitation shown by the model did not correspond exactly to any system or orthographic rules that we know of. The model produced as much facilitation, for example, for special nonwords like *SLNT*, which are clearly irregular, as it did for matched regular nonwords like *SLET*. Thus, it is not correct to say that the model exactly mimicked the behavior we would expect to emerge from a system which makes use of explicit orthographic rules. However, neither do human subjects. Just like the model, they showed equal facilitation for vowelless strings like *SLNT* as for regular nonwords like *SLET*. Thus, human perceptual performance seems, in this case at least, to be characterized only approximately by rules.

Some people have been tempted to argue that the behavior of the model shows that we can do without linguistic rules. We prefer, however, to put the matter in a slightly different light. There is no denying that rules still provide a fairly close characterization of the performance of our subjects. And we have no doubt that rules are even more useful in characterizations of sentence production, comprehension, and grammaticality judgments. We would only suggest that parallel distributed processing models may provide a mechanism sufficient to capture lawful behavior, without requiring the postulation of explicit but inaccessible rules. Put succinctly, our claim is that PDP [parallel distributed processing] models provide an alternative to the explicit but inaccessible rules account of implicit knowledge of rules.

We can anticipate two kinds of arguments against this kind of claim. The first kind would claim that although certain types of rule-guided behavior might emerge from PDP models, the models simply lack the computational power needed to carry out certain types of operations which can be easily handled by a system using explicit rules. We believe that this argument is simply mistaken. We discuss the issue of computational power of PDP models elsewhere in this work, with some applications to sentence processing. The second kind of argument would be that the details of language behavior, and, indeed, the details of the language acquisition process, would provide unequivocal evidence in favor of a system of explicit rules.

It is this latter kind of argument we wish to address in the present chapter. We have selected a phenomenon that is often thought of as demonstrating the acquisition of a linguistic rule. And we have developed a parallel distributed processing model that learns in a natural way to behave in accordance with the rule, mimicking the general trends seen in the acquisition data.

The Phenomenon

The phenomenon we wish to account for is actually a sequence of three stages in the acquisition of the use of past tense by children learning English as their native tongue. Descriptions of development of the use of the past tense may be found in Brown (1973), Ervin (1964), and Kuczaj (1977).

In Stage 1, children use only a small number of verbs in the past tense. Such verbs tend to be very high-frequency words, and the majority of these are irregular. At this stage, children tend to get the past tenses of these words correct if they use the past tense at all. For example, a child's lexicon of past-tense words at this stage might consist of *came, got, gave, looked, needed, took,* and *went.* Of these seven verbs, only two are regular—the other five are generally idiosyncratic examples of irregular verbs. In this stage, there is no evidence of the use of the rule—it appears that children simply know a small number of separate items.

In Stage 2, evidence of implicit knowledge of a linguistic rule emerges. At this stage, children use a much larger number of verbs in the past tense. These verbs include a few more irregular items, but it turns out that the majority of the words at this stage are examples of the *regular* past tense in English. Some examples are *wiped* and *pulled.*

The evidence that the Stage 2 child actually has a linguistic rule comes not from the mere fact that he or she knows a number of regular forms. There are two additional and crucial facts:

· The child can now generate a past tense for an invented word. For example, Berko (1958) has shown that if children can be convinced to use *rick* to describe an action, they will tend to say *ricked* when the occasion arises to use the word in the past tense.

· Children now *incorrectly* supply regular past-tense endings for words which they used correctly in Stage 1. These errors may involve either adding *ed* to the root as in *comed* /kṁd/, or adding *ed* to the irregular past tense form as in *camed* /kʌmd/[1] (Ervin 1964; Kuczaj 1977).

Such findings have been taken as fairly strong support for the assertion that the child at this stage has acquired the past-tense "rule." To quote Berko (1958):

If a child knows that the plural of *witch* is *witches,* he may simply have memorized the plural form. If, however, he tells us that the plural of *gutch* is *gutches,* we have evidence that he actually knows, albeit unconsciously, one of those rules which the descriptive linguist, too, would set forth in his grammar. (p. 151)

In Stage 3, the regular and irregular forms coexist. That is, children have regained the use of the correct irregular forms of the past tense, while they continue to apply the regular form to new words they learn. Regularizations persist into adulthood—in fact, there is a class of words for which either a regular or an irregular version are both considered acceptable—but for the commonest irregulars such as those the child acquired first, they tend to be rather rare. At this stage there are some clusters of exceptions to the basic, regular past-tense pattern of English. Each cluster includes a number of words that undergo identical changes from the present to the past tense. For example, there is *ing/ang* cluster, an *ing/ung* cluster, an *eet/it* cluster, etc. There is also a group of words ending in /d/ or /t/ for which the present and past are identical.

Table 24.1 summarizes the major characteristics of the three stages.

Variability and Gradualness

The characterization of past-tense acquisition as a sequence of three stages is somewhat misleading. It may suggest that the stages are clearly demarcated and that performance in each stage is sharply distinguished from performance in other stages.

In fact, the acquisition process is quite gradual. Little detailed data exists on the transition from Stage 1 to Stage 2, but the transition from Stage 2 to Stage 3 is quite protracted and extends over several years (Kuczaj 1977). Further, performance in Stage 2 is extremely variable. Correct use of irregular forms is never completely absent, and the same child may be observed to use the correct past of an irregular, the base+ed form, and the past+ed form, within the same conversation.

Other Facts About Past-Tense Acquisition

Beyond these points, there is now considerable data on the detailed types of errors children make throughout the acquisition process, both from Kuczaj (1977) and more recently from Bybee and Slobin (1982). We will consider aspects of these findings in more detail below. For now, we mention one intriguing fact: According to Kuczaj (1977), there is an interesting difference in the errors children make to irregular verbs at different points in Stage 2. Early on, regularizations are typically of the base+ed form, like *goed;* later on, there is a large increase in the frequency of past+ed errors, such as *wented.*

Table 24.1 Characteristics of the three stages of past-tense acquisition

Verb Type	Stage 1	Stage 2	Stage 3
Early verbs	Correct	Regularized	Correct
Regular	—	Correct	Correct
Other irregular	—	Regularized	Correct or regularized
Novel	—	Regularized	Regularized

The Model

The goal of our simulation of the acquisition of past tense was to simulate the three-stage performance summarized in Table 24.1, and to see whether we could capture other aspects of acquisition. In particular, we wanted to show that the kind of gradual change characteristic of normal acquisition was also a characteristic of our distributed model, and we wanted to see whether the model would capture detailed aspects of the phenomenon, such as the change in error type in later phases of development and the change in differences in error patterns observed for different types of words.

We were not prepared to produce a full-blown language processor that would learn the past tense from full sentences heard in everyday experience. Rather, we have explored a very simple past-tense learning environment designed to capture the essential characteristics necessary to produce the three stages of acquisition. In this environment, the model is presented, as learning experiences, with pairs of inputs—one capturing the phonological structure of the root form of a word and the other capturing the phonological structure of the correct past-tense version of the word. The behavior of the model can be tested by giving it just the root form of a word and examining what it generates as its "current guess" of the corresponding past-tense form.

Structure of the Model

The basic structure of the model is illustrated in Figure 24.1. The model consists of two basic parts: (a) a simple *pattern associator* network similar to those studied by Kohenen (1977, 1984) which learns the relationships

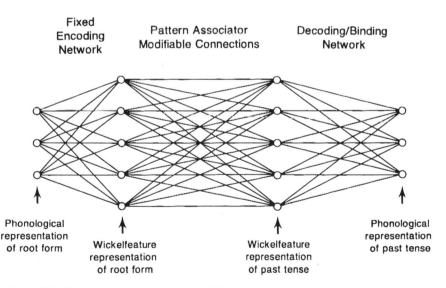

Figure 24.1 The basic structure of the model.

between the base form and the past-tense form, and (b) a decoding network that converts a featural representation of the past-tense form into a phonological representation. All learning occurs in the pattern associator; the decoding network is simply a mechanism for converting a featural representation which may be a near miss to any phonological pattern into a legitimate phonological representation. Our primary focus here is on the pattern associator.

Units The pattern associator contains two pools of units. One pool, called the input pool, is used to represent the input pattern corresponding to the root form of the verb to be learned. The other pool, called the output pool, is used to represent the output pattern generated by the model as its current guess as to the past tense corresponding to the root form represented in the inputs.

Each unit stands for a particular feature of the input or output string. The particular features we used are important to the behavior of the model, so they are described in a separate section below [omitted in this edition—Ed.].

Connections The pattern associator contains a modifiable connection linking each input unit to each output unit. Initially, these connections are all set to 0 so that there is no influence of the input units on the output units. Learning involves modification of the strengths of these interconnections, as described below.

Operation of the Model
On test trials, the simulation is given a phoneme string corresponding to the root of a word. It then performs the following actions. First, it encodes the root string as a pattern of activation over the input units. The encoding scheme used is described below. Node activations are discrete in this model, so the activation values of all the units that should be on to represent this word are set to 1, and all the others are set to 0. Then, for each output unit, the model computes the net input to it from all of the weighted connections from the input units. The net input is simply the sum over all input units of the input unit activation times the corresponding weight. Thus, algebraically, the net input to output unit i is

$$net_i = \Sigma_j a_j w_{ij}$$

where a_j represents the activation of input unit j, and w_{ij} represents the weight from unit j to unit i.

Each unit has a threshold, θ, which is adjusted by the learning procedure that we will describe in a moment. The probability that the unit is turned on depends on the amount the net input exceeds the threshold. The *logistic* probability function is used here as in the Boltzmann machine and in harmony theory to determine whether the unit should be turned on. The probability is given by

$$p\,(a_i = 1) = \frac{1}{1 + e^{-(net_i - \theta_i)/T}} \tag{24.1}$$

where T represents the temperature of the system. The logistic function is shown in Figure 24.2. The use of this probabilistic response rule allows the system to produce different responses on different occasions with the same network. It also causes the system to learn more slowly so the effect of regular verbs on the irregulars continues over a much longer period of time. The temperature, T, can be manipulated so that at very high temperatures the response of the units is highly variable; with lower values of T, the units behave more like *linear threshold units*.

Since the pattern associator built into the model is a one-layer net with no feedback connections and no connections from one output unit to another or from one input unit to another, iterative computation is of no benefit. Therefore, the processing of an input pattern is a simple matter of first calculating the net input to each output unit and then setting its activation probabilistically on the basis of the logistic equation given above. The temperature T only enters in setting the variability of the output units; a fixed value of T was used throughout the simulations.

To determine how well the model did at producing the correct output, we simply compare the pattern of output Wickelphone activations to the pattern that the correct response would have generated. [Wickelphones are elements of a particular scheme of phonological representation.—Ed.] To do this, we first translate the correct response into a

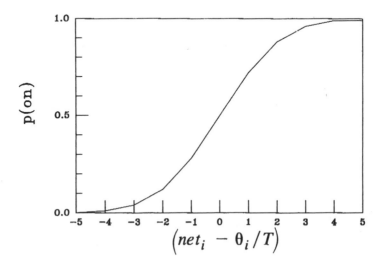

Figure 24.2 The logistic function used to calculate probability of activation. The x-axis shows values of ($net_i - \theta_i/T$), and the y-axis indicates the corresponding probability that unit i will be activated.

Rumelhart and McClelland

target pattern of activation for the output units, based on the same encoding scheme used for the input units. We then compare the obtained pattern with the target pattern on a unit-by-unit basis. If the output perfectly reproduces the target, then there should be a 1 in the output pattern wherever there is a 1 in the target. Such cases are called *hits*, following the conventions of signal detection theory (Green and Swets 1966). There should also be a 0 in the output whenever there is a 0 in the target. Such cases are called *correct rejections*. Cases in which there are 1s in the output but not in the target are called *false alarms*, and cases in which there are 0s in the output that should be present in the input are called *misses*. A variety of measures of performance can be computed. We can measure the percentage of output units that match the correct past tense, or we can compare the output to the pattern for any other response alternative we might care to evaluate. This allows us to look at the output of the system independently of the decoding network. We can also employ the decoding network and have the system synthesize a phonological string. We can measure the performance of the system either at the featural level or at the level of strings of phonemes. We shall employ both of these mechanisms in the evaluation of different aspects of the overall model.

Learning

On a learning trial, the model is presented with both the root form of the verb and the target. As on a test trial, the pattern associator network computes the output it would generate from the input. Then, for each output unit, the model compares its answer with the target. Connection strengths are adjusted using the classic *perceptron convergence procedure* (Rosenblatt 1962). The perceptron convergence procedure is simply a discrete variant of the delta rule presented earlier in this work. The exact procedure is as follows: We can think of the target as supplying a teaching input to each output unit, telling it what value it ought to have. When the actual output matches the target output, the model is doing the right thing and so none of the weights on the lines coming into the unit are adjusted. When the computed output is 0 and the target says it should be 1, we want to increase the probability that the unit will be active the next time the same input pattern is presented. To do this, we increase the weights from all of the input units that are active by a small amount η. At the same time, the threshold is also reduced by η. When the computed output is 1 and the target says it should be 0, we want to decrease the probability that the unit will be active the next time the same input pattern is presented. To do this, the weights from all of the input units that are active are reduced by η, and the threshold is increased by η. In all of our simulations, the value of η is simply set to 1. Thus, each change in a weight is a unit change, either up or down. For nonstochastic units, it is well known that the perceptron convergence procedure will find a set of weights that will allow the model to get each output unit correct, provided that such a set of weights exists. For the stochastic case, it is possible for the learning procedure to find a set of weights that will make the probability of error as low as desired. Such a set of weights exists if a set of weights exists that will always get the right answer for nonstochastic units. . . .

The Simulations

The simulations described in this section are concerned with demonstrating three main points:

· That the model captures the basic three-stage pattern of acquisition.

· That the model captures most aspects of differences in performance on different types of regular and irregular verbs.

· That the model is capable of responding appropriately to verbs it has never seen before, as well as to regular and irregular verbs actually experienced during training.

In the sections that follow we will consider these three aspects of the model's performance in turn.

The corpus of verbs used in the simulations consisted of a set of 506 verbs. All verbs were chosen from the Kucera and Francis (1967) word list and were ordered according to frequency of their gerund form. We divided the verbs into three classes: 10 high-frequency verbs, 410 medium-frequency verbs, and 86 low-frequency verbs. The ten highest frequency verbs were: *come* (k^m/), *get* (/get/), *give* (/giv/), *look* (/luk/), *take* (/tʌk/), *go* (/go/), *have* (/hav/), *live* (/liv/), and *feel* (/fɛl/). There is a total of 8 irregular and 2 regular verbs among the top 10. Of the medium-frequency verbs, 334 were regular and 76 were irregular. Of the low-frequency verbs, 72 were regular and 14 were irregular.

The Three-Stage Learning Curve
The results described in this and the following sections were obtained from a single (long) simulation run. The run was intended to capture approximately the experience with past tense of a young child picking up English from everyday conversation. Our conception of the nature of this experience is simply that the child learns first about the present and past tenses of the highest frequency verbs; later on, learning occurs for a much larger ensemble of verbs, including a much larger proportion of regular forms. Although the child would be hearing present and past tenses of all kinds of verbs throughout development, we assume that he is only able to learn past tenses for verbs that he has already mastered fairly well in the present tense.

To simulate the earliest phase of past-tense learning, the model was first trained on the 10 high-frequency verbs, receiving 10 cycles of training presentations through the set of 10 verbs. This was enough to produce quite good performance on these verbs. We take the performance of the model at this point to correspond to the performance of a child in Phase 1 of acquisition. To simulate later phases of learning, the 410 medium-frequency verbs were added to the first 10 verbs, and the system was given 190 more learning trials, with each trial consisting of one presentation of each of the 420 verbs. The responses of the model early on in this phase of training correspond to Phase 2 of the acquisition process; its ultimate performance at the end of 190 exposures to each of the 420 verbs corresponds to Phase 3. At this point, the model exhibits almost errorless performance on the basic 420 verbs. Finally, the set of 86 lower-frequency verbs were presented to the system and the transfer responses to these were recorded. During this phase, connection strengths were not adjusted. Performance of the model on these transfer verbs is considered in a later section.

We do not claim, of course, that this training experience exactly captures the learning experience of the young child. It should be perfectly clear that this training experience exaggerates the difference between early phases of learning and later phases, as well as the abruptness of the transition to a larger corpus of verbs. However, it is generally observed that the early, rather limited vocabulary of young children undergoes an explosive growth at some point in development (Brown 1973). Thus, the actual transition in a child's vocabulary of verbs would appear quite abrupt on a time-scale of years so that our assumptions about abruptness of onset may not be too far off the mark.

Figure 24.3 shows the basic results for the high frequency verbs. What we see is that during the first 10 trials there is no difference

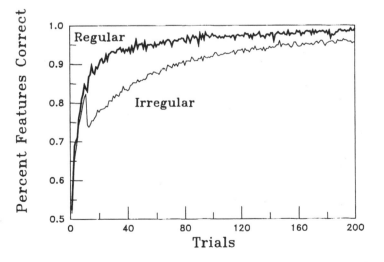

Figure 24.3 The percentage of correct features for regular and irregular high-frequency verbs as a function of trials.

On Learning the Past Tenses of English Verbs

between regular and irregular verbs. However, beginning on Trial 11 when the 410 midfrequency verbs were introduced, the regular verbs show better performance. It is important to notice that there is no interfering effect on the regular verbs as the midfrequency verbs are being learned. There is, however, substantial interference on the irregular verbs. This interference leads to a dip in performance on the irregular verbs. Equality of performance between regular and irregular verbs is never again attained during the training period. This is the so-called U-shaped learning curve for the learning of the irregular past tense. Performance is high when only a few high-frequency, largely irregular verbs are learned, but then drops as the bulk of lower-frequency regular verbs are being learned.

We have thus far only shown that performance on high-frequency irregular verbs drops; we have not said anything about the nature of the errors. To examine this question, the response strength of various possible response alternatives must be compared. To do this, we compared the strength of response for several different response alternatives. We compared strengths for the correct past tense, the present, the base+ed and the past+ed. Thus, for example with the verb *give* we compared the response strength of /gʌv/, /giv/, /givd/, and /gʌvd/. We determined the response strengths by assuming that these response alternatives were competing to account for the features that were actually turned on in the output. For present purposes, suffice it to say that each alternative gets a score that represents the percentage of the total features that it accounts for. If two alternatives both account for a given feature, they divide the score for that feature in proportion to the number of features each accounts for uniquely. We take these response strengths to correspond roughly to relative response probabilities, though we imagine that the actual generation of overt responses is accomplished by a different version of the binding network, described below. In any case, the total strength of all the alternatives cannot be greater than 1, and if a number of features are accounted for by none of the alternatives, the total will be less than 1.

Figure 24.4 compares the response strengths for the correct alternative to the combined strength of the regularized alternatives.[2] Note in the figure that during the first 10 trials the response strength of the correct alternative grows rapidly to over .5 while that of the regularized alternative drops from about .2 to .1. After the midfrequency verbs are introduced, the response strength for the correct alternative drops rapidly while the strengths of regularized alternatives jump up. From about Trials 11 through 30, the regularized alternatives together are stronger than the correct response. After about Trial 30, the strength of the correct response again exceeds the regularized alternatives and continues to grow throughout the 200-trial learning phase. By the end, the correct response is much the strongest with all other alternatives below .1.

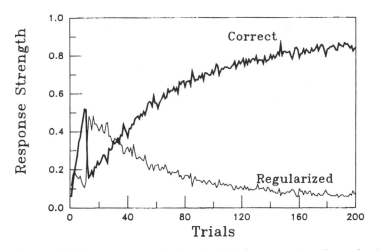

Figure 24.4 Response strengths for the high-frequency irregular verbs. The response strengths for the correct responses are compared with those for the regularized alternatives as a function of trials.

The rapidity of the growth of the regularized alternatives is due to the sudden influx of the medium-frequency verbs. In real life we would expect the medium-frequency verbs to come in somewhat more slowly so that the period of maximal regularization would have a somewhat slower onset.

Figure 24.5 shows the same data in a slightly different way. In this case, we have plotted the ratio of the correct response to the sum of the correct and regularized response strengths. Points on the curve below the .5 line are in the region where the regularized response is greater than the correct response. Here we see clearly the three stages. In the first stage, the first 10 trials of learning, performance on these high-frequency verbs is quite good. Virtually no regularization takes place. During the next 20 trials, the system regularizes and systematically makes errors on the verbs that it previously responded to correctly. Finally, during the remaining trials the model slowly eliminates the regularization responses as it approaches adult performance.

In summary, then, the model captures the three phases of learning quite well, as well as the gradual transition from Phase 2 to Phase 3. It does so without any explicit learning of rules. The regularization is the product of the gradual tuning of connection strengths in response to the predominantly regular correspondence exhibited by the medium-frequency words. It is not quite right to say that individual pairs are being stored in the network in any simple sense. The connection strengths the model builds up to handle the irregular forms do not represent these items in any separable way; they represent them in the way they must be represented to be stored along with the other verbs in the same set of connections. . . .

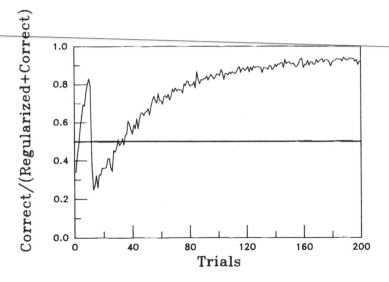

Figure 24.5 The ratio of the correct response to the sum of the correct and regularized response. Points on the curve below the .5 line are in the region where the regularized response is greater than the correct response.

Conclusions

We have shown that our simple learning model shows, to a remarkable degree, the characteristics of young children learning the morphology of the past tense in English. We have shown how our model generates the so-called U-shaped learning curve for irregular verbs and that it exhibits a tendency to overgeneralize that is quite similar to the pattern exhibited by young children. Both in children and in our model, the verb forms showing the most regularization are pairs such as *know/knew* and *see/saw,* whereas those showing the least regularization are pairs such as *feel/felt* and *catch/caught.* Early in learning, our model shows the pattern of more no-change responses to verbs ending in *t/d* whether or not they are regular verbs, just as young children do. The model, like children, can generate the appropriate regular past-tense form to unfamiliar verbs whose base form ends in various consonants or vowels. Thus, the model generates an /^d/ suffix for verbs ending in *t/d,* a /t/ suffix for verbs ending in an unvoiced consonant, and a /d/ suffix for verbs ending in a voiced consonant or vowel.

In the model, as in children, different past-tense forms for the same word can coexist at the same time. On rule accounts, such *transitional* behavior is puzzling and difficult to explain. Our model, like human children, shows a relatively larger proportion of past+ed regularizations later in learning. Our model, like learners of English, will sometimes generate past-tense forms to novel verbs which show sensitivities to the subregularities of English as well as the major regularities. Thus, the past of *cring* can sometimes be rendered *crang* or *crung.* In short, our simple learning model accounts for all of the major features of the acquisition of the morphology of the English past tense.

In addition to our ability to account for the major *known* features of the acquisition process, there are also a number of predictions that the model makes which have yet to be reported. These include:

· We expect relatively more past+ed regularizations to irregulars whose correct past form *does not* involve a modification of the final phoneme of the base form.

· We expect that early in learning, a no-change response will occur more frequently to a CVC monosyllable ending in *t/d* than to a more complex base verb form.

· We expect that the double inflection responses (/dript^d/) will occasionally be made by native speakers and that they will occur more frequently to verbs whose stem ends in /p/ or /k/.

The model is very rich and there are many other more specific predictions which can be derived from it and evaluated by a careful analysis of acquisition data.

We have, we believe, provided a distinct alternative to the view that children learn the rules of English past-tense formation in any explicit sense. We have shown that a reasonable account of the acquisition of past tense can be provided without recourse to the notion of a "rule" as anything more than a *description* of the language. We have shown that, for this case, there is no *induction problem*. The child need not figure out what the rules are, nor even that there are rules. The child need not decide whether a verb is regular or irregular. There is no question as to whether the inflected form should be stored directly in the lexicon or derived from more general principles. There isn't even a question (as far as generating the past-tense form is concerned) as to whether a verb form is one encountered many times or one that is being generated for the first time. A uniform procedure is applied for producing the past-tense form in every case. The base form is supplied as input to the past-tense network and the resulting pattern of activation is interpreted as a phonological representation of the past form of that verb. This is the procedure whether the verb is regular or irregular, familiar or novel.

In one sense, every form must be considered as being derived. In this sense, the network can be considered to be one large rule for generating past tenses from base forms. In another sense, it is possible to imagine that the system simply stores a set of rote associations between base and past-tense forms with novel responses generated by "on-line" generalizations from the stored exemplars.

Neither of these descriptions is quite right, we believe. Associations are simply stored in the network, but because we have a *superpositional* memory, similar patterns blend into one another and reinforce each other. If there were no similar patterns (i.e., if the featural representations of the base forms of verbs were orthogonal to one another) there would be no generalization. The system would be unable to generalize and there would be no regularization. It is statistical relationships among the base forms themselves that determine the pattern of responding. The network merely reflects the statistics of the featural representations of the verb forms.

We chose the study of acquisition of past tense in part because the phenomenon of regularization is an example often cited in support of the view that children do respond according to general rules of language. Why otherwise, it is sometimes asked, should they generate forms that they have never heard? The answer we offer is that they do so because the past tenses of similar verbs they are learning show such a consistent pattern that the generalization from these similar verbs outweighs the relatively small amount of learning that has occurred on the irregular verb in question. We suspect that essentially similar ideas will prove useful in accounting for other aspects of language acquisition. We view this work on past-tense morphology as a step toward a revised understanding of language knowledge, language acquisition, and linguistic information processing in general.

Acknowledgments

This research was supported by ONR Contracts N00014-82-C-0374, NR 667-483 and N00014-79-C-0323, NR 667-437, by a grant from the System Development Foundation, and by a Research Scientist Career Development Award MH00385 to the second author from the National Institute of Mental Health.

Notes

1. The notation of phonemes used in this chapter is somewhat nonstandard. It is derived from the computer-readable dictionary containing phonetic transcriptions of the verbs used in the simulations.

2. Unless otherwise indicated, the regularized alternatives are considered the base+ed and past+ed alternative. In most cases the base+ed alternative is much stronger than the past+ed alternative.

References

Bates, E. (1979). *Emergence of symbols*. New York: Academic Press.

Berko, J. (1958). The child's learning of English morphology. *Word* 14, 150–177.

Brown, R. (1973). *A first language*. Cambridge, MA: Harvard University Press.

Bybee, J. L., and D. I. Slobin (1982). Rules and schemas in the development and use of the English past tense. *Language* 58, 265–289.

Ervin, S. (1964). Imitation and structural change in children's language. In E. Lenneberg, ed., *New directions in the study of language*. Cambridge, MA: MIT Press.

Green, D. M., and J. A. Swets (1966). *Signal detection theory and psychophysics*. New York: Wiley.

Kohenen, T. (1977). *Associative memory: A system theoretical approach*. New York: Springer.

Kohonen, T. (1984). *Self-organization and associative memory*. Berlin: Springer-Verlag.

Kucera, H., and W. Francis (1967). *Computational analysis of present-day American English*. Providence, RI: Brown University Press.

Kuczaj, S. A. (1977). The acquisition of regular and irregular past tense forms. *Journal of Verbal Learning and Verbal Behavior* 16, 589–600.

McClelland, J. L., and D. E. Rumelhart (1981). An interactive activation model of context effects in letter perception: Part 1. An account of basic findings. *Psychological Review* 88, 375–407.

Pinker, S. (1984). *Language learnability and language development*. Cambridge, MA: Harvard University Press.

Rosenblatt, F. (1962). *Principles of neurodynamics*. New York: Spartan.

Rumelhart, D. E., and J. L. McClelland (1981). Interactive processing through spreading activation. In A. M. Lesgold and C. A. Perfetti, eds., *Interactive processes in reading*. Hillsdale, NJ: Erlbaum.

Rumelhart, D. E., and J. L. McClelland (1982). An interactive activation model of context effects in letter perception: Part 2. The contextual enhancement effect and some tests and extensions of the model. *Psychological Review* 89, 60–94.

25 Critique of Rumelhart and McClelland

Andy Clark

Good News and Bad News

First, the good news. PDP affords an approach to computational modeling that should be attractive to anyone engaged in what I have called causal cognitive science. That is, it should be attractive to those who seek to model the in-the-head computational causes of intelligent behavior. Its principal merits include the power of its learning algorithms, its fine-grained shading of meaning, free generalization, and the flexibility that goes with distributed representations of microfeatures.

Now the bad news. PDP affords an approach to computational modeling that should be unattractive to anyone engaged in what I have called causal cognitive science. That is, it should be unattractive to those who seek to model the in-the-head computational causes of intelligent behavior. Its principal demerits include the power of its learning algorithms, its fine-grained shading of meaning, free generalization, and the flexibility that goes with distributed representations of microfeatures.

All this is not as contradictory as it sounds. The very properties of PDP models that are advantageous in *some* problem domains are disadvantageous in others, just as being well adapted to survive underwater may be a major disadvantage when beached on dry land. [The advantages and disadvantages of PDP models are illustrated here by a particular PDP model and an influential critique of it by Steven Pinker and Alan Prince (1988).—Ed.]

The Past-Tense-Acquisition Network

The particular PDP model that Pinker and Prince use as the focus of their attack is the past-tense-acquisition network described in Rumelhart and McClelland (1986, 216–271). The point of the exercise for Rumelhart

From A. Clark, *Microcognition* (1989). Cambridge, MA: MIT Press. Reprinted by permission.

and McClelland was to provide an alternative to the psychologically realistic interpretation of theories of grammar described briefly in the previous chapter. The counter-claim made by Rumelhart and McClelland is that "the mechanisms that process language and make judgments of grammaticality are constructed in such a way that their performance is characterisable by [grammatical] rules, but that the rules themselves are not written in explicit form anywhere in the mechanism" (1986, 217).

Thus construed, the past-tense-acquisition network, would aim to provide an alternative to what I earlier called propositional psychological realism, i.e., the view that grammatical rules are encoded in a sentential format and read by some internal mechanism. But this, as we saw, is a very radical claim and is by no means made by all the proponents of conventional symbol-processing models of grammatical competence. It turns out, however, that this PDP model *in fact* constitutes a challenge even to the weaker, and more commonly held, position of structural psychological realism. Structural psychological realism is here the claim that the in-the-head information-processing system underlying grammatical competence is structured in a way that makes the rule-invoking description *exactly* true. As Pinker and Prince put it, "Rules *could* be explicitly inscribed and accessed, but they *also* could be implemented in hardware in such a way that every consequence of the rule-system holds. [If so] there is a clear sense in which the rule-theory is validated" (1988, 168).

The past-tense network challenges structural psychological realism by generating the systematic behavior of past-tense formation without respecting the information-processing articulation of a conventional model. At its most basic, such articulation involves positing separate, rule-based mechanisms for generating the past tense of regular verbs and straightforward memorization mechanisms for generating the past tense of irregular verbs. Call these putative mechanisms the nonlexical and the lexical components respectively. On the proposed PDP model, "The child need not decide whether a verb is regular or irregular. There is no question as to whether the inflected form should be stored directly in the lexicon or derived from more general principles. . . . A uniform procedure is applied for producing the past tense form in every case" (Rumelhart and McClelland 1986, 267).

One reason for positing the existence of a rule-based, nonlexical component lies in the developmental sequence of the acquisition of past tense competence. It is this developmental data that Rumelhart and McClelland are particularly concerned to explain in a novel way. The data show three stages in the development of a child's ability to correctly generate the past tense of verbs (Kuczaj 1977). In the first stage the child can give the correct form for a small number of verbs, including some regular and some irregular ones. In the second stage the child overregularizes; she seems to have learned the regular "-ed" ending for

English past tenses and can give this ending for new and even made-up verbs. But she will now mistakenly give an "-ed" ending for irregular verbs, including ones she got right at stage one. The overregularization stage has two substages, one in which the present form gets the -ed ending (e.g., "come" becomes "comed") and one in which the past form gets it (e.g., "ate" becomes "ated" and "came" becomes "camed"). The third and final stage is when the child finally gets it right, adding "-ed" to regulars and novel verbs and generating various irregular or subregular forms for the rest.

Classical models, as Pinker and Prince note, account for this data in an intuitively obvious way. They posit an initial stage in which the child has effectively memorized a small set of forms in a totally unsystematic and unconnected way. This is stage one. At stage two, according to this story, the child manages to extract a rule covering a large number of cases. But the rule is now mistakenly deployed to generate *all* past tenses. At the final stage this is put right. Now the child uses lexical, memorized, item-indexed resources to handle irregular cases and non-lexical, rule-based resources to handle regular ones.

Classical models, however, typically exhibit a good deal more structure than this bare minimum (see, e.g., the model in Pinker 1984). The processing is decomposed into a set of functional components including a lexicon of structural elements (items like stems, prefixes, suffixes, and past tenses), a structural rule system for such elements, and phonetic elements and rules. A classical model so constructed will posit a variety of mechanisms that represent the data differently (morphological and phonetic representations) with access and feed relations between the mechanisms. In a sense, the classical models here are transparent with respect to the articulation of linguistic theory. Distinct linguistic theories dealing with, e.g., morphology and phonology are paired with distinct in-the-head, information-processing mechanisms.

The PDP model challenges this assumption that in-the-head mechanisms mirror structured, componential, rule-based linguistic theories. It is not necessary to dwell in detail on the Rumelhart and McClelland model to see why this is so. The model takes as input a representation of the verb constructed entirely out of phonetic microfeatures. It uses a standard PDP pattern associator to learn to map phonetic microfeature representations of the root form of verbs to a past-tensed output (again expressed as a set of phonetic microfeatures). It learns these pairings by the usual iterated process of weight adjustments described in previous chapters. The basic structure of the model is thus: phonetic representations of root forms are input into a PDP pattern associator, and phonetic representations of past forms result as output.

The information processing structure of the classical model is thus dissolved. One kind of mechanism is doing all the work both for the regular and irregular forms (recall the quote from Rumelhart and McClelland 1986, 267). And none of the system's computational operations are explicitly defined to deal with such entities as verb stems, prefixes and suffixes (note that this is not just a lack of *labels*; the system nowhere accords any special status to the morphological chunks of words that such labels pick out). As noted by Pinker and Prince, the radical implications of such a model include

· The use of a direct phonetic modification of the root without any abstract morphological representation,

· The elimination of any process dealing specially with lexical items as a locus of idiosyncrasy,

· The use of a qualitatively identical system for regular and irregular occurrences (adapted from Pinker and Prince 1988, 95).

There is thus a quite-extensive dissolution of the structure of a classical model. Not only do we fail to find any explicit tokening of rules such as "add '-ed' to form regular past tenses," but more important, we don't even find any broad articulation of the system into distinct components, one dealing with rule-based behavior and another dealing with exceptional items.

To its undeniable credit the Rumelhart and McClelland model is able to generate much of the required behavior (e.g., the three stages of development) without any such structuring. In so doing it relies on the usual distinctive properties of PDP models, that is, on automatic shading of meaning, blending, and generalization. Thus, for example, it finally deals with new cases as if they were regular verbs because this is the correct generalization of the overall thrust of its training input data. The "-ed" ending, we might say, has by then worn down a very deep groove indeed. Nonetheless, the special context provided by inputting a known irregular root can override this groove and cause the correct irregular inflection *but only after sufficient training*. The model thus goes through a stage of overregularizing and learns in time to get it right. Most impressively, the model also produces the second kind of overregularization error observed at stage two: it also overregularizes by adding "-ed" to the *past* tense of irregular verbs, producing errors like "camed," "ated." The explanation of this must lie in the system's *blending* two known patterns from "eat" to "eated" (the regular "-ed" ending) and from "eat" to "ate," and these yield "ated" (see Pinker and Prince 1988).

The PDP model thus recapitulates the three stages of development as follows:

Stage 1. There is simple encoding of a variety of present-past pairings.

Stage 2. The automatic generalization mechanism extracts a regularity implicit in the data and then knows the standard "-ed" ending. For a while this pattern swamps the rest, and causes overregularization. Further training begins to remind the system of the exceptions. But now we find a blend of the "-ed" pattern and the exception patterns, yielding "ated"-type errors.

Stage 3. Further gradual tuning puts it all right. The exceptions and the regular patterns peacefully coexist in a single network.

All of this is just rosy, but darkness looms just around the corner.

The Pinker and Prince Critique

Pinker and Prince (1988) raise a number of objections to a PDP model of children's acquisition of the past tense. Some of these criticisms are specific to the particular PDP model just discussed, while the others are at least suggestive of difficulties with any nontrivial PDP model of such a skill. I shall only be concerned with difficulties of this last kind. Such cases can be roughly grouped into four types. These concern (1) the model's overreliance on the environment as a source of structure, (2) the power of the PDP learning algorithms (this relates to the counterfactual space occupied by such models, a space that is argued to be psychologically unrealistic), (3) the use of the distinctive PDP operation of blending, and (4) the use of microfeature representations.

Overreliance on the Environment

The Rumelhart and McClelland model, we saw, made the transition from stage 1 (rote knowledge) to stage 2 (extraction of regularity). But how was this achieved? It was achieved, it seems, by first exposing the network to a population mainly of irregular verbs (10 verbs, 2 regular) and *then* presenting it with a massive influx of regular verbs (410 verbs, 344 regular). This sudden and dramatic influx of regular verbs in the training population is the sole cause of the model's transition from stage one to stage two. Thus, "The model's shift from correct to overregularized forms does not emerge from any endogenous process: it is driven directly by shifts in the input" (Pinker and Prince 1988, 138). By contrast, some developmental psychologists (e.g., Karmiloff-Smith [1987]) believe that the shift is caused by an internally driven attempt to organize and understand the data. Certainly, there is no empirical evidence that a sudden shift in the nature of the input population must precede the transition to stage 2 (see Pinker and Prince, 1988, 142).

The general point here is that PDP models utilize a very powerful learning mechanism that, when given well-chosen inputs, can learn to produce almost any behavior you care to name. But a deep reliance on highly structured inputs may reduce the psychological attractiveness of such models. Moreover, the space of counterfactuals associated with an input-driven model may be psychologically implausible. Given a different set of inputs, these models might go straight to stage 2, or even regress from stage 2 to stage 1. It is at least not obvious that human infants enjoy the same degree of freedom.

The Power of Learning Algorithms

This is a continuation of the worry just raised. The power of PDP systems to extract statistical regularities in the input data, it is argued, is simply too great to be psychologically realistic. Competent speakers of English can't easily learn the kinds of regularity that a PDP model would find unproblematic. Such a model could learn what Pinker and Prince describe as "the quintessential unlinguistic map relating a string to its mirror-image reversal" (1988, 100). Human beings, it seems, have extreme difficulty learning such regularities. But a good explanation of language acquisition, Pinker and Prince rightly insist, must explain what we *cannot* learn as well as what we can. One way to explain such selective learning capacities is to posit a higher degree of *internal* organization geared to certain kinds of learning. Such organization is found in classical models. The price of dissolving such organization and replacing it with structured input may be a steep reduction in broader psychological plausibility.

Blending

We saw above how the model generates errors by blending two such patterns as from "eat" to "ate" and from "eat" to "eated" to produce the pattern from "eat" to "ated." By contrast a conventional rule-based account would posit a mechanism specifically geared to operate on the stems of regular verbs, inflecting them as required. If this nonlexical component were mistakenly given "ate" as a stem, it would simply inflect it sausage-machine fashion into "ated." The choice, then, is between an explanation by blending within a single mechanism and an explanation of misfeeding within a system that has a distinct nonlexical mechanism. Pinker and Prince (1988, 157) point to evidence which favors the latter, classical option.

If blending is the psychological process responsible, it is reasonable to expect a whole class of such errors. For example, we might expect blends of common middle-vowel changes and the "-ed" ending (from "shape" to "shipped" and from "sip" to "sepped"). Children exhibit no such errors. If, on the other hand, the guilty process is misfeed to a nonlexical mechanism, we should expect to find *other* errors of inflection based on a mistaken stem (from "went" to "wenting"). Children do exhibit such errors.

Microfeature Representations

The Rumelhart and McClelland model relies on the distinctive PDP device of distributed microfeature representation. The use of such a form of representation buys a certain kind of automatic generalization. But it may not be the right kind. The model, we saw, achieves its ends without applying computational operations to any syntactic entities with a projectible semantics given by such labels as "stem" or "suffix." Instead, its notion of stems is just the center of a state space of instances of strings presented for inflection into the past tense. The lack of a representation of stems as such deprives the system of any means of encoding the *general* idea of a regular past form (i.e., "stem + ed"). Regular forms can be produced just in case the stem in a newly presented case is sufficiently similar to those encountered in training runs. The upshot of this is a much more constrained generalization than that achieved within a classical model, which incorporates a nonlexical component. For the latter would do its work *whatever* we gave it as input. Whether this is good or bad (as far as the psychological realism of the model is concerned) is, I think, an open question. For the moment, I simply note the distinction. (Pinker and Prince clearly hold it to be bad; see Pinker and Prince 1988, 124).

A more general worry, stemming from the same root, is that generalization based on *pure* microfeature representation is *blind*. Pinker and Prince note that when humans generalize, they typically do so by relying on a theory of which microfeatures are *important* in a given context. This knowledge of salient features can far outweigh any more quantitative notion of similarity based simply on the number of common microfeatures. They write, "To take one example, knowledge of how a set of perceptual features was caused . . . can override any generalizations inspired by the object's features themselves: for example, an animal that looks exactly like a skunk will nonetheless be treated as a raccoon if one is told that the stripe was painted onto an animal that had raccoon parents and raccoon babies" (Pinker and Prince 1988, 177). Human generalization, it seems, is not the same as the automatic generalization according to similarity of microfeatures found in PDP. Rather, it is driven by high-level knowledge of the domain concerned.

To bring this out, it may be worth developing a final example of my own. Consider the process of understanding metaphor, and assume that a successful metaphor illuminates a target domain by means of certain features of the home domain of the metaphor. Suppose further that both the metaphor and the target are each represented as sets of microfeatures thus: $\langle MMF_1, \ldots, MMF_n \rangle$ and $\langle TMF_1, \ldots, TMF_n \rangle$ (MMF = metaphor micro-feature, TMF = target microfeature). It might seem that the necessary capacity to conceive of the target in the terms suggested by the metaphor is just another example of shading meaning according to context, a capacity that as we've seen, PDP systems are admirably suited to exhibit. Thus, just as we earlier saw how to conceive of a bedroom along the lines suggested by inclusion of a sofa, so we might now expect to see how to conceive of a raven along the lines suggested by the contextual inclusion of a writing desk.

But in fact there is a very importance difference. For in shading the meaning of bedroom, the *relevant* microfeatures (i.e., sofa) were already specified. Both the joy and mystery of metaphor lies in the lack of any such specification. It is the job of one who hears the metaphor to *find* the salient features and *then* to shade the target domain accordingly. In other words, we need somehow to fix on a salient subset of $\langle MMF_1, \ldots, MMF_n \rangle$. And such fixation must surely proceed in the light of high-level knowledge concerning the problem at hand and the target domain involved. In short, not all microfeatures are equal, and a good many of our cognitive skills depend on deciding *according to high-level knowledge* which ones to attend to in a given instance. . . .

References

Karmiloff-Smith, A. (1987). Beyond modularity: A developmental perspective on human consciousness. Draft manuscript of a talk given at the annual meeting of the British Psychological Society, Sussex, April.

Kuczaj, S. A. (1977). The acquisition of regular and irregular past tense forms. *Journal of Verbal Learning and Verbal Behavior* 16, 589–600.

Pinker, S. (1984). *Language learnability and language development.* Cambridge, MA: Harvard University Press.

Pinker, S. and A. Prince (1988). On language and connectionism: Analysis of a parallel distributed processing model of language acquisition. *Cognition* 28, 73–193.

Rumelhart, D. E., and J. L. McClelland (1986). On learning the past tenses of English verbs. In D. E. Rumelhart, J. L. McClelland, and the PDP Research Group, *Parallel distributed processing: Explorations in the microstructure of cognition,* vol. 2. Cambridge, MA: MIT Press.

26 The Mental Representation of the Meaning of Words

Philip N. Johnson-Laird

Introduction

Outside a psychological laboratory, the recognition of words is seldom an end in itself, because listeners want to understand what they hear. Comprehension requires them to know and to retrieve the meaning of the words they recognize. Lexical meanings are the ingredients from which the sense of an utterance is made up, and its syntactic structure is the recipe by which they are combined. Listeners must put together the meanings of the words they recognize according to the grammatical relations that they perceive between them. Comprehension, however, does not end there, since it transcends purely linguistic knowledge. For example, anyone who knows English can retrieve the ingredients and combine them appropriately for a sentence such as:

Do you know who those people are?

The ingredients are the sense of the word "you," the sense of the word "people," and the senses of the other words in the sentence. But, the sense of the expressions must be distinguished from their reference— the particular entities or individuals that expressions pick out in the world. Reference from the standpoint of psychology is not merely a question of individuals in the real world: human beings invent imaginary and hypothetical worlds and regularly refer to individuals within them. Unlike certain logicians, ordinary people do not treat all expressions that refer to non-existent entities as equivalent.

To grasp the sense of a phrase such as "those people" is generally a precursor to determining its reference—the particular set of individuals to whom the speaker is referring in uttering the sentence. Grasping sense is a matter of knowing the language; determining reference is a

From P. Johnson-Laird, The mental representation of the meaning of words, *Cognition* 25, 189–211 (1987). Reprinted by permission.

matter of much more since it usually depends on knowledge of the situation, knowledge of the speaker, knowledge of the conventions governing discourse, and the ability to make inferences. In the absence of these components, no-one can go from the sense of a sentence to its real significance, which depends on who or what it is about and also on why the speaker uttered it. Listeners need to determine who is referred to by "you" and "those people" in the example above and whether the speaker is asking a simple question demanding only the answer "yes" or "no," or making an indirect request for identifying information. They grasp the significance of the question only when they establish these facts.

There is, of course, no end to the process of recovering a speaker's intentions. Listeners may infer that the speaker needs to identify the relevant people, they may infer why the speaker has that need, and so on. As the processing of speech proceeds from phonology through words to comprehension, it thus becomes increasingly dependent on inferences based on the social and physical circumstances of the utterance, on a knowledge of the situation to which it refers, and on general knowledge.

This article is about the mental representation of the meaning of words, but the inferential basis of the higher orders of comprehension must be borne in mind in trying to understand lexical semantics—if only because the major phenomena apply equally to the interpretation of both speech and writing.

The plan of the article is simple. It describes five phenomena that concern the mental representation of the meanings of words, that is, their senses, since their references depend on their contexts of use. These phenomena are important clues to how the mind represents meaning. After the description of these clues, they are used to motivate a theory of the mental representation of lexical meaning. Although the theory is driven by data—in much the same way that word recognition itself proceeds, the data were not collected as a result of theory-free observations. As many philosophers of science have emphasized, it is doubtful whether any observations can be made without at least the glimmerings of some theoretical motivation. In the present case, however, the observations were made over a number of years and there is no simple unitary theory that led to them.

Consciousness and Lexical Meaning

The single most obvious phenomenon about the meanings of words is the difficulty of focusing consciousness upon them. If I ask you what does the verb "sight" mean in the sentence:

He sighted a herd of elephants on the plain

then you are immediately aware that you know the meaning of the word, and that you understand the sentence with no difficulty. You should also be able to offer a paraphrase of the word, such as:

to see something at a distance.

But the formulation of this paraphrase is not an immediate and automatic process. You cannot turn to the appropriate definition in a mental dictionary and read out the contents that you find there. It may take a second or two to formulate a definition, and in some cases, as we shall see, you may be unable to give a helpful definition at all. In short, you have an immediate awareness of knowing the sense of a word, but you have no direct introspective access to the representation of its meaning.

The importance of this simple observation is twofold. First, it presents us with the problem that is the topic of this article, because if we had a ready access to lexical representations it would hardly be necessary to advance a theory about them. Second, the very distinction between what we can and cannot be conscious of constitutes an important clue to the architecture of the mind. A good theory of linguistic processing should explain why listeners can be aware of the words and intonation that speakers use, and aware of understanding (or not understanding) what the words mean. It should also explain why listeners lack immediate introspective access to the nature of the representations that underlie the meanings of words and sentences. An answer to this question will indeed be offered in the final section of the article.

The Existence of Lexical Entries

Because theorists are in the same predicament as everyone else when it comes to introspection, they lack any immediate evidence for the existence of a mental representation of the senses of words. Indeed, a major psychological issue is whether there are lexical entries in the mind that give the meanings of words. Some theorists have assumed that the sense of a word consists of a structured set of semantic features into which its meaning is decomposed (e.g., Schaeffer and Wallace 1970; Smith et al. 1974). Others assume that the mental lexicon takes the form of a semantic network (e.g., Anderson 1976; Anderson and Bower 1973; Collins and Quillian 1969; Rumelhart et al. 1972), or a combination of network and features (Glass and Holyoak 1974/5). A third sort of theory, however, rejects the notion of semantic decomposition, and assumes that there are no semantic representations for words, only a vast set of rules of inference, or "meaning postulates" (see e.g., Fodor et al. 1975; Fodor 1977, chap. 5; Kintsch 1974). Meaning postulates in such theories specify entailments that depend on words, for example

for any x, y, if x is on the right of y, then y is on the left of x.

It is difficult to obtain crucial psychological evidence to decide amongst these theories. But, on the one hand, comprehension does not appear to call for a process of decomposition (see Fodor et al. 1975; Johnson-Laird 1983); and, on the other hand, there is evidence which, though it was designed with another issue in mind, casts doubt on the meaning postulate theories (see Johnson-Laird et al. 1978). If readers wish to participate in a single trial of the experiment, which takes only a few minutes, they should carry out each of the following instructions without looking ahead to the next instruction.

(1) Scan as quickly as possible the list of words in Table 26.1; ticking in pencil those that denote things that are both solid and ordinarily fit for human consumption, for example, tick "pear," but not "whisky" which is consumable but not solid, and not "ivory" which is solid but not consumable. This is a simple task that ordinarily takes only a few seconds.

(2) Cover up Table 1 so that it is no longer visible.

(3) Try to recall and to write down all the words in Table 26.1—every word, not just those that were ticked.

We carried out two experiments using a similar procedure, one in which the subjects listened to a brief auditory presentation of each word, and the other in which the subjects read through a list of words as quickly as possible. Both experiments showed that the more components that a word in the list had in common with the target category, the more likely it was to be remembered (see Table 26.2). Thus, a word such as "beer" which has one of the required components is more likely to be remembered than a word such as "petrol" which has neither of the key components. This result presumably reflects the amount of processing carried out on each word (Johnson-Laird et al. 1978; Ross 1981), or the number of retrieval cues provided by the target components (McClelland et al. 1981), or both. It is neutral with respect to the existence of dictionary entries. However, Table 26.2 also includes words that denote, not substances, but utensils of various sorts. We found that such words in general were not so well recalled as the substance

Table 26.1 Search down these lists of words as quickly as possible for those that denote things that are normally solid (as opposed to liquid) and fit for human consumption

sherry	knife	hammer	linoleum
ammonia	jug	ink	pippette
bucket	apple	cream	petrol
quartz	toaster	carafe	paraffin
skewer	syringe	needle	biscuit
broom	water	coal	plate
toffee	wood	veal	beer

words, yet as Table 26.2 shows there was a significant trend within them. A word such as "plate" denotes a utensil that is used for consumable solids, whereas a word such as "vase" is used for non-consumable liquids. In general, the greater the match between the type of utensil and the target category the better the recall.

If there are no lexical entires but only a vast list of meaning postulates, subjects should reject all the utensils in the same way. Suppose the target category is "consumable solids," then they should search for postulates of the form:

$$\text{For any } x, \text{ if } x \text{ is a} \begin{cases} \text{plate} \\ \text{jug} \\ \text{hammer} \\ \text{vase} \end{cases} \text{ then } x \text{ is consumable.}$$

and fail to find them. Likewise, they would succeed in finding each of the postulates:

$$\text{For any } x, \text{ if } x \text{ is a} \begin{cases} \text{plate} \\ \text{jug} \\ \text{hammer} \\ \text{vase} \end{cases} \text{ then } x \text{ is solid.}$$

Hence the postulate theory cannot explain the trend in the data. However, if there are lexical entries from which the semantic information about a word is readily accessible, then the entry for a word such as "plate" will make available the fact that plates are utensils used to serve *consumable solids*, whereas the entry for "vase" will not make available any information containing these target components. Subjects searching the list for consumable solids are therefore likely to carry out more processing in order to reject "plate" than to reject "vase," and this extra amount of processing accounts for the greater memorability of "plate." A similar explanation in terms of the cues to recall provided by "consumable" and "solid" again depends on the ease of recovering the target components from the lexical entry for "plate." The trend in the memorability for the utensil words can therefore be best explained on the assumption that there are comprehensive lexical entries containing specifications of the senses of words. The trend cannot readily be accounted

Table 26.2 The percentages of words correctly recalled in the experiment carried out by Johnson-Laird et al. (1978)

	Semantic components of the target category possessed by the words			
	Both	One	Neither	Overall
Substance words	50.0	21.5	10.6	27.4
Utensil words	16.2	10.6	8.1	11.7

for by inferences made after lexical access on the basis of independent ~~meaning postulates.~~

Context and Lexical Meanings

Linguistic context has well-known effects on the recognition of spoken and written words (see e.g., Fischler and Bloom 1979; Meyer and Schvaneveldt 1971; Schuberth and Eimas 1977; Swinney et al. 1979; Tanenhaus and Lucas 1987; Tweedy et al. 1977). It also has effects on the interpretation of words. This phenomenon is hardly surprising because words are notoriously ambiguous. There is considerable evidence which suggests that all the different senses of an ambiguous word are initially activated (Cairns and Kamerman 1975; Conrad 1974; Holmes et al. 1977; Swinney, 1979). Yet the evidence may not be decisive. Patrizia Tabossi (personal communication) has made an interesting observation using the "cross-modal lexical decision task" developed by Swinney in which subjects hear a sentence and then at some point within it have to decide whether or not a visually presented string of letters is a word in the language. Tabossi found that where the disambiguating sentential context brings to mind a salient aspect of the more frequent meaning of an ambiguous word within it, then the time to make the lexical decision is faster if the word relates to this salient feature than if it relates to the other meaning of the word. Thus, in Italian, the sentence:

Because of the terrible climate the explorers almost died in an expedition to the pole, which was long and difficult.

contains the ambiguous word, "polo," which may refer either to one of the world's poles or to the game played on horseback. The sentence not only disambiguates the word, but brings to mind a salient aspect of the world's poles, namely, their coldness. The time to decide that the string, "cold," presented visually immediately after the spoken word "polo" in the sentence, is reliably faster than the decision for the string, "horse," which relates to the other meaning of "polo." Some further results of Tabossi suggest that the effect does not arise from associative cueing by other words in the sentence. Perhaps contexts that bring to mind salient features of the main meaning of an ambiguous word eliminate the need to retrieve all of its meanings.

Listeners are normally aware of an ambiguity only if it is unresolved by the rest of the sentence. Hence the mechanism for resolving lexical ambiguities operates rapidly, automatically, and outside awareness. The standard linguistic account is that the mechanism centres on "selectional restrictions," that is, specifications of the senses of other words occurring in construction with the ambiguous word. Thus, the ambiguity of "board" is resolved in the sentence, "He sued the board," because the verb "sue" takes as its object only people and institutions: one cannot sue a plank of wood. This standard piece of lexicography was elevated into linguistic theory by Katz and Fodor (1963). Unfortunately, however, it has become clear that the crucial disambiguating component is often, not the sense of a word, but its reference. Consider the following discourse, for example:

The client received the check on Tuesday. He banked it.

The second sentence contains an ambiguous verb, which can be paraphrased as "to form a border or bank (out of some substance)," "to tilt (an aircraft) in flight," or "to deposit (money) in a bank." Yet, the sentence is unambiguous because the reference of "it" is plainly the cheque, and it is highly improbable that he formed a border or bank out of a cheque or was using it as an aircraft. For this and other reasons (Johnson-Laird 1983, 233) it seems safer to assume that disambiguation generally depends on inferences based on a knowledge of the reference of expressions.

How many different meanings are there for a verb such as "eat?" Some linguists have argued that this verb, like many others, is highly polysemous. Indeed, Weinreich (1966) claimed there are different senses of "eat" corresponding to eating soup with a spoon; eating a steak with a knife and fork; eating chop suey with chopsticks, and so on. Halff et al. (1976) have similarly claimed that words have many meanings and that a particular sense of a word is "instantiated" when it is used in context. Thus, in the sentence, "A fish attacked a swimmer," the sense of "fish" that is instantiated is likely to be equivalent to "shark." Anderson and his colleagues have reported a number of experiments in which a word corresponding to an instantiation, for example "shark," turns out to be a better recall cue to the sentence than the original word that occurred in it, e.g. "fish" (see Anderson and Ortony 1975; Anderson et al. 1976). Garnham (1979) has obtained the same effect with verbs, for example "fried" is a better recall cue than the original verb for "The housewife cooked the chips," though not, as is to be expected, for "The housewife cooked the peas."

In fact, there has been too much emphasis on polysemy and in consequence a mistaken view about the mechanism of instantiation. Linguists have formulated more accurate linguistic criteria for ambiguity (Zwicky and Sadock 1973), and the crucial psychological criterion is whether or not it is necessary to postulate more than one semantic representation for a word in order to account for the interpretations of the sentences in which it occurs. Instead of asking how many different meanings can be squeezed out of the word, psycholinguists need to ask what is the minimum number of different senses that are necessary to cope with all of its different uses. If "eat" were truly polysemous then the sentence:

He eats the food

should be highly ambiguous. It should have many wholly distinct sen-
~~ses. Yet it remains unequivocal.~~ What is true, however, is that the
sentence in common with others can be truthfully asserted of an infinite
number of different situations: "he" can refer to any male individual,
"food" can designate an indefinite number of different types of food
served in an indefinite number of different conditions, and the manner
by which the food is eaten can vary in an indefinite number of different
ways from chewing it like cud to straining it through the teeth. This
indeterminacy of reference is not sufficient to establish ambiguity because, if it were, all open-class words would be infinitely ambiguous
and their meanings could not be contained by a finite brain. Hence the
sentence above, which truly applies to a variety of situations, is referentially indeterminate, but not ambiguous. Its syntax is unambiguous,
and its words are unambiguous: they each have in ordinary usage a
single sense, but these senses suffice, as do the senses of all words, to
embrace many different situations. The sentence requires only a single
representation of its meaning.

A comparable mistake has been made in the standard interpretation
of instantiation. Context can, of course, pick out the appropriate sense
of a genuinely ambiguous word, for example "He banked the cheque."
However, the instantiation of an unambiguous word such as "fish" by
a sentential context does not depend on picking out one sense from a
long list of possibilities. A simple thought experiment, which was proposed in Johnson-Laird (1981), suggests a more plausible interpretation.
Consider the sentence:

It frightened the swimmer.

It may well be that the word "shark" would make a better recall cue
for this sentence than the original word, the pronoun "it," that functions
as its subject. However, it is obvious that this pronoun does not have
a vast set of different senses: it has a single sense that enables it to refer
to any of a potentially infinite set of entities. Its reference can depend
on its linguistic context if it is used to refer to something that is identified
elsewhere in the discourse, or it can depend directly on the reference
situation if it is used deictically. Instantiation is therefore a process, not
of eliminating senses from a list in a lexical entry, but of imagining a
more specific situation than is warranted solely by the meanings of
words (see also Gumenik 1979, for results that can be interpreted in the
same way).

All open-class words, such as "fish" and "eat," are closer to being
pronouns than is commonly recognized: they provide a relatively simple
semantic framework that can be enriched by inferences based on knowledge. These inferences concern the situation designated by the sentence, and different linguistic contexts highlight different aspects of
lexical meaning. Consider, for instance, the following sentences:

The tomato rolled across the floor.
The sun was a ripe tomato.
He accidentally sat on a tomato.

The first sentence calls to mind the characteristic shape of a tomato, the second its characteristic colour, and the third its characteristic squashiness (see Johnson-Laird 1975). Listeners know all these aspects of tomatoes, and many more, but when they initially interpret a sentence they are most unlikely to call to mind all of this information (*pace* Gibson 1971) or none of it (*pace* Fodor et al. 1975). Instead, they are likely to retrieve some information—the most relevant for imagining the state of affairs depicted by the sentence, and the rest of the sentence is one obvious cue to what is relevant.

This hypothesis has been corroborated in a number of experiments carried out by the author and his colleagues. Thus, the occurrence of a verb such as "pleased" suggests that the object of the sentence will be something that is animate, and subjects are indeed faster to detect the presence of an animate noun when it occurs in such a sentence than when it occurs in a sentence with a verb such as "soaked" (see Hodgkin 1977). The facilitation occurs even when the target noun occurs prior to the verb. Similarly, if subjects are asked a specific question that hinges on the sense of a word, such as:

Is a diamond brilliant?

then, as Tabossi and Johnson-Laird (1980) have shown, their response is faster when the question follows a sentence such as:

The mirror dispersed the light from the diamond

than when it follows a sentence that does not call to mind the relevant aspect of diamonds:

The film showed the person with the diamond.

As we expected, subjects are slower to answer the question when the preceding sentence calls to mind some other but irrelevant aspect of diamonds, such as their hardness:

The goldsmith cut the glass with the diamond.

Table 26.3 presents the mean latencies to respond correctly to the questions and the mean numbers of errors. Subsequent experiments have shown that the phenomenon is equally apparent whether the priming is a result of selectional restrictions on the sense of a word or factual inferences about its likely referent (Tabossi 1982).

For all of these experiments, independent panels of judges established that the priming sentences genuinely called to mind the relevant element of meaning, and the design made it very difficult for the subjects to guess which word in a sentence the subsequent question would be

Table 26.3 The mean latencies (ms) and mean errors (max = 12) to respond to questions about nouns in the Tabossi and Johnson-Laird (1980) experiment

	Responses after a relevant priming sentence	Responses after a non-priming sentence	Responses after an irrelevant priming sentence
Latencies	1016	1089	1142
Errors	0.54	0.88	1.33

about or what the question would be. Tabossi (1983) has even shown that there is a more general form of priming in which the initial sentence need not contain any of the nouns in the question. Thus, for example, the sentence:

The fountain pen left a spot in the desk drawer

enables subjects to respond faster to the subsequent question:

Does ink leave a stain?

than when it occurs after a neutral sentence that does not call to mind the relevant property of ink.

Linguistic context evidently has at least three different effects on the interpretation of words. First, it can enable the listener to select the appropriate sense of a truly ambiguous word. Second, it can lead to a representation of more specific referents than is strictly warranted by the sense of an unambiguous word. For example, a listener imagines a shark as an instance of the generic term, "fish," since a shark is a plausible actor in the situation described by the sentence. Third, it can call to mind particular aspects of a word's interpretation—at the expense of other aspects. Thus, it plays a major part in the interpretation of compound nouns, such as "hot dog man" (see Clark 1983). The context of a cooperative game can even lead people to a tacit negotiation of specific meanings for general nouns, such as "row" and "column" (Anderson 1983). What has sometimes been underestimated in all of these cases is the importance of reference, or more properly, its psychological correlate: the representation of specific referents, real or imaginary, in particular situations. What the context refers to can disambiguate a word; it can instantiate a more specific referent; and it can suggest an aspect of a word's meaning that is particularly relevant to what is going on.

The Acquisition of Lexical Meanings

People often do not know the meaning of a word in their language. Such ignorance may not matter. If someone says:

The explorers survived on pemmican and truffles

you may readily understand this remark, and only on being specifically questioned realize that you do not know exactly what pemmican and truffles are. The reason that an incomplete grasp of lexical meaning may be sufficient for comprehension is that you are nevertheless able to imagine the state of affairs described by the sentence. The evidence of the previous section shows that you do not necessarily retrieve all the semantic information that you possess about a word. If you lack some information, the gap may go unnoticed where it is not crucial to understanding the sentence.

Gaps in lexical knowledge are predictable. People are likely to be aware of what is important, and thus, for instance, if they know anything about the sense of a word they should know whether or not it means a substance fit for human consumption. They are similarly more likely to be aware of a perceptible property, such as whether a substance is solid or liquid, than of a more covert property, such as its provenance (whether it is natural or manmade). Graham Gibbs and I quizzed two groups of subjects about these three aspects of a set of rare words (see Johnson-Laird 1975). Typically, our subjects knew for instance that "pemmican" was consumable and that "verdigris" was not, but their knowledge of the structure and provenance of these substances was less secure. Table 26.4 presents the mean numbers of errors that the subjects made on a set of 48 rare words. The trend was reliable for both groups. Of course, exceptions to the general trend are to be expected where a particular aspect of a substance is highly salient, and such exceptions have been demonstrated by Emma Coope (in an unpublished experiment).

Gaps in lexical knowledge point to the importance of the process of acquisition, since the way in which concepts are acquired will inevitably be reflected in the form and content of lexical entries. There are two obvious processes by which you can acquire the meaning of a word: you can be told what the word means or you can infer what it means from encountering it in use. To be told the meaning of a word presupposes that it is possible to frame a useful definition of its meaning. Jerry Fodor has often claimed that there are no good definitions (see e.g., Fodor et al. 1980). The truth is—as many lexicographers would assert—there are no good definitions for *some* words. For other words, there

Table 26.4 The mean errors in categorizing 48 rare words on three semantic contrasts

	Sample 1: University students (N = 24)	Sample 2: Technical college students (N = 12)
Consumable/nonconsumable	4.7	5.0
Solid/liquid	6.7	7.3
Natural/manmade	9.1	10.0

are excellent definitions. Indeed the majority of words in the Oxford English Dictionary can only be acquired by definition because they hardly ever occur in actual discourse. Such words are in fact easy to define in a way that is genuinely informative, e.g., "an arblast is a crossbow, consisting of a steel bow fitted to a wooden shaft, furnished with a special mechanism for drawing and letting slip the bowstring, and discharging arrows, bolts, stones, etc." Other words, however, are singularly difficult to define in a way that is useful. Dr. Johnson was perhaps satirizing the futility of definition in these cases when he defined a network as "anything reticulated or decussated, at equal distances, with interstices between the intersections." Anyone who does not know the meaning of the definiens is hardly likely to be helped by the definiendum.

Is there any way of predicting the difficulty of defining the meaning of a word? Gerry Quinn and I set out to answer this question in an experimental study of definitions. We asked our subjects to try to define a series of verbs in a way that would help children or foreigners whose grasp of English was insecure. We chose four levels of semantic complexity of the verbs following the analyses of Miller and Johnson-Laird (1976), and we predicted that semantically complex verbs, such as "watch" and "lend," would be easier to define than the semantically simplest verbs, such as "see" and "own." It should be easy to break down the meaning of a complex verb into simpler components for which there are corresponding words, but it should be hard to find such components for a simple verb. Our prediction was confirmed. For the simplest of the verbs, the subjects could at best offer only synonyms, which would not be very helpful to poor speakers of the language. As for the remaining verbs, the more complex they were, the easier the subjects found the task and the more accurate their definitions (see Johnson-Laird and Quinn 1976).

The traditional account of lexical acquisition is that a child learns an association between a word and the thing that it denotes. There are many problems with this idea—establishing the set of referents for a word should not be confused with the mere conditioning of a stimulus (Harrison 1972), the word could designate any of the manifold properties of the object rather than the object itself (Wittgenstein 1953), and many words have either no perceptible referent or else are parts of speech for which the notion is irrelevant. Above all, however, children are no mere passive receivers of word-object associations: they entertain their own hypotheses about the meanings of words (Bowerman 1977), and they coin their own words if no-one provides them with a suitable term (Clark 1982). Hence, although children acquire words from observing them in use, a comprehensive theory of this process, such as might be modelled in a computer program, is a long way from being formulated. There are even theorists who are so perplexed by the process that they argue that learning has little role to play in it, and that concepts are innate and merely "triggered" by experience (Fodor 1980). Although a native endowment is crucial, the phenomena above and some that I will describe in a moment imply that a form of learning does underlie the acquisition of lexical meanings.

Conservative estimates of the rate at which children acquire words suggest that at around the age of five they are adding to their vocabulary some 20 or more words per day (see e.g., Templin 1957; Miller 1977, 1986). So rapid a rate is hardly consistent with a theory that allows only for simple associative learning. One interesting conjecture is that children can pick up elements of the meaning of a word merely from hearing it used appropriately in constructions containing words that they already understand. Til Wykes and I confirmed this conjecture in an experiment with 3- and 4-year-olds. The children listened twice to a series of stories. Each story contained a novel word that the children had not heard before. For example, one story featured the novel verb, "mib," which was used transitively with a meaning resembling "soak" and intransitively with a meaning resembling "spill"—our idea was to inhibit the children from merely substituting a familiar synonym for the nonsense syllable. After they had heard the story twice, the children were able to pick out the one entity (orange juice) that could mib from a set of four alternatives. Their performance was similar for the other three nonsense verbs, and it remained above chance one week later when they had to carry out the same task with a new set of alternatives (see Wykes and Johnson-Laird 1977). In an unpublished study, Jon Davies showed that children could also acquire elements of the meanings of nonsense *nouns* from hearing them used in constructions with verbs with which they were familiar.

There may be an analogy between acquiring a language and the implementation of a compiler for a new high level programming language. A compiler is a special program for taking programs written in the new language and translating them into the machine code that controls the actual operation of the computer. It is sensible to write part of the compiler in assembly language (which maps readily into machine code), and to write the rest of the compiler in the new language itself. The former translates the latter into machine code, and saves the designers from the chore of writing the whole of the compiler in assembly language. It is not too far-fetched to imagine that lexical learning lifts itself up by its own bootstraps in a similar way. Children first learn, or perhaps know innately, how to relate certain internal representations to states of affairs in the world. Once a fragment of the language has been mapped onto this knowledge, it becomes possible to acquire other words indirectly by inferring their meaning from the contexts in which they occur or by being given explicit definitions of them. Some words are likely to fall clearly into the category of those acquired by direct acquaintance, for example simple words like "see" and "own" that are so hard to define; other words are likely to fall clearly into the category of indirect acquisitions, for example "arblast" and "eleemosynary." Many words, however, will be of mixed acquisition; and different individuals will acquire a given word in different ways.

Meanings and Prototypes

To understand an assertion is to know how the world would be if the assertion were true. This formula does not imply that when you understand an assertion you know how to verify it, or indeed that it is possible to verify it. It is one thing to know how the world should be and quite another to know how to find out whether the world is in that condition. However, if you have no idea what constraints an assertion implies about reality, then you have no idea what it means. One striking feature of natural language is that for the language community as a whole there are lexical items (within the same syntactic category) that vary in the completeness with which their semantics specifies this information. Consider the earlier example:

He sighted a herd of elephants on the plain.

The function words and the words "sighted," "herd," and "plain," have a complete semantics, because no conceivable advance in human knowledge can force us to add to our conception of their meaning or to cause us necessarily to modify it. The way we conceive the world given the truth of this utterance is, in principle, completely specified as far as the meanings of these words are concerned. The case is different for the word, "elephant." Most speakers of English have a good idea of what an elephant is—they have seen an elephant, or a picture of one, and they know something of the nature of the beast. Yet the term is a theoretical one. It designates a set of creatures within our categorization of animals. Our knowledge of such matters is far from complete, and we are committed to the existence of the category without knowing for certain what the essentials of elephanthood actually are—indeed without knowing incontrovertibly that the class is a truly unitary one. Such words notoriously give rise to the problem of demarcating what should go into the dictionary from what should go into the encyclopedia—a problem for which there appears to be no principled solution (see Gerrig 1985). These words are "natural kind terms," and it is doubtful whether there are any necessary and sufficient conditions for defining them (Putnam 1975).

The existence of natural kind terms has important implications for the contents of lexical entries. The entry for "elephant" is likely to include information that can be used for identifying elephants and for imagining them, as well as other conceptual information (Miller and Johnson-Laird 1976). If I assert that I have sighted an elephant, then you will interpret my utterance to mean that I saw a large, four-legged mammal with tusks and a trunk. Such interpretations cannot be mediated by meaning postulates or any other form of lexical representation that implies that these attributes are necessary components of elephants. They are not; an elephant may lack any of them. They are not essential characteristics; and they are not mere inductions, since to check them inductively presupposes some independent method of first identifying elephants. In fact, they are part of our "theory" of elephants, which tells us that a prototypical member of the class has each of these attributes.

Eleanor Rosch and her colleagues have collected much evidence that is consistent with the existence of prototypes (e.g., Rosch 1976). Real objects, unlike many of the concepts studied in the psychological laboratory, have features that are correlated—if an animal has a trunk, it tends to have tusks—and such correlations will be reflected in the prototype. Likewise, not all instances of a concept are equally representative, and the speed with which instances are categorized depends on how prototypical they are (Rosch 1973). The major problem with prototypes is how they are represented in the mental lexicon. Rosch (1976) has suggested that a prototype is represented by a concrete image of an average category member. Ironically, Kant (1787) had already raised a decisive objection to this theory:

In truth, it is not images of objects, but schemata, which lie at the foundation of our pure sensuous conceptions. No image could ever be adequate to our conception of triangles in general. For the generalness of the conception it could never attain to, as this includes under itself all triangles, whether right-angled, acute-angled, etc., whilst the image would always be limited to a single part of this sphere.

The lexical entry for "elephant" must therefore consist of a schema representing the prototypical animal, and perhaps the best way to think of a schema is in terms of a mental model defined in terms of an interrelated set of "default values" (Minsky 1975), that is, specific values for variables that can be assumed in the absence of information to the contrary. Thus, default values have a different status to the normal representation of a word's contribution to the truth conditions of a sentence. Normal truth conditions support valid inferences since they are necessary components of a word's meaning. Default values place a weaker constraint on how the world should be: they hold only in the case that nothing is asserted to the contrary. Hence, your knowledge of the default values for "elephant" lead you to assume that I saw an animal with one trunk, two tusks, four legs, etc., unless you have evidence to the contrary.

Lexical entries containing default values still place constraints on the world, but they do so indirectly by way of the set of alternative prototypes governing a domain. You will not necessarily judge that I spoke falsely if the animal I saw had no trunk and one tusk. But, you will think me mistaken if, on inspection, the beast turns out to fit the ~~prototype of a rhinoceros, or alternatively~~ not to fit the prototype of an animal at all.

Towards a Theory of the Representation of Lexical Meanings

The clues of the five previous sections fit together to suggest a coherent picture of the meanings of words. This theory, which I will outline here, is intended to answer three central questions: What are the contents of lexical meanings? How are they mentally represented? And what is their role in speech and comprehension?

The evidence from the semantic search task implies that there are entries in the mental lexicon that allow ready access to the information that an individual has about the sense of a word. The contents of an entry may be incomplete in one of two distinct ways. First, the individual may have yet to acquire a complete semantics for the word; second, the word may be a theoretically based one for which there is only an incomplete semantics. There are other expressions and nonce words with meanings that depend essentially on the context in which they occur, for example, the verb "porched" as in "The newsboy porched the newspaper" (see Clark and Clark 1979; Clark 1983). Words that are acquired by direct acquaintance with their denotata are likely to have lexical entries that contain ineffable specifications of their truth conditions, that is, entries that specify how the world has to be for them to apply to it, and that are all but impossible to define. In the case of natural kind terms, a major component of the representation of sense will consist of default values.

Words with a more complex semantics may be acquired from verbal definitions, or from encountering their use in verbal expressions. Their lexical representation may accordingly relate them to other words. Most words in common usage are likely to possess elements of both sorts of information, for example, people have access to procedures for imagining elephants, and they have access to other conceptual information about elephants, which they may have acquired either from usage or from a definition, such as the fact that elephants are animals.

The theory therefore draws a basic distinction between ineffable truth conditions (akin to expressions in machine code) and verbal definitions (akin to expressions in a high level programming language). The distinction relates, of course, to the old arguments about the existence of semantic primitives. What it implies, however, is that although primitives exist they are remote from the directly expressible analyses of the meanings of words. They are unanalysable by normal cognitive mechanisms, outside conscious awareness, and presumably innate. One can advance plausible conjectures, however, about the functions that they are used to compute, for example, the perceptual representation of the world, the representation of discourse in the form of an imagined model of the state of affairs it describes, and the choice of appropriate words to describe a perceived or imaginary state of affairs. Likewise, one can begin to advance hypotheses about their role in the identification of objects (Marr 1982) and in the construction of mental models of discourse (Johnson-Laird 1983).

The specifications of verbal relations in the lexicon can be based on some mechanism akin to a semantic network or to meaning postulates, though the power of such theories is likely to make it difficult to test them empirically (see Johnson-Laird et al. 1984).

The specifications of truth conditions in the lexicon can be thought of as the ingredients necessary for the procedures that construct, modify, and manipulate mental models. Thus, the representation of, say, "on the left of" calls for a specification that will enable a verification routine to scan a mental model in the appropriate direction to verify the relation, and that will enable a construction routine to scan a mental model in the appropriate direction before adding an element to the model, and so on.

The specification of default values can depend on similar procedures, but their results in models can be undone in the light of other information. Exactly such procedures are needed in any case whenever a model is based on information that is insufficiently determinate to specify a unique situation, that is whenever a model is based on virtually any piece of discourse. I describe my office, for instance, and you form a mental model of the arrangement of the furniture, but since my description is bound to be consistent with more than one possibility, you may have a revise your model in the light of subsequent information (see Johnson-Laird 1983, for a description of computer programs using both truth conditions and default conditions of these sorts).

The dichotomy between ineffable truth conditions and verbal formulae has a number of repercussions. The logical properties of words, for instance, can arise in two distinct ways: from a representation of an explicit verbal relation ("elephants are animals") or from the consequences of the representations of their truth conditions. Hence, if you know what has to be the case for something to be an elephant, and you know what has to be the case for something to be an animal, then a simple thought experiment will lead you to the same conclusion that elephants are animals. There are a number of clear cases where the logical properties of words arise only from their truth conditions, because the vagaries of their logical behaviour are too great to be encompassed by simple verbal definitions, for example, natural language quantifiers, and spatial expressions such as "on the left of."

The contrast between verbal formulae and truth conditions also arises in the interpretation of discourse, which seems to call for a listener to construct an initial verbal representation close to the linguistic form of the utterance and then to use this representation, together with lexical entries, to construct a mental model of the discourse. Although the existence of these two levels of representation is a matter of controversy, they are borne out by the need for independent representations of sense and reference, by linguistic phenomena such as the two classes of anaphora (surface and deep), and by experimental results on the memory for discourse (see e.g. Mani and Johnson-Laird 1982; Johnson-Laird 1983).

A major problem confronting the present theory is to reconcile two important constraints on the process of comprehension. On the one hand, information from an utterance is integrated into the existing model as a function of the referential links, if any, between the utterance and the model; on the other hand, the interpretation of the sense of a sentence almost certainly depends on combining the senses of its constituent words according to the syntactic relations between them. No existing theory has yet shown how these two different demands can be met within a single unitary theory of comprehension.

One question remains: why do we lack a conscious access to the nature of lexical representations? The answer is that the truth conditions of words are intimately dependent on the mind's ability to relate representations to the world. There is a twofold evolutionary advantage in not having conscious access to such perceptual mechanisms: first, they can operate in parallel and therefore more efficiently; and, second, if you see a tiger, you take avoiding action rather than inspect the process of perception to ensure that it is operating correctly. The lexical system inherits the inaccessibility of this basic representational machinery. There is a further advantage in this lack of access: you do not become aware of a gap in lexical knowledge unless it is immediately germane to the interpretation of the discourse. If you had a conscious access to your lexical representations, then every time you encountered a word for which you possessed an incomplete semantics, you would be aware of it. You would be in a comparable state of mind to someone who looks up a word in a dictionary only to find that part of the relevant entry has been torn out. This intrusive awareness would occur even if the missing information were not actually required to construct a model of the discourse. Similarly, every time you encountered an ambiguous word, you would be aware of it—even if the ambiguity were resolved by the immediate context. Since your aim is to grasp the significance of an utterance and perhaps to act upon it, your interpretative system has no need to present these details to consciousness, just as there is no need to make the details of the perceptual process accessible. The same consideration, of course, applies to the acquisition of meaning: children can acquire a new element of meaning *en passant* without becoming aware that they are so doing, and in this way they can attend primarily to the significance of the utterance rather than the process by which they are interpreting it.

Conclusions

The present theory of lexical meanings rests on seven principal assumptions:

(1) Comprehension requires the listener to construct a model of the state of affairs described by the discourse. Words contribute to the sense of utterances, but this model depends on inferences from context about the specific referents of expressions.

(2) There is a mental dictionary that contains entries in which the senses of words are represented.

(3) A lexical entry may be incomplete as a result of ignorance or because the word is a theoretical term with an intrinsically incomplete sense.

(4) The senses of words can be acquired from definitions or from encountering instances of the word in use. The former procedure can only work with words that contain a complex semantics.

(5) Corresponding to the method of acquisition, elements of a lexical representation can consist of (a) relations to other words, which could be represented by a mechanism akin to a semantic network, and (b) ineffable primitives that are used in constructing and manipulating mental models of the world.

(6) The primitive elements in a lexical representation may specify the word's contribution to the truth conditions of the expressions in which it occurs, or else the logically weaker default values of the word.

(7) The contrast between explicit verbal relations and ineffable truth conditions is related to the way in which discourse, in turn, is represented initially in a superficial linguistic form and subsequently in the form of a model of the state of affairs that it describes.

Note

I am grateful to Lolly Tyler for forcing me to write this article and to Patrizia Tabossi and the referees for their cogent criticisms of it.

References

Anderson, A. (1983). *Semantic and social-pragmatic aspects of meaning in task-oriented dialogue.* Ph.D. dissertation, University of Glasgow, Glasgow.

Anderson, J. R. (1976). *Language, memory, and thought.* Hillsdale, NJ.: Erlbaum.

Anderson, J. R., and G. H. Bower (1973). *Human associative memory.* Washington, D.C.: Winston.

Anderson, R. C., and A. Ortony (1975). On putting apples into bottles—a problem of polysemy. *Cognitive Psychology* 7, 167–180.

Anderson, R. C., J. W. Pichert, E. T. Goetz, D. L. Schallert, K. V. Stevens, and S. R. Trollip (1976). Instantiation of general terms. *Journal of Verbal Learning and Verbal Behavior* 15, 667–679.

Bowerman, M. (1977). The acquisition of word meaning: An investigation of some current concepts. In N. Waterson and C. Snow, eds., *Development of communication: Social and pragmatic factors in language acquisition*. New York: Wiley.

Cairns, H. S., and J. Kamerman (1975). Lexical information processing during sentence comprehension. *Journal of Verbal Learning and Verbal Behavior* 14, 170–179.

Clark, E. V. (1982). The young word-maker: A case study of innovation in the child's lexicon. In E. Wanner and L. R. Gleitman, eds., *Language acquisition: The state of the art*. Cambridge: Cambridge University Press.

Clark, E. V., and H. H. Clark (1979). When nouns surface as verbs. *Language* 55, 767–811.

Clark, H. H. (1983). Making sense of nonce sense. In G.B. Flores d'Arcais and R. Jarvella, eds., *The process of understanding language*. New York: Wiley.

Collins, A. M., and M. R. Quillian (1969). Retrieval time from semantic memory. *Journal of Verbal Learning and Verbal Behavior* 8, 240–247.

Conrad, C. (1974). Context effects in sentence comprehension: A study of the subjective lexicon. *Memory and Cognition* 2, 130–138.

Fischler, I., and P. Bloom (1979). Automatic and attentional process in the effects of sentence contexts on word recognition. *Journal of Verbal Learning and Verbal Behavior* 18, 1–20.

Fodor, J. A. (1980). Fixation of belief and concept acquisition. In M. Piattelli-Palmarini, ed., *Language and learning: The debate between Jean Piaget and Noam Chomsky*. Cambridge, MA: Harvard University Press.

Fodor, J. A., M. F. Garrett, E. C. T. Walker, and C. H. Parkes (1980). Against definitions. *Cognition* 8, 263–367.

Fodor, J. D. (1977). *Semantics: Theories of meaning in generative grammar*. New York: Crowell.

Fodor, J. D., J. A. Fodor, and M. F. Garrett (1975). The psychological unreality of semantic representations. *Linguistic Inquiry* 4, 515–531.

Garnham, A. (1979). Instantiation of verbs. *Quarterly Journal of Experimental Psychology* 31, 207–214.

Gerrig, R. J. (1985). Process and products of lexical access. Unpublished MS., Department of Psychology, Yale University, New Haven.

Gibson, E. J. (1971). Perceptual learning and the theory of word perception. *Cognitive Psychology* 2, 351–368.

Glass, A. L., and K. J. Holyoak (1974/5). Alternative conceptions of semantic memory. *Cognition* 3, 313–339.

Gumenik, W. E. (1979). The advantage of specific terms over general terms as cues for sentence recall: Instantiation or retrieval? *Memory and Cognition* 7, 240–244.

Halff, H. M., A. Ortony, and R. C. Anderson (1976). A context-sensitive representation of word meanings. *Memory and Cognition* 4, 378–383.

Harrison, B. (1972). *Meaning and structure.* New York: Harper & Row.

Hodgkin, D. (1977). *An experimental study of sentence comprehension and sentence meaning.* Ph.D. thesis, University of London, London.

Holmes, V. M., R. Arwas, and M. F. Garrett (1977). Prior context and the perception of lexically ambiguous sentences. *Memory and Cognition* 5, 103–110.

Johnson-Laird, P. N. (1975). In A. Kennedy and A. Wilkes, eds., *Studies in long term memory.* London: Wiley.

Johnson-Laird, P. N. (1981). Mental models of meaning. In A. K. Joshi, B. L. Webber, and I. A. Sag, eds., *Elements of discourse understanding.* Cambridge: Cambridge University Press.

Johnson-Laird, P. N. (1983). *Mental models: Towards a cognitive science of language, inference, and consciousness.* Cambridge: Cambridge University Press/Cambridge, MA: Harvard University Press.

Johnson-Laird, P. N., G. Gibbs, and J. de Mowbray (1978). Meaning, amount of processing, and memory for words. *Memory and Cognition* 6, 372–375.

Johnson-Laird, P. N., D. Herrmann, and R. Chaffin (1984). Only connections: A critique of semantic networks. *Psychological Bulletin* 96, 292–315.

Johnson-Laird, P. N., and J. G. Quinn (1976). To define true meaning. *Nature* 264, 635–636.

Kant, I. (1787). *The critique of pure reason,* 2d ed. Translated by J. M. D. Meiklejohn. London: Dent (1934).

Katz, J. J., and J. A. Fodor (1963). The structure of a semantic theory. *Language* 39, 170–210.

Kintsch, W. (1974). *The representation of meaning in memory.* Hillsdale, N.J.: Erlbaum.

McClelland, A. G. R., R. E. Rawles, and F. E. Sinclair (1981). The effects of search criteria and retrieval cue availability on memory for words. *Memory and Cognition* 9, 164–168.

Mani, K., and P. N. Johnson-Laird (1982). The mental representation of spatial descriptions. *Memory and Cognition* 10, 181–187.

Marr, D. (1982). *Vision,* San Francisco: Freeman.

Meyer, D. E., and R. W. Schvaneveldt (1971). Facilitation in recognizing pairs of words: Evidence of a dependence between retrieval operations. *Journal of Experimental Psychology* 90, 227–234.

Miller, G. A. (1977). *Spontaneous apprentices: Children and language.* New York: Seaburg Press.

Miller, G. A. (1986). Dictionaries in the mind. *Language and Cognitive Processes* 1, 171–185.

Miller, G. A., and P. N. Johnson-Laird (1976). *Language and perception.* Cambridge, MA: Harvard University Press/Cambridge: Cambridge University Press.

Minsky, M. (1975). Frame-system theory. In R. C. Schank and B. L. Nash-Webber, eds., *Theoretical issues in natural language processing.* Preprints of a conference at MIT. Reprinted in P. N. Johnson-Laird and P. C. Wason, eds., *Thinking: Readings in cognitive science.* Cambridge: Cambridge University Press (1977).

Putnam, H. (1975). The meaning of 'meaning'. In K. Gunderson, ed., *Language, mind and knowledge.* Minnesota Studies in the Philosophy of Science, vol. 7. Minneapolis: University of Minnesota Press.

Rosch, E. (1973). On the internal structure of perceptual and semantic categories. In T. M. Moore, ed., *Cognitive development and the acquisition of language.* New York: Academic Press.

Rosch, E. (1976). Classification of real-world objects: origins and representations in cognition. In S. Ehrlich and E. Tulving, eds., La mémoire sémantique. *Bulletin de Psychologie,* Paris. Reprinted in P. N. Johnson-Laird and P. C. Wason, eds., *Thinking: Readings in cognitive science.* Cambridge: Cambridge University Press (1977).

Ross, B. (1981). The more, the better? Number of decisions as a determinant of memorability. *Memory and Cognition* 9, 23–33.

Rumelhart, D. E., P. H. Lindsay, and D. A. Norman (1972). A process model for long-term memory. In E. Tulving and W. Donaldson, eds., *Organization and memory.* New York: Academic Press.

Schaeffer, B., and R. Wallace (1970). The comparison of word meanings. *Journal of Experimental Psychology,* 86, 144–152.

Schuberth, R. E., and P. D. Eimas (1977). Effects of context in the classification of words and non-words. *Journal of Experimental Psychology: Human Perception and Performance* 3, 27–36.

Smith, E. E., E. J. Shoben, and L. J. Rips (1974). Structure and process in semantic memory: A featural model for semantic decisions. *Psychological Review* 81, 214–241.

Swinne, D. A. (1979). Lexical access during sentence comprehension: (re)consideration of context effects. *Journal of Verbal Learning and Verbal Behavior* 6, 645–659.

Swinney, D. A., W. Onifer, P. Prather, and M. Hirshkowitz (1979). Semantic facilitation across sensory modalities in the processing of individual words and sentences. *Memory and Cognition* 7, 159–165.

Tabossi, P. (1982). Sentential context and the interpretation of unambiguous words. *Quarterly Journal of Experimental Psychology* 34A, 79–90.

Tabossi, P. (1983). *Interpreting words in context.* D.Phil. Thesis, University of Sussex.

Tabossi, P., and P. N. Johnson-Laird (1980). Linguistic context and the priming of semantic information. *Quarterly Journal of Experimental Psychology* 32, 595–603.

Tanenhaus, M. K., and M. M. Lucas (1987). Context effects in lexical priming. *Cognition* 25, 213–234.

Templin, M. C. (1957). *Certain language skills in children: Their development and interrelationships*. Minneapolis: University of Minnesota Press.

Tweedy, J. R., R. H. Lapinksy, and R. W. Schvaneveldt (1977). Semantic context effects on word recognition: Influence of varying the proportion of items presented in an appropriate context. *Memory and Cognition* 5, 84–98.

Weinreich, U. (1966). Explorations in semantic theory. In T. A. Sebeok, ed., *Current Trends in Linguistics*, vol. 3. The Hague: Mouton.

Wittgenstein, L. (1953). *Philosophical investigations*. New York: Macmillan.

Wykes, T., and P. N. Johnson-Laird (1977). How do children learn the meanings of verbs? *Nature* 268, 326–327.

Zwicky, A., and J. M. Sadock (1973). Ambiguity tests and how to fail them. *Working Papers in Linguistics*. Ohio State University.

27 Brain and Language

Antonio R. Damasio and Hanna Damasio

What do neuroscientists talk about when they talk about language? We talk, it seems, about the ability to use words (or signs, if our language is one of the sign languages of the deaf) and to combine them in sentences so that concepts in our minds can be transmitted to other people. We also consider the converse: how we apprehend words spoken by others and turn them into concepts in our own minds.

Language arose and persisted because it serves as a supremely efficient means of communication, especially for abstract concepts. Try to explain the rise and fall of the communist republics without using a single word. But language also performs what Patricia S. Churchland of the University of California at San Diego aptly calls "cognitive compression." It helps to categorize the world and to reduce the complexity of conceptual structures to a manageable scale.

The word "screwdriver," for example, stands for many representations of such an instrument, including visual descriptions of its operation and purpose, specific instances of its use, the feel of the tool or the hand movement that pertains to it. Or there is the immense variety of conceptual representations denoted by a word such as "democracy." The cognitive economies of language—its facility for pulling together many concepts under one symbol—make it possible for people to establish ever more complex concepts and use them to think at levels that would otherwise be impossible.

In the beginning, however, there were no words. Language seems to have appeared in evolution only after humans and species before them had become adept at generating and categorizing actions and at creating and categorizing mental representations of objects, events and relations. Similarly, infants' brains are busy representing and evoking concepts and generating myriad actions long before they utter their first well-

From A. Damasio and H. Damasio, Brain and language, *Scientific American* 267, 88–95 (September, 1992). Reprinted with permission. Copyright © 1992 by Scientific American, Inc. All rights reserved.

selected word and even longer before they form sentences and truly use language. However, the maturation of language processes may not always depend on the maturation of conceptual processes, since some children with defective conceptual systems have nonetheless acquired grammar. The neural machinery necessary for some syntactic operations seems capable of developing autonomously.

Language exists both as an artifact in the external world—a collection of symbols in admissible combinations—and as the embodiment in the brain of those symbols and the principles that determine their combinations. The brain uses the same machinery to represent language that it uses to represent any other entity. As neuroscientists come to understand the neural basis for the brain's representations of external objects, events and their relations, they will simultaneously gain insight into the brain's representation of language and into the mechanisms that connect the two.

We believe the brain processes language by means of three interacting sets of structures. First, a large collection of neural systems in both the right and left cerebral hemispheres represents nonlanguage interactions between the body and its environment, as mediated by varied sensory and motor systems—that is to say, anything that a person does, perceives, thinks or feels while acting in the world.

The brain not only categorizes these nonlanguage representations (along lines such as shape, color, sequence or emotional state), it also creates another level of representation for the results of its classification. In this way, people organize objects, events and relationships. Successive layers of categories and symbolic representations form the basis for abstraction and metaphor.

Second, a smaller number of neural systems, generally located in the left cerebral hemisphere, represent phonemes, phoneme combinations and syntactic rules for combining words. When stimulated from within the brain, these systems assemble word-forms and generate sentences to be spoken or written. When stimulated externally by speech or text, they perform the initial processing of auditory or visual language signals.

A third set of structures, also located largely in the left hemisphere, mediates between the first two. It can take a concept and stimulate the production of word-forms, or it can receive words and cause the brain to evoke the corresponding concepts.

Such mediation structures have also been hypothesized from a purely psycholinguistic perspective. Willem J. M. Levelt of the Max Planck Institute for Psycholinguistics in Nijmegen has suggested that word-forms and sentences are generated from concepts by means of a component he calls "lemma," and Merrill F. Garrett of the University of Arizona holds a similar view.

The concepts and words for colors serve as a particularly good example of this tripartite organization. Even those afflicted by congenital color blindness know that certain ranges of hue (chroma) band together and are different from other ranges, independent of their brightness and saturation. As Brent Berlin and Eleanor H. Rosch of the University of California at Berkely have shown, these color concepts are fairly universal and develop whether or not a given culture actually has names to denote them. Naturally, the retina and the lateral geniculate nucleus perform the initial processing of color signals, but the primary visual cortex and at least two other cortical regions (known as V2 and V4) also participate in color processing; they fabricate what we know as the experience of color.

With our colleague Matthew Rizzo, we have found that damage to the occipital and subcalcarine portions of the left and right lingual gyri, the region of the brain believed to contain the V2 and V4 cortices, causes a condition called achromatopsia. Patients who previously had normal vision lose their perception of color. Furthermore, they lose the ability even to imagine colors. Achromatopsics usually see the world in shades of gray; when they conjure up a typically colored image in their minds, they see the shapes, movement and texture but not the color. When they think about a field of grass, no green is available, nor will red or yellow be part of their otherwise normal evocation of blood or banana. No lesion elsewhere in the brain can cause a similar defect. In some sense, then, the concept of colors depends on this region.

Patients with lesions in the left posterior temporal and inferior parietal cortex do not lose access to their concepts, but they have a sweeping impairment of their ability to produce proper word morphology regardless of the category to which a word belongs. Even if they are properly experiencing a given color and attempting to retrieve the corresponding word-form, they produce phonemically distorted color names; they may say "buh" for "blue," for example.

Other patients, who sustain damage in the temporal segment of the left lingual gyrus, suffer from a peculiar defect called color anomia, which affects neither color concepts nor the utterance of color words. These patients continue to *experience* color normally: they can match different hues, correctly rank hues of different saturation and easily put the correct colored paint chip next to objects in a black-and-white photograph. But their ability to put names to color is dismally impaired. Given the limited set of color names available to those of us who are not interior decorators, it is surprising to see patients use the word "blue" or "red" when shown green or yellow and yet be capable of neatly placing a green chip next to a picture of grass or a yellow chip next to a picture of a banana. The defect goes both ways: given a color name, the patient will point to the wrong color.

At the same time, however, all the wrong color names the patient uses are beautifully formed, phonologically speaking, and the patient has no other language impairment. The color-concept system is intact, and so is the word-form implementation system. The problem seems to reside with the neural system that mediates between the two.

The same three-part organization that explains how people manage to talk about color applies to other concepts as well. But how are such concepts physically represented in the brain? We believe there are no permanently held "pictorial" representations of objects or persons as was traditionally thought. Instead the brain holds, in effect, a record of the neural activity that takes place in the sensory and motor cortices during interaction with a given object. The records are patterns of synaptic connections that can re-create the separate sets of activity that define an object or event; each record can also stimulate related ones. For example, as a person picks up a coffee cup, her visual cortices will respond to the colors of the cup and of its contents as well as to its shape and position. The somatosensory cortices will register the shape the hand assumes as it holds the cup, the movement of the hand and the arm as they bring the cup to the lips, the warmth of the coffee, and the body change some people call pleasure when they drink the stuff. The brain does not merely represent aspects of external reality; it also records how the body explores the world and reacts to it.

The neural processes that describe the interaction between the individual and the object constitute a rapid sequence of microperceptions and microactions, almost simultaneous as far as consciousness is concerned. They occur in separate functional regions, and each region contains additional subdivisions: the visual aspect of perception, for example, is segregated within smaller systems specialized for color, shape and movement.

Where can the records that bind together all these fragmented activities be held? We believe they are embodied in ensembles of neurons within the brain's many "convergence" regions. At these sites the axons of feedforward projecting neurons from one part of the brain converge and join with reciprocally diverging feedback projections from other regions. When reactivation within the convergence zones stimulates the feedback projections, many anatomically separate and widely distributed neuron ensembles fire simultaneously and reconstruct previous patterns of mental activity.

In addition to storing information about experiences with objects, the brain also categorizes the information so that related events and concepts—shapes, colors, trajectories in space and time, and pertinent body movements and reactions—can be reactivated together. Such categorizations are denoted by yet another record in another convergence zone. The essential properties of the entities and processes in any interaction are thus represented in an interwoven fashion. The collected knowledge that can be represented includes the fact that a coffee cup has dimensions and a boundary; that it is made of something and has parts; that if it is divided it no longer is a cup, unlike water, which retains its identity no matter how it is divided; that it moved along a particular path, starting at one point in space and ending at another; that arrival at its destination produced a specific outcome. These aspects of neural representation bear a strong resemblance to the primitives of conceptual structure proposed by Ray Jackendoff of Brandeis University and the cognitive semantic schemas hypothesized by George P. Lakoff of the University of California at Berkeley, both working from purely linguistic grounds.

Activity in such a network, then, can serve both understanding and expression. The activity in the network can reconstruct knowledge so that a person experiences it consciously, or it can activate a system that mediates between concept and language, causing appropriately correlated word-forms and syntactical structures to be generated. Because the brain categorizes perceptions and actions simultaneously along many different dimensions, symbolic representations such as metaphor can easily emerge from this architecture.

Damage to parts of the brain that participate in these neural patterns should produce cognitive defects that clearly delineate the categories according to which concepts are stored and retrieved (the damage that results in achromatopsia is but one example of many). Elizabeth K. Warrington of the National Hospital for Nervous Diseases in London has studied category-related recognition defects and found patients who lose cognizance of certain classes of object. Similarly, in collaboration with our colleague Daniel Tranel, we have shown that access to concepts in a number of domains depends on particular neural systems.

For example, one of our patients, known as Boswell, no longer retrieves concepts for any unique entity (a specific person, place or event) with which he was previously familiar. He has also lost concepts for nonunique entities of particular classes. Many animals, for instance, are completely strange to him even though he retains the concept level that lets him know that they are living and animate. Faced with a picture of a raccoon, he says, "It is an animal," but he has no idea of its size, habitat or typical behavior.

Curiously, when it comes to other classes of nonunique entities, Boswell's cognition is apparently unimpaired. He can recognize and name objects, such as a wrench, that are manipulable and have a specific action attached to them. He can retrieve concepts for attributes of entities: he knows what it means for an object to be beautiful or ugly. He can grasp the idea of states or activities such as being in love, jumping or swimming. And he can understand abstract relations among entities or events such as "above," "under," "into," "from," "before," "after" or "during." In brief, Boswell has an impairment of concepts for many entities, all of which are denoted by nouns (common and proper). He has no problem whatsoever with concepts for attributes, states, activities and relations that are linguistically signified by adjectives, verbs, functors (prepositions, conjunctions and other verbal connective tissue) and syntactic structures. Indeed, the syntax of his sentences is impeccable.

Lesions such as Boswell's, in the anterior and middle regions of both temporal lobes, impair the brain's conceptual system. Injuries to the left hemisphere in the vicinity of the sylvian fissure, in contrast, interfere with the proper formation of words and sentences. This brain system is the most thoroughly investigated of those involved in language. More than a century and a half ago Paul Broca and Carl Wernicke determined the rough location of these basic language centers and discovered the phenomenon known as cerebral dominance—in most humans language structures lie in the left hemisphere rather than the right. This disposition holds for roughly 99 percent of right-handed people and two thirds of left-handers. (The pace of research in this area has accelerated during the past two decades, thanks in large part to the influence of the late Norman Geschwind of Harvard Medical School and Harold Goodglass of the Boston Veterans Administration Medical Center.)

Studies of aphasic patients (those who have lost part or all of their ability to speak) from different language backgrounds highlight the constancy of these structures. Indeed, Edward Klima of the University of California at San Diego and Ursula Bellugi of the Salk Institute for Biological Studies in San Diego have discovered the damage to the brain's word-formation systems is implicated in sign-language aphasia as well. Deaf individuals who suffer focal brain damage in the left hemisphere can lose the ability to sign or to understand sign language. Because the damage in question is not to the visual cortex, the ability to see signs is not in question, just the ability to interpret them.

In contrast, deaf people whose lesions lie in the right hemisphere, far from the regions responsible for word and sentence formation, may lose conscious awareness of objects on the left side of their visual field, or they may be unable to perceive correctly spatial relations among objects, but they do not lose the ability to sign or understand sign language. Thus, regardless of the sensory channel through which linguistic information passes, the left hemisphere is the base for linguistic implementation and mediation systems.

Investigators have mapped the neural systems most directly involved in word and sentence formation by studying the location of lesions in aphasic patients. In addition, George A. Ojemann of the University of Washington and Ronald P. Lesser and Barry Gordon of Johns Hopkins University have stimulated the exposed cerebral cortex of patients undergoing surgery for epilepsy and made direct eletrophysiological recordings of the response.

Damage in the posterior perisylvian sector, for example, disrupts the assembly of phonemes into words and the selection of entire word-forms. Patients with such damage may fail to speak certain words, or they may form words improperly ("loliphant" for "elephant"). They may, in addition, substitute a pronoun or a word at a more general taxonomic level for a missing one ("people" for "woman") or use a word semantically related to the concept they intend to express ("headman" for "president"). Victoria A. Fromkin of the University of California at Los Angeles has elucidated many of the linguistic mechanisms underlying such errors.

Damage to this region, however, does not disrupt patients' speech rhythms or the rate at which they speak. The syntactic structure of sentences is undisturbed even when there are errors in the use of functor words such as pronouns and conjunctions.

Damage to this region also impairs processing of speech sounds, and so patients have difficulty understanding spoken words and sentences. Auditory comprehension fails not because, as has been traditionally believed, the posterior perisylvian sector is a center to store "meanings" of words but rather because the normal acoustic analyses of the word-forms the patient hears are aborted at an early stage.

The systems in this sector hold auditory and kinesthetic records of phonemes and the phoneme sequences that make up words. Reciprocal projections of neurons between the areas holding these records mean that activity in one can generate corresponding activity in the other.

These regions connect to the motor and premotor cortices, both directly and by means of a subcortical path that includes the left basal ganglia and nuclei in the forward portion of the left thalamus. This dual motor route is especially important: the actual production of speech sounds can take place under the control of either a cortical or a subcortical circuit, or both. The subcortical circuit corresponds to "habit learning," whereas the cortical route implies higher-level, more conscious control and "associative learning."

For instance, when a child learns the word-form "yellow," activations would pass through the word-formation and motor-control systems via both the cortical and subcortical routes, and activity in these areas would be correlated with the activity of the brain regions responsible for color concepts and mediation between concept and language. In time, we suspect, the concept-mediation system develops a direct route to the basal ganglia, and so the posterior perisylvian sector does not have to be strongly activated to produce the word "yellow." Subsequent learning of the word-form for yellow in another language would again require participation of the perisylvian region to establish auditory, kinesthetic and motor correspondences of phonemes.

It is likely that both cortical "associative" and subcortical "habit" systems operate in parallel during language processing. One system or the other predominates depending on the history of language acquisition and the nature of the item. Steven Pinker of the Massachusetts Institute of Technology has suggested, for example, that most people acquire the past tense of irregular verbs (take, took, taken) by associative learning and that of regular verbs (those whose past tense ends in -*ed*) by habit learning.

The anterior perisylvian sector, on the front side of the rolandic fissure, appears to contain structures that are responsible for speech rhythms and grammar. The left basal ganglia are part and parcel of this sector, as they are of the posterior perisylvian one. The entire sector appears to be strongly associated with the cerebellum; both the basal ganglia and the cerebellum receive projections from a wide variety of sensory regions in the cortex and return projections to motor-related areas. The role of the cerebellum in language and cognition, however, remains to be elucidated.

Patients with damage in the anterior perisylvian sector speak in flat tones, with long pauses between words, and have defective grammar. They tend in particular to leave out conjunctions and pronouns, and grammatical order is often compromised. Nouns come easier to patients with these lesions than do verbs, suggesting that other regions are responsible for their production.

Patients with damage in this sector have difficulty understanding meaning that is conveyed by syntactic structures. Edgar B. Zurif of Brandeis University, Eleanor M. Saffran of Temple University and Myrna F. Schwartz of Moss Rehabilitation Hospital in Philadelphia have shown that these patients do not always grasp reversible passive sentences such as "The boy was kissed by the girl," in which boy and girl are equally likely to be the recipient of the action. Nevertheless, they can still assign the correct meaning to a nonreversible passive sentence such as "The apple was eaten by the boy" or the active sentence "The boy kissed the girl."

The fact that damage to this sector impairs grammatical processing in both speech and understanding suggests that its neural systems supply the mechanics of component assembly at sentence level. The basal ganglia serve to assemble the components of complex motions into a smooth whole, and it seems reasonable that they might perform an analogous function in assembling word-forms into sentences. We also believe (based on experimental evidence of similar, although less extensive structures in monkeys) that these neural structures are closely interconnected with syntactic mediation units in the frontoparietal cortices of both hemispheres. The delineation of those units is a topic of future research.

Between the brain's concept-processing systems and those that generate words and sentences lie the mediation systems we propose. Evidence for this neural brokerage is beginning to emerge from the study of neurological patients. Mediation systems not only select the correct words to express a particular concept, but they also direct the generation of sentence structures that express relations among concepts.

When a person speaks, these systems govern those responsible for word-formation and syntax; when a person understands speech, the word-formation systems drive the mediation systems. Thus far we have begun to map the systems that mediate proper nouns and common nouns that denote entities of a particular class (for example, visually ambiguous, nonmanipulable entities such as most animals).

Consider the patients whom we will call A.N. and L.R., who had sustained damage to the anterior and midtemporal cortices. Both can retrieve concepts normally: when shown pictures of entities or substances from virtually any conceptual category—human faces, body parts, animals and botanical specimens, vehicles and buildings, tools and utensils—A.N. and L.R. know unequivocally what they are looking at. They can define an entity's functions, habitats and value. If they are given sounds corresponding to those entities or substances (whenever a sound happens to be associated with them), A.N. and L.R. can recognize the item in question. They can perform this task even when they are blindfolded and asked to recognize an object placed in their hands.

But despite their obvious knowledge, they have difficulty in retrieving the names for many of the objects they know so well. Shown a picture of a raccoon, A.N. will say: "Oh! I know what it is—it is a nasty animal. It will come and rummage in your backyard and get into the garbage. The eyes and the rings in the tail give it away. I know it, but I cannot say the name." On the average they come up with less than half of the names they ought to retrieve. Their conceptual systems work well, but A.N. and L.R. cannot reliably access the word-forms that denote the objects they know.

The deficit in word-form retrieval depends on the conceptual category of the item that the patients are attempting to name. A.N. and L.R. make fewer errors for nouns that denote tools and utensils than for those naming animals, fruits and vegetables. (This phenomenon has been reported in similar form by Warrington and her colleague Rosaleen A. McCarthy of the National Hospital for Nervous Diseases and by Alfonso Caramazza and his colleagues at Johns Hopkins University.) The patients' ability to find names, however, does not split neatly at the boundary of natural and man-made entities. A.N. and L.R. can produce the words for such natural stimuli as body parts perfectly, whereas they cannot do the same for musical instruments, which are as artificial and as manipulable as garden tools.

In brief, A.N. and L.R. have a problem with the retrieval of common nouns denoting certain entities regardless of their membership in particular conceptual categories. There are many reasons why some entities might be more or less vulnerable to lesions than others. Of necessity, the brain uses different neural systems to represent entities that differ in structure or behavior or entities that a person relates to in different ways.

A.N. and L.R. also have trouble with proper nouns. With few exceptions, they cannot name friends, relatives, celebrities or places. Shown a picture of Marilyn Monroe, A.N. said, "Don't know her name but I know who she is; I saw her movies; she had an affair with the president; she committed suicide; or maybe somebody killed her; the police, maybe?" These patients do not have what is known as face agnosia or prosopagnosia—they can recognize a face without hesitation—but they simply cannot retrieve the word-form that goes with the person these recognize.

Curiously, these patients have no difficulty producing verbs. In experiments we conducted in collaboration with Tranel, these patients perform just as well as matched control subjects on tasks requiring them to generate a verb in response to more than 200 stimuli depicting diverse states and actions. They are also adept at the production of prepositions, conjunctions and pronouns, and their sentences are well formed and grammatical. As they speak or write, they produce a narrative in which, instead of the missing noun, they will substitute words like "thing" or "stuff" or pronouns such as "it" or "she" or "they." But the verbs that animate the arguments of those sentences are properly selected and produced and properly marked with respect to tense and person. Their pronunciation and prosody (the intonation of the individual words and the entire sentence) are similarly unexceptionable.

The evidence that lexical mediation systems are confined to specific regions is convincing. Indeed, the neural structures that mediate between concepts and word-forms appear to be graded from back to front along the occipitotemporal axis of the brain. Mediation for many general concepts seems to occur at the rear, in the more posterior left temporal regions; mediation for the most specific concepts takes place at the front, near the left temporal pole. We have now seen many patients who have lost their proper nouns but retain all or most of their common nouns. Their lesions are restricted to the left temporal pole and medial temporal surface of the brain, sparing the lateral and inferior temporal lobes. The last two, in contrast, are always damaged in the patients with common noun retrieval defects.

Patients such as A.N. and L.R., whose damage extends to the anterior and midtemporal cortices, miss many common nouns but still name colors quickly and correctly. These correlations between lesions and linguistic defects indicate that the temporal segment of the left lingual gyrus supports mediation between color concepts and color names, whereas mediation between concepts for unique persons and their corresponding names requires neural structures at the opposite end of the network, in the left anterior temporal lobe. Finally, one of our more recent patients, G.J., has extensive damage that encompasses all of these left occipitotemporal regions from front to back. He has lost access to a sweeping universe of noun word-forms and is equally unable to name colors or unique persons. And yet his concepts are preserved. The results in these patients support Ojemann's finding of impaired language processing after electrical stimulation of cortices outside the classic language areas.

It appears that we have begun to understand fairly well where nouns are mediated, but where are the verbs? Clearly, if patients such as A.N. and L.R. can retrieve verbs and functor words normally, the regions required for those parts of speech cannot be in the left temporal region. Preliminary evidence points to frontal and parietal sites. Aphasia studies performed by our group and by Caramazza and Gabriele Miceli of Catholic University of the Sacred Heart, Milan, and Rita Berndt of the University of Maryland show that patients with left frontal damage have far more trouble with verb retrieval than with noun retrieval.

Additional indirect evidence comes from positron emission tomography (PET) studies conducted by Steven E. Petersen, Michael I. Posner and Marcus E. Raichle of Washington University. They asked research subjects to generate a verb corresponding to the picture of an object— for example, a picture of an apple might generate "eat." These subjects activated a region of the lateral and inferior dorsal frontal cortex that corresponds roughly to the areas delineated in our studies. Damage to these regions not only compromises access to verbs and functors, it also disturbs the grammatical structure of the sentences that patients produce.

Although this phenomenon may seem surprising at first, verbs and functors constitute the core of syntactic structure, and so it makes sense that the mediation systems for syntax would overlap with them. Further investigations, either of aphasic patients or of normal subjects, whose brain activity can be mapped by PET scans, may clarify the precise arrangement of these systems and yield maps like those that we have produced to show the differing locations of common and proper nouns.

During the past two decades, progress in understanding the brain structures responsible for language has accelerated significantly. Tools such as magnetic resonance imaging have made it possible to locate brain lesions accurately in patients suffering from aphasia and to correlate specific language deficits with damage to particular regions of the brain. And PET scans offer the opportunity to study the brain activity of normal subjects engaged in linguistic tasks.

Considering the profound complexity of language phenomena, some may wonder whether the neural machinery that allows it all to happen will ever be understood. Many questions remain to be answered about how the brain stores concepts. Mediation systems for parts of speech other than nouns, verbs and functors, have been only partially explored. Even the structures that form words and sentences, which have been under study since the middle of the 19th century, are only sketchily understood.

Nevertheless, given the recent strides that have been made, we believe these structures will eventually be mapped and understood. The question is not if but when.

28 Meaning, Other People, and the World

Hilary Putnam

As he was the first to theorize in a systematic way about so many other things, so Aristotle was the first thinker to theorize in a systematic way about meaning and reference. In *De interpretatione* he laid out a scheme which has proved remarkably robust. According to this scheme, when we understand a word or any other "sign," we associate that word with a "concept." This concept determines what the word refers to. Two millennia later, one can find the same theory in John Stuart Mill's *Logic*, and in the present century one finds variants of this picture in the writings of Bertrand Russell, Gottlob Frege, Rudolf Carnap, and many other important philosophers. Something like this picture also appears to be built into the English language. Etymologically, *meaning* is related to *mind*. To *mean* something was probably, in the oldest usage, just to *have it in mind*. Be this as it may, the picture is that there is something in the mind[1] that picks out the objects in the environment that we talk about. When such a something (call it a "concept") is associated with a sign, it becomes the meaning of the sign.

This picture, whether we trace it back to Aristotle or to the metaphysics built into our language, is worth looking at closely. Let us write down the assumptions that constitute the picture for the purpose of inspection. (In writing them down, instead of the word "concept" I shall use the currently popular term "mental representation," because the idea that concepts are just that—*representations in the mind*—is itself an essential part of the picture.)

1. Every word he uses is associated in the mind of the speaker with a certain mental representation.

2. Two words are synonymous (have the same meaning) just in case they are associated with the *same* mental representation by the speakers who use those words.

From H. Putnam, *Representation and reality* (1988). Cambridge, MA: MIT Press. Reprinted by permission.

3. The mental representation determines what the word refers to, if anything.

These assumptions are likely to seem self-evident, but I believe that they are in fact *false*, and it is necessary to appreciate the extent to which they are false before we can make progress in any discussion having to do with meaning or mental representation.[2]

To say that they are false is to say that there cannot be such things as "mental representations" which simultaneously satisfy all three of these conditions. I do not deny that there are, in some sense, mental representations. We often think with the aid of words and pictures and other signs, and it may be that unconscious thought is even richer in the use of representations than we know. Certainly computational models of the mind/brain rely heavily on the idea of processing representations. But remember that the Aristotelian theory of meaning with which we have been stuck these two thousand–plus years doesn't *just* say that we think in terms of mental representations. It is essential to the theory that sameness and difference of these representations is what *sameness of meaning* is about; that when we say that two words do or do not have the same meaning, what we are saying is that they are or are not associated with the same mental representation. It is also part of the Aristotelian picture with which we have been stuck these two thousand-plus years that sameness and difference of the associated mental representations is what determines whether two words do or do not *refer* to the same things. Both of these latter assumptions, I shall argue, are false.

A way of seeing what is at issue, perhaps, is this: the Aristotelian model is what I spoke of (earlier) as a Cryptographer model of the mind. Everyone recognizes that sameness and difference of meaning are not the same things as sameness and difference of *word* (or sign). The French word *chat* is not the same word as the English word *cat*, but the two words have the same meaning. Again, sameness and difference of reference are not the same things as sameness and difference of word (or sign). Phonetically, at least, "he" is the same sign in Hebrew and in English; but in Hebrew "he" means *she!* Again, "bonnet" is phonetically (and in spelling) the same word in American English and in British English, but in British English "bonnet" can denote the hood of a car, whereas it cannot in American English. Moreover, Hebrew "he" and English "he" are both personal pronouns, and (of course) American "bonnet" and English "bonnet" are both concrete nouns. In each case the two words are indistinguishable at the level of *syntax*. So A and B can be syntactically and phonetically the same word in two different languages (or in two different dialects or idiolects of the *same* language) and yet have different reference. Conversely, there are, of course, many examples of words with different phonetic shape but exactly the same reference.

These things are so obvious that no thinker has ever supposed that sameness and difference of meaning are the same thing as sameness and difference of the syntactic properties (including spelling and phonetic shape) of the sign. But the Cryptographer model—the model of sign understanding as "decoding" into an innate *lingua mentis*—postulates that at a deeper level there is an identity between sign and meaning (this is the fundamental idea of the model, in fact). The idea is that in the *lingua mentis* each sign has one and only one meaning. Two words in human spoken or written languages which have the same meaning are simply two different "codes" for the same item (the same "concept") in the *lingua mentis.*

Even in the *lingua mentis,* on the other hand, it is supposed to be possible for two different representations to have the same *reference* (denotation). For example, "rational animal" and "featherless biped" are two different "concepts" which have the same reference (a popular example of Greek philosophers). But each sign in *lingua mentis* picks out a set of things and it picks it out unambiguously in each possible world. In some versions of the theory, what makes the concepts *rational animal* and *featherless biped* different concepts, even though the same things fall under both of them, is simply that there is *some* possible world in which there are rational animals which are not featherless bipeds and/or featherless bipeds which are not rational animals. Thus the *lingua mentis* is pictured as a kind of Ideal Language in which different signs always differ in meaning and in which different signs also differ in reference, not necessarily in the actual world, but at least in some possible world. If we succeed in decoding a message sent in our local natural language back into the *lingua mentis,* then by inspecting the resulting "translation" (in "clear," as cryptographers say) we shall see at once which words in the message have the same meaning and which have different meanings, which words have the same reference in all possible worlds and which words differ in reference in at least some possible worlds.

By this point we should be quite suspicious. What makes it plausible that the mind (or brain) thinks (or "computes") using representations is that all the thinking we know about uses representations. But none of the methods of representation that we know about—speech, writing, painting, carving in stone, etc.—has the magical property that there *cannot be* different representations with the same meaning. None of the methods of representation that we know about has the property that the representations *intrinsically* refer to whatever it is that they are used to refer to. All of the representations we know about have an association with their referent which is contingent, and capable of changing as the culture changes or as the world changes. This by itself should be enough to make one highly suspicious of theories that postulate a realm of "representations" with *such* unlikely properties. (As we shall see, the mental representations postulated by Fodor and Chomsky do not have property 3. Thus they avoid some of the problems avoided by the traditional view. But not all—the same representation always has the same "content" on their view, even when the speakers have grown up in radically different environments. What problems this poses for their view is a topic to which I shall return.)

I already suggested earlier that if there were a *lingua mentis* and we *could* translate our local natural language into it, we would not have solved any of the problems connected with meaning or reference; precisely the same problems would simply rearise for the *lingua mentis* itself. In particular, I want to argue that to the extent that we *do* think using mental representations, those representations cannot satisfy assumptions 1, 2, and 3 above.

The Division of Linguistic Labor

The word "robin" does not refer to the same species of bird in England and in the United States. (Neither does the word "sparrow.") Suppose that you are an American who is unaware of this fact, and you simply know that "Robins have a red breast." Suppose Jones is an Englishman who is unaware of this fact, but who also knows that robins have red breasts. Then Jones and you may very well be in the same mental state in all semantically relevant respects with respect to the word "robin." Every neurological parameter that could have anything to do with fixing the way you understand the word "robin" may have the same value in your brain and in Jones's brain. Yet the word simply does not refer to the same species on your lips and on Jones's lips. The mental representation associated with the word "robin" may be the same in Jones's brain (or in Jones's mental imagery, etc., if you do not wish to assume that this is reducible to something in the brain), yet the reference is not the same. If there is a word, say "XYZ," associated with "robin" in your *lingua mentis*, then "XYZ" has a different extension in your *lingua mentis* (call it "American deep English") and in Jones's *lingua mentis* (call it "British deep English"). Moreover, the reason is not hard to explain. *Reference is a social phenomenon.* Individual speakers do not have to know how to distinguish the species Robin from other species reliably, or how to distinguish elms from beeches, or how to distinguish aluminum from molybdenum, etc. They can always rely on experts to do this for them. Even in the case of so important a metal as gold, the average person is highly unreliable (in distinguishing gold from brass, etc.) and knows that he is unreliable. That is why he goes to a jeweler (or even to a chemist or a physicist) if he has to "make sure" that some item really is gold.

Let us stick to the word "gold" for a moment. Gareth Evans (1982) suggested that the average man doesn't really know the meaning of such words as "gold," that he only knows part of the meaning of such words. But what then is the whole meaning of the word "gold?" Is the whole meaning of the word "gold," "Element with atomic number 79?" This would be a fantastic theory. Has any linguist or philosopher ever suggested that it is *analytic* that gold has atomic number 79? In point of fact, if we should find out that some incredible scientific error has been made, and that the atomic weight of the metal jewelers and ordinary people call "gold" is not 79, we would not say that that metal wasn't really gold, but we would say that gold didn't have the atomic number 79. The chemist who knows that the atomic number of gold is 79 doesn't have a better knowledge of the *meaning* of the word "gold," he simply knows more *about* gold.

What of jewelers, metallurgists, and so on? They know a variety of tests by which they can tell whether or not something is gold. In Locke's time, a favorite test involved being "soluble in aqua regia" (a weak solution of nitric acid, I believe). Is it possible that it is the jewelers who know the whole meaning of the word "gold," and that laymen (and even the scientists, who know the atomic number but don't know the tests used by jewelers) know only *part* of the meaning of the word "gold?" But what if the tests used by jewelers are not the same in different parts of the United States, or if they are not the same in the United States and in England, or not the same in different decades? If jewelers on the West Coast are acquainted with one test for being gold and jewelers on the East Coast are acquainted with a different test, we wouldn't conclude that the word "gold" had one *meaning* on the East Coast (known, in full, only to jewelers on the East Coast) and a different *meaning* on the West Coast (known, in full, only to jewelers on the West Coast).

In any case, the move of saying that the *whole* meaning of the word "gold" is known only to some group of experts, however we decide which group that is, and of saying that the rest of us know only part of the meaning of the word "gold," is not available to mentalists (although Gareth Evans would have disagreed).[3] For the whole aim of mentalism is to identify the meaning of a word with something that is in the brain/mind of *every* speaker who knows how to use the word. It is a constraint on mentalistic theories of meaning that meanings must be *public.* A theory of meaning which makes meaning the, so to speak, property of a group of experts would not explain what thinkers like Fodor and Chomsky want to explain.

What is going on here? If different experts are acquainted with different criteria for being gold, and the person on the street is not acquainted with any very good criterion at all, but has to rely on the experts, then how can we even speak of the word "gold" as having a meaning?

According to the view that I have put forward (Putnam 1975), the answer to this question has two parts. First, what is in people's brains or minds, their mental representations or mental descriptions or mental pictures, does not in general determine the reference of a word that they know how to use. In the case of most of us, our mental representation doesn't do much beyond telling us that gold is a yellow precious metal to help determine the reference of the word "gold." It certainly doesn't pick out the reference of the word "gold" exactly. In the case of "sparrow" or "robin" the mental representation does even less, and in the case of "elm" and "beech" the mental representation is hopeless (at least if it's *my* mental representation). But what this shows isn't that these words fail to refer, but that the mental representation isn't what picks out their reference, or at least that the mental representation of the typical speaker isn't what picks out their reference. As long as we stick with Aristotle's assumption that the word "hooks on to the world" because it is associated with a mental representation which hooks on to the world, we will be blind to facts which are, so to speak, under our noses. We will keep thinking that the mental representation *must* pick out the referents of the word, because if it doesn't then what *could*? If we have equated the mental representation with the "meaning" of the word from Square One, then we shall simply take it for granted that the *meaning* of a sign must simultaneously (1) be something mental and (2) "hook on to the world." (As Wittgenstein often pointed out, a philosophical problem is typically generated in this way: certain assumptions are made which are taken for granted by *all* sides in the subsequent discussion.)

Suppose we abandon these assumptions. Then we are free to grant that reference exists and is important and interesting, and that mental representations exist and are, perhaps, important and interesting, but we don't have to *identify* problems of reference and problems of mental representation any more. (As I mentioned above, this is a point of which Fodor and Chomsky are perfectly aware.)

Let us look and see what happens if we separate the problems. To begin with, let us look at the problem of reference. We shall see later that it is difficult—I suggest, in fact, impossible—to give a *reductive* theory of reference. But if what we ask is not a reduction of the notion of reference to other notions regarded as metaphysically more basic, or a theory of "how language hooks on to the world," but simply a working characterization of how it is that words like "robin" and "gold" and "elm" manage to refer, then it is not difficult to give one. The fact is that some people know a good deal about certain kinds of things. These "experts" as I have been calling them may pick out these classes by different criteria. That doesn't matter as long as the criteria in fact pick out the same class. If experts in one country determine whether something is gold by seeing whether it is soluble in aqua regia and experts in another country determine whether it is gold by seeing whether it passes some other test, provided the two tests agree (or agree apart from borderline cases), then communication can proceed quite well. There is no reason to think of any one test as "the meaning" of the word. Indeed, the very same community may change from one test to another without anyone being aware of this (each expert may be unaware that almost all of the other experts have changed over to the new test).

But, it will be objected, this only accounts for how experts can use the word. However, there is no problem about how nonexperts can use the word: in doubtful cases, they can always consult the local experts! There is a *linguistic division of labor*. Language is a form of cooperative activity, not an essentially individualistic activity. Part of what is wrong with the Aristotelian picture is that it suggests that everything that is necessary for the use of language is stored in each individual mind; but no actual language works that way.

In sum, reference is *socially* fixed and not determined by conditions or objects in individual brains/minds. Looking inside the brain for the reference of our words is, at least in cases of the kind we have been discussing, just looking in the wrong place.

(If this is accepted, then a new puzzle may arise: why have a notion of meaning at all? If we can account for how our words refer to the things they do without appealing to the idea that they are associated with fixed "meanings" which determine their reference, then why should we have such a notion as meaning at all? But this is not really such a puzzle: the best way to get along with people who speak a different language—or, on occasion, even to get along with people who speak one's "own" language in a different way—is to find an "equivalence" between the languages such that one can expect that—after due allowance for differences in beliefs and desires—uttering an utterance in the other language in a given context normally evokes responses similar to the responses one would expect if one had been in one's own speech community and had uttered the "equivalent" utterance in one's own language. As a "definition" of sameness of meaning this would not satisfy a skeptical philosopher like Quine: it would not satisfy him because, for one thing, the identification of contexts as "the same" presupposes the very "translation scheme" which is being tested for adequacy, and because the identification of beliefs and desires likewise presupposes translation. But in the real world, our problem is not the theoretical problem of "underdetermination"—the problem of the existence of alternative schemes which satisfy the criterion of adequacy equally well—but the difficulty of finding even *one* which does the job. That we do succeed in finding such schemes in the case of all human languages is the basic anthropological fact upon which the whole notion of "sameness of meaning" rests.)

Elms, Beeches, and Searle

John Searle (1983) has vigorously attacked the above argument. (In discussion,[4] however, he has admitted that mental representations do not satisfy assumption 2, above. Thus his attack is not incompatible

Meaning, Other People, and the World

with my position, although his writings suggest the contrary.) What he defends are assumptions 1 and 3. He contends that we have mental representations which determine the referents of common nouns, pronouns, and so on. Why does the argument from the division of linguistic labor not refute this? According to Searle, the way in which I am able to have a representation of elms which does in fact single out elms from all other species, even though I cannot identify elms, is this: my own personal "concept" of an elm is simply *tree which belongs to a species which experts on whom I rely (at this time) call by the name "elm."*

Searle does not, of course, claim that people consciously (or even unconsciously) think, "When I say 'elm' I intend to refer to the trees which experts on whom I rely at this time call by the name 'elm.'" What he believes is that this is their "intention" whether they formulate it to themselves in words (or unconscious representations) or not. That there are "intended" conditions of reference is a fundamental assumption of his theory. Moreover, this claim is accompanied in Searle's writing (Searle 1984) by a strange metaphysical story about how language hooks on to the world: the capacity of a concept in my mind to refer to something outside my mind is, Searle says, *explained by the brain's chemistry.* For the time being I want to avoid discussing metaphysical questions about how a language-world connection is possible at all;[5] but some of the considerations against the possibility of reducing reference to computational cum physical relations also apply against the possibility of a direct reduction of reference to physics and chemistry of the kind Searle seems to envisage.

As I mentioned, Searle has conceded that concepts, in his sense, cannot be identified with *meanings.* But it is worth seeing why.

No philosopher, certainly not Searle, has ever maintained that it is *analytic* that elms are called by the name "elm" (by English speakers, or by me, or by experts on whom I rely, etc.). For example, suppose the meaning of the word "elm" (in English) were *species of tree which is called by the name "elm" by English speakers* (or by English experts). By parity of reasoning, the meaning of the German word "Ulme" (the German word for elms) must be *species of tree which is called by the name "Ulme" by German speakers* (or by German experts), and the meaning of the French word "orme" (the French word for elms) must be *species of tree which is called by the name "orme" by French speakers* (or by French experts). On this theory, it would be a *mistake* to translate the English word "elm" by the German word "Ulme" or by the French word "orme." Indeed, the three words differ in *meaning,* on this theory, just as much as "elm," "beech," and "maple" do! Moreover, since German has no word for *species of tree which is called by the name "elm" by English speakers,* there would be no way (except by using some such cumbersome locution as *Art von Baum die englisch sprechende Leute «elm» nennen*) to translate the English word "elm." A myriad common English nouns would be translatable into German only with immense difficulty. (And if one did translate, say, an English novel into German using these cumbersome locutions, a German speaker would not be able to understand the result!)

The fact is that *tree that English speakers call "elm,"* or rather *Art von Baum die englisch sprechende Leute «elm» nennen,* is not a *translation* of the word "elm" at all. That elms are called "elms" is not part of the concept of an elm, it is simply something very important to me as an English speaker. Few things could be more important, in fact, to an English speaker who wants to talk about the species than to know its name; but the importance of the fact doesn't make it part of the meaning of the name "elm" that these trees have that name in English. An important part of the purpose of the notion of *meaning* is precisely to *abstract away from* the phonetic shape of the name. To say that the phonetic shape of the name ("elm," or "Ulme," or "orme") is essential to the meaning is to confuse precisely what we want to abstract away from in meaning talk.

Some may retort that meaning talk is, after all, just a piece of folk psychology and we should drop the whole notion, at least in science. Quine has argued such a position for many years. Be that as it may, if we want to give a correct account of the notion of meaning—whether in the end we want to retain it or not—then we have to say that in meaning talk we equate "elm," and "Ulme," and "orme."

In fact, Searle's view has even more radical consequences if we equate his mental representations (or "intensions," as he calls them, using a traditional term for *meanings*) with meanings. As Searle is aware, it is perfectly possible that different English speakers use the word "elm" to refer to different species of tree, without my necessarily being aware of this. (Remember that something similar actually happens in connection with the words "robin" and "sparrow.") For this reason, Searle would say that what I mean (the "intension" with an *s*) when I use the word "elm" is not *tree which belongs to a species which is called "elm" in English* (i.e., by experts about common deciduous trees who speak English), but rather *tree which belongs to a species which is now called "elm" in English by the experts on whom I rely right now.* The reference to *me* is necessary because, as I said, the elms that I am talking about may not be the same as the elms someone else (say, Jones in Nova Scotia) is talking about. My *concept* of an elm (on Searle's theory) is the same as Jones's (just as "I" is the same concept, on Searle's view, whether I think it or Jones thinks it), but the *reference* may be different. Moreover, it may be that at some future time in my life I and the experts on whom I rely will use the word "elm" to refer to a species of tree different from the species we now call by that name. My intention in talking about elms right now (and also the intension of the word, according to Searle) is not to refer to the trees which are called "elms" by any experts at any place in the universe, or by any experts on whom I shall ever rely in my life, but to refer to the trees which are called "elms" now by the experts on whom I am prepared to rely right now. Thus, the intension of the word "elm" must contain both an indexical referring to myself and an indexical referring to the present time.[6]

The point is important enough to deserve restatement: I *can* incorporate my knowledge of the division of linguistic labor into my description of what I am referring to by using a phrase like *species of tree which is called "elm" by such and such experts*. Indeed, one sometimes *has* to fall back on such a description when a word does not have a synonym in the language one is speaking. For example, if there is a kind of bird which is called a *chooc* in a language spoken in the Amazon jungle, say Natool, and I have no name for that species in English, then I may have to explain what is meant by *chooc* (i.e., what sort of thing the word is used to refer to) by saying, "Well, they use the word to refer to a species of bird that they call a *chooc*." But such descriptions as *species of bird that the Natool call "chooc"* do not give us synonyms for the words whose use is so explained; rather, they are a way of bypassing the need for a synonym. Once again what we see is the impossibility of identifying meanings with the descriptions that speakers "have in their heads," i.e., of identifying the notions of *meaning* and *mental representation*.

Against this argument, it is sometimes contended that our mental representations of an elm and a beech *must* be different since we *know* that elms and beeches are different species. This counterargument is, however, fallacious. I do know that elms and beeches belong to different species; thus it is included in my "mental representation" of an elm that it is not a beech (whatever sort of tree a beech may be) and it is included in my "mental representation" of a beech that it is not an elm (whatever sort of tree an elm may be). But what this *amounts to* is that my mental representation of an elm includes the fact that there *are* characteristics which distinguish it from a beech, and my mental representation of a beech includes the fact that there *are* characteristics which distinguish it from an elm. The situation is totally symmetrical. It remains the case that the only difference between my "mental representation" of an elm and my "mental representation" of a beech is my knowledge that the former species is *called* "elm" and the latter species is *called* "beech." Apart from the differences in the phonetic shapes of the names (which, as we have seen, cannot be a part of the *meaning* of the names), there is no difference between my "mental representation" of a beech and my "mental representation" of an elm. Knowing that there are two different "species" is knowing that there *exist* distinguishing characteristics; one can know this without its being the case that those distinguishing characteristics are themselves included in the "mental representations." If the distinguishing characteristics were themselves included in the mental representations, then indeed the representations of an elm and a beech would be different, even apart from my knowledge of the phonetic shapes of the names;

but the mere knowledge of the *existence* of (unspecified) distinguishing characteristics does not make the representations different, except in the trivial way mentioned.

A different move, one that I have heard Fodor make many times, is to "bite the bullet" and say that *in one sense of "meaning"*—he calls this sense of "meaning" *narrow content*—the meaning of "elm" and "beech" is exactly the same, and that this sense of "meaning" is the one that is of interest to psychology. But meaning, we should recall, if it is anything, is what we try to preserve in translation. The one thing we *don't* do in translation is translate "elm" as "beech" (or as "Buche," if we are translating into German). It may be that *something* of psychological interest which is associated with the word "elm" is the same, for example the "stereotype." My stereotype of an elm is that of a common deciduous tree, and this is also my stereotype of a beech. But to call stereotypes "contents" (or "narrow contents") is not to offer a theory of meaning, but rather to change the subject. This is a point to which I shall return. (Note also that stereotypes are not just "images"; they are, at least in part, beliefs stated in *words*. Thus even if we decide that stereotypes are a "component" of meaning, the identification of this component is parasitic on the *ordinary* notion of "meaning.")

The elm-beech case (and also the case of gold) enabled us to see two things: first, that what is preserved in translation isn't *just* "mental representations," and second, that "mental representations" don't suffice to fix reference.[7]

The Contribution of the Environment

I have discussed the division of linguistic labor and the special role played by experts of different sorts, such as people who know how to identify gold and people who know how to tell a beech from an elm. But there is a factor that I have so far neglected—an all-important one. This is the role of the environment itself (of the things we are referring to themselves). This is, perhaps, easiest to see in the case of substance terms, such as "gold" and "water." In Putnam (1975) I illustrated the way in which the reference of the term "water" is partly fixed by the substance itself with the aid of a thought experiment involving "Twin Earth." We imagine that the year is 1750 (both on Earth and on Twin Earth) and that Daltonian chemistry has not yet been invented. We also imagine that the people on Twin Earth have brains identical with ours, a society virtually identical with ours, and so on. In fact, the only relevant difference between Earth and Twin Earth in my thought experiment was that the liquid that plays the role of water on Twin Earth was supposed not to be H_2O but a different compound, call it XYZ. On Twin Earth it does not rain H_2O but it rains XYZ, people drink XYZ, the lakes and rivers are full of XYZ, and so on. The claim I made in "The Meaning of 'Meaning'"—a claim which has provoked a great deal of subsequent discussion—is that one should say, imagining this case to be actual, that the term "water" did not have the same *reference* (even in 1750) in Earth English and in Twin Earth English. The reference of the word "water" on Earth, according to me, was the stuff *we* call water, the stuff we have discovered to be H_2O. The stuff that they called "water" on Twin Earth in 1750 (and call "water" now as well) is the stuff that fills the lakes and rivers on Twin Earth, the stuff that they later discovered (when they developed sophisticated chemistry) to be XYZ. Not only does the word "water" have a different reference *now*— now that we know that "water is H_2O" and they know that "water is XYZ"—it had (according to me) a different reference *then*.

Why do I say this? Here it is useful to recall a number of things about the way in which we view water (and, to some extent, substances generally).[8] In ancient and medieval times, water was thought of as a pure substance (in fact, it was thought of as an element by many of the ancient thinkers and by most of the medievals). Part of the notion of a pure substance is that any bit of it is expected to exhibit the same behavior as any other bit of it. People two thousand years ago, people in 1750, and people now after the rise of modern chemistry, all expected any sample of pure water to behave the same way as any other sample of pure water. If you had asked a person living in 1750 the hypothetical question, "Suppose that I gave you a glass containing 50 percent normal water and 50 percent some substance which is not found as a constituent of normal water, but you couldn't tell this by the appearance or taste or aftereffects, or by washing clothes in it, or anything like that (apart from using a still); would that mixture then simply *be* water?" I think that even in 1750 a typical person would have answered, "No, I wouldn't say it was water, I would say it was a mixture of water and something else." Of course, if it had turned out that normal water was itself a mixture, and that it contained an indefinite number of different "pure" constituents, then the answer might have been different. But we might say that our intention, even in 1750, was somewhat as follows: On the assumption that normal water is in fact a pure substance, then we do not intend the description "water" to be true *tout court* of anything which consists to a significant extent (say, 20 percent or more) of any other substance.

Now, Earth water and Twin Earth "water" were different substances even in 1750; it's just that no one on Earth or Twin Earth had yet noticed this—in fact, they didn't even know of the existence of the other substance in each case. Someone on Earth in 1750, if he had been taken to Twin Earth on a spaceship by a more advanced civilization, would have *taken* Twin Earth water for water, but he would have been making a mistake; he would have been thinking that it was the *same* substance that he knew by the name "water" on Earth. Similarly, someone from Twin Earth would have been mistaken in thinking that Earth water was what his community called "water." No one on Earth or on Twin Earth would have noticed that the word had a different meaning in 1750, but in my view they *would* have had a different meaning. The "mental representations" of Earth speakers and Twin Earth speakers were not in any way different; we may suppose that they were exactly the same, even if we include "mental representations" in the heads of the chemists; the reference was different because the *substances* were different. This illustrates how the reference is particularly fixed by the environment itself. This is the phenomenon that I have called *the contribution of the environment*.

In Putnam (1975) I expressed this by saying that even in 1750 what the word "water" referred to in Earth English was H_2O (give or take impurities). The word "water" in Twin Earth English referred to XYZ (give or take impurities). To say that this is what the word "water" referred to in the two dialects is just to say that this is what the word *denoted* or was true of; it is not to say that Earth speakers in 1750 *knew* that the word "water" referred to H_2O or that Twin Earth speakers knew that their word "water" referred to XYZ. But then, some have objected, it seems that I am saying that we "didn't know the meaning of the word 'water'" until we developed modern chemistry.

This objection simply involves an equivocation on the phrase "know the meaning." To know the meaning of a word may mean (*a*) to know how to translate it, or (*b*) to know what it refers to, in the sense of having the ability to state explicitly what the denotation is (other than by using the word itself), or (*c*) to have tacit knowledge of its meaning, in the sense of being able to use the word in discourse. The only sense in which the average speaker of the language "knows the meaning" of most of his words is (*c*). In that sense, it was true in 1750 that Earth English speakers knew the meaning of the word "water" and it was true in 1750 that Twin Earth English speakers knew the meaning of their word "water." "Knowing the meaning" in this sense isn't literally knowing some *fact*.

Another objection that I have sometimes encountered to my Twin Earth example is the following: people have supposed that if XYZ plays the role of water on Twin Earth, then it must exhibit *exactly* the same behavior as water on Earth, at least at the "observable" level. But this is simply a mistake. The average English speaker in 1750 was aware of only a very limited range of observable properties of water. Even the chemists in 1750 were aware of only a limited range of properties. They knew, for example, the boiling point of water (although not with present-day accuracy). They knew the density of water. They certainly did not know *all* of the chemical reactions into which water enters. However, H_2O and XYZ are supposed to be different compounds. Thus, there has to be some third substance S such that H_2O chemically reacts with S in one way (perhaps in the presence of catalyst C, or in the presence of heat, etc.) and XYZ reacts with S in a different way (perhaps in the presence of catalyst C, or in the presence of heat, etc.). For example, it may be that when water is mixed with S and C is added and the mixture is heated, then the mixture turns green and drops a yellow precipitate, whereas when Twin Earth water is mixed with S and C is added and the mixture is heated, then one gets a tremendous explosion. (Or it might simply be that Twin Earth water fails to react with S at all, or reacts only with a different catalyst.) This phenomenon (and many other similar ones) would show that Earth water and Twin Earth water are two different substances. But that does not mean that the "mental representations" were different in 1750, because neither Earth speakers of English nor Twin Earth speakers of English knew of these facts back in 1750. In short, the "mental representations" were the same in 1750, and yet the reference was different, and moreover this difference in reference *could* have been shown to Earth people and to Twin Earth people who were alive in 1750 notwithstanding the "sameness of their mental representations."

An Indexical Component

What makes this possible is what I have called the *indexicality* of our criteria for being water (for being a sample of a particular substance). There is a "property" which people have long associated with pure water and which distinguishes it from Twin Earth water, and that is the property of *behaving like any other sample of pure water from* our *environment*. To use a term suggested by Alan Berger (1988), when we teach the meaning of the word "water," we *focus* on certain samples. A substance which doesn't behave as *these* examples do will be counted as not the same substance (barring a special explanation). But the "property" of "behaving the way *this* stuff does" isn't what philosophers call a purely "qualitative" property. Its description involves a particular example—one given by pointing, or by "focusing" on something. Now, if the water I am focusing on looks and tastes just like the "water" that Twin Earth Hilary is focusing on, then my "mental representation" of my example may be "qualitatively" identical with Twin Earth Hilary's representation of his example. But the *stuff* is different, and so the *property* of being-pretty-much-like-*this* is a different property when I define it that way from the property of being-pretty-much-like-*this* which Twin Earth Hilary defines that way. Property terms of this kind, property terms which contain words like "this" or "here" or "now," can refer to different properties in different circumstances of use. In short, we *had* a criterion in 1750 which distinguished Earth water from Twin Earth "water"; it was not a qualitative criterion, but an indexical criterion.[9] That indexical criterion was associated with exactly the same mental representation that Twin Earth speakers of English would have used (had Twin Earth actually existed) to distinguish Twin Earth water from Earth "water." It is because the two different criteria were both indexical that they could be associated with *identical* mental representations in the heads of speakers in the two different communities and still pick out *different* substances (just as the mental representation *the conductor of this bus* may be ever so identical in quality in two different heads and still pick out different individuals).

Other Natural Kinds

Once the point is grasped in the case of substances, it can easily be extended to other natural kinds. Using the fiction of Twin Earth once again to illustrate the point, it could be that the mental representation associated with "cat" on Twin Earth in 1750 was exactly the same as the mental representation associated with that word on Earth in 1750 although Twin Earth cats are a totally different biological species (have different DNA, are not cross-fertile with Earth cats, and so on). What our discussion shows is that an ideal interpreter could not know whether the Earth term "water" and the Twin Earth Term "water" have the same meaning (should be translated in the same way) without knowing a certain amount about both Earth and Twin Earth chemistry; that he could not know whether the Earth term "cat" and the Twin Earth term "cat" have the same meaning without knowing a certain amount about both Earth and Twin Earth biology; and so on.

In certain ways, the case of biological species is different from the case of pure substances, however. Pure substances are a somewhat special case. The belief that any sample of a pure substance will exhibit the same behavior as any other sample of the same substance is only one of the beliefs which help us to fix the reference of terms which refer to such substances. Another, equally ancient, belief is that any two such samples have the same ultimate constitution. (I don't think, however, that this is really a totally different criterion from the "same behavior" criterion. For we expect differences in ultimate constitution to show up as differences in behavior and differences in behavior to be "grounded" in differences in ultimate constitution).[10] Thus the fact that Twin Earth water was *not* water, not even by the standards of 1750, even if one would have had difficulty finding a way of proving this in 1750 (unless one were a genius), is overdetermined. Twin Earth water violates (and always violated) two conditions for being called "real" water: it neither has the same ultimate constitution as "our" water nor exhibits exactly the same behavior.

I have dwelt at length on this case because I think it is in certain ways simpler than the other cases, but I think that similar principles apply to other natural kinds. We do not expect any two members of a biological species to exhibit the same behavior or to have exactly the same appearance (Siamese cats do not have exactly the same appearance as European cats); but we do have the expectation that (with occasional exceptions) two members of a species who are of opposite sex and who are biologically fertile will be able to mate and to have fertile offspring.

If Twin Earth "cats" were never able to mate with Earth cats (and produce fertile offspring), then not only biologists but laymen would say that Twin Earth cats are another species. They might, of course, say that they were another species of *cat*; but if it turned out that Twin Earth cats evolved from, say, pandas rather than felines, then in the end we would say that they were not really cats at all, and Twin Earthers would similarly say that Earth cats were not really cats at all.

Moreover, in the case of what look to be biological species, questions of ultimate constitution may also enter. If we suppose that Twin Earth cats look exactly like Earth cats and behave exactly like Earth cats, but it turns out upon detailed scientific examination using sophisticated theory and technology that they are really robots remotely controlled from Sirius, not only will we say that they are not really cats (in the Earth sense), but we will say that they are not really *animals* in the Earth sense at all. Whether they are "animals" in the Twin Earth sense will depend on whether the Twin Earth dogs, lions, tigers, etc., are or are not also remotely controlled from Sirius. If all "animals" (except people) on Twin Earth turn out to be robots remotely controlled from Sirius, then a Twin Earthian might well say, "That's what animals *are*," whereas an Earthian will say, "They aren't really animals."

Still another case is that of highly impure kinds, such as mixtures of one sort or another. We do not expect any two samples of *milk* to exhibit exactly the same behavior—some milk has higher butterfat content, some milk tastes of clover while other milk does not, and so on. There may even be a small percentage of constituents in some milk that do not occur in some other milk. But if something does not consist at least 50 percent of the constituents that we find in "normal" milk, then even if it tastes like milk, we will say that it is not "really milk" (although we might say that it "contains milk"). The point of all these examples is the same. The description given by both the Earthians and the Twin Earthians of X, where X is gold, or cats, or water, or milk, or whatever, may be the same (apart from the difference in the reference of the indexicals "we," "here," "this," etc.); the mental representations may be qualitatively the same; the description given by the experts at a given stage of scientific development may be the same; but it may turn out, because of the difference between the Earth and Twin Earth environments, that the *referents* are so different that Earth speakers would not regard the Twin Earth gold as gold at all, or regard the Twin Earth water as water at all, or regard the Twin Earth cats as cats at all, etc. *Meaning is interactional. The environment itself plays a role in determining what a speaker's words, or a community's words, refer to.*

Reference and Theory Change

We must now take a closer look at how reference is fixed. In the last section I said that the reference of a word like "gold" is fixed by criteria known to experts, and that it doesn't matter if the experts use different criteria, as long as the same stuff (apart from borderline cases) passes the various tests that these experts use. This is compatible, as I said, with East Coast experts using different tests from West Coast experts, or American experts using different tests from Asian experts, or experts in the twentieth century using different tests from experts in the nineteenth century, etc. If this were all there is to say about the fixation of reference, then when the different tests do not exactly agree, the cases on which they disagree would be correctly classified as vague cases, or ambiguous cases, or something of that kind. We could then say that something is gold if it passes *all* the tests used by experts in all the centuries and all the places; that it is not gold if it fails all the tests used by experts in any century and any place; and that it is a "borderline case" if it fails some tests and passes others. But in view of what I have just said, we can see that this would be wrong. For it makes sense to say that some of the tests are not *correct*.

If the tests for gold in use prior to Archimedes could have been passed by some stuff that did not in fact have the same density as gold, then those tests were incorrect, and Archimedes found a way of showing that those tests were incorrect and of correcting their results. He did this by relying on the principle I mentioned, that any sample of pure gold should exhibit the same behavior as any other sample of pure gold. By finding out how to determine the density of metals, he found a way to investigate the behavior of samples with respect to a parameter no one previous to him knew how to measure. Now that we have developed ways of determining the atomic constitution of a substance, and even the constitution at the subatomic level, we have still better means of determining when and how our tests fail. If people at some previous time would have accepted some alloy as gold, that does not mean that it was gold, in the sense in which the word "gold," or "chrysos," or whatever, was used at that time; it means that the people at that time did not have a way of *knowing* that they were dealing with something that had neither exactly the same behavior nor exactly the same constitution as the paradigm examples of gold. They did not know that the alloy was not really gold. But what they meant by "gold" (or "chrysos," etc.) was what we mean by "gold." The fact is that no set of operational criteria can totally fix the meaning of the word "gold"; for as we develop better theories of the constitution of gold and more elaborate tests for the behavior of substances (including the behavior in respects that we were not previously able to measure), we can always discover defects in the tests that we had before.

The same thing goes for natural kinds which are not substances. Suppose the Martians are able to build robots that look exactly like animals—they even have organic bodies, and their brains are full of stuff that looks to present-day scientists exactly like brain matter (although it doesn't really *function* as such)—but these "animals" are really directed by signals received by a miniaturized radio receiver implanted in the pineal gland. (The "brain" is just an elaborate fake.) Suppose a few of these have been smuggled in among the "normal" animal population, but most animals are the naturally evolved organisms we take them to be. Then when we develop the scientific resources to detect the fakes, we shall say that the fakes in question are not really animals (and not really cats, or whatever); even though up to this point, they may have passed all of our operational tests for being animals (and for being cats, etc.). Thus the fact that the environment itself contributes to the fixing of reference is also one of the reasons that naive operationalism and naive verificationism are wrong as an account of the meaning of natural-kind terms.

Meaning and "Mental Representation"

So far I have suggested that traditional mentalistic accounts of meaning and reference fail in two different ways. On the one hand, they neglect the division of linguistic labor. On the other hand, they neglect the way in which the paradigms that are supplied by our environment contribute to the fixing of reference. Because of these oversights, the traditional theorist is unable to imagine how two speakers or two communities could associate the very same "mental representations" with terms and yet use the terms to refer to different species, substances, etc.

This does not mean that descriptions, including descriptions "in our minds," play no role in fixing reference. Both nonindexical descriptions (the descriptions of the behavior and/or composition of gold that an expert might give) and indexical descriptions ("stuff that behaves like and has the same composition as *this*," said by someone who is "focusing" on a particular sample of a substance) do help to fix the reference of our terms. Indexical descriptions can be extremely important in fixing reference, but, as we have seen, they are not what we preserve in translation. The term "gold" is not *synonymous* with "stuff that passes the following test," or with "stuff that has the same behavior and ultimate composition as this." In fact, the effect of my account, as of Saul Kripke's (in Kripke 1980),[11] is to separate the question of how the reference of such terms is fixed from the question of their conceptual content.[12]

In the face of the difficulties I have been describing, some authors, reluctant to give up the whole of the Aristotelian picture, have tried to see if they could retain at least two of the three assumptions. I have already mentioned the case of John Searle, who has indicated that he, at least, is prepared to give up assumption 2 in my list of Aristotelian assumptions (this is the assumption that sameness of mental representation just *is* sameness of meaning, or "synonymy"), in order to hang on to the other assumptions. I have also mentioned in passing that Fodor (and at times Chomsky) would hold on to 1 and 2 while giving up 3 (the assumption that mental representation is what fixes reference).[13] Before we examine this suggestion, it will be useful to take a closer look at a notion I have so far been employing uncritically (the way, I fear, many psychologists now employ it), the notion of a *mental representation*.

At a surface level mental representations do not differ very much from representations by means of spoken sounds, or by means of writing, or from other signs. Just as one can write the words, "There are a lot of cats in the neighborhood," so one can say them, one can store them on a floppy disk, and one can also think them without speaking out loud. The notion that unspoken thought is simply sub-vocalization may be an extreme bit of reductionism, but it has a point. There is not much difference between *words* in one medium—even a mental medium—and words in another, just as words. However it is that words like "cat" and "neighborhood" manage to refer, it is not just by having a certain spelling or a certain sound—not even a certain spelling or sound "in one's mind." These surface representations— spoken thoughts—cannot be the concepts that Aristotle referred to, nor are they the "mental representations" that modern mentalists are talking about. The representations spoken of in 1, 2, and 3 were supposed to be representations which *determine* the meaning of words, not words themselves, and they were supposed to be the same whether one uses the word "elm" or the word "orme" to refer to elms.

Distinguishing between surface mental representations ("sub-vocalized" thoughts) and deep mental representations does not affect our criticisms of the Aristotelian Theory, because if someone is totally ignorant of the differences between an elm and a beech (he only knows that there *are* differences), then this ignorance must extend all the way down; we cannot suppose that although his surface representations do not distinguish between elms and beeches, his "deep" representations somehow do, for he has never *learned* the difference. No matter what we postulate in the way of "deep," or "underlying," or "unconscious" mental representations, we can reasonably suppose that at every level, no matter how deep, *my* mental representation of an elm is identical with my mental representation of a beech, except as concerns my knowledge of the different phonetic shapes of the names "elm" and "beech"; and similarly, we can suppose that my mental representation of a beech could be the same at every level as a Frenchman's mental representation of an "orme," apart from phonetic properties.

The problem with mental representations at the level of conscious thought—which are the only mental representations of whose existence we have any sure knowledge—is that they badly violate principle 2. The Frenchman's surface mental representation of an elm is not literally the same as my surface mental representation of an elm. His mental representation, at the surface level, is *arbre qu'on appelle "orme"*; my mental representation, at the surface level, is *tree that one calls an "elm."*

These are not literally (syntactically) the same object. We could decide in certain contexts to treat them as the same: we might just decide to *identify* mental representations that are synonymous. Such a maneuver would buy us nothing. The idea that what synonymy *is* is being associated with the same mental representation assumed that we had a notion of *identity of mental representation* independent of the notion of synonymy. If the very notion of having the *identical* mental representation is really just a *façon de parler* for "having mental representations with the same meaning," then assumption 2—the assumption that synonymous expressions are associated with identical mental representations—becomes trivially true. (Expressions with the same meaning are, among other things, associated with *themselves*, and they themselves are mental representations with the same meaning.) It is for this reason that Fodor has to postulate a *lingua mentis*, often called "Mentalese" in his writing, and a Cryptographic Model of the mind, according to which when a Frenchman thinks (at the surface level), *Les ormes sont arbres*, this gets transcribed into a formula or sentence in Mentalese which is exactly the same—identical by a *syntactic* criterion of identity[14]—as the formula in Mentalese which the Cryptographer in my brain encodes in English as *elms are trees*. If Fodor's theory is right, Aristotelian assumption 2 is correct, and assumption 2 is no tautology.

Assumption 2 is not a tautology, in Fodor's theory, precisely because the identity (or equivalence) relation between mental representations in Mentalese is supposed to be defined *syntactically*.

What of assumption 3? We have just seen that even if Fodor's theory is correct, it cannot be supposed that identity of "mental representation" always guarantees identity of referent (e.g., the elm/beech case, as well as the case of Earth water and Twin Earth water). Fodor concedes this point. His response in a number of papers (see Fodor 1981) is to say that the ordinary notion of meaning is referentially *ambiguous*.[15] One referent ("narrow content") is mental representation at the deepest level (the "semantic representation" in "Mentalese"). Another referent ("broad content") is the function which gives the referent(s) in each possible world.

The notion of "broad content" evidently depends on the notion of *reference*. This notion (reference) Fodor hopes to explicate with the aid of the notion of *causality*. Projects of this kind—attempts to explicate the notion of reference—will occupy our attention in the remaining chapters of this work. For this reason, I shall not discuss the notion of "broad content" further now.

Given that Fodor does not intend his work as a conceptual analysis of the notion of *meaning*, but rather as an empirical theory about the workings of the human mind, it might appear puzzling at first blush that he thinks that the "Mentalese" hypothesis has anything to do with our topic. If his theory claimed that "mental representations" somehow fixed reference, then if his theory were scientifically spelled out and scientifically verified, it would constitute a vindication of the entire Aristotelian view. But by separating "narrow content" from "broad content" and admitting that the "narrow content" of a term does not determine its "broad content" (for just the reasons we have given above), Fodor blocks this defense of the philosophical significance of his theory.

Suppose the theory is right; then, when the Frenchman thinks (in French), *Il y'a beaucoup des ormes dans le voisinage*, he thinks a sentence which encodes a formula in Mentalese, as it might be "φ©ηΔΔι." When I think (in English), *There are a lot of elms in the neighborhood*, this is simply the way my brain encodes the same formula, "φ©ηΔΔι" (or an "equivalent" formula, under some *syntactically* definable equivalence relation). To take a simpler example, when I think the word *cat*, then according to Fodor's theory, the Cryptographer in my brain "decodes" this as, say, "*#@å," and when a Thai speaker thinks the word *meew*, this is simply the code used by the Cryptographer in *his* brain for "*#@å." This is fascinating if true, and a contribution to our understanding of the way the brain works (if true), and, perhaps, very important in psychology (if true), but what is its relevance to a discussion of the *meaning* of *cat, meew*, or "*#@å"?

Notes

1. In a variant of the picture—one that represents the, so to speak, legacy of Plato rather than that of Aristotle—"concepts" are not in the mind, but rather form a realm of abstract entities (sometimes called "Platonic heaven" by detractors of the picture) independent both of the mind and of the world. Such a Platonism was, for example, defended by the great logician Kurt Gödel. Even in these "Platonistic" versions, however, speakers are supposed to be able to direct their mental attention *to* concepts by means of something akin to perception, and, if A and B are different concepts, then attending to A and attending to B are different mental states. So even in these theories, the mental state of the speaker determines which concept he is attending to, and thereby determines what it is he refers to.

2. I first argued this at length in Putnam 1975.

3. Evans's view (as I understand it), as applied to the case of "gold," would be that the "concept" of gold is simply the ability to single out gold. This is possessed by all the experts I described above, and it is the *same* ability (since it is the ability to pick out the *same* stuff). Although Evans calls himself a mentalist, this is not mentalism in the sense of Fodor and Chomsky, since concepts are individuated by *stuff-involving* and *object-involving* abilities, not by the "syntax" of representations *inside* the mind/brain. My own theory is like Evans's in holding that the concept is partly individuated by the *stuff in the world* or *objects in the world* it applies to; but I reject the view that one must be able to identify the stuff *oneself* to be said to have the concept.

4. Including a public discussion following the reading of a paper by myself (titled "Why Meanings Aren't in the Head") at Rutgers University on March 13, 1986.

5. I do discuss these questions at length in Putnam 1981 and 1983.

6. To see vividly what this means, imagine that somehow in Nova Scotia the words "elm" and "beech" have gotten switched. Then, on Searle's theory, it is wrong to say that the word "elm" in American English has the same intension as the word "beech" in Nova Scotian English and the word "beech" in American English has the same intension as the word "elm" in Nova Scotian English. In less technical language, what Searle can't say is, "In Nova Scotia 'elm' means *beech* and 'beech' means *elm*."

7. The case of the Thai word for cat ("meew") shows, on the other hand, that even the kind of mental representation we have considered—perceptual prototype—needn't be precisely preserved in translation. What we ask in translation, even when perceptual prototypes are relevant, is not that they be the same but that they be sufficiently similar.

8. I am indebted here to Jaak van Brakel, although I have not been able to accept his own view that it is constancies in the "phenomenological" properties—e.g., the melting point and the freezing point—that fix the reference of substance terms.

9. Tyler Burge (1979) objected to my expressing this (in Putnam 1975) by saying that natural-kind terms have an "indexical component," on the grounds that they are not *synonymous with descriptions containing indexical words*. But I never claimed that they were.

10. This point was first emphasized by David Wiggins (1980).

11. This account was developed independently of my own. My own was first presented in lectures at Harvard in 1967–1968, and at lectures at Seattle and at the University of Minnesota the following summer; neither Kripke nor I published our accounts until a few years later.

12. The reader interested in problems having to do with modal contexts, counterfactuals, etc., will observe that I have discussed only the question of the reference of these words in the *actual* world. I believe that a similar account can be given of their reference in all *physically possible* worlds; Kripke's claim that the account extends even farther, to the fixing of reference in what he calls "metaphysically possible worlds" (which may not obey the same laws of nature as the actual world), now appears problematic to me.

13. However, in a recent paper (Fodor 1986), Fodor has backslid on this point—in this paper he speaks of the *function* from context to referent (e.g., the function that assigns H_2O to the word "water" on Earth and XYZ to the word "water" on Twin Earth) as being in the speaker's "head," and *this*—the function—is now identified with the "narrow content." This resembles Searle's view, and is open to exactly the same objections.

14. I write "identity" here and not "equivalence" to simplify the exposition. Strictly speaking, what Fodor's theory requires is not that sentences with identical meaning have numerically the *same* underlying "semantic representation," but that there be some *syntactically definable* (and computationally effective) *equivalence relation* that holds between two expressions in "Mentalese" when and only when they are synonymous.

15. The term "ambiguous" is misleading here, as a report of Fodor's view (which is why I write "*referentially* ambiguous"). The term might suggest that Fodor's is really a conceptual claim, and Fodor does not intend his work as a conceptual analysis, but as a scientific theory. The claim that "meaning" refers to two different things (if Fodor is right) should be understood as an empirical claim, not a conceptual one.

References

Berger, A. (1988). *Terms and truth.* Cambridge, MA: MIT Press.

Burge, T. (1979). Individualism and the mental. In P. French, T. Uehling, and H. Wettstein, eds., *Midwest studies in philosophy,* vol. 4. Minneapolis: University of Minnesota Press.

Evans, G. (1982). *Varieties of reference.* Oxford: Oxford University Press.

Fodor, J. A. (1981). *Representations.* Cambridge, MA: MIT Press.

Fodor, J. A. (1986). Banish disContent. In J. Butterfield, ed., *Language, mind, and logic.* Cambridge: Cambridge University Press.

Kripke, S. A. (1980). *Naming and necessity.* Cambridge, MA: Harvard University Press.

Putnam, H. (1975). The meaning of "meaning." In K. Gunderson, ed., *Language, mind, and knowledge* (Minnesota Studies in Philosophy of Science, vol. 7). Minneapolis: University of Minnesota Press.

Putnam, H. (1981). *Reason, truth, and history.* Cambridge: Cambridge University Press.

Putnam, H. (1983). *Realism and reason: Philosophical papers, vol. 3.* Cambridge: Cambridge University Press.

Searle, J. R. (1983). *Intentionality.* Cambridge: Cambridge University Press.

Searle, J. R. (1984). *Minds, brains, and science.* Cambridge, MA: Harvard University Press.

Wiggins, D. (1980). *Sameness and substance.* Oxford: Blackwell.

VI

Ethics

29 Ethics and Cognitive Science

Alvin I. Goldman

Findings and theories in cognitive science have been increasingly important in many areas of philosophy, especially philosophy of mind, epistemology, and philosophy of language. The time is ripe to examine its potential applications to moral theory as well. This article does not aspire to a comprehensive treatment of the subject. It merely aims to illustrate the ways in which research in cognitive science can bear on the concerns of moral philosophers. For present purposes the label 'cognitive science' is used fairly broadly, encompassing, for example, the study of emotion or 'hot' cognition as well as 'cold' cognition.

This article examines three problem areas of relevance to moral theory to which cognitive science has made or can make contributions. The first topic concerns the cognitive materials deployed by moral judges or evaluators in thinking about moral matters. The language of morals includes words like *good, right, fair, honest, just,* and so forth. What do users of these words mentally associate with them? How are the concepts of fairness and justice represented? Further, are such representations wholly determined by the cultural environment, or are there perhaps innate structures that dispose cognizers toward certain conceptions of fairness or just distribution, toward reactions of distaste or opprobrium vis-à-vis certain types of action, and so forth?

The second topic concerns hedonic states and preferences, which play a particularly crucial role in ethical theory. A wide range of moral theories invoke such notions as *happiness, well-being, utility, preference-satisfaction,* or *welfare* as critical determinants of the rightness or justice of actions and social policies. What can cognitive science tell us about the nature and determinants of these states? To what extent, for example, is your happiness affected by comparing your own condition with that of others, or by comparing your present with your past condition? Answers to these questions have a bearing on the extent to

From A. Goldman, Ethics and cognitive science, *Ethics* 103, 337–360 (1993), published by the University of Chicago Press. © 1993 by The University of Chicago. All rights reserved. Reprinted by permission.

which economic prosperity or other substantive endowments determine levels of happiness.

The third topic concerns one of the psychological mechanisms or processes that may play a particularly crucial role in moral feeling and moral choice. Ethical theorists often devote the bulk of their attention to the process of reasoning or practical deliberation. In this paper I give special attention to the phenomenon of empathy. Empathy may play a significant role in motivation, in people's ability to act benevolently or altruistically. It may also strongly influence people's conception of a proper moral code. The phenomenon of empathy is one which cognitive science is starting to study more intensively. The prospective impact of such research on moral theory is the final topic on our agenda.

The Mental Structure of Moral Cognition

We begin with the question about the nature of moral cognition. In discussing moral cognition we set aside ontological issues about morality—whether there are such things as moral 'facts'—as well as epistemological questions of whether there is perceptual or intuitive access to such facts. We restrict ourselves to the way that ordinary people *think* about moral attributes, whether or not such thought 'corresponds' or 'answers to' some sort of independent reality.

It used to be assumed in many areas of philosophy that words are susceptible of strict definitions: definitions that specify *individually necessary and jointly sufficient conditions* for the application of the word. Stephen Stich (in press) points out that this kind of assumption seems to have been made by Plato in his treatment of moral terms. In the dialogue *Euthyphro* we find the following passage concerning piety.

Socrates. And what is piety, and what is impiety? . . . Tell me what is the nature of this idea, and then I shall have a standard to which I may look, and by which I may measure actions, whether yours or those of any one else, and then I shall be able to say that such and such an action is pious, such another impious.
Euthyphro. I will tell you, if you like. . . . Piety . . . is that which is dear to the gods, and impiety is that which is not dear to them.
Socrates. Very good Euthyphro, you have now given me the sort of answer which I wanted. But whether what you say is true or not I cannot as yet tell. (Plato 1892 386–388)

According to Euthyphro, being dear to the gods is a *necessary condition* for being pious and a *sufficient condition* as well.

This general approach to concepts—the approach that expects to find necessary and sufficient conditions—is called in cognitive science the *classical view* of concepts. This old and influential approach, however, has recently run into rough sledding. True, some concepts seem to conform to the classical view: *Grandmother* seems to be definable as someone who is female and is the parent of a parent. But the collective work of psychologists, linguists, and philosophers has recently challenged the applicability of this view to many other concepts, especially *natural kind* concepts, such as *dog, daisy, fruit*, or *bird* (see Fodor et al. 1980; E. Smith 1990; Putnam 1975; Rosch 1973, 1977).

One experimental finding is that people can reliably order the instances of natural kind concepts with respect to how 'typical' or 'representative' they are of the concept. For the concept *fruit*, for example, apples and peaches are considered typical, raisins and figs less typical, and pumpkins and olives atypical. These ratings predict performance in a wide variety of tasks. If subjects are asked to decide as quickly as possible if an item is an instance of a concept (for example, "Is a fig a fruit?"), they are faster the more typical the instance. Another task is memory retrieval. If asked to generate from memory all instances of a concept, subjects retrieve typical before atypical instances.

These typicality effects seem inhospitable to the classical view. They suggest that not all instances of a natural kind concept are equal; yet equality is what one might expect if every instance met the same definition of the necessary-and-sufficient-conditions type. This argument is strengthened by the additional finding that virtually all the properties listed by subjects as relevant to a concept are not strictly necessary, for example, the property of being sweet for *fruit* or the properties of flying and singing for *bird*. (Penguins don't fly and vultures don't sing.) Similar findings apply to other concepts, including artifact concepts such as *furniture* or *clothing*.

The typicality findings have led to a slightly different view of concepts: Concepts are represented in terms of properties that need not be strictly necessary but are frequently present in instances of the concept. These properties are weighted by their frequency, or perhaps by their perceptual salience. A collection of such properties is called a *prototype*. Under the prototype view, an object is categorized as an instance of a concept if it is sufficiently similar to the prototype, similarity being determined (in part) by the number of properties in the prototype possessed by the instance and by the sum of their weights. The prototype view can explain many of the typicality findings discussed earlier. For example, typical instances are categorized faster than atypical instances because categorization involves determining that an item exceeds some critical level of similarity to the prototype, and the more similar the item to the prototype the faster this determination can be made (see E. Smith and Medin 1981).

How does the way concepts are represented bear on moral philosophy? In many areas of moral philosophy there is much controversy over whether a certain item is an instance of a certain concept. For example, on the issue of abortion it is controversial whether or not a fetus is an instance of a person (or a human life). Often people try to settle this issue by trying to find necessary and sufficient conditions for being a person. This seems to presuppose, however, that such a definition is in principle forthcoming, that we (tacitly) represent the concept of a person in terms of necessary and sufficient conditions. It may be, however, that our representation of this concept, like many other concepts, has a prototype structure. This might support a conclusion that the fetus is an instance of person but a highly atypical instance. No such conclusion could directly settle the abortion controversy, of course, but it may significantly affect our theoretical reflections on the issue.

A proper understanding of concepts and conceptualization may be even more important to moral philosophy by serving to forestall hasty meta-ethical conclusions. Some moral philosophers (e.g., Ayer 1936), seeing that it is difficult to give 'classical' or 'reductive' definitions of moral terms, have concluded that descriptivism in ethics should be replaced by emotivism. But once it is appreciated that very few words have classical or reductive definitions, we can see that it is a mistake to infer from the absence of such definitions that moral words lack descriptive content. (This point is due to Holly Smith, personal communication.)

Another proposal for dealing with the previously cited experimental results hypothesizes that concepts are (sometimes) represented by one or more of their specific exemplars, or instances, that the cognizer has encountered (Medin and Schaffer 1978; Estes 1986). Thus I might represent *dog* by the set of dogs I have encountered, or by some specific dogs encountered when I first learned the term. On this 'exemplar' view, categorization occurs by activating the mental representations of one or more exemplars of the concept and then assessing the similarity between the exemplars and the item to be categorized.

The exemplar theory is particularly intriguing from the standpoint of moral theory, as Stich (in press) points out. Moral theorists often assume that people's usage of moral terms is underpinned by some sort of rules or principles they learn to associate with those terms: rules governing honesty, for example, or fairness. The exemplar theory suggests, however, that what moral learning consists in may not be (primarily) the learning of rules but the acquisition of pertinent exemplars or examples. This would accord with the observable fact that people, especially children, have an easier time assimilating the import of parables, myths, and fables than abstract principles. A morally suitable role model may be didactically more effective than a set of behavioral maxims. If this is correct, it is an important lesson for moral philosophy, which often tries to reconstruct the nature of ordinary moral judgment. Ordinary moral thinking may consist more in comparing contemplated actions with stored exemplars of good and bad behavior than with the formulation and deduction of consequences from abstract principles (cf. Dworkin 1992; Johnson 1993; H. Smith 1992). Of course, it is open to the moral theorist to spurn common patterns of moral thought, to try to replace them with something preferable. Before such a revisionary move is considered, however, we may want to have the facts straight about how 'folk morality' proceeds.

One context in which appeal is often made to ordinary practices of moral thought is 'slippery slope' arguments (see van der Burg 1991). People sometimes argue against policies allowing certain actions, such as abortion or euthanasia, by saying that the probable effect of allowing these actions is that we will be prone to accept some further, highly objectionable actions as well (such as infanticide). An argument of this sort might be bolstered by appeal to some sort of psychological principle of moral thinking or categorization. It might say that if we (the community) categorize abortion or euthanasia as morally permissible, we will also come to categorize other forms of killing as morally permissible. To the extent that moral categorization is driven by considerations of similarity or analogy between cases, there may be some plausibility in such contentions. The precise extent to which similarity or analogy *does* drive categorization is therefore an important issue, to which cognitive science can certainly contribute (cf. E. Smith 1990; Rips 1989).

Innate Constraints on Moral Thinking

Let us return now to the widely held view that moral thought somehow includes material of a rule-like nature. The method of uncovering the system of rules underlying intuitive moral judgments may then be compared, as John Rawls (1971) has done, to the method of modern linguistics. Following Noam Chomsky, linguists typically assume that speakers of a natural language have internalized a system of generative grammatical rules, which play a central role in language production and comprehension, and in the production of 'intuitions' by speakers about the grammaticality of sentences presented to them. In attempting to discover what a speaker has internalized, linguists construct systems of generative rules and check them against speakers' intuitions.

Stich (in press) points to a further possible analogy between grammatical and moral theory. Chomsky has long maintained that grammatical rules are so complex that they could not be learned from the limited data available to the child if the child were using 'unbiased', general-purpose learning algorithms. The stimuli are too 'impoverished', according to Chomsky, to permit this explanation. Instead, there must be innate constraints on learning that guide the acquisition of grammars. Such constraints would imply that the range of grammars it is possible for a child to learn is a small and highly structured subset of the set of logically possible grammars. All the grammars of actual languages, of course, fall within this subset. An intriguing possible analogy is that there may be innate constraints on moral thinking that similarly restrict the range of 'humanly possible' moral systems to a relatively small subset of the logically possible systems.

One popular candidate for an innate moral constraint is a predisposition against incest. Most cultures have taboos against sexual intercourse among close relatives; and even when taboos are lacking, incest is typically infrequent. The low rate of incest is often said to result from a genetic propensity to refrain from sexual relations with those with whom one has been reared. The thesis appears to have some empirical support, though it encounters difficulties when examined in detail (see van den Berghe 1983; Kitcher 1985).

The case of incest involves a putatively innate predisposition concerning a specific type of act. Constraints on moral thinking, however, may have a more abstract structure. Precisely this idea has been suggested by Alan Fiske (1991, in press). On the basis of a wide survey of anthropological, sociological, and psychological findings, Fiske postulates the existence of four elementary forms of sociality, four elementary models out of which people construct 'approved' styles of social interaction and social structure. The four elementary models are: (1) communal sharing, (2) authority ranking, (3) equality matching, and (4) market pricing. Because these four structures seem to be found to some extent in all cultures, and since they emerge in all the major domains of social life, Fiske suggests as a plausible inference that they are rooted in structures of the human mind.

To get a sense of Fiske's theory, let us look at the four models in a little detail. Under communal sharing, relationships are based on a model of all group members being equivalent and undifferentiated. Given a criterion for group membership, possessions of the group are then conferred on all group members equally, whatever their individual contributions may be. For example, in many hunting and gathering societies, people share the meat of game animals across the whole band: The hunter who killed the animal may get less than many others, and people give food, tools, and utensils to anyone who asks for them. In most societies this kind of sharing of material things is common among close kin and sometimes among other associates. At a commensal meal, no one keeps track of who eats how much. Other manifestations of the communal sharing (CS) structure are holding land in commons and organizing production so that people work collectively without assessing individual inputs or assigning distinct responsibilities.

The role of material things in authority ranking (AR) relationships is quite different. When people transfer things from person to person in an AR mode, higher ranking people get more and better things, and get them sooner, than their subordinates. Higher-ranking people may preempt rare or valuable items, so that inferior people get none at all. Subjects may have to pay goods in tribute to rulers, or authorities may simply appropriate what they want. Conversely, a principle of noblesse oblige usually obtains in AR relations, so that authorities have an obligation to be generous and to exercise pastoral responsibility to protect and sustain their subordinates. Fiske interprets much of religion as a manifestation of the AR model. He sees the prominence of AR in so many religions as evidence that humans have a proclivity for projecting this schema on the world, as a way of interpreting, judging, and validating experience.

Social scientists have tended to treat hierarchical relationships as if they were ultimately based on pure force or coercive power. Fiske instead postulates a psychological receptivity toward authority relationships. He points out that authority ranking, like communal sharing, emerges in a great variety of domains of social action, thought, and evaluation. Linear orderings are prominent in exchange, distribution, the organization of work, the significance of land, and so forth. The congruence of structure across such diverse contexts and cultures suggests to him that the structure is the product of the one thing that is constant across them all: the human mind.

The third elementary form of relationship is equality matching (EM), sometimes called 'balanced reciprocity.' This is an egalitarian, one-for-one exchange, exemplified in our culture by the exchange of Christmas gifts. For the purpose of such interchanges, people ignore the differentiating qualities that might make one object more desirable or valuable than another. Similarly, a dinner party matches a dinner party—within a range of possibilities that the culture defines rather precisely. In order to count and match in such cases, equivalence classes have to be defined. Once they are, however, categorical equivalence permits relationships to be balanced despite differences that actually exist between the entities exchanged. Anthropologists have pointed out that balanced reciprocity is often used as a way of establishing relationships between strangers, or reestablishing amicable relations among former enemies.

Market pricing (MP) relationships are based on a model of proportionality in social relations, in which people attend to ratios and rates. People in a market pricing relationship usually reduce all the relevant features and components under consideration to a single value or utility metric, which allows the comparison of many qualitatively and quantitatively diverse factors. This model is extremely prevalent, of course, in our society and needs no further elaboration.

Fiske emphasizes that his four hypothesized models are rarely used alone. Two friends may share tapes and records freely with each other (CS), work on a task at which one is an expert and imperiously directs the other (AR), divide equally the cost of gas on a trip (EM), and transfer a bicycle from one to the other for a market-value price (MP). He also emphasizes that culture is decisive in selecting which models are to be implemented in which relationships, and in fixing relevant parameters. But the basic models themselves, he postulates, have a psychological origin. Whether this large-scale theory can be substantiated is much too early to decide; many difficult questions obviously arise. However, it at least provides an illustration of the way in which psychological constraints may help fix extant systems of morality.

Let us now shift gears and turn to our second set of questions that bear on moral theory: questions concerning utility, welfare, and hedonic states. Most modern moral theories, especially those in the utilitarian tradition, assign an important place to the concepts of happiness, utility, welfare, or well-being. Morally good actions or social policies are widely thought to be ones that promote the general welfare, or encourage an appropriate distribution of welfare. The exact nature of happiness, welfare, or well-being, however, needs detailed investigation, and this is a topic to which cognitive psychology is making interesting contributions.

Although it is often assumed that wealth and other external conditions of life promote happiness or satisfaction, it is unclear a priori just how strong a correlation there is. We therefore need better measures of well-being. To this end, social science researchers have devised survey techniques in which respondents are asked to report how happy and satisfied they are with their life-as-a-whole and with various life domains. These so-called subjective social indicators are used as measures of subjective well-being. As Angus Campbell (1981, 23) points out, the "use of these measures is based on the assumption that all the countless experiences people go through from day to day add to . . . global feelings of well-being, that these feelings remain relatively constant over extended periods, and that people can describe them with candor and accuracy." These assumptions, however, have proved problematic. The relationship between individuals' objective life conditions and their subjective sense of well-being was found to be weak and sometimes counterintuitive. Poor people are sometimes happier than rich ones; patients three years after a cancer operation were found to be happier than a healthy control group; and paralyzed accident victims were happier with their life than one might expect on the basis of the event. Moreover, measures of well-being have been shown to have a low test-retest reliability (consistency), usually hovering around .40, and these measures were found to be quite sensitive to influence from preceding questions in a questionnaire or interview.

Cognitive social psychologists seek to understand these findings. From their perspective, reports about happiness and satisfaction with one's life are not necessarily valid read-outs of an internal state of personal well-being. Rather, they are constructions to a particular question posed at a particular time and subject to a variety of transient influences. Norbert Schwarz and Fritz Strack (1991) report their own and other psychologists' research into the question of how people go about trying to answer the survey queries.

Suppose you are a respondent asked the question: "Taking all things together, how would you say things are these days? Would you say you are very happy, pretty happy, not too happy?" Unfortunately, "taking all things together" is a difficult mental task. Indeed, as an instruction to think about all aspects of one's life, it requests something impossible. Thus, say Schwarz and Strack, you are unlikely to retrieve all information that potentially bears on this judgment, but are likely to truncate the search process as soon as enough information comes to mind to form the judgment with a reasonable degree of subjective certainty. Thus, the judgment reflects the implications of the information that comes to mind most easily.

How is accessible information used? It has been found that such use depends heavily on the standard of comparison that is momentarily established, which can be a function of salient information about one's own previous experiences or about other people and their experiences. In an experiment by Strack, Schwarz and Gschneidinger (1985), subjects in one group were instructed to recall and write down a very negative event in their lives; subjects in another group were instructed to recall and write down a very positive event in their lives. Within each group, half of the subjects were asked to recall a present event, and half were asked to recall a past event. Subjects were then asked to rate their well-being on a 10-point scale. This procedure yields a 2 by 2 design in which the recalled event was either positive or negative, in the present or in the past. For the events in the present, the results were hardly surprising. Recalling a positive present event made people feel good, whereas thinking about a negative present event made people feel less happy. The results for past events were more surprising: Ratings of well-being were higher for those who recalled a past negative event than for those who recalled a past positive event. It thus appears that the effect of comparison to one's past is quite substantial. Similar effects have been observed by Strack, Schwarz, and colleagues concerning comparisons with others. Subjects evaluated their own life more favorably when they met a handicapped experimental confederate, or listened to such a confederate describe how a severe medical condition interferes with his enjoyment of life. In the last example, the impact of the confederate's description was also found to be more pronounced when the seating arrangements rendered the confederate visible at the time of the later happiness report, a finding that emphasizes the role of temporary accessibility in the choice of comparison standards.

Endowment and Contrast in Judgments of Well-being

Building partly on the work of Schwarz and Strack (1991), Amos Tversky and Dale Griffin (1991) have constructed a model of hedonic judgments using the notions of 'endowment' and 'contrast.' The endowment effect of an event represents its direct contribution to one's happiness or satisfaction. Events also exercise an indirect contrast effect on the evaluation of subsequent events. A positive experience makes us happy, but also renders similar experiences less exciting. A negative experience makes us unhappy, but it also helps us appreciate subsequent experiences that are less bad. Thus, the hedonic impact of an event reflects a balance of its endowment and contrast effects. A simple example illustrates the point. A professor from a small midwestern town attends a conference in New York and enjoys dinner at an outstanding French restaurant. This event contributes to her endowment, but it also gives rise to a contrast effect. A later meal in the local French restaurant becomes somewhat less satisfying by comparison with the great meal in New York.

Tversky and Griffin use their endowment-contrast model to explain some of Strack et al.'s (1985) findings. Recall that one of these findings was the following 'reversal': ratings of well-being were higher for subjects who recalled a past negative event than for those who recalled a past positive event. The endowment-contrast scheme explains this as follows. For events in the present there is no room for contrast, hence we get a positive endowment effect for the positive event and a negative endowment effect for the negative event. The recall of past events, however, introduces a contrast with the present, which is positive for past negative events and negative for past positive ones. Because present events are more salient than past events, the endowment effect is greater for present than past events. For past events, the contrast component offsets the endowment component of these events and produces the observed reversal.

Students of well-being focus on judgments of satisfaction or happiness. Another paradigm for the study of welfare, dominant in economics, focuses on choice rather than judgment. In this paradigm, a person is said to be better off in State A than in State B if he or she chooses State A over State B. The concept of utility has been used in economics and decision theory in two different senses: (a) experience value, the degree of satisfaction associated with the actual experience of an outcome, and (b) decision value, the choice-worthiness of a prospective outcome. Tversky and Griffin, having drawn this distinction, point out that in many situations experience values, as expressed in self-rating, diverge from decision values, as inferred from choice. One obvious point of divergence is that we often choose options that don't actually make us happy; they just don't turn out as we expect them to. Even if judgments of well-being are restricted to anticipated satisfaction, however, choices and judgments of prospective well-being can produce different evaluations. When people are asked to assess the hedonic value of some future states (e.g., employment situations) they try to imagine what it would feel like to experience those states. But when asked to choose among these states, they tend to search for reasons or arguments to justify their choice. The resultant evaluations may well differ.

To illustrate this choice-judgment discrepancy, Tversky and Griffin (1991, 114) gave the following information to subjects:

Imagine that you have just completed a graduate degree in Communications and you are considering one-year jobs at two different magazines.

(A) At Magazine A, you are offered a job paying $35,000. However, the other workers who have the same training and experience as you do are making $38,000.

(B) At Magazine B, you are offered a job paying $33,000. However, the other workers who have the same training and experience as you do are making $30,000.

Approximately half the subjects were asked "Which job would you choose to take?" while the other half were asked "At which job would you be happier?" The results confirmed the prediction that the salary would dominate the choice whereas the comparison with others would loom larger in judgment. Eighty-four percent of the subjects given the choice question preferred the job with the higher absolute salary and lower relative position, while 62 percent of the subjects given the happiness-prediction question anticipated higher satisfaction in the job with the lower absolute salary but higher relative position.

The choice-judgment discrepancy raises an intriguing question: which is the correct or more appropriate measure of well-being? Tversky and Griffin suggest that both choice and judgment provide relevant data for the assessment of well-being, although neither one is entirely satisfactory. Notice that the judgment criterion, however, raises doubts about the most basic principle of welfare economics: Pareto optimality. Pareto optimality says that an allocation of resources is acceptable if it improves everybody's lot. Viewed as a choice criterion, this principle is irresistible. It is hard to object to a policy that improves your lot just because it improves the lot of someone else even more. But Tversky and Griffin point out that this focuses exclusively on endowment and neglects contrast altogether. Contrast effects can create widespread unhappiness. Consider a policy that doubles the salary of a few people in an organization and increases all other salaries by 5 percent. Even though all salaries rise (conforming with Pareto optimality), it is doubtful that this change will make most people happier. There is a great deal of evidence that people's reported satisfaction depends largely on their relative position, not only on their objective situation (Brickman 1975; Brickman and Campbell 1971). Surveys indicate that wealthier people are slightly happier than people with less money, but substantial increases in everyone's income and standard of living do not raise the reported level of happiness (Easterlin 1974).

These findings and considerations might be taken as grounds for abandoning judgments of subjective well-being as criteria for the measurement of welfare or happiness. Why not rely, therefore, on the more tractable notion of 'fulfillment of desire or preference' as an account of happiness or welfare? Surely the notion of preference is on a theoretically sounder footing. Unfortunately, recent psychology of choice has also raised doubts about the existence of well-defined preference orderings. Researchers have found reasons to hold that people often do not have well-defined values or preferences. Expressed preferences are not simply read off from some stored master list; they are actually constructed in the process of being elicited. Different elicitation procedures highlight different aspects of options, which may give rise to inconsistent responses.

An example of this research is Paul Slovic's (1975) study of the relationship between 'matching' and 'choice'. Slovic gave subjects two options, each involving two dimensions. For instance, a subject could choose between a gift package A, involving a certain amount of cash and a coupon book with a stated monetary value, and gift package B, involving a smaller amount of cash but a more valuable coupon book. To make the choice difficult, Slovic allowed the subjects themselves to construct the second option so that it was equally attractive to the first. Their first option was described as $20 in cash and a coupon book worth $18. The second gift package was not fully described: it would contain $10 in cash, but the subjects were invited to specify a coupon book value that would make the second package 'match' the first. After equating various pairs of options, subjects made choices from among the equated pairs. Given this task, one would expect subjects to make their choices fairly randomly. Instead, subjects consistently selected the option that was superior on the more important dimension (*viz.*, cash). It appears, then, that choice processes are different from matching processes: the judgments of value elicited by the request to match options were different from the judgments of value elicited by a request to choose among options.

In another demonstration of the influence of task, Slovic, Griffin, and Tversky (1990) asked subjects to predict the judgments of a college admissions committee regarding several applicants. For each applicant the subjects received two items of information: a rank on verbal Scholastic Aptitude Test (SAT) score and the presence or absence of strong extracurricular activities. The subjects were told that the admissions committee ranks all 500 applicants and accepts about the top fourth. Half of the subjects were required to predict the rank assigned to each applicant (a numerical task), whereas the other half were asked to predict whether each applicant was accepted or rejected (a categorical task). The difference between the tasks proved to be highly significant. The subjects given the numerical task made much more use of the numerical SAT score, whereas the categorical data (presence or absence of strong extracurricular activities) had more impact on the subjects who were given the categorical task. Thus, subtle aspects of how problems are posed, questions are phrased, and responses are elicited can have a substantial effect on people's expressed judgments and preferences. This leads some researchers to doubt whether, in general, there are stable and precise values or preferences antecedent to an elicitation procedure (Fischhoff et al. 1980; Slovic 1990).

Empathy and Morality

I turn now to our third general topic: the possible role of empathy in influencing altruistic behavior and moral codes. The phenomenon of empathy has been characterized in a number of closely related but different ways. Paradigm cases of empathy, however, consist first of taking the perspective of another person, that is, imaginatively assuming one or more of the other person's mental states. Such perspective taking might be instigated by observing that person's situation and behavior, or by simply being told about them, as when one reads a history or a novel. The initial 'pretend' states are then operated upon (automatically) by psychological processes, which generate further states that (in favorable cases) are similar to, or homologous to, the target person's states. In central cases of empathy the output states are affective or emotional states rather than purely cognitive or conative states like believing or desiring. Standardly the empathizer is aware of his or her vicarious affects and emotions as representatives of the emotions or affects of the target agent. Thus, empathy consists of a sort of 'mimicking' of one person's affective state by that of another. This characterization accords with at least some of the definitions in the psychological literature. Mark Barnett (1987), for example, defines empathy as "the vicarious experiencing of an emotion that is congruent with, but not necessarily identical to, the emotion of another individual."

Although almost everyone experiences empathy at one time or another, it remains to be shown how fundamental and robust a phenomenon it is and whether the description given above is psychologically sustainable. Does it even make sense, for example, to construe empathic states as 'similar', 'congruent', or 'homologous' to genuine affective states of the target agent? What exactly are the respects of similarity or congruence?

At this point in time researchers cannot specify the precise respects of similarity between original and vicarious affective states. This is insufficient reason, however, to deny the existence of significant similarities. We also cannot precisely specify how visual imagery resembles actual visual perception. Nonetheless, there is ample demonstration of significant respects of similarity between the two domains (Finke and Shepard 1986; Kosslyn 1980, 1990). If comparable experimental creativity is invested in the field of vicarious affect, it would not be surprising to find analogous points of similarity.

Meanwhile, there are plenty of experimental demonstrations of mimicking, 'tracking', or resonating to the mental states of others, which make such phenomena appear to be quite pervasive features of the human organism. Some of these may be primitive precursors of empathy rather than strict empathy under our definition. The fact that many of these phenomena are developmentally very early also suggests the presence of an innate mechanism, or several such mechanisms.

One phenomenon of interest is 'joint visual attention,' the propensity of infants to follow the gaze of another person. Butterworth and colleagues (Butterworth 1991; Butterworth and Cochran 1980) studied 6-month old babies and found that when the mother turns and visually inspects a target, her 6-month old baby will look to the same side of the room to which the mother is attending, and will be pretty accurate in locating the object referred to by the mother's change of gaze. Here we have one early phenomenon of 'tracking' or 'mimicking' another person's mental orientation. An even more striking type of 'mimicking' has been studied by Andrew Meltzoff and colleagues (Meltzoff and Moore 1977, 1983), who found that babies as young as one day old (in fact one subject was only 42 *minutes* old) engage in facial imitation of adults, such as lip protrusion, mouth opening, and tongue protrusion.

Another phenomenon, more pertinent to affect, is 'emotional contagion', familiar to all of us through the infectious effects of smiles and laughter. The primitive basis of emotional contagion has been experimentally studied in the reactive crying of newborns. M. L. Simner (1971) presented 2- to 4-day old infants with 6-minute tapes of various auditory stimuli, including (i) spontaneous crying by a 5-day-old neonate, (ii) spontaneous crying by a 5½-month-old, (iii) a computer-synthesized replication of a newborn cry, (iv) the baby's own spontaneous crying (previously recorded), and (v) white noise that was equivalent in sound intensity. Simner found that the sound of neonatal crying ((i) and (iv)) produced significantly more reactive crying in these newborns than did either white noise, the 5½-month-old cry, or the synthetic cry.

Another example of resonant emotion occurs in the context of 'social referencing.' M. Klinnert (1981) presented 12- and 18-month old infants with novel and somewhat forbidding toys in a laboratory playroom in their mothers' presence. Mothers were instructed to pose facial expressions conveying either fear, joy, or neutral emotion. For those infants who regularly referenced the mother, that is, looked at her to "check" on her attitude, maternal facial expressions had a profound effect. Infants were significantly more likely to move away from mother to approach the toy when the mother was smiling, but to retreat to the mother when she was displaying fear. There is additional evidence that such behavior was mediated through the arousal of a resonant emotion in the children, who themselves showed negative affect.

The foregoing cases of emotional contagion may not be paradigmatic cases of empathy, because they may not involve the stage of perspective taking. There is, however, also experimental work in which congruent emotion is plausibly produced by means of perspective taking. S. M.

Berger (1962) had subjects observe a target person performing a task. He led them to believe that the target was either receiving electric shock or not, after which the target person either jerked his or her arm or did not. All observers were told that they themselves would not be shocked during the study. Berger reasoned that both a painful stimulus in the environment (shock) and a distress response (movement) would lead observers to infer that the target person was experiencing pain. Berger found that observers informed of both shock and movement were themselves more physiologically aroused than observers in the other three conditions. Although Berger's manipulations did not directly address perspective taking, it is plausible to suppose that the observers did indeed engage in perspective taking.

An experiment of Ezra Stotland (1969) explicitly addressed imaginative projection. All of Stotland's subjects watched someone else whose hand was strapped in a machine that they were told generated painful heat. Some were told just to watch the man carefully, some were told to imagine the way he was feeling, and some were told to imagine themselves in his place. Using both physiological and verbal measures of empathy on the part of the subjects, the experimental results clearly showed that the deliberate acts of imagination produced a greater response than just watching.

It is noteworthy that these results are not restricted to painful or distressing experiences. In the study reported by Stotland, subjects who witnessed another person experiencing what they perceived to be pleasure reported, relative to controls, that they found participating in the study to be a pleasant experience. Similarly, Dennis Krebs (1975) found that participants reported feeling relatively bad when watching someone whom they thought was about to receive an electric shock and relatively good when watching someone about to receive a reward.

An insightful observation of 'positive' empathy is presented by Adam Smith, whose book *The Theory of Moral Sentiments* (1759/1976) contains some brilliant early discussions of empathy (which he called 'sympathy').

When we have read a book or poem so often that we can no longer find any amusement in reading it by ourselves, we can still take pleasure in reading it to a companion. To him it has all the graces of novelty; we enter into the surprise and admiration which it naturally excites in him, but which it is no longer capable of exciting in us; we consider all the ideas which it presents rather in the light in which they appear to him, than in that in which they appear to ourselves, and we are amused by sympathy with his amusement which thus enlivens our own. (1759/1976, 14)

Empathy and Descriptive Ethics

Let us assume, then, that empathy is a genuine and fairly pervasive facet of human life. What are the consequences for moral theory? And what relevance can further empirical investigation of empathy have to moral theory? Let me first divide moral or ethical theory into two components: descriptive and prescriptive ethics. Descriptive ethics in turn has two branches. Branch 1 would seek to describe and explain the acceptance of the various moral codes in different cultures and sub-cultures. Branch 2 of descriptive ethics would seek to describe and explain the extent of conformity with each code by people who subscribe to it. This second branch would focus heavily on motivational factors. What enables or inhibits an agent from acting on her moral creed? Prescriptive ethics would, of course, be concerned with the formulation and justification of a 'proper' or 'correct' moral system.

The empirical study of empathy is relevant to all of these branches and sub-branches of ethics. Historically, a key role for empathy in descriptive ethics was championed by Schopenhauer (1841/1965). The primary ethical phenomenon, according to Schopenhauer, is compassion, which he characterized as the vicarious 'participation' in the suffering of another. He divided ethical duties (as formulated in many codes) into duties of justice and duties of philanthropy. Duties of justice are 'negative' duties to refrain from injuring others, which are ultimately based on feelings of compassion. Duties of philanthropy are 'positive' duties to help, also based on compassion. Finally, Schopenhauer assigns compassion a critical place in explaining the cross-cultural display of moral behavior in human life.

[T]he foundation of morals or the incentive to morality as laid down by me is the only one that can boast of a real, and extensive, effectiveness. . . . [D]espite the great variety of religions in the world, the degree of morality, or rather immorality, shows absolutely no corresponding variety, but is essentially pretty much the same everywhere. . . . [Unlike the ineffectiveness of religion] the moral incentive that is put forward by me [viz., compassion] . . . displays a decided and truly wonderful effectiveness at all times, among all nations, in all the situations of life, even in a state of anarchy and amid the horrors of revolutions and wars. (Schopenhauer 1841/1965, 170, 172)

Schopenhauer is far from saying, of course, that compassion is the predominant motivation in our lives. Nonetheless, he views it as the source of moral principles and the ultimate root of compliance with such principles. A similar line is taken by Rousseau, who writes:

Mandeville has rightly recognized that, with all their morality, men would never have been anything but hideous monsters, had not nature given them compassion as a support for their faculty of reason. But he did not see that from this one quality spring all the social virtues that he wishes to deny men. In fact, what are generosity, clemency, and humanity if not compassion that is applied to the weak, the guilty, or even the entire human race? Properly understood, benevolence and even friendship are the result of a constant pity that is fixed on a particular object. . . . The commiseration will be the more energetic, the more intimately the spectator identifies himself with the sufferer. (In Schopenhauer 1841/1965, 185)

It is not implied, of course, that compassion or empathy plays an exclusively direct or simple role in influencing moral codes or eliciting compliant behavior. Even Schopenhauer grants that compassion commonly operates indirectly, by means of principles.

The task of descriptive ethics, we have said, is to identify and explain the moral systems that are found in various cultures. In recent years, however, many writers point to differences in moral systems or orientations even within a single culture. In particular, they claim to find gender differences in moral orientation. Carol Gilligan's *In a Different Voice* (1982) is probably the most influential statement of such a hypothesis. The question of whether there are such differences, and if so what is their source, is a good example of a subject ripe for empirical inquiry. Gilligan claims that women have a moral orientation that focuses on 'caring' and 'connecting' rather than abstract rights or justice. This thesis, however, has been criticized on empirical grounds. In a series of studies, Lawrence Walker and his colleagues (Walker 1984; Walker and DeVries 1985) found no statistically significant gender differences as measured within Lawrence Kohlberg's widely used moral stage framework. In a more recent study, Walker, DeVries, and Trevethan (1987) did find that females are more likely to choose personal over impersonal dilemmas as problems to talk about, and problems they claimed to confront. Moreover, personal dilemmas were more likely to elicit a 'care' response rather than a 'justice' or 'rights' response. Controlling for dilemma content, however, sex differences were still not found to be significant.

Gilligan's thesis, and similar theses advanced by other feminist writers, is particularly relevant to us because a focus on 'caring' and 'connecting' might stem from more frequent or more salient empathy. Indeed, Gilligan quotes with approval Norma Haan's (1975) and Constance Holstein's (1976) research, which indicates "that the moral judgments of women differ from those of men in the greater extent to which women's judgments are tied to feelings of empathy and compassion" (Gilligan 1982, 60). This naturally raises the question of whether there is a psychological difference between the genders in the incidence or strength of empathy, which common sex stereotypes, of course, suggest. This is a heavily researched topic, but the results are complex and inconclusive.

Randy Lennon and Nancy Eisenberg (1987; cf. Eisenberg and Lennon 1983) survey the field as follows. A principal complication in empathy research is the variety of measures used in its detection. The most popular method of assessing empathy in young children uses picture/story stimuli and operationalizes empathy as the degree of match between self-report of emotion and the emotion appropriate to the protagonist in the vignette. In 28 studies using this measure, most found no significant gender differences. In studies of school-age children and adults the most widely used index is a self-report questionnaire. In 16 studies of this sort females scored significantly higher in all. These differences may, however, be due to biases in self-reports. Females are expected to be more concerned with others as well as more emotional than males, so both females and males may respond in ways consistent with sex-role stereotypes. Other measures of empathy include facial-gestural and vocal measures of empathy as well as physiological measures of empathy. Eisenberg and Lennon conclude that no significant gender differences are found on these measures.

Empathy and Prescriptive Ethics

Let me turn now to prescriptive ethics. Although the meta-constraints on prescriptive ethics are of course highly controversial, most writers would agree that a satisfactory prescriptive theory should be firmly rooted in human nature. It would be hard to defend any moral system as prescriptively valid that did not make important contact with human moral psychology. Much of ethical theory has focused on the human capacity for reason, a tradition most vividly exemplified by Kant. In recent literature, there is also a tendency to associate moral rationalism with highly universalistic moral norms and to associate emotionalism (as the contrasting approach might be dubbed) with a particularist point of view. Universalism requires the moral agent to consider everyone's pleasure or pain equally and impartially. By contrast, particularism allows the agent to display some degree of partiality toward individuals with whom one has a personal affinity such as family members, friends, students, or comrades. If we now consider the prospects of an empathy-based view of morality, it might seem natural for it to tilt toward particularism, as Lawrence Blum (1980, 1987), for example, suggests. This is because empathy inclines an agent toward actions that are responsive to those with whom he empathizes, and these are most likely to be people with whom personal contact is established.

It is not clear, however, that an emphasis on empathy or sympathy necessarily dictates a particularist or 'agent-centered' morality. A universalist may point out that empathy can be extended beyond personal contacts, for example, to characters in fiction or history. In fact, we can readily think of sympathy-based theories that are quite universalistic. Hume's theory of justice, at least as reconstructed by Rawls (1971, 185–186), is both sympathy-based and highly universalistic. Again, R. M. Hare's (1963) highly universalistic theory acknowledges the instrumental value of sympathetic imagination in people's readiness to universalize.

Let me turn now to a more concrete way in which psychological facts may impinge on prescriptive ethics, *viz.*, by setting constraints of realism or feasibility. A moral code that is psychologically unrealizable by human beings, or just too demanding or difficult for people to satisfy, might be rejected on meta-ethical grounds. Not all moral theorists would accept this constraint, as Samuel Scheffler (1986) points out. Nonetheless, it is plausible to impose a constraint like Owen Flanagan's (1991) Principle of Minimal Psychological Realism: "make sure when constructing a moral theory or projecting a moral ideal that the character, decision processing, and behavior prescribed are possible . . . for creatures like us" (Flanagan 1991, 32). Moral theories like utilitarianism may fail to satisfy this principle because they require more altruistic behavior, or more universalism, than is feasible for human beings.

This raises the question of people's capacities for altruism, and their capacities for serving everyone's welfare equally, as opposed to their own welfare or that of specially related others. Here empathy again becomes particularly relevant, because it seems to be a prime mechanism that disposes us toward altruistic behavior. The question then arises: what exactly is the potential scope, extent, or power of empathy? Can we empathize with everyone equally? This problem worried Hume (1739/1988): "We sympathize more with persons contiguous to us, than with persons remote from us: With our acquaintances, than with strangers; With our countrymen, than with foreigners" (1739/1988, 581). There is also research evidence that empathy tends to be biased, as Martin Hoffman (1987) points out. Observers are more empathic to victims who are familiar and similar to themselves than to victims who are different. Second, people are more apt to be empathically aroused by someone's distress in the immediate situation than by distress they know is being experienced by someone elsewhere. But these issues need much more empirical investigation. More generally, cognitive science needs to give us a systematic account of the properties of the empathizing process. What targets and circumstances encourage the initiation of empathy? What variables affect the vividness or strength of empathic feelings? How do empathic feelings combine with other cognitions to influence an agent's conduct? These and other parameters concerning empathy need to be better understood.

I have said that psychological realism might be relevant to prescriptive ethics by excluding moral systems that are too demanding. But equally, psychological realism may help exclude moral or social systems that are not sufficiently constraining. Hume (1777/1972) remarks that institutions of justice would not be necessary at all if the human mind were "so replete with friendship and generosity, that every man has the utmost tenderness for every man, and feels no more concern for his own interest than for that of his fellows" (1777/1972, sec. 146). In our actual state, there do seem to be limits to our benevolence, and our empathic powers. These limits create the need for legal and political institutions that will be sufficiently constraining to shape the conduct of creatures like us.

Finally, to the extent that both descriptive and prescriptive ethics should seek to place human moralizing within the context of human biology, it is instructive to inquire into the evolutionary origins of moral psychology (cf. Gibbard 1990). Empathy might well figure centrally in an evolutionary account. Empathizing with one's kin or one's neighbor would promote mutual aid and inhibit injurious behavior, thereby contributing to biological fitness.

Moral theory needs to be sensitive, then, to the phenomenon of empathy. (For further discussions of this topic, see Boer and Lycan 1986, chap. 7; Brandt 1976; Eisenberg and Strayer 1987; Rescher 1975; and Wispe 1991.) The precise impact that the phenomenon should have on moral theory, however, depends on specific properties of empathy, properties which can only be firmly identified and established through psychological research. Thus, moral theory stands to benefit from the work of cognitive science, on this topic as well as all the others I have discussed.

References

Ayer, A. J. (1936). *Language, truth, and logic.* London: Gollancz.

Barnett, M. (1987). Empathy and related responses in children. In N. Eisenberg and J. Strayer, eds., *Empathy and its development.* Cambridge: Cambridge University Press.

Berger, S. M. (1962). Conditioning through vicarious instigation. *Psychological Review* 69, 450–466.

Blum, L. (1980). *Friendship, altruism, and morality.* London: Routledge and Kegan Paul.

Blum, L. (1987). Particularity and responsiveness. In J. Kagan and S. Lamb, eds., *The emergence of morality in young children.* Chicago: University of Chicago Press.

Boer, S., and W. G. Lycan (1986). *Knowing who.* Cambridge, MA: MIT Press.

Brandt, R. B. (1976). The psychology of benevolence and its implications for philosophy. *Journal of Philosophy* 73, 429–453.

Brickman, P. (1975). Adaptation level determinants of satisfaction with equal and unequal outcome distributions in skill and chance situations. *Journal of Personality and Social Psychology* 32, 191–198.

Brickman, P., and D. T. Campbell (1971). Hedonic relativism and planning the good society. In M. H. Appley, ed., *Adaptation level theory.* New York: Academic Press.

Butterworth, G. E. (1991). The ontogeny and phylogeny of joint visual attention. In A. Whiten, ed., *Natural theories of mind.* Oxford: Blackwell.

Butterworth, G. E. and E. Cochran (1980). Towards a mechanism of joint visual attention in human infancy. *International Journal of Behavioral Development* 19, 253–272.

Campbell, A. (1981). *The sense of well-being in America.* New York: McGraw-Hill.

Dworkin, G. (1992). Unprincipled ethics. Unpublished manuscript, Department of Philosophy, University of Illinois at Chicago.

Easterlin, R. A. (1974). Does economic growth improve the human lot? Some empirical evidence. In P. A. David and M. W. Reder, eds., *Nations and households in economic growth*. New York: Academic Press.

Eisenberg, N., and R. Lennon (1983). Sex differences in empathy and related capacities. *Psychological Bulletin* 94, 100–131.

Eisenberg, N., and J. Strayer, eds. (1987). *Empathy and its development*. Cambridge: Cambridge University Press.

Estes, W. (1986). Array models for category learning. *Cognitive Psychology* 18, 500–549.

Finke, R. A., and R. N. Shepard (1986). Visual functions of mental imagery. In K. R. Boff, L. Kaufman, and J. P. Thomas, eds., *Handbook of perception and human performance*. New York: Wiley.

Fischhoff, B., P. Slovic, and S. Lichtenstein (1980). Knowing what you want: Measuring labile values. In T. Wallsten, ed., *Cognitive processes in choice and decision behavior*. Hillsdale, NJ: Erlbaum.

Fiske, A. P. (1991). *Structures of social life: The four elementary forms of human relations*. New York: Free Press.

Fiske, A. P. (in press). The four elementary forms of sociality. *Psychological Review*.

Flanagan, O. (1991). *Varieties of moral personality: Ethics and psychological realism*. Cambridge, MA: Harvard University Press.

Fodor, J. A., M. Garrett, E. Walker, and C. M. Parkes (1980). Against definitions. *Cognition* 8, 263–367.

Gibbard, A. (1990). *Wise choices, apt feelings*. Cambridge, MA: Harvard University Press.

Gilligan, C. (1982). *In a different voice*. Cambridge, MA: Harvard University Press.

Haan, N. (1975). Hypothetical and actual moral reasoning in a situation of civil disobedience. *Journal of Personality and Social Psychology* 32, 255–270.

Hare, R. M. (1963). *Freedom and reason*. Oxford: Clarendon Press.

Holstein, C. (1976). Development of moral judgment: A longitudinal study. *Child Development* 47, 51–61.

Hoffman, M. (1987). The contribution of empathy to justice and moral judgment. In N. Eisenberg and J. Strayer, eds., *Empathy and its development*. Cambridge: Cambridge University Press.

Hume, D. (1739/1988). *A treatise of human nature*. Ed., L. A. Selby-Bigge. Oxford: Clarendon Press.

Hume, D. (1777/1972). *Enquiry concerning the principles of morals*, 2d ed. Ed. L. A. Selby-Bigge. Oxford: Clarendon Press.

Johnson, M. (1993). *Moral imagination: Implications of cognitive science for ethics.* Chicago: University of Chicago Press.

Kitcher, P. (1985). *Vaulting ambition: Sociobiology and the quest for human nature.* Cambridge, MA: MIT Press.

Klinnert, M. (1981). Infants' use of mothers' facial expressions for regulating their own behavior. Paper presented at the meeting of the Society for Research in Child Development, Boston.

Kosslyn, S. M. (1980). *Image and mind.* Cambridge, MA: Harvard University Press.

Kosslyn, S. M. (1990). Mental imagery. In D. N. Osherson, S. M. Kosslyn, and J. M. Hollerbach, eds., *Visual cognition and action.* Cambridge, MA: MIT Press.

Krebs, D. (1975). Empathy and altruism. *Journal of Personality and Social Psychology* 32, 1134–1146.

Lennon, R., and N. Eisenberg (1987). Gender and age differences in empathy and sympathy. In N. Eisenberg, ed., *Empathy and its development.* Cambridge: Cambridge University Press.

Medin, D. L., and M. M. Schaffer (1978). A context theory of classification learning. *Psychological Review* 85, 207–238.

Meltzoff, A. N., and A. K. Moore (1977). Imitation of facial and manual gestures by human neonates. *Science* 198, 75–78.

Meltzoff, A. N., and A. K. Moore (1983). Newborn infants imitate adult facial gestures. *Child Development* 54, 702–709.

Plato (1892). *The dialogues of Plato,* vol. 1, trans. B. Jowett. New York: Random House.

Putnam, H. (1975). The meaning of 'meaning'. In K. Gunderson, ed., *Language, mind, and knowledge.* Minneapolis: University of Minnesota Press.

Rawls, J. (1971). *A theory of justice.* Cambridge, MA: Harvard University Press.

Rescher, N. (1975). *Unselfishness: The role of the vicarious affects in moral philosophy and social theory.* Pittsburgh: University of Pittsburgh Press.

Rips, L. (1989). Similarity, typicality, and categorization. In S. Voisniadou and A. Ortony, eds., *Similarity, analogy, and thought.* New York: Cambridge University Press.

Rosch, E. (1973). Natural categories. *Cognitive Psychology* 4, 328–350.

Rosch, E. (1977). Human categorization. In N. Warren, ed., *Studies in cross-cultural psychology,* vol. 1. London: Academic Press.

Scheffler, S. (1986). Morality's demands and their limits. *Journal of Philosophy* 83, 531–537.

Schopenhauer, A. (1841/1965). *On the basis of morality.* Trans. A. F. J. Payne. Indianapolis: Bobbs-Merrill.

Schwarz, N., and F. Strack (1991). Evaluating one's life: A judgment model of subjective well-being. In F. Strack, M. Argyle, and N. Schwarz, eds., *Subjective well-being.* Oxford: Pergamon.

Simner, M. L. (1971). Newborn's response to the cry of another infant. *Developmental Psychology* 5, 136–150.

Slovic, P. (1975). Choice between equally valued alternatives. *Journal of Experimental Psychology: Human Perception and Performance* 1, 280–287.

Slovic, P. (1990). Choice. In: D. N. Osherson and E. E. Smith, eds., *Thinking.* Cambridge, MA: MIT Press.

Slovic, P., D. Griffin, and A. Tversky (1990). Compatibility effects in judgment and choice. In R. M. Hogarth, ed., *Insights in decision making: Theory and applications.* Chicago: University of Chicago Press.

Smith, A. (1759/1976). *The theory of moral sentiments.* Eds., D. D. Raphael and A. L. Macfie. Oxford: Clarendon Press.

Smith, E. E. (1990). Categorization. In D. N. Osherson and E. E. Smith, eds., *Thinking.* Cambridge, MA: MIT Press.

Smith, E. E., and D. L. Medin (1981). *Categories and concepts.* Cambridge, MA: Harvard University Press.

Smith, H. (1992). Are there any moral principles? Unpublished manuscript, Department of Philosophy, University of Arizona, Tucson.

Stich, S. P. (in press). Moral philosophy and mental representation. In M. Hechter, L. Nadel, and R. E. Michod, eds., *The origin of values.* Hawthorne, NY: Aldine de Gruyter.

Stotland, E. (1969). Exploratory studies in empathy. In L. Berkowitz, ed., *Advances in experimental social psychology,* vol. 4. New York: Academic Press.

Strack, F., N. Schwarz, and Gschneidinger (1985). Happiness and reminiscing: The role of time perspective, mood, and mode of thinking. *Journal of Personality and Social Psychology* 49, 1460–1469.

Tversky, A., and D. Griffin (1991). Endowment and contrast in judgments of well-being. In F. Strack, M. Argyle, and N. Schwarz, eds., *Subjective well-being.* Oxford: Pergamon.

Van den Berghe, P. (1983). Human inbreeding avoidance: Culture in nature. *Behavioral and Brain Sciences* 6, 91–123.

Van der Burg, W. (1991). The slippery slope argument. *Ethics* 102, 42–65.

Walker, L. J. (1984). Sex differences in the development of moral reasoning: A critical review. *Child Development* 55, 677–691.

Walker, L. J. and B. DeVries (1985). Moral stages/moral orientations: Do the sexes really differ? Paper presented at the Symposium on Gender Differences in Moral Development, American Psychological Association, Los Angeles.

Walker, L. J. B. DeVries, and S. D. Trevethan (1987). Moral stages and moral orientations in real-life and hypothetical dilemmas. *Child Development* 58, 842–858.

Wispe, L. (1991). *The psychology of sympathy.* New York: Plenum.

30 The Contribution of Empathy to Justice and Moral Judgment

Martin L. Hoffman

Few psychologists or philosophers can agree as to whether any moral principles are universal. Three broadly held principles, however, are often viewed as universal:

1. the principle of justice or fairness, essentially distributive justice and written about extensively by Immanuel Kant and his followers, which states that society's resources (rewards, punishments) should be allocated according to a standard equally applicable to all;

2. the principle of impartial benevolence, associated mainly with writers in the Utilitarian tradition, especially David Hume and Adam Smith, which states a moral act is one that takes into account all people likely to be affected by it—at the face-to-face level this has become a principle of caring about the well-being of others, including their need for self-respect, dignity, and avoidance of pain; and

3. the principle of maintaining the social order, derived largely from Hobbes's view that, without society, the individual would be constantly embattled, hence nothing.

The advocates of one principle do not deny the importance of the other two, but view them as subordinate.[1]

I think of these principles not as mutually exclusive precepts, but as "ideal types," any or all of which may be relevant in a given situation. When more than one are applicable, they are usually compatible—caring and justice, for example, reinforce each other in the case of honest, hard-working farmers who lose their farms because of economic forces beyond their control. However, these principles may be incompatible in some situations, as in voting for tenure when a candidate's performance is not quite up to the expected standard. If one likes the candidate and knows that one of his/her children is chronically ill, caring may move one to vote in his/her favor. At the same time, justice, may argue for a negative vote, or one might vote negatively to affirm one's commitment to the tenure system. One might even see the relevance of all three principles and be confused about how to vote, the issue finally turning on the intensity of one's feeling for the candidate and one's commitment to caring as a principle, versus one's commitment to distributive justice and to the tenure system.

Many psychologists have been concerned with justice/fairness and caring/consideration. Notions of justice are at the heart of Kohlberg's moral theory, which has been criticized for being overly cognitive and ignoring affect. Caring has been the focus of people like me who are interested in affect, especially empathy. The notion of maintaining the social order has been virtually ignored by psychologists, and I will say nothing more about it.

I have long been working on a scheme for the development of empathy, which I define as an affective response more appropriate to someone else's situation than to one's own.[2] I have described the scheme in detail (Hoffman 1984); summarized evidence for empathy's status as a moral motive, that is, in contributing to prosocial behavior (Hoffman 1978); theorized about empathy's role in moral internalization (Hoffman 1983); traced empathy's roots in Western philosophy (Hoffman 1982a); and speculated on its biological evolutionary beginnings (Hoffman 1981). I have also investigated sex differences and the contribution of female sex-role socialization to empathy and to an empathy-based, humanistic moral orientation (Hoffman 1970, 1975b, 1977). I believe that empathy as elaborated in my developmental scheme may provide the basis for a comprehensive moral theory, although to formulate such a theory one would have to expand the scheme in several directions. This chapter is a beginning attempt at such an expansion.

First, I briefly describe the scheme to pave the way for my argument, ending with five empathy-based moral affects: empathic distress, sympathetic distress, guilt, empathic anger, and empathic injustice. I then discuss how these affects may contribute to caring and justice principles, the role they may play in moral judgment and decision making, and the problem of empathic bias and how to reduce it. Finally, I speculate about the stabilizing effect that moral principles, as "hot cognitions," may have on empathy. Although I have long suggested a link between empathy, moral principles, and judgment (Hoffman 1970, 1980, 1982b, 1984a), this is my first attempt to argue systematically for such a link.

Development of Empathic Moral Affect

The scheme for empathic distress, an empathic affective response to another person's distress, starts with a simple innocent-bystander model—in which one encounters someone in pain, danger, or deprivation—and generates five empathic affects that are mediated by social cognitive development and various causal attributions or inferences.

The scheme includes five hypothesized modes of empathic affect arousal (I.A–E in Table 30.1), which have been described in detail and documented elsewhere (Hoffman, 1984b). I make four points about them here. First, they do not form a strict sequence of stages in the sense of subsequent modes encompassing and replacing preceding modes. The first mode typically drops out after infancy, owing to controls against crying; however, adults may feel sad when they hear a cry and some adults may even feel like crying themselves, although they usually control it. The fifth mode, being deliberate, may be relatively infrequent—for example, it may be used by parents and therapists who believe they can be more effective if they experience some of their child's or patient's feelings. The intermediate three modes enter at various points in development and may continue to operate throughout life.

Second, the existence of five arousal modes suggests that empathy may be overdetermined and hence may be a reliable affective response to another's distress. Thus, if only expressive cues (facial, vocal, postural) from someone in distress are provided, mimicry is available to arouse empathic distress in observers. If only situational cues are provided, conditioning and association are available. Ordinarily, the victim is present and all modes may be brought into play, which mode is dominant depending on which cues are salient. Even if the victim is not present, information about his or her distress communicated by someone else can produce empathy in an observer (through arousal modes I.D–E in Table 30.1).

Third, empathy may be self-reinforcing. Every time we empathize with someone in distress, the resulting cooccurrence of our own distress and distress cues from the other may increase the strength of the connection between cues of another's distress and our own empathic response and thus increase the likelihood that future distress in others will be accompanied by empathic distress in ourselves.

Fourth, most arousal modes require rather shallow levels of cognitive processing (e.g., sensory registration, simple pattern matching, conditioning) and are largely involuntary. Thus it should not be surprising that empathy appears to be a universal, largely involuntary response— if one attends to the relevant cues one responds empathically—that may have had survival value in human evolution (Hoffman 1981).

Although empathy may usually be aroused by these simple involuntary mechanisms, its subjective experience is rather complex. Mature empathizers know the affect aroused in them is due to stimulus events impinging on someone else, and they have an idea of what that person is feeling. Young children who lack the self-other distinction may be empathically aroused without this knowledge. This suggests that the development of empathic distress corresponds to the development of a cognitive sense of others, the four broad stages of which are indicated

Table 30.1 Scheme for the development and transformation of empathic distress

I. Modes of empathic affect arousal; operate singly or in combinations

    (*Automatic—nonvoluntary*)
    A. Primary circular reaction; neonate cries to sound of another's cry
    B. Mimicry; automatic imitation plus afferent feedback
    C. Conditioning and direct association

        (*Higher-level cognitive*)
    D. Language-mediated association
    E. Putting self in other's place; other-focused and self-focused

II. Development of a cognitive sense of others

    A. Self-other fusion
    B. Object permanence; other is physical entity distinct from self
    C. Perspective taking; other has independent internal states
    D. Personal identity; other has experiences beyond the immediate situation, own history, and identity

III. Developmental levels of empathy (coalescence of I and II)

    A. Global empathy
    B. "Egocentric" empathy
    C. Empathy for another's feelings
    D. Empathy for another's experiences beyond the immediate situation, general condition, future prospects
        1. Empathy for an entire group

IV. Partial transformation of empathic into sympathetic distress

    Begins to occur in transition from III.A to III.B; subsequently, one's affective response to another's distress has a pure empathic component and a sympathetic component

V. Causal attribution and shaping of empathy into related moral affects

    A. If victim is cause of distress, he/she may no longer be seen as a victim, so basis for empathy is removed.
    B. *Sympathetic distress*: Victim has no control over cause of victim's distress
    C. *Guilt*: Observer is cause of victim's distress
        Guilt over inaction: Observer, though not the cause, does nothing and therefore views self as responsible for continuation of victim's distress
        Guilt by association: Observer's group is cause of victim's distress (observer's or group's relative advantage may increase guilt further)
    D. *Empathic anger*: Someone else is cause of victim's distress
        1. Empathic anger may be reduced and/or turned toward victim, depending on context (e.g., if culprit was previously harmed by victim)
        2. If culprit represents society, empathic anger may lead to social criticism and moral/political ideology
    E. *Empathic injustice*: Contrast between victim's plight and character

in II.A–D in Table 30.1 (see Hoffman 1975a, for evidence for these stages):

1. fusion, or at least a lack of clear separation between the self and the other;

2. awareness that others are physical entities distinct from the self.

3. awareness that others have feelings and other internal states independent of one's own; and

4. awareness that others have experiences beyond the immediate situation and their own history and identity as individuals.

Empathic affect is presumably experienced differently as the child progresses through these stages.

The resulting coalescence of empathic affect and social-cognitive development yields four levels of empathic distress (III.A–D in Table 30.1), which I now describe briefly (see Hoffman 1984b, for details).

1. *Global empathy.* Infants may experience empathic distress through the simplest arousal modes (I.A–C in Table 30.1) long before they acquire a sense of others as physical entities distinct from the self. For most of the first year, then, witnessing someone in distress may result in a global empathic distress response. Distress cues from the dimly perceived other are confounded with unpleasant feelings empathically aroused in the self. Consequently, infants may at times act as though what happened to the other happened to themselves. An 11-month-old girl, on seeing a child fall and cry, looked as though she was about to cry herself, then put her thumb in her mouth and buried her head in her mother's lap, as she does when she herself is hurt. (For other examples, see Hoffman 1975a; Kaplan 1977; and Zahn-Waxler et al. 1979.)

2. *"Egocentric" empathy.* With object permanence and the gradual emergence of a sense of the other as physically distinct from the self, the affective portion of the child's global empathic distress may be transferred to the separate image-of-self and image-of-other that emerge. The child may now be aware that another person and not the self is in distress, but the other's internal states remain unknown and may be assumed to be the same as one's own. An 18-month-old boy fetched his own mother to comfort a crying friend although the friend's mother was also present—a behavior that, although confused, is not entirely egocentric because it indicates that the child is responding with appropriate empathic effect.

3. *Empathy for another's feelings.* With the onset of role taking, at about 2–3 years, one becomes aware that other people's feelings may differ from one's own and are based on their own needs and interpretations of events; consequently one becomes more responsive to cues about what the other is actually feeling. Furthermore, as language is acquired, children become capable of empathizing with a wide range of increas-

ingly complex emotions. Empathizing with a victim's distress, children may also eventually become capable of empathizing with the victim's anxiety about the loss of self-esteem, hence with the desire *not* to be helped. Finally, children can be empathically aroused by information about someone's distress even in that person's absence. This leads to the fourth, most advanced level.

4. *Empathy for another's life condition.* By late childhood, owing to the emerging conception of oneself and others as continuing people with separate histories and identities, one becomes aware that others feel pleasure and pain, not only in the immediate situation but also in their larger life experience. Consequently, although one still responds empathically to another's immediate distress, one's empathic response may be intensified when one realizes that the other's distress is not transitory but chronic. Thus, one's empathically aroused affect is combined with a mental representation of another's general level of distress or deprivation. As one acquires the ability to form social concepts, one's empathic distress may also be combined with a mental representation of the plight of an entire group or class of people (e.g., the poor, oppressed, outcast, or retarded). (This empathic level can provide a motive base, especially in adolescence, for the development of certain moral and political ideologies that are centered around alleviation of the plight of unfortunate groups; see Hoffman 1980, 1989.)

When one has advanced through these four levels and encounters someone in pain, danger, or distress, one is exposed to a network of information about the other's condition. The network may include verbal and nonverbal expressive cues from the victim, situational cues, and one's knowledge about the victim's life beyond the immediate situation. These sources of information are processed differently: Empathy aroused by nonverbal and situational cues can be mediated by largely involuntary, cognitively shallow processing modes (mimicry; conditioning). Empathy aroused by verbal messages from the victim or by one's knowledge about the victim requires more complex processing, such as language-mediated association or putting oneself in the other's place.

The various cues, arousal modes, and processing levels usually contribute to the same affect, but contradictions may occur—for example, between different expressive cues, such as facial expression and tone of voice, or between expressive and situational cues. If one's knowledge of the other's life condition conflicts with the other's immediate expressive cues, the expressive cues may lose much of their force for an observer who knows they reflect only a transitory state. Imagine someone who does not know that he or she has a terminal illness laughing and having a good time. A young child might respond with empathic joy, whereas a mature observer might experience empathic sadness or a mingling of sadness and joy. Similarly, a mature observer's empathic distress (but not a child's) might decrease if the other person is known to have a generally happy life and the immediate distress is a short-lived exception. Clearly, the most advanced empathic level involves some distancing—responding partly to one's mental image of the other rather than only to the others' immediate stimulus value. (See Hoffman 1986 for a more general discussion of the interaction of sensory, perceptual, and higher-order cognitive processes in generating affect.) This fits my definition of empathy, not as an exact match of another's feelings, but as an affective response that is more appropriate to the other's situation than to one's own.

Partial Transformation of Empathic into Sympathetic Distress

The transition from global to "egocentric" empathy (IV in Table 30.1) may involve an important qualitative shift in feeling: Once children are aware that others are distinct from themselves, their own empathic distress, which is a parallel response—a more or less exact replication of the victim's presumed feeling of distress—may be transformed, at least in part, into reciprocal concern for the victim. That is, they may continue to respond in a purely empathic manner—feeling uncomfortable and highly distressed themselves—but they may also experience a feeling of compassion, or "sympathetic distress," for the victim, along with a conscious desire to help, because they feel sorry for the victim, not just to relieve their own empathic distress.

Evidence for this shift comes from observational research (Murphy 1937; Zahn-Waxler et al. 1979) and from anecdotes such as those cited earlier, which show that: (1) children progress developmentally, first responding to someone's distress by seeking comfort for the self and later trying to help the victim rather than the self; and (2) a transitional stage, in which children feel sad and comfort both the victim and the self, seems to occur at about the same time that they first become aware that others are distinct from themselves.

What developmental processes account for this shift? I suggested earlier that the unpleasant, vicarious affect that is experienced as a part of the child's initial global, undifferentiated self is transferred to the separate image-of-self and image-of-other that emerge during the self-other differentiation process. It seems likely that the wish, which is not necessarily conscious, to terminate the unpleasant affect is also similarly transferred to the emerging image-of-other and image-of-self. (See Hoffman 1984, for a more detailed discussion.) Consequently, the child's empathic response now includes two components: a wish to terminate the other's distress—the sympathetic distress component—and a more purely empathic wish to terminate distress in the self. The last three empathy development levels (III.B–D) may therefore describe the development of an affective response that has both an empathic distress and a sympathetic distress component.

A question may arise as to whether the pure empathic component is egoistic rather than prosocial. I have argued that it is both and may therefore be an important bridge between these two personality dimensions (Hoffman 1981). In any case, it functions prosocially, because the other's distress must be alleviated if one's own distress is to end; this component must therefore be distinguished from the usual, primarily self-serving egoistic motives. The sympathetic distress component is obviously prosocial.

Causal Attribution, Empathy, and Related Moral Affects

People are always making causal attributions, and there is evidence that they do this spontaneously (Weiner 1985). It therefore seems reasonable to suppose that, when one encounters someone in distress, one will often make attributions about the cause, and the particular attribution made may determine how empathic affect is experienced. Consider now some causal attributions and the resulting affects (V.A–D in Table 30.1).

Sympathetic Distress   One may respond to another's distress without making a causal attribution when the other's plight is salient, there are no causal situational cues powerful enough to draw one's attention from the other's plight, and one has no prior information about the cause. These conditions often exist when young children witness someone in distress, and were therefore assumed in my discussion of early developmental levels of empathy and its transformation into sympathetic distress. One may also feel sympathetic distress when there are cues or one has information indicating that victims have no control over their plight, as in serious illness or accidental injury. Sympathetic distress in mature observers may also be part of a complex ambivalent response, as when one condemns a man in the electric chair for his crimes while sympathizing with him because of information indicating that early experiences over which he had no control played an important role in his life.

Empathic Anger   If the cues indicate that someone else caused the victim's plight, one's attention may to some extent be diverted from the victims to the culprit. One may feel anger at the culprit, partly because one sympathizes with the victim and partly because one empathizes with the victim and feels oneself vicariously attacked.[3] One's feelings may also alternate between empathic and sympathetic distress and empathic anger; or empathic anger may crowd out one's empathic and sympathetic distress entirely. Note that John Stuart Mill (1979) suggested that empathic anger, which he described as "the natural feeling of retaliation . . . rendered by intellect and sympathy applicable to . . . those hurts which wound us through wounding others [serves as the] guardian of justice." A simple example of empathic anger is that of the

17-month-old boy in the doctor's office who, on seeing another child receive an injection, responds by hitting the doctor in anger.[4]

Empathic anger may also occur in complex contexts in which it is shifted from one target to another, along with the accompanying empathic and sympathetic distress. For example, if one discovers the victim did harm to the culprit on an earlier occasion, one's empathy for the victim may decrease, and one may begin to feel empathic and sympathetic distress for the culprit because of the hurt that led to the culprit's aggression in the first place; one may even empathize with the culprit's anger. Alternatively, one might discover that the victim has a history of being mistreated in his or her relationship with the culprit. In this case, one may assume the victim had a choice (why else would he or she continue the relationship?) and is therefore responsible for his or her own plight and thus is not a victim. One's empathic and sympathetic distress for the victim and empathic anger at the culprit may then decrease sharply. The empathic anger of young children is apt to miss these nuances, and if children's perceptions are confined to the immediate situation, they may respond in all these situations with simple empathic anger directed at the visible culprit.

A particularly relevant case here is one in which the observer blames the victim's plight—say, extreme poverty—on someone who is absent, especially when that someone represents the larger society or a powerful group within it. For example, one may see the victim's basic material needs as not being met because of society's neglect or the lack of an adequate "safety net." One may then feel empathic and sympathetic distress for the victim and empathic anger toward the powerful group or society as a whole.

Guilt Feeling   The observer thus far in our analysis is an innocent bystander. If one is not innocent but the cause of the other's distress, the conditions may be ripe for feeling guilty,[5] that is, for a combination of empathic and sympathetic distress and a self-blame attribution. I have suggested that this combination may originate in discipline encounters in which parents point up the harmful consequences of the child's actions for others (Hoffman 1983). Blaming oneself for another's distress may often result in empathic anger that is directed toward the self and thus may intensify the guilt feeling. Even if one is an innocent bystander but for some reason does not help, one may feel guilty because one blames oneself, not for *causing* the other's plight, but for contributing to its continuation by not intervening to help—the guilt is over inaction.

When one reaches the most advanced level of empathy development, one can not only categorize victims into groups but can also categorize oneself as a member of a group. One may then have a feeling of guilt by association if one's group is seen as causing the victim's distress or benefiting from the same social system that disadvantages the victim. And, finally, I have suggested elsewhere (Hoffman 1980) that one may feel guilty if one simply sees oneself as being in a relatively advantaged position vis-à-vis the victim. I call this "existential guilt" because one has done nothing wrong but feels culpable owing to life circumstances beyond one's control.

Empathic Injustice   Other information beside that pertaining to the cause of the victim's distress may shape one's empathic response. I just mentioned that the contrast between the victim's plight and one's own good fortune may produce guilt feelings. Other contrasts are possible, such as that between the victim's plight and other people's good fortune. If one observes highly disadvantaged people in a context in which the extravagant life-style of others is salient, one may feel empathic injustice. Perhaps more important for our present purposes is the contrast between the victim's plight and his or her own general conduct or character. Thus if the victim is viewed as bad, immoral, or lazy one may conclude that his or her fate was deserved, and one's empathic and sympathetic distress might decrease. If the victim is viewed as basically good, however, or at least not bad, immoral, or lazy, one might view his or her fate as undeserved or unfair. One's empathic distress (or sympathetic distress, guilt, or empathic anger—whichever is appropriate) might then be expected to increase. Furthermore, the empathic affect may be transformed in part into a feeling that has elements in common with guilt and empathic anger but appears subtly different enough to be given a new name: empathic injustice.

An example of empathic injustice is found in the case of the 14-year-old Southern male "redneck" described by Coles (1986). After several weeks of joining his friends in harassing black children trying to integrate his school, this boy, a popular athlete,

began to see a kid, not a nigger—a guy who knew how to smile when it was rough going, and who walked straight and tall, and was polite. I told my parents, "It's a real shame that someone like him has to pay for the trouble caused by all those federal judges."

Then it happened. I saw a few people cuss at him. "The dirty nigger," they kept on calling him and soon they were pushing him in a corner, and it looked like trouble, bad trouble. I went over and broke it up. . . . They all looked at me as if I was crazy. . . . Before [everyone] left I spoke to the nigger . . . I didn't mean to. . . . It just came out of my mouth. I was surprised to hear the words myself: "I'm sorry." (pp. 27–28)

After this incident, he began talking to the black youth, championing him personally, while still decrying integration. Finally, he became the black youth's friend and began advocating "an end to the whole lousy business of segregation." When pressed by Coles to explain his shift, he attributed it to being in school that year and seeing "that kid behave himself, no matter what we called him, and seeing him insulted so bad, so real bad. Something in me just drew the line, and something in me began to change, I think" (pp. 28).

The boy clearly seemed to experience sympathetic distress, empathic anger, and guilt. But what really seemed to move him was the contrast between the black youth's admirable conduct and the way he was being treated—it was as if the boy felt that this was a fine person who deserved better. Empathic injustice may be important because it seems closer than other empathic affects to bridging the gap between simple empathic distress and moral principle.

Complex Combinations   Here is an example of the complex combination of empathic affects possible in moral encounters: A shabbily dressed man is observed robbing an obviously affluent person on the street. A young child might feel empathic and sympathetic distress for the victim and anger at the immediate, visible culprit. Mature observers might have these same feelings, but a variety of other empathic affects as well. They might feel guilty over not helping the victim. If they are ideologically liberal, they might empathize and sympathize not only with the victim but also with the culprit because of his poverty. The observers might view the culprit as a victim of society and feel empathic anger toward society. Furthermore, if the observers are affluent as well as liberal, they might feel guilty over being relatively advantaged persons who benefit from the same society. Ideologically conservative observers might not sympathize with the culprit but might respond with unalloyed empathic anger instead. They might also feel empathic anger toward society, but in this case because they view the victim, not the culprit, as a victim of society (because of inadequate law enforcement and citizen protection).

To summarize, the empathic reaction to someone's distress produces two basic affects: empathic distress and sympathetic distress. In addition—depending on various causal and other attributions—empathic anger, several types of guilt, and a feeling of empathic injustice may be generated. There is considerable research evidence that empathic and sympathetic distress (the research does not separate them) and guilt feelings function as motives for moral action (Hoffman 1978, 1982b). Empathic anger has not yet been researched, but it seems reasonable to suppose that such anger includes a disposition to intervene and protect the victim in some way (although egoistic motives like fear may result in inaction). Also, since anger has long been known to "mobilize one's energy and make one capable of defending oneself with great vigor and strength" (Izard 1977, 333), it seems reasonable to expect empathic anger to be an energizer of moral action, as suggested in this quotation from a letter to the *New York Times:*

The picture of starving children in Ethiopia are heartwrenching but feeling sad isn't enough . . . we send a check, the pictures disappear from TV screens, and soon we forget that millions are dying. . . . Instead we should feel outraged that in a world of plenty hunger still exists. Outrage produces action . . . etc. (February, 1985)

Research is needed to see if the letter writer is correct, not only in stating that empathic anger leads to action but that empathic anger is more likely to lead to action than is sympathetic distress.

Thus far, I have presented a scheme for empathy and empathy-related moral affects that may be aroused when the instigating stimulus is someone in pain or an otherwise distressing situation. If this scheme is to provide the basis for a comprehensive moral theory, these empathic affects, though generated by a bystander model, must be arousable in other types of moral encounters as well. Furthermore, these empathic affects must be congruent with the major moral principles. That is, the feelings, thoughts, and action tendencies associated with the affects must fit in with a principle's meaning and intent. Under these conditions, it would be reasonable to suppose that in the course of a person's development empathic affects will become meaningfully associated with moral principles, so that when empathic affect is aroused in a moral encounter this will activate the moral principles. The principles, along with the empathic affect, might then help guide the individual's moral judgment, decision making, and action. In some instances, the sequence might be reversed—the principle might be activated first and then its associated empathic affect elicited. The remainder of this chapter is concerned with these issues.

Empathic Arousal in Moral Encounters

Empathic affects may be aroused not only in bystander situations but also in most other types of moral encounters. The reasons are as follows:

1. Human beings have the capacity for representation, and represented events can evoke affect, as shown in the voluminous mood-induction research in which all manner of affects are generated by imagining oneself in a relevant situation that one experienced in the past or simply made up (e.g., Harris and Siebel 1975).

2. Human beings are capable of transposing stimuli and of imagining that stimuli impinging on someone else are impinging on oneself, and transposed stimuli can evoke empathic affect (Stotland, 1969).

3. The semantic meanings of events can become conditioned stimuli for autonomic arousal and therefore, presumably, for affect (Razran 1971; Zanna et al. 1970).

Thus, empathic affects should be arousable through the mediation of language and role taking (I.D–E in Table 30.1). The victim need not be present; one need only be informed about the victim.

Consequently, the bystander model can be intended to include instances in which one hears about victims second- or third-hand—from parents, teachers, newspapers, or television. The model's essential features may also obtain when one is talking, arguing, or merely thinking about contemporary moral issue such as racial segregation, abortion, whether doctors should tell people how seriously ill they are, whether doctors should terminate life-support systems for brain-dead people, or how society should distribute its resources. If, in the course of these activities, relevant victims come to mind or are pointed up by others, one is then in the bystander's position of observing or imagining someone in distress. These situations are often more complex than the simple bystander model. At times they include competing principles and conflicting motives as well as pragmatic concerns, and the complexity may limit the vividness and salience of the imagined event, hence the intensity of empathic affects aroused. Nonetheless, these affects may still influence the moral judgments made in the situation.

Potential victims may also come to mind or be suggested by others when one is not in the bystander position but is contemplating an action that may directly or indirectly affect the welfare of others, with or without one's knowledge. One may be thinking of ways to resolve a conflict, break bad news to someone, go back on a promise, or simply satisfy some material need that at first may seem to have no bearing on the concerns of others. Or, one may be engaged in a task that clearly and explicitly requires making a moral judgment and decision. Consider the task of writing a recommendation for tenure. The instigating stimulus for engaging in the task is not the distress of someone, but a request from a colleague in another university. One might simply write a letter indicating, as objectively as possible, one's judgment of the candidate's competence. On the other hand, one might think about the candidate, imagining how he or she would feel and what would happen if tenure were denied, or one might imagine how one would feel if one were in the candidate's place. The empathic and sympathetic distress (or, more strictly, the anticipatory empathic and sympathetic distress) that one might feel as a result of this role taking might then influence the tone and content of the letter.

Writing tenure letters is one of many moral encounters that may be readily transformed into situations involving victims or potential victims. Indeed, it is difficult to imagine moral encounters in everyday life that do *not* involve potential victims and therefore are not likely to be so transformed. The likelihood that one's actions will affect someone's welfare is another important reason—along with the human tendency to react empathically to victims, whether physically present or imagined—for expecting empathy to play a significant role in a comprehensive moral theory. I now discuss a third reason: the congruence between empathy and the principles of caring and of justice.

Congruence between Empathy and Moral Principles

Moral principles are often presented as abstractions. When they are concretized in actual life events, however, the victims and potential victims often stand out, and empathic affects become relevant.

Empathy and Caring

The link between empathic affects, especially sympathetic distress, and the caring principle appears rather direct and obvious: The empathic affects and caring operate in the same direction—that is, toward considering the welfare of others. This link appears to be reflected in the empathic moral reasoning that often accompanies people's behavior when they encounter someone in distress. Consider this example from the book *Uncle Tom's Cabin*, reported by Kaplan (1989), in which an affluent, politically uninvolved housewife whose empathy for slaves she knew, who "have been abused and oppressed all their lives," leads her to oppose a newly passed law against giving food, clothes, or shelter to escaping slaves. Arguing with her husband, who supports the law on pragmatic and legal grounds, she verbalizes what amounts to a general principle of caring—"the Bible says we should feed the hungry, clothe the naked, and comfort the desolate," adding that "people don't run away when they're happy, but out of suffering." She becomes so intensely opposed to that "shameful, wicked, abominable" law that she vows to break it at the earliest opportunity.

This episode is reminiscent of Huckleberry Finn's moral conflict between his empathic feeling for Miss Watson's slave Jim, whom he helped escape, and both Missouri law and church teaching at the time, which strongly opposed helping slaves escape. In a famous passage, Huck first writes a letter exposing Jim's hiding place, but then, after a great deal of agonizing soul-searching in which his moral thinking is driven by conflicting moral feelings—sympathetic distress and guilt over the consequences for Jim if he is exposed, and the feeling of how awful a "sin" it would be to keep Jim's whereabouts a secret—he tears the letter up and says to himself, "All right then, I'll *go* to hell." As powerful as that passage is, the episode from *Uncle Tom's Cabin* goes beyond it for our purposes because it indicates that empathy may lead to a response that transcends the immediate, individual victim. More specifically, the episode suggests that the combination of empathic and sympathetic distress and empathic anger in a particular situation may provide the motive for affirming a general caring principle, which may then serve as a premise for the moral judgment that laws violating it are morally wrong.

Empathy and Distributive Justice

Although the link between empathy and justice is less obvious and less direct than that between empathy and caring, it does exist, as I hope to show in this section. To begin, there are at least three distinct, and seemingly mutually exclusive, principles of distributive justice:

1. *Need*—Society's resources should be allocated according to what people need: Those who need more should receive more; those who need less should receive less.

2. *Equality*—Each person has the same intrinsic worth, in some larger religious or philosophical sense (e.g., in the sense of Bentham's principle, "Everyone to count for one and nobody for more than one"), and therefore society's resources should be divided equally.

3. *Equity*—People should be rewarded according to how much they produce (their output) or according to how much effort they expend.

It seems obvious that choosing one of these abstract principles of justice becomes transformed into an empathy-relevant task as soon as one imagines the consequences of various distribution systems for certain people. If one imagines the consequences and empathizes with poor people, one may conclude that any truly moral distribution system must guarantee everyone at least a minimal level of well-being and may end up affirming the principle of need or of equality. In other words, need and equality appear to have a caring component that may be activated when one empathizes with people whose welfare may be adversely affected by a distribution system, thus transforming the distributive justice issue, in part, into a caring issue.

Alternatively, one might empathize with the needs and expectations of people who work hard and save for their families, and as a result one might affirm the principle of distributing resources according to *effort*. Consider this response of a 13-year-old male research subject to the question, "Why is it wrong to steal from a store?" "Because the people who own the store work hard for their money and they deserve to be able to spend it for their family. It's not fair; they sacrifice a lot and they make plans and then they lost it all because somebody who didn't work for it goes in and takes it." In this response, the subject has transformed an abstract moral question into an empathy-relevant one by imagining a particular victim. The response has a clear empathic-identification component: One empathizes with the other's effort, sacrifice, plans, and expectations about enjoying the fruits of his or her labor and with the other's disappointment and loss. There also appears to be an empathic-anger component, as well as a feeling of empathic injustice. The response thus suggests that effort, like need and equality, has a caring component, which in this case may be activated when one empathizes with people who work hard. Empathic affect may thus contribute to one's receptivity to the principle of equity based on effort.

The size of the contribution depends on the extent of one's tendency to empathize with hard-working people rather than to derogate or compete with them or to empathize with the poor instead. Only research can provide the answer.

The principle of equity based on *output* is a different matter. Distributing resources on the basis of output seems to imply that the individual's welfare and internal state are irrelevant considerations. This would seem to rule out a direct link between empathy and output. There are at least two possible indirect links, however:

1. If output is assumed to reflect effort, as it often is, then my argument about the contribution of empathy to effort may also apply to output.

2. If distribution systems based on output motivate people to produce more, as many people believe, then there is more to go around and everyone benefits, including the poor (this reflects the trickle-down idea).[6]

It may thus be possible for empathic identification with the poor to lead one to affirm equity of output as a moral principle, but the route is circuitous and it seems far more likely that empathic identification with the poor will incline one toward the need or equality principles. A recent study of adults by Montada, Schmitt, and Dalbert (1986) supports this expectation. They found a positive correlation between a questionnaire measure of empathy and a preference for need, and a negative correlation between empathy and equity based on output. I found the same thing in an unpublished study of college students. When the subjects were asked to explain their choices, the high-empathy subjects tended to give explanations that included a concern for those who might be disadvantaged under other systems.

Need, equality, and equity are not mutually exclusive and may occur in different combinations. One principle may be dominant, the others playing a constraining role, as exemplified by the moral philosopher Rashdall (1907), who insisted that "equality is the right rule for distributive justice in the absence of any special reason for inequality" (p. 225); among the "special reasons" are need, output, and effort. Alternatively, a distribution system may be based on equity of output but may be regulated so that no one suffers if low output is due to forces beyond one's control (effort); no one, regardless of output, is excessively deprived (need); and vast discrepancies in wealth are not permitted (equality).

As an example of complexity, consider the first two drafts of the "Bishops Pastoral Letter on Catholic Social Teaching and the U.S. Economy" (1984, 1985). The analysis of the American economy in these documents appears to have been transformed into a situation relevant to empathic distress by imagining the economy's consequences for poor people. Thus the documents proclaim the Church's "tradition of compassion for the poor." Included are numerous statements describing in eloquent detail and empathic tone the plight of the poor—their "home-lessness," "feelings of despair," "vulnerability," "the daily assaults on their dignity." The statement concludes that "gross inequalities are morally unjustifiable, particularly when millions lack even the basic necessities of life," and it characterizes present levels of unemployment and poverty as "morally unacceptable." In other words, the bishops' statement is an argument that starts with the expression of empathy and the compassion for the suffering poor. It attributes that suffering to the country's system of distributing resources. It then affirms need as a principle of justice and argues that the system is morally wrong because it is insensitive to so many people's needs. However, the statement also notes that absolute equality in distribution of resources, or distribution strictly according to need, is not necessary. In the end, it supports the principle of equity, pleads that equity be tempered with need and equality. The statement thus illustrates an important point: Empathy is more likely to operate in combination with other factors (economic, political, pragmatic) in deriving the complex moral principles pertaining to distributive justice in modern society.

To summarize, in contemplating how society's resources should be distributed, one might focus on the implications for oneself and on the implications for others. For highly egoistic people, their own welfare is paramount and they are apt to be most receptive to distributive justice principles that coincide with their own condition: equity based on output if one is a higher producer, need or equality if one produces little. For empathic people, the welfare of others may be important and they may opt for need or equality even if they are high producers. Or, as seems more likely, a person's egoistic and empathic proclivities may both operate, the result being a distributive-justice orientation that combines the two—output tempered by need and equality, for example.

I have used the term *link* and suggested that empathic people opt for certain principles, but what exactly is the nature of the relation between empathy and moral principles and when and how does it become established? I comment only briefly on these matters. First, it seems obvious that, developmentally, empathic affects become part of most people's affective and motivational structures long before moral principles are seriously considered. At some point in late childhood or adolescence the individual is exposed to various moral principles, usually in a loose, scattered fashion. The "cafeteria" model seems appropriate here: The more empathic one is, the more receptive one should be to caring, need, equality, and perhaps effort.

Apart from this *developmental receptivity* to moral principles there is also the *activation* of moral principles already in one's repertoire. I have suggested that empathic affect arousal may activate related moral principles. It also seems likely that because of the congruence between empathy and principle discussed earlier, the two may be elicited independently. Either way, the resulting co-occurrence of empathy and principle may be expected to strengthen the bond between them, increasing the likelihood that both will be operative and will affect moral judgment in future situations. The influence of principles on moral judgment has been taken for granted (e.g., Kohlberg 1969). Consider now the impact of empathic affects.

Empathy and Moral Judgment

Empathy's potential contribution to moral judgment is more complex than its contribution to principles, because here the relationship is mediated by complex reasoning in particular moral encounters. This reasoning is presumably based on moral principles, and it would simplify matters if there were a universal moral principle from which to derive the logically correct moral judgment for each situation. But, as I noted earlier, there are no universally accepted moral principles. We must therefore ask not only how people derive judgments from principles, but what determines which principle, if any, one chooses in the first place, that is, which principle is activated in a situation; and, when two principles are in conflict, what determines which one wins out. My thesis is that empathy plays a key role in all these situations.

David Hume (1957) suggested more than 200 years ago that moral judgment ultimately depends on empathy. That is, moral judgment is based on feelings of satisfaction, pain, uneasiness, or disgust that result from the observer's empathy with the feelings of the person whose action is being appraised and with the feelings of those who are affected by this action. Hume's argument is as follows: First, it is obvious that we all applaud acts that further our own well-being and condemn acts that may harm us. Therefore, if we empathize with others we should applaud or condemn acts that help or harm others; and, unless we are abnormally callous, we will feel indignant (empathic anger) when someone willfully inflicts suffering on others. Empathy may thus guide the moral judgments we make about others. Furthermore, since people may be presumed to respond empathically to similar events in similar ways, empathy may thus provide the common informational input that impartial observers need to reach a consensus on moral judgments. Finally, Hume points out, we talk to one another about these events and respond empathically to each other's descriptions of the relevant acts and their consequences; these empathic responses provide further help in our efforts to reach a consensus. Although Hume does not discuss justice, my notion of empathic injustice can be used to apply Hume's argument to justice: We obviously feel indignant when we do not receive what we deserve because of our efforts or our output; it follows that, if we empathize with others, we should feel indignant when someone else does not receive what he or she deserves because of their effort or output.

Hume's view that empathy provides a reliable basis for consensus in moral judgment has been criticized by Rawls (1971), who argues that empathy lacks the situational sensitivity necessary for achieving a rational consensus. My own empathy scheme, summarized earlier, may solve this problem in part by assuming that at the most advanced empathic level one processes a network of cues that includes a knowledge of the other's life condition beyond the immediate situation. Mature empathy thus reflects a sensitivity to subtle differences in the severity and quality of the consequences that different actions might have for different people. It thus seems clear that empathy can contribute to informed moral judgments. Hume's claim that empathy provides the ultimate basis for reaching *consensus* on moral judgments is another matter, one that requires empirical testing.

Empathy's contribution to moral judgment can be illustrated by anecdotes and hypothetical illustrations. The examples I cited earlier are cases in point. The woman in *Uncle Tom's Cabin* not only affirmed a general caring principle but also used it as the basis for making the moral judgment that a law that violates this principle is morally wrong. The Bishops' Pastoral Letter not only affirmed a justice principle that incorporated need and appears to have been a direct outcome of empathic reasoning based on identification with the poor, but it also used that principle as the basis for the moral judgment that the country's allocation system is morally wrong because it creates many victims. Furthermore, the white Southern schoolboy incident not only illustrates empathic injustice, but also shows how empathic identification with a particular victim can, over time, foster a change in attitude toward a previously accepted social institution—racial segregation—with the result that one now judges that the institution is wrong.

In the research on moral judgment and decision making, subjects are typically asked how someone facing a particular moral dilemma should act and why such action would be better or worse than other actions. Or they may be asked to identify the moral issue in the dilemma. The situation is different in real life. To be sure, some occupations may require people to make judgments of others and decide whether they should receive certain punishments or rewards (such as a promotion or pay increase). For the most part, however, people's moral encounters do not begin with such a cognitive task. More likely, one's moral precepts are apt to be activated when one encounters someone in danger or distress and feels a conflict between the desire to help that individual and the desire to continue to pursue one's own goals of the moment; when one feels outraged by someone's inhumane or unjust treatment of another; when one discovers that one's actions have harmed another or that one's contemplated action may harm someone; when one realizes that one's contemplated action on behalf of someone may operate to the detriment of someone else; when one is tempted, or under external pressure, to act in a way that violates another's reasonable expectations (e.g., by breaking a promise, violating a trust, telling a lie).[7] Culture plays a role in all this, as does history. Deciding whether to have an abortion has recently become a moral dilemma (in which personal needs are placed against the violent consequences to the fetus) for some people who in the past might have considered it a moral dilemma (in which personal needs are placed against the physical danger to oneself). Advances in medical technology have added an element of moral complexity to the medical practitioner's former, relatively simple goal of prolonging life: Organ transplants save lives, but cost-benefit analysis may show that more lives could be saved if the money were spent differently.

There are many variations on these themes. What impresses me is that most moral dilemmas seem to involve victims or potential victims (and beneficiaries) of one's own actions. This means that in the course of thinking about what to do in these situations one may often be confronted with the image, or idea, of someone being helped or harmed by one's own action. This appears to be true even when one is not the actor but is compelled to judge or evaluate the action of others. It follows that empathy may often be aroused in moral judgment and decision making in life; and the empathy aroused, if my previous argument for a link between empathy and moral principles is correct, may not only have a direct effect on moral judgment and reasoning, but may also serve to activate one's moral principles and bring them to bear in the moral reasoning process, more or less along the lines indicated in the examples cited throughout this chapter.

In sum, I am arguing that most moral dilemmas in life may arouse empathy because they involve victims—seen or unseen, present or future. Since empathy is closely related to most moral principles, the arousal of empathy should activate moral principles, and thus—directly, and indirectly through these principles—have an effect on moral judgment and reasoning. This may also be true of moral reasoning in abstract situations, such as Kohlberg's moral dilemmas, provided the person making the judgment empathically identifies with relevant characters in them. Here are some examples of subjects' responses to moral questions that seem to reflect empathic identification operating in the service of moral judgment (Hoffman 1970). The moral dilemma is an adaptation of Kohlberg's story about two men—Al, who broke into a store and stole $500, and Joe, who lied to a known benefactor about needing $500 for an operation. The subjects were asked who did worse, and why. Most answers, as expected, pertained to the need for law and order, the Ten Commandments, and the possibilities of getting caught. Although the item did not highlight a victim, one quarter of the subjects, who ranged from 11 years to middle age, seemed to transform it into one involving empathic identification with a victim—either an immediate victim of one of the men's actions or potential future victims.

For example, Joe's action was said to be worse because he made the benefactor feel betrayed by someone he trusted, because he made the benefactor lose faith in people and become bitter, because he misused the benefactor's faith and pity, or because people who really needed help would no longer be able to get it. Al's action was said to be worse because the storeowner worked hard for the money, saved for his family, and needed the money—this is the kind of response I described in discussing equity of effort. Note that these empathic-identification responses more than doubled in frequency when the focus of the question changed from the actor ("Who did worse?") to the observer ("Which would make you feel worse, if you did it?"). The empathic-identification responses in which Joe's act was deemed worse might appear to reflect a simple liking for the kind benefactor—a personal bias or halo effect rather than a moral judgment—but this is not the case. When asked "what kind of person" the benefactor was, the subjects who gave these empathic-identification responses were as likely as the other subjects to criticize him for being foolish or naive. In other words, they empathized with him and felt it was wrong to deceive him, although they were critical of him. These responses are more convincing as *moral* judgments because they transcend personal feeling for the person harmed.

Empathic Bias and How to Reduce It

The case for empathy thus far looks rather strong. There are problems, however, that might appear to limit empathy's contribution to all but the simplest of situations. One is that empathy may be biased in several ways. First, there is research evidence that observers are more empathic to victims who are familiar and similar to themselves than to victims who are different, although, I hasten to add, they are usually empathic to victims who are different—just less so (Feshbach and Roe 1968; Klein 1971; Krebs 1970). Second, it seems that people are more apt to be empathically aroused by someone's distress in the immediate situation than by distress that they know is being experienced by someone somewhere else or that is likely to be experienced in the future. There is no empirical evidence for such a here-and-now bias, but it seems likely in view of the fact that several of the arousal processes noted in Table 30.1, especially the involuntary processes (conditioning, association, mimicry) are dependent on immediate situational and personal cues. These cues are absent when someone's distress occurs somewhere else or when it is likely to occur in the future.

These biases constitute a flaw in empathic morality and raise questions about its applicability in situations involving conflicting moral claims, that is, situations in which one must make a moral judgment and decision and the welfare of several people or groups depends on one's action, but only some of these people are familiar or present in the immediate situation. First, is it a fatal flaw? The answer depends on two things: whether there is an alternative morality that is bias-free, and whether the bias in empathic morality can be eliminated or minimized. Regarding the first point, the most likely alternative is cognitive morality in the Kohlberg tradition, which states that one can solve moral dilemmas by applying the universal principle of justice to the particular situation and by reasoning out the solution. There are problems with this formulation. As I noted, it is unlikely that justice can be considered universal; in any case, there are several other principles beside justice, and justice itself has several variants. The question that follows is what determines which of these principles is chosen, or activated, in a particular moral dilemma? One's socialization into a particular culture or subgroup would seem to be a reasonable answer, as would one's needs and predilections of the moment, contextual cues, and perhaps the empathic affect that may be aroused along the lines I suggested. The principle chosen may also serve as a rationalization, not necessarily conscious, for one's own interests, as long suggested by philosophers in the tradition of emotive theory (Ayer 1936; Brandt 1979; Edwards 1955).

Aside from these biases in choosing a moral principle, decades of research on ethnic and racial prejudice suggest that one's principles may be applied differentially to members of one's own group and members of other groups. Within one's group, one's moral principles are likely to be applied differentially to people who are present or absent, as I suggested may also be true of empathy. Moreover, the reasoning process, too, is open to question. There is considerable evidence that reasoning based on factual knowledge about the physical world is often unreliable, partly because of the human tendency to employ "availability" and other error-producing heuristics (Tversky Kahneman 1973). Surely the same must be true of reasoning in the moral domain. Thus, although this notion may seem counterintuitive, there are no a priori grounds for assuming that cognitive morality is any freer of bias than empathic morality. Whether it is freer of bias is an empirical question that awaits research.

The second question about the applicability of empathic morality is whether empathic bias can be reduced to a manageable level. The answer here is more complex. First, a correction for bias toward the here and now is built into my empathy scheme, as I illustrated earlier with the terminally ill person who is happy in the immediate situation. However, in order to be able to empathize with the victim's plight beyond the immediate situation, the observer requires information about the victim's condition in other situations, and this information must enter the observer's consciousness at the appropriate time. If the observer lacks the necessary information, it must be given to him or her; if the observer has it stored in memory, something in the situation must prime it so that it will be recalled. Furthermore, the observer must be sufficiently advanced developmentally to be able to process the information and realize that it may be a more compelling index of the victim's welfare than the victim's contradictory current behavior.

This brings us to the question of the role of moral education in reducing empathic bias, which I can only comment on briefly here. One thing moral education can do is teach people a simple rule of thumb: Look beyond the immediate situation and ask questions such as "What kind of experiences does the other person have in various situations beyond the immediate one?" "How will my action affect him or her, not only now but in the future?" and "Are there other people, present or absent, who might be affected by my actions?" If children learn to ask these questions, they should be able to enhance their awareness of all those who may be affected by their actions, whether present or not. In addition, to compensate for the here-and-now bias in intensity of empathic affect, children might be encouraged to imagine how they would feel in the place of those others. And, finally, a positive value might be placed on spatial and temporal impartiality, and children might be encouraged, insofar as possible, to give equal consideration to all of those who may be affected by their actions. Children cannot be expected to engage in this laborious process all the time (nor can adults), but with such moral education their empathic responses should at least be less exclusively confined to the here and now and should more closely approach the ideal of spatial and temporal neutrality.

As for the familiarity-similarity bias, Hume (1957) declared that it was perfectly natural for people to empathize more with their kin than with strangers and that doing this was not necessarily incompatible with being moral. He also said that efforts must be made to minimize this bias and suggested that society can be organized so as to minimize it: People, each having a particular bias and knowing about their own and the other's bias, can devise systems of social rules that minimize bias and encourage impartiality. To this I would add a moral education curriculum that stresses the common humanity of all people and includes efforts to raise people's levels of empathy for outgroup members. Such efforts might include direct face-to-face cultural contact and training in role-taking procedures that are vivid enough to generate empathic feeling for people in circumstances that are different from their own. The combination of rule systems and empathy-enhancing moral education should expand the range of people to whom individuals can respond empathically, thus reducing familiarity-similarity bias.

How empathic bias may be reduced in life can be illustrated in the task of writing a letter of recommendation for a former student. When composing such a letter, we may empathize with the student, to whom we feel close. Thus when negative things about the student come to mind, we may experience a moral conflict in trying to decide whether to include this negative information and hurt his chances or withhold it and violate both our standards of honesty and our commitment to the collegial system of evaluating job applications. Our empathy for the student may lead us to withhold the information and tolerate the resulting guilt feeling. Or, we may also empathize with our peer colleagues, who need the information and are counting on us to be objective and tell the truth. Obviously the moral conflict would be more complex if in addition one had to consider whether one might be betraying the trust of these unseen colleagues.[8] We may even go one step further and empathize with people whom we do not know at all and who will probably never see our letter but whose welfare may nevertheless be affected by it, namely, the other applicants for the job. This situation would further complicate the moral conflict. Regardless of our final decision, the multiple empathizing, which clearly contributes to the moral conflict, may also reduce the potency of our initial empathic bias in favor of the particular student.

Here is an even more complex example adapted from an illustration used by Noddings (1984). In considering whether to sponsor a favorite graduate student's research proposal that requires deception, a professor might empathize with the student's pride in a well-written proposal, the student's fear that months of work will be wasted if the professor rejects the proposal, and the student's eagerness to get on with the job. This empathy for the student may be strong enough to motivate the professor to sponsor the proposal. So far, there appears to be no moral conflict. But the situation may be transformed into a moral conflict if the professor's belief that deception is wrong is activated. Deception may be too abstract a concept to elicit enough affect to compete with the professor's empathy for the student. But if the professor is aware of this fact and also of his or her empathic bias, he or she may try to compensate for the bias and penetrate the abstractness by thinking about subjects being harmed by the research—by imagining how a hypothetical subject, perhaps a person he or she cares about very much, might respond to the experimental manipulation. If the danger perceived is great enough, the professor's anticipatory empathic distress may be so intense that despite his or her empathy for the graduate student (and the fact that the proposal is otherwise satisfactory), the professor might refuse to sponsor the student's research. The professor's empathic revulsion might even be so great as to compel him or her to propose guidelines for the control of all research requiring deception. This example illustrates how the combination of biases—for the familiar and the here and now, all favoring the student—may be overcome by a more or less deliberate effort to empathize with exemplars of other people whose welfare may be affected by one's action.

As in the letter-of-recommendation example, the professor might go a step further and empathize with people who are unseen and perhaps unknown but whose welfare may be indirectly at stake—namely, other researchers whose careers might be jeopardized by excessive constraints on research or other people who may ultimately benefit from the research. As a result of this multiple empathizing, the professor might refuse to sponsor the student's research but might refrain from making rules that will bind other investigators. The outcome may be entirely different, of course, but whatever it is, the process illustrates, first, how one's initial empathic response may be biased toward familiar individuals and toward the here and now, and second, how the effects of that bias may be counteracted by empathizing with people who are not present but whose welfare may nevertheless be affected by one's actions.

This all sounds like traditional utilitarian moral reasoning: Consider the future as well as immediate consequences of one's action for people who are absent as well as present. But we should not lose sight of the role of empathy in providing both substantive input and motivation at various points in the reasoning process. In any case, it seems reasonable to conclude that although empathic morality may be flawed because of certain biases, it may be no more flawed than the most apparent alternative, cognitive morality in the Kohlberg tradition. Furthermore, empathic bias appears to be controllable, although to control it one may have to add a cognitive perspective that attempts to give equal weight to all people whose welfare may be affected by one's actions. With this perspective, empathy may not only contribute to moral principles but may also play a constructive role in complex moral judgments and decision making.

Moral Principles as "Hot Cognitions"

I have suggested that empathy contributes to caring and most principles of justice through empathic identification with victims and potential victims of society and its institutions. What are the circumstances in which this process occurs? One possibility is that it occurs in the normal course of development in children who have been socialized to be empathic. Empathic socialization begins in early childhood (Hoffman 1982b), but it is not until late childhood or early adolescence that children are able to comprehend the meaning of moral principles. It follows from my previous argument, then, that, to the degree that children are empathic, they should be receptive to the principles of caring, need-based justice, equality, and perhaps effort-based justice. In this cafeteria model, people are disposed to select from the moral principles available in society, those that fit their empathic dispositions. One internalizes the principles with little external pressure, because they are in keeping with one's empathic leanings.

The moral encounters one has through life may also play a significant role, because of the empathic affects often aroused. These empathic affects are most likely to be aroused in bystander situations in which victims are salient from the start. But they may also be aroused, as I suggested, in other situations in which victims do not become apparently until later on (e.g., when writing a letter of recommendation). In either case, the empathic affects may dispose one to act on the victim's behalf; such a response would be in opposition to one's egoistic motives in the situation and thus would instigate one type of moral conflict.[9]

A moral conflict is essentially a conflict between alternative courses of action. Therefore it seems reasonable to assume that, when one experiences a moral conflict, one inevitably wonders what to do, considers alternative actions, and anticipates consequences for others. Such thoughts may not only bring to mind victims and potential victims, thus arousing empathic affects, but may also bring to mind the guidelines to action, including relevant moral principles (caring, need, etc.) and associated norms to which one has been previously exposed and that have been stored in memory. The empathic affect and moral principles may be evoked independently, or empathic affect may be aroused first and then may prime the moral principles. Either way, the cooccurrence of a principle and empathic affect should produce a bond between them (or strengthen any existing bond). The result may be that the principle, even if learned initially in a "cool," didactic context (e.g., abstract intellectual discourse in which victims are not salient), acquires an affective charge. An interesting reversed sequence may then become possible: In future cool contexts, for example, in answering moral judgment research questions, the abstract principle may be activated first and this may trigger empathic affect. Such a sequence may explain the emotionality in my subject's explanation of why it is wrong to steal (see the section Empathy and Distributive Justice). In other words, as a consequence of being coupled with empathic affect in moral encounters, a moral principle may be encoded and stored as an affectively charged representation—as a "hot" cognition or category.

What exactly is represented in such a "hot" category? Probably anything that has been associated with the principle and its accompanying empathic affects in life, including verbal descriptions of the principle's content, as well as events in which the principle is violated—events involving victims, culprits, and actions that conform or violate the principle. These representations are apt to be charged with the empathic affects associated with them in one's experiences; and when one subsequently encounters an instance fitting one of these representations, one may be expected to respond to it with the category's affect (as is assumed to occur in general when hot categories are activated; see Fiske 1982; Hoffman 1986). Empirical evidence that moral principles are encoded as hot categories is lacking, but a study by Arsenio and Ford (1985) suggests that single instances of the violation of a moral principle may be so encoded. The findings—young children experienced negative affect when told stories in which a child acts inconsiderately toward another, and their later recall of these stories was aided by the induction of negative affect—suggest that violations of particular principles may be encoded as hot cognitions. Perhaps the same is true of categories of violations.

A potentially important implication of all this is that a person's affective and cognitive responses in moral encounters are due not only to the immediate stimulus event (cues from the situation and from the victim), but also to the affectively charged moral principles that one's action and other aspects of the stimulus event may activate. The empathic affect elicited in moral encounters may thus have a stimulus-driven component and a component driven by the activated, affectively charged principle. This may have important implications for prosocial action. In some situations, for example, the empathic affect elicited by the stimulus event alone may be too weak, perhaps because of a paucity of relevant cues from victims, to override the egoistic motives that may also be operating. But if one's caring principle were activated, its associated empathic affect might be released. This category-driven component, alone or in combination with the stimulus-driven component, may be powerful enough to exceed the threshold needed to override the egoistic motives. Activating one's moral principles may thus provide an additional source of empathic affect, with a resulting increase in one's overall motivation for moral action. The obverse side to this should also be mentioned. In some situations, the empathic affect elicited by the stimulus event alone may be so intense that it produces the disruptive effects of "empathic overarousal" (Hoffman 1978). In these cases, if one's caring principle were activated and the stimulus event assimilated to it, the category-driven component might *reduce* empathic affect intensity to a more manageable level. Thus, the activation of an affectively charged moral principle may have a heightening or leveling effect and in general might function to stabilize one's level of empathic affect arousal in different situations.

In sum, empathy may play a significant role in determining whether one becomes committed to a moral principle by giving the principle an affective base. But once the principle is in place, activating it in future moral encounters may increase or decrease the intensity of one's empathic affective response. Moral principles may thus make it more likely that moral conflict will lead to effective moral action.

The hot-cognition concept also has implications for memory, as there is reason to believe that both affect and cognition contribute to memory. Recent research suggests that affect in general is an extremely powerful retrieval cue (Bower 1981). In addition, I have argued that empathic affect associated with moral concepts acquired in early discipline encounters contributes to remembering (and internalizing) these moral concepts (Hoffman 1983). The Arsenio and Ford (1985) study supports this view. On the cognitive side, a moral principle is, in part, a semantically organized category of knowledge (or prototype). Like other categories, it encompasses many instances and is shaped and made more complex over time in the process of accommodating to new instances. The fact that categorical knowledge is highly enduring in memory, for reasons spelled out by Tulving (1972), should therefore apply to moral principles. Thus, both the affective and cognitive components of a moral principle should help maintain it in memory, keeping it available for activation in future moral encounters.

Concluding Remarks

My aim in this chapter has been to demonstrate the possible role of empathy in a comprehensive moral theory. To this end I have argued as follows:

1. When one witnesses someone in distress, one may respond empathically, that is, with affect more appropriate to the other's situations than to one's own. The most likely response is empathic or sympathetic distress, but, depending on the available cues and one's prior knowledge about the victim, one may make certain causal and other attributions that may transform these feelings into empathic anger, guilt, and empathic injustice.

2. The essential features of this bystander model, including the five empathic affects it can generate, do not require a victim to be physically present because human beings have the capacity for representation and represented events have the power to evoke empathic as well as direct affect. What is required is that a victim or potential victim be imagined, as may occur when one is told or reads about someone's plight, is engaged in conversation or argument about moral issues, or even makes moral judgments about hypothetical situations in a research project. Occasions like these, though cognitively and motivationally more complex than most bystander situations, may arouse empathic affects in a similar way. In other situations, one's own actions are at issue, and when one acts or contemplates acting in a way that may affect other people's welfare, imagining the consequences for them may be expected to arouse empathic affect. Thus many, perhaps most, moral encounters appear to involve victims and potential victims (and beneficiaries, although I focus on victims) and can be counted on to evoke empathic affects.

3. Empathic affects are by and large congruent with caring and most forms of justice. These are the prevailing moral principles in Western society and may be assumed to be the part of people's knowledge structures that are most often brought to bear in moral encounters. The content of these principles also makes them relevant, in varying degrees, to issues involving victims. The moral principles may therefore be activated either by the empathic affects aroused in a moral encounter or by the relevance of their content to the victim dimension of the moral encounter. Either way, the resulting cooccurrence of the empathic affect and moral principle creates a bond between them that is strengthened in subsequent cooccurrences. Moral principles, even when initially learned in 'cool" didactic contexts, may in this way acquire an affective charge and take on the characteristics of a hot cognition.

4. An important implication of the hot-cognition concept is that when a moral principle is subsequently activated even in didactic or research contexts, empathic affect may be aroused. Another implication is that empathic affects aroused in moral encounters may have a stimulus-driven and a category-driven component. The category-driven component may have a heightening or leveling effect on the intensity of the stimulus-driven component in any given moral encounter. The overall result may be to help stabilize the individual's level of empathic affective reactions in different situations over time.

5. Empathic affect may also make important contributions to moral judgment and decision making. The contribution may be direct, or it may be mediated by the moral principles activated by the affects. In either case, the contribution may be limited by empathic bias toward the familiar or toward the here and now. However, these biases may be reduced by socialization that highlights the commonalities among human groups, places high value on impartiality, and trains people in the techniques of multiple empathizing, that is, empathizing not only with people in the vicinity who may be affected by one's actions, but also with people who are absent.

A neglected question in morality research is that of why a person applies one principle and not another in a moral encounter. Cognitive moral theories have difficulty answering this question because they lack affective and motivational concepts. My suggestion that empathic affect may shed some light on this question may seem counter intuitive. Why should affect influence the selection of a principle? This is not a simple, unadorned affect, however, as I hope I have made clear, but an empathic affect informed by one's cognitive sense of others, one's relevant causal attributions, and, in the ideal case, one's knowledge of the importance of being impartial. Furthermore, the affects may be subject to conscious efforts to correct their characteristic biases, efforts such as empathically identifying with people who are absent as well as present, which may provide a number of relevant empathic affective inputs that are then worked into the moral reasoning and judgment process. These inputs, when congruent with one another, may lead directly to the final moral judgment or decision. When the inputs are contradictory (e.g., empathic joy on contemplating an action that will make someone who is present happy versus empathic distress on recognizing that the same action may harm someone who is absent), one must somehow weight the relative importance of each. This may be a cognitive weighing, or one may base one's moral judgment on the input that includes the most intense affect, as in my example of the professor whose empathic concern for future research subjects finally outweighed his empathic concern for his graduate student.

My theoretical argument does not extend to this final phase of the moral reasoning process in which the importance of various inputs is weighed—not only empathic inputs but also moral principles and pragmatic considerations. Rather, my objective is to make sure that all relevant inputs, including empathy-based inputs, are taken into account. In this sense, my approach, as noted earlier, fits squarely in the long Utilitarian tradition in Western philosophy, which states that what is good is what benefits most people. Utilitarians often say that in any moral encounter one should consider the potential harm or benefit an action might have for all people—present or absent. I suggest that empathic affect makes an important contribution toward this end.

Before concluding, I want to correct a statement I made at the beginning of the chapter. There *is* an overriding principle on which there may be close to universal agreement, at least in Western philosophy. However, it has no particular content, but simply states that, whatever one's moral principle it must be applied impartially—to strangers as well as kin, to people who are absent as well as present, and to the future as well as the present implications of action.[10] This principle has been implicit throughout my argument.

Finally, I am *not* saying that empathic affects are an adequate substitute for moral principles or that actions guided by empathic affects automatically qualify as moral actions, as Blum (1980) and Gilligan (1982) seem to imply. According to Gilligan, an empathy-based caring morality is equal, and in many ways superior, to an equal-rights-based justice morality—even though justice morality proceeds from the premise that everyone should be treated the same, whereas caring morality does not require such impartiality. Gilligan's examples of caring do not reflect the complexities of having to care for two or more people, when one can only care for one and must make a choice, nor does she deal with familiarity and here-and-now-biases. Consider a doctor who cares for and goes out of the way to give all of his or her consulting time to a particular patient, but neglects others who are equally in need of attention. This doctor is obviously empathic and cares a lot, to the point of setting aside personal needs, but I would have difficulty calling this moral behavior. On the other hand, I do not go as far as Kohlberg and others, who seem to consider acts moral only if they derive from moral principles. The issue is complex, and I do not have an answer except to suggest a development criterion. The doctor in question may not be acting morally, but a young child, who, out of sympathetic distress, goes out of his or her way to help someone, may be acting morally.

I *am* saying that empathic affect may contribute to acceptance of moral principles in relevant situations and to the motivation to act in accordance with moral principles. Empathic affects may also contribute inputs to moral reasoning based on principles, and thus to moral decision making and moral judgment. My argument is not foolproof, as it is based mainly on anecdotal and hypothetical examples showing that people's moral reasoning and judgment sometimes have a quality of personal concern for others that seems to reflect an underlying empathic identification with them. There is also the research mentioned earlier showing that empathy correlates positively with a preference for need-based equity and negatively with a preference for output-based equity as principles of distributive justice. This research is encouraging but limited in applicability because causal inferences cannot be made (although empathy obviously predates moral principles developmentally and may therefore be the more likely antecedent). Furthermore, the research says nothing about process. We need experimental studies of how empathic and sympathetic distress, guilt, and empathic anger affect one's receptivity to certain moral principles as well as the moral reasoning and judgment used in applying these principles. Longitudinal research is also needed to explain how these empathic affects contribute developmentally to an internalized commitment to moral principles and to the moral reasoning and judgments based on them.

Notes

1. Utilitarians, for example, may view both justice and the social order as subprinciples instrumental in attaining impartial benevolence.

2. This definition differs from others, which require a close match between the affective response of the target person and that of the observer. The advantages of my definition have been discussed elsewhere (Hoffman 1982c).

3. Empathic anger should be distinguished from the type of self-righteous indignation that serves to tout one's own moral superiority.

4. I thank Inge Bretherton for this example.

5. This type of guilt feeling should be distinguished from Freudian guilt, which results not from awareness of harming someone in the present, but from activation of early repressed childhood anxieties about losing parental love; it is often unconscious and may be experienced when no one else is involved (masturbation guilt).

6. There is reason to question this assumption. Though output-oriented societies apparently produce more than other societies, such comparisons may ignore important uncontrolled variables. Experimental research by Deutsch (1985), in which relevant variables were controlled, raises serious questions about whether distribution of resources on the basis of output actually does produce greater overall output. If it does not, is there any other reason for considering output equity a justice principle?

7. We may feel guilty about violating the expectations of others intentionally, or unwittingly, owing to our normal habits. We are apt to feel far guiltier, however, about breaking an actual promise, because in this case we not only violate another's expectations but we are responsible for having created those expectations in the first place. (We may, of course, feel an obligation to keep a promise even if no one will be injured if we don't; this type of moral feeling appears to fall outside the domain of empathic morality.)

8. I stress the role of empathy in all of these examples, but we may be concerned about honesty and fairness without empathizing.

9. Other types of moral conflict involve opposition between principles, in which one's egoistic needs may not be an issue.

10. A contemporary Western philosopher who plays down the importance of impartiality is Blum (1980), who argues that it is morally appropriate to favor one's friends.

References

Arsenio, W. F., and M. E. Ford (1985). The role of affective information in social-cognitive development: Children's differentiation of moral and conventional events. *Merrill-Palmer Quarterly* 31, 1–17.

Ayer, A. J. (1936). *Language, truth and logic.* London: Gollancz.

Bishops' pastoral letter on Catholic social teaching and the U.S. economy: First draft (1984). *Origins,* 14, Nos. 22, 23.

Bishops' pastoral letter on Catholic social teaching and the U.S. economy: Second draft (1985). *Origins* 15, No. 17.

Blum, L. A. (1980). *Friendship, altruism and morality.* London: Routledge & Kegan Paul.

Bower, G. H. (1981). Mood and memory, *American Psychologist* 36, 129–148.

Brandt, R. A. (1979). *A theory of the good and the right.* New York: Oxford University Press.

Coles, R. (1986). *The moral life of children.* Boston: Atlantic Monthly Press.

Deutsch, M. (1985). *Distributive justice: A social psychological perspective.* New Haven, CT: Yale University Press.

Edwards, P. (1955). *The logic of moral discourse.* New York: Free Press.

Feshbach, N. D., and K. Roe (1968). Empathy in six- and seven-year olds. *Child Development* 39, 133–145.

Fiske, S. T. (1982). Schema-triggered affect: Applications to social perception. In S. Fiske and M. Clark, eds., *Cognition and affect: The Carnegie-Mellon Symposium.* Hillsdale, NJ: Erlbaum.

Gilligan, C. (1982). *In a different voice.* Cambridge MA: Harvard University Press.

Harris, M. B., and C. E. Siebel (1975). Affect, aggression, and altruism. *Developmental Psychology,* 11, 623–627.

Hoffman, M. L. (1970). Conscience, personality, and socialization techniques. *Human Development* 13, 90–126.

Hoffman, M. L. (1975a). Developmental synthesis of affect and cognition and its implications for altruistic motivation. *Developmental Psychology* 11, 607–622.

Hoffman, M. L. (1975b). Sex differences in moral internalization. *Journal of Personality and Social Psychology* 32, 720–729.

Hoffman, M. L. (1977). Sex differences in empathy and related behaviors. *Psychological Bulletin,* 84, 712–722.

Hoffman, M. L. (1978). Empathy, its development and prosocial implications. In C. B. Keasey, ed., *Nebraska Symposium on Motivation,* vol. 25. Lincoln: University of Nebraska Press.

Hoffman, M. L. (1980). Moral development in adolescence. In J. Adelson, ed., *Handbook of adolescent psychology.* New York: John Wiley & Sons.

Hoffman, M. L. (1981). Is altruism part of human nature? *Journal of Personality and Social Psychology* 40, 121–137.

Hoffman, M. L. (1982a). Affect and moral development. In D. Cicchetti, ed., *New directions in child development.* San Francisco: Jossey-Bass.

Hoffman, M. L. (1982b). Development of prosocial motivation: Empathy and guilt. In N. Eisenberg, ed., *Development of prosocial behavior.* New York: Academic Press.

Hoffman, M. L. (1982c). Measurement of empathy. In C. Izard, ed., *Measurement of emotions in infants and children.* New York: Cambridge University Press.

Hoffman, M. L. (1983). Affective and cognitive processes in moral internalization: An information processing approach. In E. T. Higgins, D. Ruble, and W. Hartup, ed., *Social cognition and social development: A socio-cultural perspective.* New York: Cambridge University Press.

Hoffman, M. L. (1984a). Empathy, its limitations, and its role in a comprehensive moral theory. In J. Gewirtz and W. Kurtines, eds., *Morality, moral development, and moral behavior.* New York: John Wiley.

Hoffman, M. L (1984b). Interaction of affect and cognition in empathy. In C. Izard, J. Kagan, and R. Zajonc, eds., *Emotions, cognition, and behavior.* New York: Cambridge University Press.

Hoffman, M. L. (1986). Affect, cognition, and motivation. In R. M. Sorrentino and E. T. Higgins, eds., *Handbook of motivation and cognition: Foundations of social behavior.* New York: Guilford.

Hoffman, M. L. (1989). Empathy and prosocial activism. In N. Eisenberg, J. Reykowski, and E. Staub, eds., *Social and moral values.* Hillsdale, NJ: Erlbaum.

Hume, D. (1957). *An inquiry concerning the principles of morals,* vol. 4. New York: Liberal Arts Press. (Original work published 1751).

Izard, C. E. (1977). *Human emotions.* New York: Plenum Press.

Kaplan, E. A. (1989). Women, morality, and social change: A historical perspective. In N. Eisenberg, J. Reykowski, and E. Staub, eds., *Social and moral values.* Hillsdale, NJ: Erlbaum.

Kaplan, L. J. (1977). The basic dialogue and the capacity of empathy. In N. Freedman and S. Grand, eds., *Communicative structures and psychic structures.* New York: Plenum.

Klein, R. (1971). Some factors influencing empathy in six- and seven-year-old children varying in ethnic background. Ph.D. dissertation, University of California, Los Angeles, 1970. *Dissertation Abstracts International* 31, 3960A. (University Microfilms No. 71–3862).

Kohlberg, L. (1969). The cognitive developmental approach. In D. A. Goslin, ed., *Handbook of socialization theory and research.* Chicago: Rand McNally.

Krebs, D. L. (1970). Altruism: An examination of the concept and a review of the literature. *Psychological Bulletin* 73, 258–303.

Mill, J. S. (1979). *Utilitarianism.* Cambridge, MA: Hackett (original work published 1861).

Montada, L., M. Schmitt, & C. Dalbert (1986). Thinking about justice and dealing with one's privileges: A study on existential guilt. In H. W. Bierhoff, R. Cohen, and J. Greenberg, eds., *Justice in social relations.* New York: Plenum Press.

Murphy, L. B. (1937). *Social behavior and child personality.* New York: Columbia University Press.

Noddings, N. (1984). *Caring.* Berkeley: University of California Press.

Rashdall, H. (1907). *The theory of good and evil.* New York: Oxford University Press.

Rawls, J. A. (1971). *A theory of justice.* Cambridge, MA: Harvard University Press.

Razran, G. (1971). *Mind in evolution.* Boston: Houghton Mifflin.

Stotland, E. (1969). Exploratory investigations of empathy. In L. Berkowitz, ed., *Advances in experimental social psychology,* vol. 4. New York: Academic Press.

Tulving, E. (1972). Episodic and semantic memory. In E. Tulving and W. Donaldson, eds., *Organization of memory.* New York: Academic Press.

Tversky, A. and D. Kahneman (1973). Availability: A heuristic for judging frequency and probability. *Cognitive Psychology* 5, 207–232.

Weiner, B. (1985). "Spontaneous" causal thinking. *Psychological Bulletin* 97, 74–84.

Zahn-Waxler, C., M. Radke-Yarrow, and R. A. King (1979). Childrearing and children's prosocial initiations towards victims of distress. *Child Development* 50, 319–330.

Zanna, M. P., C. A. Kiesler, and P. A. Pilkonis (1970). Positive and negative affect established by classical conditioning. *Journal of Personality and Social Psychology* 14, 321–328.

31 Situations and Dispositions

Owen Flanagan

Character and Coercion

In a controversial and widely discussed series of *New Yorker* articles, subsequently published as a book, *Eichmann in Jerusalem: A Report on the Banality of Evil* (1963), Hannah Arendt wrote that "in certain circumstances the most ordinary decent person can become a criminal" (p. 253). The "certain circumstances" Arendt had in mind were not the fantastic circumstances of Plato's Lydian shepherd who held the magical ring which afforded him complete license. The "certain circumstances" were the actual social circumstances that became the structures of everyday life during the Nazi era.

The circumstances under which "the most ordinary decent person can become a criminal" might be of several different kinds. It might be that the circumstances cause certain ordinary traits to come undone. Or it might be that the circumstances cause people to reveal that they lack a trait we expected them to have. Or the circumstances might be such that they expose the limited range of a disposition—for example, compassion—which we thought had a wider scope.

Milgram's "One Great Unchanging Result"

Stanley Milgram's studies yielded frightening and intuitively unexpected support for Arendt's hypothesis. He showed that one did not need to plant otherwise decent people in a whole socioeconomic environment gone off the deep end to get them to act badly. An isolated psychological experiment of the right kind could easily bring about this result.

From O. Flanagan, *Varieties of moral personality: Ethics and psychological realism* (1991). Cambridge, MA: Harvard University Press. Reprinted by permission. Copyright © 1991 by the President and Fellows of Harvard College.

Milgram studied over one thousand subjects during a three-year period (1960–1963). The paradigm experiment ran as follows. Subjects (aged twenty to fifty and of various socioeconomic and educational backgrounds) were recruited and paid to participate (it is perhaps not insignificant that the fee, $4.50, was a nontrivial amount of money at the time). The stated purpose of the study was to examine the effects of punishment on learning. There were three roles in the experiment: Experimenter (E), Teacher (T), and Learner (L). E and L were confederates, the subjects were all Ts. T's job was, first, to read word pairs to L and then, second, to read only the first member of each pair with four possible associations. L was to choose the correct partner from the original list. T was to administer an electric shock for each error. The shock generator consisted of a panel with thirty levers, each with an associated voltage rating of 15 to 450 volts. Ts were instructed to move up the voltage ladder after each error. It was arranged that Ls would get one question in four right, so three-quarters of the time Ts were required to raise the shock level. Engraved on the panel at various intervals were labels indicating slight shock, moderate, strong, very strong, intense, extreme intensity, danger, and severe shock. The last two levers were simply marked XXX.

Before the experiment began, the confederate L asked about the process, and E told both L and T that although the shocks could be extremely painful, they would not cause tissue damage. If during the experiment T expressed concern—and virtually all did—E said, "Please go on." "The experiment requires you to continue." "It is essential that you continue." "You have no other choice, you must go on."

Across a variety of similar protocols 65 percent of the subjects went all the way to 450 volts, even though L was pounding the walls at 300 volts. Indeed, even in variations where administration of the shock required T forcibly to place L's hand on the shock plate, Ts did so in almost 60 percent of the cases. These studies were replicated in a half dozen countries with the same degree of compliance and with no gender differences. Furthermore, and perhaps most surprisingly once one accepts the original findings of high compliance rates, there were no significant differences on standard personality measures between the maximally obedient subjects and the maximally rebellious ones (Elms and Milgram, 1966). Roger Brown describes the Milgram compliance rate as "one great unchanging result" (1986, 4).

It is not simply that lay personality theory leaves us unprepared for the Milgram results. Even our more refined theories fail to prepare us for a situation of this sort with such a dramatic effect. In one study Milgram (1974) had a group of thirty-nine Yale psychiatrists, thirty-one college students, and forty middle-class adults predict their own maximum level of compliance. Everyone was sure he or she would break off very early. When asked to predict how far a diverse group of Americans would go, the psychiatrists predicted, on average, that fewer than 50 percent would still be obedient at the tenth level (150 volts), fewer than four in a hundred would reach the twentieth level, and fewer than one in a thousand would administer the maximum shock. It is remarkable that psychiatrists, who are trained to perceive subtle force fields in the social environment, and who are also well aware of dark, seamy, and destructive urges, could be so far off the mark here.[1]

It is important to keep in mind that a significant minority—fully one-third of the participants—did refuse to obey. Whatever hopefulness this engenders, however, is mitigated by the fact that not *one* subject in any obedience experiment brought the experiments to the attention of higher authorities. The question arises, What causes people to comply and not to comply? And what relevance does this study have to questions of the unity of character, trait globality and consistency, situation sensitivity, and the power of social pressures and constraints?

It would be a mistake, and an unnecessary and tactically unwise one at that, for the defender of traits to claim that those who comply lack some global trait which those who refuse possess. The members of both groups have all sorts of psychological dispositions which are thrown into complex interaction with the Milgram situation. Which traits they have, and how exactly they are characterized and put together—both individually and collectively—differs dramatically from person to person. The personalities of members of both groups are situation sensitive. They are simply sensitive in different ways. We should not be so naive as to think that the main variable differentiating compliant souls from noncompliant ones is some single unyielding trait, and certainly not one made up exclusively of moral fiber.

To see this, consider the following variation on the Milgram experiment. The subject sees a person (as usual a confederate of the experimenter) in distress from a low shock, a person who the subject thinks has had a traumatic shock experience early in life. Some subjects describe themselves as identifying with the person being shocked and as experiencing concern and compassion. Others describe themselves as distressed, upset, and worried. Not surprisingly, members of the first group choose to help, sometimes even expressing willingness to trade places. Members of the second group choose to escape. The differences in affective dispositions help, in such cases, to explain differences in behavior. But the fact that certain persons tend to feel empathic while others feel distress in such extreme situations, although predictive of behavior *in such situations,* does not entail that greater helpfulness *in general* can be expected from the former types than from the latter. Nor should it make us think that feeling empathy is a virtue and feeling distress is a vice. This will depend on how the disposition figures in the overall psychological economy of an individual person across multifarious situations.

The question remains, what is it about persons in the Milgram situation that explains the high compliance rate? In an attempt to provide an answer Lee Ross, himself a leading situationist, writes:

Perhaps the most obvious and recognized feature of Milgram's specific paradigm was the gradual step-wise character of the teacher's complicity. The teacher did not obey a single, simple command to deliver a powerful shock to an innocent victim. At first, all he undertook to do was to deliver mild negative reinforcements—feedback really—to a learner who had willingly agreed to receive such feedback as an aid in performing his task. He also agreed, as did the learner, to a procedure in which the level of the negative reinforcements would increase slightly after each error; but he did so without ever imagining the long-term implications of that initial agreement. The step-wise progression continued, and with every increment in shock level, the teacher's psychological dilemma became more difficult. In a sense, the teacher had to find a justification (one satisfactory to himself, to the experimenter, and perhaps even to the learner) that would explain why he had to desist *now*, when he hadn't desisted earlier; how it could be illegitimate to deliver the next shock but legitimate to have delivered one of only slightly less magnitude moments before. Such justification is difficult to find. Indeed, it is clearly available at only one point in the proceedings—the point at which the learner withdraws his implied consent to receive the shocks and continue in the learning experiment—and, significantly, it is precisely this point that subjects were most likely to refuse to obey. (1988, 102–103)

Four important points are raised here. (1) There is the significance of the stepwise character of the situation. A request to administer 450 volts right off to a recalcitrant learner will gain virtually no compliance. But administering the first shock to a volunteer is hardly in itself a matter of major significance even for the morally most scrupulous. (2) Once the experiment has begun, the gradual stepwise character of the situation creates a justification problem for the subject. He has to "find a justification . . . that would explain why he had to desist *now*, when he hadn't desisted earlier; how it could be illegitimate to deliver the next shock but legitimate to have delivered one of only slightly less magnitude moments before." A sort of moral sorites problem exists here. (3) The subject is himself in an interpersonally and morally complex situation. He has agreed, after all, to abide by an experimental setup that has been made clear enough both to him and to the other (supposed) volunteer. So he confronts both the problem of looking foolish, as if he had not really understood what should have been very clear, and in addition the matter of breaking his word and failing to abide by what he had agreed to do. (4) Finally, there is the fact that, when they try to quit, the subjects are told that they are *not allowed to*. Almost invariably this occurs, if not before, at the point where L tries (also *always* unsuccessfully) to withdraw his consent. Ross writes that "many subjects essentially said 'I quit,' only to be confronted with perhaps the most important yet subtle feature of the Milgram paradigm, the difficulty of translating an intention to discontinue participation into effective action. We should recognize that from the subjects' viewpoint, they did confront the experimenter and refuse to continue, often quite forcefully, just not *effectively*" (p. 103).

Ross predicts—although the experiment cannot be done—that had the shock board included a red button marked with a clear message from the Institutional Review Board informing the subjects that pressing it for any reason whatsoever would terminate the experiment, most subjects would have gotten out pretty early. This seems exactly right. It is consistent with the behavior of Milgram's subjects as well as with what we know about the important causal variables here.

In the present context it is important to stress that Ross's analysis claims relevance for both certain features of the situation as in 1 and 4 and in certain expectable dispositions of persons as in 2 and 3. These include the disposition to maintain consistency, to be able to rationalize one's behavior over time, to abide by voluntary agreements, and to give weight to what persons in positions of authority say one can and cannot do. Indeed, there is no intelligible way of discussing the Milgram experiments which does not assume that almost all subjects are disposed to stop shocking at some point or other in the experiment. The interesting and worrisome thing is that such a widely shared and in many cases powerful disposition could be neutralized so easily by certain subtle environmental manipulations.

Coercion and Rebellion in Groups

These last reflections, which stress the fact that Milgram's subjects wanted out and were disposed to get out but were not allowed out, are especially important. It also turns out to be important that they were alone in the situation. It is hard to rebel when one is alone. Indeed, some experimental evidence shows that Milgram-like attempts to coerce people subtly to do what they do not want to do, and in particular to do what they have reason to believe is morally problematic, work less well when persons are in groups, and when they are able to share or convey mutual misgivings via body language or in discussion. There is, as we say, strength in numbers.

The classic study showing this effect was done by Gamson, Fireman, and Rytina (1982) and is known in the literature as the MHRC Encounter. Manufacturer's Human Relations Consultants (MHRC) was a front which advertised for subjects to participate in paid market research. In an imaginative end run around principles restricting depictive research, prospective subjects were asked if they were willing to participate in any or all of the following: (1) research on brand recognition; (2) research on product safety; (3) research in which they would be misled about the purpose until afterwards; (4) research on community standards. (If subjects thought these choices were all of a kind, they were making what Ryle has named a "category mistake.") Once subjects agreed to these terms, they were falsely told (remember they had agreed to participate in research in which they were misled about the purpose) that only research on 4, community standards, was being currently conducted.

Subjects assembled in a hotel conference room in which there was a U-shaped table and nine places. A research coordinator and assistant introduced themselves and then distributed a questionnaire asking for opinions on large oil companies, employee rights, and extramarital sex, as well as a statement authorizing videotaping of later discussion, with tapes to be the sole property of MHRC. After this was done, and with a video recorder on, the coordinator gave the project name and asked each subject to introduce himself or herself. The camera was then turned off, and the coordinator read a summary of a court case concerning the firing of a service station owner for cohabitation and moral turpitude. The service station owner had filed a countersuit for invasion of privacy. The coordinator then asked, "Would you be concerned if you learned that the manager of your service station had a life style like Mr. X? Please discuss why you feel the way you do." The coordinator turned on the video recorder, left for five minutes, returned, and turned the recorder off. Next, he designated three people to argue as if they were offended by Mr. X and turned the camera back on. After five minutes he designated three more to do so (two-thirds were now doing so). Finally, the coordinator announced that each person would be given time on camera to speak as one offended by Mr. X. After this each participant was asked to sign an additional release allowing court use of the videos. Breaks were spaced at several points in the procedure, during which time participants had a chance to talk informally.

Actually this is not really a description of what did in fact happen. It is what would have happened if the coercion had been successful. It wasn't. Only one group in thirty-three came close to going all the way. In eight groups a majority did sign the final release, but in half of these there was refusal by a significant minority, as well as acceptance by the majority that this was legitimate. In twenty-five groups there was unanimous or majority refusal.

A number of significant variables enter here. One essential dissimilarity with the Milgram experiment involves the lack of gradualism, or at any rate the significantly lesser amount of gradualism. As in the Milgram task, however, but even more obviously so, the situation here starts in a morally unobjectionable way. Once involved, however, subjects are asked to perform tasks which in the context of the situation appear to be ethically suspect and to fly in the face of principles of procedural justice. The widespread belief in procedural fairness is enough to motivate the desire to rebel, or at least to generate some rebellious thoughts in anyone with the proper sort of suspicions about the exercise. But perhaps such suspicions are misguided, based on a false impression of what is going on.

We know from the Milgram experiments that even when the suspicions that the situation is as it seems are firm, the ensuing disposition to rebel is not sufficient to produce actual or effective rebellion. This is where the numbers matter. What is significant is not merely that one is not alone. What matters is that at least some of the additional others are also thinking of rebelling, or are similarly disposed to rebel, and, furthermore, that questions can be raised and views shared about what is in fact going on. In this way confidence in one's interpretation of the situation is raised, as is one's assurance that the ethical issues one believes to be both important and at stake are in fact important and at stake. Finally, in groups one has reason to believe that whatever price there is to be paid for rebellion will be shared among several persons and will not all accrue to oneself.

It is necessary to emphasize that the claim here is a restricted one. It is that being with a number of other people has a considerable effect on whether one gains the courage to rebel and whether one succeeds at rebelling in situations in which, like the Milgram experiment, there is the presumption of strong prior motivation to resist.

The presence of others, however, is well known to quash rebellious impulses and make rebellion more frightening when others do not share, or cannot be persuaded to share, one's cause. Such cases are not only the familiar ones in which the costs of singular rebellion are very high or in which one has second thoughts about complex moral issues. In situations where there is little or nothing ethical at stake and where the truth is plain to see, we can be surprisingly compliant. In Solomon Asch's (1956) famous studies of conformity in perceptual judgments, subjects were asked to determine which of two lines in a series of pairs was longer. The correct choices were sufficiently unambiguous so that members of control groups performed perfectly. But in groups where the subject was sixth or seventh in line after persons intentionally making the wrong choice, one-third conformed to absurd, perceptually unconscionable judgments.

Situations and Samaritans

There are some rough and overarching generalizations which can help us understand in a unified way all three of these outcomes: the MHRC Encounter results, in which rebellious activism spread in groups in which individual members were disposed to rebel; the Asch results, in which there was a tendency to conform one's own judgments to the absurd judgments of others; and the Milgram results, which showed a high rate of compliance to demands to which an individual had a strong disposition to rebel but no social support for so doing.

The so-called Law of Social Impact (it is not, of course, a law in any strict sense) says that, ceteris paribus, the intensity of social impact is a function of the strength *(S)*—that is, the power, status, persuasiveness, and so on—of those creating a force; the immediacy *(I)*—that is, the proximity in space and time—of the force; and the number *(N)* of people presenting the force (Latané 1981; R. Brown 1986). More formally, intensity of social impact = *f(SIN)*.

There are two other principles which help fix the interpretation of the Law of Social Impact. The first—call it the Principle of the Decreasing Marginal Effectiveness of Adding Numbers over Two—says that the effect of adding numbers to the source of social impact increases at a decreasing rate, and in particular, that adding a second person to an individual source of influence has a greater effect than adding a third person to a group of two, and this a greater effect than adding a fourth to three, and so on. The third principle—call it the Principle of the Diffusion of Social Impact—says that the intensity of impact is (experienced as) diffused over, possibly simply divided by, the number of persons at whom it is directed. The light of social pressure is most intense when it is directed on one person and diffuses as it (the same amount of force) is spread over numbers of individuals.

These principles shed some unified explanatory light on the results we have seen. In the Milgram situation, the values of *S* and *I* are very high, even though *N* is low. Furthermore, there is no diffusion of impact since there is only one *T*. In the Asch situation, *I* and *N* are high while *S* is only moderate, and again there is no diffusion of impact. In the MHRC case, there are two force fields, one generated by the MHRC staff, the other by the group of participants. Rebellion, where it occurs, comes from the larger *N* of the participant group, as well as from the fact that the high intensity of feeling coopted outweighs the intensity of the pressure to do what the MHRC staff wanted. There is also, in this case, the diffusion of impact, given that each is only one of (up to) nine rebelling.

These principles, rough-hewn as they are, also help explain the important results on samaritanism. The broad findings of the innumerable studies of samaritanism can be brought out by looking at two classic studies.

In a truly mischievous experiment, Darley and Batson (1973) used as subjects seminarians at Princeton Theological Seminary. The seminarians were randomly assigned to prepare a short talk on either the parable of the Good Samaritan or the issue of job opportunities for seminary graduates. Subsequent to preparing the notes for their talks, each seminarian was sent from the preparation site ("Jerusalem") to the site where they were to give their talk ("Jericho"). Half the students in each group were told that they were running late and should hurry to the delivery site. A student confederate was slumped over in some distress along the route, and the dependent variable was simply whether the student stopped to help or not. Did the seminarians stop with any frequency? No. Was their stopping in any way related to the content of the talk they were about to give? No, not at all. The only variable of any significance was whether the seminarian was in a rush! The less the subjects were rushed, the more likely they were to help.

This sort of study is often taken as strong support for the situationist position. To be sure, it shows the powerful effect of the situational variable of being rushed. Showing this, however, has no implications whatsoever for the general issue of whether there are personality traits or dispositions or about whether the content of one's occurrent thoughts and feelings exert an influence on behavior. In fact, the study can be faulted for making it seem as if one group of seminarians was put in a position of having instrumental thoughts and the other noninstrumental and devout ones just prior to the samaritanism test, which thoughts, even when combined with the compassion and benevolence we might have thought to be typical of seminarians, have no effect on behavior. The first point is that it is very much an open question whether compassion and benevolence are dimensions along which seminarians differ from the rest of the population. Second, we can easily imagine that the members of both groups were so focused on the demand to give a talk on short notice—on the performance demand—that they did not really, as it were, get into the spirit of the content of their talk. On this interpretation the results show nothing about the relation between two different kinds of occurrent thoughts—that is, devout versus instrumental ones—and helping behavior since there is no overwhelming reason to think that the groups were actually having these different kinds of thoughts.[2]

In the second study Latané and Darley (1970) constructed the following realistic scenario with the help of the management of a liquor store. A confederate of the experimenter's waited until the attendant (also a confederate) was in the stockroom and then, with a certain amount of bravado and clear intent (so that the subject would be sure to notice and make the proper surmise), proceeded to steal a case of beer. They found, first, that only 20 percent of the subjects reported the theft spontaneously. Second, 50 percent of the remainder were forthcoming only if the attendant, upon returning, asked, "Where did that other guy go?" Third, in total only 60 percent reported the theft under either circumstance. Fourth, the probability of reporting the theft was much higher in cases in which the subject was the only onlooker than when he was one of two.

It may seem inconsistent that the probability of helping is higher if one is alone, whereas the probability of rebelling is lower if one is alone. But a unified account can be given along the following lines. In the helping case there is the perception that if anyone is going to help, it is going to have to be me, and the feeling of responsibility associated with this perception. These thoughts and feelings provide a motivational source which is, in many cases, strong enough to overcome the competing feelings of awkwardness, the thoughts that one should mind one's own business, that one may have misinterpreted the situation, and so on. In the rebellion case the motivation to act may be as strong or stronger, but the countervailing pressures are much greater and their force is heightened by one's aloneness.

In any case, the Latané and Darley results are the same in experiments involving theft and property loss as in those involving persons in distress. The greater the number of onlookers, the smaller the individual probability of helping. Roger Brown (1986) thinks that these results are in clear violation of our commonsense understanding:

the layman's approach to bystander behavior seems to me to be the same as the layman's approach to all behavior: The unit of lay psychology is personality, and the main determinants of behavior are aspects of personality—traits, values, abilities, and so on. Helping in an emergency then should occur or not, according to the strength of some trait like helpfulness or some value like altruism or social responsibility. Individual differences are to be expected in all aspects of personality, and so individuals ought to vary in their threshold for helping in an emergency. The larger the sample of individuals (number of onlookers), the greater the probability that at least one will help, that there will be at least one for whom the situation is "above the threshold." *It is perfectly correct that the probability of finding an individual of a given type must increase with the size of the group;* that is simple mathematics. Indeed the lay analysis as a whole is sound so long as one disregards social forces, but social forces are precisely what cannot be disregarded in the bystander situation. Because two or more onlookers together create the social force called "diffusion of responsibility," the effective individual probability of helping in a group is lower than the probability that an individual alone will help, and *even that is usually lower for a group than for an individual alone.* (p. 73)

I think Brown is too accepting here of the way certain situationists characterize lay personality theory. Surely the supposed violation of commonsense psychology is mitigated somewhat by recognizing that it is also part of both our commonsense psychological and prudential theories that if someone else is already helping, this lowers the effective probability that one either will or should help oneself. One, after all, might make matters worse by getting in the way or by bungling a situation which requires expertise. This belief—actually it is a constellation of beliefs involving views about situation sensitivities, about what is helpful and what is not helpful, and about expertise—gives a partial explanation of the fact that when an emergency arises, there are often large numbers of people looking on and only one or two actually attending to the victim. It also helps explain why we would be hesitant to come to the aid of a person in distress if there were others around. We hope that someone will understand the situation better than we do or will know the victim, that someone will have the requisite expertise and stomach to handle the situation.

What is unexpected, and worth knowing, is that this tendency to hold back can, in the aggregate, actually lower the overall probability that help will be given! This is due to the fact that once the process is rolling, people are reinforcing one another's behavior, modeling appropriate responses, and so on. When a person in a position to help holds back, his holding back raises doubts in the observer's mind that the proper interpretation of the situation is that of a *real emergency*. As the number of persons holding back rises, each individual's confidence in his own initial interpretation of the situation diminishes (in the MHRC case the exact same effect is operative: as the number inclined to rebel increases and information is passed back and forth, the group motive to rebel rises). Although ordinary people are not totally naive about unintended consequences, it seems clear that this result would not be predicted by ordinary reasoners.

Latané and Darley summarize as follows the main causes for what I have heard called, but which is surely a misnomer, bystander apathy.

We have suggested four different reasons why people, once having noticed an emergency, are less likely to go to the aid of the victim when others are present: (1) Others serve as an audience to one's actions, inhibiting him from doing foolish things. (2) Others serve as guides to behavior, and if they are inactive, they will lead the observer to be inactive also. (3) The interactive effect of these two processes will be much greater than either alone; if each bystander sees other bystanders momentarily frozen by audience inhibition, each may be misled into thinking the situation must not be serious. (4) The presence of other people dilutes the responsibility felt by any single bystander, making him feel that it is less necessary for himself to act. (1970, p. 125)

. . . What lessons should the defender of psychological realism, the proponent of the Principle of Minimal Psychological Realism, draw from the psychological research discussed in this chapter? [Flanagan's Principle of Minimal Psychological Realism says: "make sure when constructing a moral theory or projecting a moral ideal that the character, decision processing, and behavior prescribed are possible . . . for creatures like us."—Ed.] The remarks just made suggest a moderated response. Traits are real and predictive, but no credible moral psychology can focus solely on traits, dispositions, and character. Good lives cannot be properly envisaged, nor can they be created and sustained, without paying attention to what goes on outside the agent—to the multifarious interactive relations between individual psychology and the natural and social environments.

This point has some important consequences, for it is surely a legitimate charge against many recent forays in the revival of virtue ethics or an ethics of character that the virtues are seen as what steels "the good person" against any circumstantial pressures. All the results discussed here should make us skeptical of this picture of the good person as one with the psychological apparatus which readies him or her to withstand the pressures of all situations and temptations.

In a deep, and immensely provocative, discussion of Euripedes' *Hecuba*, Martha Nussbaum (1986) examines the classical statement—in some sense the contrary of Glaucon's point in the parable of the Lydian shepherd—of the thesis that the noble character is incorruptible. Despite the loss of her city, her husband, and most of her children, Hecuba maintains her nobility. Even the death of one of her two remaining children, Polyxena, is accompanied by pride on her part, for Polyxena shows great courage and dignity as she is sacrificed by Odysseus to appease Achilles. But, in the end, even this finest of persons, who has withstood what seems to be the worst that life can offer, cannot but come undone. When her friend Polymestor betrays her trust and kills her last beloved child, Polydorus, Hecuba becomes the empty, nihilistic, and vengeful person—a murderer of innocent children herself—that she seemed to have absolutely no tendencies whatsoever to become. Even for the very best and most resilient characters there are situations in which the center cannot hold and things fall apart.

Although I do not take up in this book the important question of the effects of psychological work on the issue of responsibility, the work discussed here suggests that there may be reason to think of certain kinds of situations, often not the obvious ones, as more mitigating than they seem intuitively. This work also suggests a basis for understanding better the grounds for many of the more common ethical mistakes we tend to make, including trusting first impressions too much, favoring one's own group, self-servingness, lack of courage in certain situations, failure to take responsibility, and so on. Does psychological realism also imply that we must tolerate and accept these foibles, given this clearer and deeper understanding of them? The answer, it seems to me, is yes and no. On the one hand, it would be foolish and naive, as well as disappointing and potentially wrenching, not to tolerate a certain amount of what one can expect inevitably to find. But, on the other hand, all this psychological work suggests a variety of responses to our characteristic foibles.

First, knowledge of the situational factors which in interaction with certain characteristic dispositional configurations result in morally problematic behavior gives us information which can be exceedingly valuable if we want and are able to put our minds to the project of keeping such situations from occurring. Second, and relatedly, the same thing is true on the dispositional side. Not all persons are equally prone to underestimate the modular organization of moral personality, or systematically to display problematic attributional tendencies. The evidence of the Oriya, who shy away from general trait ascriptions and favor very definite descriptions, is the possibility proof that we could understand one another under descriptions with richness and specificity (Shweder and Bourne 1984). But perhaps, in addition to our deep-seated lay personality theory, the absolute number of people with whom we interact makes this less feasible for us.

Furthermore, thanks to the studies of Tec (1986), London (1970), Oliner and Oliner (1988), and Koonz (1987), we now know something about some of the etiological and dispositional sources of resistance to the ethically repulsive. These include more than simply strong moral fiber, but also surprising characteristics such as adventurousness, strong identification with a morally good parent, and a sense of being socially marginal. Further work in developmental and personality psychology, especially if these were to enter into more productive relations with social psychology, could conceivably yield great advances in our knowledge. Kohlbergians claim that higher-stage reasoners are most likely to resist Milgram-like coercion and to engage in samaritanism. The overall adequacy of Kohlberg's stage theory to one side, this is an important claim if true. Because higher-stage reasoners are the best educated, and often have actually studied ethics, one strategy suggests itself for setting up the required dispositions for overcoming a certain common moral shortfall—namely, better education in general, and ethical education in particular. Relatedly, there are the hopeful data pointing to the efficacy, albeit only moderate, of direct instruction on our attributional and other biases as a way of overcoming them.

Knowing that there may be a link between gaining self-esteem and establishing a strong ego, on the one hand, and devaluing certain others, on the other hand, is, as I said, sad if true. But, assuming that such a link does exist, awareness of it is better than ignorance. In the first place, locating a foible in a strong tendency in our nature may diminish to a certain extent some of the moralistic posturing that emanates from those self-righteous souls who claim to have succeeded in avoiding the foible in question. Second, locating the source of certain countermoral tendencies puts us in a position to construct social life in ways that weaken the tendencies, and thereby keep them from realizing their damaging potential. Happily, knowledge in the human sciences—knowledge of ourselves as fallible beings with all manner of quirks—gives us a certain amount of control over the nature, structure, and quality of our lives.

Notes

1. In a related experiment Miller et al. (1974) told subjects about the original Milgram results and then showed them slides of subjects. Maleness and attractiveness were main variables in lay predictions of shock behavior, with males expected to shock to higher levels and attractive people to lower levels (on the powerful relation between judgments of physical attractiveness and moral goodness, see Dion et al. 1972). Furthermore, self-predictions of women are extraordinarily low even though there are no gender differences in the original Milgram experiments. See A. Miller (1986) for an excellent critical retrospective of the Milgrim experiments and their progeny.

2. There is some related work about whose proper interpretation I am completely bewildered but which if true certainly scores points for the situationists. Isen and Levin (1972) examined the connection between mood and helpfulness. They planted dimes in phone booths at a mall and then had a confederate drop a manila folder holding loose papers in front of those persons who had just found the extra dime, as well as in front of those who had looked (everyone does) but had not found one. Fourteen out of fifteen of those who had had the minor good fortune helped, whereas only two out of the twenty-four who had not found a dime helped (see R. Brown 1986, 60)!

References

Arendt, H. (1963). *Eichmann in Jerusalem: A report on the banality of evil.* New York: Viking.

Asch, S. E. (1956). Studies of independence and conformity: A minority of one against a unanimous majority. *Psychological Monographs* 70, no. 9.

Brown, R. (1986). *Social psychology.* 2d ed. New York: Free Press.

Darley, J. M., and C. D. Batson (1973). From Jerusalem to Jericho: A study of situational and dispositional variables in helping behavior. *Journal of Personality and Social Psychology* 27, 100–108.

Dion, K., E. Berscheid, and E. Walster (1972). What is beautiful is good. *Journal of Personality and Social Psychology* 24, 285–290.

Elms, A. C., and S. Milgram (1966). Personality characteristics associated with obedience and defiance toward authoritative command. *Journal of Experimental Research in Personality* 1, 282–289.

Gamson, W. A., B. Fireman, and R. Rytina (1982). *Encounter with unjust authority.* Homewood, IL: Dorsey.

Isen, A. M., and H. Levin (1972). Effect of feeling good on helping: cookies and kindness. *Journal of Personality and Social Psychology* 21, 384–388.

Koonz, H. (1987). *Mothers in the fatherland: Women, the family, and Nazi politics.* New York: St. Martin's.

Latané, B. (1981). The psychology of social impact. *American Psychologist* 36, 343–356.

Latané, B., and J. Darley (1970). *The unresponsive bystander: Why doesn't he help?* Englewood Cliffs, NJ: Prentice-Hall.

London, P. (1970). The rescuers: Motivational hypotheses about Christians who saved Jews from the Nazis. In J. R. Macaulay and L. Berkowitz, eds., *Altruism and helping behavior.* New York: Academic Press.

Milgram, S. (1974). *Obedience to authority: An experimental view.* New York: Harper & Row.

Miller, A. G. (1986). *The obediance experiments: A case study of controversy.* New York: Praeger.

Miller, A. G., B. Gillen, C. Schenker, and S. Radlove (1974). The prediction and perception of obedience to authority. *Journal of Personality* 42, 23–42.

Nussbaum, M. (1986). *The fragility of goodness: Luck and ethics in Greek tragedy and philosophy.* New York: Cambridge University Press.

Oliner, S. P., and P. M. Oliner (1988). *The altruistic personality: Rescuers of Jews in Nazi Europe.* New York: Free Press.

Ross, L. (1988). Situationist perspectives on the obedience experiments: Review of A. G. Miller (1986). *Contemporary Psychology* 33, 101–104.

Shweder, R. A., and E. Bourne (1984). Does the concept of the person vary cross-culturally? In R. A. Shweder and R. LeVine, eds., *Culture theory: Essays on mind, self, and emotion.* New York: Cambridge University Press.

Tec, N. (1986). *When light pierced the darkness: Christian rescue of Jews in Nazi-occupied Poland.* Oxford: Oxford University Press.

VII

Conceptual Foundations

32 Autonomous Psychology and the Belief-Desire Thesis

Stephen P. Stich

A venerable view, still very much alive, holds that human action is to be explained at least in part in terms of beliefs and desires. Those who advocate the view expect that the psychological theory which explains human behavior will invoke the concepts of belief and desire in a substantive way. I will call this expectation *the belief-desire thesis*. Though there would surely be a quibble or a caveat here and there, the thesis would be endorsed by an exceptionally heterogeneous collection of psychologists and philosophers ranging from Freud and Hume, to Thomas Szasz and Richard Brandt. Indeed, a number of philosophers have contended that the thesis, or something like it, is embedded in our ordinary, workaday concept of action.[1] If they are right, and I think they are, then in so far as we use the concept of action we are *all* committed to the belief-desire thesis. My purpose in this paper is to explore the tension between the belief-desire thesis and a widely held assumption about the nature of explanatory psychological theories, an assumption that serves as a fundamental regulative principle for much of contemporary psychological theorizing. This assumption, which for want of a better term I will call the *principle of psychological autonomy*, will be the focus of the first of the sections below. In the second section I will elaborate a bit on how the belief-desire thesis is to be interpreted, and try to extract from it a principle that will serve as a premise in the argument to follow. In the third section I will set out an argument to the effect that large numbers of belief-desire explanations of action, indeed perhaps the bulk of such explanations, are incompatible with the principle of autonomy. Finally, in the last section, I will fend off a possible objection to my argument. In the process, I will try to make clear just why the argument works and what price we should have to pay if we were resolved to avoid its consequences.

From S. Stich, Autonomous psychology and the belief-desire thesis, *Monist* 61, 573–591 (1978). Copyright © 1978, THE MONIST, La Salle, Illinois 61301. Reprinted by permission.

Perhaps the most vivid way of explaining the principle I have in mind is by invoking a type of science fiction example that has cropped up with some frequency in recent philosophical literature. Imagine that technology were available which would enable us to duplicate people. That is, we can built living human beings who are atom for atom and molecule for molecule replicas of some given human being (cf. Putnam 1973, 1975). Now suppose that we have before us a human being (or, for that matter, any sort of animal) and his exact replica. What the principle of autonomy claims is that these two humans will be psychologically identical, that any psychological property instantiated by one of these subjects will also be instantiated by the other.

Actually, a bit of hedging is needed to mark the boundaries of this claim to psychological identity. First, let me note that the organisms claimed to be psychologically identical include any pair of organisms, existing at the same time or at different times, who happen to be atom for atom replicas of each other. Moreover, it is inessential that one organism should have been built to be a replica of the other. Even if the replication is entirely accidental, the two organisms will still be psychologically identical.

A caveat of another sort is needed to clarify just what I mean by calling two organisms "psychologically identical." For consider the following objection: "The original organism and his replica do not share *all* of their psychological properties. The original may, for example, remember seeing the Watergate hearings on television, but the replica remembers no such thing. He may think he remembers it, or have an identical "memory trace", but if he was not created until long after the Watergate hearings, then he did not see the hearings on television, and thus he could not remember seeing them." The point being urged by my imagined critic is a reasonable one. There are many sorts of properties plausibly labeled "psychological" that might be instantiated by a person and not by his replica. Remembering that p is one example, knowing that p and seeing that p are others. These properties have a sort of "hybrid" character. They seem to be analyzable into a "purely psychological" property (like seeming to remember that p, or believing that p) along with one or more non-psychological properties and relations (like p being true, or the memory trace being caused in a certain way by the fact that p). But to insist that "hybrid" psychological properties are not psychological properties at all would be at best a rather high handed attempt at stipulative definition. Still, there is something a bit odd about these hybrid psychological properties, a fact which reflects itself in the intuitive distinction between "hybrids" and their underlying "purely psychological" components. What is odd about the hybrids, I think, is that we do not expect them to play any role in an explanatory psychological theory. Rather, we expect a psychological theory which aims at explaining behavior to invoke only the "purely psychological" properties which are shared by a subject and its replicas. Thus, for example, we are inclined to insist it is Jones's *belief* that there is no greatest prime number that plays a role in the explanation of his answering the exam question. He may, in fact, have *known* that there is no greatest prime number. But even if he did not know it, if, for example, the source of his information had himself only been guessing, Jones's behavior would have been unaffected. What knowledge adds to belief is psychologically irrelevant. Similarly the difference between really remembering that *p* and merely seeming to remember that *p* makes no difference to the subject's behavior. In claiming that physical replicas are psychologically identical, the principle of psychological autonomy is to be understood as restricting itself to the properties that can play a role in explanatory psychological theory. Indeed, the principle is best viewed as a claim about what sorts of properties and relations may play a role in explanatory psychological theory. If the principle is to be observed, then the only properties and relations that may legitimately play a role in explanatory psychological theories are the properties and relations that a subject and its replica will share.

There is another way to explain the principle of psychological autonomy that does not appeal to the fanciful ideas of a replica. . . . Jaegwon Kim (1978) has explicated and explored the notion of one class of properties *supervening* upon another class of properties. Suppose S and W are two classes of properties, and that S# and W# are the sets of all properties constructible from the properties in S and W respectively. Then, following Kim, we will say that the family S of properties supervenes on the family W of properties (with respect to a domain D of objects) just in case, necessarily, any two objects in D which share all properties in W# will also share all properties in S#. A bit less formally, one class of properties supervenes on another if the presence or absence of properties in the former class is completely determined by the presence or absence of properties in the latter.[2] Now the principle of psychological autonomy states that the properties and relations to be invoked in an explanatory psychological theory must be supervenient upon the *current, internal physical* properties and relations of organisms (i.e., just those properties that an organism shares with all of its replicas).

Perhaps the best way to focus more sharply on what the autonomy principle states is to look at what it rules out. First, of course, if explanatory psychological properties and relations must supervene on *physical* properties, then at least some forms of dualism are false. The dualist who claims that there are psychological (or mental) properties which are not nomologically correlated with physical properties, but which nonetheless must be invoked in an explanation of the organism's behavior, is denying that explanatory psychological states supervene upon physical states, However, the autonomy principle is not inimical to all

Autonomous Psychology and the Belief-Desire Thesis

forms of dualism. Those dualists, for example, who hold that mental and physical properties are nomologically correlated need have no quarrel with the doctrine of autonomy. However, the principle of autonomy is significantly stronger than the mere insistence that psychological states supervene on physical states.[3] For autonomy requires in addition that certain physical properties and relations are psychologically irrelevant in the sense that organisms which differ *only* with respect to those properties and relations are psychologically identical.[4] In specifying that only "current" physical properties are psychologically relevant, the autonomy principle decrees irrelevant all those properties that deal with the history of the organism, both past and future. It is entirely possible, for example, for two organisms to have quite different physical histories and yet, at a specific pair of moments, to be replicas of one another. But this sort of difference, according to the autonomy principle, can make no difference from the point of view of explanatory psychology. Thus remembering that p (as contrasted with having a memory trace that p) cannot be an explanatory psychological state. For the difference between a person who remembers that p and a person who only seems to remember that p is not dependent on their current physical state, but only on the history of these states. Similarly, in specifying that only *internal* properties and relations are relevant to explanatory psychological properties, the autonomy principle decrees that relations between an organism and its external environment are irrelevant to its current (explanatory) psychological state. The restriction also entails that properties and relations of external objects cannot be relevant to the organism's current (explanatory) psychological state. Thus neither my seeing that Jones is falling nor my knowing that Ouagadougou is the capital of Upper Volta can play a role in an explanatory psychological theory, since the former depends in part on my relation to Jones, and the latter depends in part on the relation between Ouagadougou and Upper Volta.

Before we leave our discussion of the principle of psychological autonomy, let us reflect briefly on the status of the principle. On Kim's view, the belief that one set of properties supervenes on another "is largely, and often, a combination of metaphysical convictions and methodological considerations" (Kim 1978). The description seems particularly apt for the principle of psychological autonomy. The autonomy principle serves a sort of regulative role in modern psychology, directing us to restrict the concepts we invoke in our explanatory theories in a very special way. When we act in accordance with the regulative stipulation of the principle we are giving witness to the tacit conviction that the best explanation of behavior will include a theory invoking properties supervenient upon the organism's current, internal physical state.[5] As Kim urges, this conviction is supported in part by the past success of theories which cleave to the principle's restrictions, and in part by some very fundamental metaphysical convictions. I think there is much to be learned in trying to pick apart the various metaphysical views that support the autonomy principle, for some of them have implications in areas quite removed from psychology. But that is a project for a different paper.

The Belief-Desire Thesis

The belief-desire thesis maintains that human action is to be explained, at least in part, in terms of beliefs and desires. To sharpen the thesis we need to say more about the intended sense of *explain*, and more about what it would be to explain actions *in terms of beliefs and desires*. But before trying to pin down either of these notions, it will be useful to set out an example of the sort of informal belief-desire explanations that we commonly offer for our own actions and the actions of others.

Jones is watching television; from time to time he looks nervously at a lottery ticket grasped firmly in his hand. Suddenly he jumps up and rushes toward the phone. Why? It was because the TV announcer has just announced the winning lottery number, and it is the number on Jones's ticket. Jones believes that he has won the lottery. He also believes that to collect his winnings he must contact the lottery commission promptly. And, needless to say, he very much wants to collect his winnings.

Many theorists acknowledge that explanations like the one offered of Jones rushing toward the phone are often true (albeit incomplete) explanations of action. But this concession alone does not commit the theorist to the belief-desire thesis as I will interpret it here. There is considerable controversy over how we are to understand the 'because' in "Jones rushed for the phone because he believed he had won the lottery and he wanted . . ." Some writers are inclined to read the 'because' literally, as claiming that Jones's belief and his desire were the *causes* (or among the causes) of his action. Others offer a variety of non-causal accounts of the relation between beliefs and desires on the one hand and actions on the other.[6] However, it is the former, "literal," reading that is required by the belief-desire thesis as I am construing it.

To say that Jones's belief that he had won the lottery was among the causes of his rushing toward the phone is to say of one specific event that it had among its causes one specific state. There is much debate over how such "singular causal statements" are to be analyzed. Some philosophers hold that for a state or event S to be among the causes of an event E, there must be a law which somehow relates S and E. Other philosophers propose other accounts. Even among those who agree that singular causal statements must be subsumed by a law, there is debate over how this notion of subsumption is to be understood. At the heart of this controversy is the issue of how much difference there can be between the properties invoked in the law and those invoked in the description of the event if the event is to be an instance of the law.[7] Given our current purposes, there is no need to take a stand on this quite general metaphysical issue. But we will have to take a stand on a special case of the relation between beliefs, desires, and the psychological laws that subsume them. The belief-desire thesis, as I am viewing it, takes seriously the idea of developing a psychological theory couched in terms of beliefs and desires. Thus, in addition to holding that Jones's action was caused by his belief that he had won the lottery and his desire to collect his winnings, it also holds that this singular causal statement is true in virtue of being subsumed by laws which specify nomological relations among beliefs, desires and action.[8]

There is one further point that needs to be made about my construal of the belief-desire thesis. If the thesis is right, then action is to be explained at least in part by appeal to laws detailing how beliefs, desires and other psychological states effect action. But how are we to recognize such laws? It is, after all, plainly not enough for a theory simply to invoke the terms 'belief' and 'desire' in its laws. If it were, then it would be possible to convert any theory into a belief-desire theory by the simple expedient of replacing a pair of its theoretical terms with the terms 'belief' and 'desire'. The point I am laboring is that the belief-desire thesis must be construed as the claim that psychological theory will be couched in terms of beliefs and desires *as we ordinarily conceive of them*. Thus to spell out the belief-desire thesis in detail would require that we explicate our intuitive concepts of belief and desire. Fortunately, we need not embark on that project here.[9] To feel the arguments I will develop in the following section, I will need only a single, intuitively plausible, premise about beliefs.

As a backdrop for the premise that I need, let me introduce some handy terminology. I believe that Ouagadougou is the capital of Upper Volta, and if you share my interest in atlases then it is likely that you have the same belief. Of course, there is also a perfectly coherent sense in which your belief is not the same as mine, since you could come to believe that Bobo Dioulasso is the capital of Upper Volta, while my belief remains unchanged. The point here is the obvious one that beliefs, like sentences, admit of a type-token distinction. I am inclined to view belief tokens as states of a person. And I take a state to be the instantiation of a property by an object during a time interval. Two belief states (or belief tokens) are of the same type if they are instantiations of the same property and they are of different types if they are instantiations of different properties.[10] In the example at hand, the property that both you and I instantiate is *believing that Ouagadougou is the capital of Upper Volta*.

Now the premise I need for my argument concerns the identity conditions for belief properties. Cast in its most intuitive form, the premise is simply that if a particular belief of yours is true and a particular belief of mine is false, then they are not the same belief. A bit more precisely: If a belief token of one subject differs in truth value from a belief token of another subject, then the tokens are not of the same type. Given our recent account of belief states, this is equivalent to a sufficient condition for the non-identity of belief properties: If an instantiation of belief property p_1 differs in truth value from an instantiation of belief property p_2 then p_1 and p_2 are different properties. This premise hardly constitutes an analysis of our notion of sameness of belief, since we surely do not hold belief tokens to be of the same type if they merely have the same truth value. But no matter. There is no need here to explicate our intuitive notion of belief identity in any detail. What the premise does provide is a necessary condition on any state counting as a belief. If a pair of states can be type identical (i.e., can be instantiations of the same property) while differing in truth value, then the states are not beliefs as we ordinarily conceive of them.

Before putting my premise to work, it might be helpful to note how the premise can be derived from a quite traditional philosophical account of the nature of beliefs. According to this account, belief is a relation between a person and a proposition. Two persons have the same belief (instantiate the same belief property) if they are belief-related to the same proposition. And, finally, propositions are taken to be the vehicles of truth, so propositions with different truth values cannot be identical. Given this account of belief, it follows straightforwardly that belief tokens differing in truth value differ in type. But the entailment is not mutual, so those who, like me, have some suspicions about the account of belief as a relation between a person and a proposition are free to explore other accounts of belief without abandoning the intuitively sanctioned premise that differences in truth value entail difference in belief.

The Tension between Autonomy and the Belief-Desire Thesis

In this section I want to argue that a certain tension exists between the principle of psychological autonomy and the belief-desire thesis. The tension is not, strictly speaking a logical incompatibility. Rather, there is an incompatibility between the autonomy principle and some assumptions that are naturally and all but universally shared by advocates of the belief-desire thesis. The additional assumptions are that singular causal statements like the ones extractable from our little story about Jones and the lottery ticket are often true. Moreover, they are true because they are subsumed by laws which invoke the very properties which are invoked in the characterization of the beliefs and desires. A bit less abstractly, what I am assuming is that statements like "Jones's belief that he had won the lottery was among the causes of his rushing toward the phone" are often true; and that they are true in virtue of being subsumed by laws invoking properties like *believing that he had just won the lottery*. The burden of my argument is that if we accept the principle of autonomy, then these assumptions must be rejected. More specifically, I will argue that if the autonomy principle is accepted then there are large numbers of belief properties that cannot play a role in an explanatory psychological theory. My strategy will be to examine four different cases, each representative of a large class. In each case we will consider a pair of subjects who, according to the autonomy principle, instantiate all the same explanatory psychological properties, but who have different beliefs. So if we accept the principle of psychological autonomy, then it follows that the belief properties our subjects instantiate cannot be explanatory psychological properties. After running through the examples, I will reflect briefly on the implications of the argument for the belief-desire thesis.

Case 1: Self-referential Beliefs[11]

Suppose, as we did earlier, that we have the technology for creating atom for atom replicas of people. Suppose, further, that a replica for me has just been created. I believe that I have tasted a bottle of Chateau d'Yquem, 1962. Were you to ask me whether I had ever tasted a d'Yquem, 1962, I would reply, "Yes, I have." An advocate of the belief-desire thesis would urge, plausibly enough, that my belief is among the causes of my utterance. Now if you were to ask my replica whether he had ever tasted a d'Yquem, 1962, he would likely also reply, "Yes, I have." And surely a belief-desire theorist will also count my replica's belief among the causes of *his* utterance. But the belief which is a cause of my replica's utterance must be of a different type from the one which is a cause of my utterance. For his belief is false; he has just been created and has never tasted a d'Yquem, nor any other wine. So by the premise we set out in section II, the belief property he instantiates is different from the one I instantiate. Yet since we are replicas, the autonomy principle entails that we share all our explanatory psychological properties. It follows that the property of believing that I have tasted a Chateau d'Yquem, 1962, cannot be one which plays a role in an explanatory psychological theory. In an obvious way, the example can be generalized to almost all beliefs about oneself. If we adhere to the principle of autonomy, then beliefs about ourselves can play no role in the explanation of our behavior.

Case 2: Beliefs about One's Spatial and Temporal Location

Imagine, to vary the science fiction example, that cryogenics, the art of freezing people, has been perfected to the point at which a person can be frozen, stored, then defrosted, and at the end of the ordeal be atom for atom identical with the way he was at the beginning of the freezing process. Now suppose that I submit myself to cryogenic preservation this afternoon, and, after being frozen, I am transported to Iceland where I am stored for a century or two, then defrosted. I now believe that it is the twentieth century and that there are many strawberry farms nearby. It would be easy enough to tell stories which would incline the belief-desire theorists to say that each of these beliefs is serving as a cause of my actions. I will leave the details to the reader's imagination. On being defrosted, however, I would presumably still believe that it is the twentieth century and that there are many straw-berry farms nearby. Since my current beliefs are both true and my future beliefs both false, they are not belief tokens of the same type, and do not instantiate the same belief property. But by hypothesis, I am, on defrosting, a replica of my current self. Thus the explanatory psychological properties that I instantiate cannot have changed. So the belief property I instantiate when I now believe that it is the twentieth century cannot play any role in an explanatory psychological theory. As in the previous case, the example generalizes to a large number of other beliefs involving a subject's temporal and spatial location.

Case 3: Beliefs about Other People

Hilary Putnam (1973, 1975) has made interesting use of the following fanciful hypothesis. Suppose that in some distant corner of the universe there is a planet very much like our own. Indeed, it is so much like our own that there is a person there who is my doppelganger. He is atom for atom identical with me and has led an entirely parallel life history. Like me, my doppelganger teaches in a philosophy department, and like me has heard a number of lectures on the subject of proper names delivered by a man called "Saul Kripke." However, his planet is not a complete physical replica of mine. For the philosopher called "Saul Kripke" on that planet, though strikingly similar to the one called by the same noun on our planet, was actually born in a state they call "South Dakota," which is to the north of a state they call "Nebraska." By contrast, our Saul Kripke was born in Nebraska—our Nebraska, of course, not theirs. But for reasons which need not be gone into here, many people on this distant planet, including my doppelganger, hold a belief which they express by saying "Saul Kripke was born in Ne-braska." Now I also hold a belief which I express by saying "Saul Kripke was born in Nebraska." However, the belief I express with those words is very different from the belief my doppelganger expresses using the same words, so different, in fact, that his belief is false while mine is true. Yet since we are doppelgangers the autonomy principle dictates that we instantiate all the same explanatory psychological properties. Thus the belief property I instantiate in virtue of believing that Saul Kripke was born in Nebraska cannot be a property invoked in an explanatory psychological theory.

Case 4: Natural Kind Predicates

In Putnam's doppelganger planet stories, a crucial difference between our planet and the distant one is that on our planet the substance which we call "water," which fills our lakes, etc. is in fact H_2O, while on the other planet the substance they call "water" which fills their lakes, etc. is in fact some complex chemical whose chemical formula we may abbreviate XYZ. Now imagine that we are in the year 1700, and that some ancestor of mine hears a story from a source he takes to be beyond reproach to the effect that when lizards are dipped in water, they dissolve. The story, let us further suppose, is false, a fact which my ancestor might discover to his dismay when attempting to dissolve a lizard. For the belief-desire theorist, the unsuccessful attempt has as one of its causes the belief that lizards dissolve in water. Now suppose that my ancestor has a doppelganger on the far off planet who is told an identical sounding story by an equally trustworthy raconteur. However, as it happens that story is true, for there are lizards that do dissolve in XYZ, though none will dissolve in H_2O. The pattern should by now be familiar. My ancestor's belief is false, his doppelganger's is true. Thus the belief tokens instantiate different belief properties. But since *ex hypothesi* the people holding the beliefs are physically identical, the belief properties they instantiate cannot function in an explanatory psychological theory.[12]

This completes my presentation of cases. Obviously, the sorts of examples we have looked at are not the only ones susceptible to the sort of arguments I have been using. But let us now reflect for a moment on just what these arguments show. To begin, we should note that they do *not* show the belief-desire thesis is false. The thesis, as I have constructed it here, holds that there are psychological laws which invoke various belief and desire properties and which have a substantive role to play in the explanation of behavior. Nothing we have said here would suffice to show that there are no such laws. At best, what we have shown is that, if we accept the principle of psychological autonomy, then a large class of belief properties cannot be invoked in an explanatory psychological theory. This, in turn, entails that many intuitively sanctioned singular causal statements which specify a belief as a cause of an action cannot be straightforwardly subsumed by a law. And it is just here, I think, that our argument may serve to undermine the belief-desire thesis. For the plausibility of the thesis rests, in large measure, on the plausibility of these singular causal statements. Indeed, I think the belief-desire thesis can be profitably viewed as the speculation that these intuitively sanctioned singular causal statements can be cashed out in a serious psychological theory couched in terms of beliefs and desires. In showing that large numbers of these singular causal statements cannot be cashed out in this way, we make the speculation embodied in the belief-desire thesis appear idle and unmotivated. In the section that follows, I will consider a way in which an advocate of the belief-desire thesis might try to deflect the impact of our arguments, and indicate the burden that this escape route imposes on the belief-desire theorist.

A Way Out and Its Costs

Perhaps the most tempting way to contain the damage done by the arguments of the previous section is to grant the conclusions while denying their relevance to the belief-desire thesis. I imagine a critic's objection going something like this: "Granted, if we accept the autonomy principle, then certain belief properties cannot be used in explanatory theories. But this does nothing to diminish the plausibility of the belief-desire thesis, because the properties you have shown incompatible with autonomy are the *wrong kind* of belief properties. All of the examples you consider are cases of *de re* beliefs, none of them are *de dicto* beliefs. But those theorists who take seriously the idea of constructing a belief-desire psychological theory have in mind a theory invoking *de dicto* beliefs and desires. *De re* beliefs are a sort of hybrid; a person has a *de re* belief if he has a suitable underlying *de dicto* belief, *and* if he is related to specific objects in a certain way. But it is only the underlying *de dicto* belief that will play a role in psychological explanation. Thus your arguments do not cast any serious doubt on the belief-desire thesis."[13]

Before assessing this attempt to protect the belief-desire thesis, a few remarks on the *de dicto/de re* distinction are in order. In the recent philosophical discussion of *de re* and *de dicto* beliefs, the focus has been on the logical relations among various sorts of belief attributions. Writers concerned with the issue have generally invoked a substitution criterion to mark the boundary between *de dicto* and *de re* belief attributions. Roughly, a belief attribution of the form

S believes that *p*

is *de re* if any name or other referring expression within *p* can be replaced with a co-designating term without risk of change of truth value; otherwise the attribution is *de dicto*.[14]

But now given this way of drawing the *de re/de dicto* distinction, my imagined critic is simply wrong in suggesting that all of the examples I used in my arguments are cases of *de re* belief. Indeed, just the opposite is true; I intend all of the belief attribution in my examples to be understood in the *de dicto* sense, and all my arguments work quite well when they are read in this way. Thus, for example, in Case 3 I attribute to myself the belief that Saul Kripke was born in Nebraska. But I intend this to be understood in such a way that

Stich believes 'Φ' was born in Nebraska

might well be false if 'Φ' were replaced by a term which, quite unbeknownst to me, in fact denotes Saul Kripke.

There is, however, another way the critic could press his attack that sidesteps my rejoinder. Recently, a number of writers have challenged

Autonomous Psychology and the Belief-Desire Thesis

the substitutional account of the *de dicto/de re* distinction. The basic idea underlying their challenge is that the term *'de re'* should be used for all belief attributions which intend to ascribe a "real" relation of some sort between the believer and the object of his belief. The notion of a real relation is contrasted with the sort of relation that obtains between a person and an object when the object happens to satisfy some description that the person has in mind.[15] Burge, for example, holds that "a *de dicto* belief is a belief in which the believer is related only to a completely expressed proposition *(dictum),*" in contrast to a *de re* belief which is "a belief whose correct ascription places the believer in an appropriate, *nonconceptual, contextual* relation to the objects the belief is about."[16] Thus, if Brown believes that the most prosperous Oriental rug dealer in Los Angeles is an Armenian, and if he believes it simply because he believes all prosperous Oriental rug dealers are Armenian, but has no idea who the man may be, then his belief is *de dicto*. By contrast, if Brown is an intimate of the gentleman, he may have the *de re* belief that the most prosperous Oriental rug dealer in Los Angeles is an Armenian. The sentence

Brown believes that the most prosperous Oriental rug dealer in Los Angeles is an Armenian.

is thus ambiguous, since it may be used either in the *de re* sense to assert that Brown and the rug dealer stand in some "appropriate, non-conceptual, contextual relation" or in the *de dicto* sense which asserts merely that Brown endorses the proposition that the most prosperous rug dealer in Los Angeles (whoever he may be) is an Armenian.

The problem with the substitutional account of the *de dicto/de re* distinction is that it classifies as *de dicto* many belief attributions which impute a "real" relation between the believer and the object of his belief. In many belief attributions the names or definite descriptions that occur in the content sentence do a sort of double duty. First, they serve the function commonly served by names and descriptions; they indicate (or refer to) an object, in this case the object to which the believer is said to be related. The names or descriptions in the content sentence *also* may serve to indicate how the believer conccives of the object, or how he might characterize it. When a name or description serving both roles is replaced by a codesignating expression which does *not* indicate how the believer conceives of the object, then the altered attribution (interpreted in the "double duty" sense) will be false. Thus the substitutional account classifies the original attribution as *de dicto*, despite its imputation of a "real" relation between believer and object.[17]

Now if the *de dicto/de re* distinction is drawn by classifying as *de re* all those belief attributions which impute a "real" relation between believer and object, then the critic conjured in the first paragraph of this section is likely right in his contention that all of my arguments invoke examples of *de re* beliefs. Indeed, the strategy of my arguments is to cite an example of a *de re* (i.e., "real relation") belief, then construct a second example in which the second believer is a physical replica of the first, but has no "real relation" to the object of the first believer's belief. However, to grant this much is not to grant that the critic has succeeded in blunting the point of my arguments.

Let me begin my rejoinder with a fussy point. The critic's contentions were two: first, that my examples all invoked *de re* belief properties; second, that *de re* belief properties are hybrids and are analyzable into *de dicto* belief properties. The fussy point is that even if both the critic's contentions are granted, the critic would not quite have met my arguments head on. The missing premise is that *de dicto* belief properties (construed now according to the "real relation" criterion) are in fact compatible with the principle of psychological autonomy. This premise may be true, but the notion of a "real" relation, on which the current account of *de dicto* belief properties depends, is sufficiently obscure that it is hard to tell. Fortunately, there is a simple way to finesse the problem. Let us introduce the term *autonomous beliefs* for those beliefs that a subject must share with all his replicas; and let us use the term *non-autonomous* for those beliefs which a subject need not share with his replica.[18] More generally, we can call any property which an organism must share with its replicas an *autonomous property*. We can now reconstrue the critic's claims as follows:

1. All the examples considered in section III invoke non-autonomous belief properties.

2. Non-autonomous belief properties are hybrids, analyzable into an underlying autonomous belief property (which can play a role in psychological explanation) plus some further relation(s) between the believer and the object of his belief.

On the first point I naturally have no quarrel, since a principle purpose of this paper is to show that a large class of belief properties are non-autonomous. On the second claim, however, I would balk, for I am skeptical that the proposed analysis can in fact be carried off. I must hasten to add that I know of *no argument* sufficient to show that the analysis is impossible. But, of course, my critic has no argument either. Behind my skepticism is the fact that no such analysis has ever been carried off. Moreover, the required analysis is considerably more demanding than the analysis of *de re* belief in terms of *de dicto* belief, when the distinction between the two is drawn by the substitutional criterion. For the class of autonomous beliefs is significantly smaller than the class of *de dicto* beliefs (characterized substitutionally).[19] And the most impressive attempts to reduce *de re* beliefs to *de dicto* plainly will not be of much help for the analysis my critic proposes.[20] But enough, I have already conceded that I cannot prove my critic's project is impossible. What I do hope to have established is that the critic's burden is the burden of the belief-desire theorist. If the reduction of non-autonomous

Autonomous Psychology and the Belief-Desire Thesis

beliefs to autonomous beliefs cannot be carried off, then there is small prospect that a psychological theory couched in terms of beliefs and desires will succeed in explaining any substantial part of human behavior.

A final point. It might be argued that, however difficult the analysis of non-autonomous beliefs to autonomous ones may be, it must be possible to carry it off. For, the argument continues, a subject's non-autonomous beliefs are determined in part by the autonomous psychological properties he instantiates and in part by his various relations to the objects of the world. Were either of these components suitably altered, the subject's non-autonomous beliefs would be altered as well. And since non-autonomous beliefs are jointly determined by autonomous psychological properties and by other relations, there must be some analysis, however complex, which specifies how this joint determination works. Now this last claim is not one I would want to challenge. I am quite prepared to grant that non-autonomous beliefs admit of some analysis in terms of autonomous psychological properties plus other relations. But what seems much more doubtful to me is that the autonomous properties invoked in the analysis would be *belief properties*. To see the reasons for my doubt, let us reflect on the picture suggested by the examples in section III. In each case we had a pair of subjects who shared all their autonomous properties though their non-autonomous beliefs differed in truth value. The difference in truth value, in turn, was rooted in a difference in reference; the beliefs were simply about different persons, places or times. In short, the beliefs represented different states of affairs. If the non-autonomous belief properties of these examples are to be analyzed into autonomous psychological properties plus various historical or external relations, then it is plausible to suppose that the autonomous psychological properties do not determine a truth value, an appropriate reference or a represented state of affairs. So the state of exhibiting one (or more) of these autonomous properties itself has no truth value, is not referential, and does not represent anything. And this, I would urge, is more than enough reason to say that it is not a belief at all. None of this amounts to an *argument* that non-autonomous beliefs are not analyzable into autonomous ones. Those who seek such an analysis are still free to maintain that there will be at least one autonomous belief among the autonomous properties in the analysans of each non-autonomous belief property. But in the absence of an argument for this claim, I think few will find it particularly plausible. The ball is in the belief-desire theorist's court.[21]

Appendix

A bit more needs to be said about the premise urged at the end of section II. The premise, it will be recalled, was this:

If a belief token of one subject differs in truth value from a belief token of another subject, then the tokens are not of the same type.

A number of helpful critics have pointed out to me that we actually have a variety of intuitively sanctioned ways to decide when two belief tokens are of the same type. Moreover, some of these patently violate my premise. Thus, for example, if Jones and Smith each believes that he will win the next presidential election, there would be no intuitive oddness to the claim that Jones and Smith have the same belief. Though, of course, if Jones's belief is true, Smith's belief is false. It would be equally natural in this case to say that Jones and Smith have different beliefs. So I cannot rest my premise on our intuitive judgments; the intuitions will not bear the weight.

I think the best way of defending the premise is to make clear how it is related to a certain view (actually a category of views) about what beliefs are. The views I have in mind all share two features in common:

(i) they take belief to be a relation between a believer and a type of abstract object;

(ii) they take the abstract objects to be representational—that is, the abstract objects are taken to picture the world as being a certain way, or to claim that some state of affairs obtains. Thus the object, along with the actual state of the believer's world, determines a truth value.

For example, certain theorists take belief to be a relation between a person and a proposition; a proposition, in turn, determines a truth value for every possible world—truth for those worlds in which it is true and falsity for those worlds in which it is false. A person's belief is true if the proposition is true in his or her world. Rather more old fashioned is the theory which holds belief to be a relation between a person and an image or a mental picture. The belief is true if and only if the mental picture correctly depicts the believer's world.

Now on views such as these which take belief to be a relation between a person and an abstract object, the most natural way of determining when a pair of belief tokens are of the same type is by appeal to the abstract objects. A pair of subjects' belief tokens are of the same type when the subjects are related to the same abstract object. Thus when subjects are in the same possible world, their belief tokens are of the same type only if they are identical in truth value. And this, in effect, was the premise advanced in section II. The thesis of this paper is best taken to be that the principle of psychological autonomy is in conflict with the belief-desire thesis, *when beliefs are construed as in (i) and (ii)*. Let me add a final observation. A number of theorists have taken belief to be a relation between a person and a sentence or sentence-like object. For example, Jerry Fodor (1975) holds that belief is a relation between a person and a sentence in "the language of thought." It is interesting to ask whether a theory like Fodor's is at odds with the principle of psychological autonomy. The answer, I think, turns on whether the sentences in the language of thought are taken to have truth values, and whether their referring expressions are taken to determine a referent in a given world, independent of the head in which they happen to be inscribed. If sentences in the language of thought are taken to be analogous to Quine's eternal sentences, true or false in a given world regardless of who utters them or where they may be inscribed, then Fodor's view will satisfy (i) and (ii) and will run head on into the principle of psychological autonomy. For Fodor, I suspect, this would be argument enough to show that the sentences in the language of thought are not eternal.

Notes

1. The clearest and most detailed elaboration of this view that I know of is to be found in Goldman 1970. The view is also argued in Brandt and Kim 1963, and in Davidson 1963. However, Davidson does not advocate the belief-desire thesis as it will be construed below (cf. n. 8).

2. Kim's account of supervenience is intentionally non-committal on the sort of necessity invoked in the definition. Different notions of necessity will yield different, though parallel, concepts of supervenience.

3. This weaker principle is discussed at some length in Kim 1977.

4. Note, however, that physical properties that are irrelevant in this sense may nonetheless be *causally* related to those physical properties upon which psychological properties supervene. Thus they may be "psychologically relevant" in the sense that they may play a role in the explanation of how the organism comes to have some psychological property.

5. It has been my experience that psychologists who agree on little else readily endorse the autonomy principle. Indeed, I have yet to find a psychologist who did not take the principle to be obviously true. Some of these same psychologists also favored the sort of belief-desire explanations of action that I will later argue are at odds with the autonomy principle. None, however, was aware of the incompatibility, and a number of them vigorously resisted the contention that the incompatibility is there.

6. For a critique of these views, cf. Goldman 1970, chap. 3; Alston 1967b.

7. For discussion of these matters, see Kim 1973. Kim defends the view that the property invoked in the description must be identical with the one invoked in the law. For a much more liberal view see Davidson 1967.

8. Thus Davidson is not an advocate of the belief-desire thesis as I am construing it. For on his view, though beliefs and desires may be among the causes of actions, the general laws supporting the causal claims are not themselves couched in terms of beliefs and desires (cf. Davidson 1970). But Davidson's view, though not without interest, is plainly idiosyncratic. Generally, philosophers who hold that beliefs and desires are among the causes of behavior also think that there are psychological laws to be found (most likely

probabilistic ones) which are stated in terms of beliefs and desires (cf. Hempel 1965, 463–487; Alston 1967a, 1967b; Goldman 1970, chaps. 3 and 4).

We should also note that much of recent psychology can be viewed as a quest for psychological laws couched in terms of beliefs and/or desires. There is, for example, an enormous and varied literature on problem solving (cf. Newell and Simon 1972) and on informal inference (cf. Nisbett and Ross 1980) which explores the mechanisms and environmental determinants of belief formation. Also, much of the literature on motivation is concerned with uncovering the laws governing the formation and strength of desires (cf. Atkinson 1964).

9. For an attempt to explicate our informal concepts of belief and desire in some detail, see Stich (1983).

10. For more on this way of viewing states and events, cf. Kim 1969 and 1976. I think that most everything I say in this paper can be said as well, though not as briefly, without presupposing this account of states and events.

11. The examples in Case 1 and Case 2, along with my thinking on these matters, have been influenced by a pair of important papers by Castañeda 1966 and 1967.

12. We should note that this example and others invoking natural kind words work only if the extension of my ancestor's word 'water' is different from the extension of the word 'water' as used by my ancestor's doppelganger. I am inclined to agree with Putnam that the extensions are different. But the matter is controversial. For some support of Putnam's view, see Kripke 1972 and Teller 1977; for an opposing view cf. Zemach 1976. Incidentally, one critic has expressed doubt that my doppelganger and I could be physically identical if the stuff called 'water' on the far off planet is actually XYZ. Those who find the point troubling are urged to construct a parallel example using kinds of material not generally occurring within people.

13. The idea that *de dicto* beliefs are psychologically more basic is widespread. For a particularly clear example, see Armstrong 1973, 25–31. Of the various attempts to analyze *de re* beliefs in terms of *de dicto* beliefs, perhaps the best known are to be found in Kaplan 1968 and Chisholm 1976.

14. The substitutional account of *de re/de dicto* distinction has a curious consequence that has been little noted. Though most belief sentences of the form

S believes that Fa

can be used to make either *de re* or *de dicto* attributions, the substitutional account entails that some can only be used to make *de re* attributions. Consider, for example.

(i) Quine believes that the Queen of England is a turtle.

The claim of course, is false. Indeed, it is *so* false that it could not be used to make a *de dicto* belief attribution. For in all likelihood, there is *no* name or definite description Φ denoting Elizabeth II such that

Quine believes that Φ is a turtle

is true. Thus 'Quine believes that the Queen of England is a turtle' is false and cannot be turned into a truth by the replacement of 'the Queen of England' by a codesignating expression. So on the substitutional account, this sentence can be used to make only *de re* attributions. A parallel problem besets Quine's well known substitutional account of a *purely referential position* (Quine 1960, 142 ff.) In (i), the position occupied by 'the Queen of England' can only be regarded as purely referential.

15. For more on the distinction between "real" relations and mere "satisfaction" relations, cf. Kim 1977.

16. Burge 1977, 345 and 346; last emphasis added.

17. For more on this "double duty" view of the role of names and descriptions in content sentences, see Loar 1972.

18. Of course when the notion of a "real relation" has been suitably sharpened it might well turn out that the autonomous/non-autonomous distinction coincides with the "real relation" version of the *de dicto/de re* distinction.

19. For example, when I say, "I believe that Kripke was born in Nebraska," I am attributing to myself a belief which is substitutionally *de dicto*, but not autonomous.

20. Kaplan's strategy, for example, will be of no help, since his analysans are, for the most part, non-autonomous substitutionally *de dicto* belief sentences (cf. Kaplan 1968; Burge 1977, 350 ff.).

21. I am indebted to Robert Cummins, Jaegwon Kim, William Alston and John Bennett for their helpful comments on the topics discussed in this paper. After completing this paper, I was delighted to discover a very similar view in Perry 1979. Fodor 1980 defends a version of the principle of psychological autonomy.

References

Alston, W. P. (1967a). Motives and motivation. *The encyclopedia of philosophy*. New York: MacMillan.

Alston, W. P. (1967b) "Wants, Actions and causal explanations." In H. N. Castañeda, ed., *Intentionality, minds and perception*. Detroit: Wayne State University Press.

Armstrong, D. M. (1973). *Belief, truth and knowledge*. Cambridge: Cambridge University Press.

Atkinson, J. W. (1964). *An introduction to motivation*. New York: Van Nostrand.

Brandt, R. B., and Jaegwon Kim (1963). Wants as explanations of actions. *Journal of Philosophy* 60, 425–435.

Burge, T. (1977). Belief de re. *Journal of Philosophy* 74, 338–362.

Castañeda, H. N. (1966). 'He': A study in the logic of self-consciousness. *Ratio* 8, 130–157.

Castañeda, H. N. (1967). Indicators and quasi-indicators. *American Philosophical Quarterly* 4, 85–100.

Chisholm, R. (1976). *Person and object*. LaSalle, IL: Open Court.

Davidson, D. (1963). Actions, reasons and causes. *Journal of Philosophy* 60, 685–700.

Davidson, D. (1967). Causal relations. *Journal of Philosophy* 64, 691–703.

Davidson, D. (1970). Mental events. in L. Foster and J. W. Swanson, eds., *Experience and Theory*. Amherst: University of Massachusetts Press.

Fodor, J. (1975). *The Language of Thought*. New York: Crowell.

Fodor, J. (1980). Methodological solipsism considered as a research strategy in cognitive psychology. *Behavioral and Brain Sciences* 3, 63–73.

Goldman A. (1970). *A Theory of Human Action*. Englewood Cliffs, NJ: Prentice-Hall.

Hempel, C. G. (1965). *Aspects of Scientific Explanation*. New York: Free Press.

Kaplan, D. (1968). Quantifying in. *Synthese* 19, 178–214.

Kim, J. (1969). Events and their descriptions: Some considerations. In N. Rescher et al., eds., *Essays in Honor of C. G. Hempel*. Dordrecht, Holland: Reidel.

Kim, J. (1973). "Causation, nomic subsumption and the concept of event." *Journal of Philosophy*, 70, 217–236.

Kim, J. (1976). Events as property-exemplifications. In M. Brand and D. Walton, eds., *Action Theory*. Dordrecht, Holland: Rcidel.

Kim, J. (1977). Perception and reference without causality. *Journal of Philosophy* 74, 606–620.

Kim, J. (1978). Supervenience and nomological incommensurables. *American Philosophical Quarterly* 15, 2, 149–156.

Kripke, S. (1972). Naming and necessity. In D. Davidson and G. Harman, eds., *Semantics and Natural Language*. Dordrecht, Holland: Reidel.

Loar, B. (1972). Reference and propositional attitudes. *Philosophical Review* 80, 43–62.

Newell, A., and H. A. Simon (1972). *Human Problem Solving*, Englewood Cliffs: Prentice-Hall.

Nisbett, R., and L. Ross (1980). *Human Inference: Strategies and Shortcomings of Social Judgment*, Englewood Cliffs, NJ: Prentice-Hall.

Perry, J. (1979). The problem of the essential indexical. *Noûs* 13, 3–21.

Putnam, H. (1973). Meaning and reference. *Journal of Philosophy* 70, 699–711.

Putnam, H. (1975). The meaning of 'meaning'. In K. Gunderson, ed., *Language, Mind and Knowledge*. Minneapolis: University of Minnesota Press.

Quine, W. V. O. (1960). *Word and Object*. Cambridge: MIT Press.

Stich, S. (1983). *From Folk Psychology to Cognitive Science.* Cambridge, MA: Bradford Books/ MIT Press.

Teller, P. (1977). Indicative introduction. *Philosophical Studies* 31, 173–195.

Zemach, E. (1976). Putnam's theory on the reference of substance terms. *Journal of Philosophy* 83, 116–127.

33 Individualism and Psychology

Tyler Burge

Recent years have seen in psychology—and overlapping parts of linguistics, artificial intelligence, and the social sciences—the development of some semblance of agreement about an approach to the empirical study of human activity and ability. The approach is broadly mentalistic in that it involves the attribution of states, processes and events that are intentional, in the sense of 'representational'. Many of these events and states are unconscious and inaccessible to mere reflection. Computer jargon is prominent in labeling them. But they bear comparison to thoughts, wants, memories, perceptions, plans, mental sets and the like—ordinarily so-called. Like ordinary propositional attitudes, some are described by means of that-clauses and may be evaluated as true or false. All are involved in a system by means of which a person knows, represents, and utilizes information about his or her surroundings.

In the first part of this paper, I shall criticize some arguments that have been given for thinking that explanation in psychology is, and ought to be, purely "individualistic." In the second part of the paper, I shall discuss in some detail a powerful psychological theory that is not individualistic. The point of this latter discussion will be to illustrate a non-individualistic conception of explanatory kinds. In a third section, I shall offer a general argument against individualism, that centers on visual perception. What I have to say, throughout the paper, will bear on all parts of psychology that attribute intentional states. But I will make special reference to explanation in cognitive psychology.

Individualism is a view about how kinds are correctly individuated, how their natures are fixed. We shall be concerned primarily with individualism about the individuation of mental kinds. According to individualism about the mind, the mental natures of all a person's or animal's mental states (and events) are such that there is no necessary or deep individuative relation between the individual's being in states

From T. Burge, Individualism and psychology, *Philosophical Review* 95, 3–45 (1986). Reprinted by permission.

of those kinds and the nature of the individual's physical or social environments.

This view owes its prominence to Descartes. It was embraced by Locke, Leibniz, and Hume. And it has recently found a home in the phenomenological tradition and in the doctrines of twentieth century behaviorists, functionalists, and mind-brain identity theorists. There are various more specific versions of the doctrine. A number of fundamental issues in traditional philosophy are shaped by them. In this paper, however, I shall concentrate on versions of the doctrine that have been prominent in recent philosophy of psychology.

Current individualistic views of intentional mental states and events have tended to take one of two forms. One form maintains that an individual's being in any given intentional state (or being the subject of such an event) can be *explicated* by reference to states and events of the individual that are specifiable without using intentional vocabulary and without presupposing anything about the individual subject's social or physical environments. The explication is supposed to specify—in non-intentional terms—stimulations, behavior, and internal physical or functional states of the individual. The other form of individualism is implied by the first, but is weaker. It does not attempt to explicate anything. It simply makes a claim of *supervenience:* an individual's intentional states and events (types and tokens) could not be different from what they are, given the individual's physical, chemical, neural, or functional histories, where these histories are specified non-intentionally and in a way that is independent of physical or social conditions outside the individual's body.

In other papers (Burge 1979, 1982a, 1982b, 1986a, 1986b) I have argued that both forms of individualism are mistaken. A person's intentional states and events could (counterfactually) vary, even as the individual's physical, functional (and perhaps phenomenological) history, specified non-intentionally and individualistically, is held constant. I have offered several arguments for this conclusion. Appreciating the strength of these arguments, and discerning the philosophical potential of a non-individualist view of mind, depend heavily on reflecting on differences among these arguments. They both reinforce one another and help map the topography of a positive position.

For present purposes, however, I shall merely sketch a couple of the arguments to give their flavor. I shall not defend them or enter a variety of relevant qualifications. Consider a person *A* who thinks that aluminum is a light metal used in sailboat masts, and a person *B* who believes that he or she has arthritis in the thigh. We assume that *A* and *B* can pick out instances of aluminum and arthritis (respectively) and know many familiar general facts about aluminum and arthritis. *A* is, however, ignorant of aluminum's chemical structure and micro-properties. *B* is ignorant of the fact that arthritis cannot occur outside of joints.

Now we can imagine counterfactual cases in which A and B's bodies have their same histories considered in isolation of their physical environments, but in which there are significant environmental differences from the actual situation. A's counterfactual environment lacks aluminum and has in its places a similar-looking light metal. B's counterfactual environment is such that no one has ever isolated arthritis as a specific disease, or syndrome of diseases. In these cases, A would lack "aluminum thoughts" and B would lack "arthritis thoughts." Assuming natural developmental patterns, both would have different thoughts. Thus these differences from the actual situation show up not only in the protagonist's relations to their environments, but also in their intentional mental states and events, ordinarily so-called. The arguments bring out variations in obliquely (or intensionally) occurring expressions in literal mental state and event ascriptions, our primary means of identifying intentional mental states.[1]

I believe that these arguments use literal descriptions of mental events, and are independent of conversational devices that may affect the form of an ascription without bearing on the nature of the mental event described. The sort of argument that we have illustrated does not depend on special features of the notions of arthritis or aluminum. Such arguments go through for observational and theoretical notions, for percepts as well as concepts, for natural-kind and non-natural kind notions, for notions that are the special preserve of experts, and for what are known in the psychological literature as "basic categories." Indeed, I think that, at a minimum, relevantly similar arguments can be shown to go through with any notion that applies to public types of objects, properties, or events that are typically known by empirical means.[2]

I shall not elaborate or defend the arguments here. In what follows, I shall presuppose that they are cogent. For our purposes, it will be enough if one bears firmly in mind their conclusion: mental states and events may in principle vary with variations in the environment, even as an individual's physical (functional, phenomenological) history, specified non-intentionally and individualistically, remains constant.

A common reaction to these conclusions, often unsupported by argument, has been to concede their force, but to try to limit their effect. It is frequently held that they apply to common-sense attributions of attitudes, but have no application to analogous attributions in psychology. Non-individualistic aspects of mentalistic attribution have been held to be uncongenial with the purposes and requirements of psychological theory. Of course, there is a tradition of holding that ordinary intentional attributions are incapable of yielding any knowledge at all. Others have held the more modest view that mentalistic attributions are capable of yielding only knowledge that could not in principle be systematized in a theory.

I shall not be able to discuss all of these lines of thought. In particular I shall ignore generalized arguments that mentalistic ascriptions are deeply indeterminate, or otherwise incapable of yielding knowledge. Our focus will be on arguments that purport to show that non-individualistic mentalistic ascriptions cannot play a systematic role in psychological explanation—*because* of the fact that they are not individualistic.

There are indeed significant differences between theoretical discourse in psychology and the mentalistic discourse of common sense. The most obvious one is that the language of theoretical psychology requires refinements on ordinary discourse. It not only requires greater system and rigor, and a raft of unconscious states and events that are not ordinarily attributed (though they are, I think, ordinarily allowed for). It also must distill out descriptive-explanatory purposes of common attributions from uses that serve communication at the expense of description and explanation. Making this distinction is already common practice. Refinement for scientific purposes must, however, be systematic and meticulous—though it need not eliminate all vagueness. I think that there are no sound reasons to believe that such refinement cannot be effected through the development of psychological theory, or that effecting it will fundamentally change the nature of ordinary mentalistic attributions.

Differences between scientific and ordinary discourse survive even when ordinary discourse undergoes the refinements just mentioned. Although common sense discourse—both about macro-physical objects and about mental events—yields knowledge, I believe that the principles governing justification for such discourse differ from those that are invoked in systematic scientific theorizing. So there is, *prima facie*, room for the view that psychology is or should be fully individualistic—even though ordinary descriptions of mental states are not. Nevertheless, the arguments for this view that have been offered do not seem to me cogent. Nor do I find the view independently persuasive.

Before considering such arguments, I must articulate some further background assumptions, this time about psychology itself. I shall be taking those parts of psychology that utilize mentalistic and information-processing discourse pretty much as they are. I assume that they employ standard scientific methodology, that they have produced interesting empirical results, and that they contain more than a smattering of genuine theory. I shall not prejudge what sort of science psychology is, or how it relates to the natural sciences. I do, however, assume that its cognitive claims and, more especially, its methods and presuppositions are to be taken seriously as the best we now have in this area of inquiry. I believe that there are no good reasons for thinking that the methods or findings of this body of work are radically misguided.

I shall not be assuming that psychology *must* continue to maintain touch with common sense discourse. I believe that such touch will almost surely be maintained. But I think that empirical disciplines must find their own way according to standards that they set for themselves. Quasi-*apriori* strictures laid down by philosophers count for little. So our reflections concern psychology as it is, not as it will be or must be.

In taking psychology as it is, I am assuming that it seeks to refine, deepen, generalize and systematize some of the statements of informed common sense about people's mental activity. It accepts, for example, that people see physical objects with certain shapes, textures, and hues, and in certain spatial relations, under certain specified conditions. And it attempts to explain in more depth what people do when they see such things, and how their doing it is done. Psychology accepts that people remember events and truths, that they categorize objects, that they draw inferences, that they act on beliefs and preferences. And it attempts to find deep regularities in these activities, to specify mechanisms that underly them, and to provide systematic accounts of how these activities relate to one another. In describing and, at least partly, in explaining these activities and abilities, psychology makes use of interpreted that-clauses and other intensional constructions—or what we might loosely call "intentional content."[3] I have seen no sound reason to believe that this use is merely heuristic, instrumentalistic, or second class in any other sense.

I assume that intentional content has internal structure—something like grammatical or logical structure—and that the parts of this structure are individuated finely enough to correspond to certain individual abilities, procedures, or perspectives. Since various abilities, procedures, or perspectives may be associated with any given event, object, property, or relation, intentional content must be individuated more finely than the entities in the world with which the individual interacts. We must allow different ways (even, I think, different primitive ways) for the individual to conceive of, or represent any given entity. This assumption about the fine-grainedness of content in psychology will play no explicit role in what follows. I note it here to indicate that my skepticism about individualism as an interpretation of psychology does not stem from a conception of content about which it is already clear that it does not play a dominant role in psychology.[4]

Finally, I shall assume that individualism is *prima facie wrong* about psychology, including cognitive psychology. Since the relevant parts of psychology frequently use attributions of intentional states that are subject to our thought experiments, the language actually used in psychology is not purely individualistic. That is, the generalizations with counterfactual force that appear in psychological theories, given their standard interpretations, are not all individualistic. For ordinary understanding of the truth conditions, or individuation conditions, of the relevant attributions suffices to verify the thought experiments. Moreover, there is at present no well-explained, well-understood, much less

well-tested, individualistic language—or individualistic reinterpretation
of the linguistic forms currently in use in psychology—that could serve
as surrogate.

Thus individualism as applied to psychology must be revisionistic. It
must be revisionistic at least about the language of psychological theory.
I shall be developing the view that it is also revisionistic, without good
reason, about the underlying presuppositions of the science. To justify
itself, individualism must fulfill two tasks. It must show that the language of psychology should be revised by demonstrating that the presuppositions of the science are or should be *purely* individualistic. And
it must explain a new individualistic language (attributing what is sometimes called "narrow content") that captures genuine theoretical commitments of the science.

These tasks are independent. If the second were accomplished, but
the first remained unaccomplishable, individualism would be wrong;
but it would have engendered a new level of explanation. For reasons
I will mention later, I am skeptical about such wholesale supplemen-
tation of current theory. But psychology is not a monolith. Different
explanatory tasks and types of explanation co-exist within it. In questioning the view that psychology is individualistic, I am not *thereby*
doubting whether there are some sub-parts of psychology that conform
to the strictures of individualism. I am doubting whether all of psychology as it is currently practiced is or should be individualistic. Thus
I shall concentrate on attempts to fulfill the first of the two tasks that
face someone bent on revising psychology along individualistic lines.
So much for preliminaries.

I

We begin by discussing a general argument against non-individualistic
accounts. It goes as follows (cf. Stich 1983, chap. 8). The behavior of
the physiologically and functionally identical protagonists in our
thought experiments is identical. But psychology is the science (only)
of behavior. Since the behavior of the protagonists is the same, a science
of behavior should give the *same* explanations and descriptions of the
two cases (by some Ockhamesque principle of parsimony). So there is
no room in the discipline for explaining their behavior in terms of
different mental states.[5]

The two initial premises are problematic. To begin with the first: it is
not to be assumed that the protagonists are behaviorally identical in the
thought experiments. I believe that the only clear, general interpretation
of 'behavior' that is available and that would verify the first premise is
'bodily motion'. But this construal has almost no relevance to psychology as it is actually practiced. 'Behavior' has become a catch-all term in
psychology for observable activity on whose description and character
psychologists can reach quick "pretheoretical" agreement. Apart from

methodological bias, it is just not true that all descriptions that would count as "behavioral" in cognitive (social, developmental) psychology would apply to both the protagonists. Much behavior is intentional action; many action specifications are non-individualistic. Thought experiments relevantly similar to those which we have already developed will apply to them.

For example, much "behavioral" evidence in psychology is drawn from what people say or how they answer questions. Subjects' utterances (and the questions asked them) must be taken to be interpreted in order to be of any use in the experiments; and it is often assumed that theories may be checked by experiments carried out in different languages. Since the protagonists' sayings in the thought experiments are different, even in non-transparent or oblique occurrences, it is *prima facie* mistaken to count the protagonists "behaviorally" identical. Many attributions of non-verbal behavior are also intentional and non-individualistic, or even relational: she picked up the apple, pointed to the square block, tracked the moving ball, smiled at the familiar face, took the money instead of the risk. These attributions can be elaborated to produce non-individualist thought experiments. The general point is that many relevant specifications of behavior in psychology are intentional, or relational, or both. The thought experiments indicate that these specifications ground non-individualist mental attributions. An argument for individualism cannot reasonably *assume* that these specifications are individualistic or ought to be.

Of course, there are non-individualistic specifications of behavior that are unsuitable for any scientific enterprise ('my friend's favorite bodily movement'). But most of these do not even appear to occur in psychology. The problem of providing reasonable specifications of behavior cannot be solved from an armchair. Sanitizing the notion of behavior to meet some antecedently held methodological principle is an old game, never won. One must look at what psychology actually takes as "behavioral" evidence. It is the responsibility of the argument to show that non-individualistic notions have no place in psychology. Insofar as the argument assumes that intentional, non-individualistic specifications of behavior are illegitimate, it either ignores obvious aspects of psychological practice or begs the question at issue.

The second step of the argument also limps. One cannot assume without serious discussion that psychology is correctly characterized as a science (only) of behavior. This is, of course, particularly so if behavior is construed in a restrictive way. But even disregarding how behavior is construed, the premise is doubtful. One reason is that it is hardly to be assumed that a putative science is to be characterized in terms of its evidence as opposed to its subject matter. Of course, the subject matter is to some extent under dispute. But cognitive psychology appears to be about certain molar abilities and activities some of which are propositional attitudes. Since the propositional attitudes attributed do not seem to be fully individuable in individualistic terms, we need a direct argument that cognitive psychology is not a science of what it appears to be a science of.

A second reason for doubting the premise is that psychology seems to be partly about relations between people, or animals, and their environment. It is hard to see how to provide a natural description of a theory of vision, for example, as a science of behavior. The point of the theory is to figure out how people do what they obviously succeed in doing—how they see objects in their environment. We are trying to explain relations between a subject and a physical world that we take ourselves to know something about. Theories of memory, of certain sorts of learning, of linguistic understanding, of belief formation, of categorization, do the same. It is certainly not obvious that these references to relations between subject and environment are somehow inessential to (all parts of) psychological theory. They seem, in fact, to be a large part of the point of such theory. In my view, these relations help motivate non-individualistic principles of individuation (cf. Section II). In sum, I think that the argument we have so far considered begs significant questions at almost every step.

There is a kindred argument worth considering: the determinants of behavior supervene on states of the brain. (If one is a materialist, one might take this to be a triviality: "brain states supervene on brain states.") So if propositional attitudes are to be treated as among the determinants of behavior, they must be taken to supervene on brain states. The alternative is to take propositional attitudes as behaviorally irrelevant.[6]

This argument can, I think, be turned on its head. Since propositional attitudes are among the determinants of our "behavior" (where this expression is as open-ended as ever), and since propositional attitudes do not supervene on our brain states, not all determinants of our "behavior" supervene on our brain states. I want to make three points against the original argument, two metaphysical and one epistemic or methodological. [The epistemic point is omitted in this edition.—Ed.] Metaphysics first.

The ontological stakes that ride on the supervenience doctrine are far less substantial than one might think. It is simply not a "trivial consequence" of materialism about mental states and events that the determinants of our behavior supervene on the states of our brains. This is because what supervenes on what has at least as much to do with how the relevant entities are individuated as with what they are made of. If a mental event m is individuated partly by reference to normal conditions outside a person's body, then, regardless of whether m has material composition, m might vary even as the body remains the same.

Since intentional phenomena form such a large special case, it is probably misleading to seek analogies from other domains to illustrate the point. To loosen up the imagination, however, consider the Battle of Hastings. Suppose that we preserve every human body, every piece of turf, every weapon, every physical structure and all the physical interactions among them, from the first confrontation to the last death or withdrawal on the day of the battle. Suppose that, counterfactually, we imagine all these physical events and props placed in California (perhaps at the same time in 1066). Suppose that the physical activity is artificially induced by brilliant scientists transported to earth by Martian film producers. The distal causes of the battle have nothing to do with the causes of the Battle of Hastings. I think it plausible (and certainly coherent) to say that in such circumstances, not the Battle of Hastings, but only a physical facsimile would have taken place. I think that even if the location in Hastings were maintained, sufficiently different counterfactual causal antecedents would suffice to vary the identity of the battle. The battle is individuated partly in terms of its causes. Though the battle does not supervene on its physical constituents, we have little hesitation about counting it a physical event.

Our individuation of historical battles is probably wrapped up with intentional states of the participants. The point can also be made by reference to cases that are clearly independent of intentional considerations. Consider the emergence of North America from the ocean. Suppose that we delimit what count as constituent (say, micro-) physical events of this larger event. It seems that if the surrounding physical conditions and laws are artfully enough contrived, we can counterfactually conceive these same constituent events (or the constituent physical objects' undergoing physically identical changes in the same places) in such a way that they are embedded in a much larger land mass, so that the physical constituents of North America do not make up any salient part of this larger mass. The emergence of North America would not have occurred in such a case, even though its "constituent" physical events were, in isolation, physically identical with the actual events. We individuate the emergence of continents or other land masses in such a way that they are not supervenient on their physical constituents. But such events are nonetheless physical.

In fact, I think that materialism does not provide reasonable restrictions on theories of the role of mentalistic attributions in psychology. The relation of physical composition presently plays no significant role in any established scientific theory of mental events, or of their relations to brain events. The restrictions that physiological considerations place on psychological theorizing, though substantial, are weaker than those of any of the articulated materialisms, even the weak compositional variety I am alluding to. My point is just that rejecting individualistic supervenience does not entail rejecting a materialistic standpoint. So materialism *per se* does nothing to support individualism.[7]

The second "metaphysical" point concerns causation. The argument we are considering in effect simply assumes that propositional attitudes (type and token) supervene on physico-chemical events in the body.

But many philosophers appear to think that this assumption is rendered obvious by bland observations about the etiology of mental events and behavior. It is plausible that events in the external world causally affect the mental events of a subject only by affecting the subject's bodily surfaces; and that nothing (not excluding mental events) causally affects behavior except by affecting (causing or being a causal antecedent of causes of) local states of the subject's body. One might reason that in the anti-individualistic thought experiments these principles are violated insofar as events in the environment are alleged to differentially "affect" a person's mental events and behavior without differentially "affecting" his or her body: only if mental events (and states) supervene on the individual's body can the causal principles be maintained.

The reasoning is confused. The confusion is abetted by careless use of the term 'affect', conflating causation with individuation. Variations in the environment that do not vary the impacts that causally "affect" the subject's body may "affect" the individuation of the information that the subject is receiving, of the intentional processes he or she is undergoing, or of the way the subject is acting. It does not follow that the environment causally affects the subject in any way that circumvents its having effects on the subject's body.

Once the conflation is avoided, it becomes clear that there is no simple argument from the causal principles just enunciated to individualism. The example from geology provides a useful countermodel. It shows that one can accept the causal principles and thereby experience no bewilderment whatsoever in rejecting individualism. A continent moves and is moved by local impacts from rocks, waves, molecules. Yet we can conceive of holding constant the continent's peripheral impacts and chemically constituent events and objects, without holding identical the continent or certain of its macro-changes—because the continent's spatial relations to other land masses affect the way we individuate it. Or take an example from biology. Let us accept the plausible principle that nothing causally affects breathing except as it causally affects local states of the lungs. It does not follow, and indeed is not true, that we individuate lungs and the various sub-events of respiration in such a way as to treat those objects and events as supervenient on the chemically described objects and events that compose them. If the same chemical process (same from the surfaces of the lungs inside, and back to the surfaces) were embedded in a different sort of body and had an entirely different function (say, digestive, immunological, or regulatory), we would not be dealing with the same biological states and events. Local causation does not make more plausible local individuation, or individualistic supervenience.

The intended analogy to mental events should be evident. We may agree that a person's mental events and behavior are causally affected by the person's environment only through local causal effects on the person's body. Without the slightest conceptual discomfort we may individuate mental events so as to allow distinct events (types or tokens) with indistinguishable chemistries, or even physiologies, for the subject's body. Information from and about the environment is transmitted only through proximal stimulations, but the information is individuated partly by reference to the nature of normal distal stimuli. Causation is local. Individuation may presuppose facts about the specific nature of a subject's environment.

Where intentional psychological explanation is itself causal, it may well presuppose that the causal transactions to which its generalizations apply bear some necessary relation to some underlying physical transactions (or other). Without a set of physical transactions, none of the intentional transactions would transpire. But it does not follow that the kinds invoked in explaining causal interactions among intentional states (or between physical states and intentional states—for example, in vision or in action) supervene on the underlying physiological transactions. The same physical transactions in a given person may in principle mediate, or underly, transactions involving different intentional states— if the environmental features that enter into the individuation of the intentional states and that are critical in the explanatory generalizations that invoke those states vary in appropriate ways. . . .

II

. . . The heart of my case is the observation that psychological theories, taken literally, are not purely individualistic, that there are no strong reasons for taking them non-literally, and that we currently have no superior standpoint for judging how psychology ought to be done than that of seeing how it *is* done. One can, of course, seek deeper understanding of non-individualistic aspects of psychological theory. Development of such understanding is a multi-faceted task. Here I shall develop only points that are crucial to my thesis, illustrating them in some detail by reference to one theory.

Ascription of intentional states and events in psychology constitutes a type of individuation and explanation that carries presuppositions about the specific nature of the person's or animal's surrounding environment. Moreover, states and events are individuated so as to set the terms for specific evaluations of them for truth or other types of success. We can judge directly whether conative states are practically successful and cognitive states are veridical. For example, by characterizing a subject as visually representing an X, and specifying whether the visual state appropriately derives from an X in the particular case, we can judge whether the subject's state is veridical. Theories of vision, of belief formation, of memory, learning, decision-making, categorization, and perhaps even reasoning all attribute states that are subject to practical and semantical evaluation *by reference to standards partly set by a wider environment.*

Psychological theories are not themselves evaluative theories. But they often individuate phenomena so as to make evaluation readily accessible *because* they are partly motivated by such judgments. Thus we judge that in certain delimitable contexts people get what they want, know what is the case, and perceive what is there. And we try to frame explanations that account for these successes, and correlative failures, in such a way as to illumine as specifically as possible the mechanisms that underly and make true our evaluations.

I want to illustrate and develop these points by considering at some length a theory of vision. I choose this example primarily because it is a very advanced and impressive theory, and admits to being treated in some depth. Its information-processing approach is congenial with mainstream work in cognitive psychology. Some of its intentional aspects are well understood—and indeed are sometimes conceptually and mathematically far ahead of its formal (or syntactical) and physiological aspects. Thus the theory provides an example of a mentalistic theory with solid achievements to its credit.

The theory of vision maintains a pivotal position in psychology. Since perceptual processes provide the input for many higher cognitive processes, it is reasonable to think that if the theory of vision treats intentional states non-individualistically, other central parts of cognitive psychology will do likewise. Information processed by more central capacities depends, to a large extent, on visual information.

Certain special aspects of the vision example must be noted at the outset. The arguments that I have previously published against individualism (cf. note 1) have centered on "higher" mental capacities, some of which essentially involve the use of language. This focus was motivated by an interest in the relation between thought and linguistic meaning and in certain sorts of intellectual responsibility. Early human vision makes use of a limited range of representations—representations of shape, texture, depth and other spatial relations, motion, color, and so forth. These representations (percepts) are formed by processes that are relatively immune to correction from other sources of information; and the representations of early vision appear to be fully independent of language. So the thought experiments that I have previously elaborated will not carry over simply to early human vision. (One would expect those thought experiments to be more relevant to social and developmental psychology, to concept learning, and to parts of "higher" cognitive psychology.) But the case against individualism need not center on higher cognitive capacities or on the relation between thought and language. The anti-individualistic conclusions of our previous arguments can be shown to apply to early human vision. The abstract schema which those thought experiments articulate also applies.

The schema rests on three general facts. The first is that what entities in the objective world one intentionally interacts with in the employment of many representational (intentional) types affects the semantical properties of those representational types, what they are, and how we individuate them.[8] A near consequence of this first fact is that there can be slack between, on the one hand, the way a subject's representational types apply to the world, and on the other, what that person knows about, and how he or she can react to, the way they apply. It is possible for representational types to apply differently, without the person's physical reactions or discriminative powers being different. These facts, together with the fact that many fundamental mental states and events are individuated in terms of the relevant representational types, suffice to generate the conclusion that many paradigmatic mental states and events are not individualistically individuated: they may vary while a person's body and discriminative powers are conceived as constant. For by the second fact one can conceive of the way a person's representational types apply to the objective world as varying, while that person's history, non-intentionally and individualistically specified, is held constant. By the first fact, such variation may vary the individuation of the person's representational types. And by the third, such variation may affect the individuation of the person's mental states and events. I shall illustrate how instances of this schema are supported by Marr's theory of vision.[9]

Marr's theory subsumes three explanatory enterprises: (a) a theory of the computation of the information, (b) an account of the representations used and of the algorithms by which they are manipulated, and (c) a theory of the underlying physiology. Our primary interest is in the first level, and in that part of the second that deals with the individuation of representations. Both of these parts of the theory are fundamentally intentional.

The theory of the computation of information encompasses an account of what information is extracted from what antecedent resources, and an account of the reference-preserving "logic" of the extraction. These accounts proceed against a set of biological background assumptions. It is assumed that visual systems have evolved to solve certain problems forced on them by the environment. Different species are set different problems and solve them differently. The theory of human vision specifies a general information processing problem—that of generating reliable representations of certain objective, distal properties of the surrounding world on the basis of proximal stimulations.

The human visual system computes complex representations of certain visible properties, on the basis of light intensity values on retinal images. The primary visible properties that Marr's theory treats are the shapes and locations of things in the world. But various other properties—motion, texture, color, lightness, shading—are also dealt with in some detail. The overall computation is broken down into stages of increasing complexity, each containing modules that solve various subproblems.

The theory of computation of information clearly treats the visual system as going through a series of intentional or representational states. At an early stage, the visual system is counted as representing objective features of the physical world.[10] There is no other way to treat the visual system as solving the problem that the theory sees it as solving than by attributing intentional states that represent objective, physical properties.

More than half of Marr's book is concerned with developing the theory of the computation of information and with individuating representational primitives. These parts of the theory are more deeply developed, both conceptually and mathematically, than the account of the algorithms. This point is worth emphasizing because it serves to correct the impression, often conveyed in recent philosophy of psychology, that intentional theories are regressive and all of the development of genuine theory in psychology has been proceeding at the level of purely formal, "syntactical" transformations (algorithms) that are used in cognitive systems.

I now want, by a series of examples, to give a fairly concrete sense of how the theory treats the relation between the visual system and the physical environment. Understanding this relation will form essential background for understanding the non-individualistic character of the theory. The reader may skip the detail and still follow the philosophical argument. But the detail is there to support the argument and to render the conception of explanation that the argument yields both concrete and vivid.

Initially, I will illustrate two broad points. The *first* is that the theory makes essential reference to the subject's distal stimuli and makes essential assumptions about contingent facts regarding the subject's physical environment. Not only do the basic questions of the theory refer to what one sees under normal conditions, but the computational theory and its theorems are derived from numerous explicit assumptions about the physical world.

The *second* point to be illustrated is that the theory is set up to explain the reliability of a great variety of processes and sub-processes for acquiring information, at least to the extent that they are reliable. Reliability is presupposed in the formulations of the theory's basic questions. It is also explained through a detailed account of how in certain specified, standard conditions, veridical information is derived from limited means. The theory explains not merely the reliability of the system as a whole, but the reliability of various stages in the visual process. It begins by assuming that we see certain objective properties and proceeds to explain particular successes by framing conditions under which success would be expected (where the conditions are in fact typical). Failures are explained primarily by reference to a failure of these conditions to obtain. To use a phrase of Bernie Kobes, the theory is not success-neutral. The explanations and, as we shall later see, the kinds of theory presuppose that perception and numerous subroutines of perception are veridical in normal circumstances.

Example 1: In an early stage of the construction of visual representation, the outputs of channels or filters that are sensitive to spatial distributions of light intensities are combined to produce representations of local contours, edges, shadows, and so forth. The filters fall into groups of different sizes, in the sense that different groups are sensitive to different bands of spatial frequencies. The channels are primarily sensitive to sudden intensity changes, called "zero-crossings," at their scales (within their frequency bands). The theoretical question arises: How do we combine the results of the different sized channels to construct representations with physical meaning—representations that indicate edge segments or local contours in the external physical world? There is no *a priori* reason why zero-crossings obtained from different sized filters should be related to some one physical phenomenon in the environment. There is, however, a physical basis for their being thus related. This basis is identified by *the constraint of spatial localization.* Things in the world that give rise to intensity changes in the image, such as changes of illumination (caused by shadows, light sources) or changes in surface reflectance (caused by contours, creases, and surface boundaries), are spatially localized, not scattered and not made up of waves. Because of this fact, if a zero-crossing is present in a channel centered on a given frequency band, there should be a corresponding zero-crossing at the same spatial location in larger-scaled channels. If this ceases to be so at larger scales, it is because a) two or more local intensity changes are being averaged together in the larger channel (for example, the edges of a thin bar may register radical frequency changes in small channels, but go undetected in larger ones); or b) because two independent physical phenomena are producing intensity changes in the same area but at different scales (for example, a shadow superimposed on a sudden reflectance change; if the shadow is located in a certain way, the positions of the zero-crossings may not make possible a separation of the two physical phenomena). Some of these exceptions are sufficiently rare that the visual system need not and does not account for them—thus allowing for possible illusions; others are reflected in complications of the basic assumption that follows. The spatial coincidence constraint yields *the spatial coincidence assumption:*

If a zero-crossing segment is present in a set of independent channels over a contiguous range of sizes, and the segment has the same position and orientation in each channel, then the set of such zero-crossing segments indicates the presence of an intensity change in the image that is due to a single physical phenomenon (a change in reflectance, illumination, depth, or surface orientation).

Thus the theory starts with the observation that physical edges produce roughly coincident zero-crossings in channels of neighboring sizes. The spatial coincidence assumption asserts that the coincidence of zero-crossings of neighboring sizes is normally sufficient evidence of a real physical edge. Under such circumstances, according to the theory, a representation of an edge is formed.[11]

Example 2: Because of the laws of light and the way our eyes are made, positioned, and controlled, our brains typically receive similar image signals originating from two points that are fairly similarly located in the respective eyes or images, at the same horizontal level. If two objects are separated in depth from the viewer, the relative positions of their image signals will differ in the two eyes. The visual system determines the distance of physical surfaces by measuring the angular discrepancy in position (disparity) of the image of an object in the two eyes. This process is called stereopsis. To solve the problem of determining distance, the visual system must select a location on a surface as represented by one image, identify the same location in the other image, and measure the disparity between the corresponding image points. There is, of course, no *a priori* means of matching points from the two images. The theory indicates how correct matches are produced by appealing to three *Physical Constraints* (actually the first is not made explicit, but is relied upon): (1) the two eyes produce similar representations of the same external items; (2) a given point on a physical surface has a unique position in space at any given time; (3) matter is cohesive— separated into objects, the surfaces of which are usually smooth in the sense that surface variation is small compared to overall distance from the observer. These three physical constraints are rewritten as three corresponding *Constraints on Matching:* (1) two representational elements can match if and only if they normally could have arisen from the same physical item (for example, in stereograms, dots match dots rather than bars); (2) nearly always, each representational element can match only one element from the other image (exceptions occur when two markings lie along the line of sight of one eye but are separately visible by the other—causing illusions); (3) disparity varies smoothly almost everywhere (this derives from physical constraint (3) because that constraint implies that the distance to the visible surface varies, approximately continuously except at object boundaries, which occupy a small fraction of the area of an image). Given suitable precisifications, these matching constraints can be used to prove the *Fundamental Theorem of Stereopsis:*

If a correspondence is established between physically meaningful representational primitives extracted from the left and right images of a scene that contains a sufficient amount of detail (roughly 2% density for dot stereograms), and if the correspondence satisfies the three matching constraints, then that correspondence is physically correct— hence unique.

The method is again to identify general physical conditions that give rise to a visual process, then to use those conditions to motivate constraints on the form of the process that, when satisfied, will allow the process to be interpreted as providing reliable representations of the physical environment.[12]

These examples illustrate theories of the computation of information. The critical move is the formulation of general physical facts that limit the interpretation of a visual problem enough to allow one to interpret the machinations of the visual system as providing a unique and veridical solution, at least in typical cases. The primary aim of referring to contingent physical facts and properties is to enable the theory to explain the visual system's reliable acquisition of information about the physical world: to explain the success or veridicality of various types of visual representation. So much for the first two points that we set out to illustrate.

I now turn to a *third* that is a natural corollary of the second, and that will be critical for our argument that the theory is non-individualistic: the information carried by representations—their intentional content—is individuated in terms of the specific distal causal antecedents in the physical world that the information is about and that the representations normally apply to. The individuation of the intentional features of numerous representations depends on a variety of physical constraints that our knowledge of the external world gives us. Thus the individuation of intentional content of representational types, presupposes the verdicality of perception. Not only the explanations, but the intentional kinds of the theory presuppose contingent facts about the subject's physical environment.

Example 3: In building up informational or representational primitives in the primal sketch, Marr states six general physical assumptions that constrain the choice of primitives. I shall state some of these to give a sense of their character: (a) the visible world is composed of smooth surfaces having reflectance functions whose spatial structure may be complex; (b) markings generated on a surface by a single process are often arranged in continuous spatial structures—curves, lines, etc.; (c) if direction of motion is discontinuous at more than one point—for example, along a line—then an object boundary is present. These assumptions are used to identify the physical significance of—the objective information normally given by—certain types of patterns in the image. The computational theory states conditions under which these primitives form to carry information about items in the physical world (Marr 1982, 44–71). The theory in Example 1 is a case in point: conditions are laid down under which certain patterns may be taken as representing an objective physical condition; as being edge, boundary, bar, or blob detectors. Similar points apply for more advanced primitives.

Example 4: In answering the question "what assumptions do we reasonably and actually employ when we interpret silhouettes as three-dimensional shapes?" Marr motivates a central representational primitive by stating physical constraints that lead to the proof of a theorem. *Physical Constraints:* (1) Each line of sight from the viewer to the object grazes the object's surface at exactly one point. (2) Nearby points on the contour in an image arise from nearby points on the contour generator on the viewed object. (That is, points that appear close together in the image actually are close together on the object's surface.) (3) The contour generator lies wholly in a single plane. Obviously, these are conditions of perception that may fail, but they are conditions under which we seem to do best at solving the problem of deriving three-dimensional shape descriptions from representations of silhouettes. *Definition:* A *generalized cone* is a three-dimensional object generated by moving a cross section along an axis; the cross section may vary smoothly in size, but its shape remains the same. (For example footballs, pyramids, legs, stalagmites are or approximate generalized cones.) *Theo-*

rem: If the surface is smooth and if physical constraints (1)–(3) hold for all distant viewing positions in any one plane, then the viewed surface is a generalized cone. The theorem indicates a natural connection between generalized cones and the imaging process. Marr infers from this, and from certain psychophysical evidence, that representations of generalized cones–that is, representations with intentional content concerning, generalized cones—are likely to be fundamental among our visual representations of three-dimensional objects (Marr 1982, 215–225).

Throughout the theory, representational primitives are selected and individuated by considering specific, contingent facts about the physical world that typically hold when we succeed in obtaining veridical visual information about that world. The information or content of the visual representations is always individuated by reference to the physical objects, properties, or relations that are seen. In view of the success-orientation of the theory, this mode of individuation is grounded in its basic methods. If theory were confronted with a species of organism reliably and successfully interacting with a different set of objective visible properties, the representational types that the theory would attribute to the organism would be different, regardless of whether an individual organism's physical mechanisms were different.

We are now in a position to argue that the theory is not individualistic: (1) The theory is intentional. (2) The intentional primitives of the theory and the information they carry are individuated by reference to contingently existing physical items or conditions by which they are normally caused and to which they normally apply. (3) So if these physical conditions and, possibly, attendant physical laws were regularly different, the information conveyed to the subject and the intentional content of his or her visual representations would be different. (4) It is not incoherent to conceive of relevantly different physical conditions and perhaps relevantly different (say, optical) laws regularly causing the same non-intentionally, individualistically individuated physical regularities in the subject's eyes and nervous system. It is enough if the differences are small; they need not be wholesale. (5) In such a case (by (3)) the individual's visual representations would carry different information and have different representational content, though the person's whole non-intentional physical history (at least up to a certain time) might remain the same. (6) Assuming that some perceptual states are identified in the theory in terms of their informational or intentional content, it follows that individualism is not true for the theory of vision.

I shall defend the argument stepwise. I take it that the claim that the theory is intentional is sufficiently evident. The top levels of the theory are explicitly formulated in intentional terms. And their method of explanation is to show how the problem of arriving at certain veridical representations is solved.

The second step of the argument was substantiated through Examples 3 and 4. The intentional content of representations of edges or generalized cones is individuated in terms of *specific* reference to those very contingently instantiated physical properties, on the assumption that those properties normally give rise to veridical representations of them.

The third step in our argument is supported both by the way the theory individuates intentional content (cf. the previous paragraph and Examples 3 and 4), and by the explanatory method of the theory (cf. the second point illustrated above, and Examples 1–2). The methods of individuation and explanation are governed by the assumption that the subject has adapted to his or her environment sufficiently to obtain veridical information from it under certain normal conditions. If the properties and relations that *normally* caused visual impressions were regularly different from what they are, the individual would obtain different information and have visual experiences with different intentional content. If the regular, law-like relations between perception and the environment were different, the visual system would be solving different information-processing problems; it would pass through different informational or intentional states; and the explanation of vision would be different. To reject this third step of our argument would be to reject the theory's basic methods and questions. But these methods and questions have already borne fruit, and there are presently no good reasons for rejecting them.

I take it that step four is a relatively unproblematic counterfactual. There is no metaphysically necessary relation between individualistically individuated processes in a person's body and the causal antecedents of those processes in the surrounding world.[13] (To reject this step would be self-defeating for the individualist.) If the environmental conditions were different, the same proximal *visual* stimulations could have regularly had different distal causes. In principle, we can conceive of some regular variation in the distal causes of perceptual impressions with no variation in a person's individualistically specified physical processes, even while conceiving the person as *well adapted* to the relevant environment—though, of course, not uniquely adapted.

Steps three and four, together with the unproblematic claim that the theory individuates some perceptual states in terms of their intentional content or representational types, entail that the theory is non-individualistic.

Steps two and three are incompatible with certain philosophical approaches that have no basis in psychological theory. One might claim that the information content of a visual representation would remain constant even if the physical conditions that lead to the representation were regularly different. It is common to motivate this claim by pointing out that one's visual representations remain the same, whether one is perceiving a black blob on a white surface or having an eidetic hallucination of such a blob. So, runs the reasoning, why should changing the distal causes of a perceptual representation affect its content? On this view, the content of a given perceptual representation is commonly given as that of "the distal cause of *this* representation," or "the property in the world that has *this* sort of visual appearance." The content of these descriptions is intended to remain constant between possible situations in which the micro-physical events of a person's visual processes remain the same while distal causes of those processes are regularly and significantly different. For it is thought that the representations themselves (and our experiences of *them*) remain constant under these circumstances. So as the distal antecedents of one's perceptual representations vary, the reference of those representations will vary, but their intentional content will not.[14]

There is more wrong with this line than I have room to develop here. I will mention some of the more straightforward difficulties. In the first place, the motivation from perceptual illusion falls far short. One is indeed in the same perceptual state whether one is seeing or hallucinating. But that is because the intentional content of one's visual state (or representation) is individuated against a background in which the relevant state is *normally* veridical. Thus the fact that one's percepts or perceptual states remain constant between normal perception and hallucinations does not even tend to show that the intentional visual state remains constant between circumstances in which different physical conditions are the normal antecedents of one's perceptions.

Let us consider the proposals for interpreting the content of our visual representations. In the first place both descriptions ('the distal cause of *this* representation' *et al.*) are insufficiently specific. There are lots of distal causes and lots of things that might be said to appear "thus" (for example, the array of light striking the retina as well as the physical surface). We identify the relevant distal cause (and the thing that normally appears thus and so) as the thing that we actually see. To accurately pick out the "correct" object with one of these descriptions would at the very least require a more complex specification. But filling out the descriptive content runs into one or both of two difficulties: either it includes kinds that are tied to a specific environment ('the convex, rough textured object that is causing this representation'). In such case, the description is still subject to our argument. For these kinds are individuated by reference to the empirical environment. Or it complicates the constraints on the causal chain to the extent that the complications cannot plausibly be attributed to the content of processes in the early visual system.

Even in their unrevised forms, the descriptions are over-intellectualized philosophers' conceits. It is extremely implausible and empirically without warrant to think that packed into every perceptual representation is a distinction between distal cause and experiential effect, or between objective reality and perceptual appearance. These are distinctions developed by reflecting on the ups and downs of visual perception. They do not come in at the ground, animal level of early vision.

A further mistake is the view that our perceptual representations never purport to specify particular physical properties *as such*, but only via some relation they bear to inner occurrences, which are directly referred to. (Even the phrase 'the convex object causing this percept' invokes a specification of objective convexity as such.) The view will not serve the needs of psychological explanation as actually practiced. For the descriptions of information are too inspecific to account for specific successes in solving problems in retrieving information about the actual, objective world.

The best empirical theory that we have individuates the intentional content of visual representations by specific reference to specific physical characteristics of visible properties and relations. The theory does not utilize complicated, self-referential, attributively used role descriptions of those properties. It does not individuate content primarily by reference to phenomenological qualities. Nor does it use the notions of cause or appearance in specifying the intentional content of early visual representations.[15]

The second and third steps of our argument are incompatible with the claim that the intentional content of visual representations is determined by their "functional role" in each person's system of dispositions, non-intentionally and individualistically specified. This claim lacks any warrant in the practice of the science. In the first place, the theory suggests no reduction of the intentional to the non-intentional. In the second, although what a person can do, non-visually, constitutes evidence for what he or she can see, there is little ground for thinking that either science or common sense takes an individual person's non-visual abilities fully to determine the content of his or her early visual experience. A person's dispositions and beliefs develop by adapting to what the person sees. As the person develops, the visual system (at least at its more advanced stages—those involving recognition) and the belief and language systems affect each other. But early vision seems relatively independent of these non-visual systems. A large part of learning is accommodating one's dispositions to the information carried by visual representations. Where there are failures of adaptation, the person does not know what the visual apparatus is presenting to him or her. Yet the presentations are there to be understood. . . .

III

Although the theory of vision is in various ways special, I see no reason why its non-individualistic methods will not find analogs in other parts of psychology. In fact, as we noted, since vision provides intentional input for other cognitive capacities, there is reason to think that the methods of the theory of vision are presupposed by other parts of psychology. These non-individualistic methods are grounded in two natural assumptions. One is that there are psychological states that represent, or are about, an objective world. The other is that there is a scientific account to be given that presupposes certain successes in our interaction with the world (vision, hearing, memory, decision, reasoning, empirical belief formation, communication, and so forth), and that explains specific successes and failures by reference to these states.

The two assumptions are, of course, interrelated. Although an intention to eat meat is "conceptually" related to eating meat, the relation is not one of entailment in either direction, since the representation is about an objective matter. An individual may be, and often is, ignorant, deluded, misdirected, or impotent. The very thing that makes the non-individualistic thought experiments possible—the possibility of certain sorts of ignorance, failure, and misunderstanding—helps make it possible for explanations using non-individualistic language to be empirically informative. On the other hand, as I have argued above, some successful interaction with an objective world seems to be a precondition for the objectivity of some of our intentional representations.

Any attempt to produce detailed accounts of the relations between our attitudes and the surrounding world will confront a compendium of empirically interesting problems. Some of the most normal and mundane successes in our cognitive and conative relations to the world must be explained in terms of surprisingly complicated intervening processes, many of which are themselves partly described in terms of intentional states. Our failures may be explained by reference to *specific* abnormalities in operations or surrounding conditions. Accounting for environmentally specific successes (and failures) is one of the tasks that psychology has traditionally set itself.

An illuminating philosophy of psychology must do justice not only to the mechanistic elements in the science. It must also relate these to psychology's attempt to account for tasks that we succeed and fail at, *where these tasks are set by the environment and represented by the subject him- or herself.* The most salient and important of these tasks are those that arise through relations to the natural and social worlds. A theory that insists on describing the states of human beings *purely* in terms that abstract from their relations to any specific environment cannot hope to provide a completely satisfying explanation of our accomplishments. At present our best theories in many domains of psychology do not attempt such an abstraction. No sound reason has been given for thinking that the non-individualistic language that psychology now employs is not an appropriate language for explaining these matters, or that explanation of this sort is impossible.

Notes

A version of this paper was given at the Sloan Conference at MIT in May 1984. I have benefited from the commentaries by Ned Block, Fred Dretske, and Stephen Stich. I have also made use of discussion with Jerry Fodor, David Israel, Bernie Kobes, and Neil Stillings; and I am grateful to the editors for several suggestions.

1. The aluminum argument is adapted from an argument in Hilary Putnam (1975). What Putnam wrote in his paper was, strictly, not even compatible with this argument. But the aluminum argument lies close to the surface of the argument he does give. The arthritis argument raises rather different issues, despite its parallel methodology.

2. On basic categories, cf., e.g., Rosch, Mervis, Gray, Johnson, and Boyes-Graem (1976). On the general claim in the last sentence, cf. Burge (1986b) and the latter portion of this paper [not included in the present edition—Ed.].

3. Our talk of intentional "content" will be ontologically colorless. It can be converted to talk about how that-clauses (or their components) are interpreted and differentiated— taken as equivalent or non-equivalent—for the cognitive purposes of psychology. Not all intentional states or structures that are attributed in psychology are explicitly propositional. My views in this paper apply to intentional states generally.

4. Certain approaches to intensional logic featuring either "direct reference" or some analogy between the attitudes and necessity have urged that this practice of fine-structuring attitudinal content be revised. I think that for purely philosophical reasons these approaches cannot account for the attitudes. For example, they do little to illumine the numerous variations on Frege's "paradox of identity." They seem to have even less to recommend them as prescriptions for the language of psychology. Some defenses of individualism have taken these approaches to propositional content to constitute the opposition to individualism. I think that these approaches are not serious contenders as accounts of propositional attitudes and thus should be left out of the discussion.

5. Although I shall not discuss the unformulated Ockhamesque principle, I am skeptical of it. Apart from question-begging assumptions, it seems to me quite unclear why a science should be required to explain two instances of the same phenomenon in the same way, particularly if the surrounding conditions that led to the instances differ.

6. I have not been able to find a fully explicit statement of this argument in published work. It seems to inform some passages of Jerry Fodor (1981), e.g., pp. 228–232. It lies closer to the surface in much work influenced by Fodor's paper (cf., e.g., McGinn (1982, 207–216). Many who like McGinn concede the force of the arguments against individualism utilize something like this argument to maintain that individualistic "aspects" of intentional states are all that are relevant to psychological explanation.

7. In Burge (1979, 109–113), I argue that token *identity* theories are rendered implausible by the non-individualistic thought experiments. But token identity theories are not the last bastion for materialist defense policy. Composition is what is crucial.

It is coherent, but I think mistaken, to hold that propositional-attitude attributions non-rigidly pick out physical events: so the propositional attributions vary between the actual and counterfactual protagonists in the thought experiments, though the ontology of mental event tokens remains identical. This view is compatible with most of my opposition to individualism. But I think that there is no good reason to believe the very implausible thesis that mental events are not individuated ("essentially" or "basically") in terms of the relevant propositional-attitude attributions (cf. ibid.). So I reject the view that the same mental events (types or tokens) are picked out under different descriptions in the thought experiments. These considerations stand behind my recommending, to the convinced materialist, composition rather than identity as a paradigm. (I remain unconvinced.)

8. 'Representational type' (also 'intentional type') is a relatively theory-neutral term for intentional content, or even intentional state-kinds. Cf. note 3. One could about as well speak of concepts, percepts, and the representational or intentional aspects of thought contents—or of the counterpart states.

9. In what follows I make use of the important book, Marr 1982. Marr writes:

The purpose of these representations is to provide useful descriptions of aspects of the real world. The structure of the real world therefore plays an important role in determining both the nature of the representations that are used and the nature of the processes that derive and maintain them. An important part of the theoretical analysis is to make explicit the physical constraints and assumptions that have been used in the design of the representations and processes . . . (p. 43).

It is of critical importance that the tokens [representational particulars] one obtains [in the theoretical analysis] correspond to real physical changes on the viewed surface; the blobs, lines, edges, groups, and so forth that we shall use must not be artifacts of the imaging process, or else inferences made from their structure backwards to the structures of the surface will be meaningless (p. 44).

Marr's claim that the structure of the real world figures in determining the nature of the representations that are attributed in the theory is tantamount to the chief point about representation or reference that generates our non-individualist thought experiments— the first step in the schema. I shall show that these remarks constitute the central theoretical orientation of the book.

Calling the theory Marr's is convenient but misleading. Very substantial contributions have been made by many others; and the approach has developed rapidly since Marr's death. Cf. for example, Ballard et al. (1983). What I say about Marr's book applies equally to more recent developments.

10. It is an interesting question when to count the visual system as having gone intentional. I take it that information is in a broad sense, carried by the intensity values in the retinal image; but I think that this is too early to count the system as intentional or symbolic. I'm inclined to agree with Marr that where zero-crossings from different sized filters are checked against one another (cf. Example 1), it is reasonable to count visual processes as representational of an external physical reality. Doing so, however, depends on seeing this stage as part of the larger system in which objective properties are often discriminated from subjective artifacts of the visual system.

11. Marr (1982, 68–70); cf. also Marr and Hildreth (1980), where the account is substantially more detailed.

12. Marr (1982, 111–116); Marr and Poggio (1979); Marr (1982, 205–212); Ullman (1979).

13. As I have intimated above, I doubt that all biological, including physiological, processes and states in a person's body are individualistically individuated. The failures of individualism for these sciences involve different, but related considerations.

14. Descartes went further in the same direction. He thought that the perceptual system, and indeed the intellect, could not make a mistake. Mistakes derived from the will. The underlying view is that we primarily perceive or make perceptual reference to our own

perceptions. This position fails to account plausibly for various visual illusions and errors that precede any activity of the will, or even intellect. And the idea that perceptions are in general what we make perceptual reference to has little to recommend it and, nowadays, little influence. The natural and, I think, plausible view is that we have visual representations that specify external properties specifically, that these representations are pre-doxastic in the sense they are not themselves objects of belief, and that they sometimes fail to represent correctly what is before the person's eyes: when they result from abnormal processes.

15. Of course, at least in the earliest stages of visual representation, there are analogies between qualitative features of representations in the experienced image and the features that those representations represent. Representations that represent bar segments are bar-shaped, or have some phenomenological property that strongly tempts us to call them "bar-shaped." Similarly for blobs, dots, lines and so forth. (Marr and Hildreth 1980, 211, remark on this dual aspect of representations.) These "analogies" are hardly fortuitous. Eventually they will probably receive rigorous psychophysical explanations. But they should not tempt one into the idea that visual representations in general make reference to themselves, much less into the idea that the content of objective representation is independent of empirical relations between the representations and the objective entities that give rise to them. Perhaps these qualitative features are constant across all cases where one's bodily processes, non-intentionally specified, are held constant. But the information they carry, their intentional content, may vary with their causal antecedents and causal laws in the environment.

References

Ballard, D., G. Hinton, and T. Sejnowski (1983). Parallel vision computation. *Nature* 306, 21–26.

Burge, T. (1979). Individualism and the mental. In P. French, T. Uehling, and H. Wettstein, eds., *Midwest studies in philosophy*, vol. 4. Minneapolis: University of Minnesota Press.

Burge, T. (1982a). Other bodies. In A. Woodfield, ed., *Thought and object*. Oxford: Oxford University Press.

Burge, T. (1982b). Two thought experiments reviewed. *Notre Dame Journal of Formal Logic* 23, 284–293.

Burge, T. (1986a). Cartesian error and the objectivity of perception. In P. Pettit and J. MacDowell, eds., *Subject, thought, and context*. Oxford: Oxford University Press.

Burge, T. (1986b). Intellectual norms and foundations of mind. *Journal of Philosophy* 83, 697–720.

Fodor, J. (1981). Methodological solipsism considered as a research strategy in cognitive psychology. In J. Fodor, *Representations*. Cambridge, MA: MIT Press.

McGinn, C. (1982). The structure of content. In A. Woodfield, ed., *Thought and object*. Oxford: Oxford University Press.

Marr, D. (1982). *Vision*. San Francisco: Freeman.

Marr, D., and E. C. Hildreth (1980). Theory of edge detection. *Proceedings of the Royal Society of London* B 207, 187–217.

Marr, D., and T. Poggio (1979). A computational theory of human stereo vision. *Proceedings of the Royal Society of London* B 204, 301–328.

Putnam, H. (1975). The meaning of 'meaning'. In K. Gunderson, ed., *Language, mind, and knowledge* (Minnesota Studies in the Philosophy of Science, vol. 7). Minneapolis: University of Minnesota Press.

Rosch, E., C. B. Mervis, W. D. Gray, D. M. Johnson, and P. Boyes-Braem (1976). Basic objects in natural categories. *Cognitive Psychology* 8, 382–439.

Stich, S. (1983). *From folk psychology to cognitive science.* Cambridge, MA: MIT Press.

Ullman, S. (1979). *The interpretation of visual motion.* Cambridge, MA: MIT Press.

34 The Co-evolutionary Research Ideology

Patricia S. Churchland

The Division of Research Labor

According to the functionalist research ideology, the task of cognitive psychology is to determine what "programs" the mind-brain runs in virtue of which it has certain cognitive capacities, and the job of neuroscience is to find out whether the brain really implements the hypothesized programs. Moreover, this ideology recommends that cognitive psychology is to be *autonomous* with respect to neuroscience, in the sense that neurobiological data are irrelevant to figuring out the cognitive "program" the mind-brain runs.

Five general reasons speak against the autonomy ideology and in favor of embracing an ideology of co-evolutionary development:

1. Our mental states and processes *are* states and processes of our brains.

2. The human nervous system evolved from simpler nervous systems.

3. Brains are by far the classiest information processors available for study. In matters of adaptability, plasticity, appropriateness of response, motor control, and so forth, no program has ever been devised that comes close to doing what brains do—not even to what lowly rat brains do. If we can figure out how brains do it, we might figure out how to get a computer to mimic how brains do it.

4. If neuroscientists are working on problems such as the nature of memory and learning, studying cellular changes, synaptic changes, the effects of circumscribed lesions, and so forth, it is perverse for a cognitive scientist trying to understand memory and learning to ignore systematically what the neuroscientists have discovered.

From P. Churchland, *Neurophilosophy: Toward a unified science of the mind/brain* (1986). Cambridge, MA: MIT Press. Reprinted by permission.

5. Categories at any level specifying the fundamental *kinds* may need to be revised, and the revisionary rationales may come from research at any level.

Philosophers are sometimes fond of arguing that certain things are possible *in principle,* and in this context it may be argued that it is in principle possible for psychology to hew out a functionalist cognitive theory without interleaving itself with neuroscience. I don't know whether this is true, and I have no sense of how to assess the claim. My guess is that it shares a flaw with many other philosophical thought-experiments: too much thought and not enough experiment. What I think is clear is that the history of science reveals that co-evolution of theories has typically been mutually enriching. In practice at least, psychology as a discipline has nothing to gain from adopting an isolationist methodology. In what follows I shall explain the competing research ideology, namely the co-evolution of research, drawing on examples outside the fields at issue. Then, using the case of research on memory and learning, I shall indicate why psychology should prefer the co-evolutionary ideology.

The Benefits of Co-evolutionary Development

The case of thermodynamics and statistical mechanics displays especially well the mutual benefits of concordant development. Our understanding of the nature of temperature, equilibrium, and entropy was expanded and readjusted as discoveries were made at *both* the macro and the micro levels. Hooker's swift synopsis of the co-evolution of the two gives the flavor:

First, the mathematical development of statistical mechanics has been heavily influenced precisely by the attempt to construct a basis for the corresponding thermodynamical properties and laws. For example, it was the discrepancies between the Boltzmann entropy and thermodynamical entropy that led to the development of the Gibbs entropies, and the attempt to match mean statistical quantities to thermodynamical equilibrium values which led to the development of ergodic theory. Conversely, however, thermodynamics is itself undergoing a process of enrichment through the injection "back" into it of statistical mechanical constructs, e.g. the various entropies can be injected "back" into thermodynamics, the differences among them forming a basis for the solution of the Gibbs paradox. More generally, work is now afoot to transform thermodynamics into a generally statistical theory, while retaining its traditional conceptual apparatus, and there is some hope that this may eventually allow its proper extension to non-equilibrium processes as well. (1981:49)

The value of co-evolution can also be seen in the development of physics and chemistry, of astronomy and dynamics, of the theory of infectious disease and microbiology, of classical genetics and molecular genetics, and more recently of nonequilibrium thermodynamics and biology, and of immunology and genetic engineering. In these instances discoveries at one level often provoke further experiments and further corrections at the other level, which in turn provoke questions, corrections, and ideas for new explorations.

It may be objected that the example of classical genetics and molecular genetics is in fact a bad example of what I wish to show, because it conflicts with the idea that co-evolution will lead to reduction. The trouble, it will be said, is that molecular genetics has not succeeded in reducing "gene" to a structural basis, and there is well-reasoned skepticism that it never will do so. (See especially Hull 1974.) This case is worth a closer look because of the analogies between it and the case of psychology and neurobiology.

Reduction and Co-evolution

In classical genetics genes are the units of hereditary transmission, mutation, and recombination. Their role in the theory is to explain why there is a given output (phenotypic traits) given a certain input (fertilization), and they are specified essentially in terms of their causal properties. Looked at in this way, a gene is a set of functional properties. The problem for molecular genetics was to find what structural mechanism in the organism could be identified as the gene for a particular phenotypic trait. The early expectations were that it would be some identifiable segment of a chromosome, and later, some identifiable strip of DNA. It became evident that matters were exceedingly complex and that many mechanisms and many biochemical conditions contributed to the expression of a trait. Not that the complexity by itself was thought to frustrate reduction, but what did seem discouraging was the discovery that differences in the structure of the DNA did not always result in differences in the phenotype, owing to compensating biochemical circumstances; and conversely that the same DNA base could yield distinct phenotypic traits, again owing to divergent matters in the biochemical surround. In short, instead of the coveted one-to-one relation between genes as functionally specified and genes as structurally specified, there is a *many-to-many* relation between the genes of classical genetics and the genetic material of molecular genetics. And perhaps, it has been suggested, it may be so bad as to be a many-to-(indefinitely)many relation. As Philip Kitcher puts it, "There is no molecular biology of the gene. There is only molecular biology of the genetic material" (1982:357).

Importantly, those who have rejected reduction in genetics as a hopeless cause have not wished to claim that molecular genetics cannot explain the input-output phenomena described by transmission genetics, or that transmission genetics is an autonomous science, or that molecular genetics is irrelevant to transmission genetics. On the contrary, they typically agree with reductionists in arguing exactly the

The Co-evolutionary Research Ideology

reverse. The heart of the disagreement, then, concerns the significance of one-to-one mappings between the functional units of the molar theory and the structural units of the molecular theory. This issue is of central importance to those who see the reductionist program in neuroscience blocked by the possibility that psychological categories will not map one to one onto neurobiological categories. Now from the reductionist viewpoint, this possibility does not look like an obstacle to reduction so much as it predicts a fragmentation and reconfiguration of the psychological categories. Indeed, there are already signs of a fragmentation of the folk psychological category of memory. To show why the reductionist's course is reasonable, I shall explore the issue more fully.

When a property of a system is postulated on the basis of the input-output profile of the system, the natural expectation is that there is a (unitary) mechanism for accomplishing the effect, and the reasonable research strategy is to try to find that unitary mechanism. However reasonable the expectation and the research, it is a frustrating truth that functions postulated at the input-output level do not always map onto unitary structures. This is especially likely to be so when the system is complex—that is, when there is a long and complicated route between input and output. The following simple but compelling example from Dewan 1976, described by Hooker, makes this sort of situation clear.

Consider a set of electrical generators G, each of which produces alternating current electrical power at 60Hz but with fluctuations in frequency of 10% around some average value. Taken singly, the frequency variability of the generators is 10%. Taken joined together in a suitable network, their collective frequency variability is only a fraction of that figure because, statistically, generators momentarily fluctuating behind the average output in phase are compensated for by the remaining generators, and conversely, generators momentarily ahead in phase have their energy absorbed by the remainder. The entire system functions, from an input/output point of view, as a single generator with a greatly increased frequency reliability, or, as control engineers express it, with a single, more powerful, "virtual governor." The property "has a virtual governor of reliability f" is a property of the system as a whole, but of none of its components. Does this render it irreducible? Yes, and no. For, once the mechanism of the system's operation is understood, it is seen that this property's being a property of this system is entailed by the conjunction of laws for the individual generators plus specification of system structure. Its being so is not, however, entailed by the laws of the component generators alone. In this sense, the property *is* irreducibly a property of the whole system—the system *structure* obtaining is essential to *its* obtaining. But from an ontological point of view, there is nothing to the system over and above its components and the physical relations between them (however physically realized). This latter point is driven home by enquiring "*what thing* is the virtual governor?" (a real governor, one on each component generator, is an actual physical device), "*where* is the virtual governor?" and so on. The answers must be that, in the sense of the questions, there is no thing which is the virtual governor, so "it" cannot be localized more closely than the system as a whole. (This is why engineers refer to it as a virtual governor.) (Hooker 1981, 509)

Genes, it appears, are more like the virtual governor in the example than like a distinct component such as a generator. One way to describe the situation in genetics, therefore, is to say that there really are no genes, *in the sense specified* by such questions as "What thing in the DNA is a gene?" or "Where are the genes?" The assumption that there is a single structural unit is an assumption that has to be dropped. Instead, there is a complex set of conditions and mechanisms, some of which are themselves functionally specified at some level down from the top, and DNA segments figure prominently but not exclusively in that set.

The many-to-many tangle will resolve into a one-to-one pattern so long as the micro half of the relation is permitted to include things beyond the DNA configuration, things like the biochemical milieu. (Unless of course, the system's macro properties are indeterministic with respect to its biochemical properties, but neither party to the debate makes this implausible claim.) Moreover, given the levels of organization to be found in organisms, part of the story may involve specification of middle-range input-output functions that are in turn explained by lower-level mechanisms. As to the macro half of the relation, it is evident that input-output characterizations of the system as a whole and of subsystems at various levels within modify and are modified by molecular as well as high-level discoveries. For example, the specification of what is a phenotypic trait is not theory-neutral either and has itself undergone modifications to reflect deeper understanding in both classical and molecular genetics. (For example, Benzer's modification 1957; see discussions in Philip Kitcher 1982; Hull 1974.)

Very roughly, reduction will still have been accomplished if the input-output effects described by a suitably evolved macrogenetic theory can be explained by molecular goings-on. Following Hooker here, the crux of what is required is that the laws (in general, the true sentences) of the evolved transmission genetics have an "image" in the theorems of the reducing theory. A bit more specifically, this requires that (1) initial macrolevel inputs are identified with initial states of mechanisms, (2) final macrolevel outputs are identified with final states of mechanisms, and (3) for every macrolevel input-to-output function there is a class of mechanisms nomically relating the relevant input and output states (1981, 516).[1]

If such a reduction were to emerge, notice that we could describe it as occupying a place on the revisionary end of the spectrum if we think of Mendel's theory (his laws and his specification of "factor" (= gene) and "dominance") as the theory that is reduced/replaced. Alternatively, given the co-evolution of transmission genetics and molecular genetics, future historians of science might prefer to say that what was reduced

The Co-evolutionary Research Ideology

was the *evolved* macrotheory T*, that it was essentially retained by the evolved microtheory M*, and that the reduction was smooth, macrolevel properties having been identified with microlevel complex conditions. The first reading seems rather perverse because it does not acknowledge the historical fact of co-evolution of the theories preceding reduction. However, on the second reading the important addendum is that one effect of the co-evolution of transmission and molecular genetics will have been to revise rather radically the causal mainstay of Mendelian genetics as the macro- and microtheories approached reductive integration.

If anything, genetics is an especially good case rather than a problematic one to consider as we view the prospects for co-evolution and reduction of psychology and neuroscience.[2] Three major themes resonate through Hooker's analysis of the genetics case, all of which are here applicable: (1) input-output functional properties are not always subserved by unitary mechanisms, but are the outcome of the orchestration of diverse mechanisms, no one of which can be suitably identified as the realization of the macrolevel property, (2) this tends to be the case the more levels of organization there are in the system and the more complex the route between input and output, and (3) because of these and other factors, the characterization of input-output functions and input-output laws will be revised to mesh more closely with lower-level discoveries.

Co-evolution of Research on Memory and Learning

A predictable outcome of the co-evolution of psychology and neuroscience is that some types of mental state, specified by folk psychology in terms of their presumed causal properties, will turn out to be "virtual governors." It is of enormous philosophical interest that this is already happening in the case of two interconnected categories whose role is quite central in folk psychology, namely memory and learning. "Memory," as a category characterized within folk psychology, is at least as bad as a virtual governor.

As indicated earlier "learning" does not define a single kind of business; among the various kinds can already be distinguished habituation, sensitization, imprinting, one-trial learning, classical conditioning, instrumental conditioning, and place-learning. Suppose these to be "basic" kinds of plasticity, the list must then be expanded to include so-called higher learning, and here too the general catchall category appears ready to fragment into a number of distinct classes with distinct underlying neuronal systems. Perceptual-motor skills may differ along certain dimensions from "purely" cognitive skills, and the mechanisms subserving language learning appear to be different from those subserving facial recognition or cognitive mapping. And some of the research raises deep problems for the commonsense conception of "control" in human mental life, and for the role of consciousness. The theoretical future of a unified folk psychology category, "memory," or "learning," looks bleak because the domain of input-output phenomena is itself undergoing redescription and reclassification. And the interconnected set of categories "consciousness," "awareness," and "attention" are themselves evolving and may in time be transformed rather radically.

Moreover, the research on memory and learning illustrates very well the mutual benefits of co-evolution at all levels of research. Having shed the confining Skinnerian dogma that knowledge of the internal mechanisms would contribute nothing to understanding behavioral plasticity, and taking advantage of recent electronic and micro technology, the memory and learning field has in the last twenty-odd years become a classical exhibit of productive research on a nervous system capacity at many levels at once. Research influences go up and down and all over the map. Though I cannot give anything like a review of the enormous relevant literature, I want to provide a few samples to illustrate the interdisciplinary nature of the research program.

At the cellular and molecular level Kandel and his colleagues (Kandel 1976; Hawkins and Kandel 1984) have discovered much concerning the neurobiological basis for habituation, sensitization, and classical conditioning in the invertebrate *Aplysia Californica*. These discoveries are truly remarkable both because they represent a landmark in the attempt to understand the neurobiological basis of plasticity and because they show that memory and learning can, despite the skepticism, be addressed neurobiologically. Quinn and his colleagues (Quinn and Greenspan 1984) have found a complementary account to explain why certain mutant populations of *Drosophila* are learning disabled, and thus a connection has been made between specific genes and the production of an enzyme known to have a causal role in learning. The neurobiological basis of imprinting in the chick is slowly coming into focus (Horn 1983), as are the neural circuitry underlying classical conditioning in the mammalian brain (McCormick 1984) and the neural circuitry underlying song learning in the canary (Nottebohm 1981).

The discovery that bilateral surgical removal of the medial temporal lobe, amygdala, and hippocampus in humans resulted in profound amnesia for events occurring after surgery (Scoville and Milner 1957; see the discussion below) led to intensive study of the role of those structures in animal models. Some of this work has involved complex testing of residual capacities after making circumscribed lesions at various sites, and some has involved recording from specified areas in the hippocampus.

In one of the latter experimental attempts Berger, Thompson, and their associates found that after training there was a sort of cellular representation of the behavioral response in the hippocampus, and this "representation" developed during the training phase of classical conditioning (Berger and Thompson 1978; Berger et al. 1980). In the performance of the learned response, it occurred prior to the onset of the behavioral response. Interestingly, however, lesioning of the hippocampus does not prevent classical conditioning, though lesioning of the interpositus nuclei of the cerebellum does. Anatomical studies reporting pathways and connections have formed the basis for hypotheses to explain the effects, and these hypotheses were important to those studying humans and those studying animal models. Zipser (1985) has developed a theoretical model to explain hippocampal learning during classical conditioning that draws on some principles found to apply in *Aplysia*. Vertebrate nervous systems are much more complicated than those of invertebrates, but the *Aplysia* research has provided a framework of hypotheses that structures research on the cellular basis of habituation, sensitization, and classical conditioning in the vertebrate brain.

The amnesic syndromes found in Korsakoff's patients, whose intellectual degeneration is correlated with many years of alcohol abuse, and in Alzheimer's patients, patients who have undergone electroconvulsive therapy, and patients with tumors or with other lesions have been intensively studied and compared both at the performance level and in terms of the underlying pathology. Important differences have emerged, and the data have suggested to some neuropsychologists that there are at least two distinct physiological systems subserving higher long-term learning and memory.

One line of evidence in favor of the hypothesis depends on showing that the two capacities are dissociable, and the most striking example of such dissociation is displayed by Milner's patient, H.M. At age 27 H.M. underwent surgery as a means of last resort to control his intractable epilepsy. The surgery involved bilateral resectioning of the medial temporal lobe and hippocampal structures (Scoville and Milner 1957). In tests following the surgery an unexpected side effect was discovered: H.M. has profound anterograde amnesia and can recall virtually nothing of any events that have happened since the surgery. As Scoville and Milner have observed, he appears to forget everything as soon as it happens. He cannot remember what he had for lunch or whether he had lunch, he cannot recall having met the hospital staff he sees many times a day or how to get to the bathroom. Nor can he recall being told that his favorite uncle has died, and each time he inquires about his uncle and is told of his death, his grief is renewed. His IQ was slightly above average preoperatively and is still so postoperatively. H.M. has quite good retrograde memory, especially for events a year or so before surgery, and he easily recalls events from his early life. Eventually H.M. came to understand that something was very wrong in his life, and he commented,

Right now, I'm wondering. Have I done or said anything amiss? You see, at this moment everything looks clear to me, but what happened just before? That's what worries me. It's like waking from a dream; I just don't remember. (Milner 1966:115)

Despite his severe anterograde memory deficit, it has been found that H.M. does have a retained capacity for learning certain kinds of things. For example, Milner (1966) showed that he could learn a mirror tracing task, and Corkin (1968) showed that he could learn rotary pursuit and manual tracking. Although these achievements might be considered merely noncognitive, sensorimotor skills, it is remarkable that H.M. has also mastered, at a normal rate, the Tower of Hanoi puzzle. That is, when presented with the puzzle, H.M. can solve it in the optimal number of steps, and he can proceed to the end if started anywhere in the middle (Cohen and Corkin 1981). This is a nontrivial intellectual feat.

More puzzling still, on each occasion when he is asked to attempt the puzzle, he does not recall having learned how to do it, and he does not even recall having encountered it before. That is, he has no conscious recognition of the puzzle that he can verbally report. When, having solved the puzzle in the optimal number of steps, H.M. is asked to explain his expertise, he shrugs it off with a confabulatory explanation, such as that he is good at puzzles, this one is easy, and so forth. He has acquired an impressive cognitive-cum-motor skill, yet so far as he is able to *tell* us, the puzzle is always a complete novelty. Control is therefore also problematic here because H.M. can initiate and successfully complete an extended, intellectually demanding task, even though he has no awareness that he has the knowledge or that he is executing his knowledge on the task at hand. If H.M. has no awareness of his skill, how, one wonders, does the nervous system execute the long sequence of steps necessary for the puzzle's solution? The point is, in some sense H.M. is not aware of what he is doing, yet what he is doing is cognitive, complex, and, should we say, intentional. To put it crudely, it is as though some part of H.M.'s nervous system knows what it is doing and has the relevant complex intentions, but H.M. does not. What does H.M. think he is doing? Thus the problem of control. (See also Warrington and Weiskrantz 1982.)

It is this unpredicted dissociation of capacities that has moved some neuropsychologists to postulate two memory systems, each with its own physiological basis. In attempting to key onto the criterial features of the lost and the retained capacities of H.M., Squire and Cohen (1984) propose that the distinction be made as follows: "descriptive memory" is the capacity to verbally report recollections, and "procedural memory" is the capacity to exhibit a learned skill. Although this way of framing the distinction is useful in some measure, it is acknowledged by Squire and Cohen to be a preliminary and imprecise taxonomy, and much remains to be discovered about the range and nature of each capacity, assuming there are indeed two.

Studies of animal models tend to confirm the fractionation of memory components (Weiskrantz 1978; Mishkin and Petri 1984; Zola-Morgan 1984), but interpretive questions remain concerning which anatomical structures explain the observed deficits and the degree to which animal models illuminate the human cases. Anatomical studies are certainly important in determining whether there are distinct anatomical structures subserving dissociable memory systems and in suggesting further ways to test amnesic patients in order to determine just which capacities are retained and which are lost. It could be that PET and cerebral blood flow scans will help resolve some of the issues currently in dispute. (For a cautionary discussion concerning the Squire version of the two-systems hypothesis, see Weiskrantz 1985).)

At the same time, of course, psychologists have collected immense amounts of data concerning learning and remembering in the intact human. Learning curves, forgetting curves, distinctions between unaided recall, cued recall, and recognition, and the role of attention, for example, have been enormously useful and have been employed at other levels of investigation. Some psychologists have framed a "two-systems" hypothesis but have drawn the boundaries quite differently from the neuropsychologists. Tulving (1972, 1983) distinguishes episodic from semantic memory (neither of which encompasses cognitive skills), and Kinsbourne and Wood (1975) have used this distinction in their research on amnesia. Others (Norman and Rumelhart 1970) have distinguished between memory for item and memory for context, and this rather different taxonomy has also been used in interpreting data on amnesics (Huppert and Piercy 1976).

The assorted more-than-one-system hypotheses have provoked widespread testing of intact humans and have occasioned new studies on skills (Kolers 1975; Rumelhart and Norman 1982), the role of consciousness in the various kinds of memory (Posner 1984; Poulos and Wilkinson 1984), and so forth, in order to try to discover the nature of the two capacities, if such there really be, and whether there is theoretical justification for postulating yet other capacities. What is striking about the research on memory and learning is its interdisciplinary character. Researchers working at one level are always on the lookout for, and are often successful in finding, results elsewhere that can help them in devising useful experiments or in reconfiguring the memory-learning taxonomy.

One hope concerning the research in memory and learning is that the explanation of the biological basis of relatively simple plasticity such as habituation in *Aplysia* can be used as a scaffolding for addressing the neurobiology of other kinds of learning and for figuring out the neurobiology both of habituation and (eventually) of other kinds of plasticity in humans. The current classification of kinds of learning may well be reconfigured even further in unpredictable ways as the research at all levels continues. There is a sense in which, so far as higher learning is concerned, we cannot be at all sure yet what the explananda are. For example, we do not have a principled way to characterize either the capacity that is preserved in H.M. or the capacity that is lost.

One response to those who advocate the autonomy of psychology is therefore this: it would be simply boneheaded for a cognitive psychologist working on learning and memory to refuse to care about animal models, pathway research, clinical cases, imprinting in chicks, song learning in canaries, and habituation in *Aplysia*. We simply don't know remotely enough yet to know what is not relevant. And learning and memory are not some recherché capacities of tangential connection to intelligent behavior; they are as central to cognitive psychology as anything could be. . . .

Are Sentential Attitudes Important to Theorizing in Psychology?

Sentential attitudes and *logical* inference occupy center stage in the disagreement between those who defend autonomy and those who defend co-evolution and interdependence. But are the sentential attitudes really so very important in folk psychology or in cognitive psychology? Would thoroughgoing revision of their theory be so very revolutionary?

The answer to both questions is a resounding yes. Beliefs, desires, thoughts, intentions, and the like, are invariably assumed to mediate between input and output and to have a crucial role in the causation of behavior. Moreover, to echo an earlier remark, it is only in the case of the sentential attitudes that we have something approaching a systematic theory both of the nature of the representations and of the rules that govern the transitions between representations. Most of the generalizations routinely used in the explanation of human behavior advert to sentential attitudes and their interplay. One of the beauties of sentential attitudes as a theoretical postulate is that they can also be given a role in nonconscious processes and hence can be invoked to describe cognitive business a long way down. Additionally, we can exploit deductive logic and such inductive logic and decision theory as are available to extend our theory of the rules followed by internal states. Dismantle sentential attitude theory, and we no longer have any idea how to explain behavior—we no longer have any idea of what is going on inside. Fodor (1975) grittily describes the situation: it's the only theory we've got.

The theoretical blessings of sentential attitude psychology are undeniably rich, and it is entirely reasonable to try to develop a scientific psychology by extending and pruning the sentential attitude base. Consequently, the suggestion that substantial revisions to this base resulting from co-evolution are likely will fall on ungrateful ears. It is of course no defense of the truth of a theory that it's the only theory we've got.

(Compare some fictional Aristotelian, circa 1400: "It's the only theory we've got.") What the lack of alternatives implies is that one has no choice but to *use* the available theory, and this is consistent with its falsity and with trying to construct a better competing theory. In view of the continual harping on the theme of revision, the advocates of theory interdependence must finally square up to this question: is the prospect of revision to sentential attitude psychology serious or frivolous? That is, does it rest on substantial grounds, or is it just a pie-in-the-sky possibility?

We have already seen in Stich's (1983) research compelling reason to suppose that the folk psychological categories of belief, desire, and so forth, will require substantial revision. In addition, there are substantial reasons for predicting that at best inference and sentence-like representations will have a small role in the theory of information processing, and for predicting quite radical revisions in folk psychology. These matters will be discussed in the next section.

Information Processing and the Sentential Paradigm

The Sentential Manifesto

An information-processing theory is *sentential* if it adheres to the following tenets (Patricia S. Churchland 1980):

1. Like beliefs and desires, the cognitively relevant internal states are states that have content, where the content is identified via a sentence. The identification is presumed to be possible by virtue of an isomorphism holding between the states of the person (his brain) and the relevant sentences of a set.

2. The theoretically important relations between cognitive states are characterized by means of the resources of logic. These obtain in virtue of the aforementioned isomorphism. (Various theories of logic will be variously favored by cognitive scientists.)

3. The transitions between states are a function of the logical relations holding between the sentences identifying the states, which in the most straightforward case will consist of inference, abductive and deductive. Again, by virtue of the isomorphism.

4. The evaluation of the cognitive virtue (rationality) of a system is a function of the extent to which it succeeds in doing what the favored theory of state transition (i.e., theory of logic) says it ideally should do.

Any sentential theory needs a theory of how it is that internal states have content, since it is plainly ad hoc to suppose it a lucky accident that the relevant isomorphisms systematically obtain. Fodor's theory (1975, 1981) is that sentential attitudes (alias propositional attitudes) are relational states, where one of the relata is a sentence in the organism's *language of thought.* Thus, if Smith has the thought that gulls' eggs are delicious, then he stands in a certain relation to a sentence in his language of thought, namely, the sentence whose English translation is "Gulls' eggs are delicious." Broadly speaking, the information processing is manipulation of representations, and representations are symbols of the language of thought. Thinking is, to put it crudely, sentence-crunching, and the machine analogy underwrites the intended sense of symbol manipulation.

Within cognitive science there is considerable loose talk about cognitive representations, where the question of the nature and status of representations is left conveniently vague. Fodor's theory makes explicit what is an implicit commitment in sentential/representational hypotheses generally. There are, it should be emphasized, many cognitive psychologists who do not adhere to the sentential theory and who investigate cognitive capacities while awaiting the development of a nonsentential theory of representations.

The foregoing is just a thumbnail sketch of the main features of a sentential theory of information processing, but the finer points and the in-house disputes can for now be set aside.

Cognition and Sentence-Crunching

How plausible are the framework assumptions of the sentential paradigm? The theme of the ensuing section is that as an approach to cognitive activity in general, they have serious flaws. Language is a social art, and linguistic behavior serves a communicative function. We may stand to enhance our cognitive repertoire as a result of acquiring linguistic skill, inasmuch as such a skill structures and enables certain cognitive capacities. On the other hand, there is something deeply mystifying in the idea that all of our cognitive activity, including cognitively dependent perception, pattern recognition, and the cognitive activity of infants, is language-like, in the sense that it consists of sentence manipulation.

If we think of linguistic behavior as something that evolved because it provided for a quantum jump in the information available to organisms by allowing for complex exchange between individuals, then the enthusiasm for cognition as sentence-crunching seems insensitive to evolutionary considerations. Sentence-crunching is certain to have been a cognitive latecomer in the evolutionary scheme of things, and it must have knit itself into the preexisting nonsentential cognitive organization, or, perhaps one should say, it must have evolved out of preadaptive nonsentential structures. To be sentence-crunching "all the way down" implies either that cognition must have been sentence-crunching "all the way back," which is implausible, or that sentence-crunchers have no cognitive heritage from earlier species, which is also implausible given the evolution of the brain.

The objections in the literature to the sentential paradigm condense around several prominent problems, which I shall consider briefly in turn.

The Infralinguistic Catastrophe

It is a problem for the sentential paradigm that intelligent behavior is displayed by organisms who have no overt linguistic capacity. Consider the case of a nonverbal deaf-mute who was committed to an asylum for the insane as a result of misdiagnosis (and some malice). He made his escape after what must have been elaborate planning, deception, and arranging, and the escape must be considered intelligent by any standard. The behavior of chimpanzees in getting what they want or where they want is also as obviously intelligent as much behavior of the overtly verbal human (Menzel 1974). The orangutans who make umbrellas of jungle leaves have an intelligent solution to a comfort problem. The octopi who unscrew mason jars to get the food inside, the macaques who wash their sandy potatoes in the sea, and the rooks who drop stones on would-be invaders all display a solution that is in some degree intelligent (Griffin 1984). Nonverbal human infants learn the language of their peers, a cognitive feat of monumental proportions.

Short of conceding that there is substantial nonsentential representation, two solutions are possible. (1) One can argue that behavior in the infralinguistic organism is not really a cognitive product. Language learning by the toddler, on this view, is not in fact cognitive in the intended sense. (2) One can argue that since the behavior in question is cognitive, then the infraverbal organisms have a language of thought in which they reason, solve problems, etc. (Fodor 1975).

The first alternative in effect defines a cognitive process as a sentence-crunching process. Accordingly, it becomes true *by definition* that cognition is essentially sentence-crunching, but this leaves it entirely open whether much of the information processing subserving intelligence is cognitive in this special sense.

The second alternative suffers from diminished credibility. It is a strain to see the justification for supposing that orangutans, infant humans, and all the rest have a language of thought, Mentalese, in which they frame hypotheses, test them against the evidence, draw deductive inferences, and so forth. Mentalese, as Fodor (1975) depicts it, is a full-fledged language, with a syntax, a semantics, and a finite vocabulary—as indeed it must be if it is to be the wherewithal for sentence-crunching. An additional difficulty that Fodor himself draws out concerns how the infant uses Mentalese to learn the language of his peers. If the infant learns English by hypothesizing what chunks of English can be correlated with concepts in Mentalese, then he can only acquire English concepts for which there are Mentalese correlates. This means that there is no such thing as real concept learning, in the sense that wholly new concepts are added to the conceptual repertoire.

This consequence is sufficiently unacceptable to be a reductio of the Mentalese hypothesis. For it entails that the ostensibly new concepts evolving in the course of scientific innovation—concepts such as atom, force field, quark, electrical charge, and gene—are lying ready-made in the language of thought, even of a prehistoric hunter-gatherer. It is difficult to take such an idea seriously, even supposing there is something like a language of thought in linguistically accomplished humans. The concepts of modern science are defined in terms of the theories that embed them, not in terms of a set of "primitive conceptual atoms," whatever those might be. To suppose they are ready-made in Mentalese is to suppose the embedding theory is somehow (miraculously) ready-made in Mentalese. This cannot be right. (For a fuller discussion, see Patricia S. Churchland 1980.) If it is not, then however learning of a first language is accomplished, it is not by sentence-crunching in the language of thought. Something entirely different is going on.

The Problem of Tacit Knowledge

Under the lens of philosophical analysis, the concept of belief as it lives in folk psychology shows serious theoretical defects, and if the theory cannot be modified to correct the problems, then radical revision of the theory may have to be considered. The philosophical analysis can be understood as a testing of the internal coherence of the theory, and some of the results are very puzzling. Tacit beliefs are a case in point. (See especially Dennett 1975, 1984; Lycan 1986).

Some of the things Smith believes are things he is dwelling on right now, as for example when he says silently to himself, "My fern needs water." Other things are allegedly not part of his current silent monologue, but were part of past monologues, such as what he said to himself as he drove to work, namely, "Flin Flon is on the migration route of polar bears." What else does Smith believe? Well, suppose we determine the range of what he believes by querying him. We ask, "Is Medicine Hat on the migration route of polar bears?" and when he says no, we can add the negation of our question to the list of what he believes. Why not ask him the same question about Tallahassee, Dallas, and so forth? Why not ask him whether polar bears are made of sand, of salt, of spaghetti, . . .? Again, with additions to the belief-list. Why not ask him, for every number n greater than 7, whether he believes that polar bears are less than n meters tall? Since he will answer yes each time, his answers to these questions can also be added. The trouble is, things are getting out of hand, and the modest Smith is now credited with an infinite number of beliefs.

Philosophers have tried to augment and exploit the resources of folk theory to save it from the extravagance of infinite belief stores. Call "tacit" any belief that one really has but has not explicitly entertained. The problem then is how to specify conditions under which someone does really have "P" as a tacit belief, where the conditions are not so broad as to entail that we all have an infinity of beliefs. The problem seems manageable enough at first blush, but it turns out to be stubbornly resistant to solution.

The austere solution is simply to cut out tacit beliefs altogether. The price of that solution is that the consequences of one's beliefs—even the dead obvious consequences—are no longer things one believes. Smith believes that all men are mortal, and he believes that Trudeau is a man, but, busy with other things, he has never troubled to explicitly draw the conclusion: Trudeau is mortal. But it is an obvious consequence of his beliefs, he would assent in a flash if asked, and it can be shown to have a causal role in his behavior if we set up the right circumstances. (Suppose Smith is a prairie socialist who attends the opposition's rally and hears an Ottawa Liberal say, "Trudeau will live forever." Smith, ever forthright and voluble, unhesitatingly shouts out, "Trudeau is mortal.") Given these considerations, it seems reasonable to say that Smith all along believed that Trudeau is mortal, notwithstanding the implicit status of the belief. The austere solution looks unacceptable.

The trick is to find a principled way of dividing, among the sentences Smith will assent to, those that are really tacit beliefs, with real causal effects, and those that are not. If an extrapolator-deducer mechanism is postulated, this explains how Smith (really) has the belief that Trudeau is mortal (it gets deduced from other beliefs in the store), but it also brings additional problems. Are *all* the consequences of all of Smith's beliefs things he believes? Alas, no, since no one will assent to every such consequence, and some, such as theorems of mathematics, will not even be recognized, let alone assented to. Nor will it do to take all the *obvious* consequences of Smith's beliefs as what he tacitly believes, because what is obvious depends on who the person is, and there is no independent measure. What was obvious to Gödel is not obvious to me (Field 1977). Moreover, all of us—irrationally, one might say—can fail on occasion to see the "obvious" consequences of our beliefs (Nisbett and Ross 1980). On the other side of the coin, even some of the far-flung consequences Smith does assent to are not plausible candidates as tacit beliefs if they were assented to on the spot, so to speak, rather than having been cranked out by the extrapolator-deducer working behind the scenes (see especially Lycan 1986).

Moreover, when we look closely at how the extrapolator-deducer mechanism might be expected to operate, there are intractable problems. How does it "know" what beliefs in the store are relevant to deducing an answer to a particular question? Does it have its own store of beliefs about what is relevant to what questions? Is there a higher-order extrapolator-deducer mechanism to handle that? And what of *its* beliefs? (See Dennett 1975.) In many examples it is not evident either what could be the input to the extrapolator-deducer or what the chain of reasoning might have been. For example, I suppose it must be said that I believe that the computer on which I now enter this word will not blow up in the next ten seconds. But that is not a belief that until this moment figures in my speech, silent or overt, so it must be deducible from my other beliefs. Like what? That computers never blow up? (I don't know if I believe that.) That North Star computers never blow up? That computers only blow up if . . . if what? I really don't have the faintest idea. (See also Dreyfus 1979, 1981.)

With the failure of internal solutions to the problem of tacit beliefs, it must be suspected that there is a framework mistake somewhere, perhaps infecting the statement of the problem itself. Thus, the supposition that the knowledge store is a sentence (belief) store comes to be regarded as untenable. Abandoning that supposition, we can try instead the idea that tacit knowledge is not (mainly not) a corpus of tacit beliefs. It may be that on some occasions sentences are stored, as for example when the exact words of Macbeth's death speech are burned into memory, but verbatim storage may be the exception rather than the rule.

What is stored is generally something else, something that may be verbally encoded on demand, but need not be verbally encoded to be cognitively engaged. Accordingly, even those sentences that have been explicitly assented to or that figured in silent speech are generally not stored as sentences. If such information is nonconsciously used in the course of solving a problem, or if it serves as a background assumption, there is no reason to assume it must first acquire a sentential encoding. Sometimes the background assumptions that affect behavior and problem solving can be verbalized only with immense effort or perhaps not at all. Think, for example, of social knowledge, or of a farmer's "bovine knowledge," or of a woodsman's "bush knowledge."[3] The scope of sentential representation and sentential manipulation now looks more limited than the sentential paradigm assumes. Other sorts of representational structures will need to be postulated; hence the interest in nonsentential representations such as prototypes (Rosch 1973), images (Kosslyn 1975), and frames (Minsky 1975).

The Problem of Knowledge Access

An organism's knowledge store is a waste of resources unless it can be used, and that means that the right bits must be available at the right times. For motile creatures, survival and reproductive success depend upon being able to use the stored information for fleeing, fighting, feeding, and reproducing. It does a bull moose no good to know what a female moose looks like if that information remains untapped during rutting season. Notice too that the point holds whether the information is innate or acquired. So much, I think, is obvious. What is not obvious is how an information-processing system knows which of the many things in its store is relevant to the problem at hand. If everything in the store is accessed, then the system will be swamped and unable to make a speedy decision (starving to death while it continues to canvass information), but if relevant information is unavailable, the organism's environment will make it pay. As noted earlier, something akin to this question troubled Peirce profoundly, and the form it took for him was how humans happen to light upon relevant hypotheses to explain an event.

At first encounter the problem of relevant access might seem merely a philosopher's curiosity, but it turns out to be much more. This becomes most clearly visible in the context of artificial intelligence (AI), where the problem is to program a robot that can interact with the world using a knowledge store. Consider the following example, adapted from Dennett 1984. The robot's task is to survive, and it is told that the spare battery it needs is in a room where a time bomb is set to explode soon. Suppose that the battery is on a wagon, and, having entered the room, the robot pulls the wagon out of the room. The bomb explodes and destroys both the battery and the robot, because the bomb, it turns out, was also on the wagon. Apparently the robot knew that but failed to see an obvious consequence of its behavior, so its program must be improved to allow for that.

Having modified the program, we try again. This time the robot goes into the room and, after pulling out the wagon, begins to crank out the consequences of its behavior, and the consequences of the consequences, including such things as "Some heat will be generated by the action of the wheels on the floor" and "Pulling out the wagon will not change the color of the walls," and the bomb explodes while it is still cranking.

The defect, it seems, is that the robot needs to distinguish between relevant and irrelevant consequences, and what it needs is a mechanism for lighting on the relevant ones. Our parents would say to us, "Use your common sense: the color of the walls does not matter, but the bomb's still being on the wagon does." But how do we translate our parents' advice into an instruction the robot can follow? Should it have the following instruction in its store: if you are trying to get your battery away from a bomb, make sure they are not both on the same wagon, and all else is irrelevant? This is both too specific and too general. Many other things could indeed be relevant, such as: if there is water nearby, don't put the battery in that; if there is apple juice nearby, don't put the battery in that; don't put the bomb in a fire; don't let yourself be near the bomb; if the bomb can be switched off, do that; and so on and drearily on. Moreover, it seems too specific if it is to mimic human knowledge, since we do not have explicit instructions for what to do when finding bombs and babies on wagons, yet we would typically behave successfully.

Suppose, on the other hand, we give the robot the more general instruction, "If you find a hazard situated close to your battery, separate them by a good distance." More will still be needed, however—namely, a list of what to count as hazards, and how close "close" is, and how far a "good" distance is. Part of the trouble is that the last measure varies as a function of the hazard, and even what counts as a hazard depends on what else is around. A meter is far enough from a sharp knife, "in the cottage" is far enough from a bear, two feet is far enough from a smoldering camp fire but not far enough from a roaring one.

It is now deeply puzzling how the robot might be instructed so as not to be a fool, a problem that in AI research is called the *frame problem* (McCarthy and Hayes 1969).[4] How do humans manage not to be fools? What does our "common sense" or "intelligence" consist in? The more we try to solve the robot's problem of sensible behavior, the more it becomes clear that *our* behavior is not guided by explicit sentential instructions in our store of knowledge (Dennett 1984). Specifying the knowledge store in sentences is a losing strategy. We have knowledge, all right, but it does not consist in sets of sentences. We know about moving babies away from hazards without having detailed lists of what counts as a hazard and how far to move the baby. Our "relevant-access mechanism" is imperfect, since we are tripped up from time to time, and tort law is full of instances of such imperfection. The right things do not always occur to us at the right times. Nevertheless, we manage on the whole to survive, reproduce, and do a whole lot more.

Somehow, nervous systems have solved the problem of knowledge access. Once that solution is understood, we may be amazed at how different it is from what we imagined, and we may find that we had even naively misconceived the problem itself. It is of course no mere trifle that can be isolated as we get on with understanding the rest of cognition. It is the problem of explaining how an organism can behave intelligently, and it is therefore at the very heart of questions concerning learning, memory, attention, problem-solving, and whatever else of a smart sort the mind-brain does.

Even relatively simple nervous systems have solved the problem of knowledge access, insofar as past experiences modify their behavior. The evolution of increasingly complex nervous systems must involve increasingly complex solutions to the problem of knowledge use. One strategy for coming to understand what is going on is to study learning, memory, and knowledge use in simpler systems and to see how Nature in fact solved the problem. The answers found at that level may well be illuminating for more complex nervous systems. Ethologists learning ever more about the nature of animal behavior, such as imprinting and song learning, and neuroscientists finding mechanisms that subserve that behavior (Kandel 1976; Horn 1983; Nottebohm 1981) can thus put a squeeze on the questions.

The co-evolution of ethology and neuroscience is already well under-way, and the two have coalesced at some points in what goes by the name of *neuroethology*. (See for example Horn 1983; Nottebohm 1981; Hoyle 1984.) The complaint that the simpler nervous systems do not display intelligence is premature: we will not know what intelligence is until we have a solution to the problem of knowledge use. In any event, if there are grades of intelligence, understanding the lower grades may be essential to understanding the higher grades.[5]

The problems of tacit knowledge and knowledge access are not unrelated, and together with the infralinguistic problem they make an impressive case for assessing the sentential paradigm as unsound. The sententialist is of course right about this much: if cognition is not *in general* the manipulation of sentences, then we don't know what is going on. The antecedent of this conditional seems to me inescapable, and since my extrapolator-deducer is in good order, I conclude that indeed we do not know what is going on. Not, however, that I see that as cause for despair; it is what we would expect for a science in *statu nascendi*. Compare the lament of the vitalist in the nineteenth century: if there is no such thing as vital spirit, then we do not have any idea what makes living things alive and different from nonliving things. Biochemistry eventually changed all that. . . .

Notes

1. This is just a partial specification of what is needed; for Hooker's complete account, see Hooker 1981, part III. The rest is not unimportant, but I think it need not be set out here.

2. For a discussion of the opposite view, see Patricia Kitcher 1980, 1982.

3. This idea has been intensively explored by Dreyfus (1979, 1981).

4. As I understand it, the frame problem refers to a rather more circumscribed problem within AI, and hence I felt bound to select "knowledge access" as the name for this more general problem. For my purposes the differences are not important. The research on the problem in AI has been crucial in bringing the problem itself into clear focus.

5. Since Menzel (1983) is surely right when he says that no animals are simple, I should clarify that by "simpler system" I here mean any organism lower on the phylogenetic scale than *Homo sapiens*. Thus, the term obviously includes a lot of profoundly complex brains. Rhesus monkey brains are scarcely less complex than ours, but they are more researchable. The nervous system of *Aplysia californica* is considerably less complex than that of a monkey, but even so it is a wonder of complexity.

References

Benzer, S. (1957). The elementary units of heredity. In W. McElroy and B. Glass, eds., *The chemical basis of heredity*. Baltimore: John Hopkins University Press.

Berger, T. W., R. I. Latham, and R. F. Thompson (1980). Hippocampal unit-behavior correlations during classical conditioning. *Brain Research* 193, 483–485.

Berger, T. W., and R. F. Thompson (1978). Identification of pyramidal cells as the critical elements in hippocampal neuronal plasticity during learning. *National Academy of Sciences of the United States of America. Proceedings. Biological Sciences* 75, 1572–1576.

Churchland, P. S. (1980). Language, thought, and information processing. *Nous* 14, 147–170.

Cohen, N. J., and S. Corkin (1981). The amnesic patient. H. M.: Learning and retention of cognitive skill. *Society for Neuroscience Abstracts* 7, 517–518.

Corkin, S. (1968). Acquisition of motor skill after bilateral medial temporal-lobe excision. *Neuropsychologia* 6, 255–265.

Dennett, D. C. (1975). Brain writing and mind reading. In K. Gunderson, ed., *Language, mind, and knowledge*. (Minnesota Studies in the Philosophy of Science, vol. 7.) Minneapolis: University of Minnesota Press.

Dennett, D. C. (1984). Cognitive wheels: The frame problem of artificial intelligence. In C. Hookway, ed., *Minds, machines, and evolution*. Cambridge: Cambridge University Press.

Dewan, E. M. (1976). Consciousness as an emergent causal agent in the context of control system theory. In G. Globus, G. Maxwell, and I. Savodnik, eds., *Consciousness and the brain*. New York: Plenum.

Dreyfus, H. L. (1979). *What computers can't do*. 2nd. ed. New York: Harper and Row.

Dreyfus, H. L. (1981). From micro-worlds to knowledge representation: AI at an impasse. In J. Haugeland, ed., *Mind design*. Cambridge, MA: MIT Press.

Field, H. (1977). Logic, meaning, and conceptual role. *Journal of Philosophy* 74, 379–408.

Fodor, J. A. (1975). *The language of thought*. New York: Crowell.

Fodor, J. A. (1981). *Representations*. Cambridge, MA: MIT Press.

Griffin, D. R. (1984). *Animal thinking*. Cambridge, MA: Harvard University Press.

Hawkins, R. D., and E. R. Kandel (1984). Steps toward a cell-biological alphabet for elementary forms of learning. In G. Lynch, J. L. McGaugh, and N. M. Weinberger, eds., *Neurobiology of learning and memory*. New York: Guilford.

Hooker, C. A. (1981). Towards a general theory of reduction. Part I: Historical and scientific setting. Part II: Identity in reduction. Part III: Cross-categorial reduction. *Dialogue* 20, 38–59, 201–236, 496–521.

Horn, G. (1983). Information storage in the brain: A study of imprinting in the domestic chick. In J.-P Ewart, R. Capranica, and D. J. Ingle, eds., *Advances in vertebrate neuroethology: Proceedings of a NATO Advanced Study Institute*. New York: Plenum.

Hoyle, G. (1984). The scope of neuroethology. *Behavioral and Brain Sciences* 7, 367–412.

Hull, D. (1974). *Philosophy of biological science*. Englewood Cliffs, NJ: Prentice-Hall.

Huppert, F. A., and M. Piercy (1976). Recognition memory in amnesia patients: Effect of temporal context and familiarity of material. *Cortex* 12, 3–20.

Kandel, E. R. (1976). *Cellular basis of behavior: An introduction to behavioral neurobiology.* San Francisco: W. H. Freeman.

Kinsbourne, M., and F. Wood (1975). Short-term memory processes and the amnesic syndrome. In D. Deutsch and J. A. Deutsch, eds., *Short-term memory.* New York: Academic Press.

Kitcher, Patricia (1980). How to reduce a functional psychology? *Philosophy of Science* 47, 134–140.

Kitcher, Patricia (1982). Discussion: Genes, reduction, and functional psychology. *Philosophy of Science* 49, 633–636.

Kitcher, Philip (1984). Genes. *British Journal for the Philosophy of Science* 33, 337–359.

Kolers, P. (1975). Specificity of operation in sentence recognition. *Cognitive Psychology* 7, 289–306.

Kosslyn, S. M. (1975). Information representation in visual images. *Cognitive Psychology* 7, 341–370.

Lycan, W. G. (1986). Tacit belief. In R. J. Bogdan, ed., *Belief.* Oxford: Oxford University Press.

McCarthy, J., and P. Hayes (1969). Some philosophical problems from the standpoint of Artificial Intelligence. In B. Meltzer and D. Michie, eds., *Machine intelligence,* vol. 4. New York: Harper and Row.

McCormick, D. (1984). Cerebellum: Essential involvement in a simple learned response. Doctoral dissertation, Stanford University.

Menzel, E. W. (1974). A group of young chimpanzees in a one-acre field. In A. M. Schrier and F. Stollnitz, eds., *Behavior of nonhuman primates,* vol. 5. New York: Academic Press.

Menzel, E. W. (1983). Parlez-vous baboon, Bwana Sherlock? (Commentary on Dennett 1983). *Behavioral and Brain Sciences* 6, 371–372.

Milner, B. (1966). Amnesia following operation on the temporal lobes. In C. W. M. Whitty and O. Zangwill, eds., *Amnesia.* London: Butterworth.

Minsky, M. (1975). Frame-system theory. In R. Schank and B. Nash-Webber, eds., *Theoretical issues in natural language processing.* (Reprinted in P. Johnson-Laird and P. Wason, eds., *Thinking: Readings in cognitive science.* Cambridge: Cambridge University Press.)

Mishkin, M., and H. L. Petri (1984). Memories and habits: Some implications for the analysis of learning and memory. In L. R. Squire and N. Butters, eds., *Neuropsychology of memory.* New York: Guilford.

Nisbett, R. E., and L. Ross (1980). *Human inference: Strategies and shortcomings of social judgment.* Englewood Cliffs, NJ: Prentice-Hall.

Norman, D. A., and D. E. Rumelhart (1970). A system for perception and memory. In D. A. Norman, ed., *Models of human memory*. New York: Academic Press.

Nottebohm, F. (1981). Laterality, seasons and space governing the learning of a motor skill. *Trends in Neurosciences*. 4/5, 104–106.

Posner, M. I. (1984). Selective attention and the storage of information. In G. Lynch, J. L. McGaugh, and N. M. Weinberger, eds., *Neurobiology of learning and memory*. New York: Guilford.

Poulos, C. X., and D. A. Wilkinson (1984). A process theory of remembering: Its application to Korsakoff amnesia and a critique of context and episodic-semantic theories. In L. R. Squire and N. Butters, eds., *Neuropsychology of memory*. New York: Guilford.

Quinn, W. G., and R. J. Greenspan (1984). Learning and courtship in *Drosophila*: Two stories with mutants. *Annual Review of Neuroscience* 7, 67–93.

Rosch, E. (1973). On the internal structure of perceptual and semantic categories. In T. Moore, ed., *Cognitive development and the acquisition of language*. New York: Academic Press.

Rumelhart, D. E., and D. A. Norman (1982). Simulating a skilled typist: A study of skilled cognitive-motor performance. *Cognitive Science* 6, 1–36.

Scoville, W. B., and B. Milner (1957). Loss of recent memory after bilateral hippocampal lesions. *Journal of Neurology, Neurosurgery, and Psychiatry* 20, 11–21.

Squire, L. R., and N. J. Cohen 91984). Human memory and amnesia. In G. Lynch, J. L. McGaugh, and N. M. Weinberger, eds., *Neurobiology of learning and memory*. New York: Guilford.

Stich, S. P. (1983). *From folk psychology to cognitive science: The case against belief*. Cambridge, MA: MIT Press.

Tulving, E. (1972). Episodic and semantic memory. In E. Tulving and W. Donaldson, eds., *Organization of memory*. New York: Academic Press.

Tulving, E. (1983). *Elements of episodic memory*. Oxford: Clarendon Press.

Warrington, E. K., and L. Weiskrantz (1982). Amnesia: A disconnection syndrome? *Neuropsychology* 20, 233–248.

Weiskrantz, L. (1978). A comparison of hippocampal pathology in man and other animals. In *Functions of the septo-hippocampal system*. Ciba Foundation Symposium (new series). 58, 373–406. Amsterdam: Elsevier, Excepta-Medica, North-Holland.

Weiskrantz, L. (1985). On issues and theories of the human amnesic syndrome. In N. M. Weinberger, J. L. McGaugh, and G. Lynch, eds., *Memory systems of the brain: Animal and human cognitive processes*. New York: Guilford.

Zipser, D. (1985). A theoretical model of hippocampal learning during classical conditioning. *Behavioral Neuroscience*.

Zola-Morgan, S. (1984). Toward an animal model of human amnesia: Some critical issues. In L. R. Squire and N. Butters, eds., *Neuropsychology of memory*. New York: Guilford.

35 On the Proper Treatment of Connectionism

Paul Smolensky

Introduction

In the past half-decade the connectionist approach to cognitive modeling has grown from an obscure cult claiming a few true believers to a movement so vigorous that recent meetings of the Cognitive Science Society have begun to look like connectionist pep rallies. With the rise of the connectionist movement come a number of fundamental questions which are the subject of this target article. I begin with a brief description of connectionist models.

Connectionist Models

Connectionist models are large networks of simple parallel computing elements, each of which carries a numerical *activation value* which it computes from the values of neighboring elements in the network, using some simple numerical formula. The network elements, or *units*, influence each other's values through connections that carry a numerical strength, or *weight*. The influence of unit i on unit j is the activation value of unit i times the strength of the connection from i to j. Thus, if a unit has a positive activation value, its influence on a neighbor's value is positive if its weight to that neighbor is positive, and negative if the weight is negative. In an obvious neural allusion, connections carrying positive weights are called *excitatory* and those carrying negative weights are *inhibitory*.

In a typical connectionist model, input to the system is provided by imposing activation values on the *input units* of the network; these numerical values represent some encoding, or *representation*, of the input. The activation on the input units propagates along the connections until some set of activation values emerges on the *output units*; these activation values encode the output the system has computed from the input. In between the input and output units there may be other units, often called *hidden units*, that participate in representing neither the input nor the output.

The computation performed by the network in transforming the input pattern of activity to the output pattern depends on the set of connection strengths; these weights are usually regarded as encoding the system's knowledge. In this sense, the connection strengths play the role of the program in a conventional computer. Much of the allure of the connectionist approach is that many connectionist networks *program themselves*, that is, they have autonomous procedures for tuning their weights to eventually perform some specific computation. Such learning procedures often depend on training in which the network is presented with sample input/output pairs from the function it is supposed to compute. In learning networks with hidden units, the network itself "decides" what computations the hidden units will perform; because these units represent neither inputs nor outputs, they are never "told" what their values should be, even during training.

In recent years connectionist models have been developed for many tasks, encompassing the areas of vision, language processing, inference, and motor control. Numerous examples can be found in recent proceedings of the meetings of the Cognitive Science Society; *Cognitive Science* (1985); Feldman et al. (1985); Hinton and Anderson (1981); McClelland et al. (1986); Rumelhart et al. (1986).

Goal of this Target Article

Given the rapid development in recent years of the connectionist approach to cognitive modeling, it is not yet an appropriate time for definitive assessments of the power and validity of the approach. The time seems right, however, for an attempt to articulate the goals of the approach, the fundamental hypotheses it is testing, and the relations presumed to link it with the other theoretical frameworks of cognitive science. A coherent and plausible articulation of these fundamentals is the goal of this target article. Such an articulation is a nontrivial task, because the term "connectionist" encompasses a number of rather disparate theoretical frameworks, all of them quite undeveloped. The connectionist framework I will articulate departs sufficiently radically from traditional approaches in that its relations to other parts of cognitive science are not simple.

For the moment, let me call the formulation of the connectionist approach that I will offer *PTC*. I will not argue the scientific merit of PTC; that some version of connectionism along the lines of PTC constitutes a "proper description of processing" is argued elsewhere (e.g., in Rumelhart et al. 1986; McClelland et al. 1986). Leaving aside the scientific merit of connectionist models, I want to argue here that PTC offers a "Proper Treatment of Connectionism": a coherent formulation of the connectionist approach that puts it in contact with other theory in cognitive science in a particularly constructive way. PTC is intended as a formulation of connectionism that is at once strong enough to constitute a major cognitive hypothesis, comprehensive enough to face a number of difficult challenges, and sound enough to resist a number of objections in principle. If PTC succeeds in these goals, it will facilitate the real business at hand: Assessing the scientific adequacy of the connectionist approach, that is, determining whether the approach offers computational power adequate for human cognitive competence and appropriate computational mechanisms to accurately model human cognitive performance.

PTC is a response to a number of positions that are being adopted concerning connectionism—pro, con, and blandly ecumenical. These positions, which are frequently expressed orally but rarely set down in print, represent, I believe, failures of supporters and critics of the traditional approach truly to come to grips with each other's views. Advocates of the traditional approach to cognitive modeling and AI (artificial intelligence) are often willing to grant that connectionist systems are useful, perhaps even important, for modeling lower-level processes (e.g., early vision), or for fast and fault-tolerant implementation of conventional AI programs, or for understanding how the brain might happen to implement LISP. These ecumenical positions, I believe, fail to acknowledge the true challenge that connectionists are posing to the received view of cognition; PTC is an explicit formulation of this challenge.

Other supporters of the traditional approach find the connectionist approach to be fatally flawed because it cannot offer anything new (since Universal Turing machines are, after all, "universal"), or because it cannot offer the kinds of explanations that cognitive science requires. Some dismiss connectionist models on the grounds that they are too neurally unfaithful. PTC has been designed to withstand these attacks.

On the opposite side, most existing connectionist models fail to come to grips with the traditional approach—partly through a neglect intended as benign. It is easy to read into the connectionist literature the claim that there is no role in cognitive science for traditional theoretical constructs such as rules, sequential processing, logic, rationality, and conceptual schemata or frames. PTC undertakes to assign these constructs their proper role in a connectionist paradigm for cognitive modeling. PTC also addresses certain foundational issues concerning mental states.

I see no way of achieving the goals of PTC without adopting certain positions that will be regarded by a number of connectionists as premature or mistaken. These are inevitable consequences of the fact that the connectionist approach is still quite underdeveloped, and that the term "connectionist" has come to label a number of approaches that embody significantly conflicting assumptions. PTC is *not* intended to represent a consensus view of what the connectionist approach is or should be.

It will perhaps enhance the clarity of the article if I attempt at the outset to make my position clear on the present value of connectionist models and their future potential. This article is not intended as a defense of all these views, though I will argue for a number of them, and the remainder have undoubtedly influenced the presentation. On the one hand, I believe that:

(1) a. It is far from clear whether connectionist models have adequate computational power to perform high-level cognitive tasks: There are serious obstacles that must be overcome before connectionist computation can offer modelers power comparable to that of symbolic computation.

b. It is far from clear that connectionist models offer a sound basis for modeling human cognitive performance: The connectionist approach is quite difficult to put into detailed contact with empirical methodologies.

c. It is far from clear that connectionist models can contribute to the study of human competence: Connectionist models are quite difficult to analyze for the kind of high-level properties required to inform the study of human competence.

d. It is far from clear that connectionist models, in something like their present forms, can offer a sound basis for modeling neural computation: As will be explicitly addressed later, there are many serious gaps between connectionist models and current views of important neural properties.

e. Even under the most successful scenario for connectionist cognitive science, many of the currently practiced research strategies in cognitive science would remain viable and productive.

On the other hand, I believe that:

(1) f. It is very likely that the connectionist approach will contribute significant, long-lasting ideas to the rather impoverished theoretical repertoire of cognitive science.

g. It is very likely that connectionist models will turn out to offer contributions to the modeling of human cognitive performance on higher-level tasks that are at least as significant as those offered by traditional, symbolic, models.

h. It is likely that the view of the competence/performance distinction that arises from the connectionist approach will successfully heal a deep and ancient rift in the science and philosophy of mind.

i. It is likely that connectionist models will offer the most significant progress of the past several millenia on the mind/body problem.

j. It is very likely that, given the impoverished theoretical repertoire of computational neuroscience, connectionist models will serve as an excellent stimulus to the development of models of neural computation that are significantly better than both current connectionist models and current neural models.

k. There is a reasonable chance that connectionist models will lead to the development of new somewhat-general-purpose self-programming, massively parallel analog computers, and a new theory of analog parallel computation: They may possibly even challenge the strong construal of Church's Thesis as the claim that the class of well-defined computations is exhausted by those of Turing machines.

Levels of Analysis

Most of the foundational issues surround the connectionist approach turn, in one way or another, on the level of analysis adopted. The terminology, graphics, and discussion found in most connectionist papers strongly suggest that connectionist modeling operates at the neural level. I will argue, however, that it is better *not* to construe the principles of cognition being explored in the connectionist approach as the principles of the neural level. Specification of the level of cognitive analysis adopted by PTC is a subtle matter which consumes much of this article. To be sure, the level of analysis adopted by PTC is lower than that of the traditional, symbolic paradigm; but, at least for the present, the level of PTC is more explicitly related to the level of the symbolic paradigm than it is to the neural level. For this reason I wll call the paradigm for cognitive modeling proposed by PTC the *subsymbolic paradigm*.

A few comments on terminology. I will refer to the traditional approach to cognitive modeling as the *symbolic paradigm*. Note that I will always use the term "symbolic paradigm" to refer to the traditional approach to cognitive *modeling*: the development of AI-like computer programs to serve as models of psychological performance. The symbolic paradigm in cognitive modeling has been articulated and defended by Newell and Simon (1972; Newell 1980), as well as by Fodor (1975, 1987), Pylyshyn (1984), and others. The fundamental hypotheses of this paradigm embrace most of mainstream AI, in addition to AI-based systems that are explicitly offered as models of human performance. The term "symbolic paradigm" is explicitly *not* intended to encompass competence theories such as the formal theory of grammar; such competence theories bear deep relations to the symbolic paradigm but they are not a focus of attention in this paper. In particular, much of the work in formal linguistics differs from the symbolic paradigm in cognitive modeling in many of the same ways as the connectionist approach I will consider; on a number of the dimensions I will use to divide the symbolic and subsymbolic paradigms, much linguistics research falls on the subsymbolic side.

I have found it necessary to deal only with a subset of the symbolic and connectionist approaches in order to get beyond superficial, syntactic issues. On the symbolic side, I am limiting consideration to the Newell/Simon/Fodor/Pylyshyn view of cognition, and excluding, for example, the view adopted by much of linguistics; on the connectionist side, I will consider only a particular view, the "subsymbolic paradigm," and exclude a number of competing connectionist perspectives. The only alternative I see at this point is to characterize the symbolic and connectionist perspectives so diffusely that substantive analysis becomes impossible.

In calling the traditional approach to cognitive modeling the "symbolic paradigm," I intend to emphasize that in this approach, cognitive descriptions are built of entities that are symbols both in the semantic sense of referring to external objects and in the syntactic sense of being operated upon by symbol manipulation. These manipulations model fundamental psychological processes in this approach to cognitive modeling.

The name "subsymbolic paradigm" is intended to suggest cognitive descriptions built up of entities that correspond to *constituents* of the symbols used in the symbolic paradigm; these fine-grained constituents could be called *subsymbols*, and they are the activities of individual processing units in connectionist networks. Entities that are typically represented in the symbolic paradigm by symbols are typically represented in the subsymbolic paradigm by a large number of subsymbols. Along with this semantic distinction comes a syntactic distinction. Subsymbols are not operated upon by symbol manipulation: They participate in numerical—not symbolic—computation. Operations in the symbolic paradigm that consist of a single discrete operation (e.g., a memory fetch) are often achieved in the subsymbolic paradigm as the result of a large number of much finer-grained (numerical) operations.

Since the level of cognitive analysis adopted by the subsymbolic paradigm for formulating connectionist models is lower than the level traditionally adopted by the symbolic paradigm, for the purposes of relating these two paradigms, it is often important to analyze connectionist models at a higher level; to amalgamate, so to speak, the subsymbols into symbols. Although the symbolic and subsymbolic paradigms each have their preferred level of analysis, the cognitive models they offer can be described at multiple levels. It is therefore useful to have distinct names for the levels: I will call the preferred level of the symbolic paradigm the *conceptual level* and that of the subsymbolic paradigm the *subconceptual level*. These names are not ideal, but will be further motivated in the course of characterizing the levels. A primary goal of this article is to articulate a coherent set of hypotheses about the subconceptual level: the kind of cognitive descriptions that are used, the computational principles that apply, and the relations between the subconceptual and both the symbolic and neural levels.

The choice of level greatly constrains the appropriate formalism for analysis. Probably the most striking feature of the connectionist approach is the change in formalism relative to the symbolic paradigm. Since the birth of cognitive science, *language* has provided the dominant theoretical model. Formal cognitive models have taken their structure from the syntax of formal languages, and their content from the semantics of natural language. The mind has been taken to be a machine for formal symbol manipulation, and the symbols manipulated have assumed essentially the same semantics as words of English.

The subsymbolic paradigm challenges both the syntactic and semantic role of language in formal cognitive models. The next section formulates this challenge. Alternative fillers are described for the roles language has traditionally played in cognitive science, and the new role left to language is delimited. The fundamental hypotheses defining the subsymbolic paradigm are formulated, and the challenge that nothing new is being offered is considered. Next I consider the relation between the subsymbolic paradigm and neuroscience; the challenge that connectionist models are too neurally unfaithful is addressed. A later section presents the relations between analyses of cognition at the neural, subconceptual, and conceptual levels. . . .

In this target article I have tried to typographically isolate concise formulations of the main points. Most of these numbered points serve to characterize the subsymbolic paradigm, but a few define alternative points of view; to avoid confusion, the latter have been explicitly tagged by the phrase, *To be rejected*.

Formalization of Knowledge

Cultural Knowledge and Conscious Rule Interpretation
What is an appropriate formalization of the knowledge that cognitive agents possess and the means by which they use that knowledge to perform cognitive tasks? As a starting point, we can look to those knowledge formalizations that predate cognitive science. The most formalized knowledge is found in sciences like physics that rest on mathematical principles. Domain knowledge is formalized in linguistic structures such as "energy is conserved" (or an appropriate encryption), and logic formalizes the use of that knowledge to draw conclusions. Knowledge consists of axioms, and drawing conclusions consists of proving theorems.

This method of formulating knowledge and drawing conclusions has extremely valuable properties:

(2) a. *Public access*: The knowledge is accessible to many people.

  b. ~~*Reliability*: Different people~~ (or the same person at different times) can reliably check whether conclusions have been validly reached.

  c. *Formality, bootstrapping, universality*: The inferential operations require very little experience with the domain to which the symbols refer.

These three properties are important for science because it is a cultural activity. It is of limited social value to have knowledge that resides purely in one individual (2a). It is of questionable social value to have knowledge formulated in such a way that different users draw different conclusions (e.g., can't agree that an experiment falsifies a theory) (2b). For cultural propagation of knowledge, it is helpful if novices with little or no experience with a task can be given a means for performing that task, and thereby a means for acquiring experience (2c).

There are cultural activities other than science that have similar requirements. The laws of a nation and the rules of an organization are also linguistically formalized procedures for effecting action which different people can carry out with reasonable reliability. In all these cases, the goal is to create an abstract decision system that resides outside any single person.

Thus, at the cultural level, the goal is to express knowledge in a form that can be executed reliably by different people, even inexperienced ones. We can view the top-level conscious processor of individual people as a *virtual machine*—the *conscious rule interpreter*—and we can view cultural knowledge as a program that runs on that machine. Linguistic formulations of knowledge are perfect for this purpose. The procedures that different people can reliably execute are explicit, step-by-step linguistic instructions. This is what has been formalized in the theory of *effective procedures* (Turing 1936). Thanks to property (2c), the top-level conscious human processor can be idealized as universal: capable of executing any effective procedure. The theory of effective procedures— the classical theory of computation (Hopcroft and Ullman 1979)—is physically manifest in the von Neumann (serial) computer. One can say that the von Neumann computer is a machine for automatically following the kinds of explicit instructions that people can fairly reliably follow—but much faster and with perfect reliability.

Thus we can understand why the production system of computation theory, or more generally the von Neumann computer, has provided a successful model of how people execute instructions (e.g., models of novice physics problem solving such as that of Larkin et al. 1980). In short, when people (e.g., novices) consciously and sequentially follow rules (such as those they have been taught), their cognitive processing is naturally modeled as the sequential interpretation[1] of a linguistically formalized procedure. The rules being followed are expressed in terms of the consciously accessible concepts with which the task domain is conceptualized. In this sense, the rules are formulated at the conceptual level of analysis.

To sum up:

(3) a. Rules formulated in natural language can provide an effective formalization of cultural knowledge.

b. Conscious rule application can be modeled as the sequential interpretation of such rules by a virtual machine called the conscious rule interpreter.

c. These rules are formulated in terms of the concepts consciously used to describe the task domain—they are formulated at the conceptual level.

Individual Knowledge, Skill, and Intuition in the Symbolic Paradigm

The constraints on cultural knowledge formalization are not the same as those on individual knowledge formalization. The intuitive knowledge in a physics expert or a native speaker may demand, for a truly accurate description, a formalism that is not a good one for cultural purposes. After all, the individual knowledge in an expert's head does not possess the properties (2) of cultural knowledge: It is not publicly accessible or completely reliable, and it is completely dependent on ample experience. Individual knowledge is a program that runs on a virtual machine that need not be the same as the top-level conscious processor that runs the cultural knowledge. By definition, conclusions reached by intuition do not come from conscious application of rules, and intuitive processing need not have the same character as conscious rule application.

What kinds of programs are responsible for behavior that is not conscious rule application? I will refer to the virtual machine that runs these programs as the *intuitive processor*. It is presumably responsible for all of animal behavior and a huge portion of human behavior: Perception, practiced motor behavior, fluent linguistic behavior, intuition in problem solving and game playing—in short, practically all skilled performance. The transference of responsibility from the conscious rule interpreter to the intuitive processor during the acquisition of skill is one of the most striking and well-studied phenomena in cognitive science (Anderson 1981). An analysis of the formalization of knowledge must consider both the knowledge involved in novices' conscious application of rules and the knowledge resident in experts' intuition, as well as their relationship.

An appealing possibility is this:

(4) a. The programs running on the intuitive processor consist of linguistically formalized rules that are sequentially interpreted. (*To be rejected.*)

This has traditionally been the assumption of cognitive science. Native speakers are unconsciously interpreting rules, as are physics experts when they are intuiting answers to problems. Artificial intelligence systems for natural language processing and problem solving are programs written in a formal language for the symbolic description of procedures for manipulating symbols.

To the syntactic hypothesis (4a) a semantic one corresponds:

(4) b. The programs running on the intuitive processor are composed of elements, that is, symbols, referring to essentially the same concepts as the ones used to consciously conceptualize the task domain. (*To be rejected.*)

This applies to production system models in which the productions representing expert knowledge are compiled versions of those of the novice (Anderson 1983; Lewis 1978) and to the bulk of AI programs.

Hypotheses (4a) and (4b) together comprise:

(4)   The unconscious rule interpretation hypothesis: (*To be rejected.*) The programs running on the intuitive processes have a syntax and semantics comparable to those running on the conscious rule interpreter.

This hypothesis has provided the foundation for the symbolic paradigm for cognitive modeling. Cognitive models of both conscious rule application and intuitive processing have been programs constructed of entities which are *symbols* both in the syntactic sense of being operated on by symbol manipulation and in the semantic sense of (4b). Because these symbols have the conceptual semantics of (4b), I am calling the level of analysis at which these programs provide cognitive models the *conceptual level*.

The Subsymbolic Paradigm and Intuition

The hypothesis of unconscious rule interpretation (4) is an attractive possibility which a connectionist approach to cognitive modeling rejects. Since my purpose here is to formulate rather than argue the scientific merits of a connectionist approach, I will not argue against (4) here. I will point out only that in general, connectionists do not casually reject (4). Several of today's leading connectionist researchers were intimately involved with serious and longstanding attempts to make (4) serve the needs of cognitive science.[2] Connectionists tend to reject (4) because they find the consequences that have actually resulted from its acceptance to be quite unsatisfactory, for a number of quite independent reasons, including:

(5) a. Actual AI systems built on hypothesis (4) seem too brittle, too inflexible, to model true human expertise.

   b. The process of articulating expert knowledge in rules seems impractical for many important domains (e.g., common sense).

c. Hypothesis (4) has contributed essentially no insight into how knowledge is represented in the brain.

What motivates the pursuit of connectionist alternatives to (4) is a hunch that such alternatives will better serve the goals of cognitive science. Substantial empirical assessment of this hunch is probably at least a decade away. One possible alternative to (4a) is:

(6)   The neural architecture hypothesis: (*To be rejected.*)
        The intuitive processor for a particular task uses the same architecture that the brain uses for that task.

Whatever appeal this hypothesis might have, it seems incapable in practice of supporting the needs of the vast majority of cognitive models. We simply do not know what architecture the brain uses for performing most cognitive tasks. There may be some exceptions (such as visual and spatial tasks), but for problem solving, language, and many others (6) simply cannot do the necessary work at the present time.

These points and others relating to the neural level will be considered in more detail later. For now the point is simply that characterizing the level of analysis of connectionist modeling is not a matter of simply identifying it with the neural level. While the level of analysis adopted by most connectionist cognitive models is not the conceptual one, it is also not the neural level.

The goal now is to formulate a connectionist alternative to (4) that, unlike (6), provides a viable basis for cognitive modeling. A first, crude approximation to this hypothesis is:

(7)   The intuitive processor has a certain kind of connectionist architecture (which abstractly models a few of the most general features of neural networks). (To be elaborated.)

Postponing consideration of the neural issues, we now consider the relevant kind of connectionist architecture.

The view of the connectionist architecture I will adopt is the following (for further treatment of this viewpoint, see Smolensky 1986). The numerical activity values of all the processors in the network form a large *state vector*. The interactions of the processors, the equations governing how the activity vector changes over time as processors respond to one another's values, is an *activation evolution equation*. This evolution equation governing the mutual interactions of the processors involves the connection weights: numerical parameters which determine the direction and magnitude of the influence of one activation value on another. The activation equation is a differential equation (usually approximated by the finite difference equation that arises from discrete time slices). In learning systems, the connection weights change during training according to the learning rule, which is another differential equation: the *connection evolution equation*.

Knowledge in a connectionist system lies in its connection strengths. Thus, for the first part of our elaboration on (7) we have the following alternative to (4a):

(8) a. The connectionist dynamical system hypothesis:
The state of the intuitive processor at any moment is precisely defined by a vector of numerical values (one for each unit). The dynamics of the intuitive processor are governed by a differential equation. The numerical parameters in this equation constitute the processor's program or knowledge. In learning systems, these parameters change according to another differential equation.

This hypothesis states that the intuitive processor is a certain kind of *dynamical system*: Like the dynamical systems traditionally studied in physics, the state of the system is a numerical vector evolving in time according to differential evolution equations. The special properties that distinguish this kind of dynamical system—a *connectionist dynamical system*—are only vaguely described in (8a). A much more precise specification is needed. It is premature at this point to commit oneself to such a specification, but one large class of subsymbolic models is that of quasilinear dynamical systems, explicitly discussed in Smolensky (1986) and Rumelhart, Hinton, and Williams (1986). Each unit in a quasilinear system computes its value by first calculating the weighted sum of its inputs from other units and then transforming this sum with a nonlinear function. An important goal of the subsymbolic paradigm is to characterize the computational properties of various kinds of connectionist dynamical systems (such as quasilinear systems) and thereby determine which kinds provide appropriate models of various types of cognitive processes.

The connectionist dynamical system hypothesis (8a) provides a connectionist alternative to the syntactic hypothesis (4a) of the symbolic paradigm. We now need a semantic hypothesis compatible with (8a) to replace (4b). The question is: What does a unit's value *mean*? The most straightforward possibility is that the semantics of each unit is comparable to that of a word in natural language; each unit represents such a concept, and the connection strengths between units reflect the degree of association between the concepts.

(9)   The conceptual unit hypothesis. (*To be rejected*.)
Individual intuitive processor elements—individual units—have essentially the same semantics as the conscious rule interpreter's elements, namely, words of natural language.

But (8a) and (9) make an infertile couple. Activation of concepts spreading along degree of association links may be adequate for modeling simple aspects of cognition—such as relative times for naming words or the relative probabilities of perceiving letters in various contexts—but it cannot be adequate for complex tasks such as question answering or grammaticality judgments. The relevant structures cannot even be feasibly represented in such a network, let alone effectively processed.

Great computational power must be present in the intuitive processor to deal with the many cognitive processes that are extremely complex when described at the conceptual level. The symbolic paradigm, based on hypothesis (4), gets its power by allowing highly complex, essentially arbitrary, operations on symbols with conceptual-level semantics: simple semantics, complex operations. If the operations are required to be as simple as those allowed by hypothesis (8a), we cannot get away with a semantics as simple as that of (9).[3] A semantics compatible with (8a) must be more complicated:

(8) b. The subconceptual unit hypothesis:
      The entities in the intuitive processor with the semantics of conscious concepts of the task domain are complex patterns of activity over many units. Each unit participates in many such patterns.

(See several of the papers in Hinton and Anderson 1981; Hinton et al. 1986; the neural counterpart is associated with Hebb 1949; Lashley 1950, about which see Feldman 1986.) The interactions between *individual units* are simple, but these units do not have conceptual semantics: they are *subconceptual*. The interactions between the entities with conceptual semantics, interactions between complex patterns of activity, are not at all simple. Interactions at the level of activity patterns are not directly described by the formal definition of a subsymbolic model; they must be computed by the analyst. Typically, these interactions can be computed only approximately. In other words, there will generally be no precisely valid, complete, computable formal principles at the conceptual level; such principles exist only at the level of individual units— the *subconceptual level*.

(8) c. The subconceptual level hypothesis:
      Complete, formal, and precise descriptions of the intuitive processor are generally tractable not at the conceptual level, but only at the subconceptual level.

In (8c), the qualification "complete, formal, and precise" is important: Conceptual-level descriptions of the intuitive processor's performance can be derived from the subconceptual description, but, unlike the description at the subconceptual level, the conceptual-level descriptions will be either incomplete (describing only certain aspects of the processing) or informal (describing complex behaviors in, say, qualitative terms) or imprecise (describing the performance up to certain approximations or idealizations such as "competence" idealizations away from actual performance). Explicit examples of each of these kinds of conceptual-level descriptions of subsymbolic systems will be considered in a subsequent section [omitted here—Ed.].

Hypotheses (8a–c) can be summarized as:

(8)   The subsymbolic hypothesis:
      The intuitive processor is a subconceptual connectionist dynam-
      ical system that does not admit a complete, formal, and precise
      conceptual-level description.

This hypothesis is the cornerstone of the subsymbolic paradigm.[4]

The Incompatibility of the Symbolic and Subsymbolic Paradigms
I will now show that the symbolic and subsymbolic paradigms, as
formulated above, are incompatible—that hypotheses (4) and (8) about
the syntax and semantics of the intuitive processor are not mutually
consistent. This issue requires care, because it is well known that one
virtual machine can often be implemented in another, that a program
written for one machine can be translated into a program for the other.
The attempt to distinguish subsymbolic and symbolic computation
might well be futile if each can simulate the other. After all, a digital
computer is in reality some sort of dynamical system simulating a von
Neumann automaton, and in turn, digital computers are usually used
to simulate connectionist models. Thus it seems possible that the symbolic and subsymbolic hypotheses (4) and (8) are *both* correct: The intuitive processor can be regarded as a virtual machine for sequentially
interpreting rules on one level *and* as a connectionist machine on a
lower level.

This possibility fits comfortably within the symbolic paradigm, under
a formulation such as:

(10)   Valid connectionist models are merely implementations, for a
       certain kind of parallel hardware, of symbolic programs that
       provide exact and complete accounts of behavior at the concep-
       tual level. (*To be rejected.*)

However (10) contradicts hypothesis (8c), and is thus incompatible with
the subsymbolic paradigm. The symbolic programs that (4) hypothesizes for the intuitive processor could indeed be translated for a connectionist machine; but the translated programs would *not* be the kind of
subsymbolic program that (8) hypothesizes. If (10) is correct, (8) is
wrong; at the very least, (8c) would have to be removed from the
defining hypothesis of the subsymbolic paradigm, weakening it to the
point that connectionist modeling does become mere implementation.
Such an outcome would constitute a genuine defeat of a research program that I believe many connectionists are pursuing.

What about the reverse relationship, where a symbolic program is
used to implement a subsymbolic system? Here it is crucial to realize
that the symbols in such programs represent the activation values of
units and the strengths of connections. By hypothesis (8b), these do

not have conceptual semantics, and thus hypothesis (4b) is violated. The subsymbolic programs that (8) hypothesizes for the intuitive processor can be translated for a von Neumann machine, but the translated programs are *not* the kind of symbolic program that (4) hypothesizes.

These arguments show that unless the hypotheses of the symbolic and subsymbolic paradigms are formulated with some care, the substance of the scientific issue at stake can easily be missed. It is well known that von Neumann machines and connectionist networks can simulate each other. This fact leads some people to adopt the position that the connectionist approach cannot offer anything fundamentally new because we already have Turing machines and, following Church's Thesis, reason to believe that, when it comes to computation, Turing machines are everything. This position, however, mistakes the issue for cognitive science to be the purely syntactic question of whether mental programs are written for Turing/von Neumann machines or connectionist machines. This is a nonissue. If one cavalierly characterizes the two approaches *only syntactically*, using (4a) and (8a) alone, then indeed the issue—connectionist or not connectionist—appears to be "one of AI's wonderful red herrings."[5]

It is a mistake to claim that the connectionist approach has nothing new to offer cognitive science. The issue at stake is a central one: Does the complete formal account of cognition lie at the conceptual level? The position taken by the subsymbolic paradigm is: No—it lies at the subconceptual level.

Representation at the Subconceptual Level

Having hypothesized the existence of a subconceptual level, we must now consider its nature. Hypothesis (8b) leaves open important questions about the semantics of subsymbolic systems. What kind of subconceptual features do the units in the intuitive processor represent? Which activity patterns actually correspond to particular concepts or elements of the problem domain?

There are no systematic or general answers to these questions at the present time; seeking answers is one of the principal tasks for the subsymbolic research paradigm. At present, each individual subsymbolic model adopts particular procedures for relating patterns of activity—activity vectors—to the conceptual-level descriptions of inputs and outputs that define the model's task. The vectors chosen are often values of fine-grained features of the inputs and outputs, based on some preexisting theoretical analysis of the domain. For example, for the task studied by Rumelhart and McClelland (1986), transforming root phonetic forms of English verbs to their past-tense forms, the input and output phonetic strings are represented as vectors of values for context-dependent binary phonetic features. The task description at the conceptual level involves consciously available concepts such as the words "go" and "went," while the subconceptual level used by the model involves a very large number of fine-grained features such as "roundedness preceded by frontalness and followed by backness." The representation of "go" is a large pattern of activity over these features.

Substantive progress in subsymbolic cognitive science requires that systematic commitments be made to vectorial representations for individual cognitive domains. It is important to develop mathematical or empirical methodologies that can adequately constrain these commitments. The vectors chosen to represent inputs and outputs crucially affect a model's predictions, since the generalizations the model makes are largely determined by the similarity structure of the chosen vectors. Unlike symbolic tokens, these vectors lie in a topological space in which some are close together and others far apart.

What kinds of methodologies might be used to constrain the representation at the subconceptual level? The methodology used by Rumelhart and McClelland (1986) in the past-tense model is one that has been fairly widely practiced, particularly in models of language processing: Representational features are borrowed from existing theoretical analyses of the domain and adapted (generally in somewhat ad hoc ways) to meet the needs of connectionist modeling. This methodology clearly renders the subsymbolic approach dependent on other research paradigms in the cognitive sciences and suggests that, certainly in the short term, the subsymbolic paradigm cannot *replace* these other research paradigms.

A second possible theoretical methodology for studying subconceptual representation relates to the learning procedures that can train hidden units in connectionist networks. Hidden units support internal representations of elements of the problem domain, and networks that train their hidden units are in effect learning effective subconceptual representations of the domain. If we can analyze the representations that such networks develop, we can perhaps obtain principles of subconceptual representation for various problem domains.

A third class of methodology views the task of constraining subconceptual models as the calibration of connectionist models to the human cognitive system. The problem is to determine what vectors should be assigned to represent various aspects of the domain so that the resulting behavior of the connectionist model matches human behavior. Powerful mathematical tools are needed for relating the overall behavior of the network to the choice of representational vectors; ideally, these tools should allow us to *invert* the mapping from representations to behavior so that by starting with a mass of data on human performance we can turn a mathematical crank and have representational vectors pop out. An example of this general type of tool is the technique of *multidimensional scaling* (Shepard 1962), which allows data on human judgments of the similarity between pairs of items in some set to be turned nto vectors for representing those items (in a sense). The subsymbolic paradigm needs tools such as a version of multidimensional scaling based on a connectionist model of the process of producing similarity judgments.

Each of these methodologies poses serious research challenges. Most of these challenges are currently being pursued, so far with at best modest success. In the first approach, systematic principles must be developed for adapting to the connectionist context the featural analyses of domains that have emerged from traditional, nonconnectionist paradigms. These principles must reflect fundamental properties of connectionist computation, for otherwise, the hypothesis of connectionist computation is doing no work in the study of mental representation. In the second methodology, principles must be discovered for the representations learned by hidden units, and in the third methodology, principles must be worked out for relating choices of representational vectors to overall system behavior. These are challenging mathematical problems on which the ultimate success of the subsymbolic paradigm rests.

The next two sections discuss the relation between the subconceptual level and other levels: The relation to the neural levels is addressed in the next section, and the relation to the conceptual level is taken up in the following one.

The Subconceptual and Neural Levels

The discussion in the preceding section overlooks an obvious methodology for constraining subconceptual representations—just look at how the brain does it. This brings us back to the parenthetical comment in (7) and the general issue of the relation between the subconceptual and neural levels.[6]

The relation between the subconceptual and neural levels can be addressed in both syntactic and semantic terms. The semantic question is the one just raised: How do representations of cognitive domains as patterns of activity over subconceptual units in the network models of the subsymbolic paradigm relate to representations over neurons in the brain? The syntactic question is: How does the processing architecture adopted by networks in the subsymbolic paradigm relate to the processing architecture of the brain?

There is not really much to say about the semantic question because so little is known about neural representation of higher cognitive domains. When it comes to connectionist modeling of say, language processing, the "just look at how the brain does it" methodology doesn't take one very far towards the goal of constructing a network that does the task at all. Thus it is unavoidable that, for the time being, in subsymbolic models of higher processes, the semantics of network units are much more directly related to conceptual level accounts of these processes than to any neural account. Semantically, the subconceptual

On the Proper Treatment of Connectionism

level seems at present rather close to the conceptual level, while we have little ground for believing it to be close to the neural level.

This conclusion is at odds with the commonly held view that connectionist models are neural models. That view presumably reflects a bias against semantic considerations in favor of syntactic ones. If one looks only at processing mechanisms, the computation performed by subsymbolic models seems much closer to that of the brain than to that of symbolic models. This suggests that syntactically, the subconceptual level is closer to the neural level than to the conceptual level.

Let us take then the syntactic question: Is the processing architecture adopted by subsymbolic models (8a) well-suited for describing processing at the neural level? Table 35.1 presents some of the relations between the architectures. The left column lists currently plausible features of some of the most general aspects of the neural architecture, considered at the level of neurons (Crick and Asanuma 1986). The right column lists the corresponding architectural features of the connectionist dynamical systems typically used in subsymbolic models. In the center column, each hit has been indicated by a + and each miss by a −.

In Table 35.1 the loose correspondence assumed is between neurons and units, between synapses and connections. It is not clear how to make this correspondence precise. Does the activity of a unit correspond to the membrane potential at the cell body? Or the time-averaged firing rate of the neuron? Or the population-averaged firing rate of many neurons? Since the integration of signals between dendritic trees is probably more like the linear integration appearing in quasilinear dynamical systems than is the integration of synaptic signals on a dendrite, would it not be better to view a connection not as an individual synaptic contact but rather as an aggregate contact on an entire dendritic tree?

Given the difficulty of precisely stating the neural counterpart of components of subsymbolic models, and given the significant number of misses, even in the very general properties considered in Table 35.1, it seems advisable to keep the question open of the detailed relation between cognitive descriptions at the subconceptual and neural levels. There seems no denying, however, that the subconceptual level is significantly closer to the neural level than is the conceptual level: Symbolic models possess even fewer similarities with the brain than those indicated in Table 35.1.

The subconceptual level ignores a great number of features of the neural level that are probably extremely important to understanding how the brain computes. Nonetheless, the subconceptual level does incorporate a number of features of neural computation that are almost certainly extremely important to understanding how the brain computes. The general principles of computation at the subconceptual level—computation in high-dimensional, high-complexity dynamical systems—*must* apply to computation in the brain; these principles are likely to be necessary, if not sufficient, to understand neural computa-

Table 35.1 Relations between the neural and subsymbolic architectures

Cerebral cortex		Connectionist dynamical systems
State defined by continuous numerical variables (potentials, synaptic areas, . . .)	+	State defined by continuous numerical variables (activations, connection strengths)
State variables change continuously in time	+	State variables change continuously in time
Interneuron interaction parameters changeable; seat of knowledge	+	Interunit interaction parameters changeable; seat of knowledge
Huge number of state variables	+	Large number of state variables
High interactional complexity (highly nonhomogeneous interactions)	+	High interactional complexity (highly nonhomogeneous interactions)
Neurons located in 2 + 1-d space have dense connectivity to nearby neurons; have geometrically mapped connectivity to distant neurons	− − −	Units have no spatial location uniformly dense connections
Synapses located in 3-d space; locations strongly affect signal interactions	−	Connections have no spatial location
Distal projections between areas have intricate topology	−	Distal projections between node pools have simple topology
Distal interactions mediated by discrete signals	−	All interactions nondiscrete
Intricate signal integration at single neuron	−	Signal integration is linear
Numerous signal types	−	Single signal type

tion. And while subconceptual principles are not unambiguously and immediately applicable to neural systems, they are certainly more readily applicable than the principles of symbolic computation.

In sum:

(11)   The fundamental level of the subsymbolic paradigm, the subconceptual level, lies between the neural and conceptual levels.

As stated earlier, on semantic measures, the subsymbolic level seems closer to the conceptual level, whereas on syntactic measures, it seems closer to the neural level. It remains to be seen whether, as the subsymbolic paradigm develops, this situation will sort itself out. Mathematical techniques like those discussed in the previous section may yield insights into subsymbolic representation that will increase the semantic distance between the subconceptual and conceptual levels. There are already significant indications that as new insights into subsymbolic computation are emerging, and additional information processing power is being added to subsymbolic models, the syntactic distance between the subconceptual and neural levels is increasing. In the drive for more computational power, architectural decisions seem to be driven more and more by mathematical considerations and less and less by neural ones.[7]

Once (11) is accepted, the proper place of subsymbolic models in cognitive science will be clarified. It is common to hear dismissals of a particular subsymbolic model because it is not immediately apparent how to implement it precisely in neural hardware, or because certain neural features are absent from the model. We can now identify two fallacies in such a dismissal. First, following (11): Subsymbolic models should not be viewed as neural models. If the subsymbolic paradigm proves valid, the best subsymbolic models of a cognitive process should one day be shown to be some reasonable higher-level approximation to the neural system supporting that process. This provides a heuristic that favors subsymbolic models that seem more likely to be reducible to the neural level. But this heuristic is an extremely weak one given how difficult such a judgment must be with the current confusion about the precise neural correlates of units and connections, and the current state of both empirical and theoretical neuroscience.

The second fallacy in dismissing a particular subsymbolic model because of neural unfaithfulness rests on a failure to recognize the role of individual models in the subsymbolic paradigm. A model can make a valuable contribution by providing evidence for general principles that are characteristic of a broad class of subsymbolic systems. The potential value of "ablation" studies of the NETtalk text-to-speech system (Sejnowski and Rosenberg 1986), for example, does not depend entirely on the neural faithfulness of the model, or even on its psychological faithfulness. NETtalk is a subsymbolic system that performs a complex task. What happens to its performance when internal parts are damaged? This provides a significant clue to the general principles of degradation in *all* complex subsymbolic systems: Principles that will apply to future systems that are more faithful as models.

There are, of course, many neural models that do take many of the constraints of neural organization seriously, and for which the analogue of Table 35.1 would show nearly all hits. But we are concerned here with connectionist models for performing cognitive tasks, and these models typically possess the features displayed in Table 35.1, with perhaps one or two deviations. The claim is not that neural models don't exist, but rather that they should not be confused with subsymbolic models.

Why is it that neural models of cognitive processes are, generally speaking, currently not feasible? The problem is not an insufficient quantity of data about the brain. The problem, it seems, is that the data are generally of the wrong kind for cognitive modeling. Our information about the nervous system tends to describe its structure, not its dynamic behavior. Subsymbolic systems are dynamical systems with certain kinds of differential equations governing their dynamics. If we knew which dynamical variables in the neural system for some cognitive task were the critical ones for performing that task, and what the "equations of motion" were for those variables, we could use that information to build neurally faithful cognitive models. But generally what we know instead are endless static properties of how the hardware is arranged. Without knowing which (if any) of these structures support relevant dynamical processes, and what equations govern those processes, we are in a position comparable to someone attempting to model the solar system, armed with voluminous data on the colored bands of the planets but with no knowledge of Newton's Laws.

To summarize:

(12) a. Unlike the symbolic architecture, the subsymbolic architecture possesses a number of the most general features of the neural architecture.

b. However, the subsymbolic architecture lacks a number of the more detailed but still quite general features of the neural architecture; the subconceptual level of analysis is higher than the neural level.

c. For most cognitive functions, neuroscience cannot provide the relevant information to specify a cognitive model at the neural level.

d. The general cognitive principles of the subconceptual level will probably be important contributors to future discoveries of those specifications of neural computations that we now lack.

Reduction of Cognition to the Subconceptual Level

The previous section considered the relationship between the fundamental level of the subsymbolic paradigm—the subconceptual level— and the neural level. The remainder of this article will focus on relations between the subconceptual and conceptual levels; these have so far only been touched upon briefly (in (8c)). Before proceeding, however, it is worth summarizing the relationships between the levels, including those that will be discussed in the remainder of the article. [Much of this is omitted in the present edition.—Ed.]

Imagine three physical systems: a brain that is executing some cognitive process, a massively parallel connectionist computer running a subsymbolic model of that process, and a von Neumann computer running a symbolic model of the same process. The cognitive process may involve conscious rule application, intuition, or a combination of the two. According to the subsymbolic paradigm, here are the relationships:

(13) a. Describing the brain at the neural level gives a neural model.

b. Describing the brain approximately, at a higher level—the sub-conceptual level—yields, to a good approximation, the model running on the connectionist computer, when it too is described at the subconceptual level. (At this point, this is a goal for future research. It could turn out that the degree of approximation here is only rough; this would still be consistent with the subsymbolic paradigm.)

c. We can try to describe the connectionist computer at a higher level—the conceptual level—by using the patterns of activity that have conceptual semantics. If the cognitive process being executed is conscious rule application, we will be able to carry out this conceptual-level analysis with reasonable precision, and will end up with a description that closely matches the symbolic computer program running on the von Neumann machine.

d. If the process being executed is an intuitive process, we will be unable to carry out the conceptual-level description of the connectionist machine precisely. Nonetheless, we will be able to produce various approximate conceptual-level descriptions that correspond to the symbolic computer program running on the von Neumann machine in various ways.

For a cognitive process involving both intuition and conscious rule application, (13c) and (13d) will each apply to certain aspects of the process. . . .

The relationships in (13) can be more clearly understood by reintroducing the concept of "virtual machine." If we take one of the three physical systems and describe its processing at a certain level of analysis, we get a virtual machine that I will denote "system$_{level}$". Then (13) can be written:

(14) a. brain$_{neural}$ = neural model

b. brain$_{subconceptual}$ $\simeq$ connectionist$_{subconceptual}$

c. connectionist$_{conceptual}$ $\simeq$ von Neumann$_{conceptual}$ (conscious rule application)

d. connectionist$_{conceptual}$ $\sim$ von Neumann$_{conceptual}$ (intuition)

Here, the symbol $\simeq$ means "equals to a good approximation" and $\sim$ means "equals to a crude approximation." The two nearly equal virtual machines in (14c) both describe what I have been calling the "conscious rule interpreter." The two roughly similar virtual machines in (14d) provide the two paradigms' descriptions of the intuitive processor at the conceptual level.

Table 35.2 indicates these relationships and also the degree of exactness to which each system can be described at each level—the degree

Table 35.2 Three cognitive systems and three levels of description

Level	(process)	Cognitive system		
		Brain	Subsymbolic	Symbolic
Conceptual	(intuition)	?	rough approximation $\gtrsim$	exact
	(conscious rule application)	?	good approximation $\approx$	exact
Subconceptual		good approximation $\approx$	exact	
Neural		exact		

On the Proper Treatment of Connectionism

of precision to which each virtual machine is defined. The levels included in Table 35.2 are those relevant to predicting high-level behavior. Of course each system can also be described at lower levels, all the way down to elementary particles. However, levels below an exactly describable level can be ignored from the point of view of predicting high-level behavior, since it is possible (in principle) to do the prediction at the highest level that can be exactly described (it is presumably much harder to do the same at lower levels). This is why in the symbolic paradigm any descriptions below the conceptual level are not viewed as significant. For modeling high-level behavior, how the symbol manipulation happens to be implemented can be ignored—it is not a relevant part of the cognitive model. In a subsymbolic model, exact behavioral prediction must be performed at the subconceptual level, but how the units happen to be implemented is not relevant.

The relation between the conceptual level and lower levels is fundamentally different in the subsymbolic and symbolic paradigms. This leads to important differences in the kind of explanations the paradigms offer of conceptual-level behavior, and the kind of reduction used in these explanations. A symbolic model is a *system* of interacting processes, all with the same conceptual-level semantics as the task behavior being explained. Adopting the terminology of Haugeland (1978), this *systematic explanation* relies on a *systematic reduction* of the behavior that involves no shift of semantic domain or *dimension*. Thus a game-playing program is composed of subprograms that generate possible moves, evaluate them, and so on. In the symbolic paradigm, these systematic reductions play the major role in explanation. The lowest-level processes in the systematic reduction, still with the original semantics of the task domain, are then themselves reduced by *intentional instantiation*: they are implemented exactly by other processes with different semantics but the same form. Thus a move-generation subprogram with game semantics is instantiated in a system of programs with list-manipulating semantics. This intentional instantiation typically plays a minor role in the overall explanation, if indeed it is regarded as a cognitively relevant part of the model at all.

Thus cognitive explanations in the symbolic paradigm rely primarily on reductions involving no dimensional shift. This feature is not shared by the subsymbolic paradigm, where accurate explanations of intuitive behavior require descending to the subconceptual level. The elements in this explanation, the units, do *not* have the semantics of the original behavior: that is the content of the subconceptual unit hypothesis, (8b). In other words:

(15)   Unlike symbolic explanations, subsymbolic explanations rely crucially on a semantic ("dimensional") shift that accompanies the shift from the conceptual to the subconceptual levels.

The overall dispositions of cognitive systems are explained in the subsymbolic paradigm as approximate higher-level regularities that emerge from quantitative laws operating at a more fundamental level with different semantics. This is the kind of reduction familiar in natural science, exemplified by the explanation of the laws of thermodynamics through a reduction to mechanics that involves shifting the dimension from thermal semantics to molecular semantics.

Indeed the subsymbolic paradigm repeals the other features that Haugeland identified as newly introduced into scientific explanation by the symbolic paradigm. The inputs and outputs of the system are not quasilinguistic representations but good old-fashioned numerical vectors. These inputs and outputs have semantic interpretations, but these are not constructed recursively from interpretations of embedded constituents. The fundamental laws are good old-fashioned numerical equations.

Haugeland went to considerable effort to legitimize the form of explanation and reduction used in the symbolic paradigm. The explanations and reductions of the subsymbolic paradigm, by contrast, are of a type well-established in natural science.

In summary, let me emphasize that in the subsymbolic paradigm, the conceptual and subconceptual levels are not related as the levels of a von Neumann computer (high-level-language program, compiled low-level program, etc.). The relationship between subsymbolic and symbolic models is more like that between quantum and classical mechanics. Subsymbolic models accurately describe the microstructure of cognition, whereas symbolic models provide an approximate description of the macrostructure. An important job of subsymbolic theory is to delineate the situations and the respects in which the symbolic approximation is valid, and to explain why. . . .

Constituent Structure of Mental States

Fodor and Pylyshyn have argued (e.g., Fodor 1975; Pylyshyn 1984) that mental states must have constituent structure, and they have used this argument against the connectionist approach (Fodor and Pylyshyn 1988). Their argument applies, however, only to ultra-local connectionist models (Ballard and Hayes 1984); it is quite inapplicable to the distributed connectionist systems considered here. A mental state in a subsymbolic system is a pattern of activity with a constituent structure that can be analyzed at both the conceptual and the subconceptual levels. In this section I offer a few general observations on this issue; the connectionist representation of complex structures is an active area of research (Smolensky 1987; Touretzky 1986), and many difficult problems remain to be solved (for further discussion see Smolensky 1988).

At the conceptual level, a connectionist mental state contains constituent subpatterns that have conceptual interpretations. Pylyshyn, in a debate over the connectionist approach at the 1984 meeting of the Cognitive Science Society, suggested how to extract these conceptual constituents with the following example: The connectionist representation of *coffee* is the representation of *cup with coffee* minus the representation of *cup without coffee*. To carry out this suggestion, imagine a crude but adequate kind of distributed semantic representation, in which the interpretation of *cup with coffee* involves the activity of network units representing features like brown liquid with flat top surface, brown liquid with curved sides and bottom surface, brown liquid contacting porcelain, hot liquid, upright container with a handle, burnt odor, and so forth. We should really use subconceptual features, but even these features are sufficiently low-level to make the point. Following Pylyshyn, we take this representation of the interpretation of *cup with coffee* and subtract from it the representation of the interpretation of *cup without coffee*, leaving the representtion of *coffee*. What remains, in fact, is a pattern of activity with active features such as brown liquid with flat top surface, brown liquid with curved sides and bottom surface, brown liquid contacting porcelain, hot liquid, and burnt odor. This represents *coffee*, in some sense—but *coffee in the context of cup*.

In using Pylyshyn's procedure for determining the connectionist representation of *coffee*, there is nothing sacred about starting with *cup with coffee*: why not start with *can with coffee, tree with coffee,* or *man with coffee,* and subtract the corresponding representation of *X without coffee*? Thinking back to the distributed featural representation, it is clear that each of these procedures produces quite a different result for "the" connectionist representation of *coffee*. The pattern representing *coffee* in the context of *cup* is quite different from the pattern representing *coffee* in the context of *can, tree,* or *man*.

The pattern representing *cup with coffee* can be decomposed into conceptual-level constituents, one for *coffee* and another for *cup*. This decomposition differs in two significant ways from the decomposition of the symbolic expression *cup with coffee*, into the three constituents, *coffee, cup,* and *with*. First, the decomposition is quite approximate. The pattern of features representing *cup with coffee* may well, as in the imagined case above, possess a subpattern that can be identified with *coffee*, as well as a subpattern that can be identified with *cup*; but these subpatterns will in general not be defined precisely and there will typically remain features that can be identified only with the interaction of the two (as in brown liquid contacting porcelain). Second, whatever the subpattern identified with *coffee*, unlike the symbol *coffee*, it is a context-dependent constituent, one whose internal structure is heavily influenced by the structure of which it is a part.

These constituent subpatterns representing *coffee* in varying contexts are activity vectors that are not identical, but possess a rich structure of commonalities and differences (a family resemblance, one might say). The commonalities are directly responsible for the common processing implications of the interpretations of these various phrases, so the approximate equivalence of the *coffee* vectors across contexts plays a functional role in subsymbolic processing that is quite close to the role played by the exact equivalence of the *coffee* tokens across different contexts in a symbolic processing system.

The conceptual-level constituents of mental states are activity vectors, which themselves have constituent structure at the subconceptual level: the individual units' activities. To summarize the relationship between these notions of constituent structure in the symbolic and subsymbolic paradigms, let's call each *coffee* vector the (connectionist) symbol for coffee in the given context. Then we can say that the context alters the internal structure of the symbol; the activities of the subconceptual units that comprise the symbol—its subsymbols—change across contexts. In the symbolic paradigm, a symbol is effectively contextualized by surrounding it with other symbols in some larger structure. In other words:

(16)   Symbols and context dependence:
         In the symbolic paradigm, the context of a symbol is manifest around it and consists of other symbols; in the subsymbolic paradigm, the context of a symbol is manifest inside it and consists of subsymbols. . . .

Notes

I am indebted to Dave Rumelhart for several years of provocative conversations on many of these issues; his contributions permeate the ideas formulated here. Sincere thanks to Jerry Fodor and Zenon Pylyshyn for most instructive conversations. Comments on earlier drafts from Geoff Hinton, Mark Fanty, and Dan Lloyd were very helpful, as were pointers from Kathleen Akins. Extended comments on the manuscript by Georges Rey were extremely helpful. I am particularly grateful for a number of insights that Rob Cummins and Denise Dellarosa have generously contributed to this paper. This research has been supported by NSF grant IST-8609599 and by the Department of Computer Science and Institute of Cognitive Science at the University of Colorado at Boulder.

1. In this target article, when *interpretation* is used to refer to a process, the sense intended is that of computer science: the process of taking a linguistic description of a procedure and executing that procedure.

2. Consider, for example, the connectionist symposium at the University of Geneva held Sept. 9, 1986. The advertised program featured Feldman, Minsky, Rumelhart, Sejnowski, and Waltz. Of these five researchers, three were major contributors to the symbolic paradigm for many years (Minsky 1975; Rumelhart 1975, 1980; Waltz 1978).

3. This is an issue that divides connectionist approaches. "Local connectionist models" (e.g., Dell 1985; Feldman 1985; McClelland and Rumelhart 1981; Rumelhart and McClelland 1982; Waltz and Pollack 1985) accept (9), and often deviate significantly from (8a). This approach has been championed by the Rochester connectionists (Feldman et al. 1985). Like the symbolic paradigm, this school favors simple semantics and more complex

operations. The processors in their networks are usually more powerful than those allowed by (8); they are often like digital computers running a few lines of simple code. ("If there is a 1 on this input line then do X else do Y," where X and Y are quite different simple procedures; e.g., Shastri 1985). This style of connectionism, quite different from the subsymbolic style, has much in common with techniques of traditional computer science for "parallelizing" serial algorithms by decomposing them into routines that can be run in parallel, often with certain synchronization points built in. The grain size of the Rochester parallelism, although large compared to the subsymbolic paradigm, is small compared to standard parallel programming: The processors are allowed only a few internal states and can transmit only a few different values (Feldman and Ballard 1982).

4. As indicated in the introduction, a sizeable sample of research that by and large falls under the subsymbolic paradigm can be found in the books, *Parallel Distributed Processing: Explorations in the Microstructure of Cognition*: Rumelhart et al. 1986; McClelland et al. 1986. While this work has since come to be labelled "connectionist," the term "PDP" was deliberately chosen to distinguish it from the localist approach, which had previously adopted the name "connectionist" (Feldman and Ballard 1982).

5. The phrase is Roger Schank's, in reference to "parallel processing" (Waldrop 1984). Whether he was referring to a connectionist system I do not know; in any event, I don't mean to imply that the grounds for his comment are addressed here.

6. In this section the disclaimer in the introduction is particularly relevant: The arguments I offer are not intended to represent a consensus among connectionists.

7. For example, two recently discovered learning rules that allow the training of hidden units, the Boltzmann machine learning procedure (Hinton and Sejnowski 1983) and the back-propagation procedure (Rumelhart et al. 1986), both involve introducing computational machinery that is motivated purely mathematically; the neural counterparts of which are so far unknown (unit-by-unit connection strength symmetry, alternating Hebbian and antiHebbian learning, simulated annealing, and backwards error propagation along connections of identical strength to forward activation propagation).

References

Anderson, J. R. (1981). *Cognitive skills and their acquisition*. Hillsdale, NJ: Erlbaum.

Anderson, J. R. (1983). *The architecture of cognition*. Cambridge, MA: Harvard University Press.

Ballard, D. H., and P. J. Hayes (1984). Parallel logical inference. *Proceedings of the Sixth Conference of the Cognitive Science Society*.

Crick, F., and Asanuma, C. (1986). Certain aspects of the anatomy and physiology of the cerebral cortext. In J. L. McClelland, D. E. Rumelhart, and the PDP Research Group, *Parallel distributed processing: Explorations in the microstructure of cognition*, vol. 2. Cambridge, MA: MIT Press.

Dell, G. S. (1985). Positive feedback in hierarchical connectionist models: Applications to language production. *Cognitive Science* 9, 3–23.

Feldman, J. A. (1985). Four frames suffice: A provisional model of vision and space. *Behavioral and Brain Sciences* 8, 265–289.

Feldman, J. A. (1986). Neural representation of conceptual knowledge. Technical Report 189, Department of Computer Science, University of Rochester.

Feldman, J. A., and Ballard, D. H. (1982). Connectionist models and their properties. *Cognitive Science* 6, 205–254.

Feldman, J. A., D. H. Ballard, C. M. Brown, and G. S. Dell (1985). Rochester connectionist papers: 1979–1985. Technical Report 172, Department of Computer Science, University of Rochester.

Fodor, J. A. (1975). *The language of thought*. New York: Crowell.

Fodor, J. A. (1987). *Psychosemantics*. Cambridge, MA: MIT Press.

Fodor, J. A., and Z. W. Pylyshyn (1988). Connectionism and cognitive architecture: A critical analysis. *Cognition* 28, 3–71.

Haugeland, J. (1978). The nature and plausibility of cognitivism. *Behavioral and Brain Sciences* 1, 215–226.

Hebb, D. O. (1949). *The organization of behavior*. New York: Wiley.

Hinton, G. E., and J. A. Anderson, eds. (1981). *Parallel models of associative memory*. Hillsdale, NJ: Erlbaum.

Hinton, G. E., J. L. McClelland, and D. E. Rumelhart (1986). Distributed representations. In McClelland, D. E. Rumelhart, and the PDP Research Group, *Parallel distributed processing: Explorations in the microstructure of cognition*, vol. 2. Cambridge, MA: MIT Press.

Hinton, G. E., and T. J. Sejnowski (1983). Analyzing cooperative computation. *Proceedings of the Ninth Annual Cognitive Science Society Conference*. Hillsdale, NJ: Erlbaum.

Hopcroft, J. E., and J. D. Ullman (1979). *Introduction to automata theory, languages, and computation*. Reading, MA: Addison-Wesley.

Larkin, J. H., J. McDermott, D. P. Simon, and H. A. Simon (1980). Models of competence in solving physics problems. *Cognitive Science* 4, 317–345.

Lashley, K. (1950). In search of the engram. In *Psychological mechanisms in animal behavior*, Symposia of the Society for Experimental Biology, No. 4. New York: Academic Press.

Lewis, C. H. (1978). *Production system models of practice effects*. Unpublished Ph.D. dissertation, University of Michigan, Ann Arbor.

McClelland, J. L., and D. E. Rumelhart (1981). An interactive activation model of context effects in letter perception: Part 1. An account of the basic findings. *Psychological Review* 88, 375–407.

McClelland, J. L., D. E. Rumelhart, and the PDP Research Group (1986). *Parallel distributed processing: Explorations in the microstructure of cognition*, vol. 2, *Psychological and biological models*. Cambridge, MA: MIT Press.

Minsky, M. (1975). A framework for representing knowledge. In P. H. Winston, ed., *Computers and thought*. New York: McGraw-Hill.

Newell, A. (1980). Physical symbol systems. *Cognitive Science* 4, 135–183.

Newell, A., and H. A. Simon (1972). *Human problem solving*. Englewood Cliffs, NJ: Prentice-Hall.

Pylyshyn, Z. (1984). *Computation and cognition: Toward a foundation for cognitive science*. Cambridge, MA: MIT Press.

Rumelhart, D. E. (1975). Notes on a schema for stories. In D. G. Bobrow, and A. Collins, eds., *Representation and understanding*. New York: Acdemic Press.

Rumelhart, D. E. (1980). Schemata: The building blocks of cognition. In R. Spiro, B. Bruce, and W. Brewer, eds., *Theoretical issues in reading comprehension*. Hillsdale, NJ: Erlbaum.

Rumelhart, D. E., G. E. Hinton, and R. J. Williams (1986). Learning internal representations by error propagation. In D. E. Rumelhart, J. L. McClelland, and the PDP Research Group, *Parallel distributed processing: Explorations in the microstructure of cognition*, vol. 1. Cambridge, MA: MIT Press.

Rumelhart, D. E., and J. L. McClelland (1982). An interactive activation model of context effects in letter perception: Part 2. The contextual enhancement effect and some tests and extensions of the model. *Psychological Review* 89, 60–94.

Rumelhart, D. E., and J. L. McClelland (1986). On learning the past tense of English verbs. In J. L. McClelland, D. E. Rumelhart, and the PDP Research Group, *Parallel distributed processing: Explorations in the microstructure of cognition*, vol. 2. Cambridge, MA: MIT Press.

Rumelhart, D. E., J. L. McClelland, and the PDP Research Group (1986). *Parallel distributed processing: Explorations in the microstructure of cognition*, vol. 1: *Foundations*. Cambridge, MA: MIT Press.

Sejnowski, T. J., and C. R. Rosenberg (1986). NETtalk: A parallel network that learns to read aloud. Technical Report JHU/EECS-86/01, Department of Electrical Engineering and Computer Science, Johns Hopkins University.

Shastri, L. (1985). Evidential reasoning in semantic networks: A formal theory and its parallel implementation. Technical Report TR 166, Department of Computer Science, University of Rochester.

Shepard, R. N. (1962). The analysis of proximities: Multidimensional scaling with an unknown distance function. I and II. *Psychometrica* 27, 125–140, 219–246.

Smolensky, P. (1986). Neural and conceptual interpretations of parallel distributed processing models. In J. L. McClelland, D. E. Rumelhart, and the PDP Research Group, *Parallel distributed processing: Explorations in the microstructure of cognition*, vol. 2. Cambridge, MA: MIT Press.

Smolensky, P. (1987). On variable binding and the representation of symbolic structures in connectionist systems. Technical Report Cu-CS-355-87, Department of Computer Science, University of Colorado at Boulder.

Smolensky, P. (1988). The constituent structure of connectionist mental states: A reply to Fodor and Pylyshyn. *Southern Journal of Philosophy*, 26, Supplement, 137–161.

Touretzky, D. S. (1986). BoltzCONS: Reconciling connectionism with the recursive nature of stacks and trees. *Proceedings of the Eighth Conference of the Cognitive Science Society*.

Turing, A. (1936). On computable numbers with an application to the Entscheidungs problem. *Proceedings of the London Mathematical Society* (Ser. 2) 42, 230–265 and 43, 544–546.

Waldrop, M. M. (1984). Artificial intelligence in parallel. *Science* 115, 608–610.

Waltz, D. L. (1978). An English language question answering system for a large relational database. *Communications of the Association for Computing Machinery* 21, 526–539.

Waltz, D. L., and J. B. Pollack (1985). Massively parallel parsing: A strongly interactive model of natural language interpretation. *Cognitive Science* 9, 51–74.

Connectionism and Cognitive Architecture

Jerry A. Fodor and Zenon W. Pylyshyn

Classical psychological theories appeal to the constituent structure of mental representations to explain three closely related features of cognition: its productivity, its compositionality and its inferential coherence. The traditional argument has been that these features of cognition are, on the one hand, pervasive and, on the other hand, explicable only on the assumption that mental representations have internal structure. This argument—familiar in more or less explicit versions for the last thirty years or so—is still intact, so far as we can tell. It appears to offer something close to a demonstration that an empirically adequate cognitive theory must recognize not just causal relations among representational states but also relations of syntactic and semantic constituency; hence that the mind cannot be, in its general structure, a Connectionist network.

Productivity of Thought

There is a classical productivity argument for the existence of combinatorial structure in any rich representational system (including natural languages and the language of thought). The representational capacities of such a system are, by assumption, unbounded under appropriate idealization; in particular, there are indefinitely many propositions which the system can encode.[1] However, this unbounded expressive power must presumably be achieved by finite means. The way to do this is to treat the system of representations as consisting of expressions belonging to a generated set. More precisely, the correspondence between a representation and the proposition it expresses is, in arbitrarily many cases, built up recursively out of correspondences between parts of the expression and parts of the proposition. But, of course, this strategy can operate only when an unbounded number of the expres-

From J. Fodor and Z. Pylyshyn, Connectionism and cognitive architecture: A critical analysis, *Cognition* 28, 3–71 (1988). Reprinted by permission.

sions are non-atomic. So linguistic (and mental) representations must constitute *symbol systems.* So the mind cannot be a PDP.

Very often, when people reject this sort of reasoning, it is because they doubt that human cognitive capacities are correctly viewed as productive. In the long run there can be no a priori arguments for (or against) idealizing to productive capacities; whether you accept the idealization depends on whether you believe that the inference from finite performance to finite capacity is justified, or whether you think that finite performance is typically a result of the interaction of an unbounded competence with resource constraints. Classicists have traditionally offered a mixture of methodological and empirical considerations in favor of the latter view.

From a methodological perspective, the least that can be said for assuming productivity is that it precludes solutions that rest on inappropriate tricks (such as storing all the pairs that define a function); tricks that would be unreasonable in practical terms even for solving finite tasks that place sufficiently large demands on memory. The idealization to unbounded productive capacity forces the theorist to separate the finite specification of a method for solving a computational problem from such factors as the resources that the system (or person) brings to bear on the problem at any given moment.

The empirical arguments for productivity have been made most frequently in connection with linguistic competence. They are familiar from the work of Chomsky (1968) who has claimed (convincingly, in our view) that the knowledge underlying linguistic competence is generative—i.e., that it allows us *in principle* to generate (/understand) an unbounded number of sentences. It goes without saying that no one does, or could, *in fact* utter or understand tokens of more than a finite number of sentence types; this is a trivial consequence of the fact that nobody can utter or understand more than a finite number of sentence tokens. But there are a number of considerations, which suggest that, despite de facto constraints on performance, one's knowledge of one's language supports an unbounded productive capacity in much the same way that one's knowledge of addition supports an unbounded number of sums. Among these considerations are, for example, the fact that a speaker/hearer's performance can often be improved by relaxing time constraints, increasing motivation, or supplying pencil and paper. It seems very natural to treat such manipulations as affecting the transient state of the speaker's memory and attention rather than what he knows about—or how he represents—his language. But this treatment is available only on the assumption that the character of the subject's performance is determined by interactions between the available knowledge base and the available computational resources.

Classical theories are able to accommodate these sorts of considerations because they assume architectures in which there is a functional distinction between memory and program. In a system such as a Turing machine, where the length of the tape is not fixed in advance, changes in the amount of available memory *can be affected without changing the computational structure of the machine;* viz., by making more tape available. By contrast, in a finite state automaton or a Connectionist machine, adding to the memory (e.g., by adding units to a network) alters the connectivity relations among nodes and thus does affect the machine's computational structure. Connectionist cognitive architectures cannot, by their very nature, support an expandable memory, so they cannot support productive cognitive capacities. The long and short is that if productivity arguments are sound, then they show that the architecture of the mind can't be Connectionist. Connectionists have, by and large, acknowledged this; so they are forced to reject productivity arguments.

The test of a good scientific idealization is simply and solely whether it produces successful science in the long term. It seems to us that the productivity idealization has more than earned its keep, especially in linguistics and in theories of reasoning. Connectionists, however, have not been persuaded. For example, Rumelhart and McClelland (1986, 119) say that they "do not agree that [productive] capabilities are of the essence of human computation. As anyone who has ever attempted to process sentences like 'The man the boy the girl hit kissed moved' can attest, our ability to process even moderate degrees of center-embedded structure is grossly impaired relative to an ATN [Augmented Transition Network] parser. . . . What is needed, then, is not a mechanism for flawless and effortless processing of embedded constructions. . . . The challenge is to explain how those processes that others have chosen to explain in terms of recursive mechanisms can be better explained by the kinds of processes natural for PDP networks."

These remarks suggest that Rumelhart and McClelland think that the fact that center-embedding sentences are hard is somehow an *embarrassment* for theories that view linguistic capacities as productive. But of course it's not since, according to such theories, performance is an effect of interactions between a productive competence and restricted resources. There are, in fact, quite plausible Classical accounts of why center-embeddings ought to impose especially heavy demands on resources, and there is a reasonable amount of experimental support for these models (see, for example, Wanner and Maratsos 1978).

In any event, it should be obvious that the difficulty of parsing center-embeddings can't be a consequence of their recursiveness per se since there are many recursive structures that are strikingly easy to understand. Consider: 'this is the dog that chased the cat that ate the rat that lived in the house that Jack built.' The Classicist's case for productive capacities in parsing rests on the transparency of sentences like these.[2] In short, the fact that center-embedded sentences are hard perhaps shows that there are some recursive structures that we can't parse. But what Rumelhart and McClelland need if they are to deny the productivity of linguistic capacities is the much stronger claim that there are no recursive structures that we can parse; and this stronger claim would appear to be simply false.

Rumelhart and McClelland's discussion of recursion (pp. 119–120) nevertheless repays close attention. They are apparently prepared to concede that PDPs can model recursive capacities only indirectly—viz., by implementing Classical architectures like ATNs; so that *if* human cognition exhibited recursive capacities, that would suffice to show that minds have Classical rather than Connectionist architecture at the psychological level. "We have not dwelt on PDP implementations of Turing machines and recursive processing engines *because we do not agree with those who would argue that such capacities are of the essence of human computation*" (p. 119, our emphasis). Their argument that recursive capacities *aren't* "of the essence of human computation" is, however, just the unconvincing stuff about center-embedding quoted above.

So the Rumelhart and McClelland view is apparently that if you take it to be independently obvious that some cognitive capacities are productive, then you should take the existence of such capacities to argue for Classical cognitive architecture and hence for treating Connectionism as at best an implementation theory. We think that this is quite a plausible understanding of the bearing that the issues about productivity and recursion have on the issues about cognitive architecture.

However, we propose to view the status of productivity arguments for Classical architectures as moot; we're about to present a different sort of argument for the claim that mental representations need an articulated internal structure. It is closely related to the productivity argument, but it doesn't require the idealization to unbounded competence. Its assumptions should thus be acceptable even to theorists who—like Connectionists—hold that the finitistic character of cognitive capacities is intrinsic to their architecture.

Systematicity of Cognitive Representation

The form of the argument is this: Whether or not cognitive capacities are really *productive*, it seems indubitable that they are what we shall call 'systematic'. And we'll see that the systematicity of cognition provides as good a reason for postulating combinatorial structure in mental representation as the productivity of cognition does: You get, in effect, the same conclusion, but from a weaker premise.

The easiest way to understand what the systematicity of cognitive capacities amounts to is to focus on the systematicity of language comprehension and production. In fact, the systematicity argument for combinatorial structure in *thought* exactly recapitulates the traditional Structuralist argument for constituent structure in sentences. But we pause to remark upon a point that we'll re-emphasize later; linguistic capacity is a paradigm of systematic cognition, but it's wildly unlikely that it's the only example. On the contrary, there's every reason to believe that systematicity is a thoroughly pervasive feature of human and infrahuman mentation.

What we mean when we say that linguistic capacities are *systematic* is that the ability to produce/understand some sentences is *intrinsically* connected to the ability to produce/understand certain others. You can see the force of this if you compare learning languages the way we really do learn them with learning a language by memorizing an enormous phrase book. The point isn't that phrase books are finite and can therefore exhaustively specify only *non*-productive languages; that's true, but we've agreed not to rely on productivity arguments for our present purposes. Our point is rather that you can learn *any part of a phrase book without learning the rest*. Hence, on the phrase book model, it would be perfectly possible to learn that uttering the form of words 'Granny's cat is on Uncle Arthur's mat' is the way to say (in English) that Granny's cat is on Uncle Arthur's mat, and yet have no idea at all how to say that it's raining (or, for that matter, how to say that Uncle Arthur's cat is on Granny's mat). Perhaps it's self-evident that the phrase book story must be wrong about language acquisition because a speaker's knowledge of his native language is never like that. You don't, for example, find native speakers who know how to say in English that John loves the girl but don't know how to say in English that the girl loves John.

Notice, in passing, that systematicity is a property of the mastery of the syntax of a language, not of its lexicon. The phrase book model really does fit what it's like to learn the *vocabulary* of English since when you learn English vocabulary you acquire a lot of basically *independent* capacities. So you might perfectly well learn that using the expression 'cat' is the way to refer to cats and yet have no idea that using the expression 'deciduous conifer' is the way to refer to deciduous conifers. Systematicity, like productivity, is the sort of property of cognitive capacities that you're likely to miss if you concentrate on the psychology of learning and searching lists.

There is, as we remarked, a straightforward (and quite traditional) argument from the systematicity of language capacity to the conclusion that sentences must have syntactic and semantic structure: If you assume that sentences are constructed out of words and phrases, and that many different sequences of words can be phrases of the same type, the very fact that one formula is a sentence of the language will often imply that other formulas must be too: in effect, systematicity follows from the postulation of constituent structure.

Suppose, for example, that it's a fact about English that formulas with the constituent analysis 'NP Vt NP' are well formed; and suppose that 'John' and 'the girl' are NPs and 'loves' is a Vt. It follows from these assumptions that 'John loves the girl,' 'John loves John,' 'the girl loves the girl,' and 'the girl loves John' must all be sentences. It follows too that anybody who has mastered the grammar of English must have linguistic capacities that are systematic in respect of these sentences; he *can't but* assume that all of them are sentences if he assumes that any of them are. Compare the situation on the view that the sentences of English are all atomic. There is then no structural analogy between 'John loves the girl' and 'the girl loves John' and hence no reason why understanding one sentence should imply understanding the other; no more than understanding 'rabbit' implies understanding 'tree.'[3]

On the view that the sentences are atomic, the systematicity of linguistic capacities is a mystery; on the view that they have constituent structure, the systematicity of linguistic capacities is what you would predict. So we should prefer the latter view to the former.

Notice that you can make this argument for constituent structure in sentences without idealizing to astronomical computational capacities. There are productivity arguments for constituent structure, but they're concerned with our ability—in principle—to understand sentences that are arbitrarily long. Systematicity, by contrast, appeals to premises that are much nearer home; such considerations as the ones mentioned above, that no speaker understands the form of words 'John loves the girl' except as he also understands the form of words 'the girl loves John'. The assumption that linguistic capacities are productive "in principle" is one that a Connectionist might refuse to grant. But that they are systematic *in fact* no one can plausibly deny.

We can now, finally, come to the point: the argument from the systematicity of linguistic capacities to constituent structure in sentences is quite clear. *But thought is systematic too,* so there is a precisely parallel argument from the systematicity of thought to syntactic and semantic structure in mental representations.

What does it mean to say that thought is systematic? Well, just as you don't find people who can understand the sentence 'John loves the girl' but not the sentence 'the girl loves John,' so too you don't find people who can *think the thought* that John loves the girl but can't think the thought that the girl loves John. Indeed, in the case of verbal organisms the systematicity of thought *follows from* the systematicity of language if you assume—as most psychologists do—that understanding a sentence involves entertaining the thought that it expresses; on that assumption, nobody *could* understand both the sentences about John and the girl unless he were able to think both the thoughts about John and the girl.

But now if the ability to think that John loves the girl is intrinsically connected to the ability to think that the girl loves John, that fact will somehow have to be explained. For a Representationalist (which, as we have seen, Connectionists are), the explanation is obvious: Entertaining thoughts requires being in representational states (i.e., it requires tokening mental representations). And, just as the systematicity of language shows that there must be structural relations between the sentence 'John loves the girl' and the sentence 'the girl loves John,' so the systematicity of thought shows that there must be structural relations between the mental representation that corresponds to the thought that John loves the girl and the mental representation that corresponds to the thought that the girl loves John,[4] namely, the two mental representations, like the two sentences, *must be made of the same parts*. But if this explanation is right (and there don't seem to be any others on offer), then mental representations have internal structure and there is a language of thought. So the architecture of the mind is not a Connectionist network.[5]

To summarize the discussion so far: Productivity arguments infer the internal structure of mental representations from the presumed fact that nobody has a *finite* intellectual competence. By contrast, systematicity arguments infer the internal structure of mental representations from the patent fact that nobody has a *punctate* intellectual competence. Just as you don't find linguistic capacities that consist of the ability to understand sixty-seven unrelated sentences, so too you don't find cognitive capacities that consist of the ability to think seventy-four unrelated thoughts. Our claim is that this isn't, in either case, an accident: A linguistic theory that allowed for the possibility of punctate languages would have gone not just wrong, but *very profoundly* wrong. And similarly for a cognitive theory that allowed for the possibility of punctate minds.

But perhaps not being punctate is a property only of the minds of language users; perhaps the representational capacities of infraverbal organisms do have just the kind of gaps that Connectionist models permit? A Connectionist might then claim that he can do everything "up to language" on the assumption that mental representations lack combinatorial syntactic and semantic structure. Everything up to language may not be everything, but it's a lot. (On the other hand, a lot may be a lot, but it isn't everything. Infraverbal cognitive architecture mustn't be so represented as to make the eventual acquisition of language in phylogeny and in ontogeny require a miracle.)

It is not, however, plausible that only the minds of verbal organisms are systematic. Think what it would mean for this to be the case. It would have to be quite usual to find, for example, animals capable of representing the state of affairs aRb, but incapable of representing the state of affairs bRa. Such animals would be, as it were, aRb sighted but bRa blind since, presumably, the representational capacities of its mind affect not just what an organism can think, but also what it can perceive. In consequence, such animals would be able to learn to respond selectively to aRb situations but quite *unable* to learn to respond selectively to bRa situations. (So that, though you could teach the creature to choose the picture with the square larger than the triangle, you couldn't for the life of you teach it to choose the picture with the triangle larger than the square.)

It is, to be sure, an empirical question whether the cognitive capacities of infraverbal organisms are often structured that way, but we're prepared to bet that they are not. Ethological cases are the exceptions that prove the rule. There *are* examples where salient environmental configurations act as 'gestalten'; and in such cases it's reasonable to doubt that the mental representation of the stimulus is complex. But the point is precisely that these cases are *exceptional;* they're exactly the ones where you expect that there will be some special story to tell about the ecological significance of the stimulus: that it's the shape of a predator, or the song of a conspecific . . . etc. Conversely, when there is no such story to tell you expect structurally similar stimuli to elicit correspondingly similar cognitive capacities. That, surely, is the least that a respectable principle of stimulus generalization has got to require.

That infraverbal cognition is pretty generally systematic seems, in short, to be about as secure as any empirical premise in this area can be. And, as we've just seen, it's a premise from which the inadequacy of Connectionist models as cognitive theories follows quite straightforwardly; as straightforwardly, in any event, as it would from the assumption that such capacities are generally productive.

Compositionality of Representations

Compositionality is closely related to systematicity; perhaps they're best viewed as aspects of a single phenomenon. We will therefore follow much the same course here as in the preceding discussion: first we introduce the concept by recalling the standard arguments for the compositionality of natural languages. We then suggest that parallel arguments secure the compositionality of mental representations. Since compositionality requires combinatorial syntactic and semantic structure, the compositionality of thought is evidence that the mind is not a Connectionist network.

We said that the systematicity of linguistic competence consists in the fact that "the ability to produce/understand some of the sentences is intrinsically connected to the ability to produce/understand certain of the others". We now add that which sentences are systematically related is not arbitrary from a semantic point of view. For example, being able to understand 'John loves the girl' goes along with being able to understand 'the girl loves John', and there are correspondingly close semantic relations between these sentences: in order for the first to be true, John must bear to the girl the very same relation that the truth of the second requires the girl to bear to John. By contrast, there is no intrinsic connection between understanding either of the John/girl sentences and understanding semantically unrelated formulas like 'quarks are made of gluons' or 'the cat is on the mat' or '2 + 2 = 4'; it looks as though semantical relatedness and systematicity keep quite close company.

You might suppose that this covariance is covered by the same explanation that accounts for systematicity per se; roughly, that sentences that are systematically related are composed from the same syntactic constituents. But, in fact, you need a further assumption, which we'll call the 'principle of compositionality': insofar as a language is systematic, a lexical item must make approximately the same semantic contribution to each expression in which it occurs. It is, for example, only insofar as 'the' 'girl', 'loves' and 'John' make the same semantic contribution to 'John loves the girl' that they make to 'the girl loves John' that understanding the one sentence implies understanding the other. Similarity of constituent structure accounts for the semantic relatedness between systematically related sentences only to the extent that the semantical properties of the shared constituents are context-independent.

Here it's idioms that prove the rule: being able to understand 'the', 'man', 'kicked' and 'bucket' isn't much help with understanding 'the man kicked the bucket', since 'kicked' and 'bucket' don't bear their standard meanings in this context. And, just as you'd expect, 'the man kicked the bucket' is *not* systematic even with respect to syntactically closely related sentences like 'the man kicked over the bucket' (for that matter, it's not systematic with respect to 'the man kicked the bucket' read literally).

It's uncertain exactly how compositional natural languages actually are (just as it's uncertain exactly how systematic they are). We suspect that the amount of context induced variation of lexical meaning is often overestimated because other sorts of context sensitivity are misconstrued as violations of compositionality. For example, the difference between 'feed the chicken' and 'chicken to eat' must involve an *animal/food* ambiguity in 'chicken' rather than a violation of compositionality since if the context 'feed the . . .' could *induce* (rather than select) the meaning *animal,* you would expect 'feed the veal', 'feed the pork' and the like.[6] Similarly, the difference between 'good book', 'good rest' and 'good fight' is probably not meaning shift but syncategorematicity. 'Good NP' means something like NP *that answers to the relevant interest in NPs:* a good book is one that answers to our interest in books (viz., it's good to read); a good rest is one that answers to our interest in rests (viz., it leaves one refreshed); a good fight is one that answers to our interest in fights (viz., it's fun to watch or to be in, or it clears the air); and so on. It's because the meaning of 'good' is syncategorematic and has a variable in it for relevant interests, that you can know that a good flurg is a flurg that answers to the relevant interest in flurgs without knowing what flurgs are or what the relevant interest in flurgs is (see Ziff 1960).

In any event, the main argument stands: systematicity depends on compositionality, so to the extent that a natural language is systematic it must be compositional too. This illustrates another respect in which systematicity arguments can do the work for which productivity arguments have previously been employed. The traditional argument for compositionality is that it is required to explain how a finitely representable language can contain infinitely many nonsynonymous expressions.

Considerations about systematicity offer one argument for compositionality; considerations about entailment offer another. Consider predicates like '. . . is a brown cow'. This expression bears a straightforward semantical relation to the predicates '. . . is a cow' and '. . . is brown'; viz., that the first predicate is true of a thing if and only if both of the others are. That is, '. . . is a brown cow' severally entails '. . . is brown' and '. . . is a cow' and is entailed by their conjunction. Moreover—and this is important—this semantical pattern is not peculiar to the cases cited. On the contrary, it holds for a very large range of predicates (see '. . . is a red square,' '. . . is a funny old German soldier,' '. . . is a child prodigy;' and so forth).

How are we to account for these sorts of regularities? The answer seems clear enough; '. . . is a brown cow' entails '. . . is brown' because (a) the second expression is a constituent of the first; (b) the syntactical form '(adjective noun)$_N$' has (in many cases) the semantic force of a conjunction, and (c) 'brown' retains its semantical value under simplification of conjunction. Notice that you need (c) to rule out the possibility that 'brown' means *brown* when it modifies a noun but (as it might be) *dead* when it's a predicate adjective; in which case '. . . is a brown cow' wouldn't entail '. . . is brown' after all. Notice too that (c) is just an application of the principle of composition.

So, here's the argument so far: you need to assume some degree of compositionality of English sentences to account for the fact that systematically related sentences are always semantically related; and to account for certain regular parallelisms between the syntactical structure of sentences and their entailments. So, beyond any serious doubt, the sentences of English must be compositional to some serious extent. But the principle of compositionality governs the semantic relations between words *and the expressions of which they are constituents.* So compositionality implies that (some) expressions *have* constituents. So compositionality argues for (specifically, presupposes) syntactic/semantic structure in sentences.

Now what about the compositionality of mental representations? There is, as you'd expect, a bridging argument based on the usual psycholinguistic premise that one uses language to express ones thoughts: Sentences are used to express thoughts; so if the ability to use some sentences is connected with the ability to use certain other, semantically related sentences, then the ability to think some thoughts must be correspondingly connected with the ability to think certain other, semantically related thoughts. But you can only think the

Fodor and Pylyshyn

thoughts that your mental representations can express. So, if the ability to think certain thoughts is interconnected, then the corresponding representational capacities must be interconnected too; specifically, the ability to be in some representational states must imply the ability to be in certain other, semantically related representational states.

But then the question arises: *how could* the mind be so arranged that the ability to be in one representational state is connected with the ability to be in others that are semantically nearby? What account of mental representation would have this consequence? The answer is just what you'd expect from the discussion of the linguistic material. Mental representations must have internal structure, just the way that sentences do. In particular, it must be that the mental representation that corresponds to the thought that John loves the girl contains, as its parts, the same constituents as the mental representation that corresponds to the thought that the girl loves John. That would explain why these thoughts are *systematically* related; *and, to the extent that the semantic value of these parts is context-independent, that would explain why these systematically related thoughts are also semantically related.* So, by this chain of argument, evidence for the compositionality of sentences is evidence for the compositionality of the representational states of speaker/hearers.

Finally, what about the compositionality of infraverbal thought? The argument isn't much different from the one that we've just run through. We assume that animal thought is largely systematic: the organism that can perceive (hence learn) that $a\mathbf{R}b$ can generally perceive (/learn) that $b\mathbf{R}a$. But, systematically related thoughts (just like systematically related sentences) are generally semantically related too. It's no surprise that being able to learn that the triangle is above the square implies being able to learn that the square is above the triangle; whereas it would be *very* surprising if being able to learn the square/triangle facts implied being able to learn that quarks are made of gluons or that Washington was the first President of America.

So, then, what explains the correlation between systematic relations and semantic relations in infraverbal thought? Clearly, Connectionist models don't address this question; the fact that a network contains a node labelled X has, so far as the constraints imposed by Connectionist architecture are concerned, *no implications at all* for the labels of the other nodes in the network; in particular, it doesn't imply that there will be nodes that represent thoughts that are semantically close to X. This is just the semantical side of the fact that network architectures permit arbitrarily punctate mental lives.

But if, on the other hand, we make the usual Classicist assumptions (viz., that systematically related thoughts share constituents and that the semantic values of these shared constituents are context independent) the correlation between systematicity and semantic relatedness follows immediately. For a Classicist, this correlation is an 'architectural' property of minds; it couldn't but hold if mental representations have the general properties that Classical models suppose them to.

What have Connectionists to say about these matters? There is some textual evidence that they are tempted to deny the facts of compositionality wholesale. For example, Smolensky (1988) claims that: "Surely . . . we would get quite a different representation of 'coffee' if we examined the difference between 'can with coffee' and 'can without coffee' or 'tree with coffee' and 'tree without coffee'; or 'man with coffee' and 'man without coffee' . . . context insensitivity is not something we expect to be reflected in Connectionist representations."

It's certainly true that compositionality is not generally a feature of Connectionist representations. Connectionists can't acknowledge the facts of compositionality because they are committed to mental representations that don't have combinatorial structure. But to give up on compositionality is to take 'kick the bucket' as a model for the relation between syntax and semantics; and the consequence is, as we've seen, that you make the systematicity of language (and of thought) a mystery. On the other hand, to say that 'kick the bucket' is aberrant, and that the right model for the syntax/semantics relation is (e.g.) 'brown cow', is to start down a trail which leads, pretty inevitably, to acknowledging combinatorial structure in mental representation, hence to the rejection of Connectionist networks as cognitive models.

We don't think there's any way out of the need to acknowledge the compositionality of natural languages and of mental representations. However, it's been suggested (see Smolensky 1988) that while the principle of compositionality is false (because content isn't context invariant) there is nevertheless a "family resemblance" between the various meanings that a symbol has in the various contexts in which it occurs. Since such proposals generally aren't elaborated, it's unclear how they're supposed to handle the salient facts about systematicity and inference. But surely there are going to be serious problems. Consider, for example, such inferences as

(i)   Turtles are slower than rabbits.
(ii)   Rabbits are slower than Ferraris.
....
(iii) Turtles are slower than Ferraris.

The soundness of this inference appears to depend upon (a) the fact that the same relation (viz., *slower than*) holds between turtles and rabbits on the one hand, and rabbits and Ferraris on the other; and (b) the fact that that relation is transitive. If, however, it's assumed (contrary to the principle of compositionality) that 'slower than' means something different in premises (i) and (ii) (and presumably in (iii) as well)—so that, strictly speaking, the relation that holds between turtles and rabbits is *not* the same one that holds between rabbits and Ferraris—then it's hard to see why the inference should be valid.

Talk about the relations being 'similar' only papers over the difficulty since the problem is then to provide a notion of similarity that will guaranty that if (i) and (ii) are true, so too is (iii). And, so far at least, no such notion of similarity has been forthcoming. Notice that it won't do to require just that the relations all be similar in respect of their *transitivity*, i.e., that they all be transitive. On that account, the argument from 'turtles are slower than rabbits' and 'rabbits are furrier than Ferraris' to 'turtles are slower than Ferraris' would be valid since 'furrier than' is transitive too.

Until these sorts of issues are attended to, the proposal to replace the compositional principle of context invariance with a notion of "approximate equivalence . . . across contexts" (Smolensky 1988) doesn't seem to be much more than hand waving.

The Systematicity of Inference

Earlier we saw that, according to Classical theories, the syntax of mental representations mediates between their semantic properties and their causal role in mental processes. Take a simple case: It's a 'logical' principle that conjunctions entail their constituents (so the argument from $P\&Q$ to P and to Q is valid). Correspondingly, it's a psychological law that thoughts that $P\&Q$ tend to cause thoughts that P and thoughts that Q, all else being equal. Classical theory exploits the constituent structure of mental representations to account for both these facts, the first by assuming that the combinatorial semantics of mental representations is sensitive to their syntax and the second by assuming that mental processes apply to mental representations in virtue of their constituent structure.

A consequence of these assumptions is that Classical theories are committed to the following striking prediction: inferences that are of similar logical type ought, pretty generally,[7] to elicit correspondingly similar cognitive capacities. You shouldn't, for example, find a kind of mental life in which you get inferences from $P\&Q\&R$ to P but you don't get inferences from $P\&Q$ to P. This is because, according to the Classical account, this logically homogeneous class of inferences is carried out by a correspondingly homogeneous class of psychological mechanisms: The premises of both inferences are expressed by mental representations that satisfy the same syntactic analysis (viz., $S_1\&S_2\&S_3\& \ldots S_n$); and the process of drawing the inference corresponds, in both cases, to the same formal operation of detaching the constituent that expresses the conclusion.

The idea that organisms should exhibit similar cognitive capacities in respect of logically similar inferences is so natural that it may seem unavoidable. But, on the contrary: there's nothing in principle to preclude a kind of cognitive model in which inferences that are quite similar from the logician's point of view are nevertheless computed by quite different mechanisms; or in which some inferences of a given logical type are computed and other inferences of the same logical type are not. Consider, in particular, the Connectionist account. A Connectionist can certainly model a mental life in which, if you can reason from *P&Q&R* to *P*, then you can also reason from *P&Q* to *P*. For example, the network in figure 36.1 would do:

But notice that *a Connectionist can equally model a mental life in which you get one of these inferences and not the other.* In the present case, since there is no structural relation between the *P&Q&R* node and the *P&Q* node (remember, all nodes are atomic; don't be misled by the node *labels*) there's no reason why a mind that contains the first should also contain the second, or vice versa. Analogously, there's no reason why you shouldn't get minds that simplify the premise *John loves Mary and Bill hates Mary* but no others; or minds that simplify premises with 1, 3, or 5 conjuncts, but don't simplify premises with 2, 4, or 6 conjuncts; or, for that matter, minds that simplify only premises that were acquired on Tuesdays . . . etc.

In fact, the Connectionist architecture is *utterly indifferent* as among these possibilities. That's because it recognizes no notion of syntax according to which thoughts that are alike in inferential role (e.g., thoughts that are all subject to simplification of conjunction) are expressed by mental representations of correspondingly similar syntactic form (e.g., by mental representations that are all syntactically conjunctive). So, the Connectionist architecture tolerates gaps in cognitive capacities; it has no mechanism to enforce the requirement that logically homogeneous inferences should be executed by correspondingly homogeneous computational processes.

But, we claim, you don't find cognitive capacities that have these sorts of gaps. You don't, for example, get minds that are prepared to

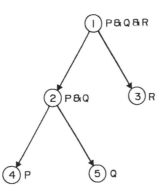

Figure 36.1 A possible Connectionist network which draws inferences from P&Q&R to P and also draws inferences from P&Q to P.

Fodor and Pylyshyn

infer *John went to the store* from *John and Mary and Susan and Sally went to the store* and from *John and Mary went to the store* but not from *John and Mary and Susan went to the store*. Given a notion of logical syntax—the very notion that the Classical theory of mentation requires to get its account of mental processes off the ground—it is a *truism* that you don't get such minds. Lacking a notion of logical syntax, it is a *mystery* that you don't.

Summary

It is perhaps obvious by now that all the arguments that we've been reviewing—the argument from systematicity, the argument from compositionality, and the argument from inferential coherence—are really much the same: If you hold the kind of theory that acknowledges structured representations, it must perforce acknowledge representations with *similar* or *identical* structures. In the linguistic cases, constituent analysis implies a taxonomy of sentences by their syntactic form, and in the inferential cases, it implies a taxonomy of arguments by their logical form. So, if your theory also acknowledges mental processes that are structure sensitive, then it will predict that similarly structured representations will generally play similar roles in thought. A theory that says that the sentence 'John loves the girl' is made out of the same parts as the sentence 'the girl loves John', and made by applications of the same rules of composition, will have to go out of its way to explain a linguistic competence which embraces one sentence but not the other. And similarly, if a theory says that the mental representation that corresponds to the thought that *P&Q&R* has the same (conjunctive) syntax as the mental representation that corresponds to the thought that *P&Q* and that mental processes of drawing inferences subsume mental representations in virtue of their syntax, it will have to go out of its way to explain inferential capacities which embrace the one thought but not the other. Such a competence would be, at best, an embarrassment for the theory, and at worst a refutation.

By contrast, since the Connectionist architecture recognizes no combinatorial structure in mental representations, gaps in cognitive competence should proliferate arbitrarily. It's not just that you'd expect to get them from time to time; it's that, on the 'no-structure' story, *gaps are the unmarked case*. It's the *systematic* competence that the theory is required to treat as an embarrassment. But, as a matter of fact, inferential competences are *blatantly* systematic. So there must be something deeply wrong with Connectionist architecture.

What's deeply wrong with Connectionist architecture is this: Because it acknowledges neither syntactic nor semantic structure in mental representations, it perforce treats them not as a generated set but as a list. But lists, qua lists, have no structure; any collection of items is a possible list. And, correspondingly, on Connectionist principles, any collection of (causally connected) representational states is a possible mind. So, as far as Connectionist architecture is concerned, there is nothing to prevent minds that are arbitrarily unsystematic. But that result is *preposterous*. Cognitive capacities come in structurally related clusters; their systematicity is pervasive. All the evidence suggests that *punctate minds can't happen*. This argument seemed conclusive against the Connectionism of Hebb, Osgood and Hull twenty or thirty years ago. So far as we can tell, nothing of any importance has happened to change the situation in the meantime.[8]

A final comment to round off this part of the discussion. It's possible to imagine a Connectionist being prepared to admit that while systematicity doesn't *follow from*—and hence is not explained by—Connectionist architecture, it is nonetheless *compatible* with that architecture. It is, after all, perfectly possible to follow a policy of building networks that have *a*R*b* nodes only if they have *b*R*a* nodes . . . etc. There is therefore nothing to stop a Connectionist from stipulating—as an independent postulate of his theory of mind—that all biologically instantiated networks are, de facto, systematic.

But this misses a crucial point: It's not enough just to stipulate systematicity; one is also required to specify a mechanism that is able to enforce the stipulation. To put it another way, it's not enough for a Connectionist to agree that all minds are systematic; he must also explain *how nature contrives to produce only systematic minds*. Presumably there would have to be some sort of mechanism, over and above the ones that Connectionism per se posits, the functioning of which insures the systematicity of biologically instantiated networks; a mechanism such that, in virtue of its operation, every network that has an *a*R*b* node also has a *b*R*a* node . . . and so forth. There are, however, no proposals for such a mechanism. Or, rather, there is just one: The only mechanism that is known to be able to produce pervasive systematicity is Classical architecture. And, as we have seen, Classical architecture is not compatible with Connectionism since it requires internally structured representations. . . .

Notes

1. This way of putting the productivity argument is most closely identified with Chomsky (e.g., Chomsky 1965; 1968). However, one does not have to rest the argument upon a basic assumption of infinite generative capacity. Infinite generative capacity can be viewed, instead, as a consequence or a corollary of theories formulated so as to capture the greatest number of generalizations with the fewest independent principles. This more neutral approach is, in fact, very much in the spirit of what we shall propose below. We are putting it in the present form for expository and historical reasons.

2. McClelland and Kawamoto (1986) discuss this sort of recursion briefly. Their suggestion seems to be that parsing such sentences doesn't really require recovering their recursive structure: "the job of the parser [with respect to right-recursive sentences] is to spit out

phrases in a way that captures their *local* context. Such a representation may prove sufficient to allow us to reconstruct the correct bindings of noun phrases to verbs and prepositional phrases to *nearby* nouns and verbs" (p. 324; emphasis ours). It is, however, by no means the case that all of the semantically relevant grammatical relations in readily intelligible embedded sentences are local in surface structure. Consider: '*Where* did the man who owns the cat that chased the rat that frightened the girl say that he was going to move to (X)?' or '*What* did the girl that the children loved to listen to promise your friends that she would read (X) to them?' Notice that, in such examples, a binding element (italicized) can be arbitrarily displaced from the position whose interpretation it controls (marked 'X') without making the sentence particularly difficult to understand. Notice too that the 'semantics' doesn't determine the binding relations in either example.

3. See Pinker (1984, chap. 4) for evidence that children never go through a stage in which they distinguish between the internal structures of NPs depending on whether they are in subject or object position: i.e., the dialects that children speak are always systematic with respect to the syntactic structures that can appear in these positions.

4. It may be worth emphasizing that the structural complexity of a mental representation is not the same thing as, and does *not* follow from, the structural complexity of its propositional content (i.e., of what we're calling "the thought that one has"). Thus, Connectionists and Classicists can agree to agree that *the thought that P&Q* is complex (and has the thought that *P* among its parts) while agreeing to disagree about whether mental representations have internal syntactic structure.

5. These considerations throw further light on a proposal we discussed earlier. Suppose that the mental representation corresponding to the thought that John loves the girl is the feature vector $\{+John\text{-}subject; + loves; +the\text{-}girl\text{-}object\}$ where '*John-subject*' and '*the-girl-object*' are atomic features; as such, they bear no more structural relation to '*John-object*' and '*the-girl-subject*' than they do to one another or to, say, '*has-a-handle*'. Since this theory recognizes no structural relation between '*John-subject*' and '*John-object*', it offers no reason why a representational system that provides the means to express one of these concepts should also provide the means to express the other. This treatment of role relations thus makes a mystery of the (presumed) fact that anybody who can entertain the thought that John loves the girl can also entertain the thought that the girl loves John (and, mutatis mutandis, that any natural language that can express the proposition that John loves the girl can also express the proposition that the girl loves John). This consequence of the proposal that role relations be handled by "role specific descriptors that represent the conjunction of an identity and a role" (Hinton, 1987) offers a particularly clear example of how failure to postulate internal structure in representations leads to failure to capture the systematicity of representational systems.

6. We are indebted to Steve Pinker for this point.

7. The hedge is meant to exclude cases where inferences of the same logical type nevertheless differ in complexity in virtue of, for example, the length of their premises. The inference from $(A \lor B \lor C \lor D \lor E)$ and $(-B \& -C \& -D \& -E)$ to A is of the same logical type as the inference from $A \lor B$ and $-B$ to A. But it wouldn't be very surprising, or very interesting, if there were minds that could handle the second inference but not the first.

8. Historical footnote: Connectionists are Associationists, but not every Associationist holds that mental representations must be unstructured. Hume didn't, for example. Hume thought that mental representations are rather like pictures, and pictures typically have a compositional semantics: the parts of a picture of a horse are generally pictures of horse parts.

On the other hand, allowing a compositional semantics for mental representations doesn't do an Associationist much good so long as he is true to this spirit of his Associationism. The virtue of having mental representations with structure is that it allows for structure sensitive operations to be defined over them; specifically, it allows for the sort of operations that eventuate in productivity and systematicity. Association is not, however, such an operation: all *it* can do is build an internal model of redundancies in experience by altering the probabilities of transitions among mental states. So far as the problems of productivity and systematicity are concerned, an Associationist who acknowledges structured representations is in the position of having the can but not the opener.

Hume, in fact, cheated: he allowed himself not just Association but also "Imagination", which he takes to be an 'active' faculty that can produce new concepts out of old parts by a process of analysis and recombination. (The idea of a unicorn is pieced together out of the idea of a horse and the idea of a horn, for example.) Qua associationist Hume had, of course, no right to active mental faculties. But allowing imagination in gave Hume precisely what modern Connectionists don't have: an answer to the question how mental processes can be productive. The moral is that if you've got structured representations, the temptation to postulate structure sensitive operations and an executive to apply them is practically irresistible.

References

Chomsky, N. (1965). *Aspects of the theory of syntax*. Cambridge, MA: MIT Press.

Chomsky, N. (1968). *Language and mind*. New York: Harcourt, Brace and World.

Hinton, G. E. (1987). Representing part-whole hierarchies in connectionist networks. Unpublished manuscript.

McClelland J. L., and A. H. Kawamoto (1986). Mechanisms of sentence processing: Assigning roles to constituents. In J. L. McClelland, D. E. Rumelhart and the PDP Research Group, *Parallel distributed processing: Explorations in the microstructure of cognition*, vol. 2. Cambridge, MA: MIT Press.

Pinker, S. (1984). *Language learnability and language development*. Cambridge, MA: Harvard University Press.

Rumelhart, D. E., and J. L. McClelland (1986). PDP models and general issues in cognitive science. In D. E. Rumelhart, J. L. McClelland, and the PDP Research Group, *Parallel distributed processing: Explorations in the microstructure of cognition*, vol. 1. Cambridge, MA: MIT Press.

Smolensky, P. (1988). On the proper treatment of connectionism. *Behavioral and Brain Sciences* 11, 1–74.

Wanner, E. and M. Maratsos (1978). An ATN approach to comprehension. In M. Halle, J. Bresnan, and G. A. Miller, eds., *Linguistic theory and psychological reality*. Cambridge, MA: MIT Press.

Ziff, P. (1960). *Semantic analysis*. Ithaca, NY: Cornell University Press.

37 The Computer Model of the Mind

Ned Block

Functional Analysis

. . . The paradigm of defining or explicating intelligence in cognitive science is a methodology sometimes known as *functional analysis*. Think of the human mind as represented by an intelligent being in the head, a "homunculus." Think of this homunculus as being composed of smaller and stupider homunculi, and each of these being composed of still smaller and still stupider homunculi, until you reach a level of completely mechanical homunculi. (This picture was first articulated in Fodor 1968; see also Dennett 1974 and Cummins 1975.)

Suppose one wants to explain how we understand language. Part of the system will recognize individual words. This word recognizer might be composed of three components, one of which has the task of fetching each incoming word, one at a time, and passing it to a second component. The second component has a dictionary, that is, a list of all the words in the vocabulary, together with syntactic and semantic information about each word. This second component compares the target word with words in the vocabulary (perhaps executing many such comparisons simultaneously) until it gets a match. When it finds a match, it sends a signal to a third component, whose job it is to retrieve the syntactic and semantic information stored in the dictionary. Of course, this is only a small part of a model of language understanding; it is supposed to illustrate the process of explaining part of a cognitive competence via simpler cognitive competences, in this case the simple mechanical operations of fetching and matching.

The idea of this kind of explanation of intelligence comes from attention to the way computers work. Consider a computer that multiplies the number m by the number n by adding m to itself n times. Here is a program for doing this. Think of m and n as represented in the

From N. Block, The computer model of the mind, in D. N. Osherson and E. E. Smith, eds., *Thinking: An invitation to cognitive science*, vol. 3 (1990). Cambridge, MA: MIT Press. Reprinted by permission.

registers M and N in figure 37.1. Register A is reserved for the answer, a. First, a representation of 0 is placed in register A. Second, N is examined to see whether it contains (a representation of) 0. If the answer is yes, the program halts and the correct answer is 0. (If n = 0, m times n = 0.) If no, N is decremented by 1 (so the value of register N is now n − 1), and m is added to the answer register, A. Then the procedure loops back to the second step. Register N is checked once again to see whether its value is 0; if not, it is again decremented by 1, and m is again added to register A. This procedure continues until N finally has the value 0, at which time m will have been added to the answer register exactly n times. At this point register A contains a representation of the answer.

This program multiplies via a "decomposition" of multiplication into other processes, namely, addition, subtraction of 1, setting a register to 0, and checking a register for 0. Depending on how these things are themselves done, they may be the fundamental bottom-level processes, known as *primitive processes.*

The cognitive science definition or explication of intelligence is analogous to this explication of multiplication. Intelligent capacities are understood via decomposition into a network of less intelligent capacities, ultimately grounded in totally mechanical capacities executed by primitive processors.

The concept of a primitive process is very important; the next section is devoted to it.

Primitive Processors

What makes a processor primitive? One answer is that for primitive processors, the question "How does the processor work?" is *not a question for cognitive science to answer.* The cognitive scientist answers "How does the multiplier work?" in the case of the multiplier described above

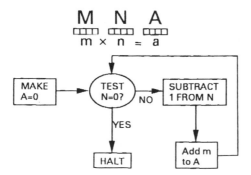

Figure 37.1 Program for multiplying. One begins the multiplication by putting a representation of the numbers m and n, the numbers to be multiplied, in registers M and N. At the end of the computation the answer, a, will be found in register A. See the text for a description of how the program works.

by giving the program or the information flow diagram for the multiplier. But if certain components of the multiplier—say, the gates of which the adder is composed—are primitive, then it is not the cognitive scientist's business to answer the question of how such a gate works. The cognitive scientist can say, "That question belongs in another discipline, electronic circuit theory." We must distinguish the question of *how something works* from the question of *what it does*. The question of *what* a primitive processor does is part of cognitive science, but the question of *how* it does it is not.

This idea can be made a bit clearer by looking at how a primitive processor actually works. The example will involve a common type of computer adder, simplified so as to handle only one-digit addends.

To understand this example, you need to know the following simple facts about binary notation: 0 and 1 are represented alike in binary and normal (decimal) notation, but the binary representation that corresponds to decimal 2 is 10.[1] Our adder will solve the following four problems:

$0 + 0 = 0$

$1 + 0 = 1$

$0 + 1 = 1$

$1 + 1 = 10$

The first three equations are true in both binary and decimal, but the last is true only if understood in binary.

The second item of background information is the notion of a *gate*. An *and* gate is a device that accepts two inputs and emits a single output. If both inputs are 1s, the output is a 1; otherwise, the output is a 0. An *exclusive or* gate is a "difference detector": it emits a 0 if its inputs are the same ($1, 1$ or $0, 0$), and it emits a 1 if its inputs are different ($1, 0$ or $0, 1$).

This talk of 1 and 0 is a way of thinking about the "bistable" states of computer representers. These representers are made so that they are always in one or the other of two states, and only momentarily in between. (This is what it is to be bistable.) The states might be a 4-volt and a 7-volt potential. If the two input states of a gate are the same (say, 4 volts), and the output is the same as well (4 volts), and if every other combination of inputs yields the 7-volt output, than the gate is an *and* gate, and the 4-volt state realizes 1. A different type of *and* gate might be made so that the 7-volt state realized 1. The point is that 1 is conventionally assigned to whatever bistable physical state of an *and* gate it is that has the role described in the sentence before last. And all that counts about an *and* gate from a computational point of view is its input-output function, not how it works or whether 4 volts or 7 volts realizes 1. Note the terminology: one speaks of a physically described state (4-volt potential) as "realizing" a computationally described state (having the value *1*). This distinction between the computational and physical levels of description will be important in what follows.

The adder works as follows. The two digits to be added are connected both to an *and* gate and to an *exclusive or* gate as illustrated in figures 37.2a and 37.2b. Let's look first at figure 37.2a. The digits to be added are *1* and *0*, and they are placed in the input register, which is the top pair of boxes. The *exclusive or* gate, which is a difference detector, sees different things and therefore outputs a *1* to the rightmost box of the answer register, which is the bottom pair of boxes. The *and* gate outputs a *0* except when it sees two *1*s, and so it outputs a *0*. In this way, the circuit computes 1 + 0 = 1. For this problem, as for 0 + 1 = 1 and 0 + 0 = 0, the *exclusive or* gate does all the real work. The role of the *and* gate in this circuit is *carrying*, and that is illustrated in figure 37.2b. The digits to be added, *1* and *1*, are again placed in the top register. Now, both inputs to the *and* gate are *1*s, and so the *and* gate outputs a *1* to the leftmost box of the answer (bottom) register. The *exclusive or* gate makes the rightmost box a *0*, and so we have the correct answer, *10*.

The borders between scientific disciplines are notoriously fuzzy. No one can say exactly where chemistry stops and physics begins. Since the line between the upper levels of processors and the level of primitive processors is the same as the line between cognitive science and one of the "realization" sciences such as electronics or physiology, the boundary of the level of primitives will have the same fuzziness. Nonetheless, in this example it seems clear that it is the gates that are the primitive processors. They are the largest components whose operation must be explained, not in terms of cognitive science, but rather in terms of electronics or mechanics or some other realization science. That is,

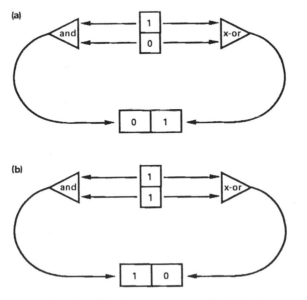

Figure 37.2 (a) Adder doing 1 + 0 = 1. (b) Adder doing 1 + 1 = 10.

assuming that the gates are made in the common manner described in the next section. It would be *possible* to make an adder each of whose gates was a *whole computer*, with its own multipliers, adders, and normal gates. It would be silly to waste a whole computer on such a simple task as that of an *and* gate, but it could be done. In that case the real level of primitives would be, not the gates of the original adder, but rather the (normal) gates of the component computers.

Primitive processors are the only computational devices for which *behaviorism is true*. Two primitive processors (such as gates) count as computationally equivalent if they have the same input-output function (that is, the same behavior), even if one works hydraulically and the other electrically. But computational equivalence of *non*primitive devices is not to be understood in this way. Consider two multipliers that work via different programs. Both accept inputs and emit outputs only in decimal notation. One, however, converts inputs to binary, does the computation in binary, and then converts back to decimal. The other does the computation directly in decimal. These are not computationally equivalent multipliers despite their identical input-output functions.

What is the functional analysis of the human mind? What are its primitive processors? These are the questions that functional analysis of human intelligence aims at.

The Mental and the Biological

One type of electrical *and* gate consists of two circuits with switches arranged as in figure 37.3. The switches on the left are the inputs. When only one or neither of the input switches is closed, nothing happens, because the circuit on the left is not completed. Only when both switches are closed does the electromagnet go on, and that pulls the switch on the right closed, thereby turning on the circuit on the right. (The circuit on the right is only partially illustrated.) In this example a switch being closed realizes *1*; it is the bistable state that obtains as an output if and only if two of them are present as an input.

Another *and* gate is illustrated in figure 37.4. If neither of the mice on the left (mouse₁ and mouse₂) is released into the part of their cages that have the cheese, or if only one of the mice is released, the cat does

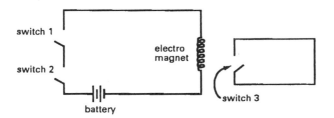

Figure 37.3 Electrical *and* gate.

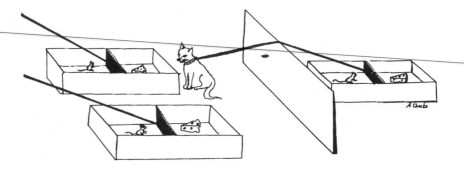

Figure 37.4 Cat and mouse *and* gate.

not strain hard enough to pull the leash. But when both mouse$_1$ and mouse$_2$ are released into the cheese part and are thereby visible to the cat, the cat strains enough to lift mouse$_3$'s gate, letting it into the cheese part of its box. So we have a situation in which a mouse getting cheese is output if and only if two cases of mice getting cheese are input.

The point illustrated here is the irrelevance of hardware realization to computational description. These gates work in very different ways, but they are nonetheless computationally equivalent. And of course, it is possible to think of an indefinite variety of other ways of making a primitive *and* gate. How such gates work is no more part of the domain of cognitive science than is the nature of the buildings that hold computer factories. This reveals a sense in which the computer model of the mind is profoundly *unbiological*. We are beings who have a useful and interesting biological level of description, but the computer model of the mind aims for a level of description of the mind that abstracts away from the biological realizations of cognitive structures. As far as the computer model goes, it does not matter whether our gates are realized in gray matter (which is actually gray only when preserved in a bottle), switches, or cats and mice.

Of course, this is not to say that the computer model is in any way incompatible with a biological approach. Indeed, cooperation between the biological and computational approaches is vital to *discovering* the program of the brain. Suppose one were presented with a computer of alien design and set the problem of ascertaining its program by any means possible. Only a fool would choose to ignore information to be gained by opening the computer up to see how its circuits work. No doubt, one would put information at the program level together with information at the electronic level, and likewise, in finding the program of the human mind, one can expect biological and cognitive approaches to complement one another.

Nonetheless, the computer model of the mind has a built-in antibiological bias, in the following sense. If the computer model is right, we should be able to create intelligent machines in our image—our *computational* image, that is. If we can do this, we will naturally feel that the most compelling theory of the mind is one that is general enough to apply to both them and us, and this will be a computational theory, not a biological theory. A biological theory of the *human* mind will not apply to these machines, though the biological theory will have a complementary advantage: namely, such a biological theory will encompass us together with our less intelligent biological cousins and thus provide a different kind of insight into the nature of human intelligence.

It is an open empirical question whether or not the computer model of the mind is correct. Only if it is *not* correct could it be said that psychology, the science of the mind, is a *biological* science. I make this obvious and trivial point to counter the growing trend toward supposing that the fact that we have brains that have a biological nature shows that psychology is a biological science.

Intelligence and Intentionality

Our discussion so far has centered on computer models of one aspect of the mind, intelligence. But there is a different aspect of the mind that we have not yet discussed, one that has a very different relation to the computer model—namely, intentionality.

For our purposes, we can take intelligence to be a capacity, a capacity to do various intelligent activities such as solving mathematics problems, deciding whether to go to graduate school, and figuring out how spaghetti is made.

Intentionality is aboutness. It is the property possessed most clearly by mental states or events such as beliefs, thoughts, or "cognitive perception" (for instance, seeing that there is a cat on the sofa). Intentional states represent the world as being a certain way. For example, a thought might represent an earthquake as having an intensity of 6.1 on the Richter scale. If so, we say that the *intentional content* of the thought is *that the earthquake has an intensity of 6.1 on the Richter scale.* A single intentional content can have very different behavioral effects, depending on its relation to the person who has the content. For example, the fear that there will be nuclear war might inspire one to work for disarmament, but the belief that there will be nuclear war might influence one to emigrate to Australia. (Don't let the spelling mislead you: intending is only one kind of intentional state. Believing and desiring are others.) Intentionality is an important feature of many mental states, but it is controversial whether it is "the mark of the mental." Pain, for example, would seem to be a mental state that has no intentional content.

The features of thought just mentioned are closely related to features of language. Thoughts represent, are about things, and can be true or false; and the same is true of sentences. The sentence *Bruce Springsteen was born in the USSR* is about Springsteen, represents him as having been born in the Soviet Union, and is false. In the light of this similarity between the mental and the linguistic, it is natural to try to reduce two problems to one problem by reducing the content of thought to the content of language or conversely.

Before we go any further, let's try to see more clearly just what the difference is between intelligence and intentionality. That there is such a distinction should be clear to anyone who attends to the matter, but the precise nature of the distinction is controversial.

One way to get a handle on the distinction between intelligence and intentionality is to note that in the opinion of many writers on this topic, it is possible to have intentionality without intelligence. Thus, John McCarthy (1980) (the creator of the artificial intelligence language LISP) holds that thermostats have intentional states in virtue of their capacity to represent and control temperature. And there is a school of thought that assigns content to tree rings in virtue of their representing the age of the tree. But no school of thought holds that the tree rings are actually intelligent. An intelligent system must have certain intelligent capacities, capacities to do certain sorts of things, and tree rings can't do these things.[2]

Moreover, there can be intelligence without intentionality. Imagine that an event with negligible (but importantly, nonzero) probability occurs: in their random movement, particles from the swamp come together and by chance result in a molecule-for-molecule duplicate of you. The swamp creature will have all the capacities (behavioral capacities) that you have, and they will be produced by the same sort of physiological processes as occur in you. So it will arguably be intelligent. But there are reasons for denying that it has the intentional states that you have, and indeed, for denying that it has any intentional states at all. The swamp creature says, as you do, "Gorbachev influenced Thatcher on his trip to England." But unlike you, it has never seen Gorbachev or Thatcher (or anything else) on TV, or read about them in the papers. (It was created only seconds ago.) The swamp creature has had no causal contact of any sort with them or with any case of anyone meeting or influencing anyone. No signals from the Soviet Union or Britain have reached it in any way, no matter how indirectly. Its utterance is not in any way causally affected by Gorbachev, Thatcher, or England, or by Gorbachevian or Thatcherian or English states of the world, so how can it be regarded as being *about* Gorbachev or Thatcher or England? The swamp creature is simply mouthing words. Had its molecules come together slightly differently, it would be uttering "Envelopes sir tattoo Eisenhower on Neptune." Much more must be said to be convincing on this point, but I hope you can see the shape of the case to be made that the swamp creature has intelligence without intentionality.

The upshot is this: what makes a system intelligent is what it can do. What makes a system an intentional system is a matter of its states' representing the world—that is, having aboutness. Even if you are not convinced that either can exist without the other, you can still agree that intelligence and intentionality are very different kettles of fish.

Now let's see what the difference between intelligence and intentionality has to do with the computer model of the mind. Notice that the method of functional analysis that explains intelligent processes by reducing them to unintelligent mechanical processes *does not explain intentionality*. The parts of an intentional system can be just as intentional as the whole system. (See Fodor 1981 on Dennett on this point.) In particular, the component processors of an intentional system can manipulate symbols that are about just the same things that the symbols manipulated by the whole system are about. Recall that the multiplier of figure 37.1 was explained via a decomposition into devices that add, subtract, and the like. The multiplier's states were intentional in that they were about numbers. The states of the adder, subtractor, and so on, are also about numbers and are thus similarly intentional.

There is, however, an important relation between intentionality and functional decomposition. The level of primitive processors is the *lowest intentional level*. That is, though the inputs and outputs of primitive processors are about things, primitive processors do not contain any parts that have states that are themselves about anything. That is why the internal operation of primitive processors is in the domain of a "realization" science (such as electronics or physiology) rather than in the domain of cognitive science.

The explication of intentionality is more controversial (this is an understatement) than the explication of intelligence, but one aspect of the matter is relatively straightforward, namely, the explication of rational *relations* among intentional states. It is widely (but not universally) agreed that part of what it is for a state to have a certain intentional content is for it to have certain relations to other contentful states. Thus, if a person makes claims of the form "If x then y," but infers from this conditional and y to x, and never from the conditional and x to y, other things being equal it would be reasonable to conclude that the person's claims of this form do not express beliefs to the effect that if x, then y. Let us explore the computer model of the mind's approach to relations among intentional states by returning to the adder depicted in figures 37.2a and 37.2b. The cognitive science account of these rational relations among intentional states hinges on the idea of the brain as a syntactic engine, which is the topic of the next section.

The Brain as a Syntactic Engine Driving a Semantic Engine

To see the idea of the brain as a syntactic engine, it is important to see the difference between the number 1 and the symbol (in this case a numeral or digit) *1*. (Note the use of roman type in referring to the number and italics in referring to the symbol.) Certainly, the difference between the city, Boston, and the word *Boston* is clear enough. The former has bad drivers in it; the latter has no people or cars at all but does have six letters. No one would confuse a city with a word, but the distinction may seem less clear in the case of a symbol denoting a number and the number itself. The point to keep in mind is that many different symbols can denote the same number (say, *II* in Roman numerals and *two* in alphabetical writing), and one symbol can denote different numbers in different counting systems (as *10* denotes one number in binary and another in decimal).

With this distinction in mind, we can see an important difference between the multiplier and the adder discussed earlier. The algorithm used by the multiplier in figure 37.1 is *notation-independent*: "Multiply the number n by the number m by adding n to itself m times" works in any notation. And the program described for implementing this algorithm is also notation-independent. As we saw in the description of this program, the program depends on the properties of the numbers represented, not the representations themselves. By contrast, the internal operation of the adder described in figures 37.2a and 37.2b depends on binary notation, and its description speaks of numerals (note the italic type). Recall that the adder exploits the fact that an *exclusive or* gate detects differences, yielding a *1* when its inputs are different digits, and a *0* when its inputs are the same digits. This gate gives the right answer all by itself so long as no carrying is involved. The trick used by the *exclusive or* gate depends on the fact that when we add two digits of the same type (*1* and *1* or *0* and *0*), the rightmost digit of the answer is the same. This is true in binary, but not in other standard notations.

The inputs and outputs of the adder must be seen as referring to numbers. One way to see this is to note that otherwise one could not see the multiplier as exploiting an algorithm involving multiplying numbers by adding numbers. But once we go inside the adder, we must see the binary states as referring to the *symbols themselves*. This fact gives us an interesting additional characterization of primitive processors. Typically, as we functionally decompose a computational system, we reach a point where there is a shift of subject matter from things in the world to the symbols themselves. The inputs and outputs of the adder and multiplier refer to numbers, but the inputs and outputs of the gates refer to numerals. Typically, this shift occurs when we have reached the level of primitive processors. The operation of the higher-level components such as the multiplier can be explained in two ways: (1) in terms of a program or algorithm manipulating numbers, or (2) in terms of the functional decomposition into networks of gates manipulating numerals. But the operation of the gates cannot be explained in terms of number manipulation; it must be explained in symbolic terms (or at lower levels—say, in terms of electromagnets). At the most basic computational level, computers are symbol-crunchers, and for this reason the computer model of the mind is often described as the symbol manipulation view of the mind.

Seeing the adder as a syntactic engine driving a semantic engine requires noting two functions: one maps numbers onto other numbers, and the other maps symbols onto other symbols. The symbol function is concerned with the numerals as symbols—without attention to their meanings. Here is the symbol function:

0, 0 → 0

0, 1 → 1

1, 0 → 1

1, 1 → 10

This symbol function is mirrored by a function that maps the numbers represented by the numerals on the left onto the numbers represented by the numerals on the right. This function will thus map numbers onto numbers. We can speak of this function that maps numbers onto numbers as the *semantic* function (semantics being the study of meaning), since it is concerned with the meanings of the symbols, not the symbols themselves. (It is important not to confuse the notion of a semantic function in this sense with a function that maps symbols onto what they refer to.) Here is the semantic function (in decimal notation— we must choose *some* notation to express a semantic function):

0, 0 → 0

0, 1 → 1

1, 0 → 1

1, 1 → 2

Notice that the two specifications just given differ in that the first maps italicized entities onto other italicized entities. The second has no italics. The first function maps symbols onto symbols; the second function maps the numbers referred to by the arguments of the first function onto the numbers referred to by the values of the first function. (A function maps arguments onto values.) The first function is a kind of linguistic "reflection" of the second.

The key idea behind the adder is that of a correlation between these two functions. The designer has joined together (1) a meaningful notation (binary notation), (2) symbolic manipulations in that notation, and (3) rational relations among the meanings of the symbols. The symbolic manipulations correspond to useful rational relations among the meanings of the symbols—namely, the relations of addition. The useful relations among the meanings are captured by the semantic function above, and the corresponding symbolic relations are the ones described in the symbolic function above. It is the correlation between these two functions that explains how it is that a device that manipulates symbols manages to add numbers.

Now the idea of the brain as a syntactic engine driving a semantic engine is just a generalization of this picture to a wider class of symbolic activities, namely, the symbolic activities of human thought. The idea is that we have symbolic structures in our brains, and that nature has seen to it that there are correlations between causal interactions among these structures and rational relations among the meanings of the symbolic structures. The primitive mechanical processors "know" only the "syntactic" form of the symbols they process (for instance, what strings of zeros and ones they see), and not what the symbols mean. Nonetheless, these meaning-blind primitive processors control processes that "make sense"—processes of decision, problem solving, and the like. In short, there is a correlation between the meanings of our internal representations and their forms. And this explains how it is that our syntactic engine can drive our semantic engine.[3]

The last paragraph referred to a correlation between causal interactions among symbolic structures in our brains and rational relations among the meanings of the symbol structures. This way of speaking can be misleading if it encourages the picture of the neuroscientist opening the brain, just *seeing* the symbols, and then figuring out what they mean. Such a picture inverts the order of discovery and gives the wrong impression of what makes something a symbol.

The way to discover symbols in the brain is to first map out rational relations among states of mind and then identify aspects of these states that can be thought of as symbolic in virtue of their functions. Function is what gives a symbol its identity, even the symbols in English orthography, though this can be hard to appreciate because these functions have been made rigid by habit and convention. In reading unfamiliar handwriting, we may notice an unorthodox symbol, someone's weird way of writing a letter of the alphabet. How do we know which letter of the alphabet it is? By its function! Th% function of a symbol is som%thing on% can appr%ciat% by s%%ing how it app%ars in s%nt%nc%s containing familiar words whos% m%anings w% can gu%ss. You will have little trouble figuring out, on this basis, what letter in the last sentence was replaced by %. . . .

Notes

I am grateful to Susan Carey, Jerry Fodor, and Stephen White for comments on an earlier draft. This work was supported by the National Science Foundation grant DIR8812559.

1. The rightmost digit in binary (as in familiar decimal) is the 1s place. The second digit from the right is the 2s place (corresponding to the 10s place in decimal). Next is the 4s place (that is, 2 squared), just as the corresponding place in decimal is the 10 squared place.

2. I should mention that functionalists (including myself) are more skeptical than proponents of the views just mentioned about the possibility of intentionality without intelligence. The functionalist point of view will be explained later.

3. The idea described here was first articulated to my knowledge in Fodor 1975, 1980. See also Dennett 1981, to which the terms *syntactic engine* and *semantic engine* are due and Newell 1980. More on this topic can be found in Dennett 1987 by looking up *syntactic engine* and *semantic engine* in the index.

References

Cummins, R. C. (1975). Functional analysis. *Journal of Philosophy* 72, 741–765.

Dennett, D. C. (1974). Why the law of effect will not go away. *Journal for the Theory of Social Behavior.* 5, 169–187.

Dennett, D. C. (1981). Three kinds of intentional psychology. In R. Healy, ed., *Reduction, time and reality.* Cambridge: Cambridge University Press.

Dennett, D. C. (1987). *The intentional stance.* Cambridge, MA: MIT Press.

Fodor, J. A. (1968). The appeal to tacit knowledge in psychological explanation. *Journal of Philosophy* 65, 627–640.

Fodor, J. A. (1975). *The language of thought.* New York: Crowell.

Fodor, J. A. (1980). Methodological solipsism considered as a research strategy in cognitive psychology. *Behavioral and Brain Sciences* 3, 417–424.

Fodor, J. A. (1981). Three cheers for propositional attitudes. In J. A. Fodor, *Representations.* Cambridge, MA: MIT Press.

McCarthy, J. (1980). Beliefs, machines and theories. *Behavioral and Brain Sciences* 3, 435.

Newell, A. (1980). Physical symbol systems. *Cognitive Science* 4, 135–183.

The Critique of Cognitive Reason

John R. Searle

Introduction: The Shaky Foundations of Cognitive Science

For over a decade, really since the beginnings of the discipline, I have been a practicing "cognitive scientist." In this period I have seen much valuable work and progress in the field. However, as a discipline, cognitive science suffers from the fact that several of its most cherished foundational assumptions are mistaken. It is possible to do good work on the basis of false assumptions, but it is more difficult than need be; and in this chapter I want to expose and refute some of those false assumptions. They derive from the pattern of mistakes that I described earlier.

Not everybody in cognitive science agrees on the foundational principles, but there are certain general features of the mainstream that deserve a separate statement. If I were a mainstream cognitive scientist, here is what I would say:

Neither the study of the brain as such nor the study of consciousness as such is of much interest and importance to cognitive science. The cognitive mechanisms we study are indeed implemented in the brain, and some of them find a surface expression in the consciousness, but our interest is in the intermediate level where the actual cognitive processes are inaccessible to consciousness. Though in fact implemented in the brain, they could have been implemented in an indefinite number of hardware systems. Brains are there, but inessential. The processes which explain cognition are unconscious not only in fact, but in principle. For example, Chomsky's rules of universal grammar (1986), or Marr's rules of vision (1982), or Fodor's language of thought (1975) are not the sort of phenomena that could become conscious. Furthermore, these processes are all computational. The basic assumption behind cognitive science is that the brain is a computer and mental processes are computational. For that reason many of us think that artificial intelligence (AI) is the heart of cognitive science. There is some dispute among us as to whether or not the brain is a digital computer

From J. Searle, *The rediscovery of the mind* (1992). Cambridge, MA: MIT Press. Reprinted by permission.

of the old-fashioned von Neumann variety or whether it is a connectionist machine. Some of us, in fact, manage to have our cake and eat it too on this question, because we think the serial processes in the brain are implemented by a parallel connectionist system (e.g., Hobbs 1990). But nearly all of us agree on the following: Cognitive mental processes are unconscious; they are, for the most part, unconscious in principle, and they are computational.

I disagree with just about every substantive claim made in the previous paragraph, and I have already criticized some of them in earlier chapters, most notably the claim that there are mental states that are deep unconscious. The main aim of this chapter is to criticize certain aspects of the computational claim.

I think it will help explain what makes the research program seem so implausible to me if we nail the question down to a concrete example right away: In AI great claims have been made for programs run on SOAR.[1] Strictly speaking, SOAR is a type of computer architecture and not a program, but programs implemented on SOAR are regarded as promising examples of AI. One of these is embodied in a robot that can move blocks on command. So, for example, the robot will respond appropriately to the command "Pick up a cube-shaped block and move it three spaces to the left." To do this, it has both optical sensors and robot arms, and the system works because it implements a set of formal symbol manipulations that are connected to transducers that receive inputs from the optical sensors and send outputs to the motor mechanisms. But my problem is: What has all that got to do with actual human behavior? We know for example many of the details about how a human being does it in real life. First, she must be *conscious*. Furthermore she must *hear and understand* the order. She must *consciously see* the blocks, she must *decide* to carry out the command, and then she must perform the *conscious voluntary intentional action* of moving the blocks. Notice that these claims all support counterfactuals: for example, no consciousness, no movement of blocks. Also we know that all this mental stuff is caused by and realized in the neurophysiology. So before we ever get started on computer modeling, we know that there are two sets of levels: mental levels, many of them conscious, and neurophysiological levels.

Now where are the formal symbol manipulations supposed to fit into this picture? This is a fundamental foundational question in cognitive science, but you would be amazed at how little attention is paid to it. The absolutely crucial question for any computer model is, "How *exactly* does the model relate to the reality being modeled?" But unless you read skeptical critics like the present author, you will find very little discussion of this issue. The general answer, which is supposed to evade the demand for more detailed specific answers, is that between the level of intentionality in the human (what Newell [1982] calls "the knowledge level") and the various neurophysiological levels, there is an intermediate level of formal symbol manipulation. Now our question is, empirically speaking, what could that possibly mean?

If you read books about the brain (say, Shepherd 1983; or Bloom and Lazerson 1988), you get a certain picture of what is going on in the brain. If you then turn to books about computation (say, Boolos and Jeffrey 1989), you get a picture of the logical structure of the theory of computation. If you then turn to books about cognitive science (say, Pylyshyn 1984), they tell you that what the brain books describe is really the same as what the computation books were describing. Philosophically speaking, this does not smell right to me and I have learned, at least at the beginning of an investigation, to follow my sense of smell.

Strong AI, Weak AI, and Cognitivism

The basic idea of the computer model of the mind is that the mind is the program and the brain the hardware of a computational system. A slogan one often sees is: "The mind is to the brain as the program is to the hardware."[2]

Let us begin our investigation of this claim by distinguishing three questions:

1. Is the brain a digital computer?

2. Is the mind a computer program?

3. Can the operations of the brain be simulated on a digital computer?

In this chapter, I will be addressing 1, and not 2 or 3. In earlier writings (Searle 1980a, 1980b, and 1984), I have given a negative answer to 2. Because programs are defined purely formally or syntactically, and because minds have an intrinsic mental content, it follows immediately that the program by itself cannot constitute the mind. The formal syntax of the program does not by itself guarantee the presence of mental contents. I showed this a decade ago in the Chinese room argument (Searle 1980b). A computer, me for example, could run the steps in the program for some mental capacity, such as understanding Chinese, without understanding a word of Chinese. The argument rests on the simple logical truth that syntax is not the same as, nor is it by itself sufficient for, semantics. So the answer to the second question is demonstrably "No."

The answer to 3 seems to me equally demonstrably "Yes," at least on a natural interpretation. That is, naturally interpreted, the question means: Is there some description of the brain such that under that description you could do a computational simulation of the operations of the brain. But given Church's thesis that anything that can be given a precise enough characterization as a set of steps can be simulated on a digital computer, it follows trivially that the question has an affirmative answer. The operations of the brain can be simulated on a digital computer in the same sense in which weather systems, the behavior of the New York stock market, or the pattern of airline flights over Latin America can. So our question is not, "Is the mind a program?" The answer to that is, "No." Nor is it, "Can the brain be simulated?" The answer to that is, "Yes." The question is, "Is the brain a digital computer?" And for purposes of this discussion, I am taking that question as equivalent to "Are brain processes computational?"

One might think that this question would lose much of its interest if question 2 receives a negative answer. That is, one might suppose that unless the mind is a program, there is no interest to the question of whether the brain is a computer. But that is not really the case. Even for those who agree that programs by themselves are not constitutive of mental phenomena, there is still an important question: Granted that there is more to the mind than the syntactical operations of the digital computer; nonetheless, it might be the case that mental states are *at least* computational states, and mental processes are computational processes operating over the formal structure of these mental states. This, in fact, seems to me the position taken by a fairly large number of people.

I am not saying that the view is fully clear, but the idea is something like this: At some level of description, brain processes are syntactical; there are so to speak, "sentences in the head." These need not be sentences in English or Chinese, but perhaps in the "language of thought" (Fodor 1975). Now, like any sentences, they have a syntactical structure and a semantics or meaning, and the problem of syntax can be separated from the problem of semantics. The problem of semantics is: How do these sentences in the head get their meanings? But that question can be discussed independently of the question: How does the brain work in processing these sentences? A typical answer to that latter question is: The brain works as a digital computer performing computational operations over the syntactical structure of sentences in the head.

Just to keep the terminology straight, I call the view that all there is to having a mind is having a program, Strong AI, the view that brain processes (and mental processes) can be simulated computationally, Weak AI, and the view that the brain is a digital computer, cognitivism. This chapter is about cognitivism.

The Primal Story

Earlier I gave a preliminary statement of the assumptions of mainstream cognitive science, and now I want to continue by trying to state as strongly as I can why cognitivism has seemed intuitively appealing. There is a story about the relation of human intelligence to computation that goes back at least to Turing's classic paper (1950), and I believe it is the foundation of the cognitivist view. I will call it the primal story:

We begin with two results in mathematical logic, the Church-Turing thesis and Turing's theorem. For our purposes, the Church-Turing thesis states that for any algorithm there is some Turing machine that can implement that algorithm. Turing's thesis says that there is a universal Turing machine that can simulate any Turing machine. Now if we put these two together, we have the result that a universal Turing machine can implement any algorithm whatever.

But now, why was this result so exciting? Well, what made it send shivers up and down the spines of a whole generation of young workers in artificial intelligence was the following thought: Suppose the brain is a universal Turing machine.

Well, are there any good reasons for supposing the brain might be a universal Turing machine? Let us continue with the primal story:

It is clear that at least some human mental abilities are algorithmic. For example, I can consciously do long division by going through the steps of an algorithm for solving long-division problems. It is furthermore a consequence of the Church-Turing thesis and Turing's theorem that anything a human can do algorithmically can be done on a universal Turing machine. I can implement, for example, the very same algorithm that I use for long division on a digital computer. In such a case, as described by Turing (1950), both I, the human computer, and the mechanical computer are implementing the same algorithm. I am doing it consciously, the mechanical computer nonconsciously. Now it seems reasonable to suppose that there might be a whole lot of other mental processes going on in my brain nonconsciously that are also computational. And if so, we could find out how the brain works by simulating these very processes on a digital computer. Just as we got a computer simulation of the processes for doing long division, so we could get a computer simulation of the processes for understanding language, visual perception, categorization, etc.

"But what about the semantics? After all, programs are purely syntactical." Here another set of logico-mathematical results comes into play in the primal story:

The development of proof theory showed that within certain well-known limits the semantic relations between propositions can be entirely mirrored by the syntactic relations between the sentences that express those propositions. Now suppose that mental contents in the head are expressed syntactically in the head, then all we would need to account for mental processes would be computational processes between the syntactical elements in the head. If we get the proof theory right, the semantics will take care of itself; and that is what computers do: they implement the proof theory.[3]

We thus have a well-defined research program. We try to discover the programs being implemented in the brain by programming computers to implement the same programs. We do this in turn by getting the mechanical computer to match the performance of the human computer (i.e., to pass the Turing test) and then getting the psychologists to look for evidence that the internal processes are the same in the two types of computer.

In what follows I would like the reader to keep this primal story in mind. Notice especially Turing's contrast between the conscious implementation of the program by the human computer and the nonconscious implementation of the program, whether by the brain or by the mechanical computer. Notice also the idea that we might *discover* programs running in nature, the very same programs that we put into our mechanical computers.

If one looks at the books and articles supporting cognitivism, one finds certain common assumptions, often unstated, but nonetheless pervasive.

First, it is often assumed that the only alternative to the view that the brain is a digital computer is some form of dualism. I have discussed the reasons for this urge earlier. Rhetorically speaking, the idea is to bully the reader into thinking that unless he accepts the idea that the brain is some kind of computer, he is committed to some weird antiscientific views.

Second, it is also assumed that the question of whether brain processes are computational is just a plain empirical question. It is to be settled by factual investigation in the same way that such questions as whether the heart is a pump or whether green leaves do photosynthesis were settled as matters of fact. There is no room for logic chopping or conceptual analysis, because we are talking about matters of hard scientific fact. Indeed, I think many people who work in this field would doubt that the question I am addressing is an appropriate philosophic question at all. "Is the brain really a digital computer?" is no more a philosophical question than "Is the neurotransmitter at neuromuscular junctions really acetylcholene?"

Even people who are unsympathetic to cognitivism, such as Penrose (1989) and Dreyfus (1972), seem to treat it as a straightforward factual issue. They do not seem to be worried about the question of what sort of claim it might be that they are doubting. But I am puzzled by the question: What sort of fact about the brain could constitute its being a computer?

Third, another stylistic feature of this literature is the haste and sometimes even carelessness with which the foundational questions are glossed over. What exactly are the anatomical and physiological features of brains that are being discussed? What exactly is a digital computer? And how are the answers to these two questions supposed to connect? The usual procedure in these books and articles is to make a few remarks about 0's and 1's, give a popular summary of the Church-Turing thesis, and then get on with the more exciting things such as computer achievements and failures. To my surprise, in reading this literature I have found that there seems to be a peculiar philosophical hiatus. On the one hand, we have a very elegant set of mathematical results ranging from Turing's theorem to Church's thesis to recursive function theory. On the other hand, we have an impressive set of electronic devices that we use every day. Since we have such advanced mathematics and such good electronics, we assume that somehow somebody must have done the basic philosophical work of connecting the mathematics to the electronics. But as far as I can tell, that is not the case. On the contrary, we are in a peculiar situation where there is little theoretical agreement among the practitioners on such absolutely fundamental questions as, What exactly is a digital computer? What exactly is a symbol? What exactly is an algorithm? What exactly is a computational process? Under what physical conditions exactly are two systems implementing the same program?

The Definition of Computation

As there is no universal agreement on the fundamental questions, I believe it is best to go back to the sources, back to the original definitions given by Alan Turing.

According to Turing, a Turing machine can carry out certain elementary operations: It can rewrite a 0 on its tape as a 1, it can rewrite a 1 on its tape as a 0, it can shift the tape 1 square to the left, or it can shift the tape 1 square to the right. It is controlled by a program of instructions and each instruction specifies a condition and an action to be carried out if the condition is satisfied.

That is the standard definition of computation, but, taken literally, it is at least a bit misleading. If you open up your home computer, you are most unlikely to find any 0's and 1's or even a tape. But this does not really matter for the definition. To find out if an object is really a digital computer, it turns out that we do not actually have to look for 0's and 1's, etc.; rather we just have to look for something that we could *treat as* or *count as* or that *could be used to* function as 0's and 1's. Furthermore, to make the matter more puzzling, it turns out that this machine could be made out of just about anything. As Johnson-Laird says, "It could be made out of cogs and levers like an old fashioned mechanical calculator; it could be made out of a hydraulic system through which water flows; it could be made out of transistors etched into a silicon chip through which electric current flows; it could even be carried out by the brain. Each of these machines uses a different medium to represent binary symbols. The positions of cogs, the presence or absence of water, the level of the voltage and perhaps nerve impulses" (Johnson-Laird 1988, 39).

Similar remarks are made by most of the people who write on this topic. For example, Ned Block (1990) shows how we can have electrical gates where the 1's and 0's are assigned to voltage levels of 4 volts and 7 volts respectively. So we might think that we should go and look for voltage levels. But Block tells us that 1 is only "conventionally" assigned to a certain voltage level. The situation grows more puzzling when he informs us further that we need not use electricity at all, but we can use an elaborate system of cats and mice and cheese and make our gates in such as way that the cat will strain at the leash and pull open a gate that we can also treat as if it were a 0 or a 1. The point, as Block is anxious to insist, is "the irrelevance of hardware realization to computational description. These gates work in different ways but they are nonetheless computationally equivalent" (p. 260). In the same vein, Pylyshyn says that a computational sequence could be realized by "a group of pigeons trained to peck as a Turing machine!" (1984, 57)

But now if we are trying to take seriously the idea that the brain is a digital computer, we get the uncomfortable result that we could make a system that does just what the brain does out of pretty much anything. Computationally speaking, on this view, you can make a "brain" that functions just like yours and mine out of cats and mice and cheese or levers or water pipes or pigeons or anything else provided the two systems are, in Block's sense, "computationally equivalent." You would just need an awful lot of cats, or pigeons or water pipes, or whatever it might be. The proponents of cognitivism report this result with sheer and unconcealed delight. But I think they ought to be worried about it, and I am going to try to show that it is just the tip of a whole iceberg of problems.

First Difficulty: Syntax Is Not Intrinsic to Physics

Why are the defenders of computationalism not worried by the implications of multiple realizability? The answer is that they think it is typical of functional accounts that the same function admits of multiple realizations. In this respect, computers are just like carburetors and thermostats. Just as carburetors can be made of brass or steel, so computers can be made of an indefinite range of hardware materials.

But there is a difference: The classes of carburetors and thermostats are defined in terms of the production of certain *physical* effects. That is why, for example, nobody says you can make carburetors out of pigeons. But the class of computers is defined syntactically in terms of the *assignment* of 0's and 1's. The multiple realizability is a consequence not of the fact that the same physical effect can be achieved in different physical substances, but that the relevant properties are purely syntactical. The physics is irrelevant except in so far as it admits of the assignments of 0's and 1's and of state transitions between them.

But this has two consequences that might be disastrous:

1. The same principle that implies multiple realizability would seem to imply universal realizability. If computation is defined in terms of the assignment of syntax, then everything would be a digital computer, because any object whatever could have syntactical ascriptions made to it. You could describe anything in terms of 0's and 1's.

2. Worse yet, syntax is not intrinsic to physics. The ascription of syntactical properties is always relative to an agent or observer who treats certain physical phenomena as syntactical.

Now why exactly would these consequences be disastrous?

Well, we wanted to know how the brain works, specifically how it produces mental phenomena. And it would not answer that question to be told that the brain is a digital computer in the sense that stomach, liver, heart, solar system, and the state of Kansas are all digital computers. The model we had was that we might discover some fact about the operation of the brain that would show that it is a computer. We wanted to know if there was not some sense in which brains were *intrinsically* digital computers in a way that green leaves intrinsically perform photosynthesis or hearts intrinsically pump blood. It is not a matter of us arbitrarily or "conventionally" assigning the word "pump" to hearts or "photosynthesis" to leaves. There is an actual fact of the matter. And what we were asking is, "Is there in that way a fact of the matter about brains that would make them digital computers?" It does not answer that question to be told, yes, brains are digital computers because everything is a digital computer.

On the standard textbook definition of computation, it is hard to see how to avoid the following results:

1. For any object there is some description of that object such that under that description the object is a digital computer.

2. For any program and for any sufficiently complex object, there is some description of the object under which it is implementing the program. Thus for example the wall behind my back is right now implementing the Wordstar program, because there is some pattern of molecule movements that is isomorphic with the formal structure of Wordstar. But if the wall is implementing Wordstar, then if it is a big enough wall it is implementing any program, including any program implemented in the brain.

I think the main reason that the proponents do not see that multiple or universal realizability is a problem is that they do not see it as a consequence of a much deeper point, namely that "syntax" is not the name of a physical feature, like mass or gravity. On the contrary they talk of "syntactical engines" and even "semantic engines" as if such talk were like that of gasoline engines or diesel engines, as if it could be just a plain matter of fact that the brain or anything else is a syntactical engine.

I do not think that the problem of universal realizability is a serious one. I think it is possible to block the result of universal realizability by tightening up our definition of computation. Certainly we ought to respect the fact that programmers and engineers regard it as a quirk of Turing's original definitions and not as a real feature of computation. Unpublished works by Brian Smith, Vinod Goel, and John Batali all suggest that a more realistic definition of computation will emphasize such features as the causal relations among program states, programmability and controllability of the mechanism, and situatedness in the real world. All these will produce the result that the pattern is not enough. There must be a causal structure sufficient to warrant counterfactuals. But these further restrictions on the definition of computation are no help in the present discussion *because the really deep problem is that syntax is essentially an observer-relative notion. The multiple realizability of computationally equivalent processes in different physical media is not just a sign that the processes are abstract, but that they are not intrinsic to the system at all. They depend on an interpretation from outside.* We were looking for some facts of the matter that would make brain processes computational; but given the way we have defined computation, there never could be any such facts of the matter. We can't, on the one hand, say that anything is a digital computer if we can assign a syntax to it, and then suppose there is a factual question intrinsic to its physical operation whether or not a natural system such as the brain is a digital computer.

And if the word "syntax" seems puzzling, the same point can be stated without it. That is, someone might claim that the notions of "syntax" and "symbols" are just a manner of speaking and that what we are really interested in is the existence of systems with discrete physical phenomena and state transitions between them. On this view, we don't really need 0's and 1's; they are just a convenient shorthand. But, I believe, this move is no help. A physical state of a system is a computational state only relative to the assignment to that state of some computational role, function, or interpretation. The same problem arises without 0's and 1's because *notions such as computation, algorithm, and program do not name intrinsic physical features of systems.* Computational states are not *discovered within* the physics, they are *assigned to* the physics.

This is a different argument from the Chinese room argument, and I should have seen it ten years ago, but I did not. The Chinese room argument showed that semantics is not intrinsic to syntax. I am now making the separate and different point that syntax is not intrinsic to physics. For the purposes of the original argument, I was simply assuming that the syntactical characterization of the computer was unproblematic. But that is a mistake. There is no way you could discover that something is intrinsically a digital computer because the characterization of it as a digital computer is always relative to an observer who assigns a syntactical interpretation to the purely physical features of the system. As applied to the language of thought hypothesis, this has the consequence that the thesis is incoherent. There is no way you could discover that there are, intrinsically, unknown sentences in your head because something is a sentence only relative to some agent or user who uses it as a sentence. As applied to the computational model generally, the characterization of a process as computational is a characterization of a physical system from outside; and the identification of the process as computational does not identify an intrinsic feature of the physics; it is essentially an observer-relative characterization.

This point has to be understood precisely. I am not saying there are a priori limits on the patterns we could discover in nature. We could no doubt discover a pattern of events in my brain that was isomorphic to the implementation of the vi-editor program on my computer. But to say that something is *functioning as* a computational process is to say something more than that a pattern of physical events is occurring. It requires the assignment of a computational interpretation by some agent. Analogously, we might discover in nature objects that had the same sort of shape as chairs and that could therefore be used as chairs; but we could not discover objects in nature that were functioning as chairs, except relative to some agents who regarded them or used them as chairs.

To understand this argument fully, it is essential to understand the distinction between features of the world that are *intrinsic* and features that are *observer relative*. The expressions "mass," "gravitational attraction," and "molecule" name features of the world that are intrinsic. If all observers and users cease to exist, the world still contains mass, gravitational attraction, and molecules. But expressions such as "nice day for a picnic," "bathtub," and "chair" do not name intrinsic features of reality. Rather, they name objects by specifying some feature that has been assigned to them, some feature that is relative to observers and users. If there had never been any users or observers, there would still be mountains, molecules, masses, and gravitational attraction. But if there had never been any users or observers, there would be no such features as being a nice day for a picnic, or being a chair or a bathtub. The assignment of observer-relative features to intrinsic features of the world is not arbitrary. Some intrinsic features of the world facilitate their use as chairs and bathtubs, for example. But the feature of being a chair or a bathtub or a nice day for a picnic is a feature that only exists relative to users and observers. The point I am making here, and the essence of this argument, is that on the standard definitions of computation, computational features are observer relative. They are not intrinsic. The argument so far, then, can be summarized as follows:

The aim of natural science is to discover and characterize features that are intrinsic to the natural world. By its own definitions of computation and cognition, there is no way that computational cognitive science could ever be a natural science, because computation is not an intrinsic feature of the world. It is assigned relative to observers.[4] . . .

Further Difficulty: The Brain Does Not Do Information Processing

In this section I turn finally to what I think is, in some ways, the central issue in all of this, the issue of information processing. Many people in the "cognitive science" scientific paradigm will feel that much of my discussion is simply irrelevant, and they will argue against it as follows:

There is a difference between the brain and all of the other systems you have been describing, and this difference explains why a computational simulation in the case of the other systems is a mere simulation, whereas in the case of the brain a computational simulation is actually duplicating and not merely modeling the functional properties of the brain. The reason is that the brain, unlike these other systems, is an *information processing* system. And this fact about the brain is, in your words, "intrinsic." It is just a fact about biology that the brain functions to process information, and as we can also process the same information computationally, computational models of brain processes have a different role altogether from computational models of, for example, the weather.

So there is a well-defined research question: Are the computational procedures by which the brain processes information the same as the procedures by which computers process the same information?

What I just imagined an opponent saying embodies one of the worst mistakes in cognitive science. The mistake is to suppose that in the sense in which computers are used to process information, brains also process information. To see that that is a mistake contrast what goes on in the computer with what goes on in the brain. In the case of the computer, an outside agent encodes some information in a form that can be processed by the circuitry of the computer. That is, he or she provides a syntactical realization of the information that the computer can implement in, for example, different voltage levels. The computer then goes through a series of electrical stages that the outside agent can interpret both syntactically and semantically even though, of course, the hardware has no intrinsic syntax or semantics: It is all in the eye of the beholder. And the physics does not matter, provided only that you can get it to implement the algorithm. Finally, an output is produced in the form of physical phenomena, for example, a printout, which an observer can interpret as symbols with a syntax and a semantics.

But now contrast that with the brain. In the case of the brain, none of the relevant neurobiological processes are observer relative (though of course, like anything they can be described from an observer-relative point of view), and the specificity of the neurophysiology matters desperately. To make this difference clear, let us go through an example. Suppose I see a car coming toward me. A standard computational model of vision will take in information about the visual array on my retina and eventually print out the sentence, "There is a car coming toward me." But that is not what happens in the actual biology. In the biology a concrete and specific series of electrochemical reactions are set up by the assault of the photons on the photo receptor cells of my retina, and this entire process eventually results in a concrete visual experience. The biological reality is not that of a bunch of words or symbols being produced by the visual system; rather, it is a matter of a concrete specific conscious visual event—this very visual experience. That concrete visual event is as specific and as concrete as a hurricane or the digestion of a meal. We can, with the computer, make an information processing model of that event or of its production, as we can make an information processing model of the weather, digestion, or any other phenomenon, but the phenomena themselves are not thereby information processing systems.

In short, the sense of information processing that is used in cognitive science is at much too high a level of abstraction to capture the concrete biological reality of intrinsic intentionality. The "information" in the brain is always specific to some modality or other. It is specific to thought, or vision, or hearing, or touch, for example. The level of information processing described in the cognitive science computational models of cognition, on the other hand, is simply a matter of getting a set of symbols as output in response to a set of symbols as input.

We are blinded to this difference by the fact that the sentence, "I see a car coming toward me," can be used to record both the visual intentionality and the output of the computational model of vision. But this should not obscure the fact that the visual experience is a concrete conscious event and is produced in the brain by specific electrochemical biological processes. To confuse these events and processes with formal symbol manipulation is to confuse the reality with the model. The upshot of this part of the discussion is that in the sense of "information" used in cognitive science, it is simply false to say that the brain is an information processing device. . . .

Notes

1. SOAR is a system developed by Alan Newell and his colleagues at Carnegie Mellon University. The name is an acronym for "State, Operator, And Result." For an account see Waldrop 1988.

2. This view is announced and defended in a large number of books and articles many of which appear to have more or less the same title, e.g., *Computers and Thought* (Feigenbaum and Feldman, eds., 1963), *Computers and Thought* (Sharples et al. 1988), *The Computer and the Mind* (Johnson-Laird 1988), *Computation and Cognition* (Pylyshyn 1984), "The Computer Model of the Mind" (Block 1990), and of course, "Computing Machinery and Intelligence" (Turing 1950).

3. This whole research program has been neatly summarized by Gabriel Segal (1991) as follows: "Cognitive science views cognitive processes as computations in the brain. And computation consists in the manipulation of pieces of syntax. The content of the syntactic objects, if any, is irrelevant to the way they get processed. So, it seems, content can

The Critique of Cognitive Reason

figure in cognitive explanations only insofar as differences in content are reflected in differences in the brain's syntax" (p. 463).

4. Pylyshyn comes very close to conceding precisely this point when he writes, "The answer to the question what computation is being performed requires discussion of semantically interpreted computational states" (1984, 58). Indeed. And who is doing the interpreting?

References

Block, N. (1990). The computer model of the mind. In D. N. Osherson and E. E. Smith, eds., *Thinking: An invitation to cognitive science*, vol. 3. Cambridge, MA: MIT Press.

Bloom, F. E., and A. Lazerson (1988). *Brain, mind, and behavior*, 2d ed. New York: W. H. Freeman.

Boolos, G. S., and R. C. Jeffrey (1989). *Computability and logic*. Cambridge: Cambridge University Press.

Chomsky, N. (1986). *Knowledge of language: Its nature, origin and use*. New York and Philadelphia: Praeger Special Studies.

Dreyfus, H. L. (1972). *What computers can't do*. New York: Harper and Row.

Feigenbaum, E. A., and J. Feldman, eds. (1963). *Computers and thought*. New York: McGraw-Hill.

Fodor, J. A. (1975). *The language of thought*. New York: Crowell.

Hobbs, J. R. (1990). Matter, levels, and consciousness. *Behavioral and Brain Sciences* 13, 610–611.

Johnson-Laird, P. N. (1988). *The computer and the mind*. Cambridge, MA: Harvard University Press.

Marr, D. (1982). *Vision*. San Francisco: W. H. Freeman.

Newell, A. (1982). The knowledge level. *Artificial Intelligence* 18, 87–127.

Penrose, R. (1989). *The emperor's new mind*. Oxford: Oxford University Press.

Pylyshyn, Z. W. (1984). *Computation and cognition: Toward a foundation for cognitive science*. Cambridge, MA: MIT Press.

Searle, J. R. (1980a). Intrinsic intentionality: Reply to criticisms of Minds, Brains, and Programs. *Behavioral and Brain Sciences* 3, 450–456.

Searle, J. R. (1980b). Minds, brains, and programs. *Behavioral and Brain Sciences* 3, 417–424.

Searle, J. R. (1984). *Minds, brains, and science: The 1984 Reith lectures*. Cambridge, MA: Harvard University Press.

Segal, G. (1991). Review of Garfield, J., *Belief in psychology*. *Philosophical Review* 100, 463–466.

Sharples, M., D. Hogg, C. Hutchinson, S. Torrence, and D. Young (1988). *Computers and thought: A practical introduction to artificial intelligence*. Cambridge, MA: MIT Press.

Shepherd, G. M. (1983). *Neurobiology*. Oxford: Oxford University Press.

Turing, A. (1950). Computing machinery and intelligence. *Mind* 59, 433–460.

Waldrop, M. M. (1988). Toward a unified theory of cognition; and SOAR: A unified theory of cognition. *Science* 241, 27–29, 296–298.

Name Index

Salmon, Wesley, 154
Schachter, S., 362
Schacter, D., 419
Schank, R., 154
Schopenhauer, A., 638
Scoville, W. B., 752
Searle, John, 279, 321, 332, 368, 603–607
Shallice, T., 434
Shoemaker, S., 232, 393
Siebel, E., 658
Simon, Herbert, 373, 774
Singer, J., 362
Slobin, D. I., 539
Slovic, Paul, 634
Smith, Adam, 637, 647
Smith, Holly, 109
Smolensky, Paul, 780, 812
Sosa, Ernest, 97, 101
Squire, L. R., 426, 753
Stampe, D., 312
Stich, Stephen, 103–104, 278, 293, 627,
    724, 756
Stotland, Ezra, 637, 658
Stratton, G. M., 399

Thagard, Paul, 153
Thompson, B. (Count Rumford), 495
Thompson, R. F., 751
Tranel, D., 421
Tulving, E., 415, 423, 426, 673, 754
Turing, A., 836, 839
Tursky, B., 360
Tversky, Amos, 70, 74, 109–110, 111, 631,
    634

Ullman, J. D., 776

van Fraasen, Bas, 154
Vendler, Z., 285
Von der Heydt, R., 393
Von Humboldt, Wilhelm, 515

Walzer, M., 398
Weiner, B., 654
Weinreich, U., 567
Wellman, H. M., 329, 369
Wexler, Kenneth, 532
Williams, R. J., 780
Wilson, T., 372, 373
Winograd, T., 425
Wittgenstein, Ludwig, 366, 386, 524, 602

Woodruff, G., 369
Wright, L., 312

Ziff, P., 809
Zipser, D., 752

Subject Index

Cognitive penetrabililty, 134, 335, 408
diachronic, 134, 148
inverting lenses, 145
neurophysiological evidence, 147–150
relation to objectivity, 141–142
socialization and training, 146–147
synchronic, 134
visual illusions, 143–145
Cognitive science, 512
assumptions of, 838–839
central problems of language, 517–518,
524, 527–528
and co-evolution, 745–746
and computers, 515 (*see also* Computer
model of the mind)
critique of, 833–845
fundamental principles, 833–834
motivation behind, 837
task of, 820–821
Coherence, 65. *See also* Explanatory
coherence
various notions, 155
Color constancy, 500
Color illusion
simultaneous contrast, 496–498, 501
viewing angle, 502
Color mixing, 498
Color reflectivism, 504–505
Compositionality, 284–285, 808–813
and entailment, 810
and infraverbal thought, 811
principle of, 809
of representations, 810–811
and systematicity, 809
Computation, 776, 835, 839–840
Computer model of the mind
and the brain, 827–830, 844–845
computers as symbol manipulators, 822–
823, 828
critique of, 835–836, 841–845
and intentionality, 825–827
and language understanding, 819
primitive processors, 820–824
semantic functions, 828–830
unbiological nature, 824–825
Cones (photoreceptors), 494
Conjunction fallacy, 54–64, 109–110
Connectionism, 769–795
architecture, 779
and compositionality, 811–812, 815–816
conceptual level (symbolic paradigm),
773–775, 782–783, 789–793
connectionist models, 540–550, 769–770
critique of, 801–816

and explanatory coherence, 161–180
and inference, 814
goals, 770–773
levels of analysis, 773–775
Parallel distributed processing (PDP),
537, 540–550, 553–560, 802
Proper treatment of connectionism
(PTC), 770–773
and structure of mental states, 793–795
subconceptual level (subsymbolic
paradigm), 773–774, 778–793, 835
Conscious awareness system (CAS), 424
conceptions of, 429–430
neuroanatomy and neuropsychology of,
430–433
Conscious rule interpreter, 776
Consciousness 382, 415–35, 834. *See also*
Qualia
conscious awareness system (CAS), 424,
429–433
and dissociable interactions, 422–435
and implicit memory, 417–420
and introspection, 372–374
and lexical meaning, 562–563
neurophysiological evidence, 415–435
Constituency. *See* Compositionality
Content-addressing memory retrieval, 110
Counting model of numerical knowledge,
218
compared to accumulator theory, 218–
222
Covariation, detection of, 81–88
Cryptographer model of the mind, 598–
599

Data clusters, 192
De dicto beliefs, 709–711
De re beliefs, 709–711
Default hierarchy of deductive rules, 36
Derivational theory of complexity, 523
Descriptive ethics, 637–640
Developmental Psychology, 211–212, 214–
216, 318–322, 338, 461–477, 531–532,
538–539
habituation/dishabituation method, 211,
451
information processing concerns, 328–
330
interpretation of evidence, 322–324
joint visual attention, 636
object perception, 451–459
understanding one's own mind, 324–328
DICE (Dissociable Interactions and
Conscious Experience)

and infants, 211, 214–216
and non-human animals, 212–214

Object constancy, bias in favor of, 72
Object perception, 514. *See also* Cognitive
  penetrability
  effect of object complexity, 18
  extension to scene perception, 18
  in infancy, 451–459
  modifiability of, 449–451
  partial objects, 17
  recognition-by-components, 12–21, 105–
    107
  when does an object become
    unrecognizable, 18
Obligation schema, 34
Observation/inference distinction, 119
  consequences, 139
  meaning holism, 122–124
  ordinary language argument for, 121–122
  psychological arguments against, 125–
    137, 139
  ways that it fails, 140
Ontological commitments, 283, 462, 474,
  477
  ontological category features, 483
  prior to word learning, 463–464
  presuppositions of natural language,
    481–484

Parallel distributed processing (PDP), 802
  blending, 558
  critique of, 553–560
  described, 537
  and implicit knowledge, 534–536
  learning, 543–544
  microfeature representations, 558–560
  overreliance on the environment, 557
  pattern associator, 540
  perceptron convergence procedure, 543
  power of learning algorithms, 558
  predictions, 549
  simulations, 544–547
  Wickelphones, 542
Parsing language, 131–133
Past tense acquisition 535–550, 553–560
  connectionist model. (*see* Parallel
    distributed processing)
  empirical phenomena, 538–539
  stages of development, 538–9, 556–557
Pattern recognition, 9
Perception, 518

Permission schema, 28
Phenomenal properties, 386. *See also*
  Qualia
Physicalism
  and color subjectivism, 494
  defined, 233
Physics and syntax, 841
Plasticity
  conceptual, 150
  sensational, 150
Plato's problem, 516, 518, 528
Pragmatic anaphors, 481
Pragmatic reasoning schemas, 27–40
  abstract rule training and concrete
    example training, 31
  causal schema, 38
  obligation schema, 34
  permission schema, 28
  purely formal versus pragmatically based
    training, 30
  training based on a pragmatic schema,
    33
Prescriptive ethics, 640–642
  principle of minimal psychological
    realism, 641, 691
Primitive processors, 820–823
  hardware realization of, 823–824
Principle of minimal psychological
  realism, 641, 691
Problem of other minds, 257
Production systems, 194
Productivity, 284–285, 801–804
Proper treatment of connectionism (PTC),
  770
  contributions of, 772–773
  difficulties with, 772
Propositional attitudes, 257–258, 699, 703–
  709, 756–757
  anti-realism about, 274–276
  beliefs, 726
  and causality, 727–728
  and functionalism, 276–279
  and infra-linguistic animals, 758
  instrumentalist view of, 274–275
  and mental representations, 272–276
  and monadic functional states, 279–284
  and propositions, 281
  and psychological theorizing, 755–756
  and qualia, 364–367
  realism about, 273–374, 282–384
  and truth-conditions, 290–394
Propositions and propositional attitudes,
  281